W9-AWU-081

Schroeder's Collectible
TOYS
Antique to Modern
Price Guide

Edited by Sharon and Bob Huxford

COLLECTOR BOOKS
A Division of Schroeder Publishing Co., Inc.

The current values in this book should be used only as a guide. They are not intended to set prices, which vary from one section of the country to another. Auction prices as well as dealer prices vary greatly and are affected by condition as well as demand. Neither the Editors nor the Publisher assumes responsibility for any losses that might be incurred as a result of consulting this guide.

Searching For A Publisher?

We are always looking for knowledgeable people considered to be experts within their fields. If you feel that there is a real need for a book on your collectible subject and have a large comprehensive collection, contact us.

COLLECTOR BOOKS
P.O. Box 3009
Paducah, Kentucky 42002-3009

On The Cover:
Stacking Cans, Wee-Kin Baby Toy, Chad Valley, metal lithographed tin, EX, $75.00. Courtesy of Kay Smith.
Celluloid Cowboy on tin lithographed horse, windup, Alps, EX, $150.00. Courtesy of Rhonda Blackburn.
Toy Sewing Machine, Sew Master, Kayanee Corp., 6½"hx8¼"w, $60.00. Courtesy of Glenda Thomas.
Addams Family Lunch Box, King Seeley, 1974, with Thermos, EX, $85.00. Courtesy of Sharon Huxford.
Cadillac, turquoise, Japan, 11", $125.00. Courtesy of Sharon Huxford.

Research and Editorial Assistants: Michael Drollinger, Nancy Drollinger, Patty Durnell, Linda Holycross, Donna Newnum, Loretta Woodrow
Cover Design: Beth Summers
Layout: Terri Stalions and Beth Ray

Additional copies of this book may be ordered from:

COLLECTOR BOOKS
P.O. Box 3009
Paducah, Kentucky 42002-3009

@$17.95. Add $2.00 for postage and handling.

Copyright: Schroeder Publishing Co., Inc. 1995

This book or any part thereof may not be reproduced without the written consent of the Editors and Publisher.

Introduction

What Depression Glass was to the late sixties, Fiesta to the seventies, and cookie jars to the eighties, toys are to the nineties. No one even vaguely involved in the field can have missed all the excitement toys have stirred up among many, many collectors. If you've been using *Schroeder's Antiques Price Guide*, you know that we try very hard not to omit categories where we find even a minor amount of market activity — being collectors ourselves, we know how frustrating it can be when you are unable to find any information on an item in question. But we are limited to a specific number of pages, and as we watched the toy market explosion taking place, we realized that if we were to do it justice, we would have to publish a companion guide devoted entirely to toys. And following the same convictions, we decided that rather than to try to zero in on only the larger, more active fields, we'd try to represent toys of all kinds, from the 19th century up to today. This was the format we pursued. Taking into consideration space needed for photos, narratives, directories, and advertising and knowing we needed to limit the size of the book, we decided to try for 24,000 listings. We found out that when it comes to the toy market, that only begins to scratch the surface. We entered data for about three months and had we turned around and immediately started data entry on a second edition, we could have easily found that many fresh listings. And basically that's what we will do for our second edition. Just as we have always done, we will offer our readers fresh listings in every issue.

Our next step was to contact more than 900 dealers around the country to solicit their help and input. Response was fantastic. We had hundreds respond, many offering advice, photographs, their 'for sale' lists — help of all kinds. Toy collectors are super people. We can't say enough good about them. One collector explained it this way: Most aren't in it for profit but for pleasure. Whatever the reason, their support and enthusiasm carried us through what turned out to be an even more monumental task than our antiques and collectibles guide.

The biggest decision we had to make was organization. Collectors were quick to tell us that unlike antiques, toys can't be sorted by manufacturer. So we had to devise a sort that would not only be easy to use but one that our staff could work with. With this in mind, we kept many of our categories very broad and general. We took the simplest approach we could come up with. But nothing's written in stone; we can and will make changes on the recommendations of our readers. We view this guide (and hope you will too) as only the groundwork for future editions. Let us hear from you with your suggestions. We are always quick to say that whatever success we have achieved with *Schroeder's* is due to those hundreds of people who serve on our advisory board. The only credit we take is for knowing we couldn't do it without them.

What we want to stress is that our values are not meant to set prices. Some of them are prices realized at auction. You'll be able to recognize auction prices by the 'A' at the end of the description line. Others were taken from dealer's selling lists; these are also coded so as to identify the dealer — we'll explain this later. The listings that have neither the 'A' code or a dealer code were either sent to us by very knowledgeable collectors who specialize in specific types of toys or were originally dealer coded but altered at the suggestion of an advisor who felt that the stated price might be misleading. There are so many factors that bear on the market that for us to attempt to set prices is not only presumptuous, it's ludicrous. The foremost of these factors is the attitude of the individual collector — his personal view of the hobby. We've interviewed several by telephone; everyone has his own opinion. While some view auction prices as useless, others regard them as actual selling prices and prefer them to asking prices. And the dealer who needs to keep turning his merchandise over to be able to replenish and freshen his stock will of necessity sell at lower prices than a collector who will buy an item and wait for the most opportune time to turn it over for maximum profit. So we ask simply that you arrive at your own evaluations based on the information we've provided.

Let us hear from you — we value your input. Until next time — happy hunting! May you find that mint in the box #1 Barbie or if you prefer that rare mechanical bank that has managed to so far elude you. But even if you never do, we hope that you'll find a generous measure of happiness and success, a treasure now and then, and new friends on every journey.

The Editors

Advisory Board

The editors and staff take this opportunity to express our sincere gratitude and appreciation to each person who has contributed their time and knowledge to help us in what turned out to be our biggest undertaking ever! Because we were working on a very tight schedule, many others who had volunteered to help simply couldn't coordinate their available time with our deadlines. We're looking forward to the second edition knowing that with the groundwork we've already laid, we'll be able to get our category printouts out to our advisors much earlier next year and so have better response from them. We want to stress that even if an advisor is credited in a category narrative, that person is in no way responsible for errors. Errors are our responsibility. While some advisors sent us listings and prices, others provided background information, checked printouts, or simply answered our questions. All are listed below. Each name is followed by their code, see the section called *Dealer and Collector Codes* for an explanation of how these are used in the listings.

If you feel that you are qualified to advise us on a particular topic and have the time to work with us, let us hear from you. We still have categories that we need advisors for.

Jane Anderson (A2)

Aquarius Antiques (A3)

Bob Armstrong (A4)

Richard Belyski (B1)

Bojo (B3)

Dick Borgerding (B4)

Danny Bynum (B7)

Joe Bodnarchuk (B9)

Bill Campbell

Casey's Collectible Corner (C1)

Mark E. Chase (C2)

Arlan Coffman (C4)

Joe Corea (C5)

Mike Czerwinski (C8)

Marilyn Cooper (C9)

Allen Day (D1)

Marl Davidson (D2)

Larry DeAngelo (D3)

Doug Dezso (D6)

Ron & Donna Donnelly (D7)

George Downes (D8)

Allan Edwards (E3)

Paul Fink (F3)

Mike Fredericks (F4)

Steve Fisch (F7)

Mark Giles (G2)

Bill Hamburg (H1)

George Hardy (H3)

Jacquie & Bob Henry (H7)

Roger Inouye (I1)

Terri Ivers (I2)

Trina & Randy Kubeck (K1)

David Kolodny-Nagy (K2)

Tom Lastrapes (L4)

Kathy Lewis (L6)

Terry & Joyce Losonsky (L7)

John McKenna (M2)

Steven Meltzer (M9)

Natural Way (N1)

Roger Nazeley

Dawn Parrish (P2)

John & Sheri Pavone (P3)

Gary Pollastro (P5)

John Rammacher (R1)

Jim Rash (R3)

Robert Reeves (R4)

Charlie Reynolds (R5)

Craig Reid (R9)

Bill Stillman (S6)

Nate Stroller (S7)

Steve Santi (S8)

John Thurmond (T1)

Richard Trautwein (T3)

Norm & Cathy Vigue (V1)

Randy Welch (W4)

Henri Yunes (Y1)

Acknowledgments

A very special thank you to the dealers of The Old Tyme Toy Mall in James Dean's hometown, Fairmount, Indiana. We visited them for several days last fall and photographed hundreds of items from their booths. If you're passing through the area, it's a stop you should make.

Besides our advisory board, several more people helped us in various ways, perhaps offering advice or sending material or photographs. We want to acknowledge their assistance and express our appreciation to them as well. And if your name should be here and isn't, we do apologize and hope you'll forgive us. The omission was unintentional.

Larry Blodget (B2)
Stanley A. & Robert S. Block (B8)
Bill Bruegman (T2)
Ken Clee (C3)
Cotswold Collectibles (C6)
John DeCicco (D4)
Gordy Dutt (D9)
Dunbar Gallery (D9)
Lee Garmon
Colleen Garmon Barnes
Robert Goforth (G3)
Ellen Harnish (H4)

Lee Harris (H5)
Phil Helley (H6)
Henry Yunes
Art & Judy Turner (H8)
Dana Johnson Enterprises (J3)
Mike's General Store (M5)
The Mouse Man Ink (M8)
Gary Metz (M10)
Philip Norman (N2)
Olde Tyme Toy Mall (O1)
Parkway Furniture & Gift Shop (P1)
Bill Bruegman (T2)

How to Use This Book

Concept. Our design for this book is two-fold. Primarily it is a market report compiled from many sources, meant to be studied and digested by our readers, who can then better arrive at their own conclusion regarding prices. Were you to ask ten active toy dealers for their opinion as to the value of a specific toy, you would no doubt get ten different answers, and who's to say which is correct? Quite simply, there are too many variables to consider. Condition is certainly subjective, prices vary from one area of the country to another, and probably the most important factor is how you personally view the market — how much you're willing to pay and at what price you're willing to sell. So use this as a guide along with your observations at toy shows, flea markets, toy auctions, and elsewhere to arrive at an evaluation that satisfies you personally.

The second function of this book is to put buyers in touch with sellers who deal in the type of toys they want to purchase. Around the first of the year, we contacted dealers all over the country asking them to send us their 'for sale' lists and permission to use them as sources for some of our listings, which we coded so as to identify the dealer from whose list the price and description were taken. Even though much of their merchandise will have sold since we entered our data early last spring, many of them tell us that they often get similar or even the same items in over and over, so if you see something listed you're interested in buying, don't hesitate to call any of them. Remember, though, they're not tied down to the price quoted in the book, since their asking price is many times influenced by what they've had to pay to restock their shelves. Let us know how well this concept works out for you.

Toys are listed by name. Every effort has been made to list a toy by the name as it appears on the original box. There have been very few exceptions made, and then only if the collector-given name is more recognizable. For instance, if we listed 'To-Night Amos 'n' Andy in Person' (as the name appears on the box lid), very few would recognize the toy as the Amos 'n' Andy Walkers. But these exceptions are few.

Descriptions and sizes may vary. When we were entering data, we often found the same toy had sold through more than one auction gallery or was listed in several dealer lists. So the same toy will often be described in various ways, but we left descriptions just as we found them, since there is usually something to be gleaned from each variation. We chose to leave in duplicate lines when various conditions were represented so that you could better understand the impact of condition on value. Depending on the source and who was doing the measuring, we found that the size of a given toy might vary by an inch or more. Not having the toy to measure ourselves, we had to leave dimensions just as they were given in auction catalogs or dealer lists.

Lines are coded as to source. As we said before, collectors have various viewpoints regarding auction results. You will have to decide for yourself. Some feel they're too high to be used to establish prices while others prefer them to 'asking' prices that can sometimes be speculative. We must have entered about 8,000 auction values, and here is what we found to be true: the really volatile area is in the realm of character collectibles from the '40s, '50s, and '60s — exactly where there is most interest, most collector activity, and hot competition when the bidding starts. But for the most part, auction prices were not far out of line with accepted values. Many times, compared to the general market place, toys in less-than-excellent condition actually sold under 'book.' Because the average auction-consigned toy is in especially good condition and many times even retains its original box, it will naturally bring higher prices than the norm. And auctions often offer the harder-to-find, more unusual items. Without taking these factors into consideration, prices may seem high, when in reality, they may not be. Prices may be driven up by high reserves, but not all galleries have reserves. Whatever your view, you'll be able to recognize and consider the source of the values we quote and factor that into your evaluation. Each line that represents an auction-realized price will be coded 'A' at the end, just before the price. Other letter/number codes identify the dealer who sent us that information. These codes are explained later on.

Categories that have priority. Obviously there are thousands of toys that would work as well in one category as they would in another, depending on the preference of the collector. For instance, a Mary Poppins game would appeal to a games collector just as readily as it would to someone who bought collector-related toys of all kinds. The same would be true of many other types of toys. We tried to make our decisions sensibly and keep our sorts as simple as we possibly could, not only for the sake of our staff (none of whom are toy specialists) but with the reader in mind as well. To help you know where to look for some of these cross-over categories, here is what we decided to do.

These categories have precedence over Character:

Battery-Operated Toys (also specific man-
    ufacturers)
Bubble Bath Containers
Character and Promotional Drinking
    Glasses
Character Clocks and Watches
Corgi
Dakins
Dolls, Celebrity
Fisher-Price
Halloween Costumes

Lunch Boxes
Model Kits
Nodders
Paper Dolls
Pez Dispensers
Pin-Back Buttons
Snow Domes
Sports Collectibles
View-Master
Windups, Friction, and Other Mechanicals

Be sure to read the narratives at the beginning of each section; we've tried to direct you to other categories when there was some overlap. If you're having trouble locating an item, look in the index. It's as detailed as we know how to make it.

Price Ranges. Once in awhile, you'll find a listing that gives a price range. These result from our having found varying prices for the same item. We've taken a mid-range — less than the highest, a little over the lowest, if the original range was too wide to really be helpful. If the range is still coded 'A' for auction, all the prices we averaged were auction-realized prices.

Condition, how it affects value, how to judge it. The importance of condition can't be stressed enough. Unless a toy is exceptionally rare, it must be very good or better to really have much collector value. But here's where the problem comes in: though each step downward on the grading scale drastically decreases a toy's value, as the old saying goes, 'beauty is in the eye of the beholder.' What is acceptable wear and damage to one individual may be regarded by another as entirely too much. Criteria used to judge condition even varies from one auction company to the next, so we had to attempt to sort them all out and arrive at some sort of standardization. Please be sure to read and comprehend what the description is telling you about condition; otherwise you can easily be mislead. Auction galleries often describe missing parts, repairs, and paint touchups, summing up overall appearance in the condition code. When losses and repairs were noted in the catalog, we noted them as well. Remember that a toy even in mint restored condition is never worth as much as one in mint original condition. And even though a toy may be rated otherwise 'EX' after losses and repairs are noted, it won't be worth as much as one with original paint and parts in excellent condition. Keep this in mind when you use our listings to evaluate your holdings.

These are the condition codes we have used throughout the book and their definitions as we have applied them:

M — mint. Unplayed with, brand new, flawless.
NM — near mint. Appears brand new except on very close inspection.
EX — excellent. Has minimal wear, very minor chips and rubs, a few light scratches
VG — very good. Played with, loss of gloss, noticeable problems, several scratches.
G — good. Some rust, considerable wear and paint loss, well used.
P — poor. Generally unacceptable except for a filler.

Because we do not use a three-level pricing structure as many of you are used to and may prefer, we offer this table to help you arrive at values for toys in conditions other than those that we give you. If you know the value of a toy in excellent condition and would like to find an approximate value for it in near mint condition, for instance, just run your finger down the column under 'EX' until you find the approximate price we've listed (or one that easily factors into it), then over to the column headed 'NM.' We'll just go to $100.00, but other values will be easy to figure by addition or multiplication. Even though at auction, toys in very good to excellent condition sometimes bring only half as much as a mint condition toy, the collectors we interviewed told us that this was not true of the general market place. Our percentages are simply an average based on their suggestions.

G	VG	EX	NM	M
40/50%	55/65%	70/80%	85/90%	100%
5.00	6.00	7.50	9.00	10.00
7.50	9.00	11.00	12.50	15.00
10.00	12.00	15.00	18.00	20.00
12.00	15.00	18.00	22.00	25.00
14.00	18.00	22.50	26.00	30.00
18.00	25.00	30.00	35.00	40.00
22.50	30.00	37.50	45.00	50.00
27.00	35.00	45.00	52.00	60.00
32.00	42.00	52.00	62.00	70.00
34.00	45.00	55.00	65.00	75.00
35.00	48.00	60.00	70.00	80.00
40.00	55.00	68.00	80.00	90.00
45.00	60.00	75.00	90.00	100.00

Condition and value of original boxes and packaging. When no box or packaging is referred to in the line or in the narrative, assume that the quoted price is for the toy only. Please read the narratives! In some categories (Corgi, for instance), all values are given for items mint and in original boxes. Conditions for boxes (etc.) are in parenthesis immediately following the condition code for the toy itself. In fact, any information within parenthesis at that point in the line will refer to packaging. Collector interest in boxes began several years ago, and today many people will pay very high prices for them, depending on scarcity, desirability, and condition. The more colorful, graphically pleasing boxes are favored, and those with images of well-known characters are especially sought after. Just how valuable is a box? Again, this is very subjective to the individual. We asked this question to several top collectors around the country, and the answers they gave us ranged from 20% to 100% above mint-no-box prices.

Advertising. You'll notice display ads throughout the book. We hope you will contact these advertisers if they deal in the type of merchandise you're looking for. If you'd like your ad to appear in our next edition, please refer to the advertising rate chart in the back of the book for information.

Listing of Standard Abbreviations

These abbreviations have been used throughout this book in order to provide you with the most detailed descriptions possible in the limited space available. No periods are used after initials or abbreviations. When two dimensions are given — height is noted first. When only one measurement is given, it will be the greater height if the toy is vertical, length if it is horizontal. Remember that in the case of duplicate listings representing various conditions, we found that sizes often varied as much as an inch or more.

Am	American	MOC	mint on card
att	attributed to	MOT	mint on tree
bk	back	mt, mtd	mount, mounted
bl	blue	NM	near mint
blk	black	NP	nickel plated
brn	brown	NRFB	never removed from box
bsk	bisque	NRFP	never removed from package
c	copyright	orig	original
ca	circa	o/w	otherwise
cb	cardboard	P	poor
CI	cast iron	Pat	patented
compo	composition	pc	piece
dbl	double	pg, pgs	page, pages
dk	dark	pk	pink
dtd	dated	pkg	package
emb	embossed	pnt	paint, painted
EX	excellent	prof	professional
F	fine	rfn	refinished
fr	frame, framed	rnd	round
ft, ftd	foot, feet, footed	rpl	replaced
G	good	rpr	repaired
gr	green	rpt	repainted
hdl	handle, handled	rstr	restored
hdw	hardware	sq	square
illus	illustrated, illustration	sz	size
litho	lithographed	turq	turquoise
lt	light, lightly	unmk	unmarked
M	mint	VG	very good
MBP	mint in bubble pack	wht	white
MIB	mint in box	w/	with
mc	multicolored	w/up	windup
MIP	mint in package	yel	yellow
mk	marked		

Activity Sets

Activity sets once enjoyed by so many as children — the Silly Putty, the Creepy Crawlers, and those Mr. Potato Heads — are finding their way back to some of those same kids, now grown up, more or less, and especially the earlier editions are carrying pretty respectable price tags when they can be found complete or reasonably so. The first Thingmaker/Creepy Crawler (Mattel, 1964) in excellent but played-with condition will sell at around $65.00. Activity books with punch-out figures and accessories from the fifties through the seventies were published by Saalfield, Whitman, and Golden Press, and when these are found complete (but used) and in excellent condition, most are priced from $20.00 to $50.00, with a few even higher. If in your wildest dreams you ever thought you might like to make candles to look like your favorite monster, you could. But to do it today could be pretty pricey (See the listings!). You'll find more of these sets in the category called Character Collectibles.

Adam's Magic Set, includes several tricks, 1950s, in 11x14" box, sealed, NMIB, A $190.00
Adventure w/Weather, 1959, orig 11x15" box, VG, N2 ..$30.00
Automotive Illustrator's Paint-by-Number Set, AMT, 2 numbered pictures, pnts & brushes, 1960s, MIB.............$50.00
Casting Race Car Set, Master Caster, 1974, EX+ (VG box), T1..$35.00
Casting Set, Rapco, 1969, orig box, VG, T1.....................$24.50
Chandu White King of Magic Trick Set, 10 tricks w/instruction booklet, coin missing, 1930s, 11x14", EX+ (EX+ box), A $133.00
Colorforms Set, including cavemen & many dinosaurs, 1960, 8x12" box, M (EX box), T2.......................................$32.00
Creeple Peeple Thingmaker, Mattel, molds & plastic goop, hair & feathers, 1965, 9x12x4" box, EX (EX box), T2 .....$70.00
Creepy Crawlers, Mattel, 1st series, 1964, EX, T1 ....$65.00
Creepy Crawlers, Mattel, 2nd series, 1966, EX, T1...........$55.00
Creepy People Thingmaker, Mattel, 1966, T1..................$45.00
DC Super Heroes Plaster Molding Set, Toy Biz, M, E3 ....$20.00
Ding-Dong School Finger Paints, Milton Bradley, 1950s, M (NM box)..$30.00
Ding-Dong School Peg-a-Picture, Whitman, 1953, EX....$28.00
Drawing Made Easy for Little Folks, McLoughlin, heavy paper w/animals for kids to trace, 1887, 5x7", NM (EX box), A $30.00
Famous Monsters Candle Making Set, complete, NMIB..$180.00
Famous Monsters Creature Casting Set, RAPCO, MIP, E3 ..$180.00
Fighting Men Thingmaker, Mattel, complete, extra pcs, EX (EX box)..$40.00
Fighting Men Thingmaker, Mattel, NMIB $70.00
Foto-Fun Printing Kit, Fun-Built, transfer photo images to paper, 1958, 10x4" box, unused, MIB, T2............................$40.00
Frosty Freeze Ice Cream Maker, Hasbro, NMIB..............$35.00
Gangly Dangly Mold Set, Mattel, loose $20.00
Great Foodini Magic Set, Pressman, paper mask, magic tricks & book, orig box, 20", VG-EX, A $110.00
Holster, Indian Leathercraft, 1950s, MIB, T1.................$125.00
Incredible Edibles, Mattel, MIB $50.00

Hocus-Pocus Magic Set, Adams, 1962, unused, NM (EX box), A, $85.00.

Incredible Edibles, Mattel, missing goop, EX (VG box)...$35.00
Jack Frost Paint Set, Hasbro, sketches, pnts & crayons, 1950s, 12x16" box, sketches colored (EX- box), T2 ....$30.00

Jimmy Dodd Magic Slate, ca 1954, 6½x9", NM, $36.00.

Joe Thomas' Magic Kit, Cardes Co, 1940, 11x15" box filled w/magic tricks, NM (EX box), A $50.00
Johnny Toy Maker, Topper, NM......................................$40.00
Jon Gnagy Four-in-One Master Art Set, oils, pastels & watercolors, drawing & sketching, 1950s, M (EX+ box), A....$50.00
Kenner Easy Bake Oven, 1964, NM (EX+ box) $40.00
Kodatoy, Westman Kodak, w/several movie reels, 12x11", EX (G box), A...$50.00
Kookey Kakes, Mattel, MIB..$50.00
Looney Tunes Cartoon-O-Graph, 7 cartoons to copy (1 torn), in orig 14x19" box, EX (VG box), T6 ....$20.00
Looney Tunes Soap-Making Kit, 3 character molds, missing instructions, orig box, G-VG, T6 ....$5.00
Magic Wand, Porter Chemical, contains vials & equipment, lid shows boy being watched by genie, 1928, EX (EX box), A...$158.00
Marvel Comic Artists Inking & Coloring Kit, Marvel Comics, 18 8x11" illus, complete, 1969, MIB, scarce, A $81.00
Mini Dragons Thingmaker, Mattel, molds & plastic goop to make dragons, sm set (9x12x4" box) w/no heater, 1967, EX, T2...$70.00
Mosaic Paint-by-Number, Transogram, 1959, NMIB.......$25.00
Motorized Monster Maker Basic Set, Topper, NMIB.....$125.00

Mr Machine, Ideal, 1st edition, MIB.............................$650.00

Mysto Magic Set, Gilbert, complete & unused, 10x18", NM (EX box), A...$105.00

Pee Wee's Colorforms Play Set, Herman Toys, 1987, MIB, $25.00.

Picadoo's Thingmaker, Mattel, molds, goop, glue, booklet & accessories, 1967, MIB, from $40 to............................$55.00

Play Poster Paints, Kenner, 1972, complete, MIB $15.00

Power Shop, Mattel, 95% complete, EX-NM, T1 ....$75.00

Senior Magic Set, USA, contains 20 unused tricks, 8x12" box, NM (EX box), A $115.00

Shaker Maker Pictures, Ideal, MIB.....................................$25.00

Silly Putty, Silly Putty Co, yel & wht plastic egg w/contents, 1950, on 5x7" foil card, M (EX+ card), A $37.00

Snoopy Sno-Cone Machine, Playskool, MIB.....................$25.00

Space Fleet Set, casting & coloring set, Handi-Craft, complete, unused, 1950s, NM (EX+ box), A $144.00

Spirograph, Kenner, 2 lg transparent plastic rings w/18 sm wheels & 2 racks, complete, 1968, NM (EX+ box), A............$36.00

Strange Change Machine, Mattel, complete $40.00

Super Cartoon Maker, Mattel, MIB................................$140.00

Super Magic, Sherms Creations, box lid features magician boy doing tricks for children, complete, NM (VG box), A...$144.00

Super Thingmaker, Mattel, NMIB....................................$50.00

Tarzan Thingmaker Mold, Mattel, 1966, EX+, T1 ....$50.00

Thingmaker Fright Factory Pack, Mattel, 1966, EX, T1...$50.00

Tissage Des Perles, many pcs in wooden box to be used to perform tricks, 13¼x9x2¾", EX, A $300.00

Toot Sweet, Mattel, NMIB...$45.00

Vac-U-Form Car & Truck Mold Set, Mattel, MIB...........$15.00

Wonder Box Magic, Royal, 1954, features 24-pg instruction booklet & several boxed tricks, 13x18", NM (EX box), A $171.00

Zoofie Goofie Play Pak, Mattel, MIP (sealed)..................$75.00

Zoofie Goofies Thingmaker, Mattel, 1 mold missing, used pipe cleaners, orig box, EX, H4 ....$40.00

Advertising

The assortment of advertising memorabilia geared toward children is vast — plush and cloth dolls, banks, games, puzzles, trucks, radios, watches, and much, much more. And considering the popularity of advertising memorabilia in general, when you add to it the crossover interest from the realm of toys, you have a real winning combination! Just remember to check for condition very carefully; signs of play wear are common. Think twice about investing much money in soiled items, especially cloth or plush dolls. Stains are often impossible to remove.

For more information we recommend *Advertising Character Collectibles* by Warren Dotz; *Advertising Dolls Identification & Value Guide* by Joleen Ashman Robinson and Kay Sellers; *Huxford's Collectible Advertising* by Sharon and Bob Huxford; and *Pepsi-Cola Collectibles, Vols I, II, and III*, by Bill Vehling and Michael Hunt. Our advisors for this category are John and Sheri Pavone (P3) and Jim Rash (R3), who specializes in advertising dolls. See also Character Collectibles; Radios; Telephones.

Actigall, squeeze toy, 1990, 4" or 8", R3, ea.....................$20.00

Alka-Seltzer, bank, Speedy, molded vinyl, Canada, 5", EX $150.00

Alka-Seltzer, bank, Speedy, molded vinyl, 1960s, 5½", NM..$250.00

Alka-Seltzer, squeeze toy, Speedy, molded vinyl, 8", R3 .$500.00

Allied Van Lines, doll, printed cloth, minor discoloration $22.00

Allied Van Lines, tin truck, MIB, D10, $325.00.

Alpo Dog Food, doll, Dan the Dog, plush, w/collar, M, D4..$10.00

Alpo Dog Food, frisbee, red & wht, M, D4 ....$4.00

American Steel & Wire Co, jigsaw puzzle, farm landscape divided by fences & giant boots..., 1933, 9x12", EX, F6 ....$35.00

Armstrong's Quaker Rugs, jigsaw puzzle, boy & girl playing on rug w/blocks spelling out company name, 1930s, EX, F6 ....$45.00

Atlantic Premium Gas, bank, gas pump, tin, red & wht w/red, wht, bl & blk lettering, bl bottom, 5", NM, A...........$45.00

Atlas Battery, bank, V6 battery, EX $35.00

Atlas Van Lines, doll, Atlas Annie, cloth, 15", EX $20.00

Aunt Jemima, dolls, Aunt Jemima, Uncle Moses, Wade & Diana, stuffed cloth, 12½" to 8¾", set of 4, EX........$625.00

Aunt Jemima, mask, Aunt Jemima's head wrapped in scarf, diecut cb, cutouts for eyes & nose, 13x12", M, A....$200.00

Aunt Jemima, puzzle, 2 product images on string attached to image of Aunt Jemima, diecut cb, 4x5", EX............$125.00

Baby's Dy-Dee Service, squeeze toy, delivery truck w/crowned infant sitting atop, rubber, 1950s, 4x5", VG, A.........$35.00

Bazooka Gum, Exploding Battleship, orig mailer, MIP, V1 ....$30.00

Beech-Nut Gum, bendee, Multi-Toys, 1967, R3............$150.00

Beech-Nut Gum, squeeze toy, open pack of peppermint gum w/silvered tip, rubber, 1960s, VG, A.........................$37.00

Big Boy, bank, vinyl figure, 1970s, EX, T1 ....$20.00

Black Jack Gum, jigsaw puzzle, shows domineering woman putting pc of gum into husband's mouth, 1933, 7x10", EX, F6 ....$40.00

Blue Bonnet Margarine, doll, Dutch girl, hard plastic, 8", MIB..$8.50

Boker Coffee, bank, can shape, tin, 1970s, NM, T1 ....$15.00

Bond Bread, company wagon w/horse & driver, Schoenhut, all orig, rare promotional toy, EX, A............................$330.00

Borden, bendee, Elsie the Cow, 3¾", M, H4.....................$20.00

Borden, board game, Elsie's Milkman Game, complete w/box, 1963, EX, A $87.00

Borden, book, Adventures w/Elsie the Famous Cow, Elsie's travels from 1939-1964 World's Fairs, hardbound, 60 pgs, P6..$65.00

Borden, book, Elsie & the Looking Club, hardbound, 1946, P6...$25.00

Borden, bowl, Elsie dancing in flowers, Cambridge, M, P6 .$180.00

Borden, doll, Elsie, stuffed fabric w/rubber head, premium, VG, A..$180.00

Borden, early milk truck, pnt CI, wht w/Borden's Milk Cream lettered in red, flat roof, rubber wheels, 6", EX, A...$800.00

Borden, Elsie's Good Food Line Train, punch-out cb for constructing 7-car train, orig mailer, 1940s, 37x25", M, P6 ....$245.00

Borden, place mat, full-color image of Elsie, 11x16¾", M, P6 ....$12.00

Borden, pull toy, Elsie Jumped Over the Moon, 1944, NMIB...$175.00

Borden, push-button puppet, Elsie on gr base, wood & paper, moos when pressed, 1950s, 5", NM..........................$200.00

Borden, toy bottle, Elsie's Milk Bottle, contains clothespins & beads, plastic, 1956, MIP, P6......................................$65.00

Borden, watch, wht plastic border & numbers around raised head of Elsie, missing link bands, 1950s, 1" dia, G, A $18.00

Borden's Farm Products, pull toy, Rich Toys, horse-drawn wagon, pnt wood w/decals, 32" L, EX...................$1,050.00

Boscul Coffee, bank, coffee tin w/One Hour Fresh & Vacuum Packed above & below product name, 2¼x2½" dia, EX, A $20.00

Bounce Fabric Softener, doll, Montgomery Moose, brn plush, knit shirt & corduroy pants, logo on shoe, 1985, 15", EX...$15.00

Brach's, doll, scarecrow, cloth body, vinyl head, 1972, 16", EX $25.00

Brach's, doll, Wile E Coyote, brn plush body w/beige head & chest, 1989, 16½", M..$15.00

Brim Coffee, jigsaw puzzle, General Foods, jar, can & coupon graphics, 100-pc, 1977, 10x13", VG+, T6 ....$25.00

Buick, puzzle, Best Buy & Buick lettered on blk & wht plastic sliding tiles in sq fr, EX $25.00

Buster Brown, Amusement Park balloon inflator head and cape, D10, $650.00.

Buster Brown, bank, No Parents Allowed, vinyl, 11", R3.$40.00

Buster Brown, color transfer kit, Time Machine-68, M4..$10.00

Buster Brown, Crazy Scopes, M4 ....$10.00

Buster Brown, figure, Germany, pnt bsk, jtd arms, 1920s, 3½", NM $260.00

Buster Brown, game, Pin the Tie & Tail on Buster & Tige, 1967, M4 ....$25.00

Buster Brown Shoes, mask, upper portion of Buster Brown's head in red hat, stiff diecut paper, ca 1905, 8x10", VG, A.$75.00

Butternut Bread, clip-bk badge featuring the Cisco Kid, EX, J2 ....$30.00

C&H Sugar, doll, Hawaiian girl, stuffed cloth, 15", MIP, H4 ....$5.00

Cadbury Chocolate, hand puppet, Clovis Cow, wht & brn plush, inside lined w/nylon, 12", M....................................$13.00

Calumet Baking Powder, bank, Edward Barnes, tin, child atop can, orange & bl, Pat 9/16/1924, EX, A...................$300.00

Cambell's Soups, squeeze toys, vinyl boy & girl, R3, pr $30.00

Campbell's Soups, bank, can shape w/Campbell's Vegetable Garden label showing Campbell Girl, 4½", EX $950.00

Campbell's Soups, child's electric mixer, Mirro, pictures Campbell Kids on sides, 1960s, rare, MIB $225.00

Campbell's Soups, child's fork, Campbell Kid's head eng above M-m-m Good on hdl, EX..$5.00

Campbell's Soups, child's tea set, plastic, includes 4 plates, cups, tray, bowl & utensils, shows Campbell Kids, MIB $65.00

Campbell's Soups, coloring book, A Story of Soup, unused, 1976, 14x11", M $20.00

Campbell's Soups, doll, Campbell Girl, stuffed cloth, bl bibs w/red & wht checked shirt, ca 1973, 15½", EX $65.00

Campbell's Soups, dolls, Campbell Kids as Paul Revere & Betsy Ross, vinyl, 1973, 10", MIB..................................$200.00

Campbell's Soups, jigsaw puzzle, All Aboard, #319, 28-pc, 1986, VG $30.00

Campbell's Soups, lunch box w/thermos, metal, bl, shows kid at play, red & wht thermos w/logo, 1973, 7x9x3½", G...$275.00

Campbell's Soups, lunch box w/thermos, metal, domed top, brn, 1968, VG $250.00

Campbell's Soups, story book, Rand McNally, Campbell Kids on front, 1954, 8x6½", VG.................$25.00

Campbell's Soups, truck, wht cab w/red trailer promoting Campbell's products, Truck Load of Good Food, 1985, 5x18", NM.................$95.00

Campbell's Soups, warming dish, Grace Dayton, Campbell Kids, girl cries/boy has candy, 1930s, 7½" dia, from $75 to..$90.00

Campbell's Soups, word game, cb canister w/tin lid, pictures Campbell Kids, contains red plastic letters, EX $22.00

Cap'n Crunch Cereal, bank, plastic, R3.................$25.00

Cap'n Crunch Cereal, booklet, Scratch 'N Sniff, 1975, NM $15.00

Cap'n Crunch Cereal, kaleidoscope, cb cylinder w/paper label showing 6 characters, 1970s, 7x2" dia, VG+, A $10.00

Cap'n Crunch Cereal, puzzle, cb fr-tray type, M.................$25.00

Cap'n Crunch Cereal, Sea-Cycle, rubber-band powered kit, figures in boat, plain brn mailer, 1979, MIB, P4 ....$35.00

Caravelle Candy Man, wire-armed, 7", R3 ....$150.00

Carr's Biscuits, tin container, London Transport Bus, Chad Valley, England, litho tin, tin wheels, 10", G+, A $500.00

Charlie Tuna, squeeze toy, vinyl, 1974, 8", R3 ....$50.00

Chase & Sanborn Coffee, jigsaw puzzle, Ceylon girl picking tea, G $30.00

Cheetos, game, electronic; Chester Cheetah Paw Play, MIB,T1 ....$65.00

Cheetos, tumbler, Chester Cheetah graphics on plastic, NM, M4 ....$6.00

Chevrolet, bank, yel, bl & wht folding cb picturing car, truck & logo, orig envelope, EX.................$20.00

Chevrolet, figure, Popeye-type w/mechanic's smock & hat, 1930s, VG, T1 ....$325.00

Chevron, truck w/driver, Tonka, #XR101, tan & wht w/bl & red Chevron logo, 15¾" L, MIB.................$185.00

Chicken of the Sea, doll, mermaid, cloth, 1992, NM, T1 .$15.00

Chiclets, puzzle, plastic, 12-pc, orig Chiclets box, 6x3", EX, T6.................$8.00

Chiffon Margarine, doll, Mother Nature, cloth, in package, M.$20.00

Chiquita Bananas, doll, Olympic Raccoon, printed cloth w/wht plastic vest, 1980, M.................$10.00

Chocks Vitamins, doll, Chocks man, stuffed cloth, 20", EX, H4.................$28.00

Chrysler, bank, Mr Fleet, vinyl, 1973, 9", R3 ....$300.00

Clark Candy Bars, squeeze toy, Clark boy holding candy bar, molded vinyl, Beatrice Foods, 1960s, 8½", M $90.00

Clicquot Club Ginger Ale, bank, plaster half-figure of Eskimo boy holding lg bottle, 7x5½x4", EX, A $345.00

Coca-Cola, bank, dispenser, Marx, wht on red w/2 clear front panels showing 3 glasses, battery-op, 1950s, EX+, M5 ....$440.00

Coca-Cola, bank, red cb & tin can w/wht lettering, Drink Coca-Cola In Bottles, Delicious & Refreshing, 3", EX, M5 .$32.00

Coca-Cola, bank, red plastic house w/wht lettering, bottler's premium, EX+.................$16.00

Coca-Cola, bank, upright dispenser w/paper cup, plastic, wht decal w/red lettering at top, orig box, 1960s, VG, M5 ....$85.00

Coca-Cola, bank, upright vending machine, plastic, flat top, Play Refreshed, 5¢, EX, A.................$25.00

Coca-Cola, bank, upright vending machine, plastic, red w/wht Drink Coca-Cola above, Ice Cold below, NM, M5 ...$65.00

Coca-Cola, bubble blower, red bottle-shaped machine gun, w/orig soap & instructions, NM, A $250.00

Coca-Cola, can, GE, Coke lettered vertically & horizontally w/wht contour logo, NM, A $30.00

Coca-Cola, crayons, box of 4, M $5.00

Coca-Cola, cribbage board, w/instructions, 1930-40s, orig box, EX+, A.................$40.00

Coca-Cola, cutout for children, Circus (w/clown holding Coke glass), lt cb, 1 lg sheet, 1932, VG+, A.................$40.00

Coca-Cola, cutout for children, Circus Miniature..., lt cb, 1 lg sheet, fr, 1927, VG+, A.................$45.00

Coca-Cola, cutout for children, Fontaine Fox Toonerville Town, lt cb, 1 lg sheet, 1930s, VG+, A $170.00

Coca-Cola, cutout for children, Uncle Remus Story, lt cb, 1 lg sheet, 1931, VG, A.................$60.00

Coca-Cola, dart board, numbers border rnd target on sq board w/silhouette girl & disk logos at corners, 1940s, EX+, A.................$90.00

Coca-Cola, dart board, numbers run vertically through center of bull's-eye target, logos at corners, 1950s, EX+, A $45.00

Coca-Cola, darts, wood w/feathered ends, box of 3, 1940s-50s, NM, A.................$90.00

Coca-Cola, dbl-decker bus, Japan, red w/2 flags flanking banner reading Welcome to Japan, 17½", NM (EX box), A .$225.00

Coca-Cola, delivery truck, Buddy L, 1960s, NM, $150.00.

Coca-Cola, dispenser, red & wht plastic, Drink... on side panels, logo & images of 2 glasses above spigot, EX, M5 ....$40.00

Coca-Cola, dispenser, red plastic, Drink Coca-Cola logo on sides, Hey Kids!..., w/orig glasses & box, 1950s, EX+, M5.................$60.00

Coca-Cola, doll, Buddy Lee, plastic, cap bill, tie & belt rpl, 1950s, 12", EX, A $425.00

Coca-Cola, doll, Christmas elf, stuffed felt w/vinyl hands & feet, 1980s or earlier, 12", EX, A $45.00

Coca-Cola, doll, Santa w/bottle, stuffed cloth, red suit w/blk boots & wht mittens, 1960s, NM, A.................$60.00

Coca-Cola, domino set, yel box w/red & blk graphics, Coke bottles on domino pcs, complete, EX, M5.................$55.00

Coca-Cola, game, Robin Hood Bo-Arro, complete w/orig card, 1920s-30s, NM, A $190.00

Coca-Cola, game, Shanghai, 1957, NMIB, A $10.00

Coca-Cola, game, Steps to Health, complete, 1938, 26x11", NM, M5 ....$150.00

Coca-Cola, game board, Milton Bradley, Winko Baseball, 1940s-50s, VG+, A $45.00

Coca-Cola, games, chess, checkers, dominos & backgammon, Milton Bradley, w/instructions & box, NM (VG+ box), A $80.00

Coca-Cola, jigsaw puzzle, Canadian, party scene w/pennants, bottles on ice & Sprite boy below, 1950s, 12x18", EX, M5 ....$80.00

Coca-Cola, kite, High Flyer, Coca-Cola in script above 6-oz bottle, EX+, A $140.00

Coca-Cola, marbles, bottler's premium, 1960s, MIP $16.00

Coca-Cola, paddle & ball, wood, ball attached w/rubber band, In Bottles Only, NM, A $55.00

Coca-Cola, playing cards, Coca-Cola Adds Life to Everything Nice, complete, 1976, NMIB, sealed, M10 ....$16.00

Coca-Cola, playing cards, Cola-Clan Convention, Alexandria, complete, 1980, M $40.00

Coca-Cola, playing cards, couple resting under unplanted tree, Things Go Better..., complete, 1963, MIB, sealed, A .$30.00

Coca-Cola, playing cards, Elaine seated w/folded parasol at knee, plain edge, complete, orig box, 1915, EX, A $2,039.00

Coca-Cola, playing cards, gr & gold w/blk stripe, Drink...in Bottles, complete, orig box, rare, 1938, EX, A $357.00

Coca-Cola, playing cards, ice skater being offered a bottle, Through The Years, complete, orig box, 1956, NM, A $130.00

Coca-Cola, pop gun, Santa airborne in wht sleigh, Coca-Cola logo on bk, 4½x7½", NM, A $15.00

Coca-Cola, puzzle, 2-pc bent wire, The Pause That Refreshes mk on both sides, 1940s-50s, NM, A $10.00

Coca-Cola, puzzle maze, Memphis TN Bottling Co, Get the BB's in the Eyes of the Sprite Boy, 1950s, EX+, A $20.00

Coca-Cola, race car, tin, 1970s, NMIB, A $85.00

Coca-Cola, shopping cart, masonite, shows various products & prominent Coca-Cola carton, 1950s, EX+, A $500.00

Coca-Cola, table tennis, orig box, 1930s-40s, NM (VG+ box), A $50.00

Coca-Cola, top, wood, bright gold & red Drink Coca-Cola logo, rare, NM, A $803.00

Coca-Cola, toy, upright vending machine, plastic, slightly arched top, Work Refreshed, EX, A $65.00

Coca-Cola, toy dishes, My Dolly Loves a Party, orig box, NM (EX+ box), A $80.00

Coca-Cola, train, tin w/up, side of base features graphics of Coca-Cola truck in busy street scene, W Germany, EX+, A $450.00

Coca-Cola, transformer, can-shaped robot, 1980s, MIB...$45.00

Coca-Cola, truck, Buddy L, carrier has sodas, cooler, etc, 1989, 14", NRFB (EX+ box), P3 ....$25.00

Coca-Cola, truck, Buddy L, late model w/enclosed cargo bed, contour logo all around, dolly attached to side, EX+, A $30.00

Coca-Cola, truck, Buddy L, yel metal, dbl-decker open cargo bed w/center ad panel, 1960s, VG, A $45.00

Coca-Cola, truck, Japan, plastic & tin, 1970s, 3½", EX, A, $50.00.

Coca-Cola, truck, Japan, tin & plastic, 2 bottles & disk logo on sides of enclosed cargo bed, friction, 1970s, EX+, A..$50.00

Coca-Cola, truck, Japan, yel metal, dbl-decker bed, Delicious...Refreshing center ad panel, friction, 1956, 8", EX+, M5 ....$250.00

Coca-Cola, truck, Lincoln Toys, red w/wht Drink Coca-Cola on door, open bed holds 15 stamped blocks, 16", EX, A $355.00

Coca-Cola, truck, Marx, metal, yel w/red grill & trim, dbl-decker open cargo bed, wheel-well covers, 12", EX+, M5 ....$270.00

Coca-Cola, truck, Marx #22, metal, yel w/Sprite boy on side panels around open cargo bed, rubber wheels, EX+, A...$475.00

Coca-Cola, truck, Metalcraft, A-frame cargo bed w/10 orig bottles, reads Every Bottle Sterilized, 1930s, EX, M5....$550.00

Coca-Cola, truck, Metalcraft, flat roof, reads Every Bottle Sterilized, w/10 orig bottles, rubber wheels, 1930s, G-, A $190.00

Coca-Cola, truck, pnt & pressed steel, plastic & varnished wood trim, yel & red, modern, 26", M, A $575.00

Coca-Cola, truck, red & wht late model w/enclosed cargo bed, contour logo w/tilted bottle, battery-op, EX+, A $25.00

Coca-Cola, truck, Rosco, yel w/decaled cargo bed showing 4 tiers of cases, friction, 8", EX, M5..............................$90.00

Coca-Cola, truck, wht over red cab & enclosed cargo bed, orig box, battery-op, 1950s, EX+ (VG+ box), M5..........$425.00

Coca-Cola, truck, yel metal, dbl-decker open cargo bed w/center ad panel, 1960s, EX+, M5 ....$150.00

Coca-Cola, truck, yel metal & plastic late model w/sq cab, open stair-step cargo bed, center red ad panel, 4", NM, M5 ....$72.00

Coca-Cola, truck, yel plastic w/enclosed cargo bed, red Drink... logo on sides, red ad panel atop, 1949, 11", VG, M5...........$110.00

Coca-Cola, van, Corgi #437, Lieferwagon Camionnette, w/orig box, 1978, M (VG box)...$60.00

Coca-Cola, van, Flip-O-Matic, plastic, bottle lever on rear, contour logo on sides, friction, 1970s-80s, NM, A $45.00

Coca-Cola, van, yel metal w/red trim, bottle & disk logo on top, 1 from set of 12, friction, 1960, 4", EX+, M5............$90.00

Coca-Cola, wagon, bottle-case body w/wheels & handle, 1960, NM, A $125.00

Coca-Cola, whistle, plastic, Merry Christmas, Coca-Cola Bottling Memphis Tenn, EX $15.00

Coca-Cola, whistle, wood, 1920s, NM, A $40.00

Coca-Cola, yo-yo, Bolo, maroon, 1920s-30s, NM, A $60.00

Coca-Cola, yo-yo, bottle cap form, 1960s, EX $15.00

Coca-Cola, yo-yo, mc inlay, 1920s-30s, NM, A................$40.00

Cocomalt, jigsaw puzzle, Faith, full-color boy & dog, complete in orig envelope, 6½x10", EX, P6 ....$60.00

Continental Trailways, bus, metal, 7", M4 ....$150.00

Cracker Jack, cradle, metal, 1930s-40s, ½x1¼", E1............$3.00

Cracker Jack, cruise ship, metal, 1930s-40s, ½x1½", E1 .....$7.50

Cracker Jack, drawing book, Cracker Jack boy on front cover, 1930s, premium, 2¼x1¼", VG $25.00

Cracker Jack, fortune wheel, litho tin, 1933, VG $60.00

Cracker Jack, frying pan, metal, 1930s-40s, 1¼x¾", E1 ......$4.00

Cracker Jack, Halloween cat, metal, 1930s-40s, 1x¾", E1 ..$7.50

Cracker Jack, Indy racer, metal, 1930s-40s, ¾x1", E1 ....$2.50

Cracker Jack, iron, metal, 1930s-40s, ¾x1¼", E1................$2.50

Cracker Jack, Key to My Heart, metal, 1930s-40s, ¾x1¾", E1..$2.00

Cracker Jack, lg racehorse, metal, 1930s-40s, 1x2", E1 ....$4.00

Cracker Jack, lunch box, EX+, T1.....................................$32.50

Cracker Jack, periscope, MIB $35.00

Cracker Jack, pin, Future Pilot wings, metal, no pin, 1930s-40s, ¾x2", E1 ....$9.00

Cracker Jack, sitting cat charm, metal, 1930s-40s, ¾" sq, E1..$3.50

Cracker Jack, top hat, metal, ½x¾", E1..............................$3.00

Crawford & Sons, biscuit tin, dbl-decker bus, litho passengers in lower deck, top opens for biscuits, 10½", A..........$5,000.00

Crawford's Aeroplane A-One, biscuit tin, gold & blk, w/wheels, movable prop, British flag on wing, orig box, 16", A $3,400.00

Crayola Crayons, necklace, gr crayon on plastic cord, EX ..$4.50

Cream of Wheat, doll, Rastus, printed cotton, lacking his chef's hat, some soil, VG+, P6..$85.00

Crest Toothpaste, lunch box w/thermos, plastic, M, T1...$35.00

Crown Premium Motor Oil, bank, can form, Crown lettered on stylized wing emblem above Premium Motor Oil, 3", EX, A...$18.00

Del Monte, pineapple doll, 1984, 11", $12.00.

Curad Bandages, doll, Curad Kid, 7", M............................$25.00

Dad's Root Beer, teddy bear, 8½", EX $12.50

Del Monte, bank, Big Top Bonanza, clown figure, 1985, 7", H4..$16.00

Del Monte, doll, Pineapple, stuffed cloth, 1983, M $12.00

Del Monte, doll, Reddy Tomato, Country Yumpkins series, red plush w/felt eyes, leaves on head, 1984, 11", M $8.00

Del Monte, doll, Sweet Pea, gr pea-pod form, 1991, M $8.00

Diamond Dyes, paper doll, chomolitho, blond girl w/pk party dress, 5¼", EX..$8.00

Dick Graves Nugget Hotel & Casino, squeeze toy, Nugget Sam, rubber, 1950s, 12", VG+...$35.00

Domino's Pizza, bendee, Donnie or Dotty, M, ea..............$15.00

Domino's Pizza, doll, The Noid, stuffed cloth, 12", EX.....$15.00

Donald Duck Orange Juice, bank, cb w/metal ends, Donald saying 'Start Your Day, Drink OJ...,' 4", NM, A...........$250.00

Dow Bathroom Cleaner, squeeze toy, Scrubbing Bubble, molded vinyl, 1989, 3½", M, minimum value........................$10.00

Dunkin' Donuts, child's tea set, plastic, 1970s, MIB, P6 ..$90.00

Dutch Boy Paints, hand puppet, cloth body w/soft vinyl head, felt hands missing some fingers, 1956, VG+, A $24.00

Dutch Boy Paints, trailer truck, tin, Japan, MIB, D10, $325.00.

Dynamo Detergent, doll, dinosaur, gr w/yel lid from detergent bottle, 1990, 11", M..$15.00

Electrolux, bank, lt bl hard plastic Model G vacuum cleaner, spring action, missing 1 wheel, 1950s, EX..................$25.00

Ellis Foods, truck, tin, friction, 1950s, NM, T1 ....$225.00

Endicott Shoes, whistle, tin..$20.00

Esso, bank, saluting Esso man on rnd base, red plastic w/Esso emb on chest, 6½", EX, A $110.00

Esso, bank, tanker truck, red plastic, Save at Your Esso Dealer, 1950s or 1960s, VG, A $40.00

Esso, bank, tiger figure, vinyl, mk Humble Oil, 1969, EX+, T1 ....$35.00

Esso, coloring book, Happy Motoring, features the oil-drop boys & girls through US landmarks, 24 pgs, 1963, NM, A.$28.00

Esso, toy, tiger, hard plastic, w/up, EX, P6.........................$65.00

Essolube Motor Oil, jigsaw puzzle, Dr Seuss drawing of family driving through forest w/animals, 11x17", EX, F6 ....$100.00

Eveready Batteries, bank, blk cat, hard plastic, 1981, NM.$22.00

Eveready Batteries, jigsaw puzzle, boy in bedroom w/flashlight, 'Is That You, Santa Claus?,' ca 1931, 9x12", EX, F6..$50.00

Eveready Batteries, squeeze-light flashlight, Energizer Bunny, vinyl, 4", MOC, H4 ....$10.00

Fig Newtons, doll, vinyl w/movable arms & head, yel dress, orange apron & shoes, copyright 1983, 4½", VG, A .$42.00

Fischer's Vitamin D Bread, jigsaw puzzle, shows mother serving soup & bread to 4 seated children, 7x9½", EX, F6.....$25.00

Flavor Kist, truck, Tonka, NM (G box), A, $700.00.

Flintstones Vitamins, Flintmobile, car, plastic, rubber-band powered, 3½", MIB, P4 ....$20.00

Flying A Oil Co, bank, Axelrod plastic figure, missing cover, NM................$35.00

Folger's Coffee, jigsaw puzzle, in canister picturing sailing ships, premium, unopened, EX $20.00

Franco American Teddy O's, doll, teddy bear, tan plush, logo on chest, M $15.00

Franklin Finance Company, doll, Doc Dollar w/bag of bills, slot in head may be cut out to make bank, 1950s, 5", NM, A $44.00

Franklin Life, bank, Ben Franklin figure, plastic, 1970s, EX-EX+, T1 ....$15.00

Fruit Roll-Ups, bendee, Rollupo the Wizard, 6", H4 ....$12.00

Fruit Stripe Gum, bendee, Yipe Stripe, M..................$45.00

GE, doll, Mr Magoo, vinyl head on stuffed body, 14", EX+, H4................$99.00

General Electric, jointed wood figure, Bandy, Cameo Doll Co., ca 1920s, 18", EX, D10, $750.00.

GE, kite, Topflite, red, yel & blk graphics on wht paper, Spring Specials on GE Appliances..., 1960s, 32x27", EX......$15.00

General Mills Boo Berry Cereal, doll, vinyl, 8", R3 ....$35.00

General Mills Boo Berry Cereal, pencil sharpener, Boo Berry figure, MOC, H4.........................$6.00

General Mills Cinnamon Toast Crunch Cereal, bank, plastic, musical, 1988, 6", NM.............$10.00

General Mills Count Chocula Cereal, doll, vinyl, 8", R3.$35.00

General Mills Frankenberry Cereal, doll, Frankenberry, soft vinyl, 8", EX.............$35.00

General Mills Frankenberry Cereal, pencil sharpener, Frankenberry figure, MOC, H4..........$6.00

Gerber, doll, Gerber baby, Sun Rubber, sculpted hair, w/bib, 1955, 12"..............$45.00

Gerber, teddy bear, lt tan plush w/logo at neck, 1988, 22", M $25.00

Gibson Refrigerators, jigsaw puzzle, man delivering ice to lady who has purchased a refrigerator, ca 1931, 9x12", EX, F6..............$45.00

Good Humor Ice Cream, truck, Langcraft KTS Japan, friction, 11", EX (EX box), A, $540.00.

Good Humor, slot car, Aurora, the Good Humor truck given away to introduce the new 'Wild Huckleberry' flavor, MIP $50.00

Good Humor, squeeze toy, Good Humor Bar w/bite missing, molded vinyl, 1975, 8", M..................$400.00

Gorton's, squeeze toy, Gorton Fisherman, vinyl, 1975, 7", R3 ....$125.00

Grandma's Cookies, bank, plastic, 7", R3 ....$35.00

Green Giant, doll, Green Giant, vinyl, R3 ....$75.00

Green Giant, doll, Little Sprout, vinyl, 1980s, EX, T1.....$15.00

Green Giant, dolls, Jolly Green Giant & Little Sprout, stuffed cloth, in orig mailer bag, 26", 10", M, H4...........$38.00

Green Giant, Halloween costume, Jolly Green Giant, Kuskan, 1960s, MIB, H4...........$49.00

Green Giant, jump rope, Little Sprout, plastic w/figural hdls, ca 1979, M, P4...........$5.00

Green Giant, kite, in orig mailer envelope, M.................$15.00

Green Giant, puzzle, fr-tray; Jolly Green Giant in cornfield, cb, VG+, T6...........$25.00

Green Giant, puzzle, jigsaw; Jolly Green Giant, 204-pc, 24x36", EX, T6 ....$15.00

Harley-Davidson, doll, Harley Hog, pk plush, blk hat shirt, Harley license tags, M, A3 ....$10.00

Havoline Motor Oil, bank, football form, porc, NM $50.00

Hawaiian Punch, beach raft, yel canvas w/wht roping, colorful image of Punchy, Let's Get Together..., 1970s, 34x19", EX $15.00

Hawaiian Punch, board game, MIB, H4 ....$20.00

Heinz, charm bracelet, silvered brass links hold 5 product charms including gr pickle, 1940s or earlier, EX, A...$47.00

Heinz, jigsaw puzzle, children playing store w/all Heinz 57 Varieties displayed on shelves, 10x12", EX, F6 ....$35.00

Heinz Ketchup, bendee, Heinz Ketchup Ant, M, H4 ....$10.00

Heinz Ketchup, truck, Mini Toy, Canadian, 22", VG-, M5, $300.00.

Hershey's, wristwatch, Jordache, 1980s, MIB, T1 ....$25.00

Hershey's Kisses, doll, Kiss form, plush w/embroidered face, 8", EX $8.00

Hershey's Syrup, bank, can shape, pottery, silver & brn pnt, P6 ....$35.00

Homart, kaleidoscope, 1964, EX, T1 ....$15.00

Hood's Sarsaparilla, jigsaw puzzle, horse-drawn buggy carrying doctor away from lab & factory, cb, 10x15", VG, A..$95.00

Howard Johnson's Restaurant, bank, plastic, P6 ....$25.00

Humble Oil & Refining Co, bank, tiger form, hard orange vinyl w/wht & brn accents, 5½", EX, A $28.00

Hurd Shoes, whistle, metal rectangular form w/advertising, They're Tops above rnd logo, For Boys & Girls, EX, A $20.00

Hush Puppies Shoes, bank, basset hound, pnt hard vinyl, 7¼", EX $25.00

Icee Developers Inc, bank, Icee Bear holding lg Icee, molded vinyl, 8", M $25.00

Insti-Print Wizard, figure, plastic, 7", R3 ....$150.00

Jack Frost Sugar Co, doll, Jack Frost, stuffed cloth, bl & wht w/yel hair, 17", EX $35.00

Jell-O, puppet, Mr Wiggle, soft vinyl, comes w/2 sample boxes, scarce, 6", EX, A $360.00

Jewel Coffee, jigsaw puzzle, breakfast scene plus manufacturing process of coffee, 9½x12½", EX, F6 ....$35.00

Jif Peanut Butter, Jifaroo Kite, yel paper, 1959, 27x19", NM, A $30.00

John P Squire & Co, Boston, jigsaw puzzle, drawing of pig w/different cuts of meat, 1899, 11x7", EX, F6.................$150.00

Joy Ice Cream Cone, doll, girl in denim pants & red stockinette w/logo, yel yarn hair w/ponytails, 1989, 12", EX........$12.00

Karo Syrup, doll, Karo Princess, pnt compo, body is ear of corn covered by gr husks, rare, 1930s, 10½", VG, A $1,152.00

Keebler, squeeze toy, Keebler Elf, rubber, 7", NM, M5 .....$20.00

Kellogg's, cutout on canvas, Krinkle the Cat, lt fold mks, 1935, NM, M5 ....$45.00

Kellogg's, jigsaw puzzle, boy on skooter, 1933, G $45.00

Kellogg's, doll, Alligator, 10½", $40.00.

Kellogg's, pillow doll, Bingo (from Banana Splits), 1969, 14", EX $60.00

Kellogg's Corn Flakes, Mini 110 Camera, Canadian issue, working, 1990, MIB, F1 ....$5.00

Kellogg's Frosted Flakes, bank, Tony the Tiger figure, EX .$60.00

Kellogg's Frosted Flakes, bicycle horn, Tony the Tiger graphics, MIB..$45.00

Kellogg's Frosted Flakes, bowl & spoon, Tony the Tiger graphics & USA Olympic logos, 1992, NM, P3 ....$9.00

Kellogg's Frosted Flakes, doll, Tony the Tiger, plush, 1970s, 16", EX, T1 ....$25.00

Kellogg's Frosted Flakes, doll, Tony the Tiger, printed cloth, 14", M..$20.00

Kellogg's Frosted Flakes, frisbee, Tony the Tiger Flyer, late 1980s, 3¾" dia, NM, T6..$3.00

Kellogg's Frosted Flakes, game, Astronaut Breakfast, Tony the Tiger graphics, complete, H4 ....$12.00

Kellogg's Fruit Loops, doll, Toucan Sam, 1964, 8½", EX..$20.00

Kellogg's Fruit Loops, push-button puppet, Toucan Sam, 1984, 4", M..$15.00

Kellogg's OKs Cereal, game, Huckleberry Hound Flip Face, from bk of cereal box, 1960, EX+ $18.00

Kellogg's Pop Tarts, bank, Milton the Toaster, plastic, 1980, 5", M $55.00

Kellogg's Rice Krispies, bath toy, Snap! seated in rowboat, Talbot Toys, vinyl, M (EX box), A $35.00

Kellogg's Rice Krispies, canteen, Snap!, Crackle! & Pop! graphics, w/assembly instructions, 4½" dia, H4.................$5.00

Kellogg's Rice Krispies, coloring book, 50 Years With Snap!, Crackle! & Pop!, unused, 1978, 11x8", M.................$25.00

Kellogg's Rice Krispies, doll, Snap!, cloth, w/orig illus mailer, 1950s, M, V1 ....$40.00

Kellogg's Rice Krispies, doll, Snap!, plastic w/jtd arms & legs, red hair, 1984, 4½", MIP $15.00

Kellogg's Rice Krispies, push-button puppet, Crackle! on red base, plastic, 1984, 4", MIP, H4 ....$18.00

Kellogg's Rice Krispies, squeeze toy, Crackle!, vinyl, 1975, 8", EX..$20.00

Kelly Nylon Tires, child's cup & saucer, tire graphic on cup, china, EX..$50.00

Kool-Aid, child's cup, Freckleface Stawberry, 1960s, EX+..$10.00

Kool-Aid, doll, Kool-Aid Kid, 9", NRFB, H4 ....$12.00

Kool-Aid, 'Jetsons the Movie' theater giveaway, spaceship w/Judy, Elroy & Astro figures inside, plastic & vinyl, H4 ....$8.00

Kool-Aid, mechanical bank, red Kool-Aid pitcher on yel base, plastic, 1970s, M $25.00

Kraft, bendee, Cheesosaurus, H4 ....$7.00

Kraft Cheese & Macaroni, wristwatch, Kraft/Regis Marketing, Cheese & Macaroni Club promo, yel & bl band, MIP, P4 ....$15.00

Kraft Theater, Camera Man sitting on camera stand running camera mk w/letter K, 1960s, H4 ....$95.00

Land O' Lakes Butter, bank, wood, G $25.00

Lennox Furnace Co, bank, Lennie Lennox w/hand to ear, ceramic, 1949, 7½", NM $150.00

Lerner Newspaper, doll, Newsdog, cloth, EX $15.00

Life Savers, truck, Marx, red plastic cab w/10 packs of orig Life Savers on gr & yel cargo bed, 1950s, 9", NMIB, A $215.00

Lime-Away, doll, kitten, wht plush, 1990, 10", M............$10.00

Little Debbie Snack Cakes, doll, Little Debbie, porc, MIB ..$40.00

Lucas Paints & Varnishes, jigsaw puzzle, giant painter holding house & paint can kneeling among homes, 5½x7", EX, F6 ....$85.00

McKesson's Pharmaceutical Products, jigsaw puzzle, druggists, Quality for Over 100 Years, 1933, 14x11", EX..........$30.00

Meyer Milk, bottle topper, paper, Mickey Mouse offering membership in MM Globe-Trotters Club, 1938, 8x11", EX+, A $183.00

Michelin, playing cards, reproduction of early Montaut racing scene, MIB (sealed) $15.00

Miller High Life, puzzle, in unopened canister, 5", $8.00.

Mohawk Carpet, doll, Tomy, cloth, 16", EX....................$20.00

Mount Penn Stoves, Heaters & Ranges, toy skillet, CI, interior emb Mount Penn...Reading PA, 2½" dia, EX............$24.00

Mountain Dew, doll, Hillbilly, vinyl head, hands & feet w/cloth body, 24", rare, NM $195.00

Mr Bubble, bank, pk plastic Mr Bubble w/bl lettering, 9½", M $75.00

Mr. Bubble & Super Friends Bubble Bath, super heroes on front, MIB (sealed), $40.00.

Mayflower, moving van, Linemar, tin, MIB, D10, $350.00.

Mr Goodbar, wristwatch, Jordache, 1980s, MIB, T1 ....$25.00
Munsingwear, doll, penguin, vinyl, ca 1970, 7", EX $18.00
Nabisco, Honey Bee figure, plastic, 1960s, 2", EX $25.00

Nabisco Junior Mints, cloth doll, Fonz of Happy Days, Paramount Pictures, 1976, 16", NM, $32.00.

Nabisco Pretzels, doll, Mr Salty, stuffed cloth, 11", EX $10.00
Nabisco Shredded Wheat Juniors Cereal, bead-in-the-hole skill
    game, Rin Tin Tin graphics, 1950s, M......................$12.00
Nestle Crunch, bendee, Multi-Products, 1967, 7", R3 ...$150.00
Nestle Quik, booklet, Magic Tricks, premium, 1978, NM,
    P3..$5.00
Nestle Quik Chocolate Syrup, bendee, Nestle bunny, 6",
    H4 ....$12.00
Nestle's Swiss Chocolate, doll, Swiss man in original outfit w/red
    rooted-hair mustache, vinyl, 1969, 13", H4..............$69.00
New Idea Farm Equipment Co, jigsaw puzzle, farm scene
    w/machinery, 7½x16", EX, F6 ....$35.00
Northern Bath Tissue, doll, plush & vinyl, 1986, M $42.00

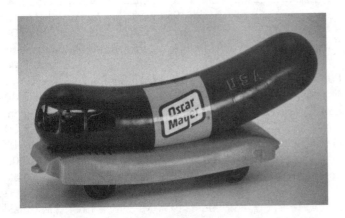

Oscar Mayer, bank, Weinermobile w/USA Olympic logo, plastic, 9¾" long, NM, $15.00.

Oreo Cookies, doll, vinyl w/movable head & arms holding
    Oreo cookie, pk dress & Oreo hat, copyright 1983, 4½",
    VG, A $56.00
Oreo Cookies, frisbee, blk soft plastic, no date, NM, T6 ..$14.00
Orkin Exterminating Co, bank, Otto the Orkin Man standing
    on gr base, papier-mache, 1960s, 8", EX $400.00
Oscar Mayer, bank, Weinermobile w/USA Olympic logo, plas-
    tic, 9¾", NM..$15.00
Oscar Mayer, coloring book, Little Oscar & the Bandit, 1 pg col-
    ored, 1962, EX+ $20.00
Oscar Mayer, Weinermobile, Little Oscar rises & falls when
    pushed or pulled, plastic, 1950s, 10", VG $173.00
Oscar Mayer, Weinermobile, 1/25 scale, plastic, 1990, H2 ..$16.00
Oscar Mayer, whistle, red plastic weiner shape w/red & yel band,
    1950s, 2", EX, A..$13.00
Oven-Kist Biscuits, truck, very early van w/advertising on side
    panels, 4x7½", G, M5..$300.00
Pan-Am Gasoline & Motor Oils, jigsaw puzzle, children
    pumping gas into auto & motor boat, 1933, 10x13½", EX,
    F6..$45.00
Panadol, figure, Panadol Bear, plastic, 2", R3 ....$10.00
Pappy Porker, figure, bl or brn, 5", R3, ea $20.00
Pau Cola, jigsaw puzzle, boy dispensing drink to mother & child,
    ca 1890, 6x8", EX, F6..$60.00

Pennzoil, 1955 Ford stretch panel truck, custom made, M, A, $225.00.

Pepsi-Cola, bank, compo cooler form w/Pepsi-Cola Ice Cold
    Sold Here, 3¾x3", G, A $55.00
Pepsi-Cola, bank, gull-wing cooler w/Pepsi-Cola logo, 1940s, NM,
    A..$240.00
Pepsi-Cola, checkers game, wood, Pepsi & Mountain Dew cans
    on checkerboard, 1970s, 14x14", NMIB, A.............$100.00

Pepsi-Cola, dispenser bank, Linemar, lithographed and painted tin, battery operated, original box, 9¾", VG, A, $400.00.

Pepsi-Cola, doll, elf, plush w/yel felt hat, gr shirt & red pants, logo on blk plastic belt, 20", NM $35.00

Pepsi-Cola, hot dog wagon, Cass Toys, wood & metal pull type w/bear, striped umbrella, 1945, EX, A $525.00

Pepsi-Cola, hot dog wagon, Ideal, plastic w/detachable man & umbrella, bottle logo on sides of wagon, 1940s, NMIB, A $925.00

Pepsi-Cola, ice cream shop, in orig box mk My Merry Ice Cream Shop, unused, VG, 6x7", M5.....................................$21.00

Pepsi-Cola, toy soda-fountain dispenser, wht plastic w/slanted bottle cap & Pepsi-Cola in print, 1950s, NMIB, A ..$100.00

Pepsi-Cola, truck, Canada, yel metal w/open cargo bed holding 2 cb 6-pack cartons, scarce, 8x18", EX+, M5.............$500.00

Pepsi-Cola, truck, Japan, plastic & tin, red w/Fresh Drink bottle & rnd logo on enclosed cargo bed, 1960s, 4", NM, A $80.00

Pepsi-Cola, truck, Marx, wht plastic, open bed holds cases w/early script logo, bottle caps on doors, 1950s-60s, NMIB, A $550.00

Pepsi-Cola, truck, metal, 2-tone cab & divided cargo bed, bottle cap logo on ea end, 6", NM, A...............................$500.00

Pepsi-Cola, truck, Ny-lint, heavy tin, various logos in divided open cargo bays, enclosed top & bk, 1958, 16", VG, A..$100.00

Pepsi-Cola, truck, Ny-lint, pressed steel, MIB, A, $325.00.

Pepsi-Cola, upright 5¢ vending machine, Marx, plastic, emb Drink Ice Cold w/oval Pepsi-Cola logo, 1945, 7", EX+, A...$110.00

Pepsi-Cola, van, Buddy L, composition, long-nose w/Railway Express & Pepsi-Cola decals, 1930s-40s, 16", VG, A $1,450.00

Pepsi-Cola, van, tin, 3-color, bottle & rnd logo on flat roof, Pepsi-Cola on all sides, friction, 1950s, 4", EX+, A.$210.00

Pepto-Bismol, bank, 24-Hour Bug, molded vinyl, 1970s, 7", EX, H4 ....$70.00

Peter Pan Peanut Butter, coloring book, unused..............$15.00

Philco Lazy-X Radio, jigsaw puzzle, woman sitting in chair w/dog at feet listening to the radio, 10x13", EX, F6.............$35.00

Phillips 66, bank, emb glass block, Phill Up w/Phillips 66, See What You Can Save, 1940s-50s, 5x5", EX+, A $75.00

Pillsbury, bank, Poppin' Fresh, ceramic, 1987, 7½", MIB .$25.00

Pillsbury, doll, Cupcake the Dough Bear, stuffed, orig box shows minor wear, H4 ....$70.00

Pillsbury, doll, Poppie Fresh, vinyl w/jtd head, 1972, 6", EX .$15.00

Pillsbury, doll, Poppin' Fresh, soft vinyl w/jtd head, 7", EX..$8.00

Pillsbury, doll, Poppin' Fresh, stuffed cloth, 1970s, 14½", VG..$9.00

Pillsbury, finger puppet, Poppie Fresh, vinyl, 3½", EX......$15.00

Pillsbury, playhouse, tall-peaked vinyl house containing Bun Bun, Popper, Poppie & Poppin' Fresh, 1974, 14x11x3", VG, A $232.00

Pillsbury Funny Face, ramp walker, Coo Coo Cherry, Goofy Grape, etc, plastic, 3", M, ea, from $35 to..................$55.00

Pizza Hut, bank, Pizza Hut man, 7", EX, J2 ....$20.00

Planters, belt buckle, Mr Peanut & guns motif, tan plastic, child sz, EX...$45.00

Planters, bendee, Mr Peanut, H4.......................................$10.00

Planters, charm bracelet, 1938 World's Fair, NM, V1 ......$40.00

Planters, coloring book, Book No 3, Around the World w/Mr Peanut, 7x10", EX, M5 ....$14.00

Planters, doll, Mr Peanut, cloth, EX................................$15.00

Planters, doll, Mr Peanut, New York World's Fair, jtd strung wood, bl top hat, 1939-40, 8½", NM, P4 ....$375.00

Planters, doll, Mr Peanut, plush, 26", MIP, H4................$26.00

Planters, figural dispenser/bank, red Bakelite base, 1940s, EX+, T1 ....$165.00

Planters, marbles, shows Mr Peanut on 3x5" header card, 25 marbles, 1950s-60s, MIP.....................................$20.00

Planters, mechanical pencil, Mr Peanut, MIP, S1 ....$15.00

Planters, pop gun, paper, shows Mr Peanut in oval grip, Bang! for Planters Peanuts, rare, 5x8¾", VG, A $200.00

Planters, ramp walker, Mr Peanut, plastic, 1984, 3", M $30.00

Planters, toy, Mr Peanut driving peanut car, plastic, 2½x2x5", EX, A $500.00

Planters, train set, battery-op, 1970s, NMIB, T1 ....$125.00

Poll Parrot Shoes, whistle $20.00

Popsicle, boot ring, red & wht plastic boot shape w/compass & magnifying glass, 1951, EX $95.00

Post Bran Cereal, doll, Cali Quail, cloth, colorful logo on bk, 1986, 6", M $10.00

Post Cereals, car, F&F Mold, 1950 Ford, 4-door, orange, NM+, B2 ....$80.00

Post Cereals, car, F&F Mold, 1954 Ford Club Coupe, Sierra Brn, NM+, B2 ....$35.00

Post Cereals, car, F&F Mold, 1954 Ford Ranch Wagon, Sierra Brn, NM+, B2 ....$35.00

Post Cereals, car, F&F Mold, 1954 Ford Sunliner, Cameo Coral, NM+, B2 ....$50.00

Post Cereals, car, F&F Mold, 1954 Ford Thunderbird, Goldenrod Yel, NM+, B2 ....$75.00

Post Cereals, car, F&F Mold, 1954 Mercury convertible, Goldenrod Yel, NM+, B2 ....$150.00

Post Cereals, car, F&F Mold, 1954 Mercury XM/800, Bloomfield Gr, posts rpr, B2 ....$20.00

Post Cereals, car, F&F Mold, 1954 Mercury 4-Door, Bloomfield Gr, NM+, B2 ....$50.00

Post Cereals, car, F&F Mold, 1955 Ford Country Sedan, Goldenrod Yel, NM, B2 ....$5.00

Post Cereals, car, F&F Mold, 1955 Ford Crown Victoria, Aquatone Bl, faded, NM, B2..$12.00

Post Cereals, car, F&F Mold, 1955 Ford Thunderbird, Sea Sprite Gr, NM, B2..$8.00

Post Cereals, car, F&F Mold, 1955 Ford Tudor Customline, Aquatone Bl, NM+, B2..$10.00

Post Cereals, car, F&F Mold, 1955 Ford Tudor Customline, Torch Red, NM, B2..$5.00

Post Cereals, car, F&F Mold, 1957 Ford Country Sedan ambulance, NM+, B2..$10.00

Post Cereals, car, F&F Mold, 1957 Ford Custom 300 fire chief car, NM, B2..$10.00

Post Cereals, car, F&F Mold, 1957 Ford Custom 4-Door highway patrol car, Dresden Bl, NM, B2..$10.00

Post Cereals, car, F&F Mold, 1957 Ford Sunliner, Flame Red, single molding, extremely rare, NM, B2..$45.00

Post Cereals, car, F&F Mold, 1957 Ford Sunliner, Silver Mocha, extremely rare, NM+, B2..$75.00

Post Cereals, car, F&F Mold, 1959 Ford Thunderbird convertible, Cordovan, NM+, B2..$12.00

Post Cereals, car, F&F Mold, 1959 Ford Thunderbird hardtop, Flamingo, NM, B2..$10.00

Post Cereals, car, F&F Mold, 1960 Plymouth Fury convertible, Sky Bl, NM, B2..$7.00

Post Cereals, car, F&F Mold, 1960 Plymouth Fury sport coupe, Chrome Gr, NM, B2..$13.00

Post Cereals, car, F&F Mold, 1960 Plymouth Suburban, Twilight Bl, NM, B2..$10.00

Post Cereals, car, F&F Mold, 1961 Ford Thunderbird, convertible Starlight Bl, NM+, B2..$12.00

Post Cereals, car, F&F Mold, 1961 Ford Thunderbird convertible, Monte Carlo Red, NM, B2..$8.00

Post Cereals, car, F&F Mold, 1961 Ford Thunderbird hardtop, Monte Carlo Red, NM, B2..$7.00

Post Cereals, car, F&F Mold, 1961 Ford Thunderbird Sports roadster, Mint Gr, NM, B2..$10.00

Post Cereals, car, F&F Mold, 1961 Thunderbird Sports roadster, Starlight Bl, NM+, B2..$15.00

Post Cereals, car, F&F Mold, 1966 Ford Mustang convertible, Signal-Flare Red, NM, B2..$7.00

Post Cereals, car, F&F Mold, 1966 Ford Mustang hardtop, Arcadian Bl, NM, B2..$6.00

Post Cereals, car, F&F Mold, 1966 Ford Mustang hardtop, Springtime Yel, NM, B2..$5.00

Post Cereals, car, F&F Mold, 1966 Ford Mustang 2+2 GT, Signal-Flare Red, NM, B2..$10.00

Post Cereals, car, F&F Mold, 1966 Ford Mustang 2+2 GT, Springtime Yel, NM+, B2..$12.00

Post Cereals, car, F&F Mold, 1967 Mercury Cougar, Fawn, NM+, B2..$10.00

Post Cereals, car, F&F Mold, 1967 Mercury Cougar, Jamaican Yel, NM+, B2..$8.00

Post Cereals, car, F&F Mold, 1967 Mercury Cougar, Tiffany Bl, extremely rare, NM+, B2..$10.00

Post Cereals, car, F&F Mold, 1969 Mercury Cougar, yel or med bl, NM, B2..$10.00

Post Cereals, car, F&F Mold, 1969 Mercury Marquis, red, NM, B2..$9.00

Post Cereals, car, F&F Mold, 1969 Mercury Maurader, med bl or med lime, NM, B2..$10.00

Post Cereals, truck, F&F Mold, 1956 Ford furniture van, orange, NM, B2..$15.00

Post Cereals, truck, F&F Mold, 1956 Ford gasoline transport, yel, NM, B2..$15.00

Post Cereals, truck, F&F Mold, 1956 Ford volume van, orange, wht tires, NM, B2..$18.00

Post Crispy Critters Cereal, Colorforms set, Linus the Lion-hearted, circus theme, scarce, NM..$45.00

Post Sugar Crisp Cereal, bowl, yel plastic w/emb Indians, M, P6..$35.00

Post Wheat Puffs Cereal, doll, Sugar Bear, stuffed cloth, MIB..$30.00

Purina, doll, scarecrow, cloth body w/vinyl head, 1972, NM..$25.00

Putnam Dyes, jigsaw puzzle, General Putnam on horse waving to cavalry, inscribed Norman E Bohn..., 5½x6½", EX, F6..$85.00

Quaker Muffets Cereal, puzzle, steel canister w/plastic lid, place balls in holes on clowns, premium, EX..$14.00

Quaker Oats, doll, Quaker man, stuffed cloth, 1965, 10", scarce, NM, A..$60.00

Quaker Oats, jigsaw puzzle, Quaker man feeding little girl, 5x6½", EX, F6..$45.00

Quaker Oats, pencil sharpener ring, radio premium, 1930s, VG+, T1..$20.00

Quisp, comic, Kite Tale, VG+..$55.00

Raid, bug figure, w/up, working, rare, EX+..$195.00

Raid, remote control bug, works, 1 of 3000 made, very rare, NM, H4..$750.00

Ralston Purina, Space Patrol Space-O-Phones, bl & yel plastic w/Space Patrol in raised letters, NM (VG+ mailer), A..$129.00

RCA Radiotrons, Cameo Doll Co, jtd wood, pnt, RCA logos, 16", VG+, A..$250.00

RCA, Radiotrons Man, jointed wood, Cameo Doll Co., 1920s, 16", M, D10, $1,500.00.

Realemon, lemon figure w/arms & legs, PVC, H4 ....$8.00

Red Goose Shoes, bank, Red Goose on red base w/emb lettering, plastic, 1960s, 5", M..........................$15.00

Reddy Kilowatt, bank, Reddy against background of bl & wht clouds, plastic, rare, 1960s, 5x6½", VG, A $1,605.00

Revlon, doll, Little Miss Revlon, 1950, 10", EX $30.00

Richfield Gasoline, early truck, American National, blk pnt sheet metal w/yel & red lettering, front crank, 27", VG, A $1,400.00

Ritz, charm, brass-plated replica of Ritz box, 1970s or early '80s, 2", EX, A $12.00

Ritz, wristwatch, Olympic quartz, Ritz logo in center, rnd chrome case, chrome & gold-tone link band w/clasp, EX, M5 ....$34.00

Rival Dog Food, bank, tin, VG.................................$14.00

Rold Gold Butter Pretzels, jigsaw puzzle, boy & girl playing w/toys on floor & eating pretzels, 1931, 8x10", EX, F6...$85.00

Rusco Brake Lining, jigsaw puzzle, couple hanging from tree after auto stops at edge of cliff, 1933, 8½x11", EX, F6.........$40.00

Salamander Children's Shoes, squeeze toy, Lurchi the Salamander, vinyl, 1980s, Germany, 4½", M.........................$25.00

Scott's Emulsion, booklet, colorful alphabet, poetry & quaint views of children, 16 pgs, 4x6", EX $15.00

Scuffy's Shoe Polish, ring, plastic, mk Truth Virtue, unused, NM (EX box), A $180.00

Sea Host, Ossie Oyster push-button puppet, Made in Hong Kong, 1969, 4¾", M, $30.00.

Sea Host, push-button puppet, Mr Bid the Shrimp, missing 1 set of arms on 1 side, 1969, 3", H4.................................$19.00

Sea Host, push-button puppet, Ossie Oyster, plastic, 1969, 4½", EX+ $22.00

Sealtest Ice Cream, hand puppet, Mr Cool, walrus head, 1962, EX $48.00

Sears, Roebuck & Co, semi-truck, Linemar, tin, mk Hauler & Van Trailer on box, friction, 12½", NM (EX box), A $175.00

Shell, tanker truck, Tootsietoy, pressed steel w/emb logos flanking shell image, 1¾x6", EX, T1 ....$75.00

Sinclair, Dino, inflatable vinyl, 1960s, 12", M.................$20.00

Sinclair, figure, Dinoland tyrannosaurus, red wax, NM $42.00

Sinclair, soap, Dino figure, 1950s, MIB, T1 ....$18.50

Singer Sewing Machine, jigsaw puzzle, Indians in front of tepee using treadle machine, 7x10", EX, F6......................$35.00

Sirloin Stockade, bank, ceramic cow, NM, T1 ....$25.00

Sony, squeeze toy, Sony boy, soft vinyl, 1965, 8", R3 .....$300.00

South Bend Watch Co, jigsaw puzzle, drawing of inside workings of lg pocket watch, 1911, 7½x9½", EX, F6 ....$100.00

Spaghetti-O's, figure, Wizard of O's, R3.......................$20.00

Sprite, talking doll, Lymon, molded vinyl, battery-op, 1988, MIB, T1 ....$15.00

Square Deal Bread, badge, Safety Club, silvered brass, 1930s, EX $9.00

Starkist Tuna, bank, Charlie Tuna surrounded by stacks of coins on tuna-can base, ceramic, 1988, 9½", M $20.00

Starkist Tuna, doll, Charlie Tuna, M, D4.......................$15.00

Starkist Tuna, squeeze toy, Charlie Tuna, soft vinyl, 1973, 8", MIB, H4 ....$80.00

Sugar Crisp Cereal, yo-yo, cereal premium, MIP $3.50

Sun Maid, California Raisin Fun Kit, orig mailer, M........$85.00

Sunbeam Bread, doll, Miss Sunbeam, Eegee, plastic body w/vinyl head, dimples, eyes moves, 1968, 17", VG, P4...........$35.00

Sunoco, bank, gas pump, tin, bl, yel & red w/Blue Sunoco logo bottom center, lift-off top, 1950s-60s, 4", EX, A $35.00

Sunshine Biscuit, card set, Space Game, 1950s, V1.........$20.00

Tab Soda, miniature tool set, 10 pcs come in simulated Tab can, M (VG+ box) $35.00

Tagamet, bendee, pk, 1980s, EX, T1 ....$25.00

Tang, figure, Tang Lips, PVC, 1980s, 3", M.........................$2.00

Tastee-Freez, bendee, Oreo Cookie Man, 1988, 4½", NM..$60.00

Tastee-Freez, hand puppets, set of 5: TC Chicken, Tasty Dog, Bear of a Burger, Frenchy Fry, Little T, complete, rare, EX $125.00

Texaco, race car, plastic, friction, 1970s, EX, T1 ....$5.00

Texaco, toy, Service Station, steel and plastic, MIB (sealed), $550.00.

Texaco Fire Chief, fireman's helmet, red hard plastic, 1960s, NM...$68.50

Texaco, ventriloquist doll, painted composition hands and head, green uniform, 25", G, A, $100.00.

Westinghouse, doll, Cozy Glow Kid, nude boy holding towel, 12½", EX, A $35.00

Winnipeg Supply, tanker truck, Mini Toy, scarce, 24", VG, M5, $350.00.

Wonder Bread, bank, loaf of bread, miniature, G **$35.00**
Wonder Bread, miniature loaf, foam w/removable wrapper, 1970s, M **$18.00**
Wrigley's Doublemint Gum, wristwatch, gr vinyl, digital, 1980s, MOC **$15.00**
Wrigley's Hubba-Bubba Bubble Gum, wristwatch, bl vinyl, digital, 1980, MOC...**$15.00**
7-Up, squeeze toy, Fresh-Up Freddie w/bottle of 7-Up, molded vinyl, 1959, 9", NM.......................................**$200.00**

Aeronautical

Toy manufacturers seemed to take the cautious approach toward testing the waters with aeronautical toys, and it was well into the second decade of the 20th century before some of the European toy makers took the initiative. The earlier models were bulky and basically inert, but by the fifties, Japanese manufacturers were turning out battery-operated replicas with wonderful details that advanced with whirring motors and flashing lights. Because of our format, you'll find more airplanes in other sections of our book. See also Battery Operated; Cast Iron, Airplanes; Windups, Friction and Other Mechanicals; Model Kits; and other specific categories.

Air France Travel Jetliner, display model, 1970s, T1 .....**$325.00**
Airplane, Mecanno, w/pilot, single engine & wing, 20" wingspan, VG+, M5 ....**$225.00**
Akron Zeppelin, Steelcraft, silver, scratches, rpr, 25", G, A .**$130.00**
B-58 Hustler, Bachmann, #8365, 1/260 scale, VG, P4 .....**$12.00**
Blimp, on wheels, tin w/silver pnt, 8", G, A **$100.00**
Bomber Plane, Renwal #777, plastic, wing decals, props spin, 7x9", in combat-illus box, 1950s, NM (EX box), A...**$125.00**
C-119 Flying Boxcar, Bachmann #8345, 1/280 scale, clamshell doors open, VG, P4...**$15.00**
Coastguard Sea Plane, Ohio Art, MIB........................**$120.00**
DC-10 McDonnell-Douglas Desk Promotional Model, 1980s, T1 ....**$125.00**

Thermo Anti-Freeze, bank, can shape w/snowman graphics above product name lettered on band, EX, A **$14.00**
Timkin Oil Burner, jigsaw puzzle, comic-book format showing people complaining about existing furnace..., 9x9", EX, F6 ....**$35.00**
Tommy Tipee Cup, squeeze toy, Teddy bear, 5", R3 ....**$30.00**
Tootsie Roll, bank, early 1980s, 7x7½" dia, NM, T6..........**$9.00**
Torrito Coyote, figure, hard plastic & vinyl, 5", R3..........**$15.00**
Toys R Us, doll, Geoffry (giraffe), plush, yel floppy legs & lg feet & shoes, store logo, 1986, 20", M..............................**$20.00**
Travel Lodge, doll, Sleepy Bear, vinyl, M **$40.00**
Trix Cereal, figure, Trix rabbit, vinyl, 10", EX, H4 ....**$29.00**
Trop-Artic All-Weather Motor Oil, bank, can form, shield logo, EX, A **$12.00**
United Airlines, color-&-send cards from Disneyland to Hawaii, M4 ....**$4.00**
United Airlines, Stick-A-State playbook, 8x11", M4.........**$7.00**
Veedol Heavy Duty Plus Motor Oil, bank, can shape w/winged-V logo, EX, A...**$10.00**
Vicolized Gasoline, jigsaw puzzle, man & woman in roadster driving through countryside, 1931, 10x13½", EX, F6........**$50.00**
Victor Talking Machine Co, jigsaw puzzle, record shape w/pictures & names of recording stars, 1908, 8¼" dia, EX, F6 ....**$90.00**
Victrola, jigsaw puzzle, couple listening to Victrola w/miniature musicians & singers about, 1922, 8x9", EX, F6 ....**$75.00**
Vlasic, beach ball, rebate premium, orig mailer, late 1980s, MIP, T6 ....**$7.00**
Wanamaker Stores, bank, 2-story Swiss chalet, litho tin, stairway leads to 2nd floor, coin slot on roof, 3¼", NM, A.....**$300.00**
Westinghouse, bank, pig standing wearing hat, bl plastic, 5", EX, H4 ....**$5.00**

Dual Cockpit Airplane, Steelcraft, pressed steel, rpt, 21" wingspan, EX, A $495.00

Emery Air Freight Jet, 8½x7", complete w/stand, MIB $15.00

Empire Express Monoplane, mk USA, silver w/red wing (removable), #550 on tail, ltweight tin, 20x18" wingspread, pnt P, A $90.00

F-104 Starfighter, Bachmann, #8304:69, 1/210 scale, NMIB, P4...$10.00

F-7U Cutlass, Pyro Plastics, 1960s, T1 ....$10.00

Fighter Plane, Renwal, plastic, single prop w/machine guns on decaled wings, orig box mk #47, 1950s, NM (EX box), A..$94.00

German ME-109, Pactra Aero-Flex Stunt Plane, styrofoam w/nose weight, 1960, about 8", MOC (shrink-wrapped), P4...$5.00

Good Year Zeppelin, pnt pressed steel, silver w/stenciled letters, rpt, scratches, 29½", G, A $130.00

Graf Zeppelin, Boycraft, pnt steel w/silver finish, metal wheels, 1931, 25", P, A $275.00

Gyroplane, Wells, England, litho tin, silver, gyroscope balanced & powered, 11", EX (VG box), A.........................$250.00

Junkers JU-88, Bachmann, #8327:69, 1/170 scale, NMIB, P4...$10.00

Kranich Airplane #310, litho tin w/up, 14" wingspan, MIB..$140.00

Messerschmitt ME-109, Bachmann, #8002:59, 1/160 scale, MIB, P4..$25.00

Monoplane, Boycraft, painted pressed steel, gray with red wheels and tail, 22½", VG-, A, $200.00.

Monoplane, pnt pressed steel, blk body, orange wings, wood wheels, scratches, 12", G, A $95.00

Navy Fighter Bomber Squadron Set, Hubley #53, 5 foldable-wing aircraft, NM (VG+ box), A...........................$450.00

P-38 Fighter, Hubley #881, diecast metal, manual spinning prop, wheels come down as landing gear, 9x12", NM (EX box), A..$270.00

P-38 Lightning Fighter Plane, Renwal, plastic, mk Lockheed, manually spinning props, 1950s, 5x7", NM (G+ box), A...$90.00

P-40 Flying Tiger, Bachmann, #8001:59, 1/160 scale, MIB, P4...$20.00

P-40 Flying Tiger, Pactra Aero-Flex Stunt Plane, styrofoam w/nose weight, 1960, MOC (shrink-wrapped), P4.......$5.00

PAA China Clipper, Wyandotte, metal props, wood wheels, 13", NM, A $360.00

Pan Am Airliner, painted pressed steel with decals, silver, 4-engine, separate stair platform, 21½", EX, A, $250.00.

Pan Am Airliner, pnt pressed steel w/decals, silver, 4 engines, separate stair platform, 21½", EX, A $250.00

Passenger Biplane, litho tin, orange w/gray tin wheels & lg pnt rudder, free-spinning prop, w/up, working, 10", VG, A....$300.00

Pathfinder Trimotor Airplane, Katz, USA, litho tin (or ltweight steel), yel & red, props rotate, 17½", VG, A $715.00

Seaplane, Mecanno, w/pilot, dbl-winged, 20" wingspan, VG+, M5 ....$300.00

Sikorsky HH-3E Jolly Green Giant, Bachmann, #8338:69, 1/260 scale, VG, P4...$8.00

Sopwith Camel, Bachmann, #8320:69, 1/90 scale, olive drab, VG (worn box), P4...$8.00

Stuka JU-87 G, Bachmann, #8331:69, 1/160 scale, NMIB, P4 ....$20.00

Trimotor Airplane, American, Kingsbury, pressed steel w/up mechanism, gold pnt, 15" wingspan, G, A...............$220.00

Turn-Over Zeppelin, European, various materials, gravity operated, 8½" L, G+, A...$143.00

US Mail Plane, Steelcraft, pnt pressed steel, orange & blk, rubber tires, belt & pulley-driven props, working, 23", G, A...$600.00

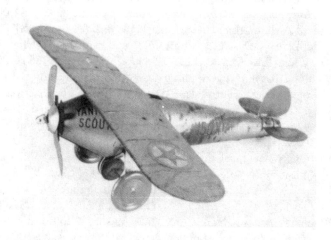

Yankee Scout Airplane, Ideal, removable 19½" wing, all in gold, replaced vertical stabilizer, G-, $200.00.

Wright Plane #20, tin, bl w/yel wings, red/yel tail, balloon tires, metal wheels (1 rpl), 7½x29", 27" wingspan, G, A....**$400.00**

Zeppelin, American, Little Giant, pressed steel, moving wheels activate props, 26" L, G-, A **$165.00**

Zeppelin, Marklin, pnt tin, clockwork mechanism, 10" L, VG+, A...**$2,310.00**

Zeppelin, Los Angeles, Dent, polished aluminum, two simulated motors and rear gondola, 12½", EX, A, $290.00.

Banks

The impact of condition on the value of a bank cannot be overrated. Cast iron banks in near-mint condition with very little paint wear and all original parts are seldom found, and might bring twice as much (if the bank is especially rare, up to five times as much) as one in average, very good original condition with no restoration and no repairs. Overpainting and replacement parts (even screws) quickly continue the downward slide. Mechanicals dominate the market, and some of the hard-to-find examples in outstanding, near-mint condition — for example the Reclining Chinaman by J&E Stevens and the Organ Grinder and Bear by Kyser & Rex — will sell in the $9,000.00 to $12,000.00 range. Still banks are widely collected as well, with more than 3,000 varieties having been documented. Beware of modern reproductions, especially of the mechanicals. Watch for paint that is too bright and castings that do not fit together well.

For more information we recommend *The Dictionary of Still Banks* by Long and Pitman; *The Penny Bank Book* by Moore; *The Bank Book* by Norman; and *Penny Lane* by Davidson. See also Advertising; Character Collectibles; Reynolds Toys; Diecast Collector Banks.

Mechanical Banks

Always Did 'Spise a Mule, J&E Stevens, pnt CI, boy on bench, working, 10", VG, A **$700.00**

Artillery, J&E Stevens, pnt CI, Union Army variation, 6", EX, w/VG pnt, A **$3,200.00**

Bad Accident, J&E Stevens, pnt CI, bench posts cracked, trap missing, 10¼", VG, A **$1,600.00**

Boy in Cabin, substantial pnt loss, 3½x3x4½", G, A **$175.00**

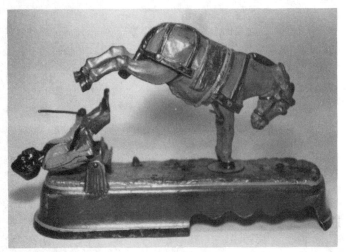

Always Did 'Spise a Mule, boy on bench, painted cast iron, J&E Stevens, NM, D10, $2,550.00.

Boy Robbing Bird's Nest, J&E Stevens, pnt CI, left bird incomplete, base missing, working, 7¾", VG-EX, A **$900.00**

Bulldog, J&E Stevens, pnt CI, glass eyes, working, 7⅝", G, A **$1,500.00**

Cabin, J&E Stevens, pnt CI, working, missing trap, 4¼", G-VG, A..**$375.00**

Chief Big Moon, J&E Stevens, frog jumps for fish held by Indian lady by tepee, EX, from $2,750 to **$3,000.00**

Circus Elephant, Chein, litho tin, gray, yel, red & bl, trunk receives coin, missing trap, 5⅛", G, A **$55.00**

Columbian Magic Savings, Columbian Expo Administration Building, trick penny drop, 5", G-VG, A...................**$75.00**

Creedmore, J&E Stevens, pnt CI, Pat 1877, 10", EX-NM..**$1,700.00**

Cupola, Diedrich Diekmann, J&E Stevens, pnt CI, gr building w/red roof, 7", G pnt, A **$4,950.00**

Darktown Battery, J&E Stevens, pnt CI, 3 animated figures, minor rpt, 10", EX-...**$2,300.00**

Darktown Battery, J&E Stevens, pnt CI, 3 animated figures, 1 arm missing, 10", G-, A **$1,700.00**

Darktown Battery, painted cast iron, Pat 1888, complete and original with only minor paint wear, NM, D10, $7,500.00.

Dinah, John Harper, England, pnt CI, brn shirt w/short sleeves, arm lifts, eyes roll (loose), 6¼", G-VG, A $350.00

Eagle & Eaglets, J&E Stevens, pnt CI, 6", NM $1,450.00

Eagle & Eaglets, J&E Stevens, pnt CI, 6", VG, from $550 to...$725.00

Eagle & Eaglets, J&E Stevens, pnt CI (worn), rpl eyes, squeaker missing, 6", A...$275.00

Frog on Rock, Kilgore, pnt CI, gr, yel & red, working, missing trap, 2¾", G-, A..$95.00

Frog on Round Base, J&E Stevens, pnt CI, gr, gold & wht, latticework on base, working, 4½" dia, EX, A $1,400.00

Frog on Round Base, J&E Stevens, pnt CI, traces of gr & wht, rpl screw, 4½", G-, A...$350.00

Hall's Liliput, pnt CI, yel w/red roof, man w/tray turns to deposit coin, Pat 1875, 4½x3x3¼", EX, A $675.00

Horse Race, with straight base, painted cast iron, J&E Stevens, white, green, and red variation, VG paint with partial possible repaint to horses, A, $3,080.00.

Humpty Dumpty, Shepard Hdw, pnt CI, rpt, working, 7½", VG...$550.00

Humpty Dumpty, Shepard Hdw, pnt CI, rpt & chips, working, 7½", G-, from $150 to $225.00

Indian Shooting Bear, J&E Stevens, pnt CI, shoots coin into bear, feather headdress fits in Indian's shirt, 10", VG.........$865.00

Jolly 'N,' John Harper, J&E Stevens, 6½", EX, from $750 to $800.00

Jolly 'N,' pnt aluminum, straight bow tie, top hat, ears move, working, 6½", G, A...$35.00

Jolly 'N,' pnt CI, red shirt, yel bow tie, wht top hat, ears move, working, 8¼", G, from $200 up to...........................$300.00

Jonah & the Whale, Shepard Hdw, pnt CI, 10¼", G, A ...$1,000.00

Kiltie, John Harper, English, pnt CI, working, rust on top hat, 6¾", VG, A...$1,700.00

Leap Frog, Shepard Hdw, 1 boy jumps over 2nd, deposits coin into tree trunk, 7½", EX- $2,900.00

Lion & 2 Monkeys, Kyser & Rex, pnt CI, monkey (brass arms) drops coin into lion's mouth, 1883, 9", NM, A....$2,500.00

Magic Bank, J&E Stevens, pnt CI, door pulls down to reveal cashier, worn, 5¼", P, A...$578.00

Magic Bank, J&E Stevens, pnt CI, lt gr w/orange trim, pull door opens to reveal cashier, working, 5¼", EX, A.......$3,200.00

Magician, J&E Stevens, pnt CI, figure lifts coin from table, disappears when he lifts hat, working, rpt, 8", G, A .$1,050.00

Magician, J&E Stevens, pnt CI, figure lifts coin from table, disappears when he lifts hat, EX...............................$6,500.00

Mammy & Child, Kyser & Rex, pnt CI, working, broken lever, rpt, trap missing, 7½", G-, A..............................$1,600.00

Milking Cow, painted cast iron, J&E Stevens, 1880s, EX+, D10, $11,000.00.

Milking Cow, J&E Stevens, cow kicks & boy falls bk & dumps milk bucket on his head, NM $12,000.00

Minstrel, tin, Black face emb on arched top above lever, tongue receives coin, 6⅞", VG, A...$750.00

Monkey, Hubley, pnt CI, key lock trap, working, 8¾", VG, A.$375.00

Mule Entering Barn, J&E Stevens, pnt CI, gray w/red trim, sm hairline crack, working, 8½", VG, A.....................$1,000.00

New Bank, pnt CI, brass soldier in door of gr building, red & gr trim w/bl chrome, working, 5¾", VG, A $2,400.00

Organ Bank, Monkey, Cat & Dog; Kyser & Rex, pnt CI, working, slight wear, 5¼", A..$1,980.00

Owl, CI, yel eyes, turns head, 7¼", G+, A.....................$270.00

Paddy & the Pig, J&E Stevens, pnt CI, brn coat, non-working, missing pig's movable leg & trap, 8", G-, A.............$350.00

Paddy & the Pig, J&E Stevens, pnt CI, pig tosses coin, Paddy catches & swallows it, rolls eyes, 8", NM, A $3,200.00

Penny Pineapple Hawaii, pnt CI, bust of 'human' pineapple, place coin in hand to receive in mouth, 8¼", EX, A...........$100.00

Pistol Bank, Elliot, plated CI, working, 5½", EX, A....$1,650.00

Pistol Bank, Elliot, plated pressed steel, working, 6", VG, A...$210.00

Punch & Judy, Shepard Hdw, pnt CI, Punch moves forward w/club as Judy deposits coin, 7", VG-EX, from $1,200 to....$1,500.00

Rabbit in Cabbage, Kilgore Toy, CI, 1925, VG..............$650.00

Rooster, Keyser & Rex, pnt CI, red, yel & blk, 6⅜", G+, A..$175.00

Santa Claus, Shepard Hdw, pnt CI, partial base, working, 5¾", G-, A...$675.00

Speaking Dog, J&E Stevens, pnt CI, working, trap missing, 7⅛", EX, from $825 to $1,000.00

Speaking Dog, Shepard Hdw, girl deposits coin, dog wags tail & speaks, NM..................................$3,000.00

Tabby Bank, CI, cat resting atop egg shape emb w/name, ped base, 4¼", G-, A.....................................$225.00

Tammany Bank, J&E Stevens, pnt CI, gray pants & blk coat, sliding trap, 5¾", VG+ $525.00

Teddy & Bear, J&E Stevens, pnt CI, bear pops up from tree, 7", VG, A $1,800.00

Teddy and the Bear, painted cast iron, ca 1904, NM, D10, $2,650.00.

Trick Dog, Hubley, pnt CI, yel w/brn base, 8¼" L, EX-, A...$525.00

Trick Dog, Shepard Hdw, pnt CI, maroon & yel base, some pnt chipping, 8½", A..................................$1,495.00

Trick Pony, Shepard Hdw, pnt CI, crazing & flaking, 7⅛", G, A $425.00

Two Frogs, J&E Stevens, pnt CI, sm frog drops coin into mouth of lg frog, 8", NM, A $1,495.00

Uncle Sam, Shepard Hdw, pnt CI, coin drops into carpetbag, eagle & banner emb on base, 11½", G-, A $850.00

Uncle Sam, Shepard Hdw, pnt CI, coin drops into carpetbag, 11½", EX-NM, A.................................$2,500.00

Uncle Tom, Kyser & Rex, pnt CI, press button on bk of neck, eyes roll & tongue thrusts out for coin, 5", VG, A ..$805.00

William Tell, Book of Knowledge, M, C5 ....$150.00

William Tell, J&E Stevens, pnt CI, apple removes from boy's head, ringing bell, working, 10½", EX, A $800.00

William Tell, J&E Stevens, pnt CI, apple removes from boy's head, ringing bell, rpl trap, 10½", G, A $460.00

Wireless, CI, tin & wood, 4⅞", G, A $130.00

World's Fair, J&E Stevens, pnt CI, Indian extends pipe to Columbus, working, 8¼", G-VG, A..................$475.00

World's Fair, J&E Stevens, pnt CI (possible retouch), Indian extends pipe to Columbus, 8", EX, A......................$750.00

Registering Banks

Bean Pot, 5¢, CI, 3-ftd w/wire hdl, 3", VG, A $95.00

Beehive 10¢, AM Mfg, pnt CI, lt wear, 5½" $440.00

New York Worlds Fair (1964-65) daily dime bank, orig package, EX...$95.00

Phoenix 10¢ (trunk), Piaget, plated CI, working, 5", VG, A..$50.00

Puzzle Bank, CI, resembles a bushel basket of fruit, 2¾", VG, A $230.00

Uncle Sam's, Durable Toy & Novelty, pnt rolled steel, blk w/gold trim, non-working, sm chips, 6¼", G+, A......$15.00

Uncle Sam's, Durable Toy & Novelty, pnt rolled steel, red w/gold, receives 3 coins, VG-EX, from $20 to $40.00

White City Barrel, #3, CI, 5⅛", G-, A $90.00

Still Banks

Bank Building, painted cast iron, Kenton (?), 1920s, 5", M, D10, $225.00.

Baby Asleep, diecast metal, 1940s, EX, T1 ....$87.50

Barrel on Victorian Pedestal, AC Williams, 3⅞", VG, A.$175.00

Bear Begging, CI, standing on hind legs, smooth body, opens vertically down middle, 5⅜", G-VG, from $30 up to.$60.00

Bear on Hind Legs, pnt CI, emb fur, mouth open, 6⅛", G-VG, from $35 to...$60.00

Beauty (horse), Arcade, blk w/gold hooves, 4¾", G, A $35.00

Bell, lead, emb floral design, coin slot on side, loop hdl on top, 5¾", G, A..$130.00

Bird's Nest, lead, bird & nest emb on side of roofed structure, ftd, key-locked trap, retains key, 3½", VG+, A $450.00

Birth Bank, wht metal, NP, rnd w/nursery images, padlock, 2⅝", VG, A..$200.00

Black Boy (2-faced), AC Williams, pnt CI, blk, gold, wht & red, rpl screw, 4⅛", VG, A $120.00

Boxer, pnt CI, gold, 4½", VG, A..$50.00

Boy Scout, AC Williams, pnt CI, gold, 5⅞", P, A...........$55.00

Boy w/Barrel on Back, wht metal & NP lead, 2¾", G+, A .$250.00

Buffalo, Arcade, pnt CI, 4⅜", G, A...............................$85.00

Buffalo, standing, brn pnt, pull tail out, head comes off, late, 6x8¾", EX, A...$550.00

Buffalo, gold-painted cast iron, Arcade, ca 1920s, 4⅜" long, EX, D10, $185.00.

Buster Brown & Tige, AC Williams, pnt CI, bl w/red collar, 5¼", G-EX, from $160 to...$200.00

Camel, Hubley, pnt CI, gold w/red & brn details, 4¾", G+, A $60.00

Cat on Tub, AC Williams, pnt CI, gold, 4⅞", G-, A $75.00

City Bank w/Chimney, Thomas Swan designer, Pat 1873, pnt CI, some chipping, 6½", A...................................$1,650.00

Coal Scuttle, NP metal, 3¼", VG, A..............................$120.00

Coin Bank, CI, sq shape w/emb design, Coin Bank emb on key-locked trap, 4¼", G, A $130.00

Cradle, wht metal, allover floral design, 3", VG+, A $250.00

Crosley Radio, pnt CI, red, 4¼", EX $650.00

Crosley Radio, pnt CI, red, 4¼", G, A...........................$110.00

Crown, pnt CI, yel & red, worn, rpl screw, 3", A $105.00

Darky (Sharecropper), AC Williams, pnt CI, gold w/blk & red, 5½", G, A...$85.00

Deer, pnt CI, gray figure mtd on oval base, 9¾", G, A $40.00

Dog on Tub, AC Williams, pnt CI, gold, 4⅛", VG, A...$100.00

Donkey (San Gabriel), lead, hinged saddle, padlock, 3⅝", G+, A...$50.00

Doughboy, Grey Iron Casting, khaki w/red hat band, 7", VG-EX, A...$500.00

Duck, AC Williams, pnt CI, gold, 4⅞", VG, A.............$100.00

Elephant on Tub, AC Williams, pnt CI, silver, red & gold, 5⅜", EX, A...$215.00

Elephant w/Howdah, AC Williams, pnt CI, gray w/gold & silver, 6¾", G, A..$65.00

Elephant w/Howdah, Hubley, pnt CI, gray w/red & gold, 4¾", G, A...$75.00

Electric R.R. Trolley, painted cast iron, removable motor man, roof repair, small crack, some restoration, 8", VG, A, $900.00.

Every Copper Helps (half-figure of London bobby), pnt CI, mc, worn, 5⅝", A...$44.00

Fido (no pillow), pnt CI, head cocked, ears stand out, 3¼", G-, A $20.00

Fido on Pillow, pnt CI, mc, minor wear, 5¼", A, from $200 to...$300.00

George Washington, pnt CI, red building w/bl roof, statue atop, chips & crazing, 9", G-VG, A.............................$1,300.00

Girl at Automat Machine, NP lead, key-locked trap, 4½", VG, A $425.00

Globe on Arc, brass, minor dents, 7⅛", G+, A...............$50.00

Globe on Arc, Grey Iron Casting, pnt CI, 5¼", EX........$285.00

Globe on Arc, Grey Iron Casting, pnt CI, 5¼", G+, A $55.00

Globe Savings Fund, Kyser & Rex, pnt CI, red & gold, combination lock door, 7⅛", EX, A...................................$1,150.00

Golliwog, John Harper, pnt CI, red & wht, 6⅛", VG, A.$425.00

Good Luck Horseshoe w/Buster Brown & Tige, Arcade, pnt CI, gold & blk, partial orig label, 4¼", VG, A..............$130.00

Good Luck Horseshoe w/Buster Brown & Tige, Arcade, pnt CI, much wear, 4¼", A...$80.00

Goodyear Zeppelin Hanger — Duralumin, CI, 2¼", EX, A..$280.00

Goose, pnt CI, gold over traces of silver, worn, 5", A.....$149.00

Green Taxi, glass body w/tin roof & wheels, 4⅛", VG, A..$475.00

Hamburg Steamship, wht metal, key-locked trap, retains key, 4", G+, A $230.00

Happyfats on Drum, glass, 4½", VG, A..........................$160.00

Holstein Cow, pnt CI, 2½", G-, A $70.00

I Made Chicago Famous Pig, JM Harper, pnt CI, blk, 4⅛", P, A...$80.00

Independence Hall, Sandwich glass, sm chip, crack, 7" VG, A..$75.00

Independence Hall Tower, pnt CI, bronze, some wear, 9½", A..$578.00

Indian w/Tomahawk, pnt CI, brn w/red headdress & gold trim, 5⅞", VG, A...$350.00

Indian With Tomahawk, painted cast iron, Hubley, 1920s, VG, D10, $350.00.

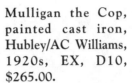

Junior Safe Deposit, CI, blk w/yel traces, 4⅝", A..............$50.00
Kelvinator Refrigerator, pnt CI, 4¼", VG, A....................$60.00
Lamb, pnt CI, gold, 5¼", VG, A $65.00
Limousine, tin body w/glass windows & wheels, 4" L, G, A..$125.00
Lion (tail right), pnt CI, gold, 6¼", VG, A.....................$35.00
Lion on Tub, AC Williams, pnt CI, gold & bl, 7½", EX, A...$215.00

Lion (with tail left), painted cast iron, Hubley, 3¾x5⅜", EX, D10, $185.00.

Main Street Trolley, AC Williams, pnt CI, gold, 6½", EX, A $300.00
Middy Bank, pnt CI, blk, minor wear, 4⅜", A................$105.00
Money Bag ($100,000), CI, key-locked trap, 3⅝", G-, A .$250.00
Monkey on Wooden Cage, compo, 5", VG, A $180.00

Mourner's Purse, lead w/brass handle, emb design, 5", G, A $85.00

Mulligan the Cop, painted cast iron, Hubley/AC Williams, 1920s, EX, D10, $265.00.

Mutt & Jeff, AC Williams, pnt CI, gold, 5⅛", VG, from $150 to..$200.00
Noah's Ark, compo, key-locked trap, 5½" L, G+, A.........$50.00
North Pole Bank (ice cream freezer), pnt CI, 4¼", G, A.$160.00
Paddle Boat, copper, key-locked trap, 5¼", VG, A.........$190.00
Parlor Stove, CI, allover emb design, ftd, 6¼", G+, A ...$400.00
Pet Stove, Turpin, CI, 'Pet' emb on oven door, ftd, 2¼", G+, A $10.00
Pig (seated), pnt CI, American, EX...............................$95.00
Rabbit (seated), Arcade, pnt CI, gold, rpl screw, 3⅝", VG, A...$55.00

Rabbit, painted cast iron, Grey Iron, ca 1940s, MIB, D10, $650.00.

Rabbit (standing), pnt CI, gold, 5⅜", G-, A $70.00
Radio Bank, pnt CI, 3 dials & 'Radio Bank' emb on front, lg, 3½", VG, A...$140.00

Red Goose Shoes, painted cast iron, Arcade, 1920s, EX, D10, $150.00.

Rooster, pnt CI, blk w/red & silver, 4¾", EX, A............$285.00
Rooster on Basket, compo, 5½", G+, A.........................$210.00
Roper Stove, pnt CI, 4", G-, A..$60.00
Saddle Horse, CI, gold, minor wear, 2⅞", A..................$116.00
Safe Bank, CI, on rollers, EX.......................................$175.00
Save for Ice (icebox), pnt CI, 4¼", G-, A.....................$300.00
State Bank, pnt CI, dk brn w/gold & copper trim, key-lock door, 6", VG, A..$120.00
Stein Bank, NP metal, padlock, 3⅞", VG, A..................$325.00
Strong Box, tin, pyramid shape w/flat hinged top, emb rivets, w/padlock, 3⅝", VG+, A..........................$110.00
Suitcase, CI, key-locked trap, 3⅜", VG, A $110.00
Swan, lead, bk of swan lifts up, 4¼", VG+, A................$350.00
Thomas Edison, bust w/script signature at base, L5 ....$135.00
Three Birds in Nest, lead, 3 3-D bird's heads atop rnd nest resembling ball of yarn, key-locked trap, 3¾", G, A..$35.00

Tower Bank, painted cast iron, John Harper, England, ca 1902-11, 9½", EX, D10, $750.00.

Time Is Money, New Haven Clock Co, lead, clock face inserted on front of money bag, trap missing, loose face, G-, A.....$110.00
Treat 'Em Rough Tank, litho tin, 5¼" L, G+, A $50.00
Upright Piano, clear glass w/backing, chipped, 2⅞", VG, A..$30.00
US Mail on Victorian Base, pnt CI, US Mail & eagle emb on front, slot mk Pull Down, 7⅞", G, A $525.00
US Savings Mailbox, pnt CI, wall-mt type w/name emb on front, latch broken, 6¾", G $130.00
US Tank Bank 1918, pnt CI, 2⅜", G+, A $50.00

Victorian Roof Bank, gold-painted cast iron, J&E Stevens, NM, $325.00.

Westinghouse Automeal, wht metal, 2⅛", G, A...............$55.00
White City Barrel on Cart, #1, CI, 5" L, VG, A.............$375.00
Windmill, wht metal, Art Nouveau style, pedestal ft, 5⅞", G+, A $300.00
Wise Pig, pnt CI, wht, pk & gray, chipping, 6¾", G-, A ..$60.00

Miscellaneous

Bank, Ohio Art, marching child, signed Fern Bisel Peat, M $35.00
Benjamin Franklin Thrift Bank, Marx, Franklin & bank lithoed on sides 4", EX (G box), A.....................................$130.00
Bird in House, Germany, tin, 1950s, MIB.....................$125.00
Brink's Armored Truck, cast metal, complete window decals featuring iron bars & guards at wheel, 8½", G+, A $120.00
Clown, Chein, litho tin, tongue moves to receive coin, 5", VG, A $45.00
Coffin Bank, Japan, litho tin w/up, coffin w/plastic skeleton that reaches up to snatch coin, #243, 6", EX, A...............$50.00
Coffin Bank, plastic & cb, lid opens & skeleton's hand grabs coin, bobbing head, 2½x6", EX, D9 ....$9.00
Drinker's Savings Bank, Illfelder, battery-op, 1960s, 9", L4..$125.00

Fingers Coin Bank, Frankonia, coffin form w/extended hand, MIB, from $35 to $50.00

Globe (wood base), litho paper on metal, 4¼", G+, A.....$55.00

Grandfather Clock, mk British Made, lacquered wood w/floral decal (damaged), paper clock face, 12½", G-VG, A..$30.00

Hand From Uncle, Spesco, plastic, shaped as Uncle Sam's hat, hand snatches coin from slot, NM (EX+ box), A......$55.00

Happy Day, Chein, litho tin, 1930s, EX............................$75.00

Hello Kiddies! Moneybox, litho tin, phone booth w/girl on phone & dog looking out door, 5¾", G+, A..............$40.00

Hole-In-One Bank, battery-op, unmk, 1960s, MIB, L4..$200.00

Home Town Fire House, Marx, w/firemen & vehicles, ladder truck, phone booth & 2 firemen included, 1930s, NM (EX box), A..$525.00

Home Town Saving Bank, Marx, #183, litho tin bank w/separate pc showing 2 tellers, customers, & counter, 1930s, NMIB, A..$280.00

Home Town Woolworth Store, Marx, #182, 3x3x5", w/accessories: Toys & Candy counter, 2 customers, 1930, NM (EX box), A......$375.00

Kick-Inn Mule, Wilder, St Louis MO, wood w/paper litho graphics, orig paper tag on base, rare, VG.........................$350.00

Monkey Tips Hat, Chein, litho tin, 5¼", VG, A, from $35 to $45.00

Pepsi-Cola Dispenser Bank, pnt & litho tin, battery-op, lights & sounds, orig box, 9¾", VG, A...................................$400.00

Pope County State Bank, airplane form, cast aluminum, 7½" G, A $45.00

Santa, unmk, litho tin, mc, oval w/Christmas scenes, 3", VG, A...$170.00

Santa on House, HTC/Japan, battery-op, 1960, EX, C8...$95.00

Spaceman, ceramic, 1960s, VG+, T1 ....$17.50

Telephone Booth, Japan, pnt tin, gray, red & bl, orig box (incomplete flaps), 6½", G-VG, A.............................$65.00

Treasure Chest Bank, Illfelder, 1960s, MIB, L4..............$150.00

Barbie and Friends

No one could argue the fact that vintage Barbies are holding their own as one of the hottest areas of toy collecting on today's market. Barbie was first introduced in 1959, and since then her face has changed three times. Her hair has been restyled over and over, she's been blond and brunette, and it's varied in length from above her shoulders to the tips of her toes. She's worn high-fashion designer clothing and pedal pushers. She's been everything from an astronaut to a veterinarian, and no matter what her changing lifestyle required, Mattel (her 'maker') has provided it for her.

Though even Barbie items from recent years are bought and sold with fervor, those made before 1970 are the most sought after. You'll need to do lots of studying and comparisons to learn to distinguish one Barbie from another, but it will pay off in terms of making wise investments. There are several books available; we recommend them all: *The Wonder of Barbie* and *The World of Barbie Dolls* by Paris and Susan Manos; and *The Collector's Encyclopedia of Barbie Dolls and Collectibles* by Sibyl DeWein and Joan Ashabraner. Our advisor for this category is Marl Davidson (D2).

Remember that unless the box is mentioned in the line (orig box, MIB, MIP, NRFB, etc.), values are given for loose items.

Dolls

Allan, pnt red hair, orig bl swim trunks, str legs, 1964, hair rubs/stains on upper arms, G, A $18.00

Allan, pnt red hair, orig bl swim trunks & striped jacket, str legs, 1964, VG (G box), A..$50.00

Barbie #1, brunette, MIB, D2, $4,000.00 minimum value.

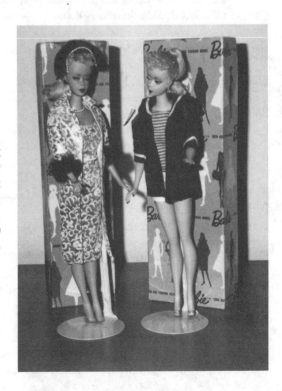

Barbie #1, Evening Splendor and Resort Barbie, both MIB, D2, $5,000.00 each, minimum value.

Barbie, #1, 1958-59, 11½", M $2,500.00

Barbie, #3, nurse uniform, 1960, 11½", M $500.00

Barbie, #9694, Stars 'N Stripes US Navy, Black, Special Edition, 1990, MIB, P4...$20.00

Barbie, American Girl, blond hair, orig 1-pc swimsuit, bendable legs, 1964, scratches on torso/swimsuit worn, G, A.$145.00

Barbie, American Girl, brunette, bendable legs, 1965, MIB, D2 ....$1,250.00

Barbie, Back to School, 1992, NRFB, D2 ....$25.00

Barbie, Barbie for President, Black, 1991, NRFB, D2 ....$30.00

Barbie, bendable legs, 1965, 11½", M, minimum value..$300.00

Barbie, Benefit Performance 1967, porc, limited edition in 1988, NRFB, A...$300.00

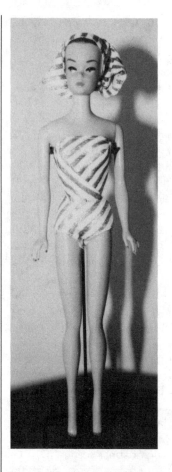

Barbie, Fashion Queen, #141, 1962, M, D2, $500.00 minimum value.

Barbie, Black Color Magic, plastic box, NRFB, D2, $4,000.00 minimum value.

Barbie, Bubble Cut, blond hair, turq silk sheath dress, str legs, 1964, faded dots on bk of legs, VG, A.........................$75.00

Barbie, Bubble-Cut, blond hair, orig 1-pc red nylon swimsuit, str legs, 1961-62, reglued neck split, VG, A....................$60.00

Barbie, Bubble-Cut, red hair, MIB, D2 ....$325.00

Barbie, Color Magic, red hair, orig 1-pc checked swimsuit, bendable legs, 1966, belt missing, VG, A $300.00

Barbie, Color Magic, 1966, retains bl ribbon won at The Winter Wonderland in 1987, NRFB, D2 ....$1,550.00

Barbie, Cool Times, 1988, NRFB, D2 ....$20.00

Barbie, Deluxe Quick Curl, 1975, M..................................$75.00

Barbie, Dramatic Living, red hair, nude, EX, D2 ....$65.00

Barbie, Empress, Bob Mackie orig, 1992, MIB, T1 ....$225.00

Barbie, Evening Enchantment, Sears, 1989, NRFB, D2 ...$25.00

Barbie, Fashion Jeans, 1981, NRFB, D2 ....$25.00

Barbie, Fashion Queen, molded brunette hair, orig swimsuit & turban, includes wig stand & 3 wigs, 1964, G, A.......$60.00

Barbie, Feelin' Groovy, 1986, NRFB, D2.........................$175.00

Barbie, Friday Nite Date outfit, 1961, M $500.00

Barbie, Gay Parisienne, porc, limited edition in 1991, NRFB, A...$100.00

Barbie, Happy Holidays, European Edition, 1988, NRFB, A..$225.00

Barbie, Happy Holidays, 1988, NRFB, A.........................$225.00

Barbie, Happy Holidays, 1990, NRFB, A $90.00

Barbie, Happy Holidays, 1991, NRFB, A $55.00

Barbie, Irish, International series, 1983, NRFB, A $55.00

Barbie, Live Action, blond hair, rooted eyelashes, orig 2-pc outfit w/fringe, bendable legs, G, A $15.00

Barbie, Live Action, NRFB, D2 ....$150.00

Barbie, Mardi Gras, 1987, NRFB, A..................................$55.00

Barbie, Movie Date outfit, 1963, M $300.00

Barbie, Neptune Fantasy, Bob Mackie, 1992, NRFB, D2 .$190.00

Barbie, Night Sensation, FAO Schwarz, 1991, NRFB, A.$55.00

Barbie, Olympic Skating Star, 1987, NRFB, D2 ....$40.00

Barbie, Oriental, International Series, box date 1980, NRFB, A $75.00

Barbie, Paint 'N Dazzle, 1993, NRFB, D2 ....$20.00

Barbie, Peach Blossom, 1992, NRFB, D2 ....$25.00

Barbie, Peaches 'N Cream, 1984, NRFB, D2 ....$25.00

Barbie, Perfume Pretty, 1987, NRFB, D2 ....$15.00

Barbie, Plantation Bell, porc, Walt Disney limited edition, 1992, NRFB, D2 ....$450.00

Barbie, Platinum, Bob Mackie, 1991, MIB, A $145.00

Barbie, Ponytail #4, brunette hair in topknot, orig 1-pc striped swimsuit & pearl earrings, 1960, VG, A $160.00

Barbie, Ponytail #6, lt blond hair in topknot, orig 1-pc red nylon swimsuit & pearl earrings, NM (G box), A $385.00

Barbie, Quick Curl Miss America, blond hair, orig gown w/Miss America sash, bendable legs, 1974, G, A..................$20.00

Barbie, Quick Curl Miss America, blond hair, 1972, M (worn box), A $40.00
Barbie, Show 'N Ride, 1988, NRFB, D2 ....$50.00

Side Part Barbie, NRFB, D2, $4,000.00 minimum value.

Barbie, silver & pk gown, limited edition by Applause, 1991, NRFB, A $50.00
Barbie, Sophisticated Lady, porc, 1990, NRFB, D2 ....$195.00
Barbie, Spanish, International Series, 1982, NRFB, A $45.00
Barbie, Spanish Talking, brunette hair, 1969, very rare, NRFB, D2 ....$350.00
Barbie, Sterling Wishes, Spiegel Special, 1991, NRFB, A .$55.00
Barbie, Super-Size w/Super Hair, blond hair w/growing pc, orig wht nylon dress/shoes (overskirt missing), 1979, NM, A $50.00
Barbie, Swedish, International Series, 1982, NRFB, A $40.00
Barbie, Swirl Ponytail, blond hair in orig style, orig 1-pc red swimsuit, 1964, NM (G box), A $225.00
Barbie, Talking, blond hair, orig 3-pc swimsuit, 1969, NM, D2 ....$125.00
Barbie, Talking, blond hair pulled to 1 side, rooted lashes, series 1880 Winter Brocade dress, bendable legs, 1968, G, A..$70.00
Barbie, Talking, brunette hair tied w/pk ribbons, #1479 Leisure Leopard dress, bendable legs, 1969, G, A...................$50.00
Barbie, Talking, titian hair in orig curl set, rooted eyelashes, Talking PJ's floral dress, 1970, non-working, VG, A.$60.00
Barbie, Talking Busy, blond hair, orig lt bl swimsuit w/flowers, rooted lashes, bendable legs & arms, 1973, G-, A $30.00
Barbie, Twist 'N Turn, 1969-70, M.................................$195.00

Barbie, Winter Fantasy, FAO Schwarz, 1990, M (G box), A $115.00
Brad, bendable legs, NRFB, D2 ....$135.00
Brad, New Talking, NRFB, D2..$135.00
Casey, Twist 'N Turn, blond hair, rooted eyelashes, nude, bendable legs, 1967, yel spots on leg, G, A $43.00
Christie, Live Action, 1968, M $140.00
Christie, Pink 'N Pretty, 1981, NRFB, D2 ....$25.00
Christie, Sun Lovin' Malibu, 1978, NRFB, D2 ....$15.00
Courtney, Baby-Sitter, 1990, NRFB, D2 ....$25.00
Francie, blond hair, bendable legs, MIB, D2 ....$250.00
Francie, Growin' Pretty Hair, blond w/bun & braid, rooted eyelashes, orig dress, bendable legs, 1971, VG, A $50.00
Francie, Hair Happenin', nude but still has her 2 hairpieces, EX, D2 ....$75.00
Francie, Twist 'N Turn, 1969, 11½", M $325.00
Jamie, Walking, brunette hair, NRFB, D2 ....$375.00
Jamie, Walking, titian hair, rooted eyelashes, orig knit dress w/belt, bendable legs, 1970, hair has been cut, G-, A.$20.00
Ken, Army, MIB, T1...$15.00
Ken, brn flocked hair, gr pants & short-sleeve shirt, str legs, 1961, VG, A $25.00
Ken, brn flocked hair, orig swim trunks & striped jacket, str legs, 1961, G- (worn box), A $120.00
Ken, Day 'N Night, Black, 1984, NRFB, D2 ....$15.00
Ken, Fashion Jeans, 1981, NRFB, D2 ....$20.00
Ken, flocked hair, wearing Campus Hero outfit, 1961, 12", M..$225.00
Ken, Gold Medal Skier, 1974, NRFB, D2 ....$50.00
Ken, Live Action, 12", M $95.00
Ken, pnt blond crew cut, orig red swim trunks & striped jacket, str legs, 1962, ink dots on bk/leg, VG, A $35.00
Ken, Roller Skating, 1980, NRFB, D2 ....$25.00
Ken, Ski Champion, 1963, 12", M..................................$250.00
Ken, Sun Valley, 1973, NRFB, D2 ....$50.00
Ken, Sunsational Malibu, Black w/red Afro, 1981, NRFB, D2 ....$50.00
Ken, Talking, pnt brn hair, newer shorts, striped shirt & bl windbreaker, bendable legs, 1969, VG, A..................$28.00
Midge, blond flipped-up hair, orig orange pants & striped shirt, str legs, 1964, G, A $25.00
Midge, blond flipped-up hair, orig swimsuit, 1964, MIB, D2 ....$125.00
Midge, blond flipped-up hair, Party Date dress & gold clutch purse, 1964, hair sparse on left side/bk, G-, A...........$20.00
Midge, brunette flipped-up hair, orange Belle dress, str legs, 1964, eyeliner/lip rubs, VG, A $40.00
Midge, brunette flipped-up hair, side-glancing eyes, Movie Date dress, str legs, 1963, G-, A $25.00
Midge, molded red hair w/orange headband, nude, str legs, 1965, indentions on toes, VG, A $35.00
Midge, Sea Holiday, 1992, NRFB, D2...............................$25.00
Midge, titian hair in orig set w/ribbon headband, orig 1-pc striped swimsuit, bendable legs, 1965, NMIB, A $425.00
Nan & Fran, Pretty Pairs, NRFB, D2 ....$295.00
PJ, New & Groovin' Talking, NRFB, D2........................$165.00
PJ, Talking, blond hair retied on sides, rooted eyelashes, 1-pc satin sheath gown, bendable legs, 1969, G, A $35.00

PJ, Talking, blond pigtails, beaded hair ornaments in bag, rooted eyelashes, nude, bendable legs, 1970, VG, A..............$35.00

PJ, Talking, 1959, M..$125.00

PJ, Twist 'N Turn, NRFB, D2 ....$210.00

Ricky, pnt red hair, nude, str legs, 1965, VG, A $25.00

Ricky, pnt red hair, orig bl swim trunks & jacket, str legs, 1965, jacket slightly discolored, NM, A......................................$40.00

Scott, Skipper's Boyfriend, 1979, NRFB, D2 ....$40.00

Skipper, Baby-Sitter, Black, 1990, NRFB, D2....................$25.00

Skipper, Baton Twirling, 1992, NRFB, D2 ....$18.00

Skipper, Beach Blast, 1989, NRFB, D2 ....$10.00

Skipper, blond hair, orig 1-pc red & wht swimsuit, str legs, 1964, VG (G box), A $70.00

Skipper, Dramatic New Living, NRFB, D2 ....$95.00

Skipper, Growing Up, 1975, NRFB, D2.............................$40.00

Skipper, Quick Curl, 1972, M (worn box), A $28.00

Skipper, Ship Ahoy dress, 1965, M $155.00

Skipper, Sun Gold Malibu, 1983, NRFB, D2 ....$18.00

Skipper, Twist 'N Turn, blond banana curls, NRFB, D2 .$395.00

Skooter, titian hair in orig pigtails, orig 2-pc swimsuit, str legs, 1965, NMIB, A...$130.00

Stacey, Talking, red hair, 1967, NRFB, D2 ....$350.00

Stacey, Talking, 1968, M...$275.00

Stacey, Twist 'N Turn, long red hair, rooted eyelashes, Zokko dress only, bendable legs, 1968, dots on ankle/leg, G, A $40.00

Stacey, Twist 'N Turn, short blond hair, 1967, NRFB, D2 .$495.00

Steffie, Talking Busy, blond hair, rooted eyelashes, #3438 Peasant Dressy dress, bendable legs, 1972, G, A $45.00

Steffie, Walk Lively, NRFB, D2 ....$275.00

Todd, 1965, NRFB, D2..$150.00

Todd, 1973, MIB, D2..$70.00

Tutti, blond or brunette hair, 1965, NRFB, D2 ....$150.00

Whitney, Jewel Secrets, 1986, NRFB, D2 ....$35.00

Whitney, Style Magic, 1988, NRFB, D2............................$18.00

Cases

Barbie & Francie, bl, rnd, 1965, rare, EX+, D2.................$40.00

Barbie & Francie, wht w/picture of Barbie & Francie in Color Magic outfits, 1965, G-, D2 ....$10.00

Barbie & Ken, bl w/picture of Barbie in Party Date & Ken in Friday Night Date, 1964, NM, D2 ....$25.00

Barbie & Ken, red w/picture of Barbie in Enchanted Evening & Ken in Tuxedo, 1963, 1 drawer missing/scuffs, G, A .$13.00

Barbie & Midge Travel Pals, wht, round, rare, 1964, G-, D2...$25.00

Barbie & Midge Travel Pals, wht, sq, 1963, EX, D2 ....$50.00

Barbie & Steffie Sleep 'N Keep, pk w/Barbie & Steffie surrounded by flowers, fold-down bedroom on lid, G, A $20.00

Barbie Fashion, pk & wht vinyl, 1982, EX, T1 ....$12.00

Barbie Goes Traveling, salmon, 1965, rare, G, D2 ....$135.00

Barbie Goes Traveling, yel, 1965, rare, EX, D2 ....$175.00

Francie, wht w/picture of Francie in gold slacks & top w/bl sash belt, rnd w/zipper, 1965, rare, EX+, D2 ....$50.00

Ken, purple w/lg picture of Ken in Rally Dally outfit, 2 drawers & hanger rack, 1962, few scuff mks, G, A..................$50.00

Skipper & Skooter, salmon, 1965, G, D2...........................$20.00

Tutti, orange flower design w/window, 1965, VG, D2......$15.00

Tutti, wht w/picture of Tutti in Swing-a-Ling outfit, 1965, rare, EX, D2..$25.00

Tutti & Chris, wht, 1965, G, D2 ....$15.00

Tutti & Chris, yel, w/window, 1967, VG, D2 ....$20.00

Clothing

All About Plaid, Barbie, 3400 series, 3-pc, A $45.00

American Airline Stewardess, Barbie, #984, complete, M, D2...$70.00

American Airlines, Ken, #779, jacket & hat only, NM, D2..$35.00

Arabian Nights, Barbie, #874, NRFB, A $250.00

Ballet Class, Skipper, #1905, 1963, NRFB, A $60.00

Barbie Color Coordinates, #1832, MOC, D2....................$75.00

Barbie in Holland, 6-pc, complete, G, A $35.00

Barbie in Mexico, #820, complete, EX, D2 ....$45.00

Barbie Shoe Wardrobe, #1833, MOC, D2 ....$150.00

Bells, Francie, #1275, NRFB, A $160.00

Benefit Performance, Barbie, 1600 series, 6-pc, complete, NM, A...$300.00

Bermuda Holidays, Barbie, #1810, 1967-68, complete, M, $85.00.

Bold Gold, Ken, #1436, complete, NM, D2......................$25.00

Bouncy Flouncy, Barbie, #1805, complete, NM, D2 ......$125.00

Bridal Brocade, Barbie, 3400 series, 2-pc, NM, A...........$65.00

Bride's Dream, Barbie, #947, complete, EX+, D2 ....$75.00

Campus Corduroys, Ken, #1410, NRFB, D2 ....$75.00

Campus Hero, Ken, #770, complete, NM, D2 ....$25.00

Candy Striper Volunteer, Barbie, #889, rpl knife, fork & spoon, o/w complete, NM, D2...$175.00

City Sparkler, Barbie, #1457, complete, NM, D2 ....$40.00

Clam Diggers, Francie, 4-pc, VG, A................................$28.00

Concert in the Park, Francie, 5-pc, G, A $40.00

Cookie Time, Skipper, 4-pc, complete, G, A.....................$30.00
Country Clubbin', Ken, #1400, NRFB, D2.....................$135.00
Crisp 'N Cool, Barbie, #1604, complete, EX, D2 ....$40.00
Dancing Stripes, Barbie, #1843, complete, NM, D2.........$95.00
Denims On!, Francie, 5-pc, complete, A $85.00
Dinner at 8, Barbie, #946, NRFB, D2 ....$195.00
Disco Dater, Barbie, 1800 series, 3-pc, complete, NM, A.$140.00
Dream Ins, Skipper, 1971, NRFB, A $28.00
Dreamtime, Skipper, #1909, NRFB, A..............................$80.00
Entertainer, Francie & Friends, #1763, complete, M, D2.$35.00
Evening Splendour, 900 series, 6-pc, complete, VG, A $35.00
Extravaganza, Barbie, 1800 series, gown only, NM, A......$35.00
Fashion Editor, Barbie, 1600 series, 3-pc, G, A................$75.00
First Things First, Francie, 5-pc, NM, A $28.00
Floating Gardens, Barbie, 1600 series, 6-pc, complete, M,
    A..$300.00
Floating In, Francie & Friends, #1207, complete, NM, D2.$110.00
Flower Girl, Skipper, #1904, complete, NM, D2 ....$40.00
Flower Shower, Barbie, 1993, NRFB, D2 ....$25.00
Furry-Go-Round, Francie, Sears Exclusive, 4-pc, complete, NM,
    A..$270.00
Garden Wedding, Barbie, 1600 series, complete, NM, A.$75.00
Goin' Hunting, Ken, #1409, complete, NM, D2 ....$40.00
Goin' Sleddin', Skipper, #3475, NRFB, D2 ....$50.00
Gold Rush, Francie & Friends, #1222, complete, NM, D2 .$45.00
Golden Elegance, Barbie, 900 series, 4-pc, complete, NM,
    A $45.00
Golden Girl, Barbie, #911, complete, NM, D2 ....$50.00
Groovin' Gauchos, Barbie, #1057, complete, EX+, D2 ..$125.00
Here Comes the Bride, Barbie, 1600 series, 4-pc, complete, G-,
    A...$65.00
Holiday, Ken, #1414, NRFB, A.......................................$90.00
Hollywood Premier, Barbie, 1992, NRFB, D2..................$25.00
Ice Breaker, Barbie, #942, complete, EX, D2 ....$45.00
Ken in Holland, #0777, 1964, NRFB, A..........................$130.00
Ken in Switzerland, #776, NRFB, A $175.00
King Arthur, Ken, 9-pc, complete, G, A...........................$65.00
Leather Limelight, Francie, 6-pc, complete, G, A $50.00
Little Bow Pink, Barbie, #1483, dress only, EX, D2 ....$15.00
Little Leaguer, Ricky #1504, NRFB, A $65.00
Lola Paloozas, Skipper, #1946, complete, M, D2 ....$55.00
London Tour, Barbie, 1600 series, 2-pc, G-, A.................$40.00
Long 'N Short of It, Skipper, 1970, NRFB, A...................$55.00
Loungin' Around, Ken, 1962, MOC, D2 ....$15.00
Mad About Plaid!, Talking Barbie, Sears Exclusive, 5-pc, com-
    plete, M, A...$275.00
Masquerade, Ken, 6-pc, complete, VG, A.........................$20.00
Matinee Fashion, Barbie, #1640, 4-pc, G-, A $105.00
Midi Magic, Barbie, #1869, 1967, NRFB, A.....................$85.00
Midi Plaid, Barbie, #3444, complete, M, D2.....................$25.00
Miss Teenage Beauty, Francie, #1284, NRFB, A.........$2,100.00
Music Center Matinee, Barbie, 1600 series, 6-pc, complete, NM,
    A..$350.00
Night Scene, Ken, #1496, 1969, NRFB, A $35.00
Nightly Negligee, Barbie, #965, complete, EX, D2 ....$25.00
Orange Blossom, Barbie, #987, Japanese version, extremely rare,
    complete, NM, D2 ....$550.00
Orange Cozy, Francie, 2-pc, NM, A.................................$40.00

Outdoor Art Show, Barbie, 1600 series, dress only, G, A.$50.00
Outdoor Casuals, Skipper, 5-pc, complete, G, A $25.00
Party Fun Pak, Ken, 1963, MOC, D2...............................$225.00
Play It Cool, Ken, #1433, complete, NM, D2 ....$25.00
Polka Dots 'N Raindrops, Francie, 3-pc, complete, M, A.$28.00
Pretty as a Picture, Barbie, #1652, NRFB, A $225.00
Puddle Jumpers, Tutti, #3601, complete, EX+, D2 ....$15.00
Rally Day, Ken, #788, 1961, NRFB, A.............................$45.00
Registered Nurse, Barbie, #991, NRFB, D2 ....$210.00
Rik Rak Rah, Skipper, #1733, NRFB, D2 ....$40.00
Roman Holiday, Barbie, #968, NRFB, D2 ....$2,750.00
Romantic Ruffles, 1800 series, 3-pc, complete, G, A........$45.00
Ruffles 'N Swirls, Barbie, #1783, NRFB, D2 ....$75.00
Sailor, Ken, 6-pc, complete, NM, A.................................$35.00
Saturday Matinee, Barbie, 1600 series, 3-pc, G, A $175.00
Saturday Night, Ken, #786, complete, NM, D2 ....$40.00
Saturday Show, Ricky, 1964, NRFB, A.............................$40.00
School Girl, Skipper, 4-pc, complete, NM, A $18.00
Senior Prom, 900 series, 1 shoe mk Japan, 3-pc, complete, NM,
    A..$50.00

Senior Prom, Barbie, #951, 1963-64, complete, M, $65.00.

Shimmering Magic, 1900 series, dress only, slightly discolored, G,
    A...$85.00
Ship Ahoy!, Skipper, #1918, NRFB, A.............................$100.00
Shoe Ins, Ken, 1970, MOC, D2 ....$10.00
Skater's Waltz, Barbie, #1629, complete, NM, D2 ....$130.00
Skater's Waltz, Barbie, #1629, NRFB, D2 ....$250.00
Slacks Are Back, Ken or Brad, 1969, MOC, D2 ....$5.00
Slumber Party, Barbie, 1600 series, 8-pc, G, A $45.00
Snappy Snoozers, Francie, #1238, 1969, NRFB, A $60.00
Sorority Meeting, 900 series, 5-pc, complete, NM, A.......$30.00
Sport Shorts, Ken, #783, NRFB, D2................................$65.00
Style Setters, Francie, #1268, Montgomery Ward's Exclusive,
    NRFB, A..$300.00

Style Setters, Francie, #1268, Montgomery Ward's Exclusive, complete, G, A $140.00
Sugar Sheers, Francie & Friends, #1229, NRFB, D2 ......$195.00
Sunday Visit, Barbie, #1675, complete, NM, D2............$175.00
Sunny Slacks, Francie & Friends, #1761, NRFB, D2........$45.00
Sweater Girl, Barbie, #976, complete, NM, D2 ....$45.00
Togetherness, Barbie, #1842, NRFB, D2 ....$110.00
Touchdown, Ken, 7-pc, complete, VG, A $30.00
Travel Togethers, Barbie, #1688, NRFB, A....................$275.00
Tunic 'N Tights, Barbie, #1859, complete, NM, D2 ......$125.00
Tuxedo, Ken, 8-pc, complete, M, D $35.00
Tweed-Somes, Francie, #1286, NRFB, A $275.00
Under Pretties, Skipper, #1900, NRFB, D2 ....$50.00
Velvet 'N Lace, Skipper, #1948, NRFB, D2 ....$150.00
Velvet Venture, Barbie, #1488, NRFB, D2......................$125.00
Wedding Day, Barbie, #972, complete, EX, D2 ....$125.00

Furniture and Rooms

Barbie's First Dream House, MIB, D2, $95.00.

Barbie's Fashion Shop, M, D2, $400.00 minimum value (NRFB, $500.00 minimum value).

Barbie Dream Bed, #5641, 1982, NRFB, D2 ....$12.00
Barbie Dream Furniture Armoire, #2471, 1978, NRFB, D2.$10.00
Barbie Dream Furniture Desk & Seat, #2467, 1978, NRFB, D2 ....$5.00
Barbie Dream Kitchen, #9119, 1984, NRFB, D2 ....$12.00
Barbie Dream Kitchen Dinette, 1965, complete, EX+, D2 .$450.00
Barbie Room Fulls Firelight Living Room, #7406, 1974, NRFB, D2 ....$50.00
Barbie Room Fulls Studio Bedroom, #7405, 1974, NRFB, D2 ....$50.00
Barbie's New Dream House, 1966, complete, NM, D2...$375.00

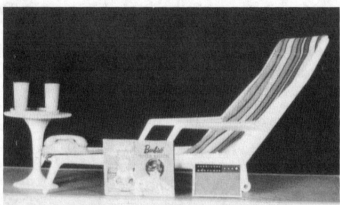

Go-Together Chair, #0410, 1964-65, M, $125.00.

Susy Goose Canopy Bed, pk & wht candy-striped pattern, 1965, NM, D2 ....$25.00
Susy Goose Jeweled Wardrobe, #418, 1965, NRFB, D2 .$135.00
Suzy Goose Grand Piano, wht w/gold trim, red velvet seat cover, sheet music missing/music box not working, G-, A ...$90.00

Gift Sets

Ballerina on Tour, 1976, MIB $85.00
Barbie, Ken & Skipper gift set by Disney, #3177, 1991, D2 .$45.00
Barbie & Francie Color Magic Fashion Designer, #4040, 1965, NRFB, D2 ....$395.00
Barbie & Friends, Disney, 1991, NRFB, D2 ....$45.00
Barbie Baby-Sits, #953, bottle gone, o/w complete, EX+, D2 ....$115.00
Barbie Beautiful Blues, includes blond Twist 'N Turn, extra outfit & accessories, stand & brochure, 1966, EX+ (VG box), A $700.00
Barbie Beautiful Blues, 1967, M $350.00
Barbie Dressing Fun, 1993, NRFB, D2 ....$32.00
Barbie Foaming Beauty Bath, 1960s, MIB $110.00
Barbie Loves To Read, 1992, NRFB, D2 ....$30.00
Barbie's Color 'N Curl, #4035, 1964, complete, NM, D2 .$95.00
Barbie Secret Hearts, 1993, MIB, D2 ....$35.00
Barbie Twinkle Town, 1968, MIB...................................$500.00
Casey Goes Casual, 1967, M $400.00
Cool City Blues, 1989, MIB...$45.00
Dance Magic, 1985, MIB..$65.00
Fashion Queen Barbie & Her Friends, 1964, M.............$250.00

Francie Rise 'N Shine, 1971, M $175.00
Gold & Lace Barbie, Target, 1989, MIB $25.00
Kissing Barbie, 1978, MIB $65.00

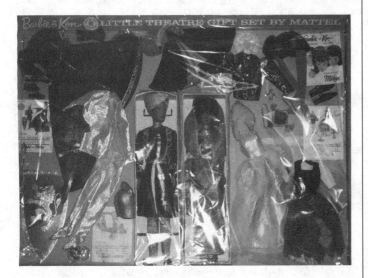

Little Theater Gift Set, rare, MIB, D2, $3,500.00 minimum value.

Living Barbie Action Accents, 1970, MIB $450.00
Loving You Barbie, 1983, MIB.................................$30.00
Malibu Ken Surf's Up, 1971, MIB..............................$250.00
Mink Barbie, w/real mink coat & Lucite case, only 500 made by
  Takara, 1989, NRFB, D2......................................$995.00
Pink & Pretty Barbie, 1981, MIB $85.00
Pose 'N Play Skipper & Her Swing-a-Rounder Gym, #1179,
  1971, MIB, D2...$250.00
Pretty Changes Barbie, 1978, MIB $45.00
Skipper Party Time, 1964, MIB................................$450.00
Skooter Cut 'N Button, 1967, MIB............................$500.00
Stacie & Butterfly Pony, 1993, NRFB, D2......................$32.00
Tropical Barbie Deluxe, 1985, MIB $45.00
Tutti Nighty Night Sleep Tight, 1965, MIB....................$175.00
Twirly Curls Barbie, 1982, MIB $45.00
Wedding Party Midge, 1990, NRFB, D2.........................$125.00

Vehicles

Barbie's First Car, MIB, D2, $200.00 minimum value.

Barbie Dream Carriage, from France, box date 1982, M (worn
  box), A $40.00
Country Camper, 1st ed, 1970, MIB $40.00
Dune Buggy, Barbie & Ken & All Their Friends, 1970, w/orig
  sticker, G, D2..$25.00
Ferrari, red plastic, 1987, MIB, A $20.00
Mercedes, gr, 1963, orig cb box, NM, D2......................$150.00
Moped, pk, 1988, NM, T1.......................................$8.50
Starcycle, #2149, 1978, MIB, D2..............................$10.00
Sun 'N Fun Buggy, orange, w/stickers, 1970, EX+, D2 .....$10.00
Sun Sailor, #9106, 1975, NRFB, D2............................$20.00
1957 Belair Chevy, aqua, 1st edition, 1989, M, D2 ....$50.00

Miscellaneous

Barbie's Color 'N Curl, NRFB, A, $550.00.

Bath Powder Mitt, Barbie, 1960s, MIB $110.00
Book, Barbie Dictionary, red, 1964, VG+, D2 ....$35.00
Book, Barbie Goes to a Party, Wonder, 1964, D2 ....$5.00
Book, Barbie Party Cookbook, EX...............................$10.00
Book, Barbie's Adventures, paperback, 1964, EX................$5.00
Book, Little Golden, 1974, VG, T1.............................$6.00
Booklet, Face the World of Barbie, #1, Mattel, M, D2 .....$10.00
Booklet, Lively World of Barbie, D2 ....$30.00
Booklet, Living Barbie as Full of Life as You Are, D2 ....$5.00
Booklet, Skipper, Skooter & Ricky, D2.........................$8.00
Box, for Barbie #850, discolored, stained, no inserts, VG,
  A $100.00
Box, for blond or brunette str-leg Midge, EX, D2 ....$40.00
Box, for Malibu Barbie, 1975, M, D2...........................$5.00
Box, for 2nd edition of str-leg Ken, VG, D2 ....$20.00
Coloring Book, Barbie & Skipper Dressed in Masquerade, Whit-
  man, 1973, M, D2..$25.00
Coloring Book, Barbie Sweet 16, dot-to-dot, Whitman,
  1974, M, D2...$8.00
Coloring Book, Quick Curl Barbie, 1975, VG, T1 ....$10.00
Dish Set, Friendship Stewardess, 1973, M (worn box), D2.$15.00
Display Case, clear acrylic on wht base, Barbie logo in pk on
  front sticker, orig cb box, 9x14" sq, M, A $50.00
Display Case, clear plastic on pk base, Barbie logo, mirror-type
  bk, 3 stands w/attached velcro, 13½x22", NM, A $80.00

Drawing Set, Barbie & Skipper Fashion Designer, electric, Lakeside, 1960s, EX (VG box) $20.00

Drawing Set, Dramatic New Living Barbie, #8279, electric, 1970, MIB, D2 ....$25.00

Drawing Set, Francie & Barbie Fashion Designer, #8272, electric, Lakeside, 1966, EX, D2 ....$25.00

Game, Barbie Miss Lively Livin', Mattel, 1970, G (G box) .$25.00

Game, Barbie Miss Lively Livin', Mattel, 1971, complete, EX $25.00

Game, Barbie Queen of the Prom, Mattel, 1960, EX+, C1 .$36.00

Gum Card Set, Dart/Pani, 1991, series 1, 196 cards, complete, M1 ....$30.00

Jewelry Box, red, 1963, VG, D2 ....$25.00

Lunch Box, blk w/picture of Barbie & Midge, no thermos, 1965, EX, D2 ....$15.00

Magazine, Barbie Bazaar, Oct, 1988, D2 ....$75.00

Magazine, Barbie Bazaar, Sept-Oct, 1989, D2...................$25.00

Necklace, Barbie Sweet 16 mail-in offer, 1974, EX $15.00

Ornament, Hallmark, 1993, MIB $49.00

Paper Dolls, Barbie & Ken, Whitman, 1970, uncut, M $28.00

Paper Dolls, Barbie Boutique, Whitman, 1973, MIP, D2 ...$5.00

Pencil Case, blk, 1961, M, D2 ....$75.00

Perfume Maker, Barbie #2740, 1978, NRFB, D2.................$5.00

Plate, #B4072, Barbie Bride-To-Be by Susie Morton, blond ponytail model, 1990, in styrofoam container, M $45.00

Plate, #B4072, Barbie Enchanted Evening by Susie Morton, brunette ponytail model, 1990, in styrofoam container, M $45.00

Plate, #B4072, Barbie Solo in the Spotlight by Susie Morton, blond ponytail model, 1990, in styrofoam container, M...........$45.00

Plate, child's, plastic, illus of bubble-cut & ponytail Barbies, EX, set of 12 ....$100.00

Puzzle, Barbie's Keys to Fame, 1963, NRFB, D2.............$65.00

Puzzle, jigsaw; Whitman, Barbie, Ken & Midge at school play, 1962, 9x11" box, rpr split/crease, o/w EX, T2 ....$20.00

Record, Barbie Sings!, 45 rpm, Barbie & Instant Love, orig paper jacket faded, NM, A $18.00

Tea Set, Barbie, 25th Anniversary, 1984, complete, NM (EX box)..$75.00

Telephone w/intercom, Duram Industries, 1976, NRFB, D2 ..$35.00

Trading Cards, Barbie, Deluxe First Edition, 1990, NRFB, A..$30.00

Wallet, Barbie in Winter Holiday outfit, bl or red, 1962, G, D2 ....$30.00

Wallet, 3 photos of Barbie on front, blk, no coin holder, 1961, G, D2...$25.00

Watch, Barbie, by Bradley, 1973, MIB, D2 ....$75.00

Battery Operated

From the standpoint of being visually entertaining, nothing can compare with the battery-operated toy. Most (probably as much as 95%) were made in Japan from the forties through the sixties, though some were distributed by American companies, who often sold them under their own names. Even big American toymakers, Marx, Ideal, and Daisy, for instance, sold Japanese-made battery-ops as their own; so even if they're marked, sometimes it's just about impossible to identify the actual manufacturer. Though batteries had been used to power trains and pro-

vide simple illumination in earlier toys, the Japanese toys could smoke, walk, talk, drink, play instruments, blow soap bubbles, and do just about anything else humanly possible to dream up and engineer. Generally the more antics the toy performs, the more collectible it is. Rarity is important as well, but first and foremost to consider is condition. Because of their complex mechanisms, many will no longer work. Children often stopped them in mid-cycle, rubber hoses and bellows aged and cracked, and leaking batteries caused them to corrode, so very few have survived to the present intact and in good enough condition to interest a collector. Though it's sometimes possible to have them repaired, unless you can buy them cheap enough to allow for the extra expense involved, it is probably better to wait on a better example. Original boxes are a definite plus in assessing the value of a battery-op and can be counted on to add from 30% to 50% (and up), depending on the box's condition, of course, as well as the toy's age and rarity.

We have made every attempt to list these toys by the name as it appears on the original box. Some will sound very similar. Many toys were reissued with only minor changes and subsequently renamed. For more information we recommend *Collecting Toys* by Richard O'Brien (Books Americana). Our advisor for this category is Mike Czerwinski (C8). See also Robots and Space Toys; Marx; Strauss; Lehmann; Chein.

#26 Racer, Japan, mc litho tin, working, 6¼", G-VG, A..$50.00

#301 Racer, MT, driver w/vinyl head, Indy-style car, flashing lights, sounds, 18", EX, A $260.00

ABC Accordion Bear, rare, EX, L4 ....$575.00

Acro Chimp Porter, Y-M/Japan, working, 1960s, EX, C8 $75.00

Aerial Ropeway, EX (EX box), L4 ....$165.00

Air Mail Helicopter, KO, tin & plastic, 3-D pilot at controls moves head & arms, 2 spinning rotors, 10", NM (EX box), A..$175.00

Air Mail Helicopter, MIB, L4 ....$225.00

Airplane, Schuco, 4-prop, tin w/red, wht, bl & gray, bright colors, working, 16½x19½", EX, A $150.00

Albino Gorilla, MIB, L4..$525.00

All Stars Mr Baseball Jr, Japan, litho tin, baseball batter's torso turns, he hits the ball, Japan, 8", NM (NM box), A............$1,150.00

American Air 747, TN, silver, red, wht & bl, engines light as plane moves, 14x12", NM, A $85.00

American Airlines, Japan, tin & plastic w/4 propellers, 1960s, T1...$225.00

American Airlines Electra II, tin & plastic, 16", EX+-NM, T1 ....$175.00

American Airlines Jet-Powered Prop Plane, Linemar, inset wing lights, Electra Flagship markings, working, 19", EX, A $345.00

Andy Gard Electric ICBM Interceptor #351, orange plastic, fires missiles, remote control, 1950s, 14", MIB, P4..........$125.00

Animated Santa on Rotating Globe, HTC, 5 actions, 1950s, M, L4...$350.00

Anti-Aircraft Jeep, Cragstan, 5 actions, 1950s, M (VG box), C8 ....$250.00

Anti-Aircraft Jeep, TN, 6 actions, antenna & rear man missing, NM, C8..$375.00

Anti-Aircraft Unit No 1, Linemar, 6 actions, 1950s, NM, C8 ....$225.00

Antique Gooney Car, Alps, 4 actions, 1960s, MIB, C8 .$150.00

Army Radio Jeep, Linemar, 4 actions, 1950s, 7", NM, C8 ..$160.00

Arthur-A-Go-Go, Japan, tin, cloth & vinyl drummer w/Beatles hairdo, sways & plays lighted drum, 9½", EX-, A $260.00

Atom Civilian Motorcycle, MT, litho tin w/helmeted rider, advances w/noise & lights, 12", NM, A $568.00

Atom Motorcycle, MT, 5 actions, 1950s, 12", VG, C8 ..$400.00

Atomic Armored Train Set, MIB, L4 ....$265.00

Atomic Radiation Detection Geiger Counter, 1950s, NMIB $75.00

Atomic Reactor, Linemar, litho tin, NMIB...................$400.00

Auto Studebaker, Italy, MIB..$480.00

Automatic Take-Off & Landing Jet, MIB, L4 ....$375.00

B-Z Fork Lift, Modern Toys, mc litho tin, working, orig box, 7¾", VG-EX, A..$40.00

B-Z Porter Baggage Truck, MT, 2 actions, missing tin luggage, 1950s, EX, C8 ....$210.00

Baby Carriage, NMIB, L4 ....$175.00

Ball-Blowing Clown, Japan, litho tin, w/cloth outfit, only air mechanism working, orig box, 11", VG+, from $225 to $275.00

Ball-Blowing Train #7021, TN, 3 actions, 1950s, NM, C8..$95.00

Ball-Playing Dog, Linemar, tin & plush, throw ball & hit dog's racket, he hits ball, eyes roll, 9", EX (NM box), A..$194.00

Balloon Bunny, rare, L4...$375.00

Balloon Vendor, Japan, tin, cloth & vinyl clown w/balloons & bell, 1961, 11", EX (EX box), A..............................$165.00

Balloon Vendor, MIB, L4..$300.00

Balloon-Blowing Monkey, Alps, 5 actions, 1950s, 11", C8.$100.00

Balloon-Blowing Teddy Bear, Alps, 5 actions, 1950s, NM, C8 ....$150.00

Balloon-Blowing Teddy Bear, MIB, L4 ....$200.00

Barbecue Rotisserie, Japan, tin, 1950s style w/chicken that is inserted over grill, w/utensils & towel, 7½", NMIB, A $120.00

Barber Bear, Linemar, plush and lithographed tin, 11", NM (EX box top, no bottom), A, $515.00.

Barber Bear, Linemar, plush & litho tin, bear barber simulates cutting action on nodding baby bear, 11", EX (EX box), A.........$370.00

Barney Bear Drummer Boy, Cragstan, 10½", NM (EX box), $150.00.

Barney the Drumming Bear, Alps, 1950s, MIB, L4 ....$195.00

Bart Simpson w/Skateboard, Mattel, 6½" figure on 6" skateboard, remote control, missing batteries, K1 ....$25.00

Bartender, TN, 6 actions, 1960s, MIB, from $85 to..........$95.00

Bartender, TN/Japan, working, 1962, EX, C8...................$40.00

Batmobile, bl w/red striping, box shows Batman & Robin in their car, 3½x12", NM (EX box), A $125.00

Batmobile, Taiwan, litho tin w/vinyl-headed Batman & Robin riders, engine noise & blinking lights, 10", NM (EX box), A....$120.00

Batmobile w/Fire-Lighted Engine, ASC, flashing light, engine noise, vinyl-headed Batman, 11", NM (EX box), A.$700.00

Bear the Cashier, MT, plush bear sits behind litho tin desk working adding machine, 7", EX (VG box), A........$276.00

Bear the Cashier, MT, 5 actions, 1950s, M (EX box), C8/L5, from $385 to $400.00

Beechcraft Airplane, MIB, L4 ....$275.00

Begging Puppy, Y/Japan, working, 1960s, G, C8..............$25.00

Bell-Ringer Choo-Coo, MT, lights & sounds, late 1950s, 6x10", MIB $80.00

Bell-Ringing Santa Claus, Japan, 1950s, EX, C8/T1, from $75 to $85.00

Bell-Ringing Santa Claus, Taiwan, plastic, 1970s, M, C8 .$15.00

Big Dipper #316, Technofix/W Germany, three 2" litho tin cars travel roller coaster, 20", EX (NM box), A..............$400.00

Big John Indian Chief, Alps, 4 actions, 1960s, M, C8....$150.00

Big Machine Bump 'N Go, all tin, 1966, MIB, T1............$65.00

Big Machine Race Car, NMIB, L4 ....$175.00

Big Ring Circus Truck, MT, 3 actions, EX, L4 ....$250.00

Billy & Betsy Jolly Riding in Their Old Fashion Car, Craftoy, 3 actions, M (EX box) $295.00

Black Smithy Bear, TN, 4 actions, rare, 1950s, 9", NM, C8 ....$320.00

Blacksmith Bear, 6 actions, 1950s, 9½", MIB, C8 ....$400.00

Blushing Cowboy, Y, 4 actions, 1960s, NM, C8 ....$125.00

Blushing Frankenstein, Japan, litho tin, 13", NM $135.00

Blushing Frankenstein, Japan, NMIB, L4 ....$275.00

Blushing Willie, Y/Japan, working, 1960s, 10", EX, C8....$40.00

Blushing Willie, Y/Japan, 10", NMIB, L4 ....$95.00

Boaterific Shark Pack, 1960s, MIB, T1 ....$25.00

Bobby Drinking Bear, Yonezawa, 6 actions, remote control, 1940s, scarce, 10", EX (NM box), A $395.00

Boeing 737 CP Air, TN, stop-&-go action, sounds, flashing lights, 14x12", NMIB, A $120.00

Boeing 737 Jet, TN, tin & plastic, travels w/stop-&-go action, engine & wing tips light, 14", MIB, A $139.00

Boeing 747, Sears (Japan), plastic w/see-through fuselage, hostesses walk as jet moves to & fro, 15", NM (EX+ box), A $83.00

Bongo Drumming Monkey, Alps, 3 actions, 1950s, MIB, L4 ....$250.00

Bouncing Army Jeep, MT, 4 actions, 1950s, NM, C8 ....$120.00

Boy on Hand Car, MT, 3 actions, 1950s, M, C8 ....$250.00

Brave Eagle, TN, 4 actions, 1960s, NM-M $150.00

Bristol Bulldog Airplane, S&E, litho tin, mk T360, spinning prop & automatic stop-&-go action, 11", EX (EX box), A.$167.00

Broadway Trolley, MT, tin, working, 1950s, EX, C8 ....$95.00

Bruno the Accordion Bear, Y, 5 actions, 1950s, MIB, L4.$575.00

Bubble-Blowing Boy, Yonezawa, litho tin, boy w/bending body dips wand into dish of bubbles, 7½", NM (EX box), A $232.00

Bubble-Blowing Kangaroo, MT, 3 actions, rare, 1950s, NMIB, C8 ....$450.00

Bubble-Blowing Lion, MT, 4 actions, 1950s, NMIB, from $185 to..$220.00

Bubble-Blowing Monkey, Alps, 4 actions, 1950s, NMIB, from $150 to $180.00

Bubble-Blowing Musician, Y, 3 actions, 1950s, soap dish missing, NM, C8..$250.00

Bubble-Blowing Popeye, Linemar, litho tin, 12", EX, A..$500.00

Bubble-Blowing Popeye, Linemar, mc litho tin figure, yel & bl base, arm raises, pipe lights, orig box, 12¼", VG-EX, A...$1,050.00

Bubble-Blowing Train C-162, MT, 3 actions, 1950s, EX, C8 ....$55.00

Bubble-Blowing Washing Bear, rpl washtub, VG, L4.....$125.00

Bubble-Blowing Washing Bear, Y, plush bear on litho tin base scrubs laundry, complete w/bubbles, 7x8", NMIB, A..$375.00

Buick LeSabre Convertible, Ideal, bl, futuristic style, trunk & hood opens, non-working, 16", EX, M5 ....$95.00

Buick Sedan, Japan, pnt tin, red, working, 8½", EX, A $40.00

Buick Special, Japan, pressed tin, lt & dk gr, litho tin interior, rubber tires, power pack missing, 8¼", G, A $45.00

Bulldog Tank, Remco, plastic w/aluminum barrel, rubber treads, fires shells & ejects casings, 1959-60, 23", M (EX+ box) $150.00

Bulldozer, Japan, litho tin, yel, gray & red, non-working, 5½", G+, A $15.00

Bunny the Magician, Alps, litho tin & plush, turns head & tips hat while doing a card trick, 14", NM (EX box), A..$397.00

Bunny the Magician, Alps, 5 actions, 1950s, VG, C8....$250.00

Burger Chef, Yonezawa, litho tin, vinyl & cloth, chef dog holding frying pan over lighted stove, 10", NM (VG box), A.$255.00

Burger Chef, Yonezawa, litho tin, 8 actions, 1950s, NM, C8...$185.00

Busy Housekeeper, MIB, L4 ....$375.00

Busy Secretary, Linemar, litho tin w/vinyl head & hands, types & paper rolls up & down, sounds, 8", NMIB, A $400.00

Busy Secretary, Linemar, mc litho tin & pnt rubber head, lighted moving typewriter, working, orig box, 7½", VG, A..$170.00

Busy Secretary, Linemar, mc litho tin & pnt rubber head, 7 actions, 1950s, NM, C8..$250.00

Busy Shoe-Shining Bear, Alps, 5 actions, 1950s, NM, C8.$225.00

Call Me Baby, NMIB, L4...$275.00

Bubble-Blowing Popeye, Linemar, copyright King Features Syndicate, 12", NMIB, from $1,500.00 to $2,000.00.

Calypso Joe, Linemar, lithographed tin, fabric, rubber and glass, 11½", EX (damaged box), A, $425.00.

Camaro, Toyio, working, 1960s, orig box, EX, C8............$45.00

Cap-Firing Tank, Cragstan, litho tin & plastic, camouflage pnt, cap action, working, orig box, 8¾", VG-EX, A..........$30.00

Capitol Airlines, Japan, tin w/4 props, remote control, 1960s, T1 ....$225.00

Capitol Airlines Viscount, W Germany, instrument panel controls props, runway speed, takeoff & landing, etc, EX, A $500.00

Cappy the Baggage Porter Dog, Alps, 4 actions, 1960s, 12", EX, C8 ....$150.00

Captain Blushwell, Y, tin, vinyl & cloth, hat bounces, pours drink, blushes & eyes roll, non-working, 11", EX (NM box)....$65.00

Captain Blushwell, Y, 11", MIB, L4 ....$160.00

Captain Blushwell, Y, 6 actions, 1960s, 11", NM $100.00

Captain Kidd Pirate Ship, Frankonia Toys/Japan, litho tin, bump-&-go action, 1960s, 13x12", NM (EX+ box), scarce, A $259.00

Caterpillar, VG+, L4 ....$95.00

Champion Racer 301, MIB, L4 ....$675.00

Change-a-Channel TV Set, Kenner, hard plastic w/16" screen, shows motorized movie cartridges, 1966, MIB (Sears box), A $111.00

Chaparral 2F, Alps, 5 actions, 1960s, 11", MIB, L4........$275.00

Charlie the Drumming Clown, M, L4............................$175.00

Charlie Weaver Bartender, TN, MIB, L4 ....$100.00

Charlie Weaver Bartender, TN, scarce version w/no mustache, face reddens, ears smoke, body sways, 12", EX (EX box), A.$135.00

Charlie Weaver Bartender, TN, working, 1960s, 12", EX, C8 ....$50.00

Chef Cook, Y, 5 actions, MIB, L4 ....$275.00

Chemical Fire Engine, HTC, litho tin hose plates, 2 plastic extinguisher containers, fireman, 1950s, 10", NMIB, A.......$185.00

Chevrolet Corvette, MIB, L4 ....$150.00

Chimpy the Drumming Monkey, Alps, 6 actions, 1950s, 9", NM, C8 ....$140.00

Chippy the Chipmunk, Alps, 1950s, 12", MIB, L4.........$250.00

Chirping Woodstock (Peanuts), Concept 2000, MIB $25.00

Circus Elephant w/Blowing Ball & Parasol, TN, rare, MIB..$325.00

Circus Fire Engine, MT, vinyl-head clown, rears up & down, clanging noise, 1960s, 11", MIB, A..........................$265.00

Circus Jet, TN, 1950s, MIB, L4...................................$185.00

Circus Lion, Rock Valley, plush over tin, touch 1 side of carpet to activate, other to turn off, 11", NM (EX+ box), A.......$425.00

Circus Lion, Rock Valley, 4 actions, missing cane & carpet, 1950s, 11", EX, C8...$285.00

Circus Lion, Rock Valley/Japan, no carpet or cane, working, 1950s, VG+ $135.00

Climbing Donald on Fire Engine, Linemar, mc litho tin, friction engine, Donald climbs ladder, working, 18", VG, A .$900.00

Climbing Linesman, TPS, 3 actions, rare, 1950s, NM, C8..$350.00

Clown & Lion, MT, litho tin & vinyl, clown holding on to metal rod is startled by a lion, 12", EX, A.................$273.00

Clown & Monkey Car, MT, 3 actions, 1960s, NM, C8 .$260.00

Clown Car, Alps, mostly plastic, car bounces, marble-eyed headlights roll, sounds, 12", NM, A...................................$110.00

Clown Circus Car/Charlie the Funny Clown, MT, 5 actions, missing broom, 1960s, EX, C8.................................$380.00

Clown Drummer, clown w/yel hair & bow tie sitting at drums in red jacket & blk & wht striped pants, 9", EX+, M5..$160.00

Clown on Roller Skates, tin, Japan, EX+, J2 ....$220.00

Clown the Magician, Alps, cloth, vinyl & litho tin, sways, tips hat & does card trick, 11½", NM (EX box), A........$395.00

Clown the Magician, Alps, cloth, vinyl & litho tin, working, orig box, 11", EX, A...$270.00

Clown w/Lion, TN, 4 actions, 1950s, 12", NM, C8........$380.00

Cock-A-Doodle-Doo Rooster, Mikuni, VG+, L4 ....$50.00

Cock-A-Doodle-Doo Rooster, Mikuni, 4 actions, 1950s, NM (EX box), C8 ....$160.00

Cola Drinking Bear, Alps, working, 1950s, VG, C8.........$55.00

Cola Drinking Bear, Alps, 3 actions, rare yel version, 1950s, NM (VG box), C8 ....$185.00

Collie, Alps, working, 1950s, MIB, from $75 to $90.00

Combat Jeep, MIB, L4...$225.00

Communication Truck, pnt metal, sends Morse code, orig box, L5 ....$350.00

Coney Island Penny Machine, Remco, 1950s, NMIB, L4 .$225.00

Corvette Sting Ray, Ichida, tin w/plastic steering wheel & windshield, bump-&-go action, 1960s, 12", EX (NM box), A $550.00

Cragstan Anti-Aircraft Tank, MIB, L4..........................$225.00

Cragstan Bullfighter, TN, tin, working, 1950s, EX, C8 ....$95.00

Cragstan Cannon, MIB $195.00

Cragstan Circus Jet, NMIB...$185.00

Cragstan Crane with Magnetic Shovel, remote control, M (worn box), $100.00.

Cragstan Crapshooter, Y/Japan, working, 1950s, 9½", VG-EX, C8...$45.00

Cragstan Crapshooter, Y/Japan, 4 actions, 1950s, M (NM box), from $150 to $200.00

Cragstan Crapshooting Monkey, Alps, NM, from $75 to.$85.00

Cragstan Crapshooting Monkey, Alps, 4 actions, 1950s, MIB, from $125.00 to $150.00.

Cragstan El Toro Bullfighter, TN, 4 actions, 1950s, NM, C8 ....$180.00

Cragstan Flying Plane w/Control Tower, 1950s, MIB, L4 .. $395.00

Cragstan Freight Train, complete w/track, working, ca 1950s, NMIB $200.00

Cragstan Inflatable Vinyl Speed Boat w/Battery-Powered Outboard, MIB, L4 ....$185.00

Cragstan Milk-Drinking Dog, Y, 3 actions, 1950s, NM, C8. $110.00

Cragstan One-Armed Bandit, Y, 1960s, MIB, L4 .... $275.00

Cragstan Playboy, 5 actions, 1960s, EX, C8 .... $150.00

Cragstan Roulette Man, Y, 5 actions, 1960s, M, C8 ...... $300.00

Cragstan's Sniffy Dog, Hong Kong, plastic & fur, working, 1960s, G (torn box), C8 ....$25.00

Cragstan Telly Bear, SE, 6 actions, 1950s, M, C8 .... $300.00

Cragstan Tugboat, SAN, 3 actions, 12¾", MIB, L4 .... $225.00

Cragstan Two-Gun Sheriff, Y, 5 actions, 1950s, EX (G box), C8 ....$200.00

Cragston Playboy, M, L4 ....$185.00

Cross Country Express, Japan, litho tin, dashboard & tunnel w/heliport, plastic cars, not working, 13" L, NM (NM box), A $61.00

Custom Roadster, M-T, 4 actions, 1960s, NMIB, C8 ..... $120.00

Cycling Daddy, Bandai, 1960s, 10", MIB, L4 .... $250.00

Daisy Jolly Drumming Duck, Alps, plush duck plays drum set, eyes light, mouth opens & closes, 9", NM, A $183.00

Daisy/matic No 60 Tractor 'N Trailer, MIB, L4 .... $165.00

Daisy/matic No. 61 Cement Mixer Truck, plastic, with original tag, 11" long, M (VG box), $75.00.

Dancing Merry Chimp, CK/Kuramochi, plush, vinyl & tin, switches on base for 16 combined actions, 11½", M (EX box), C8 ....$180.00

Dandy the Drumming Dog, NM, L4 ....$175.00

Dennis the Menace Playing Xylophone, Made in Japan for Sears, mc litho & cloth, working, orig box, 9", EX, A $165.00

Dennis the Menace Playing Xylophone, Rosko, 3 actions, 1950s, MIB, from $250 to $350.00

Dentist Bear, S&E, litho tin, plush, cloth outfit, 7 actions, working, 10", NMIB, A $575.00

Dentist Bear, S&E, 7 actions, mirror missing, 1950s, EX, C8 ....$380.00

Desert Patrol Jeep, MT, 4 actions, 1960s, 11", NM, C8 . $150.00

Dice-Throwing Monkey, Alps, plush & plastic, orig accessories, non-working, hat missing, 11", VG-EX, A $25.00

Dippie the Whale, Japan, litho tin, spouts water, working, 13", VG (EX box) $225.00

Dippie the Whale, Japan, litho tin, spouts water, 13", M (EX box), from $450 to $550.00

Disney Acrobat, Linemar, Donald, pnt celluloid figure swings on litho tin & wire fr, orig box, 9", EX, A $450.00

Disney Acrobat, Linemar, Pluto, 1950s, 9", MIB, L4 ..... $875.00

Disney Haunted House, MIB, L4 ....$275.00

Dodge Postal Savings Truck, tin, 7", EX, J2 ....$45.00

Dolly Dressmaker, TN, 10 actions, rare, 1950s, 7", NM, C8 ....$280.00

Donald Duck Climbing Fireman, Linemar, friction drive, battery action, non-working, VG-, A, $275.00.

Donny the Smiling Bulldog, Tomy, plush body, rubber face moves, barks & walks, 8", EX (NM box), A $100.00

Dozo the Steaming Clown, TN, litho tin & cloth, plush w/rubber face, felt hat, non-working, orig box, 14", VG-, A $185.00

Dozo the Steaming Clown, TN, 5 actions, hat missing, 1960s, 14", EX, C8 ....$250.00

Dreamboat Hot Rod Racer, Japan, 1950s, 7" long, M, D10, $250.00.

Drinking Bear on Barrel, RTV/Japan, working, 1960s, VG, C8 ....$48.00

Drinking Captain, S&E, litho tin, cloth, rubber & plastic, working, orig box, 12½", G, A $70.00

Drinking Captain, S&E, litho tin, cloth, rubber & plastic, 12½", MIB, from $185 to $220.00

Drinking Dog, Y, 4 actions, 1950s, NM, C8 ....$150.00

Drinking Man, M, S1 ....$75.00

Drumming Bunny, MIB, L4 ....$125.00

Drumming Mickey Mouse, Linemar, plush & cloth w/tin face, tin & paper drum, remote control, orig box, 10½", VG-EX, A $850.00

Electric Cable Car, MIB, L4 ....$125.00

Electric Cable Train, Japan, litho tin, blk w/red & gold trim, non-working, orig box, 9½", G-VG, A $15.00

Electrical Emergency Service, complete, M (EX box) $375.00

Electro Powered Monorail Santa & Reindeer, Japan, Santa & deer made of soft material, 1960, EX (EX box), A ..$350.00

Electro Toy Fire Engine, MIB, L4 ....$175.00

Electro Toy Sand Loader w/Conveyor, MIB, L4 ....$225.00

Electromobile, Japan, pnt tin body, bl, litho tin interior, working, orig box, 8¼", EX, A $150.00

Electromobile Taxi, Marusan, 8", M, D10, $325.00.

Electromobile Taxi, Japan, litho tin, working, orig box, 8½", EX, A $230.00

Electromobile Taxi, Japan, mc litho tin, working, separate light switch, 8¼", VG, A $130.00

Electronic Fighter Jet, Ideal, 10 actions, 1959, MIB $325.00

Electronic Periscope, Cragstan, 1950s, MIB $90.00

Elektro Radiant Plane, Schuco/W Germany, mc litho tin, Pan Am 4-motor plane, cast pilots, orig box, 19", EX, A .$625.00

Exploration Train, Japan, litho tin, bl, silver, red & yel, flashing light & sound, w/track, orig 12" box, G-VG, A $600.00

Express Line Train, TN, 3 actions, 1950s, EX, C8 ....$95.00

Fairy Land Train #0741, Daiya, 3 actions, 1950s, NM, C8 .$65.00

Fairy Train, MT, 3 actions, ca 1955-58, MIB $170.00

Farm Truck (Pinkee the Farmer), TN, 3 actions, 1950s, NM, C8 ....$200.00

Feeding Baby Bear, EX, L4 ....$175.00

Feeding Baby Bear, VG, L4 ....$95.00

Feeding Bird Watcher, Linemar, 5 actions, 1950s, NM, C8 ...$420.00

Feeding Bird Watcher, Linemar, 5 actions, 1950s, 9", MIB ..$525.00

Ferrari Convertible, Bandai, tin litho interior, rubber tires w/fancy hubcaps, working headlights, 11", EX, A $289.00

Ferrari 250 GT, China, tin w/litho interior, rubber tires, working horn & lights, 1960s, 9½", NM (EX box), A $503.00

Fido the Xylophone Player, Alps, 6 actions, 1950s, 8¾", EX, C8 ....$180.00

Fighting Bull, Japan, 1960s, MIB, T1 ....$65.00

Filling Station w/Studebaker, Distler, litho tin Shell station w/attached hose & plastic Studebaker, NM (EX box), A $260.00

Fire Bird III, Alps, litho tin, wht & red, flashing lights & sound, working, orig box, 11½", VG-EX, A $500.00

Fire Chief Car, SKK, tin w/plated trim, working, 1970s, EX (VG box), C8 ....$45.00

Fire Chief Mystery Car, TN, 4 actions, 1950s, 9¾", NM, C8 ..$175.00

Fire Chief 62 Ford, Taiyo, tin, 1960s, G, C8 ....$45.00

Fire Command Car, TN, 4 actions, 1950s, M (EX box), C8 ...$250.00

Fire Dept Car #12, TN, 4 actions, 1950s, NM, C8 ....$175.00

Fire Dept Car #7, MT, 3 actions, 1950s, NM, C8 ....$165.00

Fishing Bear, Alps, 6 actions, straw hat missing, 1950s, NM, C8 ....$220.00

Fishing Bear's Bank, Wonderful Toys, 6 actions, 1950s, VG, C8 ....$250.00

Fishing Polar Bear, Alps, 6 actions, 1950s, MIB, L4 ....$325.00

Flintstones Motorized Sports Car & Trailer, MIB, L4 ....$265.00

Flipper Spouting Dolphin, MIB, L4 ....$125.00

Flying Circus, Tomiyama/Japan, litho tin, 2 bears swing bk & forth above net, 17", NM (EX+ box), A $1,350.00

Flying Dutchman, Remco, 1960s, NMIB, T1 ....$125.00

Flying Man, Japan, scarce, M (EX box), A $1,250.00

Flying Police Car, rare, NM, L4 ....$375.00

Flying Tiger Line Cargo Plane, TN, tail opens to lighted cargo area, 14x14", NMIB, A $220.00

Ford Big T, Hong Kong, plastic, working, 1970s, EX (G box), C8 ....$40.00

Ford Model T, Japan, 3 actions, 1950s, NM, C8 ....$120.00

Ford Model T Convertible, Nihonkogei, 4 actions, 1950s, MIB, C8 ....$260.00

Ford Mustang, Japan, Shaggy Doggie barks when car stops automaticaly, w/driver, orig box, 13½", EX, A $650.00

Ford Mustang, Taiyo, tin w/litho interior, bump-&-go, 10", EX+ (EX+ box), A $120.00

Ford Mustang 2X2, AMF, bl, rusty battery box, NM (EX+ box), M5 ....$130.00

Ford Stunt Mustang, Japan, 1969, MIB, D10, $125.00.

Ford Skyliner, TN, w/driver & retractible roof, NMIB, L4 ....$375.00

Fork-Lift S-1002, NM, L4................................$145.00

Frankenstein Monster, TN, 4 actions, 1960s, 14", NM, C8 ....$250.00

Frankie the Rollerskating Monkey, Alps, working, 1960s, 12", VG, C8...$75.00

Frankie the Rollerskating Monkey, Alps, 1960s, MIB, L4 .$225.00

Frankie the Rollerskating Monkey, Alps, 1960s, orig box, EX, T1 ....$185.00

Fred Flintstone's Bedrock Band, Alps, lithographed tin, rubber (head), paper (on drum) and plush (clothing), 9", NM (EX box), A, $1,100.00.

Fred Flintstone Bedrock Band, Alps, 4 actions, 1962, G, C8..$250.00

Fred Flintstone Bedrock Band, Alps, 9", EX- (VG box), A...$775.00

Friendly Puppy, MIB, L4..................................$35.00

Frontline Army Jeep, MIB, L4.........................$150.00

Funland Cup Ride, Sonsco, 3 actions, 7", MIB, L4.........$375.00

Future Fire Car, Japan, litho tin, red, wht, yel & bl, mc lights & sounds, working, orig box, 9½", G-VG, A...............$230.00

F14A Jet Fighter Tom Cat, MIB, L4.................$275.00

G-AHKN.57 Helicopter, Alps, litho tin, rubber tires, working, NMIB $175.00

General Train W-20 W&ARR, SAN, 3 actions, stack rpl, 1950s, EX, C8 ....$75.00

Genie Bottle, Hobby Craft, like Jeannie's (I Dream of Jeannie), smokes, working, 1960s, M (EX box), H4...................$49.00

Gino Neapolitan Balloon Blower, Tomiyama, 5 actions, 1960s, M (EX box), C8/L4 ....$225.00

Gino Neopolitan Balloon Blower, Tomiyama, working, missing soap tray, 1960s, G, C8...$55.00

GMC Firebird III, Alps, bump-&-go, flashing red & gr lights in bk, engine noise, driver & passenger, 12", NM (EX box), A..$725.00

Golden Jubilee Car, TN, 4 actions, 1950s, NM, C8.......$185.00

Goodtime Charlie, MT, 1960s, EX, L4 ....$125.00

Goodtime Charlie, MT, 7 actions, 1960s, NM (EX box), C8 ....$220.00

Gorilla, looks like King Kong, remote control, fur w/plastic hands & feet, runs on wheels, pounds chest, 11", VG, A......$125.00

Gorilla, TN, litho tin w/fur covering, orig box, non-working, 9", EX, A...$154.00

Gorilla, TN, tin & plush, walks, raises arms as eyes light, screams, 9", NM (EX box), A.................................$365.00

Grand Prix Remote-Controlled Auto Raceway, NMIB, L4 ....$375.00

Grandpa Bear in Rocking Chair, Alps, 5 actions, glasses & book missing, NM, C8..$220.00

Grandpa Car, Y, working, 1950s, EX, C8.........................$65.00

Grandpa Car, Y, 4 actions, 1950s, MIB, C8..................$150.00

Great Western Train, MT, 3 actions, 1950s, EX, C8........$85.00

Green Caterpiller, Daiya, plush & mc litho tin, inches along as eyes light up, remote control, 17", EX+ (EX box), A..$154.00

Greyhound Bus, Japan, MIB, A, $280.00.

Greyhound Bus, Japan, bl & wht w/rubber tires, working headlights & horn, orig box, 16½", VG-EX, A $140.00

Growing Walking Lion, Ichida/Rosko, 4 actions, 1960s, MIB, C8 ....$150.00

Grumman Cougar Navy Fighter, K, 3 actions, EX, L4 ...$200.00

Gypsy Fortune Teller, Ichida, insert coin, she moves crystal ball, nods, arm raises, card appears, 10", M (EX box), A.....$1,450.00

Gypsy Fortune Teller, Ichida, 1950s, 10", EX, L4..........$675.00

Hamburger Chef, Japan, vinyl & cloth chef sits at litho tin counter, fry pan moves & bounces, 8" wide, MIB, A.$200.00

Happy 'N Sad Magic Face Clown, Y, 1960s, MIB $300.00

Happy 'N Sad Magic Face Clown, Y, 5 actions, 1960s, NM..$220.00

Happy 'N Sad Magic Face Clown, Y/Japan, tin & cloth, moves, plays accordion, sounds, face changes, 10", EX (NM box), A...$176.00

Happy Clown Theater, Y, litho tin, pnt wood & rubber, plush w/cloth outfit, 3 actions, working, 10", G, A.............$70.00

Happy Clown Theater, Y, w/Pinocchio puppet, 3 actions, 1950s, M, C8..$360.00

Happy Clown Theater, Y, 10", EX, L4 ....$225.00

Happy Drumming Santa, Alps, metal w/cloth clothing, 1960s, orig box, 9", EX...$225.00

Happy Fiddler Clown, Alps, 4 actions, 1950s, MIB, L4 .$595.00
Happy Fiddler Clown, Alps, 4 actions, 1950s, NM, C8 .$400.00
Happy Naughty Chimp, MIB, L4 ....$95.00
Happy Santa (walking), Alps, MIB, L4 ....$325.00
Happy Santa (walking), Alps, 5 actions, 1950s, 11", EX-.$200.00
Happy Santa One-Man Band, Alps, 1950s, MIB, L4 .....$295.00
Hi-Speed Racer, MIB, L4 ....$275.00
High Jinks of the Circus, Cragstan, cloth, plastic & tin, clown pushes
 chimp w/cymbals on ladder, 10", EX (EX box), A..........$255.00
High Jinks of the Circus, TN, 6 actions, 1950s, VG, C8 .$150.00
Hightechnical Rider, TPS, litho tin & plastic 33 Honda
 w/driver, moves in circles & does tight spin, 11", NM (NM
 box), A $126.00
Highway Drive, TN, 1950s, MIB, L4 ....$125.00
Highway Drive, TN, 5" litho tin car on obstacle course
 w/printed paper track, you steer, 15", NMIB, A $85.00
Highway Patrol Car, Japan, tin, w/shooting action, 6", MIB,
 J2 ....$65.00
Highway Patrol Police Car, Taiyo, 1960s, MIB, C8 ....$85.00
Hobo, Alps, litho tin, plush w/cloth outfit, pnt plastic face,
 working, orig box, 10½", EX, A $200.00
Hobo Accordion Player w/Monkey, MIB, L4 ....$575.00
Hobo Accordion Player w/Monkey (playing cymbals), Alps, 6
 actions, 1950s, EX (NM box), C8............................$450.00
Honda Accord, Alps, tin & plastic, 1970s, MIB..............$45.00

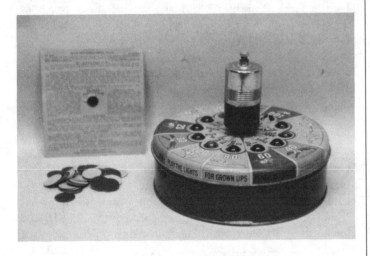

Horse Race Gambling Game, Midwell, D10, $225.00.

Hot Rod, Japan, orange litho tin w/mc trim, erratic action &
 shaking engine, working, orig box, 10", VG-EX, A.$190.00
Hot Rod, Japan, red & bl litho tin w/blk rubber tires, bk-&-forth
 action, pistons vibrate, w/driver, 8½", EX+, A $110.00
Hot Rod Assembly Kit, Unger, plastic, snaps together, unused,
 7", in 19x11" litho box, NM (EX box), A..................$70.00
Hot Rod Custom T, Alps, 4 actions, 1960s, M, C8 ....$380.00
Hot Rod Limousine, Alps, 4 actions, 1960s, NMIB, C8.$350.00
Housekeeping Rabbit, MIB, L4 ....$425.00
Huey Helicopter, MIB, L4...$100.00
Hungry Baby Bear, Yonezawa, plush & tin, mother feeds baby
 who kicks & cries when bottle is gone, 9", EX, A ...$200.00
Hungry Baby Bear, Yonezawa, plush & tin, 9", NMIB, L4.$275.00

Hot Rod Racer, Japan, 1950s, 8", MIB, D10, $325.00.

Hungry Hound Dog, Y, working, rare, VG, C8.................$95.00
Hungry Hound Dog, Y, 6 actions, 1950s, rare, EX, C8...$220.00
Hy-Que the Amazing Monkey, TN, litho tin w/rubber, cloth
 outfit, 6 actions, orig box, 6½", EX, A $150.00
Hysterical Harry, SH, 1960s, VG, L4 ....$125.00
Ice Cream Loving Bear, MT, 3 actions, 1950s, 9½", EX,
 C8 ....$300.00
Indian Joe, Alps, 4 actions, working, 1960s, 12", VG, C8 .$45.00
Indian Joe, Alps, 4 actions, 1960s, 12", NM, C8 ....$100.00
International Agent Car, MIB, L4 ....$195.00

Jaguar XKE, Bandai, 10", M, $200.00.

Jake-the-Shake Shaking Car, Y, 4 actions, 1950s, M (NM box),
 C8 ....$225.00
Japanese Bullet Train, MIB, L4 ....$175.00
Jeep, Bandai, mostly tin, steers, w/blinkers, working,
 EX, C8 ....$45.00
Jimmy Jet, Deluxe Reading, plastic cockpit w/flight simula-
 tor screen, dial & levers, working, 1960, 24x22x14", EX,
 A $225.00
Jocko the Drinking Monkey, Linemar, working, 1950s, 9", VG-
 EX, C8 ....$75.00
Jocko the Drinking Monkey, Linemar, 4 actions, 1950s, NM,
 C8..$150.00
John's Farm Truck, TN, 7 actions, 1950s, MIB, L4 ....$325.00
Jolly Bambino, Alps, candy pours from cantainer into hand, eats
 candy, legs kick, squeals, complete, 9", MIB, A.......$500.00

Jolly Bear Peanut Vender, TN, 5 actions, 1950s, 8", EX, C8 ....$350.00

Jolly Bear the Drummer Boy, K, 7", NMIB, L4...............$250.00

Jolly Daddy Elephant, Marusan, 4 actions, 1950s, NM, C8....$300.00

Jolly Pianist, Marusan, 5 actions, 1950s, 8", NM, C8.....$180.00

Jolly Santa on Snow, Alps, 1950s, MIB, L4....................$400.00

Jumbo the Bubble-Blowing Elephant, Y, 3 actions, soap dish missing, 1950s, NMIB, C8 ....$150.00

Jumbo the Bubble-Blowing Elephant, Y/Japan, working, but doesn't blow bubbles, 1950s, MIB, C8 ....$95.00

Jungle Lion, MT, 4 actions, 1950s, MIB, C8 ....$150.00

Jungle Trio, Linemar, litho tin, vinyl & rubber, monkeys w/drum & cymbals, elephant blows whistle, 8", EX (EX- box), A ..$1,000.00

Knitting Grandma, TN, 3 actions, 1950s, 8½", M, L4 ...$250.00

Ladder Fire Engine, Linemar, bell rings, mystery actions, 1950s, M (EX box)...$285.00

Lady Pup Tending Her Garden, Cragstan, litho tin & cloth, 5 actions, 8", NMIB, A...$385.00

Lady Pup Tending Her Garden, Cragstan, litho tin & cloth, 5 actions, 1950s, 8", NM, C8 ....$250.00

Laffun Head Indian Squaw, M, L4 ....$150.00

Lion, Linemar, plush, remote control, advances w/lighted eyes & roaring sound, 10", EX (VG box), A $140.00

Lincoln-Continental Mark V, Japan, 11", M (EX box), $350.00.

Lite-O-Wheel Go Kart, MIB, L4 ....$185.00

Little Black Box, MIB, L4 ....$135.00

Lockheed Electra II, TN, red, wht, silver & bl, engines fire in sequence, cabin lights up & plane moves, 14x12", EX-, A................$220.00

Loop the Loop Monkey, MIB, L4....................................$85.00

Loop the Loop Power Plane, litho tin, M (EX box), T1.$175.00

Love Bug, VW Beetle, 1960s, MIB, T1 ....$75.00

Lucky Car, rare, VG+, L4...$250.00

Lumber Jack Sitting on Stump Drinking & Holding Ax, Alps, 3 actions, 1980s, MIB, C8 ....$75.00

Lumber Jack Sitting on Stump Smoking & Reading Book, Alps, 3 actions, 1980s, MIB, C8 ....$75.00

Luncheonette Counter, Japan, mc litho tin counter, rubber figure w/cloth clothes, plastic props, lights, 8", VG-EX, A ...$65.00

Loop the Loop Clown, TN, 10½", MIB, $100.00.

M-35 Tank, K/Japan, moves w/rotating turret, makes gun noise, 9", NMIB, A $129.00

Mac the Turtle, Y, litho tin w/rubber bands & head, 5 actions, working, orig box (damaged top), 7½", EX, A.........$110.00

Mac the Turtle, Y, litho tin w/rubber hands & head, 5 actions, 1960s, MIB, C8...$240.00

Magic Bulldozer, TN, 3 actions, 1950s, MIB, L4 ....$175.00

Magic Man Clown, Marusan, 1950s, MIB, L4 ....$625.00

Magic Snow Man, MT, 4 actions, 1940s, orig box, 11¼", EX, L4...$275.00

Magnum PI Rough Riders Torture Trail, LJN, side-wheel action, working lights, 1982, M (NM box), C1 ....$36.00

Major Tooty, MIB, L4 ....$275.00

Mama Bear Feeding Baby, Japan, working, 1960s, G, C8.$90.00

Mama Feeding Baby Bear, plush, mama in bl dress w/wht dots & red & wht checked apron, working, EX+, M5.........$165.00

Mambo the Jolly Drumming Elephant, Alps, 6 actions, 1950s, 9½", C8...$225.00

Maracas Playing Turnover Pup, Japan, working, 1960s, M (worn box), C8 ....$65.00

Marshal Wild Bill, Yonezawa, remote control, w/tin hat, 11", NM (EX box), A $275.00

Maxwell Coffee Loving Bear, TN, 5 actions, 1960s, NM, C8.$200.00

McGregor, TN, smokes cigar, MIB, from $175 to $195.00

McGregor, TN, working, 1960s, VG-EX, C8....................$95.00

Mercedes-Benz C111, remote control, MIB, L4 ....$150.00

Mercedes-Benz 250 SE, Ichida, travels in 'V' pattern, radio antenna raises & lowers, 13½", NM (EX box), A ...$400.00

Mercury Cougar Police Car, MIB, L4.............................$100.00

Merry-Go-Round Truck, litho tin, red truck w/mc carousel & figures, dual function lever & sound, working, 11", VG-EX, A $250.00

Mickey & Donald Fire Engine, Japan, emb litho tin w/pnt rubber, flashing light & bell, working, orig box, 16", EX, A ..$275.00

Mickey Mouse, Tow Truck, Andy Gard Toys, red & wht molded plastic, red figures, remote control, orig box, 7½", EX, A.......$120.00

Mickey Mouse Flying Saucer, MIB, L4 ....$275.00

Mickey Mouse Locomotive, MT, 4 actions, 1960s, NM (VG box), C8...$200.00

Mickey Mouse Loop the Loop, MIB, L4 ....$175.00

Mickey Mouse on Handcar, MT, 1960s, MIB, L4 ....$525.00

Mickey Mouse on Space Scooter, M+, 4 actions, 1960s, NM, C8 ....$300.00

Mickey Mouse Spaceship, M+, 3 actions, MIB, C8........$125.00

Mickey the Acrobat, Linemar, celluloid Mickey performs on highbar, 9", NMIB, A...$545.00

Mickey the Acrobat, Linemar, litho tin w/pnt celluloid figure, working, orig box, 9", EX, A $400.00

Mighty Explorer, tin, w/piston action, NMIB, J2 ....$325.00

Mighty Mike the Barbell Lifter Bear, Japan, litho tin & plush, working, orig box, 10½", EX, A $170.00

Mighty Mike the Barbell Lifter Bear, K/Japan, brn plush bear in yel gym trunks w/barbell, M (EX+ box), A..............$358.00

Military Command Car, TN, 5 actions, 1950s, NM, C8.$280.00

Military Patrol Jeep, TN, tin, w/radio & machine gun, working, 1960s, EX, C8 ....$95.00

Million Bus, KKK, Japan, lithographed tin, forward & reverse actions, ca 1950s, 12" long, EX (EX box), A, $1,950.00.

Mischief Monkey, litho tin, gr & brn w/rubber monkey, working, orig box, 9", EX, A $325.00

Mischievous Monkey w/Bulldog, TN, 4 actions, 1950s, MIB, C8...$460.00

Miss Friday the Typist, TN, lithographed tin, rubber and cloth, 8½", M (NM box), $225.00.

Miss Friday the Typist, TN, litho tin, rubber & cloth, bell & typing actions, orig box, 8½", VG-EX, A $140.00

Miss Friday the Typist, TN, litho tin, rubber & cloth, bell & typing actions, NMIB, L4...$225.00

Mom's Turn, NM, L4 ....$125.00

Monkey Artist, Alps, 5 actions, 1950s, VG, C8 ....$200.00

Monkey on a Picnic, Alps, litho tin, plush, cloth & rubber, working, orig box, 9¾", VG-EX, A $245.00

Mother Bear Sitting & Knitting in Her Old Rocking Chair, MT, 4 actions, 1950s, MIB, from $360 to $390.00

Mountain Cable Car, MIB, L4 ....$150.00

Mountain Special Express, MIB, L4 ....$60.00

Mr Baseball Jr, Japan, mc litho tin figure & base, automatic batting action, working, orig box, 7½", VG-EX, A $375.00

Mr Fox the Magician Blowing Magical Bubbles, Cragstan, gr & red attire, Uncle Sam hat, 9½", NM (EX box), from $250 to .$350.00

Mr MacPooch Smoking Pipe, SAN, 4 actions, 1950s, NM (EX box), C8...$240.00

Mr MacPooch Smoking Pipe, SAN/Japan, working, 1950s, VG, C8 ....$75.00

Mr Magoo Car, Hubley, pnt & litho tin, cloth & pnt vinyl, 1961, 9", NM (EX+ box), from $300 to.................$400.00

Mr Magoo Car, Hubley, pnt & litho tin, plastic, cloth & pnt vinyl, sounds, working, 9", VG+, A.......................$200.00

Mr Magoo Car, Hubley, lithographed tin, car sways with forward and reverse actions, NMIB, A, $345.00.

Mr Magoo Car, Japan, tin, 1961, M, T3 ....$225.00

Mr Strong Pup, MIB, L4..$475.00

Multi-Act DC-7C Airplane American Airlines, AHI/Japan, Flagstaff CA, passengers appear/disappear, 24", EX+ (EX box), A.$675.00

Mumbo Jumbo the Hawaiian Drummer, Alps, 3 actions, 1960s, NM, C8 ....$150.00

Musical Bulldog, SAN, 1950s, 8½", M, L4 ....$875.00

Musical Cadillac, Irco, red litho tin, 1950s, 9", M (VG box).$500.00

Musical Clown, TN, clown playing xylophone mk New Adventures of Clown, plays London Bridge, EX (VG box), A...........$700.00

Musical Clown, TN, plays xylophone mk New Adventures of Clown, missing cover over base & 1 hinge on battery box, EX, M5 ....$160.00

Musical Clown, TN, 1960s, 9", MIB, L4.........................$875.00

Musical Jolly Chimp, CK, 1960s, MIB, L4......................$95.00

Musical Jolly Chimp, CK, 5 actions, 1960s, M (EX box), C8..$80.00

Musical Marching Bear, Alps, 1950s, 11", MIB, L4........$675.00

Musician, Japan, litho tin, bl cloth suit & plastic horn, working, orig box, 10", EX, A.......................................$130.00

Mustang Convertible, Yonezawa, tin, 1960s, NMIB, T1.$225.00

My Fair Dancer, Haji, 1950s, 10½", MIB, L4..................$275.00

Mystery Action Jeep, MIB, L4..$100.00

Mystery Antique Car, TN, 3 actions, 1950s, M, C8......$145.00

Mystery Car, Alps, pnt & litho tin, red & wht, working, orig box (worn), 12", EX, A $850.00

Mystery Fire Chief, Sanshin, 1950s, MIB $225.00

M35, Tank, MIB, L4..$175.00

M4 Tank, MIB, L4...$225.00

Nautilus Periscope, MIB, L4...$225.00

New Flippity Flyer, MIB, L4..$135.00

New Ford, MIB, L4..$185.00

Non-Stop Action Tiny Tank, MIB, L4.............................$65.00

Non-Stop Boat, MIB, L4..$225.00

Northwest DC-7C, Cragstan, engines start, plane moves, passengers leave, door opens, reveals stewardess, 23x21", EX, A..$300.00

Nosey the Sniffy Dog, Mego, plastic & fur, working, 1960s, MIB, C8...$45.00

Nutty Mad Car, MIB, L4...$675.00

Nutty Mad Car, VG+, L4...$195.00

Nutty Navy Submarine, 1960s, M, T1 ....$15.00

Nutty Nibs, Linemar, painted tin, retains 3 metal balls, 12", EX (EX box), A, $850.00.

Ol' Sleepy Head Rip, Y, litho tin, cloth & vinyl, features Rip in bed w/bird on headboard, 9" , EX (EX box), A........$275.00

Ol' Sleepy Head Rip, Y, MIB, L4 ....$495.00

Ol' Sleepy Head Rip, Y, 7 actions, 1950s, EX, C8..........$220.00

Old Fashioned Car, MIB, L4 ....$150.00

Old Fashioned Car, SH, 4 actions, 1950s, NM, C8 ....$80.00

Old Fashioned Fire Engine, MT, 4 actions, 1950s, NM, C8..$200.00

Old Fashioned Shaking Model T Ford Car, Japan, tin & plastic, working, 1960s, EX, C8...$75.00

Old Fashioned Telephone Bear, MT, 4 actions, 1950s, NM, C8..$200.00

Old Ford Model T Rocking Chair, Japan, tin, radiator lights & goes in & out, working, 1960s, EX, C8 ....$75.00

Old Ford Touring Car, Z, 4 actions, 1950s, MIB, C8 .....$120.00

Old Grandpa Model T Car, 5 actions, 1960s, M, C8......$125.00

Old Time Autoball, Car-Y, tin, 1950s, EX, C8................$95.00

Old Time Automobile, M-T, 3 actions, 1950s, MIB, C8..$200.00

Old Timer Car, Cragstan, 3 actions, 1950s, G, C8 ....$80.00

Old Timer Car, Yonezawa, litho tin, elderly man at wheel, changes direction on impact, 9½x8", NM (VG box), A..............$125.00

Old Timer Sunday Driver, Daiya, 4 actions, 1960s, MIB, C8..$200.00

Old Timer Taxi, Alps, mostly tin, hot rod style w/silhouettes at windows, shakes, moves & smokes, 10", EX (M box), A...$141.00

Oldsmobile Toronado, Taiyo, tin, working, 1960s, M, C8..$85.00

Overland Express Train, MT, 1950s, MIB, L4 ....$60.00

Overland Stagecoach, Cragstan, mc litho tin, galloping sound & action, working, orig box, 14", EX, from $130 to $165.00

Overland Stagecoach, MT, litho tin w/plastic driver & horses, horses gallop w/clop noise, 18", EX (NM box), A...$165.00

Pacific Choo Choo Express, Kanto, 4 actions, 1950s, NM, C8..$145.00

Pan Am Airlines 747, TN, red, wht, bl & silver, 4 engines light as plane moves, 14x12", NM , A...............................$95.00

Pan American World Airways Plane, TN, Seven Seas, 4 tin props, Douglas DC-7C on tail, lights work, 19" , EX (EX box), A..$450.00

Passenger Bus, Japan, mc litho tin w/rubber tires, working lights, door opens, orig box, 15¾", VG-EX, A....................$175.00

Patrol Helicopter, MT, mostly tin, bump-&-go action, blades spin, sounds, w/pilot & co-pilot, 17", EX (NM box), A.....$166.00

Pelican w/Fish in Mouth, Y, 4 actions, 1960s, EX, C8......$85.00

Pepi Tumbling Monkey, Yanoman, working, 1960s, EX, C8..$55.00

Pepi Tumbling Monkey, Yanoman, 1960s, MIB, L4.......$100.00

Performing Lion, MIB, L4 ....$575.00

Pet Turtle, NM, L4..$125.00

Peter the Drumming Rabbit, Japan, w/remote control, MIB..$200.00

Peter the Drumming Rabbit, Japan, working, 1950s, G, C8..$69.00

Phantom Raider, Ideal, complete, working, 1963, NMIB..$200.00

Picnic Bear, Alps, 5 actions, 1950s, M (EX box), C8.....$180.00

Picnic Bear, MT, 4 actions, rare yel version, 1950s, NMIB, C8..$185.00

Picnic Monkey, Alps, 5 actions, 1950s, NM, C8............$120.00

Piggy Cook, Japan, working, missing egg, 1950s, VG, C8..$65.00

Piggy Cook, Y, 5 actions, 1950s, NM, C8......................$220.00

Pinky the Clown, Rock Valley, M, L4 ....$375.00

Pinky the Juggling Clown, Alps, litho tin w/plastic face & plush hair, blows whistle, working, orig box, 10", EX, A ..$300.00

Pirate Ship, MT, Japan, tin with heavy paper sails, 13" long, original box, EX, A, $425.00.

Pistol Pete, Marusan, lithographed tin and cloth, 11", EX (EX box), A, $240.00.

Piston Bulldozer, SH, tin & plastic, w/driver, working, 1970s, EX, C8 ....$45.00

Playful Puppy, MT, 4 actions, 1950s, NM, C8................$180.00

Pluto, Japan, litho tin, yel plush & rubber, remote control, 4 motions, working, 10½", VG-EX, A $90.00

Police Auto Cycle, Bandai, pnt tin, wht, silver & blk, rubber figure, remote control, working, orig box, 11¾", VG, A$85.00

Police Car, Arnold, pnt tin, manual remote control, steering mechanism, working, orig box, 10", EX, A $100.00

Police Car, 1959 Olds, Ichiko, blk & wht, red trim, PD above rear wheel, speedometer on trunk, non-working, 13", VG, M5..$180.00

Police Car No 5, TN, 4 actions, 1950s, MIB, C8 ....$220.00

Police Patrol Car, TN, 4 actions, 1950s, NMIB, C8.......$225.00

Police Patrol Jeep, TN, 4 actions, 1950s, EX (EX box), C8...$200.00

Policeman on Honda Motorcycle, EX, L4 ....$225.00

Policeman w/Machine Gun, Japan, 1960s, EX, T1.........$225.00

Police Car #5, Alps, NM (VG box), $185.00.

Popcorn Vendor Truck, TN, 3 actions, 1960s, MIB, from $300 to...$350.00

Popeye Rollover Tank, litho tin, dk army gr w/Popeye figures on all sides, working, slightly sluggish, 4", EX+, M5.....$350.00

Porsche, tin, red bump-&-go car w/decals, flashing lights, working, 10", VG, M5 ....$59.00

Porsche 911, 1960, Bandai, M, $135.00.

Porsche 911 News Service Car, TPS, Japan, litho tin, camera & man atop car, orig box, 9½", EX+ (EX box), A $529.00

Porsche 911 R, Schuco #356-218, plastic, red & yel, comes w/4 tires, jack, wrench, etc, 10", complete, EX+ (EX box), A........$203.00

Portable Mixmaster, MIB, L4 ....$65.00

Poverty Pup Bank, Poynter, 3 actions, NM, C8..............$100.00

Pretty Boy the Singing Canary, AHI/Japan, w/on-&-off switch, orig box, L5...$115.00

Princess the French Poodle, Alps, 5 actions, 1950s, EX, C8..$50.00

Professor Owl, ET, 5 actions, 1950s, 8", EX, C8 ....$250.00

Professor Owl, Japan, mc litho w/blackboard, non-working, w/2 learning disks, orig box, 8¼", NM, A.....................$375.00

Queen Mary River Boat, NM, L4...................................$125.00

Queen of the Sea, MT, MIB, L4......................................$775.00

Rabbits Carriage, S&E, mother pushing baby in buggy, 6 actions, 1950s, EX (VG box), C8 ....$320.00

Radar Jeep, MIB, L4 ....$225.00

Radar Police Jeep, MIB, L4 ....$150.00

Radar Tank, MT, bl litho tin w/red, yel & wht accents, red dome light, clicking engine noise, 8", NM (EX+ box), A ...$208.00

Radar Tractor, EXIB, L4...$495.00

Radicon Benz 230 SL, MT, MIB.................................$900.00

Radicon Boat, rare, MIB, L4 ....$895.00

Railway Yard, ATC, litho tin locomotive & car travel 29" track, engine releases car & circles bk to station, MIB, A.$147.00

Rambling Ladybug, MIB, L4......................................$95.00

Randy the Walking Monkey, NMIB, L4......................$175.00

Ranger Jeep, MIB, L4 ....$175.00

Reading Bear, Alps, 5 actions, 1950s, 9", EX, C8..........$175.00

Ricki the Begging Poodle, VIA/Japan, working, 1960s, VG-EX, C8...$25.00

Ricki the Poodle, Alps, 3 actions, eyes light, mid-1950s, 8", EX (VG box) $55.00

Rifle w/Screen Scope, MIB, L4 ....$225.00

Road Roller the Steam Roller, MT, 4 actions, 1950s, M (NM box), C8..$150.00

Rock 'N Roll Monkey, Alps, litho tin, plush & cloth, plastic hat, working, orig box, 11½", G-VG, A $150.00

Rock 'N Roll Monkey, Alps, plush face, strums guitar & dances while singing into lighted microphone, 12", NMIB, L4...........$295.00

Roger Rabbit Bopper, Epoch, Japan, sounds, 15", MIB, D1 ....$800.00

Roulette Gambling Man, sways w/facial expressions, drops ball, shakes money bag, w/instructions, 10", NM (EX box), A $220.00

Rowing Snoopy, Concept/UFS, plastic, rowing Snoopy & Woodstock in red & bl boat, orig box, 8½", NM+, A $65.00

Rusher Mach 1 Mustang, Japan, 1969, D10, MIB, $125.00.

Sammy Wong the Tea Totaler, TN, 4 actions, 1950s, EX, C8.$260.00

Sand Buggy, Taiyo, tin & plastic, working, 1960s, MIB, C8 .$65.00

Santa Bank, Trim-A-Tree, HTC, 4 actions, 1960s, EX, C8.$250.00

Santa Claus on Reindeer Sleigh, MT, tin & vinyl, advances, lights & sounds, 17", EX (NM box), A....................$550.00

Santa Claus on Scooter, MT, 4 actions, 1960s, M (NM box), C8.$220.00

Santa Claus Phone Bank, rare, EX, L4...........................$495.00

Santa Copter, MT, 3 actions, 1960s, M (NM box), C8/L4.$150.00

Santa on Globe, Japan, cloth w/vinyl face, litho tin globe & base, lights & lifts gifts, partly working, 14", VG, A..$85.00

Santa on Roof, MIB, L4 ....$225.00

Santa Bank, Trim-A-Tree, HTC, NM (EX box), L4, $300.00.

School Bus, Japan, litho tin, bl, yel & red w/rubber tires, sounds, working, orig box, 20¼", EX, A $100.00

Sea Plane, Remco, working propeller, 1960s, NMIB........$40.00

Shaking Antique Car, MIB, L4 ....$125.00

Shaking Classic Car, TN, 4 actions, 1960s, M, C8.........$120.00

Shaking Old-Timer Car, TN, tin, working, 1960s, EX, C8.$85.00

Shark-U-Control Racing Car, Remco, 1961, NMIB, L4 ..$95.00

Sheriff's Car, TN, 4 actions, 1950s, NM (EX box), C8 ..$220.00

Shoe Maker Bear, TN, 3 actions, 1960s, NM, C8 ....$200.00

Shoe Maker Monkey, rare, MIB, L4..............................$675.00

Shoe Shine Bear, TN/Japan, litho tin, plush, rubber & pnt plastic, pipe lights, non-working, orig box, 9", VG+, A ..$85.00

Shoe Shine Bear, TN/Japan, 5 actions, 1950s, NM, C8.$200.00

Shoe Shine Joe, Alps, 6 actions, 1950s, NM, C8...........$200.00

Shooting Bear, Marusan, plush & litho tin, remote control, shoots rifle & smoke comes from barrel, 10½", EX, A $200.00

Shooting Cowboy, Japan, mc litho tin, sounds, working, orig box, 8¼", VG, A..$725.00

Shooting Fighter, MIB, L4 ....$150.00

Shooting Gallery Roaring Gorilla, MIB, L4...................$350.00

Showboat, Remco, 1960s, EX, T1 ....$125.00

Showboat w/Whistle & Smoke, MIB, L4.......................$225.00

Shutterbug, TN, Japan, lithographed tin, NM (EX box), from $575.00 to $650.00.

Shuttling Switcher Freight Train, Cragstan, bk-&-forth action, dumps & receives logs, brakeman signals, MIB, A ..$130.00

Sightseeing Bus, Alps, 3 actions, 1960s, M (NM box), C8 ....$125.00

Single Seat Fighter (airplane), Schuco, Radiant-5600, 4-motor, mk KLM, very clean, minor scuffing, 16½x18½", A..$100.00

Skipping Monkey, TN, 2 actions, 1960s, NM (EX box), C8 ....$100.00

Sky Patrol, Japan, pnt & litho tin, red, wht & bl, lights & sounds, working, orig box, 7¼" dia, VG-EX, A..........$70.00

Sleeping Baby Bear, Linemar, 6 actions, 1950s, NM, C8..$350.00

Slurpy Pup, TN, 4 actions, 1960s, NM, C8..................$100.00

Smokey the Bear, SAN, tin, cloth & plush, complete w/hat & shovel, walks, smokes pipe, 9", EX (NM box), A $325.00

Smokey the Bear Jeep, Japan, pnt & litho tin w/rubber tires, lights & horn sounds, working, orig box, 10½", VG, A........$650.00

Smokey the Bear Jeep, rare, EX, L4..................$675.00

Smoking & Shoe Shining Bear, Alps, litho tin, plush & plastic, cloth outfit, working, orig box, 10", EX, A $160.00

Smoking & Shoe Shining Panda Bear, Alps, plush bear seated on litho tin brick bench, 10", NM (EX box), A $257.00

Smoking Bunny, SAN, cloth & tin, walks, lifts lighted pipe to mouth, blows smoke, 9", MIB, L4 ....$250.00

Smoking Grandpa, SAN, in rocking chair, 4 actions, 1950s, M (VG box)..................................$275.00

Smoking Papa Bear, SAN, 4 actions, 1950s, MIB, C8/L4, from $175 to................................$200.00

Smoking Popeye, Linemar, lithographed tin, EX (EX box), A, $1,500.00.

Smoky Bill on Old Fashioned Car, TN, 4 actions, 1960s, MIB, C8..................................$250.00

Smoky Joe Fancy Mobile, TN, 4 actions, 1950s, EX, C8.$150.00

Smurf Train, Peyo, 1970s, orig box, EX, T1 ....$30.00

Snake Charmer, Linemar, litho tin & cloth w/plastic props, musical flute & smoke, working, orig box, 7½", VG+, A.$325.00

Snake Charmer & Casey the Trained Cobra, Linemar, 4 actions, 1950s, EX, C8 ....$300.00

Sneezing Bear, Linemar, plush, lifts tissue to nose, 10", VG+..............................$182.00

Sneezing Bear, Linemar, 5 actions, 1950s, M, C8..........$360.00

Sniffing Dog, Alps, tin & fur, working, 1960s, VG, C8....$35.00

Snoopy Driving Space Scooter, NMIB, J2 ....$325.00

Spanking Bear, Linemar, 6 actions, 1950s, EX, C8.........$250.00

Sparky the Seal, Linemar, 4 actions, 1950s, MIB $150.00

Sparky the Seal, M, L4.....................................$95.00

Strange Explorer, DSK, 4 actions, 1960s, MIB, L4.........$300.00

Streamliner, Japan, mc litho tin, non-working, orig 11½" box (torn), EX, A $60.00

Struttin' Sam, Japan, mc litho tin, emb features, working, 11", MIB, from $500 to................................$600.00

Stunt Plane, TPS, MIB, L4................................$275.00

Sunday Driver, MT, 4 actions, M (EX box), C8.............$200.00

Sunny Andy Ferry Pull Toy, litho tin, gr, yel, red & wht, lights, 13¾", G-G+, A..............................$45.00

Super Control Anti-Aircraft Jeep, S&E, 6 actions, 1950s, NM (VG box), C8 ....$245.00

Super Greyhound Bus, MIB, L4 ....$275.00

Super Power Hot Rod Racer, Japan, 10" long, EX, D10, $250.00.

Super Susie, Linemar, plush bear on litho tin advertising base behind cash register, 9x5", NM (NM box), A $700.00

Super Susie, Linemar, 6 actions, rare, 1950s, EX, C8 .....$450.00

Surrey Jeep, TN, litho tin w/fabric-fringed top, MIB......$185.00

Swinging Monkey, Iwaya, working, 1970s, EX, C8...........$35.00

Switchboard Operator, Linemar, litho tin, vinyl-headed operator, moves hands, board lights, 7", MIB...................$800.00

Switchboard Operator, Linemar, 4 actions, 1950s, NM, C8 ....$500.00

Synchromatic 5700 Packard Hawk Convertible, Schuco, steer w/ wheel, on/off on dash, 10½", EX (EX box), A $880.00

Talk-a-Vision, 1950s, M (VG box)................................$225.00

Talking Parrot, TN, parrot perched on tree branch on tree-trunk base, repeats messages, 17", EX+, M5 ....$375.00

Teddy the Artist, Japan, missing plates, VG+, L4 ....$125.00

Teddy the Artist, Japan, w/1 plate, MIB, L4....................$325.00

Teddy the Artist, Japan, w/9 drawing plates, book & crayons, orig box, 8½", EX, A................................$350.00

Teddy the Artist, Y, 3 actions, w/9 plates, 1950s, MIB, C8 ....$450.00

Teddy the Boxing Bear, Japan, tin litho & plush, swings at punching bag, movable head & eyes, 7x9", NM (EX box), A..........$385.00

Teddy the Boxing Bear, Y, 5 actions, 1950s, EX, C8......$220.00

Telephone Bear, MT, 4 actions, 1950s, NM, C8...........$350.00

Telephone Bear, TN, plush bear seated at litho tin desk mk I May Look Busy, 8x5x7", EX+ (EX+ box), A...........$300.00

Telephone Bunny, MIB, L4..$275.00

Tempo VI Speedboat, MIB, L4.....................................$165.00

Thunder Jet Boat, VG+, L4..$150.00

Thunderbird Speedster, pnt & litho tin, plastic driver, lights & door opens, non-working, orig box, 10¾", VG-EX, A............$500.00

Tin Can Alley, MIB, L4...$125.00

Tinkling Trolley, MT, 4 actions, 1950s, MIB, L4...........$195.00

Tom & Jerry Handcar, MT, 3 actions, 1960s, MIB, C8 .$300.00

Tom & Jerry Helicopter, rare, EX, L4............................$375.00

Tractor, Japan, litho & pnt tin, red, gray & silver w/rubber treads, 1 broken tread, working, orig box, 9½", VG, A........$230.00

Traffic Policeman, Japan, litho tin w/pnt plastic head, bl cloth outfit, working, orig box, 14", VG, A......................$160.00

Traffic Policeman, Japan, 13½", EX (EX box)................$295.00

Traveler Bear, brn plush in red & wht checked pants w/suitcase, works partially, needs adjustment, 7", EX+ (G+ box), M5........$150.00

Tric-Cycling Clown, MT, 5 actions, 1960s, rare, MIB, L4..$1,000.00

Trik-Trak Cross Country Road Rally, Transogram, complete w/track & accessories, 1964, MIB..........................$45.00

Trumpet Playing Monkey, Alps, 4 actions, 1950s, EX (EX box), from $275 to $300.00

Tugboat, Cragstan, mc litho tin, smokes, working, orig box, 12½", VG-EX, A...$80.00

Tumbling Monkey, MIB, L4..$125.00

Tumbling Popeye, Linemar, 4½", NMIB+, A, $1,600.00.

Turn-O-Matic Gun Jeep, TN, 1960s, NMIB, L4............$175.00

Turn-O-Matic Gun Patrol Car, MIB, L4 ....$225.00

TWA Jet Plane, TN/Japan, working, 1960s, EX, C8........$45.00

Twin Racing Cars, MIB, L4..$875.00

U-Turn Cadillac, Japan, mc litho tin, working, orig box (damaged), 9", VG-EX, A...$160.00

U-Turn Cadillac, MIB, L4..$225.00

United Airlines Jet, Japan, litho tin, metallic bl, red, wht & silver, friction (prop spins), lights, 14½", VG, A........$170.00

United Airlines 747 Jet, T/Japan, tin & plastic, working, 1960s, MIB, C8..$75.00

Veteran Car, TN, 3 actions, 1950s, MIB, C8.................$185.00

Vibraphone, S&E, 1950s, MIB, L4................................$150.00

VIP Busy Boss Bear, S&E, plush & cloth bear sitting behind litho tin desk, dial phone for action, VG (VG box), A.....$232.00

VIP Busy Boss Bear, S&E, 6 actions, 1950s, NM, C8.....$380.00

Voice Control Kennedy Airport, orig box, EX, L4.........$150.00

Volkswagen Bus, Japan, pnt & litho tin, red & wht, pnt plastic driver, 8 motions, working, orig box, 9½", EX, A...$300.00

Volkswagen w/Visible Engine, KO, 1960s, MIB, L4......$175.00

VW Police Van, MIB, L4..$175.00

Wacky Droopy Snoopy, dog, 1970s, NMIB, T1...............$35.00

Waitress Shaking Cocktail, Japan, 1970, MIB, T1...........$74.50

Walking & Barking Dog, Japan, working, 1950s, EX, C8.$25.00

Walking & Barking Lg Dog, Japan, working, 1960s, VG, C8..$35.00

Walking Donkey, MT, tin & fur, working, 1950s, G, C8.$25.00

Walking Gorilla, Linemar, remote control, in red hat, red & wht striped overalls, plush & tin, 7½", NMIB, A...........$470.00

Walking Mule, MT, tin, missing rider, working, 1950s, G, C8..$30.00

Warpath Indian, Alps, 3 actions, 1950s, EX, C8............$120.00

Wen-Mac Cargo Ship Dolphin, AMF, plastic, 26", MIB .$75.00

Western Bad Man, Japan, litho tin, pnt plastic, cloth outfit, w/plastic props, working, orig box, 9¾", EX, A........$475.00

Western Special Locomotive, Modern Toys, MIB...........$65.00

Westland G-AMHK Helicopter, EX, L4.........................$195.00

Whirlybird, Remco, NMIB...$78.00

Wild West Rodeo, bubble blower, bull & rider on litho tin base, working, missing bubble cap, VG+, M5...................$135.00

Windy the Circus Elephant, TN, EX, L4 ....$125.00

Windy the Circus Elephant, TN, plush w/tin base, waves her feet while spinning umbrella etc, 10", EX (EX box), A...$200.00

Wizard of Oz Tin Man, Remco, 21", MIB, L4 ....$375.00

Worried Mother Duck & Baby, TN, litho tin, mother quacks & turns to check on baby, hat missing, 10", NM (EX box), A.......$95.00

Yo-Yo Monkey, MIB, L4 ....$425.00

Bicycles

The most interesting of the vintage bicycles are those made between 1920 and the 1960s, though a few even later models are collectible as well. Some from the fifties were very futuristic and styled with sweeping Art Deco lines, others had wonderful features such as built-in radios and brake lights, and some were decked out with saddle bags and holsters to appeal to fans of Hoppy, Gene, and other western heroes. Watch for reproductions.

Condition is everything when evaluating bicycles, and one worth $2,500.00 in excellent or better condition might be worth as little as $50.00 in unrestored, poor condition. But here are a few values to suggest a range. Our advisor for this category is Richard Trautwein (T3).

Boy's, French, aluminum w/9" rubber wheels, 1930s, EX+, M5..$125.00

Evans, maroon & wht, w/combination headlight & horn on front fender, G...$180.00

Donald Duck Bike, two-wheeled boy's style, repainted, 58" long, VG, A, $250.00. (The same in excellent, restored condition would be worth a minimum of $1,500.00.)

Fleetwing, pnt red & bl fr, chrome wheels & fenders, shock-absorber springs in front fork, 70", G, A $120.00

George N Pierce, blk fr w/chrome handlebars, NP forks, wood wheel rims, ornate pedals, oil lamp, rstr, 72", EX, A $1,950.00

JC Higgins (Sears), maroon w/gold tank, shock-absorber springs, rstr, EX+..$400.00

Monarch, blk & cream, shock-absorber springs, all orig, EX..$650.00

Roadmaster, Cleveland Welding, bl & wht fr, chrome wheels, pnt faded, wheels pitted, 70", G, A $70.00

Roadmaster, women's, bl & cream, chrome wheels, w/out shock-master forks, pre-1948, G+ $125.00

Schwinn Hornet, headlight on fender, 26", G $70.00

Schwinn Stingray, 5-speed, mag wheels, w/orig booklet, NM $350.00

Sears Elgin Bluebird, bl w/red trim, built-in speedometer in top of tank, all orig, G $240.00

Shelby's Donald Duck, c Walt Disney, Donald's head at front, eyes light, horn quacks, fender skirts, 20", NM orig........$2,600.00

Black Americana

Black subjects were commonly depicted in children's toys as long ago as the late 1870s. Among the most widely collected today are the fine windup toys made both here and in Germany. Early cloth and later composition and vinyl dolls are favorites of many, and others enjoy ceramic figurines. Many factors enter into evaluating Black Americana, especially in regard to the handmade dolls and toys, since quality is subjective to individual standards. Because of this you may find wide ranges in dealers' asking prices. In order to better understand this field of collecting, we recommend *Black Collectibles Sold in America* by P.J. Gibbs. See also Books; Battery-Operated Toys; Windups, Friction and Other Mechanicals.

Acrobatic Balancing Toys, Anchor Toy, 5 diecut wooden pcs featuring Black porter, 1920s, 5¼", MIP, P6............$175.00

Birthday Card, amimated pop-up, Don't Be Melon-Cholic Honey..., boy at fence looking at watermelons, full-color, EX, P6 ....$22.00

Book, Beloved Belindy, MA Donahue & Co, written & illus by Johnny Gruelle, Belindy waving on cover, 1930s, 9x6", EX+, P6..$125.00

Book, diecut in form of Golliwog in red jacket, bl striped pants w/cane, Holland, Golliwog & Friends, 13½", EX, P6 .$110.00

Book, Ezekiel, written & illus by Elvira Garner, 1st edition, 1937, EX, P6 ....$75.00

Book, How Come Christmas, by Roak Bradford, c 1938 & 1948, 8¼x5¾", EX, P6 ....$79.00

Book, Little Black Sambo, color w/blk & wht illus by Nina R Jordan, 1932, 6¼x5", EX, P6 ....$110.00

Book, Little Black Sambo, Harter, illus by Fern Bisel, Sambo w/folded umbrella, hard-bound, 16 pgs, 1931, EX, P6..$85.00

Book, Little Black Sambo, Mary Perks, illus by Fern Bisel Peat, Sambo pulls on Tiger, hard-bound, 1943, 13x10", EX, P6.............$99.00

Book, Little Black Sambo, Saalfield Pub Co, full-color illus by Ethel Hays, boy w/umbrella, cloth-like, dtd 1942, EX, P6 ....$79.00

Book, Little Black Sambo's Jungle Band, written & narrated by Paul Wing, w/2 45 rpm records, 20 pgs, 1939-50, EX, P6 ....$110.00

Book, Little Black Sambo Story Book, 1962 edition by Platt & Munk w/6 orig stories, hard-bound, 54 pgs, VG+, P6 ..$85.00

Book, Little Brown KoKo, 1st edition, hard-bound w/dust jacket intact, 96 pgs, 1940, 11x8", EX, P6 ....$75.00

Book, Little Brown KoKo's Pets & Playmates, by Blanche Seal Hunt, 1st edition, 1959, 7½x5", EX $36.00

Book, Noddy Goes to School, by Grid Blyton, full-color illus by Beek, hard-bound, dust jacket intact, 60 pgs, M, P6..$32.00

Book, Petuni Be Keerful, by Anne Christopher, illus by Inez Hogan, Whitman, 1st edition, 1934, EX, P6 ....$69.00

Book, Picaninny Twins, written & illus by Lucy Fitch Perkins, school reader for grades 3-4, 149 pgs, 1931, EX, P6...$79.00

Book, Pop-Up Little Black Sambo, color cover & pop-ups, 1934, VG-EX, A...$260.00

Book, Six Little Bunkers at Mammy June's, by Laura Lee Hope, 1st edition, hard-bound, 1922, EX, P6 ....$59.00

Book, SoJo the Story of Little Lazy Bones, Erick Berry, full-color cover w/blk & wht illus, 38 pgs, 1934, 9x7", EX, P6..$65.00

Book, Stephen Foster & His Little Dog Tray, by Opal Wheeler, blk & wht illus, hard-bound, 173 pgs, 1943, EX, P6 ..$45.00

Book, Story Book of Clothes, by Maud & Miska Petersham, John C Winston Co, hard-bound, 1947, 8x8", EX, P6 ....$39.00

Book, Twin Lids, by Inez Hogan, 6th printing, hard-bound, very rare, 1938, EX, P6 ....$75.00

Book, Uncle Tom's Cabin, Young Folk's Edition, #182 MA Donohue & Co, Uncle Tom & Eva on cover, illus, 50 pgs, EX, P6 ....$65.00

Bucilla Needlework Kit, Sambo doll, stamped fabrics for body & clothes, unopened pkg, 1950s, M, P6 ....$65.00

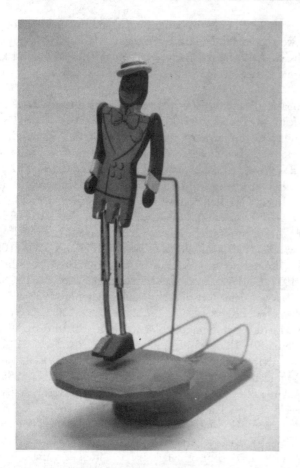

Dancing Dandy, wooden phonograph jigger, EX, D10, $225.00.

Dancing Sambo Magic Trick, by Joe Stuthard, jtd cb figure, in orig envelope, 1940s, 11½", M (EX envelope), P6 ....$75.00

Doll, blk felt w/felt features & yarn hair, red organdy dress, wht hat & red ribbon, 1930s, 8", EX, P6 ....$55.00

Doll, brn-skinned Kewpie, celluloid, true to orig Rosie O'Neill Kewpie tradition, very rare, 1920s, 5", M, P6 ....$135.00

Doll, Golliwog, blk stuffed cloth w/plush hair, orange shirt, red pants, hard plastic eyes, 12", EX, P6 ....$45.00

Doll, Goo Goo Eye, plastic, Watch My Eyes Wink, in unopened package, 1950s, EX, P6 ....$25.00

Doll, handmade Black & White topsy-turvy, stuffed cotton, Black girl in red, White girl in bl, 1930s, 12", EX, P6.$95.00

Doll, papier-mache shoulder head, molded hair/glass eyes, voice box (inoperable), wood hands/feet, orig clothes, 13", G, A...$50.00

Doll, terra cotta, sgn on back W&H USA, hand-painted facial features, movable arms & legs, bl dress, 1920s, 17", EX $79.00

Game, Jolly Darkie Target Game, Milton Bradley, ball toss, EX/NM, A $175.00

Game, Sambo Five Pins, Parker Bros, bowling game, roll ball at 5 diecut cb Sambos, 1921, scarce, EX (VG box), A $363.00

Goose Boy, Rievo, pnt molded plastic, Black boy chased by 2 geese, spring action, working, 8", EX, A $70.00

Greeting Card, shows little angel w/sheet music, All God's Chillen Got Wings, full-color, 4¼x3¼", EX, P6........$16.00

Head Toy, tin, pull string & bug eyes spin, 1910s, 3" dia, M $55.00

contest, $75 1st prize, dtd 1941, EX, P6...................$35.00

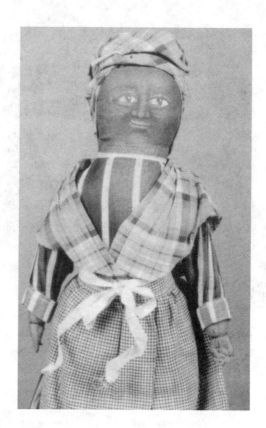

Mammy cloth doll, hand painted, unmarked, early, 12", NM, $200.00.

Man w/Uncle Sam Hat, celluloid, holds bouquet of flowers, pre-war Japan, 7", NM, A $45.00

Mechanical Pencil, alligator form w/Black man's head protruding from mouth, celluloid, very rare, 1930s, M, P6 ....$95.00

Minstrel Figures, set of 3 blk-skinned chenille figures on wooden stands w/chenille palm trees, 3¼", M, P6...................$49.00

Noisemaker, litho tin, brn-skinned man in hand-clapping & dancing pose on front, 1940s, EX, P6.........................$45.00

Noisemaker, wood paddle w/2 balls attached to wires, imprinted w/2 humorus Black figures, 8¾", 1930s, EX, P6 ....$39.00

Paper Doll, Our Gang's Stymie figure, full-color litho, fr, 1930s, 10½x9", NM, P6 ....$69.00

Phonograph Toy, animated boxing figures & dancer to attach to turntable on early disk player, NM, P6 ....$395.00

Phonograph Toy, Sambo dancer, EX, L5 ....$250.00

Playing Cards, Old Maid w/Black Sambo, 35 cards, original box lid (no bottom) $65.00

Playing Cards, Old Maid w/Sassity Sal & Steppin' Sam, 43 cards, EX $50.00

Playing Cards, 2 kittens surprised by Golliwog Jack-in-the-box, dbl deck in hinged box, NM, P6 ....$135.00

Puppet Theater, Little Black Sambo Playette, heavy cb, push-out Sambo puppet, w/book, dtd 1942, MIB, P6.......$225.00

Puzzle, fr-tray; Little Black Sambo & Tiger in jungle w/Sambo under umbrella wiping brow, Sifo, 1966, 8x10", EX, P6............$38.00

Puzzle, jigsaw; Golliwog poses in front of train named Fuzzy while dressed-up animals sit at their easels, 6x8", EX, P6 ......$49.00

Puzzle, jigsaw; wood, sgn Woof, White girl doll & Black boy doll playing w/Jack-in-the-box, orig box, 5¾x8", EX, P6..$59.00

Ramp Walker, Wilson Walkie, wood Mammy clad in red & wht dress & head scarf, 1930s, EX, P6.............................$95.00

Snowflakes and Swipes pull toy, Nifty, ca 1920s, 8", EX+, D10, $1,850.00.

Roly Poly, marked Germany, papier-mache, M, with original tag, 7", $250.00.

Stacking Blocks, set of 5 litho storybook blocks featuring Sambo & Tiger, blocks nest when inverted, 1940s, EX, P6..$125.00

Valentine, musician blowing trumpet on heart shape, Jest Horning In on Valentine's Day..., EX, P6 ....$19.00

Bliss

Bliss toys were made in Massachusetts during the last quarter of the 19th century. The company made a good variety of toys that today have a special charm for collectors, though very few have survived. For the most part they were made of wood with applied paper lithographs. See also Noah's Arks; Doll Houses; Games.

Battleship Conquerer, paper on wood, 7 cannons, 2 stacks, 2 masts, flags & lifeboats, crow's nest, 20", EX, A...$1,700.00

Battleship Terror, litho paper on wood, paper damage, rpl flags, 22", G-, A $220.00

Building Blocks, ABCs & animals, paper litho, in box, VG...$225.00

Circus Cart w/Rider, paper litho on wood, 9½", VG $275.00

Doll Chair, paper litho of seated old man in lg hat on wood, man's legs form front apron, w/rockers, 13" $400.00

Fire House, wood w/litho bricks, clanging bell in steeple, mk Bliss over front doors, 12½x10x3½", EX, A.............$775.00

Gunboat, Spanish & American War, shoots wooden shells, 1890s, some damage & paper loss, rpl foghorns, 32", A.....$1,200.00

Gunboat Kearsage, ca 1895, some damage & paper loss, some sm parts rpl, 38" $1,750.00

Horse Barn, rtcl metal fence sides, hayloft door opens, cvd wood horse w/pnt features, litho paper cart, 11", G, A $275.00

Ocean Liner St Louis, lg blk hurl, twin stacks, 6 lifeboats, wheelhouse, masts & flags, on wheels, 1985, 34½", EX, A..$3,000.00

Parlor Croquet Set, VG $100.00

Piano, pine w/paper litho cherubs on front panel, wood keys, 6½x7¼", G, A...$175.00

Rough and Ready No. 2 Hook and Ladder Horse-Drawn Fire Engine, lithographed paper on wood, missing rear fireman, driver's seat cracked, ca 1895, 30" long, A, $3,400.00.

Ship, Cincinnati, lithographed paper on wood, 8", EX, D10, $1,250.00.

Torpedo Boat Rover, paper on wood, red, bl & yel w/lt beige hull, 1 stack, 1 mast, 3 guns (working), 20", VG, A $1,495.00

Trolley Car, paper on wood, 2 horses, 28", VG $1,100.00

Boats

Though some commercially made boats date as far back as the late 1800s, they were produced on a much larger scale during WWI and the decade that followed and again during the years that spanned WWII. Some were scaled-down models of battleships measuring nearly three feet in length. While a few were actually seaworthy, many were designed with small wheels to be pulled along the carpet or out of doors on dry land. Others were motor-driven windups, and later a few were even battery operated. Some of the larger manufacturers were Bing (Germany), Dent (Pennsylvania), Orkin Craft (California), Liberty Playthings (New York), and Arnold (West Germany). Richard Trautwein (T3) and Dick Borgerding (B4) are our advisors for this category. See also Bliss; Cast Iron, Boats; Battery-Operated Toys; Windups, Friction, and Other Mechanicals; Tootsietoys; and other specific manufacturers.

Counterclockwise: Steamer, painted tin, Carette, clockwork, with key, some chipping, small parts missing, 17½", A, $1,650.00; Paddle Wheeler Priscilla, cast iron, Dent, good paint, row boat damaged, 10⅜", A, $220.00; Torpedo Boat, painted steel, Bing, clockwork, worn pnt, key missing, 16¾", A, $785.00.

Air Boat, Ernst Planck, painted tin windup, 2-tone green with red folding pontoons and uniformed pilot, some paint loss, 11½", A, $1,800.00.

#3012 Destroyer, Ives, pnt tin, dk gr & olive-gr, clockwork, working, lifeboats & deck parts missing, 12", G-G+, A....$350.00

Adirondack Paddle-Wheeler, Dent, poor rpt, 5½x3¼x14½", A $325.00

America Ferry, Milton Bradley, litho on wood, 1870s, 20", G, A $990.00

Battleship, Bing, blk/gray, ram front, 2 stacks, 6 cannons, clockwork, partial rpt, rpl flags, losses/damage, 16", A.....$700.00

Battleship, Bing, gray, ram front, 3 stacks, 8 cannons, 2 lifeboats, clockwork (sprung), rpt/losses, 16", G-, A $175.00

Cabin Cruiser, Orkin Craft, 32", EX, B4 ....$1,500.00

City of New York Paddle-Wheeler, Reed, paper litho on wood, top & compartments rpl, 19", G, A $330.00

Cruise Liner, Fleishmann, pnt tin, clockwork, rpt, lifeboats missing, 21", G, A $247.50

Cruiser, Orkin, pressed steel, heavy-duty clockwork mechanism, rpt hull, 24", G, A $440.00

Cruiser, tin, clockwork, canopy in front, rail all around side, 1 stack, clockwork, rpt/missing accessories, 6x19", A.$400.00

Destroyer, Ives, pnt tin, 2-tone gr w/silver trim, clockwork, working, pnt flaking, parts missing, 12", G-, A........$300.00

Dingy, Orkin Craft, 22", EX, B4.................................$250.00

Diving Submarine, Japan, pnt & stenciled tin, gray & wht, working, orig box (torn lid), 10", EX $150.00

Esso Tanker, Fleischmann, pnt tin, red & blk, w/catwalk, cabins, 1 stack, flags, 1940s, 20", VG, A $800.00

Fireboat, Liberty Playthings, 22", B4.............................$300.00

Flare Craft Power Driven Model Boat, Japan, wooden speedboat w/windshield & striped awning, 11", NMIB, A.......$145.00

Flotilla, Japan, battleship (7") w/2 sm ships (2¼"), pnt wood, orig box, VG-EX, A..$40.00

Freighter, Liberty Playthings, 27", EX............................$300.00

Gunboat, Carette, litho tin, inertia drive, 9½", G, A.....$121.00

Gunboat, Ives (mk on deck), gray, 2 stacks, 1 cannon, 2 masts, clockwork, 10", VG-EX, A................................$350.00

Gunboat, Ives (mk on deck), gray, 2 stacks, 1 cannon (incomplete), 2 masts, clockwork (needs rpr), 12½", VG, A .$125.00

Hornby Speedboat, Meccano, pnt tin, yel & wht w/Swift decal, clockwork, working, 12½", VG, A...........................$130.00

Indiana Battleship, Converse, litho tin, 2 stacks, 1 main mast, 10 wood gun emplacements, extras, 32", A..........$1,300.00

Italian Battleship, Ventura, Italy, pnt wood, plastic & metal, gr & gray w/tan deck, 2 masts, battery-op, 26", EX, A.$250.00

King Tugboat, Ives, pnt tin, red & blk w/tan deck & brn structures, clockwork, working, parts missing, 10½", G-, A $600.00

Lady Live Steam Paddle-Wheeler, Alessi Models, pnt tin w/emb bow ornament, brass boiler, wire railings, 19", EX, A.$350.00

Libertania Ocean Liner, Liberty Playthings, 27", EX, B4 ....$700.00

Los Angeles Battleship, Ventura, Italy, pnt wood, plastic & metal, gr & gray w/2 masts, battery-op, crack, 34", VG, A ...$275.00

Merchant Marine Ship, Ives, tin w/up, 1 passenger deck+wheelhouse mtd on 2-tone gray hull, mast & flags, chipped, 13", A $800.00

Miss America, Mengel, wood w/metal accessories, decal lettering ea side, 1930s, 15", G+, A $140.00

Mystery Boat, tin, steam-op, total rpt, 3x8¾", G (P box), A $250.00

New Jersey Battleship, Orkin, tinplate & wood, dk gray & gr, 3 stacks, cannon, gun turrets, w/up, 1920, 35", VG, A..**$1,265.00**

New York Ocean Liner, Ives, red/blk w/tan deck, 2 stacks, 2 lifeboats, clockwork (needs rpr), rpt/rpl, 13½", G-, A ...**$275.00**

New York Ocean Liner, Ives, tin, maroon, blk & beige, 2 stacks, 2 lifeboats & flags, w/up, orig box, 1915, 13", VG, A ...**$800.00**

New York Paddle-Wheeler, pnt CI, wht hull & sides w/yel deck, gold & gr trim, moving working beam, 14¼", G-VG, A **$850.00**

Ocean Liner, Arnold, pnt tin, red, blk & wht, 1 stack, clockwork, working, lt crazing, mast missing, 6", VG, A ...**$70.00**

Ocean Liner, Arnold, red & wht, 1 stack, clockwork, working, single blade missing from screw, lt chips, 8½", G-VG, A ..**$75.00**

Ocean Liner, Arnold, US Zone, pnt tin, red, blk & wht, 1 stack, clockwork, non-working, orig box, 8", VG-EX, A...**$225.00**

Ocean Liner, Arnold, US Zone, wht w/red & bl trim, 2 stacks, clockwork, working, orig box, 14", EX, A................**$385.00**

Ocean Liner, Arnold, W Germany, red, wht & yel, 2 stacks, clockwork, working, 18", VG-EX, A........................**$120.00**

Ocean Liner, att Falk, Germany, pnt tin, red & wht w/tan decks, 3 stacks, w/up, working, flaking pnt, 12", VG, A.....**$500.00**

Ocean Liner, Bing, pnt tin, red, wht, bl & orange w/litho tin deck, 2 stacks, clockwork, working, orig box, 6", G-VG, A **$400.00**

Ocean Liner, Fleischmann, litho tin, clockwork, 11½", EX, T3 ....**$1,200.00**

Ocean Liner, Fleischmann, pnt tin, red & blk hull, 2 stacks, w/wht superstructure, clockwork, working, 10½", VG, A..........**$200.00**

Ocean Liner, Germany, pnt tin, 2 stacks, 2 lifeboats, orig masts & flags, dent in hull, w/up, working, 15½", EX, A ..**$850.00**

Ocean Liner, Ives, gray w/cream deck, 1 stack, 2 masts, clockwork (needs work), 5½x2¼x10½", G, A **$200.00**

Ocean Liner, Marklin, unmotorized, for display purposes only, 2 stacks, 3rd stack+sm items missing, orig pnt, 37", A.**$12,000.00**

Ocean Queen Paddle-Wheeler, Reed, paper on wood, 2 stacks, 2 paddle wheels w/overload water pumps, wear/loss, 23", A..**$1,495.00**

Out Board, Orkin Craft, 22", EX, B4 ....**$700.00**

Paddle-Wheeler, Carette, Germany, pnt tin, passengers under canopy, 1 stack, clockwork, working, orig box, 13", VG, A.......**$4,000.00**

Paddle-Wheeler, Carette, pnt tin, w/open wheels, pnt loss, clockwork, non-working, 8", G **$302.50**

Paddle-Wheeler, Germany, pnt tin, red, blk & wht hull, cream deck & cabins, 2 stacks, 15½", VG, A..................**$1,800.00**

Paddle-Wheeler, Germany, pnt tin, w/side-wheelhousings, clockwork, rpt, tabs joining deck to hull missing, 8", G, A...**$104.50**

Paddle-Wheeler Steamboat, Buckman, pnt tin, red w/2 blk side wheels, steam engine in open cockpit, 1972, 11", A ..**$2,300.00**

Pennsylvania Battleship, Orkin, rolled steel, dual deck, lt/dk gray, gr hull, 1-stack, lifeboats, etc, 1914, 30", VG, A **$1,000.00**

Perfection Submarine, Japan, orig box, 13", L5 ....**$450.00**

Pirate Ship, Ideal, missing crow's nest & wheel, G5.........**$90.00**

Plane Carrier, Liberty Playthings, 27", EX, B4................**$400.00**

Power Boat, Bing, pnt tin, bl & wht hull, cream & wht top, flags missing, frozen motor, 10", G-VG, A........................**$600.00**

Priscilla Paddle-Wheeler, Dent, CI w/G pnt, rowboat damaged, 10⅜", A...**$220.00**

Q Boat Set, Arnold, pnt tin, red & blk, 3 interchangeable superstructures, clockwork, working, orig box, 8", VG-EX..**$295.00**

Q Boat Set, Arnold, pnt tin, red & blk hull w/3 interchangeable superstructures, clockwork, working, 8", VG-EX- ...**$195.00**

Priscilla Ocean-going Yacht, Marklin, steam powered, red and cream cabin and wheelhouse, all accessories, professionally restored, 20½", $14,000.00.

Runabout, Orkin Craft, 22", EX, B4 ....**$300.00**

Sailboat, Carette, litho tin w/litho cb sail, 6½", VG+, A .**$297.00**

Sailboat, Gescha, US Zone, pnt tin hull, red w/plated tin sail & litho tin deck, clockwork, working, G-, A **$20.00**

Sea Scooter, Liberty Playthings, 14", EX, B4..................**$200.00**

Side-Wheeler, Germany, painted tin with twin stacks, red, black and white hull, cream deck and cabins, working, 15½", VG, A, $1,800.00.

Skipper, Orkin Craft, 22", EX, B4 ....**$250.00**

Sparking Warship, Arnold, US Zone, red & 2-tone gray, clockwork w/sparking gun, working, orig box, 10", EX, A...**$475.00**

Speed Board w/Outboard, Liberty Playthings, 16", EX, B4 ...**$135.00**

Speedboat, early '30s style, mahogany-stained wood w/gr hull, live steam, Boucher plant, Type 6 gear, 36", NM, A.....**$1,100.00**

Speedboat, Hess, litho tin, gray, yel & red, friction, working, 11½", G, A...**$95.00**

Speedboat, Jacrim, wood hull, w/up motor, 20", VG, A.**$247.50**

Speedboat, Japan, pnt & lacquered wood, maroon & wht w/blk trim, battery-op w/light, non-working, orig box, 12", G-VG, A **$70.00**

Speedboat #44, Lionel, ivory & gr, 'mahogany' planking, 2 drivers aft, 12-cylinder engine, w/up, 17", VG, from $700 to ..**$900.00**

Speedster, Orkin Craft, 27", EX, B4.............................$700.00
Sportster, Liberty Playthings, 16", EX, B4.....................$125.00
SS America, Wyandotte, tin ship on wood wheels, 1930s, VG..$150.00
Steam Launch, Schonner, pnt tin, w/live steam engine, some pnt loss, lacking burner, 15", G, A............................$550.00
Steamship, Carette, pnt tin, clockwork, G pnt, some chipping, sm parts missing, 17½", A....................................$1,650.00
Steamship, Hess, litho tin, red, wht & bl, weighted flywheel mechanism, working, 9½", VG, A..............................$50.00
Submarine, Bing, tin, gr & blk, top side gun turret & flag, on blk-pnt wood stand, w/up, 1912, 10½", VG, A........$460.00
Submarine, Germany, pnt metal, olive gr, orange & blk, clockwork, non-working, pnt scrapes, missing parts, 10¼", P, A....$325.00
Submarine, Ives, pnt tin, clockwork, 10", G+, A...........$176.00
Super Catapult Plane Carrier, Saunders, #38, plastic, complete w/5 2" planes, 1950s, 12", EX (EX box), A................$73.00
Tender, Orkin Craft, 30", EX, B4 ....$1,000.00
Torpedo, Bing, pnt steel, clockwork, pnt loss, key missing, 16¾", A...$785.00
Torpedo Boat Destroyer, Liberty Playthings, 25", EX, B4.$275.00
Tugboat, Germany, pnt tin, brn & blk, clockwork, working, masts missing, 7", VG, A..$75.00
Tugboat, Germany, pnt tin, red & bl w/litho tin deck, 2 stacks, clockwork, working, minor crease, 6", G, A..............$45.00
Tugboat, Tudor Rose, London, plastic w/wheels, G5.......$15.00
Tugboat & Scow, Liberty Playthings, 24", EX, B4..........$125.00
Twin Cockpit Speed Boat, Liberty Playthings, 14", EX, B4 ....$175.00
United States Ocean Liner, Japan, mc litho tin, lights, non-working, battery trap missing, orig box, 19", G-VG, A $190.00
US Navy Battleship, Wyandotte, tin w/metal wheels, 1930s, EX...$90.00
Warship, Bing, pnt tin, gray & blk, 2 stacks, Vlastny automatic gun, clockwork, working, old rpt, 19", VG, A.........$550.00
Warship, Hess, litho tin, red, wht & gray w/gold trim, weighted flyweel, working, orig box, 9½", VG+, A................$325.00
Water Taxi, Orkin Craft, 30", EX, B4..............................$650.00
Whiz Powered Boat, CK Japan, litho tin w/2 figural sailors, w/sterno heater & gas can, 12½", EX (EX+ box), A..$600.00
4-Stack Destroyer, Liberty Playthings, 27", EX, B4 ....$275.00

Books

Books have always captured and fired the imagination of children, and today books from every era are being collected. No longer is it just the beautifully illustrated Victorian examples or first editions of books written by well-known children's authors but more modern books as well.

One of the first classics to achieve unprecedented success was *The Wizard of Oz* by author L. Frank Baum — such success, in fact, that far from his original intentions, it became a series. Even after Baum's death, other authors wrote Oz books until the decade of the 1960s for a total of more than forty different titles. Other early authors were Beatrix Potter, Kate Greenaway, Palmer Cox (who invented the Brownies), and Johnny Gruelle (creator of Raggedy Ann and Andy). All were acomplished illustrators as well.

Everyone remembers a special series of books they grew up with, the Hardy Boys, Nancy Drew Mysteries, Tarzan — there were countless others. And though these are becoming very collectible today, there were many editions of each and most are very easy to find. Generally the last few in any series will be most difficult to locate, since fewer were printed than the earlier stories which were likely to have been reprinted many times. As is true of any type of book, first editions or the earliest printing will have more collector value.

Big Little Books came along in 1933 and until edged out by the comic book format in the mid-1950s, they sold in huge volumes, first for a dime and never more than 20¢ a copy. They were printed by Whitman, Saalfield, Goldsmith, Van Wiseman, Lynn, and World Syndicate, and all stuck to Whitman's original format — thick hand-sized sagas of adventure, the right-hand page with an exciting cartoon, well illustated and contrived so as to bring the text on the left alive. The first hero to be immortalized in this arena was Dick Tracy, but many more were to follow. Some of the more collectible today feature well-known characters like G-Men, Tarzan, Flash Gordon, Little Orphan Annie, Mickey Mouse, and Western heroes by the dozens. Our specialist advisors on Big Little Books are Ron and Donna Donnelly (D7).

Little Golden Books were first published in 1942, by Western Publishing Co. Inc. The earliest had spines of blue paper that were later replaced with gold foil. Until the 1970s the books were numbered from 1 to 600, while later books had no numerical order. The most valuable are those with dust jackets from the early forties or books with paper dolls and activities. The three primary series of books are Regular (1-600), Disney (1-140), and Activity (1-52). Books with the blue or gold paper spine (not foil) often sell at $8.00 to $15.00. Dust jackets alone are worth $20.00 and up in good condition. Paper doll books are generally valued at about $30.00 to $35.00, and stories about TV Western heroes at $12.00 to $18.00. First editions of the 25¢ and 29¢ cover price books can be identified by a code (either on the title page or the last page); '1/A' indicates a first edition while a number '/Z' will refer to the twenty-sixth printing. Condition is important but subjective to personal standards. For more information we recommend *Collecting Little Golden Books, Vols 1 and 2*, by our advisor, Steve Santi (S8). The second edition also includes information on Wonder and Elf books.

Big Little Books

Ace Drummond, #1177, VG $12.00
Adventures of Pete the Tramp, #1082, VG.......................$8.00
Adventures of Tim Tyler, #1053, VG $18.00
Adventures of Tiny Tim, 1935, EX $25.00
Alice in Wonderland, Whitman, blk & wht illus from 1934 Paramount Pictures w/Charlotte Henry as Alice, 1935, EX, P6............$45.00
Alley Oop & Dinny, #763, VG $10.00
Aquaman, Scourge of the Sea; 1968, EX, T6 ....$7.00
Arizona Kid on the Bandit Trail, #1192, 1936, NM........$27.00
Barney Baxter in the Air w/the Eagle Squadron, Whitman, ca 1938, NM...$30.00
Beasts of Tarzan, 1937, EX...$40.00

Billy the Kid, #773, NM $42.00

Black Silver & His Pirate Crew, Whitman #1414, VG $15.00

Blaze Brandon w/the Foreign Legion, Whitman #1447, 1938, EX $30.00

Boss of the Chisholm Trail, #1153, NM+ $34.00

Brad Turner in Transatlantic Flight, EX $20.00

Bringing Up Father, #1133, EX $40.00

Bronc Peeler, Lone Cowboy; #1417, NM.....................$40.00

Buck Rogers & the Depth Men of Jupiter, 1935, EX+ $80.00

Buck Rogers & the Planetoid Plot, #1197, EX.................$40.00

Buck Rogers Big Big Book, Whitman, blk & wht illus, 1934, 9x7", EX, A..$100.00

Buck Rogers in the War w/Planet Venus, 1938, G $20.00

Buck Rogers in the 25th Century AD, Cocoamalt premium, 1933, VG...$30.00

Buck Rogers on the Moons of Saturn, premium, 1934, G .$35.00

Buffalo Bill Plays a Lone Hand, #1199, EX $18.00

Captain Easy, Soldier of Fortune; #1128, EX $19.00

Chester Gump, City of Gold; #1146, VG+ $15.00

Chuck Malloy, Railroad Detective; #1453, EX.................$12.00

Dan Dunn, Crime Never Pays; #1116, VG $20.00

Dan Dunn & the Border Smugglers, Whitman #1481, ca 1938, NM $45.00

Danger Trails in Africa, #1151, EX $18.00

Desert Eagle, The Hidden Fortress; EX $25.00

Detective Higgins of the Rocket Squad, #1484, VG $20.00

Dick Tracy, Detective; premium, 1933, G $50.00

Dick Tracy, FBI Operative; Whitman, Better Little Book, 1936, EX, A...$60.00

Dick Tracy & the Boris Arson Gang, #1163, EX+ $45.00

Dick Tracy on Voodoo Island, EX, P6 ....$58.00

Dick Tracy Solves the Penfield Mystery, VG, $28.00.

Dirigible & the Disappearing Zeppelin, ZR90, #1464, VG.$15.00

Don Winslow, USN; #1107, VG...................................$23.00

Donald Duck, Silly Symphony Featuring Donald Duck; #1169, 1937, G, A $15.00

Donald Duck & Ghost Morgan's Treasure, 1946, G-VG, A $20.00

Donald Duck & the Mystery of the Double X, 1949, VG, A.....$20.00

Donald Duck Headed for Trouble, #1430, 1942, G+, A...$20.00

Donald Duck Hunting for Trouble, 1938, G....................$15.00

Donald Duck in America on Parade, 1975, EX.................$8.00

Donald Duck Lays Down the Law, 1948, G-VG, A..........$15.00

Donald Duck Says Such Luck, Whitman, 432 pgs, 1941, EX+-NM...$80.00

Donald Duck Takes It on the Chin, 1941, G...................$25.00

Erik Noble & the Forty-Niners, #772, EX......................$15.00

Felix the Cat, Whitman, 1936, VG-, $30.00; *Li'l Abner in New York,* Whitman, VG, from $18.00 to $24.00.

Fighting Heroes, Battle for Freedom; #1401, EX.............$15.00

Flash Gordon & Ice World of Mongo, ca 1940, EX+ $30.00

Flash Gordon & the Monsters of Mongo, #1166, VG- $35.00

Flash Gordon & the Planet Mongo, 1934, EX $60.00

Flash Gordon & the Power Men, 1943, EX $40.00

Flash Gordon & the Tournaments of Mongo, #1171, EX+..$60.00

Flying the Sky Clipper w/Winsie Atkins, 1936, EX+ $28.00

Foreign Spies, Doctor Doom; #1460, VG.......................$15.00

G-Men on the Job, #1168, EX+ $20.00

Gang Busters Step In, 1939, EX $20.00

Gene Autry in the Law of the Range, #1453, EX-............$28.00

Goofy in Giant Trouble, Whitman, 1968, M.....................$3.50

Hairbreadth Harry in Dept QT, #1101, EX......................$25.00

Hall of Fame of the Air, #1159, EX.................................$20.00

In the Name of the Law, 1937, EX.................................$28.00

Jackie Cooper Movie Star of Skippy & Sooky, G, $15.00.

Jane Withers in Keep Smiling, #1463, VG+.....................$22.00
Jim Starr Border Patrol, #1428, EX.............................$20.00
Jimmy Allen in Airmail Robbery, 1936, EX $25.00
Jr G Men, #1442, EX...$26.00
Jungle Jim, #1138, EX..$45.00
Li'l Abner in New York #1198, VG+..............................$18.00
Little Annie Rooney & the Orphan House, #1117, EX ...$24.00
Little Jimmy's Gold Hunt, #1087, VG $10.00
Little Orphan Annie, $1,000,000 Formula; #1186, NM...$70.00
Little Orphan Annie, Punjab the Wizard; #1162, EX+ $60.00
Little Orphan Annie & the Ghost Gang, Whitman, 1936, EX+,
   C1 ....$31.00
Little Orphan Annie in the Thieves' Den, 1948, VG-EX,
   A $15.00
Lone Ranger, Menace of Murder Valley; #1465, VG $20.00
Lone Ranger & His Horse Silver, #1181, VG...................$18.00
Mac of the Marines in Africa, #1189, EX........................$25.00
Men of the Mounted, #775, VG..................................$8.00
Men of the Mounted, Whitman, Cocomalt premium, 1934,
   VG $18.00
Mickey Mouse & Bobo the Elephant, 1935, EX $40.00
Mickey Mouse & Pluto the Racer, 1936, VG-EX, A $40.00
Mickey Mouse & the Bat Bandit, #1153, 1935, VG, A....$25.00
Mickey Mouse & the Foreign Legion, Whitman, Better Little
   Book series, 1940, EX+-NM $75.00
Mickey Mouse & the Magic Lamp, 1942, G, A................$15.00
Mickey Mouse & the Pirate Submarine, 1939, G $15.00
Mickey Mouse & the Seven Ghosts, Whitman, Better Little
   Book series, 1940, EX-NM $75.00
Mickey Mouse in Blaggard Castle, #762, 1934, VG $30.00

Mickey Mouse Runs His Own Newspaper, 1937, EX, A ..$35.00
Mickey Mouse Sails for Treasure Island, premium, 1935, VG,
   A $25.00
Mickey Mouse the Detective, premium, 1934, VG- $20.00
Mickey Mouse the Mail Pilot, #731, 1933, VG, A $30.00
Mickey Rooney & Judy Garland, #1493, VG $15.00
Moon Mullins, Plushbottom Twins; #1134, VG+ $12.00
Moon Mullins & Kayo, #746, 1933, VG.......................$15.00
Mutt & Jeff, #1167, VG..$34.00
Myra North, Special Nurse & Foreign Spies; EX $30.00
Og, Son of Fire; #1115, EX $15.00
Oswald the Lucky Rabbit, 1934, VG, A.........................$20.00
Pat Nelson, Ace of Test Pilots; Whitman #1445, 1937, VG,
   T6 ....$7.00
Phantom & the Sky Pirates, Whitman #1468, 1948, VG+ .$12.00
Pioneers of the Wild West, 1933, VG...........................$7.00
Popeye & Castor Oyl the Detective, 1941, G, A..............$20.00
Popeye Sees the Sea, 1936, VG.................................$20.00
Popeye the Spinach Eater, Whitman, 1940, Better Little Book,
   EX $30.00
Prairie Bill & the Covered Wagon, #758, NM $75.00
Radio Patrol Outwitting the Gang Chief, Whitman #1496,
   1939, EX $20.00
Radio Patrol Trailing the Safeblowers, #1173, EX............$18.00
Red Barry, Undercover Man; #1426, EX.......................$20.00
Sequoia, 1935, VG...$10.00
Silver Streak, #1155, NM......................................$40.00
Skeezix at Military Academy, #1408, EX.......................$24.00
Skeezix in Africa, #1112, EX...................................$21.00
Skippy, #761, VG+...$18.00
Smilin' Jack, Stratosphere Ascent; #1152, VG $15.00
Smokey Stover, Foo Fighter; Whitman, #1421, EX..........$25.00
Sombrero Pete, #1136, EX.....................................$15.00
SOS Coast Guard, #1191, EX...................................$22.00
Story of Jackie Cooper, #W714, EX $12.00
Tailspin Tommy, Great Air Mystery; #1184, VG.............$45.00
Tailspin Tommy in the Famous Pay-Roll Mystery, Whitman, ca
   1933, VG $11.00
Tarzan Escapes, #1182, NM....................................$90.00
Tarzan of the Apes, #744, 1933, G.............................$20.00

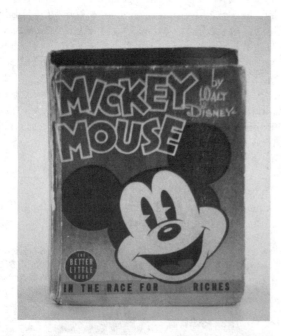

Mickey Mouse in the Race for Riches, Walt Disney, Better Little Book, ca 1938, VG, $30.00.

Mickey Mouse in Race for Riches, Whitman, 1938, NM.$75.00
Mickey Mouse in the Treasure Hunt, Whitman, 1941, EX+,
   A $30.00

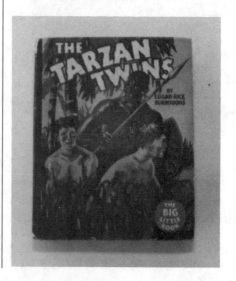

Tarzan Twins, Edgar Rice Burroughs, 1935, 1st edition, rare, NM, $120.00.

Tarzan of the Screen, Story of Johnny Weismuller; Whitman #778, VG...............................$30.00
Tarzan Twins, #770, 1935, VG..................$47.00
Tiny Tim, #767, VG.............................$12.00
Tiny Tim of the Mechanical Men, 1937, EX.............$35.00
Tom Mix, Fighting Cowboy; premium, EX+.............$65.00
Tom Mix, Stranger from the South; #1183, NM.............$52.00
Treasure Island, Jackie Cooper, #1141, VG.............$10.00
Two-Gun Montana, #1104, EX+.............$25.00

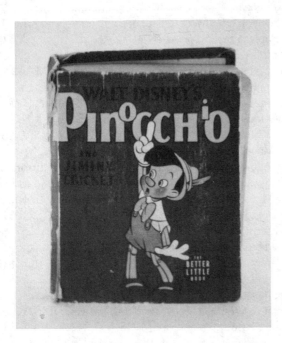

Walt Disney's Pinocchio and Jiminy Cricket,
Better Little Book, 1940, G-, $15.00.

Walt Disney's Snow White & Seven Dwarfs, Whitman #1460, ca 1938, complete, VG.............$15.00
Zane Gray, King of the Royal Mounted-Northern Treasure; #1179, VG+.............$12.00
Zane Gray's Tex Thorne, 1937, VG.............$10.00

Big Golden Books

Adventures of Mr Toad, Disney, 1949, VG, N2.............$19.00
Alice in Wonderland, Disney, 1978, VG, N2.............$6.00
Aristocats, Disney, 1970, EX.............$10.00
Baby's Mother Goose, 1968, VG, N2.............$9.00
Bambi, Disney, 1972, VG.............$3.00
Big Brown Bear, 1948, VG.............$10.00
Flintstones, Golden Press, hardcover, 48-pg, 1960, 8x10", NM, A.............$35.00
Frosty the Snowman, 1979, VG.............$3.00
Hamilton Duck, 1972, EX.............$4.00
Huckleberry Hound, 1960, damaged spine, T6.............$12.00
Huckleberry Hound & Yogi Bear, Golden Press, hardcover, 48-pg, 1960, 8x10", EX+, A.............$29.00
Lassie Finds a Way, 1957, VG, N2.............$8.00
Mickey Mouse in Hideaway Island, Disney, 1980, VG, N2.............$6.00

Pinocchio, Disney, 1978, EX.............$2.00
Quick Draw McGraw, 1961, M.............$20.00
Road Runner in a Very Scary Lesson, 1979, EX.............$10.00
Savage Sam, Disney, 1963, EX.............$15.00
Snow White, Disney, 1952, VG, N2.............$7.00
Surprise Package, Disney, rpr spine, 1948, VG.............$12.00
Top Cat, 1963, M.............$20.00
True Story of Smokey Bear, 1971, VG, N2.............$10.00
Winnie Pooh in a Tight Squeeze, Disney, 1972, VG, N2.............$7.00
Winnie Pooh in Eeyore's Birthday, Disney, 1974, EX, N2..$12.00
Wonders of the Seasons, 1966, VG.............$10.00
Yogi Bear, A Christmas Visit; 1961, EX.............$15.00

Little Golden Books

ABC Rhymes, 11th printing, VG+.............$1.00
Alice in Wonderland Finds the Garden of Live Flowers, Disney, 1951, G, T6.............$6.00
Animals & Their Babies, 1st edition, orig 25¢ price, no wheel, VG.............$5.00
Aristocats, 1970, EX.............$8.00
Babes in Toyland, Disney, 1961, EX.............$10.00
Babes in Toyland, Disney, 3rd edition, 1961, VG.............$6.00
Barbie, 1st printing, 1974, EX.............$8.50
Barbie & the Missing Wedding Dress, 1986, EX, N2.............$6.00
Bedknobs & Broomsticks, Disney, 1st edition, 1971, NM.$10.00
Bozo & the Hide & Seek Elephant, orig 39¢ price, 1973, VG.............$4.00
Bozo the Clown, 3rd edition, 1961, VG.............$3.00
Brave Eagle, 1st edition, 1957, VG+.............$12.00
Brave Eagle, 1957, EX.............$18.00
Buck Rogers & the Children of Hopetown, 1979, EX-, T6..$4.00
Bugs Bunny, 1949, VG+.............$7.00
Bugs Bunny at the Easter Party, 1953, EX.............$10.00
Bullwinkle & Rocky, 1962, EX.............$15.00
Cabbage Patch Kids & Xavier's Birthday, 1987, EX.............$3.00
Captain Kangaroo, 1956, VG.............$8.00
Captain Kangaroo & the Panda, 1st edition, orig 25¢ price, VG.............$8.00
Chicken Little, orig price 29¢, 1960, EX.............$6.00
Chitty Chitty Bang Bang, Disney, 1968, EX.............$10.00
Christmas Carols, orig 25¢ price, tape rpr spine, VG.............$4.00
Cinderella, Disney, 1950 (1961 printing), EX, T6.............$2.00
Cinderella, 1st edition, 1986, NM.............$2.00
Cinderella's Friends, 1950, NM.............$12.00
Cinderella's Friends, 1950, VG+, T6.............$6.00
Daniel Boone, 1st edition, 1956, EX.............$10.00
Darby O'Gill, Disney, 1959, EX, T6.............$12.00
David & Goliath, 3rd printing, EX.............$2.00
Davy Crockett, Disney, 1st edition, 1955, VG, N2.............$10.00
Davy Crockett, Disney, 1955, VG.............$10.00
Davy Crockett, King of the Wild Frontier; 1955, VG.............$10.00
Dennis the Menace, A Quiet Afternoon; ca 1960, VG.............$6.00
Dennis the Menace, 1st edition, orig 25¢ price, VG.............$6.00
Dennis the Menace & Ruff, ca 1959, VG.............$6.00
Dinosaurs, 1st edition, 1959, VG.............$4.00
Disneyland on the Air, 1st edition, 1955, EX.............$15.00
Donald Duck, Lost & Found; 1959, VG.............$7.00

Donald Duck & Santa Claus, 1959, VG $6.00
Donald Duck & the Witch, 1953, EX...............................$18.00
Donald Duck in America on Parade, 1975, EX, M8 ....$8.00
Donald Duck in Disneyland, 1960, EX................................$8.00

Donald Duck's Adventure, Disney, ca 1950, VG, $7.00. (Photo courtesy of Steve Santi.)

Donald Duck's Toy Boat, 3rd edition, 1954, EX, M8..........$6.00
Donald Duck's Toy Sailboat, Disney, 1954, VG $7.00
Donald Duck's Toy Train, 1950, EX $12.00
Donald Duck's Toy Train, 2nd printing, EX+ $10.00
Donnie & Marie & the Top Secret Project, 1st edition, 1977, NM...$5.00
Dumbo, Disney, 1969, 29th printing, EX, T6 ....$1.00
Exploring Space, 2nd edition, 1958, NM $5.00
Forest Hotel, 5th edition, EX..$2.00
Frosty the Snow Man, orig 29¢ price, EX.........................$5.00
Gene Autry & Champion, #267, 1956, EX......................$18.00
Golden Book of Flowers, 2nd edition, 1944, EX..............$15.00
Golden Egg Book, 8th printing, EX....................................$1.00
Golden Goose, 1st edition, 1954, VG $6.00
Goodbye Tonsil, orig 49¢ price, 1979, EX.........................$2.00
Gunsmoke, 1958, EX $17.50
Hansel & Gretel, orig 39¢ price, EX..................................$1.00
Hansel & Gretel, 2nd edition, 1945, VG $6.00
Happy Birthday, 2nd edition, 1960, EX, N2 ....$12.00
Heidi, 11th printing, EX $2.00
Herbie the Love Bug's Special Friend, orig 49¢ price, 1974, VG..$8.00
Howdy Doody & the Princess, 1952, EX+ $18.00
Howdy Doody's Circus, 1st edition, 1950, EX, P6 ....$20.00
Howdy Doody's Lucky Trip, 1962, EX+ $15.00
Huckleberry Hound, 1960, EX $12.00
Huckleberry Hound Builds a House, 1959, EX $12.00
It's Howdy Doody Time, missing title & 1st pg, VG, T6....$3.00
Johnny Appleseed, 3rd printing, 1949, EX, M8 ....$6.00
Jungle Book, 1st edition, 1967, EX....................................$7.00
Land of the Lost, 1st edition, EX+....................................$7.00
Land of the Lost, 1975, EX $7.00

Lassie & Her Day in the Sun, 1958, EX, T6......................$4.00
Life & Legend of Wyatt Earp, 1958, VG $8.00
Life & Legend of Wyatt Earp, 24-pg, full-color art each pg, 1958, 7x8", EX-..$15.00
Lippy the Lion & Hardy Har Har, 1963, EX $12.00
Little Golden Book of Dogs, 1st edition, 1952, EX $7.00
Little Lulu, 24-pg, 1962, EX- $8.00
Little Red Hen, 15th printing, EX......................................$2.00
Lone Ranger & the Talking Pony, 1st edition, orig 25¢ price, VG, N2..$9.00
Loopy de Loop Goes West, 1st ed, orig 25¢ price, VG, N2...$12.00
Lucky Puppy, orig 25¢ price, NM $10.00
Mad Hatter's Tea Party, 1951, VG $8.00
Mary Poppins, 2nd edition, orig price 29¢, 1964, NM-M ...$7.00
Mary Poppins & a Jolly Holiday, 1964, EX, from $4 to $8.00
Mary Poppins & the Magic Compass, 1963, EX+ $17.50
Mickey Mouse & His Space Ship, 1st ed, 1952, EX, M8 ..$14.00
Mickey Mouse & Pluto Pup, 1953, VG+, T6 ....$5.00
Mickey Mouse & the Missing Mouseketeers, 1956, EX-, T6..$12.00
Mickey Mouse Goes Christmas Shopping, 1st edition, 1953, EX $12.00
Mickey Mouse's Picnic, Disney, 3rd edition, 1950, VG, T6..$4.00
Mister Dog, 1st edition, 1952, EX $18.00
New Kittens, 1st edition, 1957, EX $8.00
Pepper Plays Nurse, 1st edition, 1964, VG......................$18.00
Peter Pan & the Indians, Disney, 1st edition, 1952, VG ..$10.00
Peter Pan & the Indians, 1958, EX+ $16.00
Peter Pan & the Pirates, 1958, VG $12.50
Peter Pan & Wendy, Disney, 1968, 6th printing, EX, T6...$2.00
Pinocchio, Disney, 2nd edition, 1948, VG, N2 ....$12.00
Poky Little Puppy, 1st edition, 1942, EX-, w/dust jacket .$100.00
Rescuers, 1977, EX, M8 ....$5.00
Rin-Tin-Tin & the Outlaw, 1st edition, 1957, VG $8.00
Rin-Tin-Tin & the Outlaw, 1957, EX $15.00
Road Runner & a Very Scary Lesson, 1st edition, 1974, EX..$4.00
Road Runner & a Very Scary Lesson, 4th edition, 1981, EX..$1.00
Robin Hood, 1973, EX..$5.00
Rocky & His Friends, 1973, VG, N2................................$15.00
Rootie Kazootie, Baseball Star, 28-pg, 1954, 7x8", EX+ ...$20.00
Rootie Kazootie, Baseball Star; 1954, VG........................$14.00

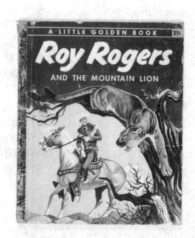

Roy Rogers & the Mountain Lion, #231, 1st edition, EX, $18.00. (Photo courtesy of Steve Santi.)

Scuffy the Tugboat, 14th printing, EX $1.00
Seven Dwarfs Find a House, 1st edition, 1960s, EX, M8 ..$12.00
Shaggy Dog, Disney, 1959 (1st printing), VG, T6..............$7.00
Shari Lewis, Party in Shariland; 1959, VG+.....................$10.00
Shazam's Circus Adventure, 1953, VG-EX.........................$4.00

Snow White, original price 25¢, 1st edition, 1948, VG, $18.00. (Photo courtesy of Steve Santi.)

Tonka, Disney, 1959, EX-...$12.00
Touche Turtle, 1962, M..$18.00

Uncle Remus, 1st edition, 1947, VG, $9.00. (Photo courtesy of Steve Santi.)

Underdog & the Disappearing Ice Cream, 1st printing, 1975, EX $10.00
Visit to the Children's Zoo, 12th printing, EX.................$1.00
Waltons & the Birthday Present, 1st edition, 1975, EX $4.00
White Bunny & His Magic Nose, 2nd edition, 1957, EX.$10.00

Woody Woodpecker at the Circus, 1976, EX.....................$4.00
Woody Woodpecker Joins the Circus, 1958, EX................$8.00
Yogi Bear, 1960, M...$15.00
Yogi Bear & a Christmas Visit, 2nd edition, 1961, EX $15.00

Tell-a-Tale Books

Barbie & Skipper Go Camping, 1973, EX, N2....................$7.00
Bedknobs & Broomsticks, Visit to Naboombu; 1971, EX, T6..$4.00
Bozo the Clown, King of the Ring; Whitman, 1960, VG, T6 .$2.00
Bugs Bunny in Something Fishy, 1955, EX, T6...................$2.00
Bugs Bunny Keeps a Promise, 1951, G, T6.........................$1.00
Bugs Bunny's Birthday Surprise, VG+, T6 ....$3.00
Captain Kangaroo's Picnic, Whitman, 1959, EX, T6 ....$4.00
Corey Baker of Julia & His Show & Tell, 1970, VG+, T6..$3.00
Donald Duck in Frontierland, 1957, EX.............................$6.00
Donald Duck on Tom Sawyer Island, 1950, VG, N2..........$6.00
Donald Duck's Lucky Day, 1951, EX..................................$4.00
Donny & Marie & the State Fair Mystery, 1977, VG.........$5.00
Especially From Thomas, 1965, VG $2.00
Fat Albert & the Cosby Kids, 1975, EX $8.00
Gene Autry, Makes a New Friend, hardcover, mc illus, 1962, 6x7", NM, T2...$15.00
Gene Autry & the Lost Dogie, 1953, G-.............................$3.00
Goofy & the Tiger Hunt, 1954, G+ $3.00
Gumby & Gumby's Pal Pokey, 1968, M............................$10.00
Gumby & Gumby's Pal Pokey, 1968, VG, T6....................$6.00
Hooray for Lassie, 1964, EX, N2......................................$10.00
Howdy Doody & the Magic Lamp, 1953, EX....................$15.00
HR Pufinstuff, 1970, VG, N2...$8.00
I Like the Farm, 1961, VG..$2.00
Lassie & the Firefighters, 1968, EX...................................$7.00
Lassie & the Kittens, 1956, NM $7.00
Lassie Finds a Friend, 1960, VG $7.00
Lassie's Brave Adventure, 1958, VG $7.00
Little Beaver, 1954, G-VG, N2..$10.00
Little Black Sambo, Whitman, mk MCML, VG $15.00
Little Lulu, Lucky Landlady; 1973, EX+-NM, C1.............$14.00
Little Lulu Has an Art Show, VG $10.00
Little Lulu Has an Art Show, Whitman, 1964, NM.........$20.00
Little Lulu Uses Her Head, 1955, VG $10.00
Little Red Hen, 1953, EX...$3.00
Mickey Mouse & the Really Neat Robot, 1970, VG $4.00
Mushmouse & Punkin' Puss & the Country Cousins, 28-pg, 1964, 6x7", EX...$20.00
Nancy & Sluggo in the Big Surprise, 1974, VG.................$6.00
Parade for Chatty Baby, 1965, NM-M, N2 ....$15.00
Peter Potamus, 1965, EX...$15.00
Pinocchio, Disney, 1961, EX, N2 ....$8.00
Ricochet Rabbit, 1965, M..$17.50
Rinty & Pals, Whitman, 1957, NM-, C1 ....$18.00
Road Runner in Tumblewood Trouble, 1971, EX..............$5.00
Roy Rogers & a Surprise for Donny, 1954, VG, N2 ....$15.00
Rubbles & Bamm-Bamm, 1965, VG $20.00
Ruff & Ready, 1958, VG, N2..$8.00
Sleeping Beauty, Disney, 1959, EX..................................$10.00

Snow White, Disney, 1957, EX, N2 ....$8.00
Three Bears, 1952, VG $3.00
Tom & Jerry & the Toy Circus, Whitman, 1953 (probably later printing), EX, T6 ....$6.00
Tom's (Tom & Jerry) Happy Birthday, 1955, VG+, T6 .....$5.00
Tweety & Sylvester & a Visit to the Vet, 1987, EX $2.00
Tweety & Sylvester at the Farm, 1978, VG $5.00
Underdog, 1966, NM-M, N2 ....$10.00
Wally Gator, 1965, EX $15.00
Wally Gator in Guess Who's Hiding at the Zoo, 1963, EX.$15.00
Where Timothy Lives, 1958, VG $3.00
Yellow Cat & Fuzzy Wuzzy, 1952, EX, N2 ....$15.00

Wonder Books

Bambi's Children, 1951, rpr spine, VG, N2 ....$4.00
Blondie's Family, 1954, EX $17.50
Casper in Ghostland, 1965, VG $12.00
Cinderella, 1954, NM-M $5.00
Deputy Dawg & the Space Man, 1961, EX $18.00
Fred Flintstone, The Fix-It Man; 1976, EX $10.00
Heckle & Jeckle, 1957, M..$8.00
Jabberjaw Out West, rpr spine, 1977, VG $8.00
Kewtie Bear, Santa's Helper; 1945, VG $7.00
Lassie's Long Trip, 1957, NM $6.00
Little Cowboy's Christmas, 1951, VG............................$15.00
Mighty Mouse, 1953, EX $10.00
Peter Rabbit, 1947, VG, N2 ....$4.00
Popeye Goes on a Picnic, 1958, EX................................$10.00
Raggedy Ann, 1952, EX..$15.00
Sonny the Lucky Bunny, 1952, VG.................................$4.00
Soupy Sales & the Talking Turtle, 1965, EX $10.00
Surprise Doll, 1949, VG $20.00
Tom Corbett's Trip to the Moon, 1953, M......................$10.00
Tom Terrific's Greatest Adventure, 1959, EX+ $15.00
Valley of the Dinosaurs, 1975, EX $8.00
Visit to the Dentist, 1974, EX..$3.00
Yogi Bear & Playtime in Jellystone Park, 1976, EX $6.00
Yogi Bear & the Baby Skunk, 1976, VG $6.00

Miscellaneous

For coloring and activity books and other character-related books, see Character. See also Black Americana; Comic Books.

Bow-Tie Book, Lilia & Co, linen pgs, 1942, M................$15.00
Ceiling Zero, based on Warner Bros movie, 1936, G-VG, A..$35.00
Chimpsey at Play, by Ruth A Roche, Action Play Book, 1945, VG+, A $5.00
Ding Dong School, Dressing Up, by Miss Frances, 1953, EX..$5.00
Ding Dong School, Looking Out the Window, by Miss Frances, VG+ $5.00
Ding Dong School, Magic Wagon, by Miss Frances, 1955, VG+..$5.00
Ding Dong School, My Daddy Is a Policeman, by Miss Frances, 1956, EX...$5.00
Elf Book, Burl Ives Sailing on a Very Fine Day, Rand McNally, 1954, VG..$7.00

Elf Book, Super Circus, w/Mary Hartline & Claude Kirchner, Rand McNally, 1955, VG- $15.00
Elf Book, Superliner, United States; Rand McNally, 1953, EX $15.00
Elf Book, Three Billy Goats Bruff, 1957, VG $4.00
Elf Book, Tom Thumb, 1954, VG, N2..............................$15.00
Elf Book, Wynken, Blynken & Nod; 1956, VG, N2.........$10.00
Grimm's Fairy Tales, set of sm books in box that folds out to display theater, Nordic Paper Denmark, NM, M5..........$60.00
Gulliver's Travels, Random House, 1939, EX $50.00

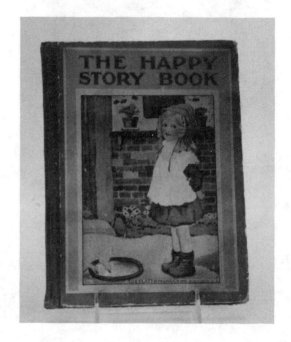

The Happy Story Book, Platt & Munk, ca 1910, VG+, $10.00.

Hiawatha Primmer, dtd 1898, VG, I2 ....$19.00
Just Kids, Saalfield, 1934, VG.......................................$25.00
Little Nemo in Slumberland, Rand McNally, 1951, EX ...$70.00
Mother Goose Picture Book, Merrill Publishing, 1958, M..$22.50

The Night Before Christmas, Whitman, 1943, NM, $15.00.

No School Today, Sparkie (radio show); Treasure Book, 1955, missing card game section, VG-, T6............................$4.00

Peculiar Penguins, Walt Disney, 1934, VG-EX, A $110.00

Princess of Oz, Random House Jr Books, 1939, M $40.00

Robber Kitten, Disney Studios, 1935, EX, A $160.00

Special Book w/Picture, Rhyme & Sound; FAO Schwarz, MIG, pull pin, activate animal noise, early, loose pgs, 12x9", A $200.00

Teddy Bears on a Toboggan, 1907, Reilly Britton, 7x5½", EX, $48.00.

Three Little Wolves, Walt Disney Picture Book, 1937, G-VG, A..$35.00

Three Orphan Kittens, Disney Studios, 1935, EX, A $140.00

Tiny Nonsense Books, complete set in orig box, 4½x4½", NM..$75.00

Tortoise & the Hare, Disney Studios, 1935, EX, A $140.00

'Twas the Night Before Christmas, Merrill Publishing, 1942, linen, 13x10", M...$25.00

Who's Afraid of the Big Bad Wolf, Walt Disney, 1933, EX, A..$55.00

Wise Little Hen, Disney Studios, 1935, EX, A $180.00

Breyer

    Breyer collecting seems to be growing in popularity, and though the horses dominate the market, the company also made dogs, cats, farm animals and wildlife figures as well. They've been in continuous production since the fifties, all strikingly beautiful and likelike in both modeling and color. Earlier models were glossy, but since 1968 a matte finish has been used. Condition and rarity are the most important worth-assessing factors. Our advisor for this category is Terri Mardis-Ivers (I2).

Adbullah Famous Takehner, 1989 Limited Edition #817, MIB..$34.00

American Indian Pony, #710, 1989, MIB $34.00

Appaloosa Scratching Foal, blk & wht, #168, EX, T2......$19.00

Appaloosa Standing Mare, 8x11", $19.00.

Appaloosa Stock Horse Stallion, #232, EX, T2 ....$16.00

Arabian Foal, dapple gray, unmk, probably Breyer, A3 ....$15.00

Arabian Foal, Family series, glossy gray w/spots on bk half, blk points, EX, T2 ....$15.00

Arabian Foal, wht glossy finish, A3.................................$20.00

Arabian Mare, Family series, EX, T2 ....$7.00

Arabian Mare, proud, gray glossy Appaloosa, w/matching stallion & foal, 3-pc set...$120.00

Arabian Stallion, Family series, wht, gray points, EX, T2...$12.00

Balking Mule, dk brn w/halter, EX.................................$100.00

Bassett Hound, #326, EX, T2 ....$14.00

Bay Nursing Foal, lt brn w/dk brn points, EX, T2 ....$14.00

Bay Stallion, jumping over wall, #300, EX, T2 ....$29.00

Black Angus Bull, 5½x10", EX..$26.00

Black Beauty Stallion, right front sock, running, #89, EX, T2..$16.00

Black Tennessee Walker Stallion, #60, EX $23.00

Brahma Bull, glossy, #70, EX, T2 ....$30.00

Buckskin Foal, lying down, #166, EX, T2 ....$23.00

Buckskin Mustang Stallion, blk mane, tail & hooves, pk nose, some dk spots, #87, EX, T2..$35.00

Buffalo, few scuffs, EX, T2 ....$19.00

Cinnamon Baby Bear, EX...$20.00

Clydesdale Dapple Gray Stallion, glossy, #85, EX $60.00

Clydesdale Foal, #84, EX, T2 ....$10.00

Clydesdale Mare, red & wht bobs in mane, EX, T2..........$14.00

Colt, brn, running, 4¾", EX...$4.00

Deer, doe, ears worn, VG, T2 ....$9.00

Elk Bull, 1987, MIB...$34.00

Fighting Stallion, wht w/gray hooves, pk muzzle, EX, T2.$25.00

Fighting Stallion, woodgrain, NM....................................$75.00

Five Gaiter Sorrell Stallion, #52, VG, T2 ....$14.00

Davy Crockett, 7" figure with accessories on 8" long horse, original box, EX, $500.00.

Foundation Stallion, blk, #64, EX-.....................................$25.00
Lady Phase, #40, EX, T2...$17.00
Legionario III Famous Andalusian, #68, MIB, T2 ....$30.00
Leopard Appaloosa Stallion, prancing, slip-on saddle, chain
    reins, pk ears & nose, #115, EX, T2 ....$25.00
Little Bits Quarter Horse Buckskin Stallion, saddle, EX,
    T2 ....$4.00
Man O' War Stallion, #47, EX, T2 ....$16.00
Marguerite Henry's Misty, EX, T2 ....$9.00

Moose, $30.00.

Old Timer Gray Mare, harness & binders, glossy, #205, EX-,
    T2 ....$25.00
Palomino Mare, Family series, lt, glossy, #5, EX, T2.........$11.00
Palomino Mare, grazing, lt to med color, pk muzzle & ears,
    EX..$30.00

Palomino Prancing Arabian Stallion, 1988, MIB, T2 ......$31.00
Palomino Stallion, Family series, glossy caramel, w/saddle, EX,
    T2 ....$12.00
Poodle, silver, EX..$35.00

Quarter Horse buckskin mare, 8x11", $50.00.

Red Roan Running Stallion, EX.....................................$75.00
Shetland Pony, tan & wht spotted, glossy, mk on belly, EX,
    T2 ....$8.00
Smokey the Cow Horse, #69, EX $36.00
Spanish Fighting Bull, EX...$65.00
Texas Longhorn Steer, EX...$40.00
Western Horse, blk w/snap-on saddle, lg, EX...................$50.00
Western Palomino, glossy orange, chain reins, snap-on saddle,
    EX..$19.00
Western Pony, blk or wht, w/saddle, sm, EX...................$35.00
Western Pony, caramel, chain reins, brn snap-on saddle, sm,
    EX..$25.00
Western Pony, Dodge City KS on sticker at rump, w/saddle, sm,
    EX..$35.00
Yellow Mount Stallion, no spot on leg, glossy face, lt pk nose,
    EX, T2..$17.00

Bubble Bath Containers

Since back in the sixties when the Colgate-Palmolive Company produced the first Soaky, hundreds of different characters and variations have been marketed, bought on demand of the kids who saw these characters day to day on TV by parents willing to try anything that might make bath-time more appealing. Purex made their Bubble Club characters, and Avon and others followed suit. Most Soaky bottles came with detachable heads made of brittle plastic which cracked easily. Purex bottles were made of a softer plastic but tended to loose their paint. Remember, value is affected to a great extent by condition. Our advisor for this category is John Thurmond (T1).

Alvin Chipmunk, in red or yel, 1960s, from $15 to..........$25.00
Atom Ant, 1960s $40.00
Augie Doggie, EX+ $35.00
Baba Looie, M w/orig sleeve, T1.....................................$25.00
Bambi, VG, N2 ....$12.00
Batman, Tsumara/TM & DC Comics, Kid Care, 1991, 10",
    M...$6.00
Batman, 1960s, T1 ....$65.00
Beatles, Ringo Starr, Colgate-Palmolive, name emb on base,
    1965, 9½", VG+, from $50 to.....................................$60.00
Beatles Paul McCartney, 1960s, NM, from $100 to $125.00
Bozo the Clown, 1960s, EX-NM, from $21 to..................$28.00
Brutus, 1960s, NM, C1 ....$40.00

Bullwinkle, Colgate-Palmolive, light brown with dark brown antlers, 11 fluid ozs., NM, from $30.00 to $40.00.

Bullwinkle, brn w/red & yel-striped turtleneck, 1960s, NM,
    from $30 to..$40.00
Bullwinkle, Fuller Brush, lg yel antlers & feet, red & wht
    bathing suit, 1970, NM, scarce, C1............................$72.00
Casper the Friendly Ghost, vinyl, hard plastic head, 10",
    M...$25.00
Creature, rare, M $100.00
Deputy Dawg, 1960s, NM, from $15 to............................$25.00
Dick Tracy, 1960s, from $30 to $45.00
Droop Along Coyote, 1960s, from $28 to $35.00
Dum Dum, Purex, H4..$28.00
Elmer Fudd, in red & blk hunting outfit, NM-M, C1 ......$25.00
ET, Avon, c 1983, M (EX box) $15.00
Felix Flatty, 1980s, T1 ....$15.00
Felix the Cat, bl w/trick bag, 1960s, NM $35.00
Flintstones Bubble Club Fun Bath, Purex, cb, Fred scrubbing Pebbles &
    Bamm-Bamm, orig 39¢, 1968, rare, NMIB (sealed), A.....$172.00
Frankenstein, 1960s, from $50 to $75.00

Godzilla, NM $50.00
Gumby, Perma Toy, No Tears Shampoo, 1987, 9½", M.....$6.00
Hulk Hogan, M, from $5 to $10.00
Lippy the Lion, Colgate-Palmolive, from $30 to............$35.00
Lucy (from Charlie Brown), Avon, EX $5.00
Mad Hatter, Avon, 8", NM $30.00
Marrocco Mole, EX $22.50
Mickey Mouse, Avon, 1971, from $15 to $20.00
Mighty Mouse, 1960s, EX, from $20 to $25.00
Mr Magoo, M, from $20 to $30.00
Mushmouse, Colgate-Palmolive, MIB...............................$35.00
Muskie, in red, 1960s, T1 ....$20.00
Peter Potamus, M w/orig sleeve, from $25 to $35.00
Pinocchio, Colgate-Palmolive, M, from $15 to.................$20.00
Popeye, non-removable head (not regular Soaky), H4 .....$20.00
Popeye, 1960s, from $25 to...$35.00
Porky Pig, Colgate-Palmolive, EX, from $10 to $15.00
Princess Leia (Star Wars), full, NM, O1 ....$20.00
Punkin' Puss, Colgate-Palmolive, M, from $25 to $35.00

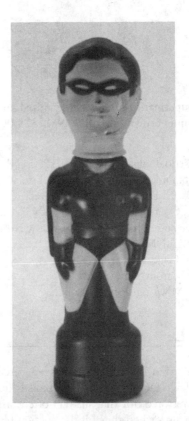

Robin, black and red painted costume, 9¾", EX, from $75.00 to $100.00.

Rocky Squirrel, M...$35.00
Santa Claus, EX, H4 ....$8.00
Silverhawks, 1960s, from $5 to.......................................$10.00
Smokey Bear w/Bubble Bath sign & shovel, 1960s, 12", from
    $15 to $25.00
Snow White, Colgate-Palmolive, movable arms, EX, from $15
    to...$18.00
Spouty Whale, M w/orig sleeve, T1 ....$25.00
Sylvester, NM $15.00

Superman, red and blue painted costume, brown hair, 10", NM, $75.00.

Tennessee Tuxedo, Colgate-Palmolive, 1960s, NM $25.00
Theodore Chipmunk, Colgate-Palmolive, EX $15.00
Top Cat, 1960s, NM $35.00
Touche Turtle, Colgate-Palmolive, full body, EX.............$30.00
Touche Turtle, Purex, lt gr molded plastic w/red pnt feather on
    hat, 5½x9½", NM, from $25 ....$30.00
Tweety Bird on Cage, 1960s, T1 ....$15.00
Wolfman, 1960s, from $75 to..$100.00
Yakky Doodle, M w/orig sleeve, T1 ....$25.00

Buddy L

First produced in 1921, Buddy L toys have escalated in value over the past few years until now early models in good original condition (or restored, for that matter) often bring prices well into the four figures when they hit the auction block. The business was started by Fred Lundahl, founder of Moline Pressed Steel Co., who at first designed toys for his young son, Buddy. They were advertised as being 'Guaranteed Indestructible,' and indeed they were so sturdy and well built that they just about were. Until wartime caused a steel shortage, they were made of heavy gauge pressed steel. Many were based on actual truck models; some were ride-ons, capable of supporting a grownup's weight. Fire trucks with hydraulically activated water towers and hoisting towers that actually worked kept little boys entertained for hours. After the war, the quality of Buddy Ls began to decline, and wood was used to some extent. Condition is everything. Remember that unless the work is done by a professional

restorer, overpainting and amateur repairs do nothing to enhance the value of a toy in poor condition. Professional restorations may be expensive, but they may be viable alternatives when compared to the extremely high prices we're seeing today. In the listings that follow, toys are all pressed steel unless noted. See also Advertising; Trains.

Airplanes

Catapult Airplane, orange & blk w/Buddy L sticker, +2-door
    hanger (6x8x12"), lever opens door/catapults 7" plane, EX,
    A $900.00
Double Airplane Hangar #5010, tan w/dbl hinged doors & red
    trim, scratched decal, 1930-31, 20¼", VG, A.........$358.00
Monocoupe, blk body, orange wings, decal on fuselage, 10",
    w/hanger #2007, dbl doors, 1930-31, 12¼", G-, A ..$715.00

Cars and Busses

Convertible #471, wood, maroon pnt, wood wheels, NP hubcaps
    & headlights, trunk opens, top retracts, 18¾", G, A .$220.00
Convertible #499, wood, metallic bl pnt, ivory roof retracts, Bakelite
    wheels, NP grille/electric headlights, 18", VG, A $825.00
Express Bus #209 Coach, gr w/all decals, some corrosion, 29",
    VG, A $2,900.00

Flivver Coupe, 1920s, 12", EX, D10, $950.00.

Greyhound Bus, painted pressed steel, windup with battery-operated lights, some staining, 16½", VG, A, $400.00.

Greyhound Bus #481, wood, ivory, bl & gray pnt, wood wheels, chrome hubcaps, metal trim, 18¼", G, A $550.00

Greyhound Bus #855, w/up, bl & wht, battery-op light, blk rubber tires, door opens, bell rings, '39, 16", EX (G+ box), A ..$600.00

Greyhound Bus #855, w/up, bl & wht, battery-op light, door opens, bell rings, orig box, 16½", VG, A $325.00

Greyhound Bus #855, w/up, bl & wht, battery-op light, door opens, non-working, 16½", EX-NM, A.....................$413.00

Long Distance Bus, orig gr now rpt red, steers, doors open, 28½", G-, A..$1,450.00

Model A Flivver, break to fender/slight rpr, much pnt loss to roof, overall G pnt, 6½x11", VG, A $500.00

Passenger Bus, pressed steel, original paint distressed toward rear, ca 1929, 29", A, $3,600.00.

Scarab #211, red w/plated bumper, headlights & hood trim, decals on sides, unpowered, 1941, 10½", M, A........$495.00

Woody #371, wood, maroon pnt w/cream trim, Station Wagon decal on tailgate, whitewall tires, chrome hubcaps, 19", EX-, A $715.00

Construction

Cement Mixer, on 4 CI wheels, w/boiler, mixing trough, chute, gears, etc, 13½x16", VG, A......................................$400.00

Cement Mixer #32, yel fr, gr wheels, red chute & hopper w/gr trim, decals, hand-crank mechanism, 7½", G-, A ...$242.00

Derrick #240, red on spoked CI blk base, needs restringing, 1921-32, 13" w/20" boom, G, A..............................$550.00

Contractor's Dump Truck, pressed steel, light wear to paint, 1920s, 11", EX, D10, $1,150.00.

Dredge, lg front bucket, 4 wheels, body turns, 15" body, 22½" crane (up), some wear/scratches, EX, A...................$350.00

Hoisting Tower #350, bucket carries load up tower to chutes, chutes missing, no rigging, rust, 38", G, A...............$300.00

Hoisting Tower #350, dk gr w/red, gold & blk decals, crank mechanism lowers chute, w/3 adjustable chutes, 38", EX-NM, A $1,265.00

Junior Excavator Model #601 Rider, Type II, bl & orange, rubber tires, 6" tall at seat, 17½", NM, A.....................$165.00

Lift Scoop-N-Dump Truck, pressed steel with 'Buddy L-East Moline' tires, movable front scoop, raising bed and rear gate, 16", NM (EX box), A, $325.00.

Pile Driver, w/wheels, flaking pnt on floor, 22", VG, A .$300.00

Road Roller, curved top, spoked wheels, orig pnt & parts, 9½x19", VG, A $4,600.00

Road Roller #290, steers, roller wheels, red cab top, rpl gears & steering chain, worn pnt, 1929-31, 19⅜", VG, A $3,410.00

Sand Screener, buckets on chain deposit dirt in hopper w/screen, hand crank, 4 CI wheels, worn/pnt loss, 22x24", G, A .$500.00

Steam Shovel, pressed steel, paint scratches, mechanism needs repair, 24", VG+, A, $500.00.

Steam Shovel #220, blk w/red roof & fr, Quality Toys decals on floor & sides, winch mechanism, 20½", VG-EX, A.$303.00

Steam Shovel #2205, blk w/maroon roof, ca 1930s, mechanism needs rpr, 24", VG+, A $500.00

Truck & Steam Shovel #848, bl & gray cab, Bakelite wheels, bl & orange shovel, crank mechanism, ca 1948, 20½", EX, A.$660.00

Firefighting

Aerial Ladder Truck, adjustable ladders on rear, surface rust/chips/scratches, 2 ladders gone, 9x33", A $350.00

Aerial Ladder Truck, open, 4-prong expanding ladder can be raised & lowered, turning front wheels, 1935, 37", A................$1,000.00

Aerial Ladder Truck #205B, red, solid red wheels, spring-powered elevation mechanism, 1927-29, orig box, 29½", NM, A..$2,420.00

Aerial Ladder Truck #27 Rider, red, steel wheels, rubber tires, spring-powered mechanism, 1933-34, 29½", VG, A...............$1,210.00

Fire Pumper #205A-B, red w/solid wheels, professionally rstr, 1929, 23⅜", M, A...$1,705.00

Fire Pumper #29 Rider, red, rubber tires, electric headlights, orig steering wheel, 26", VG, A $3,410.00

Fire Truck, battery-op lights, red w/sticker logos, rubber tires, 2 ladders, '30s style, 9½x21½", VG-EX, A..................$275.00

Fire Truck, red w/plated grille, wood wheels, decals on sides, red ladder, sm pnt chip/lt rust on grille, 12", o/w NM, A..$66.00

Fire Truck, w/hose reel, 2 ladders, turning front wheels, bell & railings, all orig, 1928, 26", A $1,265.00

Fire Truck, wood, red pnt, decal on hood, rpl headlights, missing ladder, 12⅞", o/w EX, A $33.00

Fire Truck #436, red w/NP grille, electric headlights, hard rubber wheels, decals, missing ladders, 20¼", EX-, A $215.00

Fire Water Tower, reaches 36" when activated hydraulically, grille belt, disk wheels, 46", VG, A......................$3,680.00

Ladder Truck with hydraulic lift, professionally restored, 40", $2,500.00.

Hook & Ladder Fire Truck #205, red, solid red wheels, orig pull cord, hose & nozzel, complete, 1923, 25¾", EX, A..$3,190.00

Steam Pumper, 1925, VG, T3 ....$725.00

Water Tank Truck, bl cab, red chassis, gr tank, rubber tires, steers, doors open, spigot works, parts missing, 24", G, A.....$575.00

Trains

Locomotive, wood, red pnt, blk wheels & roof, yel headlight, smokestack & sand dome, smiling face on boiler, 23", EX-, A.................$275.00

Passenger Coach #208, lt gr w/gold trim, steers, doors open, dual rear wheels, ca 1937-32, 29⅛", EX, A $5,720.00

Railroad Caboose, red, 19", EX, A $1,210.00

Railroad Set, locomotive, tender, 2 cars & caboose, 5 couplers, w/track for display, G, A $2,860.00

Railroad Set, 25" steam engine, 8-wheel coal car, 21" boxcar, 20" tanker, +4 more, w/track, EX, A $4,000.00

Railroad Set, 4-6-2 locomotive, tender, 3 cars (1 rpl) & caboose, couplers missing, G-VG, A $4,000.00

Railroad Stock Car, red, 22", EX, A $1,100.00

Round House #80, dk gr w/decals, made for industrial train, 3 bays, 1 side open, 1929-32, P, A $110.00

Union Pacific Railroad, engine, tender & tanker, rpt, parts missing, 59", G-VG, A $500.00

Union Pacific Railroad, stock car, coal car & caboose, rpt, 58", VG, A...$500.00

Trucks and Vans

Air Mail Truck, blk cab, red chassis, enclosed body, Firestone tires on red wheels, #68502, decal 22", P, A............$660.00

Air Mail Truck #2004J, blk cab, red body & chassis, dual rear tires, headlights, sm pnt chips, 1930-32, EX, A....$3,520.00

Army Truck, olive drab w/silver grille, wood wheels, Army on cloth canopy, emb mks on sides, 17¼", EX, A.........$132.00

Army Truck, olive gr w/plated grille, blk rubber tires, w/orig cannon (working), 19¾", M, A $253.00

Army Truck #342, wood, dk olive pnt, blk wheels, red hubcaps, yel headlights, decal on hood, 12⅞", M (G box), A.$248.00

Army Truck #360, wood, olive pnt, yel headlights, red hubcaps, Buddy L Army Transport decals, sm chips, 15½", EX, A..$28.00

Artillery Unit Half Track Truck, dk olive w/plated grille, plastic wheels, cannon w/spring mechanism, 13", NM, A..$264.00

Baggage Truck, red & gray cab, silver grille, yel bed, wood wheels, orig bl steel baggage ladder, 17¼", EX-, A ..$182.00

Baggage Truck #203B, blk cab, yel stake sides, red chassis & wheels, worn wheel bushings, ca 1927-29, 25⅞", G-VG, A......$2,090.00

Butterfingers/Baby Ruth, yel & gr tractor, 2 yel & red trailers (9½x12"), '30s vintage, G-G-, A $600.00

Circus Truck #484, wood, red & yel cab, mc circus wagon, Bakelite wheels, decals, w/animals, 24", orig box, M, A.$1,815.00

City Dray #2000J, blk cab, yel stake sides, red chassis, rubber tires, doors open, dual rear wheels, 1930-32, 24", G, A...$1,650.00

City Dray #439, yel w/gr trim, electric headlights, International Harvester-type grille, orig hand truck, 19⅜", EX, A.$715.00

Coal Truck, missing part of chute, bent axle, needs rstr, rpt, 12x25½", A...$650.00

Dairy Truck #2002J, blk cab, gr stake sides, front bumper, rubber tires w/rear duals, doors open, 1930, 24", pnt G, A..$2,200.00

Delivery Truck, blk cab, dk gr body & red chassis, steers, 1 door missing, 24½", VG, A..$325.00

Dump Truck, blk body w/red chassis, hydraulic dump bed (working), partial rpt, scratches, 24", G, A $500.00

Dump Truck, brn & yel w/yel grille, orange dump bed w/decals on sides, 17¼", G-VG, A...$94.00

Dump Truck, open cab, blk w/red chassis, chain-drive action, much wear, 24", A $400.00

Dump Truck, open cab, blk w/red fenders, orig Buddy L tires, overall rust/chipping/scratches, 25", VG, A $450.00

Dump Truck, wood, brn pnt cab & chassis, yel fenders, red headlights & hubcaps, decals, rpl tailgate, 14¾", G, A $72.00

Dump Truck, yel & bl cab w/wht grille, orange bed, pointed nose style, emb mks on bed, 17¼", NM, A $187.00

Dump Truck, yel cab, fenders & chassis, NP grille, dummy headlights, red bed, blk wheels, late '40s mks, 20¼", EX+, A.............$83.00

Dump Truck, yel cab, fenders & chassis, 4 open windows, plated grille, red bed, wood wheels, late '40s, 12¼", EX+, A .$143.00

Dump Truck #2001J, blk cab, red body & wheels, rubber tires, doors open, crank dump bed, ca 1930, 23¾", G, A .$688.00

Dump Truck #201, blk on red chassis & wheels, hand-crank dump mechanism, ca 1923-29, 24¼", EX, A........$1,210.00

Dump Truck #201, blk on red chassis w/red wheels, rope hoist mechanism, missing pnt on bed, ca 1921-22, 24⅝", VG, A......$578.00

Dump Truck #201A, blk, red chassis & solid wheels, hydraulic spring-action mechanism, ca 1926-29, 24¼", EX, A ..$1,100.00

Dump Truck #312, red cab & bed, gray bed w/Sand & Gravel decal, plated grille, blk rubber tires, 1949, 13¼", MIB, A..........$220.00

Dump Truck #34, Rider, blk cab, red bed, 1-pc rubber wheels, electric lights, hydraulic mechanism, 24⅞", VG, A .$770.00

Dump Truck #34, yel cab & chassis, red bed w/decals, stamped mk on bed, electric headlights, orig box, 19½", NM, A...$523.00

Dump Truck #434, red & yel cab, red bed, pnt grille, dummy headlights, blk wheels w/red centers, 1937, 19½", G, A.........$198.00

Dump Truck #434, yel cab & chassis, red bed, NP grille, electric headlights, decals & emb mks, 1935, 19½", VG-EX, A..$193.00

Dump Truck #5312, red w/plated grille, wht bed w/Sand & Gravel decal, plastic wheels, 1956, 13⅛", NM (VG box), A..$231.00

Dump Truck #634, yel w/bl trim, Buddy L Farm Supplies decals, dummy silver headlights, NP grille, 1950-51, 21", NM, A $231.00

Dump Truck #902 Rider, Type II, bl & wht, red wheels w/rubber tread, bent axle, missing seat & hdl, 1948, 25⅞", VG, A $825.00

Dump Truck Rider #803, bl & orange on bl chassis, dummy headlights, rubber tires w/duals, ca 1948, 20¾", EX, A $550.00

Express Body Truck, 1920s, 24", EX, D10, $1,500.00.

Express Line Moving Van #204, blk cab, gr body w/red wheels, dbl-latch rear doors, w/hand truck, 1924-25, 24¾", NM, A...$4,620.00

Express Line Truck, red cab w/gr trailer, rubber tires, dump gate, 23", G+, A $275.00

Express Line Truck, standard van-type body, overall wear/scratching, rear doors rpl/rpt, 11x7½x25", o/w VG, A $725.00

Express Truck, 1-Ton; closed cab w/open body in rear, areas of touch-up, lt wear, rare, 6½x14", EX, A.................$2,100.00

Express Truck #200, blk on red chassis, spoked wheels, non-dumping bed, rectangular decal, ca 1921-29, EX, A........$1,320.00

Express Truck Tractor & Trailer #34, red & gr, electric headlights, complete w/orig batteries, 1933, 23⅝", EX-NM, A.........$330.00

Flivver Series, open cab w/sm dump body, partial rpt to hood/fenders, 4½x5¼x12½", G, A $1,000.00

Flivver Series Pickup, partial rpt, 7x5¼x12", G, A.........$700.00

Huckster Model T Truck, working steering, right rear axle bent, lt pnt loss & rust, 14½", G, A $1,350.00

Ice Truck, blk cab, yel bed, red chassis & wheels, repro ice & tongs, orig canvas & pull cord, 1926-29, 26¼", VG, A $1,815.00

Ice Truck, lt yel & gr, dummy headlights, pnt grille, hard rubber tires, emb mks/decals, canvas cover, 1952, 21", EX, A..............$242.00

Ice Truck #357, wood, red & wht pnt, blk wood wheels, Buddy L Pure Ice decals, orig tongs & ice blocks, orig box, EX, A $385.00

Ice Wagon #12 Rider, blk cab, yel body, red bumper & wheels, removable saddle, decals, ice block, tongs gone, 27", G, A $990.00

International Delivery Truck Rider, gray w/red & gold stripe, bl fenders, red & silver grille, 22", EX, A......................$500.00

Little Elf Pickup, blk & red w/wood van body, missing radiator & ornament, worn pnt, ca 1923-28, sm, A............$1,155.00

Lumber Truck #365, wood, blk & yel w/red hubcaps, decals on sides of trailer & hood, 1943-45, 25⅛", EX-NM, A..$242.00

Mail Truck, blk body w/dk gr cage & red chassis, steers, 1 rear door missing, 24½", G, A $275.00

Maintenance Truck #450, gr & gray, Telephone Maintenance decals, hard rubber tires, trailer/poles, 1952, NM (VG box), A...$935.00

Market Truck, wht & orange, plated grille, dummy headlights, Bakelite wheels (1 rpl), missing divider, 21⅝", EX, A .$66.00

Market Truck #325, wht w/plated grille, blk tires, complete w/10 merchandise pkgs, 1952, 13¼", M (G rstr box), A ..$385.00

Market Truck #461, wht w/yel trim, electric headlights, emb mks, International Harvester grille, 1952, 20¼", EX, A ...$281.00

McCormick-Deering Red Baby Express Truck, spoked aluminum wheels, decals, rpl fender, 1923, 24", G, A...........$2,310.00

Merry-Go-Round Truck, pnt body, wood & plastic revolving carousel, sm scratches, 12½", G, A............................$55.00

Milk Truck, wood w/fiberboard sides, blk & red pnt, Buddy L Milk Farms decals, sliding doors, sm chips, 13⅛", VG, A...$468.00

Milk Truck #872, Type II, wood, cream & red pnt, chrome hubcaps, w/milk carrier & bottles, 1948-49, 12⅞", VG-EX, A......$550.00

Milk Truck #872, Type III, wood, cream & red pnt, Buddy L Farm decals, Bakelite wheels, 1948-49, 12⅞", G, A .$330.00

Moving Van #366, wood, orange & blk, decals on sides & hood, sm pnt chips, 1 rpl hubcap, 1945, 27⅝", G-VG, A..$154.00

Moving Van #413, red cab w/plated grille, removable cream van w/gray roof & decals, rubber tires, ca '50, 20", VG-EX, A............$176.00

Oil Corporation Junior Tank Truck #2003, blk cab, gr fillable tank, dual rear wheels, filler caps, ca '30, 24", VG, A..........$3,190.00

Oil Tanker, blk w/red trim, orig pnt, 90% decal, dents in rear fender/tap resoldered/no straps, mid-1920s, 26", M5 ...$1,150.00

Railway Express #204A, dk gr, screen-sided body (removable), ca 1928-29, 24⅞", G, A...$990.00

Railway Express Agency Tractor Trailor, red cab & chassis w/separate gr trailer, electric lights, ca '30s, VG, A.$660.00

REA Truck #763, Kelly Gr w/American Dairy decals, dummy headlights, rubber tires, removable roof, 1952, 22¼", VG, A.$275.00

Riding Academy Horse Van, missing horses & clear plastic dome, late 1950s, EX+, A3..$60.00

Robotoy Dump Truck #75, red & gr on blk chassis, remote control w/110-volt cord, steers, cable missing, 21⅝", G-VG, A..$303.00

Sand & Gravel Truck #202A, blk, red chassis & wheels, rubber treads, doors open, rstr, ca 1930-32, 25", NM $3,080.00

Sand & Gravel Truck #202A, blk w/red wheels, hopper doors open, worn decal, ca 1926-29, 25½", G, A...........$1,430.00

Sand & Stone Dump Truck, yel w/gr decal on cab door, ca 1950s, 15", EX...$195.00

Shell Pickup & Delivery #313, yel w/Shell decals, plated grille, w/Shell can bank, 1950-51, 13⅜", M (VG box), A.$468.00

Shell Pickup & Delivery #3513, yel w/decals, emb rubber wheels, plated grille, w/hole for chain, 1953-55, 13", G, A.....$72.00

Shell Truck, red stencil on orange and red truck, Buddy L in raised letters on both doors, 1940s, paint chipped, no dents, 21", $240.00.

Speedster Rider, red w/NP International Harvester-style grille, electric headlights, missing saddle, '32, 18¾", EX, A.$303.00

Tank Truck, water sprinkler w/blk closed cab & gr water tank, logo on side, some spots w/wear, 12½x25", EX, A$1,450.00

Tank Truck #206A, blk cab w/dk gr tank & red wheels, missing pnt on cab roof, 23¾", VG, A.................................$825.00

Tanker Truck, turning front wheels, original tank cap and rear spigot, minor wear, 25", M5, $1,600.00.

Texaco GMC Tanker, 1950s, 24", VG, A4....................$125.00

Truck, blk w/logo stickers, made for peddling fruits/veggies ca 1920s, all blk, open bed w/top & side stakes, 14", EX, A........$2,800.00

Truck, Jr Series, closed cab & opening doors, headlights, rubber tires, closed box body, total rpt, 1930s, 22", A $650.00

Truck & Tandem Trailer #52, yel & gr cab, red & yel detachable trailer, decals, electric headlights, 1936-37, 39", VG, A..$990.00

Truck & Trailer, blk & orange, headlights on fenders, removable van, Long Distance Moving decals, late '40s, 30", G, A.........$275.00

Truck #51 Rider, red w/NP grille, electric headlights, Bakelite wheels, missing saddle, rpl axle, 1935, 24½", G, A.................$1,100.00

Truck #803 Rider, bl & wht, dummy headlights, rubber tires w/duals, missing saddle, 1945, 23", EX, A.................................$825.00

Wrecker, restored, 1920s, 24", D10, $2,850.00.

Wrecker, blk open cab, red chassis, hook & crane, labels partially torn, 12x25½", overall EX, A.....................$1,700.00

Wrecker, lt yel & brn, NP grille, dummy headlights, stamped & emb mks, blk wheels w/yel centers, late '40s, G-, A ..$99.00

Wrecker #3317, yel w/red boom, plated grille, rubber tires, decals, 1949-52, 12½", M (VG box), A...................$275.00

Wrecker #358, Type I, wood, brn & gr pnt, yel headlights & hubcaps, decals, w/hook, missing crank hdl, 17¾", VG+, A..........$165.00

Wrecker #358, Type III, wood, brn & turq pnt, yel lights & hubcaps, orig tow hook, split but complete, 1945, 18", VG, A $110.00

Wrecker #437, wht w/red boom, NP grille, electric headlights, decals & emb mks, orig box, 1935, 20⅜", VG, A....$660.00

Wrecking Truck #209, blk cab w/red bed & wheels, ca 1928-29, missing lg gears, 27⅞", G, A $1,100.00

Miscellaneous

Jeep #354, wood, red & yel pnt, blk wheels, natural bumper, Buddy L Wood Toys decal, w/red trailer, 17", EX, A $50.00

Navigation Co Tugboat #3000, gr hull w/gray deck & superstructure, compressed air motor, 1928-29, 27½", VG, A...$6,160.00

Super Hero Motorcycle Gift Set, diecast, MIB, T1...........$75.00

Tank #362, wood, drab olive pnt w/red turret & headlights, blk cannons (1 rpl), noisemaker, pnt loss, 11⅝", G, A....$33.00

Tool Chest #1, blk & red wood w/decal, contents list for #4 set, orig tray, rare orig apron, 1927-29, 23x11", G, A....$198.00

Tool Chest #1, red & blk wood, metal corners & hdls, decal on top, w/canvas tool apron (repro), 23x11x6⅝", G, A .$66.00

Traffic Light, battery-op, NMIB.....................................$40.00

Building Blocks and Construction Toys

Toy building sets were popular with children well before television worked its mesmerizing influence on young minds; in fact, as early as 1880, Richter's Anchor (Union) Stone Building Blocks were patented in both Germany and the USA. Though the company produced more than 600 different sets, only their New Series is commonly found today (these are listed below). Their blocks remained popular until WWI, and Anchor sets were the first toy to achieve international 'brand name' acceptance. They were produced both as basic sets and supplement sets (identified by letters A, B, C, or D) which increased a basic set to a higher level. There were dozens of competitors, though none were very successful. During WWI the trade name Anchor was lost to A.C. Gilbert (Connecticut) who produced Anchor blocks for a short time. Richter responded by using the new trade name 'Union' or 'Stone Buiilding Blocks,' sets considered today to be Anchor blocks despite the lack of the Richter's Anchor trademark. The A.C. Gilbert Company also produced the famous Erector sets which were made from the about 1913 through the late 1950s. Our advisors for blocks are Arlan Coffman (C4) and (Richter's blocks specialist) George Hardy (H3).

Note: Values for Richter's blocks are for sets in very good condition.

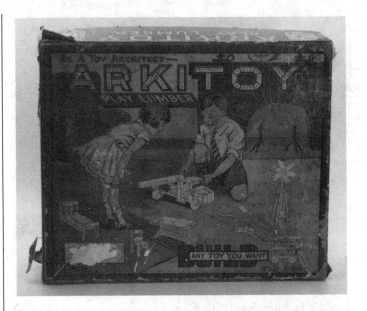

GB Lewis Co, Arkitoy #3, wood, 1930s, EX (G- box), $125.00.

Ideal Skyscraper, plastic, 1968, MIB, $85.00.

American Novelty Works, Architect Building Blocks, 1920s, EX+, T1..$125.00
Auburn, Flexible Building Bricks, G5 ....$40.00
Banner Plastic Corp, Build Your Own 5-Story Apartment, tin w/plastic furniture, orig boxes, NM, A.....................$225.00
Block City #B-500, complete w/roofing, 1950s, EX+, T1 .$45.00
Block City Set #B-300, 152-pc, no roofing, 1950s, EX+, T1 ....$40.00
Blockcraft Essential Toys, Primary Blocks, cloth bag, VG+, P3 ....$15.00
Constructive Thinking Building Set, 1950s-60s, boxed, EX+, T1..$45.00
Crandall, Heavy Artillery, wood, 1875, EX.................$2,175.00
Crandall, interlocking pcs to assemble entire alphabet, 1876, in orig 13x6½x2¼" box, VG, A $450.00
Elgo Plastics, American Plastic Bricks, #745, G5..............$70.00
Erector, #10051, Electric Engine set, 1959, EX...............$120.00
Erector, #10254, near complete, orig box, EX+ $25.00
Erector, #6½, 1956, complete..$145.00
Erector, A World To Build, 364-pc, cb box, T1 ....$35.00
Erector, Action Conveyor Set, NMIB $185.00
Erector, Action Helicopter Set #10181, 1959, NM........$125.00
Erector, Cape Canaveral, appears about complete, w/instructions, 1950s, orig metal box & motor, T1 ....$95.00
Erector, Cape Canaveral, 1960s, metal box, EX+, T1 ......$65.00
Erector, Conveyor Set #10063, 1957, EX $120.00
Erector, Five-in-One Military Vehicles, MIB $65.00
Erector, Powerline Set, w/motors & orig box, T1 ....$35.00
Halsam, American Bricks, lg set, EX+, T1 ....$50.00
Hasbro, Astrolite Building Set, build futuristic city & light up w/base, orig box, EX, T1 ....$65.00

Kenner, Girder & Panel Building Set, plastic pcs to assemble stores & other buildings, 1957, appears complete, EX+, T2............$80.00
Kenner, Girder & Panel Set, sq tube, 1970s, EX-, T1.......$25.00
Kenner, Girder & Panel Set #8, w/motor, 1960, EX.........$55.00
Kenner, Girder & Panel Set #9, complete, 1950s, EX+, T1....$95.00
Kenner, Girder Magic Building Set #32, complete, NMIB ..$40.00
Kobler, Construction set, Swiss made, rare, 1940s, MIB..$375.00
Lincoln Logs, Western Log & Metal Figure Game, 5 lead figures, logs to build cabin, 1950s, 12x17", NM (EX box), A .$70.00
Log Cabin Play Houses, pnt wood logs & panels, pnt shutters & doors, 12x8½" wood box w/paper label, VG, A $230.00
Marklin, bolt-together plates & girders, orig parts, list & instructions, orig 20x14" wood & cb box, G-VG, A $50.00
Meccano, complete, 1950s, orig wood box, EX..............$150.00
Metalcraft, Spirit of St Louis, never assembled, MIB, A..$525.00
Metalcraft, Spirit of St Louis Kit #810, in 8x14" box w/Statue of Liberty etc, EX (EX+ box), A $250.00

Metalcraft, Spirit of St Louis, builds over 25 airplanes, complete, EX, $250.00.

Skyline Building Set, 1950s, EX+, T1 ....$50.00
Tinkertoys, #146, 180 pcs, 1969, orig 12" canister, MIB, M4 ....$20.00
Tinkertoys, Curtain Wall Builder #630, metal & plastic, 1950s,
    M (M canister) $35.00
Toy Tinkers, #610, 82-pc, MIB $75.00
Toy Tinkers, #620, 123-pc, MIB $80.00
Toy Tinkers, #640, 317-pc, MIB......................................$125.00
Toy Tinkers #630, 197-pc, MIB..$100.00
Trix Construction Set, late 1940s-early '50s, MIB............$50.00

U Bilda Fort, metal, ca 1920s, $325.00. (Photo courtesy Continental Hobby House.)

WS Reed Co, ABC Windmill, wood, 1900, EX $805.00
WS Reed Co, Grand Exhibition, w/figures & wagon, wood,
    1878, EX $1,495.00

Richter Anchor Stone Building Sets

DS, Set #E3, w/metal parts & roof stones, H3 ....$45.00
DS, Set #11, w/metal parts & roof stones, H3 ....$675.00
DS, Set #11A, w/metal parts & roof stones, H3 ....$300.00
DS, Set #13A, w/metal parts & roof stones, H3 ....$325.00
DS, Set #15, w/metal parts & roof stones, H3 ....$1,300.00
DS, Set #15A, w/metal parts & roof stones, H3 ....$475.00
DS, Set #17A, w/metal parts & roof stones, H3 ....$475.00
DS, Set #19A, w/metal parts & roof stones, H3 ....$900.00

DS, Set #21A, w/metal parts & roof stones, H3 ....$975.00
DS, Set #23A, w/metal parts & roof stones, H3 ....$750.00
DS, Set #25A, w/metal parts & roof stones, H3 ....$1,300.00
DS, Set #27, w/metal parts & roof stones, H3 ....$5,000.00
DS, Set #3A, w/metal parts & roof stones, H3..................$50.00
DS, Set #5, w/metal parts & roof stones, H3 ....$100.00
DS, Set #5A, w/metal parts & roof stones, H3 ....$150.00
DS, Set #7, w/metal parts & roof stones, H3 ....$250.00
DS, Set #7A, w/metal parts & roof stones, H3 ....$175.00
DS, Set #9A, w/metal parts & roof stones, H3 ....$250.00
Fortress Set #402, H3 ....$90.00
Fortress Set #402A, H3 ....$115.00
Fortress Set #404, H3 ....$200.00
Fortress Set #404A, H3 ....$225.00
Fortress Set #406, H3 ....$400.00
Fortress Set #406A, H3 ....$400.00
Fortress Set #408, H3 ....$800.00
Fortress Set #408A, H3 ....$800.00
Fortress Set #410, H3 ....$1,600.00
Fortress Set #410A, H3 ....$750.00
Fortress Set #412A, H3 ....$1,300.00
Fortress Set #414, H3 ....$3,650.00
GK-NF, Great Castle, H3 ....$9,950.00
GK-NF, Set #10, H3..$275.00
GK-NF, Set #10A, H3..$120.00
GK-NF, Set #12, H3..$400.00
GK-NF, Set #12A, H3..$195.00
GK-NF, Set #14A, H3..$200.00
GK-NF, Set #16, H3..$800.00
GK-NF, Set #16A, H3..$240.00
GK-NF, Set #18A, H3..$375.00
GK-NF, Set #20, H3..$1,400.00
GK-NF, Set #20A, H3..$450.00
GK-NF, Set #22A, H3..$450.00
GK-NF, Set #24A, H3..$500.00
GK-NF, Set #26A, H3..$1,125.00
GK-NF, Set #28, H3..$3,875.00
GK-NF, Set #28A, H3..$1,000.00
GK-NF, Set #30A, H3..$1,125.00
GK-NF, Set #32B, H3..$1,600.00
GK-NF, Set #34, H3..$6,000.00
GK-NF, Set #6, H3...$90.00
GK-NF, Set #6A, H3...$90.00
GK-NF, Set #8, H3..$180.00

Buy Sell Trade

Also sold as **UNION, COMET, EAGLE** and **ORION** Some sets without any brand name
Information about the **Club of Anchor Friends**
George F. Hardy, 1670 Hawkwood Ct,
Charlottesville, VA 22901

GK-NF, Set #8A, H3 ....$95.00
KK-NF, Set #11, H3 ....$275.00
KK-NF, Set #11A, H3 ....$275.00
KK-NF, Set #13A, H3 ....$300.00
KK-NF, Set #15A, H3 ....$450.00
KK-NF, Set #17A, H3 ....$750.00
KK-NF, Set #19A, H3 ....$1,500.00
KK-NF, Set #21, H3 ....$3,500.00
KK-NF, Set #5, H3 ....$45.00
KK-NF, Set #5A, H3 ....$55.00
KK-NF, Set #7, H3 ....$100.00
KK-NF, Set #7A, H3 ....$90.00
KK-NF, Set #9, H3 ....$100.00
Modern House & Country House Set #206, H3 ....$600.00
Modern House & Country House Set #208, H3 ....$600.00
Modern House & Country House Set #210, H3 ....$600.00
Modern House & Country House Set #301, H3 ....$200.00
Modern House & Country House Set #301A, H3 ....$450.00
Modern House & Country House Set #303, H3 ....$650.00
Modern House & Country House Set #303A, H3 .....$2,000.00
Modern House & Country House Set #305, H3 ....$2,500.00
Neue Reihe, Set #102, H3 ....$75.00
Neue Reihe, Set #104, H3 ....$100.00
Neue Reihe, Set #106, H3 ....$150.00
Neue Reihe, Set #108, H3 ....$240.00
Neue Reihe, Set #110, H3 ....$425.00
Neue Reihe, Set #112, H3 ....$500.00
Neue Reihe, Set #114, H3 ....$800.00
Neue Reihe, Set #116, H3 ....$1,325.00

California Raisins

The California Raisins made their first TV commercials in the fall of 1986. The first four PVC figures were introduced in 1987, the same year Hardy's issued similar but smaller figures, and three 5½" Bendees became available on the retail market as well. In 1988 twenty-one more Raisins were made for retail as well as promotional efforts in grocery stores. Four were graduates identical to the original four characters except standing on yellow pedestals and wearing blue graduation caps with yellow tassels. Hardy's increased their line by six.

In 1989 they starred in two movies: *Meet the Raisins* and *The California Raisins — Sold Out*, and eight additional characters were joined in figurine production by five of their fruit and vegetable friends from the movies. Hardy's latest release was in 1991, when they added still four more. All Raisins issued for retail sales and promotions in 1987 and 1988 (including Hardy's) are dated with the year of production (usually on the bottom of one foot). Of those released for retail sales in 1989, only the Beach Scene characters are dated, and these are actually dated 1988. Hardee's 1991 series are also undated. For more information, see *The Flea Market Trader, Revised Ninth Edition*, by Sharon and Bob Huxford. Our advisor for this category is Larry DeAngelo (D3).

Beach Theme Edition, mk 1988 CALRAB-Applause, set of 4, M, D3..$40.00
Bendees, flat bodies, set of 3, D3 ....$35.00

Christmas Issue, Santa, marked 1988 CALRAB, red cap, green sneakers, M, D3, $18.00.

Christmas Issue, Sunglasses, mk 1988 CALRAB, gr glasses, red sneakers, holding candy cane, M, C3 ....$18.00
First Commercial Issue, Guitar, mk 1988 CALRAB, red guitar, M, C3 ....$8.00
First Commercial Issue, Singer, mk 1988 CALRAB, microphone in left hand not connected to face, M, C3 ....$8.00
First Commercial Issue, Sunglasses 1, aqua glasses glued on, eyes visible, M, C3...$16.00
First Commercial Issue, Sunglasses 2, mk 1988 CALRAB, aqua sunglasses glued on, eyes can't be seen, M, C3.............$8.00
First Commercial Issue, Winky, mk 1988 CALRAB, winking, right hand in hitchhike position, M, C3 ....$8.00
First Key Chains, Hands, mk 1987 CALRAB, both hands up, thumbs touch head, M, C3 ....$8.00
First Key Chains, Microphone, mk 1987 CALRAB, right hand points up, microphone in left hand, M, C3 ....$8.00
First Key Chains, Saxophone, mk 1987 CALRAB, gold sax, no hat, M, C3 ....$8.00
First Key Chains, Sunglasses, mk 1987 CALRAB, orange glasses, index fingers touch face, M, C3 ....$8.00
Graduate Key Chains, Hands, mk 1988 CALRAB 'Lic Applause Lic,' both hands up, thumbs touch head, M...............$25.00
Graduate Key Chains, Microphone, mk 1988 CALRAB 'Lic Applause Lic,' right hand points, left hand holds microphone, M.....$25.00
Graduate Key Chains, Saxophone, mk 1988 CALRAB 'Lic Applause Lic,' gold sax, no hat, M $25.00
Graduate Key Chains, Sunglasses, mk 1988 CALRAB 'Lic Applause Lic,' orange glasses, index fingers touch face, M................$25.00
Graduates from First Commercial Issue, Singer, mk 1988 CALRAB w/Clamation on bottom of yel plastic base, M, C3 ....$40.00
Graduates from Post Raisin Bran Issue, Hands, mk 1988 CALRAB w/Clamation on bottom of yel plastic base, M, C3 ....$40.00
Graduates from Post Raisin Bran Issue, Saxophone, mk 1988 CALRAB w/Clamation on bottom of yel plastic base, M, C3 ....$40.00

Graduates From First Commercial Issue, Conga Dancer with blue shoes, marked 1988 CALRAB with Clamation on bottom of yellow plastic base, M, D3, $40.00.

Graduates from Post Raisin Bran Issue, Sunglasses, mk 1988 CARAB w/Clamation on bottom of yel base, M, C3 ..**$40.00**

Hardee's 1st Promotion, Hands, mk 1987 CALRAB, both hands up, thumbs touch head, sm sz, M, C3 ....**$4.00**

Hardee's 1st Promotion, Microphone, mk 1987 CALRAB, right hand points up, microphone in left hand, sm sz, M, C3 ..**$4.00**

Hardee's 1st Promotion, Saxophone, mk 1987 CALRAB, gold sax, no hat, sm sz, M, C3 ....**$4.00**

Hardee's 1st Promotion, Sunglasses, mk 1987 CALRAB, orange glasses, index fingers touch face, sm sz, M, C3 ....**$4.00**

Hardee's 2nd Promotion, Captain Toonz, mk Mfg Applause Inc, bl boom box, yel glasses & sneakers, sm sz, M, C3 ....**$5.00**

Hardee's 2nd Promotion, FF Strings, mk Mfg Applause Inc 1988, bl guitar, orange sneakers, sm sz, M, C3 ....**$5.00**

Hardee's 2nd Promotion, Rollin' Rollo, mk Mfg Applause Inc 1988, roller skates, yel sneakers & hat mk H, sm sz, M, C3 ....**$5.00**

Hardee's 2nd Promotion, SB Stuntz, mk Mfg Applause Inc, yel skateboard, bl sneakers, sm sz, M, C3 ....**$5.00**

Hardee's 2nd Promotion, Trumpy Trunote, mk Mfg Applause Inc 1988, w/trumpet, bl sneakers, sm sz, M, C3............**$5.00**

Hardee's 2nd Promotion, Waves Weaver, mk Mfg Applause Inc 1988, yel surfboard, red glasses & sneakers, sm sz, M, C3 .**$5.00**

Hardee's 4th Promotion, Alotta Stile, mk 1992 CALRAB-Applause, shopping bags & violet heels, MIP, D3 .....**$12.00**

Hardee's 4th Promotion, Anita Break, mk 1992 CALRAB-Applause, w/boom box & pk boots, MIP, D3 ....**$12.00**

Hardee's 4th Promotion, Benny, mk 1992 CALRAB-Applause, w/bowling ball & bag, MIP, D3 ....**$12.00**

Hardee's 4th Promotion, Buster, mk 1992 CALRAB-Applause, blk & yel sneakers & skateboard, MIP, D3 ....**$12.00**

Meet the Raisins 1st Edition, Lick Broccoli, mk CALRAB-Applause, gr & blk, red & orange guitar, M, C3 ....**$15.00**

Meet the Raisins 1st Edition, Piano, mk CALRAB, issued May 1989, red hair, bl piano, gr sneakers, M, C3..............**$20.00**

Meet the Raisins 1st Edition, Banana White, marked Clamation-Applause, yellow dress, M, D3, $15.00.

Meet the Raisins 1st Edition, Rudy Bagaman, mk Clamation-Applause, vegetable cigar, purple shirt, flipflops, M, C3 ..**$15.00**

Meet the Raisins 2nd Edition, AC, mk CALRAB-Applause, gimme -5 pose, tall pompadour, red sneakers, M, C3.**$50.00**

Meet the Raisins 2nd Edition, Cecil Thyme, mk Clamation-Applause, orange carrot-like, M **$50.00**

Meet the Raisins 2nd Edition, Leonard Limabean, mk Clamation-Applause, purple coat, bl hat, M **$50.00**

Meet the Raisins 2nd Edition, Mom, mk CALRAB-Applause, yel hair, pk apron, M **$50.00**

Post Raisin Bran Issue, Hands, mk 1987 CALRAB, left hands points up, right hand points down, M, C3 ....**$4.00**

Post Raisin Bran Issue, Microphone, mk 1987 CALRAB, right hand in fist, microphone in left hand, M, C3 ....**$4.00**

Post Raisin Bran Issue, Saxophone, mk 1987 CALRAB, inside of sax pnt blk, M, C3 ....**$4.00**

Post Raisin Bran Issue, Sunglasses, orange glasses, right hand points up, left points down, M, C3 ....**$4.00**

Refrigerator Magnets, mk 1988 CALRAB-Applause, set of 4, M D3...**$40.00**

Sandwich Music Box, Hands, mk 1987 CALRAB, both hands out to side w/fingers pointing, M..................................**$15.00**

Sandwich Music Box, Microphone, mk 1987 CALRAB, both hands out as if to hug, M **$15.00**

Sandwich Music Box, Sunglasses, mk 1987 CALRAB, both hands out as if to hug, M **$15.00**

Second Commercial Issue, Bass Player, mk 1988 CALRAB-Applause, gray slippers, MIP, D3.................................**$25.00**

Second Commercial Issue, Drummer, mk 1988 CALRAB-Applause, w/set of drums, blk hat w/yel feather, MIP, D3 ....**$25.00**

Second Commercial Issue, Girl Singer, Ms Sweet, mk 1988 CALRAB, hot pink shoes & bracelet, M, C3 ....**$16.00**

Second Commercial Issue, Girl w/Tambourine, Ms Delicious, mk 1988 CALRAB-Applause, yel shoes, holding tambourine, M, C3...**$16.00**

Second Key Chains, Hip Band Hip Guitarist (Hendrix), mk 1988 CALRAB-Applause, headband, yel guitar, sm sz, M, C3 ....$25.00

Second Key Chains, Hip Band Microphone-Female, mk 1988 CALRAB-Applause, yel shoes & bracelet, sm sz, M..$15.00

Second Key Chains, Hip Band Microphone-Male, mk 1988 CALRAB-Applause, left hand extended w/open palm, sm sz, M..$15.00

Second Key Chains, Hip Band Saxophone, mk 1988 CALRAB-Applause, blk beret, bl eyelids, sm sz, M $15.00

Special Edition, Michael, mk 'Lic by Applause Lic,' silver microphone, stud belt, M, D3...$20.00

Special Lovers Issue, Female, mk 1988 CALRAB-Applause, holding 'Be Mine' heart, M, C3.................................$8.00

Special Lovers Issue, Male, mk 1988 CALRAB-Applause, same as Winky, holding 'I'm Yours' heart, M, C3.................$8.00

Unknown Promotion, Blue Surfboard, marked 1988 CALRAB, surfboard in right hand connected to right foot, M, D3, $50.00.

Special Raisin Club Issue, Tambourine Female, marked 1988 CALRAB-Applause, green shoes and bracelet, tambourine held down, M, D3, $12.00.

Third Commercial Issue, Hip Band Microphone-Female, mk 1988 CALRAB-Applause, yel shoes & bracelet, M, C3........$12.00

Third Commercial Issue, Hip Band Microphone-Male, mk 1988 CALRAB-Applause, left hand extended w/open palm, M, C3 ....$12.00

Third Commercial Issue, Hip Band Saxophone, mk 1988 CALRAB-Applause, blk beret, bl eyelids, M, C3......$12.00

Third Commercial Issue, Hip Band Hip Guitarist (Hendrix), mk 1988 CALRAB-Applause, headband, yel guitar, M, D3..$25.00

Unknown Promotion, Blue Surfboard, mk 1987 CALRAB, same as Sunglasses but w/board horizontal in right hand, M $35.00

Candy Containers

As early as 1876, candy manufacturers used figural glass containers to package their candy. They found the idea so successful that they continued to use them until the 1960s. The major producers of these glass containers were Westmoreland, West Bros., Victory Glass, J.H. Millstein, J.C. Crosetti, L.E. Smith, and Jack and T.H. Stough. Some of the most collectible and sought after today are the character-related figurals such as Amos 'n Andy, Barney Google, Santa Claus, and Jackie Coogan, but there are other rare examples that have been known to command prices of $1,000.00 and more. Some of these are Black Cat for Luck, Black Cat Sitting, Quick Firer Cannon (with original carriage), and Mr. Rabbit with Hat (that books for $1,500.00 even in worn paint). There are many reproductions; know your dealer. For a listing of these reproductions, refer to *Schroeder's Antiques Price Guide* by Sharon and Bob Huxford. Our advisor for this category is Doug Dezso (D6).

'L' numbers in the listings that follow refer to *An Album of Candy Containers, Vols 1 and 2*, by Jennie Long; 'E&A' numbers correlate with *The Compleat American Glass Candy Containers Handbook* by Eikelberner and Agadjanian, revised by Adele Bowden.

Airplane, U.S. Army B-5-1; paper wings, L #591, from $85.00 to $90.00.

Airplane, Passenger; L #323 (E&A #7) $275.00
Amos 'N Andy, L #77 (E&A #21), EX pnt $450.00

Amos 'N Andy, E&A #21, NM pnt, 4½", $600.00.

Auto w/Tassels #3, L #362.......................................$400.00
Basket, flower design, L #223 (E&A #81).........................$30.00
Basket, ruby flashed, L #225 ....$35.00
Black Cat Sitting, L #5......................................$1,000.00
Bureau, L #125 (E&A #112) $200.00
Candy Cane, Mercury Glass; L #613 ....$20.00
Cannon, Quick Firer; orig carriage, L #537 ....$1,000.00
Car, Electric Coupe #1; L #354 (E&A #49) $60.00
Chicken, fancy closure, L #9 ....$500.00
Chicken in Sagging Basket, L #8 (E&A #148) $65.00
Chicken on Oblong Basket, closure, gr, L #10 (E&A #147) .$45.00
Clock, Alarm; #11, L #549 ....$110.00
Coal Car, w/tender, L #402 (E&A #170) $225.00
Decorettes, L #655...$250.00
Esther Coach, all orig, L #397 (E&A #165) $400.00
Felix by Barrel, L #85 (E&A #211), G pnt $750.00

Gas Pump, metal base, L #316, 4½", $225.00.

Horn, Millsteins, L #282 (E&A #311) $20.00
House, orig pnt, closure, L #75 (E&A #324) $165.00
Ice Truck, all orig, L #458 (E&A #784).........................$775.00
Kiddies' Band, complete, L #277 (E&A #314) $275.00
Lantern, beaded globe, L #560 (E&A #449).........................$35.00
Lantern, brass cap, L #184 (E&A #403) $20.00
Limousine, Westmoreland Specialty, L #351 (E&A #45) $175.00
Little Express, L #405 ....$875.00
Locomotive, no wheels, L #395 (E&A #485) $150.00
Maud Muller Milk Carrier, L #69................................$175.00
Naked Child, Victory Glass, L #94, (E&A #546).............$40.00
Nurser Bottle, Waisted; L #71 (E&A #548) $25.00
Peter Rabbit, L #55 (E&A #618) $25.00
Poodle Dog, glass head, L #471.................................$30.00

Fire Engine, Victory Glass, 5¼", L #386, $15.00.

Fish, L #34 ....$500.00
Gun, cork closure, L #540......................................$25.00

Pumpkin-Head Policeman, Large; NM, $2,000.00. (Photo courtesy Doug Dezso.)

Rabbit in Eggshell, gold-painted top, L #48, 5½", $75.00.

Rabbit, aluminum ears, L #487...$425.00
Rabbit, Stough's, closure, L #54, (E&A #617)..................$40.00
Rabbit Nibbling Carrot, L #53 (E&A #609).....................$35.00
Rabbit on Dome, gold pnt, L #46 (E&A #607) $450.00

**Refrigerator, NM gold paint, $3,500.00.
(Photo courtesy Doug Dezso.)**

Refrigerator, Victory Glass Co, L #266 (E&A #650)..$3,500.00
Rooster Crowing, orig pnt, L #56 (E&A #151), EX $225.00

**Soldier by Tent, WWI, EX original paint,　$3,000.00.
(Photo courtesy Doug Dezso.)**

Spark Plug, dated 1923, 3", G- pnt, $100.00.

Taxi, 12 vents, L #366, 1½x4¼", $90.00.

Spirit of Goodwill Airplane, pnt glass, silver wings, red pilot & wheels, tin prop, 4½", EX, A $160.00

Telephone, Redlich's No 3, L #294 (E&A #752) $400.00

Toonerville Trolley, L #111 (E&A #767) $700.00

Trunk, L #218 (E&A #789) $150.00

Volkswagon, L #373 (E&A #58) $40.00

Willy's Jeep Scout Car, L #391 (E&A #350) $30.00

Cast Iron

Realistically modeled and carefully detailed cast-iron toys enjoyed their heyday from about the turn of the century (some companies began production a little earlier) until about the 1940s when they were gradually edged out by lighter weight toys, less costly to produce and to ship (some of the cast irons were more than 20" in length and very heavy). Many were vehicles faithfully patterned after actual models seen on city streets at the time. Horse-drawn carriages were phased out when motorized vehicles came into use.

Some of the larger manufacturers were Arcade (Illinois), who by the 1920s was recognized as a leader in the industry; Dent (Pennsylvania); Hubley (Pennsylvania); and Kenton (Ohio). In the 1940s Kenton came out with a few horse-drawn toys which are collectible in their own right, but naturally much less valuable than the older ones. In addition to those already noted, there were many minor makers; you will see them mentioned in the listings. Character-related cast-iron toys will be found in the Character category.

For more detailed information on these companies, we recommend *Collecting Toys* by Richard O'Brien (Books Americana). Our advisor for this category is John McKenna (M2).

Airplanes

America, rpl motors & propellers, wing is aluminum rpl, pnt poor, 13½x17", A $450.00

America Tri-Motor, Hubley, gray & red, 2 pilots, worn pnt, rpl tires, 1931, 17" wingspan, A $2,700.00

Lindy, Hubley, bl, plated wheels w/rubber, aluminum prop, working, 10¼", EX, A..$825.00

Lindy, Hubley (sticker on tail section), wear/scratches/dirt, rust on prop, NP wheels worn, 9x10", A...........$600.00

Lindy Glider, Hubley, red & yel, w/pilot & plated wheels, 6", VG, A $925.00

Lindy-type Single Engine, NP motor & running gear, stars ea side of wing, wear/chipping, 2½x6", A......................$275.00

Los Angeles Dirigible, Dent, yel w/bl letters & trim, 2½", EX, A $320.00

Lucky Boy, Dent, silver w/red accents, wheels, blk radial engine & single prop, orig Dent sample room tag, 12x11", VG, A..$2,000.00

Sea Gull Single Engine, rpr to tail section, rpl prop, 7¾x8¼", A..$325.00

Spirit of St Louis, Hubley, Lindy emb on wing, rubber tires, prop turns as wheels move, rpl tires, decal worn, 11x13", A........$1,950.00

Spirit of St Louis, rpr fuselage, rpt wing/fuselage, rpl wheel, 1 wheel missing, 10½x13¼", A $475.00

UX 166 Monoplane, red w/NP engine, prop & wheels, sm pnt chips, 6", G+-EX..$200.00

Boats

Battleship, Kearsarge, rpt, 14", VG, A $121.00

Gun Boat Big Bang, gray w/blk trim, 2 blk turrets w/cannons, compartment for flint or alcohol, 2½x2½x9", G, A $125.00

Paddle Wheeler, Arcade, allover NP is worn, 3½x2¼x7½", A $80.00

Paddle Wheeler, wht hull w/orange trim & yel deck, fixed working beam, chipped pnt, 7¼", VG, A $625.00

Paddle Wheeler Adirondack, Dent, very poor rpt, 5½x3¼x14½", A..$325.00

Paddle Wheeler Puritan, Harris, rpt, 4½x3x10½", EX, A $160.00

Paddle Wheeler Puritan, orig pnt, wht w/red trim & gray top, 4x10½", VG, A..$400.00

Rowers in Racing Shell, Ideal, 8 action rowers, brn shell w/gr water, 4 fancy wheels, 1 oar rpl, 14½", EX, A $3,400.00

Showboat, Arcade, raised letters on side, pnt stripped off/some rust, needs rstr, 4¼x3x12", P, A $275.00

Lindy Monoplane, Hubley, blue with plated wheels, aluminum propeller, geared rear wheel, 10¼" wingspan, EX, A, $825.00.

Sidewheeler Riverboat, Hubley, worn paint, ca 1910, 5¾" long, D10, $350.00.

Circus

Band Wagon, pnt w/scrollwork decoration in relief, red & gold trim, 7 band members & driver, 4 horses, 29½", G-, A.......**$1,850.00**

Calliope Wagon, Hubley, bl/gold/red, 2 wht horses w/red harness, rpt driver/passenger, makes 'music,' 8x4½x16", EX, A.....**$2,500.00**

Calliope Wagon, Hubley, 2 wht horses, driver on bl & gold wagon, red cast wheels, pnt worn, 13½", A.............**$600.00**

Elephant & Clown Chariot, Kenton, gr elephant w/red blanket, red cart on yel wheels, independent clown, 9", G, A.................**$700.00**

Ferris Wheel, Hubley, 6 gondolas w/2 people ea, entirely rpt, 14" dia, A.............**$200.00**

Monkey on Trapeze Wagon, Hubley, 2 brn/gold horses, gr & red ornate mirrored wagon, sliding rear panel, driver, 12", A.............**$900.00**

Overland Circus Band Wagon, Kenton, wht horses, ea w/rider in red, red & yel wagon w/6 musicians, early, 15", VG, A.**$435.00**

Overland Circus Band Wagon, w/driver & 2 horses, ca 1950s, 7¼x15½", EX-NM, A.............**$375.00**

Overland Circus Band Wagon, Kenton, 1930s, 14" long, NM, D10, $950.00.

Overland Circus Calliope Wagon, Kenton, red & yel wagon w/2 men & 1 driver, 2 wht horses w/riders, 14½", A......**$985.00**

Overland Circus Wagon, Kenton, red w/gold trim & yel wheels, 2 wht horses, wht bear in cage, 13¾", VG-EX, A....**$170.00**

Overland Circus Wagon, red & yel, 2 wht horses, 2 rpl figures, rpt, roof damaged, 14", G-, A.............**$90.00**

Royal Circus Cage w/Bear, Hubley, red & wht cage w/sliding rear door, driver atop, 2 wht horses, chipping, 13", A.....**$485.00**

Royal Circus Cage w/Two Lions, Hubley, gray & red 4-wheel cage, 2 cast lions w/in, 2 gray horses, driver, worn, 16", A.....**$1,900.00**

Royal Circus Giraffe Wagon, Hubley, gr w/gray horses, giraffe's head sticks out top, some rpt, 15½", G, A.............**$1,400.00**

Construction

Austin Auto Craft Road Roller, Arcade (has sticker), missing driver, chipping/scratching, 3x7½", VG-EX, A.........**$95.00**

Buckeye Ditch Digger, Kenton, crank-op chain drive w/scoops on chain belt, crack on side, 6½x12", EX, A........**$1,050.00**

Buckeye Ditch Digger, Kenton, gathers buckets of dirt w/simulated engine, buckets/chains rusty, 6½x12½", G, A.**$325.00**

Buckeye Ditch Digger, Kenton, NP gears, buckets & wheels, some rusting on wheels & buckets, 5½x9", VG-EX, A.......**$300.00**

Cement Mixer, Hubley, on CI fr, NP drum & wheels, imp Wonder, 2½x3½", VG-EX, A.............**$60.00**

Cement Mixer Truck, Kenton, NP drum, orig rubber tires, some rust, rpr rear plate, pnt fairly G, 3¼x7¼", A.............**$250.00**

Cement Mixer Truck, Kenton, NP mixer revolves, rear gate cracked, rubber tires/hubs rpl, pnt overall EX, 4x3x9", A........**$1,000.00**

Cement Mixer Truck, Kenton, silver cab & chassis, NP chute & drum, 5x2½x8", VG-EX, A.............**$700.00**

Galion Master Road Roller, Kenton, orig box is ripped, M, EX, A..**$300.00**

General Steam Shovel, Hubley, gr & red, rubber tires, NP shovel, rpr chassis, 9½", G, A.............**$275.00**

Huber Road Roller, Hubley, gr w/red wheels, w/driver, totally rstr, 4x5x14", A.............**$750.00**

Huber Road Roller, Hubley, tar roller, orange w/blk star, man on bk, boiler & levers, NP wheels, 5¼x7½", EX, A......**$325.00**

Jaeger Cement Mixer, Kenton, all red w/NP wheels, CI chute & mixing drum, worn pnt/fr rpr, 5½x5x6", G, A.........**$100.00**

Jaeger Cement Mixer, Kenton, orange, aluminum dump chute & mixing container, 4 wheels, hand crank, 6x6½", VG, A........**$200.00**

Jaeger Cement Mixer, Kenton, orange, red, gr & silver, rubber tires, sm pnt chips, 9½", VG, A.............**$250.00**

Jaeger Cement Mixer, Kenton, orange & gr, aluminum dump chute & mixing bowl, ea w/crank, chain drive, 9½", G, A.....**$125.00**

Jaeger Cement Mixer, Kenton, red w/NP mixing drum, molded driver, rubber tires, 4x3¼x9¼", EX, A.....**$725.00**

Panama Digger, Arcade, gr Mack truck w/red shovel, 2 molded-in figures, 8 wheels, 1 tire missing/others poor, 13", EX, A..**$1,350.00**

Road Roller, Arcade, Austin Roll-A-Plane, gray, NP driver/rollers/hydraulic plunger, sm pc gone, 2½x7½", EX, A .**$100.00**

Road Roller, Arcade, Austin Roll-A-Plane, hydraulic plunger & driver missing, needs cleaning, 2½x7½", VG, A **$30.00**

Road Roller, Hubley, gr w/gold trim, red wheels, NP steering wheel, w/driver (rpt?), NP water tank, 4x5x14", EX, A...........**$550.00**

Road Roller, Hubley, typical, all orange, standing NP driver in rear, 5¼x3½x7¾", VG, A **$325.00**

Road Roller, Hubley, orange with standing nickel-plated driver in rear, 8" long, D10, M, $1,100.00.

Road Scraper, Kenton, w/driver, 2-bar chassis, 3x7¾", NMIB..$200.00

Scraper, Arcade, bl w/NP wheels (lt rust), w/driver, 2¾x6", VG-EX, A..$60.00

Steam Shovel, red, NP shovel, pnt chips, 4½", G, A $30.00

Horse-Drawn

Bakery Wagon, '20s era, wht w/blk horse & red harness, Bakery on side, 5¾x12½", VG, A $200.00

City Truck, Harris, w/driver, 3 wooden barrels, 1880s, 15", P, A...$1,200.00

Coach, bl, red & yel, w/driver & passenger, 1 wht horse, 16", VG, A..$200.00

Coach, Hubley, blk w/gold trim, yel spoked wheels, 2 wht horses, coachman, 17", EX, A............................$4,300.00

Contractor's Dump Wagon, gr w/blk horses, rust, 14", G-, A...$80.00

Cupid in Horse-Drawn Slipper, Kenton, NP Cupid on toe of lg 2-wheeled slipper, blk horse, 1910, 10½", A $365.00

Delivery Wagon, detailed driver, gate opens at rear, rods on wheels cause 2 horses to gallop, 13½", G-, A $135.00

Doctor's Wagon, Wilkins, driver in bl coat & top hat, blk 2-wheel rig pulled by tan trotter, pnt wear, 10½", A ..$625.00

Dray Wagon, 2 blk horses (no pnt), gray wagon missing stake rack, w/driver, minor rpt/surface rust/dirty, 8x4x17", A $350.00

English Trap, Kenton, 1895, blk & yel, 4-wheeled, w/driver, lady & dog, 2 wht horses, pnt chipped, 14", A $2,900.00

Farm Wagon, Arcade, gr w/2 blk horses, top of wagon comes off, rope hole broken out, 4¼x12", A.............................$200.00

Fire Engine #320, Kenton, ca 1940s, 10", MIB, D10, $350.00.

Fire Engine, Kenton, 3 horses & molded-in figure, 4x2¼x10", MIB, A $185.00

Fire Engine Boiler, 3 horses, blk/wht pnt (partial rpt), incorrect rear wheels/figures missing/needs rstr, 8x23", A $300.00

Fire Hose Reel, Dent, brn, gold & red w/2 firemen, 2 blk/1 wht galloping horses on eccentric wheels, 1900, 25", EX+, A.......$2,700.00

Fire Hose Reel, 1880-90 era, fireman driver, 2 orig horses, star on reel, missing wires that move horses, 18", G-, A.......$400.00

Fire Ladder Wagon, Hubley (?), 1 blk/1 wht horse, driver, wagon missing NP, now rusty, 8x26", G, A........................$125.00

Fire Ladder Truck, Hubley, ca 1900, 26", EX, D10, $1,850.00.

Fire Ladder Wagon, Ives (Phoenix on shaft), w/driver, 1 of 2 horses & 2nd man missing, 2 lanterns, little pnt, 8x24", A......$450.00

Fire Ladder Wagon, red w/yel wheels, 1 blk & 1 silver horse, driver not orig, 20", G, A $100.00

Fire Ladder Wagon, red w/3 blk & silver horses, rpl ladders & wheels, pnt chips, 18", P, A.......................................$100.00

Fire Ladder Wagon, yel & red, 2 blk & wht horses, rpl driver, pnt chips, missing parts, 18", P, A.............................$55.00

Fire Ladder Wagon (Phoenix on shaft), 2 horses move up/down, +2 ladders, rpl driver/no 2nd man, pnt loss/rust, 8x26", A...$250.00

Fire Patrol Wagon, Ives, wht horse, blk wagon, articulated, firemen/driver missing, minor losses, dirty, 6¼x4x18", A...$400.00

Fire Patrol Wagon, stencil: Fire Patrol, 1 blk/1 wht horse, missing firemen, incorrect driver, 7x21", G-, A $800.00

Fire Patrol Wagon, 1 blk horse/2 NP, 6 firemen sit in bk, driver, wheel/axle rpl, worn, 8x19½", G, A.........................$500.00

Fire Pumper, Hubley, 2 blk/1 silver horse, NP boiler, red hitch, w/driver, missing hitch chains, 6½x3¾x20", G, A ..$275.00

Fire Pumper, Hubley, 2 horses (1 w/heavy pnt loss), bell rings when pulled, missing 2 wheels/chains, 7¼x20", G, A...........$125.00

Fire Pumper, Ives (Phoenix on shaft), 2 horses, clockwork pumper (non-working), needs rpt/rpr, 7x18", A......$350.00

Fire Pumper, NP pumper, red wheels, 2 brn & silver horses w/gold trim, rpr pumper, 14½", G-, A......................$140.00

Fire Pumper, NP pumper on red chassis & wheels, 2 blk & wht horses, pnt chips, rpr/rpt, 21", G-, A........................$190.00

Fire Pumper, Pratt & Letchworth, bell rings when pulled, some rpt/rust, wrong driver, no chains, needs rpr, 6½x17", A $375.00

Fire Pumper, red wagon chassis & wheels, 2 blk horses, partial NP boiler, 14½", G, A...$150.00

Fire Pumper, yel & silver pumper, 3 blk & wht horses w/gold trim, pnt chips, partial rpt, 21", G-VG, A $800.00

Fire Pumper, 2 blk+1 gray horse, yel hitch/wheels, red boiler, gold trim, molded-in fireman, bad rpr/retouch, 5x3x13", A...$70.00

Goat Cart, Wilkins, red & yel 2-seater, wht goat, hole in driver's arm, random pnt nicks, o/w EX, 9½", A...............$1,600.00

Hansom Cab, Pratt & Letchworth, blk & yel, rear top-hatted driver, tan horse, missing horse's wheel/chipping, A .$985.00

Hay Cart, yel & orange pnt, 1 donkey harnessed by swing shaft, 10½", G-, A...$80.00

Hook & Ladder Wagon, Dent, chrome body w/red wheels, 3 horses, 2 firemen & 4 ladders, some chipping & rust, 30½", A...$1,300.00

Hansom Cab, Pratt & Letchworth, black and yellow with brown horse, ca 1890s, 13½", EX, D10, $1,850.00.

Hook & Ladder Wagon, Dent, 1 blk/1wht horse, yel wagon, 2 firemen drivers, pnt crazing on wood ladders, 1915, 27", A $2,300.00

Hook & Ladder Wagon, Ives (Phoenix on shaft), 2 blk & 2 wht horses, red & blk wagon, 4 ladders, bucket, men, 28", G, A $1,000.00

Hook & Ladder Wagon #5, Ives, blk & red w/2 drivers, 1 blk/1 wht horse on eccentric wheel, some crazing, 1885, 28", A $1,800.00

Hose Reel Fire Wagon, Ives (Phoenix on shaft), 1 blk/1 wht horse, very little pnt, needs cleaned, 7x4x18", A $425.00

Ice Wagon, Dent, red & yel w/brn horse, w/driver & accessories, pnt worn, 15", A...$745.00

Lady's Phaeton, blk horse, red & yel 4-wheel open phaeton w/lady in bl dress, some wear, o/w EX, 17", A $3,400.00

Lady's Phaeton, carriage w/tufted seat bk & lady driver w/articulated arms, red w/yel wheels, 1 blk horse, 18", G, A.$550.00

Log Cart, Kenton, 2 blk & wht oxen pull 4-wheel log cart, Blk driver sits sideways on log, 15½", A.......................$1,000.00

McCormick-Deering Thresher, Arcade, gray over red, pitting, missing parts, 10", P, A..$70.00

Milk Wagon, '20s era, wht w/red hitch, blk horse, 5¾x12½", VG, A $225.00

Patrol Wagon, bl w/red wheels, notched seats for 4 passengers, 3 blk & wht horses, rpl figures, pnt loss, 20½", G, A..$130.00

Patrol Wagon, Shimer, NP, rpr horse leg, pnt traces, some rpt, 21", A...$1,750.00

Sand & Gravel Wagon, gr w/red wheels & hitch, 1 blk/1 wht horse, w/driver, lever-op, 4½x14½", VG-EX, from $150 to $300.00

Sleigh, Dent, gray horse pulls curved gr sleigh, NP driver, yel runner, 1905, 16", A $1,150.00

Stake Wagon, red & gr, 1 blk horse, missing driver, rpt, pnt chips, 11", G, A $45.00

Sulky Racer, red w/blk horse, rpr, pnt loss, 7", G-, A........$35.00

Sulky w/Driver, Pratt & Letchworth, blk w/red wheels, separate driver, lt chips, rpr driver, 7⅞", VG-EX, A..............$300.00

Surrey w/Driver, Hubley, 2 horses, gr & red 4-wheel surrey, lady in rear seat, 1900, 12½", A $750.00

Surrey Wagon, ca '40s, fringe on top, 2 horses, driver/lady passenger, orig fringe, 4½x3x12", EX, A $70.00

Surrey, Pratt & Letchworth, 1880s, 15" long, EX, D10, $2,450.00.

Threshing Machine, Arcade, gray & red w/cream wheels, plated parts, orig box (torn), 6¾", VG, A..........................$900.00

Transfer Wagon, att Buffalo Toys, 2 horses (1 missing leg), all blk, incorrect driver, all rpt, needs rstr, 5x17", A $90.00

Wagon, gr, 1 wht horse, rpt, rust, 13", G-, A $30.00

Wagon, Pratt & Letchworth, blk w/yel wheels, wood barrel in rear bed, 1 horse, w/driver, lt pnt wear, 16", A........$800.00

Wagon, 2 blk horses w/gold trim pull open gr wagon w/red hitches, w/driver, 6¾x15", VG, A...........................$110.00

Water Tower Truck, Wilkins, gr & blk wagon w/gold striping, red wheels, 3 horses, articulated driver, 44", from $6,500 to..$7,000.00

Motor Vehicles

#13 Trolley, Dent, yel, chipped pnt, 5", G-, A.................$60.00

#2 Racer, Vindex, red w/gold exhaust pipes, rubber tires, w/Vindex label, pnt chips, 11", VG, A...........................$1,800.00

#5 Racer, red, bl & wht, disk wheels, dual-opening hood, NP grille, pnt chips, rpr chassis, 9¼", G, A....................$900.00

Ahrens Fox-Fire Engine, Hubley, red & silver, rubber tires, NP features, rpt, rpl wheels & ladders, 11½", G, A $925.00

Automobile, AC Williams, roaring '20s style, lt bl-gr (strong/some chips), spare tire rpl, no people, 3½x2½x9", A $475.00

Automobile, Kenton, '05, 2-seater, tiller operated, rear engine, gr w/beige, silver wheels & yel driver, worn, 6", A..$230.00

Automobile, Kenton, '06, fenderless runabout, tiller steering, no driver, wrong wheels, 3¼x3½x6", VG, A $80.00

Automotive Pumper, Hubley, red w/gold trim, rubber tires, missing driver, 11", VG, A...$170.00

Bell Telephone Cable Layer Truck, Hubley, C Mack front end, hook on rear, orig tires, winch, tools, 5x9", VG, A.$450.00

Bell Telephone Truck, Arcade, gr, 9", +bl pole trailer, 8", winch digger, +2 ea (rpl ?) ladders/shovels, EX, A $700.00

Bell Telephone Truck, Hubley, C Mack cab, molded-in driver, no tools, rpl tires/hubs, crack in body, EX pnt, 4x8", A ..$150.00

Bell Telephone Truck, Hubley, C Mack cab, molded-in driver, no tools, 3½x2¼x6¾", overall VG, A $200.00

Bell Telephone Truck, Hubley, C Mack cab, telephone gr, molded-in driver, some wear, 3x2x5", EX, A..........$200.00

Bell Telephone Truck, Hubley, C Mack cab, telephone gr, slight wear, 2x1¾x3¾", EX, A $125.00

Bell Telephone Truck and Trailer, Hubley, ca 1930, 19" long, NM, D10, $1,650.00.

Boat-Tail Racer, orange, pnt chips, surface rust, 5½", G, A $45.00

Borden's Milk Truck, Hubley, totally rpt, 3⅜x2⅛x5¾", A $450.00

Bulldog Mack Dump Truck, Arcade, w/driver, working dump gate, lift mechanism incomplete, rpl wheels, rpt, 11½", G-, A...$300.00

Bulldog Mack Hook & Ladder, Arcade, red & gold, rubber tires, rpl driver, ladders & ladder holders, 21", G+, A......$190.00

Bus, Arcade, orange w/gold belt rail sides & bk, NP driver, rubber tires, 2 side mts, EX pnt/lt rpt, 3½x13", A......$1,750.00

Bus, bl w/NP wheels, pnt chips, 6", G, A $50.00

Bus, Dbl-decker; Arcade, snub-nose '37, gr w/blk tires, 3 CI riders atop, molded-in driver, label, 3½x2½x8", EX, A......$500.00

Bus, Dbl-decker; Arcade, 1927 5th Ave style, rear stair platform, driver+6 lead passengers, orig label, 2½x8", EX, A .$700.00

Bus, Dbl-decker; Kilgore, turq bl w/orange stripe, 7 seats in open top area, rear stairs, pnt worn/rust, 6", A $625.00

Bus, Sight-Seeing; Kenton, emb Seeing New York 1899, open-air type, w/driver/4 passengers (3 rpl), yel-orange, 10", G, A......$2,700.00

Bus Line School Bus, Dent, orange w/blk trim & letters, blk hubs & NP wheels, 8½", EX, A...$250.00

Car Carrier, A.C. Williams, red cab, green trailer, 12½", EX, D10, $850.00.

Car Carrier, Arcade, '28, gr tractor (heavy pnt loss), red flat bed, +4 CI 5" cars: 2 ea Models T & A, 24½", EX, A $650.00

Car Carrier, Arcade, gr tractor, orange pressed steel trailer, +4 3" cars, some rpl rubber wheels, 3x2x11", EX, A..........$150.00

Car Carrier, Arcade, gr tractor/red (rpt?) pressed steel flat bed, +2 sm Austin cars/1 stake-body truck, 3x14", EX, A $350.00

Car Carrier, Arcade, gr tractor/steel 2-level trailer, +sm truck/wrecker/2 cars, 4½x3x15¼", NM, A $675.00

Car Carrier, Arcade, red 2-level trailer/tractor, rubber tires, +sedan/coupe/wrecker/truck (some rpl tires), 10", EX, A..$250.00

Car Carrier, Nucar Transport, '30s, w/driver, rpl rubber tires, +2 sm race cars, coupe, convertible, 4x3x16", EX, A ..$1,000.00

Champion Dump Truck, red w/bl dump bed, rpl tires, 4¾", G-, A..$35.00

Champion Motorcycle Cop, bl, integral rider in red coat, rubber tires, rpt, 7", G, A...$120.00

Champion Motorcycle Cop, bl, rubber tires, 5", G, A......$70.00

Chevrolet Utility Stake Truck, Arcade, blk w/gray stake-rack body, w/driver, 4x3x8¾", EX, minimum value.....$2,000.00

Chevy Coupe, Arcade, blk & gray, solid wheels, mk w/stamp on grille, ink stamp on tire, 8", EX, A......................$2,400.00

Chevy Coupe, Arcade, blk & gray, w/spare tire, considerable pnt loss to roof, axle w/crack, 4x8", G, A.......................$475.00

Chevy Coupe, Arcade, blk w/rpl driver, 6¾", VG, A.....$900.00

Chevy Sedan, Arcade, '28, blk w/gold belt rail trim, NP wheels w/blk hubs, silver radiator, 4x3x8½", EX, A.........$1,000.00

Chevy Superior Coupe, Arcade, no driver, overall wear/chipping, rpl radiator wire mesh grille, 3½x2¾x6¾", A $900.00

Chevy Superior Sedan, Arcade, 4-door, blk, incorrect driver, 3¾x6¾x2¾", EX, A $1,100.00

Chevy Superior Touring Sedan, blk w/NP driver, rpt, rpl wire mesh grille, 3¾x2½x6¾", A...$1,000.00

Chrysler Convertible & Clipper Trailer, Sehloff, silver & blk car w/silver trailer, signed, orig boxes, 24", M, A $550.00

City Ambulance, Arcade (has sticker in bk), all bl, EX pnt w/chipping around roof & sides, 2½x5¾", EX, A $375.00

Coast to Coast Bus, Arcade, red & wht, plated slant front & bk, wht rubber wheels, 9", VG, A $450.00

Coupe, Arcade, blk w/orange & wht wheels, NP driver, most of the blk bottom & cab is rpt, 4¼x3½x8½", A $900.00

Coupe, Arcade, 2-door, low roof, blk, no driver, 3½x6¾", EX, A $250.00

Coupe, Arcade, 2-door, 6-window, no driver, possible touch-up to pnt, 3¾x6½", G, A...$275.00

Coupe, Hubley, gr w/gold headlights, molded-in driver in gr shirt & gold cap, 3¼x6½", EX, A $675.00

Coupe, Hubley, 2-door, blk w/silver grille, headlights & wheels, 3½x2¾x7", EX, A...$200.00

Coupe, Kilgore, 2-door, all red w/NP wheels, 3½x2¼x6¼", EX, A...$225.00

Delivery Truck, Freidag (mk inside), all wht w/molded-in driver, panel style, some chipping, 3½x7½", EX, A $850.00

Dump Truck, Arcade, crank & hoist dump mechanism, plated wheels, driver missing, rpt, 10¾", G-VG, A $200.00

Dump Truck, Arcade, red, rpl driver & lift mechanism parts, pnt loss, 10½", G, A...$160.00

Dump Truck, Freidag, molded-in driver, red cab, orange dump, rpr break, pnt chipped on roof & body, 3⅝x8", VG, A $700.00

Dump Truck, red & gr, rubber tires, rpr front, 6½", G, A.$45.00

Dump Truck #676, Arcade (orig label), open style, w/driver, some touch-up, 5" to top of driver, 6½", A $300.00

Fageol Safety Coach, Arcade, purple & blk rpt, NP driver, 12", G-,
    A $120.00
Fire Engine Boiler, orig pnt, quite worn, 5", M5 ....$46.00
Fire Patrol Truck, Hubley, bl w/gold trim, yel wheels, w/hose
    reel bracket, missing figures, 14½", G, A..............$1,050.00
Fire Patrol Wagon, Hubley, bl w/yel wheels, molded-in driver+3
    men, 3x6½", EX, A......................................$110.00
Fire Patrol Wagon, Kenton, bl, missing driver & fireman, pnt
    touch-up, 3¼x6½", G, A $35.00
Fire Pumper, Hubley, '38, 2 men, NP boiler/fr, rpl rubber tires,
    chips/scrapes, 3¾x3x8½", EX, A.........................$175.00
Fire Pumper, Kenton, molded-in driver, NP wheels, minor pnt
    touch-up, 4¾x2¼x7½", G, A $95.00
Fire Pumper, Kenton, molded-in driver, red w/rubber tires,
    3½x7", VG-EX, A...$80.00
Fire Pumper, Kenton, red w/gold trim, partial rpt to boiler,
    wheel rpl, 5½x2¼x9¼", G-, A $35.00

**Ford Stake Truck, Arcade, ca 1928-32, 8" long, NM,
D10, $750.00.**

Globe Police Motorcycle, red w/silver handlebars, driver in blk,
    rare, 8½", EX, A $2,100.00
Greyhound Bus, Arcade, bl & wht w/blk rubber tires, 9", G-VG,
    A $220.00
Greyhound Bus, Arcade, bl & wht w/plated slant front & rear,
    wht rubber wheels, pnt chips, 9", VG-EX, A...........$325.00
Greyhound Bus, Arcade, later model, some rpt/touch-up,
    2¾x8¾", A...$200.00
Harley-Davidson Motorcycle, Hubley, allover red, driver
    w/swivel head, 7", NM, A $1,000.00
Harley-Davidson Motorcycle, orange, rubber tires, integral civil-
    ian rider, pnt chips, 6", G, A...........................$225.00
Harley-Davidson Motorcycle & Sidecar, Hubley, red cycle &
    driver, gr sidecar, w/passenger, rpl tires, 5½", EX+, A.$700.00
Harley-Davidson Motorcycle Cop, bl uniform, bl cycle, rpt,
    4x6", A..$95.00
Harley-Davidson Motorcycle Cop, Hubley, olive gr w/gold-trim
    rider w/swivel head, NP wheels, 7", EX, A $750.00
Harley-Davidson Motorcycle Cop, Hubley, red, integral rider
    w/swivel head, rubber tires, 7", VG, A....................$140.00
Harley-Davidson Motorcycle Cop, orange w/NP wheels, pnt
    chips, 5½", G, A $70.00

**Fire Pumper, Kenton, red with gold trim, white rubber tires,
ca 1927, 10" long, EX, D10, $1,100.00.**

Fire Pumper, red, blk & silver, NP boiler, solid wheels, rubber
    tires, rpt, 4½", G, A $65.00
Fire Pumper, red, rubber tires, sm pnt chips, 4½", VG-EX,
    A $30.00
Fire Pumper, red & blk, NP pumper & grille, spoked wheels,
    rubber tires, 6¼", G, A $120.00
Fire Truck, Arcade, late '30s style, molded-in driver & fireman,
    NP grille/bumper, rubber balloon tires, 9½", EX, A .$275.00
Fire Truck, Hubley, red, 2 molded-in drivers, turning front
    wheel section, emb gold eagle, wood ladders, 1920s, 16",
    A $460.00
Fire Truck, Kenton, no pnt, no driver, 2¼x5¾", o/w VG-EX,
    A $35.00
Ford Coupe, silver, rpr wheel, pnt chips, 6½", G-, A........$75.00
Ford Rumble-seat Roadster, Arcade, red w/NP grille, rubber
    tires, 1934, 2½x2¼x6½", EX, A $600.00
Ford Sedan, Arcade, 4-door, red w/NP wheels, pnt chips, 5", VG,
    A $375.00
Ford Stake Body Truck, Arcade, NP driver, 4x8½", EX pnt,
    A $900.00

**Harley-Davidson Parcel Post Motorcycle, Hubley, 9½", EX,
D10, $2,650.00.**

Harley-Davidson Motorcycle w/Sidecar, Hubley, olive gr w/silver handlebars, 2 figures, rubber tires, 9", G-, A $475.00

Harley-Davidson Motorcycle w/Sidecar, w/passenger, rpl tires, 5½", EX+, A $700.00

Harley-Davidson Racer, bl & gold, integral rider, blk engine & tank, rubber tires, rpr, 6½", G-, A $375.00

Hook & Ladder Truck, Hubley, red & gold, rpt wheels, rpl ladders, 15", G, A $425.00

Hook & Ladder Truck, red w/gold trim, silver & yel wheels, driver missing, rpl ladder & brackets, 13", VG, A ...$170.00

Hose Reel Ladder Truck, Hubley, 2 molded-in drivers, NP grille, rubber tires, missing some ladders, 2x6½", VG-EX, A $55.00

Ice Truck, Arcade, bl w/gold letters & nickel grille, rubber tires, 6¾", VG-EX, A $450.00

Ice Truck, Arcade, stub nose, bl w/NP grille, rubber tires, integral driver, some wear/pnt chipping, 3¼x6¾", EX, A $200.00

Indian Crash Car Motorcycle Delivery, Hubley, 3-wheel, w/driver & wagon in bk, rubber tires, 3½x6½", G-, A $450.00

Indian Motorcycle, red w/silver handlebars & light, driver in blk, w/clicker, 9¼", EX+, A $1,450.00

Indian Motorcycle Cop, Hubley, red cycle w/NP engine, separate officer in bl, w/clicker, rpl guide tires, 9½", EX-, A..$1,350.00

Indian Say It w/Flowers Delivery Van, Hubley, w/clicker, rpl rear door, lt pnt wear, 10½", EX, A $16,000.00

Indian Traffic Car, Hubley, red w/gr trailer, swivel-head driver, unplayed with, 9", A $1,600.00

Indian US Air Mail Delivery Cycle, Hubley, red w/blk & wht logo, w/clicker, 8½", EX, A $2,500.00

International Dump Truck, Arcade, '40s, red w/silver body, rubber tires, some touch-up, VG-, A $350.00

International Dump Truck, Arcade, '40s style, red cab & chassis, silver spring-loaded dump, dual wheels, 11", EX, A..$550.00

International Dump Truck, Arcade, red, w/dumping mechanism, allover chipping, rpl crank, radiator cap gone, 4⅜x10", A $400.00

International Dump Truck, Arcade, all red, 10¾", EX+, $650.00.

Ladder Truck, Arcade, red w/yel ladders (2 rpl), NP driver, rubber tires, 4¼x4x18", EX, A $500.00

Ladder Truck, Champion, all red, 2 firemen, NP wheels, 3¼x7½", G, A $100.00

Ladder Truck, driver & fireman standing on rear, 3 ladders, 6x16½", EX, A $600.00

Ladder Truck, Hubley, '20s-30s, cast-in spotlight, NP ladder/racks, spoke wheels/rubber tires, 5½x13", EX, A $900.00

Ladder Truck, Hubley, missing driver/2 stanchions/ladders, heavy wear, 5x3¼x13¼", A $75.00

Ladder Truck, Hubley, red, w/driver, rpl rubber tires, some wear, 3x8", G, A $35.00

Ladder Truck, Hubley, transitional (motorized front on horse-drawn rear), mc w/some gold, minor losses, 23", EX, A..........$800.00

Ladder Truck, Kenton, all red, w/driver, rpl wood ladders/racks, crack in front spring hanger, 5½x11¾", G, A..........$150.00

Ladder Truck, Kenton, driver old but rpl (?), poor ladder rpr, broken fender, 5x3¾x17½", G-, A $200.00

Ladder Truck, Kenton, w/driver & NP boiler, pc broken off front fender, pnt faded but good, no hoses, 7½x14", G, A .$300.00

Limousine, Kenton, red w/yel wheels, open chauffeur's compartment, closed rear quarters, early, 7¾", VG, A $575.00

Lincoln Zepher, Hubley, '39, all gr w/NP grille & bumper, rpl rubber tires/hubs, possible rpt, 2¼x2½x7", EX, A ...$300.00

Long Distance Bus, red w/NP wheels pnt chips, 4¾", G-, A **$55.00**

Mack Dump Truck, Arcade, NP driver & rubber tires, blk, red & gold rpt, 12", G-VG, A................................$300.00

Mack Dump Truck, gr, part of mechanism missing, driver rpl, entirely rpt, 5x4¼x12", A...............................$165.00

Mack Dump Truck, Hubley, gr cab w/red bed, NP wheels, spring-loaded lever release, Hubley label, 8¼", EX-VG, A $350.00

Mack Dump Truck, Hubley, gr cab/chassis (rpt), red dump box (rpt), 6 rubber tires (rpl), 5x5½x11", EX, A $400.00

Mack Dump Truck, pnt CI & sheet metal, hinged tailgate, dual rear wheels, dump mechanism missing, rpt, 12", G-VG, A $225.00

Mack Gasoline Truck, Arcade, all CI including tank, orig wheels, needs rstr, broken rear spring hanger, 5x13", P, A $525.00

Mack 6 Bus, Arcade, rubber tires, dual rear wheels, side-mtd spare, rpt, 12¾", VG, A $2,700.00

Model A Stake Body Truck, Arcade, red w/decal logo, VG+ pnt, 3¼x2½x7¼", A...$450.00

Model T Coupe, Arcade, high hip roof, no driver, possible rpt, minor scratches/chips, 3¾x6½", A..........................$200.00

Model T Coupe, 2-door; Arcade, '22, blk, allover chipping, heavy pnt loss to roof, 3¾x3x6½", G, A $150.00

Model T Coupe, 2-door; Arcade, '24, bl, some chips, especially heavy on roof, 3¾x3x6½", VG, A $250.00

Model T Coupe, 2-door; Arcade, red w/NP wheels, no driver, 3½x3x7", EX, A.......................................$425.00

Model T Coupe, 2-door; unknown mfg, '26, gr, 3½x3x6¾", EX, A $600.00

Model T Coupe, 4-door; Arcade, red w/NP wheels, much chipping, 3¾x3x6½", G, A $275.00

Model T Sedan, center door; Arcade, blk w/gold trim, NP wheels, missing driver, rpt, 6½", G, A $425.00

Model T Sedan, center door; Arcade, 2-tone blk & brn, 3¾x3x6¼", EX, A..$200.00

Model T Sedan, 2-door; Arcade, '25, gr w/gold belt rail, NP wheels, some chipping to fenders/roof, 3¾x6½", EX, A...........$350.00

Model T Sedan, 4-door; Arcade, blk w/silver belt rail, NP wheels, typical chipping, 3¾x3x6½", VG...............$200.00

Model T Wrecker, Arcade, with driver, red and green, 10", EX, D10, $1,350.00.

Motorcycle, Speed; lt bl w/NP wheels, pnt chips, 3⅝", G+,A $110.00

Motorcycle, Streamline; orange, rubber tires, 4⅛", G-, A $290.00

Motorcycle, Vindex Excelsior-Henderson, 4-cylinder, w/driver & clicker, rare, 8½", EX, A.....................$2,000.00

Motorcycle Cop, Champion, dk bl w/wht rubber tires, 5", EX+, A $225.00

Motorcycle Cop, Hubley, bl & wht w/integral rider, 6¼", VG-EX, A $75.00

Motorcycle Cop, red, rubber tires, lt pnt loss, 4", VG, A .$45.00

Motorcycle Cop, red w/gold trim, rubber tires, headlight mechanism (missing), pnt chips, 6", VG, A.....................$110.00

Motorcycle Cop, red w/NP wheels, 4", VG, A................$70.00

Motorcycle Cop, yel, rubber tires, headlight mechanism (missing), pnt loss, pitting, 6¼", G-, A $70.00

Motorcycle Cop w/Sidecar, Champion, red cycle, blk sidecar w/passenger, scarce, 6¼", EX+, A $800.00

Motorcycle Cop w/Sidecar, Hubley, red w/gold engine, separate officer figure, w/clicker & orig label, 8¼", VG, A .$1,150.00

Motorcycle Cop w/Sidecar, red w/NP wheels, pnt chips, 4", G+, A $75.00

Motorcycle Traffic Car, Hubley, allover red, spoked wheels, w/driver, average pnt wear, 4¾", G, A...................$250.00

Nash Sedan, Kenton, bl w/blk fenders & running boards, 6 windows, spare tire, lt pnt chipping, 3½x8", EX, A ...$5,200.00

National Transit Co Trolley, Dent, yel w/2 NP drivers, rpl wood tip on boom, 11½", G, A..$350.00

Packard Sedan, Hubley, doors/engine hood open, bl (rare)/blk, w/driver, steering wheel & motor, license #608, 11", EX, A..$25,000.00

Patrol Wagon, bl w/gold trim, silver wheels, 4 integral figures, pnt chips, 6½", G+, A $185.00

Patrol Wagon, Kenton, dk bl w/gold trim, disk wheels, pnt chips, figures missing, 8¾", G, A $275.00

Patrol Wagon, Kenton, gr w/yel spoked wheels, driver & 3 integral figures, lt pnt chips, 6½", VG, A.....................$130.00

Pickup Truck, Arcade, red w/gold wheels, 75% orig pnt, early, 8½", EX+, M5 ....$250.00

Pickup Truck, att Freidag, gr w/spoked hubs & wht simulated tires, closed cab, open body w/driver, 3½x7½", G, A $1,100.00

Pickup Truck, 1-Ton; Arcade, NP driver, minor possible touch-up, 4x8¼", EX, A $800.00

Pontiac Sedan, Arcade, bl w/NP grille, rubber tires, some chipping, strong pnt, 2x2x6½", EX, A.....................$1,200.00

Pontiac Ladder Truck, Arcade, yellow ladders, black rubber tires, very rare, 9½", NM, D10, $575.00.

#5 Red Devil Racer, Hubley, 9½" long, EX, D10, $2,500.00.

Rumble Seat Coupe, Arcade, gr w/NP wheels, rpl rumble seat, rpr, 6¾", G, A $525.00

Rumble Seat Roadster, Kilgore, dk maroon, NP wheels, molded-in spare tire, driver missing, 2¾" Wx8", EX, A........$250.00

Runabout, Wilkins, blk w/red & gold trim, silver wheels, 3¾", VG, A $190.00

Runabout, yel w/red wheels, missing driver, pitted & rpt wheels, 7½", G-, A $35.00

Runabout Roadster, Kenton, w/driver, mustard gold w/maroon details, 2-seater, pnt crazed, early, 6½", A $175.00

Sedan, blk w/gr, pnt chips, missing part, 7½", G-, A......$250.00

Sedan, Kenton, dk maroon w/blk fenders & running board, NP wheels, molded-in spare tire, 3¼x2¼x6¼", EX, A ..$500.00

Sedan, red w/gold trim & blk top, disk wheels, 7½", EX, A..$625.00

Sedan, 4-door; AC Williams, yel cab/hood, o/w blk, take-apart series, rpt, poor tires, 2¾x2¼x7", A $70.00

Special Delivery Cycle, Kilgore, 3-wheeler, allover red, w/driver, 4½", EX+, A $525.00

Stake Body Truck, Arcade, all gr w/NP grille, pnt strong w/worn spots, orig but poor tires, 2½x2½x6½", A $575.00

Stake Truck, 10-ton; Hubley, '30s, orange cab & chassis, NP grille & body, orig rubber tires, 2⅝x2¾x8¼", EX, A...........$350.00

Streamline Racer, Hubley, silver w/red grille, rubber tires, pnt chips, 7¼", G, A $200.00

Toonerville Trolley, Dent, gr w/red & orange trim, plated wheels, orig box, 4½", EX...$700.00

Touring Car, Arcade, red w/NP wheels, no driver, wear/chipping, some touch-up, 4x2⅜x6¼", EX, A.................$250.00

Touring Car, Dent, metal wheels, 2 passengers, no driver, pnt poor w/touch-up, structurally sound, 3½x2½x9½", A $300.00

Touring Car, open; Kenton, all bl, driver & 2 passengers, rpt, possible rpl, wear/chipping, 3½x2¼x9", EX, A........$400.00

Touring Car, Sedan, gr w/wht trim on door, yel hubs for wheels, rpt spare tire, molded-in driver, 3x6", EX-VG, A....$600.00

Touring Car, Williams, red w/gold trim, spoked wheels, 3 silver figures, 9½", EX, A $850.00

Tractor-trailer Cattle Car, Kenton, all gr w/wear & typical chips/scratches, missing 4 wheels/hubs, 2x2x9", A..$175.00

Trailways Bus, '39, red & cream w/NP grille & rear panel, rubber tires loose (1 flat), pnt scratches, 9", A....................$750.00

Trolley Car, Harris, bl & red w/gold letters, 2 integral figures, lt pnt chips, 7½", G-VG, A.............................$200.00

US Airmail Motorcycle, Hubley, red w/US Airmail sidecar, rider w/orange hat, incomplete, arm broken, 9½", G-, A...**$1,850.00**

White Delivery Van, Arcade, Lammerts on side, white rubber tires, ca 1928, 14", EX, D10, $18,000.00.

World's Fair Greyhound Bus, Arcade, bl & wht, rubber tires, varnished, 10¼", G-, A...............................$80.00

World's Fair People Mover, bl & orange tractor w/driver, 3 cars w/litho tin canopies, 16", EX, A..............................$400.00

World's Fair Sightseeing Bus, Arcade, bl, wht & orange, plated trim, blk rubber wheels, 10½", EX...................$500.00

Wrecker, bl & purple, rubber tires w/wood hubs, rpl front tires, parts missing, 7¼", G-, A...............................$45.00

Yellow Cab, allover varnish, blk pnt VG, heavy flaking to yel, 3⅝x8", A..$775.00

Yellow Cab, Arcade, solid disk wheels, pnt driver, rear spare, cowl lights, 9", VG, A...................................$1,265.00

Yellow Cab, Arcade, yel w/blk top, hood & fenders, NP driver & steering wheel, rpl radiator screen, 4½x9", from $900 to...$1,200.00

Yellow Cab, Arcade, yel w/blk top windows, fenders & running gear, wheels w/yel hubs, 2½x2x5½", EX-, A............$725.00

Yellow Cab, Arcade, 2-tone orange-yel & blk, solid wheels, driver missing, rpr/rstr, 7¾", P, A.....................$150.00

Yellow Cab, Hubley, '39, w/driver & removable rear luggage rack, rpl rubber tires, EX, 8½", A........................$1,150.00

Yellow Cab, Sky View, Hubley, 8" long, M, D10, $1,450.00.

Yellow Cab Taxi, Freidag, 8", NM, D10, $1,850.00.

Yellow Coach Bus, Arcade, brn & blk, sheet metal seats & rubber tires, rear staircase broken, missing 1 seat, 12¼", G, A $1,300.00

Miscellaneous

Cannon, Young American Rapid Fire, Pat Feb 1907, turn crank, shoots pellet, no pnt, 7x16", VG, A.......................$135.00

Dog Cart, Wilkins, blk cart on 2 red wheels, bl-suited driver, lg yel-wht dog, pnt worn, 9½", A...............................$980.00

Evening News & Baby Quieter, J&E Stevens, man reclines on chaise w/paper, baby on knee, pnt loss/rpl bell, 1890, 8", A...$1,950.00

GE Refrigerator, Hubley, '20s style, condenser on top half, 3⅝x7", G, A..$20.00

I Always Did 'Spise a Mule, Stevens, same action & inscription as the bank, mk #2, on wood base, 9½", EX, A $715.00

Push Toy, Wilkins, horse & jockey in red jacket on axle between lg spoked wheels, 1910, some pnt chipped, 29" overall, A $230.00

Gas Pump, Arcade, 7",
EX, D10, $450.00.

Bobby's Adventures in Structoland, Structo Toys, 1956,
EX, $25.00.

Catalogs

In any area of collecting, old catalogs are a wonderful source for information. Toys collectors value buyers' catalogs, those from toy fairs, and Christmas 'wish books.' Montgomery Ward issued their first Christmas catalog in 1932, and Sears followed a year later. When they can be found, these 'first editions' in excellent condition are valued at a minimum of $200.00 each. Even later issues may sell for upwards of $75.00, since it's those from the fifties and sixties that contain the toys that are now so collectible.

American Flyer, 1933, missing pages, O1 ....$5.00
American Flyer Lines Caboose #24627, NM, O1 ....$19.00
American Flyer Trains, Erector...; EX-EX+, O1................$35.00
American Toy & Furniture, 1976, Toy Fair, 20-page, M4 ..$10.00
AMF Juvenile Wheel Goods, 1974, Toy Fair, 28-page, M4....$15.00
AMF Roadmasters, 1973, Toy Fair, 20-page, M4..............$15.00
Amsco, 1974, Toy Fair, 20-page, M4 ....$10.00
Animal Fair, Most Wanted; 1972, Toy Fair, 30-page, M4.$20.00
Auburn Rubber, 1957 ....$25.00
Aurora AFX Model Motoring, 1972, Toy Fair, 20-page,
	M4 ....$20.00
Aurora Games, 1972, Toy Fair, 14-page, M4 ....$20.00
Aurora Hobby Kits, 1974, Toy Fair, 30-page, M4.............$20.00
Aurora Toys, 1972, Toy Fair, 6-page, M4 ....$10.00
Avalon Crafts & Activities, 1971, Toy Fair, 14-page, M4.$10.00
Bachmann Electric Trains, 1973, Toy Fair, 32-page, M4 .$25.00
Bachmann Mini-Planes, 1971, Toy Fair, pocket size, M4.$20.00
Barbie Dolls, 1962, VG..$25.00
Bendy Toys, Silver Jubilee; 1973, Toy Fair, 10-page, M4 .$10.00
Breyer Animal Creations, 1976, Toy Fair, 12-page, M4 ...$20.00

Brownie Scout, 1951, VG...$25.00
Buddy L, Fine Products Since 1912; 1973, Toy Fair, 28-page,
	M4...$75.00
Buddy L, GMC Trucks, 1957-58 ....$30.00
Buddy L New Fun World, 1968, Toy Fair, 28-page, M4 ...$75.00
Buddy L Train Sets, 1976, Toy Fair, 4-page, M4..............$50.00
Cadaco Great Games, 1976, Toy Fair, 24-page, M4 ....$10.00
California Stuffed Toys, 1971, Toy Fair, 4-page, M4........$10.00
Carter Tru-Scale, farm toys, ca 1967-69, EX....................$15.00
Cass Toys Sales Company's 75th Anniversary, 1972, Toy Fair,
	30-page, M4 ....$10.00
CG Wood, 1976, Toy Fair, 8-page, M4 ....$5.00
Character Easter Bunnies, 1976, Toy Fair, 2-page folder,
	M4 ....$10.00
Child Guidance, Platt & Munk, Tinkertoy; 1973, Toy Fair, 40-
	page, M4...$40.00
Chilton Toys, 1975, Toy Fair, 14-page, M4 ....$15.00
Coleco Toys, Games & Sporting Goods; 1972, Toy Fair, 52-
	page, M4 ....$20.00
Colorforms, 1973, Toy Fair, 28-page, M4.........................$10.00
Commonwealth Toy & Novelty, 1975, Toy Fair, 16-page,
	M4...$20.00
Connor Toy, 1973, Toy Fair, 34-page, M4........................$20.00
Corgi, 1966 or 1967, Toy Fair, NM, F5 ....$22.50
Corgi, 1969, includes Beatles' Yel Submarine, Chitty Chitty Bang
	Bang & others, 48-page, 6x7", NM, from $15 to..........$25.00
Corgi, 1970..$20.00
Corgi, 1972, from $9 to...$12.00
Corgi, 1973, Toy Fair, pocket size, M4 ....$10.00
Corgi, 1979, NM, F5 ....$8.50
Corgi, 1981...$7.50
Creative Playthings, 1970, Toy Fair, 42-page, M4............$20.00
Creative Playthings, 1971, Toy Fair, 18-page, M4............$10.00
Daisy Country, 1973, Toy Fair, 14-page, M4 ....$10.00
Dakin & Co, A Wild & Wonderful Collection; 1973, Toy Fair,
	16-page, M4 ....$10.00
Davis Grabowski Toy Imports, 1976, Toy Fair, 44-page, M4..$20.00
Dolly Toy, 1972, Toy Fair, 20-page, M4 ....$10.00

Dorfan, Modern Electric Trains; VG-EX, O1 ....$5.00

Eagle for the Fun Times, 1974, Toy Fair, 28-page, M4 .....$10.00

Ed-U-Cards Corp, 1972, Toy Fair, 24-page, M4 ....$10.00

Effanbee Dolls That Touch Your Heart, 1974, Toy Fair, 12-page, M4 ....$20.00

Ertl Land, 1971, Toy Fair, 28-page, M4 ....$100.00

Fable Toys, 1971, Toy Fair, 14-page, M4 ....$10.00

Fisher-Price Rainy Day Toy Promotion, 1974, Toy Fair, 6-page, M4 ....$40.00

Fisher-Price Toy Center, 1973, Toy Fair, 34-page, M4.....$90.00

Fisher-Price Toys, 1966, Toy Fair, pocket sz, M4.............$15.00

Fisher-Price Toys, 1975, Toy Fair, 16-page, MIP (sealed), M4..$170.00

Fisher-Price Toys, 1975, Toy Fair, 16-page, M4 ....$90.00

Fisher-Price Toys Make Learning Fun, 1968, Toy Fair, 24-page, M4 ....$100.00

Furga Dolls, 1970, Toy Fair, 38-page, M4 ....$50.00

Gabriel, The Lone Ranger; 1975, Toy Fair, 6-page, M4 ...$10.00

Gabriel Erector, Science & Crafts; 1975, Toy Fair, 20-page, M4 ....$20.00

Gabriel Learning Toys & Games, 1976, Toy Fair, 24-page, M4 ....$20.00

Gabriel Wannabees, 1976, Toy Fair, 3-page, M4..............$10.00

General Merchandise Co, Christmas 1962, EX $35.00

Gilbert, Keys to Tomorrow; 1970, Toy Fair, 18-page, M4 .$20.00

Golden Press, Fall 1967, Toy Fair, 36-page, M4...............$50.00

Golden Press, Spring 1976, Toy Fair, 12-page, M4 ....$5.00

Golden Press, 1973, Toy Fair, 64-page, M4......................$50.00

Golden Press, 1976, Toy Fair, 46-page, M4......................$50.00

Golden Press Bicentennial Books, 1975, Toy Fair, 64-page, M4 ....$50.00

Guillows Airplane Models, 1965 ....$25.00

Hall's Lifetime Toys, 1971, Toy Fair, 12-page, M4 ....$10.00

Halsam Products Co, 1968, Toy Fair, 20-page, M4...........$15.00

Hampshire, The Hottest Sun 'N Fun Line; 1973, Toy Fair, 28-page, M4..$10.00

Hasbro, 1975, Toy Fair, 96-page, M4 ....$150.00

Hasbro Action Toys (GI Joe), 1972, Toy Fair, 32-page, M4..$200.00

Hasbro Games, Toys & Crafts; 1973, Toy Fair, 76-page, M4...$50.00

Hasbro Romper Room, 1972, Toy Fair, 20-page, M4........$50.00

Hedstrom Play Products, 1972, Toy Fair, 22-page, M4.....$10.00

Hi-Ho Products, 1973, Toy Fair, 12-page, M4 ....$10.00

Howdy Doody Merchandise, Kagran, 20-page pamphlet, 1955, NM, A $60.00

Hubley, 1970, Toy Fair, 30-page, M4 ....$25.00

Ideal, 1972, Toy Fair, 84-page, M4..................................$75.00

Ideal (Evel Knievel), 1974, Toy Fair, 70-page, M4 ....$75.00

Ideal Doll, 1957...$20.00

Ideal Model Airplanes, 1928 ....$100.00

Janex Corporation, 1975, Toy Fair, 8-page, M4...............$10.00

Jaymar Pianos, 1957..$20.00

Juro's Cast of Celebrity Dolls, 1976, Toy Fair, 2-page, M4..$10.00

Karmar's 21st Edition, Fall 1972, Toy Fair, 30-page, M4..$10.00

Kenner, Getting Greater Every Year; 1974, Toy Fair, 98-page, M4..$75.00

Kenner, Six Million-Dollar Man; 1976, Toy Fair, 98-page, M4..$100.00

Knickerbocker, 1972, Toy Fair, 24-page, M4 ....$65.00

Kohner, 1972, Toy Fair, 31-page, M4................................$10.00

Kusan Toys, 1968, Toy Fair, 14-page, M4 ....$25.00

Lewis Galoob Co Toys, 1972, Toy Fair, 24-page, M4 ....$30.00

Lincoln Logs by Playskool, 1976, Toy Fair, 2-page, M4....$10.00

Lionel Trains, 1954, G..$30.00

Lionel Trains, 1968, Toy Fair, M4....................................$20.00

Lionel Trains, 1972, Toy Fair, M4....................................$20.00

Little Golden Books, 1972, Toy Fair, 28-page, M4...........$10.00

Madame Alexander Dolls, 1968, Toy Fair, 16-page, M4 ..$80.00

Madame Alexander Dolls, 1971, Toy Fair, 16-page, M4 ..$70.00

Madame Alexander Dolls, 1979, Toy Fair, 16-page, M4 ..$50.00

Madame Alexander Dolls, 1982, Toy Fair, 16-page, M4 ..$30.00

Marx, Presidents of the US; NM+, F5.............................$8.50

Marx Toys, 1964, Toy Fair, 80-page, EX+, F5 ....$249.50

Marx Toys, 1965, Toy Fair, 72-page, EX+, F5 ....$249.50

Marx Toys, 1966, 70-page, M, scarce, A $245.00

Marx Toys, 1969, Toy Fair, 72-page, EX, F5 ....$219.50

Marx Toys, 1972, Toy Fair, 72-page, M4 ....$100.00

Marx Toys, 1974, Toy Fair, 54-page, M4 ....$100.00

Marx Toys, 1975, Toy Fair, 48-page, M4 ....$100.00

Matchbox Collector's Catalog, 1968, NM, F5 ....$18.50

Matchbox Fighting Furies, 1974, Toy Fair, 30-page, M4..$75.00

Matchbox Miniature Scale Model, 1970, Toy Fair, 26-page, M4 ....$175.00

Matchbox Series 1-75, 1976, Toy Fair, 20-page, M4 ....$75.00

Matchbox Stunt Machine, 1972, Toy Fair, 20-page, M4.$175.00

Mattel, Movin' Mattel; 1976, Toy Fair, 72-page, M4 .....$100.00

Mattel Games, Crafts & Hobbies; 1971, Toy Fair, 12-page, M4..$50.00

Mattel Toys, 1968, Toy Fair, 64-page, M4......................$150.00

Mattel Toys, 1975, Toy Fair, 68-page, M4......................$100.00

Mattel Toys & Hobbies, 1972, Toy Fair, 56-page, M4 .....$75.00

Mayfair Toys, 1964-65 ....$30.00

Mego, Follow the Yellow Brick Road; 1975, Toy Fair, 10-page, M4..$250.00

Mego Super Stars (Super Heroes), 1974, Toy, 34-page, M4..$250.00

Milton Bradley Games Numerical Listing, 1976, Toy Fair, M4 ....$15.00

Milton Bradley Games & Puzzles, 1970, Toy Fair, 50-page, M4 ....$50.00

Mirro Aluminum Toys, 1957..$25.00

Monogram Hobby Kits, 1969, Toy Fair, 32-page, M4.......$10.00

Monogram Models, Collectors Showcase Silver Anniversary; 1974, Toy Fair, M4 ....$30.00

Monogram Models, 1957 ....$20.00

Murray Bicycles & Wheel Goods, 1973, Toy Fair, 20-page, M4 ....$10.00

NFL Merchandise, 1974, Toy Fair, 64-page, M4...............$10.00

Nylint, 1967, Toy Fair, 14-page, M4 ....$35.00

Nylint Turbo Power, 1971, Toy Fair, 18-page, M4 ....$35.00

Ohio Art, World of Toys; 1972, Toy Fair, 16-page, M4 ...$25.00

Ohio Art Toys, 1957..$20.00

Parker Bros, 1972, Toy Fair, 70-page, M4 ....$125.00

Parker Bros Games, 1968, Toy Fair, 54-page, M4...........$150.00

Parker Bros Games, 1971, Toy Fair, 72-page, M4...........$125.00

Parker Bros Games & Toys, 1976, Toy Fair, 40-page, M4 .$80.00

Parris Mfg, 1971, Toy Fair, 4-page, M4 ....$10.00

Pillsbury Playthings, 1972, Toy Fair, 2-page, M4..............$15.00
Play-Doh, 1971, Toy Fair, 34-page, M4 ....$10.00
Playskool, 1968, Toy Fair, 48-page, w/Lincoln Log insert,
    M4...$100.00
Playskool, 1970, Toy Fair, 48-page, M4 ....$90.00
Playskool, 1974, Toy Fair, 54-page, M4 ....$70.00
Playthings, Preview Edition; 1975, Toy Fair, M4..............$20.00
Pressman Toy Factory, 1957......................................$25.00
Pressman Toy Factory, 1976, Toy Fair, 22-page, M4 ....$10.00
Remco, 1975, Toy Fair, 6-page, M4 ....$10.00
Remco, 1976, Toy Fair, 18-page, M4 ....$15.00
Revell Model Kits, 1975, Toy Fair, 40-page, M4 ....$75.00
Rushton Toys, 1957..$30.00
Schmid Bros, 1974, Toy Fair, 32-page, M4 ....$10.00
Schoenhut Humpty Dumpty Circus, 1918, EX, A..........$300.00
Sears, Christmas 1968, NM $90.00
Sears, Fall & Winter 1953 ....$30.00
Sears, Spring & Summer 1939..$35.00
Sears, Spring & Summer 1949..$10.00
Sechow & Righter Games, 1957 ....$20.00
Sechow & Righter Games, 1976, Toy Fair, 48-page, M4 .$10.00
Sidley, 1976, Toy Fair, 6-page, M4..................................$10.00

Official Space Patrol Christmas Catalog, fold-out pamphlet with approximately 15 items to order, 1950s, 9x16", NM, A, $35.00.

Spear Electronics for the Young, 1973, Toy Fair, 4-page,
    M4 ....$10.00
Sportrite Catalog, 1973, Toy Fair, 6-page, M4..................$10.00
Steiff, Catalog E; 1966, soft cover w/spiral bk, 76-page, M4 .$175.00
Steiff, New Items for Easter; 1974, Toy Fair, 6-page, M4 .$20.00
Steiff Program '71, 1971, Toy Fair, 48-page, M4 ....$150.00
Steven, 1975, Toy Fair, 36-page, M4 ....$10.00
Strombecker Tootsietoy 100th-Year Anniversary, 1976, Toy
    Fair, 20-page, M4...$100.00
Structo, 1956, Toy Fair, 3½x5½", M4 ....$20.00
Superior Toy & Mfg, 1973, Toy Fair, 4-page, M4.............$10.00
Tomy Corp, 1976, Toy Fair, 20-page, M4 ....$10.00
Tonka Toys, Introducing Tonka; 1968, Toy Fair, 26-page,
    M4 ....$150.00
Tonka Toys, 1960, Toy Fair, 16-page, M4 ....$35.00
Tonka Toys, 1962, Toy Fair, 16-page, 5x3¼", M4...........$35.00
Tonka Toys, 1967, Toy Fair, 14-page, 5½x3½", M4.........$35.00
Tonka Toys, 1971, Toy Fair, 26-page, M4 ....$150.00
Tonka Toys, 1972B, Toy Fair, 3½x5½", M4 ....$25.00

Tonka Toys, 1976, Toy Fair, 30-page, M4 ....$40.00
Topper Toys, 1971, Toy Fair, 98-page, M4 ....$35.00

Toy Fair Catalog, Kewley Brothers, 1954-55, 30 color pages, 8x11", NM, A, $50.00.

Toys, Toy Fair Edition; 1975, M4....................................$20.00
Transogram, 1969, Toy Fair, 48-page, M4 ....$75.00
Tyco Ho-Scale Electric Trains, 1971, Toy Fair, 30-page, M4 .$25.00
Tyco Train Sets, 1975, Toy Fair, 16-page, M4...................$25.00
Uneeda Doll Co, Inc; 1975, Toy Fair, 20-page, M4..........$10.00
View-Master Film & Photo Products, 1973, Toy Fair, 38-page,
    M4...$40.00
View-Master Pictoral Products, 1976, Toy Fair, 40-page,
    M4 ....$40.00
Vogue, Dolls, 1975, Toy Fair, 10-page, M4.......................$25.00
Walt Disney Merchandise Selection, 1974, Toy Fair, 76-page,
    M4...$150.00
WB Conkey, Christmas 1897, VG, I2..............................$35.00
Western Consumers Product Catalog, 1976, Toy Fair, 50-page,
    M4...$35.00
Western Stamping, 1974, 4-page, M4 ....$10.00
Wham-O, 1976, Toy Fair, 14-page, M4 ....$10.00
Whiting by Milton Bradley, 1976, Toy Fair, 14-page, M4.$15.00
Whitney Bros, 1972, Toy Fair, 16-page, M4 ....$20.00
Wolverine, 1957 ....$20.00
Wolverine Toys, 1973, Toy Fair, 30-page, M4...................$20.00
Wonder Sells Happiness, 1971, Toy Fair, 8-page, M4 ......$20.00
Wonder 25th-Anniversary, 1974, Toy Fair, 16-page, M4.$25.00
Wood Products Co, 1971, Toy Fair, 16-page, M4.............$10.00
Worcester Toys, 1971, Toy Fair, 16-page, M4 ....$10.00
Zee Toys, 1976, Toy Fair, 28-page, M4 ....$10.00

Cereal Boxes

This is an area of collecting with crossover interest from fans of advertising as well as character-related toys. What makes a cereal box interesting? Look for Batman, Huckleberry Hound, or a well-known sports figure like Larry Bird or Roger Marris. They don't have to be old to be collectible, but the basic law of supply and demand dictates that the older ones are going to be expensive! After all, who saved cereal boxes from 1910? By chance if Grandma did, the 1910 Corn Flakes box with a printed-on baseball game could get her $750.00. Unless you're not concerned with bugs, it will probably be best to empty the box and very carefully pull apart the glued flaps. Then you can store it flat. Be sure to save any prize that might have been packed inside. Unless noted, our values are for boxes in mint condition, whether full or folded. John Thurmond (T1) is our advisor for this category.

Cap'n Crunch, Halloween Cereal, 1990, from $5 to $15.00
Cheerios, Muppet stickers, 1983 ....$20.00
Cheerios, San Diego Chicken on front, 1982 ....$65.00
Cheerios, Star Wars poster, 1978 ....$55.00

Cheerios, Lone Ranger on front, Frontier Town building punch-out model on back, General Mills, 1948, EX, A, $375.00.

Cocoa Puffs, Battlestar Galactica offer, 1978, from $25 to..$35.00
Corn Flakes, Dennis the Menace cereal bowl offer, 1962 ...$55.00
Corn Flakes, Hanna-Barbera cartoon character spoon offer, 1962 ....$35.00
Corn Flakes, Hopalong Cassidy game, 1940s, from $100 to $200.00
Corn Flakes, Huckleberry Hound on front, 1961.............$50.00
Corn Flakes, Miss America on front, 1973, from $25 to...$30.00
Corn Flakes, rooster & free masks offer on front, mask of Pixie the Mouse on bk, 16-oz, EX, M5 ....$25.00
Corn Flakes, Yogi Bear on front, 1962, from $45 to $65.00
Corn Flakes, 75th-Anniversary edition, 1980, from $10 to...$15.00
Corn Flakes, 85th-Anniversary edition, 1990, from $5 to ..$10.00
Corny Snaps, 1975..$65.00
Count Chocula, Bela w/Star of David.............................$25.00
Croonchy Stars, Swedish Chef of Muppets on front.......$10.00
Dinersaurs, Ralston, 1988, from $10 to $15.00
Dunkin' Donuts, 1988, from $10 to...............................$15.00
Frankenberry, 1971 ....$35.00
Freakies, 1987, from $5 to...$10.00
Froot Loops, giant display box, 1991 ....$25.00

Ghostbusters, Porsche offer...$20.00
Ghostbusters, set of 3 hologram boxes............................$50.00
GI Joe, w/sailor & parrot, 1985, from $25 to....................$35.00
Gremlins, Gizmo offer, 1985, from $35 to........................$45.00
Gummi Bears, 1987, from $10 to....................................$15.00
Honey Nut Cheerios, Star Trek stickers, 1987 ....$25.00
Honeycomb, Superman poster, 1978................................$65.00
Ice Cream Cones, 1987, from $5 to..................................$10.00
King Vitaman, Quaker, 1980s $10.00
Krumbles, 1940s...$25.00
Lucky Charms, Christmas 1990 ....$8.00
Magic Crunch, Mickey Mouse, 1990, from $5 to.............$10.00
Mr T Cereal, 1984, from $15 to.......................................$25.00
Ok's, Yogi Bear on front, 1960, NM-M, scarce, A..........$325.00
Pebbles, mirror offer, 1970s..$65.00

Pep Whole Wheat Flakes, Superman comic strip on back, Kellogg's, 1948, rare, EX+, A, $675.00.

Pro Stars, Wayne Gretsky on front, 1990.........................$22.50
Quake Cereal, special edition, 1990.................................$25.00
Quaker Puffed Rice, Quaker man & cereal exploding from cannon on front, flatware offer on bk, EX, M5................$40.00
Rice Crispies, 60th-Anniversary edition, 1991, NM, from $5 to..$10.00
Rice Krispies, Back to the Future cards, 1990 ....$15.00
Rice Krispies, blk lettering & red images of Snap!, Crackle! & Pop! on front, bracelet offer on bk, 1950s, 5.5-oz, M5 .$15.00
Rice Krispies, Fernando Valenzuela & Nolan Ryan on front, baseball cards, 1982 ....$125.00
Rice Krispies, Roger Rabbit on front, 1987, from $40 to ..$50.00
Rice Krispies, Snap! w/spoon & bowl of cereal on front, Krispie Quicks recipe on bk, top missing, EX+, M5 ....$10.00
Rice Krispies, 75th Anniversary edition, 1981..................$10.00
Rocky Road, 1987, from $18 to $20.00
Shredded Wheat, Jane Fonda workout offer, 1988 ....$10.00
Shredded Wheat, Rin-Tin-Tin rifle pen offer, 1950s $65.00
Smores Crunch, General Mills, 1988, from $10 to $15.00
Star Wars C-3PO's, w/mask, 1984, from $35 to...............$40.00
Sugar Crisp, w/Batman cards, 1990 ....$25.00
Sugar Pops, cowboys on front, 1970s...............................$25.00

Sugar Pops, Woody Woodpecker on front, Canadian distribution, 1968, rare, M, A.................................$250.00
Super Sugar Crisp, Archies on bk, 1969..........................$25.00
Wheaties, Dallas Cowboys Championship, 1992, M........$10.00

Wheaties, Larry Bird on front, General Mills, 1993, M, $25.00.

Wheaties, Michael Jordon on front, full-color photo w/product, 1990, 8x12x3", unused file copy, M, T2.....................$12.00

Character and Promotional Drinking Glasses

Once given away from fast-food chains and gas stations, a few years ago, you could find these at garage sales everywhere for a dime or even less. Then, when it became obvious to collectors that these glass giveaways were being replaced by plastic, as is always the case when we realize no more (of anything) will be forthcoming, that's when we all decide we want it. Since many were character-related and part of a series, we felt the need to begin to organize these garage-sale castaways, building sets and completing series. Out of the thousands available, the better ones are those with super heroes, sports stars, old movie stars, Star Trek, and Disney and Walter Lantz cartoon characters. Pass up those whose colors are worn and faded. Unless another condition or material is indicated in the description, values are for glass tumblers in mint condition. Cups are plastic unless noted otherwise.

There are some terms used in our listings that may be confusing if you're not familiar with this collecting field. 'Brockway' style tumblers are thick and heavy, and they taper at the bottom. 'Federal' is thinner, and top and diameters are equal. Our advisor for this category is Mark E. Chase (C2). See also Clubs and Other Publications.

Alice in Wonderland, Disney Movies, Pepsi, rnd bottom, 6", A...$23.00
Alvin & the Chipmunks, Simon, 1985, EX, N2.................$3.00
Apollo 11 Man on the Moon, 1969, EX, N2......................$9.00
Aquaman, Pepsi, 1973, T1..$10.00
Arby's Thought Factory, 1982, 4¾", set of 4, A..............$15.00
Archie Bunker for President, gr goblet, lg, A...................$7.00
Archies, Archie Taking the Gang for a Ride, 1971, T6......$3.00
Archies, Betty & Veronica Give a Party, 1973, T6............$3.00
Archies, Friends Are for Sharing, 1973, T6.....................$3.00

Archies, Gets a Helping Hand and Having a Jam Session, 4¼", $3.00 each.

Archies, Hot Dog Goes to School, red, yel & bl on clear, 1971, sm, T6...$3.00
Archies, Jughead Wins the Pie Eating Contest, gr & red on clear, 1973...$3.00
Archies, Mr Weatherbee Drops In, 1973.........................$3.00
Archies, Sabrina Calls the Play, 1973............................$3.00
Archies, Sabrina Cleans Her Room, 1971.......................$3.00

Boris and Natasha, Snidely Whiplash, Pepsi, $19.00 each.

Baby Huey, Harvey Cartoons, 12-oz, NM, C1 ....$12.00

Barney Bear, Pepsi, T1 ....$8.00

Batgirl, Pepsi, 1973, T1...$15.00

Batman, unmk, cased plastic w/glitter inside, 1960s, 4½" ...$6.00

Batman or Superman, Super Heroes Series, 1978, Brockway, 16-oz, A...$7.00

Beaky Buzzard, Pepsi, 1973, T1...$6.00

Boris & Natasha, PAT Ward/Pepsi, wht letters, 16-oz, A .$19.00

Bugs Bunny, 50th Anniversary, Warner Bros, Canadian issue, 1990, set of 4, C2 ....$16.00

Bullwinkle, w/fishing Pole, Pizza Hut, CB lingo, 1977, C2 .$65.00

Burger King, Where Kids Are King; pedestal base, 1975-76, 5½", A...$2.00

Burgerilla Falls Head Over Heels in Love, Burger Chef, 1977, C2 ....$45.00

Camp Snoopy, McDonald's, set of 4.....................................$5.00

Cinderella, leaving at midnight, WDP, 1950s, T1............$15.00

Civil War Bicentennial, any of 4, ea, A $3.00

Cleveland Browns, 1986 AFC Central Division Champions, T1 ....$5.00

Cool Cat, Pepsi, 1973, T1...$5.00

Creature of the Black Lagoon, Anchor Hocking, gr & yel wraparound scene, 1963, 7", A...................................$63.00

Daffy Duck, Pepsi, 1973, N2/T1 ....$5.00

Davy Crockett, Crockett in Canoe..., 1950s, lg, T1 ....$12.50

Davy Crockett, Crockett in Canoe..., 1950s, sm, T1 ....$10.00

Davy Crockett, yel on clear, fighting bear or Indian, 1950s, T1 ....$10.00

Dick Tracy, Domino's Pizza, A...$110.00

Domino's Pizza, $1,000,00 in Savings; champagne sz, 1985, A...$10.00

Dudley Do-Right, Pepsi, no action, 12-oz $15.00

Dudley Do-Right, Pepsi, wht or blk letters, no action, 16-oz, A...$10.00

Dudley Do-Right in Canoe, PAT Ward/Pepsi, shows action, 12-oz, A...$13.00

Elmer Fudd, Pepsi, 1973, T1 ....$5.00

Empire Strikes Back, Darth Vader, Coca-Cola/Burger King, 5½", T6 ....$8.00

Endangered Species, Panda, Burger Chef, A $4.00

Felix the Cat, Monkeys of Melbourne, 2 illus on wht frost, 1992, NM-M, C1 ....$31.00

Flash, DC Comics Moon Series, 1976, 6¼", A $12.00

Flintstones, Bedrock Pet Show, Fred on bottom, 1964 ......$6.00

Flintstones, Fred & Barney Go Hunting, Welch's, Dino on bottom $6.00

Flintstones, Fred & His Pal at Work, Welch's, Barney on bottom $6.00

Flintstones, Fred at the Beach, Welch's, Pebbles on bottom.$6.00

Flintstones, Fred Builds a Doll Cave, Welch's, Wilma on bottom $6.00

Flintstones, Fred's Newest Invention, Welch's, Betty on bottom $6.00

Flintstones, Fred's Sports Car, Welch's, Pebbles on bottom.$6.00

Flintstones, Hanna-Barbara/Pepsi, 1977, 6¼", A.............$23.00

Flintstones, Having a Ball, Welch's, Betty on bottom $6.00

Flintstones, Pebbles Babysitter, Welch's, Fred on bottom ..$6.00

Flintstones, Pebbles Lands a Fish, Welch's, Wilma on bottom .$6.00

Flintstones, Pebbles with Dino and Wilma, Welch's, $6.00 each.

Flintstones, 30th Anniversary, Hardee's, 1991, set of 4, C2.$12.00

Foghorn Leghorn, Marc Antony & doghouse; Warner Bros/Pepsi, action series, 1976, 6¼", A $39.00

Foghorn Leghorn, Pepsi, 1973, T1......................................$6.00

Frankenstein, Anchor Hocking, wraparound scene, 1963, 7", NM-M, A $55.00

Gloria, from Little Lulu comic strip.................................$50.00

Go-Go-Gophers, Leonardo TTV/Pepsi, 6¼", A $15.00

Goonies, Data on Waterslide, Godfather's Pizza/Coca-Cola, 1985, 5⅝", A...$5.00

Goonies, Sloth & Goonies, Godfather's Pizza/Coca-Cola, 1985, 5⅝"...$5.00

Granny, Sylvester & Tweety; Warner Bros/Pepsi, action series, 1976, 6¼", A...$46.00

Great Muppet Caper, Miss Piggy, 1981, T6 ....$3.00

Green Lantern, Pepsi Super Heroes 'Moon' Series, 1976, $25.00.

Happy Birthday Mickey, 50 Years, A $13.00

Happy Days, Fonzie, Dr Pepper/Pizza Hut, 1976, C2 ....$12.00

Happy Days, Ralph or Richie, Dr Pepper/Paramount, 1977, 6⅛",
A...$12.00

Henry Hawk, Warner Bros/Pepsi, Brockway, wht letters, 1973,
16-oz, A...$27.00

Holly Hobbie, mk #1 of 4, Christmas 1977, A $5.00

Hopalong Cassidy, blk Hoppy & lasso on milk glass, EX, A..$20.00

Hot Sam, NM, A...$20.00

Hot Stuff, Harvey Cartoons/Pepsi, shows action, 12-oz....$10.00

Howard the Duck, c Marvel Comics Group/7-11, 1977, 5½",
A...$15.00

Howdy Doody, at circus, Welch's, Professor on bottom, 1950s,
from $10 to...$12.00

Howdy Doody, fishing, Welch's, Flub-a-Dub on bottom, 1950s,
from $10 to...$12.00

Howdy Doody, Hip Hip Hooray Welch's Leads the Parade Each
Day, 1963, 4⅛", A...$10.00

Howdy Doody, marching band, Welch's, Flub-a-Dub on bottom,
1950s, from $10 to $12.00

Howdy Doody, on train, Welch's, Howdy on bottom, 1950s,
from $10 to...$12.00

Howdy Doody, weightlifter, Welch's, Clarabelle on bottom,
1950s, from $10 to $12.00

Howdy Doody, weightlifter, Welch's, Dilly Dally on bottom,
1950s, from $10 to $12.00

Howdy Doody, weightlifter, Welch's, Flub-a-Dub on bottom,
1950s, from $10 to $12.00

Huckleberry Hound & Yogi Bear, Hanna-Barbera/Pepsi, 1977,
6¼", A...$18.00

Inch-High Private Eye, orange & yel w/3 illus, 1973, scarce,
C1...$27.00

Indianapolis 500, 1951, A...$16.00

Joker, Pepsi, 1973, T1..$20.00

Josie & the Pussycats, Hanna-Barbera/Pepsi, 1977, 6¼", A.$19.00

Jungle Book, Rama, 1977, 6¼", A.....................................$30.00

King Kong, Coca-Cola, 1976, 5½", set of 4, A.................$12.00

Li'l Abner, w/2 shmoos, 1949 ....$20.00

LK's Pierre the Bear, Fall 1977, A $4.00

Love Is, 1980s, T1..$1.00

McDonald's Nutcracker, test market issue, 1990, set of 4, C2..$20.00

Mickey's Christmas Carol, 1982, 6⅛", set of 3, A.............$15.00

Morris the Cat, 9 Lives Cat Food $15.00

Mr Munch, Pizza Time Theatre, A.....................................$21.00

Mr Peabody, PAT Ward/Pepsi, wht letters, 16-oz, A........$20.00

Mummy, Anchor Hocking, gr, blk & wht wraparound scene in
tomb, 1963, 7", NM-M, A..$55.00

National Flag Foundation, Coca-Cola, 1976, set of 12 glasses
w/pitcher, C2 ....$145.00

National Flag Foundation, First Stars & Stripes, A $3.00

Ohio Indians, Blue Jacket, A...$6.00

Oklahoma Indians, Hen-Toh, Wyandot; frosted, 15-oz, A.$6.00

Olive Oyl, Popeye's Chicken, 1970s, T1...........................$15.00

Pac-Man, Speedy, Army & Air Force Exchange Service, 1980,
A...$5.00

Penguin, Pepsi, DC Comics Moon Series, 1976, 6¼", A..$17.00

Pepe Le Pew, Warner Bros/Pepsi, Federal, wht letters, 1973,
16-oz, A...$5.00

Petunia Pig, Warner Bros/Pepsi, Federal, wht letters, 1973, 16-oz,
A...$5.00

Pittsburgh Steelers Hall of Fame, set of 4, A....................$10.00

Popeye, Popeye's Chicken, 1980s, T1 ....$15.00

Popeye Kollect A Set, Brutus, 1975, 5⅞", A $5.00

Popeye's 10th Anniversary, Olive Oyl, Popeye's Chicken/Pepsi,
1982, 5⅝", A..$10.00

Porky Pig, Pepsi, no action, 1973, 6¼", from $3 to $5.00

Porky Pig & Daffy Duck, w/pot & ladle, Warner Bros/Pepsi,
shows action, 1976, 6¼", A $29.00

Post Cereal, 75th Anniversary, A.......................................$3.00

Psych Out, Sports Collector Series, A...............................$5.00

Ralph, Sheep & Wile E Coyote; Warner Bros/Pepsi, action
series, 1976, 6¼", A..$38.00

Rescuers, Bernard, c 1977 WDP/Pepsi, 6¼", A................$10.00

Rescuers, Evinrude, Pepsi, 1977.......................................$10.00

**Rescuers, Penny or Brutus and Nero, c 1977, WDP/
Pepsi, $10.00 each.**

Rescuers, Rufus, Pepsi, 1977, EX, N2 ....$35.00

Return of the Jedi, Coca-Cola/Burger King, 1983, T6 ....$5.00

Riddler, Pepsi, DC Comics Moon Series, 1976, 6¼", A ...$25.00

Ringling Bros, Felix & 99 Clowns, Federal, 1975, 6¼", A.$12.00

Road Runner, Pepsi, 1973, T1 ....$5.00

Robin, Pepsi, DC Comics Moon Series, 1976, 6¼", from $10
to $12.00

Rocky Squirrel, Pepsi, 1973, 16-oz, T1 ....$15.00

Shazam, Pepsi, DC Comics Moon Series, no action, 1976,
6¼" $10.00

Shazam, Pepsi, Super Heroes Series, Brockway, shows action,
1978, 16-oz, A $7.00

Slow Poke, Warner Bros/Pepsi, Brockway, blk letters, 1973, 16-oz,
A...$38.00

Snidley Whiplash, PAT Ward/Pepsi, 11-oz, A $15.00

Sonic, girl on skates, Pepsi, EX, N2..................................$20.00

Speedy Gonzales, Warner Bros/Pepsi, Federal, blk letters, 1973,
11-oz, from $3 to $5.00

Spock Lives, Star Trek III; Taco Bell/Paramount Pictures, 1984, 5⅝"...$5.00

Star Trek, Kirk, Dr Pepper, 1976, 6⅛", A $15.00

Star Wars Empire Strikes Back, Burger King, 1980, set of 4, NM-M, C1 ....$25.00

Steelers Hall of Fame, McDonald's, 1990, set of 4, C2 .....$16.00

Sunday Funnies, Terry & the Pirates, c 1976, 5⅝", A $12.00

Super Mario 2, 1990, T1 ....$2.00

Superman, Pepsi, DC Comics Moon Series, no action, 1976, 6¼", from $10 to $12.50

Superman, The Movie: Superman to the Rescue; 1978, 5⅝", A...$9.00

Superman, The Movie: The Characters; rnd bottom, 1978, 5⅝", A $7.00

Sylvester Cat & Tweety, sawing limb, Pepsi, Brockway, 1976, 16-oz...$5.00

Tasmanian Devil, Warner Bros/Pepsi, Brockway, blk letters, 16-oz, A...$12.00

Tasmanian Devil Chasing Porky..., Looney Tunes/Welch's, T1...$2.00

Truckline, 1970s, T1 ....$1.00

Tuffy, MGM/Pepsi, Brockway, 16-oz, T1 ....$8.00

Tweety Bird, Warner Bros/Pepsi, Brockway, no action, 1973, 6¼", T1 ....$5.00

Tyrannasaurus Rex, Welch's, 1980s, T1 ....$1.25

USA Moonshot Apollo, tall pedestal base, rocket form, 1969, 6", T1 ....$10.00

Wile E Coyote, Warner Bros/Pepsi, Brockway, 1973, T1 ...$5.00

Wile E Coyote, Warner Bros/Pepsi, Federal, blk letters, A .$7.00

Wile E Coyote Heads for a Big Finish, 1974, T6.................$4.00

Winnie the Pooh, Winnie & friend, Sears, A.....................$4.00

Wizard of Oz, Emerald City, mk S & Co, Brockway, 5", T6..$15.00

Wizard of Oz, 1950s, T1...$15.00

Wolfman, Anchor Hocking, brn, bl & gr wraparound scene in cemetery, 1963, 7", NM-M, A..................................$65.00

Wonder Woman, Pepsi, 1976, 16-oz, from $8 to $10.00

Woody Woodpecker w/butterfly, Pepsi, 1970s, NM-M, C1 .$15.00

Yosemite Sam, Pepsi, 1973, T1 ....$5.00

Ziggy, looking at sun, Pizza Hut, 1980s, T1 ....$2.00

Ziggy, Smile, Pizza Hut, 1989, T1 ....$2.00

1982 Knoxville World's Fair, flared top, A $3.00

Character and Promotional Plastic Cups

Batman, 7-11, 1973, T1 ....$5.00

Batman Returns, McDonald's, complete set, M, E3..........$12.00

Batman the Movie, Taco Bell, complete, set, M, E3 ....$20.00

Black Bolt, 7-11, 1975, M..$6.00

Conan, 7-11, 1977, M...$5.00

Cosmic Boy, 7-11, 1973, T1...$5.00

Dick Grayson, 7-11, 1973, T1...$5.00

Doc Savage, 7-11, 1973, T1..$5.00

Dr Doom, 7-11, 1973, T1..$5.00

Dr Strange, 7-11, 1977, M...$8.00

Dracula, 7-11, 1973, T1 ....$5.00

Dracula, 7-11, 1977, M..$8.00

Family Circus, girl on 2 cartoon panels, 1980s, T1 ....$2.00

Galactus & the Fantastic Four, 7-11, 1977, M...................$8.00

Hercules, 7-11, 1973, T1..$5.00

Inhumans, 7-11, 1977, M...$8.00

Invisible Girl, 7-11, 1973, T1...$5.00

Iron Fist, 7-11, 1977, M $5.00

Kull, 7-11, 1973, T1 ....$5.00

Master of Kung Fu, 7-11, 1977, M $5.00

Medusa, 7-11, 1975, M..$6.00

Mr Fantastic, 7-11, 1973, T1..$5.00

Nova, 7-11, 1977, M..$5.00

Odin, 7-11, 1975, M..$6.00

Penguin, 7-11, 1973, T1...$5.00

Red Sonja, 7-11, 1977, M $5.00

Robin, 7-11, 1973, T1..$5.00

Shazam, 7-11, 1973, T1 ....$5.00

Thing, 7-11, 1973, T1..$5.00

Triton, 7-11, 1975, M..$6.00

Universal Monsters Creature, Getty's, M, E3.....................$8.00

Valkyrie, 7-11, 1973, T1...$5.00

Character and Promotional Mugs

Amazing Spiderman, allover mc illus, 1977, EX, T6...........$4.00

Astro Boy, ceramic, emb Astro & Uran on front, rocket hdl, M, C1 ....$19.00

Batman, milk glass, 1966, from $15 to $20.00

Bear (movie), AMC, T1 ....$10.00

Brutus, pnt ceramic, MIB, D4 ....$5.00

Buck Stops Here, ceramic, T1 ....$3.50

Darkseid, Burger King, T1..$5.00

Davy Crockett, Beacon, plastic, 1950s, EX $15.00

Davy Crockett Famous Frontiersman 1786-1836, blue paint on milk glass, 3", $17.00.

Dennis the Menace, EX, N2 ....$15.00

Dig 'Em, plastic w/feet, Kellogg's, 1981, EX, N2 ....$10.00

Dopey, Disney, red plastic w/hdl, VG+, T6.......................$3.00

Dukes of Hazzard, plastic w/photos, 1981, EX, from $3 to $6.00

Felix the Cat, 1960s, T1 ....$15.00

Flintstones' Bamm-Bamm, Flintstones Vitamins premium, 1972, EX, T6...$4.00

Flintstones' Fred, 1982, M...........................$5.00

Flintstones' Fred, Flintstones Vitamins premium, 1968-69, from $10 to $12.00

Flintstones' Pebbles, 1972, VG, N2 ....$7.00

Garfield, I'd Like Mornings Better..., A............$4.00

Hopalong Cassidy, milk glass, bl Hoppy w/drawn guns, cowboy roping steer, 1950s, NM-M, C1 ....$32.00

Hopalong Cassidy, milk glass, Hoppy w/Topper on front, lunch verse on bk, 1950s, 5", from $45 to $55.00

Hopalong Cassidy, milk glass w/gr image of Hoppy shooting at rustler, name in rope, M, A $35.00

Howdy Doody, Bob Smith & Ovaltine w/Howdy on red plastic, chip at bottom, VG, A $25.00

Howdy Doody, Century Plastic/Kragran, red mug, lid w/Howdy's head, hole for straw, 3½", bright/clean (EX box), A..$200.00

Howdy Doody, Ovaltine, bl, VG, N2 ....$8.00

Jiminy Cricket, milk glass, EX, N2 ....$6.00

John Wayne, Hamilton/Republic Westerns, mc, as Fighting Kentuckian, 1990, M, F1 ....$10.00

Josie & the Pussycats, plastic w/hdl, 1971, EX, N2 ....$12.00

Keebler Elf, 1972, EX, N2 ....$9.00

Li'l Abner, heatproof glass w/Abner, Daisy, Mammy & Pappy, 1968, NM, C1 ....$15.00

Little Orphan Annie, Ovaltine premium, comic strip decals & red dome lid, EX+, M5 ....$22.00

Ludwig Von Drake, Japan, ceramic, NM...........$12.00

Lum & Abner, milk glass, NM $65.00

Mickey Mouse, wht, blk & red w/yel molded feet, lg, VG, T6..$3.00

Mickey Mouse Club, tall w/wide base, see-through bottom, no date, VG+, T6....................................$4.00

Minnie Mouse, milk glass, Pepsi, EX, N2 ....$9.00

Mr Peanut, EX, N2 ....$8.00

Nestle Quik Bunny, ear hdls, 1980s, 4½", EX, T6.............$5.00

Peanuts, Allergic to Mornings, EX, O1 ....$5.00

Peanuts, Christmas 1976, NM, O1 ....$20.00

Peanuts, Snoopy, milk glass, EX, N2 ....$5.00

Peanuts, Snoopy, trainer type, VG, O1 ....$10.00

Peanuts, Snoopy w/slice of cake, EX, O1 ......$12.50

Raggedy Ann & Andy, milk glass, T1 ....$5.00

Rainbow Brite, on parade, 1983, EX, N2.............$4.00

Roy Rogers, F&F Mold & Die, plastic, 1950s, EX, P6 ......$35.00

Scooby Doo, 1982, EX, N2 ....$6.00

Smokey Bear, milk glass........................$10.00

Space, graphics on wht milk glass, 1960s, T1 ....$15.00

Super Scout, w/Batman & Superman, 1979, T1 ....$15.00

Superman, milk glass, 1971, NM-M, C1 ....$25.00

Tony Tiger, Kellogg's, 1964, EX, N2 ....$12.00

Toucan Sam, plastic w/feet, Kellogg's premium, 1981, 6", EX, N2 ....$15.00

Winnie the Pooh & Tigger, figural, Japan, EX, P6 ....$32.00

Wizard of Oz, Tin Man & Cowardly Lion, Krystal Restaurant promotion, plastic, c 1990 Turner Entertainment, 4", M, A $50.00

Woody Woodpecker, molded Woodys all around, plastic, 1965, EX, T6 ....$6.00

Yogi Bear, plastic, 1960s, NM........................$8.00

Ziggy, milk glass, 1979, EX, N2......................$6.00

Character Clocks and Watches

Clocks and watches whose dials depict favorite sports and TV stars have been manufactured with the kids in mind since the 1930s, when Ingersoll made both a clock and a wristwatch featuring Mickey Mouse. The #1 Mickey wristwatch came in the now-famous orange box illustrated with a variety of Disney characters. The watch itself featured a second hand with three revolving Mickey figures. It was available with both a metal and leather band. Babe Ruth stared on an Exacta Time watch in 1949, and the original box contained not only the watch but a baseball with a facsimilie signature.

Collectors prize the boxes about as highly as they do the watches. Many were well illustrated and colorful, but most were promptly thrown away, so they're hard to find today. Be sure you buy only watches in very good condition. Rust, fading, scratches, or other signs of wear sharply devalue a clock or a watch. Hundreds have been produced, and if you're going to collect them, you'll need to study *Comic Character Clocks and Watches* by Howard S. Brenner (Books Americana) for more information. In the section called Watches, 'pocket' indicates pocketwatch values, all others are wristwatches. Our advisor for this category is Bill Campbell; he is listed in the section called Categories of Special Interest under Character Clocks and Watches. Advertising watches are included here as well.

Mickey Mouse, Pepsi, Walt Disney Productions, multicolor paint on milk glass, $11.00.

Clocks

Andy Panda, w/alarm, 1972, EX..............................$50.00
Batman, Janex, w/alarm, talking, complete, 1974, 7x6" ...$60.00
Big Bad Wolf, Ingersoll, w/alarm, M $400.00

**Bugs Bunny Alarm Clock, Ingraham, 1940s, 5"
square, M, D10, $375.00.**

Bugs Bunny, w/alarm, c Warner Bros, 1970, EX, P6.........$65.00
Bullwinkle, Larami, w/alarm & bank, turn knob & Rocky &
    other characters appear at top, 1969, NM, C1...........$63.00

**Charlie McCarthy Alarm Clock, Gilbert Clock
Corp., Edgar Bergen, metal casting with glass-
covered dial face, 1938, EX, A, $555.00.**

Cinderella, Bradley, w/up, 1970s, 3", MIB $75.00
Disney Castle, Japan, quartz movement, M......................$75.00

Disney's Busy Boys Alarm Clock, Germany/WDP, tin w/plastic
    Mickey & Donald on top striking alarm bell, 8", EX (M
    box), A..$366.00
Donald Duck, Bayard, Made in France, w/alarm, repro of 1930s
    model, 1960s, 4½x5", MIB...................................$250.00
Donald Duck, Bradley, LCD desk type, 1980s, MIB.........$20.00
Donald Duck, Bradley, sq form, w/alarm, AM/FM radio, quartz,
    MIB..$75.00
Donald Duck, France, arms show time as head moves w/2nd
    hand, 1972, 5", MIB, A.....................................$195.00
Donald Duck & Thumper, w/alarm, Glen Scotland, metal
    w/glass face, 1940s, 5½x5½", NMIB, A.....................$685.00
Elvis Presley, wall type, hips swing, MIB, S1...............$35.00
Ernie the Keebler Elf, EX......................................$40.00
Freakie's (cereal), wall type, 1970s, M.......................$125.00
Hamburger Helper's Helping Hand, NM, J2.....................$40.00
Heinz Aristocrat Tomato Man, w/talking alarm, plastic, on rnd
    base, 1980s, 9½", M..$150.00
Howdy Doody, It's Howdy Doody Time on face, Bozo reclining
    & juggling Howdy & supporting clock, L5................$99.00
Howdy Doody, w/talking alarm, MIB, P6......................$125.00
Land Before Time, battery-op, M, T1...........................$35.00
Little Sprout, talking, w/alarm, NM...........................$45.00
Max Headroom/Coke, over-sized wristwatch for wall, Coca-
    Cola/Chrysalis Visual, battery-op (1 AA), 1987, 57", MIB,
    P4...$45.00
Mickey & Donald, Germany w/alarm, figures w/mallets strike bell,
    M..$250.00
Mickey & Minnie, Bayard/France, both on rnd dial, 2nd hand,
    5", MIB, A..$200.00
Mickey & Pluto, mk USA/WDP, in nightcap, scarce,
    5½x4", NM, A...$195.00

**Mickey Mouse Alarm Clock, Bayard, Walt
Disney, metal with 4" diameter dial, animated
head movement, using hands for time, NM
(EX+ box), A, $125.00.**

Mickey Mouse, Bayard/France, w/alarm, repro of 1930s model,
    1960s, 4½x5", M, M4..$250.00
Mickey Mouse, Bradley, w/alarm, metal, EX....................$50.00
Mickey Mouse, Bradley/Germany/WDP, hands point to hour,
    w/alarm, 7x5", NM, A.......................................$100.00
Mickey Mouse, Bradley/Mexico/WDP, arms & legs move,
    w/alarm, 6¼", in slightly worn box, NM, A............$100.00

Mickey Mouse, Bradley/W Germany/WDP, red metal w/yel bells, plastic face w/scratches, working, 4x3", EX, T6 ....$150.00

Mickey Mouse, Elgin, quartz, w/alarm, 1970s, MIB $150.00

Mickey Mouse, Elgin, wall type, battery-op, Disneyland possible origin, 18x14", M4 ....$75.00

Mickey Mouse, General Electric Youth Electronics, w/alarm radio, 1960s, EX $50.00

Mickey Mouse, Ingersoll, w/alarm, ca 1955, M..............$150.00

Mickey Mouse, Phinney-Walker, 1960s, EX.....................$75.00

Mickey Mouse, W Germany, tin w/Mickey on face, plastic bezel, w/alarm, 1950s, 4", EX, A..............................$60.00

Mickey Mouse, W Germany/WDP, pendulum, diecut wood, 1960s, orig box, 11½", EX, P6 ....$225.00

Mickey Mouse, w/red plastic schoolhouse, electric, w/alarm, S1 ....$35.00

Minnie Mouse, Bradley, w/2 bells & alarm, 1970s, 3", NMIB $75.00

Minnie Mouse, Germany, talking, w/alarm, w/up, 1970s, MIB $180.00

Monkees, mc group photo on face, w/alarm, EX $50.00

Peanuts, Allergic to Mornings, w/alarm, NM, O1 ....$40.00

Pinocchio, Bayard/France, w/alarm, repro of 1930s model, 1960s, 4½x5", MIB, M4 ....$250.00

Pluto, France, doghouse in center, 2nd hand moves Pluto's head, 1978, 5", MIB, A $325.00

Raggedy Ann & Andy, talking, w/alarm, ca 1975, EX $25.00

Raid Bug, digital, NM $30.00

Roger Rabbit, Amblin/Happy Cow/WD, wall type, Who Framed..., oversized wristwatch, not US licensed, 35", MIB........$100.00

Roy Rogers & Trigger, w/alarm, Ingraham, metal, shows Roy & Trigger in desert, 1950s, orig box, 4½x4½", NM, A $425.00

R2-D2 & C-3PO, Bradley, figures stand by rnd clock face on rectangular base w/decal, 1980, M (EX+ box), A $65.00

R2-D2 & C-3PO, w/alarm, working, EX, I2.....................$52.00

Snow White, France, movie character for ea hour, bluebird is 2nd hand, rare, 5", MIB, A........................$215.00

Sooty the Boxing Puppet, Smith, EX $100.00

Star Trek Next Generation, w/alarm, 1991, MIB $38.00

Star Wars, w/alarm, talking, MIB $85.00

Thundercats, w/alarm, talking, quartz, M.......................$35.00

Watches

Abbott & Costello, Bradley, Oldies Series, quartz, analog, wht strap, sweep 2nd hand, orig box, 1986, M, P4............$20.00

Alice in Wonderland, Timex, Alice in flower, leather band, 1958, VG..$35.00

Alice in Wonderland, Timex, Alice written on face, display box w/5" Alice figure, 1958, w/guarantee & sleeve, M $200.00

Alice in Wonderland, US Time, rpl band, 1958, EX........$30.00

Alice in Wonderland, US Time, w/teacup in powder puff-shaped box, NMIB..$225.00

All-Star Baseball w/Mickey Mantle, Roger Marris & Willie Mays, MIB $150.00

American Tale w/Fievel, Armitron, 1986, MIP...............$30.00

Babe Ruth, Exacta Time, round face with lithograph of Babe holding bats, metal expansion band, 1949, EX, A, $200.00.

Barbie, Bradley/Mattel, ¾" figure w/articulated arms, vinyl band, 1973, VG, P4.................................$60.00

Barnabus Collins, Abbelare, M, E3 ....$65.00

Bart Simpson, Bradley, MIB $20.00

Bart Simpson, Nelsonics, LCD 5-function, Don't Have a Cow Man!, plastic, man's or woman's, K1 ....$12.00

Batman, Marx, working, orig band, 1974, NM $48.00

Batman, Quintel, 1989, MIP $15.00

Batman, unmk, blk bat on face, gold w/expansion band, dtd 1984 ....$60.00

Beauty & the Beast, limited edition, offered to Disney employees only, M...$150.00

Betty Boop, Bright Ideas, MIB....................................$35.00

Big Bad Wolf Pocket Watch, Ingersoll, 1934, MIB with all papers and packaging, D10, $2,500.00.

Big Boy, sm, NM...$100.00

Black Cauldron, Frito-Lay premium, 1985, MIB..............$45.00

Bobby Sherman, non-working, orig band, 1970s, EX $50.00

Bozo, pocket, Larry Harmon/Japan, plastic, tin & paper, toy only, 1960s, MIP, P4...$6.00

Buck Rogers, Photorific, lightning bolt hands w/spaceship 2nd hand, 1971, MIB...$450.00

Buck Rogers, pocket, mc dial w/rocket ship 2nd hand, working, VG-EX, A...$260.00

C-3PO & R2-D2, Bradley, characters on face, 1984, MIP, A.$35.00

Captain America, Nasta, 1984, MOC..............................$25.00

Captain Marvel, Fawcett/Marvel, Swiss, aluminum case, wrong hands, needs sm rpr, missing band, 1948, G..............$50.00

Charlie Chaplin, Bradley, Oldies Series, analog, Little Tramp on face, blk plastic case & band, 1985, M......................$20.00

Charlie Chaplin, Bubbles/Cadeaux, Swiss, articulated cane, lg chrome case, blk leather band, 1972........................$100.00

CHIPS Speedster Wind'n Wristwatch, Buddy L, CHIPS on cycle on band, w/up motor, pull-out launch ramp, 1981, MOC, C1.$24.00

Cinderella, Bradley, sm chrome case w/wht vinyl band, 1980, display box, MIB, P4...$55.00

Cinderella, Cinderella on face, pk band, display box w/5" plastic figure, w/shipping sleeve, 1958, MIB.......................$200.00

Cinderella, Timex, Cinderella in foreground, castle at 12 o'clock, rpl pk leather band, 1958, VG, P4.............$45.00

Clara Peller, Armitron, 1984, NM $12.50

Dale Evans, Bradley, Dale & Buttercup on rectangular face, leather band, 3-D box, 1950s, M.........................$400.00

Dale Evans, Ingraham, profile in horseshoe on tan ground, chrome case/bk, orig leather band, 1951, VG, from $85 to $100.00

Dan Dare, pocket, Ingersoll, chrome case, dbl animation, hands & rocket ship move, worn case, 1953, VG, from $300 to..$400.00

Dark Horse Comics, Image, M, E3 ....$40.00

Davy Crockett, Liberty Watch Corp, 1" dia dial w/pistol illus, orig strap w/coonskin, NMIB, A...........................$635.00

Death, DC Comics, EX+ $150.00

Dick Tracy, GTI/WD, lg thin blk case, Warren Beatty profile on dial, leather band, 3-sided box, MIB, P4.................$75.00

Dick Tracy, New Haven, 1948, NM, from $125 to........$150.00

Dizzy Dean, rectangular oval face w/full-length figure, missing 2nd hand, not running..$300.00

Donald Duck, Bradley, celebrating 50th Birthday, gold-tone face, Registered Edition, 1985, scarce, MIB, M8.....$225.00

Dr Doom, Nasta, quartz, 1984, MOC............................$22.00

Duck Tales, 1988, NMIB...$12.50

Elvis Presley, Bradley, quartz, analog, young Elvis or Las Vegas Elvis portrait, vinyl band, 1983, M, P4, ea.................$45.00

ET, Nelsonic, 1982, MIB..$25.00

Flash Gordon, Bradley, Swiss, chrome case, base metal bk, sweep 2nd hand, 1979, M, P4..$175.00

Ghostbusters, Columbia Pictures/unknown maker, purple plastic case w/logo, 1988, MIP, P4..$10.00

Girl From UNCLE, April Dancer on lt lavender face, red plastic band, working, 1967, EX+-NM, A...........................$65.00

Goofy, Helbros, backward version, orig, MIB.................$525.00

Goofy, Pedre, MIB..$125.00

Gene Autry Six Shooter Watch, New Haven, NM in 2½x6" simulated wood-grained box, A, $450.00.

Green Hornet Agent, M, E3...$65.00

Hopalong Cassidy, name lettered above bust image at 6 o'clock, red numbers, orig brn band, working, EX+, M5........$62.00

Hopalong Cassidy, US Time, chrome-plated bezel w/litho dial, leather band, working, orig box (top missing), EX, A...$125.00

Hopalong Cassidy, US Time, Good Luck From Hoppy on bk, rnd chrome case, orig western band, VG, P4 ....$90.00

Howdy Doody, Patent Watch, Swiss, chrome case, moving eyes, vinyl & leather band, 1954, VG, P4.......................$200.00

Howdy Doody Wristwatch, Ideal Watch Company, M on original stand, A, $150.00.

Hulk, gr Hulk on yel background w/blk numbers, rnd gold-tone case, blk band w/yel stitching, 1976, EX+, M5 ....$43.00

James Bond 007 Spy Watch, Gilbert, MIB $250.00

Jeff Arnold, pocket, Ingersoll, left gun hand moves, push to set, Eagle on bk, 1953, VG, from $300 to $400.00

Jessica Rabbit, Armitron, man's, suede pouch included, 1987, needs battery, o/w EX (EX box), M8 ....$50.00

Jessica Rabbit, Disney, legs are hands, discontinued due to poor workmanship, M, D1 ....$200.00

Jetsons, Judy on dial, Lewco, quartz, 5-function, 1986, MIB, from $25 to $35.00

Jetsons, The Movie; digital, 1990, MOC, I2 ....$15.00

John Wayne, authorized issue, quartz, orig leather band, MIB .$50.00

Joker, Fossel, 1989, MIB $100.00

Kiss, 1980s, T1 ....$45.00

Knight Rider, Larami, 1982, MOC, C1 ....$17.50

Labyrinth, Bradley, 1986, MIB $22.50

Little Sprout, Green Giant premium, quartz, analog, sweep 2nd hand, yel plastic case & band, M, P4 ....$15.00

Lone Ranger, Bradley, from movie, MIB.........................$125.00

Lucy, figure on wht face w/1952 & blk numbers, chrome case, lt tan leather band, 1960(?), EX, M5 ....$39.00

Lucy, Timex, articulated hands, sweep 2nd hand, wht vinyl band, 1970s, VG, P4 ....$35.00

Major Moon, Ralston Purina premium, Swiss movement, chrome case w/vinyl band, 1983, NM, P4 ....$100.00

Marilyn Monroe, pocket, portrait on blk ground, 2" dia, M $60.00

Mary Marvel, orig band, M $100.00

Mickey Mouse, Bradley, 1970s, T1................................$125.00

Mickey Mouse, Bradley, 50th Anniversary, limited edition, MIB $175.00

Mickey Mouse, Helbros, 17-jewel, 1972, M....................$300.00

Mickey Mouse, Ingersoll, metal band, box features Horace, Clarabell, Mickey & Minnie, 1933, EX (EX box), M8 ....$700.00

Mickey Mouse, Ingersoll, Mickey on face, hands keep time, 3 sm Mickeys count 2nds, diecuts on band, 1938, NM (EX box)..$700.00

Mickey Mouse, Ingersoll, 1960s, T1 ....$125.00

Mickey Mouse, Ingersoll, 1968, orig box, EX....................$75.00

Mickey Mouse, pocket, Ingersoll, c WD, complete w/instructions, fob & fob box insert, emb bk, NMIB, A $850.00

Mickey Mouse, Timex, Mickey on face, display box w/5" plastic figure, tape rpr on base, 1958, unused, M (EX+ box)..$200.00

Mickey Mouse, Timex/WDP, lg chrome case, standing Mickey, sweep 2nd hand, blk leather band, 1968, VG $60.00

Mickey Mouse, Timex/WDP, lg rnd chrome case, stainless bk, red vinyl band, 1960s, VG, P4....................................$65.00

Mickey Mouse, US Time, Mickey on rectangular face, vinyl band, 1947, orig box, EX, A $277.00

Mickey Mouse & Donald Duck, Lorus/WD, chrome case & band, sweep 2nd hand, bl box, 1986, MIB, from $90 to $150.00

Minnie Mouse, Bradley, standing Minnie faces left, flower between 12 & 1, denim & leather band, 1975, M, P4 .$60.00

Minnie Mouse, Timex, chrome case w/stainless bk, articulated hands, orig yel vinyl band, 1958, VG, P4...................$60.00

Minnie Mouse, Timex, Minnie on face, in orig box w/3-D Minnie on 4" plaque, w/guarantee & sleeve, 1958, MIB, A ...$275.00

Mickey Mouse Pocket Watch, Ingersoll, with fob, 1930s, NM, D10, $650.00.

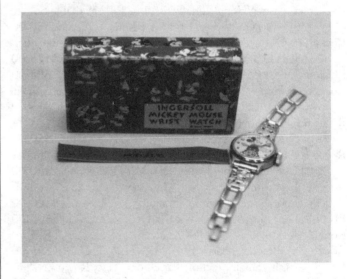

Mickey Mouse Wristwatch, Ingersoll, second hand, diecuts on metal band, ca 1933, MIB, D10, $850.00.

Miss Piggy, Picco/Henson, 7 jewels, sweep 2nd hand, striped purple band, plastic case, 1979, M.............................$40.00

Orphan Annie, New Haven, rectangular w/full-length Annie on face, leather band, 1934 (ca 1933), unused, NM (EX+ box), A $380.00

Pee Wee Herman, LCD, MIP..$35.00

Pluto, Ingersoll/US Time, Birthday Series, glow-in-dark dial & hands, gr vinyl band, 1948, VG $175.00

Pokey, Prema/Lewco, Hong Kong, quartz, 5-function, MIB, P4 ....$15.00

Popeye Pocket Watch, New Haven, second hand is Wimpy, 1935, 1¾" diameter, NM, $550.00.

Popeye, pocket, New Haven/KFS, full-figure Popeye w/hands for time, Wimpy as 2nd hand, 1935, 2" dia, EX, A $436.00
Raggedy Andy, Bradley, 1971, orig box, M4 ....$35.00
Red Ryder, commemorative issue, MIB............................$75.00
Return of Superman, Fossil, 1993, MIB............................$80.00
Robocop, wristwatch, Fada, 1989, MOC, from $15 to......$22.50
Rocketeer, Disney/Hong Kong/Swiss, 1 of 1500 available only to Walt Disney employees, 1991, M, P4 ....$350.00
Rocketeer, Disney/Mars/unknown maker, Twixt premium, rectangular case, tan leather band, 1991, MIB, P4 ....$175.00
Rocketeer, Fossil, 1991, MIB...$95.00
Rocketeer, Hope/Walt Disney, 5-function LCD, gold case, bl vinyl band, 1991, MOC, P4 ....$35.00
Roger Rabbit, Amblin/Disney, Shiraka, Swiss, bullet-hole style, wht case & band, 1987, MIB, P4..............................$50.00
Roger Rabbit, Amblin/Disney, silhouette style, Swiss quartz, gold case, blk leather band, 1987, MIB, P4................$60.00
Roger Rabbit, Amitron, set of 4, M in pouch, D1 ....$400.00
Roger Rabbit, Disney Channel promotion, M, D1 ....$100.00
Roger Rabbit, Shiraka, set of 4, MIB, D1 ....$500.00
Ronald McDonald, 1984, MOC.......................................$12.50
Roy Rogers, Bradley, quartz, 1985, MIB...........................$95.00
Roy Rogers, Ingraham, rectangular chrome case, Roy on rearing Trigger, brn leather band, 1951, VG, P4....................$90.00
Roy Rogers w/Dale & Trigger, Bradley, LCD, 1985, MOC..$30.00
Simpsons Family Dancing, Nelsonics, 5 function, LCD, plastic, man's or woman's, K1 ....$12.00
Snap!, Crackle! & Pop!; Rice Krispies premium, 1988, MIB...$30.00
Snoopy, Timex Swiss, tennis ball orbits on clear disk, articulated hands, denim band, 1970s, VG, P4 ....$75.00
Snow White & Dopey, Timex, sm rnd chrome case, rpl leather band, 1958, VG, P4 ....$90.00
Space Patrol, working, 1950s, T1 ....$185.00
Spiderman, Dabs, Super Heroes Series, 1977, MIB $135.00
Spiro Agnew, Dirty Time, NM...$58.00
Spiro Agnew, Dirty Time, 1971, MIB.................................$75.00

Smurf Wristwatch, Bradley, blue plastic band, MIB, $25.00.

Spuds McKenzie, orig Budweiser band, EX $40.00
Star Trek 20th Anniversary, 1986, MIB $40.00
Star Wars, Bradley, mk Official, MIB $125.00
Superman, Armour premium, 1987, MIB..........................$15.00
Superman, New Haven, Superman on rectangular face, leather band, 1939, EX, A $200.00
Superman, Superman in flight over lg emblem, rnd chrome case, brn leather band w/yel stitching, EX+, M5 ....$45.00
Tasmanian Devil, Bright Ideas, MIB $30.00
The Fonz, Bradley Swiss, lg gold case w/base metal bk, sweep 2nd hand, blk leather band, 1976, NM, P4...............$55.00
Three Little Pigs, Lorus, 1991, MIB $65.00
Three Little Pigs, pocket, Ingersoll, metal casing, wolf watches pigs play instruments, 1934, 2" dia, VG+, A $563.00
Tom & Jerry, Armitron, Looney Tunes 3-D Series, oversized blk acrylic case & band, 1991, MIB, P4 ....$27.00
Tom Corbett, w/up stem, orig space-graphic band, VG-EX, T1 ....$175.00
Tom Corbett, 1950s, NMOC...$415.00
Trix Rabbit, Trix Cereal premium, Trix Rabbit in center w/ears as hands, bl plastic case & band, NM........................$15.00
Voltron Time Keeper Robot, M, F1 ....$5.00
Walt Disney World 20th Anniversary, Lorus, MIB $75.00
Wayne Gretsky, digital, Gretsky in hockey uniform, blk band, needs battery, late 1980s, NM, M5 ....$42.00
Winnie the Pooh, asleep under tree, NRFB.......................$25.00
Woody Woodpecker 50th Anniversary, Lorus, 1990, MIB.$125.00
Young Astronauts, 1986, NMIB $8.50

Character Collectibles

It's the TV characters from the fifties and sixties that collectors are most avidly interested in right now, those cowboy stars and super heroes (you know them all); cartoon characters from Hanna-Barbera, Walter Lantz, and Walt Disney; Saturday morning kid show hosts; monsters and familiar faces from long-running sit-coms. Dealers we've talked with tell us that some of the seventies' TV shows, The Brady Bunch and Laverne and Shirley, for example, are not far behind. From the entertainment industry, Elvis and the Beatles are hot, so are Marilyn and Kiss. Since many of the action figures are modeled after well-known characters, they're included here as well. All in all, we've listed more than 4,000 descriptions and prices in this category, and we've only begun to scratch the surface. Had space permitted, no doubt we could have doubled its size. You'll find just about any character-related item here with these exceptions (which will be found in categories thus titled): Books, Big Little, Little Golden, Wonder; Battery-Operated Toys; Bubble Bath Containers; California Raisins; Corgi; Character and Promotional Drinking Glasses; Character Clocks and Watches; Dakins; Dolls, Celebrity; Dolls, Jem; Ertl; Fisher-Price; GI Joe; Models; Paper Dolls; Pez; Playsets; Radios; Santa Claus; Sports Collectibles; Star Trek; Star Wars; Telephones; View-Master; Windups, Friction and Other Mechanicals.

Here's our list of suggested reading material: *Stern's Guide to Disney Collectibles* by Michael Stern; *The Collector's Encyclopedia of Disneyana* by Michael Stern and David Longest; *Character Toys and Collectibles, Vols I and II*, by David Longest; *Cartoon Friends of the Baby Boom Era* by Bill Bruegman; *The Tom Mix Book* by M.G. 'Bud' Norris; *Collector's Guide to Hopalong Cassidy Memorabilia* by Joseph J. Caro; *The Beatles, A Reference & Value Guide*, by Michael Stern, Barbara Crawford, and Hollis Lamon; *Elvis Collectibles* and *Best of Elvis Collectibles* by Rosalind Cranor; and *The Official Price Guide to Peanuts Collectibles* by Freddi Margolin and Andrea Podley. Bojo (B3) is our advisor for Beatles memorabilia; Allen Day (D1) is our advisor for Roger Rabbit; Ron and Donna Donnelly (D7) are advisors for Western heroes; Robert Reeves (R4) is our advisor for Johnny West; Jim Rash (R3) advised us on character squeeze toys; Trina & Randy Kubeck (K1) are advisors on The Simpsons; and our Wizard of Oz specialist is Bill Stillman (S6).

Though most characters are listed by their own names, some may be found under the title of the movie, comic strip or dominate character they're commonly identified with. For instance, Catwoman will be found in the Batman section.

A-Team, Cobra figure, MOC, D4.............................$5.00
A-Team, game, board; Parker Bros, 1984, MIB T6...........$15.00
A-Team, game, Grenade Toss, 1983, MIB......................$15.00
A-Team, gum card set, Monty Gum, 1983, 100 cards, complete, M1 ....$15.00
A-Team, gum card set, Topps, 1983, 66 cards w/12 stickers, complete, M1 ....$9.50
A-Team, Mr T figure, Galoob, 1983, 12", MIB, C1..........$36.00
A-Team, puffy stickers, set of 6, MIP, T6......................$4.00
A-Team, Rub & Play Transfers, MIP, F1 ....$5.00
A-Team, Soldiers of Fortune Figure Set, Galoob, 1983, MOC $25.00
Abbott & Costello, figure, Sports Impressions, Who's on First, porc, limited edition, 1988, MIB, C1 ....$90.00
Action Boy, figure, Ideal, missing clothes & accessories, rpl ft,

VG, H4..$170.00
Action Boy, outfit, Super Boy jumpsuit, Ideal, missing cape, sm tear on emblem, H4...$15.00
Action Jackson, figure, Mego, mod-styled hair w/stick-on tattoos, 8", MIB, from $25 to...$29.50
Action Jackson, figure, Mego, wht w/blk hair & beard, 1974, MIB, F1..$25.00
Action Jackson, outfit, Baseball #1115, NMIB, H4 ....$8.00
Action Jackson, outfit, Jungle Safari, 1974, orig box, T1....$8.00
Action Jackson, outfit, Rescue Squad #1107, MIB, H4 ....$10.00
Action Jackson, outfit, Secret Agent, 1974, orig box, T1...$8.00
Action Jackson, outfit, Snow Mobile #1112, MIB, H4.....$10.00
Action Jackson, outfit, Surf & Scuba, Mego, for 8" figure, 1971, MIB, C1...$13.00
Action Jackson, outfit, Western #1108, MIB, H4.............$10.00
Action Jackson, Rescue Pack, Mego, MIB, F1 ....$15.00
Addams Family, bank, Thing, NM (VG-EX box), O1 ...$150.00
Addams Family, cartoon kit, Colorforms, w/instructions & box insert, 1965, 8x12" box, NM (EX box), A...............$110.00
Addams Family, doll, Aboriginal Pugsley, stuffed, complete, lt stain on face & arms, rare, 26", VG, H4.................$500.00
Addams Family, Fester figure, Remco, vinyl, 1964, EX-NM, T1..$185.00
Addams Family, figure, Playmates, Gomez, Morticia, Pugsley, Lurch, Grandma or Uncle Fester, 1992, MIP, F1, any...$10.00
Addams Family, flashlight, Ralston Purina premium, Thing, 1991, dead battery, H4..$2.00
Addams Family, game, board; Ideal, 1965, NMIB, A $275.00
Addams Family, game, board; Milton Bradley, 1974, NMIB, C1..$54.00
Addams Family, game, board; Reunion, Pressman, 1991, MIB, F1..$20.00
Addams Family, game, card; Find Uncle Fester, Pressman, 1991, MIB, F1..$15.00
Addams Family, game, Cartoons, Milton Bradley, 1973, EX+, F3..$28.00

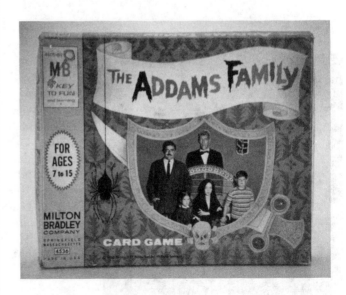

Addams Family Card Game, Milton Bradley, M (EX box), $45.00.

Addams Family, game, Ideal, 1964, complete, EX (EX box), H4 ....$100.00

Addams Family, gum card set, Topps, 1991, 99 cards w/11 stickers, complete, M1..$22.00

Addams Family, Lurch figure, Remco, vinyl, 1964, EX-NM, T1...$110.00

Addams Family, Morticia doll, Remco, hard plastic w/soft plastic head, long blk hair, 1964, 5", EX+, D9 ....$149.00

Addams Family, photo, blk & wht glossy of cast, 1965, 3½x5", NM, C1..$24.00

Addams Family, puzzle, Addams Family Mystery, Milton Bradley, 1965, complete, EX $35.00

Adventure Boy, finger puppet, Remco, in Skymobile vehicle, 1970, MIB, H4 ....$40.00

AFC Blinky, figure, Hasbro, MIP, E3 ....$6.00

Agir, figure, Bandai, vinyl, MIP, E3 ....$10.00

Airwolf, wallet, action scene, NMOC, T6 ....$7.00

Aladdin, figure, Applause, PVC, set of 4: Aladdin, Prince Ali, Gennie & Jasmine, MIP, F1 ....$12.00

Aladdin, pins, set of 5: Abu, Genie, Jasmine/Aladdin, Jafar/Yago & Sultan, 1992, M, M8 ....$100.00

Aladdin, soundtrack, 1958, sealed $15.00

Alan Ladd, gun, Schmidt, diecast pistol w/nickel finish, break-to-front, metal grips, lever release, 1950s, 10", VG, P4 ....$95.00

Alf, book, cartoon; Coleco, Alf Sounds Off!, MIP, F1........$5.00

Alf, doll, plush, 1980s, lg, NM, T1 ....$15.00

Alf, figure, Coleco, Augie, Skip or Curtis, 1986, MIP, F1, any $10.00

Alf, gum card set, Topps, 1987, 1st series, 47 cards w/22 stickers, complete, M1 ....$12.00

Alf, hand puppet, Cookin' w/Alf, chef's apron, hat & mustache, 1988, 12", NM, P3 ....$15.00

Alf, kite, MIP (sealed), D4 ....$4.00

Alf, mask, rubber, adult sz w/hair, full head, w/tags, M, P3 .$12.00

Alfred E Neuman, see MAD

Alfred Hitchcock, game, Why?, Milton Bradley, 1950-60, EX+, F3 ....$18.00

Alice in Wonderland, Alice figure, Ceramic Arts Studio, 5" on 3" dia base, M, P6 ....$125.00

Alice in Wonderland, Alice figure, Shaw Pottery, EX, P6.$650.00

Alice in Wonderland, bath towel, full color, EX, P6 ....$45.00

Alice in Wonderland, bedspread, chenille, twin sz, 1950s, EX, P6..$120.00

Alice in Wonderland, book, coloring; Saalfield, 1951, 16 pgs, 1 colored, o/w unused & EX, P6...................................$22.00

Alice in Wonderland, game, Alice Croquet, features main characters, MIP, P6 ....$60.00

Alice in Wonderland, Mad Hatter figure, Shaw Pottery, EX, P6..$475.00

Alice in Wonderland, marionette, Peter Puppet, 1950s, NM (VG box)...$200.00

Alice in Wonderland, pins, set of 3: Alice, Cheshire Cat & White Rabbit, cloisonne, 1990s, M, M8 ....$75.00

Alice in Wonderland, rabbit, Italy, ceramic figure w/heart on costume, hand to face, 5½", NM, A $10.00

Alice in Wonderland, record, Little Golden, Very Good Advice, orig sleeve, 1950s, P6..$20.00

Alice in Wonderland, record, 78 rpm, orig sleeve, 1950, EX, P6..$22.00

Alice in Wonderland, sewing cards, c Walt Disney Prod 1951, 4 cards & 2 laces, complete in orig box, EX, P6...........$60.00

Alice in Wonderland, soap dish, ceramic, full-color graphic of Alice w/flowers, 1960s, M, P6 ....$60.00

Alice in Wonderland, tea set, c Walt Disney Prod, china, 1960s, MIB, P6..$95.00

Alice in Wonderland, Tweedle Dum figure, Shaw Pottery, EX, P6..$275.00

Alien, game, board; Kenner, 1979, MIB, from $50 to.......$70.00

Alien, glow putty, Larami, 1979, MOC............................$3.50

Alien, gum card set, Topps, 1979, 84 cards w/22 stickers, complete, M1...$22.00

Alien, gum card set, 84 color photo cards from 1st movie, 1979, NM-M, C1...$31.00

Alien, puzzle, jigsaw; HG #473, 1979, in orig 7x24" box, NMIB, C1..$72.00

Alien, puzzle, 250-pc, 1979, 14½x36", VG+, T6 ....$20.00

Alien, T-shirt, Acme, M, E3...$5.00

Alien Nation, gum card set, FTCC, 1990, 60 cards, complete, M1..$12.00

Alien 3, gum card set, Star Pictures, 1992, 80 cards, complete, M1..$16.00

Aliens, Apone figure, Kenner, MIP, E3.............................$8.00

Aliens, Atax figure, Kenner, MIP, E3 ....$15.00

Aliens, Bishop figure, Kenner, MIP, E3 ....$15.00

Aliens, Bull Alien figure, Kenner, MIP, E3.......................$8.00

Aliens, Corporal Hicks figure, 1993, MOC, from $9 to....$12.00

Aliens, Drake figure, 1993, MOC, from $9 to..................$12.00

Aliens, Drake figure, Kenner, MIP, E3.............................$8.00

Aliens, Gorilla Alien figure, 1993, MOC, from $9 to......$12.00

Aliens, Hicks figure, Kenner, MIP, E3 ....$8.00

Aliens, Queen figure, Kenner, MIP, E3............................$12.00

Aliens, Sergeant Apone figure, 1993, MOC, from $9 to.$12.00

Aliens, Scorpion Alien figure, Kenner, MIP, E3................$8.00

All in the Family, game, Milton Bradley, 1972, NMIB, C1 .$24.00

All in the Family, record album, 33⅓ rpm, 1971, EX, N2 .$25.00

Alice in Wonderland Book with Cut-Out Pictures, illustrated by Julia Green (after Tenniel), London, no date, 9¾x7¾", NM, uncut, $65.00.

All My Children, game, board; TSR, mc photo of 12 stars on box, 1985, NM, T6 ....$8.00

All My Children, gum card set, Star Pics, 1991, 72 cards, complete, M1 ....$17.00

Allan Ladd, tablet, Alan on cover w/facsimile signature, 1950s, 8x10", unused, EX, T2 ....$10.00

Allan Sherman, record album, My Son the Folk Singer, Warner Bros, 33⅓ rpm, endorsements on jacket, 1962, NM, T2 .$10.00

Alley Oop, game, Tiddlewinks, NM, V1 ....$28.00

Alvin (Chipmunk), doll, stuffed, talker, 1983, 18", S1 .....$20.00

Alvin (Chipmunk), figural soap dispenser, 1978, T1 ....$8.00

Alvin & the Chipmunks, Christmas stocking, vinyl, 1963, 14", EX+, A $80.00

Alvin & the Chipmunks, record player, working, 1965, EX+ $48.00

Andy Gump, car, Arcade, CI, Andy in 348 roadster, gr & red car w/doughnut-sized wheels, 1932, 7", VG, A $1,495.00

Andy Gump #348 Car, Arcade, green and red car, steering wheel, 7" long, EX, A, $2,500.00.

Andy Gump, car, Arcade, red body w/NP Andy & wheels, 348 mk on grille, 1924, 7½" L, EX, A $2,500.00

Andy Gump, doll, jtd wood, mk Sidney Smith, ca mid-1930s, 6", EX+, A $120.00

Andy Gump, figure, German, HP bsk, sm pnt loss, 4", G+, A $20.00

Andy Panda, squeeze toy, Oak Rubber, R3 ....$50.00

Andy's Gang, squeeze toy, McConnell/Rempel, Froggy Gremlin figure, working, 1948, 5", VG, P4 ....$50.00

Angiras, figure, Bandai, vinyl, MIP, E3 ....$20.00

Annette Funicello, book, coloring; Whitman, 128-pg, 1964, many pgs colored, some creasing, T2 ....$15.00

Annie Oakley, game, board; Milton Bradley, complete, 1959, NM $55.00

Annie Oakley, game, board; Milton Bradley, 1955, NMIB, C1 ....$79.00

Annihilus, figure, Toy Biz, MIP, E3 ....$5.00

Antlar, figure, Bandai, vinyl, MIP, E3 ....$10.00

Anton Arcane, figure, Kenner, MIP, E3 ....$8.00

Apocolype, Toy Biz, MOC, D8 ....$9.00

Apple's Way, game, board; Milton Bradley, 1974, VG, T6.$25.00

Aquaman, bendee, Mego, 1974, loose, NM $32.00

Aquaman, figure, swimming posed, cereal premium, 1988, 3", M, H4 ....$8.00

Aquaman, figure, Mego, 8", MIB, H4 ....$129.00

Aquaman, figure, Toy Biz, 2nd series, rare, MOC, from $15 to $25.00

Aquanauts, game, board; Underwater Adventure, Transogram, complete, 1961, orig 9x18" box, M (EX+ box), A $55.00

Arachnophobia, Big Bob Spider, Remco, 1990, MOC $15.00

Archie Bunker, game, card; Milton Bradley, 1972, NMIB..$10.00

Archies, bendee, Jesco, 1989, 7", MOC, any $7.50

Archies, book, iron-on transfer; Golden, 1977, unused, 8½x11", NM, C1 ....$20.50

Archies, figure, Archie, stuffed w/Archies Series Comic #268, mail-order premium, 1960s, MIP, H4 ....$39.00

Archies, figure, Mattel, Archie or Jughead, vinyl, 1975, 9", MOC, H4, ea $39.00

Archies, puzzle, jigsaw; Whitman, 1972, EX, T6 ....$8.00

Archies, snare drum, litho tin & metal, character lithos, 14" dia, +stand, NMIB, A $125.00

Archies, tattoos, Topps, 2x4" wrapper w/tattoo sheet & slab of gum, Archie on wrapper, 1969, M, T2 ....$20.00

Aristocats, soundtrack, 1970, EX $8.00

Art Linkletter, game, House Party, 1968, MIB (sealed), V1..$25.00

As the World Turns, game, Transogram, 1957, EX+, F3 ..$35.00

Astro Boy, tattoo wrapper, Topps, portrait on front, tattoos on bk, 1960s, scarce, 1½x3½", NM, T2 ....$40.00

Atom Ant, book, coloring; G $20.00

Atom Ant, push-button puppet, Kohner, 1960s, EX $35.00

Attack of Killer Tomatoes, Wilbur Finletter figure, 1988, MOC, T1 ....$5.00

Auto Cat, squeak toy, Hanna-Barbera, soft vinyl, rare, 4", VG, H4 ....$16.00

Avengers, gum card box, Cornerstone Communications, empty, M, E3 ....$30.00

Avengers, T-shirt, Marvel Comics, wht cotton, 1965, child sz, mail-order premium, EX+-NM, A $184.00

Baba Looey, figure, Marx, TV Tinykin series, revival of Ricky Riccardo, 1960s, NM, C1 ....$18.00

Babes in Toyland, book, Toymaker's Helper, Whitman Tip-Top Tale, 1961, EX, T6 ....$3.00

Babes in Toyland, Colorforms, 1961, M4 ....$10.00

Babes in Toyland, Disneykin, Marx, soldier w/trumpet, 1960s, EX, M8 ....$10.00

Baby Huey, squeeze toy, Harvey, R3 ....$65.00

Back to the Future, Action Hoverport Micro Playset, Texaco Gas giveaway, MIP, F1 ....$6.00

Back to the Future, Delorian, 6", MIB, D4 ....$20.00

Back to the Future II, gum card set, Topps, 1992, 88 cards w/11 stickers, complete, M1 ....$10.00

Badfinger, sheet music songbook, 12 songs, photos, 48 pgs, 1972, EX-, T6 ....$15.00

Baloo, pin, figural Talespin, cloisonne, 1990s, M, M8 ....$6.00

Bambi, pencil sharpener, Bakelite, red, 1940s, rare, worn letters, o/w EX, M8 ....$85.00

Bambi, plaster figure, running position, Leonardi of England, 1950s, rare, 5½", EX, M8 ....$125.00

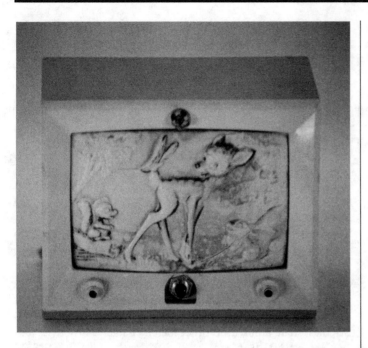

Bambi Night Light, with music box, plastic, working, 1950s, 5x6", EX, $65.00.

Bambi, print, NY Graphic Society, Bambi Meets His Friends, 1945, minor edge wear, o/w EX, M8...........................$25.00

Bambi, puppet, Marx, plastic w/push-button action, 1960s, 4", EX+, T2...$30.00

Bambi, switch plate, hard plastic, full color, 1949, MIP, P6 .$60.00

Banana Splits, Kut-Up Kit, Larami, w/scissors & stencils, 1973, NMOC, C1..$24.00

Banana Splits, ornament, Diener, 1968, NMIB..............$175.00

Banana Splits, puzzle, fr-tray; Whitman, snowmobiling to North Pole, 1969, 11x14", EX+, T2......................................$22.00

Banana Splits, puzzle, jigsaw; Whitman, 1968, G.............$35.00

Banana Splits, puzzle, jigsaw; Whitman, 1969, EX (rpr corner on box), H4..$30.00

Banana Splits, record, theme song+3 more, Hanna-Barbera/Kellogg's, 45 rpm, in 7x7" illus sleeve, 1965, NM, T2......$18.00

Banana Splits, record album, soundtrack, Decca, 33⅓ rpm, w/mc jacket, 1968, scarce, EX+, T2....................................$30.00

Banana Splits, switch plate cover, 1960s, MOC..............$40.00

Banana Splits, tambourine, 1972, MIB, T1.......................$35.00

Banshee, figure, Toy Biz, MIP, E3....................................$8.00

Baragon, figure, Bandai, vinyl, MIP, E3 ....$20.00

Baretta, game, The Street Detective, Milton Bradley, 1976, M (EX box), C1..$26.00

Barney Google, chalk board, King Features syndicate, 1950s, 16x24", EX+, T2..$50.00

Barney Google & Spark Plug, pull toy, c 1924 King Features Syndicate, litho tin, blk jockey, 7x6", NM, A......$5,700.00

Barney Miller, game, board; Parker Bros, 1976, complete, EX..$15.00

Barnyard Commandos, figure, Playmates, any from 1st or 2nd series, MIP, F1...$5.00

Bat Masterson, book, Whitman, hardcover, 1960, EX......$15.00

Bat Masterson, game, board; Lowell, 3-D playing pcs, 1958, EX, from $70 to...$85.00

Bat Masterson, playsuit, Ben Cooper/Ziv TV, vest, shirt, pants & 2-part cane (sm crack), ca 1959, NMIB, P4..............$50.00

Batman, Batcave, Toy Biz, MIB, D4.................................$35.00

Batman, Batcopter, Kenner, MIP, E3................................$18.00

Batman, Batcycle, Kenner, MIP, E3...................................$8.00

Batman, Batjet, Kenner, MIP, E3.....................................$16.00

Batman, Batman Returns Set, Ertl, 2pc: Batman w/Batmobile, MOC, F1...$10.00

Batman, Batman Thingmaker Mold, Mattel, M...............$35.00

Batman, Batmobile, Batman & Robin in seats under clear plastic dome, 8½", on lithoed 8x9" display, NM (EX card), A.$100.00

Batman, Batmobile, Kenner, Super Powers series, EX, H4 .$20.00

Batman, Batmobile, Palitoy, talking, 1977, 10", NM (VG box), C6...$65.00

Batman, Batmobile, Toy Biz, MIP, E3..............................$25.00

Batman, Batplane, Ertl #0972G, plastic, 4¼", M................$3.00

Batman, Batplane/tractor, TM & DC Comics, plastic, 1991, 3½", M..$3.00

Batman, Batring, 1960s, M, H4..$8.00

Batman, Batscope Dart Launcher, Tarco, 1966, MOC, A.$60.00

Batman, bendee, Mego, 6", EX, H4.................................$15.00

Batman, bicycle ornament, Empire, 1966, A....................$74.00

Batman, book, activity; 128-pg, 1966, VG, T6...................$7.00

Batman, book, Batman Verses 3 Villians of Doom, soft cover, 1966, EX...$20.00

Batman, book, coloring; Whitman, 80+ pgs, 1967, 8x11", unused, NM, T2...$30.00

Batman, Bruce Wayne figure, Dark Knight series, MOC, D8...$15.00

Batman, buckle, unmk, gold & silver on brass, 3", M.......$15.00

Batman, Catwoman figure, Applause, 1992, 11", M.........$18.00

Batman, Catwoman figure, diecast, 1993, 2", MOC, T1.....$5.00

Catwoman and Penguin Figures, Mego, 8", from $35.00 to $55.00.

Batman, Catwoman figure, Kenner, Batman Returns, MOC, D4 ....$10.00

Batman, character card, Topps, orange-bk series, set of 55, 1966, NM, C1...........................$131.00

Batman, Colorforms, 1976, MIB, C1..............$31.00

Batman, Custom Coupe, Kenner, Batman Returns, MIP, E3 .$25.00

Batman, Dark Knight Sonic Neutralizer, Kenner, MIB, D4.$35.00

Batman, doll, Made in China, unlicensed, highly detailed, mc box mk Bat Hero, 12", MIB, from $30 to $40.00

Batman, figure, Applause, PVC, Batman, Catwoman, or Penguin, Batman Returns (2nd movie), MIP, F1 ....$4.00

Batman, figure, Applause, PVC, from 1st movie, 3", M, F1 .$5.00

Batman, figure, Applause, w/cape, 1991, 11½" $18.00

Batman, figure, Australian, poseable, 1989, 8", MOC, T1.$55.00

Batman, figure, China, Super Powers, plastic, 1992, 10", MOC, T1 ....$10.00

Batman, figure, DC Comics, cb hanger, 1977, 36", MIP, T1.$15.00

Batman, figure, DC Comics, diecast, 2¼", M, F1 ....$5.00

Batman, figure, Kenner, blk rubber w/gold trim, missing cape, 1992, M $3.00

Batman, figure, Kenner, Dark Knight, 1st series, any of 6 different, MOC, F1..$15.00

Batman, figure, Kenner/DC Comics, plastic, gray w/blk & gold trim, 1992, 5", M...$3.00

Batman, figure, Mego, 12", MIB, from $60 to................$100.00

Batman, figure, Presents, PVC, w/bl & gray costume, MIP, F1 ....$4.00

Batman, figure, South America, Super Power, 1980s, T1.$27.50

Batman, figure, Toy Biz, 1st issue, Keaton face, 1989, MOC, from $12 to....................................$15.00

Batman, figure, Toy Biz, 2nd issue, w/sq jaw, 1989, MOC, from $12 to....................................$15.00

Batman, figure, Toy Biz, 3rd issue, w/pnt face, 1989, MOC, from $12 to....................................$15.00

Batman, figure w/parachute, CDC, metallic bl figure & working parachute on 11x9" display card, 1966, M, from $50 to $70.00

Batman, fork, stainless steel, 1960s, 6¼", EX+, T6 ....$25.00

Batman, game, Adventures of the Caped Crusader, Hasbro, 1966, VG, T1...................................$30.00

Batman, game, Batman Returns, Canadian issue, MIB.....$20.00

Batman, game, board; Hasbro, 1973, NM (EX box), C1 ..$19.50

Batman, game, board; Ideal, w/cards & chips, 1966, 6x10" box, EX (sealed box), T2.................................$60.00

Batman, game, card; Ideal, NM+, F3...............$45.00

Batman, game, Electronic Pinball, 1989, 20x12" box, NMIB, C6..$98.00

Batman, game, Exploding Bridge w/Batmobile & Activator, Mego, complete, 1976, orig 18x9" box, M (EX box), A.........$176.00

Batman, game, Milton Bradley, 1966, EX+, F3.................$35.00

Batman, game, board; TV Game, Japan, complete 1960s, 9x16" box, unused, NMIB, A $300.00

Batman, gum card box, Topps, empty red store display box w/pop-up lid, 1966, 8x4x2", NM, A.........................$250.00

Batman, gum card set, Topps, 1989, from movie, 1st series, 132 cards w/22 stickers, complete, M1 ....$18.00

Batman, gum card set, Topps, 1992, Batman Returns, 88 cards w/10 stickers, complete, M1 ....$12.50

Batman, gum cards, Zellers, 1992, 24 cards, complete, M1.$7.50

Batman, hand puppet, Ideal, 12", on water-stained display card, 1966, unused, o/w EX, T2......................$60.00

Batman, Joker bank, Mego, plastic ¾-length figure, 1974, EX+, C1..$39.00

Batman, Joker bendee, Mego, 1974, VG, loose.................$12.00

Batman, Joker Cycle, Kenner, Batman Dark Knight, 1st series, MIP, F1 ....$15.00

Batman, Joker figure, DC Comics, diecast, 2¼", MIP, F1 ...$5.00

Batman, Joker figure, Kenner, animated, MIP, E3 ....$8.00

Batman, Joker figure, Mego, NM, D8..............$40.00

Batman, Joker figure, Mego, 8", MOC (sm hole where staple was removed & written price), H4 ....$125.00

Batman, Joker figure, Toy Biz, NMOC, D4.....................$10.00

Batman Lamp, Vanity Fair Industries, Made in Taiwan, extendable arm for light, 7½", $135.00.

Batman, Life Magazine, cover & feature story, Mar 11, 1966, NM, T2.....................................$20.00

Batman, lobby card set, Zanart, Batman Returns, M, E3 ..$12.00

Batman, marble, Summit Art Glass, red & wht swirl w/decal, M $6.00

Batman, mask, Wilton/DC Comics, 1977, 4½"..................$2.00

Batman, membership & comic kit, includes record & ring, NMIB, T1 ....$145.00

Batman, mug, Applause, full face, Batman Returns, MIP, F1.$20.00

Batman, mug, Applause/TM & DC Comics, ceramic, 3½", M.$10.00

Batman, night light, shaped like Bat logo w/head of Batman between 2 Batwings, 3", 1960s, M, from $10 to........$18.00

Batman, Official Bat-Signal Stickers, Alan-Whitney, in poly bag w/header card, 1966, unused, EX+, T2.....................$20.00

Batman, Paint-By-Number, Hasbro, no pnts, 1966, VG, T1 .$35.00

Batman, pencil sharpener, DC Comics/Hong Kong, 1981, 5", M $8.00

Batman, Penguin car, Penguinmobile, #259, M, C6 ....$50.00

Batman, Penguin figure, Applause, vinyl, Batman Returns, 10", MIP, F1 ....$10.00

Batman, Penguin figure, Kenner, Super Powers, w/umbrella, MIP, from $15 to $25.00

Batman, Penguin figure, Mego, 8", MIB (cellophane w/sm pinholes & crinkles on box), H4 ....$65.00

Batman, Penguin figure, Toy Biz, MOC, D4 ....$10.00

Batman, photo, ABC TV, Batman & Robin etc, facsimile signature on bk, 1966, 3½x5½", M, T2 ....$15.00

Batman, photo, ABC TV, Bruce Wayne & Batman, facsimile inscription & signature, blk & wht, 1966, 8x10", M, T2 ....$18.00

Batman, picture, Davaco Publications, stiff cb w/full-figure portrait in action pose, 1966, 7x14", EX, T2 ....$18.00

Batman Picture Pistol, battery-operated, 1960s, MIB, M5, $450.00.

Batman, pin, unmk, foil, 2¼x1¼", M $2.50

Batman, playing cards, US Playing, Batman Returns, 1992, 52 photo cards, complete, M1 ....$4.00

Batman, postcards, Dexter Press, taken from panel from Batman Comics, 1966, M, lot of 3, T2 ....$30.00

Batman, puzzle, APC, 81-pc (1 missing), 1976, 11x11", VG, T6 ....$5.00

Batman, puzzle, Batman Returns, Penguin on Penguin Mobile, 200-pc, NM (sealed box), P3 ....$9.00

Batman, puzzle, fr-tray; Whitman, 1966, Headbusters in Spanish, Batcave scene, 11x14", NM, A $35.00

Batman, record, Power Records, 33⅓ rpm, M, E3 ....$15.00

Batman, record, Warner Brothers, theme song, 45 rpm, plain brn paper sleeve, 1966, M, T2 ....$8.00

Batman, Riddler figure, Kenner, Animated series, MOC, D4 .$10.00

Batman, Riddler figure, Toy Biz, 1989, MOC, F1 ....$15.00

Batman, rings, store display, 24 plastic figures w/extended capes, Linda/NPPI, 1966, 15x8", NM (EX card), A $226.00

Batman, Robin figure, Batman Returns series, MOC, D8 ..$10.00

Batman, Robin figure, China, plastic, 1993, 10", MOC, T1 ..$10.00

Batman, Robin figure, Jetfoil, Kenner, MIP, E3 ....$10.00

Batman, Robin figure, Mego, 1973, 8", VG (G- box), T1 .$75.00

Batman, Special Decoder, paper, for Riddler cards, w/hard plastic holder, NM, C1 ....$21.00

Batman, standee, cb display figure from 1st movie, 60", EX, H4 ....$70.00

Batman, Stunt Cycle, 1974, MOC, V1 ....$65.00

Batman, sunglasses, Nasta, 1984, MOC $10.00

Batman, temporary tattoo transfer, Coca-Cola/Hong Kong, premium, 1992, M, F1 ....$10.00

Batman, troll, National Periodical, 7", EX+, A $100.00

Batman & Robin, book, coloring; Whitman, 1966, M $30.00

Batman & Robin, game, Batman & Robin Skill Game, Hasbro, missing marble, 1966, orig 12x12" box, EX+, A $90.00

Batman & Robin, game, Shooting Arcade, Marx, plastic pistol inserted into clear plastic housing, 1966, NMIB, A .$240.00

Batman & Robin Board Game, Hasbro, 1965, EX, $25.00.

Batman & Robin, mask, cb, dbl-sided, 1966, NM, T1 ......$15.00

Batman & Robin, valentine, 1966, VG, T1 ....$10.00

Batman & Superman, cake pan set, 1977, VG (VG box), N2 ....$35.00

Batman & Superman, game, Super Powers 3-D, Parker Bros, 1984, MIB (sealed), C1 ....$36.00

Batman vs Joker, banner, wht coarse cloth w/wood rod for hanging, 1966, 17x29", NM, A $200.00

Batman vs Penguin, banner, wht coarse fabric w/wood rod for hanging, 1966, 17x29", NM, A $150.00

Battlestar Galactica, Adama figure, Mattel, 1978, 4", M (NM card), C1 ....$27.00

Battlestar Galactica, book, activity; Space Flight, 1978, EX, T6 ....$4.00

Battlestar Galactica, collector cards, Wonder Bread, 1978, 36 cards, complete, M1 ....$6.50

Battlestar Galactica, Colonial Stellar Probe, w/2" figure & laser, 1978, MIB, C1 ....$54.00

Battlestar Galactica, Cylon Raider, Mattel, missing pilot, 12 firing missiles, VG, P4 ....$20.00

Battlestar Galactica, Daggit figure, Mattel, 1978, M (NM card), C1 ....$13.50

Battlestar Galactica, game, Colonial Scarab #2534, Mattel, complete, non-firing missiles, 1978, NMIB, P4 ....$35.00

Battlestar Galactica, game, Colonial Stellar Probe #2533, Mattel, complete, 1978, NMIB, P4 ....$65.00

Battlestar Galactica, gum card set, Topps, 1978, 132 cards w/22 stickers, complete, M1 ....$35.00

Battlestar Galactica Cylon Raider, Mattel, MIB, $35.00.

Battlestar Galactica, Imperious Leader figure, Mattel, 1978, 3¾", MOC $15.00

Battlestar Galactica, Medic Kit, Mattel, MOC, F1 ....$10.00

Battlestar Galactica, Ovion figure, Mattel, 1978, MOC, H4..$18.00

Battlestar Galactica, puzzle, Viper Launch, Parker Bros, 140-pc, 1978, 14x18", EX, T6 ....$20.00

Battlestar Galactica, record album, MCA #3051, orig soundtrack, 1978, EX (EX cover), T6..................................$15.00

Battlestar Galactica, tablecloth, paper, MIP, D4.................$3.00

Battora, figure, Bandai, winged, lg, MIP, E3 ....$50.00

Battora Larva, figure, Bandai, vinyl, MIP, E3.....................$25.00

BC, Grog key chain, Field Ent/Curtis, Grog the World's 1st 4-Letter Man or Down w/Hate, 1976, 1¾", VG, P4........$6.00

Beany, book, activity; Time for Beany, 1953, EX, T6.......$35.00

Beany & Cecil, Dishonest John hand puppet, talker, working, NM..$110.00

Beany & Cecil, game, Jumping DJ, Mattel, 1950, NM (EX box)..$69.00

Beany & Cecil, guitar, w/up to play, 1961, EX..................$40.00

Beany & Cecil, hand puppet, cloth w/pull-string talking mechanism, working, 1960, 10", VG, P4 ....$65.00

Beany & Cecil, Official Beany Copter, Mattel, 1961, MOC, H4 ....$120.00

Beany & Cecil, tea set, service for 4, 1950s, MOC, V1 ....$70.00

Beatles, balloon, 1964, orig pkg (sealed), R2 ....$75.00

Beatles, banjo, Mastro, plastic, shows faces of the Beatles w/fascimile signatures, scarce, 22" L, EX+, A $800.00

Beatles, beach bag, cloth w/vinyl lining, red, bl & cream w/rope drawstring, Beatles & Yeh, Yeh, Yeh, VG, B3.........$219.00

Beatles, beach hat, bl & wht material w/blk faces & autographs, NM, B3 ....$119.00

Beatles, beach towel, Cannon, 1964, few sm brn spots, EX.$160.00

Beatles, bicycle seat, Persons, Yellow Submarine graphics on vinyl, 1968, unused, NM-M, A $300.00

Beatles, birthday card, color photo of group on orange background, EX $25.00

Beatles, birthday card, unfolds to 25x28" poster, split bottom margin/tear mks in corners, G, R2 ....$25.00

Beatles, blanket, United Kingdom, tan w/red & blk photos, instruments & names, EX, B3 ....$289.00

Beatles, book, coloring; 1964, used, EX.............................$70.00

Beatles, book, John Lennon Story, by Swenson, paperback, VG+, B3..$5.00

Beatles, book, Love Letters to the Beatles, by Bill Adler, hardcover, w/dust jacket, 1964, VG+, B3....................$21.00

Beatles, book, Original Beatles Book, 70 pgs, 1964, EX....$25.00

Beatles, book, Out of the Mouths of Beatles, Dell, paperback, 1964, VG+, B3...$20.00

Beatles, book, punch-out; King Features, Yellow Submarine Pop-Up Art Decorations, unused, 1968, M $30.00

Beatles, booklet, fan club; 1971, gr cover, 20 pgs, 8½x11", B3..$18.00

Beatles, bracelet, blk & wht ceramic photo w/She Loves You on brass bk, group photo & song titles on orig card, VG, R2..........$75.00

Beatles, brunch bag, Aladdin/Nems, zippered vinyl case w/group pictured on front, 1965, 8", NM...............................$400.00

Beatles, calendar, 1964, group photo w/some history on ea member below, March pg, 11x15", VG+ $125.00

Beatles, calendar, 1970, Yoko Ono & John on cover, NM.$15.00

Beatles, cap, Ringo, blk leather, VG, R2 ....$125.00

Beatles Carrying Case, AirFlite, vinyl with plastic handle, M, $700.00.

Beatles, coloring set, Kit Fix, United Kingdom, includes 6 colored pencils & 5 pictures, 1964, rare, B3 ....$749.00

Beatles, concert book, 1966, VG, R2 ....$40.00

Beatles, cup, Washington Pottery, United Kingdom, fired-on bl, blk & gray group photo & names, EX, B3.................$119.00

Beatles, Disk-Go record case, pk, NM.............................$95.00

Beatles, doll, Remco, John w/instrument, VG, R2 ....$120.00

Beatles, doll, Remco, Paul w/instrument, VG, R2 ....$75.00

Beatles, doll, Remco, Ringo w/instrument, VG+, R2 ....$75.00

Beatles, doll, Ringo, Remco, NMIB $150.00

Beatles, doll, Rosebud, England, Remco look-alike, w/red guitar mk Rosebud, 1964, 7".................$125.00

Beatles, drum set, Ringo Star, Selcol, drum (14" dia), w/stand & drumsticks, orig box, VG-EX, A $475.00

Beatles, flicker ring, silver, set of 4, NM $70.00

Beatles, game, Flip Your Wig, complete, EX (EX box)...$150.00

Beatles, guitar, Mastro, red & pk plastic 4-string w/faces & autographs, 21" L, NM, A $285.00

Beatles, gum cards, Diary series, #1-60, complete, EX, B3 .$95.00

Beatles, gum cards, Donruss, Sergeant Pepper's Lonely Heart Club Band, set of 66, complete, 1978, M1 ....$12.00

Beatles, gum cards, Paul McCartney & Wings, tour, set of 6, M1.................$15.00

Beatles, gumball sticker, faces & autographs in blk & gold, orig gumball capsule, 1x2", EX, B3.................$24.00

Beatles, hair bow, Burlington, bl, VG (sealed on card), R2.$275.00

Beatles, headband, Better Wear, bl, has musical notes & says Love The Beatles, orig pkg (sealed), R2.................$35.00

Beatles, headband, Better Wear, wht, blk, pk or tan, has musical notes & Love the Beatles, orig package (sealed), R2, ea.................$50.00

Beatles Kaboodle Kit, Standard Plastic Products/Nems, vinyl with black plastic handle, 7x9½", EX, A, $875.00.

Beatles, key chain, John Lennon, photo on side, promotional item for record, M.................$7.00

Beatles, key chain, Yellow Submarine, 6x2½", EX, set of 4..$65.00

Beatles, lobby card, Hard Day's Night, M $75.00

Beatles, magazine, Life, Paul w/family on cover, November 7, 1969, EX, N2 ....$10.00

Beatles, necklace, gold-plated record disk w/blk & wht group photo on gold chain, B3 ....$69.00

Beatles, notebook, Japan, LP photo on front, record on bk, 1969, unused, 8½x8", B3 ....$89.00

Beatles, notebook, Vernon Royal, spiral-bound, lined paper, 7½x5", unused, NM, B3 ....$129.00

Beatles, notebook, Westab, spiral-bound, Beatles doorway on front, 8½" paper, EX, B3.................$59.00

Beatles, Paint-By-Number Set; color photo insert of Ringo, brushes, pnts, alcohol bottle & instructions, VG+, B3...............$669.00

Beatles, pencil case, Standard Plastic Products, bl vinyl w/group & facsimile signatures, zippered, 3½x8", EX, A.......$120.00

Beatles Pillow, Nordic House, 1960s, EX, $169.00.

Beatles, pin, ceramic photo disk w/autograph on metal bk, 1¾", VG, R2 ....$50.00

Beatles, poster, Dell #1, 1964, 18x52", VG+, R2 ....$35.00

Beatles, poster, Paul, life-sz, 1964, EX $50.00

Beatles, poster, shows solo & group LPs, 1975, VG, R2 ....$15.00

Beatles, poster, Yellow Submarine, 3-sheet, EX, T1 ....$450.00

Beatles, punch-out portraits, Whitman, unused, VG+, R2 ....$150.00

Beatles, purse, Canadian, silky material w/gold metal clasp, colorful picture of John Lennon, 1970s, B3 ....$33.00

Beatles, puzzle, Beatles in Pepperland, over 650 pcs, complete, EX (EX box), B3 ....$149.00

Beatles, puzzle, Sea of Monsters, missing 2 pcs, o/w EX (G-box), R2 ....$25.00

Beatles, puzzle, Sea of Monsters, over 100 pcs, B3, NMIB (sealed) $184.00

Beatles, puzzle, United Kingdom, Beatles on stage, 340-pc, 11x17", EX (EX box), B3 ....$269.00

Beatles, record, Ebony & Ivory, 45 rpm, Paul McCartney, unused w/picture sleeve, NM, B3 ....$10.00

Beatles, record, Say Say Say, 45 rpm, Paul McCartney, unused w/picture sleeve, NM, B3 ....$10.00

Beatles, record, Woman, 45rpm, John Lennon, unused w/picture sleeve, NM, B3.................$10.00

Beatles, scarf, silky wht w/fringe, colorful photos, instruments, records, etc, NM, B3.................$42.00

Beatles, scrapbook, The Beatles, Whitman, 1964, 11½x14", NM.................$55.00

Beatles, sheet music songbook, Hard Day's Night, 12 songs, 1964, EX $12.00

Beatles, stickpin or cake decoration, plastic heart shape flasher-type, gr or purple, VG $15.00

Beatles, sunglasses, Solarex, blk plastic wraparound style w/gr lenses, stickers w/2 Beatles in ea corner, NM $250.00

Beatles Tennis Shoes, Wing Dings, MIB, $500.00.

Beatles, ticket stub, 1966, NM $75.00

Beatles, tote bag, Wako Plastics, blk & wht head shots w/illus bodies, facsimile signatures, 1960s, 13x14", NM, A .$160.00

Beatles, tray, serving; Worchester Ware, 1960s, EX, J2 ....$55.00

Beatles, tumbler, Australian, wht plastic w/group photo under clear seal, We Love the Beatles on seam, B3 ....$224.00

Beatles, tumbler, clear glass w/starbursts $150.00

Beatles, tumbler, color photo on glass, w/insulated coating around middle, VG+ $150.00

Beatles, tumbler, Paul, clear glass w/red & blk pnt, VG+, R2 ....$100.00

Beatles, tumbler, Paul, United Kingdom, clear glass w/full-color decal & gold rim, 4", EX, B3 ....$154.00

Beatles, wig, orig pkg w/header card, VG+, R2 ....$75.00

Beauty & the Beast, cookie jar, Treasure Craft, pnt ceramic Mrs Potts, 10", MIB $50.00

Beauty & the Beast, figures, Applause, PVC, Beast & 5 different Belles, MIB, F1 ....$20.00

Beauty & the Beast, gum card set, Pro Set, 1992, 75 cards w/10 stickers, complete, M1 ....$18.00

Beauty & the Beast (TV show), doorknob hanger w/Shakespeare quote & Do Not Disturb, 1988, EX, T6 ....$5.00

Bee Gees, book, 1979 Tour, 24 pgs, NM $15.00

Beetle Bailey, bendee, 1960s, 2½", EX $7.00

Beetle Bailey, puzzle, sliding tile; Roalex, 1960s, NMOC..$25.00

Beetlejuice, Adam Maitland figure, Kenner, MIP............$15.00

Beetlejuice, Exploding or Shipwreck figure, Kenner, 1989, MOC, F1, ea $10.00

Beetlejuice, Gross-Out Meter, Kenner, MIP, E3 ....$10.00

Beetlejuice, Harry figure, Kenner, MIP, E3 ....$8.00

Beetlejuice, Hungry Hog, Street Rat, or Teacher Creature, MIP, E3, ea $15.00

Beetlejuice, Old Buzzard figure, Kenner, MIP, E3 ....$15.00

Beetlejuice, Showtime or Spinhead figure, Kenner, MIP, E3, ea $5.00

Beetlejuice, Teacher Creature figure, Kenner, 1989, MOC, F1 ....$20.00

Beetlejuice, Vanishing Vault, Kenner, MIP, E3 ....$8.00

Bemler, figure, Bandai, vinyl, MIP, E3 ....$10.00

Ben Casey, diary, w/lock, 1962, NM $15.00

Ben Casey, game, board; Transogram, 1961, NM (EX box) from $25 to $40.00

Ben-Hur, book, coloring; Sampson Lowe, 1959, M $45.00

Benji, game, board; VG $15.00

Berenstain Bears, gum card set, 1992, 72 cards, complete, M, M1 ....$15.00

Bernard & Bianca, gum card set, Panini, 360 cards, complete, M1 ....$35.00

Betty Boop, bank, tin truck, 1988, MIB, T1 ....$17.50

Betty Boop, bendee, NJ Croce, 1988, 7½", M, from $7 to .$12.00

Betty Boop, Bimbo doll, compo w/rpt & crazing, good appearance, NM decal, 9", A...$200.00

Betty Boop, Bimbo figure, pnt bsk, w/accordion, Fleischer Studios, 3½", EX+, A...$70.00

Betty Boop, Christmas tree light, figural, pnt glass, Japan, 1930s, 2½", EX, A...$61.00

Betty Boop, delivery truck, Schylling Inc, Collector series, 1990, MIB, H4..$35.00

Betty Boop Doll, jointed wood and composition, Fleischer, ca 1935, EX+, $600.00.

Betty Boop, doll, jtd wood & compo figure in strapless dress, orig tag, minor crazing, 12", EX, A.................................$500.00

Betty Boop, doll, M-Toy, jtd vinyl in Mae West-type pk gown, 1986, 12", MIB, H4...$22.00

Betty Boop, doll, M-Toy, vinyl, wearing fur coat, 1986, 12", MIB, H4...$22.00

Betty Boop, doll, USA, jtd wood, ca 1932, 4½", EX, A..$120.00

Betty Boop, fan, pnt oval w/stick hdl, lg twirling eyes, 12", EX, A..$130.00

Betty Boop, Felix, Mickey & Minnie, stroller, PICO Y CIA, Spain (no logo), whiskered Mickey, Felix ea corner, 11", NM, A...$1,200.00

Betty Boop, figure, pnt bsk, w/French horn, sgn Fleischer Studios, prewar Japan, 3½", EX, A.................................$85.00

Betty Boop, figure, PVC, any of 8 different poses & outfits, 3",
MOC, H4 ....$4.00

Betty Boop, figures, Betty, Bimbo & Koko, bsk, 1930s, ea figure
approximately 3", EX (VG box), A $387.00

Betty Boop, outfit, M-Toy, High Fashion Boutique, for 12" doll,
1986, MOC, H4 ....$8.00

Betty Boop, paper dolls, Goes to Hollywood, mk KFS/BS Ltd,
cut & punch doll+5 outfits, 1984, M, P4 ....$5.00

Betty Boop, quilt, her image in center, name to right, early, very
clean, 16x12", A...$150.00

Beverly Hillbillies Coloring Book, Whitman #1137, EX, $25.00.

Betty Boop String Holder, painted plaster, ca 1920s, 10" across, M, $135.00.

Betty Boop, tambourine, Japan, litho tin featuring dancing Betty
surrounded by musical notes, 1950s, 6" dia, EX+, A..$345.00

Betty Boop, truck, Schylling, litho tin, collector series, 1990,
MIB, H4..$35.00

Betty Boop & Bimbo, ashtray, lustreware, mk FS Japan, scarce,
4½x3x3", NM, A $90.00

Beverly Hillbillies, book, coloring; Watkins, 1964, EX $30.00

Beverly Hillbillies, book, coloring; Whitman, 128 pgs, 1963, EX+,
A $30.00

Beverly Hillbillies, book, Sage of Wildcat Creek, Whitman,
hardcover, 1963, EX $12.00

Beverly Hillbillies, book, Whitman TV Book, 1963, NM,
C1 ....$22.00

Beverly Hillbillies, fan club postcard, features cast & facsimile
signatures, 1963, 3x5", unused, M, T2 ....$15.00

Beverly Hillbillies, game, card; Set Back, Milton Bradley, 1963,
NMIB, C1 ....$25.00

Beverly Hillbillies, game, Standard Toycraft, 1963, EX+,
F3 ....$45.00

Beverly Hillbillies, puzzle, fr-tray; Jaymar, car scene, 1963,
M...$30.00

Beverly Hillbillies, puzzle, fr-tray; Jaymar, Ellie May, 1963,
M...$25.00

Beverly Hills 90210, gum card set, Topps, 1991, 77 cards w/11
stickers, complete, M1 ....$17.50

Bewitched, book, activity; 1965, EX+, T6 ....$25.00

Bewitched, game, board; Game Gems, 1960s, EX............$45.00

Bewitched, game, card; Stymie, 1964, NMIB, C1............$69.00

Bewitched, sheet music, 1964, V1 ....$20.00

Bewitched, tablet, color cast photo, 1960s, unused, M, from $15
to $29.00

Big Bad Wolf Doll, Ross, with tag, rare, 14", M, D10, $2,500.00.

Big Bad Wolf, figure, bsk, 1¾", EX, P6...........................$100.00

Big Bird, Big Bird's Mystery Bank, 1970s, VG+, T1............$8.00

Big Jim, Action Set #7390, 1970s, MOC, T1......................$5.00

Big Jim, Adventure Gear #7435, 1970s, MIP, T1 ....$5.00

Big Jim, Agent 004 figure, Big Jim/James Bond series, w/6 interchangeable faces & disguises, NRFB, H4 ....$60.00

Big Jim, Air Ace figure, Space series (last), NRFB, H4 ....$70.00

Big Jim, all-terrain vehicle, Space series, NRFB, H4 ....$39.00

Big Jim, Astros figure, Team Global Command & Team Condor Force series, NRFB, H4...$70.00

Big Jim, Barron Fangg figure, Team Global Command & Team Condor Force series, NRFB, H4 ....$70.00

Big Jim, Camper Gear #8868, 1970s, MOC, T1.................$7.50

Big Jim, Camping Tent Set, NMIB $30.00

Big Jim, Captain Laser figure, Space series (last series), NRFB, H4...$99.00

Big Jim, Commander figure, Team Global Command & Team Condor Force, basic figure only, NRFB, H4..............$40.00

Big Jim, Commander figure, Team Global Command & Team Condor Force series, deluxe version, NRFB, H4........$70.00

Big Jim, Commando Jeff figure, Big Jim/James Bond series, NRFB, H4 ....$70.00

Big Jim, Corvette, Big Jim/004 Secret Agent series, w/remote control, NRFB, H4 ....$99.00

Big Jim, Dr. Alec figure, Jungle Team Leader, 1984, MIB, $80.00.

Big Jim, Explorer figure, Team Global Command & Team Condor Force series, NRFB, H4 ....$45.00

Big Jim, figure, basic version, orig red shorts, loose, H4....$16.00

Big Jim, figure, basic version in motorcycle outfit, complete w/accessories, loose, H4 ....$20.00

Big Jim, figure, Mattel, 1971, M (NM box), H4 ....$38.00

Big Jim, Frescia Rugiada (female Indian) figure, Big Jim Western series, NRFB, H4 ....$90.00

Big Jim, Gyrocopter, Big Jim/004 Secret Agent series, NRFB, H4...$18.00

Big Jim, Kung Fu Studio, NMIB...................................$45.00

Big Jim, outfit, Attack Vehicle Driver, NRFB, H4 ....$12.00

Big Jim, outfit, Basketball #8854, Adventure series, MOC, from $5 to...$10.00

Big Jim, outfit, Communications Agent, NRFB, H4 ....$12.00

Big Jim, outfit, Demolition Expert, NRFB, H4 ....$10.00

Big Jim, outfit, Equestrian #9922, complete, MIB, H4 .....$15.00

Big Jim, outfit, Grand Prix Jockey #9491, complete, MIB, H4 ....$15.00

Big Jim, outfit, Headquarters Commander, Team Global Command & Team Condor Force series, MIB, H4 ....$20.00

Big Jim, outfit, Paramedic, NRFB, H4...........................$10.00

Big Jim, outfit, Scuba Diving #8855, Action series, MOC, from $5 to $10.00

Big Jim, playset, Devil River Trip, 1970s, MIB, T1 ....$35.00

Big Jim, Professor Obb Overlord figure, Team Global Command & Team Condor Force series, in Kendo outfit, NRFB, H4...$40.00

Big Jim, Professor Obb Overlord figure, Team Global Command & Team Condor Force, deluxe version, NRFB, H4...$70.00

Big Jim, Secret Agent figure, Big Jim/James Bond series, in karate outfit, NRFB, H4 ....$50.00

Big Jim, Special Agent figure, Big Jim/James Bond series, w/reversible outfit, NRFB, H4.............................$60.00

Big Jim, Sports Camper Van, NMIB $45.00

Big Jim, Sports Camper Van, VG, H4.............................$10.00

Big Jim, US Olympic Basketball #7343, 1970s, MOC, T1 .$5.00

Big Jim, Vector figure, Team Global Command & Team Condor Force series, NRFB, H4...$70.00

Big Valley, book, Whitman, 210-pg hardback w/illus, & color cover, 1966, 5x8", EX, T2...$15.00

Big Valley, Lee Majors exhibit card, 1966, blk & wht photo, 3½x5", in plastic holder, NM, C1 ....$15.00

Bigfoot, The Giant Snow Monster, Milton Bradley, lg plastic Bigfoot w/secret footprints, 1977, 10x20" box, EX, T2......$20.00

Bill & Ted's Excellent Adventure, Bill or Ted figure, Kenner, 1991, MOC, F1, ea $10.00

Bill & Ted's Excellent Adventure, Grim Reaper figure, Kenner, 1991, 3¾", MOC (sealed)..$20.00

Bill & Ted's Excellent Adventure, gum card set, Pro Set, 1991, 140 cards, complete, M1..$15.00

Bill & Ted's Excellent Adventure, Wyld Stallions Jam Session 2, w/tape & speaker, MIB, D4 ....$10.00

Bill Cosby, record, Wonderfulness, Warner Bros, EX-, P3..$5.00

Bing Crosby, game, board; Call Me Lucky, complete, orig box, VG+, M5...$70.00

Bionic Six, Dr Scarab figure, LJN, 1986, MOC, J4 ....$8.00

Bionic Six, Helen figure, LJN, 1986, MOC, J4 ....$6.00

Bionic Six, Madame O figure, LJN, 1986, J4.....................$6.00

Bionic Six, Meg figure, LJN, 1986, MOC, J4 ....$6.00

Bionic Woman, book, Fun & Activity, Grosset & Dunlap, 1976, unused, 1976, NM, C1...$18.00

Bionic Woman, Fembot figure, Kenner, MIB, H4 ....$50.00

Bionic Woman, game, Parker Bros, features Jamie Summers, 9x19", MIB, from $20 to...$35.00

Bionic Woman, outfit, Floral Delight, 1970s, MOC, T1 ....$6.00

Bionic Woman, tattoos & stickers, Kenner, 1 sheet of 8 stickers & 1 sheet of 28 tattoos, 1976, M (NM card), D9.........$5.00

Black Beauty, game, Transogram, 1953, VG, F3...............$22.00

Black Hole, figure, Mego, Harry Booth, Dr McRae, or Dr Reinhardt, 1979, 3¾", M, C1, any.....................................$18.50

Black Hole, gum card set, Topps, 1979, 88 cards w/22 stickers, complete, M1...$12.00

Black Hole, puzzle, fr-tray; Whitman, 1979, NM, D9.........$6.00

Black Hole, record, orig movie soundtrack, M, F1............$10.00

Blackstar, figure, Galoob, w/laser light action, 1983, MOC, H4..$10.00

Blackstar, Kadray or Tongo figure, Galoob, 1983, MOC (opened & damaged card), H4...$7.00

Blackstar, spaceship, Galoob, 1983, MIB, H4...................$20.00

Blondie, Beetle Bailey, Hi & Lois, & Popeye Comic Character Card Game, Milton Bradley, 1972, lg box, EX-NM, C1..$36.00

Blondie, doll stroller, Nassau, litho tin, mc comic figures, lt pnt chips, 16", G, A...$60.00

Blondie, game, board; Sunday Funnies, Ideal, 1972, MIB, C1..$19.50

Blondie, game, Goes to Leisureland, Westinghouse, promotional item, 1940, MIP...$45.00

Blondie, game, skill; litho tin & glass, 3x4", EX, P6.........$50.00

Blondie, puzzle, jigsaw; Dagwood's in Trouble, Jaymar, 100-pc, 1960, in 8x10" box, NM, T2.................................$22.00

Blondie & Dagwood, game, Transogram, 1966, NMIB $65.00

Blues Brothers, poster, orig, M...................................$65.00

Bluto, wall hanging, emb tile, full color, 4⅛x3", M, P6....$35.00

Bob Dylan, sheet music songbook, 12 songs, 1966, VG+, T6..$25.00

Bob Newhart, record album, stand-up comedy monologue, 33⅓ rpm, 1960s, EX, T2...$10.00

Bobby Darin, iron-on patch, Picture Patches, c 1960, 3x3", MIP..$35.00

Bobo Bones, Mummy Accessory Kit, Topper, 1960s, MIB, C1..$81.00

Bonanza, book, coloring; Artcraft, 1960, EX....................$27.50

Bonanza, book, softcover, 1959, EX $25.00

Bonanza, cup, litho metal w/Ponderosa ranch house & characters, NM, T6..$9.00

Bonanza, cup, litho tin, early issue features Adam, Ponderosa on bk, 1960s, 3½" dia, EX, T2.......................................$30.00

Bonanza, doll, American Character, Hoss, vinyl, fully jtd, 8", EX (NM box), A...$145.00

Bonanza, doll, American Character, Little Joe, 8", NM, J2.$160.00

Bonanza, game, Rummy, Parker Bros, EX, F3 ....$35.00

Bonanza, horse, American Character, blk & wht w/saddle, for 9" figure, VG, H4...$30.00

Bonanza, soundtrack, Ponderosa Party Time, 1962, EX ...$30.00

Bonanza, record album, RCA #2843, Welcome to the Ponderosa, 33⅓ rpm, 1964, EX (EX jacket cover), T6.....$45.00

Bonanza, wagon w/2 figures, Marx, 1950s, VG+, T1......$125.00

Bonanza, writing tablet, early, unused, M, J2.....................$24.00

Bonanza, 4-in-1 wagon w/doll, American Character, EX, J2..$290.00

Boo-Boo from Huckleberry Hound, hand puppet, German, orig sticker, 13", NM, M5..$15.00

Boris & Natasha, doorknob hanger, I Need Someone Real Bad, Are You Real Bad?, 1987, 9½x4", EX-NM, T6...........$7.00

Boris Badinoff, bendee, Wham-O, 1960s, used, T1 ....$10.00

Boy Scout, figure, Kenner, Negro, 1974, MIB, H4...........$39.00

Bozo the Clown, balloon vending machine, litho steel, missing key, rare, EX+, T1 ....$265.00

Bozo the Clown, bank, composition, 1960s, D10, $85.00.

Bozo the Clown, bendee, Jesco, 6", K1 ....$3.95

Bozo the Clown, bendee, Knickerbocker, 1960s, MIP, T1..$50.00

Bozo the Clown, book, punch-out; Whitman, 1966, 8x12", M (EX+ cover), T2...$18.00

Bozo the Clown, book, sticker; Safari, Whitman, 8x12", some pgs stuck together (EX+ cover), T2.............................$6.00

Bozo the Clown Circus Train, Multiple Toymakers, ca 1970, MIB, $70.00.

Bozo the Clown, Bop-It, 36", M (G-VG pkg), O1 ....$85.00

Bozo the Clown, game, board; World's Most Famous Clown, Parker Bros, 1967, complete in orig box, EX, P6 ....$35.00

Bozo the Clown, game, cards; Ed-U-Cards, 1972, in 3x4" illus box, NM, T2 ....$12.00

Bozo the Clown, membership card & patch, sew-on cloth, bottom of pkg is membership card, 1970s, MOC, P4 ....$6.00

Bozo the Clown, pocket watch, Larry Harmon, plastic, tin & paper, non-working toy, 1960s, MIP, P4 ....$6.00

Bozo the Clown, puppet, talker, working, EX, O1 ....$45.00

Bozo the Clown, record, Bozo at the Circus, 78 rpm, 1950, EX $25.00

Bozo the Clown, record, I Like People & others, Little Golden, 45 rpm in 7x8" stiff paper sleeve, 1960, EX+, T2.......$15.00

Bozo the Clown, Spinikin, Kohner, Bozo on unicycle, plastic w/pnt features, pull string for action, 1960s, 4", NM, A..$17.00

Bozo the Clown, tablecloth, paper w/circus illus, orig pkg, 1950, 50x102", unused, T2 ....$30.00

Bozo the Clown, ukelele, wood w/color illus, VG+, T6....$50.00

Brady Bunch, Chess & Checkers, Larami, NMIB.............$57.50

Brady Bunch, soundtrack, Meet the Brady Bunch, 1972, EX $30.00

Branded, game, board; Milton Bradley, 1950s, G..............$25.00

Branded, game, board; Milton Bradley, 1966, MIB (sealed), A .$55.00

Branded, magazine, TV Times w/Chuck Connors, 1965, V1.$12.50

Branded, TV Guide, October 23, 1965, Chuck Conners Today, NM, C1 ....$17.50

Braniac, figure, Kenner, Super Powers, MOC (creased), F1.$25.00

Branson on Stage, gum card set, Hit Cards, 1992, country & western, 100 cards, complete, M1 ....$18.00

Bravestarr, Skull Walker figure, MIB, D4........................$8.00

Brownies, Brownie Artillery, 26 litho-on-wood people, stands, wheeled cannon & 3 balls, 10x12", EX, A $1,300.00

Brownies, Brownie Blocks, McLoughlin, litho blocks in wooden box, G color cover, 13½x11", A $985.00

Brownies, candle holder, majolica Uncle Sam, scarce, 7", NM, VG $325.00

Brownies, game, 9 figures, made to be knocked down, litho paper on wood base, c 1892, ea 12½", all but 1 is EX, A...$425.00

Bruce Lee, blk light poster, Pro Arts, collage of Enter the Dragon graphics, 1974, 21x32", EX+, A $25.00

Bruce Lee, figure, Largo, Legend of Bruce Lee, mk Deluxe Mechanized w/Action, Martial Arts Action, rare, MIB, F1.$40.00

Bruce Lee, gum card set, NGP, 12 cards, complete, M1 ...$25.00

Buccaneers, game, Transogram, from CBS TV game show, 1957, 8x16", VG (VG box)...$75.00

Buck Rogers, Ardella figure, Mego, 1979, 3¾", MOC, H4 .$15.00

Buck Rogers, badge, Solar Scouts Member Badge, Cream of Wheat premium, gold finish, appears rpr, 1935-36, VG, P4 ....$90.00

Buck Rogers, binoculars, Buck Rogers Space Glasses, Norton-Honer, 1950s, orig box missing top cover, EX, A $110.00

Buck Rogers, book, Buck Rogers in the 25th Century, Kellogg's, mc cover & illus, 1933, EX, A $100.00

Buck Rogers, book, paint; Whitman, 1935, VG-EX, A..$120.00

Buck Rogers, book, pop-up; Pleasure Books, 1935, binding frayed at bottom/cover soiled, VG, A............................$251.00

Brownie Tower, Palmer Cox, D10, $850.00.

Buck Rogers, book, pop-up; Strange Adventures in the Spider-Ship, 1935, G, A $170.00

Buck Rogers, card & sticker set, Topps, 1979, NMOC, C1 ....$15.00

Buck Rogers, Colorforms Adventure Set, 1979, MIB, C1 .$18.00

Buck Rogers, Communications Set, HG, complete except for code wheel, 1979, MIB (resealed), C1 ....$39.00

Buck Rogers, crayons, Dille, illus box mk School Crayons, 1936, ea crayon 5" L, complete in orig box, EX, A..............$96.00

Buck Rogers, Draco or Killer Kane figure, Mego, 1979, 3¾", MOC, ea $14.00

Buck Rogers, Flying Saucer, 2 rnd litho cb sections connected w/wire rim, 6" dia, NM, A...$86.00

Buck Rogers, game, Battle for the 25th Century, TSR, MIB (sealed), D4..$15.00

Buck Rogers, game, board; Game of the 25th Century, Lutz & Sheinkman, 1935, wooden pcs missing, scarce, orig box, EX, A...$601.00

Buck Rogers, game, board; Transogram, w/diecut figures, complete, 17½", EX, A..$40.00

Buck Rogers, gum card set, Topps, 1979, 88 cards w/22 stickers, complete, M1 ....$18.00

Buck Rogers, gun, Adventures in 25th Century, Transogram, 1960s, M (NM box), C1 ....$63.00

Buck Rogers, gun, Atomic Pistol & Holster Set, Daisy, 10" metal pop gun sparks, book & instruction tag, NM (EX box), A..$1,500.00

Buck Rogers, gun, Atomic Pistol U-235, Daisy, pressed steel, sounds & flashes, 1946, 9½", VG, P4........................$225.00

Buck Rogers, gun, Rocket Pistol Pop Gun, Daisy, pressed steel, mid-1930s, 9½", VG, P4...$185.00

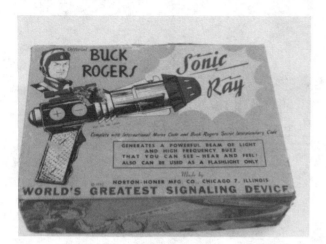

Buck Rogers Sonic Ray Gun, Norton-Honer, original box, M, A, $450.00.

Buck Rogers, gun, Super Sonic Ray, Norton-Honer, plastic, compass ea side, battery-op, 1955, 8", EX (VG box), A $162.00

Buck Rogers, gun, 25th Century, pressed steel pop gun, 1930s, 7½", VG, P4 ....$100.00

Buck Rogers, Killer Kane doll, 1970s, B, T1 ....$85.00

Buck Rogers, Killer Kane figure, Mego, 1980, 3¾", MOC, F1...$10.00

Buck Rogers, magazine ad, 1952, M $20.00

Buck Rogers, pencil box, American Lead Pencil Co, thick cb, gr w/graphics, snap-open, 1936, 10x6", EX+, T2.........$100.00

Buck Rogers, pencil box, American Lead Pencil Co, thick cb, gr w/graphics, 1935, 4x6", EX, T2 ....$80.00

Buck Rogers, pencil box, Dille, features Buck & Wilma flying through space, 1936, 8" L, VG, A $51.00

Buck Rogers, Star Fighter Command Center, Mego, for 3¾" figures, 1979, MIB (sealed), C1 ....$45.00

Buck Rogers, Strato Kite, MIP, T1.................................$100.00

Buck Rogers, Super Sonic Glasses (binoculars), MIB, T1.$125.00

Buck Rogers, Tigerman figure, Mego, 1980, 3¾", M, loose, F1...$5.00

Buck Rogers, Twiki figure, battery-op, 10", EX (orig box missing insert & cellophane window), H4 ....$20.00

Buck Rogers, Twiki figure, Mego, 1979, 3¾", MIP, minimum $8.00

Buck Rogers, walkie-talkies, Remco/Dille, plastic, 1950s, in 8x13" box, NM (EX box), A $175.00

Bucky O'Hare, figure, Hasbro, MIP, from $6 to $10.00

Bucky O Hare, figures, Hasbro, complete set of 10 different figures, M on separate cards, F1 ....$50.00

Buffalo Bill, gloves, w/orig tag, sm, M $40.00

Buffalo Bill, ring, brass, picture of Buffalo Bill, radio premium, 1950s, EX, T1 ....$50.00

Bugs Bunny, candle holder, ceramic, 1970s, NMIB, T1 ...$25.00

Bugs Bunny, Cartoon-O-Graph, NM (VG box), O1........$15.00

Bugs Bunny, doll, Mattel, talker, 1971, 12", NMIB $50.00

Bugs Bunny, doll, Mattel, wht & gray stuffed plush, vinyl face & hands, talker, 1961, 26", EX+ (EX+ box), A $225.00

Bugs Bunny, doll, talker, 25", NMIB, J2 ....$110.00

Bugs Bunny, doll, Warner Bros, cloth body w/mask face, orange collar & ears, 19", G, A $50.00

Bugs Bunny, Ertl, diecast figure in train car, MOC, D4 ......$5.00

Bugs Bunny, figure, ceramic, wearing golfer-type outfit, 1977, sm chip on nose, VG...$25.00

Bugs Bunny, game, Race in Space, Whitman, 1980, complete, EX...$12.00

Bugs Bunny, jack-in-the-box, Mattel, plastic, plays Hail Hail the Gang's All Here, 1978, EX, T6....................................$4.00

Bugs Bunny, napkin, Happy Birthday, 1972, 24 count, MIP, T6..$5.00

Bugs Bunny Pencil Holder, white metal, 1940s, M, D10, $125.00.

Buck Rogers Space Ranger Kit, ca 1952, D10, $175.00.

Bugs Bunny, puzzle, fr-tray; Jaymar, Elmer & other characters in garden scene, 11x14", EX, T2.......................................$30.00

Bugs Bunny, squeeze toy, Oak Rubber, R3 ....$50.00

Bugs Bunny, tablecloth, paper, 1972, 52x96", MIP, T6 ......$5.00

Bugs Bunny & Elmer Fudd, bank, talking, Janex, 1978, EX $85.00

Bugs Bunny & Porky Pig, print, glow-in-the-dark, c Warner Bros, 1940s, orig fr, 10¾x8¼", EX, P6.........................$40.00

Bullwinkle, castanets, Larami/Ward, wood, 1973, MOC, P4...$8.00

Bullwinkle, doll, Gund, Come Dance w/Me, elastic straps on feet, 1970, 36", NM..$135.00

Bullwinkle, figure, Jay Ward, diecast w/wiggle eyes, 1965, 6x5", MIB, P4..$25.00

Bullwinkle, figure, stuffed w/vinyl head, orange bib overalls w/B on chest, 14", EX, H4..$59.00

Bullwinkle, Make Your Badge Set #5845, Larami/Ward, plastic, 1973, MOC, P4...$20.00

Bullwinkle, spelling & counting board, Larami, 1969, NM (EX+ card), D9...$8.00

Bullwinkle, squeeze toy, Jay Ward, R3 ....$200.00

Bullwinkle, Trickie Trapeze, Larami, 1960s, M (EX card), H4..$80.00

Bullwinkle & Friends, bendee, Jesco, Gift Set w/7" Bullwinkle, 5" Rocky, 3½" Boris & 5½" Natasha, 1991, K1 ....$14.95

Bullwinkle & Friends, bendee, Jesco, Mini Gift Set w/3" Bullwinkle, 2½" Rocky, Mr Peabody & Dudly Do Right, K1..$7.95

Bullwinkle & Rocky, Cartoon Mitts, Me Too Sales Corp, w/illus header card, 1960s, 7½", NM (EX pkg), A, pr.........$110.00

Bullwinkle & Rocky, game, Transogram, 1988, complete, EX $20.00

Bullwinkle & Rocky, Towing Set, Lincoln International, 2 vehicles, gas pump & 2 figures, MOC, H4.........................$45.00

Burl Ives, book, Sailing on a Very Fine Day, Rand McNally Elf Book, 1954, VG, T6..$4.00

Buster Brown, sled, oak w/wrought iron strip runners, handles cut in sides of runners, rfn, 24", EX, A.....................$200.00

Buster Brown, yo-yo, litho tin, EX, P6 ....$30.00

Buster Brown & Tige, plate, Germany, Tige w/teapot on his nose, mk Three Crowns, 7", NM, A...........................$70.00

Butch Cassidy & the Sundance Kid, playset, wagon, complete, 1970s, MIB, T1 ....$25.00

Buzz Corry, book coloring: For Space Patroller above line for name, blk & wht, Ralston Purina, 12-pg, 11x8½", NM, A..$40.00

Cabbage Patch Kids, crayons, 1983, MOC..........................$5.00

Cabbage Patch Kids, gum card set, Coleco, astronaut theme, 6 cards, complete w/extras, M1 ....$90.00

Cabbage Patch Kids, gum card set, Coleco, circus theme, set of 6, complete w/extras, scarce, M1................................$60.00

Camelot, game, Parker Bros, 1930, EX, F3.......................$26.00

Candid Camera, magic slate, Lowe, 1963, 8x12" w/wood stylus, M, A...$30.00

Cannonball, figure, Toy Biz, pk, MOC, D8 ....$25.00

Capitol Critters, figure, Steven Bochco/20th Century/Kenner, mc plastic, 1992, MIB, ⅞", P4, any 1 of 6, ea.............$10.00

Captain Action, figure, Ideal, complete, VG $175.00

Captain Action, Ideal, plastic and vinyl, 1966, 12", MIB, from $300.00 to $350.00.

Captain Action, figure, Ideal, lt worn pnt on hair, w/emblem & all orig accessories, EX-NM, O1/H4 ....$220.00

Captain Action, Inter-Galactic Jet Mortar, Ideal, w/tripod, scanner, ammo carrier & missiles, 1967, M (EX+ box), A $259.00

Captain Action, jacket, for Green Hornet Adventure, Super Heroes series, needs snap rpr, lt fading, H4................$75.00

Captain Action, jumpsuit, Steve Canyon, Ideal, EX $15.00

Captain Action, Superman outfit, Super Hero series, complete w/accessories, EX, H4..$120.00

Captain Action, Survival Kit, Ideal, 20-pc, complete, 1967, orig 8x9" window box, M (EX+ box) $375.00

Captain Action, Weapons Arsenal, Ideal, 10-pc mtd on storage rack, 1967, orig 8x9" box, MIB $375.00

Captain Action, Working Parachute, Ideal, full-body harness, pack, crash helmet & jump boots, 1967, 48", M (NM box) $375.00

Captain America, bike plate, Marx, litho tin, 1967, 2x4", M, C1 ....$24.00

Captain America, car, Mego, for 9" figures, 1976, NM.....$58.00

Captain America, Dress-Up Accessory Playset, Toy Biz, MIB, F1..$25.00

Captain America, figure, Marvel Secret Wars series, 4", MOC, C1 ....$18.00

Captain America, figure, Mego, 12", MIB $175.00

Captain America, finger puppet, Imperial, 1978, NM $5.00

Captain America, game, board; Captain American w/Falcon & Avengers, Milton Bradley, 1977, NM (EX- box), T2 .$30.00

Captain America, game, board; Milton Bradley, missing comic, 1966, EX (NM box), C1.................................$36.00

Captain America, game, Thor, Milton Bradley, w/comic book, 1976, MIB, M4.................................$110.00

Captain America, gum card set, Comic Image, 1990, 45 cards, complete, M1.................................$20.00

Captain America, kite, Pressman, 1966, MIP.................$35.00

Captain America, T-shirt, Marvel Comics, wht cotton, mail-order premium only, 1970, child sz, NM, A.................$50.00

Captain Gallant, game, board; 1955, NMIB, C1.............$63.00

Captain Hook, Disneykin, Marx, 1st series, 1960s, in orig box, EX, M8.................................$15.00

Captain Kangaroo, book, Captain Kangaroo's Read-Aloud Book, Random House, 1962, EX, T6.................................$8.00

Captain Kangaroo, book, punch-out; Treasure House, Whitman #1943, unpunched, 1959, NM.................................$95.00

Captain Kangaroo, game, card; Noah's Ark (Old Maid), ca mid-1960s, complete, EX, T6.................................$15.00

Captain Kangaroo, game, Kangadoodles, Hasbro, 1956, M (EX sealed box), C1.................................$41.00

Captain Kangaroo, game, Treasure House, Colorforms, stick-on diecuts, background board, 1961, 12x18" box, unused, NM, T2.................................$50.00

Captain Kangaroo, magic slate, EE Fairchild, w/stylus, old store stock, 1960s, M, H4.................................$8.00

Captain Kangaroo, puzzle, fr-tray; Fairchild, Captain & Mr Green Jeans as king & court jester, 1971, sealed, M, T2.................................$20.00

Captain Kangaroo, TV Eras-O-Board Set, Hasbro, wipe-off slates, eraser & crayons, 1956, 6x9" box, unused, EX+, T2.................................$32.00

Captain Kangaroo, TV Shoebox Activity Kit, Hasbro, toys & crafts, 1956, 12x6x4" box, lt wear/writing, o/w EX+, T2.................................$30.00

Captain Kangaroo & Bunny Rabbit, Presto Slate & Stylus, Keeshan/Fairchild, 1950s, 12x8½", M, P4.................................$6.00

Captain Midnight, mug, plastic, Ovaltine premium, 4¾", $45.00.

Captain Marvel, bank, Captain Marvel's Magic Dime Saver Opens at $5, litho tin, 2⅝", G, A.................................$80.00

Captain Marvel, tie clip, 1946, EX, A.................................$50.00

Captain Midnight, manual & code book, from Ovaltine, 4½x6", NM+, A.................................$135.00

Captain Midnight, membership card, 1955-56, unused, NM, A.................................$70.00

Captain Midnight, mug, Ovaltine promotion w/portrait, red plastic, w/lid, EX.................................$45.00

Captain Midnight, Spinner Membership Token, Skelly premium, brass w/raised design, 1940s, NM, C1.................................$21.00

Captain Midnight, SQ decoder, silver plastic badge w/wht plastic code wheel on reverse, 1955-56, 2" dia, EX+, A.................................$159.00

Captain Planet, Argos Bleak figure, MOC, D4.................................$20.00

Captain Planet, Eco Sub, MIB (Spanish/English on box), F1.................................$30.00

Captain Planet, figure, Applause, 12", MIP, F1.................................$15.00

Captain Planet, figure, in pollution armour or w/color change, MOC, F1, either.................................$20.00

Captain Planet, figure, PVC, complete set of 6, M, F1.................................$20.00

Captain Planet, Geo Cruiser, MIB (Spanish/English on box), F1.................................$25.00

Captain Planet, Sly Sludge figure, MOC, D4.................................$20.00

Captain Planet, Toxic Dump, MIB (Spanish/English on box), F1.................................$15.00

Captain Power, Blastarr Ground Guardian figure, Mattel, 1987, 3¾", MOC, from $6 to.................................$8.00

Captain Power, Communication Station, Mattel, 1987, MIB, J4.................................$16.00

Captain Power, Corporal Pilot Chase figure, Mattel, 1987, 3¾", MOC, J4.................................$12.00

Captain Power, figure, Mattel, 1987, 3¾", MOC, from $5 to.................................$10.00

Captain Power, Interlocker Throne, Mattel, 1987, MIB, J4.................................$9.00

Captain Power, Lord Dread figure, Mattel, 1987, 3¾", MOC, J4.................................$5.00

Captain Power, Major Hawk Masterson figure, Mattel, 1987, 3¾", MOC, J4.................................$6.00

Captain Power, Power-On-Engergizer, Mattel, 1987, MIB, D4.................................$10.00

Captain Power, Sergeant Scout Baker figure, Mattel, 1987, 3¾", MOC, from $10 to.................................$12.00

Captain Power, Soaron Sky Sentry figure, Mattel, 1987, 3¾", MOC, J4.................................$6.00

Car 54 Where Are You?, Muldoon puppet, Allison, 1962, EX.................................$10.00

Car 54 Where Are You?, record album, Golden, Joe E Ross & Fred Gwynne cover, 1963, scarce, EX+, A.................................$58.00

Casper the Friendly Ghost, bank, ceramic w/pnt features, on base holding money sack, mk USA, 1950s, scarce, 9", NM, A.................................$288.00

Casper the Friendly Ghost, bank, pnt ceramic w/lg bag & coin, hairline crack, moderate crazing, 8¼", G, A.................................$120.00

Casper the Friendly Ghost, book, coloring; Ghostly Trio, 1968, EX, T6.................................$2.00

Casper the Friendly Ghost, book, paperback; Search-a-Word, 1975, VG, N2.................................$4.00

Casper the Friendly Ghost, bookend, ceramic, EX, H4 ....$40.00

Casper the Friendly Ghost, doll, soft cloth, w/orig ribbon, 1960s, EX+, T1 ....$65.00

Casper the Friendly Ghost, figure, ceramic, 1960s, 6½", NM, V1 ....$70.00

Casper the Friendly Ghost, figure, Mattel, hard plastic, pull-string talker, 1971, NM-, C1 ....$81.00

Casper the Friendly Ghost, game, Ideal, 1981, EX, T6 ....$7.00

Casper the Friendly Ghost, game, Milton Bradley, complete, 1959, VG+ $15.00

Casper the Friendly Ghost, Glo-Whistle, 1987, M (NM card) $5.00

Casper the Friendly Ghost, pull toy, Casper's Delivery Truck, diecut wood, paper litho, 1962, 9½", NM (EX box), A..$149.00

Casper the Friendly Ghost, pull toy, xylophone, American Pre-School Noma, diecut wood, animated arms, 9x10", G-EX, A...$200.00

Casper the Friendly Ghost, soundtrack, Haunted House Tales, EX..$12.00

Casper the Friendly Ghost, squeeze toy, Knickerbocker, R3 ....$30.00

Casper the Friendly Ghost, standee, ABC/Harvey, heavy cb for store display, 1960, 35x26", EX+, A $200.00

Cat in the Hat, doll, Eden/Dr Seuss, VG $40.00

Cat in the Hat, doll, Mattel/Dr Seuss, cloth w/plastic head, pull-string talker, working, 1970, 10", VG, P4 ....$90.00

Cat in the Hat, hand puppet, Mattel, molded vinyl head on plush body, talker, non-working, 1970, 18", EX, A ...$61.00

Cat in the Hat, jack-in-the-box, Mattel, cloth & plastic, 7", NMIB..$45.00

Cat in the Hat, puzzle, fr-tray; 1985, MIP (sealed), C1 ....$19.50

Charlie Chaplin, bank w/ash barrel, clear & pnt glass, 3¾", G, A...$100.00

Charlie Chaplin, book, coloring; Saalfield, 1930s, 36 pgs, EX+...$150.00

Charlie Chaplin, book, coloring; Saalfield, 1941, nearly all colored, G-VG, A..$40.00

Charlie Chaplin, crib toy, celluloid figure, missing string, 3½", NM, A...$90.00

Charlie Chaplin, figure, compo, 1930s, 6", EX, T1.........$195.00

Charlie Chaplin, musical jigger dances on stage, Krauss, very rare, L5 ....$1,650.00

Charlie Chaplin, postcard, English, early 1900s, V1........$29.50

Charlie McCarthy, book, paint; 1938, uncolored, VG, A .$60.00

Charlie McCarthy, figure, compo, ca 1935, 13", NM-M, L5...$325.00

Charlie McCarthy, game, Question & Answer, McCarthy Inc, 1938, NM (VG+ box), C1 ....$36.00

Charlie McCarthy, game, Topper, Whitman, 1938, NM (EX box)...$47.50

Charlie McCarthy, hand puppet, USA, pnt compo head w/blk & wht cloth outfit, orig box (tape rpr), 10½", VG, A...$85.00

Charlie McCarthy, pencil sharpener, Bakelite w/decal (sm pc of decal missing), 1¾" $55.00

Charlie McCarthy, puppet, compo head w/cloth body, rpl monocle, VG...$65.00

Charlie McCarthy, radio, Majestic, pnt wht Bakelite case, pnt seated metal figure, working, damaged case, 7", P, A $160.00

Charlie McCarthy, spoon, Dutchess silverplate, EX+, T6 .$25.00

Charlie McCarthy Ventriloquist Doll, 25", EX, D10, $350.00.

Charlie's Angels, dresser set, Fleetwood, comb w/Farrah mirror, 1977, MOC, C1 ....$31.00

Charlie's Angels, game, board; Milton Bradley, Cheryl Ladd photo on box, 1978, NM, T6 ....$18.00

Charlie's Angels, game, Milton Bradley, Farrah Fawcett on cover, complete, 1977, NM (NM box) $20.00

Charlie's Angels, Gift Book, Stafford Pemberton, England, 1977, 8x10", NM, C1 ....$31.00

Charlie's Angels, gum card set, Topps, 1977, 1st series, 55 cards, M1 ....$28.00

Charlie's Angels, gum card set, Topps, 1978, 4th series, 66 cards w/11 stickers, complete, M1 ....$22.00

Charlie's Angels, necklace, Fleetwood, 1977, MOC, C1..$17.50

Charlie's Angels, puzzle, features Farrah Fawcett in mauve swimsuit, 1977, EX (NM box) $10.00

Charlie's Angels, puzzle, HG, shows stars, 150-pc, 1977, 14x10", orig box, VG, T6...$9.00

Charlie's Angels, stickers, Topps, 1977, 1st or 2nd series, M1, ea..$2.00

Charley Weaver, nodder, NM......................................$175.00

Cheers, game, board; 1987, MIB (sealed).....................$48.00

Cher, Travel Trunk, Mego, MIB $35.00

Cheyenne, game, board; Milton Bradley, 1966, MIB, M4 .$45.00

Cheyenne Game, Milton Bradley, Warner Bros., 1957, NM in original box, A, $46.00.

Cheyenne, sheet music, Clint Walker photo, 1960, V1 ...$16.50

Chicken Man, record, Spot Records, satirical excerpts from Chicago radio show, 1966, NM (EX+ cover), A $60.00

Child's Play, Chucky doll, from 2nd movie, 1988, M, T1 .$22.50

Chilly Willy, bank, Royal Industries, vinyl, in bl hat & scarf on red skis, 1972, 8½", M............................$45.00

Chilly Willy, book, coloring; Whitman, 1957, NM..........$32.50

Chilly Willy, squeeze toy, Oak Rubber, R3 ....$50.00

China Clipper, ring, brass, pictures airplane, radio premium, 1937, EX, T1...$85.00

Chip & Dale, bendee, Just Toys, Chip or Dale as Rescue Rangers, 4½", K1, ea $4.95

CHIPS, Colorforms, 1981, MIB, C1 ....$15.00

CHIPS, gum card set, Donruss, 1979, 66 cards, complete, M1...$20.00

CHIPS, Highway Patrol Motorcycle, 1970s, MIB, T1 ......$25.00

CHIPS, Highway Patrol Van, MIB, T1.............................$75.00

CHIPS, Jimmy Squeaks or Wheels Willy figure, Mego, 3¾", MOC, D4, ea $10.00

CHIPS, motorcycle & rider, Fleetwood, plastic, removable rider w/authentic detail, ca 1978, 5", MOC (color photo)...$6.50

CHIPS, playset, Emergency Medical Kit, 25+ pcs, 1980, MIB, C1..$36.00

CHIPS, Ponch, Jon, or Sarge figure, Mego, posable, 1977, 8", MOC, any, from $25 to $30.00

CHIPS, Ponch figure, Mego, wearing uniform, 8", VG, N2.$15.00

Chitty-Chitty Bang Bang, flashlight, EX, O1 ....$22.00

Chuck Norris, figure, in any of 7 outfits, MOC, F1, ea $5.00

Chucky, doll, plush, 15", M, D4 ....$20.00

Chucky, doll, plush, 24", M, D4 ....$40.00

Cinderella, album, published in England, 6 songs, story line & colorful illus, 1950, EX, M8.....................................$50.00

Cinderella, book, New Better Little Book, 1950, cover darkened, o/w EX, M8 ....$20.00

Cinderella, Cinderella's Coach, Dinky, #111, MIB, C5 ...$30.00

Cinderella Figure, Irving W. Rice, NY, 8", $125.00.

Cinderella, pencil sharpener, Bakelite, half-length portrait facing right, rnd, scarce $65.00

Cinderella, puzzle, fr-tray; Walt Disney, w/coach & castle in background, EX+, D9.....................................$4.00

Cinderella, sheet music, The Work Song, VG, T6..........$50.00

Cinderella, soundtrack, 1965, EX....................................$10.00

Cinderella, Storybook Doll, plush w/4 faces, 12", 1980s, EX+ $5.00

Cindy Bear (Yogi's girlfriend), figure, Hanna-Barbera, vinyl, rare, T1...$45.00

Circus Boy, book, coloring; Whitman, features Mickey Dolenz, softbound, 100+ pgs, 1957, unused, 8x11", EX+ cover, T2 ....$32.00

Cisco Kid, book, coloring; 1963, NM.............................$20.00

Cisco Kid, bread photo card, Tip Top Bread, w/facsimile autographs, 1950, 3½x5½", T2.............................$18.00

Cisco Kid, gun, Chicken, cb, A $44.00

Clarabell, music box, Hurdy Gurdy, Kagran, plays It's Howdy Doody Time, 9", VG-EX, A $220.00

Clarabell, push-button puppet, Kohner, pnt wood w/plush hair on base, cracked base, 5¾", G-VG, A $60.00

Clarabell, doll, molded vinyl head w/googly eyes, red & wht striped outfit, 1950, NM $95.00

Clarabell, suction-cup toy, Stahlwood/Kagran, her head in vinyl, in 9x6" illus box, NM (G+ box), A $110.00

Clarabell, wall plaque, McGowan Wood Products, diecut figure of Clarabell riding a horse, 8x6", 1930s, EX, A..........$68.00

Clarabelle, book, Clarabelle Cow, Walt Disney Enterprises, 1938, EX, A $15.00

Clash of the Titans, book, coloring & paint; 14x20", M, F1 ....$10.00

Clash of the Titans, Calibos figure, Mattel, 1980, M........$10.00

Clash of the Titans, gum card set, Canada, 12 sq cards w/rounded corners, complete, scarce, M1 ....$36.00

Cleo the Goldfish, squeeze toy, Sun Rubber, R3..............$50.00

Close Encounters of a Third Kind, card & sticker set, 1978, NMIP, C1 ....$12.50

Close Encounters of the Third Kind, collector cards, Crown, 1978, 48 3½x5" cards, complete, M1 ....$20.00

Close Encounters of the Third Kind, collector cards, Wonder Bread, 1979, 24 cards, complete, M1 ....$5.00

Close Encounters of the Third Kind, game, board; Parker Bros, cards, playing pcs, chips & dice, 1978, EX, T2 ....$20.00

Close Encounters of the Third Kind, gum card set, Topps, 66 cards w/11 stickers, complete, 1979, M1 ....$5.00

Close Encounters of the Third Kind, puzzle, We Are Not Alone #100, 108 pcs, 11x16", EX, T6.................................$9.00

Columbo, game, Mystery Puzzle, APC, 1989, MIB (sealed), C1..$21.00

Combat, game, card; 1965, orig 6x7½" box, EX+, C1 ......$63.00

Combat, game, Ideal, features Vic Morrow & Rick Jason, 1963, G (G box) $35.00

Conan, figure, Mego, 8", MOC, H4 ....$280.00

Cookie Monster, see Sesame Street

Cool Cat, poster, 1968, M, T1 ....$10.00

Cool Ghoul, figure, Powco, MIP, E3 ....$10.00

COPS (Central Organization of Police Specialists), figure, Hasbro, Big Boss, Koo Koo or Hyena, 1988, MIP, F1, any $10.00

COPS (Central Organization of Police Specialists), figure, Hasbro, Highway, Taser, Barricade or Berserko, MIP, F1, any $15.00

Cosby Show, scrapbook, hardcover, color photos, 80 pgs, 5½x8", NM, T6 ....$7.00

Courageous Cat & Minute Mouse, book, activity; 1962, VG-, T6 ....$10.00

Crash Dummies, Daryl figure, Tyco, MIP, E3 ....$15.00

Crash Dummies, Hubcat & Bumper figures, Tyco, MIP, E3..$10.00

Crash Dummies, Larry figure, Tyco, MIP, E3.....................$25.00

Crash Dummies, Pitstop figure, Tyco, Canadian release, 1991, MOC, F1 ....$20.00

Crash Dummies, Skid the Kid figure, Tyco, MIP, E3 ....$8.00

Crash Dummies, Spare Tire figure, Tyco, MIP, E3 ....$8.00

Crash Dummies, Vince & Larry figures, together on card, MOC, J4 ....$26.00

Crash Dummies, Vince figure, Tyco, MIP, E3 ....$15.00

Creature from the Black Lagoon, figure, Hamilton, vinyl, 13", EX..$30.00

Creature from the Black Lagoon, figure, Penn-Plax, for aquarium, connects to air pump for action, 1971, 5", MIB, A $303.00

Creature from the Black Lagoon, figure, Remco, glow-in-the-dark, plastic, 1983, 3¾", MOC, C1 ....$23.00

Creature from the Black Lagoon, figure, Uncle Milton, glow-in-the-dark, MIP, E3 ....$10.00

Crystar, Ogeode figure, Remco, MIP, E3 ....$5.00

Crystar, Zardeth figure, Remco, MIP, E3............................$5.00

Curious George, doll, Knickerbocker, stuffed, 14", S1 ......$15.00

Cyndi Lauper, gum card set, Topps, 1985, 33 cards, complete, M1 ....$7.50

Daddy Warbucks, canvas bag, NY newspaper item, 1930s, EX, A...$45.00

Daffy Duck, book, coloring; Whitman, 1971, unused, NM-M, C1..$18.00

Daffy Duck, car, Etrl, diecast, 1989, MIP, F1 ....$5.00

Daffy Duck Flower Holder, 1940s, 4x5x2", D10, $125.00.

Daffy Duck, poster, color, 1969, M, T1 ....$15.00

Daffy Duck & Elmer Fudd, puzzle, fr-tray; 1977, complete, EX...$10.00

Daffy Duck & Elmer Fudd, puzzle, jigsaw; Milton Bradley, 100-pc, 1973, 14x18", EX-, T6..$8.00

Dagwood, figure, Syroco KFS, 1944, 5", NM, A $45.00

Dagwood, musical toy, Dagwood Sandwich, 6x4½", NM (VG box), A...$100.00

Daisy Duck, bendee, Applause, 5½", K1.............................$6.00

Dallas Game, Lorimar Productions, 1980, MIB, $15.00.

Dallas, game, Yaquinto, 1980, complete, NM (EX box) $5.00

Daniel Boone, book, coloring; Saalfield, featuring Fess Parker, 1964, 8x11", M, T2 ....$60.00

Daniel Boone, figure, Marx, missing primer horn & bullet loading block, w/instructions, EX (EX box), H4 ....$175.00

Daniel Boone, game, board; Trail Blazers, Milton Bradley, 1964, 10x20" box, MIB, A $110.00

Dark Crystal, puzzle, 250-pc, MIB (worn box), D4 ....$4.00

Dark Shadows, game, Barnabas Collins, Milton Bradley, 1969, NMIB, C1 ....$65.00

Dark Shadows, game, Milton Bradly, build plastic & cb skeletons, +pr of fangs for player, 1968, 10x20", NM (EX box), T2 ....$42.00

Dark Shadows, game, Whitman, NM (EX box) $25.00

Dark Shadows, Josette's Music Box, working, missing plastic lid o/w M, orig box, H4 ....$190.00

Dark Shadows, poster, House of Dark Shadows, orig, EX+, T1 ....$125.00

Dark Shadows, record, Phillips, 33⅓ rpm, 1969, EX-NM, C1 ....$45.00

Darkseid, Destroyer (vehicle), Kenner, Super Powers, MIP, F1 ....$30.00

Darkseid, figure, Kenner, Super Powers, MOC, F1 ....$15.00

Darkwing Duck, figure, Playmates, MIP, E3 ....$8.00

Darkwing Duck, Gosalyn figure, Playmates, MIP, E3 ....$8.00

Darkwing Duck, Launchpad figure, Playmates, MIP, E3 .....$8.00

Darkwing Duck, Steelbeak figure, Playmates, MIP, E3 ....$8.00

Darkwing Duck, Tuskerninni figure, Playmates, MIP, E3 ...$8.00

Dasterdly & Muttley, game, board; Milton Bradley, 1969, EX $40.00

Dating Game, Hasbro, 3rd edition, 1968, VG, T6 ....$4.00

Davy Crockett, bank, Metro Art, pottery figural, chartreuse w/flesh tones, 1950s, 7", NM, P6 ....$165.00

Davy Crockett, belt, Great Britain, elastic w/metal buckle mk WD, 1" dia pin-bk attached, NM (EX card), A $95.00

Davy Crockett, book, coloring; EX-, T6 ....$20.00

Davy Crockett, book & record set, Disney, sung by The Wellingtons, 24-pg book w/45 rpm record, EX-NM, T6 ....$5.00

Davy Crockett, boots, Graham Brown Shoe Co, box mk Designed by David Crockett's Great Grandson, 1950s, NMIB, A $800.00

Davy Crockett, boots, Yorktown Rubber Footwear, brn & tan w/illus of Davy, fringe at top, NM (EX+ box), A $130.00

Davy Crockett, candy box, Walt Disney, 1960s, VG, V1.$21.00

Davy Crockett, cooking grill, metal, Rockaway Metal Products, 1950s, orig price $2.98 on box, 4x12x12", VG (VG box), A $303.00

Davy Crockett, doll, Nancy Ann Storybook type, w/leather outfit & coonskin cap, leather tag on belt, 10", EX, H4 .$25.00

Davy Crockett, Frontiersman Girl's Playsuit, tan cloth w/brn plastic fringe, 1950s, VG, P4 ....$25.00

Davy Crockett, game, board; Disneyland's Official Davy Crockett Indian Scouting, 1955, complete, EX, P6...........$125.00

Davy Crockett, game, From Tennessee to the Alamo, Ewing, 1955, complete, NM (EX box), A $94.00

Davy Crockett, Ge-Tar & Music Box, Mattel, 14", NM (NM box)...$165.00

Davy Crockett, gun, Frontier Fighter Cork Gun, Japan, tin & wood, cigarette flint mechanism at muzzle, 1950s, 21", NM, P4 ....$65.00

Davy Crockett, gun, Marx, plastic & metal flintlock pistol w/working trigger, 11", NM (EX box), A $110.00

Davy Crockett, gun, Wyandotte, litho tin clicker type, working, sm scratches, 1950s, 8", VG, P4 ....$60.00

Davy Crockett Auto Magic Picture Gun, 1950s, MIB, D10, $165.00.

Davy Crockett, moccasin kit, Coleco, litho box lid features Davy w/the Alamo beyond, NM (EX box), A $85.00

Davy Crockett, moccasin kit, France, box depicts Davy on log pointing to lg moccasin, complete, unused, NMIB, A $330.00

Davy Crockett, night light, Cactus Craft, cb litho Conestoga wagon w/cork wheels, working, 1950s, 5" L, M, from $70 to $100.00

Davy Crockett, outfit, Eddy, complete w/cap, belt, pistol etc, box mk Walt Disney's Frontierland, EX (VG box) .$165.00

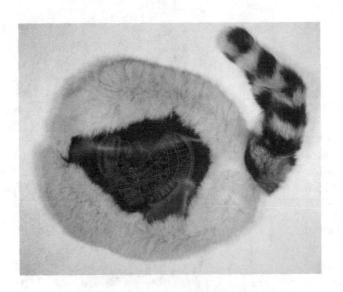

Davy Crockett Coon Skin Cap, NM, $50.00.

Davy Crockett, pocketknife, 2½", EX+, M5 ....$25.00

Davy Crockett, puzzle, jigsaw; Indian Fighter, Jaymar, 60+ pcs, 1956, 8x10" box, VG+-, T2.................................$12.00

Davy Crockett, puzzle, King of the Wild Frontier, Jaymar, 1950s, NM (EX box), C1......................................$54.00

Davy Crockett, record, Ballad of Davy Crockett, Crickett, 45 rpm, 7x7" paper sleeve, 1950s, EX-, T2.....................$15.00

Davy Crockett, record album, Disneyland #1315, 3 Adventures of Davy Crockett, 33⅓ rpm, VG (EX- box), T6........$40.00

Davy Crockett, ring, brass, pictures Davy Crockett, radio premium, 1950s, EX, T1 ....$25.00

Davy Crockett, sheet music, Ballad of Davy Crockett, Walt Disney Prod, 1954, EX, from $20 to $35.00

Davy Crockett, shoe bag, yel vinyl w/6 pouches, bl vinyl trim, 12x12" illus at top, 1950s, NM, A..............................$60.00

Davy Crockett, sunglasses, Fosta, old store display w/6 prs, 1950s, complete, M, H4..$30.00

Davy Crockett, tie, brn w/jewelled leather slide, EX, P6 ..$35.00

Davy Crockett, tie clip & cuff links, copper-tone, M, P6 .$35.00

Davy Crockett, Wagon Train, Marx, plastic coach, driver & horse pull 3 litho tin units, 14", EX+ (VG box), A $215.00

Davy Crockett, wallet, plastic w/Davy in real fur cap, w/orig ID card, calendar & certificate, 5x4", MIB, A $40.00

DC Comic Super Heros, pencil sharpeners, set of 12, MIP, T1 ....$18.00

Dean Martin & Jerry Lewis, decal, color photo, 1950s, 3x5", MIP (sealed), C1...$27.00

Dean Martin & Jerry Lewis, sheet music, Ev'ry Street's a Boulevard, 1953, NM, C1..$27.00

Dennis the Menace, Lock 'N Key, 1987, MOC, T1 ....$5.00

Dennis the Menace, napkins, 1954, NMIB, J2 ....$20.00

Dennis the Menace, playset, Mischief Kit, Hassenfeld Bros, 1953, orig 5x8" box, NM, C1 ....$72.00

Dennis the Menace, record album, Coltix, orig TV soundtrack, 33⅓ rpm w/full-color jacket, 1960, EX, T2 ....$25.00

Deputy, game, Milton Bradley, Peter Fonda on lid, 1960, NMIB...$50.00

Deputy Dawg, game, Fun & Adventure, Milton Bradley, 1960, complete, EX, H4..$25.00

DeSaad, figure, Kenner, Super Powers series, MOC, from $16 to...$20.00

Dick Tracy, badge, Official Member Crime Stoppers, w/ID card & illus sheet, M, V1..$32.00

Dick Tracy, Big Boy figure, Playmates, MIP, E3.................$8.00

Dick Tracy, book, pop-up; Capture of Boris Arson, 1935, VG, from $100 to $150.00

Dick Tracy, braces, suspenders, badge, whistle & magnifying glass, 12x6" orig box, NMIB, A..................................$95.00

Dick Tracy, Breathless Mahoney figure, Applause, 1990, 14", M..$22.50

Dick Tracy, Breathless Mahoney figure, PVC, 3", M, F1 ....$3.00

Dick Tracy, Brow figure, Playmates, MIP, E3 ....$12.00

Dick Tracy, camera, Cine-Vue, Acme, plastic, w/3 films, appears unused, 1947, orig 7½x5" box, EX+ (M box), A $200.00

Dick Tracy, camera, Seymore, blk plastic w/Tracy drawing & name on front, 2½x5½", NM, T6..............................$50.00

Dick Tracy, car, Big Boy's Getaway, MIB, F1 ....$40.00

Dick Tracy, car, Linemar, pnt & litho tin, '54 Chevy, EX.$140.00

Dick Tracy, car, Squad, Playmates, 1990, MIB, J4............$25.00

Dick Tracy, Cartoon Kit, Colorforms, 1961, NM (EX box), A $91.00

Dick Tracy Costume, Motorola premium, 1954, complete, M, D10, $175.00.

Dick Tracy, Crime Stoppers Club Kit, 1961, MIB, from $30 to $40.00

Dick Tracy, Crime Stoppers Lab, Porter Chemical, suitcase-type box w/microscope & other items, scarce, EX, A $60.00

Dick Tracy, figure, Applause, resin, limited edition (only 5000 made), 7", M, F1 ....$40.00

Dick Tracy, figure, Applause, w/stand, 8", M, F1 ....$10.00

Dick Tracy, figure, Playmates, MIP, E3 ....$5.00

Dick Tracy, flashlight, Dick Tracy image on red tin cylinder w/wht plastic light dome, 3", NM, M5.....................$25.00

Dick Tracy, Flattop or Lips Manlis figure, Playmates, MIP, E3, ea...$12.00

Dick Tracy, game, card; Whitman, instructions missing, 1937, in box, EX, A $70.00

Dick Tracy, game, Crime Stoppers, Ideal, 1963, MIB, C1 .$230.00

Dick Tracy, game, Master Detective, Selchow & Righter, 1961, 10x20" box, NM (EX box), T2.................................$32.00

Dick Tracy, game, Pinball, Marx, 1967, NMIB $125.00

Dick Tracy, gun, Marx, click pistol, metal w/facsimile Chester Gould signature, 1930s, 8", NM (EX box), A..........$245.00

Dick Tracy, gun, Power Jet Squad, Mattel, shoots water & caps, 1962, 8", C6...$210.00

Dick Tracy, handcuffs, Ja-Ru, w/trick lock, 1980s, MOC, C1 ....$21.00

Dick Tracy, Influence, Sam Catchem, or Shoulders figure, Playmates, MIP, E3, ea $8.00

Dick Tracy, Itchy, Mumbles, Pruneface, or Rodent figure, Playmates, MIP, E3, ea $10.00

Dick Tracy, magnifying glass, Larami, 1979, MOC, C1 ...$19.00

Dick Tracy, movie cards, Dandy, 1989, set of 60, MIP, C1 ....$36.00

Dick Tracy Komic Kamera, 1930s, D10, $110.00.

Dick Tracy, plate, Tracy talks on TV watch, Muggs & squad car in background, prewar, 9", NM-, A $195.00

Dick Tracy, puzzle, jigsaw; Jaymar, reviewing police lineup, 100-pc, 1961, 8x10" box, EX+, T2 ....$22.00

Dick Tracy, radio, 2-way, wrist type, w/Detective Club badge & ID, 8x4", orig card w/tape rpr, M, A $100.00

Dick Tracy, Sparkle Plenty cradle, pnt wood w/liner, VG-EX, T1 ....$85.00

Dick Tracy, Steve the Tramp figure, Playmates, 3¾", MOC, J4 ....$15.00

Dick Tracy Wrist Radio, 3½x4½", EX, $70.00.

Different Strokes, book, coloring; 1983, VG, T6 ....$4.00

Digger Doug, figure, Powco, MIP, E3 ....$10.00

Dinosaurs, Baby Sinclair, Earl, Fran, Robbie, Charlene or Mr Sinclair figure, MOC, D4, any..................................$6.00

Disney, book, paint; 1939, M, V1.................................$58.00

Disney, Disneyland Woodburning Set, American Toys, 1958, complete, 9x16", NMIB, A $66.00

Disney, game, Casey Jr, EX (EX box), O1 ....$55.00

Disney, game, Education Identification, NM (NM box), O1 ....$550.00

Disney, jack-in-the-box, Cannival, ca 1981-84, EX $30.00

Disney, puzzle, Disney on Parade, Jaymar, 1969, complete, EX...$10.00

Disney, world globe, litho tin, major characters on globe & base, Rand McNally, stained orig box, 10x8", NM, A $110.00

Disney Character TV Set, Automatic Toys, red plastic, cylinder rotates w/scenes from Peter Pan, 1949, 4x5x5", MIB, A $193.00

Disney Studio, stationery, Great Mouse Detective, 1986, M8 ....$6.00

Disney Studio, stationery, Sword in the Stone, 1960s, M8 ....$8.00

Disneykin Play Sets, Dumbo & circus figures displayed in cutout box, EX+ (VG+ box), M5 ....$89.00

Disneyland, bank, Haunted House, tin w/plastic roof, place coin at front door, light goes on, ghost pulls coin in, NM, A $150.00

Disneyland, biscuit container, Holland, litho tin w/early characters, 1938, 12" L, EX, A..$300.00

Disneyland, cake decoration, Happy Birthday Carousel, litho tin, orig box, VG-EX, A...$190.00

Disneyland, card set, Donruss, set of 66 color photo scenes to celebrate 10th anniversary, 1965, NM-M, C1 ....$81.00

Disneyland, charm bracelet, features Mickey, Tinker Bell & Sleeping Beauty castle, 1950s, MIB, P6 ....$35.00

Disneyland, raft, Ideal, MIP, V1 ....$98.00

Doc Holiday, game, Wild West, Transogram, w/4 cb figures, board & spinner, 1960, EX+, T2 ....$50.00

Don Winslow, Magic Slate Secret Code Book, premium, w/magic slate & pencil, 7x4", EX+, A........................$90.00

Donald Duck, baby feeding dish, Hankscraft, figure on bowl, 1960s, MIP, T1 ....$25.00

Donald Duck, baby rattle, celluloid, fully emb w/medium bill, 1940s, EX, P6 ....$75.00

Donald Duck Bubble Duck, Walt Disney Productions, Morris Plastic Corp., MIB, $72.00.

Donald Duck, ball, Sun Rubber, emb image of Donald, 1940s, minor wear, P6..............$38.00

Donald Duck, bank, ceramic, ca 1960s, S1 ....$30.00

Donald Duck, bank, compo, camping out in tent, 1960s, EX, T1 ....$25.00

Donald Duck, bank, compo, laying on top of gr van, 1960s, EX, T1..............$25.00

Donald Duck, bendee, Applause, 5", K1 ....$6.00

Donald Duck, bendee, Lakeside, 1970s, 6", VG, H4..........$8.00

Donald Duck, book, Donald & His Friends, Heath, 9 stories, 1939, VG, A $45.00

Donald Duck, book, Donald Duck & the Boys, Walt Disney Productions, 1948, EX, A..............$15.00

Donald Duck, book, Grosset & Dunlop, 1936, w/dust jacket, 10x11", EX, A..............$235.00

Donald Duck, book, Walt Disney's Donald Duck, Whitman, illus, 1935, 9x13", EX, A $95.00

Donald Duck, camera, Herbert George, blk, w/127 war surplus film dtd 1947, orig box (very torn), T6..............$45.00

Donald Duck, cap, Albee, straw & plastic, quacks when beak (hat brim) is squeezed, 1948, M, A $45.00

Donald Duck, diecut cb banner poster, 28x17", M4..............$100.00

Donald Duck, doll, Brio (Sweden), pnt wood, string jtd, orig box (end flaps missing), 9¾", EX, A..............$70.00

Donald Duck, doll, Knickerbocker, Band Master, stuffed, long billed, all orig w/tag, 16", NM, A..............$1,100.00

Donald Duck Band Master Doll, Knickerbocker, composition ca 1936, 11", M with tag, D10, $2,000.00.

Donald Duck, doll, Knickerbocker, cowboy attire, metal 6-guns, lambskin chaps, pnt chips, compo damage, rpr, 8¾", A..............$660.00

Donald Duck, doll, Knickerbocker, stuffed, long billed, orig hat, some soiling, 12½", A..............$250.00

Donald Duck, doll, Knickerbocker, stuffed, w/orig hat, cracks around bill & feet but strong, 36", EX, A $250.00

Donald Duck, Donald the Bubble Duck, Morris Plastics, ca 1962, MIB..............$72.00

Donald Duck, figure, American Pottery, ceramic, orig paper label, 6½", NM, A..............$85.00

Donald Duck, figure, Applause, PVC, MOC, F1 ....$3.00

Donald Duck, figure, Brayton Laguna, ceramic, prone w/chin resting on left hand, 4", NM, A $150.00

Donald Duck, figure, bsk, hands on hips, 1930s, 1¾", EX, M8..............$45.00

Donald Duck, figure, bsk, head turned to right, hands at sides, 1930s, 3¼", EX, M8..............$75.00

Donald Duck, figure, bsk, on yel skooter, 1930s, 3¾", EX+, M8..............$175.00

Donald Duck, figure, bsk, purple admiral's uniform & hat w/yel feathers, 1930s, 3", EX, M8..............$175.00

Donald Duck, figure, bsk, w/accordion, mk Walt Disney, Made in Japan on bk, 1930s, EX+, A..............$175.00

Donald Duck, figure, chalkware, carnival premium, 1930s, 13½", NM..............$200.00

Donald Duck, frozen orange juice container, 1982, M4..............$5.00

Donald Duck, game, Bean Bag Party, Parker Bros, 1939, NMIB $35.00

Donald Duck, hand puppet, VG, O1..............$25.00

Donald Duck, lamp, table; Brechner, pnt ceramic, 1950s, NM..............$200.00

Donald Duck, Nephews & Pluto; sand sifter, Ohio Art, 1930s, inside screen loose/rusting, 7¾" dia, EX, M8 ....$110.00

Donald Duck, nodder, unmk, pnt compo, red, yel, bl & wht, clockwork, working, 7½", EX, A..............$450.00

Donald Duck, paint box, Transogram, litho tin, also features Huey, Louie, Dewey & Mickey, 1946, pnts used, o/w EX, M8..............$40.00

Donald Duck, pencil sharpener, Bakelite, full-length portrait w/right hand on hip, left hand to face, rnd, scarce $85.00

Donald Duck, planter, Leeds, as Santa, 1950s, 6", EX....$195.00

Donald Duck, printing set, Canada, shows Donald on box, print stamps of Elmer, Toby Tortoise, etc, 1930s, 6x8", EX, M8 ....$45.00

Donald Duck, projector, Transogram, battery-op, w/2 cartridges, orig box, 8½", EX, A..............$25.00

Donald Duck, puppet, Gund, w/squeaker, M $40.00

Donald Duck, push toy, Gong Bell, diecut wood w/litho paper image of Donald, metal wheels, push hdl missing, 9", VG+, A $71.00

Donald Duck, push-button puppet, Kohner, pnt wood w/plastic head, orig box (tape rpr), 5¾", EX, ...$95.00

Donald Duck, push-button puppet, Kohner, 1960s, EX....$25.00

Donald Duck, sand pail, Ohio Art, litho tin, Donald at beach, sm dent, 1939, 3", EX, M8..............$145.00

Donald Duck, soap figure, Lightfoot Schultz, c WDE, some pnt loss/pc broken on foot, 4", VG (EX box), A $50.00

Donald Duck, Spinikin, Kohner, 1960s, plastic w/pnt features, pull string for action, 4", NM, A $21.00

Donald Duck, squeaker, celluloid, Donald atop 3½" circle, 1930s, not working, 5½", VG, A..............................$90.00

Donald Duck, squeeze toy, Dell, EX+, R3 ....$30.00

Donald Duck Sun Rubber Car, ca 1940s, NM, D10, $150.00.

Donald Duck Wooden Shoo-Fly, Walt Disney Productions, multicolor silk screen design, 1930s, 32", EX+, A, $600.00.

Donald Duck, wallet, girl's, Disneyland graphics, 1972, M4..$4.00

Donald Duck & Pluto, book, Moving Picture, Collins (England), 1936, 4x9", EX+, A..$210.00

Donald Duck & Pluto, car, Sun Rubber, 1950s, G, T1.....$65.00

Donald Duck & Pluto, movie book, w/5 reels, 1939, damaged binding, G-VG, A $120.00

Donald's Nephew, figure, bsk, 1930s, 2", EX, M8 ....$75.00

Donny & Marie Osmond, drum set, MIB.....................$75.00

Donny & Marie Osmond, puzzle, fr-tray; Whitman, 1977, EX, T6...$5.00

Donny & Marie Osmond, tambourine & microphone set, 1976, MOC...$15.00

Donny & Marie Osmond, Wireless Microphone/Radio, missing instructions, orig box, EX-, T6 ....$7.00

Donny Osmond, Keepsake Photo & Activity Book, Artcraft, 1973, unused, NM-M, C1..$13.00

Donny Osmond, nodder, NMIB.....................................$25.00

Dopey, bank, Dime Register, Dopey points to bank book, litho tin, 2½", G-VG, A...$120.00

Dopey, doll, stuffed w/compo head, all orig, sm holes in cloak, bright colors, no tag, 14", A $125.00

Dopey, puppet, Gund, w/squeaker, NM $25.00

Dopey, trinket box, ceramic, full-color graphics, gold trim, 1960s, 2x2x2½", EX, P6..$60.00

Doug Davis, figure, Mattel, bendable, in yel space suit w/helmet & Cat Trak, 1968, 6", EX+, T2............................$50.00

Dr Doolittle, jack-in-the-box, litho tin, NM, T1.............$65.00

Dr Doolittle, puzzle, fr-tray; Whitman, 1967, NM, C1 .....$19.50

Dr Jekyll & Mr Hyde, book, Harper & Row, paperback w/movie photos, 1976, EX+, D9..$5.00

Dr Kildare, book, Assigned to Trouble, Whitman TV Book, 1963, NM, C1 ....$14.00

Dr Kildare, game, board; Ideal, 1962, NM (EX box), C1..$41.00

Dr Kildare, nodder, resembles Richard Chamberlain, EX, HA...$99.00

Dr Kildare, note paper ring binder, plastic-sealed cover, 1962, VG+-EX, T6..$50.00

Dr Kildare, Pencil-By-Number Set, Standard Toycraft, 6 pictures w/6 pencils, 1962, 9x13", VG+, T2......................$40.00

Dr Kildare, Young Doctor Medical Kit, Hasbro, complete, NMIB...$40.00

Dr Sinister, figure, Toy Biz, MOC, D8 ....$9.00

Dr Who, Deny Fisher figure, Mego, complete outfit except scarf, 1967, 9½", NM $80.00

Dracula, doll, Drac Bat, 1985, 19", sold exclusively to Halloween stores & never in retail stores, M (M coffin box), F1.$40.00

Dracula, doll, Presents, M...$35.00

Dracula, doll, Remco, 1979, NM, J2 ....$25.00

Dracula, doll, talking; Commonwealth Toy & Novelty, NM, J2 ....$45.00

Dracula, figure, Mego, Mad Monster series, complete, 8", EX, H4...$80.00

Dracula, figure, Palmer Plastics, raising full-length cape, 1963, 3", NM, T2...$20.00

Dracula, figure, Placo/Universal Studios, 60th-Anniversary Limited Edition, 10", MIB, F1 ....$15.00

Dracula, game, board; Mystery, Hasbo, 1963, NM (NM box).$125.00

Dracula, game, I Want To Bite Your Finger, Hasbro, 1981, MIB (sealed), C1...$24.50

Dracula, movie trailer, Frances Ford Coppola, 35mm, M ..$20.00

Dracula, puzzle, APC/Universal Studios, 100-pc, 1974, NM (EX canister), C1 ....$22.00

Dracula, puzzle, fr-tray; Universal Studios, 11-pc, M, F1 ....$5.00

Dragnet, game, puzzle; Badge 714, Transogram, 1955, MIB, from $60 to $80.00

Dragnet, gun, water; Knickerbocker, blk plastic .38 Special style w/#714 shield on grip, 1960s, 6", MIP.....................$48.00

Dragnet, sheet music, Theme from Dragnet, 1953, NM, C1..$15.00

Dragnet, whistle, plastic, blk, radio premium, 1960s, EX+, T1 ....$7.00

Droop-a-Long Coyote, hand puppet, Ideal Toy Co,, 1960s, VG, H4 ....$39.00

Duck Tales, bendee, Scrooge McDuck, Just Toys, 4½", K1 .$4.95

Duck Tales, book, sticker; complete set of 140 stickers, unused, 1987, NM, M8 ....$28.00

Duck Tales, figures, PVC, set of 4, Kellogg's premium, M, D4 ....$5.00

Duck Tales (Scrooge McDuck & family), gum card set, Panini, 1988, complete, M1 ....$39.00

Dudley Do-Right, bendee, Wham-O, 1960s, MOC, T1 ...$20.00

Dudley Do-Right, book, coloring; Artcraft, 1962, EX+ $20.00

Dukes of Hazzard, bank, General Lee car w/decals, 1981, 4½x16", EX, T6...$8.00

Dukes of Hazzard, Bo Duke doll, Mego, 8", MOC, F1 .....$20.00

Dukes of Hazzard, Boss Hogg doll, Mego, 1981, 8", M (EX card), D9...$15.00

Dukes of Hazzard, carrying case, orange vinyl, holds 24 mini cars, 1981, 11x6½", T6 ....$9.00

Dukes of Hazzard, Coy Duke doll, Mego, Bo variation, 8", MOC, F1 ....$40.00

Dukes of Hazzard, Duke figure, Hasbro/Target Stores, limited edition, 12", NRFB, H4.....................$60.00

Dukes of Hazzard, folder, 1981, 10x8", EX, T6..................$4.00

Dukes of Hazzard, game, Ideal, 1981, complete, EX..........$15.00

Dukes of Hazzard, General Lee car, Ertl, diecast, 1981, 8¼", M (EX box), C1...$39.00

Dukes of Hazzard, General Lee figure, soap, MIP, F1........$10.00

Dukes of Hazzard, General Lee slot car, HO scale, 1981, EX, T6...$6.00

Dukes of Hazzard, gum cards, Donruss, 1980, 1st series, set of 66, complete, M1 ....$18.00

Dukes of Hazzard, Luke Duke figure, Mego, 3¾", MOC, F1 ....$10.00

Dukes of Hazzard, playset, HG, hat, belt, buckle, CB unit, car & photo, 1981, NMIB, C1..........................$63.00

Dukes of Hazzard, puzzle, 200 pcs, complete, 1982, EX $10.00

Dukes of Hazzard, Sheriff Roscoe figure, Mego, 1981, 3¾", MOC, C1 ....$18.50

Dumbo, doll, Cameo, pnt compo, jtd w/fabric ears & collar, orig box, 8½", EX, A $450.00

Dumbo, figure, Knickerbocker, compo w/pnt features, cloth ears, movable trunk & head, 1930s, 8", EX, A................$240.00

Dumbo, soap figure, wht, stands on cb platform, red & wht box w/Dumbo image, unused, NMIB, M5.....................$25.00

Dunbine, figure, Bandai, vinyl, MIP, E3 ....$10.00

Dune, folder, men on stairs, NM, T6.............................$4.00

Dune, game, board; Parker Bros, photo cards, character disks & many other pcs, 1984, unused, MIB, T2 ....$30.00

Dune, gum cards, Fleer, 1984, set of 132, complete, M1...$15.00

Dune, gun, Fremen, LJN, MIP, E3...................................$30.00

Dune, gun, Sardauker, LJN, MIP, E3................................$25.00

Dune, Motorized Sand Roller, LJN, battery-op, 1984, M (EX card), G1...$24.00

Dune, Paul Atreides figure, LJN, 1984, 6", MOC, J4........$25.00

Dune, Paul Atreides figure, LJN, 1984, 3¾", MOC (sealed)..$15.00

Dune, Sandworm figure, De Laurentis/LJN, posable, 1984, 15", MIB, P4..$30.00

Dune, Sardauker Warrior figure, 1980s, MOC, T1 ....$25.00

Dune, Spice Scout, De Laurentis/LJN, plastic, for use w/action figures, 1984, MIB, P4 ....$45.00

Dune, stickers, Fleer, 1984, set of 44, scarce, M1 ....$50.00

Dungeons & Dragons, Mandoom figure, LJN, 1983, 3¾", MOC $15.00

Dungeons & Dragons, Mettaflame figure, LJN, 1983, 3¾", MOC $15.00

Dungeons & Dragons, Zorgar figure, LNJ, 1983, 3¾", MOC $10.00

Ed Wynn, game, Ed Wynn's Fire Chief, Selchow & Righter, 1930s, missing instructions, VG+, F3.......................$28.00

Eddie Cantor, game, Tell It to the Judge, Parker Bros, 1930s, NM, F3...$45.00

Eddie Cantor, record, Maxie the Taxi, M $35.00

Eeyore, figure, Japan, 1960s, 3", A3..............................$10.00

Eeyore, figure, Sears exclusive, red, fuzz-covered, w/posable head, 1988, MOC, P4......................................$10.00

Eight Is Enough, puzzle, jigsaw; APC, 1978, MIB (sealed), C1...$21.00

Elmer Elephant, figural soap, Lightfoot Schultz, 1930s, age cracking to soap/box has minor wear, o/w EX, M8..$125.00

Elmer Fudd, book, coloring; Watkins, 1962, NM $25.00

Elmer Fudd, figure, ceramic, wearing brn suit & holding hat, EX $28.00

Elmer the Elephant, squeeze toy, Seiberling, R3.............$200.00

Elvira, belt, MOC, J2..$20.00

Elvira, book, comic from movie, NM $10.00

Elvira, earrings, mk Official, MOC (picture card), H4 ....$5.00

Elvira, eyelashes, MOC, H4...$5.00

Elvira, make-up kit w/earrings, MOC (picture card), H4 .$10.00

Elvis Presley Overnight Case, available in blue and brown, c 1956, EPE, from $650.00 to $850.00.

Elvira, Nightmare Nail Enamel, MOC (picture card), H4 .$6.00

Elvira, plate, Red Velvet, MIB $75.00

Elvira, poster, Mistress of the Dark Movie, M..................$12.50

Elvira, stein, Night Rose, MIB..$65.00

Elvis, game, River Group, 1977, NMIB $100.00

Elvis, gum cards, Donruss, 1978, set of 66, complete, M1.$25.00

Elvis, gum cards, Donruss, 1978, set of 67 color photos w/variant card, NM, C1 ....$39.00

Elvis, gum cards, Monty Gum, set of 50, complete, M1 ....$35.00

Elvis, gum cards, River Group, 1992, 1st or 2nd series, set of 220, complete, M1, either $40.00

Elvis, music box, plastic guitar, w/up to play Love Me Tender, late 1970s, 10", MIB $35.00

Elvis, musical hound dog, plays 6 tunes, 16", MIB, I2 ....$29.00

Elvis, ornament, Hallmark, 1992, NRFB, H4 ....$20.00

Elvis, poster, Coloring Contest, 1962, NM, T1 ....$4.00

Elvis, poster, Easy Come, Easy Go; 1967, 27x41", NM $50.00

Elvis, puzzle, side view w/microphone, 200-pc, 1977, 11x17", EX, T6 ....$9.00

Elvis, ring, Vari-Vue, flasher type, 3", NM-M, C1 ....$17.50

Elvis Presley Scrapbook, Solid Gold Memories, Ballantine Books, October 1977, $15.00.

Emergency, book, coloring; Lowe #6932, 1977, cover shows the 5 stars of the shows, unused, EX $25.00

Emergency, fire hat, plastic, 1975, EX, N2 ....$29.00

Emergency, puzzle, Casse-Tete, in can, complete, 1975, VG+, P3 ....$7.00

Emmett Kelly, doll, Willie (clown), Baby Barry Toys, hard stuffed body, vinyl head & hands, 1956, 20", NM (EX+ box), T2 ....$250.00

ET, book, autograph; 1982, M, T6 ....$5.00

ET, book, coloring; 1982, VG+, T6 ....$7.00

ET, book, Scholastic Book Services, The Extra Terrestrial, paperback, 1982, 8x11", EX, D9 ....$4.00

ET, Colorforms, MIB $25.00

ET, doll, fuzzy brn fabric, 1980s, lg, M, T1 ....$20.00

ET, doll, fuzzy pk fabric, orig tags, 1980s, M, T1 ....$15.00

ET, doll, soft, w/marble eyes, 1980s, M, T1 ....$6.50

ET, figure, LJN, set of 6, 1982, 2", MIP, F1 ....$20.00

ET, figure, LJN, w/potted plant or wearing robe & drinking beer, 1982, 2", D9, ea $4.00

ET, game, board; Parker Bros, 1982, MIB, T2 ....$20.00

ET, game, card; MIP (sealed), D4 ....$5.00

ET, gum cards, Nabisco, 1982, set of 12, M1 ....$18.00

ET, key chain, 1982, M, T6 ....$5.00

ET, napkins, set of 20, 1982, MIP (sealed), T6 ....$5.00

ET, night light, EX $8.00

ET, puzzle, Craft Master, 1982, complete, EX $6.50

ET, Shrinky Dinks Activity Set, Colorforms, 1982, NMIB, C1 ....$18.00

ET, Spaceship Launcher, LJN, push button & ET pops up, 1982, MOC, C1 ....$18.50

ET, toothbrush, Hasbro, 1983, NMIB $40.00

ET, wallet, purple w/velcro closure, 1982, MIP (seal torn), T6 ....$15.00

Eugene the Jeep (Popeye's friend), doll, jtd wood, VG decal, tail missing, cracks/scuffs, 8½", A $400.00

Eugene the Jeep (Popeye's friend), doll, Schoenhut & King Features, ca 1935, compo w/jtd wood tail, 12", VG, A .$600.00

Evel Knievel, Colorforms, 1970s, VG-EX, T1 ....$15.00

Evel Knievel, gum card, Topps, 1974, single card, M1 ....$2.50

Evel Knievel, King of Stuntman Artic Explorer Set, 1970s, MOC, T1 ....$35.00

Evel Knievel, Rocket Cycle, missing handlebar, 1970s, T1 ..$10.00

Evel Knievel, trailer, bl, w/2 ramps, 1970s, T1 ....$10.00

Eye-Gore, figure, Mattel, MIP, E3 ....$5.00

F-Troop, book, Whitman, hardcover w/mc laminated binding, 1967, NM $12.50

F-Troop, game, Ideal, complete, orig box, 1965, EX, H4 .$150.00

F-Troop, Ken Berry photo, blk & wht glossy, signed, 1966, 8x10", NM-M, C1 ....$42.00

Fabian, pillow, cloth w/printed graphics, 1950s, 11x11", EX $65.00

Falcon, figure, Mego, complete, 8", loose, H4 ....$45.00

Falcon, figure, Mego, wearing stretch jumpsuit & boots, 1974, 8", NM, C1 ....$69.00

Falcon, figure, Mego, 8", MIB, H4 ....$129.00

Fall Guy, book, activity; 1982, EX, T6 ....$6.00

Fall Guy, game, Milton Bradley, 1982, 9x19", VG+ (VG+ box) $25.00

Fall Guy, Stunt Action Toy, Fleetwood, 1982, MOC, H4 ..$10.00

Fall Guy, truck, Fleetwood, motorized, breaks apart, 1981, M (NM card), H4 ....$8.00

Fame, book, coloring; photo of 5 stars, 1983, EX, T6 ....$5.00

Family Affair, book, coloring; Whitman, 1968, EX $20.00

Family Affair, book, sticker; Mrs Beasley, 1972, EX $30.00

Family Affair, book, trace & color; Whitman #1414, cover shows Jodie & Buffy, uncolored, some tracing, 1969, VG+ $25.00

Family Affair, Buffy's Cookbook, by Jodie Cameron of Celebrity Kitchen, EX, H4 ....$15.00

Family Affair, Colorforms, missing 4 minor pcs, 1970, NM (EX), C1 ....$36.00

Family Affair, doll, Buffy & Mrs Beasley, Mattel, compo, 1967, 6", MIB, H4 ....$60.00

Family Affair, puzzle, Whitman, playing doctor scene, complete, 1970, EX $25.00

Family Affair, book, Color and Read, Whitman, 1972, NM, $9.00.

Fantasia, jack-in-the-box, NM (NM box), O1 ....$165.00
Fantasia, soundtrack, 2-album set, 1982, EX.....................$12.00
Fantastic Voyage, game, board; 1968, EX+ (VG+ box), C1 .$21.00
Father Know's Best, TV Guide, June 26, 1959, EX+, C1 .$17.00
Fauna, hand puppet w/squeaker, Gund, 1959, squeaker not
    working, o/w EX, M8 ....$30.00
Felix the Cat, bank, ceramic, 1987, MIB, T1....................$17.50

Felix the Cat Chocolate Pot, ceramic, Germany, 1920s, 5½", D10, $650.00.

Felix the Cat, bendee, Applause, 1988, 6", K1 ....$5.95
Felix the Cat, book, coloring; 1950s, M $30.00
Felix the Cat, Bop Bag, plastic, 1950s-60s, 12", NM, C1..$113.00
Felix the Cat, bowl, Monkeys of Melbourne, ceramic, 1988, 8",
    NM, C1 ....$81.00
Felix the Cat, figure, compo w/pnt details, standing w/hands
    behind bk, hollow, ca 1920, 4½", EX, A.................$150.00
Felix the Cat, figure, jtd wood, chest & foot decal 100%, 1924,
    4", NM, A..$176.00

Felix the Cat Figure, jointed wood, ca 1928, 7", D10, $350.00.

Felix the Cat, game, Target Set, Lido Toys, tin litho target
    w/plastic gun & darts, orig pkg, 11½", VG-EX, A $65.00
Felix the Cat, label, paper, advertising German drink, 5½",
    V1...$46.00
Felix the Cat, puzzle, fr-tray; NM, J2 ....$25.00
Felix the Cat, squeak toy, figural, 1962, 6¼", EX, J2 ....$60.00
Felix the Cat, walker, pnt papier-mache w/wood legs, wood plat-
    form w/instructions, 5¼", EX, A $1,050.00
Ferdinand the Bull, book, #842, Whitman, 1938, minor color
    fading/sm tear on cover, o/w EX, M8 ....$35.00
Ferdinand the Bull, figure, bsk, Japan, blk, yel & gr pnt, 3⅛", G-
    VG, A $25.00
Ferdinand the Bull, game, marble; Whitman, #2916, 1938, com-
    plete in orig box, EX, P6...$90.00
Ferngully, The Last Rain Forest; gum cards, Dart, 1992, set of
    100, complete, M1 ....$18.00
Fibber McGee & Molly, game, Wistful Vista Mystery, Milton
    Bradley, 1940, EX+, from $30 to $45.00

Fievel, American Tail II; gum cards, Impel, set of 90, complete, 1991, M1 ....$17.00

Figaro, Goebel figure, w/label, full bee mk, 1950s, 2¼", NM, M8 ....$110.00

Fish Police, bendee, Hanna-Barbera/Just Toys, Inspector Gil, Crabby, Sharkster, or Angel, 1992, MOC, P4, any......$5.00

Flash, figure, Kenner, Super Powers series, MOC, H4 ......$10.00

Flash, figure, Toy Biz, 2nd series, MOC (Flash or DC Comics card), F1 ....$15.00

Flash Gordon, book, pop-up; Tournament of Death, Pleasure, Raymond art, 1935, EX, A $585.00

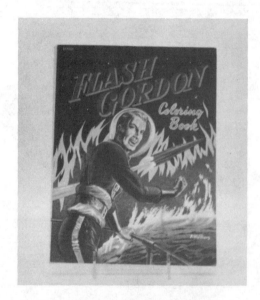

Flash Gordon Coloring Book, A. McWilliams, King Features, 1952, M, $34.00.

Flash Gordon, charm, bubble gum premium, 1950s, in clear plastic holder, NM, C1 ....$15.00

Flash Gordon, Dale or Ming figure, Mego, 1976, 9", M (NM card), C1, ea. $54.00

Flash Gordon, Dr Zarkov figure, Mattel, 1979, 3¾", MOC..$20.00

Flash Gordon, game, target; unmk, 2-sided tin, features Flash & his spaceships, 1930s, 15x12", VG, A $115.00

Flash Gordon, gum cards, English, set of 180, complete, M1 ....$45.00

Flash Gordon, gun, Air Ray, Budson, pressed steel w/rubber diaphragm (ripped), EX decal, 1950s, 10", VG, P4 .$265.00

Flash Gordon, gun, Arresting Ray, mc litho tin w/clicker trigger, working, orig box, 10", EX, A $300.00

Flash Gordon, gun, Click Ray Pistol, Marx, litho tin w/illus of Flash on either side of grips, 10", EX+ (EX box), A $750.00

Flash Gordon, gun, Nasta, battery-op, shoots 3 light beams: wht laser, bl stun & red atomic, 1976, MIP, F1 ....$20.00

Flash Gordon, gun, Signal Pistol, pressed steel, gr w/red accents, decaled sides, 1935, scarce, 7", VG+, A $293.00

Flash Gordon, gun, water pistol, Marx, plastic, name & lightning bolts on grips, 7", NM (EX box), A $350.00

Flash Gordon, hand puppet, EX, O1 ....$175.00

Flash Gordon, Ming, Lizard Woman, or Thun the Lion Man figure, Mattel, 1979, 3¾", MOC, H4, any..................$26.00

Flash Gordon, picture record, 45 rpm, City of Sea Caves, Record Guild, 1948, NM, A, from $60 to $85.00

Flash Gordon, poster, Universal, Land of the Dead, Flash Gordon Conquers the Universe, Chapter 7, 1940, 40x26", VG+, A....................$825.00

Flash Gordon, puzzle set, jigsaw; Milton Bradley, contains 3 complete puzzles, 1951, 9x12", NM (EX+ box), A..$316.00

Flash Gordon Radio Repeater Click Pistol, Marx, 1935, EX+ (EX box), A, $750.00.

Flash Gordon, serving tray, mc Flash battles lizard, 1979, 17½x13", EX, D9 ....$12.00

Flash Gordon, space outfit, Esquire, jacket & cummerbund silkscreened w/Flash riding rocket, 1952, 15x12", NM, A....................$256.00

Flash Gordon, Strato Kite, 1950s, MIP, T1 ....$85.00

Flash Gordon, viewer, Ja-Ru, w/2 boxed movies, 1981, MOC, C1....................$18.00

Flintstones, baby bottle, complete w/lid, 1977, 6", NM....$10.00

Flintstones, Baby Pebbles doll, Ideal, 1963, MIB, H4.....$149.00

Flintstones, Bamm-Bamm doll, Ideal, 12", MIB $185.00

Flintstones, Bamm-Bamm doll, w/club, tattered clothes, 1960s, 18", VG, T1 ....$45.00

Flintstones, bank, plastic, Barney w/bowling ball, 1973, EX-NM, H4 ....$20.00

Flintstones, Barney bendee, w/guitar, cereal premium, 1991, 3½", EX-NM, H4 ....$4.00

Flintstones, Barney figure, Imperial, w/pnt detail, 1976, 2½", EX, H4 ....$8.00

Flintstones, Barney finger puppet, Knickerbocker, 1972, H4 ....$4.00

Flintstones, Barney night light, Electricord, 1979, MOC, H4 ....$6.00

Flintstones, Barney's Car, D-Toys, Spain, 1985, 3¾", MOC, H4 ....$15.00

Flintstones, Betty Rubble squeeze toy, Lanco, 1960s, 5", NM (EX pkg), A....................$72.00

Flintstones, book, coloring; Whitman, 1961, NM $17.50

Flintstones, book, Fred & Barney Join the Circus, Durabooks, 1972, EX....................$10.00

Flintstones, book, Pebbles & Bamm-Bamm Go to School, Giant Durabook, 1973, VG $10.00

Flintstones, book, Take a Vacation, Durabook, 1974, EX ..$8.00

Flintstones, book, 4 stories, 79 pgs, 1978, 8x9½", T6.........$9.00

Flintstones, camera, emb Fred face fitted over lens, uses Kodak 126 film, 1976, MOC, C1..$31.00

Flintstones, cover & pillow set, Pebbles & graphics on cloth, MIP, 14¼", EX, A..$55.00

Flintstones, Dino & cavemen figure, Kreiss Co., 7", $35.00.

Flintstones, Dino bendee, Bendy, salmon foam w/pnt features & polka-dot body, 1961, 10", NM, A.............................$73.00

Flintstones, Dino on wheels (for dolls to ride), yel, 12x20", EX, J2 ....$75.00

Flintstones, Dino push-button puppet, Kohner, plastic, 4", M, from $25 to...$40.00

Flintstones, Dino Spinikin, Kohner, pull-string action, 1960s, 4", NM $35.00

Flintstones, Dino stroller, Ideal, yel plastic figure w/red accents, w/pull rope, orig box, 18½", EX+, A $316.00

Flintstones, Flintstones Kids Bedrock Airlines, MIB, D4 .$10.00

Flintstones, Flintstones Kids Dreamship Limo, MIB, D4 ....$8.00

Flintstones, Fred, Wilma, Betty, or Barney figure, Flintstones Kids, Coleco, 1986, MOC, any....................................$8.00

Flintstones, Fred bank, plastic, 10", VG, T1 ....$22.00

Flintstones, Fred push-button puppet, Kohner, M, A $35.00

Flintstones, Fred Spinikin, Kohner, pull-string action, 1960s, 4", NM..$35.00

Flintstones, game, Big Hunt, Whitman, 1962, NMIB, C1...$81.00

Flintstones, game, Break Ball, Whitman, 1962, NM (EX box), from $30 to...$45.00

Flintstones, game, Dino the Dinosaur, Transogram, EX+, from $65 to...$72.00

Flintstones, game, Giant Checkers, Empire, early 1960s, NM, C1...$63.00

Flintstones, game, Prehistoric Animal Rummy, Ed-U-Cards, 1961, NMIB, C1 ....$23.00

Flintstones, game, The Flintstones, Transogram, orig box, 17½", VG+, A...$60.00

Flintstones, gum cards, Cardz, 1993, set of 100, complete, M1 ....$25.00

Flintstones, gumball machine, Hasbro, Fred's head as dispenser, 1968, 10x5", NM, A $60.00

Flintstones, lamp, w/shade, 1960s, EX............................$185.00

Flintstones, magnetic slate, Henry Gordy, put whiskers on Fred, 1988, EX, H4...$4.00

Flintstones, motorcycle, D-Toys, Spain, 1985, 3¾", MOC, H4 ....$8.00

Flintstones, night light, plastic Fred figure, 5", M, A........$25.00

Flintstones, party hat, cone-shaped, 1969, EX $10.00

Flintstones, Pebbles and Bamm-Bamm dolls in cradle, Hanna-Barbera, plastic, 8½" each in 14½" long cradle, $110.00.

Flintstones, Pebbles & Dino, bank, gr vinyl, 1973, EX+, T1 .$35.00

Flintstones, Pebbles Mini-Movie Viewer, Gordy, w/film cartridge, 1979, MOC, C1...$27.00

Flintstones, pencil sharpeners, character on red plastic, 1983, set of 5 different, 2½", NM-M, C1.................................$65.00

Flintstones, plate, Melmac, Pebbles on Dino, Bamm-Bamm on pogo stick, & adults waving, 8", EX, T6.....................$6.00

Flintstones, playset, Flintstones Kids Town of Bedrock, MIB, D4 ....$15.00

Flintstones, playset, train & village, oval track goes through Bedrock, unassembled, MIB, A $110.00

Flintstones, puzzle, fr-tray; Warren, 1975, NM, C1 ....$27.00

Flintstones, puzzle, fr-tray; Whitman, Bamm-Bamm & Pebbles riding pet dinosaur, 1964, 11x14", EX+, T2.............$24.00

Flintstones, puzzle, jigsaw; Warren, Bedrock Rodeo, 100+ pcs, 1976, EX, T6...$9.00

Flintstones, record, Lullaby of Pebbles, Little Golden, 78 rpm, in mc stiff paper sleeve, 1962, NM, T2..........................$24.00

Flintstones, Rotodraw, England, missing 1 of 6 drawing disks, EX-, T6................................$6.00

Flintstones, Wilma & Pebbles push-button puppets, Kohner, orig 2x6x7" window box holds both, NMIB, A.......$300.00

Flintstones, Wilma push-button puppet, Kohner, NM.....$35.00

Flipper, Color-By-Number set, Hasbro, complete w/pencils, 1966, MIB (sealed) $55.00

Flipper, game, board; Flipper Flips, Mattel, 1965, M $50.00

Flipper, puzzle, Big Little Book, Whitman, 1966, NM (EX box), C1..$15.00

Flipper, puzzle, fr-tray; Whitman, 1965, EX+, T6.............$12.00

Flipper, record, soundtrack, Flipper's New Adventure, 1986, EX $20.00

Flub-A-Dub, push-button puppet, Kohner, wood on plastic base, 4½", NM, from $90 to $125.00

Flying Avengers, Human Torch, Iron Man, Thor the Mighty, or Vision figure, 1977, MOC, T1, any..........................$10.00

Flying Nun, doll, Hasbro, 12", MIB.......................$395.00

Flying Nun, figure, Hasbro, 4", MIB.......................$65.00

Flying Nun, figure, Rayline, solid plastic figure w/prop device, flies, 1970, 5", NRFB, H4 ....$50.00

Flying Nun, game, board; Milton Bradley, 1968, EX (EX box), from $35 to........................$50.00

Flying Nun, gum cards, Donruss, 1968, single unopened pkg, M1..$20.00

Flying Nun, soundtrack, 1966, EX........................$30.00

Foxy Grandpa, bank, silver, gr, red & blk pnt CI, rpt, 5½", G-, A..$25.00

Foxy Grandpa, toy, Hubley, CI, sm donkey pulls lg-headed Grandpa, pnt chipped, 1905, 6", A........................$325.00

Foxy Grandpa, whistle, pnt clay, violet, mustard, wht & brn, 3", VG, A $35.00

Frank Buck, initial ring, premium, ivory, NM, J2..........$280.00

Frankenstein, bendee, Ahi, 1974, 4", MOC.................$25.00

Frankenstein, Coppersmith picture kit, K&B Mfg, Frankenstein walking through cemetery, 1960s, 8x11" box, EX (EX box), A..$95.00

Frankenstein, figure, Ace Novelty, stuffed, MIP, E3.........$15.00

Frankenstein, figure, Kenner, MIP, E3 ....$8.00

Frankenstein, figure, Marx, EX+, J2 ....$16.00

Frankenstein, figure, Mego, Mad Monster series, complete, loose, EX, H4 ....$40.00

Frankenstein, figure, Remco, glow-in-the-dark plastic, 1980, 8", M (VG box), C1..$45.00

Frankenstein, figure, Universal Studios, nude, 1979, 9", VG, N2 ....$15.00

Frankenstein, glow putty, Larami, 1979, MOC, D9............$8.00

Frankenstein, monster ball, Illco, 1980s, MOC $4.50

Frankenstein, night light, Hamilton, ceramic head flashes, 6", EX $28.00

Frankenstein, poster, Wesco-Realtex, Bride of Frankenstein, 1982, 22x30", M $25.00

Frankenstein, puzzle, fr-tray; Universal Studios, 11-pc, M, F1 ....$5.00

Frankenstein, spoon, Zoo-Piks, plastic w/figure hdl, 5½", M.$45.00

Frankenstein, Super-8 Home Movie w/Sound, Castle, 200-ft film, Boris Karloff & Colin Clive, NM (NM box), C1 ....$31.00

Frankenstein, Wolfman, Creature, Mummy & Dracula Horrorscope Magic Drawing Slate, Lowe, 1963, c Universal,, 8x14", NM, T2..$60.00

Frankenstein Jr, Sticker Fun Book, Whitman, 1967, 11x12", EX+, A..$200.00

Freddie & the Dreamers, gum cards, Donruss, 1965, set of 66, complete, M1..$95.00

Freddy Krueger, doll, Matchbox, talker, has 5 sayings, 18", MIB, from $50 to..$62.00

Freddy Krueger, doll, posable, 1988, 12", MIB, T1 ....$25.00

Freddy Krueger, game, A Nightmare on Elm Street, MIB, F1..$25.00

Freddy Krueger, game, Cardinal, sealed, F3................$28.00

Freddy Krueger, glove, from Nightmare on Elm Street, w/bendable & movable fingers, MOC, F1 ....$25.00

Freddy Krueger, quick-change doll set, Nightmare on Elm St, Matchbox, 1989, MIB, from $15 to................$20.00

Freddy Krueger, Scary Nite Sticks, 1990s, MOC, T1........$15.00

Freddy Krueger, yo-yo, Spectra Star, MIP, F1 ....$5.00

Frosty the Snowman, record, 45 rpm, 1951, EX..............$12.00

Fuddnuddlers, puzzle, Dr Suess, NRFB, H4 ....$5.00

Fugitive, game, board; Ideal, NMIB.......................$70.00

Funny Company, Shrinking Violette figure, Mattel, talker, 1963, MIB..$100.00

Fury, puzzle, fr-tray; Whitman, 1960s, NM, C1 ....$18.00

G-Man, fingerprint set, complete w/instructions, 1936, 12x9x8", EX, A..$75.00

G-Man, ring, silver, radio premium, 1930s, EX, T1.........$15.00

Gabby Hayes, puzzle, fr-tray; NM $42.50

Gamera, figure, Bandai, vinyl, MIP, E3......................$20.00

Garbage Pail Kids, gum cards, Topps, 1st series, 1985, set of 88, complete, M1..$150.00

Garbage Pail Kids, gum cards, Topps, 2nd series, 1st or 2nd print, puzzle bks, set of 88, complete, M1................$60.00

Garbage Pail Kids, gum cards, Topps, 3rd series, set of 88, complete, M1..$18.00

Garbage Pail Kids, gum cards, Topps/Trebor (British), 1985, 1st series, set of 88, M1..$35.00

Garfield, bank, vinyl figure, 1985, VG+, T1 ....$6.50

Garfield, gum cards, Skybox, 1992, set of 100, complete, M1 ....$18.00

Garfield, lunch bag, cotton, insulated, hand & shoulder straps, VG+, w/yel Thermos, NM, P3, set........................$15.00

Gene Autry, book, Gene Autry & Red Shirt, Sandpiper, 8 chapters, 1951, 5x8", M, A..$25.00

Gene Autry, game, Built-Rite/Gene Autry, Dude Ranch, dbl game w/car race on bk, complete, 1956, orig box, VG, P4.....$75.00

Gene Autry, gun, Buzz Henry, gold-plated CI cap pistol, 1950s, 7½", M..$115.00

Gene Autry, gun, Buzz Henry, NP CI cap pistol, 1950s, 7½", EX..$115.00

Gene Autry, gun, Kenton, dummy cap pistol, CI, wht plastic grips w/90% signature, 1939, 8⅜", VG, P4.............$185.00

Gene Autry, gun, Kenton, Junior Model cap gun, CI w/simulated pearl inset hdls, ca 1939, 7", unused, w/pin-bk, NMIB, A..$275.00

Gene Autry, gun, Kenton, NP CI cap pistol, orange grips, late 1940s, EX, H1..$145.00

Gene Autry, gun, Leslie-Henry, diecast cap pistol w/blk plastic horse-head grips, break-to-front, 1950s, 9", VG, P4 . **$110.00**

Gene Autry, gun, Leslie-Henry, diecast cap pistol w/wht horse-head grips, unfired, 7¾", M, P4 .... **$120.00**

Gene Autry, gun, Leslie-Henry, 44 cap pistol, diecast w/gold finish, wht plastic horse-head grips, '50s, 10½", NM, P4 .... **$245.00**

Gene Autry, hat, cream-colored cloth w/stitching around rim, 1" band featuring his image & name in script, EX, A **$65.00**

Gene Autry, photo, Homogenized Bond premium, blk & wht, 1949, NM in plastic holder, C1 .... **$15.00**

Gene Autry, puzzle, fr-tray; orig sleeve, 12x15", EX+, J2.. **$55.00**

Gene Autry, ranch outfit box, lid features Gene waving his hat on horseback, MA Henry, 1941, 11x8", VG+ **$95.00**

Gene Autry, ring, silver face, 1950s, EX+, T1 .... **$65.00**

Gene Autry, songbook, 1950s, VG, T1 .... **$35.00**

Gene Autry Tray, Gene on Champion decal on yellow-painted metal, 15", EX, $45.00.

Gene Autry, wallet, vinyl, M4... **$20.00**

Gene Autry, writing pad, full color, sgn cover, 1950s, 9x5½", M, P6 .... **$32.00**

Gene Autry, 6-gun paper popper, advertises his TV show, 1950s, NM, T1 .... **$6.00**

Gepetto, Marx, Tinykins series, M, H4 .... **$5.00**

Gerald McBoing, record, Gerald McBoing-Boing, Cricket Records, 45 rpm, 1956, unused, M (EX+ illus sleeve), T2 .... **$20.00**

Ghidrah, figure, Bandai, vinyl, MIP, E3 .... **$35.00**

Ghostbusters, Colorforms, 1986, EX, N2 .... **$5.00**

Ghostbusters, Ecto 1A Ambulance, 1980s, MIB, T1 .... **$25.00**

Ghostbusters, Ecto 500 vehicle, Kenner, 1986-1990, MIP, F1 .... **$15.00**

Ghostbusters, Egon, Peter or Ray figure, Screaming Heroes series, MOC, D4, any **$6.00**

Ghostbusters, Fearsom Flush figure, MOC, D4 .... **$5.00**

Ghostbusters, figures, Kenner, Ecto Glow series, set of 5, MIP, rare, F1 .... **$75.00**

Ghostbusters, Ghost Grab-a-Meter weapon, Kenner, 1986-1990, MIP, F1 .... **$10.00**

Ghostbusters, Ghost Sweeper vehicle, Kenner, 1986-1990, MIP, F1 .... **$15.00**

Ghostbusters, gum cards, Panini, 1987, set of 264, complete, M1... **$35.00**

Ghostbusters, gum cards, Topps, 1989, from 2nd movie, set of 88 cards w/11 stickers, complete, M1 .... **$9.50**

Ghostbusters, Haunted Air Sickness Vehicle, MIB, D4 ..... **$5.00**

Ghostbusters, Peter, Ray, or Monster figure, Fright Features series, MOC, D4, ea **$6.00**

Ghostbusters, playing cards, Belguim, sealed deck, 1986, M **$5.00**

Ghostbusters, Proton Back Pack, Kenner, 1986-1990, MIP, F1 .... **$30.00**

Ghostbusters, Slimer figure, Kenner, w/pizza, 1986-1990, MIP, F1 .... **$30.00**

Ghostbusters, Spitballs, Entertech, MIP, E3 .... **$6.00**

Ghostbusters, Winston Zeddmore figure, Kenner, 1st series, 1987, MOC (sealed) **$12.00**

Ghouls Just Wanna Have Fun T-shirt, M, E3 .... **$5.00**

Gideon, figure, Toy Biz, MOC, D8 .... **$9.00**

Gidney the Moon Man, squeeze toy, Jay Ward, R3 .... **$200.00**

Gigan, figure, Bandai, vinyl, MIP, E3 .... **$20.00**

Giget, game, card; Milton Bradley, 1965, MIB (sealed) ... **$47.50**

Gilligan's Island, book, Whitman, hardcover, 1966, EX .. **$20.00**

Gilligan's Island, game, New Adventures, 1974, NM, C1 .... **$31.00**

Gilligan's Island, Skipper doll, Presents, very detailed, w/stand, 1991, 9", M, F1 .... **$20.00**

Gilligan's Island, tablet, full-color cover of Gilligan & the Skipper, 1965, 8x10", 1965, NM, T2 .... **$18.00**

Girl from UNCLE, soundtrack, 1967, EX **$20.00**

Gnomemobile, book, coloring; 1967, VG+, T6 .... **$7.00**

Godzilla, figure, Bandai, Kaiju series, vinyl, MIP, from $70 to **$90.00**

Godzilla, figure, Bandai, Super Deformed set, MIP, E3..... **$20.00**

Godzilla, figure, Bandai, vinyl, sm, MIP, E3 .... **$25.00**

Godzilla, figure, Bandai, vinyl, 36", MIP, E3 .... **$175.00**

Godzilla, game, board; Ideal, 1963, M **$575.00**

Godzilla, lighter, Beetland, MIP, E3 .... **$40.00**

Godzilla, Pocket Hero Set, Yutaka, MIP, E3 .... **$15.00**

Godzilla, poster, from 1985 movie, M **$10.00**

Godzilla, puzzle, HG Toys, #458-04, battle action w/Air Force, 150-pc, complete, 1978, H4 .... **$25.00**

Godzillasaurus, figure, Bandai, vinyl, MIP, E3 .... **$10.00**

Gomer Pyle, game, board; Transogram, 1966, NMIB **$65.00**

Gomer Pyle, game, Transogram, 1961, EX+, F3 .... **$35.00**

Gong Show, game, American Publishing, 1977, MIB (sealed), C1 ....$36.00

Gong Show, gum cards, Fleer, 1979, set of 66, M1 ....$22.00

Good Times, JJ Walker figure, Shindana, 1975, NMIB....$67.50

Goofy, bank, plastic head, 11", VG, N2 ....$19.00

Goofy, bendee, Applause, 6", K1 ....$6.00

Goofy Doll, Schuco, ca 1950s, 14", EX, D10, $350.00.

Goofy, figure, Cristallerie Antonia Imperatore, Italy, frosted glass, 1960s, 7", MIB, P6...$50.00

Goofy, figure, plastic, 12", missing hat, VG-EX, O1 ....$15.00

Goofy, Klock Model Kit, Lindberg, assemble working clock, red & yel plastic, 1965, 7x14" $100.00

Goofy, nodder, Marx, 1960s, EX..............................$7.50

Goofy, paint box, England, litho tin, also features Huey, Louie & Dewey, 1940s, used/brush missing, o/w EX, M8.....$55.00

Goofy, pencil sharpener, WDP, gr & wht plastic, hand crank, ca 1980, M $20.00

Goofy, Swish Game, Gardner, standee w/net for shooting baskets, early 1960s, MIB...$45.00

Goofy & Pluto, tray, Hasko, litho tin, ca 1954, 16x7½", NM, P6...$35.00

Goonies, gum cards, Topps, 1986, set of 86 w/22 stickers, complete, M1 ....$12.00

Grease, gum cards, Topps, 1978, 1st series, set of 66 w/11 stickers, M1 ....$12.00

Grease, puzzle, 150-pc, 10x14", VG, T6 ....$5.00

Green Arrow, figure, Mego, missing accessories, G, D8 ...$25.00

Green Goblin, figure, Mego, complete w/accessories, 8", loose, H4..$125.00

Green Goblin, figure, Mego, 1974, jtd plastic, wearing jumpsuit w/bag around neck, 8", NM (EX box), A.................$141.00

Green Goblin, figure, Toy Biz, MIP, from $10 to $15.00

Green Hornet, book, coloring; Green Hornet & Kato's Revenge, Watkins, 1966, EX, J2 ....$24.00

Green Hornet, book, 1989, EX, T1 ....$25.00

Green Hornet, charm bracelet, Greenway, 1966, MOC .$70.00

Green Hornet, Flasher Ruler, Vari-Vue, 1966, NM, C1...$72.00

Green Hornet, flicker disk, 1966, 3" dia, M, J2................$25.00

Green Hornet, game, Quick Switch, NMIB, H4 ....$300.00

Green Hornet, magic slate, 1960s, VG $95.00

Green Hornet, playing cards, autographed by Van Williams, 1966, M (NM box) $50.00

Green Hornet, playing cards, Ed-U-Cards, Green Hornet jokers, standard deck, 2½x3½" photo box, NMIB, from $35 to..$50.00

Green Hornet, postcard, full-color glossy, 1966, 3½x5½", unused, EX, T2...$10.00

Green Hornet, puzzle, fr-tray; Whitman, complete set of 4, 1960s, 8x10", EX (EX box)..................................$65.00

Green Hornet, stickers, Gower/Greenway Prod, pressure sensitive, in orig 3x9" pkg, NM (EX+ card), A $250.00

Green Hornet Touch of Velvet Art Stardust Set, 1966, NMIB, A, $110.00; Green Hornet Cartoon Kit, Colorforms, with illustrated booklet, 1966, NMIB, $110.00.

Green Lantern, figure, Toy Biz, 2nd series, rare, MOC, F1 .$25.00

Gremlins, card & sticker set, 1984, NMIP, C1 ....$9.00

Gremlins, Colorforms, MIB, D4 ....$10.00

Gremlins, Gizmo figure, vinyl, 1983, MIB, T1..............$19.50

Gremlins, Gizmo pin, Applause, MOC, D4 ....$3.00

Gremlins, gum cards, Topps, 1984, set of 82 w/11 stickers, complete, M1 ....$12.00

Gremlins, night light, EX $10.00

Gremlins, stickers, Topps, 1984, cereal premium, blank bk, set of 11, M1 ....$6.00

Gremlins, Stripe bendee, 5", NMOC, D4 ....$10.00

Gremlins, Stripe figure, vinyl, 1980s, 3¾", VG, T1 ....$2.00

Gremlins, transfers, Colorforms, MIP, F1 ....$5.00

Grim Reaper, tattoo wrapper, 1963, unused, NM, T2 ......$24.00

Grinch, doll, Coleco/Dr Seuss, NM $32.50

Grizzly Adams, book, coloring; Rand McNally, 1978, EX-NM, C1..$15.00

Grizzly Adams, game, Save the Animals, Waddingtons, 1978, EX, T2..$20.00

Groucho Marx, game, Groucho's You Bet Your Life, Lowell, bl, orange & yel litho box, 18¼", VG $50.00

Groucho Marx, game, Groucho TV Quiz, Pressman, litho paper board, plastic play pcs, complete, orig box, 18", EX, A..............$35.00

Growing Pains, gum cards, Topps, 1988, set of 66 w/11 stickers, complete, M1 ....$15.00

Guiron, figure, Bandai, vinyl, MIP, E3..............$20.00

Gulliver's Travels, King Little figure, compo & wood, jtd, 1939, EX $700.00

Gumby, air freshener, cb, oval, 1986, 4", M..............$2.00

Gumby, bendee, Applause, dressed as baseball player or surfer, 1989, 5", K1, either..............$4.95

Gumby, bendee, Applause, 1989, 5", K1 ....$3.95

Gumby, bendee, Playskool, 1988, 6", K1 ....$3.95

Gumby, book, Gumby's Book of Colors, hardcover, 1986, EX $8.00

Gumby, doll, stuffed w/plastic eyes & felt features, 22", S1.$18.00

Gumby, Electric Drawing Set, Lakeside, light table, drawing stand, etc in 10x15x4" box, 1966, EX- (VG+ box), T2..........$40.00

Gumby, figure, Applause, 1989, 12", MIB..............$25.00

Gumby, figure, Perma Toy, 2¾", M..............$3.50

Gumby, figure, Perma Toy, 5¾", M..............$7.00

Gumby, figure, Perma Toys/Lewco Toys, 1984, 12", M $12.00

Gumby, outfit, Lakeside, Knight, Fireman, or Space Adventure, 1965, MOC, H4, any..............$12.00

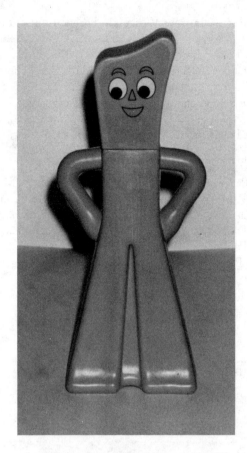

Gumby No Tears Shampoo Bottle, Perma Toy Co, 1987, 9½", full, $9.00.

Gumby, pin, cloisonne, M $5.00

Gumby, playset, Colorforms/Perma Toy, 1988, M $5.00

Gumby, playset, Construction Site, includes framed house w/cement mixer & other building props, EX $16.50

Gumby, playset, Diner Booth, includes diner booth w/table, plants & backdrop, EX..............$24.00

Gumby, playset, Gasoline Alley, exterior scene w/garbage cans, boxes, signs & hobo figure, EX $25.00

Gumby, playset, Granny's Porch, house front w/Granny sitting on porch, EX..............$20.00

Gumby, playset, Gumby & Pals Band, includes characters & instruments, EX $65.00

Gumby, playset, Kap's Laboratory, detailed interior w/scientific equipment, EX $25.00

Gumby, playset, King's Court, interior of throne room w/marble-based dais, throne & king, EX $20.00

Gumby, playset, Medieval Village, elaborate street scene complete w/flags, carts, horse, etc, EX..............$70.00

Gumby, playset, Pink Mansion, Delani's house, includes interior backdrop, front yard fountain & sports car, EX..........$40.00

Gumby, playset, Schoolroom, nostalgic interior w/desks, chairs, chalkboard & teacher, EX $25.00

Gumby, playset, Sheriff's Office, complete w/horse & carriage, EX..............$18.00

Gumby, playset, Western Hotel, 2-story exterior w/street, comes w/chairs, lamppost clock, horse & buggy, EX..........$35.00

Gumby, playset, White House, lg exterior facade of the President's home, 72x13x24", EX $40.00

Gumby Astronaut Adventure Costume, Lakeside, 1965, MIP, $12.00.

Gumby, puzzle, fr-tray; Whitman, barbecuing scene, 1965, 11x14", EX+, T2 ....$20.00

Gumby & Pokey, air freshener, cb, oval, 1987, 4", M.........$2.00

Gumby & Pokey, figures, Clay Pals, hand-sculpted, limited edition, M $975.00

Gumby & Pokey, game, board; Playful Trails, 1968, orig box, EX $95.00

Gumby & Pokey, puzzle, fr-tray; Whitman, 1968, EX $30.00

Gumby's Pal Pokey, bendee, Jesco, 10", K1 ....$12.00

Gumby's Pal Pokey, bendee, Playskool, 1988, 6", K1.........$3.95

Gumby's Pal Pokey, figure, Jesco/Perma Toy, sitting, 9", M .$12.00

Gumby's Pal Pokey, figure, Lakeside, orange rubber, from vending machine, mid-1960s, 2x2", M, T2 ....$6.00

Gumby's Pal Pokey, figure, Perma Toy, 2¼", M $3.50

Gumby's Pal Pokey, figure, Perma Toy, 4¼", M $7.00

Gumby's Pal Pokey, hand puppet, Lakeside, orange w/vinyl head, cloth body, 1965, in cellophane pkg, MIP $25.00

Gumby's Pal Pokey, stick horse, Lakeside, plastic head at top, plastic wheel on bottom, 36", long, 1965, EX+, T2 ...$30.00

Gunsmoke, ad, James Arness & Amanda Blake w/L&M cigarettes on Gunsmoke set, color, 1958, 11x13", NM, C1 ....$18.50

Gunsmoke, badge, Texas Ranger Sheriff, 1963, MOC $12.00

Gunsmoke, book, coloring; Whitman, James Arness fighting bad guy on covers, 1958, NM, C1 ....$19.50

Gunsmoke, game, board; Lowell, 1955, orig 10x20" box, NMIB (rpr box) $65.00

Gunsmoke, paperback, 1957, EX $12.00

Gunsmoke, pencil case, Hasbro, thick bl cb w/James Arness photo, 1961, 4x9", EX-, T2 ....$40.00

Gunsmoke, TV Guide, cast photo, 1960, EX+, C1 ....$15.00

Gyaos, figure, Bandai, vinyl, MIP, E3 ....$20.00

Hair Bear Bunch, Hair Bear bank, pnt ceramic, 1970s, 4", NM, C1...$21.00

Hair Bear Bunch, Hair Bear figure, Sutton, stuffed w/bendable arms, orig tag, 1971, 8", EX, H4 ....$49.00

Hair Bear Bunch, Square Bear figure, Sutton, stuffed w/bendable wire arms, 1971, 6", EX, H4..............................$49.00

Hamilton, Invaders Helmet, 1960s, MIB, T1 ....$125.00

Hansel & Gretel, Gingerbread House #985, Auburn, 1970s, MIB...$125.00

Happy Days, card set, 1st series, set of 44, NMIP, C1 ....$15.00

Happy Days, Fonzie's Cool Fun Activity Book, Grosset Dunlap, 1976, NM-M, C1 ....$19.00

Happy Days, Fonzie's Paint Set, 1979, MIB (sealed), V1 .$14.50

Happy Days, game, board; Parker Bros, 1976, MIB, from $25 to...$40.00

Happy Days, game, card; Milton Bradley, Hanging Out at Arnold's, complete, 1976, EX, T6 ....$7.00

Happy Days, gum cards, Topps, 1976, set of 44 w/11 stickers, complete, M1 ....$25.00

Happy Days, playset, 1976, MIB (sealed) $25.00

Happy Days, puzzle, HG, Arnold's place w/Richie, Fonz & Potsy, 150-pc, 1976, 14x10", EX+, T6 ....$7.00

Happy Hooligan, ashtray, porc, standing by big boot, 1900, 6x4", rare, NM+, A..$110.00

Happy Hooligan, bank, glazed brn ceramic, crazing, missing trap, 5¾", G-VG, A $30.00

Happy Hooligan, toy, Hubley, CI, 'rubber-necked' figure on 2-wheeled donkey cart, 70% orig pnt, 1910s, 6½", M5 ....$550.00

Hardcastle & McCormick, walkie-talkies, Jaru, 1983, NMOC $15.00

Hardy Boys, game, Hardy Boys Mystery, Parker Bros, 1978, complete, EX...$15.00

Harry & the Hendersons, doll, Galoob, 18", MIP, E3/T1.$25.00

Harry & the Hendersons, doll, Galoob, talking, 24", MIB..$45.00

Harry & the Hendersons, gum cards, Topps, 1987, set of 77 w/22 stickers, complete, M1 ....$12.00

Have Gun Will Travel, book, coloring; Lowe, 120+ pgs, 1960, 8x11", unused, NM.................................$95.00

Have Gun Will Travel, exhibit card, blk & wht w/facsimile autograph of Palladin, 1950s-60s, 3½x5", NM in holder, C1 ....$18.00

Have Gun Will Travel, game, board; Parker Bros, 1959, EX+ (EX+ box) $85.00

Hawaii Five-O, book, Octopus Caper, Whitman, hardcover, 1971, EX...$10.00

Hawaii Five-O, book, Top Secret, Whitman, 1969, NM-, C1 .$16.50

Hawaii Five-O, gun set, 4 mini pistols w/4 cases of ammo, unmk, MOC, H4 ....$39.00

Hawkman, figure, Toy Biz, 2nd series, rare, MOC, F1 ......$25.00

Heathcliff, bank, plastic figure, 1980s, VG, T1 ....$10.00

Heavy Metal, gum cards, Comic Images, 1991, set of 90, M1 ....$17.50

Hector Heathcote, game, Hashimoto San, The Japanese House Mouse; Transogram, 1961, NMIB, C1 ....$81.00

Hector Heathcote, game, Silly Sidney the Absent-Minded Elephant, Transogram, 1963, EX+, C1 ....$127.00

Hector Heathcote, game, The Minuteman & 1/2 Man, complete, EX (EX box), H4 ....$150.00

Hedwig Bird, squeeze toy, Mattel, talker, 1970, 10", R3...$50.00

Hee Haw, game, target; Milton Bradley, 1937, EX, F3 .....$28.00

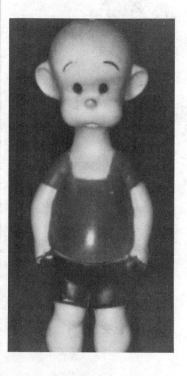

Henry Doll, early rubber vinyl with painted details, marked KF, ca 1950, NM, $30.00.

Henry, figure, Carl Anderson, Japan, pnt bsk, dtd 1934, 3½x1",
EX+, A..$100.00

Herbie Rides Again, poster, 1974, 27x40", M4.................$25.00

Hercules, book, coloring; Lowe, 1963, 8x11", unused, NM,
A..$50.00

Herman & Katnip, puzzle, fr-tray; Warren, Katnip holds Herman
in ice cream cone, 1978, EX+, D9.............................$4.00

High Chaparral, book, Apache Way, Whitman, 200+ pgs, hardback, 1969, 5x8", EX, T2...$9.00

High Chaparral, figures, Airfix, 5x6" box w/42 including
John & Victoria, Blue Boy, etc, 1969, unused, M (EX
box), T2..$30.00

Hogan's Heroes, game, Transogram, 1965, EX.................$45.00

Hogan's Heroes, record album, Sunset, Sing the Best of WWII,
cast members on jacket, 33⅓ rpm, 1967, EX+, T2 ....$30.00

Hogan's Heroes, tablet, full-color cover of Colonel Hogan, 1965,
8x10", NM, T2...$20.00

Hollywood Squares, game, Ideal, complete, 1974, EX+......$8.00

Hollywood Squares, record album, Event #6903, Zingers From
the Hollywood Squares, 1974, EX (EX cover), T6 ....$15.00

Honey I Shrunk the Kids, paperback, 1989, EX.................$6.50

Honey West, Accessories for TV's Private Eye Full, Gilbert,
1965, MOC, C1...$54.00

Honeymooners, book, comic; Triad #1, 1987, M, F1.........$6.00

Honeymooners, game, board; VIP Corp/TRS Inc, 1968, MIB
(sealed), P4..$15.00

Honeymooners, game, board; 1985, NM..........................$10.00

Honeymooners, game, board; 1986, VG, N2......................$7.00

Honeymooners, game, VCR; VIP/Mattel, VHS format, 1986,
MIB (sealed), P4..$25.00

Honeymooners, gum cards, Comic Images, 1988, set of 51,
M1...$60.00

Hong Kong Phooey, book, Fire Engine Mystery, Rand McNally
Elf Book, 1977, NM, C1...$13.00

Hong Kong Phooey, book, Fortune Cookie Caper, 1975, EX,
T6..$4.00

Hong Kong Phooey, puzzle, jigsaw; HG, 70-pc (1 missing), 1974,
10x14", VG-, T6...$5.00

Hook, Ace figure, Mattel, MIP, E3..................................$8.00

Hook, Air-Attack Peter Pan figure, Mattel, MIP, E3..........$8.00

Hook, gum cards, Topps, 1991, set of 99 w/11 stickers, M1 .$10.00

Hook, Multi-Blade Hook figure, Mattel, MIP, E3...............$8.00

Hook, Rufio figure, Mattel, MIP, E3.................................$8.00

Hook, Skull Armor Hook figure, Mattel, MIP, E3............$15.00

Hook, Swashbuckling Peter Pan figure, Mattel, MIP, E3....$8.00

Hopalong Cassidy, ad photo, for bread, 8x10", M.............$20.00

Hopalong Cassidy, bedspread, Bar-20 over Hoppy on horseback
leaping over fence, name below, 100x104", EX, from $140
to..$175.00

Hopalong Cassidy, book, coloring; partially used, 15x11", EX+,
M5...$28.00

Hopalong Cassidy, book, coloring; 24 pgs, all pages colored, EX,
M5...$15.00

Hopalong Cassidy, book, Hopalong Cassidy & Lucky at
Copper Gulch, Television Book, Crowe illus, 1950,
EX, A..$100.00

Hopalong Cassidy, book, Makes New Friends, 1950,
EX-...$12.00

Hopalong Cassidy, book, pop-up; Hopalong Cassidy Lends a
Helping Hand, EX, A..$80.00

Hopalong Cassidy, book, pop-up; Lucky at Double-R Ranch,
Garden City Publishing, 1950, 11x8", EX...............$125.00

Hopalong Cassidy, book, punch-out; Whitman, 1951,
unpunched, EX, A...$130.00

Hopalong Cassidy, book, sticker; partially used, 12x10", EX+,
M5...$28.00

Hopalong Cassidy, breakfast set, WS George, plate, mug & bowl
featuring Hopalong Cassidy, 1950, MIB, A............$499.00

Hopalong Cassidy, Bunkhouse Clothes Corral, 24" long w/3 bars
for clothes, premium, 1950s, NM, C1....................$130.00

Hopalong Cassidy Canasta Game, MIB, M5, $120.00.

Hopalong Cassidy, chalk/coloring slate, Transogram, 1950,
complete w/slate, pencils, chalk & crayons, NM (EX
box)..$285.00

Hopalong Cassidy, cookie jar, Bar 20, complete w/M decal,
V1...$385.00

Hopalong Cassidy, dental kit, w/Mr West's toothpaste, toothbrush & mirror, orig box, 8¾", EX.........................$300.00

Hopalong Cassidy, ear muffs, Bailey, Hoppy on ea, 1950s, in
scarce box, NM+ (EX box)...................................$500.00

Hopalong Cassidy, film strip viewer, Picture Gun & Theatre,
w/2 complete films, orig box, 12½", EX.................$185.00

Hopalong Cassidy, game, Chinese Checkers, Milton Bradley, paper
litho board w/glass marbles, complete, VG-EX..........$145.00

Hopalong Cassidy, game, Hopalong Canasta, scarce, orig box
w/minor discoloration, A..$65.00

Hopalong Cassidy, game, Official Hopalong Cassidy Lasso
Game, Transogram, paper, wood & plastic, complete, EX,
A...$160.00

Hopalong Cassidy, gun, Wyandotte, gold, fires caps, EX, J2 ..$250.00

Hopalong Cassidy, gun, Zoomerang, Tigrett Ent, plastic,
spring action, photo illus of Hoppy & boy on lid, EX
(EX box)..$300.00

Hopalong Cassidy, gun & holster, Wyandotte, 8" diecast
repeater, studded holster w/emb concho, 1950s, VG+,
A...$229.00

Hopalong Cassidy, gun & holster set, Wyandotte, complete, NMIB **$1,200.00**

Hopalong Cassidy Gun and Holster Pencil Case, plastic, holds pencils and crayons, 8" long, NM, A, $300.00.

Hopalong Cassidy, Hair Trainer, glass bottle, 9¾", M **$45.00**

Hopalong Cassidy, Mechanical Shooting Gallery, Automatic Toy, 1950s, 18" triangular target, instructions, NM, C1 ....**$360.00**

Hopalong Cassidy, movie poster, The Showdown, 1940, few minor tears/tack holes, o/w EX, 41x27", A **$100.00**

Hopalong Cassidy, night light, The Stagecoach, revolving, EX+ (NM box), J2 ....**$550.00**

Hopalong Cassidy, outfit, color graphics on blk cloth, plastic gun, orig box, 12½", EX..**$250.00**

Hopalong Cassidy, outfit (girls') Iskin, complete w/blouse & skirt, scarf, etc, appears unused, 1950, NM (EX box), A...**$253.00**

Hopalong Cassidy, paper plate, unknown maker, ca 1950, M, P4...**$8.00**

Hopalong Cassidy, pennant, blk cloth w/wht letters, 1950, 28", VG, P4 ....**$35.00**

Hopalong Cassidy Plate, W.S. George, 9½", $48.00.

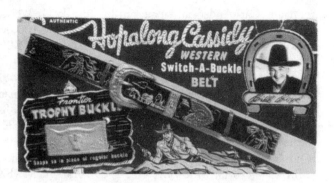

Hopalong Cassidy Switch-A-Buckle Belt, Yale Belt, M on original 7x13" illustrated card, A, $190.00.

Hopalong Cassidy, plaque, Good Luck, hangs on wall, M .**$65.00**

Hopalong Cassidy, puzzle, fr-tray; Milton Bradley, set of 4 w/Hoppy & Topper in 4 poses, 1950, 12x12", NMIB, A **$143.00**

Hopalong Cassidy, puzzle, fr-tray; photo w/horse, 1950, EX, D9...**$35.00**

ORIGINAL
HOPALONG CASSIDY
FOIL FACES FOR THE 441T ARVIN RADIO

Rare two feet in air version - $65.00

More common one foot in air, one foot on ground version - $50.00

BUY THE PAIR - $100.00 plus $3.50 P&I

I purchased the original tools & dies for the above. Included in the purchase was a quantity of foil faces for the radio. No need to call – I have plenty.

SATURDAY HEROES

SATURDAY HEROES
P.O. Box 7047
Panama City Beach, Florida 32413
(904) 234-7944
Ron & Donna Donnelly

• Western Hero Collectibles • Character Collectibles • Character Watches •
Disney • Radio & TV Premiums • Big Little Books • Movie Posters • Gone With The Wind

Hopalong Cassidy, puzzle, jigsaw; Milton Bradley, 1950, set of 2, ea 12x9", orig box, VG, A $70.00

Hopalong Cassidy, ring, face; premium, NM+, J2 ....$125.00

Hopalong Cassidy, School Slate Outfit, Transogram, 1 side for chalk, 1 for crayons, orig box, 17", EX, A $180.00

Hopalong Cassidy, viewer, Shapiro, #24, Heart of the West, contains 2 films & viewer, 1940s, NMIB, from $150 to $250.00

Hopalong Cassidy, wallet, 1950s, VG, T1 ....$45.00

Hopalong Cassidy & Topper, figures, Ideal, plastic, 1950s, 6", VG (EX+ box)...$165.00

Horace, wall plaque, McGowan Wood Products, diecut figure of Horace falling off horse, 1930s, 8x6", EX, A..............$68.00

Horton the Elephant, doll, Coleco, w/nest & egg, M $58.00

Hound Tank, figure, Popy, diecast, MIP, E3 ....$35.00

How the West Was Won, press book, from film, hardcover, A3...$5.00

Howdy Doody, acrobat, Arnold, pnt compo head w/cloth outfit, litho tin base & posts, crack in head, 11½", G, A $40.00

Howdy Doody, American History Album, Wonder Bread, 8-pg, 1950s, NM, C1...$75.00

Howdy Doody, bank, Howdy on pig's bk, red & bl pnt ceramic, 7", EX, A...$280.00

Howdy Doody, Big Prize Doodle List, 1954-55, NM.........$60.00

Howdy Doody, bubble pipe set, Lido, includes 2 plastic pipes, tin bowl & soap, scarce, unused, NM (EX box), A $210.00

Howdy Doody, Colgate store display, Bob Smith, cb litho standee, 1950s, 7", EX+, A $35.00

Howdy Doody Cowboy Pumpmobile, Nylint, cart is propelled by movement on handlebars, 1950s, 9", NM+ (EX+ box), A...$550.00

Howdy Doody, diecut, Palmolive Soap advertisement, Howdy waving, crease at neck, 6¾", VG, A............................$30.00

Howdy Doody, doll, Cameo, pnt compo & wood, string-jtd body, 12½", G-VG, A $230.00

Howdy Doody, figure, TeeVee Toys, plastic, w/moving mouth, box converts to TV set to show Howdy, 1950s, 4", NM, A $70.00

Howdy Doody, Figurine Painting Kit, Hadley, 4 plaster figures (2 have some pnt), 6 vials & 2 cups, EX (EX box), A .$173.00

Howdy Doody, game, Bean Bag, Parker Bros, 1950s, illus box, scarce, EX (EX box), A $300.00

Howdy Doody, game, board; Harett-Gilmar, Electric Carnival, unused, 1950s, 8x13", NM (EX+ box), A................$118.00

Howdy Doody, game, Howdy Doody Quiz Show, litho cb dial w/answer window, 12" dia, EX, A $190.00

Howdy Doody, game, Howdy Doody's Own Game, cb & wood, knock-down targets, 7x15", MIB, A $120.00

Howdy Doody, game, Snap-a-Wink, Kagran, cb litho, Poll Parrot premium, 1953, NM, A...$81.00

Howdy Doody, game, 3-Ring Circus, Gilmar, Clarabell's nose lights as player moves on board, working, 1950s, NM, A $81.00

Howdy Doody, hand puppet, head on red & gr-checkered cotton body, 1950s, EX+, C1 ....$27.00

Howdy Doody, Howdy Doody Crayons & Pictures, Milton Bradley, complete, uncolored, orig box, VG, A.........$35.00

Howdy Doody, life preserver, Ideal, vinyl, images of Howdy & friends, yel background, 1950s, 20", EX, A $45.00

Howdy Doody, Magic Kit, Luden's Inc mail-in premium, 1950s, complete w/instructions & mailer, 1950s, from $60 to...$75.00

Howdy Doody Marionette, Peter Puppet Playthings, 1950s, MIB, D10, $375.00.

Howdy Doody, nodder, Japan, compo, as cowboy, 1950s, VG, I2..$35.00

Howdy Doody Doodle Slate, 1950s, NM, D10, $35.00.

Howdy Doody, paint set, Milton Bradley, various pictures of Howdy & friends, complete, 12x10" box, NM (NM box), A...$258.00

Howdy Doody, photo, It's Howdy Doody Color TV Time, mc, set of 7 in paper sleeve, EX, A....................................$55.00

Howdy Doody, Princess push-button puppet, Kohner, pnt wood figure, working, 5¾", G-, A.......................................$70.00

Howdy Doody, pull toy, Howdy on wooden tricycle, legs pedal & bell jingles, Kagran, 1950s, scarce, 8½", EX+, A...$557.00

Howdy Doody, push-button puppet, Kohner, pnt wood body w/plastic head, working, broken stand, 5¾", G-VG, A.$45.00

Howdy Doody, puzzle, Howdy Doody Magic Puzzle Ball, Jolly Blinker Co Inc, orig box, 7½", VG-EX, A.................$90.00

Howdy Doody, puzzle, jigsaw; Howdy's One-Man Band, complete, 1950s, VG, I2...$19.00

Howdy Doody, puzzle, jigsaw; in 8x8" envelope from Poll Parrot, NM (EX envelope), A...$100.00

Howdy Doody, record, Howdy & the Air-O-Doodle, 78 rpm, 1949, set of 2 in mc jacket, VG-EX, A.......................$60.00

Howdy Doody, record, Howdy Doody's Christmas Party, yel vinyl, 45 rpm, set of 2 in picture sleeve, VG-EX, A ..$60.00

Howdy Doody, see also Clarabell

Howdy Doody, Sun-Ray Camera, MOC, V1 ....$68.00

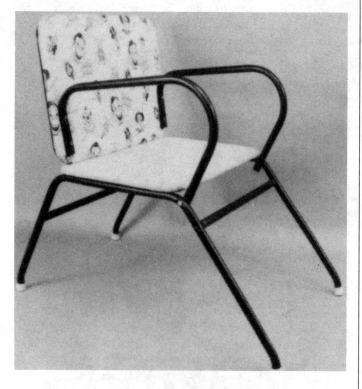

Howdy Doody TV Chair, broadcast giveaway, 1950s, from $250.00 to $300.00.

Howdy Doody, Tee Vee Puppet Show, Kagran, 4 mc plastic figures w/movable mouths, Clarabell's horn blows, 4", NMOC, C1..$240.00

Howdy Doody, ventriloquist doll, c NBC, hard rubber & cloth, 13", EX, A..$650.00

Howdy Doody, ventriloquist doll, Goldberger, 1971, 24", MIB..$135.00

Howdy Doody, wall walker, plastic figure of Howdy Doody, 1950s, 7", EX (VG+ card), A $41.00

Howdy Doody, wallet, Kagran, panels showing Howdy at circus, playing bagpipes & Dilly-Dally charming snake, 1950s, NM, A...$25.00

Howling Howard, figure, Powco, MIP, E3........................$10.00

HR Puf 'N Stuff, game, Sid & Marty Croft, Milton Bradley, EX, from $20 to...$30.00

HR Puf 'N Stuff, puzzle, fr-tray; EX, H4 ....$60.00

Huckleberry Hound, bank, plastic, VG, O1.....................$20.00

Huckleberry Hound, book, Stand-Up Story Book, 1975, EX, T6...$3.00

Huckleberry Hound, charm bracelet, Hanna-Barbera, gold chain w/6 charms, 1959, 6", MOC, P4.............................$20.00

Huckleberry Hound, cuff links & tie clasp set, Hanna-Barbera, Huck as ringmaster, 1959, MOC, P4.........................$10.00

Huckleberry Hound, doll, Knickerbocker, plush/vinyl, 1959, 18", EX+ $75.00

Huckleberry Hound, doll, plush & vinyl, orig tag, 14", NM, P6...$45.00

Huckleberry Hound, figure, ceramic, 1961, 5", M............$38.00

Huckleberry Hound, flashlight, MIP, T1 ....$20.00

Huckleberry Hound, game, board; Huckleberry Hound Bumps, Transogram, 1961, EX $48.00

Huckleberry Hound, game, board; Milton Bradley, 1981, NMIB, C1...$15.00

Huckleberry Hound, game, Flip Face, Kellogg's, from bk panels of OKs cereal, 1960, EX, T2 ....$18.00

Huckleberry Hound, game, Huck's Western Game, Milton Bradley, 1959, MIB (rpr corner on box), H4 ....$20.00

Huckleberry Hound, hand puppet, German, 13", NM, M5 ....$15.00

Huckleberry Hound, poster, 1969, M, T1 ....$15.00

Huckleberry Hound, puzzle, jigsaw; Whitman Jr, 1959, EX..$30.00

Huckleberry Hound, record album, Colpix #207, 33⅓ rpm, VG+ (VG cover), T6...$35.00

Huckleberry Hound, squeeze toy, Dell, R3......................$30.00

Huckleberry Hound, viewer, Marx, 1962, 2½", MIB........$22.50

Huckleberry Hound, yo-yo, litho tin, 1976, EX $15.00

Huckleberry Hound & Yogi Bear, night light, 1 ea side of TV w/Mr Jinx on screen, 1961, 7", NM, A $100.00

Hugh Downs, game, Chit Chat, Milton Bradley, 1963, MIB, H4..$8.00

Hulk, bank, vinyl head, 1980s, M, T1 ....$15.00

Hulk, belt, Remco, 1978, NMIB $10.00

Hulk, Break-Away Cage, Funstuff, 1978, NRFB, H4........$29.00

Hulk, card & sticker set, 88 color photo cards & 11 stickers, 1979, NMIP, C1...$31.00

Hulk, figure, Hamilton, 16", M, D4.................................$20.00

Hulk, figure, Mego, complete, loose, EX, H4 ....$12.00

Hulk, figure, Presents, posable vinyl, 18", M, F1.............$25.00

Hulk, figure, Remco, Engergized series, 1979, 12", MIB (torn flap on box), H4...$29.00

Hulk, figure, Toy Biz, 18", MIB, F1 ....$50.00

Hulk, figure, Toy Biz, 3¾", MOC, F1 ....$15.00

Hulk, figure, 3-D plastic, hangs on wall, 1979, 40", NM ..$20.00

Hulk, game, board; Incredible Hulk w/Fantastic Four, Milton Bradley, 1978, NM (EX- box), T2....................$30.00

Hulk, game, Gamma Glaster Pistol, Remco, 1978, MIB (sm tears on box), H4..$12.00

Hulk, game, Smash-Up Action, Ideal, 1978, M (NM box), C1..$36.00

Hulk, gum cards, Comic Images, 1991, set of 90, M1 ....$20.00

Hulk, gum cards, Topps, 1979, set of 88 w/22 stickers, M1 ....$16.00

Hulk, gum cards, Topps, 7 photo color cards w/1 sticker & 1 pc of gum, unopened, 1979, M, T2 ....$8.00

Hulk, lamp, EX-EX+, T1 ....$75.00

Hulk, playing cards, Nasta, MIP, F1 ....$3.00

Hulk, record, Queen City Records, Nobody Loves the Hulk, 45 rpm, mail-order premium, M (NM 7x7" cb sleeve), A...$55.00

Hulk, stickers wrapper, Philadelphia Gum Corp, once contained 5 gum card-sz stickers, 1966, NM, T2 ....$20.00

Hulk, switch plate, glow-in-the-dark plastic, 1976, MIP (sealed), C1..$13.00

Hulk, T-shirt, Marvel Comics, wht cotton, mail-order premium only, 1964, child's, scarce, EX+-NM, A...................$200.00

Hulk, Target Set, Fun Stuff, 1978, MOC....................$15.00

Human Torch, figure, Mego, 8", MOC, F1 ....$40.00

Human Torch, figure, Toy Biz, MIP, from $8 to $15.00

Hunter, Police Accessory Kit, Largo, 1984, MOC, C1 .....$13.00

I Dream of Jeannie, doll, 1960s, sm version, orig bl box, NMIB, T1..$125.00

I Dream of Jeannie, figure, Remco, 1977, 7", M (NM box), H4..$60.00

I Dream of Jeannie, game, Milton Bradley, 1965, EX, T6.$30.00

I Dream of Jeannie, outfit, Remco, dress & accessories, for 7" doll, 1977, MIB, H4/C1 ....$18.00

I Dream of Jeannie, scrapbook, 1966, EX $50.00

I Love Lucy, gum cards, Pacific, 1991, pk or silver border, set of 110, M1 ....$15.00

I Spy, game, board; Ideal, 1964, NM (NM box), from $75 to.$90.00

I Spy, Target Playset, 1960s, MOC, T1 ....$95.00

In Living Color, gum cards, Topps, 1992, set of 88 w/11 stickers, complete, M1 ....$15.00

In Living Color, Homey the Clown doll, Acme, 1992, 24", MIP, F1 ....$20.00

Inch-High Private Eye, dart gun, EX-NM, T6 ....$9.00

Indiana Jones, Belloq figure, in ceremonial robes, orig mailer, 1981, 3¾", MOC, from $10 to...........................$15.00

Indiana Jones, Cairo Swordsman figure, Kenner, MOC, H4..$14.00

Indiana Jones, coin, Indy Epic Stunt Spectacular, brass, MIB, D4 ....$8.00

Indiana Jones, Desert Convoy Truck, Kenner, 1980s, MIB, from $35 to $50.00

Indiana Jones, figure, Kenner, Sallah, MOC, H4.............$24.00

Indiana Jones, figure, missing pistol o/w complete, EX, H4..$75.00

Indiana Jones, game, board; Raiders of the Lost Ark, Parker Bros, 1982, MIB...$18.00

Indiana Jones, German Mechanic figure, Kenner, 1981, 3¾", MOC, C1 ....$22.00

Indiana Jones Figure, Kenner, 1982, 3¾", M on card, $125.00.

Indiana Jones, Giant Thuggee figure, LJN, 1984, MOC, H4..$55.00

Indiana Jones, gum card set, Topps, 88 color photo cards, complete, Raiders of Lost Ark, NM-M, C1......................$26.00

Indiana Jones, Khyber figure, bowie knife, complete w/accessories & authenticity papers, MIB, D4....................$135.00

Indiana Jones, Mola Ram figure, LJN, 1984, MOC, H4 ...$65.00

Indiana Jones, patch, Temple of Doom, M, D4..................$5.00

Indiana Jones, plates, Reed, paper, set of 8, 1981, MIP (sealed), C1..$15.00

Indiana Jones, playset, Map Room, Kenner, MIB, H4......$30.00

Indiana Jones, playset, Streets of Cairo, Kenner, MIB......$32.00

Indiana Jones, playset, Well of Souls, Kenner, 1982, NMIB (VG box) $45.00

Indiana Jones, Toth figure, Kenner, 1982, MOC, F1........$10.00

Indiana Jones, trading cards, Proset, Young Indiana Jones Chronicles, entire box of 36 pkgs, MIB, F1................$20.00

Invisible Girl, figure, Mego, complete, loose, EX, H4.......$35.00

Invisible Girl, figure, Mego, 8", MOC..............................$80.00

Invisible Man, figure, Mego, complete, loose, VG, H4.....$30.00

Ipcress File, game, Milton Bradley, complete, EX-NM (EX rpr box), H4..$25.00

Iron Man, figure, Mego, 1974, fully jtd plastic in cloth outfit w/vinyl belt & boots, 8", NM (EX box), T2 ....$80.00

Iron Man, figure, Mego, 8", MIB, H4..............................$129.00

Iron Man, figure, Toy Biz, 3¾", MIP $18.00

Isis, figure, Mego, 1976, 8", MOC $70.00

It's About Time, book, coloring; Whitman, 1967, 8x11", NM, A...$76.00

It's About Time, game, Ideal, 1967, 10x20" box, MIB, A.$200.00

Ivanhoe, figure, Mego, Super Knight series, 8", MIB (lt crushed top of box), H4 ....$80.00

Jack & Jill, game, target; Cadaco-Ellis, NMIB $22.00

Jack & the Beanstalk, Transogram, 1957, complete, EX ..$20.00

Jack Armstrong, game, Adventures w/the Dragon Talisman, General Mills premium, no spinner or game pcs, G (G envelope), A..$75.00

Jack Armstrong, ring, Egyptian whistle; radio premium, 1940s, NM+, T1..$95.00

Jackie Gleason, book, coloring; Dan, Dan, Dandy Coloring Book; Lowe, 120+ pgs, 1956, 8x11", EX+-NM, A.....$64.00

Jackie Gleason, book, Funny Book for Boys & Girls, Bonnie Books, 1956, VG-, T6..$6.00

Jackie Gleason, Bus Driver's Outfit, Empire Plastic, 1955, complete w/hat, shield, ticket puncher, etc, NM (EX box), A..$402.00

Jackie Gleason, magazine ad, Shick Shavers, EX.............$12.50

Jackson Five, pillow, VG $32.50

Jaiger, figure, Bandai, vinyl, MIP, E3.............................$20.00

Jak Pak, Inspector Gadget Periscope Dart Gun, complete w/darts, 1983, MOC, C1 ....$27.00

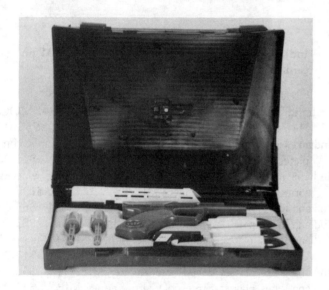

James Bond 007 Attache Case, Multiple Products, Hong Kong, cap gun, grenade pistol, rocket launcher, EX in 14x9½" case, $450.00.

James Bond, banner, wht cloth w/wood rod for hanging, 1965, 17x29", NM, A...$100.00

James Bond, car, Milton Bradley, NM-, F3 ....$48.00

James Bond, Code-O-Matic Machine, Multiple, create your own secret coded messages, NM (EX card), A..................$100.00

James Bond, doll, Ideal, 12", EX, J2................................$95.00

James Bond, Dr No figure, #10 of series, 3", MOC, H4 ....$15.00

James Bond, Electric Drawing Kit, Lakeside, 1966, NMIB, C1 ....$199.00

James Bond, figure, Gilbert, in scuba outfit, 1965, MOC, C1 ....$13.00

James Bond, game, Action Episode, EX-NM, H4 ....$5.00

James Bond, game, Message From M, Ideal, w/4 3-D territories of villains, complete, 1966, orig 22x16" box, scarce, EX+, A...$125.00

James Bond, game, Thunderball, Milton Bradley, 1965, NM (EX box), C1 ....$72.00

James Bond, game, 007 Tarot, US Games, 1973, M, F3 ...$38.00

James Bond, Goldfinger figure, Gilbert, 1965, 3", M, F1 ....$6.00

James Bond, gun, Lone Star, 100-Shot Repeater Cap Pistol w/Silencer, 1960s, NMIB, from $120 to $165.00

James Bond, gun, Secret Service Dart Gun, Imperial Toy, 1975, MOC, T1 ....$20.00

James Bond, hand puppet, Gilbert, vinyl, missing hat, 1960s, VG, H4 ....$80.00

James Bond, ID tags, Imperial, 1984, MOC, C1 ....$19.50

James Bond, M (Bond's boss) figure, Gilbert, 1965, 3", M, loose, F1 ....$6.00

James Bond, Moneypenny figure, M (VG card), O1........$15.00

James Bond, Odd Job figure, Gilbert, karate outfit w/derby hat, 1960s, M (EX box), H4 ....$275.00

James Bond, Official Secret Agent 007 Automatic Shooting Camera, Multiple Toy, 1966, missing cap plate, EX (VG box), H4...$149.00

James Bond, press kit, A View To Kill, MGM, 53 pgs, 1985, NM, C1 ....$45.00

James Bond, record, For Your Eyes Only, EX, P3 ....$6.00

James Bond, record album, Thunderball soundtrack, 1965, NM, J2 ....$20.00

James Bond, ring, 007, silver-tone, radio premium, 1960s, EX, T1 ....$35.00

James Bond, Shooting Attache Case, missing knife, sm crack in case & missing handle, T1 ....$325.00

James Bond, Shooting Attache Case, MPC, orig box, 1965, NM, A...$900.00

James Bond, swim fins, Voit, bl box illus w/Sean Connery as 007 in Thunderball, 1965, 14", NM (VG+ box), A.......$185.00

James Bond, walkie-talkies, Secret Service, Imperial, 1984, M (EX card), C1 ....$27.50

James Bond Jr, Buddy Mitchell figure, Hasbro, 1991, MIP, F1 ....$5.00

James Bond Jr, Dr Derange, Gordo Leiter or Odd Job figure, MOC, D4, ea...$4.00

James Bond Jr, Dr No figure, Hasbro, 1991, MIP, F1 ....$5.00

James Bond Jr, figure, Hasbro, 1991, MIP, F1 ....$5.00

James Bond Jr, Jaws figure, Hasbro, 1991, rare, MIP, F1 ...$10.00

James Bond 007, slot car, Aston Martin, Imai, 1/32 scale, M $135.00

James Dean, gum cards, European issue, 1990, set of 8, M1 .$10.00

James Dean, record album, Columbia, Tribute..., music from 3 movies, scarce, EX+ (EX+ cover), A.........................$50.00

Jane Mansfield, water bottle, NM $115.00

Jaws II, card & sticker set, 1978, NMIP, C1 ....$9.00

Jaws II, gum cards, Topps, 1978, set of 59 w/11 stickers, complete, M1 ....$9.50

Jerry Mahoney, ventriloquist doll, Paul Winchell, pnt compo w/wood head & hands, cloth body, 24", G-VG, A $50.00

Jesse James, puzzle, jigsaw; Jesse Robs the Train, Milton Bradley, 1965, 10x19" assembled, scarce, EX+, T2 ....$32.00

Jessica Rabbit, tray, England, litho tin, full figure on blk & wht background, 1987, 10½x13", NM, M8 ....$15.00

Jetsons, Astro Boy Squirt Gun, VG, H4 ....$12.00

Jetsons Bobbing Pull Toy, Transogram, plastic, advances with whirring sound, MOC, A, $375.00.

Jetsons, book, coloring; Rand McNally, 1986, NM, H4 .....$6.00

Jetsons, book, Sunday Afternoon on Moon, Durabook, 1972, EX $12.00

Jetsons Space Ball Game, Marx, Bagatelle game action, EX in box, A, $260.00.

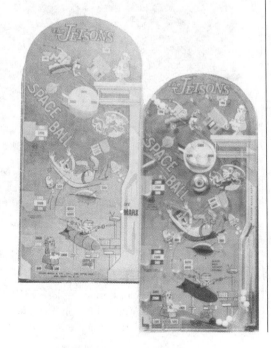

Jetsons, figure, Applause, PVC, any of 7 characters, MIP, F1, ea...$4.00

Jetsons, figure, Applause, vinyl, any of 4, 6", M, F1, ea $10.00

Jetsons, game, board; Rosie the Robot & Astro, Transogram, VG $65.00

Jetsons, George figure, Applause, 12", EX, H4..................$14.00

Jetsons, George, hand puppet, Ideal, 1960s, EX $95.00

Jetsons, modeling clay, Toycraft, complete, 1962, MIB....$55.00

Jetsons, record, Push Button Blues, Little Golden Records, in 7x8" paper sleeve, 1963, NM, T2 ....$32.00

Jetsons, Rosie Robot figure, Applause, 9", EX, H4...........$14.00

Jetsons, Slate & Chalk Set, 1960s, MIP, T1 ....$75.00

Jetsons, tote bag, Wonderland, Australia, 1987, 9x12", NM, C1 ....$27.00

Jim Lee, gum cards, Comic Images/Marvel, 1990, set of 45, M1...$22.00

Jiminy Cricket, book, Random House, 1940, VG............$15.00

Jiminy Cricket, doll, Knickerbocker, pnt compo, jtd arms & head, cloth outfit, 9½", EX, A...............................$425.00

Jiminy Cricket, figure, Argentina, pnt rubber, poseable, 1950s, 15", EX-, A..$60.00

Jiminy Cricket, figure, jtd wood, felt hat & collar, 1940s, 8½", EX, P6 ....$295.00

Jiminy Cricket Wallet, leather, EX, $25.00.

Jiminy Cricket, soundtrack, Jiminy Cricket's Add & Subtract, 1963, EX...$10.00

Jimmy Durante, ukelele, 20", VG (VG box), C6............$25.00

Jimmy Hendrix, lobby card, Woodstock, M, A...............$120.00
Joe Carioca, lamp, ceramic, Joe leaning on umbrella while smoking a cigar, no shade or wire, 6", EX+, A $113.00

Joe Carioca Figure, American Pottery Company, 1940s, M, $125.00.

Joe Hardy (Shaun Cassidy), puzzle, APC, 200-pc, 11x17", VG+, T6...$6.00
John F Kennedy, game, Exciting New Game of Kennedys, rare, NMIB, A..$300.00

John Wayne Figure, Avon, styled as Bob Seton in Dark Command, porcelain, 1985, 7⅜", $40.00.

John F Kennedy, gum cards, Rosan, set of 64, M1 ....$60.00
John F Kennedy, rocking chair, Kamar, rubber, cloth & wood, JFK reads newspaper, rocks, musical, 12x8", MIB, A........$195.00
John Wayne, belt buckle, True Grit photo, limited edition w/facsimile signature, M...$30.00
John Wayne, playing cards, NRFB $20.00
John Wayne, spoon, figure at hdl, M...............................$10.00
Johnny Apollo, figure, Marx, complete outfit & accessories, 9", H4 ....$40.00
Johnny Appleseed, book, softcover, 1969, EX....................$6.00
Johnny Carson, book, Misery Is..., hardcover, NM..........$10.00
Johnny Eagle, poster, Topper, diecut cb, 1965, 36x22", EX+, A $176.00
Johnny Quest, book, coloring; Whitman, 100+ pgs, 1965, unused, VG+, T2 ....$50.00
Johnny Quest, book, The Lost City, Durabook, 1972, VG, T6...$5.00
Johnny West, Bill Buck, figure, complete, MIB, R4, minimum value..$400.00
Johnny West, buckboard wagon, complete, MIB, R4 ....$60.00
Johnny West, buffalo, complete, MIB, R4 ....$150.00
Johnny West, Captain Maddox figure, complete, MIB, R4..$85.00
Johnny West, case, Johnny West Ranch Carry All, MIB, R4...$50.00
Johnny West, Chief Cherokee figure, complete, MIB, R4.$85.00
Johnny West, covered wagon, complete, MIB, R4 ....$60.00
Johnny West, dog, Flick or Flack, complete, MIB, R4......$80.00
Johnny West, Fighting Eagle figure, complete, MIB, R4.$125.00
Johnny West, General Custer figure, complete, MIB, R4.$85.00

Johnny West, Geronimo figure, with accessories, MIB, $85.00.

Johnny West, horse, Buckskin, complete, MIB, R4 ....$60.00
Johnny West, horse, Comanche, complete, MIB, R4 ....$50.00
Johnny West, horse, Flame, complete, MIB, R4 ....$50.00

Johnny West, horse, Pancho Pony, complete, MIB, R4 ...$40.00

Johnny West, horse, Stormcloud, complete, MIB, R4 ......$50.00

Johnny West, horse, Thunderbolt, complete, MIB, R4 ....$40.00

Johnny West, horse, Thundercolt, complete, MIB, R4 ....$35.00

Johnny West, Jamie West figure, complete, MIB, R4/M4 .$40.00

Johnny West, Jane West figure, complete, MIB, R4 ....$50.00

Johnny West, Janice West figure, complete, MIB, R4 ......$40.00

Johnny West, Jay West figure, complete, MIB, R4 ....$40.00

Johnny West, Jed Gibson figure, complete, MIB, R4, minimum value...$400.00

Johnny West, Johnny West figure, complete, MIB, R4 ....$50.00

Johnny West, Josie West figure, complete, MIB, R4 ....$40.00

Johnny West, playset, Circle X Ranch, complete, MIB, R4.$75.00

Johnny West, playset, Fort Apache, complete, MIB, R4 .$100.00

Johnny West, playset, Indian Tepee, complete, MIB, R4.$85.00

Johnny West, playset, Johnny West, Geronimo, Buckskin w/accessories, 1 hand missing, orig box, EX, A $55.00

Johnny West, playset, Johnny West Jeep Camping Set, complete $100.00

Johnny West, Princess Wildflower figure, complete, MIB, R4...$95.00

Johnny West, Sam Cobra figure, complete, MIB, R4 ....$85.00

Johnny West, Sheriff Garrett figure, complete, MIB, R4.$125.00

Johnny West, Zeb Zachary figure, complete, MIB, R4, minimum value...$150.00

Joker, see Batman

Josie & the Pussycats, puzzle, fr-tray; set of 4, MIB $50.00

Judy Garland, book, paint; 1941, EX+ $20.00

Julia, book, coloring; 1968, VG+, T6 ....$9.00

Jungle Book, game, Parker Bros, 1960, EX $20.00

Jungle Book, gum card, Costa Rican, single unopened pkg, M1...$1.00

Jungle Book, puzzle, fr-tray; Whitman, Baloo & Mowgli dancing, 1967, 11x14", NM, T2.................................$20.00

Jungle Book's Baloo the Bear, doll, plush, 1966, 6", EX, M8 ....$35.00

Jurassic Park, Alan Grant figure, Kenner, MIP, E3 ....$8.00

Jurassic Park, Ceolophysis or Dimetrodon figure, Kenner, MIP, E3, ea...$5.00

Jurassic park, Dennis Nedry or Ellie Sadler figure, Kenner, MIP, E3, ea...$8.00

Jurassic Park, gum card box, Topps, gold, empty, M, E3 ..$30.00

Jurassic Park, souvenir magazine, M, E3 ....$4.00

Jurassic Park, Young Explorer Jeep, MIB, D4 ....$20.00

Kalibak, Boulder Bomber, Kenner, Super Powers, MIP, F1.$25.00

Kalibak, figure, Kenner, Super Powers series, MOC, H4 ..$10.00

Kamen Rider, figure, Bandai, vinyl, lg, MIP, E3 ....$30.00

Kamen Rider, figure, Bandai, vinyl, sm, MIP, E3 ....$10.00

Kaptain Kool & the Kongs, puzzle, fr-tray; M $12.50

Karate Kid, playset, Remco, 1987, MIB (sealed), C1........$15.00

Katzenjammer Kids, Hans figure, Sirocco, pressed wood, 1940s, 3", EX...$45.00

Kayo, figure, German, pnt bsk, 2¼", G-, A $110.00

Kayo, suspenders, w/metal Kayo heads, 1940s, M, V1 .....$20.00

Kelly, rifle, Hubley, plastic, mk Kelly's Rifle & H (Hubley's logo), box shows Wm Bendix as Kelly, 1960, EX (VG+ box), A...$129.00

Kigmy, inflatable toy, Al Capp, NM, T1..............................$45.00

King Crab, figure, Bandai, vinyl, MIP, E3 ....$10.00

King Kong, decanter, Jim Beam, 1976, NM.......................$95.00

King Kong, game, board; Ideal, complete w/instructions, 1976, EX, H4...$10.00

King Kong, key chain, Universal, pewter, 1989, M $18.00

King Kong, salt & pepper shakers, M, pr............................$20.00

King Kong vs Godzilla, poster, 1963, 24x17", EX...........$250.00

King Leonardo, book, Royal Contest, Tip-Top Tales, 30-pg, 7x8" hardcover, 1961, EX, T2......................................$15.00

King Leonardo, puzzle, fr-tray; Jaymar, Knighting the Hunter, 1961, uncommon, 10x13", EX+, T2................$40.00

King Leonardo, puzzle, jigsaw; Jaymar, His Majesty Goes to Town, 60 pcs, 7x10" box, 1962 (EX box), T2............$40.00

Kiss, book, sheet music & photo; Almo Publishing, Rock-'n-Roll-Over, 64 pgs, 1978, EX, H4.............................$10.00

Kiss, gum cards, Donruss, 1978, 1st series, set of 66, M1...$35.00

Kiss, gum cards, Donruss, 1978, 2nd series, set of 66, M1 .$45.00

Kiss, program, 1977-78 World Tour, lg, VG, H4 ....$35.00

Kit Carson, bandana, red, wht & gr print cloth, See Bill Williams as Kit Carson, Coca-Cola premium, '50s, 20" sq, VG, P4...$55.00

Kit Carson, gun, Kilgore #40, blk plastic grips w/emb bust of Kit Carson, 1950s, MIB, H1................................$75.00

Klinger (from Hulk), figure, Durham, clings to anything, 1980, MOC, C1...$14.50

Knight Rider, bank, blk plastic, M, D4 ....$10.00

Knight Rider, book, activity; 1983, EX, T6........................$7.00

Knight Rider, Colorforms, 1982, MIB (sealed), T6 ....$10.00

Knight Rider, game, Parker Bros, 1983, MIB $25.00

Knight Rider, gum cards, Donruss, 1985, set of 66 (includes 11 variations), M1...$18.00

Knight Rider, gum cards, Monty Gum, 1985, single unopened pkg, M1...$1.00

Knight Rider, Michael Knight figure, 1982, 6", M (NM card), C1...$18.00

Knight Rider, puzzle, sliding tile; Ja-Ru, 1982, M (EX card), C1...$15.00

Knight Rider, Rub & Play Transfers, MIP, F1 ....$5.00

Knight Rider, wallet, Larami, silver plastic, 1982, MOC, C1...$12.00

Knight Rider, 2000 Turbo booster launcher, 1970s, MOC, T1...$15.00

Kojak, card set, Holland, 1977, NM, C1 ....$31.00

Kojak, game, Milton Bradley, unused, 1975, 10x20", VG (VG box)...$38.00

Kojak, gum cards, Monty Gum, set of 100 puzzle type, M1.$18.00

Krazy Ikes, figure, 1950s, MOC, T1..................................$25.00

Krazy Kat, book, Krazy Cat & Ignatz Mouse in Koko Land, Herriman, 1934, minor binding damage, G-VG, A $50.00

Kukla & Ollie, game, board; Parker Bros, cue cards & playing pcs, 1962, 10x20" box, lt wear, VG+, T2...................$40.00

Lady & the Tramp, puppy figure, Hagen-Renaker Designer Workshop, sitting on hind legs, 1950s, 1", M, M8.....$40.00

Lady & the Tramp, wallet, vinyl, emb figures on tan background, EX, P6...$30.00

Laffs, gum cards, Impel, 1991, set of 80, M1....................$8.00

Land of the Giants, book, coloring; Whitman, 1965, EX $45.00

Land of the Giants, book, Flight of Fear, Whitman, hardcover, 1969, EX.................................$20.00

Land of the Giants, book, paperback, by Murray Leinster, 1st printing, 1968, EX-NM, H4 ....$12.00

Land of the Giants, book, Whitman TV Book, M............$10.00

Land of the Giants, Colorforms, missing 1 minor pc o/w complete, NMIB, H4................................$79.00

Land of the Giants, game, Ideal, EX, from $135 to........$170.00

Land of the Giants, viewer, Chemtoy, 1969, NMOC, C1 ..$72.00

Lassie, book, Forbidden Valley, Whitman, #1508, Timmy & Lassie photo cover, 1959, VG $14.50

Lassie, book, The Sandbar Rescue, Whitman Tip-Top Tale, 1964, VG+, T6................................$3.00

Lassie, book, Trouble at Panter's Lake #1515, Whitman, 1972, VG................................$8.00

Last Action Hero, Axe Swingin' Ripper, Heat Packin' Jack, or Skull Attack Jack figure, MOC, D4, ea.................$10.00

Laugh-In, Button Making Kit, MIB (sealed).................$55.00

Laugh-In, Fickle Finger of Fate Award, wood & metal, 1967, M................................$175.00

Laugh-In, game, Squeeze Your Bippie, Hasbro, 1968, complete, EX (VG box), H4................................$60.00

Laugh-In, notebook holder, pk vinyl, 1969, EX, V1 ....$20.00

Laugh-In, record album, 33⅓ rpm, NM, V1.................$12.00

Laugh-In, ring, flasher; Vari Vue Flasher, Flying Fickle Finger, 1960s, NM, T1................................$10.00

Laugh-In, ring, flasher; Vari Vue Flasher, Here Comes the Judge, 1960s, NM, T1................................$10.00

Laugh-In, sleeping bag, 1969, EX, V1 ....$75.00

Laurel, bendee, Knickerbocker, 1960s, MIP, T1 ....$50.00

Laurel & Hardy, figures, Spain, cb, mechanical, 1940s, rare, NM, T1................................$45.00

Laurel & Hardy, game, Transogram, EX, F3 ....$35.00

Laurel & Hardy, stroller, PICO Y CIA of Spain, image of both on bk, Felix's head ea corner, rare, 11x6x5", NM, A..$1,400.00

Laurel & Hardy, toy wristwatch, Occupied Japan, tin & paper, EX+, C1 ....$36.00

Laverne & Shirley, Coloring & Activity Book, Playmore, 1983, NM-M, C1................................$13.00

Laverne & Shirley, game, board; Parker Bros, w/spinner, cards, playing pcs, 20 chips & color markers, 1977, EX+, T2................................$20.00

Laverne & Shirley, Lenny & Squiggy figures, Mego, set of 2, 1977, MIB, H4................................$110.00

Laverne & Shirley, puzzle, jigsaw; HG, 1976, NMIB, C1.$15.00

Lawman, TV Guide, July 25, 1959, NM, C1.................$13.00

Leading Edge, figure, Alien Warrior #2 Miniatures series, MIP, E3................................$15.00

Leave It to Beaver, gum cards, Pacific, 1984, set of 60, M1.$60.00

Leave It to Beaver, TV Eras-O-Picture Book, Hasbro, 12-pg, 1959, 11x9", EX+, A................................$66.00

Led Zeppelin, book, 1975 US Tour, 24-pg, NM $18.00

Legend of Big Foot, gum cards, Leesley, 1989, set of 100, M1................................$12.00

Let's Make a Deal, game, Ideal, 1970s, EX $15.00

Lex Luther, figure, Kenner, Super Powers series, complete w/accessories, loose, H4................................$4.00

Lex Luther, figure, Kenner, Super Powers series, MOC, M5 .$7.00

Lex Luther, figure, Toy Biz, MOC, D4 ....$6.00

Lex Luther, Lex Soar 7 Car, Kenner, Super Powers series, MIB, from $10 to................................$15.00

Li'l Abner, plate, ceramic, Dogpatch USA, 1970s, NM ...$25.00

Li'l Abner, plate, heavy plastic w/Dogpatch USA & characters, 1958, 12", NM, C1 ....$27.00

Lil' Abner Vendor Bar, ca 1930s, 12x11x24", M, $1,250.00.

Lieutenant (Gary Lockwood), puzzle, fr-tray; Saalfield, 1964, EX, T6................................$20.00

Linus the Lionhearted, Colorforms, Post, mail-in premium, circus animals, 1965, 6x8" backboard, NM, T2 ....$45.00

Linus the Lionhearted, doll, Post Cereals, stuffed plush w/plastic eyes, felt mouth, nylon whiskers, 1965, 12", M, A.....$83.00

Linus the Lionhearted, doll, stuffed brn plush w/vinyl face, pull-string talker, non-working, 1965, 21", NM, A.........$125.00

Little Annie Rooney, book, wishing; 1932, 10x13", VG, N2................................$15.00

Little Audry, squeeze toy, Harvey, R3 ....$70.00

Little Beaver, puzzle, fr-tray; Whitman, 1954, EX+ $40.00

Little House on the Prairie, Colorforms, NMIB.................$30.00

Little House on the Prairie, photo, by studio, 1978, 5x7", C1................................$29.00

Little Lulu, bag & jewelry, M (NM card), O1.................$10.00

Little Lulu, bank, vinyl figure, 1970, EX, T1.................$25.00

Little Lulu, book, paint; 96 pgs, 1946, EX $45.00

Little Lulu, Cartoon-a-Kit, Kits Toys, complete w/paper, crayons & fr-tray inlay, 1948, M (NM box), scarce, A.........$125.00

Little Lulu, doll, Gund, Hong Kong, stuffed, orig label, no accessories, lt stain, 20", A..$75.00

Little Lulu, puzzle, fr-tray; Tubby in a tree, Lulu & friend, 1973, 11x14", EX, T2..$14.00

Little Lulu, puzzle, jigsaw; Whitman Jr, 1956, VG............$20.00

Little Mermaid, Ariel bank, MIB, D4 ....$10.00

Little Mermaid, Ariel or Eric figure, Tyco, nonposable, 3", MOC, D4 ....$4.00

Little Mermaid, bendee, Just Toys, Ariel, Sebastian & Flounder, 2½" to 6" largest, 3-pc gift set, K1 ....$9.95

Little Mermaid, charm bracelet, mail-in premium, M $10.00

Little Mermaid, figure, Applause, PVC, set of 6: Eric, Sebastian, & 4 different Ariel figures, MIP, F1 ....$18.00

Little Mermaid, pop-up birthday party invitation, PopShots Inc, 1980s, in orig envelope, M, M8...................................$15.00

Little Orphan Annie, bank, Dime Register w/Unique Savings Tally, litho tin, 2¾", G-VG, A $160.00

Little Orphan Annie, book, All-Star Action Show Circus, premium, 1935, 10x14", VG, C1 ....$113.00

Little Orphan Annie, book, coloring; Artcraft, 80+ pgs, w/other activities, 1974, 8x11", NM, T2.................................$10.00

Little Orphan Annie, book, The Pop-Up Little Orphan Annie & Jumbo the Circus Elephant, 1935, VG+, A $150.00

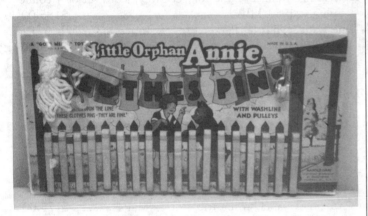

Little Orphan Annie Clothes Pins, 1930s, MOC, D10, $125.00.

Little Orphan Annie, figure, German, pnt bsk, 3⅜", VG, A..$110.00

Little Orphan Annie, figure, Knickerbocker, any of 7, 1982, 2", MOC, F1, ea $5.00

Little Orphan Annie, figure, mk Harold Gray, jtd wood, ca 1936, 5x3", EX, A..$65.00

Little Orphan Annie, game, board; Pursuit, Selchow & Righter, 1970s, in 10x20" box, MIB (sealed), T2 ....$30.00

Little Orphan Annie, game, board; 1981, VG, N2 ....$7.00

Little Orphan Annie, game, Rummy Cards #3077, Whitman, 1935-37, NMIB, P4 ....$75.00

Little Orphan Annie, game, Television, Milton Bradley, EX, F3 ....$145.00

Little Orphan Annie, handkerchief, shoulder portrait of Annie w/name & Hankies lettered below, 1930s, EX (EX box), A..$93.00

Little Orphan Annie, lamp, table; glass light-up base w/orig paper shade, S1 ....$45.00

Little Orphan Annie, motion lamp, 1982, MIB, S1 ....$40.00

Little Orphan Annie, pin, Radio Orphan Annie's Secret Society Booklet & Membership Decoder, 1936, set, NM+, A..$100.00

Little Orphan Annie Pop-Up Book, 1930s, NM, D10, $275.00.

Little Orphan Annie, Punjab figure, Sears, from Annie movie, 7", MIB (Sears box), F1 ....$15.00

Little Orphan Annie, Sandy figure, jtd wood, 4x3", EX, A..$65.00

Little Orphan Annie, tablecloth, mk Made in USA, paper w/Happy Birthday graphics, 1981, MIP......................$27.00

Little Orphan Annie & Sandy, figures, jtd wood, 5½", V1, pr...$125.00

Little Shop of Horrors, Audrey II bank, Geffen, 1986, M (NM box)..$50.00

Lizard, figure, Mego, complete w/accessories, 8", loose, H4..$65.00

Lizard, figure, Mego, 1974, 8", NRFB, from $100 to.......$150.00

Lone Ranger, accessories, The Blizzard Adventure, poncho, saddlebags, etc, 1973, 10x12", M (EX+ box), M5...........$38.00

Lone Ranger, album, orig broadcast, sealed, 1970s, M......$15.00

Lone Ranger Rocking Book, 7½x9½", EX, $40.00.

Lone Ranger, badge, Chief Scout, NM, V1......................$85.00

Lone Ranger, bendee, Lakeside, dated 1967, 6", MOC $65.00

Lone Ranger, book, Lone Ranger & the War Horse, Whitman, 1951, VG, T6..$8.00

Lone Ranger, book, paint; 1940, unused, M, J2 ....$42.00

Lone Ranger, book, Texas Renegade, Grosset & Dunlop, illus, 1938, hardcover, 24 pgs, 10x7", corners frayed o/w EX, A...$105.00

Lone Ranger, book, To the Rescue, Dell, 1939, scarce, 11½x8½", EX, A...$245.00

Lone Ranger, boot box, Endicott-Johnson, bl w/Official Lone Ranger Boots above boot image, complete & firm, VG+, A $11.50

Lone Ranger, camera, De-Luxe Cine-Vue, Acme, w/3 boxed films, orig 8x9" box, EX+ (M box), A.....................$242.00

Lone Ranger, doll, Dollcraft Novelty/TLR Inc, compo head, hands & feet, w/guns, 1938, 17", mask missing, EX, A..........$450.00

Lone Ranger, doll, Molly/TLR, stuffed w/movable vinyl head, 29", w/5" plastic clicker pistol & holster, NM (EX box), A..$245.00

Lone Ranger, figure, chalkware, carnival prize, 1930s, NM..$60.00

Lone Ranger, figure, Gabriel, 1980, 3¾", MOC, H4..........$6.00

Lone Ranger, figure, Gilbert, Legend of Lone Ranger series, 1980, MOC...$10.00

Lone Ranger First Aid Kit, White Cross Labs, tin case with items inside, 1938, 6x4", EX, A, $98.00.

Lone Ranger, game, board; Lone Ranger Silver Bullets, Whiting, 1950s, instructions missing, orig box, NM, A..........$125.00

Lone Ranger, game, board; Milton Bradley, 1938, orig 5x8" box, NM, C1...$113.00

Lone Ranger, game, Pop-up Target, Transogram, 3x19x22" box holds 2 6" diecut bad men, plastic dart gun, 1950s, NM, A...$125.00

Lone Ranger, game, target; Marx, tin standup features Lone Ranger & Silver, 1938, orig box, 9½x9½", NM, A .$175.00

Lone Ranger, gun, Kilgore, bl fr w/NP CI hammer & trigger, wht grips, 1940s, surface rust, VG, H1..........................$125.00

Lone Ranger, hairbrush, TLR, wood w/oval decal of Lone Ranger on Silver, 1930s, EX, A......................................$45.00

Lone Ranger, hairbrush & comb set, 1938, NMIB.........$125.00

Lone Ranger, harmonica, Harmonica Corp, inscribed The Lone Ranger, orig box, scarce, EX, A.................................$175.00

Lone Ranger, holster set w/Actoy guns, blk leather holster w/conchos & jewels, 1940s, rare, 1 gun inoperative, EX, H1..$395.00

Lone Ranger, key chain, bullet w/Lone Ranger figure inside, 1950s, V1...$42.00

Lone Ranger, pencil box, American Pencil Co, cb w/simulated blk leather, emb images, sliding tray, 1949, 5x9", NM, T2...$80.00

Lone Ranger, pencil box, brn cb, EX+, I2...........................$42.00

Lone Ranger, pencil sharpener, bread premium, signature on side, M...$55.00

Lone Ranger, playset, Boys-De-Lite, generic, 1930s, scarce, complete in orig box, EX, A..$90.00

Lone Ranger, playset, Hidden Rattler Adventure, Gabriel, 1973, M (EX box), C1...$23.00

Lone Ranger, playset, Rodeo Ranch, Marx, 1950s, NMIB, T1..$450.00

Lone Ranger, puppet, hand; cloth w/rubber head, 1955, scarce, 10", EX, A...$65.00

Lone Ranger, puppet, marionette, National Mask & Puppet, cloth & rubber, 1945, scarce, orig box, 12", EX, A..$175.00

Lone Ranger, puzzle, fr-tray; Whitman, Lone Ranger & Silver racing through desert, 15x11", NM, A.........................$30.00

Lone Ranger, puzzle, Lone Ranger Story, TLR, set of 4 comic photos, 1950, MIB...$185.00

Lone Ranger, puzzle, Parker Bros, 4 stories w/3 panels in ea, 1950, complete in orig box, ea panel: 17½", M, A ..$175.00

Lone Ranger, radio soundtrack, Adventures of Lone Ranger, EX $15.00

Lone Ranger, ring, Atomic Bomb, radio premium, 1930s, EX, T1...$95.00

Lone Ranger, ring, flashlight; 1950, w/bulb & orig battery, NM, A $96.00

Lone Ranger, ring, movie film; 1949, complete w/filmstrip & mailer from General Mills, NM $125.00

Lone Ranger, ring, remove cover to view 16mm film, glow-in-the-dark panel, w/filmstrip, 1951, NM, P4 ....$175.00

Lone Ranger, ring, 6-Shooter, gold w/gray pistol & silver grips, General Mills, 1947, EX, from $110 to $125.00

Lone Ranger, Signal Siren & Flashlight, metal & plastic, battery-op, w/orig code book, 7x2", MIB, A $120.00

Lone Ranger, Silver Bullet Pen Set, Everlast, 3 3" bullet-shaped pens, complete, NMIB...$150.00

Lone Ranger, Silver figure, Gabriel, Action series, for 8" figure, 1975, MIB, C1..$47.00

Lone Ranger, tie, brn w/silk-screened bust image of the Lone Ranger, 1940, EX, A...$70.00

Lone Ranger, trading cards, Ed-U-Cards, 87 from set of 120, 1950s, VG, A...$165.00

Lone Ranger & Tonto, puzzle, fr-tray; Whitman, both on horseback, 1954, 15x11", NM, A...$35.00

Lone Rider, Leslie-Henry Ranch Holster outfit, box only, EX, J2...$100.00

Looney Toons, bendee, Applause, Bugs Bunny, Daffy Duck, Sylvester & Wile E Coyote, set of 4, K1 ....$14.00

Looney Toons, tray, serving; Warner Bros, litho metal w/many characters, mc striped border, 1974, 12" dia, NM, T2 .$40.00

Lorax, figure, Coleco/Dr Seuss, MIB, H4 ....$40.00

Lost in Space, game, board; Milton Bradley, complete, orig box, EX $65.00

Lost in Space, gum card box, Topps, bl outer-space background w/Milky Way star pattern, 1966, 8x4x2", EX+, A ...$550.00

Lost in Space, gum card wrapper, Topps, 1966, any of 55, M1 ....$90.00

Lost in Space, gum cards, Topps, 1966, unopened pkg, M1 ....$185.00

Lost in Space, helmet, complete, rare, NM, T1 ....$225.00

Lost in Space, magazine, TV Weekly, Sept 19-25, NM, O1 ....$19.00

Lost in Space, note pad, 1960s, 8x10", M, C1...................$42.00

Lost in Space, tablet, features June Lockhart in flight uniform, 1965, 8x10", NM, from $25 to $35.00

Lucille Ball, decal, glossy color photo, for wood, fabric, or glass, 1950s, 4x5", MIP, C1...$45.00

Lucille Ball, game, Body Language, Milton Bradley, 1975, G+ $10.00

Lucille Ball & Bob Hope, tablet, Lucy in baseball uniform, Hope is coach, 1950s, 8x10", EX+, T2...........................$15.00

Ludwig Von Drake, doll, talker w/tape player, VG-EX, O1 .$85.00

Ludwig Von Drake, game, Ball Toss, EX+-NM, T1........$125.00

Ludwig Von Drake, pencil case, Wonderful World of Color, Hasbro, thick cb, red w/mc decal, 1961, 4x9", sealed, NM+, T2 ....$32.00

M*A*S*H, ambulance, Tristar, w/3¾" figure, 1982, NMIB, C1 ....$42.00

M*A*S*H, dog tag, 1981, MOC, H4....................................$5.00

M*A*S*H, dog tag kit, Make Your Own Dog Tags, Tristar, 2 steel chains w/tags, 1981, MOC (cast photo card), C1 ....$16.00

M*A*S*H, Father Mulcahy figure, 1980s, 4", MOC, T1.$10.00

M*A*S*H, figure, Durham, Hot Lips w/medical case or Hawkeye w/golf clubs, w/accessories, 1969, 9", MOC, C1, ea $120.00

M*A*S*H, game, Milton Bradley, 1981, EX, F3.............$15.00

M*A*S*H, gear set, Jaru, w/canteen, flashlight & lantern, MOC, C1 ....$12.00

M*A*S*H, gum card pack, Topps, unopened w/6 cards & gum, 1982, M, T2...$8.00

M*A*S*H, gum cards, Donruss, 1982, set of 66, M1 ......$15.00

M*A*S*H, Klinger figure, Tri-Star, 1980s, 4", MOC, T1/H4 ....$12.00

M*A*S*H, photo postcard, McLean Stevenson w/facsimile signature, sent to fans, 1973, 5x7", NM, C1...................$31.00

M*A*S*H, vehicle set, Kidco, set of 3: jeep, ambulance & supply carrier, 1981, M (EX card), C1 ....$36.00

M*A*S*H, 4077 Check-up Set, 1981, M (G- card)...........$4.00

MAD, Alfred E Neuman bendee, Concepts Plus, 1988, 9", K1 ....$7.95

MAD, Alfred E Neuman bust, sm $150.00

MAD, Alfred E Neuman postcard, plastic, Plan Ahead, 1958, 6x4", M, V1...$25.00

MAD, game, board; missing play money, 1979, VG, N2 ....$8.00

MAD, game, card; Milton Bradley, 1980, NMIB, C1 ....$17.00

MAD, gum card box, Lime Rock, Spy vs Spy, empty, M, E3 ....$50.00

MAD, gum card box, Lime Rock, 2nd series, empty, M, E3 ....$28.00

MAD, gum cards, Fleer, set of 128 w/64 stickers, M1 ....$65.00

MAD, gum cards, Lime Rock, commemorative issue, complete set, M, E3 ....$30.00

MAD, record, Twists Rock & Roll, EX, V1 ....$19.50

Magilla Gorilla, book, At the Art Show, Giant Durabook, 1973, EX, T6..$7.00

Magilla Gorilla, book, Magilla Gorilla & the Bananapeppers, Durabook, 1972, VG+, T6.......................................$4.00

Magilla Gorilla, figure, Ideal, stuffed cloth w/vinyl head, 24", EX $100.00

Magilla Gorilla, figure, Ideal, stuffed plush w/hard plastic head, 11", VG+...$55.00

Magilla Gorilla, figure, Ideal, vinyl head on stuffed body, bendable arms, 1960s, 8", EX, H4.................................$90.00

Magilla Gorilla, game, board; Ideal, w/spinner & 4 stand-up Magilla cb playing pcs, 1964 (EX+ box), T2 ....$100.00

Magilla Gorilla, game, Target Barrel, Ideal, 6" plastic barrel w/pop-up gorilla, pistol & darts, sm rpr/lt stains, T2..$30.00

Magilla Gorilla, hand puppet, Ideal, 1960s, VG, H4 ....$39.00

Magneto I, figure, Toy Biz, MOC, D4 ....$10.00

Magnum PI, gum card box, full w/36 pkgs, 1983, NM-M, C1 ....$27.00

Magnum PI, gum cards, Donruss, 1983, set of 66, M1 ......$10.00

Major Matt Mason, Astro Trak Vehicle, Mattel, complete, w/foam wheels, working, EX, H4................................$28.00

Major Matt Mason, binoculars or movie camera, loose, H4..$7.00

Major Matt Mason, book, coloring; Whitman, 1968, EX+.$25.00

Major Matt Mason, Callisto bendee, 1969, used, T1 ....$35.00

Major Matt Mason, Callisto figure, Mattel, w/part of weapon accessory pc, missing pc that holds string, EX, H4.....$60.00

Major Matt Mason, Cat Trak, red or wht, EX, H4...........$10.00

Major Matt Mason, crescent wrench, flare gun, or hammer, loose, ea $6.00

Major Matt Mason, Doug Davis (Black) figure, Mattel, w/helmet, no broken wires, EX, loose, H4 ....$90.00

Major Matt Mason, figure, Mattel, w/helmet, no broken wires, EX, H4 ....$45.00

Major Matt Mason, figure, Mattel, 1969, MOC $135.00

Major Matt Mason, Firebolt Space Cannon, Mattel, antennae, radar screen, Firebolt bbl, on wheels, 1966, M (EX- box), T2..$190.00

Major Matt Mason, Firebolt Space Cannon, Mattel, complete, working, EX, H4 ....$30.00

Major Matt Mason, Gamma Ray Card Pack, Mattel, w/5 gamma rays to load, 1968, 9x12" card, M (EX card), T2........$60.00

Major Matt Mason, Gamma Ray Guard Gun, Mattel, complete w/missiles, H4..$18.00

Major Matt Mason, Jeff Long figure, Mattel, w/helmet, 1 leg wire broken, EX, H4 ....$50.00

Major Matt Mason, Laser Rifle, G, H4..............................$10.00

Major Matt Mason, Recono Jet Pack, Mattel, complete, EX, H4 ....$18.00

Major Matt Mason, Satellite Launch Pack, Mattel, complete w/4 satellites, EX, H4 ....$20.00

Major Matt Mason, Satellite Locker, Mattel, carrying case, EX, H4 ....$25.00

Major Matt Mason, Sergeant Storm figure, Mattel, w/helmet, no broken wires, EX, H4..$55.00

Major Matt Mason, Space Crawler Vehicle, Mattel, working, EX, H4 ....$28.00

Major Matt Mason, Space Power Suit Pack, Mattel, w/windshield dome, claws & telescoping hammer, 1968, M (EX-card), T2 ....$70.00

Major Matt Mason, Space Shelter Pack, Mattel, w/inflatable tent & accessories, EX, H4 ....$18.00

Major Matt Mason, Space Sled, Mattel, EX, H4 ....$10.00

Major Matt Mason, Space Station, Mattel, complete w/instructions, missing box, 1966-68, EX, H4 ....$90.00

Major Matt Mason, Space Station, Mattel, plastic pcs to assemble in many ways, 1966, 16x14x5" box, M (EX box), T2 ....$300.00

Major Matt Mason, Space Travel Pack, Mattel, space sled, backpack, chemical gun, etc, 1968, on 9x12" card, M (EX box), T2 ....$60.00

Major Matt Mason, Star Seeker, Mattel, orig box, EX, H4.$79.00

Major Matt Mason, Supernaut Power Limbs, complete, EX, H4 ....$18.00

Major Matt Mason, Supernaut Power Limbs, Mattel, mechanical suit, power scope & oxygen, 1968, M (EX+ card), T2 ....$60.00

Major Matt Mason, Talking Command Console, non-working, orig box, EX, H4 ....$49.00

Major Matt Mason, Uni-Tred Space Hauler Vehicle, Mattel, complete, working, EX, H4 ....$24.00

Major Matt Mason, Uni-Tred w/Space Bubble, Mattel, ca 1966-68, EX (EX pkg), H4 ....$65.00

Mamas & Papas, Mama Cass, bendee, Hasbro, Show Biz Babies series, w/record, NMOC (opened card), H4 ....$125.00

Mamas & Papas, Michelle Phillips or Denny Doherty bendee, Hasbro, Show Biz Babies series, missing shoes, loose, H4, ea $39.00

Mammy Yokum, doll, stuffed w/vinyl head, hands & feet, orig corn cob pipe, 1950s, EX $125.00

Man From UNCLE, accessories, Gilbert, binoculars, cap pistol, rifle & attachments, 1965, MOC, H4 ....$35.00

Man From UNCLE, book, Affair of Gentle Saboteur, Whitman, hardcover, 1966, EX $12.00

Man From UNCLE, game, Automatic Shooting Arcade, Marx, 1966, complete, NM (EX box), A $600.00

Man From UNCLE, game, board; Thrush Ray Gun Affair, Ideal, complete, 1966, EX-NM (VG box), H4 ....$60.00

Man From UNCLE, game, board; UNCLE Napoleon Solo, Ideal, 1965, NM (EX box), C1 ....$63.00

Man From UNCLE, game, card; Illya Kuryakin, Milton Bradley, 1966, NM (NM box), H4 ....$45.00

Man From UNCLE, game, card; Milton Bradley, 1965, EX+ (EX- box), from $10 to $20.00

Man From UNCLE, game, card; Milton Bradley, 1966, NMIB, C1 ....$40.00

Man From Uncle, game, Pinball Affair, Marx, plastic covered bagatelle w/litho tin board, 1966, 24", EX, A $101.00

Man From UNCLE, gum card box, Topps, held 24 pkgs, 1965, rare, 8x4x2", EX+-NM, A $450.00

Man From UNCLE, gum card set, Topps, complete set of 55, blk & wht, 1965, NM, T2 ....$170.00

Man From UNCLE TV Action Figure Apparel, Gilbert, 1965, $35.00.

Man From UNCLE, gum card wrapper, Topps, fuchsia w/blk & wht image of Napoleon Solo w/UNCLE gun, 1965, EX, T2 ....$50.00

Man From UNCLE, gun, metal, mk UNCLE 7.63 MM, on orig card from Lone Star/MGM 1965, w/UNCLE badge, EX+ (VG+ card), A $123.00

Man From UNCLE, gun, plastic luger-style pop gun, orig pkg w/Illya & Napoleon on header card, unlicensed, 1965, M, T2 ....$15.00

Man From UNCLE, Illya Kuryakin figure, Gilbert, missing accessories & paperwork, 1965, 12", orig box, EX, H4 ....$160.00

Man From UNCLE, poster, Napoleon Solo, blk & wht, 1965, 24x36", M in shrink wrap, T2 ....$25.00

Man From UNCLE, puzzle, jigsaw; Milton Bradley, #4, 1966, MIB (sealed) $75.00

Man From UNCLE, record album, RCA, 33⅓ rpm, orig soundtrack, w/jacket, 1965, EX+, T2 ....$30.00

Man From UNCLE, Secret Print Putty, Colorforms, putty is stored in blk gun, has secret book, MIP $90.00

Man From UNCLE, Spy Magic Tricks Set, Gilbert, missing 4 pcs, 1965, EX (EX box), H4 ....$129.00

Mandrake the Magician, game, board; Transogram, 16 cards, X-ray eyes, spinner & 4 red markers, 1966, M (EX+-NM box), A $48.00

Manhunt, game, Milton Bradley, 1971, MIB, M4 ....$50.00

Mantis, figure, Kenner, Super Powers, MOC $25.00

Margie, game, Milton Bradley, from TV show ca Oct of 1961 to Aug of 1962, 1961, VG (VG box) $38.00

Marie Osmond, puppet, Mattel, MIB $25.00

Marilyn Monroe, demi-spoon, photo on gold, 4½", M........$8.00
Marilyn Monroe, earrings, MOC..$10.00
Marilyn Monroe, figure, 1990, 3½", M..............................$40.00

Marilyn Monroe Invitations, Hallmark, Wanna Party?, set of 8, $6.00; Spiral Notebook, A Card Co, 1981, M, $5.00.

Marilyn Monroe, Life Magazine, August 1960, VG, N2...$10.00
Marilyn Monroe, playing cards, dtd 1956, MIP (sealed)...$17.50
Marilyn Monroe, playing cards, souvenir, ca 1950, complete $10.00
Marilyn Monroe, pocket mirror, Marilyn in bathing suit, 2x3", M $5.00
Marilyn Monroe, postcard book, Marriott, Portraits of a Goddess, 1990, 5½x8½", M $7.95
Marilyn Monroe, puzzle, Golden Spotlight, 550-pc, 15½x18", NM $5.00
Marilyn Monroe, puzzle, jigsaw; 550-pc, MIB (sealed) $10.00
Marilyn Monroe & Joe DiMaggio, commerative coin, photo ea side w/dates, M..$10.00
Marlin Perkins, game, Cadaco Ellis, Zoo Parade, complete, 1965, EX (1 rpr corner on box), H4 ....$35.00
Marlin Perkins, game, Zoo Parade, MIB, V1....................$45.00
Martian Manhunter, figure, Kenner, Super Powers series, MOC $35.00
Marvel Super Heroes, Annihilus figure, Toy Biz, MOC, D4 ....$10.00
Marvel Super Heroes, Banshee figure, Toy Biz, MOC, D4 .$10.00
Marvel Super Heroes, bendee, Applause, Spiderman, Captain America & The Hulk, 6", set of 3, K1........................$15.00
Marvel Super Heroes, bendee, Just Toys, Spiderman, The Hulk, Punisher, or Captain America, 6", ea............................$4.95
Marvel Super Heroes, booklet, House of Ideas, Complete Marvel Index, 100+ pgs, 1970, NM, A....................................$18.00
Marvel Super Heroes, decal sheet, Marvel Comics Group, 20 mc decals on 12x12" sheet, Fan Club premium, scarce, M, A..$50.00
Marvel Super Heroes, figures, Sears Mailer Set: Styfe, Cable, Deadpool & Forearm, MIB, D4 ....$15.00
Marvel Super Heroes, figures, series 1, complete set of 10, MIP, F1 ....$15.00
Marvel Super Heroes, figures, series 2, complete set of 15, MIP, F1 ....$20.00

Marvel Super Heroes, figures, Toy Biz, set of 4: Mr Fantastic, The Thing, Annihilus & Venom w/flicking tongue, MIB, F1 ....$40.00
Marvel Super Heroes, gum card box, Donruss, empty yel store display w/pop-up lid, 1966, scarce, 8x4x2", EX+-NM, A..$150.00
Marvel Super Heroes, postcard book, mc, perforated, showing different heroes, 1981, EX+, D9 ....$12.00
Marvel Super Heroes, puzzle, jigsaw; Milton Bradley, 100-pc, 1966, NMIB (8x12" box), A $80.00
Marvel Super Heroes, See-A-Show Stereo Viewer Set, Kenner, rectangular, w/5 cards, MOC (8x5" card), A...........$150.00
Marvel Super Heroes, stationery set, Marvel Comics, 12 characters on 8x11" sheet, 1964-68, NMIP, A....................$75.00
Marvel Super Heroes, Training Center Playset, Toy Biz, lg, MIP, F1 ....$50.00
Marvel Super Heroes, transfers, Presto, Secret Wars, complete, NMIP, D9...$8.00
Mary Hartman, Mary Hartman; game, board; 1977, MIB (sealed)..$20.00
Mary Poppins, doll, Horsman, 1960s, 12", NMIB, T1 ....$135.00
Mary Poppins, game, Carousel #153, Parker Bros, VG $25.00
Mary Poppins, game, Whitman, 1964, 1 pc missing (EX box), H4 ....$16.00
Mary Poppins, hand puppet, Gund/Walt Disney, VG $25.00
Mary Poppins, poster, reissue, 1973, 27x40", M4.............$25.00
Mary Poppins, puzzle, fr-tray; Flying Kites, 1965, EX, T6 .$10.00
Mary Poppins, puzzle, fr-tray; Tea Party or Happy Holiday, 1964, EX, T6...$10.00
Mary Poppins, puzzle, fr-tray; Whitman, Mary w/Bambi characters, EX+, D9...$6.00
Mary Poppins, spoon holder, ceramic, 5¾", M................$75.00
Mary Poppins, sugar spoon, International Silver, 1964, EX, M8 ....$20.00
Mask, Billboard Blast & Dusy Hayes figures, MIB, D4, ea .$10.00
Mask, Bullet (street bike/hovercraft), Kenner, w/action figure, 1985, MIP, from $10 to $15.00
Mask, Raven (Corvette/armed seaplane), Kenner, w/action figure, MIP, F1 ....$15.00
Mask, Stinger & Bruno Sheppard figures, MIB, D4..........$15.00
Masquerade Party, game, from TV show, EX-NM, H4 .....$30.00
Masters of the Universe, Attack Trak, MIB, F1...............$15.00
Masters of the Universe, Blaster Hawk, MIB, F1 ....$40.00
Masters of the Universe, carrying case, for Battle Bones figures, MIB, from $5 to $10.00
Masters of the Universe, Dragon Walker, MIB, F1...........$15.00
Masters of the Universe, Electronic Skeletor Skull Staff, 36", MIB, D4 ....$12.00
Masters of the Universe, Extendar figure, MOC, F1........$10.00
Masters of the Universe, Flipshot figure, Mattel, He-Man series, MIP, F1 ....$10.00
Masters of the Universe, Flogg figure, He-Man series, MOC, D4 ....$5.00
Masters of the Universe, Fright Fighter, MIB, F1 ....$40.00
Masters of the Universe, gum cards, Panini, 1987, from movie, set of 240, M1 ....$32.00
Masters of the Universe, gum cards, Topps, set of 88 w/22 stickers, 1984, M1 ....$18.00

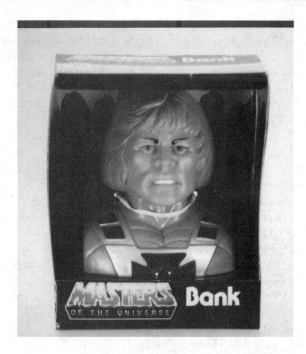

Masters of the Universe, bank, HG Toys LTD, Hong Kong, MIB, $12.00.

Masters of the Universe, Jet Sled, MIB, F1 ....$10.00
Masters of the Universe, King Hiss figure, MOC, F1........$10.00
Masters of the Universe, Land Shark, MIB, F1 ....$15.00
Masters of the Universe, Masters Weapon Pak, MIB, F1....$5.00
Masters of the Universe, Mega Laser, MIB, F1 ....$10.00
Masters of the Universe, Night Stalker, MIB, F1..............$15.00
Masters of the Universe, Ninjor figure, MOC, F1.............$15.00
Masters of the Universe, Paint & Play Set, w/diecast figures, 1980s, MIB, T1 ....$15.00

Masters of the Universe, Ram Man figure, Mattel, MIB, $35.00.

Masters of the Universe, Panthor, 1982, MIB, F1..............$25.00
Masters of the Universe, Rattlor figure, MOC, from $6 to..$10.00
Masters of the Universe, Roton Vehicle, MIB, F1 ....$20.00
Masters of the Universe, Scareglow figure, MOC, F1 ....$20.00
Masters of the Universe, Shuttle Pod, He-Man series, MIB, D4 ....$7.00
Masters of the Universe, Skeletor figure, Mattel, He-Man series, 1990, MIP $10.00
Masters of the Universe, Slime Pit, MIB, F1 ....$25.00
Masters of the Universe, Sorceress figure, MOC, F1.........$15.00
Masters of the Universe, Spydor, MIB, F1 ....$30.00
Masters of the Universe, Stonedar figure, MOC, F1.........$10.00
Masters of the Universe, Thunder Punch figure, MOC, F1 .$15.00
Matt Dillon, gun, Leslie-Henry, Marshal Dillon Gunsmoke, diecast cap pistol, pop-up magazine, late '50s, 10", VG, P4...$135.00
Maverick, book, Eras-O-Picture, Hasbro, 12 glossy cb illus, 1959, 10x9", minus crayons, EX, T2 ....$50.00
Maverick, Paint-By-Number, Hasbro, 3 numbered canvases & 24 vials in 14x18" box, 1958, M (EX box), T2........$100.00
Max Headroom, doorknob hanger, Don't Lose Your Head..., 1987, w/mc photo, NM, T6 ....$5.00
Max Headroom, figure, ventriloquist bust, vinyl w/rpl sunglasses, 12", EX, H4 ....$12.00
Max Headroom, gum cards, Topps, 1988, test market, 33 stickers w/11 foils, complete, rare, M1 ....$75.00
McHale's Navy, game, Transogram, 1962, unused, NM, V1...$40.00
McHale's Navy, gum cards, set of 66 blk & wht photos, 1966, NM, C1 ....$72.00
Mecha Ghidrah, figure, Bandai, vinyl, 14", MIP, E3 ....$55.00
Mecha Godzilla, figure, Bandai, vinyl, MIP, E3 ....$20.00
Mecha Kong, figure, Bandai, vinyl, MIP, E3 ....$20.00
Megalon, figure, Bandai, vinyl, MIP, E3 ....$20.00
Melvin the Moon Man, game, dice; Remco, 1960s, orig box, 1 figure missing, o/w EX, H4...$25.00
Mephilas, figure, Bandai, vinyl, MIP, E3 ....$10.00
Miami Vice, game, Pepper Lane Ind, full-color photos top & sides of 10x20" box, 1984, sealed, M, T2 ....$40.00
Michael Jackson, belt, 1980s, M.......................................$12.00
Michael Jackson, Billy Jean outfit, LJN, MOC $17.50
Michael Jackson, Colorforms, 1984, MIB (sealed) $27.50
Michael Jackson, doll, Powco, 6" posable plastic Zombie character, w/coffin, 1984, on 7x10" card, MOC, T2 ....$40.00
Michael Jackson, gum cards, OPC, 1984, set of 33 w/33 stickers, M1 ....$10.00
Michael Jackson, gum cards, Topps, 1984, 1st series, set of 33 w/33 stickers, M1 ....$7.50
Michael Jackson, gum cards, Topps, 1984, 2nd series, set of 33 w/33 stickers, M1 ....$10.00
Michael Jackson, Motown outfit, LJN, MOC...................$10.00
Michael Jackson, playing cards, MOC $15.00
Michael Jackson, puffy stickers, set of 4 (based on Thriller), MIP, T6...$3.00
Michael Jackson, puzzle, jigsaw; Colorforms, 500-pc, MIB (sealed)...$25.00
Michael Jackson, stickers, Topps, 1984, Super Sticker series, 5x7", set of 13, M1 ....$30.00

Mickey, Goofy, Donald & Pluto; xylophone, color-coded keys, stick missing, 1960s, EX, M8 ....$75.00

Mickey & Minnie Mouse, bookends, compo, figural, 1970s, 6½", EX, P6, pr.....................$95.00

Mickey & Minnie Mouse, canister, litho tin, w/Post Office mk at top, 6", VG, A $80.00

Mickey & Minnie Mouse, feeding set, Gorham China, also features Donald & Goofy in western scene, 1970s, MIB, P6......................$95.00

Mickey & Minnie Mouse, pillow case kit, early pie-eyed Mickey & Minnie under umbrella, ready to embroider, 1931, EX, A.......................$61.00

Mickey & Minnie Mouse, pin, Caroling, Happy Holidays, cloisonne, 1991, M, M8......................$10.00

Mickey & Minnie Mouse, plate & mug, china, Mickey presents gift & bouquet to Minnie, hearts on background, M, P2......................$55.00

Mickey & Minnie Mouse, sand pail, Ohio Art, litho tin, Mickey & Minnie behind fence waving at friends, 1938, 8x8", EX, A......................$258.00

Mickey & Minnie Mouse, sand sifter, Ohio Art, also features Clarabell, Horace & Pluto, 1 sm dent, 1930s, 8", EX, M8......................$150.00

Mickey & Minnie Mouse, tea set, lustreware, 16-pc set, 1930s, EX, M8......................$200.00

Mickey & Minnie Mouse, tea set, lustreware, 17-pc set w/6 cups & saucers, teapot, creamer & sugar, 1930s, NM, A.$443.00

Mickey & Minnie Mouse, wall pocket, lustreware, EX+, T1......................$185.00

Mickey & Minnie Mouse w/Felix, musical toy, European, litho tin cylinder w/hand crank in top, 2x2" dia, NM, A.$550.00

Mickey & Minnie Mouse w/Pluto, doll pattern, Simplicity, 1945, unused (worn pkg), P6......................$95.00

Mickey Mouse, acrobat, paper litho on wood, 8¼", VG-EX, A......................$30.00

Mickey Mouse Air Mail, Sun Rubber, 1940s, replaced wheels and propeller, 6½", VG, $100.00.

Mickey Mouse, back scratcher, mk Walt Disney World, S1 ....$5.00

Mickey Mouse, bank, ceramic, unmk French (?), head tilted, resting on his hands, pnt features, rpr, 1930s, 6", EX, A......................$330.00

Mickey Mouse, bank, emb bl cloth on metal, w/orig key, 4¼", VG-EX, A......................$65.00

Mickey Mouse, belt, Pyramid Belt Co, leather mk 1928-1978, brass buckle, 1978, MIB, P4......................$30.00

Mickey Mouse, bendee, Applause, 5", K1 ....$6.00

Mickey Mouse, bendee, Durham, 5", H4......................$8.00

Mickey Mouse, book, A Mickey Mouse ABC Story, Walt Disney, 1936, VG, A......................$230.00

Mickey Mouse, book, Adventures of Mickey Mouse Book 1, Walt Disney, title pg missing, G-, A $10.00

Mickey Mouse, book, coloring; #2165, Saalfield, 1937, EX-, M8 ....$50.00

Mickey Mouse, book, Friends Wait for the County Fair, Whitman & Walt Disney, #833, 24 illus pgs, scarce, 9x10", EX, A......................$110.00

Mickey Mouse, book, Mickey Mouse, A Stand-Out; Walt Disney Enterprises, diecut wood figure on cover, 1936, G-VG, A......................$140.00

Mickey Mouse, book, Mickey Mouse & Boy Thursday, Whitman, 96 pgs, 5x5½", M4......................$20.00

Mickey Mouse, book, Mickey Mouse Has a Busy Day, Whitman, #1077, 1937, 16 pgs, rare, VG, M8......................$90.00

Mickey Mouse, book, Mickey Mouse in Pigmy Land, Walt Disney Enterprises, 1936, VG-EX, A......................$70.00

Mickey Mouse, book, Mickey Mouse Stories #2, Walt Disney Studios, 1934, VG-EX, A......................$50.00

Mickey Mouse, book, Mickey Mouse Story Book, McKay, 60 pgs, 1931, VG, A......................$65.00

Mickey Mouse, book, Mickey Mouse the Miracle Maker, Walt Disney Productions, 1948, G-VG, A $15.00

Mickey Mouse, book, paint; Dean & Sun, Mickey showing Goofy finished painting on cover, 62 pgs, unused, 1930s, VG+, A......................$61.00

Mickey Mouse, book, pop-up; In King Arthur's Court, Blue Ribbon, 1933, 7x10" hardcover, EX, A $390.00

Mickey Mouse, book, The Mickey Mouse Fire Brigade, Walt Disney Enterprises, w/dust jacket, 1936, VG, A......................$140.00

Mickey Mouse, book, The Pop-Up Mickey Mouse, Walt Disney Enterprises, 1933, cover warped, G-VG, A $130.00

Mickey Mouse, book & record set, Brave Little Taylor, 45 rpm-sz record plays at 33⅓ rpm, NM, T6......................$5.00

Mickey Mouse, bottle, Ginger Ale, gr w/2 labels, ea w/pie-eyed Mickey saying 'Have 1 w/Me,' empty/no cap, 1930s, EX, M8 ....$700.00

Mickey Mouse, bowl, Patriot China, features Mickey as a fireman, orange rim, 1930s, EX, M8 ....$95.00

Mickey Mouse, bread advertisement, c WDE, 9½x7½", EX, in fr, A......................$225.00

Mickey Mouse, Bubble Buster, Kilgore Mfg, cast metal pump pistol w/paper label around barrel, 8", EX-NM, A $175.00

Mickey Mouse, bubble gum card, #23, 1930s, EX, M8......................$20.00

Mickey Mouse, cake decorations, Dean's Rag-type porc figures, teeth & 5 fingers, upright: 1¾", seated: 1½", NM, A, pr........$200.00

Mickey Mouse, calendar, Silly Symphony, Brown & Bigelow, complete 12-pg calendar for 1938, 16x9", VG+, A.$350.00

Mickey Mouse, camera, NM (VG-EX box), O1 ....$55.00

Mickey Mouse, carrying case, wood w/brn plastic hdl, features Mickey playing saxaphone, 1930s, 6x8x3", EX, A $138.00

Mickey Mouse, chamber pot, child's, RGK/NY & Germany, enamelware, Mickey & Minnie at piano, some chips, 3x5¾", A...$45.00

Mickey Mouse, Christmas card, stenciled paper unfolds, 1930s, tears along creases, 23x19", G, A $10.00

Mickey Mouse, Christmas tree lights, Noma, string of 8 lithoed plastic shells, illus box, 1930s, EX (EX box), A.......$300.00

Mickey Mouse, circus tent w/extra circus dining car, from Wells' 3-car Circus Train, Mickey as barker, (rpr/touch-up), EX, A...$1,000.00

Mickey Mouse, Circus Train, Wells of London, set: band car, 7" engine, 6" car, 3" stoker, EX+ (EX box), A..........$1,150.00

Mickey Mouse, Colorforms, 1970s, 12x16", NM, A $65.00

Mickey Mouse, condiment, ceramic Mickey as mustard, nephew w/arm through his on ea side as salt & pepper, 4", 2", EX, A..$500.00

Mickey Mouse, condiment, 2 side-joined ceramic Mickeys w/open bks & tails that loop above as hdls, rare, 2x3", NM..$425.00

Mickey Mouse, cork stopper, Dean's Rag-type cast Mickey figure w/5 fingers atop, missing spring tail, 5" overall, EX, A..$800.00

Mickey Mouse, decal, iron-on, 1940s, EX, M8...................$6.00

Mickey Mouse, doll, Character Novelty Corp, c WDP, stuffed, some stain on face, orig label, ca 1950s, 18", A.......$200.00

Mickey Mouse, doll, Collector series, NM, O1...............$125.00

Mickey Mouse, doll, Knickerbocker, stuffed, compo shoes, very clean, all orig, 11", EX, A...$350.00

Mickey Mouse, doll, Knickerbocker, compo 2-Gun Mickey (cowboy), all orig, missing tail, 12", NM, A.........$5,500.00

Mickey Mouse, doll, stuffed cloth w/pnt compo arms & head, lt crazing & pnt wear, 16", G, A....................................$55.00

Mickey Mouse Cowboy Doll, Knickerbocker, missing guns and tags, VG+, $1,000.00.

Mickey Mouse, doll, unmk, cowboy, cloth w/pnt compo shoes, chaps, bandana, hat & pistol, eyes missing, 11", G, A...$70.00

Mickey Mouse, drinking cup, plastic ice cream cone form, S1...$10.00

Mickey Mouse, drum, Ohio Art, mc litho tin, Disney character graphics, w/sticks, 6¼", VG, A...............................$130.00

Mickey Mouse, Electric Space Quiz, 1950s, MIB, T1 ....$25.00

Mickey Mouse, figure, Applause, PVC, MOC, F1 ....$3.00

Mickey Mouse, figure, bsk, Japan, gr shorts & brn shoes, 1¾", EX, P6..$125.00

Mickey Mouse, figure, bsk, standing w/top hat in 1 hand, cane in other, c WD, 4", NM, A...$385.00

Mickey Mouse, figure, bsk, w/French horn, bulbous head, 1930s, tail missing, 3¼", o/w EX, M8 ....$275.00

Mickey Mouse, figure, bsk, w/sword, 1930s, 3¼", VG, M8..$75.00

Mickey Mouse, figure, celluloid, French, spring arms & legs, VG, rare, T1 ....$325.00

Mickey Mouse Celluloid Figure on Hobby Horse, Japan, 5" long, rare, NM, D10, $2,250.00.

Mickey Mouse, figure, celluloid, movable arms & legs, 1950s, 4", EX, M8..$20.00

Mickey Mouse, figure, celluloid, walking w/hands on hips, 1930s, rare, 3", EX, M8...$165.00

Mickey Mouse, figure, ceramic, Dr Brechner Mfg, 1961, 5", EX, P6 ....$55.00

Mickey Mouse, figure, from Timex wristwatch gift pkg, 1969, M4 ....$125.00

Mickey Mouse, figure, Marx, solid red plastic, 6", EX-NM, H4..$6.00

Mickey Mouse, figure, Marx, wire arms & legs, 1960s, 6", EX, M8..$45.00

Mickey Mouse, figure, Marx, yel plastic, 1970, 5½", EX, M8 ....$8.00

Mickey Mouse, figure, Seiberling, latex, 1930s, VG-EX, O1..$165.00

Mickey Mouse, figure, unmk, diecut wood, Mickey giving thumbs-up sign, 15", EX, A $150.00

Mickey Mouse, figure set, Mickey & Minnie's Barrel Organ, Salco, lead figures w/organ cart & music, orig box, 3", G, A $110.00

Mickey Mouse, fire truck, diecast metal, M4 ....$30.00

Mickey Mouse, fire truck, Sun Rubber, EX $65.00

Mickey Mouse, Floating in Water Shoo-Fly, Mengel, c WDE, decal complete, 17x13x35", EX, A $750.00

Mickey Mouse, fob w/strap for Ingersoll pocket watch, 1½" dia, 3½" strap, EX, A $80.00

Mickey Mouse, game, Follow the Leader, Milton Bradley, 1971, MIB, M4 ....$40.00

Mickey Mouse, game, Funny Rummy, Russell, early 1950s, EX+ (VG+ box), C1 ....$18.00

Mickey Mouse, game, Mickey Mouse Party Game, mk By Permission of Walt Disney Enterprises, complete, 22x18", VG, A $60.00

Mickey Mouse, game, Pin the Tail on Mickey Mouse, Walt Disney & Hallmark, oilcloth, orig sleeve, 23x20", EX, A $55.00

Mickey Mouse, game, Spin 'N Win, NM (VG+ box), O1 .$85.00

Mickey Mouse Guitar, Mousegetar Jr., Mattel, plastic, 14", EX, $50.00.

Mickey Mouse, gum ball machine, G, C8 ....$15.00

Mickey Mouse, gum card, Americana, no date, set of 360, complete, M1 ....$150.00

Mickey Mouse, gum cards, Panini, set of 360, M1 ....$60.00

Mickey Mouse, gun, Pop Shot Rifle, Durham, 1977, MIB, C1 ....$27.00

Mickey Mouse, hairbrushes (2), Henry L Hughes Co, aluminum clad, box features a pie-eyed Mickey, 1936, EX, M8.$300.00

Mickey Mouse, hand puppet, Gund, cotton & vinyl, EX, P6 ....$25.00

Mickey Mouse, handkerchiefs, set of 3 w/Mickey playing instruments, pinned together w/illus sticker, NM (EX box), A $345.00

Mickey Mouse Home Foundry, contains three molds, with instructions, EX (EX box), A, $500.00.

Mickey Mouse, kaleidoscope, cb litho, 1950s, 8½", EX $45.00

Mickey Mouse, knife rest, Germany (?), ceramic bar w/Mickey on 1 end & bird on other, 3½", NM, A $100.00

Mickey Mouse, lamp, Dan Brechner Mfg, ceramic, full color, 1960s, scarce, 8½", EX, P6.......................................$175.00

Mickey Mouse, lamp, Soreng Manegold, plaster pie-eyed Mickey in easy chair, shade is period but rpl, 14" overall, NM, A $1,600.00

Mickey Mouse, lamp, table; plastic figure w/orig paper shade, S1..$35.00

Mickey Mouse, magazine, Vol 4, No 3, Ferdinand the Bull on cover, 1938, minor wear to spine & ea pg, o/w EX, M8..$50.00

Mickey Mouse, magazine, Vol 4, No 7, Ugly Duckling cover, 1939, some crayon on 3 pgs & cover, o/w VG, M8 ...$20.00

Mickey Mouse, Magic Slate Blackboard, Strathmore, ca 1943, 12½x18½", EX (worn box), P6 ....$100.00

Mickey Mouse, mask, paper, WDP premium, 1972, 14x10", M4...$8.00

Mickey Mouse, Mickey's Air Mail, Sun Rubber, late 1940s, 3½x6½", VG..$100.00

Mickey Mouse, Movie Jecktor by Movie Jecktor Co Inc, 1930s, side lamp missing, o/w complete, VG, M8.................$75.00

Mickey Mouse, movie viewer, Chemtoy, 1980, MOC........$4.00

Mickey Mouse, pencil box, #3104, Dixon, yel & blk on gr, 1930s, EX, P6...$95.00

Mickey Mouse, pencil box, Dixon, bl & yel cb w/snap-open lid, 3 in jalopy on lid, 1930s, 10x6", lt wear, EX, T2........$90.00

Mickey Mouse, pencil box, Dixon, thick cb, Donald & Pluto on bk, 1930s, 6x9", spine split/fading, o/w VG+, T2 ......$80.00

Mickey Mouse, pencil holder, Dixon, Mickey figure, minor pnt flaking, 5", EX, A..$275.00

Mickey Mouse, pencil sharpener, Bakelite, red, 1930s, EX, M8..$125.00

Mickey Mouse Pillow, store demo, 13x13", M, D10, $250.00.

Mickey Mouse, piano, Jaymar, VG-EX, O1 ....$85.00

Mickey Mouse, pin, classic pie-eyed Mickey, Pleasure Is, cloisonne, 1980s, M, M8..$6.00

Mickey Mouse, pins on display card, 12 sterling figural pins, cb display w/early image, c Ideal Films, 7x4", NM, A...$3,250.00

Mickey Mouse, pitcher, Japan knock-off, ceramic, early, ears bk, hands on sides of tummy, 4½", EX, A $75.00

Mickey Mouse, planter, china egg behind Mickey w/accordion, Germany, 1930s, 4½", EX, A $375.00

Mickey Mouse, planter, Japan knock-off, ceramic Mickey w/sax stands by flowerpot, 4x4", EX, F, A............................$10.00

Mickey Mouse, postcard, Come & Learn About Investing in Movies w/WDP, Mickey & EF Hutton, 6¼", M4 ....$5.00

Mickey Mouse, poster, Silly Symphony, RKO, 1946, EX+, T1 ....$325.00

Mickey Mouse, pouring spouts, porc pie-eyed heads w/corks, pour through mouth, possibly German, 3", 4", M, A, 2 for...$300.00

Mickey Mouse, puppet, Pelham marionette, MIB, M9, minimum value..$55.00

Mickey Mouse, purse, mesh, silver metal w/orange & blk detailing, 1930s, 3¼x2½", EX, P6 ....$425.00

Mickey Mouse, push-button puppet, Kohner, pnt wood, working, 6", EX, A..$120.00

Mickey Mouse, racing car, flat litho tin Mickey in racer #5, 3 orig rubber wheels deteriorated, 1½x4", EX, A........$450.00

Mickey Mouse, rattle, celluloid, bell hands w/red & blk beaded legs, orig string, 1930s, scarce, EX, M8 ....$100.00

Mickey Mouse, riding toy, Mickey Mouse Bus Lines, Gong Bell Mfg, litho tin & paper on masonite, bell rings, 20", G-VG, A $70.00

Mickey Mouse, ring, plastic, 1973, M4................................$2.00

Mickey Mouse, rocker, Walt Disney Productions, red, blk, wht & gr pnt wood, enclosed sides, 31", G, A....................$95.00

Mickey Mouse, sand pail, Marx, red plastic, Mickey decal on front, other characters on litho tin hdl, 1950s, EX, M8...$25.00

Mickey Mouse, scarf, dk bl wool, features Mickey skating, 1930s, rare, VG, M8..$60.00

Mickey Mouse, scoop shovel, diecast metal, M4..............$30.00

Mickey Mouse, seed packet, Mickey w/radishes, packed for 1977 season, M, T6...$4.00

Mickey Mouse, sheet music, Mickey Mouse's Birthday Party, 1936, 2" spine tear, o/w EX, M8 ....$75.00

Mickey Mouse, sheet music, The Wedding Party of Mickey Mouse, M, P6...$150.00

Mickey Mouse, sled, Flexible Flyer, SL Allen, lacquered wood on metal fr w/mc Mickey & Minnie decal, 28", G, A $180.00

Mickey Mouse, Slugaroo, NM (EX box), O1 ....$45.00

Mickey Mouse, soap figure, Lightfoot Schultz, c WDE, minor pnt loss, 4", EX (EX box), A.....................................$90.00

Mickey Mouse Soldiers, Standup, D10, $20.00 each.

Mickey Mouse, sparkler, litho tin diecut, opening in eyes & mouth, sparkling action not working, 1930s, 6", EX, A............$288.00

Mickey Mouse, Spinikin, Kohner, 1960s, plastic w/pnt features, pull string for action, 4", NM, A $24.00

Mickey Mouse, spoon, Disneyland souvenir, 1930s, M.....$22.50

Mickey Mouse, squeeze toy, Dell, R3 ....$30.00

Mickey Mouse, squeeze toy, figure on ball, celluloid, 1930s, 5", M, L5 ....$450.00

Mickey Mouse, squeeze toy, Japan, litho tin sax player, red arms/legs, never pnt on bk, rpl sax/arm, 6", EX, A .$3,000.00

Mickey Mouse, squeeze toy, Jazz Drummer, litho tin, c WD, missing only tail support, sm bend/slight discolor, 6½", A $1,750.00

Mickey Mouse, squeeze toy, Seiberling, R3......................$85.00

Mickey Mouse, squeeze toy, Sun Rubber, 1945, NM $65.00

Mickey Mouse, stroller, Ricoh of Spain, early Mickey on bk, biplane logo & RSR on seat, 1 rivet popped, 11x8x6", EX, A $450.00

Mickey Mouse, stroller, Spain, 1 wheel detached, loose rivet, bent rear axle, complete, A $250.00

Mickey Mouse, tea set, Faiencerie D'Onnaing, Art Deco styling w/mc transfers on china, rpr sugar lid, pot: 8", EX, A $1,000.00

Mickey Mouse, tea set, Nifty, Japan, Borgfeldt Distributor, porc, 15-pc, orig 9x10¾" box w/foil lining, NM, A..........$375.00

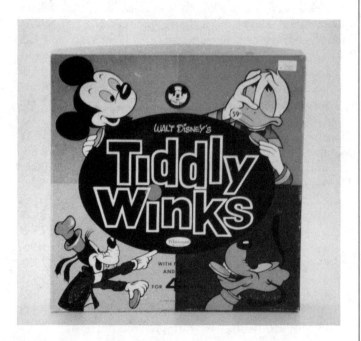

Mickey Mouse Tiddly Winks, Walt Disney Productions, Whitman, 1963, MIB, $25.00.

Mickey Mouse, toy wristwatch, Occupied Japan, paper & tin, C1...$27.00

Mickey Mouse, Transfer-O-S Album, Paas Dye Co, in 9x11" illus album, 1930s, EX-NM, A $150.00

Mickey Mouse, trapeze, mk USA/WDP, ca 1930s, 8½", M $65.00

Mickey Mouse, ventriloquist doll, EX, O1 ....$225.00

Mickey Mouse, wallet, red, 1973, M4................................$3.00

Mickey Mouse, washer, Ohio Art, litho tin, 1935, missing wood knob from crank, o/w EX, M8 ....$350.00

Mickey Mouse, washtub, Ohio Art, mc litho tin, pie-eyed Mickey & Minnie, 1 sm dent, 1930s, 2½x5¼" dia, EX, M8 ....$135.00

Mickey Mouse & Donald Duck, coat rack, wall type, VG-EX, O1 ....$10.00

Mickey Mouse & Donald Duck, crayons, Transogram, giant-sz, 1949, EX (EX box), P6 ....$50.00

Mickey Mouse & Donald Duck, pencil box, w/contents, 1950s, T1 ....$25.00

Mickey Mouse & Donald Duck, Speedway, Ideal, litho tin track w/plastic cars, working, 17½", VG-EX, A $45.00

Mickey Mouse & Donald Duck w/Goofy as Spirit of '76, tray, America on Parade, litho tin, 1976, 11" dia, NM, M8.$25.00

Mickey Mouse & Goofy, book, crossword puzzle; 1982, EX.$8.50

Mickey Mouse & Pluto, book, Mickey Mouse & Pluto the Pup, Walt Disney Enterprises, 1936, VG+, A.................$220.00

Mickey Mouse & Pluto, book, Mickey's Dog Pluto, comic pictures, 1943, EX, A...$75.00

Mickey Mouse & Pluto, bottle cap, never used, rare, 1930s, EX, M8..$30.00

Mickey Mouse & Pluto, figure, bsk, pnt features, Mickey riding Pluto, mk Japan, 1930s, complete box of 24, ea 3" L, NM, A $1,000.00

Mickey Mouse & Pluto, paint box, red & yel w/Pluto posing for Mickey Mouse, box only, 2½x6½", EX+, M5 ....$15.00

Mickey Mouse Band, drum, features Mickey, Minnie, Clarabell, Horace, Donald & Pluto, litho tin, 1930s, 5x11", EX, M8 ....$350.00

Mickey Mouse Club, bank, brn clear glass Mickey Mouse figure, MMC logo on bk, 1970s, NM, M8................$15.00

Mickey Mouse Club, book, Annette & Mystery at Moonstone Bay, Whitman, 1962, VG..$7.50

Mickey Mouse Club, doll stroller, Adco Liberty, tin, features all the gang, 1950s, 20", EX+, P6..................................$295.00

Mickey Mouse Club, drum, Noble & Cooley, litho tin, w/wood sticks, features Club regulars, 1970s, EX+, M8..........$48.00

Mickey Mouse Club, game, card; Russell, ca 1957-59, MOC...$42.50

Mickey Mouse Club, poster, Back on the Air, 1971, 36x22", M4...$75.00

Mickey Mouse Club, record, Old Yeller, 78 rpm, w/Kevin Corcoran on sleeve, VG (VG+ sleeve), T6 ....$35.00

Mickey Mouse Club, tablet, shows Scrooge McDuck on cover, unused, 5x3", EX, M8 ....$22.00

Mickey Mouse Club, tamborine, EX, O1 ....$32.50

Mickey Mouse Club, yo-yo, logo on wht, MIP.................$15.00

Mickey Mouse Club House, bank, compo, 1960s, EX, T1 .$25.00

Micronauts, Hydro Copter, MIB, D4 ....$20.00

Micronauts, Pharoid Space Warrior figure, Mego, w/time chamber, 1977, MOC, F1...$10.00

Micronauts, Time Traveler figure, 1976, 3¾", MOC, J4 ..$12.00

Midnite Mike, figure, Powco, MIP, E3 ....$10.00

Mighty Mouse, bendee, Jesco, 4½", K1.............................$4.95

Mighty Mouse, book, Mighty Mouse & the Moon Men, softcover, EX...$6.50

Mighty Mouse, book, Scared Scarecrow, Treasure Books, 1954, EX..$25.00

Mighty Mouse, book, Treasure Books, 1953, EX..............$25.00

Mighty Mouse, doll, Ideal, soft molded vinyl face on plush head, corduroy inner ears, 1953, 14", M (EX+ box), A.....$250.00

Mighty Mouse, game, board; Parker Bros, 1964, 10x20" box (EX+ box) T2 ....$50.00

Mighty Mouse, record album, Peter Pan #8200, 33⅓ rpm, 1977, VG+ (VG jacket), T6..$6.00

Mighty Mouse, Signal Lite, Larami/Terry Toon, battery-op, 1970s, NMOC, P4...$15.00

Mighty Mouse, Slide Rule Blackboard, 1960s, orig box, EX, T1 ....$45.00

Mighty Mouse, squeeze toy, Terrytoons, R3.....................$50.00

Mighty Mouse, wallet, Larami, 1978, MOC......................$10.00

Mike Hazzard, figure, w/coat & 42-pc accessory kit, sm crack at elbow, VG, loose, H4..$75.00

Milton the Monster, game, 1966, EX $28.00

Milton the Monster, puzzle, fr-tray; 1966, V1 ....$15.00

Ming (from Flash Gordon), figure, Mattel, 1979, 3¾", MOC $15.00

Minnie Mouse, bendee, Applause, Minnie 'N Me series, 2½", K1 ....$2.50

Minnie Mouse, bendee, Applause, 5", K1 ....$6.00

Minnie Mouse, bendee, Mattel, Minnie 'N Me Secret Stamp Club series, w/accessories, complete, 1990, set of 5, K1 ....$50.00

Minnie Mouse, book, pop-up; Blue Ribbon Books, 1933, minor soil/wear, o/w EX, M8..$145.00

Minnie Mouse, doll, Collector series, NM, O1 ....$125.00

Minnie Mouse Doll, Gund, black plush, jointed, painted rubber face, hands, and shoes, 24", G, A, $50.00.

Minnie Mouse, figure, Applause, PVC, MOC, F1 ....$3.00

Minnie Mouse, figure, bsk, holds mandolin, 1930s, 3½", EX.$65.00

Minnie Mouse, puppet, Pelham marionette, MIB, M9, minimum value..$55.00

Minnie Mouse, valentine card, Hallmark, full-color image, 1936, EX, P6 ....$35.00

Minya, figure, Bandai, vinyl, MIP, E3 ....$10.00

Miss Piggy, hand puppet, NM, D4 ....$5.00

Mod Squad, book, Pyramid, Sock-It-To-Em Murders, #3 in series, paperback, 1968, EX+, D9 ....$4.00

Mod Squad, book, The Hideout, Whitman TV Book, 1970, EX+, C1 ....$13.00

Mod Squad, puzzle, jigsaw; Milton Bradley, 500-pc, 15x10" box, 1969, NM, T2..$40.00

Monkees, book, Laufer, Private Picture Book, Fan Club offer, 32-pg, 8½x11", NMIP...$75.00

Monkees, bubble gum pack, Donruss, from More of the Monkees series, w/5 cards, 1968, unopened, NM, T2 ....$15.00

Monkees, charm bracelet, Raybert Prod, gold-colored metal chain w/4 1" dia portraits, 1967, on 10x4" card, M, T2 ....$40.00

Monkees, doll, Mattel, talker, 1966, 9", EX, A $90.00

Monkees, exhibit card, promotional issue, 1966, M............$4.00

Monkees, finger puppet, Davy Jones, 5", 1967, MIB, from $40 to $48.00

Monkees, finger puppet, Mickey Dolenz, Remco, plastic w/rooted hair, 'walks,' 1970s, 5", M, T2 ....$20.00

Monkees, flasher ring, Mickey at drums, 1967, M $50.00

Monkees, game, Transogram, EX+, F3............................$110.00

Monkees, Monkee-Mobile, ASC Japan, tin & plastic, friction, working, 11½", EX (EX box), A..............................$500.00

Monkees, pennant, Monkees Are the Greatest on gr felt, 20½", NM..$65.00

Monkees, postcard, fan club issue, 5½x8", NM $5.00

Monkees, puzzle, jigsaw; Fairchild, 340-pc, 1967, NMIB..$75.00

Monkees, puzzle, jigsaw; Monkees Waterskiing, Fairchild, 1967, G+ $25.00

Monkees, tambourine, 1960s, M $55.00

Moon Mullins, doll, jtd wood, mk Willard USA, 1935, 6", EX+, A...$100.00

Moon Mullins, figure, German, pnt bsk, pnt loss, 3¾", G-, A...$110.00

Moon Mullins, game, Automobile Race, Milton Bradley, EX, F3 ....$80.00

Mork Doll With Talking Spacepack, Mattel, 1979, MIB, C1, $31.00.

Mork & Mindy, Colorforms, complete w/booklet, 1979, EX-, T6..$6.00

Mork & Mindy, game, board; Parker Bros, w/cards, markers & Greebles, 1979, EX+, from $10.00 ....$20.00

Mork & Mindy, game, card; Milton Bradley, 1978, MIB (sealed),..$18.00

Mork & Mindy, gum cards, OPC, 1978, set of 99, complete, M1..$15.00

Mork & Mindy, gum cards, Topps, 1978, set of 99 w/22 stickers, complete, M1 ....$18.00

Mork & Mindy, Mork doll, Mattel, talker, 1979, 9", MIB, C1..$31.00

Mork & Mindy, Mork figure, 3¾", loose, H4 ....$2.00

Mork & Mindy, paperback, The Mork & Mindy Story, 1979, EX..$5.00

Mork & Mindy, Shrinky Dinks, Colorforms, 1979, MIB (sealed), C1..$17.00

Mortimer Snerd, decanter, Jim Beam, 1976, VG, N2.......$50.00

Mortimer Snerd Doll, Ideal, 1930s, 12", EX, D10, $375.00.

Mother Goose, blocks, McLoughlin, c 1894, mc paper litho on wood, set of 20 w/orig instructions, orig box, 13", G, A $100.00

Mother Goose, doll, Grimm, w/orig tag, 1988, M............$15.00

Mother Goose, drinking straws, M (NM box), O1 ....$18.00

Mother Goose, game, Milton Bradley, EX, F3 ....$25.00

Mother Goose, record, Mother Goose Nursery Rhymes, 1964, EX..$10.00

Mothra, figure, Bandai, winged, lg, MIP, E3 ....$50.00

Mothra, figure, Yutaka, vinyl, 4-pc set, MIP, E3 ....$15.00

Mothra Larva, figure, Bandai, vinyl, lg, MIP, E3 ....$25.00

Mothra Larva, figure, Bandai, vinyl, sm, MIP, E3 ....$10.00

Mouseketeers, television, T Cohn Inc, litho tin, plastic & wood, electric, working, orig box, 13½", EX, A $110.00

Mowgli, Disneykin, Marx, 2nd series, 1970s, EX, M8.......$35.00

Mr Ed, game, board; Parker Bros, complete, 1962, 9x18" box, M (EX+ box), A..$40.00

Mr Ed, hand puppet, Mattel, vinyl head w/plush body, pull-string talker, working, 1962, 13", VG, P4 ....$55.00

Mr Ed, TV stool, stuffed fuzzy body w/vinyl head & saddle, 1959, VG, T1..$135.00

Mr Freeze, figure, Toy Biz, 1989, MOC, F1 ....$15.00

Mr I Magination, puzzle, jigsaw; Jaymar, 400-pc, 1951, 7x10" box, EX+, T2..$60.00

Mr Magoo, book, Mr Magoo's Christmas Carol, 1977, EX .$8.00

Mr Magoo, game, Visits the Zoo, Lowe, cb figures of Magoo & zoo animals, 1961, in 10x20" box, EX-, T2 ....$80.00

Mr Magoo, record album, 33⅓ rpm, 1956, NM, C1 ....$36.00

Mr Magoo, squeeze toy, UFA, hard plastic w/gr shirt, 1958, 12", R3..$125.00

Mr Magoo, tattoos, Fleer, set of 6 different pkgs, M1........$35.00

Mr Magoo & Waldo, ring, Macman Ent, w/2 interchangeable heads, 1956, bagged on 2x4" illus card, M, T2...........$32.00

Mr Miracle, figure, Kenner, Super Powers series, missing cape, loose, H4 ....$20.00

Mr Miracle, figure, Kenner, Super Powers series, MOC, H4 ....$130.00

Mr Mxyzptlk, figure, Mego, 8", NM (VG box), T1...........$75.00

Mr Mxyzptlk, figure, Mego, 8", MOC (mk Kresge on card), H4 ....$99.00

Mr Peabody the Dog, squeeze toy, Jay Ward, R3 ....$200.00

Mr Smith (TV orangutan), puzzle, sliding tile; 1983, EX, T6..$8.00

Mummy Figure, Remco, Made in Hong Kong, fully posable, M (EX box), $35.00.

Mr T, air freshnener, M, T6..............................$3.00

Mr Wicker, figure, German, pnt bsk, 3⅝", EX, A............$70.00

Mummy, bendee, Novelty Mfg, 1979, 5¼", NMOC, D9..$23.00

Mummy, figure, Ideal, w/ring, 1978, 9", M (EX+ box) $55.00

Mummy, figure, Kenner, MIP, E3.............................$8.00

Mummy, figure, Mego, MIB, E3 ....$75.00

Mummy, figure, Placo/Universal Studios, 60th-Anniversary Limited Edition, 10", MIB $8.00

Mummy, figure, Remco, 1980, 3¾", NMOC....................$30.00

Mummy, figure, Remco/Universal Monsters, 8", MIB......$50.00

Mummy, iron-on transfer, Universal Monsters, 1964, MOC $25.00

Mummy, Mummy's Tomb Super-8 Home Movie, Castle, 200-ft, NMIB, C1 ....$21.00

Mummy, Paint-By-Number Set, Crafthouse, complete w/oil pnt & brushes, 1975, MIB (sealed) $27.50

Mummy, play case, Remco, for 3¾" figures (not included), w/mummy's tomb, creature, cage & laboratory, 1980, NM, D9....................$23.00

Mummy, poster, Warner Bros, Curse of the Mummy, Spanish text, 1950s, 14x22", EX-, A....................$25.00

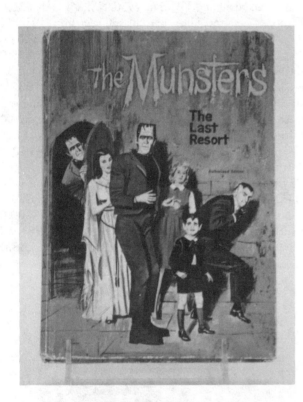

Munsters Book, The Last Resort, Whitman, VG, $15.00.

Munsters, calendar, recalled due to printing error, 12 glossy color photos, 1986, MIP (sealed), C1 ....$31.00

Munsters, Eddie doll, Ideal, molded vinyl w/movable head & jtd limbs, missing shoes, 1965, scarce, 9", A....................$81.00

Munsters, figure, Presents, PVC, 3", set of 4: Eddie, Lily, Herman & Grandpa, MIP, F1....................$12.00

Munsters, game, card; Milton Bradley, 1960s, EX+, F3 ....$45.00

Munsters, Grandpa doll, Remco, NM, T1 ....$185.00

Munsters, Grandpa doll, Remco, 1964, EX, H4..............$125.00

Munsters, Grandpa hand puppet, loose, NM, O1 ....$65.00

Munsters, Grandpa music box, Presents, limited edition, plays King of the Road, 6", MIB, F1 ....$40.00

Munsters, gum card wrapper, Leaf, features family, 1964, NM, T2....................$30.00

Munsters, Herman, Grandpa, or Eddie doll, Presents, 8", MIP, F1, ea....................$10.00

Munsters, Herman doll, Mattel, stuffed w/gr soft plastic head & hands, pull-string talker, 1964, NM (NM box), scarce, A $550.00

Munsters, Herman puppet, Mattel, gr molded soft plastic head w/cloth body & clothes, non-working talker, NM (NM box), A....................$300.00

Munsters, Lily Munster figure, Remco, 1964, 5", NM $215.00

Munsters, Lily Munster hand puppet, Ideal, cloth body, 1964, EX, H4....................$79.00

Munsters, magazine, #1, 1965, EX+, J2 ....$100.00

Munsters, puzzle, jigsaw; cast w/boiling pot, 1965, 100-pc, complete, M (VG box)....................$45.00

Munsters, puzzle, sliding tile; shows family, 2½x2½", M..$35.00

Munsters, tray, features Herman Munster, metal, NM, J2 .$40.00

Muppets, bendee, Applause, Big Bird, Elmo, Ernie, Bert, Cookie Monster, or Grover, 1991, largest 6", K1, ea $6.00

Muppets, game, Parker Bros, 1977, EX, T6 ....$15.00

Muppets, puppet, stick type, Miss Piggy or Scooter, NMOC, D4, ea $3.00

Murder She Wrote, game, Warren, 1985, EX, T6............$10.00

Mush Mouse, figure, Ideal, vinyl head w/stuffed cloth body, bendable arms & legs, missing vest, 1960s, 8", VG, H4......$60.00

Mush Mouse & Punkin' Puss, game, 1961, EX, V1...........$60.00

Mutt & Jeff, figures, Switzerland, pnt compo w/felt & cloth clothes, fully jtd, 6½" & 8", VG-EX, A....................$375.00

Mutt & Jeff, statues, early 1900s, T1, pr....................$185.00

My Favorite Martian, book, coloring; Whitman, 128 pgs, 1964, minor coloring w/EX cover, T2 ....$22.00

My Favorite Martian, game, board; Transogram, 1963, EX $45.00

My Three Sons, book, coloring; Whitman, 1963, uncolored, M $25.00

My Three Sons, figure, Remco, triplet babies, 1969, set of 3, MIB, H4....................$150.00

My Three Sons, record, promotion, Kathy Garver w/toy reindeer on cover, 1960s, EX+, C1....................$16.00

Nancy and Sluggo Dolls, Georgene, 1949, MIB, D10, $1,450.00 for the pair.

Nancy Drew Mysteries, puzzle, jigsaw; APC, 121-pc, 1978, 11x11", EX, T6...$7.00

Natasha, bendee, Wham-O, NMOC.......................$15.00

National Velvet, game, Transogram, 1961, EX+, F3 ....$30.00

Nelson Family, postcard, glossy cast photo, sent by studio, 1963, 5x7", NM, C1 ....$31.00

New Kids on the Block, Danny or Jordan figure, posable, 6", MIB, D4, ea...$5.00

New Kids on the Block, gum cards, Topps, 1990, 1st series, set of 88 w/22 stickers, complete, M1 ....$12.00

Nicodemus, figure, German, pnt bsk, 2¼", VG, A $110.00

No Time for Sergeants, game, Ideal, 1964, EX, F3............$22.00

Noble Knights & Vikings, Bravo (Sir Gordon's horse), Marx, complete, MIB, from $80 to $100.00

Noble Knights & Vikings, Erik the Viking figure, Marx, complete w/accessories & paperwork, MIB, from $150 to $200.00

Noble Knights & Vikings, Odin the Viking figure, Marx, complete, MIB, from $150 to.....................................$200.00

Noble Knights & Vikings, Odin Viking figure, Marx, fur vest, cape, spear, 2 helmets, sword, axe & horn, 1960s, EX, H4 ....$100.00

Noble Knights & Vikings, Sir Gordon the Golden Knight figure, Marx, complete w/accessories, H4.............................$65.00

Noble Knights & Vikings, Sir Gordon w/Bravo figure, Marx, complete, MIB, R4 ....$220.00

Noble Knights & Vikings, Sir Stuart the Silver Knight figure, Marx, 1 arrow & crossbow stock missing, VG, H4 ....$90.00

Noble Knights & Vikings, Sir Stuart the Silver Knight figure, Marx, silver, complete, MIB, R4..............................$125.00

Noble Knights & Vikings, Valor (Sir Stuart's horse), Marx, complete, MIB, from $80 to $100.00

Nutty Mad, game, pinball; Marx, 1964, MIB....................$40.00

Odd Job, figure, Gilbert, plastic, spring-activated arm throws derby, 1965, 12", NM (EX box), T2 ....$330.00

Oil Can Harry, bank, Looney Toons, 1950s, 14", EX, D10, $225.00.

Old King Cole, bracelet, charm; w/King, pipe, bowl & musicians charms, 1960s, NMOC......................................$17.00

Old Yeller, soundtrack, 1964, sealed $20.00

Olive Oyl, squeeze toy, Rempel, in long stride, mk King Features, late 1940s, 8x6", EX, A.................................$75.00

Oliver, bank, ceramic, figural bull, Sears, 1988, NM, M8..$20.00

Oliver, Punch-Out & Sticker Book, 1968, unused, M, V1 .$16.50

Orion, figure, Kenner, Super Powers series, MOC, H4.....$22.00

Oswald the Rabbit, squeeze toy, Sun Rubber, R3 ....$80.00

Our Gang, book, coloring; Saalfield, 1933, G+, A $40.00

Our Gang, book, Romping Through the Hal Roach Comedies, Eleanor Lewis Packer, 1939, VG-EX, A....................$45.00

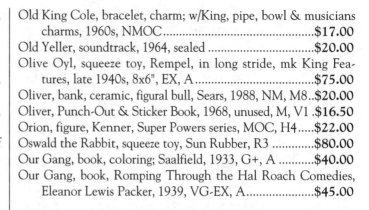

Our Gang Rowboat, Mego, plastic, 1975, 12½" long, MIB, $40.00.

Our Gang, tablet, shows classroom, 8x10", EX $10.00

Outer Limits, puzzle, Milton Bradley, 1964, orig box, EX.$295.00

Pa Winkle Branner, figure, German, pnt bsk, 4", VG, A..$110.00

Pac-Man, bank, ceramic, 1980s, EX, T1............................$5.00

Pac-Man, TV tray, 1983, VG, N2 ....$9.00

Paladin, card holder, M...$50.00

Paladin, game, Checkers, Ideal, NM (G+ Paladin header card), A $100.00

Para Demon, figure, Super Powers series, MIP, H4 ....$8.00

Partridge Family, book, coloring; Artcraft, 1970, VG, from $7 to $15.00

Partridge Family, game, board; Milton Bradley, 1971, MIB, from $40 to...$65.00

Partridge Family, magazine, Tiger Beat, 66-pg, David on cover, 1972, M, T2 ....$12.00

Pat Boone, magazine, Life, February 2, 1959, EX, N2 ....$9.00

Pathfinder, game, board; Milton Bradley, David Jensen on box, 1977, M (VG box).......................................$35.00

Patty Duke, book, The Chinese Junk, Whitman, 1966, EX.$15.00

Patty Duke, game, board; Milton Bradley, 1960s, complete, EX, from $30 to..$45.00

Paul McCartney & Wings, card set, Back to the Egg, set of 5 blk & wht photos, EX+, C1..............................$13.00

Peanuts, bank, gumball; Superior, MIB.........................$17.50

Peanuts, bank, Snoopy, as baseball player, EX, O1 ....$30.00

Peanuts, bank, Snoopy, Chex Mix, EX, O1 ....$30.00

Peanuts, bank, Snoopy, on basketball, EX, O1 ....$25.00

Peanuts, bank, Snoopy, pewter, VG+, O1 ....$45.00

Peanuts, bank, Snoopy, porc, on doghouse, NM, O1 ....$15.00

Peanuts, bath set, Christmas, red or wht towels, 3 pcs, NM, O1 ....$25.00

Peanuts, bell, Christmas 1975, NM, O1 ....$75.00

Peanuts, bottle, Avon, Snoopy, glass, NM, O1 ....$4.50

Peanuts, Charlie Brown figure, Aviva, parachuting, 3", M (EX card), H4...$5.00

Peanuts, Charlie Brown or Lucy figure, plastic, 12", VG+, O1, either $40.00

Peanuts, game, board; S&R, 4 playing pcs, tiles & dice, 1959, 10x20" box, EX+ (EX- box), T2...................................$80.00

Peanuts, game, Snoopy Come Home, Milton Bradley, 1966, EX, F3...$20.00

Peanuts Greeting Cards Store Display, Hallmark, 17½x15½" each, D10, $350.00 for complete set of six.

Peanuts, jack-in-the-box, Snoopy, VG-VG+, O1 ....$22.00

Peanuts, Linus nodder, EX, O1 ....$75.00

Peanuts, megaphone, Head Beagle, EX, O1 ....$15.00

Peanuts, music box, Aviva, Snoopy w/Woodstock sitting on doghouse, key-wound mechanism, NM, P3 ....$25.00

Peanuts, music box, Snoopy figure, works sometimes, EX+, I2..$19.00

Peanuts, ornament, Snoopy & Woodstock, 1991, NMIB, O1 ....$15.00

Peanuts, Paint-By-Numbers Set, Snoopy, Determined, 12x16" panel, vials of pnts & brush, 1971, 12x17" box, sealed, M, T2..$24.00

Peanuts, paper plates, Snoopy, Hallmark, 1971, MIP $10.00

Peanuts, Peppermint Patty doll, rag type, 14", NRFB, H4.$12.00

Peanuts, plate, Christmas 1975, NMIB, O1 ....$30.00

Peanuts, poster, Huntington North High, VG-VG+, O1.$20.00

Peanuts, pull toy, Snoopy & Woodstock, VG+, O1 ....$18.95

Peanuts, puzzle, jigsaw; Milton Bradley, 100-pc, 1976, 16x11", EX, T6 ....$11.00

Peanuts, record, Snoopy Come Home, 33⅓ rpm, 1972, EX.$15.00

Peanuts, Snoopy bendee, 5½", EX $6.00

Peanuts, Snoopy doll, w/cassette player, 14", VG-VG+, O1 .$35.00

Peanuts, Snoopy figure, UFS/Schulz, glazed ceramic, seated in chair, dtd 1966, 3½", M...$45.00

Peanuts, Snoopy, nodder, as Red Barron, EX, O1 ....$35.00

Peanuts, Snoopy or Woodstock figure, Day Dreamin', EX, O1, either $8.00

Peanuts, Snoopy Figure, Hasbro, plastic, twist sections to pose, 1966, 9", $25.00.

Peanuts, Snoopy Race Car, Aviva, red, MIB, U1 ....$12.00

Peanuts, Snoopy's Scooter Shooter, Child Guidance, broken antenna, 1970s, orig box, VG, H4 ....$15.00

Peanuts, squeak toy, Snoopy, as golfer, VG-VG+, O1 ....$3.50

Peanuts, sticker, Panini, 1987, I Love Snoopy, MIP, M1....$1.00

Peanuts, suitcase, UFS/Aviva, Snoopy & Woodstock, bl canvas w/gr trim, zipper w/lock, missing key, 1970s, VG, P4 ....$25.00

Peanuts, toothbrush, Hasbro, Snoopy, Brusha-Brusha, complete, MIB..$30.00

Peanuts, top, metal, Ohio Art, EX+, P3 ....$20.00

Peanuts, umbrella, Snoopy, ca 1965, S1 ....$26.00

Peanuts, vase, Snoopy, ceramic figural, Woodstock & food bowl on Snoopy's head, 1971, 9", EX, P3 ....$15.00

Peanuts, Woodstock figure, stuffed, 1972, VG+, O1 ....$15.00

Peanuts, Woodstock Stunt Cycle, Aviva, MIB................$12.50

Pee Wee Herman, Billy Baloney, figure, 18", NRFB, H4 .$60.00

Pee Wee Herman, Billy Baloney ventriloquist doll, 18", MIB, M5 ....$52.00

Pee Wee Herman, Chairy action figure, chair w/facial features, MOC, M5 ....$12.00

Pee Wee Herman, figure, Matchbox, w/scooter & helmet, 1988, M (NM card), D9 ....$10.00

Pee Wee Herman, figure, talking, 18", NRFB, H4............$75.00

Pee Wee Herman, King of Cartoons action figure, MOC..$12.00

Pee Wee Herman, Magic Screen, Matchbox, 1988, M (NM card), C1 ....$3.00

Pee Wee Herman, Miss Yvonne figure, Matchbox, 1988, 6", MOC , H4 ....$15.00

Pee Wee Herman, Pterri action figure, w/up, MOC, M5 ....$12.00

Pee Wee Herman, Pterri or Chairy figure, 18", NRFB, H4, ea $50.00

Pee Wee Herman, Reba or Ricardo figure, Matchbox, posable, 1988, 6", MOC, H4, ea.....................$20.00

Pee Wee Herman, scooter, Matchbox/JC Penney, 1988, child sz, MIB, H4..$200.00

Pee Wee Herman, scooter & helmet, Matchbox, 1988, M (NM card), D9 ....$10.00

Pee Wee Herman, Vance the Talking Pig, Matchbox, stuffed, 1988, MIB, F1 ....$30.00

Pegasus (from Fantasia), porc figure, Wade, 1950s, 1¾", NM, M8 ....$150.00

Pete's Dragon, gum cards, Panini, complete set, M1 ....$35.00

Pete's Dragon, soundtrack, 1977, EX $15.00

Peter Pan, doll, Duchess, hard plastic, sleep eyes, orig paper label & sword, 1950s, 7", EX, P6 ....$22.00

Peter Pan, sheet music, 1952, NM, M8 ....$10.00

Petticoat Junction, book, coloring; Whitman, 120+ pgs, 1964, 8x11", NM, A $100.00

Petticoat Junction, game, Toykraft, 1963, complete, EX $75.00

Petunia, figure, ceramic, wearing orange dress, 1985, EX $22.00

Petunia, figure, Japan, ceramic, in yel dress w/orange purse, 1977, EX $35.00

Phantom, figure, Remco, glow-in-the-dark, 1980, 3¾", M (EX card), D9 ....$14.00

Phantom, puzzle, sliding tile; Ja-Ru, 1985, MIP (sealed), C1 ....$13.00

Phantom, Rub-Ons Magic Picture Transfers, Hasbro, 3 9x10" pictures (rub-ons already applied), 1966, (EX-box), T2 ....$50.00

Phantom, water pistol, w/holster, MOC.........................$40.00

Pink Panther, bendee, Jesco, 7", K1 ....$4.95

Pink Panther, doll, plush, 1989 Anniversary on tags, w/T-shirt, 12", P3 ....$10.00

Pink Panther, gum cards, Monty Gum, bl or pk, set of 100, complete, M1 ....$25.00

Pinocchio, bank, plastic, 11", VG, N2 ....$19.00

Pinocchio, bendee, Just Toys, 1980s, 4", M.......................$9.50

Pinocchio, cookie jar, Treasure Craft, holds fishbowl, pnt ceramic, 12", MIB...$80.00

Pinocchio, doll, Applause, 10", NM...............................$10.00

Pinocchio, doll, Knickerbocker, mc pnt compo figure, jtd, cloth outfit, early, 11", NM, A $375.00

Pinocchio, doll, Knickerbocker, 1960s, NRFP, J2.............$30.00

Pinocchio, doll, Storybook series, plush, 4 faces, 1979, 11½", VG $5.00

Pinocchio, doll, unmk, molded compo head, feet & hands, cloth outfit w/checked shirt, 25", EX, A $100.00

Pinocchio, figure, bsk, Japan, 1940, 2¾", EX, M8.............$20.00

Pinocchio, figure, bsk, Japan, 1940, 4½", EX+, M8 ....$25.00

Pinocchio Doll, Knickerbocker, composition, 11", NM, $375.00.

Pinocchio, figure, compo w/pnt features, fully jtd, mk Pinocchio-Walt Disney Prod on neck, 1940s, 12", EX, A.........$248.00

Pinocchio, figure, plastic, Marx, pk, 1970, 5½", EX, M8 ....$8.00

Pinocchio, figure, PVC, Applause, set of 4, Pinocchio, Pinocchio w/Jiminy, Blue Fairy & Jiminy, MIP, F1 ....$12.00

Pinocchio, game, card; NM (EX box), O1 ....$25.00

Pinocchio, game, Pin the Nose on Pinocchio, Parker Bros, complete, minor wear, 20", EX, A....................................$90.00

Pinocchio Hoop Toss Toy, De-Ward Novelty Co., Walt Disney Productions, D10, $45.00.

Pinocchio, night light, Schmid, porc figural, fired-on pnt, 1970s, 7", M, P6 ....$85.00

Pinocchio, nodder, unmk, pnt compo, gr, red & bl outfit, yel hat w/brn shoes, clockwork, working, 7½", VG, A........$245.00

Pinocchio, pencil box, VG, T1 ....$45.00

Pinocchio, puppet, Pelham, NMIB, from $65 to $90.00

Pinocchio, record, 45 rpm, 1961, EX.............................$12.00

Pinocchio Ride-On Rocker, American, 1940s, M, D10, $165.00.

Planet of the Apes, Dr. Zaius Bank, Play Pal Plastics Inc., c 1967, 10", $28.00.

Pinocchio, soap, pnt figure, Schultz, 1950, 3½", NMIB, A.$45.00

Pinocchio, soundtrack, RCA Camden Records, EX $20.00

Pinocchio, squeaker, celluloid, Pinocchio atop 3½" dia circle, 1930s, not working, 5½", VG, A $35.00

Pirates of the Dark Water, figure, Hasbro, 1990, any of set of 8, MIP, from $6 to $10.00

Planet of the Apes, book, cut & color; Artcraft, 1974, unused, M, C1 ....$13.00

Planet of the Apes, book & record set, mc comic book w/45 rpm record, NM, T6 ....$5.00

Planet of the Apes, candy box, Phoenix Candy Co, photo of Apes on front, portrait on bk, 1967, 5x2½x1", NM, T2 ....$24.00

Planet of the Apes, Colorforms, complete, 1973, NMIB, T1..$25.00

Planet of the Apes, Colorforms, complete w/booklet, 1967, VG, T6 ....$8.00

Planet of the Apes, Cornelius figure, Mego, 1975, 8", MOC $55.00

Planet of the Apes, cup, plastic w/pictures & logo, EX, H4 .$5.00

Planet of the Apes, Dr Zaius & Galen dolls, signed, 1967, MIP, V1, pr $85.00

Planet of the Apes, Dr Zaius & Galen hand puppets, 1967, MIP, V1, pr $58.00

Planet of the Apes, Dr Zaius or Zira, figure, Mego, 8", MOC, H4, ea $55.00

Planet of the Apes, Galen figure, Dangle, MIP, V1 ....$23.00

Planet of the Apes, game, board; Milton Bradley, 1974, MIB (sealed), C1...$54.00

Planet of the Apes, General Urko figure, Mego, 8", MOC (on error Ursus card), D4 ....$75.00

Planet of the Apes, gum cards, Topps, 1975, from TV show, set of 66, complete, M1 ....$45.00

Planet of the Apes, non-sport cards, unopened box w/36 M pkgs, 1974, V1 ....$175.00

Planet of the Apes, Peter Burke figure, Mego, 8", MOC, H4..$65.00

Planet of the Apes, press book, 20th-Century Fox, ca 1974, 8½x14", NM...$7.50

Planet of the Apes, puzzle, On Patrol, HG, 96-pc, 1967, EX, from $7 to..$15.00

Planet of the Apes, Soldier Ape bendee, MOC, $15 to....$25.00

Planet of the Apes, Soldier Ape figure, Mego, 8", MOC, H4 ....$90.00

Planet of the Apes, trash can, Chienco, 1967, 16½x9" dia, NM, C1..$69.00

Planet of the Apes, Treehouse Playhouse, Mego, for 8" figures, complete, unused, 1967, NM-M, C1........................$145.00

Pluto, book, Pluto & the Puppy, Walt Disney Enterprises, 1937, VG+, A...$170.00

Pluto, figure, Sun Rubber, 1950s, 6", in window box, NM (EX box), A...$100.00

Pluto, hand puppet, VG, O1...$25.00

Pluto, jump rope, red, wht & bl, 1970s, NM.....................$12.50

Pluto, marionette, Pelham, MIB, M9 ....$95.00

Pluto, nodder, Marx, plastic, 1960s, EX.............................$8.50

Pluto, pencil sharpener, cast metal, 1930s, pnt wear, 1⅛x1½", P6 ....$140.00

Pluto, push-button puppet, Kohner, pnt wood, working, 5¼", EX, A..$80.00

Pogo Possum, Albert Alligator figure, EX, O1 ....$15.00

Pogo Possum, Beauregard Hound figure, VG-EX, O1 ....$10.00

Pogo Possum, Owl figure, VG-EX, O1 ....$10.00

Pogo Possum, Pogo figure, VG-EX, O1 ....$15.00

Pogo Possum, Porky Pine, Beauregard, Albert & Howland, figure set, Walt Kelly, ca 1969, 5½" tallest, NM-M, C1 ......$79.00

Pogo Possum, poster, World of Pogo, Springfield Museum, 1970, 17x1", V1 ....$30.00

Pokey, see Gumby's Pal Pokey

Police Academy, figure, Kenner, 2nd series, 1989, MIP, F1, any...$15.00

Popeye, bank, American Bisque, rpl pipe, orig, EX.........$950.00

Popeye, bank, Daily Dime Bank w/Savings Tally, litho tin, 2½", VG-EX, A..$50.00

Popeye, bank, Daily Quarter, USA Kalon, opens when $10 is reached, 5x3½", NM+, A...$85.00

Popeye, bank, dime register, litho tin, Wimpy & Olive on sides, rare upsidedown pipe, 2½x2½", EX, A.........................$190.00

Popeye, bank, Straits Mfg, Knockout, c King Features Syndicate 1935, 5x2x3½", NM (G box), A $2,050.00

Popeye, bank, Straits Mfg, Knockout, diecut figures on litho tin platform, insert coin for action, 4¾", G, A $225.00

Popeye, bank, vinyl, 1979, 9½", EX, P6 ....$45.00

Popeye, belt, Star Suspender & Belt Corp, Genuine Top Grain Leather, w/illus, 1929, NM (G+ card), A $160.00

Popeye, Bif Bat, c King Features Syndicate 1935, wood paddle w/rubber ball attached by rubber band, 11", NM.......$70.00

Popeye, book, pop-up; 1981, EX, T6 ....$3.00

Popeye, book, Popeye, EC Segar, 1934, EX-, A $30.00

Popeye, book, Popeye, Sweet Pea & Wimpy fishing off pier on color cover, c King Features, 1936, VG, A $35.00

Popeye, book, Popeye & the Pirates, pull-tab animation, 9½x13", EX-, A..$40.00

Popeye, book, Popeye's How To Draw Cartoons, David McKay, 1939, hard-bound, 41 pgs, EX, P6 ....$95.00

Popeye, book, Trace Erase Story Slate Book, Japan, paper litho, orig pkg, 15¼", EX, A $30.00

Popeye, bubble gum machine, Hasbro, 1963, EX+, C1.....$27.00

Popeye, cap, navy bl w/wht brim, name & portrait across front, full-figure portrait on top, M, C6 ....$145.00

Popeye, Color-By-Number, Hasbro, TV authorized edition, 1957, unused, M (NM box)..$25.00

Popeye, Color-By-Number, Hasbro, 12 pencils, sharpener & 12 sketches, 1950, 13x10" box, unused, NM, T2............$90.00

Popeye, Colorforms, Popeye the Weatherman, 1959, orig box, EX, J2 ....$45.00

Popeye, doll, EFF & Bee c 1935 Fleischaker & Baum, stuffed, orig tag, missing pipe, 17", A..................................$200.00

Popeye, figure, carnival chalk, bl shirt & hat w/silver glitter, 1930s, 11", EX+, P6..$145.00

Popeye, figure, Chein, jtd wood, w/sea bag & pipe, Chein label on foot, 1932, 8", NM+, A...................................$1,000.00

Popeye, figure, Gund, musical, plush w/vinyl face, 1950s, 10", EX, P6...$45.00

Popeye, figure, Gund, vinyl head, stuffed cloth body, talker, working, 1960s, 14", MIB, H4................................$140.00

Popeye, figure, Gund, vinyl head & arms, cloth body & clothes, turn crank & he laughs, 1960s, 22", VG, H4.............$85.00

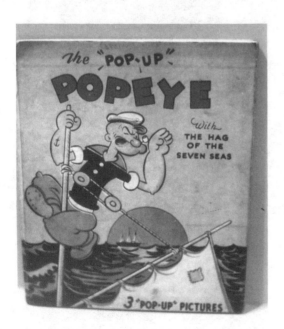

Popeye Book, Pop-Up, Hag of the Seven Seas, Blue Ribbon Press, 1935, EX, A, $250.00.

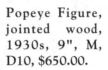

Popeye Figure, jointed wood, 1930s, 9", M, D10, $650.00.

Popeye, figure, Hamilton, PVC, 1992, 3½", set of 4, M, F1 .$15.00

Popeye, figure, jtd wood, label dtd 1935, 12x4", NM, A .$425.00

Popeye, figure, King Features, jtd wood, 6x4", NMIB, A.$110.00

Popeye, float toy, rubber, 1950s, MIP, V1 ....$38.00

Popeye, game, Ball Toss, NM (EX box), O1 ....$60.00

Popeye, game, board; Adventures of Popeye, Transogram, 1957, MIB...$130.00

Popeye, game, card; Parker Bros, complete set of 72, M1 ...$5.00

Popeye, game, Magnetic Fish Game, Transogram, 1958, VG, F3 ....$33.00

Popeye, game, Mexican Jumping Bean, 1950s, MOC, V1.$34.00

Popeye, game, Pipe Toss, stand-up Popeye, wooden target pipe & throwing rings, 11x5½", NMIB, A.........................$80.00

Popeye, game, Roly Poly Target, rifle fires cork at 6 targets, in orig cb holder, 20x9", NM A $140.00

Popeye, game, Skooz-It Pick-a-Picture, Ideal, 1963, NM (EX canister), C1 ....$54.00

Popeye Game, Sliding Boards and Ladders, King Features Syndicate, Built Rite Toy, 1958, NMIB, $25.00.

Popeye, Getar, Mattel, turn crank, plays Popeye the Sailor Man, non-working, orig box, 14", G-VG, A $25.00

Popeye, hand puppet, Gund, NM.....................................$40.00

Popeye, harmonica, King Features, dtd 1929, lt wear & scratches, 4½", EX-, A $45.00

Popeye, kazoo, Larami, plastic, 1970, MOC, C1..............$24.00

Popeye, kazoo, litho tin, EX, P6 ....$65.00

Popeye, lantern, Linemar, battery-op, glass chest, arms serve as hdl, 8x4", NM, A..$200.00

Popeye, magnets, Hamilton, set of 5, 1992, MIP, F1 ....$8.00

Popeye, marionette, 1930s, EX $95.00

Popeye, motorcycle, Hubley, CI, Popeye w/movable arms on red cycle, rpl guide-wheel tires, pnt loss, 8½", VG, A.$1,900.00

Popeye, Paddle Wagon, Corgi, pnt diecast metal w/plastic figures, orig pkg, 2¾", EX, A $70.00

Popeye, paint set, American Crayon Co, 6x4½", MIB, A .$80.00

Popeye, Paint-By-Number, Hasbro, 7x10" window box w/3 canvas panels, pnts & brush, 1958, NM, T2...................$50.00

Popeye, pamphlet, promotion for IGA & cartoons, 1930s, lg, M, scarce, V1 ....$150.00

Popeye on Motorcycle, Hubley, cast iron, Hubley embossed on rubber tires, 5x8½", EX, from $3,500.00 to $4,000.00.

Popeye, pencil, Eagle, orig box, 10½", EX, A....................$15.00

Popeye, pin, hard plastic figural, EX, P6..........................$25.00

Popeye, pipe, 1948, MOC, S1 ....$80.00

Popeye, plate, Sweet Pea twice on rim, Popeye w/fishing rod, 6", EX, A...$85.00

Popeye, playset, Jaymar, Make/Wear a Funny Face, creates over 10,000 heads, w/character masks, 1962, 11x22", NM, A...$98.00

Popeye, puzzle, fr-tray; Jaymar, Popeye & pirates w/Olive Oyl & Sweet Pea, 1950s, 11x14", EX+, T2 ....$24.00

Popeye, puzzle, jigsaw; Jaymar, Rough Waters, late 1950s-early 1960s, NMIB, C1...$21.00

Popeye Squeak Doll, Cameo, 1930s, 13½", M, D10, $400.00.

Popeye, puzzle, Saalfield/King Features, paper litho, set of 4, 1932, NMIB, P4..................$275.00

Popeye, quilt, cotton flannel, also features 12 sqs of Katzenjammer graphics, handcrafted, 43x33", M, P6 ....$80.00

Popeye, record, Popeye's Favorite Sea Songs, 45 rpm, 1959, EX (NM sleeve), C1 ....$21.00

Popeye, record, Private Treasure, mc illus, 1948, M, V1 ..$40.00

Popeye, ring, flasher; Vari-Vue Flasher, 1960s, NM, T1, ea.$5.00

Popeye, slate, Presto, cb w/images of Popeye & friends doing math problems, 1944, unused, NM, A $75.00

Popeye, soap, figural, EX, P6..................................$25.00

Popeye, Spinikin, Kohner, pnt plastic, pull-string action, 1960s, 4", NM from $28 to $45.00

Popeye, squeeze toy, Rempel, standing, facing right, flexing muscles, mk King Features, late 1940s, 12x8", NM, A.....$85.00

Popeye, Stitch-a-Story Sewing Kit, Hasbro, 1950s, NMIP, P6 ....$75.00

Popeye, tablet, King Features, dtd 1929, unused, EX+......$75.00

Popeye, toothbrush, figural, MIB, T1 ....$45.00

Popeye, train set, Larami, 1980, miniature, MOC, C1 .....$15.00

Popeye & Olive Oyl, pull toy, Stretchy Hand Car, Linemar, litho tin heads on springs, 6x6½", MIB $3,000.00

Porky Pig, book, Porky Pig's Duck Hunt, Leon Schlesinger, 1938, VG-EX, A.....................................$110.00

Porky Pig, book, Porky's Book of Tricks, Leon Schlesinger, 1942, cover damage, VG, A $30.00

Porky Pig, car, Ertl, diecast, 1989, MIP, F1/D4 ....$5.00

Porky Pig, squeeze toy, Sun Rubber, MIP $150.00

Porky Pig, squeeze toy, Sun Rubber, 1940s, EX+ $50.00

Prince Valiant Book, The Young Night, Foster art, Martin, 1945, A, $165.00; Jeweled Shield and Sword, Mattel, 11" diamater tin shield, scabbard and jeweled sword, MIB, A, $460.00.

Prince Valiant, bank, litho tin, registers dimes, 2½" sq, VG, A...$80.00

Prince Valiant, book, coloring; Saalfield, 1954, 11x14", EX+, A $110.00

Prince Valiant, book, Treasure Books, 1954, 7x8", EX+, A $25.00

Prince Valiant, comic strip, Sunday; mc full pg, 1949, matted, NM, A $55.00

Prince Valiant, game, Prince Valiant Crossbow, Parva, complete w/dart gun, belt & holster, NM (EX-NM box), A...$245.00

Prince Valiant, game, Valor, Transogram, complete, M (VG+ box), F5 ....$50.00

Prince Valiant, puzzle, fr-tray; Built Rite, 1954, 10x13", NM, A.$115.00

Punisher, figure, Toy Biz, MOC, D8................$12.99

Punkin' Puss, figure, Ideal, vinyl head w/stuffed body, bendable arms & legs, 1960s, 8", soiled, VG, H4 ....$80.00

Puss 'N Boots, puzzle, jigsaw; HG Toys, NM in canister...$12.50

Q-Bert, stickers, puffy type, 1982, MOC $3.00

Queen Hippolyte (Wonder Woman) figure, Mego, 1976, NRFB, H4................................$95.00

Quick Draw McGraw, book, On Raspberry Ridge, Durabook, 1972, EX, T6 ....$4.00

Quick Draw McGraw, doll, Hanna-Barbera/Wonderland, Australia, gray, wht & beige plush, 15", C1 ....$45.00

Quick Draw McGraw, doll, Knickerbocker, 1959, 17½", M (VG+ box).......................................$250.00

Quick Draw McGraw, doll, plush w/hat, holster & gun, 1985, 15", NM $10.00

Quick Draw McGraw Game, Moving Target, Knickerbocker, 10" wooden Quick Draw with 5" Baba Looey on back on plastic base, guns and darts included, NMIB, C1, $210.00.

Quick Draw McGraw, game, Quick Draw McGraw Private Eye, Milton Bradley, 1960, NMIB, J2 ....$28.00

Quick Draw McGraw, gun & holster set, M (EX card), O1.$75.00

Quick Draw McGraw, record album, Treasure of Sarah's Mattress, Colpix, 33⅓ rpm, 1963, EX+, T2......$32.00

Quick Draw McGraw, socks, TG (Australia), graphics on red, 1990, M, C1 ....$21.00

Quick Draw McGraw, squeeze toy, Dell, R3 ....$1.00

Quick Draw McGraw, Water Gun Hat, complete w/orig tags, 1959, M, V1 ....$40.00

Rachel, figure, German, pnt bsk, 3½", EX, A................$45.00

Raggedy Andy, doll, Knickerbocker, musical, 1960s, MIB.$115.00

Raggedy Andy, doll, Volland, cloth w/unjtd neck, blk shoe button eyes, closed smiling mouth, dressed, 15", VG, A $650.00

Raggedy Ann, cake pan, M..................................$12.50

Raggedy Ann, doll, Volland (unmk), unjtd neck, blk shoe button eyes, orig yarn hair, cb heart, orig dress, 15", VG, A..$1,050.00

Raggedy Ann, game, Magic Pebble, 1941, complete, EX, V1...$60.00

Raggedy Ann & Andy, plate, Schmid, Mother's Day, 1978, MIB...$25.00

Raiders of the Lost Ark, gum cards, OPC, 1981, set of 88, complete, M1.....................................$12.00

Raiders of the Lost Ark, gum cards, Topps, 1981, set of 88, complete, M1.....................................$20.00

Raiders of the Lost Ark, Toht figure, Kenner, MIP, E3 ...$10.00

Rainbow Brite, TV tray, 1983, VG, N2.................$9.00

Ramar of the Jungle, game, 1952, EX....................$75.00

Rambo, Combat Set, Largo, 1985, MOC, F1.......$15.00

Rambo, figure, Coleco, 1986, 6", MOC, F1 ....$10.00

Rambo, game, target; Arco, P-38 Dart Gun & Target, 1985, MOC, H4...$9.00

Rambo, gum card, Topps, 1985, set of 66 w/11 stickers, complete, M1.....................................$18.00

Rambo, gum cards, Panini, 1987, set of 240, complete, M1 .$40.00

Rambo, playset, Savage Strike Headquarters, MIB, D4 ....$20.00

Rambo, Savage Strike Cycle, Coleco, for 6" figure, 1986, MIP, F1..$10.00

Range Rider, book, coloring; Abbott, 1956, M.............$35.00

Range Rider, tablet, features Jack Mahoney, 1950s, 8x10", unused, NM, T2......................................$15.00

Range Rider, TV Chair, folding wood w/blk fabric seat & arm designs, mc cowboy scene, fringe, 1956, 24", EX, T2.$130.00

Rapunzel, puzzle, jigsaw; HG Toys, M in canister.............$12.50

Rat Finks, Bat Fink shirt decal, 1960s, MIP.................$25.00

Rat Finks, charm, plastic, from gumball machine, 1960s, 3¾", M..$7.50

Rat Finks, comb, 1960s, MOC.............................$20.00

Rat Finks, Hydro-Racer, Kenner, MIP, E3.................$10.00

Rat Finks, magazine, Confession of a Rat Fink, M, E3......$13.00

Rat Finks, Martian Finks, 1" gumball machine figure, 4 different on orig display card, M, H4...........................$10.00

Rat Finks, Rad Rod Dragnut in His Haulin' Hog, 1980s, MOC, from $10 to...$15.00

Rat Finks, Rad Rod Junkyard Kid in His Clod Hopper, 1980s, MOC, from $10 to.....................................$15.00

Rat Finks, ring, Get That Fink Official Gun & Hunting, Henal Novelties, ca 1960(?), orig card, M, P4.................$20.00

Rat Finks, ring, gumball machine prize, 1" figure on plastic base, 1960s, NM, H4......................................$5.00

Rat Finks, ring, Macman Enterprises, 1¼" detachable figure on base, 1963, orig 3x1" header card w/membership, MIP...$29.00

Rat Finks, Rockin' Roadster, Kenner, MOC, F1.............$10.00

Rat Finks, Sonic Scream figure, Kenner, MOC, F1/E3 .....$10.00

Rat Patrol, book, coloring & activity; 1966, EX-, T6.........$7.00

Rat Patrol, book, Desert Danger, paperback, EX.............$15.00

Rat Patrol, game, Transogram, missing 4 or 5 pcs, 1966, EX, H4...$40.00

Rat Patrol, insignia ring, Topps, from bubble gum cards, rare, NM-M, C1...$29.00

Real McCoys, book, Whitman, hardcover, 1960, EX $15.00

Real McCoys, Walter Brennan photo, blk & wht glossy, signed, 1961, NM, C1......................................$24.00

Red King, figure, Bandai, vinyl, MIP, E3 ....$10.00

Red Ranger, costume box, 1940s, EX, T1 ....$35.00

Red Rider, book, paint; 1947, NM $35.00

Red Ryder, gun, Christmas Story BB Gun, VG-EX, O1 ...$65.00

Ren & Stimpy Show, snack & play tray, MTV-Nicktoons/Marsh-Allan, litho metal w/folding legs, 1992, 17x12", M, P4 ....$10.00

Rescuers Down Under, bendee, Applause, Bianca, Bernard, Jake, Wilbur, Cody & Frank, set of 6, K1 ....$12.50

Rescuers Down Under, bendee, Just Toys, Bernard or Bianca, 5", K1, ea...$4.95

Restless Gun, game, board; Milton Bradley #4905, marbles & play money, 1959, VG, P4...........................$35.00

Restless Gun, TV Guide, January 18, 1958, EX+, C1.......$14.00

Revenge of the Nerds II, yo-yo, promotional item, 1987, EX+, T6...$4.00

Richard Petty, gum cards, Traks, 1991, set of 25, complete, M1 ....$5.00

Ricky Nelson, photo, facsimile signature, sent by studio to fan, 1958, 5x7", NM, C1...............................$27.00

Ricky Nelson, press book, Love & Kisses, 12-pg, 12x18", EX+,T6...$50.00

Ricochet Rabbit, book, coloring; Whitman, 1965, NM ...$25.00

Ricochet Rabbit, hand puppet, Ideal, 1960s, EX, H4 ....$39.00

Rifleman Book, Whitman, authorized edition, 1959, EX, $10.00.

Rifleman, game, board; Milton Bradley, Chuck Conners on cover, 1959, M (NM box), C1 ....$136.00

Rin Tin Tin, beanie, premium, EX+, J2 ....$50.00

Rin Tin Tin, book, One of the Family, Whitman Tip-Top Tales, 1953, G+ $6.50

Rin Tin Tin, cavalry hat, premium, NM+, J2 ....$70.00

Rin Tin Tin, Coloring Fun Set, Transogram, 4 crayon-by-number illus & wipe-off slates +more, 20x14" box, 1956, EX, T2 ....$90.00

Rin Tin Tin, game, Adventures of..., Transogram, 1955, VG+, F3 ..$42.00

Rin Tin Tin, game, Bead-in-the-Hole, Nabisco, offered in boxes of Shredded Wheat Jrs, 1950s, 1½" dia, M, T2 ....$12.00

Rin Tin Tin, game, Skill Ball, Nabisco Shredded Wheat premium, 1950s, NM, C1 ....$15.00

Rin Tin Tin, Paint-By-Number-Set, Transogram, 8 dryed pnt tubes, 2 used/7 unused drawings, no date, T6 ....$45.00

Rin Tin Tin, pennant, premium, EX+, J2 ....$85.00

Rin Tin Tin, puzzle, jigsaw; Whitman Jr, 1956, EX $25.00

Rin Tin Tin, Rusty on horse, Marx, pnt plastic, complete w/13 accessories, scarce, 1950s, 14", NM (EX box), A $261.00

Rin Tin Tin, soundtrack, Adventures of Rin Tin Tin, 1956, G+ $25.00

Ripper, figure, Mattel, MIP, E3 ....$8.00

Road Runner, figure, PVC, Shell Gas premium, MIP, D4 ..$3.00

Road Runner, game, board; Milton Bradley, 1969, NMIB, C1 ....$79.00

Robby Benson, tie clasp, enameled, NM, V1 ....$125.00

Robin Hood, Azeem figure, Kenner, MIP, E3 ....$10.00

Robin Hood, Battle Wagon (vehicle), MIB, D4 ....$10.00

Robin Hood, Dark Warrior figure, Kenner, MIP, E3 ....$16.00

Robin Hood, figure, Mego, 1st issue, complete, w/orig cloth belt, loose, H4 ....$35.00

Robin Hood, Friar Tuck figure, Kenner, Robin Hood Prince of Thieves, 1991, rare, MOC, F1 ....$20.00

Robin Hood, Friar Tuck figure, Mego, Robin Hood series, 8", MIB, H4 ....$40.00

Robin Hood, Little John figure, Kenner, MIP, E3 ....$10.00

Robin Hood, Long Bow figure, Kenner, MIP, E3 ....$5.00

Robin Hood, Net Launcher, 1980s, MIB, T1 ....$10.00

Robin Hood, poster, Walt Disney release, 1973, 27x40", M4 ....$25.00

Robin Hood, puzzle, fr-tray; Built-Rite, Richard Green & Alan Wheatley in sword fight, 1956, 11x14", EX-, T2 ....$24.00

Robin Hood, Sheriff of Nottingham figure, Kenner, MIP, from $5 to $10.00

Robin Hood, Will Scarlet figure, Kenner, MIP, E3 ....$16.00

Robocop, Claw Callahan figure, 2nd series, MOC, D4 ......$7.00

Robocop, figure, China, jtd vinyl, unlicensed, Robocop getting out of car on box, 12", MIB, from $30 to $45.00

Robocop, figure, Taiwan, full-jtd talker, unlicensed, not sold in US, 12", mc photo box, MIB, H4 ....$150.00

Robocop, Gatlin Blast Robocop figure, Kenner, 2nd series, rare, MIP, F1 ....$25.00

Robocop, Nightfighter figure, Kenner, MIP, E3 ....$10.00

Robocop, Nitro figure, MOC, D4 ....$5.00

Robocop, Robo 1 (vehicle), Kenner, MIP, F1 ....$25.00

Robocop, Robocopter, Kenner, MIP, F1 ....$30.00

Robocop, Robocycle or Skull Hog, MIB, D4, ea $10.00

Robocop II, gum cards, Topps, 1990, set of 88 w/11 stickers, complete, M1 ....$11.00

Robotech, Amoured Zent figure, Matchbox, 1985, 6", MOC, J4 ....$12.00

Robotech, Bioroid Terminator figure, Matchbox, MIP, E3 .$10.00

Robotech, book, Robotech II Illus Handbook, M, E3 ....$15.00

Robotech, Breetai figure, Matchbox, 1985, 6", MOC, J4 .$12.00

Robotech, Breetai figure, Matchbox, 8", MIP, E3 ....$15.00

Robotech, Corg figure, Matchbox, 1985, 3¾", MOC, J4 ....$5.00

Robotech, Dana's Hover Cycle, Matchbox, 1980s, MIB, T1 ..$20.00

Robotech, Dana Sterling figure, Matchbox, 1985, 3¾", MOC, from $12 to $20.00

Robotech, Exodore figure, Matchbox, 1985, 6", MOC, J4 .$12.00

Robotech, Khyron figure, Matchbox, 1985, 6", MOC, J4 .$12.00

Robotech, Khyron figure, Matchbox, 8", MIP, E3 ....$15.00

Robotech, Lisa Hayes figure, Matchbox, 12", MIP, E3 .....$30.00

Robotech, Lisa Hayes figure, Matchbox, 1985, 3¾", MOC, J4 ....$10.00

Robotech, Lynn Minmei figure, Matchbox, Harmony Gold issue, 1985, 3¾", MOC, from $50 to $70.00

Robotech, Lynn Minmei figure, Matchbox, 12", MIP, E3 .$35.00

Robotech, Max Sterling figure, Matchbox, 1985, 3¾", MOC $10.00

Robotech, Micro Zentraedi figure, Matchbox, 1985, 3¾", MOC, J4 ....$5.00

Robotech, Miriya figure, Matchbox, 1985, 6", MOC, J4 ..$15.00

Robotech, Miriya figure, Matchbox, Harmony Gold reissue, purple, 1985, 3¾", MOC, J4 ....$30.00

Robotech, Miriya figure, Matchbox, 8", MIP, E3 ....$20.00

Robotech, party invitations, MIP, D4 ....$2.00

Robotech, Rand figure, Matchbox, 1985, 3¾", MOC, from $5 to $7.00

Robotech, Rick Hunter figure, Matchbox, MIP, E3 ....$20.00

Robotech, Robotech Master figure, Matchbox, 1985, 3¾", MOC $5.00

Robotech, Rook Bartley figure, Matchbox, Harmony Gold reissue, 1985, 3¾", MOC, from $20 to $30.00

Robotech, Roy Fokker figure, Matchbox, 1985, 3¾", MOC .$12.00

Robotech, Zentraedi Warrior figure, Matchbox, MIP, E3...$7.00

Robotech, Zor Prime figure, Matchbox, 1985, 3¾", MOC .$6.00

Rock & Bubble, gum card, Dandy, 1987, 90 pkgs per box, MIB (sealed), M1 ....$48.00

Rock Lords, Boulder, Tonka, 1986, MIP, F1 ....$5.00

Rock Lords, Narliphant, Tonka, 1986, MOC, F1 ....$5.00

Rock Lords, Tombstone, Tonka, 1986, MOC, F1 ....$5.00

Rock Stars, gum card, Donruss, 1979, set of 66, complete, M1 ....$15.00

Rock Stars, gum cards, AGI, 1982, 108 cards w/12 stickers, complete, M1 ....$45.00

Rock Super Stars, gum card, Pro Set, 1991, 1st series, set of 260, complete, M1 ....$15.00

Rock Super Stars, gum card, Pro Set, 1991, 2nd series, set of 340, complete, M1 ....$20.00

Rocketeer, Airplane Bee Gee, Spectra Star, yel plastic, rubber-band powered, 1991, 16", MIB, P4 ....$25.00

Rocketeer, candy container, plastic, helmet head or half figure (waist up), 2½", M, P4, ea $3.00

Rocketeer, cookie jar, Bulldog Cafe, M $65.00

Rocketeer, gum cards, Topps, 1991, set of 99 w/11 stickers, complete, M1 ....$10.00

Rocketeer, Poster Pen Set #1921, Rose Art/Disney, complete w/2 posters & 6 markers, 1991, MOC, P4....................$30.00

Rocketeer, Premiere Blast-Off Party Passport, Buena Vista, book w/5 coupons for movie promos, Orlando edition, M, P4....................$20.00

Rocketeer, puzzle, Movie Poster, Golden & Golden, 300-pc, 1991, MIB, P4....................$12.00

Rocketeer, standee, Applause/Disney, vinyl, w/tags, 1991, 9", M, P4....................$25.00

Rocky & Bullwinkle, book, Go to Hollywood, Whitman Tip-Top Tale, 1961, VG....................$15.00

Rocky & Bullwinkle, game, Supermarket; Whitman, 1970s, VG....................$45.00

Rocky & Friends, see also Bullwinkle

Rocky & Friends, sewing cards, Whitman, set of 6 punched cards w/yarn, EX+, A....................$125.00

Rocky Jones Space Ranger, record, The Space Pirates, Columbia #MJV-154, 78 rpm, 1950, NM (VG+ color picture sleeve)....................$60.00

Rocky Squirrel, bendee, Jesco, 1980s, MOC, T1....................$10.00

Rocky Squirrel, bendee, Wham-O, 1969, MOC, T1....................$25.00

Rodan, figure, Bandai, vinyl, MIP, E3....................$20.00

Rodney Dangerfield, game, board; No Respect, 1985, NM.$10.00

Roger & Jessica Rabbit, tray, litho tin, England, 1987, 11½" dia, NM, M8....................$15.00

Roger Rabbit, ashtray, tin w/Baby Herman, MIP, D4.........$8.00

Roger Rabbit, Baby Herman bendee, LJN, 1988, MOC, J4 .$20.00

Roger Rabbit, bendee, LJN, 1987, 14", MOC, F1............$15.00

Roger Rabbit, bendee, LJN, 1987, 6", MOC, from $5 to ..$10.00

Roger Rabbit, bendee, LJN, 3", MIP, E3............$5.00

Roger Rabbit, Benny the Cab bendee, LJN, 6", declared unsafe & general recall issued, MOC, D1....................$40.00

Roger Rabbit, Benny the Cab figure, Animate series, MOC, D4....................$28.00

Roger Rabbit, book, pop-up; Budget Books, Made in Australia, hardcover, M, D1....................$75.00

Roger Rabbit, book, pop-up; Fleetway Books of England, 1988, scarce, NM, M8....................$25.00

Roger Rabbit, book, Who Censored Roger Rabbit, St Martins publishing, hardcover, M, D1....................$100.00

Roger Rabbit, cassette w/storybook, MIP, D4....................$4.00

Roger Rabbit, doll, Applause, plush, w/orig tag, 48", M, D1....................$300.00

Roger Rabbit, doll, LJN, inflatable, 1987, 36", MIP, F1 ...$10.00

Roger Rabbit, doll, Playskool, stuffed, 17", MIB (Benny the Cab box), F1....................$15.00

Roger Rabbit, doll, Playskool, talking, 14", MIB..............$15.00

Roger Rabbit, Eddie Valiant bendee, LJN, 6", MOC, D1 ...$5.00

Roger Rabbit, figure, Portable Hole series, MOC, D4.........$5.00

Roger Rabbit, figure, PVC, Applause, M, D1....................$5.00

Roger Rabbit, figure, PVC, Applause, on yel crate, M, D1 .$10.00

Roger Rabbit, game, board; Germany, MIB, D4..............$20.00

Roger Rabbit, game, board; Who Framed Roger Rabbit?, rare, MIB (sealed), D4....................$50.00

Roger Rabbit, game, Roger Rabbit Dip Flip, LJN, MIB, $12 to....................$18.00

Roger Rabbit, gum cards, Topps, 1988, 132 cards w/22 stickers, complete, M1....................$18.00

Roger Rabbit, Jessica bendee, LJN, 6", MOC, D1.............$30.00

Roger Rabbit, Judge Doom bendee, LJN, 6", MOC, D1 .....$5.00

Roger Rabbit, mug, w/Jessica photo, MIB, D4....................$5.00

Roger Rabbit, poster, Disney, orig for theater, 27x41", M, D1....................$35.00

Roger Rabbit, poster, Killian, I'm Not Bad I'm Just Drawn That Way, gold mylar, 2nd limited edition, unnumbered, M, D1....................$500.00

Roger Rabbit, poster, Killian, Time To Toon In Again, gold mylar, limited edition, unnumbered, M, D1............$400.00

Roger Rabbit, puzzle, Milton Bradley, set of 4, MIB, D1 .$200.00

Roger Rabbit, puzzle, Waddingtons, England, 300-pc, MIB, D4....................$20.00

Roger Rabbit, Smart Guy bendee, LJN, 6", MOC, D1........$5.00

Roger Rabbit, Snow Sled, Germany, M, D4....................$20.00

Roger Rabbit, Wacky Head Hand Puppet, Applause, MIP, F1....................$10.00

Roger Rabbit, yo-yo, Germany, MOC, D4....................$8.00

Rolling Stones, sheet music songbook, Big Hits, 6 pgs color photos, EX, T6....................$25.00

Rookies, cap pistol, Fleetwood, mk Official, 1975, MOC, H4....................$6.00

Rookies, Emergency Kit, Fleetwood, 1975, MOC, C1......$21.00

Rookies, game, target; Fleetwood, dart pistol w/3 targets & stands, 1975, MOC, H4....................$8.00

Rookies, Official Police Car, Fleetwood, 1975, MOC, C1.$31.00

Rookies, Target Gallery Fun Mechanism, Placo, w/suction darts & 3 targets, 1976, MIB (sealed), C1....................$37.00

Rookies, Terry figure, 1970s, 8", MOC, T1....................$30.00

Rookies, walkie-talkies, bl plastic, uses 9-volt batteries, non-working, 1973, EX, T6....................$20.00

Rootie Kazootie, puzzle, fr-tray; 1955, complete, EX $30.00

Roquefort Mouse, squeeze toy, Terrytoons, R3 ....$80.00

Roy Rogers, badge, Nellybell, tin, Post Raisin Cereal, MIP, J2....................$20.00

Roy Rogers, binoculars, w/case, 1950s, VG+, T1..............$85.00

Roy Rogers, book, Favorite Christmas Story, signed, hardcover, 1960, EX+, I2....................$19.00

Roy Rogers, book, Favorite Western Stories, Whitman, 1956, w/orig 9x11" box, EX (EX-NM box)....................$65.00

Roy Rogers, book, Rimrod Renegades, Whitman, softcover, 8x5½", 1952, VG+, A....................$25.00

Roy Rogers, box which once held football & basketball, Dubow Prod, box pictures Roy on rearing Trigger, 1950s, EX, A....................$149.00

Roy Rogers, crayon set, Toykraft, complete, 1950s, orig 11x17" paper litho box, EX (EX box)....................$75.00

Roy Rogers, flashlight, US Electric Mfg, litho tin & plastic, w/signal siren, working, w/orig cb display card, 7", EX, A....................$160.00

Roy Rogers, flashlight, Usalite, w/siren, in orig store display, orig price 98¢, 1950s, MIB....................$360.00

Roy Rogers, game, board; Roy Rogers Rodeo, 4 games in 1, 1949, has 12 of 16 cowboy figures, EX (VG box), A..........$76.00

Roy Rogers, Give-A-Show Slide Strip, Kenner, Mark of the Big Cat, w/7 35mm slides, 1962, NM, C1....................$17.50

Roy Rogers, guitar, Range Rhythm Toys, red, in orig mailing box, NM....................$350.00

Roy Rogers Guitar, also features Trigger, 28", D10, $125.00.

Roy Rogers, gun, Classy, Roy Rogers Shootin' Iron, emb design of Roy on rearing Trigger, illus card, EX (EX card), A..$152.00

Roy Rogers, gun, Kilgore, gold cap pistol w/plastic inset hdls, 8", NMOC, A $244.00

Roy Rogers, gun, Leslie-Henry, diecast cap gun, break-to-front/lever release, smoking action, unfired, 1950s, 9", NM, P4 ....$175.00

Roy Rogers, gun, Marx, gray plastic carbine repeater, pull-down cap magazine, 1950s, 26", NM (worn box), P4........$135.00

Roy Rogers, harmonica, Reed, mk w/Roy inside horseshoe, NM (VG+ portrait header card), A...................................$65.00

Roy Rogers, harmonica, 1950s, G+, T1 ....$45.00

Roy Rogers, holster outfit box, circular image & Roy tipping hat on bucking Trigger, 1950, 12x13", G.......................$150.00

Roy Rogers, holsters (2), blk & wht leather w/studs, Classy, 2 9" diecast pistols w/copper grips, early '50s, VG...........$495.00

Roy Rogers, holsters (2), brn & cream leather, Classy, 2 10" diecast guns w/copper grips, 4 wood bullets, VG, P4 .$425.00

Roy Rogers, holsters (2), leather, 1950s, VG, T1 ....$65.00

Roy Rogers Holster Set, marked with Double R Bar Ranch insignia, two leather holsters with buckles and 'jewel' studs, six bullets mounted on belt, EX in box, A, $390.00.

Roy Rogers, Horseshoe Set, Ohio Art, complete, 1950s, NM (EX box), A $156.00

Roy Rogers, Horseshoe Set, Ohio Art, facsimile signature on ea, in 7½x14" box, EX (G+ box) $115.00

Roy Rogers, neckerchief, M $35.00

Roy Rogers, outfit, shirt, pants & belt, w/orig tags, MIB, V1 ....$225.00

Roy Rogers, playset, Roy Rogers Rodeo Ranch, Marx, partially assembled, incomplete in orig box, VG, A $86.00

Roy Rogers, postcard, w/picture & signature, 1950s, NM, T1..$22.00

Roy Rogers, poster, Post Cereals, 1950s, NM+, T1..........$95.00

Roy Rogers, puppet, pnt molded rubber head w/blk cloth outfit, 13", VG-EX, A $130.00

Roy Rogers, puzzle, fr-tray; Whitman, 1953, complete, VG..$20.00

Roy Rogers, puzzle, Rohr Co, Roy & Trigger, 15x11", NM, A $30.00

Roy Rogers, puzzle, Whitman, stands by Trigger w/patriotic saddle, 1953, 15x11", EX+, A...$25.00

Roy Rogers Ranch Lantern, Ohio Art, NM (G box), A, $100.00.

Roy Rogers, ring, microscope; radio premium, 1949, NM..$95.00

Roy Rogers, scarf, 1990s, NM+, T1 ....$6.00

Roy Rogers, shirt, Frontier Shirts, plaid w/embroidered yoke featuring Roy & Trigger, 1950s, child's, NM, T2.........$100.00

Roy Rogers, story & record set, RCA-Victor, 1950, illus hardcover w/21-pg story, +2 45 rpm records, EX+, A $55.00

Roy Rogers, tin can, Nestle's Quick Chocolate Drink, Roy's testimonials, EX, A $180.00

Ruff & Ready, game, board; Circus, Transogram, 1962, NMIB, C1 ....$72.00

Ruff & Reddy, puzzle, fr-tray; Whitman, 1950s, NM, C1 .$24.00

Sad Sack, figure, Sterling Doll Co, vinyl w/cloth clothes & hat, orig tag, 16", EX, H4...$70.00

Saint, cap gun, Lone Star, diecast metal, 100-shot repeater Luger, stick-figure image of The Saint on card, EX+, A..$125.00

Sammy Davis Jr hand puppet, rubber head, 10", EX $25.00

Sammy Davis Jr Show, record album, Reprise #6188, 33⅓ rpm, EX+, T6..$35.00

Sandy, figure, German, pnt bsk, 2", VG, A.....................$110.00

Sarge (from Beetle Bailey), hand puppet, EX, J2 ....$30.00

Saturday Night Live, gum cards, Star Pics, 1992, set of 150, complete, M1 ....$20.00

Scooby Doo, book, Hanna-Barbera's Favorite Adventures, Rand McNally, 1979, VG-, T6 ....$4.00

Scooby Doo, bubble gum machine, Hasbro, 1968, NM, C1 .$27.00

Scooby Doo, doll, JS Sutton & Sons, stuffed, lt orange & brn w/dk brn accents, w/illus tag, 1970, 14", NM, T2 ......$60.00

Scooby Doo, game, Scooby Doo Where Are You, Milton Bradley, 1973, VG, F3 ....$22.00

Scooby Doo, pendant, 3" figure on chain, 1970s, MOC, C1 .$15.00

Scooby Doo, record, Mystery of Strange Paw Prints, 1976, EX $15.00

Scooby Doo, 3-D viewer, Imperial Toy/Hong Kong, Dyne Mutt cards, 1977, MOC, P4 ....$18.00

Scrappy, xylophone pull toy, Columbia Pictures Corp, wooden diecut figure on pressed steel base, 1930s, 10x10", G+, A $100.00

Scrooge McDuck, bank, Superior/WD, gumball coin machine #3253, 1989, 9½", MIB, P4 ....$20.00

Sea Hunt, Diver's Watch 'N Sunglasses, Ja-Ru, 1987, MOC, C1 ....$14.00

Seagoras, figure, Bandai, vinyl, MIP, E3 ....$10.00

Secret Agent 002, grab bag & candy, Best, illus bag, 3 plastic toys, 1966, 3½x7", M, T2 ....$8.00

Secret Sam, Shooting Cane, Topper, plastic w/sculpted lion's head, top is rifle, on photo card, 1965, 32", NM, T2 .$90.00

Sergeant Bilko, Phil Silvers, game, board; You'll Never Get Rich, Gardner, 1956, EX+ (EX+ box w/rpr corner), A $52.00

Sergeant Bilko, record, Marches, 1950s, EX+, C1 ....$36.00

Sergeant Peppers Band, card set, Donruss, 1978, NM-M, C1 ....$15.00

Sesame Street, Big Bird figure, Hasbro, 1987, 31", M $60.00

Sesame Street, Grover bendee, Muppets, Tara Toys, 3", K1 .$5.95

Sesame Street, gum cards, Idolmaker, 1992, set of 100, complete, M1 ....$15.00

Sesame Street, puzzle, fr-tray; Big Bird, 1977, complete, EX .$8.00

Sgt Preston & Yukon King, puzzle, fr-tray; Milton Bradley #4508, rare, 1954, VG+ $60.00

Sgt Preston & Yukon King, book, Rand McNally Elf Book, 1955 (possible later printing), VG, T6 ....$3.00

Shadow, book, coloring; Artcraft/Saalfield, 50+ pgs, 1974, 8½x11", unused, EX cover, T2 ....$20.00

Shaggy Dog, figures, Enesco, mk Walt Disney Productions on bottom, ea has bright gold tag, set of 3, 4", NM (EX box), A $63.00

Shari Lewis, book, Stories To Read Aloud, mid-1960s, G, T6 ....$2.00

Shari Lewis, Hush Puppy figure, Ideal, 10", M $20.00

Shazam, book, coloring; Whitman, 1967, M $35.00

Shazam, figure, Mego, 8", MIB (sm tear in cb around cellophane on box), H4 ....$99.00

Shazam, figure, Super Powers series, MOC, M5 ....$22.00

She-Ra, gum cards, Comic Images, 1987, set of 216, complete, M1 ....$35.00

Sherman (Bullwinkle), bendee, 1972, MOC, V1 ....$15.00

Shindig, game, board; Teen Shindig, Remco, 1965, 10x20" box, MIB (sealed), A $50.00

Shinkamen Rider, figure, Bandai, vinyl, lg, MIP, E3 ....$30.00

Shirley Temple, book, Favorite Tales of Long Ago, Random House, 1958, 3rd printing, missing cellophane surface, T6 ....$6.00

Shirley Temple, book, Shirley Temple Through the Day, Saalfield, 1936, photo illus throughout, cb cover, EX, P6 .$55.00

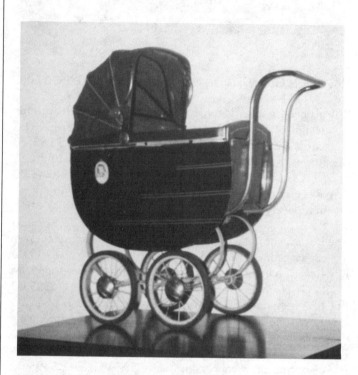

Shirley Temple Doll Buggy, buttons on the hood and hub caps all marked Shirley Temple, portrait on sides, $400.00 minimum.

Shirley Temple, figure, brn speckled pottery, EX, 6", P6 ..$45.00

Shirley Temple, sewing cards, complete but sewn, 1936, NMIB $30.00

Shirley Temple, sheet music, When I Grow Up, 1935, EX .$25.00

Shmoo, whistle pencil box, lg crayon form, mc graphics, 10½", VG, A $35.00

Shogun Warrior, book, coloring; Go!! Go!! Raideen, Mattel, M, F1 ....$5.00

Shogun Warrior, Grand Gar, Mattel, diecast, MIP, F1 .....$15.00

Shogun Warrior, poster, Grandizer, mc, 24x36", M, F1 ...$10.00

Shogun Warrior, Rydoto (vehicle), Mattel, 1978, MIP, F1 .$15.00

Shotgun Slade, puzzle, jigsaw; Milton Bradley, box shows series star on rock w/rifle, complete, 1960, NMIB, A $37.00

Shugaron, figure, Bandai, vinyl, MIP, E3 ....$10.00

Silly Symphony, book, paint; ca 1932-34, M4 ....$25.00

Silverhawks, Bluegrass & New Suit figures, Kenner, 2nd series, MOC, F1, pr $10.00

Silverhawks, figure, Molecular, Steelwill, or Windhammer, MOC, D4, any $8.00

Silverhawks, Hardware & Prowler figures, 2nd series, MOC, T1, pr $10.00

Silverhawks, Moon Stryker & Tailspin figures, Kenner, 1st series, MOC, F1, pr $10.00

Silverhawks, Silver Shadow (vehicle), 1980s, MIB, T1 ...$15.00

Simon & Simon, Walkie Talkies w/Telescoping Antennas, Gordy, 1983, MOC, C1......................................$15.00

Simpsons, activity set, Colorforms, Simpson's Deluxe Play Set, 14¼x11½", K1..$10.00

Simpsons, activity set, Rose Art, Fun Dough Model Maker, 2 molds, 1 action playmate, 3 cans dough, complete, K1.$10.00

Simpsons, activity set, Rose Art, Paint-By-Numbers, w/2 picture panels, 8 acrylic pnts, brush & instructions, K1...........$5.00

Simpsons, air mattress, Mattel, inflatable, 72x30", K1........$8.00

Simpsons, backpack, Imaginings 3, gr nylon w/zippers, Lisa & Bart's heads w/sayings, 15x13x4", K1.......................$15.00

Simpsons, Bart on skateboard, PVC, 1989, T1..................$2.00

Simpsons, Bartman, Homer, Nelson, or Marge, figure, Mattel, MOC, ea..$8.00

Simpsons, bendee, Jesco, Special 5-Pack Gift Set, 1990, K1.$17.95

Simpsons, book, Publishing International Ltd, History of TV's 1st Family, Consumers Guide, spiral bound, 8x11", K1......$7.50

Simpsons, bumper sticker, NJ Croce, Don't Have a Cow, Man!, 9x3", K1..$1.00

Simpsons, Christmas ornament, Presents, PVC figure w/candy cane stick, silver elastic hanger, 3½", P4.....................$3.50

Simpsons, decal, Randor, vinyl, set of 6, MIP, K1..............$2.00

Simpsons, doll, Bart, Dan Dee, soft vinyl w/cloth clothes, pull-string talker, 18", K1..$25.00

Simpsons, doll, Bart, Dan Dee, soft vinyl w/cloth clothes, 16", K1..$18.00

Simpsons, doll, Bart, Dan Dee, stuffed cloth w/bl shirt & pants, 11", MOC, K1..$7.50

Simpsons, doll, Really Rude Bart, Mattel, w/2 noisemakers, 18", K1..$25.00

Simpsons, earrings, NJ Croce, hard plastic diecut Lisa or Maggie, pierced w/gold wires, ¾x½", K1, pr.........................$11.00

Simpsons, flashlight, Happiness Express, plastic, battery-op, 5½", K1..$4.00

Simpsons, frisbee, Betras Plastics, wht plastic, Bart portrait w/Radical Dude, K1..$3.00

Simpsons, game, board; Cardinal, Mystery of Life, K1......$15.00

Simpsons, game, Don't Have a Cow, Milton Bradley, w/dice, K1..$15.00

Simpsons, gum cards, Topps, 1990, set of 88 w/22 stickers, complete, M1..$15.00

Simpsons, Homer figure, Mattel, w/5 interchangable quotes that attach to PVC figure, w/accessories, 5½", K1...............$7.50

Simpsons, key chain, Street Kids, Bart figure, 3", MIP, K1.$4.50

Simpsons, notebook, red vinyl w/Bart & sayings, 3-ring style, 10x11¾", K1..$3.50

Simpsons, poster, Western Graphics, Go Out for the Long Bomb, Bart!, 32x21", K1..$4.00

Simpsons, puzzle, Milton Bradley, Bart surfing, 250-pc, 16½x16½", K1..$6.00

Simpsons, stamper set, Rubber Stampede, set of 4 w/bl washable ink pad, K1..$4.00

Simpsons, sticker, Diamond, puffy style, set of 10, MIP, K1..$2.50

Simpsons, tote bag, Imaginings 3, gr or purple nylon w/blk nylon hdls, 15x12x8", K1..$12.00

Sir Lancelot, game, board; 1957, M...........................$100.00

Six Million-Dollar Man, Bionic Transport & Repair Station, Kenner, 1975, MIB (sealed), C1...............................$50.00

Six Million-Dollar Man, book, coloring & activity; 1977, EX, T6..$6.00

Six Million-Dollar Man, game, board; Parker Bros, EX, D9.$5.00

Six Million-Dollar Man, gum cards, Donruss, 1975, set of 66, complete, M1..$50.00

Six Million-Dollar Man, gum cards, Monty Gum, 1975, set of 72, complete, M1..$55.00

Six Million-Dollar Man, playsuit, Lindsay (Australia), 2-pc suit, MOC (cb display hanger), C1...................................$45.00

Six Million-Dollar Man, record, Peter Pan, 33⅓ rpm, 1976, M, F1..$10.00

Six Million-Dollar Man, record, Power Records, 33⅓ rpm, 1975, EX, H4..$5.00

Six Million-Dollar Man, Steve Austin figure, Kenner, 1975, 12½", MIB..$42.00

Skeezix, cup, Czech, ceramic w/mc decor & gold trim, 1928, 3", EX, A..$60.00

Skeleton, bendee, wht & gray, 1980s, 5", MOC................$7.50

Sky King, code writer, Spy Detecto, radio premium, 1940s, EX, T1..$55.00

Sky King, ring, Electronic Television, glow-in-the-dark image of Sky King inside, plane & horse on brass band, EX, A...$107.00

Sky King, ring, Magni-Glo Writing, gold w/fold-out pen & magnifier, secret compartment, 1949, VG, P4..................$75.00

Sky King, ring, Radar Signal, glow-in-the-dark stone in center of brass band w/wing & propeller designs, ca 1949, VG+, A..$135.00

Sky King, Secret Signalscope, 5", 1947, in orig mailer w/instruction sheet, NMIB, A..$115.00

Sky King, stamping kit, red on wht litho tin container, removable ink pad, orig mailer, EX, A...............................$45.00

Sleeping Beauty, book, Disney, hardcover, 1974, 7x9½", EX-, T6..$3.00

Sleeping Beauty, booklet, Walt Disney's Sleeping Beauty Castle, 1957, NM, M8..$60.00

Sleeping Beauty, bubble wand w/empty bubble solution packets, 1959, unopened on card, EX, M8...............................$45.00

Sleeping Beauty, Colorforms, 3 actual movie backgrounds on 1 board, 1959, few minor pcs missing, o/w EX, M8.......$40.00

Sleeping Beauty Game, Walt Disney, Parker Bros., Whitman, 1958, NM (VG box), $25.00.

Sleeping Beauty, game, Milton Bradley, 1959, complete, scarce, EX, M8 ....$50.00

Sleeping Beauty, Paint-By-Number Set, Transogram, watercolors, 6 sketches & brush, 1958, 10x17" box, EX (EX box), T2 ....$40.00

Small World, Spain or Hawaii figure, ceramic, 1972, 2¾", M4 .$15.00

Smitty, convertible, pnt diecast, gr, red, brn & blk w/gold grille, Smitty rocks as car moves, 3¼", G+, A....................$300.00

Smitty, figure, German, pnt bsk, 3½", VG-EX, A.............$70.00

Smokey Bear, badge, Junior Forest Ranger, 1950s, VG, P4.$12.00

Smokey Bear, Ideal, Official, cloth pants, Smokey on buckle, 1950s, 15", no enrollment card, EX+ (EX box), A..$125.00

Smokey Bear, nodder, MIB..$375.00

Smokey Bear, record, Peter Pan Records, 78 rpm in 7x8" illus sleeve, 1960, NM, T2 ....$15.00

Smurfs, barrettes, set of 2, 1982, MIP, T6 ....$3.00

Smurfs, card set, complete set of 2½x5" cards, 1982, NM-M, C1 ....$13.00

Smurfs, figure, Super Smurf series, MIB, D4, any..............$8.00

Smurfs, gum card, Topps, 1984, set of 55 in wax or printed cellophane wrappers, complete, M1 ....$12.00

Smurfs, pencil case, w/Smurfette, M, D4 ....$3.00

Smurfs, Peyo, figure, Smurfette Chatter Chum, plastic, 1983, 8", VG+..$10.00

Smurfs, photograph, Vanity Fair, suitcase type w/hdl, red w/ dancing Smurfs, 1983, NM insides, VG+ case, P3.....$20.00

Smurfs, puffy stickers, set of 4, MIP, D4 ....$2.00

Smurfs, Space Traveler Toy, 1978, MOC, T1...................$25.00

Smurfs, tote bag, w/Smurfette, MIP, D4 ....$5.00

Snagglepuss, game, Transogram, box features Yogi, Boo-Boo & Snagglepuss, 1961, 8x15", VG (VG box)..................$85.00

Snagglepuss, record, Snagglepuss Tells Wizard of Oz, 1965, EX $30.00

Sneezy, book, #1044, The Story of Sneezy, 1938, spine wear, o/w VG, M8 ....$32.00

Snidely Whiplash, figure, Wham-O, 1972, MOC $15.00

Sniffles the Mouse, bank, metal, standing beside barrel, missing cover, 1940s, 5", EX, T1 ....$125.00

Sniffles the Mouse, pencil holder, pnt cast metal, mk WBC on end, 5", EX+, T1 ....$125.00

Sniffles the Mouse, squeeze toy, Oak Rubber, R3 ....$50.00

Snow White, doll, Knickerbocker, compo, orig outfit: lt bl velveteen bodice, pk organdy dress, cape missing, 12", EX, A $275.00

Snow White, doll, pnt compo w/sleep eyes, ball & socket neck, jtd, yel & brn dress, eyes cracked, 15", VG, A...........$65.00

Snow White, figure, pottery, Wade, 1950s, scarce, 4x5", NM, M8..$150.00

Snow White & Dopey, print, glow-in-the-dark, full color, 1940s, orig fr, scarce, 10¾x8¾", P6 ....$90.00

Snow White & Seven Dwarfs, baby rattle, celluloid, 1938, 6½", EX, M8 ....$150.00

Snow White & Seven Dwarfs, bank, dime register, litho tin, 2½", VG, A..$100.00

Snow White & Seven Dwarfs, bank, dime register, 1939, 2½", NM, A..$250.00

Snow White & Seven Dwarfs, book, cut-out; Dean (England), 1938, 10x13", uncut, minor soiling, EX, A.............$215.00

Snow White Dairy Recipes Book, American Dairy Association, Walt Disney Productions, 1955, NM, $60.00.

Snow White & Seven Dwarfs, book, Disney Studios, set of 8, 1 about ea character, orig box, 11¼", EX, A..............$320.00

Snow White & Seven Dwarfs, Bunny figure, Brayton Laguna, ceramic, wht w/pk nose & ears, 1938, 2½", M, M8 .$250.00

Snow White & Seven Dwarfs, Doc figure, ceramic, Enesco, 1960s, 4½", NM, M8 ....$32.00

Snow White & Seven Dwarfs, dolls, Knickerbocker, compo, jtd arms, pnt faces, velvet clothes, set: 15½" & 9", EX+, A..$1,150.00

Snow White & Seven Dwarfs, figure, Bashful, Hagen-Renaker Designer Workshop, 1950s, 3¼", EX, M8...............$125.00

Snow White & Seven Dwarfs, figures, bsk, Borgfeldt/WDE, 8 pcs in orig 5x9" box, she: 3¼", 1938, EX (EX box), A....$345.00

Snow White & Seven Dwarfs, figures, Enesco, pnt ceramic, complete set of 8, M $350.00

Snow White and the Seven Dwarfs Figures, bisque, 1938, dwarfs 5", Snow White 6½", largest size set, NM, D10, $500.00.

Snow White & Seven Dwarfs, figures, Gund, Happy or Sleepy, stuffed body w/vinyl arms & cloth legs, w/tag, MIP, H4, ea...$18.00

Snow White & Seven Dwarfs, figures, Gund, stuffed body w/bendee vinyl arms & legs, 1967, 9", set of 7, MIP, rare, H4..$100.00

Snow White & Seven Dwarfs, game, Milton Bradley, pnt wood play pcs, complete, 19", VG, A $70.00

Snow White & Seven Dwarfs, gum cards, Pantini, 1987, set of 225, complete, M1 ....$35.00

Snow White & Seven Dwarfs, Happy figure, ceramic, Enesco, 1960s, 5", NM, M8 ....$35.00

Snow White & Seven Dwarfs, ladder toy, mk Formosa, paper on wood, orig 9" box, VG+, A $154.00

Snow White & Seven Dwarfs, playset, Marx, 3 props & dwarfs only, Snow White missing, 1960s, orig box, VG, M8.$45.00

Snow White & Seven Dwarfs, poster, Hallmark, features forest animals & castle, 1970s, 40x28", EX, M8 ....$12.00

Snow White & Seven Dwarfs, poster, Still the Fairest of Them All, re-release issue, crease/border tear, 41x27", A $80.00

Snow White & Seven Dwarfs, puzzle, fr-tray; Jaymar, w/other characters outside cottage, 1940s, 11x14", EX+, T2..$24.00

Snow White & Seven Dwarfs, puzzle, jigsaw; set of 2, orig box, VG, T1 ....$125.00

Snow White & Seven Dwarfs, sewing cards, Whitman, 1950s, complete, NMIB, A $95.00

Snow White & Seven Dwarfs, sheet music, Some Day My Prince Will Come, 1937, missing pg 3 & 4, o/w EX, M8 ....$8.00

Snow White & Seven Dwarfs, Sleepy, figure, bsk, 1930s, 3", EX, M8...$25.00

Snow White & Seven Dwarfs, song album, Irving Berlin, 46-pg, 1937, G $50.00

Snow White and the Seven Dwarfs Top, lithographed tin, 1940s, EX, D10, $150.00.

Snuffy Smith, game, board; Time's a-Wastin', Milton Bradley, 4 playing pcs & spinner, 1963, 8x16" box (EX box), T2..$30.00

Sons of Hercules, game, board; Milton Bradley, complete, 1965, EX+-NM, A..$45.00

Soupy Sales, Fan Club Badge, EX+-NM, T6...............$9.00

Soupy Sales, Fun & Activity Book, M $10.00

Soupy Sales, game, Soupy Sales Says Go-Go-Go, Milton Bradley, 1960s, few cards missing, o/w EX (VG box), H4...$55.00

Soupy Sales, ring, flasher; Vari Vue Flasher, 1960s, NM, T1...$15.00

Space Kidettes, magic slate, Watkins, 1968, M.............$35.00

Space Kidettes, puzzle, fr-tray; Whitman, leaving clubhouse to unknown planet, 1967, 11x14", EX, T2.................$25.00

Space Kidettes, puzzle, jigsaw; Whitman, complete, 1968, EX, H4..$18.00

Space Patrol, Official Christmas Catalog, folding pamphlet w/about 15 items to order, ca 1950, 9x16", NM, A...$80.00

Space Patrol, phones, Ralston Purina premium, w/orig string & mailer, M (EX pkg), A...$205.00

Space Patrol, puzzle, fr-tray; Milton Bradley, features crew & spaceship, 1950, 11x14", EX, A...........................$72.00

Space Patrol, record, Buzz Corry Becomes Commander-In-Chief, Decca #K-134, 78 rpm, w/sleeve, #1 of a series, rare, EX $95.00

Space Patrol, record, Buzz Corry Becomes Commander-in-Chief, Decca, 45 rpm, w/dust jacket, EX+, A $30.00

Space Patrol, stamp album, 1950, unused, 3½x6", EX+, A...$40.00

Space Patrol, Terra V Rockets Project-a-Scope Premium, Ralston Purina, complete, ca 1950, NM (EX+ mailer), A $575.00

Space 1999, Colorforms, 1976, complete, MIB, C1..........$31.00

Space 1999, Commander Koneig, figure, Mattel, complete, 1975, loose, H4...$20.00

Space 1999, Dr Russel, figure, Mattel, seated pose w/helmet, 1979, 3¾", loose, H4..$15.00

Space 1999, Dr Russell, figure, Mattel, complete, 1975, loose, H4..$20.00

Space 1999, Dr Russell (Barbara Bain) or Commander Koenig (Martin Landau) figure, Mattel, 1975, 9", MOC, C1, ea...$55.00

Space 1999, Eagle, Mattel, wht plastic, some decals worn, 1976, VG+, T6 ....$30.00

Space 1999, game, board; NMIB, D4 ....$12.00

Space 1999, gum cards, Donruss, 1976, 1st or 2nd season, set of 400, complete, M1 ....$60.00

Space 1999, gum cards, Monty Gum, set of 64, complete, very scarce, M1...$35.00

Space 1999, gum cards, set of 66 color photos from show, 1976, NM, C1..$28.00

Space 1999, playset, Moon Base Alpha Control Room & Launch Monitor Center, Mattel, for 9" figures, complete, NMIB, H4...$39.00

Space 1999, Professor Burgman figure, Mattel, 1975, MOC, H4..$40.00

Space 1999, puzzle, jigsaw; HG Toys, Commander Koenig & Dr Russel fight space creatures, 150-pc, 8x9" box, 1976, EX+, T2..$18.00

Spark Plug, pull toy, litho tin on lg base, several dents/wear spots on jockey & base, rare, 6x9", A..............$600.00

Spark Plug, pull toy, on sm base w/wood wheels, some corrosion/general wear, dents, 6x6", A.............$200.00

Spiderman, bike plate, Marx, litho tin, 1967, 2x4", M, A.$24.00

Spiderman, car, AHI, w/accelerator, 1978, MOC, T1......$15.00

Spiderman, car, diecast, 5", EX, N2...............$6.00

Spiderman, Code Breaker, 1977, MOC, T1.............$5.00

Spiderman, Daredevil, Thor, Captain America & Iron Man, gum card wrapper, Donruss, 1966, NM, T2..............$15.00

Spiderman, Energized Copter, 1978, MIB, T1.............$85.00

Spiderman, figure, China, plastic, 1993, 10", MOC, T1...$10.00

Spiderman, figure, Mego, 8", MOC, H4.............$20.00

Spiderman, figure, Presents, vinyl, w/stand, 1990, 12", MIP, H4..............$29.00

Spiderman, figure, Secret Wars series, w/shield flasher, loose, H4...........$7.00

Spiderman, figure, Toy Biz, jtd, MOC, D8...........$9.00

Spiderman, figure, Toy Biz, orig issue, MOC, D8............$25.00

Spiderman, figure, Toy Biz, shoots web, MOC, D8..........$15.00

Spiderman, figure, Toy Biz, 18", MIB, F1..............$50.00

Spiderman, game, board; Amazing Spiderman & Fantastic Four, Milton Bradley, 1977, MIB (sealed), T2..................$50.00

Spiderman, game, board; Milton Bradley, w/standee figures & dice, 1966, scarce, MIB, A.............$140.00

Spiderman, gumball dispenser, Superior Toy, plastic, lift arm to dispense gum, ca 1984, w/10 gumballs, MIP.............$8.50

Spiderman, kite, Gayla, inflates, 1985, MIP.............$15.00

Spiderman, pencil sharpener, Nasta, mc plastic figure, ca 1980, 4", MOC, from $6 to..............$10.00

Spiderman, pogo-stick, 1974, MIB..............$125.00

Spiderman, puzzle, fr-tray; Puzzleforms, 1983, 12x16", MIP (sealed), C1...........$19.50

Spiderman, puzzle, sliding; Belgium, 1978, 6½x8", EX, T6.$5.00

Spiderman, Reading Motivation Kit & Teacher's Guide, McGraw Hill Films, visual aid kit, 1975, 11x17x3" box, NM, A...........$400.00

Spiderman, record, Power Records, 33⅓ rpm, 1974, G, H4.$5.00

Spiderman, roller skates, Jotastar, 1988, MIP..............$17.50

Spiderman, scissors, Nasta, mc plastic w/figure on hdls, ca 1980, 4", MIP..............$8.50

Spiderman, Spider Bike, 4", VG, N2..............$12.00

Spiderman, Spidercopter, Buddy L, diecast, 1984, rare, MIB, F1..............$6.00

Spiderman, stickers, Comic Image, 1988, set of 50, complete, M1..............$25.00

Spiderman, stickers, Jotastar, 1988, MOC.............$10.00

Spiderman, Supervader Super Action Flyby (vehicle), Mego, for 8" figure, 1974, EX, H4..............$39.00

Spiderman, talker, Toy Biz, MIB, F1..............$20.00

Spiderman & Incredible Hulk, Color & Recolor TV Showtime Set, Avalon, 1980, MIB (sealed), C1.............$21.00

Stagecoach West, game, board; Transogram, 1961, complete, NM (EX+ box), C1..............$103.00

Star-Bellied Sneetch, figure, Coleco/Dr Seuss, MIB, H4..$45.00

Starsky & Hutch, Chopper figure, Mego, 8", MOC, F1....$40.00

Starsky & Hutch, game, board; MIB, D4.............$8.00

Starsky & Hutch, gun, Laramie, 1970s, MIP, T1.............$22.50

Starsky & Hutch, Hutch or Dobey figure, Mego, 8", MOC, D9, ea..............$20.00

Starsky & Hutch, puzzle, jigsaw; 1976, 9x7½" box, MIB (sealed), D9..............$6.00

Starsky & Hutch, Starsky or Huggy Bear figure, Mego, 1976, MOC, from $22 to..............$32.00

Starsky & Hutch, viewer, Fleetwood, w/4 film strips, 1976, M (EX card), C1..............$27.00

Steppenwolf, figure, Kenner, MIP, F1..............$10.00

Steve Canyon Air Force Game, Lowell Toy Mfg. Corp., 1960s, NMIB, A, $25.00.

Steve Canyon, membership card, w/place for photo, 1959, 3½x2½", M, T2..............$5.00

Steve Scout, figure, all orig, complete, H4..............$22.00

Steve Scout, metal detector, MOC (damaged card), H4..$16.00

Steve Scout, Mountain Medic Kit, MOC (damaged card), H4..............$16.00

Steve Scout, Ski Mobile, EX, H4..............$12.00

Steve Trevor (Wonder Woman), figure, Mego, 1976, 12", NRFB (crack in cellophane on box), H4..............$90.00

Stingray, book, coloring; Whitman, 1965, EX+..............$32.50

Stingray, puzzle, fr-tray; 1966, NM, V1..............$29.50

Stoney Smith, figure, Marx, not deluxe version, complete w/accessories, 12", M (EX box), H4..............$140.00

Stoney Smith, Paratrooper figure, Marx, complete w/insignia stickers & accessories, M (NM box), H4..............$160.00

Stoney Smith, shirt, army style, snap needs rpr, H4..........$4.00

Stoney Smith, Sky Commando figure, deluxe version, complete w/accessories, rare, NM (EX box), H4..............$190.00

Straight Arrow, puppet theatre puppets & props, Nabisco premium, paper, 1 sheet (M), w/50+ cutouts (VG), 1952, P4........$35.00

Straight Arrow, ring, picture; gold plastic w/name on base below nugget design, viewing lens on side, 1950, NM, A..$234.00

Super Heroes, dictionary, lg, VG, T1..............$35.00

Super Heroes, game, board; Strategy, Marvel Comics, NMIB, D4..............$5.00

Super Six, puzzle, jigsaw; Whitman, complete, 1969, rare, EX (G box), H4..............$15.00

Supergirl, book, activity; 1984, EX, T6 ....$5.00

Supergirl, figure, Mego, 8", MOC $300.00

Supergirl, stickers, Topps, 1985, from movie, complete set of 44, M1 ....$6.00

Superman, badge, Jr Defense, diecut brass w/Superman holding flag, pin-bk still attached, 1940s, EX, A $150.00

Superman, bank, Dime Register, litho tin, Superman breaks chains, 2½", VG, A $100.00

Superman, belt, Pioneer, plastic w/all-around decals of Superman in action poses, scarce, 1940, G+, A $105.00

Superman, book, coloring; Saalfield, 1940, some pgs colored, VG, A $80.00

Superman, book, coloring; Saalfield, 1957, uncolored, 11x14", NM, A $190.00

Superman, book, pop-up; Random House, 1979, EX, T6 ...$5.00

Superman, book, Superman, George Lowther, 1942, VG, A $40.00

Superman, book, The Gospel According to Superman, softcover, 1973, EX $10.00

Superman, bop bag, Largo, inflatable, 1978, MIB, C1 ......$19.50

Superman, candle holder, Wilton, figure w/building, for birthday cake, 1979, any of set of 5, MIP, F1, ea $5.00

Superman, card set, from movie Superman II or Superman III, complete, NM-M, C1 ....$13.00

Superman, ceiling shade, glass, wht w/mc illus, 1976, 13x13", M, T2 ....$90.00

Superman Cinematic Picture Pistol, 1940s, NM (VG box), D10, $650.00.

Superman, Color-By-Number Pencil Set, Hasbro, 1965, M, A .$60.00

Superman, cookie jar, California Originals, figure at phone booth, 12", EX $550.00

Superman, figure, Kenner, Super Powers, 1983, MOC, from $12 to $15.00

Superman, figure, Mego, 3¾", MIP, F1 ....$15.00

Superman, figure, Toy Biz, 1989, rare, MOC, F1 ....$30.00

Superman, game, Adventures of Superman, Milton Bradley, 1940, complete in orig box, 10x19", NM, A $325.00

Superman, game, Adventures of Superman, Milton Bradley, 8 game pcs & instructions, ca 1940, EX (NM box), A ..$143.00

Superman, game, card; Ideal, EX, F3 ....$45.00

Superman, game, card; Russell, complete, M1 ....$3.50

Superman, game, card; Whitman, 45 cards, MIB, from $35 to $45.00

Superman Figure, Ideal, painted wood, posable, cloth cape, 12¾", EX, A, $675.00.

Superman, game, Speed, Milton Bradley, 1940s, EX, V1..$195.00

Superman, game, Spinball, Mattel, 1978, NM $50.00

Superman, game, Superman II, 1980, EX+, C1 ....$27.00

Superman, game, Superman III, 1982, M (NM box), C1 .$21.00

Superman, gum card set, English, 1979, from the movie, 1st or 2nd series, 66 cards, complete, M1, either $30.00

Superman, gum card set, Topps, 1979, from the movie, 2nd series, 88 cards, complete, M1 ....$22.00

Superman, gum card set, Topps, 1981, from Superman II movie, 88 cards, complete, M1 ....$12.00

Superman, hairbrush, Avon, 1976, bl plastic, EX+, from $12 to $20.00

Superman, Kiddie Paddlers Swimming Fins, Super-Swim Inc, bl rubber w/mc Superman illus, 1956, M (VG+ box), T2.$50.00

Superman, Krypto-Ray Film Gun, Daisy, 7" metal gun shows Superman in flying pose, complete w/6 films, orig box, EX, A $526.00

Superman, Kryptonite Rocks, Pro Arts, gr glow-in-the-dark rocks, 1978, MIB, F1 ....$15.00

Superman, Movie Viewer, Acme, 1940, MIB, A $150.00

Superman, music box, Schmid, ceramic, 1977, MIB, T1.$150.00

Superman, necklace, 1990, MOC, T1 ....$5.00

Superman, nutcracker, wood, 1979, 10", VG, N2 ....$10.00

Superman, ornament, Hallmark, 1993, MIB $35.00

Superman, Pogo Ball, 1970s, EX, T1 ....$15.00

Superman, puzzle, jigsaw; Saalfield, 3 complete 8x10" scenes from comic books, 1940, rare, M (EX+-NM box), A $350.00

Superman Puzzle Set, Saalfield, three 7x10" puzzles (one shown), ca 1940, MIB, A, $300.00.

Superman, record, Power Records, 33⅓ rpm, 1975, G, H4..$5.00
Superman, ring, airplane, premium, 1948, NM+, J2 ......$245.00

Superman Ring, Post Toasties premium, 1976, EX, $25.00.

Superman, soundtrack, 1978, NM.....................................$12.50
Superman, stencil sheet, 10x8", VG-EX, A $30.00
Superman, sticker, Topps, 1979, from the movie, Man of Steel or reflective version, 2nd series, M1, ea.......................$3.50
Superman, sticker set, Topps, 1981, from Superman II, 22 stickers, complete, M1..$8.50
Superman, tattoo, Topps, in 1½x3½" wrapper depicting Superman snapping chains off chest, 1962, NM, T2 ....$50.00
Superman, toothbrush, Janex, battery-op, EX+ $15.00
Superman, viewer, Acme Plastics, w/3 boxes of film, 1940s, EX+ (VG+ box), A..$150.00
Superman, viewer, Chemtoy, complete w/2 movies, 1968, MOC..$32.50
Superman, viewer w/3 celluloid film strips, USA, orig paper litho box, G+, A...$120.00
Superman, whistle flashlight, Bantam-lite, 1966, MOC, C1.$36.00
Supernaturals, Mr Lucky-Heroic Ghostling figure, 1988, MOC, T1 ....$5.00

Surfside 6, game, board; Troy Donahue on box, 1960s, MIB $75.00
Swamp Thing, Bio-Glo Thing figure, 1992, MOC, T1 ....$10.00
Swamp Thing, Bog Rover (vehicle), MIB, D4.................$10.00
Swamp Thing, Camouflage Swamp Thing, 1992, MOC, T1 ....$10.00
Swamp Thing, figure, Kenner, 2nd series, 1991, MIP, F1.$15.00
Swamp Thing, Snare Arm or Snap-up, figure, Kenner, MIP, E3 ....$8.00
SWAT, Bullhorn, Fleetwood, 1976, MOC, C1 ....$18.00
SWAT, Rescue Parachute, Fleetwood, 1976, MOC, C1 ..$19.50
SWAT, Target Practice Set, 1975, MIP, T1 ....$35.00
Sweet Pea, doll, Hamilton, 10", MIP, F1........................$10.00
Sweet Pea, doll, Uneeda, cloth & vinyl, 1979, M (NM box), C1..$31.00
Sweet Pea, pin, hard plastic, figural, 1½", M, P6..............$25.00
Swiss Family Robinson, book, Whitman, illus cover, 1960, VG $6.50
Sword in the Stone, book, Disney, paperback, EX............$10.00
Sword in the Stone, puzzle, jigsaw; 1963, V1 ....$18.50
Sylvester, figure, ceramic, w/sand pail, 1977, EX $35.00
Sylvester, squeeze toy, Oak Rubber, R3..........................$50.00
Sylvester & Tweety, music box, porc, Sylvester chasing Tweety, 1979, EX...$85.00
Sylvester Stallone, figure, Over the Top, posable, 1986, M (shelf-worn box), H4 ....$50.00
Sylvester Stallone, puzzle, in gr tank top, 500-pc, 1977, 16x20", EX, T6..$7.00
Sylvester Stallone, Rocky, Bubble Fun, Stallone photo on bottle, w/pipe, 1984, M, T6...$10.00
Sylvester Stallone, Rocky II, gum cards, Topps, 1979, 99 cards w/22 stickers, complete, M1 ....$12.00
Tales of the Vikings, book, coloring; Saalfield, 100+ pgs, 1960, 8½x11", 2 pgs colored, o/w EX, T2....................$32.00
Tales of Wells Fargo, photo, sgn Dale Robertson, 1958, 8x10", NM, C1..$21.00
Tammy, puzzle, 100-pc, 1964, 14x18", EX, T6................$15.00
Tarantula, movie program, foreign printing, 1950s, 5x6", EX $25.00
Tarzan, bendee, Mego, 1974, M $32.00
Tarzan, bendee, Mego, 1972, scarce, 5", NMOC............$95.00
Tarzan, book, Tazan of the Apes, Watson-Guptill, 1972, illus, hardcover, M, A...$20.00
Tarzan, Colorforms, 1966, NM (EX box), C1 ....$38.00
Tarzan, figure, Mego, w/bodysuit, 1973, 8", EX, T1 ....$35.00
Tarzan, figure, Mego, 8", MOC, H4.................................$139.00
Tarzan, figures, Airfix, 5x6" box w/31 miniature HO scale hunters, natives & jungle animals, 1966, M (EX box), T2 ....$30.00
Tarzan, game, board; Tarzan to the Rescue, Milton Bradley, MIB (sealed), C1..$23.00
Tarzan, gum card set, Panini, 400 cards, complete, M1 ....$60.00
Tarzan, Paint & Wear Clothes & Fabric Painting Kit, Avalon, 2 reusable iron-on designs & acrylic pnt, MIB (sealed), C1.$25.00
Tarzan, party set, Amscan, paper tablecloth, cups & napkins, w/invitations, 1977, ea MIP, C1............................$14.00
Tarzan, Story Teller, book & cassette tape, Superscope, 1978, MIP (sealed), C1..$15.50

Teenage Mutant Ninja Turtles, April O'Neil Figure, Playmates, second issue, blue stripe, MOC, from $35.00 to $50.00.

Teenage Mutant Ninja Turtles Figure, Playmates, any of the four, hard plastic with jointed shoulders and hips, 4½", $8.00.

Teenage Mutant Ninja Turtles, April O'Neil, figure, Playmates, orig 1st issue, no stripe, EX-NM, H4........................$100.00

Teenage Mutant Ninja Turtles, April O'Neil, Playmates, mutating, 1988, MOC, J4 ....$12.00

Teenage Mutant Ninja Turtles, April O'Neil figure, Playmates, orange stripe, MIP, from $8 to....................................$12.00

Teenage Mutant Ninja Turtles, April O'Neil figure, Playmates, as Ninja or Ravishing, 1988, MOC, J4, ea.................$16.00

Teenage Mutant Ninja Turtles, Baxter Stockman figure, MOC (old-style card), D4...$25.00

Teenage Mutant Ninja Turtles, Footsoldier figure, movie version, MOC, F1 ....$15.00

Teenage Mutant Ninja Turtles, gum cards, Diamond, 1989, 180 cards, complete, M1...$17.50

Teenage Mutant Ninja Turtles, gum cards, Topps, from movie, 132 cards w/11 stickers, complete, 1990, M1 ....$10.00

Teenage Mutant Ninja Turtles, gum cards, Topps, from Secret of the Ooze movie, 99 cards w/11 stickers, complete, M1 ....$15.00

Teenage Mutant Ninja Turtles, gum cards, Topps, 1st cartoon series, 88 cards w/11 stickers, complete, M1 ....$10.00

Teenage Mutant Ninja Turtles, gum cards, Topps/Ireland, set of 132 cards from movie, complete, 1990, M1 ....$7.00

Teenage Mutant Ninja Turtles, gum cards, Topps/Ireland, 1990, set of 66 cartoon cards, complete, M1 ....$3.50

Teenage Mutant Ninja Turtles, Krang figure, Playmates, 1989, MOC, J4..$12.00

Teenage Mutant Ninja Turtles, Mona Lisa figure, Playmates, MIP, E3 ....$8.00

Teenage Mutant Ninja Turtles, Mondo Gecko figure, MOC, F1 ....$10.00

Teenage Mutant Ninja Turtles, Needlenose figure, MIB, D4...$10.00

Teenage Mutant Ninja Turtles, playing cards, US Playing Cards, 1990, purple or yel deck, complete, M1 ....$6.00

Teenage Mutant Ninja Turtles, postcards, Random House, 1992, set of 24, complete, M1...$5.00

Teenage Mutant Ninja Turtles, Princess Mitsu figure, Playmates, MIP, E3 ....$6.00

Teenage Mutant Ninja Turtles, Ray Fillet figure, Playmates, color change version, MIP, from $15 to.....................$20.00

Teenage Mutant Ninja Turtles, Slice 'N Dice Shredder figure, MOC, F1 ....$25.00

Teenage Mutant Ninja Turtles, Sludgemobile, MIB, D4....$5.00

Teenage Mutant Ninja Turtles, Splinter figure, Playmates, 1st issue, MIP, E3...$10.00

Teenage Mutant Ninja Turtles, Target Exclusive, set of 4, MIP, F1 ....$50.00

Teenage Mutant Ninja Turtles, Tokka figure, Playmates, lt skin version, MIP, from $10 to...$16.00

Teenage Mutant Ninja Turtles, Wacky Action Mouser figure, MOC, D4..$15.00

Tennessee Tuxedo, magic slate, Saalfield, w/lift-up erasable film sheet & wood stylus, 1963, 8x11", NM, A..............$100.00

Terminator, Randy Bowden figure, pnt vinyl, 12", M, D4...$25.00

Terminator 2, Battle Damage Terminator figure, Kenner, 1991-92, MIP, from $10 to $15.00

Terminator 2, Bio-Flesh Regenerator, Kenner, MIP $25.00

Terminator 2, doll, China, unlicensed, highly detailed, 12", MIB, F1 ....$30.00

Terminator 2, game, Rock 'Em Sock 'Em Robots, Remco, MIB..$40.00

Terminator 2, gum card set, Topps, 1991, 44 cards, complete, M1 ....$6.00

Terminator 2, John Conner figure, Kenner, MIP, E3 ....$12.00

Terminator 2, John Connor w/motorcycle, Kenner, 1991-92, MIP, F1 ....$25.00

Terminator 2, knife, United, replica, M, E3 ....$110.00

Terminator 2, make-up kit, Imagineering, MIP, E3 ....$20.00

Terminator 2, Mobile Assault Vehicle, Kenner, MIP, E3..$12.00

Terminator 2, Ultimate Terminator figure, Kenner, 1991-92, lg, MIB, F1 ....$50.00

Terry & the Pirates, game, board; Sunday Funnies, Ideal, 1972, MIB, C1 ....$29.00

Terry & the Pirates, ring, detector, gold-tone, radio premium, 1940s, EX, T1..$40.00

That Girl, book, coloring; Saalfield, 1968, M $35.00

Thor, figure, Mego, complete, loose, EX, H4..................$100.00

Thor, figure, Toy Biz, MIP, E3 ....$8.00

Thor, hand puppet, Imperial, 1978, MIP, from $15 to......$20.00

Three Caballeros, music box, litho tin, crank on top, French, 1940s, 2½x2¾" dia, EX, M8 ....$110.00

Three Little Pigs, bank, compo, pig in stone house, 1960s, EX, T1..$25.00

Three Little Pigs Bisque Figures, with instruments, 2½", MIB, D10, $450.00 for the set.

Three Little Pigs, bowl, divided; Patriot China, ea section features 1 pig, bl rim, 1930s, 7¾" dia, EX, M8..............$100.00

Three Little Pigs, pitcher, Wade Heath, emb ceramic tankard w/Big Bad Wolf as hdl, 10½", NM $750.00

Three Little Pigs, plate, Patriot China, dtd 1934, 6½", EX, A $75.00

Three Little Pigs, plate, Patriot China, pigs dancing & playing instruments, bl rim, 1930s, 6¼" dia, NM, M8............$65.00

Three Little Pigs, puzzle, fr-tray; Jaymar, 2 play, 3rd builds brick house, 1940s, 11x14", EX+, T2 ....$30.00

Three Little Pigs, sand set, Ohio Art, pail, shovel, watering can, 2 sand molds, c WD, 11" shovel, NMIB, A $450.00

Three Little Pigs, washing machine, Chein, litho tin & wood, lt pitting & scratches, 8", G+, A..............................$120.00

Three Little Pigs & Big Bad Wolf, bank, Japan, pnt compo, 1960s, EX-EX+, T1..$25.00

Three's Company, gum card set, Topps, 16 cards w/14 stickers, complete, M1 ....$21.00

Three's Company, puzzle, Suzanne Somers as Chrissy, Casse-Tete, 1978, complete (EX box), P3 ....$9.00

Three's Company, sticker set, 44 card-sized stickers w/color photos from show, 1978, NM, C1 ....$17.50

Three Stooges, book, coloring; Playmore, 1983, 2 pgs colored, H4..$12.00

Three Stooges, Christmas ornament, Hamilton, set of 3 figures, 1991, 3½", MIP, F1 ....$10.00

Three Stooges, Colorforms, missing some pcs, 1959, VG, T1..$50.00

Three Stooges, Colorforms, 1959, EX, T4 ....$75.00

Three Stooges, Curly, hand puppet, cloth w/soft vinyl head, 9", EX, A $75.00

Three Stooges, fan club kit, 1959, T4 ....$35.00

Three Stooges, finger puppets, Wilkening, pnt plastic, 1959, orig bubble pkg, unopened, VG-EX, A $500.00

Three Stooges, flicker ring, Curly, Larry, or Moe, H4, ea.$20.00

Three Stooges, folder, Mauer, cb w/2 blk & wht photos, 12x10", 1984, M, P4 ....$5.00

Three Stooges, game, board; Fun House, Lowell, 1959, 10x20" box, scarce, EX (VG+ box), A $272.00

Three Stooges, game, card; Pressman, 1986, MIP (sealed), T6..$25.00

Three Stooges, Golden Record, 78 rpm, 1959, NM (M paper sleeve), C1 ....$36.00

Three Stooges, gum card set, FTCC, 1985, 60 cards, complete, M1 ....$30.00

Three Stooges, gum card wrapper, Fleer, all 3 on orange background, 1965, EX+, T2 ....$24.00

Three Stooges, Larry, hand puppet, cloth w/soft vinyl face, 1950s, 10", VG+, A $55.00

Three Stooges, Moe ventriloquist dummy, Horsman, 1981, VG, H4..$120.00

Three Stooges, poster, Around the World, in Spanish, T1.$125.00

Three Stooges, poster, Three Stooges in Orbit, 1965, 1-sheet, T4..$40.00

Three Stooges, press book, American International, Super Stooges vs the Wonder Woman, 16-pg, 1974, 8½x14", NM..$3.50

Three Stooges, sheet music, Snow White & the Three Stooges, 1961, T4..$25.00

Three Stooges, stamp set, w/Laurel & Hardy stamps, 1974, set, T4..$25.00

Three Stooges, stein, Markowski, glazed ceramic, portraits w/gold trim, licensed, 1/500 made, 1984, 7½", M, P4 ....$135.00

Thumper, figure, American Pottery, 1940s, 4", NM, M8 .$65.00

Thumper's Girlfriend, figure, American Pottery, 1940s, 4", NM, M8 ....$65.00

Thunderbirds, book, coloring; Whitman, 1965, EX..........$55.00

Thunderbirds, game, board; Parker Bros, space graphics on cover, 1967, NMIB, from $60 to $75.00

Tick, gum cards, NEC, 1991, 32 cards, complete, M1 ......$15.00

Tigger, figure, Beswick, M, P6 ....$40.00

Tilda, figure, German, pnt bsk, chip on shoulder, 3¾", G, A..$70.00

Tim Conway, book, coloring; Rango, M, V1 ....$25.00

Time Tunnel, book, coloring; Whitman, 1968, M $75.00

Time Tunnel, game, board; Ideal, 1966, complete, EX+ (EX+ box), C1 ....$150.00

Time Tunnel, game, board; Ideal, 1966, MIB (sealed), A..$278.00

Time Tunnel, game, card; Ideal, complete w/cards & chips, orig 6x9" plastic case, 1969, scarce, NM, A $250.00

Time Tunnel, game, Spin to Win, Pressman, 1967, orig 10x16" box, EX, A $250.00

Timothy the Circus Mouse (Dumbo's pal), figure, soft vinyl, jtd head & arms, 8", EX, H4 ....$25.00

Tinkerbell, cup & saucer, also features Disneyland castle, gold rim, 1960s, scarce, NM, M8........................$50.00

Tinkerbell, doll, Duchess, hard plastic, sleep eyes, 1950s, 7", EX, P6 ....$22.00

Tinkerbell, figure, clear plastic, standing, 1960s, 3½", EX, M8 ....$25.00

Tinkerbell, handbag, pk plastic, rnd w/loop handle & zipper, Disneyland under portrait of Tinkerbell, 5" dia, EX+, M5 ....$10.00

Tinkerbell, Spinikin, Kohner, 1960s, plastic w/pnt features, pull string for action, 4", NM, A $26.00

Tiny Tim, game, Beautiful Things, Parker Bros, signed by Tiny Tim, 1960s, EX+, from $40 to $55.00

Tom & Jerry, bendees, Just Toys, 6" & 3", K1, pr $5.95

Tom & Jerry, dolls, cloth w/litho facial features, 6½" & 17½", VG, A, pr $170.00

Tom & Jerry, game, Milton Bradley, 1977, EX+, F3.........$15.00

Tom & Jerry, pull toy, Lowe, wood Tom cutout w/metal springs on hands plays Diablo, 1959, 10", NM, A $185.00

Tom & Jerry, tracing book, 1971, EX................................$12.00

Tom Corbett, binoculars, metal w/decal, VG, I2 ....$30.00

Tom Corbett, book, coloring; Saalfield, 1950, NM, C1 ...$72.00

Tom Corbett, book, Danger in Deep Space, 200-pg, 8x5½", NM, A $25.00

Tom Corbett, book, punch-out; mc, 1950, unpunched, EX, A $110.00

Tom Corbett, Cosmic Vision Helmet, Practi Cole Prod, red plastic w/emb letters, NM (EX box), A, from $225 to..$279.00

Tom Corbett, flashlight & store display, Usalite, working, w/phamphlet & box, ca 1950, NM (EX box), A $685.00

Tom Corbett, Flashlight Ray Gun & Target Set, sounds, VG, T1 ....$135.00

Tom Corbett, Kellogg's Magic Eye Disk, plastic w/photo, 1950s, EX+, C1 ....$36.00

Tom Corbett, play outfit, Yankee Boy, complete, NMIB .$550.00

Tom Corbett, Push-Outs, Saalfield, 8-pg, in 17x10" cb folder, 1952, M, A $135.00

Tom Corbett, puzzle, jigsaw; Captures the Pirates, Saalfield, 1952, orig 7x10" box, EX+, A $150.00

Tom Corbett, record, Tom Corbett Space Cadet Song & March, yel vinyl, 45 rpm, 1951, orig jacket, VG-EX, A.........$15.00

Tom Corbett Space Cadet Belt, Yale/Rockhill, punch-out space ship on card, 1950s, NM (EX card), A, $170.00.

Tom Corbett, Sparkling Machine Gun, Marx, factory sample, w/tag, needs new flint, 21", NM (G box), A $425.00

Tom Mix, game, card; Tom Mix Wild Cat, 1935, EX, J2 .$45.00

Tom Mix, Glow-in-the-Dark Compass & Magnifier, Ralston Premium, NM-M, C1 ....$72.00

Tom Mix, gun, premium, wood, EX, J2...........................$125.00

Tom Mix, horse, wood, on wheels, w/seat for rider, 16", EX, A..$450.00

Tom Mix, humming lariat, premium, never used, M, J2...$50.00

Tom Mix, ID bracelet, 1947 ....$45.00

Tom Mix, marbles, premium, orig bag, M, J2...................$75.00

Tom Mix, photo, premium, silver fr, EX $95.00

Tom Mix, ring, brass bands w/Tom Mix on ea side, aluminum slide w/whistle on top, 1949, EX, A $100.00

Tom Mix, ring, Look-Around, cereal premium, EX+, J2.$125.00

Tom Mix, ring, magnet, brass band w/logo ea side, silver magnet on top, 1947, EX-, A..$75.00

Tom Mix, Rodeo Rope, Mordt, Tom's portrait on lid, dtd 1933, 14-ft rope in 9x8" box, EX (EX box), A...................$360.00

Tom and Jerry Wooden Carrying Case, Spain, lithographed cover, 1957, scarce, NM, A, $100.00.

Tom Corbet, Space Cadet, book, coloring; Saalfield #4801, 120-pg, EX+ $60.00

Tom Corbett, binoculars, metal & plastic, in leatherette case, some decal loss, NM, A...$100.00

Tom Mix, spurs, glow-in-the-dark, premium, MIB, J2....$150.00

Tonto, book, coloring; 1957, M..$10.00

Tonto, figure, Gabriel, 3¾", MOC, D4 ....$8.00

Tonto, hand puppet, Ideal, 1966, EX $35.00

Tonto, tin, Jay Silverheels on Scout, 1950s, 6" dia, NM, A.$68.00

Top Cat, bank, Transogram, plastic, in bl trash can, w/orig paper label, 1962, 10", NM..$45.00

Top Cat, game, Whitman, 1962, orig 13½x13½" box, NM, from $150 to $200.00

Top Cat, puzzle, fr-tray; Whitman, 1961, EX, T6 ....$25.00

Top Cat, puzzle, jigsaw; Whitman, 70 pcs assemble 14x18" scene, 1961, EX+ (EX+ box), A................................$45.00

Topo Gigo, nodder, M..$150.00

Total Recall, gum card set, PTC, 1990, 110 cards, complete, M1 ....$20.00

Touche Turtle, figure, Ideal, vinyl head w/stuffed body, rpr felt hands, 1962, H4 ....$80.00

Touche Turtle, game, board; Transogram, 1962, orig box, VG $65.00

Toxic Crusaders, Apocalype Helicopter, MIB, D4 ....$12.00

Toxic Crusaders, figure, Playmates, 1991, any of 7 characters, MIP, from $5 to $10.00

Toxic Crusaders, Toxic Surf Surfer (vehicle), MIB, D4 .....$8.00

Tron, book & record, 33⅓ rpm, M, F1/C1 ....$10.00

Tron, collector card, York Peanut Butter, 1982, set of 6, complete, M1 ....$15.00

Tron, gum card set, Donruss, 1982, 66 cards w/8 stickers, complete, M1 ....$13.00

Tweetie Pie, squeeze toy, Oak Rubber, R3 ....$50.00

Tweety, bank, compo, Tweety sitting atop birdhouse, orig box, EX..$75.00

Tweety, figure, ceramic, w/life preserver & sand pail, 1977, 3"..$35.00

Tweety & Sylvester, puzzle, jigsaw; Whitman, 99-pc (2 missing), 1975, 10x13", VG-, T6 ....$5.00

Twelve O'Clock High, game, board; Ideal, 1965, A.........$75.00

Twenty-Thousand Leagues Under the Sea, puzzle, Jaymar, 1960s, MIB, H4..$18.00

Twilight Zone, book, Grosset & Dunlap, hardback w/dust jacket, contains 13 stories, 1963, 8x10", EX-, T2 ....$15.00

Two Face, figure, Toy Biz, 2nd series, rare, MOC, F1 ......$25.00

Tyr, figure, Kenner, Super Powers, MOC.....................$70.00

Tyrannosaurus Retch, Blurp Ball, Ertl, MIP, E3 ....$4.00

Ultra-Seven, figure, Bandai, vinyl, MIP, E3 ....$10.00

Ultraman, Bogun figure, Dreamworks, MIP, E3 ....$10.00

Ultraman, figure, Bandai, vinyl, MIP, E3 ....$10.00

Ultraman, Gerukidon figure, Dreamworks, MIP, E3.........$10.00

Ultraman, Majaba figure, Dreamworks, MIP, E3 ....$10.00

Ultraman, Ultraman & Blue Shindo figures, Dreamworks, MIP, E3, pr..$20.00

Uncle Remus, book, Walt Disney's Uncle Remus Stories, hardcover, 90 pgs, 1972, 13x10½", M4 ....$20.00

Uncle Scrooge, bank, Dan Brechner Mfg, ceramic, Uncle Scrooge in bed, 1961, EX, P6 ....$95.00

Uncle Scrooge, book, coloring; Dell, #130, M, P6...........$35.00

Uncle Scrooge, car, Politoys, diecast w/butler driver & Uncle Scrooge in bk, scarce, orig box, 6", EX, A................$351.00

Uncle Scrooge, squeeze toy, Dell, R3 ....$30.00

Uncle Wiggily, bank, Chein, orange, yel & bl litho, 5", VG+, A..$150.00

Uncle Wiggily, puzzle, Halloween theme, orig 10x11" box, EX+ (frayed box), A..$295.00

Underdog, bank, Play Pal, vinyl, 8½", M $45.00

Underdog, book, sticker; Whitman, 1973, NM, C1 ....$21.00

Underdog, plate, wht plastic, rescuing Sweet Polly from crocodile, 1970s, EX+, C1 ....$18.00

Underdog, puzzle, jigsaw; w/Sweet Polly & Simon Bar Sinister, 100-pc, 1975, 8x11", EX, T2 ....$32.00

Underdog, sleeping bag, c Leonardo TTV, EX................$35.00

Undersea World of Jacques Costeau, game, board; Parker Bros, 1968, NM (EX+ box), from $30 to $40.00

Universal Monsters, book, coloring; Universal Studios, M, F1 ....$5.00

Universal Monsters, booklet & trading card set, Golden Books/Universal Studios, Frightening Facts w/4 cards, 1992, M, F1..$10.00

Untouchables, game, board; Transogram, 1961, NM (EX+ box)..$130.00

Untouchables, gun, Marx, Bullet-Firing Snub-Nose Pistol, w/shoulder holster, revolving cylinder, rare, 1960, 6", VG, P4..$110.00

US Marshall & Heroes of the West, book, coloring; James & Jonathan, w/historical accounts, 1955, 8x11", NM, T2..$24.00

V, bop bag, Arco, 1984, 42" weighted plastic alien, M (VG box), C1..$63.00

V, figure, LJN, ca 1984, 12", MIB (dented cellophane window on box), H4..$25.00

V, gum card set, Fleer, 1984, 66 cards w/22 stickers, complete, M1 ....$30.00

V, puffy stickers, set of 6, 1984, MIP, T6......................$5.00

Valley of the Dinosaurs, book, 1975, EX, lg, T6 ....$5.00

Vampire, bendee, Amscam, mc, 1980, 6", M $25.00

Vampire, kit, Toys 'N Things, MIP, E3 ....$5.00

Venom, figure, Toy Biz, flicks tongue, MOC, D8 ....$15.00

Venom, figure, Toy Biz, talker, MIB, F1.......................$20.00

Vincent Van Gopher, doll, Ideal, soft molded vinyl head on stuffed body, felt hands & feet, 1961, 13", scarce, EX-NM, A..$125.00

Voltron, Battling Black Lion Vehicle, Defender of the Universe, MIP, F1..$25.00

Voltron, Coffin of Darkness, Defenders of the Universe, MIB,F1..$10.00

Voltron, figure, Defender of the Universe series, MOC, F1 .$10.00

Voltron, Haggar the Witch figure, MOC, D4 ....$6.00

Voltron, King Zarkon figure, MOC, D4 ....$6.00

Voltron, Skull Tank, MIB, D4 ....$10.00

Voltron, Zarkon Zapper figure, MIB, D4.......................$10.00

Voyage to the Bottom of the Sea, book, coloring; Watkins-Strathmore, #1851-B, 1965, colored, EX $45.00

Voyage to the Bottom of the Sea, book, coloring; Whitman, 1965, M..$55.00

Voyage to the Bottom of the Sea, book, Pyramid, paperback w/blk & wht photo cover, 1964, EX, T2 ....$12.00

Voyage to the Bottom of the Sea, fan club photo, postcard sz w/main cast members & facsimile signatures, 1950s, M, T2..$18.00

Voyage to the Bottom of the Sea, game, board; Milton Bradley, 1964, NMIB, C1 ....$63.00

Voyage to the Bottom of the Sea, gum card box, Donruss, empty store display, 1964, 8x4x2", rare, EX+-NM, A $450.00

Wagon Train, book, coloring; Whitman, 1959, VG.........$20.00

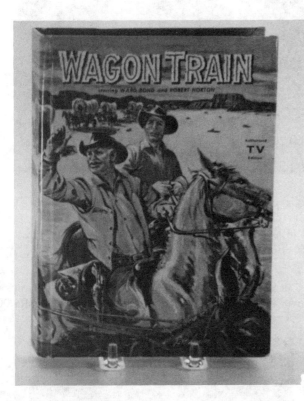

Wagon Train Book, Whitman, TV authorized edition, 1959, EX, $10.00.

Waltons, game, board; Milton Bradley, 26 cards & marker, 10x20" box, 1974, EX, T2 ....$29.00

Wanted: Dead or Alive, game, target; Marx, 1959, NM, A .$350.00

WC Fields, bank, c MGM, plastic, 7½"............................$15.00

WC Fields, battery tester, red nose lights, working, 1974, EX, I2 ....$10.00

WC Fields, bookends, plastic bust figure, 8", pr $30.00

WCW Wrestlers, bendee, Just Toys, Sting, Lex Luger, Ric Flair, Sid Vicious, Barry Windham & Arn Anderson, 6", K1, ea $3.95

WCW Wrestlers, bendee pencil hugger, Applause, Hulk Hogan or Ultimate Warrior, complete w/logo pencil, 2", K1, ea $2.25

Webster, record album, Kid Stuff #1036, Good Secrets Bad Secrets, 33⅓ rpm, 1986, M (sealed sleeve), T6 ....$8.00

Weird-Ohs, Crashmobile, Triplay, 1960s, NMOC $38.00

Weird-Ohs, Davey the Way-Out Cyclist Magic Slate, 1963, 8x11", MIP...$60.00

Weird-Ohs, gum card pkg, Fleer, 1963, 5 cards & gum, 4x2", MIP $25.00

Welcome Back Kotter, Colorforms, complete w/booklet, 1976, EX+, T6 ....$9.00

Welcome Back Kotter, Colorforms, 1976, MIB (sealed), C1 ....$18.00

Welcome Back Kotter, figure, Mattel, set of 5: Kotter, Horshack, Epstein, Barbarino & Washington, MOC (separate), C1 ....$175.00

Welcome Back Kotter, game, board; Milton Bradley, 1976, MIB..$30.00

Welcome Back Kotter, game, card; Milton Bradley, 1960s, EX+, F3 ....$18.00

Welcome Back Kotter, gum card set, 1979, complete set of 53 color photo cards, NM-M, C1 ....$15.00

Welcome Back Kotter, puzzle, fr-tray; Whitman, shows cast, 1977, EX+, D9 ....$4.00

Wendy the Good Little Witch, book, coloring; Artcraft, 1960, M $20.00

Wendy the Good Little Witch, doll, Gund, stuffed w/soft molded vinyl head, orig fabric label, 1959, 9", EX, A $30.00

Werewolf, figure, Mego, World's Greatest Super Monster series, 8", MIB...$90.00

Werewolf, firecracker label, night scene, 1960s, 8x6", A..$38.00

What's My Line, game, quiz; Lowell, 1950s, EX, F3 ....$35.00

Where's Waldo, bendee, Mattel, 1991, 5", K1, any $5.95

Where's Waldo, doll, Mattel, MIB, D4 ....$20.00

Where's Waldo, figure, Applause, PVC, MIP, F1, any of 5..$3.00

Wild Bill Hickock, gun, Leslie-Henry Young Buffalo Bill Cap Pistol, diecast, single shot, unfired, 1954, 7½", NM, P4 ....$45.00

Wild Bill Hickock, gun, Leslie-Henry 44 Cap Pistol, diecast, swing-out/side-loading, cylinder revolves, '50s, 11", M $155.00

Wild Bill Hickock, map, Treasure Guide & Map, Kellogg's premium, lg, EX, A $55.00

Wild Bill Hickock, puzzle, fr-tray; EX $22.50

Wild Kingdom, game, Marlin Perkins Zoo Parade, Cadaco Ellis, 1965, EX (EX box), H4 ....$35.00

Wile E Coyote, hand puppet, sm head on brn plastic body, 1970s, NM, C1..$16.00

William Boyd, book, coloring; Abbot, 1951, uncolored, 13x11", M, A...$60.00

Willow, Airk Thaughbauer, Rebel Trooper, Sorsha, Troll, or Death Dog, 1984, MOC, T1, ea $5.00

Willow, Death Dog, Sorsha, Madmartigan, or Nockmarr Warrior w/horse, Tonka, 1988, MIB, F1, ea......................$5.00

Willow, placemat, Kraft premium, laminated, set of 4 different, NM-M, T6 ....$10.00

Willow, Ufgood figure, Tonka, w/baby, 1988, rare, MOC, from $5 to $10.00

Wimpy, doll, jtd wood, ca 1935, USA, wear on hip, 10x6", o/w NM, A..$325.00

Wimpy, figure, jtd wood, mk King Features, mid-1930s, 4x3", EX+, A $110.00

Wimpy, soap, figural, EX, P6 ....$25.00

Wimpy, squeeze toy, Rempel, standing, arms behind bk, 8x4", NM, A $75.00

Wimpy, wall hanging, emb tile, full color, 4⅛x3", M, P6 ....$35.00

Win, Lose or Draw; game, cereal premium, 1988, MIP (sealed 3½x4½" pkg), T6 ....$3.00

Winky Dink, Clay Doodle, 20x6x2" box w/colors of modeling clay, 1950s, M (NM box), A $22.00

Winky Dink, puzzle, jigsaw; Jaymar, 60+-pc, scene w/pirate gang, 1950s, NM-M (EX box), A $40.00

Winnie the Pooh, Activity Kit, Animal Friends, Sears, 1977, M4 ....$10.00

Winnie the Pooh, book, pop-up; 1952, scarce, VG-EX........$40.00

Winnie the Pooh, bulletin board, 27x19", EX, J2 ....$20.00

Winnie the Pooh, grow chart tree, WDP, 1977, M4 ....$10.00

Winnie the Pooh, lamp, ceramic, Pooh & characters on base, missing shade, I2 ....$18.00

Winnie the Pooh, lamp, w/plastic balloons as shade, EX, I2 .$25.00

Winnie the Pooh, music box, VG-EX, O1 ....$34.00

Winnie the Pooh, nodder, 2 cracks in bk of head, VG, H4 .$20.00

Winnie the Pooh, poster, Disney Press bookstore promo, New Adventures of Winnie the Pooh, 1980s, scarce, 23x18", NM, M8 ....$12.00

Winnie the Pooh, puzzle, fr-tray; Jaymar, Pooh at table w/Christopher Robin & friends, 1964, 14½x11", NM, P6 ....$25.00

Winnie the Pooh, tie, gr clip-on w/embroidered Pooh, 1960s, EX, P6 ....$35.00

Winnie the Pooh & Tigger, record case, for 45 rpm, vinyl-coated cb, EX, P6 ....$35.00

Wizard of Id, key chain, Field Ent/Curtis, metal, The King Is a Fink, 1976, 1¾" dia, VG, P4 ....$6.00

Wizard of Oz, activity kit, Friends Industries, decoupage craft w/2 scenes, assembled, complete, 1975, EX+ (worn box), A $58.00

Wizard of Oz, beach towel, Franco, terrycloth w/artwork based on 1975 Marvel/DC Comic cover, ca 1976, 33x60", VG-EX, A $70.00

Wizard of Oz, book, coloring; Whitman, 1939 abridged edition, 48-pg, VG, A $38.00

Wizard of Oz, chair w/crystal ball (came w/Emerald City playset), Mego, 1975, M, F1 ....$10.00

Wizard of Oz, Cowardly Lion puppet, Proctor & Gamble, plastic & vinyl, ca 1965-67, 9x7", NM, A $85.00

Wizard of Oz, doll, Mego, set of 4: Tin Man, Lion, Dorothy & Scarecrow, 1975, rare, 16", M (NM box), H4 ......$1,200.00

Wizard of Oz, dolls, stuffed, mail-order premium from M-D Tissue, 1971, 17", set of 4 in orig mailer $200.00

Wizard of Oz, Dorothy, Scarecrow, Tin Man, or Lion bendee, Just Toys, 1989, 6", K1, ea $6.00

Wizard of Oz, Dorothy figure, Multi-Toy, 3¾", MOC, F1 .$10.00

Wizard of Oz, game, board; Milton Bradley, complete, w/insert card, 1968, NM (EX 9½x19" box), A $67.00

Wizard of Oz, game, Parker Bros, missing some parts & booklet, rpr & rstr box, 1939, rare, 10x19", VG, A $200.00

Wizard of Oz, General Munchkin, figure, Multi-Toy, MIB, F1 ....$15.00

Wizard of Oz, General Munchkin figure, Mego, 5", MIB, H4 ....$110.00

Wizard of Oz, Lion figure, Multi-Toy, 3¾", MOC, F1 ......$15.00

Wizard of Oz, magazine ad, Modern Romances, August 1939, 2-pg, 8½x11", VG+, A $41.00

Wizard of Oz, magazine article, Life, July 17, 1939, 2-pg color tear-sheet w/8 photos, NM, A $35.00

Wizard of Oz, Munchkin, PVC, set of 6, M, D4 ....$12.00

Wizard of Oz, Munchkin girl figure, Multi-Toys, 6", MIB, D4 ....$7.00

Wizard of Oz Mug, marked Presented by Mickey Carrol, white ceramic with facsimile signature, ca 1989, 3", M, A, $50.00. (Photo courtesy Scarfone & Stillman Vintage Oz, photo by Tim McGowan.)

Wizard of Oz, newspaper supplement song sheet, Scarecrow on cover, 1903, 10¾x14", EX, A $95.00

Wizard of Oz Cowardly Lion Valentine, ca 1940, rare, 3x5", NM, A, $113.00. (Photo courtesy Scarfone & Stillman Vintage Oz, photo by Tim McGowan.)

Wizard of Oz, playset, Mego, Emerald City, w/8" doll, crystal ball, throne, tree & yel brick road, 1975, orig box, EX, A $50.00

Wizard of Oz, record album, Disney, Songs From Wizard of Oz, 33⅓ rpm, 1969, EX, N2 ....$12.00

Wizard of Oz, records, Decca, 78 rpm, set of 4 (1 missing), w/photo booklet, 1939, EX, A..................................$150.00

Wizard of Oz, sand pail, Swift's Oz Peanut Butter, red & yel litho tin, ca 1950s, 6½", EX, A $123.00

Wizard of Oz, scarecrow jack-in-the-box, Mattel, plays music, 1967...$45.00

Wizard of Oz, sheet music, Over the Rainbow, Leo Feist, 1939, EX $20.00

Wizard of Oz, song folio, reissue of orig 1940 edition, ca 1950s, 9x12", VG, A...$78.00

Wizard of Oz, soundtrack album, Singer, premium edition, 1970, revised jacket w/new cover art, G (VG jacket), A.....$26.00

Wizard of Oz, Story-Telling Kit, Summer Weekly Reader premium, cb, complete, M, F1 ....$10.00

Wizard of Oz, tablecloth, Unique, mc paper w/movie graphics, 1975, 54x90", NMIP, A..$60.00

Wizard of Oz, Tin Man hand puppet, Proctor & Gamble, vinyl head & thin plastic body, ca 1965-67, 10", M, T2.....$24.00

Wizard of Oz, Tin Man water gun, plastic figure, 1989, EX .$5.00

Wizard of Oz, Wizard figure, Mego, 8", MIP, F1 ....$25.00

Wizard of Oz, Wizard figure, Multi-Toy, 1988, 12", MIB, from $15 to $20.00

Wolfman, bendee, Novelty Mfg, 1979, 5", M (NM card), D9 ....$23.00

Wolfman, figure, Hamilton, vinyl, 13", EX.......................$30.00

Wolfman, figure, Presents, 1992, M $35.00

Wolfman, figure, Remco, 1980, 3¾", NMOC.................$45.00

Wolfman, Monster Ball, Illco, tennis ball sz w/fur & etched features, 1980s, MOC (EX+ card), C1............................$18.00

Wolfman, pencil sharpener, UP Co, gr plastic bust on sharpener base, 1960s, 3", unused, M, T2 ....$30.00

Wolverine, bumper sticker, MCG, 1990, M.......................$5.00

Wonder Woman, cake pan, Wilton, 1978, 10x18" box, M (NM box), C1 ....$27.00

Wonder Woman, figure, Kenner, Super Powers, MOC (sm card), F1 ....$15.00

Wonder Woman, figure, Mego, 8", MIB, H4 ....$300.00

Wonder Woman, figure, Toy Biz, 1989, MOC, F1 ....$15.00

Wonder Woman, squeeze toy, Tarco, 1983, MIP, T1.......$20.00

Woody Woodpecker, book, activity; 1971, VG+, T6 ....$5.00

Woody Woodpecker, book, Whitman, 1967, EX+ $10.00

Woody Woodpecker, figure, Kay Bee, pnt plastic w/metal pole, spring-activated pecking action, 19", VG-EX, A.......$55.00

Woody Woodpecker, Flannel Board Set, 1950s, EX, T1 ..$45.00

Woody Woodpecker, kazoo, figural, premium, MIB, J2....$38.00

Woody Woodpecker, lamp, plastic, full figure, S1 ....$25.00

Woody Woodpecker, night light, red, yel, wht & blk, no date, EX, T6 ....$7.00

Woody Woodpecker, placemat, plastic-sealed illus, 1978, 12x18", EX-, T6 ....$4.00

Woody Woodpecker, planter, pnt ceramic figure w/suitcase, 1958, 7¼", EX+..$40.00

Woody Woodpecker, soundtrack, Woody Woodpecker's Talent Show, 1975, EX...$8.00

Woody Woodpecker, squeeze toy, Oak Rubber, R3.........$50.00

Wonder Woman, DC Comics, plastic with jointed waist, 1983, 14", $35.00.

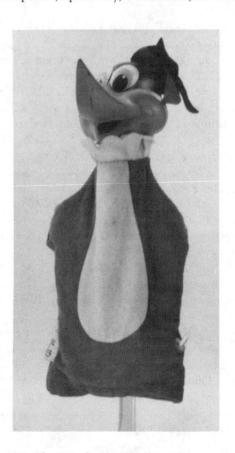

Woody Woodpecker Talking Puppet, Mattel, felt features, hard plastic head, 11", EX, $60.00.

Woody Woodpecker, TV Coloring Pencil Set, Connecticut Pencil, 1958, M (EX box), A................................$40.00

WWF Wrestling, Akeem figure, Hasbro, 1988-92, 4", MOC, F1 ....$30.00

WWF Wrestling, Andre the Giant figure, Hasbro, 1988-92, rare, 4", MOC, F1 ....$40.00

WWF Wrestling, Ax figure, Hasbro, 1988-92, 4", MOC, F1 ....$20.00

WWF Wrestling, Brutus Beefcake figure, Hasbro, MOC, D4 ....$6.00

WWF Wrestling, Gene Okerland figure, LJN, 1986-88, 8", MOC, F1 ....$20.00

WWF Wrestling, Honky Tonk Man figure, Hasbro, 1988-1992, 4", MOC, F1 ....$10.00

WWF Wrestling, Jake the Snake figure, Hasbro, 1991, MIB, F1 ....$10.00

WWF Wrestling, Jimmy Snuka figure, Hasbro, MOC, D4 ....$10.00

WWF Wrestling, Macho Man Randy Savage figure, Hasbro, orange trunks, MOC, D4 ....$15.00

WWF Wrestling, Official WWF Wrestling Ring & Championship Belt, Hasbro, MIP, F1 ....$15.00

WWF Wrestling, Rick Rude figure, Hasbro, MOC, D4....$20.00

WWF Wrestling, Slick figure, LJN, 1986-88, 8", MOC, F1 ....$20.00

WWF Wrestling, Smash figure, Hasbro, 1988-92, 4", MOC, F1 ....$20.00

WWF Wrestling, Tag Team Bushwackers figures, Hasbro, 1988-92, set of 2 on card, MOC, F1 ....$15.00

WWF Wrestling, Tag Team Nasty Boys (Brian & Jerry) figures, Hasbro, 1988-92, set of 2 on card, rare, MOC, F1 .....$20.00

WWF Wrestling, Thumb Wrestlers figures, LJN, 1986-88, set of 2 on card, MOC, F1, any..$10.00

WWF Wrestling, Ultimate Warrior figure, Hasbro, wht trunks, MOC, D4 ....$15.00

Wyatt Earp, badge, Wyatt Earp Ent/20th Century, 6-point metal star, 1959, MOC $15.00

Wyatt Earp, book, coloring; 1958, EX+ $15.00

Wyatt Earp, Color-By-Number Stencil Set, NMIB $27.50

Wyatt Earp, figure, Mego, American West series, complete w/accessories, MIB (Sears or JC Penney brn box), F1.$50.00

Wyatt Earp, game, Lowell, EX+, F3 ....$65.00

Wyatt Earp, gun, Actoy, Buntline Special, CI cap pistol w/copper finish, wht stag grips, 1950s, EX, H1..$150.00

Wyatt Earp, gun, Hubley, 1950s, fires caps, 10½" barrel, NM, H1 ....$100.00

Wyatt Earp, holster set, Hubley, 2 10¾" diecast guns w/nickel finish (fired), blk & wht leather holster, VG, P4 ....$385.00

Wyatt Earp, holsters (2), leather, 1950s, VG-EX, T1 ....$45.00

Wyatt Earp, Paint-By-Number Set, Transogram, 10 sketches, pnt, mixer tray, etc, 1958, 13x16" box, unused (VG+ box), T2 ....$90.00

Wyatt Earp, puzzle, Whitman, waist-length portrait, 1958, 15x11", NM, A $30.00

Wyatt Earp, wallet, 1957, EX $35.00

Wyatt Earp Jr, holster set, Hubley, cowhide w/2 Pet pistols & plastic badge, 1959, NM (EX card), A..$200.00

X-Force, Cable figure, Toy Biz, 2nd edition, MOC, F1 ....$15.00

X-Force, Gideon figure, Toy Biz, MOC, F1..$15.00

X-Force, Shatterstar figure, Toy Biz, MOC, F1 ....$15.00

X-Force, Super Heroes Gift Set, Toy Biz, set of 4: Forarm, Deadpool, Stryfe & Cable, MIB, F1..$40.00

X-Force, Warpath figure, Toy Biz, MOC, F1 ....$15.00

X-Men, bendee, Just Toys/Marvel Comics, Wolverine, Cyclops, Colossus, Nightcrawler, Magneto, or Juggernaut, 6", K1, any..$4.95

X-Men, Figure & Weapon Set, 1990, MIB, T1..$25.00

X-Men, Gambit figure, Toy Biz, MOC, F1..$15.00

X-Men, Magneto Magnetron Cycle w/Metallic Disk, Toy Biz, MIB, F1..$30.00

X-Men, Magneto 2 figure, Toy Biz, MOC, F1..$15.00

X-Men, playset, Cyclops Light Force Arena Danger Room, Toy Biz, MIB, F1..$30.00

X-Men, playset, Wolverine Combat Cave, Toy Biz, MIB..$28.00

X-Men, Sabertooth figure, 1990, MOC, T1..$10.00

X-Men, Storm figure, Toy Biz, MOC, F1 ....$20.00

X-Men, Super Heroes Gift Set, Toy Biz, set of 4: Sabertooth, Ice Man (rare), Wolverine 2 & Mr Sinister, MIB, F1 .....$60.00

X-Men, Tusk figure, Toy Biz, MOC, F1 ....$15.00

X-Men, Wolverine figure, 2nd edition, 1990, MOC, T1..$12.00

X-Men, Wolverine figure, 3rd edition, 1990, MOC, T1...$10.00

X-Men, Wolverine Stunt Cycle, 1991, MIB, T1 ....$20.00

Yellow Kid, rocker, oak w/clear finish, pressed & turned features, caned seat center, rstr, 30", VG-, A $325.00

Yellow Kid Goat Cart, Hubley, CI, silver goat & cart, figure w/red coat, red wheels, pnt loss & lt pitting, 6¾", G, A..$130.00

Yertle the Turtle, doll, Mattel/Dr Seuss, hard plastic w/stuffed body, talker, non-working, EX $100.00

Yertle the Turtle, figure, Coleco/Dr Seuss, MIB, H4 ....$40.00

Yertle the Turtle, game, Revell/Dr Seuss, complete, orig box, EX (VG box), H4 ....$90.00

Yogi & Boo-Boo, Mebetoys, in convertible w/fishing poles, NM, U1 ....$110.00

Yogi Bear, book, Bubble Gum Lions, 1974, EX..$8.00

Yogi Bear, book, coloring; Yogi vs Magilla for President, Hanna-Barbera, 1964, uncolored, EX, A..$30.00

Yogi Bear and Cindy Push-Button Puppets, Kohner, NM (EX box), A, $120.00.

Yogi Bear, book, No Picnic, Whitman Tip-Top Tales, 1961, VG, T6..$3.00

Yogi Bear, book, Teeny Weeny Mountain, Durabook, 1974, EX..$8.00

Yogi Bear, cake plate, musical, plays Happy Birthday, also features characters from Huckleberry Hound, 1960s, M, P6..$60.00

Yogi Bear, figure, Imperial, solid plastic w/parachute, World Champion Sky Diver, 1977, MOC, H4 ....$15.00

Yogi Bear, flashlight, 1973, MIP, T1 ....$20.00

Yogi Bear, game, Milton Bradley, complete, 1971, EX-NM.$12.00

Yogi Bear, game, Pixie & Dixie Pile-On, Whitman, 1962, in orig 7" plastic cylinder, NM, C1 ....$28.00

Yogi Bear, game, Presents Snagglepuss Fun at the Picnic #2805, Transogram, EX (EX box), P4 ....$60.00

Yogi Bear, game, Rummy, Ed-U-Cards, 1961, MIB, (sealed), T2 ....$18.00

Yogi Bear, game, Score-A-Matic Ball Toss, Transogram, 1960, EX+ (EX box), T2 ....$80.00

Yogi Bear, lamp, pnt chalkware, ca 1960, NM..................$40.00

Yogi Bear, push-button puppet, Kohner, NM, V1 ....$17.50

Yogi Bear, record, Golden Records, TV Theme Song, 78 rpm, 1961, M (NM illus paper sleeve), A..........................$46.00

Yogi Bear, squeeze toy, Dell, R3 ....$30.00

Yogi Bear, swim ring, inflatable plastic, 1960, MIB, V1 ...$20.00

Yogi Bear, valentines, Hanna-Barbera/Whitman, 36 valentines w/envelopes, plastic-sealed tray box, 1965, NMIB, P4..$10.00

Yogi Bear & Friends, playset, Irwin, plastic spoons, cups, plates & serving pot, 1962, complete, NM (EX box), A......$89.00

Yosemite Sam, air freshener, Medeo, 1990, MIP $15.00

Yosemite Sam, nodder, Looney Tunes, pnt ceramic, 8", MIB..$35.00

Yosemite Sam, transfer, Vogart, 1971, MIP $20.00

Yuri, doll, Bandai, vinyl, MIP, E3....................................$30.00

Zany Zone, Barry Dalive figure, Mattel, MIP, E3 ....$8.00

Zap, figure, Mattel, American Gladiators, MIP, E3 ....$10.00

Zero, nodder, Lego, compo w/spring-mtd head, 1961, uncommon, 8", NM, A..$182.00

Ziggy, game, board; Milton Bradley, A Day w/Ziggy, 1977, NM..$25.00

Zorro, Activity Box, Whitman, cb ranch scene w/figures, 1965, EX+ (VG+ box), C1..$49.00

Zorro, book, coloring; Whitman, 120+pgs, 1958, 8x11", EX+, A $42.00

Zorro, cap gun, Lone Star, NMOC $100.00

Zorro, cap pistol, plastic, 1960s, EX, T1 ....$35.00

Zorro, gum cards, Topps, 82 of 88 mc photo cards w/Guy Williams, 1950s, EX+, C1..$231.00

Zorro, hat, Benay-Albee, blk w/wht & blk label featuring Zorro on horse & name, 1950s, EX, M8............................$45.00

Zorro, mask, whip & lariat, 1960s, MOC, T1 ....$85.00

Zorro, Oil Paint-By-Numbers Set, Hasbro, w/12x16" canvas, plastic fr & 10 vials of pnt, 1965, M (NM box), A $139.00

Zorro, The Gay Blade, poster, George Hamilton, NM, T1 .$10.00

Zorro, puzzle, fr-tray; Whitman, #4521, 1965, orig shrink wrap, M, P6..$40.00

Zorro, puzzle, fr-tray; Whitman, Zorro in Mexican villa, 1957, 11x14", lt wear, EX-, T2 ....$32.00

101 Dalmations, bendee, Just Toys, Perdita, Pongo, Patch, Rolly, or Lucky, 1991, 5" or 3½", ea, $5 to $10.00

101 Dalmations, bendee, Just Toys, Pongo or Perdita, 1980s, M, ea..$12.50

101 Dalmations, book, hardcover, 1961, EX....................$12.00

101 Dalmations, figure, PVC, Applause, set of 4: Pongo, Cruella, Colonel & Patch, MIP, F1..$12.00

21 Jump Street, gum card set, Topps, 1988, 44 cards, complete, M1..$8.50

77 Sunset Strip, game, board; Lowell, 1960, MIB, from $50 to..$75.00

Chein

Though the company was founded shortly after the turn of the century, this New Jersey-based manufacturer is probably best known for the toys it made during the thirties and forties. Windup merry-go-rounds and Ferris wheels as well as many other carnival-type rides were made of beautifully lithographed tin even into the fifties, some in several variations. The company also made banks, a few of which were mechanical, and some that were character-related. Mechanical, sea-worthy cabin cruisers, space guns, sand toys, and some Disney toys as well were made by this giant company; they continued in production until 1979. See also Banks.

TOY SCOUTS, INC.

SPECIALIZING IN BABY-BOOM COLLECTIBLES
(1940's – 70's)

Including:
- TV, Cartoon & Comic Characters
- TV & Movie Props & Items
- Gum Cards (10,000 in stock!)
- Model Kits
- Cereal Boxes
- Disneyana
- Sci-Fi
- Superheroes
- Premiums
- Space
- Spies
- Music
- Monsters
- Westerns
- Playsets

MAIL ORDER SALES & AUCTION CATALOG

Each issue of our quarterly, 100-page illustrated catalog features approximately 1,000 vintage items which you may buy or bid on from the comfort of your home.

Send $3.00 to:

TOY SCOUTS, INC.

137 Casterton Avenue
Akron, Ohio 44303
(216) 836-0668
FAX (216) 869-8668

BUY • SELL • TRADE

Windups and Other Mechanicals

Aeroswing, litho tin, lever action, 10", EX, A $325.00

Alligator, tin, Native rider on bk, 15", NM $285.00

Army Sergeant, walker, 5x3", EX- $75.00

Band Leader, litho tin, 8¾", G-, A $190.00

Barnacle Bill, litho tin, sways side to side while moving about, 1930s, 6", EX, A $207.00

Boat, cruiser, 1940s, tin, 8½", EX $65.00

Cathedral, litho tin, plays music, EX+ $50.00

Chipper Chipmunk, Chip goes around track, treadmill turns, rpr box, M, A $120.00

Clown Floor Puncher, clown & punching bag, 1930s, 8", EX, A $545.00

Disneyland Mechanical Ferris Wheel, litho tin, c WDP, 16", M (EX box), A $400.00

Disneyland Roller Coaster, litho tin, cars w/bobbing heads travel ride, Mickey on face plate, 19", EX+ (NM box), A.$700.00

Disneyland Roller Coaster, mc litho tin, clockwork, bell rings, working, 19½", VG+, A $350.00

Dough Boy Walker, litho tin, 6", EX, A $253.00

Drummer & Cymbal Player, litho tin, beats drum & plays cymbals, 1930s, 8½", NM, A $250.00

Drummer #109, in red & bl uniform w/red helmet, yel drum, 9", unused, MIB, from $260 to..............$300.00

Ferris Wheel #172, litho tin, 6 gondolas, carnival scene on base, 17", NM (NM box), A $394.00

Happy Hooligan, lithographed tin, authorized version, 6", EX+, D10, $550.00.

Navy Frogman, lithographed tin windup, 1950s, M, D10, $275.00.

Ferris Wheel, lithographed tin windup, 16½", EX, A, $300.00; Ride-A-Rocket Carousel, lithographed tin windup, orig box, EX, A, from $500.00.

Hand-Standing Clown, purple pants w/wht circles, balances on hands, moves bk & forth, 5", EX, A..............$110.00

Hand-Standing Clown, striped pants, balances on hands, moves bk & forth, 1938, 5", EX, A..............$90.00

Happy Holligan Walker, unauthorized version, no name on hat or c on bk, litho tin, 6", NM, A $550.00

Hercules Ferris Wheel, mc litho tin, clockwork, working, 16½", EX, from $100 to $150.00

Mark I Cruiser Boat, litho tin, 1957, 8½", G $15.00

Playland Merry-Go-Round, VG $280.00

Playland Whip, litho tin, 4 cars move, heads bob, bell sounds, carnival concession at center, 11x20", EX (EX box), A.........$623.00

Popeye Heavy Hitter, c King Features, litho tin, Popeye uses sledge hammer to ring bell, bell has dulled, 12x7", NM-, A..............$4,750.00

Popeye Overhead Puncher, c 1932, some wear, fading, scratches & rubs, o/w EX, 9½x4½x4¼", A..............$1,525.00

Popeye Overhead Puncher, c 1932 King Features Syndicate, very minor rubs/scratches, bag is about M, 9½x4¼", NM, A..............$4,000.00

Popeye Overhead Punching Bag, tin and celluloid, original box, 9½", MIB, A, $4,950.00.

Rabbit, red, yel & blk litho tin, moves on 3 red wheels, 5½", EX+, A..$175.00
Rabbit Pulling Cart, M...$150.00
Race Car #52, litho tin w/driver, red & yel w/wht rubber tires, 6½", VG+, A...$166.00
Ride-A-Rocket, litho tin, orange, bl & yel, clockwork, working, orig box, 18", EX..$500.00
Roller Coaster, litho tin, 2" cars (2) w/kids move continuously, carnival scenes at base, 1930s, 19" long, NM (M box)...$425.00
Sand Mill, litho tin, cups form 2 wheels, sand makes cups spin in Ferris wheel motion, 7x11", EX, A..............................$85.00

Seaplane, lithographed tin windup, 9" long, M, D10, $275.00.

Seaside Water Pump, litho tin, place in water, lever pumping action, 14", EX, A...$241.00
Ski Boy, litho tin, moves arms, wheels hidden, working, orig box (torn flap), 7", EX, A..$175.00

Ski Boy, litho tin, working, 7", VG+, A.........................$90.00
Ski Ride, litho tin, orig box, 18", EX, A.......................$495.00
Ski Ride, litho tin, 2 skiers travel up & down w/continuous action, factory touch-up on ramp, 19", VG+ (EX box), A...$582.00
Skin Diver, tin w/plastic flippers that move propelling him through water, 11", NM (EX box), A.....................$140.00
Turtle #145, litho tin, turtle scoots around as native bounces on bk, 7", NMIB, A...$320.00
US Army Sergeant, litho tin, 5½", M (M card), A..........$78.00
Walking Pelican, litho tin, 5", EX+, A.........................$185.00
Walking Pig, litho tin, EX, J2..................................$60.00
Yellow Taxi, litho tin, yel & blk, clockwork, working, 6", EX..$250.00

Miscellaneous

Atomic Flash Space Gun, EX+....................................$65.00
Bonzo Scooter, tin pull toy, Bonzo works bar when pulled, 1930s, 7", EX, A...$335.00
Disney Melody Player, ca 1955, MIB (sealed)................$450.00
Drum, mc children's band on tin, 9" dia, w/sticks, EX......$35.00

Hercules Bulldog Mack 'C' Cab Ice Truck, ca 1930s, 20", NM, $950.00.

Hercules Motor Express, litho tin, red tractor, gr trailer, all w/litho, 4¼x15", VG, A...$325.00
Hercules Motor Express Truck, pnt tin, blk & orange w/red metal wheels, lowering rear truck tailgate, '30s, 20", A......$750.00
Ice Truck, litho tin, yel & gr, mk Ice on both sides, 1930s, 8½", EX, A...$213.00
Junior Bus, litho tin, mk 219 on door, Danger & To Pass signs emb on rear, 9", VG, A...$244.00
Krazy Kat Scooter, litho tin, orange & gr scooter, yel, bl & red cat, pull toy, 7", VG, A...$240.00
Log Truck, litho tin w/6 metal poles in bed, early mk, 8½", EX, A...$248.00
Lunar Globe, MIB...$115.00
Popeye, pnt & jtd wood & compo, decals, 10½", VG....$400.00
Tambourine, tin, parrot in litho design, EX, J2...............$45.00
Yellow Taxi, tin, never had mechanism, 8", EX, A.........$80.00

Chinese Tin Toys

China has produced toys for export since the 1920s, but most of their tin toys were made from the 1970s to the present. Collectors are buying them with an eye to the future, since right now, at least, they are relatively inexpensive.

Government-operated factories are located in various parts of China. They use various numbering systems to identify types of toys, for instance, ME (metal-electric — battery operated), MS (metal-spring — windup), MF (metal friction), PMS (plastic-metal-spring), and others. Most toys and boxes are marked, but some aren't; and since many of the toys are reproductions of earlier Japanese models, it is often difficult to tell the difference if no numbers can be found.

Prices vary greatly depending on age, condition, availability, and dealer knowledge of origin. Toys currently in production may be discontinued at any time and may often be as hard to find as the earlier toys. Records are so scarce that it is difficult to pinpoint the start of production, but at least some manufacture began in the 1970s and '80s. In the listings below, values are for mint in the box items. Our advisor for this category is Steve Fisch (F7).

#ME060, tank, remote control, 1970s, 7x4x4", F7, from $35 to $75.00

#ME086, Shanghai Bus, MIB, F7, from $85.00 to $150.00.

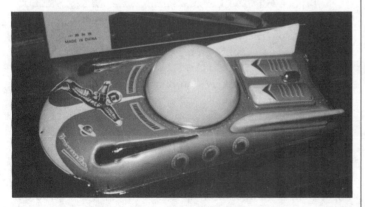

#ME089, Universe Car, MIB, F7, from $85.00 to $150.00.

#ME093, open-door trolley, current, 10x5x4", F7, from $25 to $35.00
#ME100, robot, current, 12x4x6", F7, from $35 to.........$125.00
#ME102, spaceship, blows air, current, 13x5x4", F7, from $35 to...$75.00
#ME610, hen laying eggs, current, 7x4x6", F7, from $25 to ..$50.00

#ME603, Hen and Chickens, MIB, F7, from $25.00 to $50.00.

#ME611, News Car or World Cup Car, MIB, F7, from $55.00 to $125.00.

#ME614, automatic rifle, current, 23x2x8", F7, from $25 to .$35.00
#ME677, Shanghai convertible, 1970s, 12x5x3", F7, from $60 to $100.00
#ME679, dump truck, current, 13x4x3", F7, from $25 to .$50.00
#ME699, fire chief car, current, 10x5x2", F7, from $25 to.$50.00
#ME756, Anti-Aircraft Armoured Tank, MIB, F7, from $50.00 to $100.00
#ME767, Universe boat, current, 10x5x6", F7, from $35 to.$75.00
#ME767, Universe boat, 1970s, 10x5x6", F7, from $75 to.$150.00
#ME770, Mr Duck, current, 9x7x5", F7, from $25 to $50.00

#ME809, Anti-Aircraft Armoured Car, 1970s, 12x6x6", F7, from $75 to $100.00.

#ME774, tank, remote control, 1970s, 9x4x3", F7, from $45 to $75.00

#ME777, Universe Televiboat, current, 15x4x7", F7, from $35 to $75.00

#ME777, Universe Televiboat, 1970s, 15x4x7", F7, from $75 to $150.00

#ME801, Lunar explorer, 1970s, 12x6x4", F7, from $75 to $125.00

#ME821, giant cicada, 1970s, 10x4x4", F7, from $50 to.$100.00

#ME842, camel, discontinued, 10x4x7", F7, from $35 to .$50.00

#ME895, fire engine, 1970s, 10x4x4", F7, from $50 to.....$85.00

#MF032, Eastwind sedan, current, 6x2x2", F7, from $8 to $15.00

#MF033, pickup truck, current, 6x2x2", F7, from $8 to....$15.00

#MF046, sparking carbine, current, 18x5x1", F7, from $20 to $35.00

#MF083, sedan, current, 6x2x2", F7, from $8 to...............$15.00

#MF104, passenger plane, current, 9x10x3", F7, from $15 to $25.00

#MF111, ambulance, current, 8x3x3", F7, from $15 to $20.00

#MF134, tourist bus, current, 6x2x3", F7, from $15 to $25.00

#MF136, dbl-decker train, current, 8x2x3", F7, from $15 to $20.00

#MF146, construction truck, 1970s, 7x3x5", F7, from $35 to $75.00

#MF146, Volkswagon, current, 4x2x3", F7, from $10 to ..$15.00

#MF151, Shanghai pickup, 1970s, 12x4x4", F7, from $50 to $100.00

#MF154, tractor, 1970s, 5x3x4", F7, from $25 to.............$50.00

#MF155, airplane, discontinued, 13x11x4", F7, from $15 to $35.00

#MF163, fire truck, current, 6x2x3", F7, from $8 to.........$15.00

#MF170, train, current, 10x2x4", F7, from $15 to............$25.00

#MF171, convertible, current, 5x2x2", F7, from $8 to......$15.00

#MF185, dbl-decker bus, current, 11x5x3", F7, from $15 to $25.00

#MF193, soft-cover truck, 1970s, 11x3x4", F7, from $50 to $75.00

#MF201, oil tanker, current, 14x4x4", F7, from $15 to $25.00

#MF202, jetliner, discontinued, 9x4x3", F7, from $15 to .$25.00

#MF206, panda truck, current, 6x3x2", F7, from $10 to...$20.00

#MF216, airplane, discontinued, 9x9x3", F7, from $15 to $35.00

#MF239, tiger truck, current, 10x3x4", F7, from $15 to ...$30.00

#MF249, flying boat, 1970s, 6x6x2", F7, from $35 to.......$75.00

#MF254, Mercedes sedan, current, 8x4x3", F7, from $15 to $25.00

#MF274, tank, 1970s, 3x2x2", F7, from $8 to $15.00

#MF294, Mercedes sedan, litho, current, 7x3x2", F7, from $10 to $15.00

#MF304, race car, discontinued, 10x4x3", F7, from $15 to..$35.00

#MF310, Corvette, current, 3x2x3", F7, from $10 to........$15.00

#MF316, Corvette, 1953, MIB, F7, from $20.00 to $50.00.

#MF317, Corvette convertible, current, 10x4x3", F7, from $20 to $50.00

#MF320, Mercedes sedan, current, 7x3x2", F7, from $10 to $20.00

#MF321, Buick convertible, current, 11x4x3", from $20 to $50.00

#MF135, Red Flag Convertible, MIB, F7, from $35.00 to $75.00.

#MF321, Buick Convertible, 1951, MIB, F7, from $20.00 to $50.00.

#MF322, Buick sedan, current, 11x4x3", F7, from $20 to.$50.00

#MF326, Mercedes gull-wing sedan, current, 9x3x2", F7, from $15 to..$25.00

#MF330, Cadillac sedan, current, 11x4x3", F7, from $20 to..$50.00

#MF333, Thunderbird convertible, current, 11x4x3", F7, from $20 to...$50.00

#MF340, Cadillac convertible, current, 11x4x3", F7, from $20 to...$50.00

#MF712, locomotive, current, 7x2x3", F7, from $10 to....$15.00

#MF713, taxi, current, 5x2x2", F7, from $8 to.................$15.00

#MF714, fire chief car, current, 5x2x2", F7, from $8 to....$15.00

#MF716, ambulance, 1970s, 8x3x3", F7, from $15 to.......$30.00

#MF717, dump truck, discontinued, 10x3x3", F7, from $15 to $35.00

#MF718, ladder truck, current, 10x3x4", F7, from $15 to.$35.00

#MF721, light tank, current, 6x3x3", F7, from $15 to......$20.00

#MF722, jeep, current, 6x3x3", F7, from $15 to $20.00

#MF731, station wagon, current, 5x2x2", F7, from $8 to .$15.00

#MF732, ambulance, current, 5x2x2", from $8 to $15.00

#MF735, rocket racer, current, 7x3x3", F7, from $15 to...$25.00

#MF742, flying boat, current, 13x4x4", F7, from $15 to...$35.00

#MF743, Karmann Ghia sedan, current, 10x3x4", F7, from $15 to $45.00

#MF753, sports car, current, 8x3x2", F7, from $15 to.......$25.00

#MF763, sports car, current, 8x3x2", F7, from $15 to.......$25.00

#MF782, circus truck, current, 9x3x4", F7, from $15 to ...$25.00

#MF787, Lucky open car, current, 8x3x2", from $15..$25.00

#MF798, patrol car, current, 8x3x3", F7, from $15 to.......$25.00

#MF800, race car, discontinued, 6x2x2", F7, from $10 to..$25.00

#MF804, locomotive, current, 16x3x5", F7, from $15 to..$25.00

#MF844, dbl-decker bus, current, 8x4x3", F7, from $15 to.$20.00

#MF893, animal van, current, 6x2x3", F7, from $15 to....$20.00

#MF900, police car, current, 6x3x2", F7, from $8 to $15.00

#MF910, airport limo bus, current, 15x4x5", F7, from $20 to..$35.00

#MF923, torpedo boat, current, 8x3x3", F7, from $15 to .$25.00

#MF951, fighter jet, 1970s, 5x4x2", F7, from $15 to.........$25.00

#MF956, sparking tank, current, 8x4x3", F7, from $15 to .$20.00

#MF958, poultry truck, current, 6x2x2", F7, from $15 to.$20.00

#MF959, jeep, discontinued, 9x4x4", F7, from $15 to $20.00

#MF962, station wagon, 1970s, 9x3x3", F7, from $25 to..$45.00

#MF974, circus truck, current, 6x2x4", F7, from $15 to..$20.00

#MF985, fowl transporter, current, 8x2x3", F7, from $15 to...$20.00

#MF989, noisy locomotive, 1970s, 12x3x4", F7, from $25 to...$50.00

#MF993, mini car, current, 5x2x2", F7, from $8 to...........$15.00

#MF998, sedan, current, 5x2x2", F7, from $8 to..............$15.00

#MS002, jumping frog, current, 2x2x2", F7, from $8 to ...$15.00

#MS006, pecking chick, 1970s, 2x1x1", F7, from $8 to....$15.00

#MS011, roll-over plane, current, 3x4x2", F7, from $10 to $18.00

#MS014, single-bar excerciser, 1970s, 7x6x6", F7, from $25 to...$50.00

#MS042, swimming duck, current, 4x1x2", F7, from $8 to $15.00

#MS057, horse & rider, 1970s, 6x2x5", F7, from $18 to...$35.00

#MS058, old-fashioned car, current, 3x3x4", F7, from $12 to $20.00

#MS082, jumping frog, current, 2x2x2", F7, from $8 to ...$15.00

#MS083, jumping rabbit, current, 3x3x2", F7, from $8 to.$15.00

#MS085, xylophone girl, current, 7x3x9", F7, from $18 to.$35.00

#MS134, sparking jet, current, 5x5x3", F7, from $15 to ...$30.00

#MS203, train, current, 11x2x2", F7, from $8 to.............$15.00

#MS405, ice cream vendor, current, 4x3x4", F7, from $8 to $20.00

#MS505, jumping zebra, current, 5x2x4", F7, from $8 to .$20.00

#MS565, drumming panda/wheel, current, 5x3x5", F7, from $8 to $20.00

#MS568, sparrow, current, 5x2x2", F7, from $8 to $15.00

#MS569, oriole, current, 5x2x2", F7, from $8 to $15.00

#MS575, bear w/camera, current, 6x3x4", F7, from $15 to.$35.00

#MS702, motorcycle, current, 7x4x5", F7, from $15 to....$35.00

#MS704, bird music cart, 1970s, 3x2x5", F7, from $15 to .$25.00

#MS709, cycle w/sidecar, current, 7x4x5", F7, from $15 to .$35.00

#MS710, tricycle, current, 5x3x5", F7, from $15 to..........$20.00

#MS713, washing machine, current, 3x3x5", F7, from $15 to $20.00

#MS827, sedan, steering, 1970s, 9x3x3", F7, from $50 to..$75.00

#MS858, girl on goose, current, 5x3x5", F7, from $15 to .$25.00

#PMS102, rolling cat, current, 3x2x1", F7, from $15 to...$20.00

#PMS105, jumping dog, current, 3x2x6", F7, from $15 to...$25.00

#PMS106, jumping parrot, current, 3x2x6", F7, from $15 to..$25.00

#PMS108, duck family, current, 10x2x3", F7, from $15 to .$25.00

#PMS113, Fu dog, current, 4x2x3", F7, from $15 to.........$25.00

#PMS119, woodpecker, current, 3x2x6", F7, from $15 to .$25.00

#PMS210, clown on bike, current, 4x2x5", F7, from $15 to..$25.00

#PMS212, elephant on bike, current, 6x3x8", F7, from $15 to $35.00

#PMS213, duck on bike, current, 6x3x8", F7, from $15 to....$35.00

#PMS214, lady bug family, current, 13x3x1", F7, from $15 to $25.00

#PMS215, crocodile, current, 9x3x1", F7, from $12 to.....$20.00

#PMS217, jumping rabbit, current, 3x2x6", F7, from $15 to $25.00

#PMS218, penguin, current, 3x2x6", F7, from $15 to $30.00

#PS013, boy on tricycle, current, 2x4x4", F7, from $15 to..$25.00

Circus Toys

If you ever had the opportunity to go to one of the giant circuses as a child, no doubt you still have very vivid recollections of the huge elephants, the daring trapeze artists, the clowns and their trick dogs, and the booming voice of the ringmaster, even if that experience was a half century ago. Most of our circus toys are listed in other categories. See also Battery-Operated Toys; Cast Iron, Circus; Chein, Windups; Marx, Windups; Windups; Friction and Other Mechanicals.

Circus, Webber, 5 litho-on-wood animals, clown w/cloth outfit (9"), slotted stands, 1912, NM (EX box), A............$275.00
Circus Cage Wagon, Arcade, pnt wood wagon w/CI lion bank, CI wheels & horses, rpl driver, 14", VG, A..............$120.00
Clicker, litho tin clown hits golliwog w/mallet when clicker is depressed, possibly German, 4", EX+, A..................$160.00
Clown Roly Poly, France, pnt compo w/tan & blk costume, lt crazing & pnt loss, 8", VG, A..................................$190.00
Crandall's Great Show the Acrobats, Crandall, paper litho on wood, acrobats to join, orig box, 7¾", EX, A............$275.00
Daredevil Driver on Motorcycle, Arnold, on device opposite man in spoked cage, push to revolve, 11", NM (EX box), A..$550.00
Ferris Wheel, stamped steel w/CI benches, riders & base, clockwork w/chain drive, 17", G, A $475.00
Giant Ride Ferris Wheel, Ohio Art, 17", EX, J2.............$250.00

Jackies Acrobats, National Toy Mfg. Co., wooden box and characters, ca 1920s, VG, A, $85.00.

Mammoth Circus, Britains, 8 personnel & 13 animals, w/ring & stand, in orig box, 1955, figures: 4", A..................$1,265.00
Mammoth Show Circus Wagon, Reed, paper on wood, 4-wheeled, sliding top contains 3 animals, 2 trainers, 1890, 14", A $1,900.00
Polar Bear in Horse-drawn Circus Wagon, Reed, paper on wood, 2 dapple gray horses, trainer & bear inside, 26", A..$7,400.00
Ringling Bros Circus Truck, pnt pressed steel, blk w/red lion cage & wheels, plastic trim, wood lion, 25½", EX, A $300.00
Train Car, Converse, World's Greatest Shows, wood, animal in center cage, others at window, ca 1900, 10x20", VG, A..$325.00

Ringling's Performing Animals on Circus Wagon, paper litho animals, painted metal wagon, original box, 11", VG+, A, $160.00.

Comic Books

For more than a half a century, kids of America raced to the bookstand as soon as the new comics came in for the month and for 10¢ an issue kept up on the adventures of their favorite super heroes, cowboys, space explorers, and cartoon characters. By far most were eventually discarded — after they were traded one friend to another, stacked on closet shelves, and finally confiscated by Mom. Discount the survivors that were torn or otherwise damaged over the years and those about the mundane, and of those remaining, some could be quite valuable. In fact, first editions of high-grade comics books or those showcasing the first appearance of a major character often bring $500.00 and more. Rarity, age, and quality of the artwork are prime factors in determining value, and condition is critical. If you want to seriously collect comic books, you'll need to refer to a good comic book price guide such as Overstreet's. The examples we've listed here are worth from $5.00 and up; most of the higher end prices were realized at auction.

Action Comics #94, EX-, A..$90.00
Africa, Magazine Ent #1, Powell art, 1955, EX-, A...............$50.00
Air Fighters Comics #6, VG+, A $75.00
All Star #14, features Super Heroes, VG, A $267.00
All Winners #1, 1948, G+-VG, A $140.00
All Winners #6, patriotic cover, tears on cover, some chipped pgs, G+, A $130.00
Amazing Fantasy, Marvel #15, 1st appearance of Spiderman, Aug 1962, G, A $800.00
Amazing Spiderman & Captain America in Dr Doom's Revenge, Marvel #1, limited edition, 1989, NM, P3 ...$8.00
Andy Panda, Walter Lantz, 1943, EX, A $20.00
Animal Comics, Dell #5, Kelly art, 1943, NM, A $225.00
Bat Masterson #7, w/gun in front of window, 1961, VG, N2...$10.00
Best of the West, Magazine Ent #1, features Straight Arrow, Durango Kid, etc, 1951, EX, A................................$250.00
Bill Boyd Western, Fawcett #3, 1950, NM, A $95.00
Billy the Kid, Toby #3, 1951, EX, A................................$50.00

Blue Ribbon Comics #3, scarce, EX-EX+, A $113.00

Bobby Benson's B-Bar-B Riders, Parkway #9, Frazetta art, EX, A...$80.00

Bonanza #7, Ben, Hoss & Joe in Street; 1961, VG, N2 ....$10.00

Boris Karloff, Thriller #1, 1962, EX, N2.........................$20.00

Brave & Bold #34, features 1st Hawkman story, lt worn spine, EX+-NM, A...$300.00

Buck Rogers: Mile High #1, In the 25th Century, Calkin, 1993, M, A, $2,200.00; Mile High #2, 1933, EX-, A, $225.00.

Buck Rogers #3, 1933, minor spine roll, o/w EX, A........$236.00

Bugs Bunny, Trik 'N Treet Halloween Fun Comic #3, 1955, VG+, C1 ....$27.00

Buster Crabbe, Famous Funnies #1, Nov 1951, NM, A..$225.00

Captain America, Marvel Mini, Captain America for President on cover, P3...$75.00

Captain America #53, G+-VG, A $80.00

Captain Marvel #22, 1st Mr Mind story, VG, A...............$64.00

Captain Marvel #7, VG, A...$80.00

Captain Midnight, Fawcett #1, 1942, minor fading, o/w EX-, A...$502.00

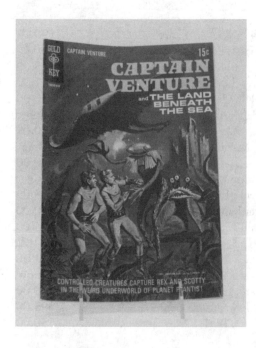

Captain Venture, Gold Key #10225-910, EX+, $16.00.

Car 54 Where Are You?, #1, 1961, VG, N2 ....$15.00

Cheyenne #734, NM $30.00

Cheyenne/Clint Walker #13, 1960, VG, N2 ....$10.00

Cisco Kid #37, 1957, VG, N2...$20.00

Close Encounters of the Third Kind, Marvel, Special Edition Supersize #1, M, F1 ....$10.00

Conan the Barbarian, Marvel #1, Oct 1970, NM, A........$88.00

Conan the Barbarian, Marvel #2, 1970, VG, N2.............$15.00

Detective #113, G+, A $50.00

Detective #61, some torn pgs, lt stain on bk, G, A..........$68.00

Detective #67, 1st Penguin cover, VG+, A $80.00

Dino (Flintstones), Charlton #13, missing cover, VG, P3.$75.00

Don Winslow of the Navy, Fawcett #1, Capt Marvel on cover, EX-F, A..$170.00

Donald Duck: Dell #178, 4-color, first Uncle Scrooge by Carl Barks, 1947, EX-, A, $185.00; Dell #203, 4-color, Carl Barks, slight tears along top edge, A, $130.00.

Gene Autry Comics, Mile High #1, Fawcett, NM, $2,000.00.

Double Life of Private Strong, Archie #1, June 1959, VG, A $85.00

Dr Kildare #4, 1962, EX, N2....................................$10.00

Earthman on Venus, Avon, 1951, EX, A.....................$375.00

Easter w/Mother Goose, Four Color #103, EX-EX+, A $24.00

Famous Feature Stories, Dell #1, features Terry & the Pirates, Tarzan, Don Winslow, etc, 1938, EX, A..................$236.00

Famous Funnies, Frazetta #212, July 1954, EX, A...........$205.00

Favorite Harvey Characters, American Airlines, 1973, EX-, P3 ....$10.00

Flash Gordon, Dell #10, Four Color, 1943, EX-, A $215.00

Flash Gordon, Harvey #1, Oct 1950, spine roll/minor creasing, o/w EX-, A $105.00

Gabby Hayes Western, Fawcett #1, 1948, EX-, A $100.00

Gene Autry March of Comics, K&K #39, 1949, EX-, A ..$50.00

Ghost #2, EX+-NM, A $130.00

Ghost #4, ½" tear on bk cover, EX+-NM, A.................$92.00

Ghost #5, ½" tear on bk cover, NM, A..........................$109.00

Ghost #6, EX+-NM, A $99.00

Ghost #9, EX+, A $45.00

Green Lantern #3, VG, A $341.00

Hopalong Cassidy, Fawcett #5, 1947, VG, A.................$45.00

Hopalong Cassidy: Mile High #1, Fawcett, 1943, NM, A, $1,900.00; Mile High #2, Fawcett, 1946, NM, A, $450.00.

Hi-Yo Silver The Lone Ranger to the Rescue, Dell, 1939, EX, A, $245.00; Heigh-Yo Silver The Lone Ranger, Whitman, 1938, EX, A, $245.00.

I Spy #3, Bill Cosby & Robert Culp standing bk to bk, 1967, EX, N2..$10.00

Jimmy Wakely, DC #1, Toth art, 1949, EX, A $135.00

John Wayne Adventure Comics, Toby Press #1, 1949, EX, A $625.00

Little Orphan Annie Sparkie Comic Book #2, 1941, EX, V1...$28.00

Lone Ranger, Dell #82, 4-color, 1945, EX-, A $70.00

Lone Ranger, Dell Giant #145, 1956, EX, A $145.00

Man From UNCLE #5, 1966, Robert Vaughn cover, EX, N2...$15.00

Mandrake the Magician #5, 1967, EX, N2 ....$6.00

Master of Kung Fu, Marvel #46, G, P3 ....$75.00

Mod Squad #1, 1969, VG, N2..$10.00

Monster #2, EX-EX+, A $73.00

Munsters, #4, NM, J2..$25.00

My Favorite Martian #1, Ray Walston in space suit, 1963, EX, N2...$25.00

New York World's Fair 1939, 1st Sandman, creased cb cover, G-, A $932.00

Out of the Night #1, 3 lt rounded edges, EX-EX+, A $160.00

Out of the Night #2, splits top & bottom of spine, lt creases, VG-, A...$20.00

Planet Comics #6, rusted staples, water stain on cover, G-, A $110.00

Pogo Parade, Dell #1, 1953, NM, A..............................$325.00

Pogo Possum, Dell, #8 and #9, 1952, both in NM condition, A, $65.00 each.

Popeye #32, fist through brick wall, 1955, G+, N2...........$10.00

Prince Valiant, Ace Comics-David McKay Publications, Feature Book #26, rare, 1937, EX, A.....................................$500.00

Prince Valiant, Street Enterprises #1, blk & wht, 1972, M, A...$25.00

Reprint Action Comics #1, Nestle Foods premium, 1987, NM, P3...$5.00

Richie Rich & Casper, Harvey #42, missing cover, VG, P3 ....$45.00

Rocket to the Moon, Avon, 1951, EX, A $456.00

Roy Rogers, Dell #124, Four Color, 1946, NM, A..........$225.00

Roy Rogers, Dell #137, Four Color, 1947, M, A.............$250.00

Roy Rogers, Dell #2, 1948, NM, A $205.00
Roy Rogers, Dell #86, Four Color, 1945, NM, A...........$275.00
Roy Rogers March of Comics #86, EX $25.00
Shadow, DC #1, Nov 1973, M, A $50.00
Shock SuspenStories, EC #1, 1952, EX, A $210.00
Shock SuspenStories #13, EX-EX+, A $85.00
Smiley Burnett Western, Fawcett #1, 1950, VG, A..........$65.00
Smokey Bear, True Story of Smokey Bear, 1969, EX, H4 ...$5.00
Snow Skiing, Bullwinkle & Rocky #5, 1971, VG, N2 ......$10.00
Snow White & the Seven Dwarfs, Dell #49, Four Color,
    1944, EX, A $101.00
Space Squadron #2, EX+-NM, A $132.00
Spiderman & the Human Torch, Marvel Team-Up #1, Mar
    1972, NM, A $50.00
Spy Thrillers, Atlas #1, 1954, EX, A............................$70.00
Star Trek, Gold Key, #7, M $10.00
Star Trek, Gold Key #1, 1967, EX, A..........................$175.00
Star Trek, Gold Key #3, Dec 1968, EX, A $85.00
Strange Tales, Marvel #101, featuring Human Torch, Oct 1962,
    minor fading, o/w EX-, A $110.00

Strange Worlds, Avon #1, Nov. 1950, VG+, A,
$185.00; Strange Worlds, Avon #3, June 1951,
EX+, A, $390.00.

Strange Worlds, Avon #4, Sept 1951, minor spine roll, o/w
    EX-, A $246.00
Super Goof, Whitman #67, EX-, P3 ....$75.00
Superman #11, 1" spine split, G-, A.............................$174.00
Superman #13, G, A..$152.00
Superman #15, G, A..$188.00
Superman #3, 4" spine tear from bottom, lt warping, scarce,
    G-G+, A $550.00
Superman #42, lt spine roll, VG-, A $75.00
Suspense Detective #1, sm tear on cover, EX-, A $71.00
Swamp Thing, DC #1, Nov 1972, M, A $33.00
Tales to Astonish #35, 2nd Ant Man, G+, A..................$70.00
Tales to Astonish #38, EX+-NM, A...............................$70.00
Tarzan, Single Series #20, Hal Foster, 1940, minor fading,
    o/w EX, A $286.00
Tom Mix, Ralston Premium #2, VG-, C1.......................$31.00
Twilight Zone #1, 1961, G+, N2..................................$10.00
Vault of Horror #15, A...$770.00

Walt Disney's Comics & Stories, K&K #40, features Donald &
    Nephews, 1944, EX, A...$95.00
Walt Disney's Davy Crockett at the Alamo, Dell, Fess Parker as
    Davy Crockett on cover, 1955, NM, A.....................$15.00
Walt Disney's Donald Duck, Dell #147, Four Color, 1947, EX,
    A $180.00
Walt Disney's Donald Duck, Dell #178, Four Color, features 1st
    Uncle Scrooge by Carl Barks, 1947, EX-, A $185.00
Walt Disney's Donald Duck, Dell #203, Four Color, 1948, EX-,
    A $130.00
Walt Disney's Vacation Parade, Dell Giant #1, 1950, NM,
    A $1,050.00
Western Hero, Fawcett #76, features Tom Mix, Monte Hall &
    Gabby Hayes, 1949, EX, A $75.00
Whiz Comics #18, 1" split on spine, G+-VG, A.............$100.00
World's Finest #7, features Green Arrow, VG-, A $160.00
Zane Grey's King of the Royal Mounted, Feature Books #1,
    McKay, 1936, VG, A...$75.00

Price Valiant Feature Book, Ace Comics #26, only Hal
Foster comic, rare, 1937, EX-, A, $500.00; Shadow
Comics, Mile High #1, 1940, NM, $5,400.00; Thunda
King of the Congo, Mile High #1, only comic done entirely
by Frazetta, all Thunda (no Cave Girl), 1½" tear, otherwise
NM, A, $975.00.

Corgi

Corgi vehicles are among the favorites of the diecast collectors; they've been made (in Great Britain) since 1956, and
they're still in production today. They were well detailed and
ruggedly built to last. Some of the most expensive Corgi's on
today's collector market are the character-related vehicles, James
Bond's (there are several variations), Batman's, and
U.N.C.L.E.'s, for instance that go for a minimum of $100.00.
Corgi Huskies were marketed exclusively through the Woolworth chain until 1970. Today most Huskies sell for $12.00 to
$20.00 if mint and in the original package; loose, mint-condi-
tion Huskies generally go for about $6.00 to $10.00 — **except** for
the ones we've listed below. After the Huskies' demise, the company produced Corgi Juniors, a 1/64 scale line.

For further information about Corgi automobiles, race cars, and
character cars we recommend our advisor Joe Corea (C5); our advisor for Corgi Huskies is Robert Reeves (R4). Values are for examples
mint and in the original packaging unless noted otherwise.

Automobiles and Race Cars

#C100, Porsche 956	$15.00
#C102, Opel Manta	$15.00
#C104, Toyota Corolla	$15.00
#C106, Saab 9000	$15.00
#C108, Chevrolet Z-28	$15.00
#C110, BMW 635	$15.00
#C113, Saab 900	$15.00
#C139, Porsche 911	$15.00
#C150, Chevrolet Camaro	$10.00
#C151, McLaren M19A Yardley	$30.00
#C152, Ferrari 312	$35.00
#C154, Lotus John Player	$40.00
#C155, Shadow F Racer	$35.00
#C156, Graham Hill's Shadow	$40.00
#C158, Elf Tyrrell Ford	$35.00
#C159, Indianapolis Racer	$35.00
#C163, Santa Pod Dragster	$60.00
#C167, USA Racing Buggy	$35.00
#C169, Starfighter Jet Dragster	$50.00
#C201, Mini 1000 Team Corgi	$20.00
#C257, Mercedes Benz 500SEC	$15.00
#C258, Toyota Celica Supra	$15.00
#C275, Mini Metro	$20.00
#C276, Triumph Acclaim	$15.00
#C277, Triumph Acclaim Driving School	$20.00
#C279, Rolls Royce	$15.00
#C279, Rolls Royce Corniche	$20.00
#C281, Metro Data Post	$20.00
#C284, Citroen SM	$40.00
#C285, Mercedes Benz 240D	$20.00
#C287, Citroen Dyane	$20.00
#C288, Minissima	$20.00
#C289, VW Polo	$20.00
#C289, VW Polo PTT	$30.00
#C291, Mercedes Benz 240 Rally	$20.00
#C293, Renault 5TS	$20.00
#C294, Renault 5TS Alpine	$15.00
#C299, Ford Sierra Ghia	$25.00
#C299, Sierra Rally	$20.00
#C300, Ferrari Daytona	$25.00
#C301, Lotus Elite Racer	$25.00
#C302, VW Polo	$20.00
#C303, Porsche 924 Racer	$20.00
#C306, Fiat Y 1.9S	$20.00
#C308, BMW M1	$15.00
#C308, Mini Cooper S	$75.00
#C309, VW Turbo	$15.00
#C310, Porsche 924 Turbo	$15.00
#C312, Ford Capri S	$15.00
#C314, Fiat X1.9	$35.00
#C314, Supercat Jaguar	$20.00
#C315, Lotus Elite	$50.00
#C318, Jaguar XJS Motul	$15.00
#C319, Lamborghini Miura	$40.00
#C323, Ferrari Daytona 365	$30.00
#C334, Ford Escort	$25.00

#C338, Rover 3500	$25.00
#C340, Rover Triplex	$15.00
#C341, Chevrolet Caprice	$15.00
#C345, Honda Prelude	$25.00
#C346, Citroen 2CV Charleston	$25.00
#C350, Toyota Celica Supra	$15.00
#C351, Ford Sierra Race Car	$15.00
#C352, BMW 325	$15.00
#C370, Ford Cobra Mustang	$25.00
#C373, Peugeot 50S	$25.00
#C374, Jaguar E 2.2 Litre	$70.00
#C374, Jaguar E 5.3 Litre	$70.00
#C378, Ferrari 308 GTS	$25.00
#C380, BMW M1 FASF	$15.00
#C381, Renault Turbo Elf	$15.00
#C382, Lotus Elite 2.2	$25.00
#C400, VW 1200 Corgi Driving School	$65.00
#C401, VW 1200 Corgi Driving School	$75.00
#C440, Porsche 944 Rally	$15.00
#C448, Jeep Renegade	$15.00
#Q330, Mini 30th-Anniversary	$20.00
#150, Surtees TS9 Formula 1	$40.00
#150, Vanwall Racer	$100.00
#151S, Lotus XI Racer	$100.00
#152S, BRM Racer	$100.00
#153, Bluebird Record Racer	$100.00
#153, Team Surtees	$40.00
#154, Ferrari Formula 1	$40.00
#155, Lotus Climax Racer	$50.00
#156, Cooper Maserati Racer	$50.00

Cooper Maserati F/1 Racer #156, 3½", VG+ (EX+ box), A, $45.00; Lotus-Climax Formula 1 Racing Car #155, 3½", MIB, A, $50.00.

#158, Lotus Climax Racer	$40.00
#159, Cooper Maserati	$50.00
#161, Elf Tyrrell	$40.00
#161, Santa Pod	$50.00
#162, Quartermaster Dragster	$60.00
#164, Wild Honey Dragster	$60.00
#165, Adams Brothers Dragster	$60.00
#166, Ford Mustang	$60.00
#170, John Woolfe Dragster	$50.00
#190, Lotus John Player	$70.00
#191, McLaren Texaco Marlboro	$70.00
#200, Ford Consul	$150.00
#200M, Ford Consul	$150.00

#201, Austin Cambridge	$150.00
#201M, Austin Cambridge	$150.00
#202, Morris Cowley	$200.00
#202M, Morris Cowley	$200.00
#203, De Tomaso Mangusta	$30.00
#203, Vauxhall Velox	$160.00
#203M, Vauxhall Velox	$160.00
#204, Morris Mini-Minor	$50.00
#204, Rover 90	$150.00
#205, Riley Pathfinder	$150.00
#205M, Riley Pathfinder	$150.00
#206, Hillman Husky Estate	$150.00
#206M, Hillman Husky Estate	$150.00
#207, Standard Vanguard III	$170.00
#207M, Standard Vanguard III	$150.00
#208M, Jaguar 2.4 Litre	$160.00
#208S, Jaguar 2.4 Litre	$130.00
#210, Citroen DS19	$130.00
#210S, Citroen DS19	$100.00
#211, Studebaker Golden Hawk	$200.00
#211M, Studebaker Golden Hawk	$160.00
#211S, Studebaker Golden Hawk	$160.00
#214, Ford Thunderbird Hardtop	$100.00
#214M, Ford Thunderbird Hardtop	$150.00
#214S, Ford Thunderbird Hardtop	$120.00
#215, Thunderbird Sport	$150.00
#216, Austin A40	$130.00
#216M, Austin A40	$200.00
#217, Fiat 1800 Saloon	$75.00
#218, Aston Martin DB4	$100.00
#219, Plymouth Suburban	$100.00
#220, Chevrolet Impala	$75.00
#222, Renault Floride	$80.00
#224, Bentley Continental	$80.00
#225, Austin 7 Mini	$90.00
#226, Morris Mini Minder	$95.00
#227, Mini Cooper Rally	$300.00
#228, Volvo P-1800	$100.00
#229, Chevrolet Corvair	$100.00
#230, Mercedes Benz Coupe	$80.00
#231, Triumph Herald	$100.00
#232, Fiat 2100	$75.00
#233, Heinkel Trojan	$75.00
#234, Ford Consul Classic	$100.00
#235, Oldsmobile Super 88	$80.00
#238, Jaguar MK10	$100.00
#238, Jaguar MK10, silver	$220.00
#239, VW Karmann Ghia	$80.00
#240, Fiat 600 Jolly	$100.00
#241, Chrysler Ghia	$75.00
#242, Fiat 600 Jolly	$75.00
#245, Buick Rivera	$80.00
#246, Chrysler Imperial, metallic color	$200.00
#246, Crysler Imperial	$125.00
#247, Mercedes Benz Pullman	$75.00
#248, Chevrolet Impala	$80.00
#249, Morris Mini Cooper	$125.00
#251, Hillman Imp	$80.00
#252, Rover 2000	$100.00
#253, Mercedes Benz Coupe	$100.00
#255, Motor School A60	$200.00
#259, Citroen Le Dandy	$100.00
#260, Renault 16TS	$60.00
#262, Lincoln Continental, lt bl & tan	$200.00
#262, Lincoln Continental, metallic gold & blk	$100.00
#263, Marlin Rambler	$70.00
#264, Oldsmobile Toronado	$60.00
#271, Ghia Mangusta de Tomaso	$45.00
#273, Honda Ballade	$50.00
#273, Rolls Royce Silver Shadow	$70.00
#274, Bentley	$80.00
#275, Rover 200TC	$90.00
#275, Royal Wedding Mini Metro	$30.00
#276, Oldsmobile Toronado	$60.00
#280, Rolls Royce Silver Shadow	$70.00
#281, Rover 2000TC	$60.00
#282, Mini Cooper Rally	$100.00
#283, DAF City Car	$40.00
#291, AMC Racer	$20.00
#300, Austin Healey 100-4	$125.00
#300, Corvette Stingray	$70.00
#301, Triumph TR2	$150.00
#302, Hillman Hunter Rally	$150.00
#302, MG MGA	$150.00
#303, Mercedes Benz 300SL, open	$100.00
#303, Roger Clark's Capri	$75.00
#303S, Mercedes Benz 300SL, open	$100.00
#304, Chevrolet Camaro	$70.00
#304, Mercedes Benz 300SL, hardtop	$100.00
#304S, Mercedes Benz 300SL, hardtop	$100.00
#305, Mini Marcos GT850	$50.00
#305, Triumph TR3	$150.00
#305S, Triumph TR3	$170.00
#306, Morris Marina	$75.00
#307, Jaguar E Type	$150.00
#307, Renault Turbo	$15.00
#309, Aston Martin DB4	$125.00
#310, Chevrolet Stingray	$75.00
#311, Ford Capri	$70.00
#312, Jaguar E Type	$120.00
#312, Marcos Mantis	$70.00
#313, Ford Cortina	$90.00
#314, Ferrari Berlinetta 250LM	$75.00
#315, Simca 1000 Sports	$80.00
#316, Ford GT70	$70.00
#316, NSU Sport Prinz	$60.00
#317, Mini Cooper Monte Carlo, 1964	$150.00
#318, Jaguar XJS	$20.00
#318, Lotus Elan	$100.00
#318, Lotus Elan S2	$150.00
#318, Mini Cooper Monte Carlo, 1965	$150.00
#319, Jaguar XJS	$35.00
#319, Lotus Elan, hardtop	$125.00
#320, Ford Mustang	$100.00
#321, Mini Cooper Monte Carlo, 1965, w/signatures	$500.00
#321, Porsche 924	$40.00

#322, Rover 2000 Monte Carlo	$180.00
#323, Citroen DS19 Monte Carlo, 1965	$180.00
#324, Ferrari Daytona Le Mans	$30.00
#324, Marcos Volvo 1800GT	$80.00
#325, Chevrolet Caprice	$30.00
#325, Ford Mustang Competition	$100.00
#327, Chevrolet Astro	$75.00
#327, MGB GT	$150.00
#328, Hillman Imp Monte Carlo, 1966	$200.00
#329, Ford Mustang	$65.00
#329, Opel Senator	$30.00
#331, Ford Capri Texaco	$30.00
#332, Lancia Fulvia Sports	$60.00
#333, Mini Cooper Sun/Rac	$350.00
#334, Mini Cooper Magnifique	$75.00
#335, Jaguar E Type	$125.00
#337, Chevrolet Stock Car	$70.00
#338, Chevrolet Camaro SS350	$100.00
#339, Mini Cooper Monte Carlo, 1967	$250.00
#340, Sunbeam Imp Monte Carlo, 1967	$150.00
#341, Mini Marcos GT850	$70.00
#342, Lamborghini P400 Miura	$60.00
#343, Ford Capri	$25.00
#343, Pontiac Firebird	$60.00
#344, Ferrari Dino	$65.00
#345, MGC GT	$120.00
#348, Mustang Pop Art	$130.00
#356, VW East African Rally	$200.00
#370, Ford Cobra Mustang	$15.00
#371, Porsche Carrera 6	$40.00
#372, Lancia Fulvia	$60.00
#375, Toyota 2000GT	$70.00
#376, Chevrolet Corvette Stock Car	$40.00
#377, Marcos 3 Litre	$50.00
#378, MGC GT	$90.00
#380, Alfa Romeo P33	$70.00
#381, VW Beach Buggy	$50.00
#382, Porsche Targa 911S	$70.00
#383, VW 1200, no decals	$70.00
#383, VW 1200 ADAC	$150.00
#383, VW 1200 Flower Power	$120.00
#383, VW 1200 Rally	$25.00
#384, Adams Brothers Probe	$60.00
#384, Renault 11GTL	$25.00
#385, Mercedes 190E	$25.00
#385, Porsche 917	$35.00
#386, Bertone Barchetta	$60.00
#386, Mercedes 2.3	$15.00
#387, Chevrolet Corvette Stingray	$75.00
#388, Mercedes Benz CIII	$60.00
#392, Bertone Shake Buggy	$60.00
#394, Datsun 240Z	$50.00
#394, Datsun 240Z East African Safari	$40.00
#396, Datsun 240Z John Morton	$50.00
#397, Porsche-Audi 917	$25.00
#399, Peugeot 205	$15.00
#402, BMW M1	$15.00
#403, Ford Escort	$15.00

#404, Rover 3500	$15.00
#420, BMW M1	$15.00
#422, Renault 5	$15.00
#423, Ford Escort	$15.00
#424, Ford Mustang	$15.00
#424, Ford Zephyr Estate	$120.00
#426, Rover Hepo Lite	$15.00
#435, Volvo 760 Turbo	$15.00
#440, Ford Cortina Estate	$175.00
#445, Plymouth Suburban Sport	$100.00
#485, Mini Countryman	$150.00
#491, Ford Cortina Estate	$100.00
#600, Ford Escort	$25.00
#601, Fiat N-9	$25.00
#602, BL Mini 1000	$25.00
#602, BL Mini 1000, chrome plated	$100.00
#603, VW Polo	$25.00
#604, Renault 5	$25.00
#605, Austin Mini Metro	$25.00

Character — Related Vehicles

Basil #865	$50.00
Basil Brush's Car #808	$200.00
Batbike #268	$50.00
Batboat #107, on trailer	$120.00
Batcopter #925	$60.00
Batmobile #267, 1st issue, photo box	$350.00
Batmobile #267, 2nd issue, window box	$200.00
Batmobile #267, 3rd issue, whizz wheels	$100.00
Beatle's Yellow Submarine #803	$50.00
Brian Snail #864	$50.00
Buck Rogers Starfighter #647	$60.00
Captain America Jetmobile #263	$40.00
Captain Marvel Porsche #262	$60.00
Charlie's Angels Chevy Van #434	$40.00
Chevrolet Kennel Truck #486	$100.00
Chipperfield Circus Animal Cage #1123	$125.00
Chipperfield Circus Booking Office #426	$250.00
Chipperfield Circus Crane & Cage #1144	$400.00
Chipperfield Circus Crane Truck #1121	$250.00
Chipperfield Circus Elephant Cage #607	$70.00
Chipperfield Circus Giraffe Transport #503	$150.00
Chipperfield Circus Horse Transporter #1130	$250.00
Chipperfield Circus Menagerie Transporter #1139	$500.00
Chipperfield Circus Parade Rover #487	$200.00
Chipperfield Circus Poodle Pickup #511	$450.00
Chitty Chitty Bang Bang, 25th-Anniversary model	$40.00
Chitty Chitty Bang Bang #266	$350.00
Citroen Alpine Rescue #513	$350.00
Citroen Olympic 1964 Winter #475	$150.00
Citroen Olympic 1968 Winter #499	$150.00
Citroen Ski Club #475	$150.00
Daily Planet Jetcopter #929	$50.00
Dick Dastardly's Car #809	$150.00
Dolphin Cabin Cruiser #104, on trailer	$50.00
Dolphinarium #1164	$80.00
Dougal #860	$50.00

Dougal's Car #807..$200.00
Dylan #868..$50.00
Ermit Rude #866..$50.00
Florence #861..$50.00
Green Hornet #268......................................$450.00

Green Hornet Black Beauty Racer, Corgi/Greenway, 1966, diecast, 5" long, VG, $150.00.

Hardy Boys #805..$250.00
Incredible Hulk Mazda Pickup #264.............$50.00
James Bond Aston Martin #270, bubble pkg.....$300.00
James Bond Aston Martin #270, silver..........$225.00
James Bond Aston Martin #271, silver............$50.00
James Bond Aston Martin DB5 #261, gold......$250.00
James Bond Citroen #272...............................$50.00
James Bond Drax Helicopter #930..................$50.00
James Bond Lotus #269...................................$75.00
James Bond Moon Buggy #811.......................$400.00
James Bond Mustang #391.............................$200.00
James Bond Space Shuttle #649.......................$60.00
James Bond Stromberg Helicopter #926...........$60.00
James Bond Toyota 2000 GT #336..................$300.00
Jean Richard Circus Booking Office #426.........$40.00
Jean Richard Circus Human Cannon Truck #1163...$50.00
Kojak Buick #290...$60.00
Lunar Bug #806..$200.00
Magic Roundabout Playground #853.............$1,200.00
Magic Roundabout Train #851.......................$350.00

Man From UNCLE Car, Oldsmobile Super 88, blue, two passengers, 4¼", NM, $125.00.

Man From UNCLE #497, bl..........................$200.00
Man From UNCLE #497, wht........................$350.00
Mini-Mostest #349.....................................$1,000.00
Monkeemobile #277.....................................$250.00
Mr McHenry's Trike & Zebedee #859.............$250.00
Mr Rusty #863...$50.00
Musical Carousel #852..................................$400.00
NASA Space Shuttle #648..............................$50.00
Noddy's Car #801, Blk-faced Golly...............$1,000.00
Noddy's Car #801, tan-faced Golly................$350.00
Noddy's Car #804...$300.00
Penguinmobile #259......................................$50.00
Popeye Paddle Wagon #802...........................$500.00
Public Address Land Rover #472...................$100.00
Saint's Jaguar #320.......................................$60.00
Saint's Volvo #201, w/o driver.....................$120.00
Saint's Volvo #258, w/Saint driver................$160.00
Spider Buggy #261..$50.00
Spiderbike #266...$40.00
Spidercopter #928..$60.00
Spiderman Chevy Van #436............................$50.00
Starsky & Hutch Ford Torino #292.................$60.00
Superman Chevy Van #435.............................$50.00
Superman Police Car #260..............................$60.00
Supermobile #265...$50.00
Tour de France Manager's Car #510..............$100.00
Vegas Ford Thunderbird #348..........................$75.00
Wildlife Safari Citroen #436.........................$120.00
Zebedee #862...$50.00

Huskies

Aston Martin DB6, metallic bronze, gray wheels, MIP, R4..$25.00
Aston Martin DB6, purple or metallic olive, metal wheels w/blk tires, MIP, R4..............................$25.00
Batmobile, MIP, R4......................................$100.00
Batmobile w/Batboat, MIP, R4.....................$150.00
Buick Electra Police Car, dk bl w/red logo, gray plastic wheels, MIP, R4................................$25.00
Buick Electra Police Car, lt bl w/red logo, gray plastic wheels, MIP, R4................................$25.00
Chitty Chitty Bang Bang Car, MIP, R4..........$100.00
Crime Busters Set, MIP, R4...........................$400.00
Hoyner Car Transporter, MIP, R4...................$50.00
James Bond Aston Martin, MIP, R4...............$100.00
Machinery Low-Loader, MIP, R4.....................$50.00
Man From UNCLE Car, MIP, R4....................$100.00
Monkeemobile, MIP, R4...............................$100.00
Removals Delivery Van, MIP, R4......................$50.00

Corgi Juniors

#1, Mercedes Benz Binz Ambulance, wht, MBP, J1............$3.00
#1, Zakespeed Ford Capri Racer, '9 Duckhams,' MBP, J1..$2.00
#10, Aston Martin DB6, yel, MBP, J1...............$3.00
#103, Ford Transit Wrecker, 'Police Wrecker,' wht, MBP, J1...$3.00
#1077, Tom & Jerry Car, MOC, T1.................$15.00

#12, Iveco Tanker Truck, 'BP Oil' on tank, gr & chrome, MBP, J1...$3.00

#121, '57 T-Bird Convertible, red, w/opening hood, MIB, J1 ....$3.00

#122, Mercedes 300SL Gullwing, silver, MBP, J1..............$2.50

#123, Mustang Hatchback, 'Ford Cobra,' wht, MIB, J1 ......$3.00

#13, Iveco Bottle Truck, 'Pepsi,' red, wht & bl, MBP, J1....$3.00

#178, 6-Wheel Container Truck, 'Dunlop,' wht, MIB, J1 ..$3.00

#18, Jaguar XJS, wht, MBP, J1..$2.50

#19, Pink Panther Motorcycle, pk, M, G3 ....$6.00

#206, '60s Buick Regal Sedan, gr, MBP, J1.......................$2.50

#23, Renault 5 Turbo, 'Elf,' dk bl, MIB, J1 ....$2.50

#24, Ford Transit Wrecker, 'BP Rescue' on boom, yel & red, MBP, J1..$3.00

#29, Mercedes 500SL Coupe, blk, MIB, J1........................$3.00

#30, BMW M3, '5 Silverstone,' yel, MIB, J1 ....$3.00

#31, Land Rover Wrecker, red & silver, MBP, J1 ....$3.50

#32, Ferrari 308 GTS, 'Ferrari' on sides, red, MBP, J1 ....$2.00

#34, Adidas Van, bl, M, G3 ....$5.00

#35, Porsche 911 Turbo, 'Shell' on sides, blk, MIB, J1 ....$3.00

#36, Ferrari Testarossa, red, MIB, J1................................$2.50

#4, Ford Transit Van, 'Porsche Kremer Racing,' wht, MBP, J1 ....$2.50

#45, Corvette, 'Vette,' red & wht, MBP, J1 ....$2.00

#45, Starsky & Hutch Police, red, M, G3..........................$6.00

#46, Pontiac Firebird, silver, MBP, J1 ....$2.00

#48, Jeep 4X4, wht w/red interior, MIB, J1 ....$2.50

#49, Army Jeep, 'USA,' army gr w/tan roof, MIB, J1 ....$3.00

#52, Refuse Truck, 'NBC,' orange, MIB, J1.......................$3.00

#58, Ford Sierra Police, 'Police,' wht, MIB, J1 ....$3.00

#58, Tom's Go-Cart, yel, M, G3..$5.00

#59, Mercedes 240D, dk bl, MIB, J1.................................$3.00

#59, Range Rover Emergency Vehicle, 'Mountain Rescue,' red, MIB, J1..$3.00

#61, Custom Van, wht, MBP, J1.......................................$3.00

#66, Centurion Tank, olive, M, G3....................................$5.00

#7, ERF Fire engine, 'Fire,' red & silver, MBP, J1 ....$3.00

#8, Simon Snorkel Fire Engine, 'Snorkel' on boom, red & wht, MBP, J1...$3.00

#80, Porsche 911, Carrera blk, MBP, J1 ....$2.50

#84, Volvo 760, silver, MIB, J1..$2.50

#86, Fiat X 1.9, MBP, J1 ....$2.50

#86, Porsche 935, '74 Lucas,' lt bl, MIB, J1 ....$3.00

#90, Mercedes 2.3, maroon, MIB, J1 ....$2.50

#91, Jaguar XJ40, dk gr, MIB, J1.....................................$3.00

#98, Porsche, Targa red, MIB, J1 ....$3.00

Dakins

Dakin has been an importer of stuffed toys as far back as 1955, but it wasn't until 1959 that the name of this San Francisco-based company actually appeared on the toy labels. They produced three distinct lines: Dream Pets (1960 - early '70s), Dream Dolls (1965 - mid-'70s) , and licensed characters and advertising figures, starting in 1968. Of them all, the latter series was the most popular and the one that holds most interest for collectors. Originally there were seven Warner Brothers

characters. Each was made with a hard plastic body and a soft vinyl head, all under 10" tall. All in all, more than 50 cartoon characters were produced, some with several variations. Advertising figures were made as well. Some were extensions of the three already existing lines; others were competely original.

Goofy Grams was a series featuring many of their character figures mounted on a base lettered with a 'goofy' message. They also utilized some of their large stock characters as banks in a series called Cash Catchers. A second bank series consisted of Warner Brothers characters molded in a squatting position and therefore smaller. In 1974 nine licensed characters were produced as squeeze toys, and the last plastic line the company produced was the Hanna-Barbera park set (1980-1982). Our advisor for this category is Jim Rash (R3).

Baby Puss, Hanna-Barbera, 1971, EX-NM, R3 ....$100.00

Baby Puss, Hanna-Barbera, 1971, MIP, R3...................$175.00

Bambi, Disney, 1960s, MIP, C1/R3...............................$36.00

Bamm-Bamm, Hanna-Barbera, 1970, MIP, R3...............$50.00

Banana Splits Fleagle Beagle the Dog, 1970, EX-NM, $100.00. (MIB, $150.00.)

Barney Rubble, Hanna-Barbera, 1970, MIP, R3 ....$50.00

Bozo the Clown, MIP..$60.00

Bugs Bunny, Warner Bros, 1971, MIP, R3 ....$30.00

Bugs Bunny, Warner Bros, 1976, MIB (cartoon threatre box), R3 ....$40.00

Bullwinkle, Jay Ward, 1976, EX-NM, R3 ....$45.00

Bullwinkle, soft vinyl & hard plastic, 1976, MIB (cartoon theater box), R3 ....$75.00

Bullwinkle, stuffed fur w/wht felt antlers & hands, red felt sweater w/gr letter B, orig tag, 1978, M, C1..............$29.00

Cool Cat, w/tag, EX, H4..............$40.00

Cool Cat, Warner Bros, 1969, MIP, R3..............$50.00

Daffy Duck, Warner Bros, 1968, EX-NM, R3..............$25.00

Daffy Duck, Warner Bros, 1976, MIB (cartoon threatre box)..............$40.00

Deputy Dawg, Terrytoons, 1977, MIP, R3..............$60.00

Dewey Duck, Disney, red shirt, MIP, R3..............$30.00

Dino Dinosaur, Hanna-Barbera, 1970, MIP, R3..............$60.00

Dino Dinosaur, hard plastic body w/soft vinyl head, name tag on collar, 1970, 8", R3..............$40.00

Dog in Suit, Goofy Gram, Have a Dog-Gone Good Time, 1971, 8", R3..............$40.00

Donald Duck, Disney, MIP, R3..............$35.00

Dudley Do-Right, Jay Ward, MIB (cartoon theater box), R3..............$75.00

Dumbo, Disney, MIP, R3..............$30.00

Elmer Fudd, in hunting outfit, missing rifle, H4..............$75.00

Elmer Fudd, in tuxedo, 1968, MIP, R3..............$40.00

Foghorn Leghorn, Warner Bros, 1970, EX-NM, R3..............$75.00

Foghorn Leghorn, Warner Bros, 1970, MIP, R3..............$125.00

Fred Flintstone, Hanna-Barbara, 1970, MIP, P6/R3..............$50.00

Fred Flintstone, missing bl felt tie, VG, H4..............$12.00

Glamour Kitty, w/gold crown & red cape, 1978, 5", R3..............$150.00

Goofy, Disney, cloth clothes, MIP, R3..............$30.00

Goofy, soft vinyl head on hard plastic body, yel molded shirt, 1978, 5", R3..............$40.00

Hokey Wolf, Hanna-Barbera, 1971, MIP, R3..............$400.00

Hoppy Hopperoo, MIP, H4..............$99.00

Huckleberry Hound, Hanna-Barbera, 1970, MIP, R3..............$100.00

Huey Duck, Disney, gr shirt, MIP, R3..............$30.00

Jack-in-the-Box, bank, 1971, 6", R3..............$40.00

Laurel or Hardy, 1968, w/orig tag, MIP, C1..............$35.00

Louie Duck, Disney, bl shirt, MIP, R3..............$30.00

Merlin Magic Mouse, Warner Bros, 1970, MIP, R3..............$40.00

Mickey Mouse, Disney, MIP, R3..............$30.00

Mighty Mouse, Terrytoons, 1977, MIP, R3..............$175.00

Mighty Mouse, w/cape, lt worn pnt, sm teeth marks, H4..............$55.00

Minnie Mouse, Disney, MIP, R3..............$30.00

Olive Oyl, King Features, cloth clothes, 1974, MIP, R3..............$60.00

Olive Oyl, molded clothes, 1976, MIB (cartoon theater box)..............$60.00

Oliver Hardy, Larry Harmon, 1974, MIP, R3..............$40.00

Pebbles, Hanna-Barbera, 1970, MIP, R3..............$50.00

Pepe LePew, Warner Bros, 1971, EX-NM, H4/R3..............$75.00

Pepe LePew, Warner Bros, 1971, MIP, R3..............$125.00

Pink Panther, Mirisch-Freleng, 1971, MIP, R3..............$50.00

Pink Panther, Mirisch-Freleng, 1976, MIB (cartoon theater box), R3..............$50.00

Pinocchio, Disney, MIP, R3..............$30.00

Pluto, Disney, MIP, R3..............$35.00

Popeye, King Features, 1974, MIP, R3..............$60.00

Popeye, King Features, 1976, MIB (cartoon theater box), R3..............$60.00

Porky Pig, Warner Bros, 1968, MIP, R3..............$30.00

Purple Poodle, Goofy Gram, It Was Sweet of You, 1971, 8", R3..............$40.00

Roadrunner, Warner Bros, 1968, MIP, R3..............$30.00

Roadrunner, Warner Bros, 1976, MIB (cartoon theater box), R3..............$40.00

Rocky Squirrel, Jay Ward, 1976, 5", EX-NM, R3..............$45.00

Hokey Wolf, 1971, EX-NM, $250.00.
(Photo courtesy Suzan Hufferd.)

Rocky Squirrel, 7", MIB, from $60.00 to $75.00.

Scooby Doo, Hanna-Barbera, 1971, EX-NM, R3 ....$75.00
Scrappy Doo, Hanna-Barbera, 1971, EX-NM, R3 ....$75.00
Seal w/Ball, bank, 1971, 8", R3......................................$40.00
Second Banana, Warner Bros, 1970, EX-NM, from $28
  to $35.00
Second Banana, Warner Bros, 1970, MIP, R3.................$50.00
Smokey Bear, 1976, MIB (cartoon theater box), R3 ....$35.00
Snagglepuss, Hanna-Barbera, 1971, EX-NM, R3 ....$100.00
Snagglepuss, Hanna-Barbera, 1971, MIP, R3 ....$150.00
Speedy Gonzales, vinyl, movable arms & legs, in gr top, wht
  pants, red scarf, yel sombrero, 1969, 8", NM, T2......$24.00
Speedy Gonzales, Warner Bros, 1976, MIB (cartoon theater
  box), R3..$40.00
Stan Laurel, Larry Harmon, 1974, MIP, R3....................$40.00
Swee' Pea, King Features, beanbag, 1974, EX-NM, R3 ...$25.00
Sylvester, Warner Bros, 1969, MIP, C1/R3 ....$30.00

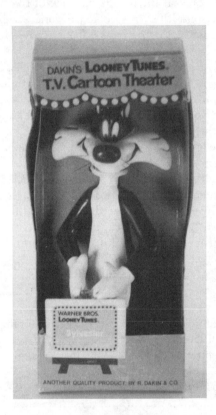

Sylvester, ca 1976, MIB, $40.00.

Tasmanian Devil, Warner Bros, mk Fun Farm, 1978, EX-
  NM, R3 ....$300.00
Tasmanian Devil, Warner Bros, mk Fun Farm, 1978, MIP,
  R3 ....$500.00
Tweety Bird, bank, Looney Tunes, EX $20.00
Tweety Bird, vinyl, yel & orange, movable arms, swivel
  head & feet, separate hair tuft, orig tag, 1969, 8", EX+,
  O1/T2 ....$32.00
Tweety Bird, Warner Bros, molded arms & hair tuft, 1969,
  MIP, R3 ....$30.00
Tweety Bird, Warner Bros, 1976, MIB (cartoon theater box),
  R3...$40.00
Uncle Bugs Bunny, Warner Bros, 1975, MIP, R3............$60.00

Tasmanian Devil, 1978, EX-NM, $300.00; Mighty
Mouse, 1977, EX-NM, $125.00. (Photo courtesy
Suzan Hufferd.)

Underdog, Leonardo TV, 1976, EX-NM, R3 ....$85.00
Underdog, Leonardo TV, 1976, MIP, R3 ....$150.00
Wile E Coyote, Warner Bros, 1968, MIP, R3 ....$30.00
Wile E Coyote, Warner Bros, 1976, MIB (cartoon theater
  box) $40.00
Wile E Coyote, wht & brn plush, w/orig tag, 1977, 11", M,
  C1/J2 ....$27.00
Yogi Bear, Hanna-Barbera, 1970, MIP, R3....................$100.00
Yosemite Sam, vinyl, posable arms & legs, in yel cloth top, bl
  pants, red scarf & blk accessories, 1969, 8", EX+......$20.00
Yosemite Sam, Warner Bros, molded clothes, 1978, EX-NM,
  R3..$20.00
Yosemite Sam, Warner Bros, 1968, MIP, R3 ....$30.00

Advertising

Bay View Eagle, 1976, EX-
NM, R3, $35.00. (Photo
courtesy Suzan Hufferd.)

Bob's Big Boy, 1974, EX-NM, R3 ....$100.00
Bob's Big Boy, 1974, MIP, R3 ....$200.00
Diaparene Baby, molded vinyl, 1980, 5", EX-NM $35.00
Freddy Fastgas, 1976, MIP, R3 ....$125.00
Glamour Kitty, 1977, EX-NM, R3 ....$150.00
Hobo Joe, 1977, EX-NM, R3 ....$150.00
Kernal Renk, American Seeds, 1977, rare, EX-NM, R3.$400.00
Li'l Miss Just Rite, 1965, EX-NM, R3 ....$60.00
Miss Liberty Belle, 1975, EX-NM, R3..........................$50.00
Miss Liberty Belle, 1975, MIP, R3 ....$125.00
Quasar Robot, 1975, MIP, R3.....................................$200.00

Sambo Boy, 1974, 8¾", $80.00.

Sambo's Tiger, 1974, EX-NM, R3 ....$200.00
Skunk, Western Railroad Goofy Gram, 1972, R3 ....$100.00
Smokey Bear, 1974, MIP, R3 ....$40.00
Woodsy Owl, 1974, EX-NM, R3....................................$50.00
Woodsy Owl, 1974, MIP, R3 ....$75.00
Woodsy Owl, w/clothes, 1960s, EX, T1 ....$25.00

Diecast

Diecast replicas of cars, trucks, planes, trains, etc., represent a huge corner of today's collector market, and their manufacturers see to it that there is no shortage. As far back as the 1920s, Tootsietoy had the market virtually by themselves, but one by one other companies had a go at it, some with more success than others. Among them were the American companies of Barclay, Hubley, and Manoil, all of whom are much better known for other types of toys. After the war, Metal Masters, Smith-Miller, and Doepke Ohlsson-Rice (among others) tried the market with varying degrees of success. Some companies were phased out over the years, while many more entered the market with fervor. Today it's those fondly-remembered models from the fifties and sixties that many collectors yearn to own. Solido produced well-modeled, detailed little cars; some had dome lights that actually came on when the doors were opened. Politoy's were cleanly molded with good detailing and finishes. Mebetoys, an Italian company that has been bought out by Mattel, produced several; and some of the finest come from Brooklyn, whose Shelby (signed) GT-350H Mustang can easily cost you from $900.00 to $1,000.00 when you can find one.

If you're interested in Majorette Toys, we recommend *Collecting Majorette Toys* by Dana Johnson; ordering information is given with Dana's listing under Diecast in the section called Categories of Special Interest in the back of the book. Other diecast makers are listed in specific categories. See also Corgi; Dinky; Diecast Collector Banks; Tootsietoy; Hot Wheels; Matchbox.

ADJ, Citroen CX Station Wagon, Fire Chief, red, MIB, L1 ....$30.00
Alezan, Alfa Romeo Evoluzion, dk red, MIB, L1 ....$75.00
AMR, Abarth 1300, limited edition, red, MIB, L1 ....$375.00
AMR, Mercedes 500SCL, off-wht, MIB, L1 ....$95.00
AMR, Morgan 2+2 Convertible, wht, MIB, L1 ....$65.00
AMR, Renault Alpine, limited edition, red, MIB, L1 ...$250.00
Autopilen/Intercar, Corvette Stingray, coral, M, L1 ......$35.00
Autopilen/Intercar, Monteverdi Hai, metallic gray, MIB, L1 ....$35.00
Autopilen/Intercar, Vauxhall Service, metallic mauve, M, L1 ....$30.00
Autoreplica, Amilcar Italiana, bl, NMIB+, L1 ....$45.00
Autoreplica, Morgan +4, wht, NMIB, L1 ....$35.00
Bandi, 1962 Volkswagen Sedan #742, MIB, L5.............$195.00
Benbros, Electric Milk Trolley #7, 1/64 scale, orange, w/driver, ca early 1950s, EX+, W1 ....$20.00
Bendros, Electric Milk Trolley #7, 1/64 scale, bl, early 1950s, NMIB...$22.50
Box, #8415 Ferrari 57, 250 GT Mille Miglia, red, MIB, L1...$22.00
Box, #8417 Ferrari, 275 GTB (street version), yel, MIB, L1...$22.00
Box, #8422 Shelby Cobra '98,' red, MIB, L1 ....$28.00
Box, #8426 Ferrari 62, 250TDF, red, MIB, L1 ....$22.00
Brooklyn, #13 Thunderbird Coupe, red, MIB, L1...........$65.00
Brooklyn, #31 Pontiac 'Modelex 92,' metallic gr, MIB, L1 ....$175.00
Brooklyn, #6 Packard Light 8 Coupe, beige & brn, MIB, L1 ....$65.00
Brooklyn, Special Version 1941 Packard Clipper, metallic bronze, 1 of 400 made, U1 ....$700.00
Brooklyn, 1930 Ford 'A' Fire Prevention Vehicle, red & bl, no printing on box, U1 ....$175.00
Brooklyn, 1933 Pierce Silver Arrow, lt bl, U1..............$160.00
Brooklyn, 1934 Chrysler Air Flow, navy bl, silver box, very rare, U1...$550.00

Brooklyn, 1935 Dodge Van 'Sears Roebuck,' navy bl, U1 .$260.00

Brooklyn, 1936 Dodge Van 'Litchfield,' U1 ....$250.00

Brooklyn, 1940 Chrysler Newport, lime gr, silver box, U1 ....$550.00

Brooklyn, 1949 Buick Roadmaster, metallic gray, U1 ...$165.00

Brooklyn, 1955 Chevy Nomad, CTCS 1987 Show, red, U1 ....$300.00

Brooklyn, 1955 Chrysler 300C, red, U1 ....$150.00

Brooklyn, 1957 Ford Fairlane Skyliner, CTCS 1991 Show, gr, U1 ....$325.00

Brumm, #r024 Fiat 500C Topolino, Fire Chief, red, MIB, L1...$15.00

Brumm, #r070 Mercedes 1937 Formula 1, W25, silver, MIB, L1 ....$15.00

Brumm, #r091 Alfa-Romeo Police, bl, MIB, L1 ....$15.00

Brumm, #r105, Jaguar XK 120, blk, MIB, L1 ....$35.00

Buccaneer, Daimler, spare tire, bl, U1 ....$80.00

Budgie, Dump Truck #18, 1/64 scale, red & gray, ca 1950s, EX, W1 ....$15.00

Budgie, Rover Squad Car Sedan #30, 1/64 scale, red rpt bl, 1950s, G, W1 ....$9.00

Budgie, VW Micro Van #12, 1/64 scale, bl, ca 1950s, G, W1 ....$20.00

Can Am, 1980 Citroen SM Presidentielle Convertible, dk silver, MIB, L1 ....$100.00

CCC, Delahaye Fire T-140, red, MIB, L1 ....$135.00

Century, #008 Mercedes 300CE Coupe, dk metallic bl, MIB, L1 ....$95.00

Century, #014 Lincoln Continental, silver & blk, MIB, L1 ....$95.00

CIJ, #3.15a Chrysler Windsor, gr, MIB, L1 ....$115.00

CIJ, #3.20 Panhard Tanker 'Energol,' gr, MIB, L1...........$95.00

CKO, Ferrari Formula I, red, U1 ....$125.00

CKO, Mercedes Taxi, 4-door, cream, U1 ....$125.00

CKO, VW Pickup, bl, U1 ....$145.00

Conquest, #1 Olds Starfire 98 Convertible, bl & wht, MIB, L1...$185.00

Conquest, #2 Buick Special Sedan, fawn & bl, MIB, L1.$185.00

Conrad, #1015 VW Santana, silver, M, L1 ....$45.00

Conrad, #1034 Mercedes Race Car Carrier, bl & silver, MIB, L1 ....$75.00

Conrad, #3053 Mercedes Tanker 'Messer Griessheim,' dk bl & wht, MIB, L1 ....$75.00

Cragstan/Sabra, Chevy Corvair Coupe, bright gr, M, L1..$45.00

Cragstan/Sabra, Chevy Impala Coupe, dk red, M, L1......$55.00

Cragston, VW Beetle, blk, U1 ....$80.00

Crescent, #1285 BRM Formula 1 Car, bright gr, MIB, L1 .$150.00

Cursor Modell, Matador Van Pickup, bl, NM, U1 ....$70.00

Cursor Modell, VW Bus, lt gray, 4", M, U1 ....$120.00

DCMT River Series, Open Lorry, Military Truck, olive drab, MIB, L1 ....$75.00

Dinkum, Ford Falcon GT, red & blk, MIB, L1 ....$95.00

Dinkum, Holden FJ Panel Van, dk bl, MIB, L1 ....$85.00

Dubray, Peugeot 402, spare tire, blk, M, L1 ....$55.00

Dubray, Renault Viva Grand Sport Convertible, bl & blk, MIB, L1 ....$55.00

Eko, #6005 Hispano Suiza Alphonso XIII Convertible, red & cream, M, L1 ....$15.00

Eko, #6010 Daimer 1911 Convertible, silver, M, L1 ....$10.00

Eligor, #1003 Delage D8 Open Cabriolet, pale bl, MIB, L1...$22.00

Eligor, #1005 Citroen Rosalie Sedan, med bl, MIB, L1 ...$22.00

Eligor, #1030 Rolls Royce Limousine, silver, MIB, L1.....$18.00

Eligor, #1044 Mercedes, Hotel Kaiserhof Limousine, brn, MIB, L1 ....$30.00

Eligor, #1048 Bentley T Saloon, navy, MIB, L1 ....$22.00

Eligor, #1080, Ford Pickup, blk, MIB, L1.....................$18.00

Eligor, #1082 Ford V8 'Trenton' Fire Department, red, MIB, L1 ....$25.00

Eligor, #1084 Ford V8 'Washington' Fire Department, red, MIB, L1 ....$25.00

Eligor, #1221 Ford Tudor Ambulance, wht, MIB, L1 ......$25.00

Erie, Packard, sky bl & gold, M (rstr), L1 ....$25.00

Esdo, Olds Omega Sedan, gold, MIB, L1 ....$65.00

Franklin Mint, 1935 Mercedes Benz 500K Roadster, red w/blk rubber tires, 1 side mirror missing, 8⅜", NM, W1 ....$49.00

Freewheels, Mercedes 190E, silver, MIB, L1 ....$10.00

FYP, Rolls Royce Phantom V Landaulet, wht & bl, MIB, L1 ....$450.00

FYP, Rolls Royce Silver Wraith 'Gulbenkian,' dk gr, MIB, L1 ....$385.00

Gad, Cadillac La Espada Convertible, yel, MIB, L1 ......$175.00

Gama, #1146 Audi Taxi, beige, MIB, L1.......................$25.00

Gama, #987 Mercedes 1928 Sportswagon, wht & blk, MIB, L1 ....$25.00

Gama, #995 Ford Taurus Coupe, orange & bl, M, L1......$65.00

Gama, BMW M 3, red, MIB, L1 ....$25.00

Gama, Opel Kadett Adac, yel, MIB, L1 ....$25.00

Goodee, Fire Engine, red w/blk rubber tires, ca 1950s, 3", NM, W1 ....$17.50

Goodee, Ford Gas Tanker Truck, yel w/blk rubber tires, 1950s, 3⅛", NM, W1 ....$17.50

Goodee, Ford Police Car, bl w/blk rubber tires, ca 1950s, 3", NM, W1 ....$17.50

Goodee, Ford Sedan, yel w/blk rubber tires, ca 1950s, 3", EX, W1 ....$15.00

Goodee, Jeep, olive-gr w/blk rubber tires, ca 1950s, 2½", NM, W1 ....$17.50

Goodee, Moving Van, bl w/blk rubber tires, ca 1950s, 3", VG, W1 ....$12.50

Goodee, Panel Truck, gr w/blk rubber tires, ca 1950s, 3", NM, W1 ....$17.50

Goodee, Studebaker Sedan, gr w/blk rubber tires, ca 1950s, 3", NM, W1 ....$17.50

Goodee, Truck, red w/blk rubber tires, ca 1950s, 3", EX+, W1 ....$15.50

Govroski, Volga Sedan, metallic bl, MIB, L1 ....$35.00

Guisval, Cadillac V16, wht, M, L1 ....$10.00

Guisval, Renault Espace 'Police,' dk bl, MIB, L1............$15.00

Heco, Rolls Royce Phantom III, limited edition, cream, MIB, L1 ....$165.00

Hubley, #452 Sedan, bl w/blk rubber tires, 1 bracket on axle broken, ca 1940, 7", EX, W1 ....$29.00

Hubley, Airflow Car, bl w/wht rubber tires, ca 1930s, 5¼", VG, W1 ....$84.50

Jet Mechanics, Lamborghini Countach, red, U1 ....$35.00

Johnny Lightning, Custom '32 Ford Roadster, MBP $10.00

Johnny Lightning, Custom El Camino Surfer, MBP........$10.00

Johnny Lightning, Custom Jaguar XKE Sports Car, MBP .$10.00

Johnny Lightning, Custom Pontiac GTO, MBP $10.00

Johnny Lightning, Moving Van, MBP............................$10.00

Johnny Lightning, Vicious Vette, MBP $10.00

Johnny Lightning, Wasp, MBP $10.00

K&R Replicas, Triumph TR6 Convertible, butterscotch,
   NMIB+, L1 ....$85.00

KDN, #412-7 Skoda 110 L Sedan, orange, MIB, L1 ....$13.00

KDN, #494 Skoda 120LS, red, MIB, L1............................$13.00

Lone Star, Cadillac Coupe de Ville, wht & bl, NM, L1 ..$95.00

Lone Star, Chevy Corvair, coral, M, L1 ....$65.00

Lone Star, Chevy Corvair, wht, wht interior, MIB (box partly
   damaged), U1 ....$90.00

Lone Star, Dodge Dart Phoenix, metallic bl, M, L1 ....$95.00

Lone Star, Ford Sunliner Convertible, pale bl, MIB, L1..$115.00

Lone Star, Military Jeep, olive drab, M, L1.....................$65.00

Lusotoys, Citroen GS Pallas 'Michelin,' yel, NM+, L1....$35.00

Macadam, Renault 1000 KG 'Valentine,' dk gr, MIB, L1.$45.00

Madison 3, Chrysler 300C Hardtop, metallic red, MIB,
   L1..$165.00

Majorette, #201, Ford Model A Van, 'Tea Shop,' metallic
   red, MBP, J1 ....$2.00

Majorette, #204, Armoured Truck, 'Bank Security,' wht, MBP,
   J1 ....$2.00

Majorette, #206, Pontiac Fiero, '3 Fiero Turbo,' wht & bl, MBP,
   J1 ....$1.00

Majorette, #207, Ladder Fire Engine, extending ladder, red &
   wht, MBP, J1 ....$1.50

Majorette, #209, Porsche 911 Turbo, 'Porsche 911,' blk, MBP,
   J1..$1.00

Majorette, #211, Ferrari GTO, red, MBP, J1 ....$1.00

Majorette, #213, Chevy Impala Taxi, 'Yellow Cab,' yel, MBP,
   J1 ....$2.00

Majorette, #215, Grand Prix Corvette, 'ZR1,' red, MBP,
   J1 ....$1.50

Majorette, #216, Toyota Van Wagon, bl, MBP, J1...........$2.00

Majorette, #217, Thunderbird Stock Car, '4 Gambler,' yel,
   MBP, J1 ....$1.50

Majorette, #220, Ford Mustang SVO, '1 Mustang,' wht, MBP,
   J1 ....$1.00

Majorette, #224, Jeep Cherokee Limited, w/surfboards, blk &
   orange, MBP, J1 ....$2.00

Majorette, #226, Road Roller, yel, blk roller, MBP, J1 ......$1.50

Majorette, #227, Mustang GT Convertible, yel, blk interior,
   MBP, J1 ....$1.50

Majorette, #228, Chevy Tow Truck, 'Emergency Road Service,'
   red, MBP, J1 ....$2.00

Majorette, #229, BMW 325I, wht, MBP, J1 ....$2.00

Majorette, #231, Mercedes 190E, '13 Turbo,' wht, MBP,
   J1 ....$1.00

Majorette, #232, Beach Buggy, 'Fun Buggy,' pk w/wht roof,
   MBP, J1 ....$2.00

Majorette, #237, Lamborghini Countach, red, MBP, J1 ....$1.00

Majorette, #240, Chevy Impala Police Car, 'Police N31,' blk &
   wht, MBP, J1 ....$2.00

Majorette, #242, Shovel Engine, yel w/blk shovel, MBP,
   J1 ....$1.00

Majorette, #243, Ford Transit Ramp Truck, '24 Hr Service,'
   red, MBP, J1 ....$2.00

Majorette, #244, Jeep CJ, Renegade, red w/blk top, MBP,
   J1 ....$1.00

Majorette, #246, Range Rover Fire Rescue, 'District 3 Fire
   Dept,' red, MBP, J1..$2.00

Majorette, #247, Garbage Truck, Hippo emblem, gr cab, gray
   dumper, MBP, J1 ....$1.50

Majorette, #255, Ambulance, 'NYC EMS Ambulance,' wht,
   MBP, J1 ....$2.00

Majorette, #257, Mazda RX-7 Daytona, '23 Mazda,' wht, MBP,
   J1..$2.00

Majorette, #258, Pro Stocker Firebird, 'Number 1,' wht, MBP,
   J1..$1.00

Majorette, #259, Ice Cream Van, metallic red, w/yel canopy,
   MBP, J1 ....$3.00

Majorette, #260, Mercedes 500SL, pearl beige, w/brn interior, MBP, J1 ....$2.00

Marklin, BMW 1600GT, purple, U1 ....$65.00

Marklin, Sprint Sportswagon, blk & silver, U1 ....$100.00

Marklin, VW K70, orange, U1......................................$75.00

Marklin, VW 411, red, U1 ....$65.00

Mebetoys, #6627 De Tomaso Pantera Gran Toros, moss gr, M,
   L1...$45.00

Mebetoys, Alfa Romeo, bl, U1.....................................$80.00

Mebetoys, Corvette Roundine Pinin Farina, metallic bl, M,
   L1...$65.00

Mebetoys, Ferrari 365 GTC 4, chartreuse, NM+, L1.......$55.00

Mebetoys, Fiat 1100, gray, M, L1 ....$35.00

Mebetoys, Fiat 124 Rome Taxi, metallic gr, NM, L1 ......$45.00

Mebetoys, Ford Mark II, bl, front/bk hoods open, NM,
   U1..$75.00

Mebetoys, Lamborghini Urraco, moss gr, MIB, L1 ....$65.00

Mebetoys, VW Beetle 'Jeans,' yel, U1............................$90.00

Mercury, Ferves Ranger, orange, M, L1 ....$48.00

Mercury, Fiat 500L, orange, M, L1................................$55.00

Mercury, Jack Demon Dragster, yel, M, L1 ....$45.00

Mercury, Maserati Racing, red, NM, L1 ....$150.00

Metal Masters, Bus, bl w/blk plastic tires, ca 1937, 7⅛", G,
   W1..$19.00

Metal Masters, Jeep, gr w/blk plastic tires, ca 1947, 5⅝", G,
   W1..$14.00

Metal 43, #1211 Delage Andreau 'Vue Totale,' gray bl, MIB,
   L1...$180.00

Metal 43, 1951 Mercedes 220 Convertible (closed), dk gr,
   MIB, L1 ....$165.00

Metosul, Citroen DS 19 Lisbon Taxi, turq & blk, M,
   L1...$38.00

Midgetoy, Army Ambulance, olive w/blk rubber tires, ca 1950s,
   3⅞", EX-, W1 ....$14.00

Midgetoy, Army Truck, olive w/blk rubber tires, ca 1950s, 4½",
   EX+, W1...$14.00

Midgetoy, Army Truck & Cannon, olive w/blk rubber tires, ca
   1950s, 4½" & 3¼", MIP, W1 ....$29.00

Midgetoy, Camping Trailer, purple w/blk plastic tires, ca 1950s,
   2⅜", VG, W1...$4.50

Midgetoy, Convertible, bl w/blk rubber tires, ca 1950s, 5⅜", EX+, W1...$19.00

Midgetoy, Corvette, gr, ca 1970s, 2", VG, W1 ....$2.50

Midgetoy, Corvette, yel, blk plastic tires, ca 1950s, 2⅞", VG, W1...$12.50

Midgetoy, El Camino, red, ca 1970s, 3", VG, W1 ....$2.50

Midgetoy, Indy-Style Race Car, silver w/blk rubber tires, ca 1950s, 3", EX, W1 ....$15.00

Midgetoy, Jeep, military gr, crimped axles, ca 1950s, 1¾", NM, W1...$5.00

Midgetoy, Jeep, red w/blk rubber tires, ca 1960s, VG, W1 .$4.00

Midgetoy, MC Sports Car, gr, ca 1960s, 2", G+, W1.........$2.50

Midgetoy, Pick-Up Jeep Cab-Over, bl w/blk rubber tires, ca 1950s, 5¾", NM, W1...$19.00

Minialuxe, Volvo 144, lt brn, M, L1...............................$35.00

Minialuxe 04, Renault Paris Madrid, red, MIB, L1...........$12.00

Minialuxe 26, Jamieson 1902, gray, MIB, L1..................$12.00

Minialuxe 31, De Dion Boulton Limousine, blk, M, L1 ..$35.00

Minialuxe 34, Peugeot Double Phaeton, wht & blk, MIB, L1..$15.00

Minialuxe/SIJP, Hotchkiss Gregoire, almond gr, M, L1 ..$50.00

Minimac, Scania Vabis 'Transalfa,' wht & red, NM+, L1 .$75.00

Minimarque, Ford 1936 Roadster, gray, MIB, L1 ....$165.00

Minimarque, Packard Caribbean Hardtop, blk & metallic red, MIB, L1..$125.00

Minitruck, Berlift 'Pomona' Delivery Van, cream & brn, MIB, L1..$350.00

Minitruck, Bernard Transport Bananier, brn & yel, MIB, L1..$425.00

Minitruck, Laffly Fire Premier Secours, red, MIB, L1....$250.00

MOG, Ferrari 400 Jankel Le Marquis Limousine, limited edition, wht & mint gr, MIB, L1 ....$165.00

Pilen of Spain, 1967 Corvette Split-Window Stingray, 1/43 scale, gr w/wire wheels & blk rubber tires, ca 1967, MIB, W1...$89.00

Plumbies, Opel P4, gray over blk, NM, U1.....................$85.00

Polistil, Ferrari 365 GTB/4 Daytona, w/decals '450,' red, U1..$25.00

Polistil, Lamborghini Countach, w/decals '67,' bl, U1 ....$25.00

Polistil, Nissan Datsun, bl, U1......................................$35.00

Politoys, BRM V8 F1, Penny Policar, bl, U1 ....$35.00

Politoys, Dragster 'Drago,' yel, NM, U1.........................$55.00

Politoys, Espada Lamborghini Mertone, gr, NM, U1......$95.00

Politoys, Ferrari Dino, silver, NM, U1............................$95.00

Politoys, Ferrari F1, Penny Policar, red, U1 ....$35.00

Precision, 1954 Corvette, out of production, powder bl, MIB, L1..$150.00

Ralstoy, Sedan, blk rubber tires, 5⅝", EX, W1................$49.00

Record, 1939 Hotchkiss Cabriolet, blk, MIB, L1............$42.00

Record, 1952 Chevy Skyline Convertible, blk, MIB, L1.$48.00

Rextoys, #001 Cadillac V16 Pope Pius XII, blk, MIB, L1.$36.00

Rextoys, #005 Cadillac V16 Coupe, bordeaux, MIB, L1 .$25.00

Rextoys, #050 Ford V8 Taxi, blk & yel, MIB, L1 ....$36.00

Rio, #003 Fiat Tipo 501 Convertible, blk & bl, M, L1....$18.00

Rio, #011 Autobiancchi Landaulet, navy, MIB, L1.........$20.00

Rio, #019 Alfa Romeo 1750, brn & cream, M, L1...........$20.00

Rio, #020 Fiat Autocar, yel, MIB, L1..............................$20.00

Rio, #041 Lancia Di Lambda Sedan, gr & blk, MIB, L1 ..$20.00

Rio, #045, Dusenberg Convertible (closed), wht & bl, MIB, L1..$20.00

Rio, #050 Lincoln Sports Phaeton, gr, MIB, L1..............$20.00

Rio, #053 Renault 40 CV, wht, MIB, L1 ....$20.00

Rio, #057 Fiat 519 Convertible, wht & red, MIB, L1......$20.00

Rio, #066 Bugatti Royale Limousine, blk & beige, MIB, L1..$22.00

Rio, #072 Rolls Royce 20 Coupe, silver & bl, MIB, L1 ...$20.00

Rio, #081 Alfa Romeo Ricotti, dk red, MIB, L1 ....$18.00

RW Modell, Clark C-500-Y40D, gr & blk, NM, U1.....$100.00

RW Modell, Hanomig Sattelschlepper, red, NM, U1 ...$100.00

Sakura, Corvette Stingray, Famous Car Series, silver, U1...$60.00

Shaback, #1018 VW Corrado, metallic gr, MIB, L1........$20.00

Shaback, #1092 Ford Orion, steel gray, MIB, L1 ....$20.00

Shaback, #1160 BMW Z1 Spyder, metallic gr, MIB, L1..$20.00

Siku, #1033 VW Rabbit Hatchback, silver, MIB, L1.........$6.00

Siku, #2918 Ford Coca-Cola, red, MIB, L $35.00

Sinsei, Studebaker, Occupied Japan, gr, U1.................$140.00

Solido, #0044 Ferrari BB, red, M, L1 ....$18.00

Solido, #0053 Ford Fiesta Coupe, silver, M, L1 ....$15.00

Solido, #0091 Renault 18 Sedan, lt metallc gr, M, L1.....$15.00

Solido, #0101 Porsche 1500 Spyder (no driver), silver, NMIB+, L1...$85.00

Solido, #0116 Cooper 1500cc3, '#12,' almond gr w/yel nose, M, L1..$75.00

Solido, #0138 Harvey Indianapolis #82, reddish orange, NM+, L1..$65.00

Solido, #0176 McLaren, '#4,' lt orange, M, L1 ....$45.00

Solido, #0187 Alfa Romeo 33/3, red, M, L1 ....$55.00

Solido, #0356 Volvo Dumpster, yel, M, L1....................$50.00

Solido, #0366 Saviem Wrecker, red, M, L1 ....$25.00

Solido, #0379 Mercedes Garbage Truck, silver, M, L1 ....$35.00

Solido, #209 AMX Tank (1st series), olive drab, M, L1..$75.00

Solido, #3106 Mack Fire Truck, red, M, L1 ....$15.00

Solido, Abarth De Record, silver, NMIB+, L1 ....$105.00

Solido, Chevy Staff Car, olive drab, MIB, L1 ....$15.00

Solido, Ferrari Daytona, Gam 2, red, U1.......................$120.00

Solido, Ferrari Daytona LeMans, red, wht & bl, U1......$150.00

Solido, Ferrari 512, Gam 2, red, U1..............................$120.00

Solido, Ford Escort, Gam 1, red, U1...............................$80.00

Solido, Ford Thunderbird, gr, U1.................................$125.00

Solido, Jaguar D, almond gr, NMIB+, L1 ....$110.00

Solido, Mercedes Moving Van, red & silver, MIB, L1.....$35.00

Solido, Richier Crane, yel, M, L1...................................$50.00

Solido, Trolleybus Chausso, red, very rare, U1.............$600.00

Spot-on, Jaguar XKSS, lt bl, U1.....................................$95.00

Starter, 1983 Thunderbird Coors (no decals), metallic beige, MIB, L1...$60.00

Supercar, Ferrari Dino 246GT, red, U1 ....$55.00

Supercar, Lamborghini Jota, red, U1 ....$55.00

Tin Wizard, 1963 Ford Thunderbird, pale mauve, MIB, L1..$165.00

Tomica, Bluebird Wagon, red, U1 ....$6.00

Tomica, Cadillac Fleetwood Brougham, metallic red, U1 .$6.00

Tomica, Nissan Skyline, red, U1......................................$6.00

Tomica, Pontiac Firebird Trans Am, yel, U1...................$6.00

Tomica Dandy, Nissan Racing Car (Mazda & #32 decals), red, wht & bl, U1...$22.00

Tomica Dandy, Schoolbus, yel, door opens, U1 ....$25.00
Tomica Dandy, VW Bug Metro Police, yel, siren & lights, U1...$25.00
Trax, Holden Monaro Coupe, metallic bl, MIB, L1 ....$25.00
Trax, Holden Pickup, moss gr, MIB, L1.............................$25.00
Vitesse, #123 BMW Convertible (closed), bl, MIB, L1...$35.00
Vitesse, Saurer 'Circus Knie,' red & yel, MIB, L1............$55.00
Western Models, Lotus 79 Mark IV Martini, gr, U1 .....$175.00
Western Models, 1935 Auburn 851 Speedster, wht, U1..$175.00
Western Models, 1953 MG TF Midget, red, tire on bk, U1 ....$125.00
Western Models, 1979 Ferrari 312 T4, red & gray, U1 .$125.00
Wiking, Man SD 200 Berlin Bus 'BVG,' beige, U1.........$42.50
Wiking, VW Beetle, red & gr, U1 ....$125.00

Diecast Collector Banks

Thousands of banks have been produced since Ertl made its first model in 1981, the 1913 Model T Parcel Post Mail Service #9647. The Ertl company was founded by Fred Ertl, Sr., in Dubuque, Iowa, back in the mid-1940s. Until they made their first diecast banks, most of what they made were farm tractors. Today they specialize in vehicles made to specification and carrying logos of companies as large as Texaco and as small as your hometown bank. The size of each 'run' is dictated by the client and can vary from a few hundred up to several thousand. Some clients will later add a serial number to the vehicle; Ertl does not. Other numbers that appear on the base of each bank are a 4-number dating code (the first three indicate the day of the year up to 365 and the fourth number is the last digit of the year, '5' for 1995, for instance.) The stock number is shown only on the box, never on the bank, so it is extremely important that you keep them in their original boxes.

Other producers of these banks are Scale Models, incorporated in 1991 (a division of the original Ertl company), First Gear Inc., and Spec-Cast, whose founders at one time all worked for the Ertl company.

In the listings that follow, unless another condition is given, all values are for banks mint and in their original boxes. (#d) indicates a bank that was numbered by the client, not Ertl.

Key:
JLE — Joseph L. Ertl   NB — not a bank

Ertl

AC Spark Plugs, 1950 Chevy Panel Truck, #2901, J1.....$35.00
AC/Delco/Rockingham, #93, Lumina, P1 ....$35.00
Alka Seltzer, 1917 Ford Model T, #9791, J1....................$40.00
Alliance Racing Team, 1913 Ford Model T, #2174, J1 ...$75.00
Alzheimers Assoc #1, 1913 Ford Model T, limited edition, #9680, J1 ....$85.00
American Quarter Horse Assoc, 1948 Diamond T Semi Tractor & Trailer, #2780, J1 ....$38.00
Amoco Motor Club, 1931 Hawkeye Truck, #9417, J1 ....$25.00
Amoco/Red Crown, 1923 Chevy ½-Ton Truck, limited edition, #1320, J1..$20.00

Amsouth, 1913 Ford Model T, #9454, J1 ....$60.00
Anheuser-Busch, Silver Spokes, 1918 Ford, #9766, H8 .$125.00
Anheuser-Busch, 1905 Ford Delivery Van, #2774, J1 .....$20.00
Apco Petroleum Products (sampler), 1931 Hawkeye, #2098, H8...$45.00
Ar-Jay Sales #4, 1938 Chevy Panel Van, #8072, J1........$25.00
Arm 'N Hammer, 1905 Ford Delivery Van, #9828, J1 ....$65.00
Arrow Dist #4, 1905 Ford Delivery Van, #7542, J1 ....$35.00
Atlanta Falcons, 1913 Ford Model T, #1248, J1..............$25.00
Atlanta/Hooters 500, T-Bird, P1 ....$35.00
Auto Palace, 1955 Chevy Camero Pickup, #2773, J1......$45.00
Auto Palace/Joe Bessey #97, Pontiac, #0384, P1............$30.00
Baltimore Gas & Electric #1, 1932 Ford Panel Truck, #9153, J1..$175.00
Banjo Matthews, 1932 Ford Panel Truck, #2191, J1 ....$95.00
Barq's Root Beer, 1913 Ford Model T, limited edition, #9826, J1..$60.00
Barq's Root Beer, 1951 Ford, NB, #1080, H8 ....$29.00
Beckman's High School (2nd edition), 1913 Ford Model T, #1656, J1..$25.00
Beer Nuts, 1950 Chevy Panel Truck, #2118, J1 ....$25.00
Bell Telephone, 1918 Ford Runabout w/ladder, #9800, J1..$45.00
Big 'A, 1917 Ford Model T, limited edition, #9772, J1 ...$30.00
Big Brothers/Sisters-Roche, 1932 Ford Panel Truck, #9853, J1..$95.00
Bill Elliot #11 Transport, premier edition, #8702, P1......$25.00
Black & Decker, 1913 Ford Model T, #9451, J1..............$45.00
Bobby Hillan (#d), 1940 Panel, chrome, GA-6021, P1...$65.00
Branson MO, Music City, 1920 International, JLE, #3044, H8...$30.00
Branson MO, Roy Clark, 1920 International, JLE, #3060, H8...$30.00
Branson MO, Willie Nelson, 1920 International, JLE, #3098, H8..$30.00
Brownies Muffler Wagon, 1950 Chevy Panel Truck, #9894, J1..$25.00
Budweiser Racing Transport '93, premier edition, #8729, P1...$35.00
Budweiser/Bill Elliot, #1, T-Bird, P1 ....$45.00
Butterfinger, 1932 Ford Panel Truck, #1318, J1 ....$25.00
California Dept of Forestry, 1926 Seagrave Pumper, #9888, P1...$25.00
Campbell's Baked Beans, 1931 Hawkeye Truck, #7665, J1..$25.00
Campbell's Soup, 1931 Hawkeye Truck, #7667, J1 ....$25.00
Campbell's Soup, 1937 Chevy, #10004, H8 ....$22.00
Campbell's Soup, 1955 Chevy, #50013, H8 ....$22.00
Canada Dry, 1918 Ford Runabout, #7680, J1 ....$35.00
Carl Budding, 1913 Ford Model T, #2106, J1 ....$75.00
Carlisle Flea Marketeers, 1931 Hawkeye Truck, #9314, J1.$30.00
Champion Fever/Davey Allison, T-Bird, P1 ....$38.00
Champlain Refining, 1930 Diamond T Tanker Truck, #9134, J1..$30.00
Charlotte Speedway/Mello Yello, Lumina, #0439, P1 .....$30.00
Chevrolet KY, 1937 Chevy Pickup, #12506, H8............$19.00
Chevrolet-'See the USA,' 1955 Chevy Camero Pickup, B070, J1..$30.00

Chevron-Employee Only, 1930 Diamond T Tanker Truck, #2968, J1 ....$35.00

Chiquita Bananas #2, 1931 Hawkeye Stake Truck, #9343, J1 ....$30.00

Cintas, Grumman's Step Van, #7776, J1 ....$75.00

Citgo, 1931 Hawkeye Tanker Truck, #9820, J1...............$30.00

Clearly Canadian (#d), 1926 Mack Truck, #9238, J1......$40.00

Clyde Beatty Circus Set, 4 Tractor Trailers, #9391, J1 .$125.00

Coca-Cola, 1920 International, #3015, H8 ....$95.00

Coca-Cola, 1931 Hawkeye Truck, #2919, J1 ....$20.00

Coca-Cola Ronald McDonald House, 1929 International, #5023, H8...$35.00

Colorado Rockies, 1923 Chevy ½-Ton Van, #3241, J1...$20.00

Congratulations Class of '92, 1905 Ford Delivery Van, #9775, J1 ....$20.00

Conoco #7, 1925 Kenworth Stake Truck, limited edition, #2778, J1 ....$25.00

Continental Oil Co, 1929 International, #4003, H8.......$23.00

Corona Extra Beer #3, 1931 Hawkeye Truck, #7549, J1 .$25.00

Country Time, 1913 Ford Model T, #1640, J1 ....$35.00

Cumberland Valley '91, 1931 Hawkeye Truck, #9393, J1 .$45.00

Dairy Queen, 1926 Seagrave Pumper, #9681, P1.............$45.00

Dairy Queen, 1950 Chevy Panel Truck, #9178, J1........$175.00

Dallas Cowboys, 1931 Hawkeye Truck, #3566, J1 ....$20.00

Danish Bakery-Publix, 1918 Ford Runabout, #9185, J1 ..$30.00

Daytona 53rd Bike Week (set of 2), 1931 Internationals, #5071-72, H8..$75.00

Detroit News, 1913 Ford Model T, #1667, J1 ....$75.00

Diamond Walnut Growers, 1931 Hawkeye Truck, #9881, J1 ....$25.00

Domino's Pizza (#d), 1913 Ford Model T, limited edition, #9458, J1 ....$45.00

Douglas City, Republicans, 1913 Ford Model T, limited edition, #9369, J1 ....$125.00

Dover Downs/Bud 500 #93, Pontiac, #0227, P1 ....$35.00

Dragich Auto Literature, 1950 Chevy Tractor & Trailer, #7682, J1...$30.00

Dubuque Coke Santa, 1920 International, #3020, H8 ..$350.00

Dubuque Golf & Country Club #2, 1913 Ford Model T, #9726, J1 ....$75.00

Dupont/Jeff Gordon, #24, Lumina, P1 ....$45.00

Dyersville Historical Society, 1918 Ford Runabout, limited edition, #9883, J1 ....$35.00

Eason Oil (sampler), 1930 International, #4034, H8 ......$45.00

Eastman #3, 1918 Ford Tanker, limited edition, #8024, J1.$35.00

Eastwood #11, 1937 Ahrens-Fox Fire Engine, #9748, P1 .$45.00

Eastwood #2, 1932 Ford Panel Truck, #9562, J1 ....$325.00

Eastwood #9, 1955 Chevy Panel Truck, #9747, J1 ....$95.00

English Pub, 1920 International, GA-3003, P1 ....$20.00

Ephrata Fair, 1950 Chevy Panel Truck, limited edition, #7541, J1 ....$25.00

Ertl Collectors Club (replica), 1950 Chevy Panel Truck, #9064, J1...$100.00

Esso (sampler), 1938 Dodge Airflow, B243, H8.............$79.00

Ethyl Gasoline (sampler), 1931 International, #4005, H8 ....$49.00

Farm Progress Show, 1930 International, #5008, H8 ......$20.00

Fathers' Days '93, 1932 Ford Panel Truck, #9451, J1.......$20.00

FDR Assoc, 1905 Ford Delivery Van, limited edition, #9378, J1 ....$50.00

Fina, 1918 Ford Runabout, limited edition, #9502, J1.....$25.00

First National Bank of Texas, 1932 Ford Panel Truck, #9208, J1 ....$35.00

Forbes (#d), 1950 Chevy Panel Truck, #9978, J1 ....$30.00

Friendship Fire Dept (Heallam), 1926 Seagrave Pumper, #9098, P1 ....$35.00

Frito Lays, Grumman Step Van, #9023, J1 ....$30.00

Gilmore Oil, 1931 Hawkeye Tanker, #9890, J1..............$45.00

Goodyear, #1, Lumina, #0318, P1.............................$75.00

Graduation Day '93, 1905 Ford Delivery Van, #9453, J1 .$20.00

Grapette Soda, 1940 Delivery, GA-6002, P1 ....$35.00

Gulf #1, 1931 Hawkeye Tanker, #7652, J1 ....$75.00

Gulf Refining #2 (#d), 1926 Mack Tanker Truck, #9158, J1 ....$60.00

Halliburton (sampler), 1931 Hawkeye, #2929, H8..........$49.00

Hamblin Oil, 1931 Hawkeye Tanker Truck, #9596, J1 ...$35.00

Happy Birthday, 1905 Ford Delivery Van, #9685, J1 ......$20.00

Hardees/Ward Burton #2, Lumina, #0413, P1 ....$35.00

Harley-Davidson #3, 1932 Ford Panel Van, limited edition, #7525, J1 ....$250.00

Harley-Davidson #5, 1931 Hawkeye Tanker Truck, limited edition, #9164, J1...$195.00

Heartbeat of America #1, 1950 Chevy Panel Truck, wht, #9873, J1...$55.00

Heartbeat of America #2, 1950 Chevy Panel Truck, blk, #9561, J1 ....$20.00

Heilig Meyers, 1926 Mack Truck, #9749, J1....................$25.00

Heinken #2, 1950 Chevy Panel Truck, #9356, J1 ....$30.00

Hemmings Motor News, 1932 Ford, Irish gr, #9669, H8.$195.00

Hemmings Motor News #2, 1950 Chevy Panel Truck, #9461, J1 ....$35.00

Henny Penny, 1950 Chevy Panel Truck, #9692, J1 ....$30.00

Hershey's, 1926 Seagrave Pumper, #7637, P1.................$30.00

Hershey's Cocoa, 1905 Ford Delivery Van, #9665, J1 .....$65.00

Hershey's Kisses, 1950 Chevy Panel Truck, silver, #2126, J1...$150.00

Hershey's Sweet Chocolate, 1931 Hawkeye Truck, #9349, J1 ....$25.00

Hinkley & Schmitt, 1913 Ford Model T, #9427, P1 ....$25.00

Hollycliff Farms #1, 1926 Kenworth Truck, #9477, J1 ....$50.00

Homestead Collectibles, 1905 Ford Delivery Van, limited edition, #9651, J1 ....$25.00

Hostess #2 (wht spokes), 1913 Ford Model T, #9422, J1.$25.00

Hwi, 1923 Chevy ½-Ton Van, #1365, J1 ....$30.00

I-70 Speedway, 1950 Chevy Panel Truck, #1319, J1 ....$25.00

IGA, 1923 Chevy ½-Ton Van, #9375, J1.........................$20.00

Imperial Oil (premier), 1931 Hawkeye Tanker Truck, #9455, J1 ....$60.00

Indian Motorcycle Warrior, 1940 Ford, JLE, silver, #6023, H8...$49.00

Iowa Hawkeye #6, 1926 Mack Truck, limited edition, #2135, J1 ....$45.00

IPCA #3, Check the Oil, 1931 Hawkeye Tanker, #9599, J1 ....$25.00

Jack Daniels, 1931 Hawkeye Stake Truck, #9342, J1 ......$35.00

JC Express, 1913 Ford Model T, unofficial, #1339, J1 .....$40.00

JC Penney, horse & wagon, #9445, J1 ....$20.00

JC Penney, 1923 Chevy ½-Ton Truck, #9447, J1 ....$25.00

JC Penney, 1938 Chevy Panel Van, #9637, J1 ....$25.00

JI Case, 1955 Chevy Camero Pickup, #4626, J1 ....$35.00

Jim Beam (District #3), 1918 Ford Runabout, #9659, J1.$30.00

Jim Beam (District #5), 1918 Ford Barrel, #2964, J1 ....$75.00

Jim Beam International #2, Kenworth Tractor Trailer, #T072, H8 ....$39.00

K&B Drugs, 1913 Ford Model T, #1656, J1 ....$25.00

Kaufman's Apple Farm, 1918 Ford Runabout, #7560, J1.$30.00

Kellogg's Anniversary, 1917 Ford, blk, #3252, H8 ....$95.00

Kendall Oil, 1931 Tanker, GA-4073, P1 ....$30.00

Key Aid Distributors, 1931 Hawkeye Stake Truck, #1332, J1 ....$25.00

Kingsport TN, #2, 1917 Ford Model T, limited edition, #9394, J1 ....$30.00

Kiwanis Club, 1905 Ford Delivery Van, 39884, J1 ....$25.00

Kodak, 1905 Ford, Gold Wheel, no camera in promo box, #9985, H8 ....$295.00

Kodak, 1905 Ford, red spokes, #9985, H8 ....$45.00

Kodak/Ernie Irvan #4, Lumina, #0344, P1 ....$35.00

Kroger, 1923 Chevy ½-Ton Truck, #7633, J1 ....$20.00

Kyle Petty (sampler), 1950 Chevy, #2881, H8 ....$75.00

LA Dodgers (#d), 1905 Ford Delivery Van, limited edition, #3247, J1 ....$20.00

Lawrys (#d), 1950 Chevy Panel Truck, limited edition, #9159, J1 ....$25.00

Lennox #6, 1923 Chevy ½-Ton Van, limited edition, #9378, J1 ....$25.00

Lepages Glue, 1913 Ford Delivery Van, limited edition, #2120, J1 ....$35.00

Linkbelt (#d), 1918 Ford Runabout, limited edition, #2107, J1 ....$35.00

Lion Oil #2, 1938 Chevy Panel Truck, #3203, J1............$35.00

Lipton Tea, 1932 Ford Panel Truck, #9087, J1 ....$35.00

Long Island Fire Dept (wht), 1926 Seagrave Pumper, #9653, P1 ....$45.00

Marathon Oil (sampler), 1929 International Tanker, #4045, H8 ....$39.00

Marshall Fields, 1913 Ford Model T, #1650, J1 ....$50.00

McCanny Oil, 1931 Hawkeye Tanker, #9594, J1 ....$45.00

McDonald's Racing Transport #93, premier edition, #8704, P1 ....$25.00

Miller High Life, 1918 Ford Barrel, #9486, J1 ....$25.00

Miller/Rusty Wallace, #2, Pontiac, #0428, P1 ....$45.00

Mobil Oil, 1955 Chevy Camero Pickup, #7521, J1 ....$30.00

Mobil One, 1931 Hawkeye Tanker, employee issue, #7540, H8 ....$95.00

Mobilgas, 1918 Ford Oil Tanker, #7519, J1 ....$30.00

Mom & Pops/Dale Earnhardt, #3, Lumina, P1 ....$35.00

Monoghans Fire Dept, 1926 Seagrave Pumper, #9719, P1..$30.00

Monroe Shocks, 1931 Hawkeye Truck, #9350, J1 ....$45.00

Montgomery Wards #4, horse & wagon, #1367, J1 ....$55.00

Morema Inc/Ken Schrader, Lumina, #0421, P1..............$35.00

Mounds (Hershey), 1923 Chevy ½-Ton Van, #7652, J1.$30.00

National Street Rod Assoc, 1937 Ford Tractor Trailer, #7504, J1 ....$75.00

National Toy Trucking, 1913 Ford Model T, #9711, J1..$25.00

New Hobby, Grumman Step Van, #9479, J1..............$25.00

New York Fire Dept, 1926 Seagrave Pumper, #7628, P1.$25.00

New York Giants, 1931 Hawkeye Truck, #3573, J1 ....$20.00

Oakland A's, 1905 Ford Delivery Van, #3242, J1 ....$20.00

Old Cars Magazine, 1950 Chevy Panel Truck, #9973, J1.$25.00

Old Milwaukee Light, 1918 Ford Barrel, #9173, J1 ....$25.00

Otasco #1, 1913 Ford Model T, #1359, J1 ....$135.00

Overnite Trucking, 1937 Ford Tractor Trailer, #9068, J1 .$95.00

Pennzoil, 1955 Chevy Pickup, #7648, J1 ....$30.00

Pennzoil (#d), 1913 Ford Model T, #9019, J1 ....$35.00

Penske Racing/Rusty Wallace '93 Transport, premier edition, #8712, P1 ....$25.00

Pepsi, 1931 Hawkeye Stake Truck, #9341, J1 ....$40.00

Perkasie Lions Club #2, 1932 Ford Panel Truck, #2162, J1..............$40.00

Pet Milk, 1913 Ford, Red Wheels, #1652, H8 ....$45.00

Phillips 66, 1929 Tanker, 75th anniversary, GA-4030, P1 ....$125.00

Phillips 66 #1 (old logo), 1931 Hawkeye Tanker, #9407, H8 ....$110.00

Phillips 66 75th Anniversary, 1917 Ford, #1326, H8 ......$17.00

Phillips 66, 1932 Ford Panel Truck, #9131, P1 ....$35.00

Phillips 66 #1 (#d), 1913 Ford Model T, #9230, J1 ....$225.00

Police, 1905 Ford Delivery Van, #1332, P1 ....$25.00

Preferred Hotels (#d), 1917 Ford Model T, limited edition, #9240, P1 ....$30.00

Publix Dairy Fresh, 1937 Ford Tractor & Tanker Trailer, #9695, P1 ....$40.00

Publix Floral, 1923 Chevy ½-Ton Van, #9182, P1........$20.00

Publix Produce, 1931 Hawkeye Stake Truck, #9186, P1.$20.00

Publix w/Reefer, 1950 Chevy Tractor Trailer, #9698, P1.$30.00

Quakertown National Bank #5, 1917 Ford Model T, #1370, P1 ....$35.00

Racing Champions #51/1st Bank, Lumina, #0317, P1....$85.00

Rain-X (#d), 1939 Dodge Air-Flow, GA-7007, P1..........$35.00

Raybestos/Sterling Marlin #8, T-Bird, #0337, P1 ....$25.00

Red Crown Gasoline #1, 1931 Hawkeye Tanker Truck, #7654, P1 ....$75.00

Reeses, 1923 Chevy ½-Ton Van, #9808, P1...................$30.00

Renningers Adamstown PA, 1932 Ford Panel Truck, limited edition, #7556, P1 ....$35.00

Richard Petty, Vintage Plane, #35003, 1992, H8............$69.00

Richard Petty, Vintage Plane, all bl, #35003, 1993, H8.$495.00

Richard Petty (sampler), 1950 Chevy, #2169, H8...........$75.00

Richard Petty #3, 1905 Ford Delivery Van, #9682, J1.....$50.00

Richard Petty/Rick Wilson, Vega Plane, bl, #363B, H8.$195.00

Richlandtown, 1926 Mack Truck, #9290, P1 ....$125.00

Riestertown Fire Dept, 1926 Seagrave Pumper, #2925, P1..............$30.00

Route 66 Anniversary (sampler), 1950 Chevy, #7625, H8..............$75.00

Royalite Oil, 1931 Hawkeye Tanker Trailer, #9568, P1..$35.00

Ryder Truck Rental, 1931 International, #5054, H8......$25.00

S&F Toys (2nd edition), 1913 Ford Model T, limited edition, #9205, P1..............$25.00

Safeguard, 1950 Chevy Panel Truck, #7508, P1.............$30.00

Safety Kleen-Parts, 1913 Ford Model T, #9506, P1.........$45.00

Sasco, 1917 Ford Model T, #9354, P1...........................$25.00

Scott Tissue (gold spokes), 1917 Ford Model T, #9652, P1 .**$75.00**

Sears, 1913 Ford Model T, #2129, M in tin box, P1 ....**$65.00**

Shamrock Oil #1, 1931 Hawkeye Tanker Truck, #9676, P1 ....**$30.00**

Shell Oil, 1955 Chevy Pickup, #7562, P1 ....**$30.00**

Shoprite, 1905 Ford Delivery Van, #9711, P1 ....**$20.00**

Shrine Circus-Kazim Temple, 1931 Hawkeye Truck, #9643, P1 ....**$50.00**

Silver Springs Speedway, 1926 Kenworth Truck, #9172, P1 ....**$35.00**

Sinclair Oil, 1918 Ford Barrel, #9483, P1 ....**$35.00**

Smokey Bear, 1937 Ford Tractor Trailer, #2147, P1 ....**$35.00**

Southern States #1, 1926 Kenworth Truck, #9199, P1 .**$275.00**

Southern States #6, 1931 Hawkeye Stake Truck, #3962, P1 ....**$28.00**

Speed Pro Sealed Power, 1905 Ford Delivery Van, limited edition, #1663, P1 ....**$25.00**

Split Fire, 1920 Panel, GA-3094, P1 ....**$50.00**

Springettsbury Fire Dept (yel), 1926 Seagrave Pumper, #9099, P1 ....**$35.00**

Spur, 1937 Ford Tractor Trailer, #3901, P1 ....**$30.00**

Steamtown USA, 1926 Mack Truck, #9167, P1 ....**$125.00**

Stevens Van Lines, 1926 Mack Truck, #9841, P1 ....**$40.00**

Storey Wrecker w/Title, 1931 Hawkeye Wrecker, #9006, P1 ....**$75.00**

STP/Richard Petty #43, Pontiac, #0346, P1 ....**$45.00**

Straits MI #2 Antique Auto Show, 1955 Chevy Pickup, #3960, P1 ....**$25.00**

Sun Holiday, 1918 Ford Runabout, #9618, P1 ....**$30.00**

Sunoco #1, 1926 Mack Tanker Truck, #9796, P1 ....**$45.00**

Sunray Oil, 1930 Diamond T Tanker, #2970, H8 ....**$55.00**

Super Value, 1932 Ford Panel Truck, #9663, P1 ....**$25.00**

Support Your Armed Forces, 1950 Chevy Panel Truck, #9466, P1 ....**$35.00**

Tabasco, 1931 Hawkeye Stake Truck, #9345, P1 ....**$30.00**

Telephone Pioneers of America, 1937 Ford Tractor Trailer, #9802, P1 ....**$40.00**

Texaco, 1929 Tanker, limited edition, GA-4028, P1....**$125.00**

Texaco #1, 1913 Ford Model T, #2128, P1 ....**$725.00**

Texaco #4 (sampler), 1905 Ford Delivery Van, #9321, P1..**$575.00**

Texaco #9, 1925 Kenworth Tanker, #9385, P1 ....**$25.00**

Tip Up Town, 1950 Chevy Panel Truck, #9034, P1 ....**$20.00**

Tisco, 1905 Ford Delivery Van, #9982, P1 ....**$125.00**

Toms Foods, Grummans Step Van, #1337, P1.................**$25.00**

Toy Tractor Times #1, 1937 Ford Tractor Trailer, #9480, P1 ....**$40.00**

Tropicana, 1932 Ford Panel Truck, #9798, P1 ....**$25.00**

True Value #10 (10th Anniversary), 1931 Hawkeye Truck, #9501, P1 ....**$20.00**

TRW, 1913 Ford Model T, #2887, P1 ....**$85.00**

United Airlines (#d), 1913 Ford Model T, limited edition, #9233, P1 ....**$30.00**

United Van Lines #2, horse & wagon, #9227, P1............**$35.00**

University of Nebraska, 1913 Ford Model T, #1330, P1..**$65.00**

US Mail, 1905 Ford Delivery Van, limited edition, #7641, P1 ....**$30.00**

US Mail, 1923 Chevy ½-Ton Van, limited edition, #1352, P1 ....**$25.00**

V&S Variety Stores #2, 1918 Ford Runabout, #7625, P1.**$25.00**

Valvoline #2, 1925 Kenworth Tanker, #9253, P1 ....**$30.00**

Valvoline #5, 1948 Diamond T Tractor & Tanker Trailer, #9321, P1 ....**$20.00**

Valvoline/Mark Martin #6, T-Bird, #0334, P1 ....**$25.00**

Virginville Fire Dept, 1926 Seagrave Pumper, #9090, P1.**$65.00**

Walgreens, 1913 Ford Model T, #9531, P1 ....**$25.00**

Watkins Glen #93, T-Bird, #0237, P1 ....**$35.00**

Weil McClain, 1905 Ford Delivery Van, #2122, P1........**$35.00**

Western Auto, 1913 Ford Model T, #1328, P1 ....**$110.00**

Western Auto/Darrell Waltrip, Lumina, P1 ....**$45.00**

Wings 'N Things, 1932 Ford Panel Truck, #9634, P1 .....**$35.00**

Winn Dixie, 1913 Ford, (red spokes), #1364, H8............**$49.00**

Winn Dixie, 1913 Ford Model T, #7694, P1 ....**$25.00**

Wireless (2nd edition), 1950 Chevy Panel Truck, #2953, P1 ....**$35.00**

Wix Filters, 1932 Ford Panel Truck, #9810, P1 ....**$35.00**

Wonder Bread #3, 1913 Ford Model T, limited edition, #9161, P1 ....**$50.00**

WSSC, 1926 Mack Tanker Truck, #7522, P1 ....**$35.00**

Yelton Trucking, 1913 Ford Model T, #9401, P1 ....**$35.00**

York #2, 1932 Ford Panel Truck, #9096, P1 ....**$45.00**

20th Street Bank, 1932 Ford Panel Truck, #2198, P1 .....**$25.00**

Scale Models

Alan Kulwicki Racing, 1940 Ford, #6021, H8.................**$79.00**

Amoco, 1929 International Tanker, JLE, #4032, H8 ......**$24.00**

Amoco #2, 1940 Ford, JLE, #6018, H8 ....**$29.00**

Amoco Motor Club #3, 1931 International Wrecker, #9000, H8 ....**$29.00**

Amoco Oil #3, 1938 Dodge Airflow, #7008, H8 ....**$34.00**

Cam-2 Motor Oil, 1931 International, #4103, H8 ....**$29.00**

CC of Tulsa, 1931 International, #5034, H8 ....**$95.00**

Champlin Refining, 1931 International, #4088, H8 ....**$29.00**

Clearkote Protector, 1940 Ford, #UP140, H8.................**$32.00**

Co-op 'The Farm Store,' 1929 International, #4089, H8 ....**$19.00**

Coca-Cola, 1929 International Tanker, #4075, H8 ....**$34.00**

Coors, Sussex Fair, 1931 International, #5002, H8 ....**$19.00**

Diamond Motor Oil, 1931 International, #4079, H8 ......**$24.00**

Drake Well, 1929 International, #4059, H8 ....**$19.00**

Eason Oil, 1931 International Tanker, #4033, H8 ....**$21.00**

Eddie Beirchwals, 1920 International, #3094, H8 ....**$65.00**

Edelbrock (sampler), 1931 International, #5055, H8 ......**$32.00**

Ethyl Gasolin, 1931 International, #4006, H8 ....**$27.00**

Exxon, 1931 International Tanker, #4067, H8 ....**$125.00**

Farm Service, 1931 International, #4052, H8 ....**$65.00**

Field of Dreams #2, 1920 International, #3046, H8 ....**$25.00**

Gilmore Oil, 1931 International Tanker, #4010, H8 ......**$22.00**

Gilmore Oil (sampler), 1931 International Tanker, #4009, H8 ....**$45.00**

Green Spot Beverage, 1931 International, #4107, H8 ....**$27.00**

Gulf Oil, 1940 Ford, #6000, H8 ....**$75.00**

Harley-Davidson of Baltimore, 1931 International, #5033 , H8 ....**$125.00**

Harley-Davidson 90th Anniversary, 1934 Mack, #8008, H8 ....**$39.00**

Harleys-R-Us #3 Schott Enterprises, 1931 International, #5063, H8 ....$49.00

Henderson Motorcycles, 1920 International, #3066, H8 .$35.00

Indian Motorcycle, Hubley Plane, #4102, H8 ....$29.00

Indian Motorcycle, 1931 International Tanker, #4068, H8 ....$75.00

Indian Motorcycle #2 Scout, 1929 International, #5022, H8 ....$115.00

JI Case, 1931 International, #0734, H8 ....$19.00

John Deere Nashville '93, 1931 International Tanker, #0962, H8 ....$245.00

Johnson Gasoline, 1920 International, #4047, H8 ....$25.00

Johnson Gasoline (sampler), 1920 International, #4046, H8 ....$39.00

K-Mart, 1931 International, #5043, H8 ....$29.00

Kendall Oil, 1929 International Tanker, #4073, H8 ....$19.00

Lake Speed, 1931 International, #5056, H8 ....$45.00

Lonestar Beer, 1920 International, #3021, H8 ....$27.00

Magnolia Oil #1, 1934 Sterling, #4022, H8 ....$25.00

Maryland Oil #1 Special, 1929 Ford, #4002, H8 ....$75.00

Maryland Oil Co, 1920 International, #3079, H8 ....$29.00

Maryland Oil Co (sampler), 1920 International, #3080, H8 ....$75.00

Michelin Tires #1, 1931 International, #5046, H8 ....$25.00

Miller Lite Beer, 1931 International, #5042, H8 ....$49.00

New York Farm Show, 1931 International, #5040, H8 ...$35.00

Pan American Air, 1931 International, #4081, H8 ....$32.00

Pepsi-Cola, 1931 International, #5027, H8 ....$44.00

Pepsi-Cola, 1940 Ford, #6039, H8 ....$29.00

Phillips 66 75th Anniversary, 1929 International, #4030, H8 ....$125.00

Pronto Oil Co, 1931 International Tanker, #4016, H8...$25.00

Rain-X, 1938 Dodge Airflow, #7007, H8........................$42.00

Road Runner Oil, 1931 International Tanker, #4064, H8..$19.00

Ronald McDonald House, 1920 International, #3083, H8 .$34.00

Seacoast HD #3, 1940 Ford, #6038, H8........................$59.00

Shell Oil, 1920 International, #3001, H8........................$65.00

Shell Petroleum (sampler), 1931 International, #4017, H8 ....$49.00

Signal Oil, 1931 International, #4015, H8 ....$19.00

Simpson Racing Equipment #1, 1940 Ford, #6012, H8 ...$69.00

Skelly Oil (sampler), 1931 International Tanker, #3036, H8 ....$45.00

Speedway Racing, 1940 Ford, #6006, H8........................$49.00

Steel City Beer, 1931 International, #5049, H8 ....$29.00

Sturgis 53rd Annual Rally, 1929 International, #5027, H8 .$34.00

Sun Oil, 1931 International, #4037, H8........................$19.00

Sunoco, 1931 International, #4102, H8 ....$29.00

Sunoco (sampler), 1931 Hawkeye Tanker, #3790, H8 ....$65.00

White Castle #1, 1931 International, #5045, H8 ....$32.00

Wilwerts Harley-Davidson #2, 1930 International, #5024, H8 ....$95.00

Wolf's Head Motor Oil, 1931 International, #4031, H8 .$19.00

Yamaha Motorcycles, 1931 International, #5063, H8 .....$27.00

Spec-Cast

Allis Chalmers, 1929 Roadster, #2000, P1......................$25.00

Amoco (bl), 1937 Tanker, #17501B, P1.........................$20.00

Amoco (silver), 1929 Tanker, #2001S, P1 ....$25.00

Amoco #1, Vintage Plane, #0801, H8 ....$85.00

Amoco #2, Vega Plane, #35001, H8 ....$49.00

Amoco Christmas, 1937 Chevy, #10001, H8 ....$19.00

Amoco-Santa #2, 1937 Cabriolet Roadster, #10001, P1 .$25.00

Atlanta Falcons, 1931 Hawkeye, #B164, H8 ....$17.00

Bell South, 1931 Ford, #1004, H8.................................$24.00

Bobby Allison, 1940 Ford, JLE, #6014, H8 ....$65.00

Bucks Motorsports, 1929 Roadster, #1020, P1 ....$45.00

Buffalo Bills, 1931 Hawkeye, #B173, H8 ....$22.00

California Highway Patrol, 1929 Ford, #2585, H8 ....$24.00

Charlotte Coca-Cola 600, 1929 Roadster, #1013, P1....$125.00

Chevy Factory Service, 1937 Chevy Sedan Delivery, #15011, H8 ....$19.00

Chicago Bears, 1931 Hawkeye, #3574, H8 ....$17.00

Cincinnati Bengals, 1931 Hawkeye, #B172, H8............$17.00

Citgo, Vega Plane, #35012, H8.....................................$29.00

Citgo, 1916 Studebaker, #27502, H8.............................$28.00

Clark Oil, 1929 Roadster, #1544, P1 ....$25.00

Coca-Cola 600, Kenworth Tractor Trailer, #30001, H8 .$49.00

Coca-Cola 600, 1929 Ford, #2711, H8 ....$75.00

Collector's Edition '92, 1929 Roadster, #1510, P1..........$25.00

Conoco Oil, 1929 Ford, #2002, H8................................$29.00

Cooper Tires #3, 1931 Panel, #2518, P1 ....$25.00

Dallas Cowboys, 1931 Hawkeye, #3566, H8 ....$49.00

Darlington Southern 500, 1929 Panel, #2707, P1 ....$55.00

Darlington 500, 1929 Ford, #2706, H8 ....$65.00

Davey Allison, 1937 Ford, #0438, H8.............................$35.00

Daytona Pepsi 500, 1929 Ford, #0255, H8 ....$24.00

Daytona Speedway, 1929 Ford, #0209, H8 ....$24.00

Daytona Speedway, 1931 Panel, #0209, P1 ....$65.00

Daytona 500 STP, 1929 Ford, #0231, H8 ....$24.00

Eastwood Auto Club #1, Vintage Plane, #1715, H8 .....$149.00

Eastwood Co, 1952 GMC Wrecker, #0109, H8...............$79.00

Eastwood Co #2, Vega Plane, #35000, H8......................$25.00

Eastwood Co #3, Stearman Bi-Plane, #21200, H8..........$35.00

Eastwood Pioneer Airport, 1916 Seagrave Pumper, #1174, P1 ....$35.00

Eastwood UK #3, 1931 Panel, #1172, P1 ....$35.00

Eastwood UK Grand Opening, 1931 Panel, #1992, P1 ...$45.00

Evers Toy Store #3, 1931 Panel, #2512, P1 ....$20.00

Fina Oil, 1929 Ford Tanker, #2004, H8.........................$19.00

Fire Chief, 1929 Roadster, #1540, P1 ....$25.00

Ford, 1929 Ford, #1551, H8 ....$17.00

Golden Rule #1, 1930 Panel, #1054, P1 ....$20.00

Goodyear, 1937 Chevy, #15001, H8...............................$15.00

Grapette Soda (sampler), 1940 Ford, #6001, H8 ....$45.00

Hank Williams Jr, 1929 Ford, #2561, H8 ....$27.00

Harley-Davidson, 1929 Ford, #1516, H8 ....$59.00

Harley-Davidson, 1929 Roadster, #1516, P1 ....$85.00

Harley-Davidson, 1931 Ford, #99194, H8 ....$55.00

Harley-Davidson #1, Vintage Plane, #0820, H8...........$275.00

Harley-Davidson #2, Vintage Plane, #9920, H8.............$89.00

Harry Gant #33, 1929 Ford, #0228, H8 ....$44.00

Heinz, HJ Co, 1929 Ford, #1018, H8 ....$19.00

Heinz Pickle #2, 1931 Stake Truck, #1027, P1 ....$20.00

Hershey's Chocolate Milk, 1916 Studebaker, #27503, H8 .$22.00

Hesston-Louisville Toy Show, 1929 Panel, #0161, P1 ....$35.00
Hooters Atlanta 500, 1929 Ford, #2709, H8 ....$75.00
Hooters 500/R Petty (#d), Kenworth Tanker, #0316, P1 .$85.00
House of Kolor, 1937 Chevy, #15013, H8 ....$32.00
Hurst Performance #6, 1931 Panel, #1164, P1.................$35.00
LA Rams, 1931 Hawkeye, #B162, H8..............................$17.00
Laconia Motorcycle Week, 1929 Ford, #2553, H8 ....$49.00
Liberty Classics, 1929 Tanker, #2000, P1 ....$35.00
Liberty Classics, 1955 Chevy Sedan Delivery, #50015, H8..$17.00
Liberty Classics (1st Bank), 1929 Roadster, #1500, P1....$95.00
Lions Club National Show, 1929 Ford, #2530, H8..........$20.00
Louisville Slugger, 1929 Panel, #1036, P1 ....$20.00
Louisville Slugger, 1931 Ford, #1036, H8 ....$25.00
Marathon Oil, 1929 International Tanker, #4044, H8....$23.00
Massey Ferguson, Kenworth Tanker Trailer, #30007, P1 .$25.00
Massey Harris, 1929 Panel, #2501, P1 ....$20.00
Mello Yello 500, 1929 Ford, #2710, H8..........................$34.00
Minneapolis Moline Farm Equipment, 1929 Roadster, #1513,
    P1 ....$20.00
Mr Gasket/Performance Pioneer #9, 1960 Tractor Trailer,
    #B020, P1 ....$35.00
Nabisco, 1929 Ford, #2508, H8......................................$19.00
NASCAR, 1929 Ford, #0314, H8....................................$22.00
NASCAR Racing '93, Kenworth Tractor Trailer, #00313,
    P1 ....$35.00
Now & Then Vehicle Club, 1929 Roadster, #1528, P1 ..$20.00
Old Car Magazine, 1929 Ford, #1526, H8 ....$23.00
Olympia Beer (Pabst), 1929 Panel, #2528, P1 ....$25.00
Pabst 100th Anniversary, 1916 Studebaker, #25001, H8 .$17.00
Pennzoil, 1929 Ford, #1557, H8......................................$22.00
Philadelphia Eagles, 1931 Hawkeye, #B159, H8..............$25.00
Piggly Wiggly Racing, Kenworth Tractor Trailer, #00303,
    P1 ....$55.00
Posies Racing, 1929 Ford, #1993, H8..............................$32.00
RC Cola, 1951 Ford Bottle Truck, NB, #1099, H8 ....$28.00
Red Crown, 1930 Tanker, #2006, P1...............................$25.00
Richmond Pontiac 400/Davey Allison, 1931 Panel, Kenworth
    Tractor Trailer, #0212 & #0213, set of 2, P1..........$125.00
Rockingham Speedway, K100E, #0211, P1.......................$55.00
Sheriff #3, 1929 Roadster, #1529, P1 ....$30.00
Spec-Tacular News, 1929 Panel, #1005, P1.....................$35.00
Sunsweet #3, 1931 Panel, #2520, P1...............................$25.00
Talladega Speedway, 1929 Ford, #0325, H8 ....$24.00
Texaco, Bruce's in Tulsa (sampler), 1931 International,
    #4101, H8 ....$95.00
Texaco #11, Vintage Plane, #0841, H8 ....$95.00
Texaco Fire Chief, 1929 Tanker, #2008, P1 ....$45.00
Texaco Havoline, 1929 Ford, #2529, H8..........................$25.00
Texaco Lubricants, 1929 International, #4028, H8 ......$105.00
Tip-up Town, 1955 Chevy Panel, #50022, H8.................$23.00
Total Performance, 1931 Ford, #1169, H8.......................$29.00
Total Performance #2, 1931 Panel, #1169, P1.................$35.00
Toy Farmer Zeke, 1929 Ford, #1532, H8 ....$25.00
True Value Green Thumb '93, 1931 Panel, #2545, P1....$25.00
Trustworthy #9, 1916 Studebaker, #2250, P1 ....$20.00
Trustworthy Hardware, 1929 Ford, #1013, H8 ....$19.00
US Mail, Vintage Plane, #8679-81, H8............................$27.00
Vic Eldebrock Sr, 1931 Roadster, #1168, P1 ....$35.00

Wix Filters, 1955 Chevy, #50001, H8 ....$29.00
Wrigleys Doublemint Gum, 1931 Panel, #2521, P1 ....$25.00

First Gear

Anheuser-Busch Eagle Snacks #1, 1951 Ford, NB, #1140,
    H8..$34.00
Anheuser-Busch Snacks #2, 1952 GMC, NB, #1140, H8 .$32.00
Chevron Gasoline, 1951 Ford, NB, #1021, H8................$27.00
Coke Classic/Diet Coke Set, 1929 International, #5020,
    H8 ....$185.00
Dad's Root Beer, 1951 Ford, NB, #1115, H8.................$35.00
Eastwood Museum, 1951 Ford, NB, #1010, H8 ....$125.00
Eastwood Museum, 1952 GMC, NB, #0115, H8 ....$49.00
Gulf Oil, 1951 Ford, NB, #1020, H8...............................$29.00
Hershey's Chocolate, 1951 Ford, NB, #1002, H8 ....$29.00
Hershey's Syrup, 1951 Ford, NB, #1079, H8 ....$28.00
Lionel Trains, B-Mack Tractor Trailer, NB, #0116, H8..$95.00
Lionel Trains #2, 1952 GMC, NB, #0108, H8 ....$39.00
Mountain Dew, 1951 Ford, NB, #1075, H8 ....$29.00
Nehi Soda, 1951 Ford, NB, #1074, H8 ....$32.00
Pennzoil, 1952 GMC, NB, #40002, H8 ....$28.00
Pepsi-Cola, 1951 Ford, NB, #1091, H8............................$39.00
Phillips 66, 1951 Ford, NB, #1026, H8............................$34.00
Police Department, 1952 GMC, NB, #1058, H8............$34.00
Red Crown Gasoline, 1951 Ford, NB, #1019, H8 ....$29.00
Rolling Thunder, 1951 Ford, NB, #1141, H8 ....$44.00
Storey Wrecker, 1952 GMC, NB, #1068, H8 ....$34.00
US Mail, 1951 Ford, NB, #1001, H8 ....$29.00
Valvoline, 1952 GMC, NB, #1060, H8 ....$28.00

Dinky

Dinky diecasts were made by Meccano (Britain) as early as 1933, but high on the list of many of today's collectors are those from the decades of the fifties and sixties. They made commercial vehicles, firefighting equipment, farm toys, and heavy equipment as well as classic cars that were the epitomy of high style, such as the #157 Jaguar XK120, produced from the mid-fifties through the early sixties. Some Dinkys were made in France; since 1979 no Dinky toys have been produced in Great Britain. In the following listings, all Dinkys were produced in Great Britain unless noted 'FR' (France).

Alfa Romeo Meccano Ltd. Red Racer #8, Made in England, 1952, 4", EX, O1, $90.00.

#60C, Air France Constellation, 8" wingspan, original box, EX, A, $95.00.

#071, Dublo VW Van, yel, MIB, C5 ....$120.00
#106, Austin Atlantic, bl, bl seats, EX-, G3 ....$30.00
#106, Austin Atlantic, bl, MIB, C5 ....$150.00
#106, Prisoner Mini Moke, MIB, C5 ....$250.00
#108, Sam's Car, metallic red, MIB, G3 ....$75.00
#112, Purdy's TR-7, yel, MIB, G3 ....$50.00
#116, Volvo 1800 S, red, MIB, C5 ....$30.00
#122, Volvo 122 DL Station Wagon, lt metallic bl, M, L1.$38.00
#123, BNC Austin Princess 2300, copper & blk, MIB, L1..$65.00
#124, Rolls Royce Phanton V, metallic bl, MIB, C5 ....$50.00
#128, Mercedes Benz 600, metallic bl, MIB, C5 ....$50.00
#130, Ford Corsair, bl, MIB, C5 ....$90.00
#131, Jaguar E Type, copper, MIB, C5 ....$100.00
#134, Triumph Vitesse, metallic bl, red interior, NM, G3.$55.00
#137, Cadillac Tourer, El Dorado, yel, MIB, C5 ....$200.00
#139, Ford Fordor, red, G-, L1 ....$40.00
#1402, Ford Galaxie (sedan), metallic gold, red interior, FR, NM, L1 ....$115.00
#1403, Matra 530, T-top, wht (scarce color), FR, M, L1.$95.00
#143, Ford Capri, turq & wht, MIB, C5 ....$120.00
#147, Cadillac 62 Sedan, metallic turq, red interior, NM, L1 ....$50.00
#150, Rolls Royce, M (VG box) $75.00
#151B, 6-Wheeled Army Wagon, EX, F2 ....$70.00
#151D, Water Tanker Trailer, M, F2 ....$35.00
#152A, Light Tank, M, F2 ....$80.00
#152B, Reconnaisance Car, olive drab, NM, L1.............$75.00
#152C, Austin 7 Military, M, F2..................................$35.00

#153, Aston Martin, silver & gray, no insert, MIB, G3...$35.00
#153, Aston Martin DB6, silver bl, M, L1 ....$65.00
#153A, US Army Jeep, NM, F2......................................$65.00
#155, Rolls Royce Silver Shadow, metallic red, MIB, C5.$80.00
#157, Jaguar, EX+...$90.00
#158, Rolls Royce, MIB..$60.00
#161, Ford Mustang, wht, missing grille decal, NM, L1 ..$65.00
#161B, Anti-Aircraft Gun (prewar), VG, F2....................$75.00
#162, Dragon Tractor Set, M F2....................................$150.00
#162, Ford Zephyr Saloon, 2-tone bl, MIB, C5 ....$140.00
#162, Triumph 1300, bl, MIB, C5 ....$90.00
#162A, Dragon Tractor, NM, F2....................................$65.00
#162B, Limber, M, F2..$45.00
#162B, Trailer, army gr, NM+, L1 ....$25.00
#162C, 18 Pounder Cannon, M, F2 ....$45.00
#163, VW Fastback, red, MIB, C5 ....$70.00
#164, Ford Zodiac, silver, MIB, C5 ....$70.00
#164, Vauxhall Cresta Salon, cream & maroon, MIB, C5.$140.00
#164, Vauxhall Cresta Salon, cream & maroon, NM, L1.$75.00
#166, Sunbeam Rapier, turq & bl, MIB, C5 ....$140.00
#167, DC Aceca Coupe, MIB..$150.00
#169, Studebaker Golden Hawk, gr & cream, MIB, C5 .$140.00
#170, Lincoln Continental, bl, MIB, C5 ....$110.00
#172, Fiat 2300 Station Wagon, dk bl & lt bl, NM, L1...$65.00
#174, Hudson Hornet, red & cream, MIB, C5 ....$175.00
#174G, Hudson Hornet Sedan, gray hubs, gray & yel, NM, L1 ....$75.00
#174H, Mercury Cougar, metallic bl, MIB, L1 ....$85.00
#176, Austin A105, cream & bl, first Dinky to have windows, MIB, C5 ....$150.00
#176, Austin A105, gray, red flashes, NM+, L1 ....$75.00
#178, Morris Mini Clubman, bronze, MIB, C5..............$40.00
#182, Porsche 356A, cream hubs, pale bl, NM+, L1 ....$95.00
#182, Porsche 356A Coupe, rpt cream, VG+, G3 ....$35.00
#185, Alfa Romeo 1900, red, NM, L1............................$55.00
#186, Mercedes Benz 220 SE, bl, MIB, C5 ....$90.00
#187, De Tomaso Magousta, pk & wht, NM, L1 ....$35.00
#187, De Tomaso Mangusta, red & ivory, MIB, C5 ....$50.00
#187, VW Karman Ghia, red & blk, MIB, C5 ....$125.00
#188, Caravan, gr & cream, NMIB, L1 ....$75.00
#188, Jensen FF Coupe, yel, blk interior, M, L1 ....$50.00
#188, Singer Gazelle, gray & gr, MIB, C5 ....$140.00
#189, Lamborghini Marzal, gr & wht, M, L1 ....$45.00
#190, Caravan, orange & cream, MIB, C5 ....$70.00
#190, Monteverdi, metallic maroon, MIB, C5...............$75.00
#191, Dodge Royal Sedan, gr, MIB, C5 ....$140.00
#192, Range Rover, bronze, MIB, C5 ....$27.00
#195, Fire Chief's Car, metallic red, MIB, C5 ....$35.00
#196, Holden Sedan, ivory & bronze, M, L1 ....$65.00
#196, Holden Sedan, turq, MIB, C5 ....$75.00
#198, Phantom V Rolls Royce, cream & lt gr, NM+, L1.$65.00
#199, Austin Countryman, bl, MIB, C5 ....$45.00
#202, Fiat Abarth 2000, orange & wht, MIB, C5............$50.00
#205, Lotus Cortina Rally, wht, MIB, G3.......................$25.00
#206, Corvette Stingray, red, MIB, G3...........................$12.00
#207, Triumph TR7 Rally, wht, bl & red, M, L1............$35.00
#208, VW Porsche 914, MIB, C5 ....$50.00
#212, Ford Cortina Rally Car, wht & blk, MIB, C5 ......$125.00

#210, Alfa Romeo 33 Tipo Le-Mans, opening doors and engine cover, M decals, 4", NMIB, A, $40.00; #23, Mercedes Benz CIII, Speedwheels, gull wing doors, molded engine, 4", NMIB, A, $40.00.

#215, Ford GT Racing Car, wht, MIB, C5 ....$50.00
#22S, Searchlight Lorry, M, F2.............................$125.00
#223, McClaren M8A Can Am, gr, MIB, C5 ....$45.00
#225, Lotus F Racing Car, red, MIB, C5.......................$32.00
#226, Ferrari 312/B2, red, MIB, C5...........................$25.00
#227, Beach Buggy, yel, EX+, G3.............................$15.00
#230, McClaren Can Am, metallic gr, MIB, C5 ....$45.00
#232, Alfa Romeo Racing Car, red, MIB, C5.................$150.00
#233, Cooper Bristol Racing Car, gr, MIB, C5..............$125.00
#237, Mercedes Racing Car, wht, MIB, C5 ....$100.00
#238, Jaguar Racing Car, turq, MIB, C5 ....$150.00
#24, Mercedes Benz CIII, red, 4", NM (NM box), A $40.00
#24A, Chrysler New Yorker, red, FR, NM, L1 ....$115.00
#24D, Plymouth Belvedere, blk & gr, FR, NM, L1 ....$115.00
#24F, Peugeot 403 Station Wagon, gr & bl, FR, NM, L1.$75.00
#24H, Mercedes 190SL, blk & ivory, FR, NM, L1 ....$115.00
#24M, VW Karman Ghia, blk & red, FR, NM, L1 ....$95.00
#24Q, Ford Vedette 49, metallic bl, FR, rare, NM, L1 ..$150.00
#24V, Buick Roadmaster, cream & bl, scarce color, FR, NM+, L1...$130.00
#24Y, Studebaker Commander, cream & orange, FR, NM, L1...$95.00
#240, Cooper Racing Car, bl, MIB, C5.........................$60.00
#242, Ferrari Racing Car, red, NM, L1 ....$35.00
#242, Ferrari Racing Car, red, MIB, C5.......................$60.00
#243, BRM Racing Car, metallic gr, MIB, C5 ....$60.00
#25V, Ford Refuse Truck, dk gr, scarce, FR, NM+, L1..$165.00
#250, Police Mini Cooper S, wht, MIB, C5 ....$100.00
#250, Streamlined Fire Engine, red, MIB, C5..............$180.00
#251, Pontiac Police Car, blk & wht, MIB, C5.............$100.00
#255, Mercy Tunnel Police, red, EX+, L1 ....$35.00
#260, Royal Mail, NM $130.00
#261, Telephone Service Van, gr, MIB, C5 ....$250.00
#263, Superior Criterion Ambulance, wht, MIB, C5 ......$75.00
#268, Range Rover Ambulance, wht, MIB, C5 ....$30.00
#269, Jaguar Police Car, wht, MIB, C5.......................$175.00
#27G, Motorcart (342), brn & dk gr, M, G3 ....$35.00
#270, Ford Police Car, turq, MIB, C5.........................$50.00
#275, Brinks Truck, gray, MIB, C5 ....$75.00
#276, Ford Ambulance, wht, MIB, C5.........................$32.00
#278, Plymouth Yellow Cab, yel, MIB, G3...................$35.00
#281, Military Hovercraft, MIB, F2............................$75.00
#282, Land Rover Fire Appliance, red, MIB, C5 ....$45.00
#283, Ford Transit Fire Appliance, red, MIB, C5..........$150.00
#285, Merry Weather Fire Tender, MIB, C5 ....$95.00
#287, Police Accident Unit, wht, MIB, C5 ....$80.00

#299, Crash Squad Set, MIB, C5 ....$50.00
#30HM, Daimler Ambulance, NM, F2.........................$125.00
#303, Commando Squad Gift Set, MIB, F2..................$110.00
#308, Leyland Tractor, bl, MIB, C5...........................$50.00
#308, Leyland Tractor, bl, no driver or stack, EX+, G3 ..$20.00
#320, Hay Trailer, red & tan, MIB, C5........................$70.00
#321, Massey Ferguson Manure Spreader, red, MIB, G3 .$30.00
#340, Land Rover, NM+......................................$55.00
#341, Land Rover Trailer, orange, MIB, C5 ....$15.00
#355, Lunar Roving Vehicle, bl, MIB, G3.....................$45.00
#357, Klingon Battle Cruiser, box has wear, MIB, G3 ....$40.00
#358, USS Enterprise, only 1 bomb, EX, G3 ....$15.00
#36B, Bently Sports Coupe, mocha & blk, rstr, M, L1 ....$85.00
#36B, Willeme Tractor Trailer, Fruehauf, red, gr & yel, FR, MIB, L1...$275.00
#361, Galactic War Chariot, gr, MIB, C5 ....$30.00
#38A, Alvis Convertible, maroon, NM, L1..................$105.00
#38F, Jaguar, 1-sided windshield, bl, gray interior, NM, L1...$65.00
#384, Convoy Fire Rescue, MIB $19.00
#40B, Triumph 1800 Renown, tan, gr wheels, NM, L1 ...$75.00
#401, Coventry Climax Fork Lift, orange & gr, NMIB, L1.$65.00
#409, Articulated Lorry, MIB $100.00
#410, Bedford Van Royal Mail, red, MIB, C5................$40.00
#411, Bedford Truck, gr, MIB, C5.............................$135.00
#416, Ford Fire Service, red, MIB, C5 ....$30.00
#416, Ford Transit Van 'Motorway Services,' yel, MIB, C5.$30.00
#416, Ford Transit Van Fire Service, red, MIB, C5.........$30.00
#435, Bedford Tipper (1st issue), wht & orange, MIB, C5..$80.00
#440, Mobile Gas Truck, MIB $180.00
#442, Esso, NM $130.00
#442, Fordson, NM..$45.00
#448, Johnston Road Sweeper, gr, MIB, C5 ....$65.00
#449, Chevy El Camino, gr & cream, EX+, G3 ....$30.00
#475, 1908 Ford Model T, bl & red, MIB, C5 ....$110.00
#477, Parsley's Car, gr, MIB, G3 ....$110.00
#480, Kodak Van, NM $100.00
#481, Ovaltine, NM+......................................$90.00
#488, Bedford Van 'Dinky Toys,' MIB, C5 ....$300.00
#516, Mercedes Benz 230SL, gray & cream, FR, MIB, C5...$125.00
#518, Renault 4L, mocha, FR, MIB, C5 ....$100.00
#520, Fiat 600D, ivory, FR, NM, L1 ....$65.00
#532, Lincoln Premiere, silver & pale bl, FR, NM, L1 ....$85.00
#543, Renault Floride, metallic gold, FR, NM, L1..........$75.00
#545, De Soto Diplomat, blk & coral, FR, NM, L1 ....$95.00
#549, Borgward Coupe, FR, MIB $155.00
#552, Chevy Corvair, pale bl, FR, NM, L1 ....$85.00
#555, Ford Thunderbird, wht, FR, M, L1 ....$145.00
#564, Elevator Loader, NM (EX- box)........................$90.00
#571, Coles Mobile Crane, 1st issue, NMIB (+insert).....$85.00
#602, Armoured Command Car, MIB, F2 ....$75.00
#604, Land Rover Bomb Disposal Unit, military gray, MIB, C5...$50.00
#609, US Howitzer, w/3-man crew, MIB, F2 ....$75.00
#615, US Jeep & 105MM Howitzer, M, F2.................$95.00
#616, AEC Transporter w/Tank, MIB, F2...................$160.00
#618, AEC Transporter w/Helicopter, MIB, F2 ....$145.00

#620, Berliet Missle Launcher, MIB, F2 ....$225.00

#621, Bedford Army Truck, Army gr, NM+, L1 ....$75.00

#622, Bren Gun Carrier, MIB, F2 ....$55.00

#622, 10-Ton Army Truck, MIB, F2 ....$125.00

#623, Army Covered Wagon, MIB, F2 ....$70.00

#626, Ford Military Ambulance, Army gr, red crosses, NM, L1 ....$60.00

#641, 1-Ton Cargo Truck, MIB, F2 ....$75.00

#642, Pressure Refueller, EX-, F2 ....$50.00

#643, Water Tanker, M, F2.......................................$75.00

#654, 155MM Mobile Gun, MIB, F2 ....$75.00

#660, Anti-Tank Transporter, MIB, F2 ....$150.00

#661, Recovery Tractor, MIB, F2 ....$150.00

#662, Static 88MM Gun w/Crew, MIB, F2 ....$85.00

#666, Corporal Missile, MIB, F2 ....$400.00

#667, Missile Servicing Platform, MIB, F2 ....$300.00

#670, Armoured Car, MIB, F2 ....$65.00

#673, Scout Car, olive, minus 1 box flap, MIB, G3 ....$35.00

#674, Austin Champ, M, F2..$35.00

#674, Coast Guard Amphibian, MIB, C5 ....$27.00

#674, Coast Guard Missle Launch, wht, MIB, from $27 to..$35.00

#675, US Army Staff Car, EX, F2 ....$70.00

#676, Armoured Personnel Carrier, MIB, F2 ....$60.00

#676, Saracen Military Blinded Car, Army gr, NM+, L1 .$50.00

#677, Task Force Set, MIB, F2 ....$80.00

#680, Ferret Scout Car, MIB, F2 ....$40.00

#683, Chieftan Tank, MIB, F2 ....$85.00

#686, 25-Pound Gun, MIB, F2 ....$60.00

#687, Convoy Army Truck, MIB, F2 ....$40.00

#688, Field Artillery Tractor, MIB, F2.........................$70.00

#690, Scorpion Tank, M, F2 ....$60.00

#691, Striker Anti-Tank Vehicle, MIB, F2 ....$85.00

#692, Leopard Tank, MIB, F2 ....$80.00

#694, Hanomag Tank Destroyer, MIB, F2 ....$90.00

#696, Leopard Anti-Aircraft Tank, M, F2 ....$75.00

#697, 25 Pound Field Gun Set, MIB, F2........................$165.00

#699, Leopard Recovery Vehicle, MIB, F2 ....$90.00

#70A, York Airliner, silver, NM, L1............................$95.00

#710, Beechcraft Bonanza, copper & yel, NM+, L1 ....$65.00

#72, Dublo Bedford, NM (VG box)...............................$65.00

#73, Dublo Rover & Horse Trailer, MIB.......................$130.00

#735, Gloster Javelin, camouflaged, NM+, L1 ....$50.00

#736, Hawker Hunter, camouflaged, NM+, L1 ....$40.00

#80B, Military Jeep, FR, MIB, F2................................$90.00

#80C, AMX 13T Tank, FR, MIB, from $85 to $95.00

#80D, Berliet 6X6, FR, MIB, F2.................................$125.00

#80F, Renault Goelette Ambulance, olive drab, FR, NM, L1 ....$115.00

#800, Renault Sinpar 4X4, FR, MIB, F2 ....$150.00

#810, Dodge Command Car, FR, MIB, F3.....................$225.00

#813, 155MM Canon Automoteur, FR, M, F2.............$150.00

#814, AML Panhard, FR, MIB, F2...............................$100.00

#815, EBR Panhard, FR, M, F2 ....$85.00

#816, Berliet Gazelle Missile Truck, EX, F2 ....$35.00

#817, AMX 13T Tank, FR, MIB, F2.............................$90.00

#818, Berliet 6X6, FR, M, F2.....................................$110.00

#819, 155MM Obusier, FR, M, F2 ....$75.00

#821, Mercedes Unimog, FR, MIB, F2 ....$125.00

#822, M-34 Half-Track, FR, MIB, F2 ....$135.00

#822, White Half-Track (type 2 w/gun), olive drab, FR, M, L1..$75.00

#823, Cuisine Marion, FR, MIB, F2..............................$80.00

#826, Berliet Wrecker, FR, M, F3 ....$175.00

#828, Jeep, w/missiles, FR, MIB, F2 ....$110.00

#829, Jeep, w/cannon, FR, MIB, F2 ....$110.00

#883, AMX Bridgelayer, FR, MIB, F2...........................$200.00

#884, Brockway Bridgelayer, FR, MIB, F2 ....$400.00

#890, Berliet Tank Transporter, FR, MIB, F2...............$285.00

#893, Trailer, Pipe Carrier, FR, MIB $260.00

#897, Trailer, 'Willeme,' FR, NM $235.00

#932, Heinz Bedford, NMIB $365.00

#949, Wayne School Bus, MIB $290.00

#952, Luxury Coach, MIB...$140.00

#952, Vega Major Luxury Coach, cream, MIB, C5 ....$200.00

#956, Bedford Turntable Fire Escape, red, NM+, L1 .....$135.00

#958, Snow Plow, MIB $285.00

#961, Blaw Know Bulldozer, red, missing 1 tread, NMIB, L1 ....$75.00

#972, Lorry Mounted Crane, MIB $150.00

#978, Refuse Wagon, MIB, C5....................................$20.00

Dollhouse Furniture

Back in the forties and fifties, little girls often spent hour after hour with their dollhouses, keeping house for their imaginary families, cooking on tiny stoves (that often came with scaled-to-fit pots and pans), serving meals in lovely dining rooms, making beds, and rearranging furniture, most of which was plastic, much of which was made by Renwal, Ideal, Marx, Irwin, and Plasco. Jaydon made plastic furniture as well, but sadly never marked it. Tootsietoy produced metal items, many in boxed sets.

Of all of these manufacturers, Renwal and Ideal are considered the most collectible. Renwal's furniture was often detailed, some pieces had moving parts. Pieces were made in more than one color, often brightened with decals. Besides the furniture, they made accessory items as well as 'dollhouse' dolls of the whole family. Ideal's Petite Princess line was packaged in sets with wonderful detail, accessorized down to the perfume bottles on the top of the vanity. Ideal furniture and parts are numbered, always with an 'I' prefix.

Arcade, kitchen furnishings, painted cast iron, 7 pieces, A, VG, $170.00.

Acme, hammock, red & bl, sm glue stains in center, T5.$15.00
Acme, sled w/dog, gr & yel w/red harness, T5 ....$20.00
Acme, stroller, pk w/bl top, M7 ....$8.00
Acme, swing, red, yel & gr, T5 ....$14.00
Acme, teeter-totter, red w/yel horse heads, M7 ....$8.00
Acme, wagon, turq w/yel wheels & pk hdl, M7 ....$15.00
Allied, sink, kitchen, w/pump, working, T5 ....$17.00
Allied, stroller, bl w/pk wheels, 3x2¼", M7 ....$8.00
Arco, sofa w/2 chairs, red w/tan trim, M7 ....$5.00
Best, bunk beds, pk w/ladder, T5 ....$10.00
Best, hobby horse, pk, M7 ....$6.00
Best, lawn rocker, yel, missing 1 rocker tip, T5.................$3.00
Ideal, baby, M7...$10.00
Ideal, bathtub, corner; bl w/bright yel hardware, M, T5 ..$15.00
Ideal, bed, ivory & lt bl, M7 ....$10.00

Ideal, Petite Princess Bed Set, M (EX box), $30.00.

Ideal, cabinet, medicine; ivory & blk, T5 ....$30.00
Ideal, card table (folding) w/4 folding chairs, ivory w/brn, 1 leg
    loose, rpr bk support, sm glue stains, T5 ....$45.00
Ideal, chair, bedroom; bl marbleized top w/ivory base, T5 .$18.00
Ideal, chair, folding, brn w/red seat, M7 ....$10.00
Ideal, chair, kitchen; ivory w/bl seat, M7 ....$4.00
Ideal, chair, living room; gr, T5...................................$5.00
Ideal, chair, lounge; red or wht, ea, T5 ....$7.00
Ideal, chair, potty; w/bowl, salmon, M, T5 ....$16.00
Ideal, china cupboard, dk brn, M7 ....$10.00
Ideal, cradle, pk, missing support pin, T5......................$5.00
Ideal, dining chair, brn w/bl seat, M7...........................$5.00
Ideal, hamper, ivory, M7 ....$4.00
Ideal, highboy, dk brn, VG, T5 ....$4.00
Ideal, highchair, folding, bl, M7..................................$15.00
Ideal, mangle, wht, M, T5 ....$12.00
Ideal, night stand, ivory & lt bl, M7 ....$5.00
Ideal, radio, brn floor model, M7 ....$8.00
Ideal, radio, console, VG, T5 ....$4.00
Ideal, secretary, brn, M, T5 ....$19.00
Ideal, sewing machine, brn, M7 ....$12.00
Ideal, sink, bl w/dk yel hardware, VG, T5 ....$8.00

Ideal, sink, kitchen; ivory w/blk, M7 ....$15.00
Ideal, stove, ivory w/blk hdls, T5 ....$6.00
Ideal, table, coffee; unmk, scratched top, T5 ....$2.00
Ideal, table, kitchen; ivory, M7 ....$6.00
Ideal, table, patio; yel, rnd w/red umbrella, missing post,
    T5 ....$1.00
Ideal, table, patio/picnic; yel w/red umbrella, no pole,
    M7 ....$15.00
Ideal, vanity, ivory w/lt bl trim & seat, lt wear, M7.........$20.00
Ideal, vanity seat, ivory & lt bl, M7 ....$5.00
Ideal, vanity w/stool, dk brn, no silver on mirror, VG, T5..$3.00
Ideal, washing machine, door w/glass, dented top, stain,
    T5 ....$4.00
Ideal Young Decorator, buffet, dk marbleized reddish-brn,
    M7 ....$15.00
Ideal Young Decorator, chair, dining; yel seat, 1 rpr leg,
    M7 ....$3.00
Ideal Young Decorator, night stand, reddish-brn, M7 .....$10.00
Irwin, watering can, shovel, rake & pitchfork, M7..........$12.00
Jaydon, buffet, reddish-brn, M7..................................$4.00
Jaydon, chair, reddish-brn or red, M7 ....$1.00
Jaydon, piano, reddish-brn, M7...................................$10.00
JP Co, hutch, dk brn, M7 ....$3.00
Marvi, Ferris wheel, mc, M7 ....$10.00
Marx, bathtub, corner; bl or dk peach, hard plastic, ¾" scale,
    M7 ....$5.00
Marx, bathtub, ivory, ½" scale, M7 ....$1.50
Marx, bed, bright yel, hard plastic, ¾" scale, M7 ....$5.00
Marx, buffet, brn, ½" scale, M7 ....$3.00
Marx, buffet, dk brn, hard plastic, ¾" scale, M7 ....$5.00
Marx, bureau, royal bl, hard plastic, ½" scale, T5 ....$2.00
Marx, chair, armless, lt bl, gr, yel, or red, ½" scale, ea,
    M7 ....$2.00
Marx, chair, living room; red, soft plastic, ¾" scale, M7....$3.00
Marx, chair, living room; gr w/rnd bk, ½" scale, M7.........$2.00
Marx, chair, living room; red or lt bl w/sq bk, ½" scale , M7.$2.00
Marx, chair, potty; pk, soft plastic, ¾" scale, M7 ....$3.00
Marx, chest of drawers, pk, hard plastic, ¾" scale, M7.......$5.00
Marx, chest of drawers, pk, soft plastic, ¾" scale, M7 ....$3.00
Marx, chest of drawers, yel or dk ivory, ½" scale, M7 ....$2.00
Marx, china cupboard, brn, hard plastic, ¾" scale, M7......$5.00
Marx, crib, peach w/emb Mickey Mouse, ½" scale, M7 .....$8.00
Marx, crib, pk, soft plastic, ¾" scale, M7........................$3.00
Marx, end table w/books, yel, soft plastic, ¾" scale, M7 ....$3.00
Marx, hamper, ivory, ½" scale, M7................................$2.00
Marx, hamper, ivory or bl, hard plastic, ¾" scale, M7 ....$5.00
Marx, highboy, yel or ivory, hard plastic, ¾" scale, M7 .....$5.00
Marx, highchair, pk, hard plastic, ¾" scale, M7................$6.00
Marx, hutch, dk brn or reddish-brn, ½" scale, M7 ....$3.00
Marx, jukebox, royal bl, hard plastic, ½" scale, T5 ....$10.00
Marx, laundry set: sink, mangle & washer, yel plastic, ½" scale,
    T5 ....$5.00
Marx, night stand, yel or dk ivory, ½" scale, M7................$2.00
Marx, night stand w/molded books, yel, hard plastic, ¾" scale,
    M7 ....$5.00
Marx, orig pkg for any ¾" scale set, paper, M7, ea............$4.00
Marx, outdoor playset: sandbox w/molded toys, seesaw, pk & bl,
    ½" scale, T5 ....$5.00

Marx, playpen, peach or pk w/emb Donald Duck, ½" scale, M7......$8.00

Marx, refrigerator, wht, ½" scale, M7......$2.00

Marx, sand pail, yel, plastic w/metal hdl, 1" scale, VG, T5.$6.00

Marx, sand shovel, yel, hard plastic, 1" scale, T5......$6.00

Marx, sandbox, yel, hard plastic, 1" scale, T5......$6.50

Marx, sink, bathroom; bl, hard plastic, ¾" scale, M7......$5.00

Marx, sink, kitchen; wht, ½" scale, M7......$2.00

Marx, sofa, red, curved, ½" scale, M7......$4.00

Marx, sofa, red or yel, soft plastic, ¾" scale, M7......$3.00

Marx, sofa, yel, hard plastic, ¾" scale, M7......$5.00

Marx, sofa w/2 chairs, lt bl, ½" scale, M7......$5.00

Marx, stool, ivory, hard plastic, ¾" scale, M7......$4.00

Marx, stove, ivory, hard plastic, ¾" scale, M7......$5.00

Marx, stove, kitchen; wht, hard plastic, ½" scale, T5/M7..$2.00

Marx, table, brn, hard plastic, ¾" scale, M7......$5.00

Marx, table, ping-pong; royal bl, soft plastic, ½" scale, T5.$10.00

Marx, television & phonograph combination, yel, hard plastic, ¾" scale, M7......$5.00

Marx, television & radio combination, royal bl, hard plastic, ½" scale, T5......$7.00

Marx, toilet, ivory, ½" scale, M7......$2.00

Marx, vanity, ivory, hard plastic, ¾" scale, M7......$5.00

Marx, washing machine, avocado, 1" scale, T5......$3.00

Mattel Littles, armoire, M7......$15.00

Mattel Littles, bathtub, M7......$15.00

Mattel Littles, chair, kitchen; set of 4, M7......$10.00

Mattel Littles, chair, M7......$8.00

Mattel Littles, cradle, M7......$5.00

Mattel Littles, dresser, M7......$15.00

Mattel Littles, sink, bathroom; M7......$8.00

Mattel Littles, sink/icebox, M7......$15.00

Mattel Littles, sofa, M7......$12.00

Mattel Littles, stove, M7......$15.00

Mattel Littles, table, drop leaf; M7......$6.00

Mattel Littles, table, tilt top, M7......$8.00

Parlor Set, scroll cut and upholstered, European, piano: 4½x5", EX, A, $250.00.

Plasco, bathtub, pk, M7......$4.00

Plasco, bedroom set: 2 beds, chest, night stand & vanity w/stool, not perfect color match, T5......$15.00

Plasco, bedspread, lt gr or dk peach, M7......$2.00

Plasco, birdbath, orig glue discoloration, T5......$6.00

Plasco, buffet, dk brn or tan, M7......$4.00

Plasco, cabinet, kitchen; wht top on bl base, T5......$7.00

Plasco, chair, dining room; tan or red w/paper seat cover, M7......$3.00

Plasco, chair, kitchen; dk bl, lt bl or dk turq, M7......$2.00

Plasco, chair, living room; gr or rose w/brn trim, M7......$6.00

Plasco, chair tufted, sea green, T5......$4.00

Plasco, couch, bl, T5......$4.00

Plasco, crib, ivory, sm glue rpr on rail, M7......$20.00

Plasco, grandfather clock, brn, M7......$10.00

Plasco, hamper, pk w/gray lid, M7......$4.00

Plasco, highboy, brn, M7......$8.00

Plasco, highboy, ivory, M7......$15.00

Plasco, hutch w/separate bookcase, brn, VG, T5......$21.00

Plasco, night stand, brn or marbleized brn, M7......$3.00

Plasco, refrigerator, pk or lt gr, no-base style, M7......$3.00

Plasco, refrigerator, wht w/bl base, M7......$5.00

Plasco, sink, bathroom; lt turq or pk, M7......$4.00

Plasco, sink, kitchen; pk or lt gr, no-base style, M7......$3.00

Plasco, sink, kitchen; wht w/bl base, M7......$5.00

Plasco, sofa, lt bl w/brn base, M7......$8.00

Plasco, stove, pk or lt gr, no-base style, M7......$3.00

Plasco, stove, wht w/bl base, M7......$5.00

Plasco, table, bl, rnd, broken centerpiece, T5......$1.00

Plasco, table, coffee; any color, M7......$3.00

Plasco, table, dining room side; dk brn, M7......$4.00

Plasco, table, kitchen; wht, M7......$5.00

Plasco, table, patio; bl w/ivory legs, missing umbrella, M7..$4.00

Plasco, television, brn, w/insert, M7......$15.00

Plasco, toilet, pk & gray, seat & lid, M7......$5.00

Plasco, vanity, dk brn or lt pk, w/sq mirror, M7......$5.00

Plasco, vanity, reddish-brn, no-mirror style, M7......$5.00

Plasco, vanity bench, blk, M7......$4.00

Renwal, baby, M7......$8.00

Renwal, baby, nursery; rubber, M7......$4.00

Renwal, baby bath, pk or bl, M7......$15.00

Renwal, baby w/crocheted dress, M7......$10.00

Renwal, bathtub, nursery; ivory, M7......$8.00

Renwal, bathtub, 2-color, M7......$6.00

Renwal, bed, brn w/ivory spread, M7......$6.00

Renwal, brother, bl w/red tie, M7......$20.00

Renwal, brother, tan, M7......$18.00

Renwal, buffet, brn, M7......$8.00

Renwal, carriage, pk w/pk wheels, M7......$20.00

Renwal, chair, barrel style, 2-color, M7......$6.00

Renwal, chair, club; bl w/brn trim, M7......$6.00

Renwal, chair, club; yel-gr w/stencil, M7......$6.00

Renwal, chair, potty; pk w/decal, decal off center, T5......$7.00

Renwal, chair, rocking; blk plastic w/stencil, T5......$15.00

Renwal, chair, rocking; pk w/bl seat, M7......$10.00

Renwal, chair, teacher's; red, M7......$10.00

Renwal, chair, 2-color, M7......$3.00

Renwal, china closet, brn, M7......$6.00

Renwal, clock, mantel; red, M7......$10.00

Renwal, crib, ivory or pk w/name, M7, ea......$6.00

Renwal, dresser, brn w/mirror, M7......$10.00

Renwal, end table, brn, rnd, M7......$5.00

Renwal, fireplace, brn & ivory, M7......$20.00

Renwal, garbage can, red w/yel lid, M7......$8.00

Renwal, hamper, ivory, M7......$2.00

Renwal, hamper, pk, lid opens, M7......$3.00

Renwal, highboy, brn, M7......$6.00

Renwal, highboy, brn w/stencil, bl or pk, M7 ....$10.00
Renwal, highchair, bl or pk, M7 ....$20.00
Renwal, hutch, cream, door opens, T5 ....$7.00
Renwal, insert w/baby, M7 ....$4.00
Renwal, ironing board, VG $35.00
Renwal, kiddie car, yel body, red wheels & tray, bl steering wheel, T5 ....$30.00
Renwal, lamp, floor; brn, red, or yel w/ivory shade, M7 ......$10.00
Renwal, lamp, table; brn or rust w/ivory shade, M7 ....$5.00
Renwal, mother, rose or red dress, M, M7 ....$20.00
Renwal, night stand/end table, bl or pk, M7 ....$3.00
Renwal, night stand/end table, brn, M7 ....$2.00
Renwal, nurse, sm chips on 3 fingers, M7 ....$20.00
Renwal, piano, brn, M7 ....$20.00
Renwal, playground slide, yel w/bl steps, M7 ....$15.00
Renwal, playpen, pk w/stencil, M7 ....$15.00
Renwal, radio, floor model, brn, M7 ....$8.00
Renwal, radio, table model, red, M7 ....$10.00
Renwal, refrigerator, ivory & blk, M7 ....$8.00
Renwal, scale, red, M7 ....$6.00
Renwal, server, brn, M7 ....$6.00
Renwal, server, lt brn or red, drawer opens, M7 ....$8.00
Renwal, sewing machine, red, yel & bl, M7 ....$20.00
Renwal, sink, bl & pk or blk & ivory, M7 ....$4.00
Renwal, sink, ivory w/red stencil, M7 ....$10.00
Renwal, sister, yel dress, M, M7 ....$20.00
Renwal, sofa, pk w/brn trim or red w/brn trim, M7 ....$10.00
Renwal, stand, smoking; ivory w/red hdl or red w/ivory hdl, M7 ....$10.00
Renwal, stool, red w/ivory seat, M7 ....$6.00
Renwal, stove, ivory & blk, M7 ....$8.00
Renwal, stove, ivory w/red stencil, M7 ....$10.00
Renwal, table, card; folding, gold, T5 ....$9.00
Renwal, table, cocktail; brn or reddish-brn, M7 ....$5.00
Renwal, table, dining; red, M7 ....$10.00
Renwal, toilet, 2-color, M7 ....$8.00
Renwal, tray, bottle; ivory, M7 ....$8.00
Renwal, tricycle, red body w/bl wheels, sm glue stain on fender, T5 ....$11.00
Renwal, vacuum cleaner, red w/yel hdl & decal, M7 ......$25.00
Renwal, vanity, brn w/mirror, M7 ....$10.00
Superior, bathtub, lt turq or yel gr, ¾" scale, M7 ....$3.00
Superior, chair, kitchen; lt or dk gr, ¾" scale, M7 ....$2.00
Superior, chest of drawers, pk, ¾" scale, M7 ....$3.00
Superior, china closet, pk, ¾" scale, M7 ....$3.00

Superior, refrigerator, lt gr, ¾" scale, M7 ....$3.00
Superior, sink, bathroom; dk gr, ¾" scale, M7 ....$3.00
Superior, sofa, yel-gr, ¾" scale, M7 ....$3.00
Superior, toilet, lt or dk gr, ¾" scale, M7 ....$3.00
Thomas, baby carriage, bl, pk top, wht wheels, VG-EX, M7.$3.00
Thomas, cradle, pk w/bl, unmk, 3x4 ½", M7 ....$4.00
Thomas, stroller, bl or pk, M7 ....$5.00

Dollhouses

Dollhouses were first made commercially in America in the late 1700s. A century later, Bliss and Schoenhut were making wonderful dollhouses that even yet occasionally turn up on the market, and many were imported from Germany. During the forties and fifties, American toy makers made a variety of cottages; today they're all collectible. See also Schoenhut.

Bliss, lithographed paper on wood, all ranging from 16" to 17", G-G+ condition, A, from $600.00 to $950.00.

Bliss, mc trim w/metal porch lattice, hinged front door, paper loss & damage, worn pnt, 16½", G, A $600.00
Bliss, mc window appointments, rpl front door, eaves & dormer damaged, overall wear, 17", G+, A $950.00
Bliss, paper litho on wood, 11", VG..............................$450.00
Bliss, turned porch balusters, hinged front door, rpt, damage to hinge, moderate paper loss, 16", G, A $800.00

Tootsietoy, Kitchen Set, 8 pieces, all painted white, EX in original box, A, $325.00.

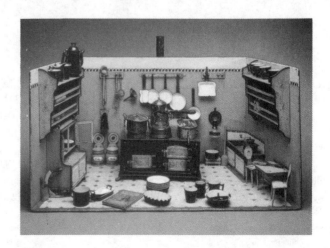

Kitchen, hand-painted, fully furnished, Marklin, ca 1900, 19x37x20", EX, A, $9,900.00.

Colonial, half-style, handcrafted, 6 rooms, open bk, 1950s, 33½x37x13", A $110.00

Converse, Horse Barn, emb & stenciled gable ends & roof, lift-off roof, w/2 pnt lead farm animals, 9½", G+, A.....$200.00

Converse, Red Robin Farm, roof lifts off, w/7 stenciled wood animals, minor damage & wear, 12", VG, A $275.00

Germany, gr w/red roof, 2 story w/delicate fretwork, open 1 side, 7 pcs wood furniture, 14½", VG, A $800.00

Marx, Suburban Colonial Home, unassembled, orig box & instructions, complete, NM $165.00

Paper litho on wood, 2-story, glass windows w/orig curtains, bl roof, yel porch floor, 3 rooms, 21x17x11", EX, A..$1,550.00

Pnt & varnished wood, collapsible, folding roof, detachable walls & interior sections, 21", VG, A $25.00

Pnt wood, gr-gray 'slate' roof, red 'brick' facade, gable ends, chimneys, front wall opens on 2 sides, 62", G+, A $1,050.00

Unmarked, painted wood with applied wooden trim, front opens on two sides, 62", G+, A, $1,050.00.

Victorian, mansard roof, front opening, 4 rooms & staircase, assorted furniture, 1900-1930s, some damage, 35x37x21", A $600.00

Victorian, pnt & heavily textured wood, gr w/wht trim, mansard roof, dormers & cupola, front wall opens, 48", G, A $950.00

Victorian setting, 2 rooms, pnt & stenciled wood, wood & upholstered furniture, Christmas tree, 33½x12", VG-EX, A .$475.00

Shops and Single Rooms

Apothecary Shop, pnt & papered wood setting, wood drawers w/40+ goods, dressed porc figure, 18x9", VG-EX, A..$975.00

Bedroom, pnt compo & wood figure overlooks bsk baby in wood cradle, portrait on wall, rocker, 14", VG-, A $250.00

Butcher's Shop, paper-on-wood setting w/cutting block, shelves & 40 pnt plaster cuts of meat, 18x9", VG-EX, A $600.00

Chocolate Shop, stenciled wood setting w/shelves & drawers, paper litho floor, 45+ goods, 27x9½", VG-EX, A...$1,450.00

Combination Grocery Store, Stirn & Lyon, Pat July 11, 1883, dyed & printed wood w/box as base, 9½x18", EX, A.........$1,100.00

Country Kitchen, pnt wood setting, bl & wht wallpaper, table & tin stove, 65+ old & new goods, 25x7", VG-EX, A.$1,800.00

Country Sitting Room, plank wood walls & floor, cloth curtains, pnt wood furniture, compo figure, 18½", VG-, A........$850.00

Entrance Hall, pnt compo & wood figure in blk dress by tilt-top candle stand, pnt panels w/stairs & furniture, 16", G+, A $300.00

Fabric Shop, pnt & stenciled wood w/shelves & drawers, 2 counters, 75+ fabric bolts, boxes of yarn, 24½x13", EX, A $1,250.00

General Store, pnt wood setting w/papered walls, filled shelves & drawers, 40 old & new miniatures, 9½x22", EX, A..$850.00

Sweets Counter, pnt wht wood counter w/gold trim & fretwork, cases, tin & brass scales, miniatures, 24x26", VG-EX, A $1,300.00

Tobacconist Shop, pnt bl wood setting, paper litho drawer fronts & columns, 31+ old & new goods, 19x7", VG-EX, A $475.00

Tobacconist Shop, Victorian w/stepped front counter & columns, tin lamps, scale & goods, w/dressed figure, 16x22", EX, A..$2,700.00

Toy Store, pnt wood setting w/shelves, counters & drawers, 65+ old & new goods, 25x9", EX, A $625.00

Toy Town Grocery Store, Parker Bros, pnt & unfinished wood w/paper litho sign & shelves, 35+ goods, 17x7¾", VG-EX, A $425.00

19th-Century Kitchen, bl & wht paper litho on wood, cupboard, tin stove, 18+ kitchen items, 15x6½", VG-EX, A $550.00

Dolls

Obviously the field of dolls cannot be covered in a price guide such as this, but we wanted to touch on some of the plastic dolls from the fifties and sixties, since so much of the collector interest today is centered on those decades. For in-depth information on dolls of all types, we recommend the many lovely doll books written by authority Pat Smith; all are available from Collector Books. See also Barbie and Friends; GI Joes.

Celebrity Dolls

Collecting dolls has been a popular hobby for many years now, but contemporary and popular celebrity dolls have lately shown a significant increase in interest as well as demand. The majority of these dolls are still available to collectors at doll shows, toy auctions, and flea markets. Most can be purchased for under $100.00, but some have already become very rare and hard to find. These are the dolls that bring back memories of childhood TV shows, popular songs, favorite movies, and familiar characters. Mego, Mattel, Remco, and Hasbro are among the largest manufacturers. In our listings, if no box is mentioned, values are for loose dolls. See also Character Collectibles. Our advisor for this category is Henri Yunes (Y1).

Andy Gibb, Ideal, complete, 1979, 8", EX (EX box), H4 .$30.00

Barry Goldwater, Remco, presses to dashboard of car, with button, 1964, MIB, $50.00.

Barry Goldwater, Remco, 1964, NM $30.00
Ben Casey, Bing Crosby Productions, 1962, 11½", NM (EX+ box), A..$200.00
Ben Casey (Vince Edwards), from 1960s TV show, rare, 11½", MIB $350.00
Beverly Hills 90210, from 1990s TV show, any of 5, MIB, ea ..$15.00
Beverly Johnson, Matchbox, #54613, 1989, MIB............$35.00
Boy George, LJN, plush, 14", NMIB $50.00
Boy George, LJN, vinyl, 1980s, scarce, 11½", NRFB $150.00
Brooke Shields, LJN, prom dress, 1982, rare, 11½", MIB..$100.00
Brooke Shields, LJN, suntan version, 11½", MIB............$50.00
Brooke Shields, regular version, 11½", MIB $30.00
Bruce Lee, Lar-Go, plastic, w/nunchaku, 1983, M (NM box), T2..$35.00
Bruce Lee, Lar-Go, w/bo stick, 1983, 6", MOC, C1 ....$45.00
Captain or Toni Tennile, Mego, 1970s, 12½", separate boxes, ea...$45.00
Cheryl Tiegs, Matchbox, #54612, 1989, MIB, P4 ....$35.00
Christie Brinkley, #54611, 1989, MIB, P4.....................$35.00

Clark Gable as Rhett Butler, World Dolls, fully jtd, limited edition, 1980, 12", M (NM box).................................$65.00
Daniel Boone, Marx, posable hard plastic, complete w/accessories & booklet, 1964, 12", NM (VG+ box), A $195.00
Davy Crockett, Uneeda, w/coonskin cap, 1950s, 14", EX, T1..$75.00
Diahann Carol as Julia, Mattel, metallic jumpsuit, talking, 1969, rare, 11½", MIB.................................$200.00
Diahann Carol as Julia, Mattel, nurse outfit, from 1969 TV show, rare, 11½", MIB.................................$140.00
Diana Ross, Mego, 1977, 12", NRFB $125.00
Diana Ross (of the Supremes), Ideal, 1969, rare, 19", MIB $200.00
Dolly Parton, Eegee, cowgirl outfit, 1987, 11½", MIB.....$60.00
Dolly Parton, Eegee/Goldberger, red pantsuit, 1980, 11½", MIB $45.00
Donny & Marie Osmond, Mattel, 1978, 11", together in box, MIB $70.00
Donny Osmond, Mattel, 1976, MIB, J2 ....$40.00
Dorothy Hamill, Ideal, Olympic outfit, 1977 skating star, 11½", MIB $75.00
Dr Kildare (Richard Chamberlin), from 1962 TV show, rare, 11½", MIB $350.00
Dukes of Hazzard, Mego, 1981 TV show, any of 4, MIB, ea.$25.00
Dwight D Eisenhower, Effanbee, Presidents series, molded hair, 1987, 16", M..$50.00

Elvis Presley, Graceland, plastic and vinyl, 1984, any of six different outfits, MIB, $70.00.

Elizabeth Taylor, Tri-Star Dolls, blk dress from Butterfield 8, 1982, 11½", M...$125.00

Elizabeth Taylor, World Dolls, in wht dress from Cat on Hot Tin Roof, 1988, 11½", M $50.00

Elvis Presley, Graceland, in any of 6 different outfits, 1982, 11½", MIB, ea...$70.00

Elvis Presley, World Dolls, Burning Love outfit, 22", MIB..$250.00

Elvis Presley, World Dolls, Phoenix outfit, 22", MIB....$200.00

Ernest, Kenner Division of Tonka Corp, cloth & vinyl, talker, 1989, 16", M...$42.00

Farrah Fawcett, Mego, wht jumpsuit, 1977, 12½", MIB ..$50.00

Farrah Fawcett as Charlie's Angel, Hasbro, 1977, 8", MOC, C1..$45.00

Flip Wilson, Shindana Toys, stuffed talker, Geraldine on other side, 1970, 16", non-working, o/w NM (EX+ box), T2...$40.00

Florence Griffith Joyner, LJN, long rooted hair, bendable knees, 1989, 11½", MIB $30.00

Flying Nun, Hasbro, 12", MIB (sealed).........................$200.00

Hardy Boys, Kenner, from 1978 TV show, 11½", MIB, ea.$40.00

Home Alone Kevin, screaming doll, 1989, MIB, T1 ....$20.00

Hulk Hogan, LJN, 1985, 16", M (NM box), I2 ....$35.00

Jimmy Osmond, Mattel, 1979, MIB...............................$50.00

Joe Namath, Mego, 1970s football star, rare, 11½", MIB.$300.00

John Travolta, Chemtoy, 1977, 12", M (EX box), I2 ......$28.00

Kiss (rock group), Mego, set of 4, 1978, 12½", separate boxes, MIB, ea $100.00

Laurel & Hardy, Goldberger, 1986, 12", MIB, ea $45.00

Laverne & Shirley, from 1970s TV show, set of 2 dolls, 12½", MIB $125.00

Lenny & Squiggy, Mego, from 1970s TV show, set of 2 dolls, 12½", MIB...$150.00

Leonard Nimoy, Mego, as Mr Spock, from Star Trek-The Movie, 1977, 12", M...$50.00

Leslie Howard as Ashley, World Dolls, 1st issue, fully jtd, limited edition, 1980, 12", M (NM box), C1................$54.00

Louis Armstrong, Effanbee, jtd, complete w/trumpet, 15", M $125.00

Lucille Ball, stuffed cloth w/vinyl face, I Love Lucy on apron, 1950s, NM...$175.00

Lyndon B Johnson, Remco, 1964, 16", NM....................$35.00

Madonna, Playmates, as Breathless Mahoney, 1990, 14", NRFB..$28.00

Mae West, Effanbee, Great Legends series, MIB (cellophane window cracked), H4 ....$120.00

Marie Osmond, Mattel, 1976, MIB...............................$40.00

Groucho Marx, Effanbee, Legend series, 1983, 17", M, $45.00.

Marilyn Monroe, Seven Year Itch Doll #7, 1982, 11½", MIB, $85.00. (Photo courtesy Lee Garmon.)

Marilyn Monroe, Tri-Star, from 1 of 8 different movies, 1983, 12", MIB, ea from $50 to..$100.00

Marilyn Monroe, Tri-Star, rooted hair w/pnt features, wht dress from Seven Year Itch, 1982, 16½", M, A..................$85.00

Marilyn Monroe, World Dolls, limited edition, 18", MIB..$200.00

MC Hammer, Mattel, 1991, 11½", MIB......................$30.00

Michael Jackson, LJN, American Music Awards outfit, 11½", NRFB..$40.00

Michael Jackson, LJN, Beat It outfit, 11½", NRFB.........$40.00

Michael Jackson, LJN, Grammy Awards outfit, 11½", NRFB..$40.00

Michael Jackson, LJN, in Thriller outfit, 1984, 11½", MIB.$40.00

Mr T, Galoob, plastic & vinyl, red shirt & bl overalls, holes in hands for tools, 1983, 12", MIB...............................$60.00

New Kids on the Block, Danny or Jordan, plush, 12", MIB, D4, ea...$12.00

New Kids on the Block, vinyl, 11½", any of 5, MIB, ea ..$15.00

Parker Stevenson, Kenner, Hardy Boys TV show, 1978, 11½", NRFB $40.00

Patty Duke, Horseman, 1965, rare, MIB.....................$450.00

Police Woman, Angie Dickinson, Horsman, 1970s, 9", M (VG box) $40.00

Princess Diana & Prince Charles, Nisbet, wedding clothing, MIB, pr...$160.00

Ricky Ricardo, Applause, 1988, 17", MIB $40.00

Ricky Ricardo, Hamilton Presents, vinyl w/stand, 1991, 15½", MIB, F1 ....$30.00

Six Million-Dollar Man & Bionic Woman, 7 dolls in set, separate boxes, ea, from $30 to $150.00

Sonny Bono, Mego, Gypsy King outfit (no doll), NRFB.$40.00

Star Wars, set of 12 dolls, 4" to 15" tallest, separate boxes, MIB, ea, from $100 to $500.00

Sylvester Stallone as Lincoln Hawks, Lewco, knob at bk moves arms, 1986, 20", M $25.00

Sylvester Stallone as Rocky, Phoenix Toys, 1986, 16", NRFB..$15.00

Twiggy, Mattel, 1967 fashion model, rare, 11½", MIB..$250.00

Vanilla Ice, THQ Toys, 3 in series, MIB, ea...................$20.00

Vanna White, Totsy Toys, limited edition, 1990, 11½", from $35 to..$65.00

Warren Beatty as Dick Tracy, Playmate, yel trench coat & hat, 1990, 15", M...$15.00

Wayne Gretzky, Mattel, hockey star, 1979, rare, 11½", MIB...$70.00

Chatty Cathy

In their new book, *Chatty Cathy Dolls, An Identification & Value Guide,* authorities Kathy and Don Lewis (L6) tell us that Chatty Cathy (made by Mattel) has been the second most popular doll ever made. She was introduced in the 1960s and came as either a blond or a brunette. For five years, she sold very well. Much of her success can be attributed to the fact that Chatty Cathy talked. By pulling the string on her back, she could respond with eleven different phrases. During her five years of fame, Mattel added to the line with Chatty Baby, Tiny Chatty Baby and Tiny Chatty Brother (the twins), and Charmin' Chatty. Singing' Chatty (1965) talked by means of changeable records, rather than the pull string. The line was brought back in 1969, smaller and with a restyled face, but it was not well received.

Carrying Case, Chatty Baby, pk or bl, L6 ....$20.00

Carrying Case, Tiny Chatty Baby, bl or pk, L6................$20.00

Charmin' Chatty, auburn or blond hair, bl eyes, 1 record, rpl glasses, L6..$95.00

Chatty Baby, open speaker, blond hair, bl eyes, L6 ....$75.00

Chatty Baby, open speaker, brunette hair, bl eyes, L6.....$80.00

Chatty Baby, open speaker, brunette hair, brn eyes, L6 ..$90.00

Early Chatty Baby, blond hair, bl eyes, ring around speaker, L6...$75.00

Early Chatty Baby, brunette hair, brn eyes, L6 ....$95.00

Early Chatty Baby, brunette hair, L6 ....$85.00

Later Issue, open speaker grille, blond hair, bl eyes, L6.$130.00

Later Issue, open speaker grille, brunette hair, L6 ....$135.00

Later Issue, open speaker grille, brunette hair w/brn eyes, L6..$145.00

Mid-Year or Transitional, blond hair, bl eyes, open speaker, L6..$120.00

Mid-Year or Transitional, brunette hair, brn eyes, L6 ...$135.00

Mid-Year or Transitional, brunette hair, L6 ....$125.00

Patent Pending, blond hair, bl eyes, cloth over speaker or ring around speaker, L6 ....$125.00

Patent Pending, brunette hair, L6.................................$130.00

Patent Pending, brunette hair w/brn eyes, L6................$140.00

Reissue Chatty Cathy, blond hair & bl eyes, L6 ....$55.00

Timey Tell, blond hair & bl eyes, L6 ....$55.00

Tiny Chatty Baby, brunette hair, bl eyes, L6 ....$80.00

Tiny Chatty Baby, brunette hair, brn eyes, L6................$90.00

Sonny and Cher, Mego, 1973, 11", 12¾",
MIB (box not shown), $40.00 each.

Tiny Chatty Baby, blond hair, blue eyes, L6, $75.00.

Tiny Chatty Brother, blond hair w/bl eyes, L6 ....$75.00
Unmarked Prototype, blond hair, bl eyes, cloth over speaker, L6...$135.00
Unmarked Prototype, brunette, L6 ....$145.00
Unmarked Prototype, brunette w/brn eyes, L6 ....$155.00

Dawn Dolls by Topper

Dawn and her friends were made by Deluxe Topper, ca 1970s. They're becoming highly collectible, especially when mint in the box. Dawn was a 6" fashion doll, part of a series sold as the Dawn Model Agency. They were issued in boxes already dressed in clothes of the highest style, or you could buy additional outfits, many complete with matching shoes and accessories. For further information we recommend our advisor, Dawn Parrish (P2).

Dawn Doll, 6", 1970, MIB, $30.00; Dawn Model Agency Dinah, 1970-71, M, $35.00, MIB, $45.00.

Cupid's Beau #8121, NRFB, P2......................................$20.00
Dawn Doll, NRFB (2nd issue box), P2 ....$20.00
Dinner Date #0610, NRFB, P2 ....$30.00
Fuchsia Flash #0612, NRFB, P2 ....$30.00
Gala Go-Go #0621, NRFB, P2 ....$30.00
Glamour Jams #8124, NRFB, P2....................................$20.00
Groovy Baby Groovy #0620, NRFB, P2 ....$30.00
Outfit, Bouffant Bubble, #711, 3-pc, complete, NM..........$5.00
Outfit, Gold Glow Swirl, #721, 5-pc, complete, EX $5.00
Outfit, Mad About Plaid, #723, 6-pc, complete, EX..........$4.00
Outfit, Neat Pleats, #710, 3-pc, complete, NM $5.00
Outfit, no name or #, long gold coat, gold shoes & necklace, NRFB, P2 ....$25.00
Outfit, Pink Slink, #8122, NRFP....................................$15.00
Outfit, Town 'N Tailored, #819, 6-pc, complete, EX+ $5.00
Outfit, Twinkle Twirl, #8144, 1970, 5-pc, NRFP............$12.00
Outfit, Wedding Belle Dream, #0815, NRFP $18.00
Pink Pussycat #0616, NRFB, P2.....................................$30.00

Flatsys by Ideal

Flatsy dolls were a product of the Ideal Novelty and Toy Company. They were produced from 1968 until 1970 in both 5" and 8" sizes. There was only one boy in the line. All were dressed in seventies' fashions, and not only clothing but accessory items such as bicycles were made as well. Our advisor for Flatsy dolls is Dawn Parrish (P2).

Bonnie Flatsy, sailing, NRFB (tear in cellophane on box), P2 ....$60.00
Candy Flatsy, Happy Birthday, NRFB, P2 ....$60.00
Casey Flatsy, engineer, only 5" boy w/molded hair, NRFB, P2 ....$75.00
Cory Fashion Flatsy, in print mini-dress, NRFB, P2 ....$60.00
Cory Fashion Flatsy, in silver eyelash pantsuit, NRFB, P2.$60.00
Dale Fashion Flatsy, in hot pk maxi, NRFB, P2...............$60.00
Dale Fashion Flatsy, in 2-pc wet-look outfit, NRFB, P2 ..$60.00

Dale Fashion Flatsy, $60.00.

Fall Mini Flatsy Collection, complete outfit, NFRB, (1 tear in cellophane on box), P2 ....$75.00
Gwen Fashion Flatsy, in peace poncho, NRFB, P2..........$60.00
Munch-Time Mini Flatsy Clock, NRFB, P2 ....$75.00
Nancy Flatsy, nurse w/baby, NRFB, P2 ....$60.00
Sandy Flatsy, in beach outfit, NRFB (faded box), P2 ......$55.00
Slumber-Time Mini Flatsy Clock, NRFB, P2 ....$75.00
Summer Mini Flatsy Collection, complete outfit, NRFB (torn cellophane on box), P2 ....$75.00
Trixy Flatsy, w/bicycle, only 5" Blk flatsy, NRFB, P2 ......$75.00

Jem Dolls and Accessories

The glamorous life of Jem mesmerized little girls who watched her Saturday morning cartoons, and she was a natural as a fashion doll. Hasbro saw the potential in 1986 when they introduced the Jem line of 12" dolls representing her, the rock stars from Jem's musical group, the Holograms, and other members of the cast, including the only boy, Rio, Jem's road manager and Jemica's boyfriend. Each doll was posable, jointed at the waist, heads, and wrists, so that they could be positioned at will with their musical instruments and other accessory items. Their clothing, their makeup, and their hairdos were wonderfully exotic, and their faces were beautifully modeled. Our values are given for mint-in-box dolls. All loose dolls are valued at about $8.00 each.

Aja, bl hair, w/accessories, complete, MIB $40.00
Ashley, curly blond hair, w/stand, 11", MIB....................$20.00
Banee, waist-length straight blk hair, w/stand, complete, MIB $20.00
Banee, 1987, NRFB, H4..$20.00
Clash, straight purple hair, complete, MIB......................$40.00
Danse, pk & blond hair, invents dance routines, MIB $40.00
Jem Roadster, AM/FM radio in trunk (working), scarce, EX $150.00
Jetta, blk hair w/silver streaks, complete, MIB................$40.00
Kimber, red hair, w/stand, cassette, instrument & poster, complete, 12½", MIB...$40.00

Jem/Jerrica, Glitter & Gold, with accessories, complete, 12½", MIB, $50.00. (Photo courtesy Lee Garmon.)

Krissie, dk skin w/dk brn curly hair, w/stand, 11", MIB...$20.00
Pizazz, chartreuse hair, w/accessories, complete, MIB......$40.00
Raya, pk hair, w/accessories, complete, MIB....................$40.00
Rio, Glitter & Gold, w/accessories, complete, 12½", MIB.$50.00

Synergy, purple doll with purple hair, MIB, $40.00. (Photo courtesy Lee Garmon.)

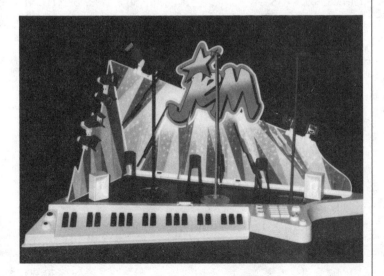

Jem Soundstage, Starlight House #17, $40.00 to $50.00. (Photo courtesy Lee Garmon.)

Roxy, blond hair, complete, MIB.....................................$40.00

Shana, purple hair, w/accessories, complete, MIB...........$40.00

Stormer, curly bl hair, complete, MIB $40.00

Video, band member who makes audio tapes, MIB $40.00

Liddle Kiddles

From 1966 to 1971, Mattel produced Liddle Kiddle dolls and accessories, typical of the 'little kid next door.' They were made in sizes ranging from a tiny ¾" up to 4". They were all posable and had rooted hair that could be restyled. Eventually there were Animiddles and Zoolery Jewelry Kiddles, which were of course animals, and two other series that represented storybook and nursery rhyme characters. There was a set of extraterrestrials, and lastly in 1979, Sweet Treats dolls were added to the assortment. Loose dolls, if complete and with all their original accessories, are worth about 25% less than the same mint in the box. Dressed, loose dolls with no accessories are worth 75% less. For more information, we recommend contacting our advisor, Dawn Parrish (P2).

Anabelle Autodiddle #3770, w/shoes & pusher, complete, P2...$40.00

Apple Blossom Kologne #3707, complete w/tag, S3........$30.00

Babe Biddle #3505, car only, S3.....................................$15.00

Babe Biddle #3505, complete, S3....................................$55.00

Baby Rockaway #3819, MOC (top 1" of card cut off), P2 .$85.00

Beddy-Bye Biddle #3748, missing bedspread & 2 bed posts, rpl hair bow, S3...$45.00

Bugs Bunny Skediddler #3822, extremely rare, MIB (cello ripped on box), P2..$85.00

Bunson Burnie #3501, complete, P2 ....$60.00

Bunson Burnie #3501, MOC, P2 ....$125.00

Calamity Jiddle #3506, complete w/horse, M, P2 ....$60.00

Calamity Jiddle #3506, orig hair set, nude, EX $10.00

Case, rectangular w/zipper, turq, M, S3 ....$40.00

Cherry Delight Sweet Treat Cookies #2818, MIP, P2.....$20.00

Cinderella Storykins, complete, S3..................................$25.00

Collector Case #3569, gr, w/insert, P2/S3........................$25.00

Collector Case #3569, pk, missing insert, P2...................$15.00

Comic Book, assorted, S3, any..$12.00

Cookin' Hiddle, #3846, orig hair set & ribbons, wearing pk panties only, EX $12.00

Cookin' Hiddle #3846, spot on dress, NMIB, P2.............$45.00

Dainty Deer #3637, w/tail, missing pin, P2......................$30.00

Donald Duck Skediddler, #3628, MOC, P2......................$75.00

Florence Niddle #3507, complete, M, P2.........................$60.00

Florence Niddle #3507, doll only, S3...............................$15.00

Flower-Bracelet Jewelry Kiddle #3747, missing doll, S3 ..$10.00

Flower-Bracelet Jewelry Kiddle #3747, MOC, P2............$25.00

Flower-Pin Jewelry Kiddle #3741, MOC, P2 ....$30.00

Flower-Pin Jewelry Kiddle #3741, pin only, P2.................$8.00

Flower-Ring Jewelry Kiddle #3744, MOC, P2 ....$30.00

Freezy Sliddle #3516, complete, w/seat belt & cord, M, P2...$25.00

Freezy Sliddle #3516, sled only, S3.................................$15.00

Frosty Mint Kone #3653, complete, S3............................$40.00

Frosty Mint Kone #3653, doll only, P2.............................$13.00

Funny Bunny #3532, aqua, MOC (price tag mark), P2 ...$40.00

Greta Grape #3728, Canadian version, MIB, P2.............$40.00

Greta Grape #3728, doll only, S3.....................................$12.00

Greta Griddle, #3508, blond hair & bl eyes, nude, VG $8.00

Greta Griddle #3508, complete w/pk table, yel chairs & accessories, M, P2...$60.00

Harriet Helididdle #3768, brunette hair, wht pnt socks, wearing Plum Pretty dress & panties, VG+............................$10.00

Harriet Helididdle #3768, missing goggles, o/w complete, P2...$35.00

Harriet Helididdle #3768, MOC, P2................................$75.00

Heart-Charm Bracelet Jewelry Kiddle #3747, MOC, P2 .$25.00

Heart-Pin Jewelry Kiddle #3741, complete, P2................$20.00

Heart-Pin Jewelry Kiddle #3741, pin only, P2 ....$8.00

Heart-Ring Jewelry Kiddle #3744, MOC, P2....................$30.00

Henrietta Horseless Carriage #3641, dressed doll w/hat, worn pnt on feet, P2..$25.00

Honeysuckle Kologne #3704, complete w/inner stand & tag, P2...$22.00

Howard Biff Boodle #3502, complete w/wht shirt & yel wagon, M, P2..$60.00

Kampy Kiddle, #3506, orig hair set, nude, EX $12.00

Kiddle Komedians w/Punch 'N Judy #3610, rare, MIB (tape rpr box), P2...$50.00

King & Queen of Hearts #3784, M (EX card), S3.........$120.00

Kola Kiddles, Olivia Orange, #3730, doll only, missing hat, EX..$4.00

Kolony #3517, G, P2..$25.00

Kosmic Kiddle, Greeny Meeny missing 1 antenna, o/w complete, M...$150.00

Kosmic Kiddles, Greeny Meeny, 1969, missing 1 antenna & lava rock, o/w EX...$75.00

Lady Crimson #A3840, MOC (hang tag missing), P2.....$75.00

Lady Lace Tea Party Kiddle #A3840, missing dome, S3..$35.00

Lady Lavender #A3840, lt faded dress, P2.......................$20.00

Lady Lavender #A3840, MOC (hang tag missing, melt mks inside cup), P2..$75.00

Lady Silver #A3840, dressed, missing accessories, P2......$45.00

Laffy Lemon #3732, Canadian version, MOC, P2...........$40.00

Larky Locket #3539, complete, NM, from $6 to..............$10.00

Laverne Locket #3718, 1976, MOC, P2 ....$25.00

Lemons Stiddle #3752, w/stand (1 melt mk), wht pitchers & glasses (detached), complete, P2...............................$60.00

Lenore Limousine #3642, doll only, S3............................$20.00

Lickety Spliddle & Her Traveliddles #3771, complete, P2 .$75.00

Lickety Spliddle & Her Traveliddles #3771, MOC, P2.$150.00

Lickety Spliddle #3674, brunette w/pk horse, S3............$45.00

Liddle Biddle Peep #3544, complete doll w/shoes, missing accessories, S3..$35.00

Liddle Biddle Peep #3544, w/all accessories except staff, P2.$65.00

Liddle Diddle #3503, complete w/checked pajamas & crib (melt mks), NM, P2..$50.00

Liddle Kiddles Kottage #3033, S3 ....$45.00

Liddle Kiddles Paper Dolls #1961, 9 dolls, uncut, M, P2...$40.00

Liddle Kiddles Talking Townhouse #5154, non-working, MIB, P2...$50.00

Liddle Middle Muffet #3545, w/rare spoon, missing book, o/w complete, P2...$75.00

Liddle Middle Muffet #3545, with book, MOC, S3, $165.00.

Liddle Red Riding Hiddle #3546, complete doll w/basket, S3 ....$40.00

Liddle Red Riding Hiddle #3546, complete w/book & variation basket, P2 ....$85.00

Lilac Locket #3540, doll w/wht hair in locket, P2 ....$18.00

Lily-of-the-Valley Kologne #3706, complete w/inner stand & tag, P2 ....$22.00

Liz Locket #3538, doll only, S3 ....$7.00

Lois Locket #3541, doll only, S3 ....$25.00

Lola Liddle #3504, complete, M, P2 ....$60.00

Lola Locket #3536, doll only, S3 ....$7.00

Lolli-Grape #3656, MOC, P2 ....$40.00

Lolli-Mint #3658, complete, S3 ....$35.00

Lolli-Mint #3658, MOC, P2 ....$40.00

Lolli-Mint, white hair, blue eyes, Mattel, 1966, M, $35.00.

Lorelei Locket #3717, 1976, MOC, P2 ....$25.00

Loretta Locket #3722, 1976, MOC, P2 ....$25.00

Lottie Locket #3719, complete, S3 ....$25.00

Lou Locket #3537, doll only, S3 ....$10.00

Louise Locket #3721, doll only, S3 ....$10.00

Luana Locket #3680, 1968, MOC, P2 ....$40.00

Lucky Lion #3635, M (NM card w/price tag mk), P2 ......$80.00

Lucky Locket Kiddles, Lorelei, #3717, blond doll, turq locket w/yel stones & orange door, clip attachment, EX.....$18.00

Lucky Locket Kiddles Box #4774, M (VG box), S3 ....$40.00

Luscious Lime Kola #3733, glitter variation, complete, S3 .$40.00

Luvvy Duvvy Animiddle #3596, S3 ....$15.00

Mickey Mouse Skediddler, #3629, MIB, P2 ....$75.00

Millie Middle #3509, missing shovel, o/w complete, S3 ..$60.00

Miss Mouse #3638, missing tail & safety pin, P2 ....$30.00

Nurse 'N Outfit #LK 7, Totsy, M (VG box missing name sticker, detached hdls), P2 ....$30.00

Olivia Orange #3730, Canadian version, MOC, P2 ....$40.00

Olivia Orange #3730, doll only, S3 ....$12.00

Orange Ice Kone #3654, MOC, P2 ....$40.00

Orange Meringue Skediddle Play Clothes, #3585, M (EX card, price tag mk, name sticker missing), P2 ....$25.00

Peter Paniddle #3547, w/Tinkerbell (no wings), missing head feather, o/w complete accessories, P2 ....$100.00

Pink Funny Bunny #3532, P2..$25.00

Playhouse Kiddles Paper Dolls, #1954, uncut, M, P2.......$40.00

Playhouse Kiddles Press-Out Book #1921, uncut, M, P2.$50.00

Plum Pretty Skediddle Play Clothes #3585, MOC, P2 ....$25.00

Posies 'N Pink Skediddle Play Clothes #3585, MOC, P2 .$25.00

Pretty Parlor #3847, NMIB, P2 ....$55.00

Pretty Priddle #3749, doll only, S3 ....$20.00

Pretty Priddle #3749, pk vanity w/matching stool, turq comb & brush, NM $12.00

Rapunzel & the Prince #3783, inner heart w/sm damage, NM, P2 ....$100.00

Record, sm, S3 ....$7.00

Romeo & Juliet #3782, inner heart w/sm damage, NM, P2.$100.00

Rosebud Kiddle Kologne, EX $25.00

Rosemary Roadster #3642, MOC, P2 ....$100.00

Santa Kiddle #3595, MOC, P2 ....$35.00

Shelia Skediddle #3765, MOC, P2 ....$50.00

Shelia Skediddle #3765, w/hair ribbon, dress & panties, P2 ....$15.00

Shirley Skediddle #3766, complete w/shoes & pusher, P2 ....$25.00

Shirley Skediddle #3766, MOC, P2 ....$50.00

Shirley Strawberry Kola #3727, missing base, S3.............$30.00

Showcase Plaque #5169, M (P card), P2..........................$20.00

Sizzly Friddle #3513, complete, S3 ....$60.00

Sizzly Friddle #3513, polka-dot outfit, missing shovel, o/w M, P2..$35.00

Sizzly Friddle #3515, blond hair, bl dress & panties, wht apron w/hot dog & hamburger print, no accessories, EX $12.00

Slipsy Sliddle #3754, complete, M, P2..............................$60.00

Slipsy Sliddle #3754, pk slide only, NM $12.00

Snap-Happy Bedroom Furniture #5172, missing bedspreads, o/w complete, P2..$15.00

Snap-Happy Patio Furniture #5171, MOC, P2 ....$35.00

Soapy Siddle #3518, missing talc & towel, o/w complete, S3 .$45.00

Soapy Siddle #3518, MOC, S3 ....$165.00

Storybook Kiddle Sweethearts Paper Doll Book #1956, M, S3..$40.00

Suki Skediddle #3767, complete w/shoes & pusher, P2....$25.00

Suki Skediddle #3767, MOC, P2 ....$50.00

Surfy Skiddle, #3517, blond hair, pk swimsuit top only, w/sunglasses & surfboard, NM...$15.00

Surfy Skiddle #3517, complete, S3 ....$65.00

Sweet Pea Kologne #3705, complete w/inner stand & tag, P2 ....$22.00

Sweet 3 Boutique #3716, Bluebell, Sweet Pea & Gardenia, MIB (faded box), P2..$200.00

Swingy Skediddle #3789, missing purse, o/w complete, S3 ....$45.00

Talking Townhouse #5154, non-talking, S3 ....$30.00

Totsy Outfit #LK6, NRFP, S3 ....$35.00

Tracy Trikediddle #3769, complete, S3 ....$45.00

Tracy Trikediddle #3769, MIB (tape on box side), P2 ....$75.00

Tracy Trikediddle #3769, w/all 4 ribbons, missing wagon, o/w complete, P2...$35.00

Trikey Triddle #3515, floral dress, MOC (water damaged card), P2...$100.00

Trikey Triddle #3515, red dress, rpl shoes, missing seat belt, P2 ....$45.00

Tutti-Frutti Kone #3655, complete w/2 stands, P2..........$25.00

Tutti-Frutti Kone #3655, MOC, P2 ....$40.00

Vanilly Lilly Sweet Treat Cookies #2819, MIP, P2.........$20.00

Violet Cologne, #3703, violet bottle w/lime gr cap & base, doll has purple hair, flowers missing, EX..........................$18.00

Windy Fliddle #3514, yel plane, missing maps, o/w complete, M, P2 ....$45.00

World of Liddle Kiddles View-Master Set #B-577, MIP, P2..$110.00

Yellow Fellow Kosmic Kiddle, missing 2 antennae, S3..$200.00

Yellow Funny Bunny #3532, P2 ....$30.00

Trolls

The first trolls to appear in America were molded from wood carvings made by Thomas Dam of Denmark. They proved to be such a huge success that several American companies began making them. Two of the most noteworthy were the Uneeda Doll Company who produced the Wishnik line and Scandia House Enterprises who named their line True Trolls. Today trolls are popular again, and the larger animals are especially collectible. Remember, trolls must be in mint condition to receive top dollar. Our advisor for this category is Roger Inouye (I1).

Bl hair w/orig tag, in silky shorts, 3", EX, H4...................$12.00

Boy bank, wht hair, gr & red outfit, 6½", I1 ....$35.00

Boy and Girl, Sun Rubber, molded vinyl, heart sticker on foot, 1964, $125.00 to $150.00 for the pair. (Photo courtesy Roger Inouye.)

Windy Fliddle, all vinyl with rooted blond hair, Mattel, 1966, MOC, S3, $145.00.

Bride-Nik, in formal outfit, Dam, 1978, MIP, T1 ....$15.00

Elephant w/blk hair, Dam, sm, EX, H4..........................$29.00

Frankenstein, Hong Kong, 3", NM $28.00
Lucky Shnook, wht hair, bl body, 1960s, 3",.....................$20.00
Neanderthal Man, Bijou Toy, pnt eyes, 1963, 7½", VG, D9 ....$32.00
No Goodniks, Wishnik series, 1970s, MOC, T1 ....$10.00
Nodder, MIB $65.00
Rain suit & hat (original felt outfit), Wishnik, 3", EX, H4 ....$12.00
Red hair pulled up w/ring ornament, wht outfit, 3", EX, H4 ....$12.00

Baby So-High #3828, orange & gr windmill, 1 bent flap, P2 ....$12.00
Down Dilly #3832, missing playland, o/w complete, P2 ....$65.00
Flossy Glossy #3827, dressed doll, hat, 'elewetter,' bucket & 1 ladder, P2 ....$50.00
Miss Information #3831, missing playland, o/w complete, P2 ....$65.00
Mother What Now #3829, missing curler & playland, o/w complete, P2 ....$55.00

Santa Claus, Chuck-O-Luck, green eyes, pink and white hair, painted-on clothes, 3½", $65.00. (Photo courtesy Roger Inouye.)

Pocus Hocus and His Dragon Wagon, $50.00.

Swedish, wood, 12", I1 ....$20.00
Tartan Girl, no hair, w/orig tag, 1964, 12", NM.............$45.00
Toronto Blue Jays, MOC...$8.00
Troll House, 11", I1 ....$15.00
Viking, wht hair, bl eyes, unmk, 3½", I1.........................$35.00
Voodoo, blk plastic w/cloth outfit, wht fuzzy hair, red ruby eyes, Japan, 1960s, M, T2. ....$15.00
Weird creature, w/real animal hair, 1960s, 3", MIP, I1....$30.00
Werewolf Monster, 1960s, 3", I1 ....$40.00
Wht hair, 3", EX, H4...$12.00

Pocus Hocus #3830, dressed doll (missing hat) & dragon wagon, P2...$50.00
Short Order From Funny Feeder #3834, complete, P2 ....$25.00
Tickle Pinkle #3825, missing bridge & playland, o/w complete, P2..$55.00
Tingle Dingle From Happy-Go-Round #3833, complete, P2 ....$22.00

Upsy Downsys by Mattel

The Upsy Downsy dolls were made by Mattel during the late 1960s. They were small, 2½" to 3½", made of vinyl and plastic, and some of the group were 'Upsies' that walked on their feet, while others were 'Downsies' that walked or rode fantasy animals while upsidedown. Our advisor for Upsy Downsys is Dawn Parrish (P2).

Farm Toys

It's entirely probable that more toy tractors have been sold than real ones. They've been made to represent all makes and models, of plastic, cast iron, and diecast metal. A few were even made of wood. They've been made in at least 1/16th scale, 1/32nd, 1/43rd, and 1/64th. If you buy a 1/16th scale replica, that small piece of equipment would have to be sixteen times larger to equal the size of the real item. Limited editions (meaning that a specific number will be made and no more) and commemorative editions (made for special events) are usually very popular with collectors. Many models on the market today are being made by the Ertl company; Arcade made cast iron models in the '30s and '40s.

Allis Chalmers Tractor and Manure Spreader, Arcade, painted cast iron, 8" long, EX, D10, $300.00.

Allis-Chalmers #12B Tractor Set, Arcade, cast iron, 1930s, 7½" long, M, D10, $650.00.

Allis-Chalmers D-19, Collectors Edition, Ertl, 1/16 scale, #2220, MIB, R1 ....$40.00
Allis-Chalmers D-19, Ertl, 1/43 scale, #2566, MIB, J5 ....$6.00
Allis-Chalmers D-19, Toy Farmer '89, Ertl, 1/16 scale, #2220, MIB, R1 ....$90.00

Allis-Chalmers #353 Tractor, Arcade, cast iron, 4", EX, D10, $145.00.

Allis-Chalmers Model C w/Roto Bailer, Ertl, 1/43 scale, #4298, MIB, J5...$11.50
Allis-Chalmers Tractor & Dump Truck, Arcade, CI, red w/gr trailer, Arcade rubber tires, 2x3x8", EX, A $75.00
Allis-Chalmers Tractor & Dump Wagon, CI, orange tractor, gr wagon, all rubber wheels, 1 rpl tire, 4x3x12½", VG-EX, A $100.00
Allis-Chalmers Tractor & Trailer, Arcade, red tractor w/gr trailer, rubber tires, pnt chips, 12", G-VG, A $60.00

Allis-Chalmers Vintage Round Baler, Ertl, 1/16 scale, #1244, MIB, R1 ....$18.00
Allis-Chalmers WC, Precision Series, Ertl, #2245, MIB, J5 .$95.00
Allis-Chalmers WD-45 & Wagon, Ertl, 1/16 scale, #1209, MIB, J5...$21.00
Ammonia Tank, Ertl, 1/64 scale, #1550, MIB, J5 ....$2.50
Antique Corn Sheller, Ertl, 1/8 scale, #4968, MIB, R1 ....$17.00
Belted Elevator, Ertl, 1/16 scale, #5609, MIB, J5 ....$18.00
Belted Elevator, Ertl, 1/64 scale, #4302, MIB, J5 ....$3.95
Case Disk, Ertl, 1/16 scale, #494, MIB, J5 ....$9.00
Case Farm Set, 5-pc, Ertl, 1/64 scale, #271, MIB, J5.........$10.95
Case Historical Tractor Set, Ertl, 1/64 scale, #4400, MIB, J5.$8.95
Case International Harvester Tractor, Ertl, 1/43 scale, #257, MIB, J5...$8.00
Case International Harvester 12 Row-Planter, 900 Series, Ertl, 1/64 scale, #656, MIB, R1....................................$4.00
Case International Harvester 1844 Cotton Picker, Ertl, 1/64 scale, #211, MIB, R1...$6.00
Case International Harvester 5130 Row Crop Tractor, 1991 Farm Show, Ertl, 1/64 scale, #229, MIB, R1 ....$10.00
Case International Harvester 5140 w/Mechanical Front Assist, Ertl, 1/64 scale, #240, MIB, R1....................................$3.85
Case L Tractor, 150 Year Collector Edition, Ertl, 1/16 scale, #252, MIB, R1...$35.00
Case Planter, Ertl, 1/64 scale, #478, MIB, J5......................$2.50
Case Plow, Ertl, 1/16 scale, #476, MIB, J5..........................$9.00
Case Spreader, Ertl, 1/16 scale, #492, MIB, J5 ....$9.00
Case VAC Antique Tractor, Ertl, 1/16 scale, #632, MIB, R1 ....$20.00
Case 500 Tractor, Ertl, 1/43 scale, #2510, MIB, R1 ....$5.25
Case 800, Ertl, 1/43 scale, #2616, MIB, J5........................$6.00
Case 800 Tractor, Collectors Edition, Ertl, 1/16 scale, #693, MIB, R1 ....$40.00
Case 800 w/Case Combine, Ertl, 1/43 scale, #4235, MIB, J5 ....$11.50
CAT 2-Ton Tractor, National Toy Truck Show, Ertl, 1/16 scale, #2438, MIB, R1 ....$65.00
Cub (wht grille), Ertl, 1/16 scale, #235, MIB, J5..............$18.55
David Brown Tractor, Ertl, 1/43 scale, #4180, MIB, J5 ....$10.00
Deutz Allis, Historical Set, Ertl, 1/64 scale, #1218, 2-pc, MIB, R1 ....$5.25
Deutz Allis Mixer Mill, Ertl, 1/64 scale #2208, MIB, R1 ....$2.25
Deutz Allis Planter, Ertl, 1/64 scale, #1212, MIB, R1 ....$3.50
Deutz Allis R-50 Combine, Ertl, 1/64 scale, #1284, MIB, R1 ....$13.00

Deutz Allis Tractor w/Loader, Ertl, 1/64 scale, #2233, MIB, J5 ....$3.95

Deutz Allis, Orlando Show Tractor, Ertl, 1/16 scale, #1280, MIB, R1 ....$190.00

English Fordson, Ertl, 1/43 scale, #2526, MIB, J5 ....$6.00

Farm Set, Hubley, metal with rubber tires, 1950s, EX (VG box), A, $65.00.

Farmall A tractor, Acrade, #7050, ca 1940s, 7", G $800.00

Farmall F-20, Ertl, 1/16 scale, #260, MIB, R1 ....$18.00

Farmall H Tractor & Wagon, Ertl, 1/16 scale, #297, MIB, J5 ....$21.00

Farmall M Tractor, Hubley, 1952 model, 1/12 scale, diecast, metal wheels w/rare shovel attachment, EX, A3 ....$95.00

Farmall M Tractor, Product Miniatures, 1947-50 model, 1/16 scale, red plastic, A3................................$130.00

Farmall Super A Tractor, Ertl, 1/16 scale, #250, MIB, R1 ....$18.00

Farmall Tractor, Precision Series, Ertl, 1/16 scale, #284, MIB, J5 ....$95.00

Farmall 300, Ertl Club Tractor, 1990 model, limited edition of 7500, 1/32 scale, MIB, A3 ....$35.00

Farmall 350, Ertl, 1/43 scale, #2244, MIB, J5 ....$6.00

Farmall 350 Tractor, Ertl, 1/16 scale, #418, MIB, R1 ....$20.00

Farmall Precision Series Tractor, Ertl, 1/16 scale, MIB, $95.00.

Farmall 350 Tractor w/Wide Front-end, Ertl, 1/43 scale, #2244, MIB, R1 ....$5.25

Flare Box Wagon, Ertl, 1/43 scale, #2845, MIB, J5 ....$4.00

Ford F Tractor, Collectors Edition, Ertl, 1/16 scale, #873, MIB, R1 ....$49.00

Ford Golden Jubilee Tractor, Ertl, 1/16 scale, #803, MIB, R1 ....$20.00

Ford Pickup w/Livestock Trailer Set, Ertl, 1/64 scale, #311, MIB, J5 ....$4.95

Ford Tractor, Ertl, 1/64 scale, #302, MIB, J5......................$2.75

Ford Tractor w/Hydraulic Scoop, Corgi, #74, MIB, C5..$100.00

Ford 7740 Row Crop, Collectors Edition, Ertl, 1/16 scale, #873, MIB, R1 ....$49.00

Ford 8N Tractor, Ertl, 1/16 scale, #843, MIB, R1 ....$17.00

Ford 8N Tractor, Product Miniatures, 1952 model, 1/12 scale, gray & red plastic, missing 3-part hitch, rpr axle, A3 ....$195.00

Ford 8N Tractor w/Loader, Ertl, 1/43 scale, #2513, MIB, R1 ....$5.25

Ford 8340 w/4-Wheel Drive, Collectors Edition, Ertl, 1/16 scale, #877, MIB, R1 ....$50.00

Ford 961 Tractor, Ertl, 1/43 scale, #2508, MIB, R1 ....$5.25

Ford/New Holland Combine, Ertl, 1/64 scale, #815, MIB, J5 ....$9.75

Fordson Model F, Ertl, 1/16 scale, #872, MIB, J5 ....$22.00

Fordson Super Major Tractor, Ertl, 1/16 scale, MIB, $30.00.

Gravity Feed Wagon, Ertl, 1/64 scale, #1864, MIB, J5........$2.50

Gravity Feed Wagon, Farm Country, Ertl, 1/16 scale, #350, MIB, J5...$14.00

Hay Wagon, Ertl, 1/16 scale, #4164, MIB, J5....................$16.00

Horses, Farm Country, Ertl, 1/32 scale, #4213, MIB, J5......$3.00

International Harvester Anhydrous Ammonia Tank, Ertl, 1/64 scale, #1345, MIB, J5.....................................$26.00

International Harvester Combine, Ertl, 1/32 scale, #443, MIB, J5 ....$30.00

International Harvester Tractor w/Loader, Ertl, 1/43 scale, #663, MIB, J5...$14.00

International Harvester Wagon & Tractor, 1950 model, Product Miniatures, plastic, A3 ....$60.00

International Row Crop, Farm Country, Ertl, 1/16 scale, #415, MIB, J5..$10.00

International Tractor & Wagon, Ertl, 1/16 scale, #5034, MIB, J5 ....$13.00

International Tractor & Wagon, Farm Country Package, Ertl, 1/32 scale, #52, MIB, J5 ....$10.00

International 1586 Tractor, Farm Country, Ertl, 1/16 scale, #463, MIB, J5 ....$17.00

International 1586 Tractor w/Loader, Ertl, 1/16 scale, #416, MIB, J5 ....$22.00

John Deere A w/Cultivators, Precision Series, Ertl, 1/16 scale, #5633, MIB, R1 ....$122.00

John Deere Ammonia Tank, Ertl, 1/16 scale, #5636, MIB, J5 ....$13.00

John Deere AMT 600, Ertl, 1/16 scale, #5597, MIB, J5 ...$11.00

John Deere Bale Throw Wagon, Ertl, 1/16 scale, #522, MIB, J5 ....$11.50

John Deere Combine, Ertl, 1/16 scale, #546, MIB, J5 ....$37.00

John Deere Combine, Ertl, 1/64 scale, #5604, MIB, J5 ....$9.75

John Deere Cotton Picker, Ertl, 1/80 scale, #1000, MIB, R1..$6.35

John Deere Crawler, Ertl, 1/32 scale, #5573, MIB, R1......$10.75

John Deere Disk Harrow, Ertl, 1/16 scale, #5602, MIB, J5..$16.00

John Deere Flare Box Wagon, Ertl, 1/16 scale, #529, MIB, J5 ....$7.50

John Deere Forage Harvester, Ertl, 1/16 scale, #509, MIB, R1 ....$12.50

John Deere Front Wheel Drive Assists Tractor w/Loader, Ertl, 1/43 scale, #5648, MIB, J5 ....$14.00

John Deere Grain Drill, Ertl, 1/16 scale, #585, MIB, J5....$19.00

John Deere Hay Bailer, Ertl, #24-T, 1962 model, diecast, A3 ....$60.00

John Deere Hay Rake, Ertl, 1/16 scale, #5686, MIB, J5....$17.00

John Deere Historical Tractor set, 1/64 scale, #5523, MIB, J5...$8.95

John Deere Hydra-Push Spreader, Ertl, 1/16 scale, #594, MIB, J5 ....$19.00

John Deere Lawn & Garden Tractor, Ertl, 1/16 scale, #5591, MIB, J5 ....$11.00

John Deere Mixer Mill, 1/64 scale, #5554, MIB, J5 ....$2.50

John Deere Model A, Ertl, 1/43 scale, #5598, MIB, J5 ....$6.00

John Deere Model A, Precision Classic, Ertl, 1/16 scale, #560, MIB $100.00

John Deere Model A w/Wagon, Ertl, 1/16 scale, #5541, MIB, J5 ....$21.00

John Deere Model D, Ertl, 1/16 scale, #5596, MIB, J5 .....$20.00

John Deere Model E Engine, Ertl, 1/16 scale, #4350, MIB, J5..$20.00

John Deere Model F Stationary Engine, Ertl, 1/16 scale, #4350, MIB, R1 ....$18.00

John Deere Model G Tractor, Ertl, 1/16 scale, #548, MIB, R1 ....$20.00

John Deere Mulch Tiller, Ertl, 1/64 scale, #578, MIB, R1 ..$2.75

John Deere Overtime Tractor, Ertl, 1/43 scale, #5607, MIB, J5..$10.00

John Deere Plow, Ertl, 1/16 scale, #525, MIB, J5..............$14.00

John Deere PTO Spreader, Ertl, 1/32 scale, #5577, battery-op, MIB, J5 ....$9.00

John Deere PTO Wagon, Ertl, 1/32 scale, #5623, battery-op, MIB, J5 ....$9.00

John Deere Skid Steer Loader, Ertl, 1/16 scale, #569, MIB, J5...$15.25

John Deere Sprayer, Ertl, 1/64 scale, #5553, MIB, J5/R1 ....$2.50

John Deere Tractor, Ertl, 1/16 scale, #31, remote controlled, MIB, J5 ....$60.00

John Deere Tractor, Ertl, 1/32 scale, #5582, battery-op, MIB, J5 ....$22.00

John Deere Tractor & Wagon, Farm Country Package, Ertl, 1/32 scale, #70, MIB, J5 ....$10.00

John Deere Tractor w/Cultivator, Precision Series, Ertl, #5633, MIB, J5...$118.00

John Deere Tractor w/Sound, Ertl, 1/64 scale, #5693, MIB, J5 ....$7.95

John Deere Utility Tractor & Wagon, Ertl, 1/16 scale, MIB, J5...$18.00

John Deere Waterloo Boy Engine, Ertl, 1/16 scale, #5645, MIB, J5...$20.00

John Deere 112 Forage Wagon, Ertl, 1965 model, 1/16 scale, diecast, A3 ....$45.00

John Deere 12-Row Planter, Ertl, 1/64 scale, #576, MIB, R1 ....$3.25

John Deere 12A Vintage Tractor, Ertl, 1/16 scale, #5601, MIB, J5...$25.00

John Deere 2640, Field of Dreams Collector, Ertl, 1/16 scale, #516, MIB, R1 ....$39.00

John Deere 2755 w/Mechanical Front Wheel Drive, Ertl, 1/16 scale, #5579, MIB, R1..$22.00

John Deere 3020 Tractor, Ertl, 1964 model, 1/16 scale, diecast, short filter, A3 ....$130.00

John Deere 4020, Precision Series #3, Ertl, 1/16 scale, #5638, MIB $99.00

John Deere 4425 Combine, Ertl, 1/50 scale, #506, MIB, R1 .$12.00

John Deere 4455 Mechanical Front Drive, Ertl, 1/16 scale, #5584, MIB, R1 ....$25.00

John Deere 630LP Tractor, Ertl, 1/16 scale, #5590, MIB, J5 .$19.00

John Deere 70 Row Crop, Ertl, 1/16 scale, #5611, MIB, J5 ...$19.00

John Derre Tractor, 1/64 scale, #5571, MIB, J5 ....$2.75

Knudson 4360 4-Wheel Drive Tractor, Ertl, 1/64 scale, #TF4360, MIB, R1 ....$17.00

Knudson 4400 4-Wheel Drive Tractor w/Duals, Ertl, 1/64 scale, #TF4400, MIB, R1 ....$20.00

Machine Trailer, Ertl, 1/16 scale, #594, MIB, J5..............$16.00

Manure Spreader, Ertl, 1/43 scale, #2846, MIB, J5 ....$4.00

Massey -Ferguson Bale Processor, Ertl, 1/64 scale, #1093, MIB, R1..$2.45

Massey-Ferguson Challenger, Ertl, 1/16 scale, #1103, MIB, R1 ....$19.00

Massey-Ferguson Tractor, Ertl, 1/64 scale, MIB, J5.............$2.75

Massey-Ferguson 3070 w/Loader, Ertl, 1/64 scale, #1109, MIB, R1 ....$5.00

Massey-Ferguson 55, National Farm Toy Show '92, Ertl, 1/43 scale, #1131, MIB, R1..$20.00

Massey-Harris 44 Special, Ertl, 1/16 scale, #1115, MIB, R1 .$18.00

Massey-Harris 55, National Toy Show '92, Ertl, 1/64 scale, #1292, MIB, R1 ....$80.00

McCormick Engine, Denton Thresher Show, 1 of 500, Ertl, 1/16 scale, #4993, MIB, R1 ....$36.00

McCormick-Deering Farm Wagon, Arcade, gr on red chassis, sliding rear axle, pnt chips, 12½", G, A $85.00

New Holland Bailer, 25th Anniversary, Ertl, 1/64 scale, #337, MIB, R1 ....$8.00

New Holland Mower Conditioner, Ertl, 1/64 scale, #322, MIB, J5 ....$2.50
New Holland Skid Loader, Ertl, 1/64 scale, #381, MIB, R1 .$4.25
Plow, Ertl, 1/43 scale, #1641, MIB, J5 ....$4.00

Threshing Machine, Arcade, cast iron, gray and red with cream wheels and plated parts, 10", EX (VG box), A, $1,000.00.

Thresher, Tru-Scale, red, 12", M...$90.00
Tractor, Arcade, CI, bl w/wht rubber tires, missing driver's head & 1 rpl tire, 3⅛", W1...$34.50
Tractor, CI w/NP wheels & red body, cast-in driver, early, 4x5¾", G-, A $95.00
Tractor, Hubley #525, MIB...$375.00

Tractor, Tru-Scale, metal with plastic tires, minor wear to paint, 8½" long, EX, $50.00.

Tractor, Turner, pnt steel, bl w/red & silver wheels, non-motorized, 15½", G, A $154.00
Waterloo Tractor Boy, Ertl, 1/16 scale, #559, MIB, J5 .....$25.00
White American 60 w/Ropes, Ertl, 1/64 scale, #4269, MIB, R1.$2.75
White American 80, Collectors Edition, Ertl, 1/64 scale, #4286, MIB, R1 ....$20.00
Wing Disk, Ertl, 1/43 scale, #1553, MIB, J5 ....$4.00

Accessories

Assorted Animals, Ertl, 1/64 scale, #4212, MIB, J5 ....$1.50
Barn & Silo Set, Ertl, 1/64 scale, #4242, MIB, J5 ....$31.00
Barnyard Accessories, Ertl, 1/64 scale, #4292, MIB, J5 ....$3.25
Boxed Accessory Set, Automated Feedbunk, Grain Bin, Propane Tank, Harvester Silo, Ertl, #4305, MIB, J5 ....$14.00
Cattle Feeding Accessories, Ertl, 1/64 scale, #4291, MIB, J5 ....$3.25
Cattle Shed Set, Ertl, #4238, MIB, J5 ....$18.00
Commercial Feed & Seed Set, Ertl, #4303, MIB, J5 ....$34.00
Cows, Ertl, 1/64 scale, #4203, MIB, J5 ....$1.50
Dairy Barn Set, Ertl, #4304, MIB, J5 ....$31.00
Deluxe Farm Set, Ertl, 1/64 scale, #4243, MIB, J5 ....$53.00
Farm House Set, Ertl, 1/64 scale, #4237, MIB, J5 ....$18.00
Hog Confinement Set, Ertl, 1/64 scale, #4236, MIB, J5 ...$18.00
Hog Feeding Accessories, Ertl, 1/64 scale, #4289, MIB, J5 .$3.25
Machine Shed, Ertl, 1/64 scale, #4241, MIB, J5 ....$18.00
Pigs, Ertl, 1/64 scale, #4227, MIB, J5 ....$1.50
Riding Stable Set, Ertl, 1/64 scale, #4217, MIB, J5...........$17.95
Shed & Barn w/Silo Sound Set, Ertl, #4219, MIB, J5.......$43.00
Silo w/Sound, Ertl, 1/64 scale, #4229, MIB, J5 ....$17.00

Fast-Food Collectibles

Fast-food collectibles are attracting lots of attention right now — the hobby is fun and inexpensive (so far), and the little toys, games, buttons, and dolls originally meant for the kids are now being snatched up by adults who're much more likely to appreciate them. They were first included in kiddie meals in the late 1970s. They're often issued in series of one to eight or ten characters; the ones you'll want to watch for are Disney characters, popular kids' icons like Barbie dolls, Cabbage Patch Kids, My Little Pony, Star Trek, etc. But it's not just the toys that are collectible. So are the boxes, store signs and displays, and promotional items (like the Christmas ornaments you can buy for 99¢). Supply dictates price. For instance, a test market box might be worth $20.00, a box from a regional promotion might be $10.00, while one from a national promotion could be virtually worthless.

Toys don't have to be old to be collectible, but if you can find them still in their original package, so much the better. Though there are exceptions, a loose toy is worth one half to two thirds the value of one mint in package. For more information we recommend *The Illustrated Collector's Guide to McDonald's® Happy Meal® Boxes, Premiums, and Promotions,©* by Joyce and Terry Losonsky, and *Tomart's Price Guide to Kid's Meal Collectibles* by Ken Clee. Both are listed under Fast-Food Collectibles in the Categories of Special Interest section of this book.

Arby's

Babar's License Plates, complete set of 4, MIP, C3 ....$11.00
Babar's Puzzles, complete set of 4, MIP, C3......................$19.00
Babar's Stampers, complete set of 3, MIP, C3..................$11.00

Babar's Squirters, 1992, complete set of 3, MIP, $10.00; Babar's Racers, 1992, complete set of 3, MIP, $11.00.

Babar's Summer Slippers, 1991 or 1992, complete set of 3, MIP, C3, either set $11.00
Babar's Vehicles, complete set of 3, MIP, C3....................$11.00
Barbar's Calendar Storybook, complete set of 3, MIP, C3 .$11.00
Classic Fairy Tales, complete set of 3, MIP, C3 ....$11.00
Looney Tunes Character Racers, MIP, H4, any.................$4.00
Looney Tunes Christmas Figures, complete set of 3, MIP, C3 ....$17.00
Looney Tunes Flat Feet,, MIP, H4, any..............................$4.00
Looney Tunes Occupations, Tasmanian Devil pilot, Sylvester fireman, or Daffy Duck student, MIP, H4, ea..............$4.00
Mr Men, loose, H4, any $3.00

Big Boy

Action Figures, complete set of 4, MIP, C3 ....$18.00
Big Boy Racers, complete set of 3, MIP, C3 ....$14.00
Sports Figures, Big Boy as baseball player, surfer, skater, or race car driver, MIP, H4, any $5.00

Burger King

Aladdin, complete set of 5, MIP, C3/F1............................$15.00
Archies, complete set of 4, MIP, F1 ....$15.00
Archies Vehicles, complete set of 4, MIP, C3 ....$10.00

Beauty and the Beast, complete set of 4, MIP, from $15.00 to $19.00.

Bonkers, complete set of 5, MIP, C3 ....$13.00
Capitol Critters, complete set of 4, MIP, from $10 to.......$15.00
Captain Planet, complete set of 4, MIP, from $10 to........$15.00
Commando Cuffs, complete set of 4, MIP, C3..................$10.00

Crayola Stencils, complete set of 6, MIP, C3...................$12.00
Cup, Teenage Mutant Ninja Turtles, set of 3, M, D4 ....$6.00
Disney Celebration Parade Trains, complete set of 4, MIP, F1..$15.00
Disney's Mickey's Toontown, complete set of 4, MIP, F1..$15.00
Disney World Surprise Celebration Parade, complete set of 4, MIP, C3 ....$12.00
Flintstones (England), complete set of 4, MIP, C3 ....$45.00
Glow-in-the-Dark Trolls, complete set of 4, MIP, C3 ......$16.00
Go-Go Gadget Gizmos, complete set of 4, MIP, C3 ....$10.00
Goof Troop, complete set of 4, MIP, from $10 to $15.00
Inspector Gadget, complete set of 4, MIP, F1 ....$15.00
It's Magic, complete set of 4, MIP, C3 ....$10.00
Little Mermaid Splash Collection, complete set of 4, MIP, C3..$12.00
McGruff Cassettes & Books, complete set of 4, MIP, C3 ....$19.00
Mickey's Toontown Disneyland, complete set of 4, MIP, C3..$12.00
Mini Sports Games, complete set of 4, MIP, C3 ....$12.00
Pinocchio, complete set of 4, MIP, C3...............................$12.00
Record Breakers, complete set of 6, MIP, C3 ....$20.00
Save the Animals, complete set of 4, MIP, C3 ....$10.00
Teenage Mutant Ninja Turtles Badges, Feb 1990, MIP, G4, any $6.00
Top Kids, complete set of 4, MIP, C3 ....$10.00
Treasure Hunt, complete set of 4, MIP, C3.......................$10.00
Water Mates, complete set of 4, MIP, C3 ....$10.00

Carl Jrs.

Addams Family, complete set of 4, MIP, C3 ....$25.00
Dino-Pour Tops, complete set of 3, MIP, C3 ....$15.00
Mix 'N Match Dinos, complete set of 4, MIP, C3 ....$27.00
Rollerblade, complete set of 4, MIP, C3.............................$24.00
Shark Attack, complete set of 4, MIP, C3 ....$24.00
Soccer Stars, complete set of 4, MIP, C3 ....$19.00
Starnaments, 1992, complete set of 5, MIP, C3................$25.00

Dairy Queen

Little Red Wagon, red plastic w/Radio Flyer & Dairy Queen on sides, 4", MIP, H4 ....$5.00
Pictionary, complete set of 3, MIP, C3..............................$11.00
Refrigerator Magnets, complete set of 3, C3 ....$11.00
Rockin' Toppers, complete set of 3, MIP, C3 ....$10.00
Sidewalk Chalk, complete set of 3, MIP, C3......................$11.00
Suction Cup Throwers, complete set of 4, MIP, C3 ....$15.00
Supersaurus Puzzles, complete set of 4, MIP, C3 ....$10.00
Tom & Jerry, complete set of 6, MIP, C3...........................$25.00

Denny's

Adventure Packs, complete set of 6, MIP, C3....................$14.00
Flintstones Fun Squirters, complete set of 6, MIP, C3......$18.00
Flintstones Fun Squirters, plastic, 2½", MIP, H4, any.........$4.00
Flintstones Glacier Gliders, complete set of 6, MIP, C3...$18.00
Flintstones Glacier Gliders, Dec 1990, MIP, H4, any $4.00

Flintstones Dino-Racers, 1991, complete set of 6, MIP, C3, $18.00.

Flintstones Mini Plush, complete set of 4, MIP, C3..........$26.00
Flintstones Rock 'N Rollers, MIP, H4, any $4.00
Flintstones Rock 'N Rollers, complete set of 6, MIP, C3..$15.00
Flintstones Stone-Age Cruisers, complete set of 6, MIP, C3 ....$18.00
Flintstones Stone-Age Cruisers, 1991, MIP, H4, any $4.00
Flintstones Vehicles, July 1990, MIP, H4, any....................$6.00
Jetsons Go Back to School, complete set of 6, MIP, C3 ...$15.00
Jetsons Puzzle Ornaments, complete set of 12, MIP, C3 ...$25.00
Jetsons Space Travel Color Books, complete set of 6, MIP, C3 ....$19.00

Hardee's

Camp California, complete set of 4, MIP, C3 ....$12.00
Cyclin' Gear, complete set of 4, MIP, C3 ....$10.00
Dinousaur in My Pocket, complete set of 4, MIP, C3.......$12.00
Fender Bender 500, complete set of 5, MIP, C3................$19.00
Finger Crayons, complete set of 4, MIP, C3......................$10.00
Flintstones' First 30 Years, complete set of 5, MIP, C3.....$19.00
Hardee's Halloween, soft toys w/plastic containers, ghost, blk cat, or goblin, MIP, H4, any $3.00
Home Alone 2, complete set of 4, MIP, C3.......................$15.00
Kazoo Crew Sailors, complete set of 4, MIP, C3 ....$13.00
Marvel Super Heroes, complete set of 4, MIP, from $16 to..$20.00
Squirters, complete set of 4, MIP, C3...............................$16.00
Surfin' Smurfs, complete set of 6, MIP, C3 ....$24.00
Tang Trio, complete set of 4, MIP, C3..............................$16.00
Treasure Trolls, complete set of 6, MIP, C3......................$15.00
Waldo's Straw Buddies, complete set of 4, MIP, C3 ....$24.00
Waldo's Travel Adventure, complete set of 4, MIP, C3 ...$10.00

International House of Pancakes

Pancake Kid Cruisers, complete set of 4, MIP, C3............$15.00
Pancake Kids, 1992, complete set of 8, w/lunch box, MIP, C3 ....$35.00

Jack-in-the-Box

Jack Pack Puzzle Books, complete set of 3, MIP, C3 ....$14.00
Junior Jack Pack Puzzles, complete set of 3, MIP, C3 ......$14.00
Magnets, complete set of 3, MIP, C3 ....$11.00
Make-a-Scene, complete set of 3, MIP, C3 ....$12.00

Long John Silvers

I Love Dinosaurs, complete set of 4, MIP, C3 ....$14.00

Once Upon a Forest, complete set of 5, MIP, C3 ....$19.00
Racing Champions, complete set of 4, MIP, C3 ....$19.00

McDonald's

African-American Heritage Series, complete set of 2, MIP $4.00
Alvin & the Chipmunks, complete set of 4, MIP, C3 ......$25.00
An American Tail Book, 1986, M, L2, any.........................$2.00
Astrosniks I, 1983, Robo (gold robot) or Snikopotamus (gr dragon), EX-NM, ea..$5.00
Astrosniks I, 1983, Scout, Thirsty, Astralia, Sport, Skater, or Lazer, EX-NM, ea...$3.00
Astrosniks II, 1984, EX-NM, any $3.00
Back to the Future, complete set of 4, MIP $5.00

Barbie, 1991, MIP, any, $3.00.

Barbie, 1992, MIP, any of 8 ....$3.00
Barbie/Attack Pack, Canadian, complete set of 4 Barbies & 4 Attack Packs, MIP...$15.00
Barbie/Hot Wheels, European, complete set of 8, MIP.....$30.00
Batman Returns Cup, complete set of 6, M $12.00
Beach Toy, 1989, MIP, any..$1.00
Beauty & the Beast, European, complete set of 4, MIP $20.00
Bedtime, 1988, MIP, any $4.00
Behind the Scenes, complete set of 4, MIP $5.00
Berenstain Bear Books, complete set of 8, MIP................$16.00

Berenstain Bears, complete set of 4, MIP $15.00

Boats 'N Floats, gr Fry Kids on floater, w/stickers, 1986, MIP $7.00

Boats 'N Floats, yel Birdie on raft, no stickers, M $7.00

Cabbage Patch Kids, MIP, any..$2.50

Camp McDonaldland, 1989, MIP, L2, any..........................$2.00

Carnival Happy Meal, 1991, MIP, H4, any.........................$5.00

Changeables, 1987, MIP, any $4.00

Chip 'N Dale Rescue Rangers, 1989, MIP, L2, any............$2.50

Cinderella Ornament Mice, 1987, MIB, L2, any $5.00

Circus Parade, complete set of 4, MIP................................$16.00

Comb, red w/Ronald, H4 ....$2.00

Connectibles, complete set of 4, MIP..................................$16.00

Cosmik Crayola, 1987, MIP, any..$5.00

Crayon Squeeze Bottle, complete set of 4, MIP $20.00

Crazy Vehicles, complete set of 4, MIP $20.00

Dink the Dinosaur, 1990, set of 6, MIP..............................$30.00

Dino-Motion, MIP, any $2.00

Dragonettes, German, complete set of 4, MIP $25.00

Ducktales, launch pad in plane, MIP, L2 ....$3.00

Farm Animals, Canadian, complete set of 8, MIP $10.00

Feeling Good, comb, any character, assorted colors, 1985, MIP, any..$30.00

Feeling Good, soap dish, Grimace w/spread arms, 1985, M .$3.00

Fitness Fun, complete set of 8, MIP......................................$8.00

Fraggle Rock, 1988, MIP, L2, any...$2.50

Friendly Skies United Airlines, complete set of 2, MIP....$10.00

Fry Benders, 1990, MIP, any..$3.00

Funny Fry Friends, 1989, MIP, L2, any................................$2.50

Garfield, Canadian, complete set of 4, MIP.......................$15.00

Garfield, 1988, MIP, any...$3.00

Garfield, 1989, MIP, any...$3.00

Good Morning, complete set of 4, MIP, C3 ....$10.00

Good Sports, puffy sticker, 1984, M $5.00

Happy Meal Band, European, complete set of 4, MIP $20.00

Happy Meal From the Heart, 1990, MIP, any.....................$2.50

Hook, complete set of 4, MIP...$10.00

Junction, Coach Car w/Birdie, 1983, MOT, L2 ....$3.00

Jungle Book, European, complete set of 4, MIP $20.00

Jungle Book, 1990, Baloo, King Louie, Shere Khan, or Kaa, MIP, any $2.50

Jungle Book, 1990, Mowgli or Junior the Elephant (for under 3 yr-old child), MIP, ea..$6.00

Ken Griffey Pins, test market, no McDonald's mk, complete set of 3, MIP $10.00

Kissyfurs, 1987, Floyd (gator w/little hair) or Joline (gator w/much hair, MIP, ea..$8.00

Lego Building Set B, tanker, 1986, MIP..............................$5.00

Little Gardner, 1989, MIP, L2, any $2.00

Little Mermaid, 1989, MIP, any $4.00

Looney Tunes, Canadian, complete set of 4, MIP $15.00

Looney Tunes Holiday Plush, Canadian, complete set of 4, MIP, C3 ....$25.00

Looney Tunes Quack-Up Cars, MIP, any.............................$2.50

Looney Tunes Super Heroes, 1991, complete set of 4, MIP .$10.00

Mac Tonight, PVC figure, complete set of 3, MIP, F1......$10.00

Magic Show, Birdie w/Magic String Trick, 1985, MIP, L2 .$3.00

McCharacters on Trikes, complete set of 4, MIP..............$16.00

McDonald's, blow-up Grimace, purple vinyl w/weighted bottom, 1978, 8", MIP..$7.00

McNugget Buddies, 1988, MIP, L2, any...............................$2.50

McRockin' Foods, European, complete set of 4, MIP $20.00

McRockin' Foods, German, complete set of 4, MIP $20.00

Mickey's Birthdayland, 1988, MIP, L2, any.........................$3.00

Mighty Mini 4x4, European, complete set of 4, MIP........$15.00

Mighty Mini 4x4, regional, 1990, MIP, L2, any.................$3.00

Mix 'Em Up Monsters, complete set of 4, MIP, C3 ....$20.00

Mix 'Em Up Monsters, 1988, MIP, any................................$5.00

Muppet Babies, Canadian, complete set of 4, MIP $8.00

Muppet Babies Storybook, 1988, M, L2, any......................$2.00

Muppet Kids, regional, lg vehicles, complete set of 4, MIP.$50.00

Mystery of the Lost Arches, January 1992, MIP, any of 4...$2.50

Mystery of the Lost Arches, Magic Lens Camera (for under 3 yr-old child), M $3.00

New Food Changeables, 1988, MIP, L2, any........................$2.50

Oliver & Co, 1988, MIP, any $2.50

Out for Fun, complete set of 4, MIP....................................$4.00

Parachute, European, complete set of 2 (Birdie & Ronald), MIP $8.00

Peanuts, Canadian, complete set of 4, MIP.......................$10.00

Peanuts, 1989, MIP, L2, any...$2.50

Piggsburg Pigs, 1990, MIP, any...$7.00

Potato Head Kids, 1992, complete set of 8, MIP, from $20 to...$25.00

Raggedy Ann & Andy, 1990, MIP, H4, any $6.00

Rescuers Down Under, European, complete set of 4, MIP.$15.00

Ronald McDonald in United Jet, Happy Meal, $8.00.

Sailors, 1987, MOT, any...$5.00

Snow White, MIP, any $3.00

Sports Ball, 1990, MIP, any $2.50

Stencils & Crayons, complete set of 2, MIP........................$4.00

Sticker Club, 1985, MIP, any $5.00

Super Looney Tunes, 1991, MIP, L2, any $2.50

Super Mario 3 Nintendo, 1990, MIP, L2, any....................$2.50

Tale Spins, European, complete set of 4, MIP.....................$15.00

Tale Spins, 1990, MIP, L2, any..$2.50
Tinosaurs, MIP, C3...$8.00
Tinosaurs, 1985, EX-NM, any $3.00
Tiny Toons Adventures Wacky Rollers, MIP, any of 8 ......$2.50
Tiny Toons Adventures Flip Cars, 1990, MIP, any............$2.50
Tonka Trucks, MIP, any $2.50
Trading Cards, All-Star Race Team, 1991, complete set of 30,
    MIP $20.00
Trading Cards, All-Star Race Team, 1992, complete set of 36,
    MIP $20.00
Trading Cards, All-Star Team Special Edition, w/date of race,
    set of 4, MIP..$10.00
Trading Cards, All-Star Team Special Edition, no date, set of
    4, MIP..$4.00
Trading Cards, Baseball, Donross, Toronto, 1992, complete set
    of 32, w/checklist, MIP, C3 ....$25.00
Trading Cards, Baseball, St Louis 100th-Anniversary, 1992,
    complete set w/book, M..$85.00
Trading Cards, Baseball, Topps, 1991, complete set of 44, MIP .$35.00
Trading Cards, Basketball, Topps, 1992, complete set of 62,
    MIP..$15.00
Trading Cards, Basketball, Upper Deck, 1993, complete set of
    50, MIP $20.00
Turbo Mac, 1988, MIP, any, from $3 to $4.00
Water Games, 1992, regional, MIP, any of 4 ....$2.50
Wild Friends, 1992, regional, realistic jtd figure w/book as base,
    MIP, any of 4..$5.00
Yo, Yogi; Canadian, complete set of 4, MIP....................$15.00
Zoo Face, 1988, MIP, any $2.00
101 Dalmations, complete set of 4, MIP $10.00

Pizza Hut

Aliens, complete set of 4, MIP, C3....................................$15.00
Beauty & the Beast Puppets, complete set of 4, MIP, C3 .$18.00
Beauty & the Beast Puzzles, complete set of 3, MIP, C3..$12.00
Eureka's Castle Puppets, complete set of 3, MIP, C3 ....$17.00
Land Before Time Dinosaurs, rubber puppets, Little Foot, Spike,
    Cera, or Ducky, MIP, H4, ea $6.00
Land Before Time Dinosaurs, rubber puppets, Petrie or Sharp-
    tooth, MIP, H4 ....$10.00
Space Aliens, bendee, H4, any $6.00
Universal Monster Cups & Holograms, complete set of 3, MIP,
    C3..$19.00
X-Men Comics, complete set of 4, MIP, C3 ....$20.00

Roy Rogers

Baseball Caps/Cups, mini, complete set of 28, MIP, C3 ...$68.00
Be a Sport Magnets, complete set of 4, MIP, C3..............$22.00
Gator Tales, complete set of 4, MIP, C3 ....$26.00
Ickky-Stickky Bugs, complete set of 16, MIP, C3 ....$59.00
Treasure Trolls/Cups, complete set of 4, MIP, C3 ....$24.00

Wal-Mart

GI Joe & Potato Head Kids, complete set of 8, MIP, C3 ..$40.00
GI Joe Kid's Meal, Warthog & Wetsuit, MIP, H4 ....$8.00

GI Joe Kids' Meal, AWE Stricker & Roadblock, MIP, H4 .$8.00
GI Joe Kids' Meal, Mobat & Grunt, MIP, H4 ....$8.00
GI Joe Kids' Meal, Persuade & Bazooka, MIP, H4 ....$8.00

Wendy's

Alien Mix-Up Characters, EX-NM (loose), any, $2.00.

Alf Tales, 1990, MIP, C3, any, $3.00.

All Dogs Go to Heaven, 1989, MIP, H4, any, $4.00.

Alf Tales, complete set of 6, MIP, C3 ....$18.00
Balls-Saurus, complete set of 4, MIP, C3 ....$16.00
Cup, Jetsons, graphics on plastic, set of 4, M, D4...............$8.00
Dino-Makers, w/interchangeable parts, MIP, H4, any........$4.00
Dinosaurs by Avis, Playskool, 1989, MIP, H4, any $4.00
Gear Up, complete set of 4, MIP, C3 ....$15.00
Jetsons, 1989, 1st series, in spaceships, MIP, H4, any $6.00
Jetsons the Movie, 1990, on scooters, MIP, H4, any..........$6.00

Kids 4 Parks, complete set of 5, MIP, C3 ....$18.00
Mighty Mouse, complete set of 6, MIP, C3......................$23.00
Super Sky Carrier, complete set of 6, MIP, C3 ....$21.00
Where's the Beef Stickers, complete set of 6, MIP, C3.....$17.00
Wild Games, complete set of 6, MIP, C3..........................$15.00
Yogi Bear, May 1990, MIP, H4, any $5.00

White Castle

Bendy Pens, complete set of 5, MIP, C3 ....$24.00
Castle Friends Bubble Makers, complete set of 4, MIP, C3.$25.00
Castle Meal Friends, 1992, complete set of 5, MIP, C3 ....$28.00
Castle Tales Storybooks, complete set of 6, MIP, C3 ....$17.00
Castleburger Dudes, w/up, complete set of 4, MIP, C3 .....$15.00
Castleburger Dudes Sports Balls, complete set of 4, MIP,
   C3...$24.00

Fat Albert and the Gang (Cosby's Kids), complete set of 4, MIP, C3, $45.00.

Glow-in-the-Dark Monsters, complete set of 3, MIP, C3.$10.00
Push 'N Go Go Go!, complete set of 3, MIP, C3..............$15.00
Silly Putty, complete set of 3, MIP, C3 ....$12.00
Tootsie Roll Express, complete set of 4, MIP, C3.............$23.00
Water Balls, complete set of 4, MIP, C3 ....$15.00

Boxes and Bags

Arby's, Barbar in Kenya, 1991 ....$2.00
McDonald's, Barbie/Hot Wheels, 1991, M, any.................$2.50
McDonald's, Beach Ball, Having a Wonderful Time, regional,
   1986, M...$7.00
McDonald's, Disney Favorites, 1987, M, L2, any...............$1.50
McDonald's, Lego Motion, 1989, M, any...........................$2.50
McDonald's, Little Engineer, complete w/sticker sheet, 1986, M,
   any...$5.00
McDonald's, Mac Tonight, regional, World Tour, 1988, M .$3.00
McDonald's, Magic Show, 1985, M, any.............................$6.00
McDonald's, McNugget Buddies, 1988, M, any $2.00
McDonald's, Mickey's Birthdayland, 1988, M, any.............$3.00
McDonald's, Mighty 4X4, regional, Desert Scene w/Cars, 1990,
   1 only, M...$3.00
McDonald's, Mix 'Em Up Monsters, regional, 1988, 1 only,
   M..$3.00

McDonald's, New Food Changeables, 1988, M, any..........$2.00
McDonald's, Oliver & Company, 1988, M, L2, any $2.00
McDonald's, On the Go, 1988, M, any $5.00
McDonald's, Rain or Shine, 1989, M, any $3.00
McDonald's, Rescuers Down Under, 1990, M, any............$2.00
McDonald's, Santa Claus the Movie, M, any....................$5.00
McDonald's, Star Trek, 1979, set of 6, M.........................$60.00
McDonald's, Super Mario 3 Nintendo, 1990, M, any $2.00
McDonald's, Tailspin, 1990, M, any..................................$2.00
McDonald's, The Little Mermaid, 1989, M, any................$3.00
McDonald's, The Real Ghostbusters, 1987, M, any $3.00
McDonald's, Tiny Toon Adventures, 1990, M, any $2.00
McDonald's, Turbo Macs, regional, Mountain Launch Ramp,
   1988, 1 only, M..$3.00
McDonald's, Zoo Face, 1988,, M any $3.00
McDonald's, 101 Dalmations, 1990, M, any $2.00

Miscellaneous

This section lists items other than those that are free with kids' meals — store displays, Christmas ornaments, and dolls, for instance, that can be purchased at the counter.

Burger King, Rodney the Reindeer, Hallmark, 1986-87, $3.00.

Burger King, Simpsons doll, stuffed cloth w/vinyl head & cb
   accessories, 1991, 10½" largest, K1, any of 5 ....$4.00
Jerry's Restaurants, flicker ring, 1960s, EX, H4 ....$20.00
McDonald's, counter display, Fraggle Rock, complete w/4
   premiums $60.00
McDonald's, counter display, Hot Wheels/Barbie 1991,
   complete w/8 Hot Wheels & 8 Barbie figures in bubble
   pkg $300.00
McDonald's, counter display, Jungle Book, complete w/4 premi-
   ums, EX, H4 ....$125.00
McDonald's, counter display, McDino Changeables, complete
   w/8 premiums, EX, H4.......................................$95.00
McDonald's, counter display, Mickey's Birthday Land, complete
   w/5 premiums...$200.00
McDonald's, counter display, Peanuts, complete w/4 premiums,
   EX, H4 ....$100.00
McDonald's, counter display, Super Looney Tunes, complete
   w/4 premiums...$45.00
McDonald's, counter display, Tailspins, complete w/4 premiums,
   EX, H4 ....$125.00

McDonald's, counter display, Tiny Toon Adventures, complete w/4 premiums..$45.00

McDonald's, display, Explore the Arts-Behind the Scenes Happy Meal w/Translight, M..................................$15.00

McDonald's, French Fry Radio, AM/FM, still available, MIB, from $20 to..$30.00

McDonald's, Frisbee, Ronald & logo on wht plastic, 8", M, L2..$4.00

McDonald's, game, tic-tac-toe; Ronald & Grimace, H4.....$5.00

McDonald's, Japanese activity booklet, 1992, 6 pages, NM, $2.50.

McDonald's, Little Mermaid Plush Ornaments, 1989, MIB, L2, any..$5.00

McDonald's, Muppet Babies stuffed doll, w/original tag, MIP, any $2.00.

McDonald's, magazine, Funtimes, The Earth Can Be Saved & Kids Can Do It!..$1.00

McDonald's, Muppet Babies stuffed doll, w/orig tag, MIP, any..$2.00

McDonald's, night light, Ronald leaning on glowing star, MIP..$3.00

McDonald's, Oliver & Co Musical Ornaments, 1988, MIB, L2, any..$5.00

McDonald's, pen, figure at top, colored plastic, MIP, any ..$6.00

McDonald's, place mat, Star Trek's Enterprise, 1979, EX-NM..$15.00

McDonald's, poster, ET w/children, M..$10.00

McDonald's, puppet, Ronald plastic glove, 1976, M..........$1.00

McDonald's, Rescuers Down Under Ornaments, 1990, MIB, L2, any..$5.00

McDonald's, Roger Rabbit Happy Halloween Gift Certificate Booklet & Puffy Sticker, 10 coupons for cones+sticker, MIP, L2..$1.50

McDonald's, Roger Rabbit Happy Halloween Poster, full color, 1989, 11¾x10¾", M, L2..$1.50

McDonald's, Ronald McDonald crayons, 1977, set of 4, MIB, L2..$3.00

McDonald's, Ronald McDonald House Poster, Snow White 50th Anniversary of Film, 1987, set of 2, M, L2..........$5.00

McDonald's, Ronald McDonald Prang crayons, 1985, set of 4, MIB..$3.00

McDonald's, Rubik's Cube, You Deserve a Break Today, MIB..$12.00

McDonald's, spoon & fork, Ronald & Grimace hdls, set of 2..$2.00

McDonald's, sunglasses, character frame w/colored lens, MIP, L2, any..$4.00

McDonald's, wrist wallet w/compartment, features Ronald, M..$1.00

Mr Softee Ice Cream Parlor, Official Membership Kit, w/button, card, & mail-in certificate for transfer decal, NM, ...$6.00

Pizza Hut, Teenage Mutant Ninja Turtles, cassette, Coming Out of Their Shells Tour, MCA, 1990, M, F1.....................$5.00

Smoky Stover, ring, plastic, EX-NM, H4..........................$20.00

Fisher-Price

The Fisher-Price Company was formed in about 1930 (in New York) and since then have done more to delight the very little tykes than nearly any other toy manufacturer. They made their toys of wood covered with vividly colored lithographed paper. Until 1949, no plastic parts were used. Because these toys held up so well, most you'll find today are in a very well played-with state. The few left around in good enough condition to attract a collector are scarce — mint in box examples extremely so. Be careful to judge condition well. Edge wear and some paint dulling is normal and to be expected, but a toy that exhibits such wear can only be described as good to excellent at best. Avoid those that are dirty or have missing parts. The most valuable Fisher-Price toys are those modeled after a well-known Disney character. For more information we recommend *Modern Toys, American Toys, 1930-1980*, by Linda Baker, and *Fisher-Price, A*

Historical, Rarity Value Guide, by John J. Murray and Bruce R. Fox (Books Americana).

Allie Gator #653, VG...$45.00
ATV Explorer, MIB, M4 ....$125.00
Bouncing Buggy, MIB, M4 ....$40.00
Bowling Game, MIB, M4...$90.00
Bunny Pulling Cart #10, 1940, 9½", EX+, A $94.00
Busy Bee #325, no pull string, wear on edges of litho paper, VG+, P3 ....$18.00
Cash Register, MIB, M4 ....$75.00
Change-a-Tune Piano, plays 3 songs, 1969, NM $25.00
Chatter Telephone, MIB, M4 ....$88.00
Chick w/Basket Cart #302, 1965, EX......................$75.00
Chug-Chug Train, 1964, EX $150.00

Gold Star Stagecoach, #175, 1954, NMIB, A, $600.00; Dr. Doodle, #477, makes quacking sound, 7x9", EX, A, $210.00.

Donald Duck Choo Choo, pull toy, 1940s, EX, D10, $275.00.

Donald Duck Xylophone #177, pull toy, paper litho on wood, 11" EX+, A $225.00
Dopey Musical Sweeper, early, 33", EX+ $90.00
Ducky Cart #11, EX $80.00
Frisky Frog, MIB, M4...$25.00
Fun Jet, 1970, VG $20.00
Go 'N Back Mule #350, complete, EX+ $325.00
Gold Star Stagecoach, hidden compartment, 15½", VG, A $150.00
Humpty Dumpty, MIB, M4 ....$40.00
Jiffy Dump Truck, MIB, M4..$25.00
Juggling Jumbo Elephant #735, wood, side crank makes balls pop through acetate trunk, 1958, NM (NM box), A $219.00
Katy Cackler Pull Toy #140, hen w/bl & wht polka dot scarf, 7x9", NMIB, A $200.00
Little Snoopy, MIB, M4..$50.00
Looky Chug-Chug #161, w/tender, VG $100.00
Mickey Mouse Choo Choo #485, ca 1949, NM $135.00
Mickey Mouse Drummer #476, 8x9", EX, A..................$116.00
Mickey Mouse Safety Patrol, NM $500.00
Mickey Mouse Xylophone, EX, A $250.00

Mickey Mouse Xylophone #798, 1939, VG, A $165.00
Molly Moo Cow, #190, paper litho on wood, tail & ears move, 1956-57, 9x10", NM, A................................$155.00
Mother Goose #164, VG $25.00
Movie Viewer, w/5 Walt Disney cartridges, MIB, M4 ......$90.00
Music Box Clock Radio, MIB, M4 ....$40.00
Music Box Pocket Radio, Twinkle-Twinkle #774, 1966, VG $8.00
Music Box Teaching Clock, MIB, M4 ....$75.00
Musical Ferris Wheel, MIB, M4 ....$67.50
Musical Sweeper #100, metal w/wood wheels & hdl, 1950-52, VG $75.00
Nifty Station Wagon #234, w/4 figures & roof, VG $100.00
Nosey Pup #445, VG...$20.00
Perky Penguin, MIB, M4...$38.00
Picnic Basket #677, 1975-79, complete..........................$12.50
Play Desk, MIB, M4...$40.00
Play Family, MIB, M4...$40.00
Play Family Action Garage, MIB, M4..............................$175.00
Play Family Airport, MIB, M4..$162.50
Play Family Bath & Utility Room, MIB, M4 ....$50.00
Play Family Camper, MIB, M4 ....$38.00
Play Family Castle, MIB, M4...$168.00
Play Family Children Hospital, MIB, M4 ....$138.00
Play Family Circus Train, MIB, M4 ....$95.00
Play Family Farm, MIB, M4...$125.00
Play Family Fun Jet, MIB, M4 ....$100.00
Play Family House, MIB, M4...$125.00
Play Family Houseboat, M (missing box), M4 ....$50.00
Play Family Kitchen Set, MIB, M4...................................$50.00
Play Family Merry-Go-Round, MIB, M4...........................$62.50
Play Family Mini Bus, MIB, M4 ....$25.00
Play Family Patio Set, MIB, M4 ....$40.00
Play Family School, MIB, M4 ....$125.00
Play Family School Bus, MIB, M4....................................$48.00
Play Family Sesame Street Clubhouse, MIB, M4...........$150.00
Play Family Village, MIB, M4...$118.00
Pocket Camera, MIB, M4 ....$25.00
Pony Chime #132, VG $30.00
Pony Chime #758, tin chime drum spins & chimes, 1948, scarce, 14", EX+-NM, A $128.00
Pop-Up-Pal Chime Phone, MIB, M4 ....$75.00

Pluto Pop-Up Kritter, pull strings from beneath, Walt Disney Enterprises, NM, $150.00.

Talking Donald Duck, #765, with voice mechanism, NM (NM box), A, from $300.00 to $400.00.

Teddy Zilo #752, advances while playing the xylophone, 1948, 9x11", EX, A..$73.00
Three Men in a Tub, M, M4 ....$25.00
Tiny Teddy, 1958, EX...$65.00
Toot-Toot Engine #641, MIB................................$45.00
Toot-Toot Engine #641, 1962, EX $18.00
Toy Wagon #131, VG $125.00
Tumble Tower, MIB, M4 ....$38.00
Two-Tone Music Box TV, MIB, M4.......................$75.00

Popeye Cowboy, #705, 10", NM, A, $700.00.

Puffy Engine #444, EX $40.00
Pull-a-Tune Xylophone #870, wood w/plastic wheels, 1978, VG..$8.00
Quacky Family, 1945, EX $85.00
Queen Buzzy Bee, MIB, M4 ....$25.00
Racing Rowboat #730, NM-M, A $100.00
Roller Chimes #123, MIB......................................$125.00
Roller Chimes #123, VG $20.00
Running Bunny w/Cart, 1960, EX...........................$85.00
Seal, pull toy, EX..$30.00
Smokie Engine, wood, 1950s, MIB, M4 ....$60.00
Squeaky Clown #777, NM-M, A $125.00
Suzy Seal, #621, EX+, A3......................................$25.00
Sweeper #700, c Walt Disney, plays Whistle While You Work, EX..$125.00
Tailspin Tabby, pop-up on base, ca 1931, EX-NM.........$150.00
Tailspin Tabby #455, VG $85.00

Uncle Timmy Turtle, #125, 1956, NMIB, A, $100.00.

Uncle Timmy Turtle #150, NM-M, A $50.00
Woofy Wowser #700, NM-M, A..................................$200.00

Furniture

Any item of furniture imaginable has been reduced to child size, and today these small scale dressers, wash stands, chairs, and tables are especially popular with doll collectors who use them to display a favorite doll. If you'd like to learn more, we recommend *Children's Glass Dishes, China, and Furniture*, by Doris Anderson Lechler.

Key:
drw — drawer   dvtl — dovetail

Amish Buggy, wood body w/vinyl walls, roll-up window, steel chassis, wood wheels, 140" (w/shaft), VG-EX, A $550.00

Buggy, wicker & wood, mtd on metal springs & wheels, rpl lining, 29", G+, A $300.00

Buggy, wicker bassinet on wood, spoked wood wheels, rpl red velvet lining, 49", VG, A $245.00

Carriage, pnt wood w/pnt scroll trim, retractable convertible top, ca 1888, rpl top & seat, 56", VG, A $300.00

Carriage, wicker w/wood fr & metal springs, lg wheels w/wood rims, 21" handle height, G, A $85.00

Chair, pnt wood, gr w/gold stencil decor, cane seat (damaged & incomplete), 14", G+, A $35.00

Chest, Empire-style walnut w/veneered fronts, 3 graduated dvtl drw w/wood pulls, rprs/rstr/wear, 18x16½", VG, A...$125.00

Chest of Drawers, scalloped crest w/rosette over 6 drws w/reeded fronts & wood knobs, made from cigar boxes, 19x11", A $80.00

Cupboard, American pine hutch w/2 graduated shelves, 1 door on bottom, scalloped top/sides, 27", EX w/G finish, A $270.00

Cupboard, stained poplar, scalloped crown, 2 doors w/glass over glass door, 2 drw, flour bin, porc knobs, 32½", EX, A...$325.00

Cupboard, walnut, step-bk style, scalloped ft & top board, 2 open shelves, 2 lower drws, 17", A..........................$250.00

Desk, oak and chestnut roll top, 15x18x9", EX, $325.00.

Dresser, oak, ornate crown & fr around mirror, 2 sm handkerchief drws over 1 long drw in base, wood knobs, 14x10", EX, A $260.00

Dresser, scalloped sides on mirror fr w/reeding & rope-twist trim, shelf under mirror, 2-drw, 17½x10", EX, A $235.00

Dresser, walnut, scrolled mirror fr & crown, sm drw over ea end of long drw, some silver damage, 15½x11", EX, A ..$240.00

Dresser, walnut & cherry, burl walnut side panels w/natural surface, fr mirror over 4 drw, 33½x17", EX, A..............$250.00

Dry Sink, walnut, top shelf & sink area, 2 bottom shelves closed w/doors, well built, EX, 15x13", A $180.00

Rocking chair, oak w/pressed bk, 35" $110.00

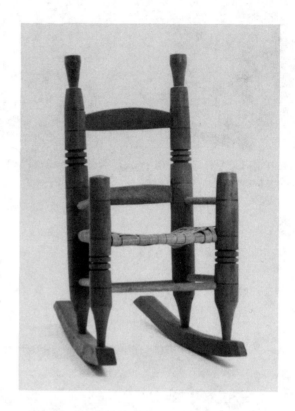

Rocking Chair, woven seat, 15", $55.00.

Rolling Chair, CI, wood seat & bk, 3 spoked wheels, wood hdl at bk of seat, guide hdl off front wheel, 51", G, A $210.00

Side chair, ladderback, pnt wood, 14", EX, A $85.00

Sideboard, oak, ornate top, upper shelf w/scrolled braces, reeded detailing, 38½x22", EX quality & condition, A $550.00

Sideboard, pine, upper shelf w/shaped braces, 2 sm shelves ea side of mirror, 2 sm+2 long drw in base, 24x18", EX, A $325.00

Sofa, Empire style, horsehair, 20x40x12", $800.00.

Sideboard, poplar w/red-brn pnt, cut-out top w/shelf & mirror, drw+2 doors, ea w/cut-out overlay, 32x20", VG, A.**$235.00**

Stroller, pnt & stenciled wood, CI brackets support retractable fringed shade, rpl vinyl lining, 31", G-G+, A..........**$190.00**

Table, brn stain, dvtl drw w/brass pull, short drop leaves, sq nails, primitive, 15x18", VG, A................**$175.00**

Tilt-Top Table, mahogany, tripod base w/latch that allows top to tilt, 7½", EX, A................**$240.00**

Vanity w/Mirror, Wolverine, pnt metal, yel w/designs, compartment under mirror, 15x13½", EX, A................**$65.00**

Victrola, may be salesman's sample, works, plays 78 rpms, orig finish, sm pc veneer missing, 25½x13", A............**$1,100.00**

Wash Stand, English style, spool legs, rpl bottom shelf, 13½", +ironstone pitcher & bowl mk M&Co, EX, A........**$225.00**

Wash Stand Set, Germany, Kate Greenaway design on bowl mk MIB & divided in 2 parts, wrought iron 17x15" stand, VG, A................**$400.00**

Wash Stand, oak w/red stain, lyre-shaped towel bar supports, 1 long drw over 2 doors, 17½x13", VG, A................**$150.00**

Games

Early games (those from 1850 to 1910) are very often appreciated more for their wonderful lithographed boxes than their 'playability,' and you'll find many collectors display them as they would any fine artwork. Many boxes and boards were designed by well-known artists and illustrators of the day. Twentieth-century games are regarded with a more nostalgic attitude by many of us who remember at least one game under the tree every Christmas morning.

When you buy a game, check to see that all pieces are there. Look on the instructions or in the box lid for a listing of contents. Value depends on rarity and condition of the box and playing pieces. Games featuring popular TV and movie characters are especially hot right now; these are included in the Character Collectibles category. Our advisor for this category is Paul Fink (F3).

$1,000,000 Chance of a Lifetime, Cardinal, 1986, EX, M6..**$20.00**

$64,000 Question Jr, Lowell, 1950, EX, M6................**$45.00**

ABC Monday Night Football, Aurora, 1972, EX, M6......**$45.00**

Above the Clouds, Milton Bradley, 1920s, VG-, M6.......**$75.00**

Acey Ducey, Parker Bros, 1940s, VG................**$75.00**

Acquire, 3-M, 1968, EX, M6................**$19.00**

Across the Board, MPH, 1975, EX+, M6................**$38.00**

Across the Continent, Parker Bros, 1952, MIB................**$60.00**

Action Baseball, Pressman, 1960s, VG-................**$30.00**

Ad Liners, Pressman, 1989, EX, M6................**$24.00**

Ad-Lib Duplicate Crossword Cubes, ES Lowe, 1976, EX, M6................**$20.00**

ADT Messenger Boy, Milton Bradley, 1909, VG, M6....**$145.00**

Advance to Boardwalk, Parker Bros, 1985, EX, M6................**$25.00**

Adventurer, Yaquinto, 1981, MIB (sealed), M6................**$25.00**

Adverteasing, Coleco, 1988, EX, M6................**$25.00**

AGGIE, Kuster Ltd, orig tube container, M, M6................**$30.00**

Aggravation, Lakeside, deluxe version, 1982, EX-, M6....**$17.00**

Aggravation, Lakeside, 1972, complete, orig box, NM.......**$8.00**

Air Assault on Crete, Avalon, 1977, EX+, M6................**$32.00**

Air Force, Avalon, 1980, EX, M6................**$22.00**

Air Mail, Milton Bradley, 1930s, EX-, D10, $345.00.

Air Raid Defense Target Dart Game, Wyandotte, litho tin combat illus board, w/dart pistol, 9½x9½", EX+ (VG box), A................**$58.00**

Air Traffic Controller, Schaper, 1974, EX-, M6................**$42.00**

Airborne!, Jag Panther, 1976, M, M6................**$35.00**

Alexander the Great, Avalon Hill, EX, M6................**$26.00**

Alfred Hitchcock's Why, 1961, EX (EX- box)................**$25.00**

All About St Cloud, All About Town, 1982, EX................**$10.00**

All-American Football, Cadaco, 1969, EX, M6................**$25.00**

All-American Football, Cadaco-Ellis, 1960, EX-, M6......**$30.00**

All-Star Baseball, Cadaco, 1969, EX................**$20.00**

All-Star Basketball, Gotham, complete w/backboard, net, ball & instructions, 1947, MIB................**$50.00**

All-Star Basketball, Whitman, 1935, EX, M6................**$65.00**

All-Star Football, Gardner, 1950s, VG, M6................**$25.00**

All-Time Greats Baseball Game, Midwest Research, 1971, EX, M6................**$32.00**

Allan Sherman's Camp Grenada, Milton Bradley, 1965, EX, M6................**$48.00**

Alley Oop, Royal Toy, 1937, orig box, VG................**$40.00**

Alpha Omega, Battleline, 1977, NM, M6................**$25.00**

Amazing Dunninger Mind-Reading Game, Hasbro, 1967, EX, M6................**$25.00**

AMOCO's Mileage Game, Cadaco, 1976, EX, M6.........**$34.00**

Amusing Game of Innocence Abroad, Parker Bros, 1888, VG-, M6................**$210.00**

Anagrams, Parker Bros, 1900s, EX++, F3................**$24.00**

Anagrams, Pressman, 1940s, NM, M6................**$25.00**

Anagrams, Transogram, 1957, VG, M6................**$20.00**

Analysis, Stuart Hoover, 1960s, EX, M6...........................$18.00

Animal Bingo, Baldwin, carnival scene on 9x10" box lid, 1930s, EX (G+ box), A...$45.00

Animal Race, Milton Bradley, 1920s, EX, F3 ....$85.00

Animal Talk, Mattel, 1963, VG, M6 ....$55.00

Animal Trap Game, Multiple, 1950s, EX, M6 ....$55.00

Anti-Monopoly II, National Games, 1977, M (EX box), M6...$34.00

Anti-Monopoly III: Star Peace; Ralph Anspach, 1987, MIB (sealed), M6..$34.00

Ants in the Pants, Schaper, 1970, VG, M6 ....$25.00

Anvil Dragoon, Jagpanther, 1976, orig envelope, VG, M6..$25.00

Anzio, Avalon Hill, 1974, M (EX box), M6 ....$30.00

APBA Baseball Master Game, APBA, 1973, MIB (sealed), M6 ....$60.00

APBA Pro-League Football, APBA, 1982, M (EX box), M6.$35.00

Apollo, A Voyage to the Moon; Traciane, 1969, M (EX box), M6..$45.00

Aquarius II, Hoi Polloi, 1973, EX (VG box), M6.............$34.00

Aquarius II, Reiss, 1973, EX (VG box), M6 ....$36.00

Aquarius 2000, Game Science, 1970, EX, M6.................$55.00

Aquire, 3M, complete, 1968, EX (VG box).....................$10.00

Arbitrage, HC Jocoby, 1986, EX, M6.............................$25.00

Ardennes Offensive, SPI, 1973, EX, M6 ....$25.00

Are You a Sacred Cow?, Beach, 1935, MIB.....................$27.00

Armada, Jeux Descartes, 1986, MIB (sealed), M6 ....$70.00

Armchair College Football, Armchair Games, 1986, EX (VG box), M6 ....$22.00

Armor at Kursk, Task Force, 1979, M (EX box), M6 ......$25.00

Arnold Palmer, Inside Golf, appears complete, 1961, EX.$30.00

Around the World in Bed, Diplomat Sales, 1969, VG, M6.$25.00

Around the World in 80 Days Travel Game, Transogram, 1957, complete, EX...$50.00

Around the World w/Nellie Bly, #4122, Milton Bradley, board & spinner, VG (G box)................................$165.00

Arrest & Trial, Transogram, 1963, VG (G box) $40.00

Assembly Line, Selchow & Righter, 1953, EX (VG box)..$50.00

Assembly Line, Selchow & Righter, 1960s, NM, F3 ....$45.00

Asteroid Pirates, Yaquinto, no date, MIB (sealed), M6....$22.00

Astro Launch Game, VG, O1 ....$25.00

Austerlitz, International Team, no date, M (EX box), M6.$55.00

Authors, Parker Bros, 1943, VG, M6 ....$25.00

Auto Dealership, Bobron Bros, 1982, EX, M6 ....$35.00

Axis & Allies, Milton Bradley, 1st edition, 1985, M (EX box), M6 ....$45.00

Baby Boomer Cards, Selchow & Righter, 1982, EX (VG box), M6 ....$30.00

Babysitters' Club, Milton Bradley, 1989, EX (VG box), M6..$20.00

Backwords, Random House, 1983, EX (VG box), M6......$20.00

Bagatelle, McLoughlin Bros, 1900, NM, $450.00.

Bagatelle, Marx, MIB...$35.00

Baha Card Game, International Games, 1989, MIB (sealed), M6 ....$10.00

Balance of Power, Hasbro, 1979, EX (VG box), M6.........$22.00

Bali, Selchow & Righter, 1969, EX, M6 ....$26.00

Bambino Baseball Game, Mansfield-Zesiger, stand-up scoreboard, attached wooden ball & bat, 1946, 10x15", NM (EX+ box), A $95.00

BAOR, SPI, 1981, orig envelope, M, M6..........................$18.00

Barbarians, Yaquinto, no date, MIB (sealed), M6............$22.00

Barbie Game, 1980, looks complete, boxed, T1 ....$6.00

Barbipapa Takes a Trip, Selchow & Righter, 1977, EX, M6.$24.00

Bargain Hunter, Milton Bradley, 1981, EX $10.00

Babe Ruth's Baseball Game, Milton Bradley, authorized edition, 1926-28, EX, $500.00.

Bart Star, Quarterback, orig box, rare, EX, A $250.00

Bas-Ket, Cadaco-Ellis, 1956, EX.......................................$35.00

Baseball Challenge, Tri Valley Games, 1980, EX, M6......$38.00

Baseball Game, Corey, NM $45.00

Baseball Game, Frantz, early 1930s, complete, EX, J2 ....$100.00

Baseball Game, MCL, EX, F3..$375.00

Baseball Game, Warren, 1970s, M (EX box), M6.............$25.00

Baseball's Greatest Moments, Ashburn IN, 1979, M (EX box), M6..$22.00

Basketball Game, Corey, EX+ $45.00

Basketball Strategy, Avalon Hill, 1974, EX, M6...............$25.00

Bats in the Belfry, Mattel, 1964, NM, A...........................$95.00

Battle Checkers: Beat the Axis; Penman, 1942, EX (G box), M6 ....$70.00

Battle Cry Command Decision Series Civil War Game, American Heritage, NM (EX+ box), C1..............................$54.00

Battle Lines, Ideal, 1963, M..$68.00

Battle of Atlanta, Southern Games, 1960, EX, M6 ....$95.00

Battle of the Bulge, Avalon Hill, 1965, EX, M6 ....$26.00

Battle of the Planets, Milton Bradley, 1979, M.................$30.00

Battle Stations, Burleson, board game, battle at sea, 1952, 12x16" box (sm rpr/lt wear), contents NM, T2 ....$50.00

Battleship, Milton Bradley, 1967, EX (VG box)...............$12.00

Battleship, Whitman, 1940, VG (G box), M6....................$40.00

Battling Spaceships Game, Ideal, 1977, M (EX box), M6...$48.00

Beachhead Invasion, Built Rite, 1950s, EX (VG box), M6.$65.00

Beat Detroit, Dynamic, 1972, EX, M6 ....$22.00

Beat Inflation, Avalon Hill, 1975, M (EX box), M6 ....$19.00

Beat the Clock, Milton Bradley, 1969, EX (VG box), M6..$25.00

Behind the 8-Ball, Selchow & Righter, 1969, EX.............$20.00

Bermuda Triangle, Milton Bradley, 1975, EX $15.00

Berzerk, Milton Bradley, 1983, EX, M6.............................$20.00

Bible Characters, Nellie Magee, 1900s, EX (G box), M6.$28.00

Bible Picture Lotto, Warner, 1950s, EX (VG box), M6 ...$18.00

Bicentennial Games, Coach House, 1975, EX (G box), M6.$17.00

Big Board, Dadan, stock market game, 12x16", 1960, VG ..$100.00

Big Board Stock Market, RJ McDonald, board game, w/cards, stocks chips have some writing, 12x18", 1958 (EX- box), T2 ....$42.00

Big League Baseball, 3M, 1967, EX, M6............................$40.00

Big Numbers: The High Rollers Game; Milton Bradley, 2nd edition, 1975, EX, M6 ....$28.00

Big Payoff, Payoff Enterprises, 1984, EX, M6 ....$20.00

Big Time Colorado Football, BJ Tall, 1983, M (VG box), M6..$25.00

Billionaire, Parker Bros, 1973, EX $20.00

Bionic Crisis Game, Parker Bros, 1976, M (EX box) $15.00

Bird Watcher, Parker Bros, 1958, EX (VG box), M6 ....$55.00

Birthday Game, Parker Bros, 1918, VG (G box), M6.......$65.00

Bits & Chips, Alfran, 1981, EX (VG box), M6 ....$22.00

Black Beauty Game, Transogram, 1958, M (EX box), M6..$48.00

Black Box, Parker Bros, 1978, EX (VG box), M6.............$26.00

Black Experience, Theme Productions, 1971, M (VG box), M6 ....$45.00

Black Hole Space Alert Game, Whitman, 1975, EX, M6...$25.00

Blacks & Whites, Psychology Today, 1970, EX, M6 ....$22.00

Blarney Stones, Parker Bros, 1940, VG, M6 ....$45.00

Blast-Off Globe, litho tin, ca 1950s, MIB $350.00

Blast-Off!, Waddingtons, 1969, EX (VG box), M6 ....$55.00

Blitzkrieg, Avalon Hill, 1975, M (EX box), M6................$28.00

Blizzard of '77, Char-Donn, 1977, EX, M6......................$22.00

Block the Clock, Ideal, 1981, VG, M6..............................$25.00

Blockade, Lakeside, 1979, EX, M6 ....$17.00

Blow Football, Made in England, NM, F3........................$65.00

Blue Line Hockey, 3M, 1970, EX (VG box), M6 ....$48.00

Boob Tube Cards, Selchow & Righter, 1987, M (EX box), M6..$20.00

Booby Trap, Parker Bros, 1965, complete, orig box, VG..$10.00

Book of Lists Game, Avalon, 1979, EX, M6 ....$25.00

Boom or Bust, Parker Bros, 1951, rare, EX (G box)........$190.00

Boot Tube Race, Milton Bradley, 13" see-through tubes w/7 levels & 8 marbles ea, 1962, unused (EX+ box), T2.......$30.00

Booth's Pro Conference Football, Sher-Co, 1977, M (VG box), M6..$28.00

Bop the Beetle, Ideal, 1962, NMIB $30.00

Boris Karloff's Monster Game, Game Gems, 1965, NM.$200.00

Boss, Ideal, 1972, VG, M6...$22.00

Boundary, Mattel, 1970, EX (VG box), M6......................$25.00

Brainsweat, Pango Enterprises, 1990, EX, M6..................$34.00

Breakout & Pursuit, SPI, 1972, EX (VG box), M6...........$30.00

Breakthru, 3M, 1965, EX, M6 ....$28.00

Brett Ball, Keltner, 1981, EX...$20.00

Bridge & Keno, Klauber, 1935, MIB.................................$32.00

Bridge for Juniors, Selchow & Righter, EX $10.00

Bridge-It, Hassenfeld, 1960, EX (VG box), M6 ....$30.00

Broadside, Milton Bradley, 1962, EX (VG box), M6........$35.00

Broadside Gang Way for Fun, Transogram, board game, 1964, complete, NM (EX+ box), T2.....................................$50.00

Broadway Game, TSR, 1981, EX, M6 ....$27.00

Brownie Auto Race, Jeannette Toy & Novelty, marble game w/2 sm cars, EX, A...$140.00

Buck-a-Roo, Ideal, 1970, EX, M6.....................................$40.00

Buckaroo, Milton Bradley, 1947, VG................................$30.00

Bugsville Games, Animate Toy, 1915, EX (VG box), M6.$185.00

Bulls and Bears, Parker Bros., 1936, EX, $130.00.

Bumper Cars, Parker Bros, 1987, EX, M6..........................$20.00
Bunco, Crestline, 1973, M (EX box), M6 ....$25.00

Bunny Rabbit (Cottontail & Peter), Parker Bros., 1928, EX, $150.00.

Burbank Power Brokers, Higgins, 1990, EX (VG box), M6.$25.00
Bureaucracy, Avalon, 1981, M (VG box), M6 ....$22.00
Burmuda Triangle, Milton Bradley, 1976, MIB $30.00
By Invitation Only, Game Works, 1987, EX, M6.............$20.00
C&O/B&O, Avalon Hill, 1969, EX, M6 ....$105.00
Cabbage Patch Kids, Parker Bros, 1984, EX, M6 ....$15.00
Cabby, Selchow & Righter, EX+, F3 ....$75.00
Cabin Boy, Milton Bradley, board bame w/spinner & counters,
     1900, 9x9" box, EX (EX- box), A..............................$75.00
Call Me Lucky, Parker Bros, 1954, EX (G box), M6 ....$35.00
Calling All Cars, Parker Bros, 1940s, VG $30.00
Camelot, Parker Bros, wood, 1931, EX $50.00
Camelot, Parker Bros, 1930s, VG, F3................................$26.00
Camp Runamuck Game, Ideal, 1965, EX (VG box), M6.$40.00
Campaign, Saalfield, 1961, EX (VG box), M6 ....$100.00
Candid Camera, Lowell, #460, 1963, VG (G box)...........$25.00

Candy Land, Milton Bradley, 1955, MIB, M4 ....$30.00
Candy Land, Milton Bradley, 1962, MIB, M4 ....$25.00
Captain Hop Across, All Fair, 1927, missing 1 apron, VG+,
     F3...$95.00
Careers, Parker Bros, 1950s, EX+, from $20 to $30.00
Careers, Parker Bros, 1970, EX, M6 ....$22.00
Careers, Tiger Electronics, 1992, EX, M6 ....$18.00
Careful: The Toppling Tower Game; Ideal, 1967, EX (VG
     box), M6 ....$24.00
Cargoes, Selchow & Righter, 1958, EX............................$50.00
Carrier Strike, Milton Bradley, 1977, M (VG box), M6...$38.00
Case of the Duplicate Door, Pearl, complete, 1940s, EX (G-
     box) $8.00
Cat & Mouse, Parker Bros, board game w/traps & plastic mice (1
     missing), 14x14" box, 1964, EX+, T2 ....$15.00
Catchphrase, Ed-U-Cards, 1975, VG, M6 ....$20.00
Catchword, Whitman, 1954, EX (G box), M6 ....$25.00
Catfish Bend Storybook Game, Selchow & Righter, 1978, EX
     (VG box), M6..$24.00
Cavalcade, Selchow & Righter, 1957, EX (VG box), M6.$45.00
Cavalcade Derby, Wyandotte, litho tin, NMIB.............$110.00
Centipede, Milton Bradley, 1983, EX, M6......................$20.00
Centurions: Power Xtreme; Parker Bros, 1986, EX (VG box),
     M6 ....$18.00
CEO, Anacom, 1984, MIB (sealed), M6...........................$22.00
Challenge Yahtzee, ES Lowe, 1974, EX, M6....................$25.00
Champion Baseball, NY Games, throw dice to determine action,
     1913, 15x12" board, VG (EX box), A........................$90.00
Championship Baseball, Milton Bradley, 1984, EX, M6 ..$28.00
Championship Fight Game, Frankie Goodman, 1940s, M
     (VG box) $30.00
Charade Game, Pressman, 1985, EX, M6.........................$25.00
Charades, Selchow & Righter, 1968, EX (VG box), M6..$20.00
Charge It!, Whitman, 1972, EX, M6.................................$35.00
Chauvinst Pigs, Tiger Games, 1991, EX, M6 ....$20.00
Cherry Ames Nursing Game, Parker Bros, 1959, VG.......$30.00
Chess Set, Peter Max, MIP...$125.00
Chevyland Sweepstakes, Milton Bradley, 1968, EX, M6..$50.00
Chicago Scene, Groovy Games, 1977, EX, M6.................$22.00
Chief Big Mouth Blowing Target Game, Marx, plastic dart
     pistols fire styrofoam balls, 1960s, 6x6x9" box, EX (G
     box), A...$275.00

Christmas Goose, McLoughlin, 1898, EX-, A, $900.00.

Chill: Black Morn Manor; Pacesetters, 1985, M (EX box), M6 ....$26.00

Chinese Checkers & Telka, Parker Bros, 1938, EX (VG box), M6 ....$38.00

Chinese Civil War, Simulation Games, 1979, MIB (sealed), M6...$35.00

Chippendales After Hours Game, Diplomat Games, 1983, M (EX box), M6...$38.00

Chit-Chat, Milton Bradley, 1963, EX+ (EX box)..............$6.00

Chopper Strike, Milton Bradley, 1976, EX, M6..............$32.00

Chutes & Ladders, Milton Bradley, 1st edition, 1943, VG .$32.00

Chutes & Ladders, Milton Bradley, 1950s, EX, F3............$22.00

Chutes Away, Gabriel, 1977, orig box, EX $35.00

Circus Comes to Town, Lowe, 1940s, complete, EX, V1..$30.00

Cities, All-Fair, 1940s, EX (VG box), M6 ....$26.00

Civil War Game, Parker Bros, 1961, 9x19", VG..............$30.00

Claim to Fame, Parker Bros, 1990, MIB (sealed), M6 ......$25.00

Class Struggle, Oilman, 1978, EX, M6 ....$25.00

Classic Derby, Doremus-Schoen, 1929, VG (G box), M6.$58.00

Clown Ring Toss, wood clown heads in dunce hats on disk base, rope rings, 11½", EX, A, pr..........................$35.00

Clue, Parker Bros, 1950, VG $30.00

Clue, Waddington, 1949, EX, M6 ....$60.00

Clue Junior, Parker Bros, 1989, MIB (sealed), M6...........$25.00

Cohorts, TSR, 1977, EX, M6......................................$28.00

Cold Feet, Ideal, 1967, EX $25.00

College Basketball, Cadaco-Ellis, 1954, M (VG box), M6 .$45.00

College Football, Sports Illustrated, 1971, EX (VG box), M6...$25.00

Colors, McLoughlin, 1888, EX
(EX box), A, $145.00.

Colossal Fossil Fight, Gabriel, 1978, VG, M6...................$25.00

Combat, Milton Bradley, board game litho on bottom of 9x15" box, EX (G+ box)...$50.00

Comical History, Parker Bros, EX+, F3 ....$35.00

Computer Vegas, Electronic Data Controls, 1971, EX, M6 .$70.00

Concentration, Milton Bradley, 1st edition, based on TV show, 1959, VG (VG box) $60.00

Concentration, Milton Bradley, 2nd edition, 1960, EX (VG box), M1...$25.00

Connect, Galt & Co, 1969, EX (VG box), M6 ....$18.00

Constellation Station, Aristoplay, 1990, MIB (sealed), M6.$40.00

Contack, Parker Bros, 1939, VG, M6............................$20.00

Cooks Tours, Selchow & Righter, 1972, EX, M6 ....$34.00

Cootie, Schaper, 1949, EX, M6...................................$25.00

Cootie, 1962, EX...$12.50

Cops & Robbers, Top Notch, 1953, VG $45.00

Count Down, Milton Bradley, 1986, EX, M6 ....$25.00

Countdown: Adventure in Space; ES Lowe, 1967, EX.....$50.00

Cowboy Roundup, Parker Bros, 1952, orig box, EX, from $22 to...$34.00

Crazy Clock, Ideal, 1960s, EX, F3................................$65.00

Crosby Derby, H Fishlove, 1947, EX (VG box), M6 ......$110.00

Crosstown Game, Milton Bradley, 1956, EX (VG box), M6...$45.00

Crow Shoot, Jaymar, complete, late 1950s, NMIB $57.50

Curly Locks, Parker Bros, EX+, F3 ....$115.00

D-Day, Avalon Hill, 1977, EX (VG box), M6.................$20.00

Daisy's Red Ryder Whirli-Crow Game, 1948, MIB $148.00

Dash Hounds Game, Cadaco, 1988, MIB (sealed), M6 ....$24.00

Daze of Our Loans, Frandzel & Share, 1988, EX (VG box), M6...$20.00

Dead Pan, Selchow & Righter, 1956, VG (G box), M6...$38.00

Dealer's Choice, Parker Bros, 1972, VG, from $10 to.......$25.00

Deck Derby Horses, Wolverine, VG, F3 ....$35.00

Deluxe Table Tennis, Pressman, MIB..........................$32.00

Derby Day, Parker Bros, 1959, EX, M6 ....$80.00

Derby Downs, Playtime House, 1940s, VG (G box), M6 .$38.00

Detective Game, Transogram, EX, F3 ....$45.00

Dinobones, Warren, 1987, EX, M6..............................$17.00

Dirty Water, Urban Systems, 1971, EX, M6 ....$46.00

Dog Race, Transogram, 1938, VG, M6...........................$55.00

Dogfight, Milton Bradley, 1962, NM $50.00

Dollars & Sense, Better Games, 1980, EX (VG box), M6.$20.00

Donkey Puzzle, Chafee & Selchow, miniature mule to 'bk in the shafts,' incomplete box, 4½", VG, A..........................$25.00

Double Decker, Pressman, 1971, EX (VG box), M6.........$22.00

Down & Out, Milton Bradley, marble game, EX+, F3......$80.00

Drac Pinball Prototype, Parker Bros (Tonka), battery-op, sounds, never marketed, unusual, 1989, NM, P4.......$55.00

Drive on Stalingrad, SPI, 1977, M (EX box), M6............$40.00

Dungeon, TSR, 1981, M (EX box), M6 ....$28.00

Dynamite Shack, Milton Bradley, 1968, EX, M6.............$40.00

Earth Satellite, Gabriel, features astronauts circling satellite on box lid, 1956, complete, NMIB, A..........................$180.00

Eastern Front Solitaire, Omega Games, 1986, EX, M6.....$20.00

Easy Money, Milton Bradley, 1936, EX+, F3 ....$35.00

Easy Money, Milton Bradley, 1940, EX..........................$12.00

Easy Money, Milton Bradley, 1956, MIB $25.00

Easy Money, Milton Bradley, 1966, MIB $25.00

Electric Bunny Run, Prentice, land on lucky spot, light-up egg will advance position, 1951, 14x16" box, EX, T2 .....$50.00

Electric Laser Battle Game, Kenner, missing AC adaptor, EX, O1..$50.00

Electronic Football, Tudor, ca 1985, EX $35.00

Electronic Intercept, Lakeside, 1978, complete, VG $15.00

Endangered Species, Teaching Concepts, 1978, EX, M6 .$22.00

Enemy Agent, 1976, complete, EX, V1..............................$16.50

Ensign O'Toole, USS Appleby, Hasbro, 1963, NMIB (sealed), A..$55.00

Ewoks Save the Trees, NM (VG- box), O1 ....$15.00

Executive Decision, 3M, 1971, M (EX box), M6..............$30.00

Eye Guess, Milton Bradley, 1963, complete, EX $15.00

Facts in 5, 3M, complete, EX (VG box) $8.00

Fairies Cauldron Tiddley Winks, Parker Bros, 1920s, EX, F3 ....$28.00

Family Feud, Milton Bradley, 2nd edition, 1977, EX, M6 .$20.00

Family Ties Game, Applestreet, 1987, EX, M6..................$30.00

Famous Paintings, Cincinnati Game Co, cards, 1897, NM, V1 ....$22.50

Fang Face, Parker Bros, complete, 1979, NM, H4...............$5.00

Fantasyland, Parker Bros, 1956, EX $28.00

Fascination Pool, Remco, 1962, EX (VG box), M6..........$20.00

Fast Attack Boats, Yaquinto, 1980, MIB (sealed), M6 .....$20.00

FBI Crime Resistance, complete, EX, V1 ....$12.50

Ferris Wheel, Columbia Mfg, 1894, fit tiny balls into grooves of Ferris wheel, litho on cb, 5x5", EX, A........................$50.00

Fic-Tio-Nar-Y, Mayfair, 1980s, MIB (sealed), M6............$25.00

Finance, Parker Bros, 1936, NM-, F3 ....$35.00

Finance, Parker Bros, 1974, MIB......................................$20.00

Finance & Fortune, Parker Bros, 1936, EX+, C1 ....$39.00

Finance & Fortune, Parker Bros, 1936, VG, M6................$25.00

Firefight, SPI, 1976, M (EX box), M6................................$34.00

Fish Bait, Ideal, MIB $95.00

Fish Game, Japan, litho tin, early 1940s, MOC................$20.00

Fish Pond, National Games, box features fishermen in canoe catching lg fish, 1950s, 9x15", VG...........................$65.00

Five Star Final, Milton Bradley, 1937, complete w/17x30" fold-out board, NM...$150.00

Flag Game, McLoughlin Bros, complete w/instructions for 47-card game, EX, A..$45.00

Flight to Paris, Milton Bradley, EX+..............................$200.00

Flinch, Flinch Card Co, 1913, w/instructions, EX+ (VG box), P3 ....$15.00

Flinch, Parker Bros, 1934, EX..$15.00

Flinch, Parker Bros, 1963, MIB..$12.50

Floating Satellite Target, SH (Japan), battery-op, litho cb w/floating ball above, dart gun, NM (EX box), A..$60.00

Flying the Beam, Parker Bros, complete, 1941, EX+, from $70 to $90.00

Fonzo - Clown Ring Game, mk Printed in USA, 1920s, 8x10" box lid w/clown litho, EX-, A.............................$100.00

Fortune 500, Pressman, 1979, M (EX box), M6..............$50.00

Foto-Electric Football, Cadaco, 1958, EX (VG box), M6 ..,..$45.00

Frisbee Horseshoes, Wham-O, 1973, NMIB....................$22.50

Funny Bones, Parker Bros, missing 2 cards, 1968, VG $4.00

Funny Face Disguise, Topper, lg face, disguises, cards, spinner & badges, 1967, 11x16" box, unopened, MIB, T2 ....$40.00

Game of Colors, McLoughlin, Gem Series, 20 counters, 2 pcs & spinner, board on box bottom, 1888, EX, A $145.00

Game of Fire Department, Milton Bradley, lg, EX+, F3 .$120.00

Game of Flowers Card Game, Cincinnati Game Co, 1899, VG $40.00

Game of Goose, Gant/England, complete, VG................$12.50

Game of India, Milton Bradley, 1910, 15x15", EX+, F3 ...$35.00

Game of India, Milton Bradley, 1932, VG (G box), M6 ..$32.00

Game of Life, Milton Bradley, 1977, EX, M6...................$18.00

Game of Poor Jenny, All-Fair, complete w/lead playing pcs & dice, 1927, 11x11", EX $100.00

Game of Round-Up, Milton Bradley, paper litho, complete, VG $85.00

Game of the States, Milton Bradley, missing 1 pc, 1954, 9x19", VG $15.00

Game of the States, Milton Bradley, 1960, VG $15.00

Game of Zoo Animals, Parker Bros, complete w/instructions, 1895, VG $28.00

Gang Way for Fun, Transogram, EX+, F3 ....$50.00

Gas Crisis, MacMillan, 1979, M (EX box), M6 ....$22.00

Gee-Wiz Racing Game, Wolverine, 1929, MIB $150.00

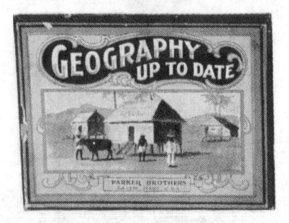

Geography Up to Date, Parker Bros., cards with geographical questions, 1890s, EX, A, $30.00.

Get My Goat, wood, slide-tile puzzle type, 1914, orig box, V1..$22.50

Parlor Foot-Ball Game, McLoughlin, spinners and markers, 1890s, EX, A, $850.00; The Fortune Teller, Milton Bradley, 1905, A, $65.00.

Giant Wheel Cowboys 'N Indians, Remco, roll-open playing board & spinning wheel, 1961, 1 cowboy missing (EX box), T2..$24.00

Gilbert Meteor Game, Gilbert, EX..................................$50.00

Gingerbread Man, Selchow & Righter, 1964, EX, M6.....$25.00

Gnip Gnop, Parker Bros, 1971, MIB, M4.......................$15.00

Go-Bang, JH Singer, tic-tac-toe-type game w/bottom of box serving as board w/markers, 5x5" box, VG+, A.........$77.00

Godfather Game, 1971, NM...$25.00

Going to Jerusalem, Parker Bros, 1955, EX.....................$35.00

Going to the Market, Ingersoll, EX+, F3........................$75.00

Gooses Wild, CO-5, 1966, EX (G- box)...........................$8.00

Gooses Wild, 1965, MIB (sealed), V1.............................$16.50

Guiness Game of World Records, Parker Bros, 1975, EX (VG box), M6...$25.00

Hangman, Milton Bradley, 1976, complete, EX..............$10.00

Harriers, Spears, track game, EX+, F3............................$75.00

Harry Lorayne Memory Game, Reiss, 1976, M (EX box), M6..$42.00

Hawaiian Punch Board Game, EX..................................$25.00

Head of the Class, Milton Bradley, 1957, EX (G- box)......$6.00

Hee Haw, game, target; Milton Bradley, 1937, EX+, F3...$28.00

Hercules, game, Sons of Hercules, Milton Bradley, 1966, MIB, M4..$50.00

Hex: The Zig-Zag Game, Parker Bros, 1950, VG (G box), M6...$26.00

Hickety Pickety, Parker Bros, 1930s, EX+, F3................$28.00

Goosy Goosy Gander, McLoughlin Bros., 1890, EX-, $550.00.

Hide and Seek, McLoughlin Bros., 1895, EX, A, $375.00.

Good Old Game of Innocence Abroad, Parker Bros. Inc., 1888, EX+, $300.00.

Goren's Bridge for Two, Milton Bradley, 1964, EX..........$10.00

Grand National, Whitman, 1937, EX (VG box)...............$50.00

Great Family Amusement, Elastic Tip Co, target game, NP pistol, arrow (tip missing), 14x10¾" (G box), A.........$220.00

Great Grape Ape, Milton Bradley, MIB (1 rpr seam on box)..$15.00

Group Therapy, GT Association, 1969, EX+, F3.............$28.00

Gruesome Mansion, Monster Bagatelle, unknown maker, EX, H4...$15.00

High Bid, 3M, missing 1 card, 1965, EX..............................$9.00
Hitch Hiker, Whitman, 1937, EX-, F3.............................$135.00
Hoc-Key, Cadaco-Ellis, 1958, VG (G box), M6..............$25.00
Home History Card Game, Milton Bradley, EX+, F3 ....$24.00
Hop Ching, Chinese Checkers, tin, orig instructions & marbles, 1980s, T1..$20.00
Hot Rod Sport Car Race, Remco, complete w/6 playing cars, early 1960s, MIB...$35.00
Hot Wheels Game, Whitman, 1982, EX, M6 ....$25.00
Hungry Henry, Ideal, 1969, EX, M6..................................$25.00
I'm a Dumbskull Stunt Game, skull & spinner, 12", EX...$38.00
Image, 3M, missing outer sleeve, 1972, EX $6.00
In the Soup, Parker Bros, EX, F3 ....$95.00
Inventors, Parker Bros, 1974, EX, M6 ....$30.00
It Takes Two, Hasbro, complete, 1970, EX+......................$5.00

Jack and the Bean Stalk, McLoughlin Bros., 1989, EX-, A, $900.00.

Jack Straws, Milton Bradley, EX+, F3 ....$18.00
Jeopardy!, Milton Bradley, 1962, VG, M6 ....$30.00
Jig Race, Game Makers, 1930s, EX, M6 ....$55.00
Jolly Robbers, Wilder, 1929, VG, M6 ....$65.00
Journey Into the Unknown, Remco, 1968, EX (VG box), M6..$140.00

Jumbo Ring Toss, Rosebud, 1940, MIB, from $30 to $48.00
Junior Combination, Milton Bradley, board game, dice & spinner, 1905, complete in orig box w/desert scene, EX, A $70.00
Just Say No Now, unused, 1960s, M..................................$10.00
Jutland, Avalon Hill, 1967, EX, M6..................................$34.00
Karter Peanut Shell Game, Morey & Neeley, 1978, M (EX box), M6...$38.00
Keep 'Em Rolling Marble Game, Mastercraft, 1942, MIB .$45.00
Kentucky Jones Horse Auction Board Game, VG $25.00
Kick-Off Soccer, Camden, 1978, M (EX box), M6...........$45.00
King Zor, board game, 1962, NM $35.00
Knockout Electronic Boxing, Northwestern Products, litho tin boxing ring w/2 5" plastic boxers, 1950, EX+ (EX box), T2...$130.00
Kreskin's ESP Advanced Edition, Milton Bradley, plastic table, cards, disks & directions, 1967, M (EX box), T2.......$30.00
Kwazy Kwilt, Kohner, 1970, EX (VG box), M6................$15.00
Last Straw, Schaper, 1966, EX, M6 ....$30.00
Leapin' Letters, Parker Bros, 1969, VG (G box), M6 ....$22.00
Let's Make a Deal, Ideal, 1974, M (VG box), M6 ....$35.00
Lie Detector Game, Mattel, player to solve murder & arrest suspect wins, complete, 15x15" window box, 1961-64, NM, A..$61.00
Life of the Party, Rosebud, 1930s, EX+, F3 ....$35.00

Lindy Hop-Off, Parker Bros., ca 1927, EX, A, $375.00.

Little Red Bushy Tail, Parker Bros, 1930, EX, F3 ....$38.00
Lobby, Milton Bradley, 1949, EX (VG box), M6..............$65.00
Logomachy, Milton Bradley, card game, EX+, F3............$35.00
Look Out Below Game, Ideal, 1968, EX, M6....................$50.00
Lost Valley of the Dinosaurs, Waddingtons, 1985, M (EX box), M6 ....$70.00
Lotto, Milton Bradley, 1932, NMIB..................................$25.00
Luck o' the Irish, Reilley & Co, 1985, EX, M6 ....$24.00
Lucky Fisherman, Whitman, 1959, orig box, EX $22.00
MacDonald's Farm Game, Selchow & Righter, EX (VG box), M6..$54.00

Mad Magazine Game, Parker Bros, complete, 1979, M $10.00

Magic Auto Race, Wolverine, action game, EX, F3 ....$75.00

Magic Realm, Avalon Hill, 1970s, M (EX box), M6 ....$17.00

Magic Robot, board, 1950s, EX+, T1 ....$35.00

Magnetic Fish Pond, McLoughlin, folding pond, 33 fish, 6 poles, 4 magnets missing, 1891, 14½" sq, A $220.00

Mail, Express, or Acommodation; McLoughlin Bros., 1895, wooden box, EX, A, $1,000.00.

Management, Avalon Hill, 1960, EX, M6 ....$50.00

Manhunt: Use the Computer To Catch the Crook; Milton Bradley, 1972, MIB..$30.00

Marble Bingo, Wolverine Supply, 1930s, EX (G box), M6 ....$70.00

Marble Game w/Oriental Motif (Jue de Va et Vient Chinois), French, litho paper on wood w/pnt tin cars, 29", EX, A $495.00

Marble Raceway, 15" 4-pc tower w/marbles, 1960s, NM, A $42.00

Master Mind, Invicta, 1972, EX, M6....................................$25.00

Masterpiece, Parker Bros, 1972, M4 ....$40.00

Mayday, GDW, 1978, M (EX box), M6 ....$18.00

Melvin the Moon Man, Remco, NMIB $125.00

Merit Magic Robot, England, robot answers questions w/wand, complete, MIB $75.00

Merry Steeple Chase, Ottman, 1910, EX+, F3.................$35.00

Mexican Jumping Bean Game, 1950s, MOC, V1 ....$34.00

Michigan Rummy, Transogram, 1960, EX, M6................$15.00

Mid-Life Crisis, Game Works, 1982, EX, M6 ....$22.00

Money Money Money, Whitman, 1957, EX (G box), M6 .$20.00

Monkey Stix, Ideal, 1960, MIB, M4..................................$12.00

Monopoly, Parker Bros, 1935 edition, EX+, F3 ....$35.00

Monopoly, Parker Bros, 1968, MIB, M4 ....$20.00

Monopoly Deluxe Edition, Parker Bros, 1968, brn box, M4 .$50.00

Monster Madness, EX, P3 ....$18.00

Monster Mansion, Milton Bradley, 1981, complete, EX ..$25.00

Monster Squad, 1977, EX, P3 ....$25.00

Moon Blast-Off Game #543, Schaper, 1970s, MIB (shrink-wrapped box), P4...$30.00

Mostly Ghostly, Cadaco, 1975, EX (EX- box), P3............$20.00

Mother Goose, Bliss, pop-up figures in houses, balls missing, 1890s, 18x11", A $950.00

Mothers Help for Rainy Days, Parker Bros, 1930, orig box, NM...$35.00

Mouse Trap, Ideal, turn crank to set off chain reaction to trap mouse, 1963, orig 15x22" box, NMIB (sealed), A ...$131.00

Mouse Trap, Ideal, 1963, EX (VG box), M6.....................$60.00

Mr Potato Head on the Farm Set, Hasbro, appears complete, orig box, EX, H4 ....$50.00

Mystery Date Game, Milton Bradley, 1965, EX (VG box), M6...$42.00

Mystic Finger, Baumgarten & Comp, EX+, F3 ....$45.00

Mystic Skull Game of Voodoo, Ideal, 1964, EX+, C1 ......$63.00

Name That Tune Bingo Game, Milton Bradley, 1959, M (EX-box), C1...$31.00

Nancy Drew Mystery Game, Parker Bros, 1957, MIB, from $75 to...$100.00

NBC Peacock Game, Selchow & Righter, 1966, M (EX box), M6...$25.00

New Frontier, Colorful Products, 1962, orig envelope, VG, M6...$50.00

New Game of American Revolution, Lorenzo Burge, board game, 1844, EX, minumum value $1,700.00

New Newlywed Game, Pressman, 1986, complete, orig box, G...$8.00

Nick the Greek's Super Roulette, 1978, M $12.50

Nine Men's Morris, Transogram, 1956, EX.....................$10.00

Nosey Ring Toss, Transogram, 1937, VG, M6..................$45.00

Nurses, Ideal, board game, 1963, complete except for cb inlay on which the playing board rests, EX, T2....................$25.00

O'Grady's Goat, Milton Bradley, 1959, EX+, F3 ....$28.00

Official Basketball, Toy Creations, 1940, EX+, F3 ....$48.00

Official Radio Football Game, Toy Creations, 1939, VG, M6...$40.00

Operation, Milton Bradley, battery-op, 1975, orig box, EX..$40.00

Orbit, Parker Bros, board game, 24 wooden disks & 2 spinners, 1959, 9x18" box (EX box), T2 ....$50.00

Organized Crime, Kowplow Games, 1974, EX, M6 ....$30.00

Outboard Motor Race, Milton Bradley, 1930s, EX, M6....$75.00

Outwit, Parker Bros, 1978, EX, M6 ....$25.00

Overland Limited, Milton Bradley, 1920s, EX (VG box), M6/F3...$130.00

Par Golf, National, F3...$35.00

Parcheesi, Selchow & Righter, 1938, EX (VG box), M6 .$32.00

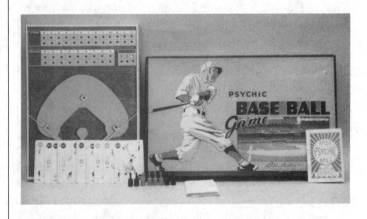

Psychic Baseball Game, Parker Bros., 1935, EX, D10, $400.00.

Park & Shop, Traffic Game, EX+, F3.................$65.00

Parlor Croquet, Bliss, 10½" mallet, orig box, NM $105.00

Parlor Football, McLoughlin Bros, complete w/spinners, markers, 1 ball pc, 1890, 11x19", EX, A.................$850.00

Password, Milton Bradley, complete, 1964, EX (EX+ box)..$7.00

Pat Moran, game, Pat Moran's Own Ball Game, dtd 1919, A.................$800.00

Pathfinder, Milton Bradley, 1954, EX $20.00

Pathfinder, Milton Bradley, 1977, EX, T6/M6.................$35.00

Peg Baseball, Parker Bros, 1917, EX+, minumum value .$100.00

Peg Chow/Telka, Parker Bros, 1962, EX, M6.................$35.00

Peter Coodles, Singer, card game, EX, F3 ....$35.00

Philip Marlow, game board; Exciting Detective Game, Transogram, 1960, complete w/box, rare, EX+ $95.00

Philmont, Nalpac, 1987, M (EX box), M6.................$45.00

Ping Pong, J Jaques & Son Ltd, 2 balls/2 hide-covered paddles & net, in wood box w/graphic litho, 19½x7¾x4", EX, A.$120.00

Ping Pong, Parker Bros, Victorian cover, EX+, F3.........$110.00

Pirate & the Traveller, Milton Bradley, 1956, MIB (sealed) $25.00

Pirates Chase Game, TeePee Toys, no date, EX, M6.........$30.00

Pit, Parker Bros, 1964, MIB, M4.................$15.00

Playboy, Victory Games, 1986, EX, M6 ....$30.00

Pocket Size Golf, Built-Rite, illus deck of cards, 1950s, 3x4" illus box, complete, NM, T2 ....$20.00

Point of Law, 3M, complete, 1972, M (VG box).................$10.00

Pollyanna, Parker Bros, 1930, EX $35.00

Pontiac Safety Drive Game, RL Polk, 1937, orig envelope, EX, M6.................$60.00

Pop-the-Bird Target Game, NN Hill, orig box, NM $105.00

Popular Game of Go Bang, Parker Bros, similar to checkers, G, A $40.00

Prediction Rod, Parker Bros, 1970, M6 ....$28.00

Pro Bowl Live Action Football, 1968, MIB.................$65.00

Probe, Parker Bros, complete, 1964, VG (G box).................$8.00

Prospecting, Selchow & Righter, 1953, complete, scarce, EX, V1.................$68.00

Psychedelic Brain Drain Game, MIP.................$25.00

Public Assistance, Hammerhead, 1980, EX, F3 ....$28.00

Punch & Judy Target, Reed, litho paper on wood, 1 pop-up target rpl, 13", G+, A.................$220.00

Qubic, Parker Bros, 1965, EX, M6.................$23.00

Quinto, 3M, complete, 1968, EX (VG box).................$6.00

Race to Planets, E-Z Game Mfg, board game w/space money, spinner, plastic missile playing pcs, 1950s, EX, A....$150.00

Rack-O, Milton Bradley, 1972, EX.................$10.00

Radar Search, Ideal, electronic, battery-op, orig box, NM.$20.00

Radio, Milton Bradley, EX+, F3 ....$55.00

Razzle, Parker Bros, 1981, EX, M6.................$25.00

Regatta, 3M, 1968, M (EX box) $20.00

Reunion, Ungame, 1979, EX, M6 ....$18.00

Revlon's $64,000 Question Quiz Game, Cowan, 1955, EX..$40.00

Rich Uncle, Parker Bros, 1955, orig box, EX $35.00

Richthofen's War, Avalon, 1972, VG (G- box) $5.00

Ripley's Believe It or Not, Milton Bradley, 1984, EX, M6.$30.00

Ripley's Believe It or Not Library of Cards Game, Ripley, 1964, complete, MIB $40.00

Risk, Parker Bros, wooden pcs, 1959, EX+ $40.00

Risk, Parker Bros, 1974, MIB.................$20.00

Road Runner Game, Milton Bradley, EX+ $35.00

Roaring '20s, Yaquinto, 1981, MIB (sealed), M6.................$24.00

Rocket (Train), Parker Bros, complete w/board & spinner, Art Deco-style box lid, 1930s, EX.................$175.00

Rockets Away Space Travel, Amsco, shoot rockets from periscope-type bomb dropper, 1950s, EX, from $120 to $135.00

Ruff-n-Ready Board Game, Transogram, 1963, NM.................$60.00

Rumbo, Selchow & Righter, 1930s, VG (G box), M6 .....$30.00

Sail Away, Howard J Mullin, 1962, EX, M6 ....$55.00

Sammy the White House Mouse Game, 1977, NM.................$8.00

Santa Claus Game, Milton Bradley, mc paper litho fireplace & stockings, spinner, wood pcs, orig box, 8½x12", VG, A.................$100.00

Score Four, Funtastic, 1968, EX.................$6.00

Scouts, Milton Bradley, w/incomplete set of markers, Indian litho on box lid, 1920, 11x22", EX, A.................$100.00

Scrabble, Selchow & Righter, 1953, EX, minumum value..$150.00

Screwball-Mad Mad, Transogram, EX+, F3 ....$65.00

Seduction, Crea Tek, complete, 1966, EX $7.00

See New York 'Round the Town, Transogram, 1964, EX.$60.00

Shanghai Trader, Panther Games, 1986, MIB (sealed), M6.................$35.00

Sheriff w/Shooting Gun Target Game, Japan, aim cork gun at litho tin sheriff's badge & hat flies off, NM (EX box), A $150.00

Shindig, Remco, 1965, M (EX box, sealed), M6.................$85.00

Sinbad, Cadaco, 1978, EX, M6.................$35.00

Sinking of the Titanic, Ideal, 1976, NM $40.00

Six-Day Bike Race, Lindstrom, metal bagetelle, EX+, F3.$65.00

Skatebirds Game, Milton Bradley, 1978, EX, M6 ....$30.00

Ski Hi, Cutler & Saleby, EX, F3.................$95.00

Skirmish, Milton Bradley, American Heritage Series, 1975, VG $30.00

Skunk, Schaper, 1953, EX, M6.................$35.00

Smog, Urban Systems, 1970, EX, M6.................$46.00

Snake Eyes, Selchow & Righter, 1930s, EX-.................$60.00

Snap Card Game, Milton Bradley, EX+, F3 ....$22.00

Solar Quest, Western Publishing, 1986, MIB (sealed), M6..$28.00

Solitaire, Milton Bradley, 1973, EX, M6.................$20.00

Sorry, Parker Bros, 1950s, EX $20.00

Sorry, Parker Bros, 1964, MIB $25.00

Space, The Game That Defies Gravity; VG, O1 ....$15.00

Space Patrol, Japan, litho tin & cb, push plunger in center, spin & score, 1950s, 2½" dia, M, A.................$45.00

Space Pilot Game, Cadaco-Ellis, complete w/Inter-Planetary Flying Field board & accessories, 1951, NM (NM+ box) ..$75.00

Spartan, SPI, 1975, M (EX box), M6 ....$70.00

Speedboat Race, Parker Bros, EX, F3 ....$75.00

Spinette, Milton Bradley, 1930s, EX+, F3.................$22.00

Spingo & Whirlette, Transogram, 1940, EX (VG box), M6.$35.00

Spoof Card Game, Milton Bradley, 1930s, EX+, F3 ....$25.00

Spudsy Hot Potato, Ohio Art, player holding Spudsy when he 'dings' is out, 1960s, 9x8x4" window box, NM (EX box), T2 ....$30.00

Spy Game of Espionage, Transogram, 1963, NMIB.........$48.00

Stampin', Rainy Day Designs, 1989, MIB (sealed), M6....$32.00

Stay Alive, Milton Bradley, 1978, EX, M6 ....$20.00

Stars and Stripes (Red, White, and Blue), McLoughlin Bros., ca 1900, EX-, $900.00.

Stock Market, Whitman, plastic quotation board indicator, stock cars & tray, etc, 1968, 10x20" box, EX $30.00

Stocks & Bonds, 3M, complete, 1964, M (EX box) $8.00

Stop & Shop, All Fair, 1920s, some pcs rpl, EX- $75.00

Stop Thief, Parker Bros, 1979, EX, M6 ....$55.00

Strange Game of Forbidden Fruit, Parker Bros, box features boy climbing tree w/angry dog behind him, 1890s, EX.....$45.00

Stratego, Milton Bradley, 1962, EX, M6 ....$20.00

Sub Attack, Milton Bradley, unused, 1965, EX $70.00

Super Toe, Ideal, complete, MIB..$17.50

Super-Ball Golf, Wham-O, 1966, NM (EX box) $22.50

Superball Dice, Wham-O, 2 superballs molded as dice on 4x6" illus card w/playing instructions, 1966, EX+ card, T2 ....$30.00

Swahili, Milton Bradley, 1968, EX, M6 ....$30.00

Swayze Board Game, Milton Bradley, ca 1954, EX+, C1 .$36.00

Tactics II, Avalon Hill, 1961, EX, M6 ....$32.00

Tantalizer, Northers Signal Co, 1960, EX, M6 ....$65.00

Tell It to the Judge, Parker Bros, 1959, VG, M6..............$45.00

The '49ers, National Games, 1950s, EX $50.00

Thing Ding Robot Game, 1960s, scarce, MIB (rpr corners), V1..$125.00

Thing-a-Tron Electronic Question & Answer Computer, Hasbro, 1960s, MIB $75.00

Third Reich Game of WWII, Avalon, 1974, NMIB........$25.00

Three Men on a Horse, Milton Bradley, 1936, VG- $45.00

Three Musketeers: A Game of Strategy; Milton Bradley, 1920s, EX $75.00

Tiddle Tennis Jr, Schoenhut, 1930s, EX+, F3..................$35.00

Time Bomb, Milton Bradley, toss bomb from player to player until it explodes, 1965, 5x8x3" box, NMIB $50.00

Tobogganing at Christmas, McLoughlin Bros., 1899, EX, $600.00.

Topple, Kenner, 1979, EX, M6..$25.00

Torpedo Shoot, Marx, 1977, EX, M6 ....$35.00

Toss Across, Ideal, 1970, EX, M6......................................$34.00

Touring, Parker Bros, NM-, F3 ....$25.00

Town & Country Traffic, Ranger Steel, fold-out board, complete, unused, NM (EX+ box), A $85.00

Toy Village, Milton Bradley, EX+, F3 ....$65.00

Train for Boston, Parker Bros., 1900, wooden box, EX, $900.00.

Trans-World Flyer, board game w/tin litho airplane, Biller, W Germany, 1950s, 22x24", EX+ (VG box), A...........$299.00

Trap-Em Alive Marble Game, Gotham, NM...................$35.00

Tri Ominoes, Pressman, 1977, EX.....................................$15.00
Trivia Adventure Plus, Pressman, 1984, M (EX box), M6..$25.00

Trip Round the World, McLoughlin Bros., 1897, EX, $500.00.

Tru-Action Football, Tudor, 1950s, MIB.........................$25.00
Turtle Hunt in the Jungle, Tudor Toys, litho tin board, paper
    litho box, complete, 19", VG, A $50.00
Twenty-One, Lowell, 1950s, EX+, F3 ....$28.00
Twixt, 3M, 1966, EX, M6...$25.00
Two for the Money, Hassenfeld, 1955, EX.....................$15.00
Two Game Combination-India & Checkers, Milton Bradley,
    #4905, 1920s, orig box w/Egyptian scene, VG...........$30.00
Tycoon, Parker Bros, 1966, EX, M6 ....$42.00

Uncle Sam's Mail, McLoughlin Bros., 1893, VG, $200.00.

Under-N-Over Marble Game, Marx, 1950, EX $50.00
Undersea World of Jacques Cousteau, Parker Bros, 1968,
    EX, M6 ....$40.00
Venture, 3M, 1979, EX, M6...$35.00
Video Village, Milton Bradley, 1960, VG.......................$20.00
Vox Pop, Milton Bradley, 1938, VG $30.00
War Bingo, Gotham Sales, 1942, EX, M6........................$45.00
Watch, MPH Games, 1970s, EX, M6...............................$20.00
Waterloo, Stoll & Einson, fold-out board shows combat scenes
    & markers, 1935, EX, A $128.00

Visit of Santa Claus, McLoughlin Bros., #605, 1899, EX, $495.00.

Waterloo - Napoleonic Campaign, Avalon Hill, 1962, 10x12"
    box, EX, T2 ....$20.00
We Play Store, Gabriel, 1930s, EX (VG box).................$40.00
What's My Line, Lowell, 1955, EX, M6 ....$48.00
What's My Name, 1974, complete, EX $12.00
When My Ship Comes In, Geo S Parker, contains 80 playing
    slips & instructions, 1888, 4x5½" box, VG+, A $51.00
Where's the Beef, Milton Bradley, 1984, EX, T6.............$25.00
Which Witch, Milton Bradley, complete, 1970, EX-NM,
    H4...$35.00

Whirling Aeroplane Race, McDowell, 1930s, 10" diameter, D10, $275.00.

Who Can Beat Nixon?; Dynamic, 1971, EX, M6 ....$60.00

Whodunit?; Selchow & Righter, 1972, EX, M6.................$20.00

Wide World Air Travel Board Game, Parker Bros, 1957, NM
(EX box), C1...$49.00

Wildcatter, RH Kesler, 1981, MIB (sealed), M6...............$80.00

Winner Spinner, Whitman, 1953, VG+ $16.00

Woman & Man, Psychology Today, 1971, EX, M6..........$25.00

Wooden Ships & Iron Men, Battle-Line, 1974, M (EX box),
M6..$45.00

World Flag Game About the United Nations, Parker Bros, 1961,
EX (VG box), M6...$44.00

World's Educator, WS Reed, teaches arithmetic, geography &
important events of 19th C, wood box, EX, A $150.00

World's Fair Game, Milton Bradley, EX+, F3 ....$28.00

Worldbeater, Intellect Games, 1975, EX, M6...................$40.00

Yesteryear, Skor-Mor, 1973, M (EX box), M6 ....$25.00

You're the Quarterback - Rose Bowl Game, Keck Ent, board
game, figural plastic players, 1949, unused, NMIB, A.$65.00

Young Folks Geographical Game, McLoughlin Bros, features
children studying globe on box lid, 1880s, EX, A $50.00

Zip Code Board Game, Lakeside, 4 letter-sorting racks, 1 dead letter box, 48 letters & dice, 1964, NM (EX- box), A $80.00

Zoography, Amway, 1972, EX (VG box), M6...................$28.00

Zoom, All-Fair, board game, instrument flight panel w/markers,
1930s, 10x14" Deco box, EX+, A..............................$95.00

10-4 Good Buddy: The CB Game; KLS-73, 1976, EX-, M6..$25.00

1776, Avalon Hill, 1st edition, 1974, EX+, M6................$25.00

1776, Dynamic, 1974, EX-, M6 ....$30.00

1776 American Revolutionary War Game, Avalon, 1974,
NMIB $20.00

1863, Parker Bros, 1961, EX, M6.....................................$55.00

1914, Avalon Hill, 1968, EX, M6......................................$60.00

4-Cyte, Milton Bradley, 1967, EX, M6..............................$22.00

6-Tag-Rannen, Holtmann VIP, 1986, EX+, C6 ....$48.00

Gasoline Powered

Two of the largest companies to manufacture gas-powered
models are Cox and Wen Mac. Since the late fifties they have
been making faithfully detailed models of airplanes as well as
some automobiles and boats. Condition of used models will vary
greatly because of the nature of the miniature gas engine and
damage resulting from the fuel that has been used. Because of
this, 'in box' gas toys command a premium. Our advisor is
Danny Bynum (B7).

Cox Action Van, yel, sm scratches, no stickers, VG, B7..$20.00

Cox Chopper, MIB..$195.00

Cox Dune Buggy, front wheels & tires, tie rods & spindles,
#3700-4, M, B7 ....$15.00

Cox E-Z Flyer Commanche, wht, NMIB, B7 ....$25.00

Cox Golden Bee, .049 engine, M, B7...............................$20.00

Cox P-40, camouflage gr, M $50.00

Cox P-51 Combat Mustang, throttle sleeve, #2374, M, B7...$2.00

Cox Pinto/Vega, chassis w/bl gas tank & front wheels,
#6572, M, B7 ....$20.00

Cox Shrike, race car, gr, crack in canopy, VG, B7 ....$40.00

Cox Sky Raider, gray, EX (EX box) $100.00

Cox Sopwith Camel, yel & bl, NM (VG box), B7 ....$40.00

Cox Spitfire, lt gr, EX stickers, VG $50.00

Cox Stuka, gr, 1 broken tail wheel mt, EX, B7 ....$60.00

Fokker Triplane, complete, 49" wingspan, M $200.00

McCoy, .35 redhead stunt engine, EX, B7 ....$20.00

OD P-40, NM, B7...$15.00

OD P-51 Mustang, G+-VG, B7...$20.00

OD Sopwith Camel, G+-VG, B7......................................$20.00

Silver Swallow, .09 diesel engine, w/wrench, MIB, B7 .....$27.00

Silver Swallow, .15 diesel engine, w/wrench, MIB, B7 .....$32.00

Testors Cosmic Wind, orange, MIB $40.00

Testors Cosmic Wind, Spirit of '76, M............................$50.00

Testors Cosmic Wind Racer, blk or orange, M, B7, ea $20.00

Testors Fly 'Em, .049 glo-fuel engine, 1 missing hand con-
troller, EX $45.00

Testors Fly 'Em, Red Albatross, NM, B7........................$25.00

Testors Fly 'Em, Sopwith Camel, EX-NM.......................$20.00

Testors Fly 'Em, Zero, M...$30.00

GI Joe

GI Joe, the most famous action figure of them all, has been
made in hundreds of variations since Hasbro introduced him in
1964. The first of these jointed figures was 12" tall; he can be
identified today by the mark on his back: GI Joe T.M. (trademark), Copyright 1964. They came with four different hair colors: blond, auburn, black, and brown, each with a scar on his
right cheek. They were sold in four basic packages: Action Soldier, Action Sailor, Action Marine, and Action Pilot. A Black
figure was included in the line, and there were representatives of
many nations as well — France, Germany, Japan, Britain,
Canada, Russia, and Australia. Talking GI Joes were issued in
1967 when the only female (the nurse) was introduced. Besides
the figures, uniforms, vehicles, guns, and accessories of many
varieties were produced. The Adventure Team series, made from
1970 to 1976, included Black Adventurer, Air Adventurer,
Talking Astronaut, Sea Adventurer, Talking Team Commander, Land Adventurer, and several variations. Joe's hard plastic
hands were replaced with rubber ones, so that he could better
grip his weapons. Assorted playsets allowed young imaginations
to run wild, and besides the doll-size items, there were wristwatches, foot lockers, toys, and walkie-talkies made for the kids
themselves. Due to increased production costs, the large GI Joe
was discontinued in 1976.

But the market was there and kids were still clamoring for
more. So in 1982, Hasbro brought out the 'little' 3¾" GI Joe figures, each with its own descriptive name. Of the first series some
characters were produced with either a swivel arm or a jointed
elbow. Vehicles, weapons, and playsets were available, and some
characters could only be had by redeeming flag points from the
backs of packages. This small version proved to be the most successful action figure line ever made. Loose items are common;
collectors value those still mint in the original packages at two
to four times higher. For more information we recommend Collectible Male Action Figures by Paris and Susan Manos. Note: all
items are American issue unless indicated otherwise.

12" GI Joe Figures and Sets

Ace, Hasbro, Hall of Fame, 3rd series, 1992-93, MIB, F1 . **$45.00**

Action Marine, auburn molded hair, dress uniform, rpl hat, broken trigger guard on rifle, H4 .... **$99.00**

Action Marine, blond molded hair, complete sabatoge outfit w/accessories, NM, H4 .... **$220.00**

Action Marine, complete w/accessories & papers, NMIB, from $270 to **$299.00**

Action Marine, molded hair, camo outfit & hat, w/boots, lt worn pnt hair, H4 .... **$69.00**

Action Pilot, molded hair, orange jumpsuit & bl fatigue hat, lt worn pnt hair, H4 .... **$79.00**

Action Pilot, w/orig paperwork, missing stickers, NM (NM box), H4 .... **$300.00**

Action Sailor, molded hair, work shirt and blue jean pants, complete with dog tag, 1964, M (EX box), H4, $260.00.

Action Sailor, molded hair, work shirt & bl jean pants, H4 .. **$75.00**

Action Sailor, w/paperwork, missing sticker sheet, M (EX box), H4 .... **$260.00**

Action Soldier, auburn hair, complete w/stickers & papers, NM (NM box), H4 .... **$220.00**

Action Soldier, Black, M (EX box), H4 .... **$750.00**

Action Soldier, Black, w/shirt, pants, hat & boots, EX, C6 .... **$579.00**

Action Soldier, fatigues, boots, dog tag, cap, manual, decals, catalog & club sheet, EX (EX box), C6 .... **$270.00**

Action Soldier, molded hair, fatigue outfit & hat, w/boots, lt worn pnt hair, EX, H4 .... **$69.00**

Action Soldier, molded hair, w/uniform & accessories, NM+, C6 .... **$175.00**

Adventure Team Set, blond hair, no beard, hard hands, silver space outfit w/accessories, complete, H4 .... **$100.00**

Adventure Team Set, brn hair, no beard, hard hands, Secret Agent outfit w/accessories, complete, H4 .... **$100.00**

Adventure Team Set, brn hair, no beard, Kung-Fu grip, rescue outfit w/accessories, missing flashlight, H4 .... **$70.00**

Adventure Team Set, brn hair & beard, hard hands, Sky Dive to Danger outfit w/accessories, papers & comic, EX, H4 .... **$130.00**

Air Cadet, MIB (sealed photo box), C6 .... **$1,200.00**

Air Force Dress, brn molded hair, w/tie, Air Police helmet, belt, holster, pistol, carbine, bayonet, & phone, EX-NM, H4 .... **$325.00**

Annapolis Cadet, blond hair, complete w/accessories, NM, H4 .... **$350.00**

Annapolis Cadet, complete w/accessories, NRFB (photo box), A **$1,250.00**

Astronaut, space suit & helmet, gloves, boots, pack & tether cord, EX, C6 .... **$145.00**

Australian Jungle Fighter, molded hair, complete with accessories and medal, no stripes or patches on jacket, H4, $200.00.

Australian Jungle Fighter, complete w/accessories, MIB (sealed), C6 ....$1,250.00

Australian Jungle Fighter, molded hair, complete w/all accessories & medal, no stripes or patches on jacket, EX, H4 ....$200.00

Basic Training Grunt, Hasbro, Hall of Fame, 2nd series, 1992-93, MIB, F1 ....$25.00

Basic Training Heavy Duty, Hasbro, 2nd series, 1992-93, MIB, F1 ....$25.00

Black Adventurer, fuzzy hair, no beard, hard hands, w/orig tan outfit, boots, shoulder holster & pistol, H4 ....$120.00

Black Adventurer, fuzzy hair, no beard, w/Kung-Fu grip, wearing camo shirt, pants, boots, H4 ....$110.00

Breeches Buoy, pnt molded hair, yel slicker top & bottom, boots, EX, C6 ....$259.00

British Commando, w/helmet, jacket, trousers & boots, M (sm box, re-shrink-wrapped), C6 ....$1,100.00

Cobra Commander, Hasbro, Hall of Fame, 1st series, 1992-93, MIB, F1 ....$45.00

Combat Marine, in camouflage outfit, helmet, boots, cartridge belt, pack, grenades & M1 rifle, NM, C6 ....$185.00

Deep Freeze, molded hair, fur parka, gold pants, snow boots, sm pull sled, goggles & flare gun, 1976, EX-NM, H4 ....$190.00

Deep Sea Diver, auburn molded hair, missing gloves, o/w complete, NM, H4 ....$150.00

Duke, Hasbro, Hall of Fame, 1st series, 1992-1993, 12", MIB, F1 ....$45.00

Duke, Hasbro, Hall of Fame, 4th series, talker, 1992-93, MIB, F1 ....$75.00

Firefighter, missing end of fire extinguisher, belt rpr, box lid only, EX+ (VG lid), M5 ....$300.00

French Resistance Fighter, molded hair, outfit w/holster & pistol, grenades, machine gun, knife & medal, NM, C6 .....$249.00

French Resistance Fighter, w/beret, sweater, jeans & boots, MIB (sealed, sm), C6 ....$1,250.00

French Resistance Fighter, w/most accessories, missing gun & medal, H4 ....$140.00

Frogman & Sea Sled Set #8050, complete, EX (EX box), C6 ....$220.00

German Soldier, complete, MIB (sealed, sm), C6 ....$1,250.00

German Soldier, molded hair, complete w/accessories & medal, EX, H4 ....$325.00

German Soldier, NMIB (rpr box), H4 ....$700.00

German Stormtrooper, uniform, helmet, belt, gun & holster, pack, grenades, Schmeisser & medal, NM, C6 ....$325.00

Green Beret, blond molded hair, complete w/accessories except scarf, EX-NM, H4 ....$190.00

Gung-Ho, Hasbro, Hall of Fame, 3rd series, 1992-93, MIB, F1 ....$45.00

Japanese Imperial Soldier, in uniform with accessories and manual, MIB (sealed), C6, $1,300.00.

Japanese Imperial Soldier, complete w/accessories & medal, EX, H4 ....$475.00

Land Adventurer, brn hair & beard, hard hands, missing clothes & accessories, H4 ....$45.00

Land Adventurer, brn hair & beard, w/Kung-Fu grip, missing clothes & accessories, H4 ....$45.00

Land Adventurer, camouflage shirt & pants, boots, dog tag, insignia, shoulder holster & pistol, M (NM box), C6.$179.00

Duke, Hasbro, Hall of Fame, Desert Storm fatigues, MIB, $45.00.

Man of Action, brn hair, no beard, hard hands, missing clothes & accessories, H4......................$45.00

Man of Action, brn hair, no beard, w/Kung-Fu grip, missing clothes & accessories, H4........................$45.00

Man of Action, shirt, pants, hat, boots, insignia & dog tag, w/hard hands, EX (VG+ box), C6............$179.00

Marine Communications, w/uniform & accessories, NM, C6......................$189.00

Marine Jungle Fighter, molded hair, complete w/orig accessories, EX, H4......................$495.00

Military Police, molded hair, uniform w/accessories, NM, C6......................$249.00

Motorcycle Police, brn molded hair, missing sunglasses, whistle, handcuffs & 2 tickets, EX+, H4..............$220.00

Navy Attack, w/uniform & accessories, NM, C6............$249.00

Race Car Driver, auburn molded hair, complete w/helmet, goggles & boots, EX+, H4......................$130.00

Rapid Fire, Hasbro, Hall of Fame, 4th series, 1992-93, MIB, F1......................$55.00

Russian Infantryman, w/fur hat, jacket, pants & boots, MIB (sm, re-shrink-wrapped), C6......................$1,250.00

Russian Soldier, auburn hair, missing grenades, binoculars & case, EX-NM, H4......................$250.00

Sea Adventurer, flocked red hair and beard, brown eyes, scar, navy blue pants, light blue top, shoulder holster (missing pistol), with boot removal instructions, NMIB, A, $125.00; Talking Adventure Team Commander, brown flocked hair, with accessories, NM (G box), A, $200.00.

Scramble Pilot, molded hair, complete w/accessories, EX, H4......................$290.00

Scuba Diver, blk molded hair, rubber wet suit top, flippers, tanks w/hoses, mask, etc, missing blk rubber hood, H4.....$220.00

Scuba Diver, orange 3-pc wet suit w/blk zipper, flippers, EX, C6......................$149.00

Scuba Diver, pnt molded hair, 3-pc blk wet suit w/flippers, EX, C6......................$175.00

Sears Exclusive Forward Observer Set, complete w/accessories, rare, MIB, H4......................$425.00

Shore Patrol, molded hair, complete w/accessories, EX, C6/H4......................$250.00

Ski Patrol, blk molded hair, complete w/boots, gloves, goggles, field pack, skis & poles, NM, H4......................$170.00

Snake Eyes, Hasbro, Hall of Fame, 1st series, 1992-93, MIB, F1......................$45.00

Snow Troops, pnt molded hair, complete w/accessories, NM, C6......................$220.00

Stalker, Hasbro, Hall of Fame, 1st series, 1992-93, MIB, F1......................$45.00

Storm Shadow, Hasbro, Hall of Fame, 3rd series, 1992-93, MIB, F1......................$45.00

Talking Action Marine, foreign head, camo outfit, complete w/accessories & papers, working, M (EX box), C6..$800.00

Talking Action Pilot, complete w/flight suit, accessories & manual, M (EX box), C6......................$895.00

Talking Action Sailor, complete, working, M (NM box), C6......................$650.00

Talking Action Soldier, blond molded hair, working, orig shirt, pants, boots, hat & dog tag, EX, from $150 to........$170.00

Talking Action Soldier, w/foreign head, working, complete, M (EX box), C6......................$450.00

Talking Adventure Team Commander, brn flocked hair/beard, jacket, pants, boots, dog tag, gun/holster, EX (VG box), C6......................$169.00

Talking Adventure Team Commander, brn hair & beard, hard hands, Dangerous Climb outfit, w/pick, H4..............$75.00

Talking Adventure Team Commander, NM (EX+-NM box), T1......................$225.00

Talking Astronaut, Adventures of GI Joe, auburn hair, working, missing insert & paperwork, 1969, NM (EX box), H4.$340.00

Talking Man of Action, brn hair, no beard, orig outfit, working, VG-EX, H4......................$70.00

Accessories for 12" GI Joe

Adventure Team Flying Rescue Action Pack, Hasbro, 1971, M (EX box), $45.00.

Action Marine Basics, dog tag, fatigue cap & boots, #7722, MIP, A $107.00

Adventure Team Search for the Abominable Snowman, complete w/accessories & comic book, NM (NM box), C6.........$295.00

Ammo Box, Russian Soldier, H4 ....$20.00

Anchor, for raft, EX, H4 ....$15.00

Armband, Medic, EX, H4 ....$15.00

Armband, Shore Patrol, w/clip fastener, EX, H4 ....$30.00

Axe, for Crash Crew Fire Truck, EX, H4 ....$45.00

Backpack, Japanese Soldier, H4 ....$20.00

Bayonet, Japanese Soldier, H4.................................$75.00

Bazooka, Action Soldier, w/2 shells, #7525, MIP, A $352.00

Bazooka, Green Beret, w/2 shells, H4........................$28.00

Beachhead Assault Tent Set, tent, poles, flame thrower, belt, first aid pounch, mess kit & manual, MIP, C6.........$300.00

Beachhead Field Pack Set, pack, M-1 rifle, grenades, belt w/pouches, trencher tool, canteen, bayonet & manual, MIP, C6 ....$270.00

Belt, Australian Soldier, H4 ....$25.00

Belt, Japanese Soldier, H4 ....$20.00

Belt, Russian Soldier, H4 ....$30.00

Belt, Weight; Deep Sea Diver, EX, H4 ....$10.00

Bivouac Sleeping Bag Set, w/M-1 rifle, bayonet, belt w/cartridges, mess kit, canteen & manual, MIP, C6 ....$200.00

Bivouac Tent Set, tent, netting, tent pegs & foliage, 1964-65, M (VG box), C6 ....$10.50

Boots, German or Russian Soldier, H4...........................$25.00

Bunk Bed Action Marine, #7723, MIP, A $739.00

Combat Field Jacket Set, M1 rifle w/bayonet, belt w/ammo pouches, grenades, MIP, C6 ....$265.00

Combat Set, #7502, complete, MIB (minor damage & moisture stain), H4...$160.00

Combat Set, complete w/first aid pouch, trenching tool, mess kit, canteen & cover, pistol, belt & manual, MIP, C6 ....$220.00

Command Post Poncho Set, w/backpack radio, field telephone, .45 gun & holster, map w/case & wire roll, M (VG box), C6...$125.00

Communications Post & Poncho Set, complete, MIB (cellophane window), C6 ....$260.00

Communications Post Flag Set, Action Marine, no helmet sticker, #7704, MIP (torn cellophane), A.................$442.00

Communications Set, Action Pilot, bl backpack radio, binoculars, clipboard, pencil, map & case, #7812, MIP, A..$273.00

Depth Gauge, fits on wrist, EX, H4 ....$18.00

Dog Tag w/Chain, Adventure Team, plastic, EX, H4 ......$15.00

Duffle Bag, mk USN, wht, VG, H4...............................$20.00

Duffle Bag, MP, gr, EX, H4.......................................$15.00

Duffle Bag, MP, no sticker, MOC, H4 ....$30.00

Entrenching Tool, Australian Soldier, H4 ....$5.00

Field Phone, Air Police, gray, EX, H4 ....$45.00

Flag, Medic, w/pole, EX, H4 ....$20.00

Flag, United States Air Force, from Communications Flag set, w/pole, EX, H4 ....$20.00

Flame Thrower, Marine, gr, EX, H4 ....$25.00

German Soldier Accessories, MOC, H4 ....$220.00

Green Beret Set, Action Soldier, w/badge, M-16 rifle & Morse radio, #7533, MIP, A...$237.00

Grenade, German Soldier, H4.....................................$8.00

Head Gear, LSO, yel cloth, EX, H4 ....$20.00

Helmet, Action Pilot Air Police, w/field telephone, rifle & bayonet, #7813, MIP, A...$400.00

Helmet, Action Soldier MP, wht, w/accessories: belt, billy club, .45 gun & holster, #7526, MIP, A $70.00

Helmet, Air Police, w/strap, EX, H4 ....$45.00

Helmet, Army or Marine, no sticker, MOC, H4 ....$40.00

Helmet, British Soldier, H4.......................................$40.00

Helmet, Japanese Soldier, H4....................................$20.00

Helmet, Medic, w/strap, EX, H4.................................$35.00

Helmet, Navy Attack, bl, w/strap, EX, H4 ....$35.00

Helmet, Ski Patrol Bear, EX, H4 ....$35.00

M-16 Rifle, Green Beret, missing strap, EX, H4 ....$28.00

Machete w/Sheath, Australian Soldier, H4.......................$4.00

Machine Gun, British Soldier, w/ammo clip, H4..............$65.00

Machine Gun, 30-cal, w/tripod & ammo box, EX, H4 .....$30.00

Machine Gun #7514, w/tripod & ammo box, w/sticker, MOC, H4...$45.00

Machine Gun Set, Action Sailor, #7618, w/bl USN ammo box, MIP, A...$213.00

Marine Demolition Set, mine detector w/blk headphones, 3 metal mines & harness, MIB (torn cellophane, sm dent), C6 ....$225.00

Medal, Australian Soldier, H4....................................$15.00

Medal, German Soldier, w/sticker, H4 ....$40.00

Medal, Japanese Soldier, no sticker, H4.......................$65.00

Mess Kit, for Action series, w/sticker, MOC, H4..............$55.00

Mine Detector Set, complete w/4 metal land mines, H4..$60.00

Mortar Set, Action Marine, #7725, MOC (unusual card w/mc marine attacking on run), A $457.00

Mountain Troops Set, wht web belt, ice axe, snowshoes, backpack, yel cord, 4 grenades & manual, MIP, C6........$185.00

Navy Attack Set, life jacket, binoculars, blinker light, semaphore flags & manual, NM (NM box), C6 ......$185.00

Paratrooper Accessory Set, Hasbro, 1964, NMIB, A, $185.00.

Pencil, Scramble & Fighter Pilot series, goes w/clipboard, EX, H4...$10.00

Pilot Survival Set, life raft, paddle, vest, pistol, anchor, rope, first aid kit, knife, scabbard & manual, MIP, C6...$1,000.00

Pistol, German Soldier, Lugar, H4 ....$20.00

Pistol, Japanese Soldier, H4 ....$25.00

Radio, Marine Communications, gr camo, EX, H4...........$15.00

Sea Rescue Set, life raft, flare pistol, anchor, rope, knife w/scabbard, first aid box & manual, MIP, C6 ....$1,000.00

Search Light, for jeep, EX, H4.......................................$15.00

Shell, for jeep cannon, EX, H4..$8.00

Shore Patrol Jumper Set, Action Sailor, complete w/tie, SP armband & cap, no helmet sticker, #7613, MIP, A.......$428.00

Shoulder Bag, Medic, EX, H4...$15.00

Sleeping Bag, no sticker, MOC, H4 ....$30.00

Stretcher, Medic, NM, H4..$30.00

Clothing for 12" GI Joe

Beret, French Soldier, H4 ....$50.00

Beret, Green Beret, w/emblem, NM, H4........................$40.00

Boots, Crash Crew, silver, EX, H4...................................$6.00

Coveralls, Action Pilot, orange, G, H4.............................$4.00

Coveralls, Scramble Pilot, EX, H4..................................$35.00

Coveralls, Silver Space, EX, H4.......................................$8.00

Hat, Air Cadet, EX, H4..$25.00

Hat, Annapolis Cadet, EX, H4.......................................$25.00

Hat, Australian Soldier, w/cloth band, H4 ....$35.00

High Voltage Escape Outfit, MIB, M5...........................$125.00

Jacket, Action Pilot, dress style w/captain's bars & wings, #7804, MIP, A...$214.00

Jacket, Action Soldier, field combat, #7505, MIP, A.....$717.00

Jacket, Action Soldier MP, Ike style, brn w/red scarf & MP armband, #7524, MIP, A...$106.00

Jacket, Adventures of Polar Explorer, red w/fur-lined hood, 1969, EX, H4 ....$30.00

Jacket, Airborne MP, gr, EX, H4...................................$150.00

Jacket, Army Field, gr, EX, H4.......................................$20.00

Jacket, field combat style, w/bayonet, belt w/ammo pouches & grenades, MIP, C6 ....$265.00

Jacket, Japanese Soldier, EX, H4...................................$10.00

Jacket, MP, brn, EX, H4...$15.00

Jacket, Tank Commander, simulated leather, lt stain, EX-NM, H4 ....$40.00

Jacket, West Point Cadet, EX, H4..................................$30.00

Jacket & Pants, Air Force Dress, no bars or wings, G, H4 .$26.00

Jacket & Pants, Marine Dress, VG, H4...........................$15.00

Jumpsuit, LSO, EX, H4..$25.00

Life Vest, Scramble Pilot, orange vinyl, EX, H4 ....$10.00

Navy Attack Life Jacket, EX+, J2...................................$20.00

Outfit, Action Sailor Rescue Set, complete w/accessories, 1967, H4..$195.00

Outfit, Action Sailor SP, complete w/accessories, H4....$150.00

Outfit, Air Force Dress, jacket, shirt, tie, shoes, hat & bars, missing wings, EX, H4 ....$150.00

Outfit, Breeches Buoy, complete w/accessories, lt stain on pant legs, H4...$220.00

Outfit, Crash Crew, silver jacket, pants, hood & boots, gloves, complete w/accessories, MIB (cellophane window), C6 ....$300.00

Outfit, Deep Sea Diving Set, w/accessories, MIB (photo box), C6 ....$1,495.00

Outfit, Flight Suit, no helmet sticker, MIP, C6.............$120.00

Outfit, High Voltage Escape, blk jumpsuit w/silver net, face mask, wrist meter, wire cutters & warning sign, MIB .$59.00

Outfit, Japanese Backyard Patrol, complete w/helmet & cream leggings, MIP, H4 ....$50.00

Outfit, Military Police, complete w/accessories & manual, M (EX box), C6..$1,000.00

Outfit, Race Car Driver, w/helmet, missing goggles, EX, H4...$45.00

Outfit, Radiation Detection, jumpsuit w/sticker, belt, uranium rock, radiation container, goggles & tool, MIB, C6...$59.00

Outfit, Scramble, gray flight suit, belt, air vest, clipboard & pencil, .45 & holster, w/manual, MIB, C6....................$485.00

Outfit, Shore Patrol Set, rare version w/shoes, MIB, C6.$1,100.00

Super Joe Adventure Team Paths of Danger Set, Hasbro, 1977, MOC, $45.00.

Pants, Action Marine, #7715, MIP, A............................$413.00

Pants, Action Marine or Action Soldier, gr, VG, H4.........$4.00

Pants, Action Soldier, combat fatigue, #7504, MIP, A.....$76.00

Pants, Action Soldier MP, Ike style, brn, #7525, MIP, A.$73.00

Pants, Air Force Dress, needs snap rpr, VG, H4 ....$10.00

Pants, Airborne MP, tan, EX, H4...................................$30.00

Poncho, Action Marine, #7702, MIP, A $293.00

Shirt, Action Marine, fatigue type, #7714, MIP, A........$413.00

Shirt, Action Soldier, combat fatigue, #7503, MOC, A..$166.00

Shorts, Australian Soldier, H4 ....$30.00
Shorts, Desert Patrol jeep driver, EX, H4..................$30.00
Socks, Australian Soldier, pr, H4 ....$45.00
Sweater, French Soldier, H4..................................$50.00

1964-1969 Paperwork

Drag Bike Instructions, full color, also illustrates 10 Action Packs, C6..$4.00
GI Joe Air Force Manual, lg, EX, H4........................$6.00
GI Joe Air Force Manual, sm, lt wear, H4..................$6.00
GI Joe Army Manual, lg, EX, H4..............................$3.00
GI Joe Army Manual, sm, came w/boxed dolls, H4 ....$4.00
GI Joe Counter Intelligence Manual, EX+, C6...............$25.00
GI Joe Flying Rescue Instructions, full color, C6 ....$4.00
GI Joe Marine Manual, lg, EX, H4............................$3.00
GI Joe Marine Manual, sm, came w/boxed dolls, EX, H4 ...$4.00
GI Joe Navy Manual, lg, EX, H4..............................$5.00
GI Joe Navy Manual, sm, EX, H4..............................$6.00
Instruction Sheet, for making chairs, rifle rack & table from cb cutout, dtd 1966, C6 ....$5.00
Offical Gear & Equipment Manual, mc pictures, EX, H4..$15.00
Underwater Explorer Instructions, mc brochure, also illustrates 10 Action Packs, C6 ....$4.00

Vehicles for 12" GI Joe

Action Soldier Jet Helicopter, Irwin, gr, complete, H4..$120.00
Action Team Sea Wolf, submarine, w/face mask & hose, viewer & squid, missing periscope top, VG+ (VG box), C6 ......$130.00
Adventure Team Capture Copter, helicopter w/claws, pontoons, winch & net, EX (VG+ box), C6 ....$100.00
Adventure Team Devil of the Deep, swamp craft, stingray & capture snare, NRFB (sealed), C6............................$170.00
Adventure Team Fate of the Trouble Shooter, complete, EX (lt moisture damage on box), H4 ....$140.00
Adventure Team Pursuit Craft, Sears Exclusive, missing 2 sm rocket attachments, EX-NM (EX box), H4 ....$200.00
Adventure Team Sea Wolf Submarine, complete, EX (torn box), H4 ....$120.00
Adventure Team Space Walk Mystery Space Capsule, complete w/blond fuzzy-haired doll, 1970, M (EX box), H4 ...$325.00
Crash Crew Truck, missing chrome railings on bk, ladder & ladder clip, o/w complete, VG, H4 ....$500.00
Desert Patrol Attack Jeep Set, w/50 cal machine gun, tripod & ring, spare tire & antenna, M (EX+ box), C6 ......$1,250.00
Motorcycle w/Sidecar, Irwin, brn, complete, no decals, VG, H4 ....$125.00
Windboat, Action Backback series, complete, EX, H4.....$18.00

3¾" Figures

Ace, as driver, w/accessories, 1983, loose, H4..................$12.00
Ace (pilot), 1983, MOC, H4..................................$25.00
Airborne, 1983, MIP (Canadian), C6..........................$40.00
Airtight, w/accessories, missing ID, 1985, loose, H4..........$7.00
Airtight, 1985, M (EX-NM pkg), C6............................$27.00
Alley Viper, 1989, MIP, C6..................................$18.00

Ambush, 1990, MIP, C6......................................$10.00
Ambush, w/accessories, missing ID, 1990, loose................$3.00
Annihilator, w/accessories, missing ID, 1989, loose, H4.....$4.00
Annihilator, 1989, MIP, C6..................................$14.00
Astro Viper, w/accessories, missing ID, 1988, loose, H4.....$5.00
Astro Viper, 1988, MIP (English), C6 ....$15.00
Avalanche, w/accessories, missing ID, 1987, loose, H4 ......$5.00
Avalanche, 1987, MIP (English), C6..........................$20.00
Backblast, w/accessories, missing ID, 1989, loose, H4........$4.00
Backblast, 1989, MIP, C6....................................$14.00
Barbecue, Slaughter's Marauders, 1989, MIP, C6 ....$20.00
Barbecue, w/accessories & ID, 1988, loose, H4 ....$7.00
Barbecue, 1983-85, MOC, H4..................................$25.00
Baron Ironblood, M (EX-NM Action Force pkg), C6 ....$5.50
Baroness, 1983, MOC, S4 ....$115.00
Baroness, 1984, MIP (India), C6.............................$25.00
Barracuda, 1992, MIP, C6....................................$6.00
BATS, 1986, MOC (Canadian), S4..............................$16.00
Bazooka, Tiger Force, 1988, MIP, C6.........................$18.00
Bazooka, w/accessories, missing ID, 1985, loose, H4..........$7.00
Bazooka, 1983-85, MOC, H4...................................$25.00
Beachhead, w/accessories, missing ID, 1986, loose, H4 ......$5.00
Beachhead, 1986, MIP, C6....................................$33.00
Big Bear, 1992, MIP, C6.....................................$5.00
Big Boa, w/accessories, missing ID, 1986, loose, H4 ....$5.00
Black Major, MIP (Action Force), C6 ....$7.50
Blaster, w/accessories, missing ID, 1987, loose, H4 ....$5.00
Blaster, 1987, MIP (English), C6............................$20.00
Blizzard, w/accessories, missing ID, 1988, loose, H4..........$5.00
Blocker, 1987, MIP (English), C6............................$20.00
Blowtorch, w/accessories, missing ID, 1984, loose, H4 ....$8.00
Blowtorch, 1984, M (EX-NM pkg), C6..........................$33.00
Budo, w/accessories & ID, 1988, loose, H4 ....$7.00
Budo, 1988, MIP (English), C6...............................$18.00
Budo, 1988, MIP (French), C6................................$15.00
Bullhorn, w/accessories, missing ID, 1989, loose, H4..........$4.00
Bullhorn, 1990, MIP, C6.....................................$14.00
Buzzer, w/accessories, missing ID, 1984, loose, H4..............$8.00
Buzzer, 1984, MOC, H4.......................................$20.00
Captain Grid Iron, w/accessories, missing ID, 1989, loose, H4..$4.00
Captain Grid Iron, 1990, MOC, C6/D4.........................$10.00
Cesspool, Eco-Warrior w/water-firing backpack, purple, MIP, C6..$10.00
Cesspool, w/accessories, 1991, loose, H4....................$3.00
Charbroil, blk eyes, 1988, MIP, C6 ....$18.00
Charbroil, w/accessories, missing ID, 1988, loose, H4 ....$5.00
Chuckles, w/accessories, missing ID, 1986, loose, H4 ....$5.00
Chuckles, 1987, MIP, C6/D4..................................$18.00
Clean Sweep, Eco-Warrior, 1991, MIP, C6 ....$6.00
Clean Sweep, w/accessories, 1991, loose, H4.................$3.00
Clutch, w/accessories, 1982, loose, H4.......................$12.00
Clutch, 1983, M (EX-NM pkg), C6.............................$33.00
Cobra, w/accessories, missing ID, 1983, loose, H4...........$10.00
Cobra Adder, 1988, MIP, C6..................................$13.00
Cobra Commander, w/accessories & ID, 1987, loose, H4...$9.00
Cobra Commander, 1987, M (EX card), S4.....................$23.00
Cobra Hiss Driver, 1982, w/ID card, MIP, H4 ....$25.00

Cobra Officer, w/accessories, missing ID, 1982, loose, H4 .$10.00
Cobra Officer, 1983, MIP (Japanese), C6 ....$20.00
Cobra Pogo, 1987, MIP, C6..$15.00
Cobra Stinger Driver, complete, 1984, loose, H4 ....$12.00
Cobra Stinger Driver, w/ID card, 1982, MIP, H4 ....$25.00
Copperhead, gr stripe on helmet, 1984, loose, H4............$10.00
Copperhead, Python Patrol, 1989, MIP, C6 ....$13.00
Copperhead, 1984, MIP, H4..$20.00
Countdown, 1989, MIP, C6 ....$18.00
Crankcase, AWE Striker Driver, w/accessories, 1985, loose,
    H4 ....$12.00
Crankcase, 1985, MIP, H4..$18.00
Crazylegs, Night Force series, w/accessories, 1987, loose,
    H4 ....$10.00
Crazylegs, 1986, MOC (lt dent in bubble on card), H4....$12.00
Crimson Guard, Python Patrol, 1989, MIP, C6.................$13.00
Crimson Guard, w/accessories, missing ID, 1985, loose, H4..$7.00
Cross Country, w/accessories, 1986, loose, H4..................$10.00
Crystal Ball, w/accessories, missing ID, 1987, loose, H4 .....$4.00
Crystal Ball, 1986, MOC, H4..$12.00
Cutter, w/accessories, 1985, loose, H4................................$10.00
Darklon, Evader driver, complete, loose, H4........................$9.00
Dee-Jay, w/accessories & ID, 1988, loose, H4 ....$7.00
Dee-Jay, 1989, MIP, C6..$13.00
Deep Six, Eco-Warrior, 1991, M (EX card), S4 ....$6.00
Deep Six, Sharc vehicle driver, w/accessories, 1984, loose,
    H4...$10.00
Deep Six, 1988, MOC, F1..$10.00
Deep Six, 1989, MIP, C6..$14.00
DEF & Headhunters Set, Australian issue only, 1992, set of 6,
    MIP, C6 ....$108.00
Destro, Despoiler driver, w/accessories, 1988, loose, H4.....$8.00
Destro, w/accessories, missing ID, 1983, loose, H4 ....$10.00
Destro, 1983, MIP (Japanese), C6......................................$22.00
Dial Tone, w/accessories & ID, 1986, loose, H4 ....$10.00
Dial Tone, 1986, MIP, C6..$32.00
Dice, w/accessories, 1991, loose, H4....................................$3.00
Dodge, Sonic Fighter, w/Sonic backpack, gr, 1990, MIP,
    C6 ....$18.00
Dojo, w/accessories, 1991, loose, H4 ....$3.00
Dojo, 1992, MIP, C6..$12.00
Downtown, w/accessories, missing ID, 1989, loose, H4 ......$4.00
Downtown, 1989, MIP (English), C6....................................$12.00
Dr Mindbender, w/accessories, missing ID, 1986, loose, H4..$5.00
Dr Mindbender, 1986, MIP, C6 ....$31.00
Duke, 1st Sergeant; w/accessories, missing ID, 1983, loose,
    H4...$10.00
Duke, 1992, MIP, C6..$10.00
Dusty, Tiger Force, 1988, MIP, C6......................................$22.00
Dusty, w/accessories, missing ID, 1985, loose, H4.............$7.00
Dusty, 1985, MIP, C6 ....$30.00
Eels, w/accessories, 1991, loose, H4 ....$3.00
Eels, 1992, MIP, C6 ....$8.00
Falcon, Super Sonic Fighter series, 1990, MOC (Canadian),
    S4 ....$7.00
Falcon, w/accessories & ID, 1987, loose, H4 ....$9.00
Falcon, 1986, MOC, H4..$15.00
Fast Draw, 1986, MOC (sm dent in bubble), H4..............$12.00

Ferret, 1988, MIP (1993 Convention), C6 ....$13.00
Firefly, Hasbro, 1986, M (EX Japan card), S4 ....$23.00
Firefly, w/accessories, 1991, loose, H4 ....$3.00
Firefly, 1984, MIP (India), C6..$20.00
Firefly, 1984, MIP (Japanese), C6......................................$32.00
Firefly, 1992, MIP, C6..$8.00
Flak-Viper, 1992, MIP, C6..$7.00
Flash, w/accessories, missing ID, 1982, loose, H4............$10.00
Flint, Eco-Warrior w/water-firing backback, bl, 1991, MIP,
    C6 ....$10.00
Flint, 1985, MIP, C6..$57.00
Flint, 1985, MIP (Japanese), C6 ....$25.00
Flint, 1985, MIP (1992 Convention), C6 ....$12.00
Footloose, Slaughter's Marauders, 1989, MIP, C6 ....$20.00
Footloose, w/accessories, missing ID, 1984, H4................$8.00
Frag-Viper, w/accessories & ID, 1989, loose, H4................$6.00
Frag-Viper, 1989, MIP, C6..$14.00
Free Fall, 1990, MIP, C6..$12.00
Frostbite, Snow Cat driver, w/accessories, 1986, loose, H4.$10.00
Frostbite, 1985, MIP, H4..$18.00
General Flagg, 1992, MIP, C6..$6.00
Globulus, w/accessories, missing ID, 1987, loose, H4..........$5.00
Gnawgahyde, 1989, MIP, C6..$20.00
Grunt, tan uniform, complete w/accessories, 1983, EX, loose,
    C6/H4...$27.00
Grunt, 1991, MIP, C6..$15.00
Gung-Ho, Marine dress blues, 1987, MIP, C6 ....$22.00
Gung-Ho, w/accessories, missing ID, 1987, loose, H4........$5.00
Gung-Ho, 1983, MIP (Canadian), C6 ....$45.00
Gung-Ho, 1983, MIP (India), C6..$10.00
Gung-Ho, 1983, MIP (Japanese), C6 ....$25.00
Gung-Ho, 1986, MOC, H4 ....$15.00
Gung-Ho, 1987, MIP (1992 Convention), C6 ....$7.00
Gyro-Viper, Cobra Mamba driver, w/accessories, 1987, loose,
    H4 ....$8.00
Hardball, w/accessories, missing ID, 1988, loose, H4..........$5.00
Hardball, 1988, MIP, C6..$18.00
Hawk, w/accessories & ID, 1986, loose, H4 ....$10.00
Hawk, 1986, MIP..$30.00
Heavy Duty, w/accessories, 1991, loose, H4........................$3.00
Heavy Duty, 1991, MIP, C6..$6.00
Heavy Metal, 1985, MIP, H4..$18.00
Heavy Metal, 1985, MIP (1992 Convention), C6.............$35.00
Hit & Run, w/accessories, missing ID, 1988, loose, H4 .....$5.00
Hit & Run, 1988, MIP, C6..$22.00
Hydro-Viper, w/accessories, missing ID, 1988, loose, H4....$5.00
Hydro-Viper, 1988, MIP, C6..$20.00
Ice Sabre, 1992, MIP, C6..$12.00
Ice Viper, 1987, MIP (1993 Convention), C6...................$19.00
Iceberg, w/accessories & ID, 1986, loose, H4 ....$10.00
Iceberg, wht male w/red & pk on chest, 1986, MIP (India),
    C6 ....$15.00
Iceberg, 1983-85, MOC, H4...$22.00
Iceberg, 1986, MIP..$25.00
Iron Grenadier, w/accessories, missing ID, 1988, loose, H4...$5.00
Iron Grenadier, 1988, MIP, C6 ....$18.00
Jinx, blk or bl insignia, MIP (1993 Convention), C6.......$25.00
Jinx, w/accessories & ID, 1987, loose, H4 ....$9.00

Jinx, 1987, MIP, H4...$14.00

Keel Haul, mail-in offer, 1989, MIP, C6 ....$12.00

Keel Haul, 1985, MIP, H4..$18.00

Knockdown, w/accessories, missing ID, 1987, loose, H4.....$5.00

Knockdown, 1989, MIP (English), C6............................$22.00

Lady Jaye, 1985, MIP, C6...$80.00

Lady Jaye, 1985, MIP (India), C6................................$15.00

Lampreys, Cobra Hydrofoil driver, w/accessories, loose, H4.$10.00

Lampreys, Sonic Fighter, w/Sonic backpack, blk, 1990, MIP, C6 ....$18.00

Laser Viper, w/accessories, missing ID, 1989, loose, H4......$4.00

Laser Viper, 1990, MIP, C6.......................................$12.00

Law & Order, w/accessories, missing ID, 1987, loose, H4...$5.00

Leatherneck, w/accessories & ID, 1985, loose, H4 ....$10.00

Leatherneck, 1986, MOC..$25.00

Lifeline, Tiger Force, 1988, MIP, C6............................$18.00

Lifeline, w/accessories, missing ID, 1985, loose, H4...........$7.00

Lift-Ticket, Tomahawk pilot, w/accessories, loose, H4.....$12.00

Lightfoot, w/accessories, missing ID, 1988, loose, H4 ....$5.00

Lightfoot, 1988, MIP, C6..$18.00

Lightfoot, 1988, MIP (English), C6 ....$15.00

Low-Light, Slaughter's Marauders, 1989, MIP, C6 ....$18.00

Low-Light, w/accessories, missing ID, 1986, loose, H4 ....$5.00

Low-Light, 1983-85, MOC, H4....................................$22.00

Low-Light, 1986, MIP, C6...$28.00

Lt Falcon, Super Sonic Fighters, 1991, MIP, C6.................$8.00

Mainframe, w/accessories & ID, 1986, loose, from $12 to $18.00

Major Bludd, Super Sonic Fighters, 1991, MIP, C6............$8.00

Major Bludd, w/accessories, missing ID, 1983, loose, H4..$10.00

Major Bludd, 1983, MIP (Japanese), C6 ....$20.00

Manta Windsurfer, mail-in offer, 1984, MIP (1993 Convention), C6...$22.00

Metal Head, 1990, MIP...$12.00

Monkey Wrench, w/accessories & ID, 1986, loose, H4 ....$10.00

Monkey Wrench, 1986, MIP, C6..................................$20.00

Motor Viper, w/accessories, 1986, loose, H4 ....$10.00

Motor Viper, 1986, MIP, H4......................................$16.00

Muskrat, 1988, MIP, C6..$18.00

Muton, Action Force, MIP, C6 ....$5.00

Mutt, w/accessories & ID, 1988, loose, H4......................$7.00

Mutt w/Junkyard, Slaughter's Marauders, 1989, MIP, C6.$20.00

Night Creeper, w/accessories, missing ID, 1989, loose, H4.$4.00

Night Creeper, 1990, MIP, C6....................................$15.00

Night Viper, w/accessories, missing ID, 1989, loose, H4.....$5.00

Nunchuk, 1992, MIP, C6...$9.00

Outback, w/accessories, missing ID, 1987, loose, H4 ....$5.00

Outback, 1st issue w/Eco-Warrior pnt, 1992, MOC, S4...$12.00

Outback, 1987, MIP, C6..$18.00

Outback, 1987, MIP (1992 Convention), C6.....................$8.00

Ozone, Eco-Warrior w/water-firing backpack, lime, 1991, MIP, C6...$10.00

Ozone, w/accessories, 1991, loose, H4 ....$3.00

Pathfinder, 1990, MIP, C6..$11.00

Psyche-Out, Super Sonic Fighters series, 1990, MOC (Canadian), S4 ....$6.00

Psyche-Out, w/accessories & ID, 1987, loose, H4 ....$9.00

Psyche-Out, 1987, MIP, C6..$22.00

Python Patrol Officer, Python Patrol series, 1989, MIP, C6...$13.00

Python Patrol Tele-Viper, 1988, MOC, H4....................$12.00

Python Patrol Trooper, 1988, MOC, H4 ....$12.00

Q-Force Aqua Trooper, Action Force, MIP, C6 ....$7.50

Q-Force Deep Sea Defender, Action Force, MIP, C6.........$7.50

Q-Force Sonar Officer, Action Force, MIP, C6 ....$7.50

Quick Kick, w/accessories, missing ID, 1985, loose, H4......$9.00

Quick Kick, 1985, MIP, C6..$25.00

Rampart, 1990, MIP, C6..$12.00

Raptor, w/accessories, missing ID, 1987, loose, H4 ....$5.00

Raptor, 1986, MOC, H4..$15.00

Recoil, w/accessories, missing ID, 1989, loose, H4.............$4.00

Recoil, 1989, MIP, C6...$15.00

Recondo, 1983-85, MOC (torn bubble on card), H4 ....$25.00

Red Dog, w/accessories, missing ID, 1987, loose, H4 ....$5.00

Red Star, 1991, MIP, C6...$8.00

Repeater, w/accessories, missing ID, 1988, loose, H4.........$5.00

Repeater, 1988, MIP..$18.00

Ripcord, w/accessories, missing ID, 1984, loose, H4 ....$8.00

Ripper, w/accessories, missing ID, 1984, loose, H4 ....$8.00

Ripper, 1985, MIP (Japanese), C6................................$15.00

Road Pig, Super Sonic Fighters series, 1990, MOC (Canadian), S4 ....$7.00

Road Pig, 1988, MIP, C6...$21.00

Roadblock, Tiger Force, 1988, MIP, C6.........................$21.00

Roadblock, w/accessories, missing ID, 1984, loose, H4.......$8.00

Roadblock, 1st issue Battle Corp, w/comic book, MOC, S4..$15.00

Roadblock, 1986, MIP (1992 Convention), C6................$10.00

Rock 'N Roll, Super Sonic Fighters, w/Sonic backpack, gr, 1991, MIP, C6...$10.00

Rock 'N Roll, 1983, MIP (Japanese), C6 ....$22.00

Rock 'N Roll, 1986, M (VG+ Japanese card), S4 ....$15.00

Rock 'N Roll, 1989, MIP, C6......................................$15.00

Rock 'N Roll, 1989, MIP (English), C6 ....$12.00

Rock-Viper, 1990, MIP, C6..$15.00

Rumbler, 1986, MIP (1992 Convention), C6 ....$8.00

Salvo, 1990, MIP, C6...$10.00

SAS Pilot, Action force, MIP, C6 ....$5.50

SAW Viper, w/accessories, 1990, loose, H4 ....$3.00

SAW Viper, 1990, MIP, C6..$12.00

Scarlett, 1983, MIP (Japanese), C6................................$35.00

Sci-Fi, w/accessories, 1991, loose, H4.............................$3.00

Sci-Fi, w/accessories & ID, 1986, loose, H4 ....$10.00

Sci-Fi, 1986, MIP, C6...$32.00

Sci-Fi, 1991, MIP, C6...$12.00

Scoop, 1989, MIP...$12.00

Scrap Iron, w/accessories, missing ID, 1984, loose, H4 ....$8.00

Sea Slug, Cobra Sea Ray driver, w/accessories, loose, H4.$10.00

Sergeant Slaughter, Slaughter's Marauders, 1989, MIP, C6...$18.00

Sergeant Slaughter, Triple-T driver, w/accessories, 1986, loose, H4 ....$8.00

Sergeant Slaughter, w/accessories & ID, mail order only, 1985, loose, H4...$30.00

Sergeant Slaughter, Wart Hog driver, w/accessories, 1988, loose, H4 ....$9.00

Serpentor w/Air Chariot, complete, 1986, loose, H4 ....$18.00

Shipwreck, 1986, M (EX+ Japan card), S4 ....$20.00

Shockwave, w/accessories, missing ID, 1988, loose, H4......$5.00

Shockwave, 1988, MIP...$20.00

Shockwave, 1988, MIP (French or English), C6 ....$15.00

Short Fuse, 1983, MIP (Canadian) $40.00

Skid Mark, Desert Fox driver, w/accessories, 1988, loose, H4..$8.00

Skystriker, 1988, MIP (1992 Convention), C6.................$40.00

Slaughter's Renegades Set: Mercer, Taurus & Red Dog; 1987, MIP, C6...$30.00

Slice, w/accessories, 1991, loose, H4 ....$3.00

Slice, 1992, MIP, C6..$15.00

Slipstream, Conquest X-30 pilot, w/accessories, 1986, loose, H4 ....$10.00

Sludge Viper, Eco-Warrior w/water-firing cannon, purple, 1991, MIP, C6...$10.00

Snake Armor, gray, MIP (India), C6.............................$35.00

Snake Eyes, blk, MIP (India), C6.................................$20.00

Snake Eyes, w/accessories, missing ID, 1982, loose, H4....$35.00

Snake Eyes, w/accessories, missing ID, 1988, loose, H4....$10.00

Snake Eyes, 1982-83, MIP (1992 Convention), C6 ....$35.00

Snake Eyes, 1989, MIP, C6.......................................$30.00

Snake Eyes, 1991, MIP, C6.......................................$18.00

Sneak Peek, Night Force series, w/accessories, 1987, loose, H4..$10.00

Sneak Peek, 1987, MIP...$18.00

Snow Job, w/accessories, missing ID, 1983, loose, H4.......$10.00

Snow Job, 1983, MIP (Japanese), C6 ....$28.00

Snow Serpent, w/accessories, missing ID, 1986, loose, H4 .$5.00

Snow Serpent, 1983-85, MOC, H4..............................$25.00

Snow Serpent, 1985, MIP (1992 Convention), C6..........$12.00

Snowstorm, 1st issue w/Eco-Warrior pnt, 1992, MOC, S4 .$12.00

Spirit, complete, 1984, EX, loose, C6............................$13.00

Stalker, 1983, MIP (Japanese), C6...............................$28.00

Stalker, 1983, MIP (1992 Convention), C6 ....$12.00

Stalker, 1989, MIP, C6...$15.00

Steel Brigade, missing 1 rifle o/w complete, mail order only, 1983, loose, H4...$20.00

Steeler, mail-in offer, 1983, MIP, C6 ....$65.00

Steeler, 1983, MIP, C6 ....$45.00

Storm Shadow, w/accessories, missing ID, 1988, loose, H4..$8.00

Storm Shadow, 1992, MIP, C6....................................$18.00

Storm Shadow, 2nd version, 1988, MIP (English), C6.....$25.00

Strato-Viper, w/accessories, 1986, loose, H4....................$10.00

Strato-Viper, 1986, MIP, H4......................................$14.00

Stretcher, 1990, MIP, C6..$15.00

Stretcher, 1992, MIP (English), C6 ....$14.00

Sub-Zero, 1990, MIP, C6/D4......................................$12.00

T'Jbang, w/accesssories, 1991, loose, H4 ....$3.00

T'Jbang, 1992, MIP, C6..$12.00

Talking Battle Commander CB, blk, complete, 1991, MIP, C6..$12.00

Talking Battle Commander Overkill, red, w/accessories, MIP, C6..$12.00

Talking Battle Commander Stalker, yel, complete, 1991, MIP, C6..$10.00

TARGAT, w/accessories, missing ID, 1989, loose, H4.......$4.00

TARGAT, 1989, MIP...$15.00

TARGAT, 1989, MIP (English) $12.00

Taurus, w/accessories, missing ID, 1985, loose, H4 ....$7.00

Taurus, w/accessories, missing ID, 1987, loose, H4 ....$5.00

Techno-Viper, w/accessories, missing ID, 1987, loose, H4 .$5.00

Techno-Viper, 1986, MOC, H4....................................$15.00

Tele-Viper, w/accessories, missing ID, 1985, loose, H4 ......$7.00

Thrasher, Deadnok Thunder Machine driver, w/accessories, 1986, loose, H4...$10.00

Thunder, w/accessories, 1984, loose, H4........................$12.00

Thunder, 1984, MIP, H4..$20.00

Toll Booth, as driver, missing sledge hammer, loose, H4....$8.00

Topside, w/accessories, missing ID, 1989, loose, H4 ....$4.00

Topside, 1990, MIP, C6/D4...$12.00

Torch, w/accessories, missing ID, 1984, loose, H4 ....$8.00

Torch, 1985, MIP (Japanese), C6.................................$15.00

Torpedo, gray & blk wet suit, 1983, MIP (India), C6.......$18.00

Torpedo, yel & blk wet suit, 1983, MIP (India), C6.........$25.00

Torpedo, 1983, MIP (Japanese), C6..............................$22.00

Torpedo, 1986, M (EX+ Japanese card), S4.....................$15.00

Toxo-Viper, Eco-Warrior, 1991, MIP, C6........................$6.00

Toxo-Viper, w/accessories, missing ID, 1988, loose, H4 .....$4.00

Toxo-Viper, 1988, MIP, C6...$19.00

Toxo-Viper, 1988, MIP (English), C6 ....$15.00

Track Viper, Cobra Hiss II driver, complete, 1987, loose, H4..$8.00

Tripwire, Tiger Force, 1988, MIP, C6 ....$18.00

Tripwire, w/accessories, missing ID, 1983, loose, H4........$10.00

Tripwire, 1983, MIP (Japanese), C6..............................$22.00

Tripwire, 1988, MIP (English), C6................................$15.00

Tunnel Rat, w/accessories & ID, 1987, loose, H4 ....$9.00

Tunnel Rat, 1986, MOC, H4.......................................$15.00

Voltar, w/accessories, missing ID, 1988, loose, H4.............$4.00

Voltar, 1988, MIP (English), C6 ....$15.00

Wet Suit, w/accessories & ID, 1986, loose, H4.................$10.00

Wet Suit, 1992, MIP, C6..$8.00

Whirlwind, Action Force, MIP, C6................................$30.00

Wild Bill, Dragonfly pilot, complete, 1984, loose, H4......$12.00

Wild Bill, 1992, MIP, C6...$5.00

Wild Weasel, as driver, w/accessories, 1984, loose, H4.....$12.00

Windmill, complete w/accessories, 1988, EX, loose, C6...$10.00

Xamot, complete, 1985, EX, loose, C6 ....$5.00

Z Force Dart, Action Force, MIP, C6............................$15.00

Z Force Infantryman, Action Force, MIP, C6 ....$7.50

Z Force Lance, Action Force, MIP, C6 ....$15.00

Z Force Radio Operator, Action Force, MIP, C6 ....$7.50

Z Force Sapper, Action Force, MIP, C6 ....$7.50

Z Force Shaft, Action Force, MIP, C6 ....$15.00

Zandar, w/accessories, missing ID, 1985, loose, H4...........$7.00

Zandar, 1986, MIP (India), C6....................................$8.00

Zanzibar, w/accessories & ID, 1987, loose, H4 ....$9.00

Zap, Super Sonic Fighters, 1991, MIP, C6 ....$8.00

Zap, 1982, MOC, H4..$55.00

Zap, 1983, MIP (Canadian), C6...................................$45.00

Zap, 1983, MIP (India), C6 ....$15.00

Zarana, missing earrings & ID, o/w complete, 1985, loose, H4..$10.00

Zarana, w/earrings, 1986, MOC, S4 ....$25.00

Zarana, w/o earrings, 1986, MIP (India), C6....................$8.00

Zarana, w/o earrings, 1986, MIP (1992 Convention), C6 ..$6.00

Zarana, w/o earrings, 2nd version, complete, 1986, EX, loose, C6 ....$6.00

Accessories for 3¾" GI Joe

Air Defense Pack, complete, 1985, loose, H4 ....$6.00

Air Defense Pack, 1985, MIP, C6 ....$14.00

Air Force Flyer Gear, complete, M, C6 ....$4.75

Backpack, Motorized Action series, Mountain Climber, Radar Station, Rope Crosser, or Anti-Aircraft Gun, loose, H4, any..$2.00

Bivoac Battle Station, 1983, loose, H4...........................$6.00

Cobra Jet Pack, 1987, MIP, C6 ....$11.00

Cobra Rifle Range, 1984-85, MIP, F1 ....$10.00

Combat Field Pack, complete, EX+, J2 ....$40.00

Compact Missile Launcher, 1987, loose, H4 ....$4.00

Conquest, Python Patrol, MIB (worn), S4.......................$6.00

Equalizer, Slaughter's Marauders, assembled, M (EX box), S4...$9.00

Green Beret Weapons, complete, 1993, M, C6..................$6.50

Light Infantry Mission Gear, complete, 1993, M, C6 ....$8.00

Machine Gun, Pac Rat, 1983, MIB, S4............................$9.00

Machine Gun Defense Unit, 1984-85, MIP, F1 ....$10.00

Missile Defense Unit, 1984, MIP, C6..............................$18.00

Mountain Howitzer, 1985, loose, H4...............................$6.00

Outfit, Edge of Adventure, Super Joe, 1977, MIP, F1.......$12.00

Outfit, Emergency Rescue, Super Joe, 1977, MIP, F1 ....$12.00

Pocket Patrol Pack, 1983, M (EX card), S4....................$9.00

Q-Force Battle Gear, Action Force, MIP, C6.....................$3.00

SAS Battle Gear, Action Force, MIP, C6...........................$3.00

SAS Parachutist Attack, Action Force, MIP, C6 ....$25.00

SLAM, 1987, NRFB (M), S4 ....$10.00

Space Force Battle Gear, Action Force, MIP, C6 ....$3.00

SWAT Assault Mission Gear, complete, 1993, M, C6.......$8.00

Z Force Battle Gear, Action Force, MIP (M), C6.............$3.00

Vehicles for 3¾" GI Joe

Adder (Cobra Twin-Missile Launcher), MIB, D4...............$8.00

Air Skiff, complete w/Zanzibar figure & ID card, loose, H4 .$18.00

APC (Amphibious Personnel Carrier), 1983, M (EX-NM pkg), C6..$46.00

Arctic Blast, D4..$15.00

Arctic Blast, w/Windchill figure, 1989, MIP, C6.............$23.00

Armadillo Mini Tank, Slaughter's Marauders, 1989, MIP (English), C6 ....$12.00

Attack Cannon, 1982, M (EX-NM pkg), C6....................$26.00

AWE Striker, w/Crankcase figure, complete w/accessories & papers, M, loose, S4 ....$25.00

AWE Striker, w/Crankcase figure, 1985, EX (EX pkg), C6 ....$42.00

Battle Copter, bl, w/Ace figure, 1992, MIP, C6 ....$7.00

Battle Force 2000 Dominator (snow tank), NRFB (EX box), S4 ....$23.00

Battle Force 2000 Pulverizer, 1989, MIP, C6...................$12.00

Battle Force 2000 Two-Pack Avalanche, w/Blaster figure, 1988, M (EX-NM pkg), C6 ....$27.00

Battle Force 2000 Two-Pack Knockdown, w/Dodger figure, 1988, MIP, C6 ....$36.00

Battle Force 2000 Two-Pack Maverick, w/Blocker figure (no visor), 1988, M (EX-NM pkg), C6 ....$27.00

Battle Force 2000 Vector (jet), NRFB (EX box), S4 ....$23.00

Battle Force 2000 Vindicator (hovercraft), NRFB (EX box), S4 ....$23.00

Cobra ASP, MIP (Action Force), C6...............................$25.00

Cobra ASP (Assault Systems Pod), 1983, loose, H4..........$6.00

Cobra Battle Copter, pk, w/Heli-Viper figure, 1992, MIP, C6 ....$7.00

Cobra FANG, 1983, loose, H4 ....$8.00

Cobra FANG, 1983, M (EX-NM pkg), C6 ....$26.00

Cobra FANG II, 1989, MIP, C6 ....$10.00

Cobra Hiss, w/driver, 1984, loose, H4 ....$20.00

Cobra Hydro Sled, w/missiles, complete, 1986, loose, H4 ..$6.00

Cobra Ice Sabre, 1990, loose, H4....................................$6.00

Cobra IMP, 1988, M (EX-NM pkg), C6 ....$11.00

Cobra Night Attack 4-Wheel Drive Stinger, w/driver & accessories, complete, 1984, loose, C6................................$31.00

Cobra Night Landing Raft, MIB (proof of purchase cut off box), H4...$20.00

Cobra Stellar Stiletto, w/Star-Viper figure & accessories, 1988, EX (EX pkg), C6...$21.00

Cobra STUN, w/Motor Viper figure, complete w/accessories, 1988, EX (EX pkg), C6...$30.00

Cobra Surveillance Port Battle Station, 1985, NRFB (EX box), S4 ....$9.00

Cobra Wolf, w/Ice Viper figure, 1985, loose, H4 ....$10.00

Despoiler, complete w/Destro figure & ID card, loose, H4..$22.00

Devilfish, 1985, MIB (proof of purchase cut off box), H4...$18.00

Dragon Fly, w/Wild Bill figure, complete, w/all paperwork, M, loose, S4 ....$35.00

Dreadnok Swampfire, loose, H4 ....$6.00

Dreadnok Swampfire, 1986, MIB $15.00

Dreadnok Thundermachine, w/Thrasher figure, complete w/accessories, 1986, EX, loose, C6 ....$30.00

Evader, complete w/Darklon figure & ID card, loose, H4.$22.00

Fang II, MIB, D4..$15.00

Flying Submarine, Action Force, w/Deep Six figure, MIP, C6 ....$35.00

HAVOC, w/Cross Country figure, complete, w/accessories, 1986, EX, loose, C6...$20.00

HISS, w/driver, MIP (Japanese), C6 ....$65.00

Hovercraft, w/Cutter figure, complete w/accessories, 1984, EX (EX pkg), C6...$65.00

Hydro Sled, MIB, F1 ....$10.00

LCV Recon Sled, complete, 1983, loose, H4 ....$5.00

LCV Recon Sled, 1986, loose, H4....................................$5.00

LCV Recon Sled, 1986, MIP, C6......................................$14.00

Locust, brn & silver, 1990, MIP, C6 ....$12.00

MC Center, w/Steamroller figure, complete w/accessories & papers, M, loose, S4 ....$55.00

Mobile Command Center, MIB, D4.................................$40.00

Mobile Missile System, w/Hawk figure, 1982, NRFB, H4..$60.00

Motorized Battle Wagon, 1991, MIP, C6.........................$32.00

Parasite, Cobra personnel carrier, 1991, loose, H4.............$8.00

Patriot, MIB, D4..$12.00

Rage (Cobra Urban Assault Tank), MIB, D4 ....$15.00
Raider, NMIB, D4...$25.00
RAM (Rapid Fire Motorcycle), 1982, MIP, C6................$34.00
Rapid-Fire, w/video tape, 1990, MIP, C6.........................$18.00
Rhino (jeep), holds 4 figures, spring-action cannon, doors open, M, C6 ....$40.00
Roboskull, skull form vehicle w/Red Wolf figure, MIP, C6..$28.00
Rolling Thunder, 1988, MIP (English), C6 ....$29.00
SAS Panther Jeep & Stalker, Action Force, MIP, C6......$50.00
Sea Lion, w/pilot, Action Force, MIP, C6........................$34.00
Serpentors Air Chariot, complete, loose, H4 ....$5.00
Shadowtrak, w/Red Vulture figure, Action Force, MIP, C6.$25.00
SHARC, w/Deep Six figure, complete w/accessories, 1984, EX, loose, C6 ....$24.00
Silent Attack Kayak, w/Recondo figure, Action Force, MIP, C6..$25.00
Sky HAVOC, 1990, MIP, C6...$25.00
Sky Hawk, 1989, MIB...$15.00
Sky Raven, 1990, MIP, C6 ....$40.00
Sky SHARC, chrome plated, figure sold separately, 1989, loose, H4 ....$5.00
Snowcat, complete w/Frostbite figure & ID card, 1985, loose, H4...$22.00
Snowcat, w/Frostbite figure, 1985, EX (EX pkg), C6........$40.00
Snowcat, 1985, MIB, H4 ....$50.00
Stinger, w/driver, 1983, MIP (Japanese), C6 ....$60.00
Tiger Cat, w/Frostbite figure, complete w/accessories & papers, M, loose, S4 ....$25.00
Tiger Fly, Action Force, w/Recondo figure, MIP, C6 ....$35.00
Tiger Paw, Tiger Force, 1988, MIP, C6.............................$17.00
Tiger Shark, Tiger Force, 1988, MIP, C6............................$22.00
Tiger Sting, complete w/all papers, M, loose, S4 ....$15.00
Triad Fighter, Action Force, w/Captain figure, MIP, C6..$25.00
Vamp, w/Clutch figure, 1983, MIP (India), C6 ....$40.00
Vamp, w/Clutch figure, 1983, MIP (Japanese), C6...........$75.00
Vamp Mark II, unassembled, MIP (1993 Convention), C6 ....$14.00
Wolverine, w/Cover Girl figure & tow hook, 1983, MIP, C6 ....$85.00

Miscellaneous

Collector Case, complete w/papers, 1983, M, loose, S4....$23.00
Collector Case, vinyl w/2 figure trays, for 3¾" figures, EX, H4...$6.00
Flying Rescue Set, 1960s, MIB, T1....................................$75.00
Game, Card; Whitman, 1965, complete, orig clear plastic box, EX-NM, H4 ....$15.00
Game, Paratrooper, Hasbro, 1960s, EX+, F3....................$28.00
Game, 1982, EX...$10.00
Life Raft, Irwin, for 12" doll, complete w/accessories, MIB..$40.00
Playset, White Tiger Hunt, GI Joe Adventure Team, unused, M (VG box), V1 ....$135.00
Postcard, Specialty Import Co, 3-D, Joe in astronaut costume, 1960s, 4x6", M, T2 ....$10.00
Puzzle, jigsaw; 1965, NMIB, J2 ....$20.00
Puzzle, MB/Hasbro, features #2-Voltar, sealed, 1988, MIB .$8.00

Ring, Arctic Force, Shuttle Crew, Artillery, Tank Corps, Infantry, or Seal, solid-color plastic, any, H4..............$2.00
Sticker, Adventure Team, factory surplus, came on clothes, rnd, M, H4 ....$5.00

Girard

Girard Model Works (Pennsylvania) produced various types of toys, notably windups and pressed steel vehicles, from the 1920s until about 1970. See also Windups, Friction, and Other Mechanicals.

Pressed Steel

Dairy Truck, red w/cream tank, blk wood wheels w/metal hubcaps, Toyland Dairy on sides, 11¼", VG, A.............$105.00
Dump Truck, red, electric headlights, blk rubber tires w/red hubcaps, complete, orig wire bail, 9¾", NM, A $198.00
Dump Truck, red cab & chassis, yel bed, blk wood wheels w/wht hubcaps, rust in bed, 10", NM, A...........................$187.00
Dump Truck, red cab w/blk running board & fenders, gr bed, plated grille, blk wood wheels, 5¼", NM, A $132.00
Fire Truck, red, lg blk rubber tires marked Girard Balloon, blk hubcaps, orig lt gr ladders, 11¼", NM, A................$286.00
Fire Truck, red w/blk rubber tires, red hubcaps & front bumper, stamped on bottom, missing ladders, 7", M, A...........$55.00
Stake Truck, red, blk rubber tires w/red spoked wheels, electric headlights w/orig bulbs, 9¾", NM-M, A $275.00
Tank Truck w/Detachable Trailer, cream, blk rubber tires, bell under cab activated by crank on axle, 11", NM, A $231.00
Wrecker, red w/gr boom, red spoked wheels, blk rubber tires, bell under cab, activated by crank winch, 9⅞", M, A $468.00

Guns

Until WWI, most cap guns were made of cast iron. Some from the 1930s were nickel-plated, had fancy plastic grips, and were designed with realistic details like revolving cylinders. After the war, a trend developed toward using cast metal, a less expensive material. These diecast guns were made for two decades, during which time the TV western was born. Kids were offered a dazzling array of weapons, endorsed by stars like the Lone Ranger, Gene, Roy, and Hoppy. Sales of space guns, made popular by Flash Gordon and Tom Corbett, kept pace with the robots coming in from Japan. Some of these early tin lithographed guns were fantastic futuristic styles that spat out rays of sparks when you pulled the trigger. But gradually the space race lost its fervor, westerns were phased out, and guns began to be looked upon with disfavor by the public in general and parents in particular. Since guns were meant to see lots of action, most will show wear. Learn to be realistic when you assess condition; it's critical when evaluating the value of a gun. Our advisor for this category is Bill Hamburg (H1). Character-related guns are listed in the Character Collectibles category.

Actoy Restless Gun, 1950s, EX, H1 ....$150.00
Actoy Wells Fargo Buntline Cap Pistol, diecast w/cream plastic
    stag grips, break-to-front, fired, 1950s, 11", VG, P4 ..$85.00
Atomic Buster, air gun, 1940s, MIB, T1 ....$165.00
Bubble Blaster, 1950s, MIB, T1 ....$50.00

Buzz Henry Lone Rider, cast metal, 8", VG, $50.00.

Captain Cap Gun, CI, 5", EX...$60.00
Carvell-Kilgore Rebel Official Cap-Firing Scatter Gun, replica
    of Johnny Yuma gun, 1961, 5½", MOC $65.00
Classy Cap Pistol, diecast, break-to-front, U-shaped lever
    release, 1950s, 10", VG, P4 ....$75.00
Clicker Ray Gun, att Nosco, 2-color hard plastic, 1950s,
    5", M, P4 ....$20.00
Cragstan Dbl-Barrel Super Command Rifle, 1960s, MIB,
    T1 ....$35.00
Daisy Bull's-Eye Cap Gun, bl fr, wood grips, 1960s, EX-,
    H1 ....$95.00
Daisy Guns of the West #1931, 23" cork dbl-barrel shotgun & 2
    8" diecast cap guns, dbl holster, NM (EX box), A $86.00
Daiya Astronaut Rocket Gun, litho tin, sm crack in red plastic
    window, trigger sticks, sparks, late '50s, 9¼", VG, P4.$35.00
Daiya Baby Space Gun, litho tin, friction siren & sparks, late
    1950s, 6", MIB, from $90 to $150.00
Esquire/Nichols 7580 UZI Automatic, plastic, battery-op (4 Cs),
    w/2 boxes caps & 5 loose rolls, 1986, 10½", VG, P4 .$35.00
Futuristic Products Strate Gun, diecast, pull grips to fire caps,
    fired, 1950s, 9", VG, P4..$135.00
Futuristic Products Strate Gun, diecast w/red trim, pull grips to
    fire caps, unfired, 1950s, 9", NM, P4......................$275.00
Geo Schmidt Buck'n Bronc Cowhand Cap Gun, 1950s,
    EX- $75.00
Girl's Dbl Holster Set, unknown maker, wht leather, red trim,
    red belt bk, hearts & jewels, 1950s, NM $75.00
Hamilton Secret Agent Hideaway Cap Gun, CI w/red grips, late
    1950s, MIB, H1...$65.00
Hawkeye Automatic Pistol, diecast, 1950s, orig box, VG,
    T1...$20.00
Hubley #1860 Colt 44 Cal Cap Pistol, diecast, orig issued as kit,
    chambers 6 2-pc bullets (not included), 13", VG....$125.00
Hubley Army 45 Cap Pistol, diecast w/wht plastic grips, pop-up
    magazine, unfired, early 1950s, 6½", M.....................$75.00
Hubley Atomic Disintegrator, #270, diecast w/red plastic grips,
    spring-load magazine, 1954, 8", VG.........................$175.00

Hubley Atomic Disintegrator Cap Pistol, 1950s, MIB, D10, $300.00.

Hubley Atomic Disintegrator, fires caps, 4x8x1" box, EX
    (NM box)..$250.00
Hubley Automatic Cap Pistol #290, diecast w/brn checkered
    grips, 1956, 6½", NM..$50.00
Hubley Chief Cap Gun, CI, 1930, 6⅛", EX, H1 ....$65.00
Hubley Colt 45, NP diecast, brass-washed cylinder, wht grips,
    14", EX...$125.00
Hubley Cowboy Cap Gun, CI w/bl fr, 1940s, EX, H1 ....$150.00
Hubley Cowboy Cap Gun #275, diecast, wht plastic grips
    w/blk steer, release on barrel, unfired, 1950s, 12", NMIP,
    P4 ....$225.00
Hubley Cowboy Jr Cap Gun #255, diecast, wht plastic cow grips,
    revolving cylinder, side loading, 9", NMIB, P4 ....$165.00
Hubley Coyote Cap Gun, diecast, 1950s, M, H1 ....$35.00
Hubley Dagger Derringer #253, diecast, dk metal finish, fired,
    4⅛", VG..$75.00
Hubley Dandy, CI, mk Police 38, Patd 1993916, revolving cylin-
    der, side loading, 1937, 5¾", VG, P4 ....$95.00
Hubley Dbl-Barreled Flintlock, metal & wood-grain plastic, fires
    caps, 1950s, 10", NM..$35.00
Hubley Dick Cap Pistol, diecast, automatic, bright nickel finish,
    fired, 1950s, 4¼", EX..$20.00

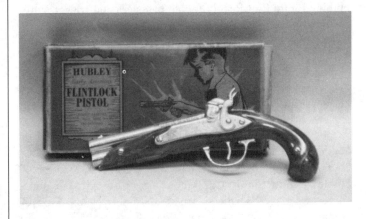

Hubley Flintlock Double-Barrel Pistol, 1950s, MIB, D10, $95.00.

Hubley Flintlock Jr Cap Pistol, diecast, single shot, dbl action,
    brn swirl plastic stock, NMIB, P4.............................$35.00
Hubley Flintlock Midget Cap Gun, diecast, 1950s, 5½", EX,
    H1 ....$20.00

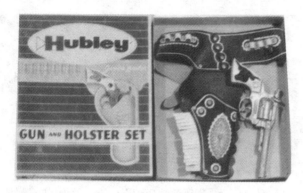

Hubley Gun and Holster Set, 1950s, MIB, A, $86.00.

Hubley Marine Automatic Holster Set #5935, w/Hubley Automatic #290, brn leather holder w/brass buckle, NMIB, P4 ....$225.00

Hubley Midget Cap Pistol, diecast w/silver finish, smallest of flintlocks, fired, 1950s, 5½", VG, P4...........................$25.00

Hubley Padlock Cap Gun, VG.................................$75.00

Hubley Panther Pistol #273, diecast, cap-firing derringer, w/blk leather wrist holster, unfired, 4", NM $50.00

Hubley Pioneer Cap Gun, CI, Navy percussion style, 1950s, M, H1...$100.00

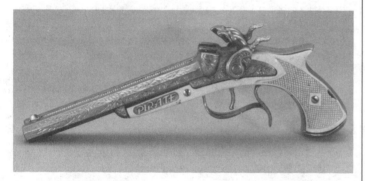

Hubley Pirate Cap Pistol, double hammers and trigger, white plastic grips, 1950s, VG, $85.00.

Hubley Pirate Cap Pistol, diecast fr w/CI dbl hammers & trigger, wht plastic grips, fired, 1950, VG, P4.........................$85.00

Hubley Pirate Dummy Cap Pistol, diecast, hammers do not reach bottom of pan, rare variation, unfired, 1950, VG, P4 ....$165.00

Hubley Red Ranger Jr, diecast, 1950s, MIB $65.00

Hubley Remington 36, blk diecast, plastic grips, EX $95.00

Hubley Remington 36 Cap Gun, diecast, blk grips, revolving cylinder, 6 2-pc bullets, 1959, 8", NM, P4...............$135.00

Hubley Ric-O-Shay 45 Cap Gun, diecast, lg fr, revolving cylinder, fires caps, sounds, unfired, 1959, 13", NM, P4..$135.00

Hubley Smokey Joe Cap Gun, dbl-holster set w/CI Texans, wht leather w/fringe & jewels, w/cuffs & spurs, 1940s, NM, H1...$550.00

Hubley Smokey Joe Cap Gun, diecast w/wht plastic steer grips, lever release, break-to-front, 1950s, 8", M, P4 ....$60.00

Hubley Smoking Texan Jr Cap Pistol, 1940s, 8", MIB ...$100.00

Hubley Sure-Shot Cap Gun, diecast, roll caps, blk steer head grips, 1950s, MIB, H1 ....$35.00

Hubley Teddy Cap Gun, CI, 1938, 5⅝", M, H1 ....$65.00

Hubley Texan Cap Gun, CI w/iron cylinder, 1940s, NMIB, H1 ....$250.00

Hubley Texan Cap Gun, CI w/nickel finish, wht plastic steer grips (hairline crack), 1940, fired, 9¼", VG, P4 ......$135.00

Hubley Texan Cap Gun, diecast, revolving cylinder, lever release, break-to-front, red star logo, 1950, 9", MIB .$150.00

Hubley Texan Jr Cap Gun, diecast, wht plastic longhorn grips, star logo, break-to-front, unfired, 9", NMIB, P4 ......$145.00

Hubley Texan 38 Cap Pistol, diecast, revolving cylinder, brn plastic steer grips, late '50s, +box of caps, 10", VG, P4 .....$175.00

Hubley Trooper Cap Pistol, diecast, blk pnt grips, pop-up cap magazine, 1950, 6½", NMIB (early litho NM box), P4 ....$65.00

Hubley Western Scout Rifle, 250-shot, lever action, 1973, 33", M4...$125.00

Hubley 2 Guns In 1 Cap Pistol #252, diecast, 4" barrel & 2" snub nose, side loading, wht grips, unfired, 1950s, NMIB $100.00

Irwin Rocket Ship Pistol, clicker flashes signals from nose, pilot in cockpit moves forward, 1950s, 7", NM (G+ box), A $130.00

Ives, Liberty, L7.1.1, japanned CI, VG $125.00

Ives Crack, C27.1, japanned CI, worn, barrel has sm crack, VG..$45.00

Ives Punch & Judy Patented, cast iron, EX, A, $450.00.

Kenton Biff Cap Gun, CI w/nickel finish, automatic, side loading, 1937, 4½", NM, P4..$90.00

Kenton Bulldog Cap Gun, CI, 1923, 5½", EX, H1 ....$85.00

Kenton Western Cap Gun, CI, 1935, 8", EX+.................$50.00

Kilgore American Cap Gun, CI cylinder, 1940s, EX, H1 .$350.00

Kilgore Big Bill Cap Gun, CI, 1930, 5¾", EX-, H1..........$45.00

Johnny Eagle Magumba (Topper/Deluxe Reading), 1965, plastic case, M, $125.00.

Kilgore Big Horn Cap Gun, CI cylinder, brn grips, 1940s, EX $450.00

Kilgore Big Horn Cap Gun, diecast, revolving cylinder, break-to-front, fires disk caps, 1950s, MIB, P4 ....$85.00

Kilgore Big Smoky, B20.1, NP, worn, VG $95.00

Kilgore Buc-a-roo Cap Pistol, CI, 1950s, NM, $40.00.

Kilgore Champion Quick Draw Timer Cap Pistol, diecast western style, w/up in grip times draw, 1959, MIB, P4...$225.00

Kilgore Clipper Automatic Cap Gun, CI, 1935, 4⅛", EX-, H1 ....$65.00

Kilgore Deputy Cap Gun, diecast, metallic purple, 1950s, 7½", M, H1 ....$15.00

Kilgore Falcon Pocket Pistol & Holster, diecast, roll caps, 1950s, MIB, H1 ....$45.00

Kilgore Grizzly Disk Cap Gun, diecast, 1950, EX, H1 ....$135.00

Kilgore Hawkeye Cap Pistol, diecast w/silver finish, automatic, side loading, unfired, 1950s, 4¼", NMIB, P4 ....$45.00

Kilgore Invincible Cap Gun, CI, 1935, 5¼", EX, H1........$65.00

Kilgore Long Tom Cap Gun, CI cylinder, 1940s, EX $450.00

Kilgore Long Tom Cap Gun, steel cylinder, late 1940s, orig box, EX, H1 ....$595.00

Kilgore Mountie Cap Gun, late 1950s, MIB, H1 ....$85.00

Kilgore Mustang Cap Gun, CI, roll caps, 1950s, MIB, H1.$80.00

Kilgore President, cast iron, ca 1925, 9", EX, $75.00.

Kilgore Presto Automatic Pocket Pistol, CI w/maroon grips, 1930s, EX, H1 ....$75.00

Kilgore Presto Cap Pistol #18, CI, red plastic grips, pop-up cap magazine, unfired, 1950, 5⅛", NM, P4.....................$75.00

Kilgore Presto Cap Pistol #18, CI w/nickel finish, brn plastic grips, unfired, 5⅛", NMIB, P4 ....$150.00

Kilgore Ranger Cap Gun, 10", MOC $77.50

Kilgore Rebel Scatter Gun Miniature, MOC...................$85.00

Kilgore 6-Shooter, CI, revolving disk, slider release, lt rust, 1934, 6½", VG, P4..$165.00

Knickerbocker Dragnet Badge 714 Cap Pistol, plastic w/diecast works, pull-down magazine, unfired, 6½", NM, P4....$55.00

Knickerbocker Mare's Laig Water Gun, wht, gold & blk plastic, missing filler cap, 1960, 15", VG, P4.........................$25.00

Kusan Western Heritage Texan Cap Gun, diecast, 1970s, MOC, H1 ....$25.00

Langson Cody Colt Paper Buster Gun, diecast, nickel finish, wht plastic steer grip, 2 boxes ammo, '50s, 7¾", NMIB, P4...$90.00

Leslie-Henry Automatic Cap Pistol, diecast, 1950s, sm, EX, H1 ....$25.00

Leslie-Henry Champion Cap Pistol, CI, 1950s, EX, H1.$150.00

Leslie-Henry Longhorn Cap Pistol, diecast, wht plastic horse-head grips, pop-up cap magazine, unfired, 1950s, 10", M $95.00

Leslie-Henry Marshal Cap Pistol, diecast, nickel finish, wht plastic grips w/blk horseshoes, 1950s, 10½", VG.............$75.00

Leslie-Henry Texas Cap Pistol, diecast, nickel finish, wht horse-head grips, break-to-front, unfired, 1950s, 9", M $75.00

Leslie-Henry Texas Ranger Cap Pistol, diecast, nickel finish, wht plastic horse-head grips, fired once, 8¼", NM, P4 ....$60.00

Leslie-Henry Wagon Train Complete Western Cowboy Outfit, rifle, pistol & leather holster, unfired, 1960, NMIB, P4...$245.00

Leslie-Henry Wagon Train Western 6-Gun #48, diecast, side loading, chambers 6 bullets, sounds, 1958, 11", NMIB, P4 ....$245.00

Let 'Er Buck Gun, Holster & Rope; World Toy House, ca 1954-57, MIB..$25.00

LM Eddy Racket Buster Holster Set, blk leather shoulder holster, ca 1960, MIB, P4..................................$35.00

Lone Star Cap-Firing Repeater, mk Made in England, 1968, M4..$45.00

Lone Star Gun Fighter Holster Set, diecast, silver finish, brn plastic grips, red & wht holster, 1960s, NMIB, P4.....$55.00

Lone Star 4-in-1 Detective Spudmatic Gun #1361, diecast, shoots water, corks, spuds & caps, 5", NM (worn box), P4.....$25.00

Luger Cap Pistol, Hong Kong, diecast, brn plastic grips, pop-up cap magazine, unfired, 1960s(?), 7½", NM, P4..........$25.00

Maco USA Machine Gun #198/250, red & yel plastic, mtd on tripod, fires plastic bullets, 1950s, 12", MIB, P4......$135.00

Marx Air Defense Laser Rifle, w/sparking action, 1970s, MIB, T1..$25.00

Marx Army Automatic Pistol #J3233, diecast w/blk pnt finish, wht plastic grips, late 1950s, 2½", NMOC, P4...........$10.00

Marx Bullet-Firing Snub-Nose Pistol, diecast, pnt blk finish, revolving cylinder, fired, 1960, 6", VG, P4.................$55.00

Marx Burp Gun #3310, gr & blk plastic, battery-op (1 D cell), 1960s, 20", NMOC, P4..................................$20.00

Marx Dbl-Holster Set, diecast, wht plastic horse & steer grips, fires cap rolls, brn vinyl holster, 1960, VG.................$75.00

Marx Derringer, fires caps, 1960s-70s, orig plastic case, NM...$35.00

Marx Derringer, Golden Guns Series, gold-colored metal w/brn plastic grips, 1960s, 4", M (EX card), T2................$30.00

Marx Famous Firearms Deluxe Edition Collectors Album, diecast & plastic, 1959, NMIB............................$100.00

Marx G-Man Machine Gun, litho tin & plastic, sparker needs flint, EX+..$75.00

Marx ISA 07-11 Gun Set, plastic w/diecast works, Luger style fires single shot cap, G, P4..............................$60.00

Marx Miniature, Wanted Dead or Alive (Mare's Laig), diecast w/blk finish, brn plastic stock, fired, 1959, 5½", VG, P4..........$20.00

Marx Miniature Bobcat Saddle Gun (Mare's Laig), Famous Firearms Collector Series, diecast, 1960s, 5½", MOC, P4..........$30.00

Marx Miniature Deluxe 4-Gun Set, diecast & plastic w/nickel finish, 1960s, NMOC, P4................................$65.00

Marx Miniature Sharps Carbine, Famous Firearms Collector Series, diecast, 1960s, 7½", MOC, P4.................$20.00

Marx Miniature 6-Shooter Cap Pistol, diecast, wht steer grips, 1960, 3¼", MOC, P4..................................$20.00

Marx Secret Agent, diecast, 1969, orig box, EX+, T1, pr.$45.00

Marx Security Pistol, w/sound action, MOC, T1..............$20.00

Marx Wanted Dead or Alive Mare's Laig Saddle Rifle, plastic w/diecast works, 19", VG, P4.......................$145.00

Marx 357 Magnum, Historical Gun Series, dk bl hard plastic w/brn handles, +3 lockers to store caps, 1974, 6", EX, T2...$40.00

Mattel Agent Zero-M Radio Rifle, blk & silver plastic portable radio opens to become rifle, orig 9x23x2" box, M, T2..$150.00

Mattel Agent Zero-M Snap-Shot Camera Pistol, plastic w/diecast works, unfired, 1964, 7½", NM, P4............$35.00

Mattel Agent Zero-M Snap-Shot Gun, MIB, $100.00.

Mattel Burp Gun Cap Machine Gun, plastic w/diecast works, fires roll caps by crank hdl, unfired, 1957, 17", M, P4.$45.00

Mattel Colt 6-Shooter Rifle, plastic w/31" cartridge holder for bullets, revolving cylinder, 1960, EX (VG box), A.$150.00

Mattel Cowboy in Africa Cap Gun & Holster, Black Fanner 50, emb antelope head on stag grips, 1960s, EX...............$75.00

Mattel Fanner 50 Cap Gun, diecast, late 1950s, EX (worn box), H1...$150.00

Mattel Fanner 50 Cap Gun, diecast, w/swivel holster & belt, late 1950s, MIB...$235.00

Mattel Fanner 50 Marshal Gun & Holster Set, NMIB...$140.00

Mattel Fanner 50 Smoking Cap Pistol #543, diecast, revolving cylinder w/6 bullets, unfired, 1957, 10½", NMIB, P4..$150.00

Mattel Official Winchester Saddle Rifle, plastic & metal w/secret trigger, holds 8 bullets, 33", NM (EX box), A.............$250.00

Mattel Shootin' Shell Buckle Gun Western Belt Set #632, shoots caps & bullets, w/instructions, 1958, 3", NM (G box), P4..$75.00

Mattel Shootin' Shell Fanner Cap Pistol #608, diecast, revolving cylinder, fires 2-pc cartridges, 1958, 9", MIB, P4.....$265.00

Mattel Shootin' Shell Snub Nose 38 Cap Gun, w/shoulder holster, no cartridges, late 1950s, EX, H1.....................$95.00

Mattel Shootin' Shell 45 Cap Gun, diecast, late 1950s, EX-, H1...$225.00

Mattel Tommy-Burst Jungle Fighter, plastic w/diecast works, fires burst, single shot or caps, ca 1960, 25", VG, P4.$75.00

Mattel-O-Matic Tri-Pod Machine Gun, fires caps, VG (VG box)..$35.00

Mauser 7.63mm 1932 Schneffleur Machine Pistol Replica, unknown maker, diecast & wood, working, w/clips & holster, VG, P4...$275.00

Midwest Long Tom Dart Gun #PD-1, blk pnt pressed steel, missing darts, 1950s, 11", NMIB, P4..........................$35.00

National Cap Gun, CI, 1925, 5¼", M, H1.......................$85.00

Nichols Buccaneer Shell-Firing Derringer #210, diecast, flintlock-style shoots plastic bullets, 1958, 3½", MOC, P4...$125.00

Nichols Colt Special Cap Gun, diecast, chrome w/blk plastic grips, fired, 1950s, 7", G, P4..................................$25.00

Nichols Dyna-Mite Derringer w/Clip, diecast, loads 2-pc Nichols bullet, w/3 bullets, 1950s, orig box, 3¼", MIB, P4 ....**$50.00**

Nichols Luger 50-Shot Cap Firing Repeater, plastic w/diecast works, entire works lift out, unusual, unfired, 9", M, P4 ....**$35.00**

Nichols Mustang 500 Cap Gun, MIB **$300.00**

Nichols Paint Cap Pistol, diecast, flip-out cylinder, fires standard 2-pc Nichols bullet, 1950s, 3½", MOC, P4 ....**$45.00**

Nichols Shell-Firing Derringer #212, diecast, hinged barrel loads 3-pc bullet, w/2 extra bullets, 1958, 4", VG **$50.00**

Nichols Spitfire #100, diecast, cap cartridge, hip mini rifle style, plastic stock, 1950s, 9", MIB, P4 ....**$35.00**

Nichols Stallion Cap Gun #41-40, diecast, late 1950s, MIB **$375.00**

Nichols Stallion 22 Cap Pistol, diecast, revolving cylinder, w/5 2-pc cartridges, single action, w/tag, '50s, 7", M, P4 ..**$65.00**

Nichols Stallion 22 Dbl-Action Cap Pistol, wht plastic grips, unfired, 1950s, 7", VG, P4 ....**$85.00**

Nichols Stallion 32 6-Shooter, diecast w/bright nickel finish, blk grips, revolving cylinder, 1955, 8", NMIB **$95.00**

Nichols Stallion 38 Cap Pistol, diecast, w/strip of 6 2-pc cartridges & box of caps, 1951, 9½", VG **$75.00**

Nichols Stallion 38 Cap Pistol, diecast, wht plastic grips, 6 2-pc cartridges, '55, 9½", NMIB **$125.00**

Nichols Stallion 45 Cap Pistol, diecast w/chrome finish, revolving cylinder, 6 2-pc bullets, 1950, 12", VG **$125.00**

Nichols Stallion 45 Mk II Cap Pistol, blk stag plastic grips w/extra set wht grips, 6 2-pc bullets, 1950s, 12", VG **$150.00**

Nichols/Kusan Detective Snub-Nose Special #685, diecast, brn plastic grips, side loading, 5", MOC, P4 ....**$15.00**

Official Space Guard Holster, unknown maker, heavy blk plastic w/space motif, belt loops, ca 1950, 7¼x4¼", VG, P4..**$75.00**

Ohio Art Astro Ray Laser-Lite Beam Dart Gun #563, red & wht plastic, Morse code on grips, +4 darts, 1960s, 10", NMIB, P4...**$175.00**

Ohio Art Sheriff's Derringer, red & silver metal, separate cap-loading bullet, 3x2", MOC, A **$60.00**

P-38 Clicker Pistol, blk steel, 1930s, 8", lt stain on orig box, M, A **$60.00**

Palmer Ray Gun Water Pistol, translucent gr or orange, solid yel or copper, 1950s, 5½", M, P4, ea **$20.00**

Park Plastics Luger Water Pistol, brn & blk plastic, 2 removable water magazines & belt clip, comic book, 1956, MIB, P4 ....**$35.00**

Park Space Squirt Gun, plastic, 5", NM **$20.00**

Parris Mfg M-1 Kadet Training Rifle, metal & wood, working bolt, clicker action, trigger guard, fired, '60s, 32", VG, P4 ....**$35.00**

Parris Pirate Pistol, diecast w/wood hdl, shoots caps, 1960s, VG-EX, T1...**$15.00**

Parris Western Man #210 Derringer & Holster Set, w/bullets, fires caps, 1970s, MOC, T1 ....**$15.00**

Pirate Pistol Son of a Gun, diecast, 1970s, MOC, T1.......**$15.00**

Plawner/Dah Yang Secret Ultra Gun, bl plastic space gun, fires caps & darts (2 included), 1970s(?), NMIB, P4.........**$55.00**

Product Engineering Frontier Smoker Cap Pistol, diecast, mk Zamak, fires roll caps, 9½", NMIB, P4 ....**$80.00**

Product Engineering 45 Smoker Cap Gun, aluminum single-shot, 1940s, EX, H1 ....**$85.00**

Radar Clicker Ray Gun, unknown maker (probably US), rose plastic w/gr spaceman, 1950s, 6¼", M, P4.................**$30.00**

Randall Space Pilot Super Sonic Gun, plastic battery-op shines light in 3 colors, 9", M (EX box), A........................**$220.00**

Remco Electronic Space Gun, plastic battery-op, futuristic, sounds, 9", in 8x12" illus box, NM (EX+ box), A ...**$110.00**

Remco Hamilton Invader Pistol, shoots caps, w/grenade launcher, 1959, MIB, T1 ....**$65.00**

Remco Jupiter 4-Color Signal Gun #600, blk plastic w/red trim, internal color wheel, 1950s, 9", MIB, P4 ....**$75.00**

Remco Space Gun Set, red & gray, 1960s, VG, T1, pr.....**$25.00**

Renwal #120, USA Pat Pend, red, blue, and yellow plastic, 11", NM, $350.00.

Renwal 6-Shooter #128, red, yel & bl plastic, spring loading cylinder, w/5 bullets+2 doz MIP, 1950s, NMIB, P4...**$55.00**

Ring Bros Tecumseh Indian Fighter Gun, Holster, Belt & Knife Set; ca 1955, MIP **$32.00**

Satellite & Rocket Pistol, unknown maker, Hong Kong, gr plastic, fires yel darts or saucers, 1960s, 5", NMOC, P4..**$35.00**

Secret Agent, cap pistol, metal, bl & silver, smokes, used roll caps, 5½", MIB, A...**$40.00**

Shackman Siren-Spark Jet Gun #A3590, litho tin, sparks, 1960s, 5½", M (worn header card & bag), P4 ....**$35.00**

Shudo Astro Ray Gun, litho tin, friction, sparks, sm dent on side, 1960s, 5⅞", VG, P4 ....**$30.00**

Space Dart Gun, unknown maker, hard plastic, 1 side wht/other blk, star & lightning motifs, w/1 dart, 1950s, VG, P4.**$35.00**

Space Jet Pistol, Japan, litho tin, MIB **$115.00**

Space Outlaw Atomic Water Pistol, lg plastic ray type, 1950s, MIP (illus header card), V1 ....**$35.00**

Space Patrol Pistol, gr plastic, 6", M **$250.00**

Space Products Official Space Patrol Auto-Sonic Rifle, shoots rubber balls, ca 1950, 25", NMIB **$500.00**

Space Ray Gun, Japan, 10", MIB......................................**$65.00**

Space Ray Gun, tin & plastic, working, 16", NM, M5 .....**$30.00**

Space Rifle, Japan, litho tin, 15", EX **$75.00**

Space Sparking Ray Gun, litho tin, brn w/yel, silver & red trim, plastic windows, sm scratches, 5", NM, P4.................**$25.00**

Space Universe Gun, unknown maker, Japan, marked T, litho tin, sparks, 1960s, 4", NMIP, P4...................................**$30.00**

Special Agent Pistol, red & silver metal, separate cap-loading bullet, England, 3x2", MOC, A....................................$55.00

Spinray Blast Pistol, unknown maker, cast aluminum, stamped metal trigger activates mechanism, sounds, 6½", A.$175.00

Spitfire Cap Cartridge Loading Hip Gun, 1950s, MIB, D4.$30.00

Stevens Big Scout Toy Cap Pistol, NP CI, Tenite hdls w/cowboy, horse & guns, ca 1940, unused, 8", VG+ (M box), A $138.00

Stevens Billy the Kid Cap Gun, metal w/emb Billy the Kid, buffaloes on grips, unused, 7½", NM, A......................$110.00

Stevens Buddy Cap Gun, CI, 1930s, 6¼", EX, H1............$65.00

Stevens Cap Gun, SN45.1, blk pnt CI, G $225.00

Stevens Cap Pistol, CI, single shot, worn nickel finish, fired, rust on barrel, 1885, 4¾", P4 ....$125.00

Stevens Cosmic Ray/Space Police Cap-Firing Ray Gun, 1949-52, 10½", VG...$125.00

Stevens Deadshot, D8.1, NP, G $160.00

Stevens Echo 3.34 Cap Gun, CI, 1930s, NM, H1 ....$45.00

Stevens Hero, H8.3.2, NP, VG $25.00

Stevens Jet Jr Space Cap Gun, diecast w/silver finish, sliding door for loading, fired, 1949, 6⅜", VG, P4 ....$245.00

Stevens Peace Maker, P8.1, gold tinted NP, VG.............$65.00

Stevens Peace Maker Cap Pistol, CI, break-to-front, lever release, wht figural grips, rpl screw, fired, 1940, VG..$50.00

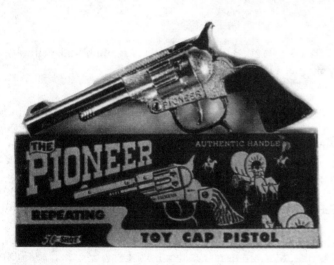

Stevens Pioneer Cap Gun, metal, unfired, 8", MIB, $45.00.

Stevens Rapid Load 6-Shot Cap Gun, CI, w/cutout in chamber to load caps into cylinder, 1925, 6½", EX, A $90.00

Stevens Sheriff Cap Pistol, nickeled CI w/Tenite wht plastic grips & red jewels, unfired, 8½", MIB $125.00

Stevens 49er Cap Gun, CI w/gold wash, wht grips w/red jewels, worn orig box, NM $275.00

Stevens 49er Cap Gun, CI w/gold wash, 1940s, MIB, H1..$400.00

Stevens 6-Shot, S2.1.3, unfinished CI, VG $200.00

Superior Rocket Dart Gun, plastic, 3 barrels shoot darts, for use w/Superior Dart Game, 1950s, 8", VG, P3.................$30.00

Superior Rocket Gun, silver, NM...................................$68.00

Tigrett Atom Flash Zoomeray Space Gun, red plastic gun, rolled paper Space Missile of Tomorrow, '50s, 7", M (NM box), P4 ....$45.00

Topper Johnny Eagle Lieutenant Carbine Rifle, WWII carbine w/bolt action & removable clip, 1965, 36", scarce, EX+, A $165.00

Topper Johnny Eagle Lieutenant 45 Cal Pistol, dk bl plastic, removable bullet clip, w/carrying case, 1965, EX+, A.$184.00

Topper Johnny Eagle Magumba Pistol, plastic, single action, removable clip magazine, 11", VG, P4 ....$45.00

Topper Johnny Eagle Red River Bullet-Firing Rifle, plastic, fires 2-pc bullets, unfired, 1965, 36", NM, P4..................$75.00

Topper Johnny Seven OMA Combat Set, plastic w/diecast works, missing pcs, 1964, 36", VG (VG box), P4 ......$75.00

Topper Multi-Pistol 09, plastic, fires 4 different missiles, 1965, w/case (screws missing), NMIB, P4........................$100.00

Topper Sixfinger, plastic, fits between fingers, fires 6 different missiles, 1965, 3½", NMOC, P4 ....$55.00

Webb Electric Atom Blaster Ray Gun, NMIB................$125.00

Webb Electric Atom Buster Mystery Gun, plastic w/side portholes, includes target sheet, 1950s, 7x11", NM (EX+ box), A $149.00

Wham-O Air Blaster, plastic, rubber diaphragm shoots air blast, 1960s, 10", VG, P4 ....$75.00

Whistle Clicker Ray Gun, unknown maker, 2-color plastic w/space motifs, gun bk is whistle, 1950s, 5", M, P4 ...$20.00

Wyandott Cork Gun, VG-EX, O1 ....$85.00

Wyandotte Dart Gun, pressed steel w/chrome, 1940s, VG, T1..$10.00

Wyandotte Me & My Buddy Pistol, pressed steel, squeeze trigger & tin cowboy's arm moves, clicker, 8", NM (G box), A $145.00

Wyandotte Red Ranger Cap Pistol, diecast w/brn plastic grips, break-to-front, lever release, unfired, 9", NM, P4......$55.00

Wyandotte Red Ranger Jr Cap Pistol, diecast, wht horse grips, break-to-front, lever release, early '50s, 7½", M, P4 ..$65.00

Wyandotte Western Gun, red pressed steel, VG, T1........$25.00

X-15 Machine Gun, litho tin sparkler, sounds, 12x7", MIB, A $55.00

Yank-a-Matic, wood w/rubber band action, 1940s, VG-EX, T1..$15.00

20th-Century Products Super Site Magic Bullet Gun, plastic, telescopic gunsight & whistle in grip, '50s, 9", VG, P4 ....$30.00

BB Guns

Daisy Buzz Barton BB Gun, VG-EX, O1 ....$115.00

Daisy Buzz Barton Special #195, metal rpt blk, varnished stock, missing sight tube, 1936-41, G, P4............................$45.00

Daisy CO2-200 Semi-Automatic Gas Pistol, 177 cal, metal w/brn plastic grips, w/BB tube & CO2 cartridge, 11" MIB $65.00

Daisy Red Ryder Rifle 1938B, steel w/carved wood stock, loads through end of barrel, 1980s, 35½", NM, P4 ....$35.00

Daisy Targeteer BB Pistol, pressed steel, chrome finish, spring fired, muzzle load, slide barrel, '50s, 10½", NM, P4 ...$55.00

Kentucky Rifle, NM (EX box), O1 ....$175.00

King BB Gun, VG-EX, O1 ....$65.00

Mattel Indian Scout Rifle, complete, MIB....................$300.00

Skell CO2 Gun, NM (EX box), O1 ....$275.00

Miscellaneous

Gun rack, Tales of Wells Fargo, unknown maker, diecast w/wood, 3-tier w/horseshoes & wood pegs, 1959, 20x22", VG, P4 ....$125.00

Gun toothbrush, unknown maker, bl plastic, mk Pat Pend Made in USA, 1950s, 6½", VG, P4.....................................$10.00

Holster, dbl, blk leather w/fancy studs & rhinestones, 1950s, VG, T1 ....$45.00

Holster, Pilgrim Leather Goods Ruff Rider, brn leather, dbl holders w/red jewels & 12 plastic bullets, NMIB, P4 ....$100.00

Holster, plastic, Fast Draw, in orig box, 1940s, EX, T1.....$45.00

Mattel Greenie Stickem' Caps, orig box, 1950s, NMIB, T1 .$5.00

Mattel Shootin' Shell Bullets, 1950s, MIP, T1 ....$25.00

Roll Caps #1505, perforated, 1500 shots, 1969, MIB (sealed), M4...$10.00

Wyandotte Texas Ranger Holster, brn leather, separate belt, single red jewel, 9", VG, P4...$30.00

Halloween

Halloween was originally a pagan holiday celebrated by the Druids of Great Britain, who began their New Year on the first of November. They believed that as the old year came to an end, the devil would gather up all the demons and evil in the world and take them back to Hades with him. Witches were women who had sold their souls to the devil. By 700 A.D., the Roman Catholic Church came into power and changed the holiday to a religious one which they called 'All Saints Day' or 'Allhallows.' The evening of October 31 became 'Allhallow's Eve' or 'Halloween.' But the holiday has long since evolved into what is now simply a fun-filled event, and the masks, noisemakers, and jack-o'-lanterns of earlier years are sought-after collectibles. See also Halloween Costumes.

Candy Container, chick bellhop, Germany, 7½", NM...$180.00

Candy Container, daddy quacker, Germany, 7½", EX ...$180.00

Candy Container, jack-o'-lantern, plastic, open top, 4½", EX $25.00

Candy Container, pumpkin shape, cb, W Germany, 5", M .$85.00

Candy Container, witch & jack-o'-lantern, plastic, M.....$20.00

Clicker, blk cats & jack-o'-lantern shape, EX $25.00

Clicker, owl, blk cat & moon shape, T Cohn, 3", EX.......$22.00

Clicker, owl, moon & devil shape, 2", EX.......................$15.00

Clicker, owl, quarter moon & witch shape, Kirchof, 4½", EX...$20.00

Clicker, owl shape, US Metal Toy, EX............................$17.50

Clicker, witch, tin, Kirchof, 2", NM...............................$14.00

Clicker, witch, tin, T Cohn, 2", VG+.............................$15.00

Diecut, bat & moon, Germany, EX $85.00

Diecut, blk cat, foil, US, 8x14", EX...............................$20.00

Diecut, blk cat, Germany, 1920s, 6", NM $80.00

Diecut, cat, cb, Merri-Lei, 13", unused, M.....................$28.00

Diecut, cat, goblin & owl, glow-in-the-dark, M, pkg of 3.$20.00

Diecut, howling blk cat & quarter moon, 9", NM $52.00

Diecut, owl, Germany, 1920s, 15", VG $95.00

Diecut, owl, HE Luhrs, 9", NM $20.00

Diecut, pumpkin, cb, 8x8", unused, M $20.00

Diecut, scowling blk cat & lantern, 9", EX $50.00

Diecut, skeleton, Beistle, 12", VG+ $18.00

Diecut, skeleton, Beistle, 32", EX..................................$28.00

Diecut, witch, cb, Merri-Lei, 8x8", NM $28.00

Diecut, witch in haunted house, HE Luhrs, 8", unused, M .$25.00

Horn, blk cat, devil & witch, litho, 6", EX $68.00

Horn, jack-o'-lantern, cats & witches, US Metal Toy, 11", NM...$22.00

Lamp, plastic Frankenstein head w/hat, mk UP, 1960s, 12", EX, A $75.00

Lantern, skull shape, 4-sided, EX+ $95.00

Candy Container, jack-o'-lantern with hat, Germany, 5", M, D10, $150.00.

Lantern, devil's head, pressed cardboard, American, M, D10, $150.00.

Lantern, witch & blk cat, 4-sided, US, old store stock, 1930s, 6"...$55.00

Noisemaker, litho tin can w/hdl, Kirchof, NM.................$15.00

Noisemaker, metal w/clown face, wood hdl, Kirchof, 4" dia, VG+, P3...$20.00

Noisemaker, ratchet type, blk cat & jack-o'-lantern, US Toys, EX..$22.00

Noisemaker, ratchet type, tin, Spanish dancer, EX..........$10.00

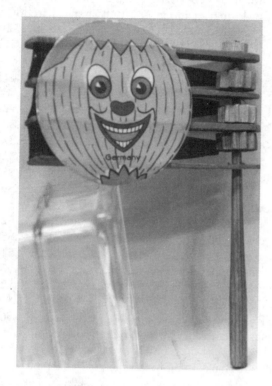

Noisemaker, jack-o'-lantern, ratchet type, 1920s, D10, $265.00.

Sparkler, Old Witch, American, 1950s, MOC, D10, $125.00.

Noisemaker, ratchet type, tin, clown musician, EX.........$10.00

Noisemaker, ratchet type, tin, goblins & witch, EX.........$20.00

Noisemaker, ratchet type, witch, owl & jack-o'-lantern, US Toys, VG...$12.00

Paper Hat, w/cats, Germany, 13x6", M..........................$25.00

Paper Hat, w/witches, Germany, 13x6", M......................$25.00

Paper Hat, witch, blk cat & jack-o'-lantern, 14", EX.......$16.00

Pin, jack-o'-lantern w/blinking eye, MOC......................$32.00

Pirate Hat, skull & crossbones, 14", M.........................$15.00

Tambourine, blk cat face, T Cohn, 7", EX......................$78.00

Tambourine, blk cats & moon over fence, tin, 6", EX......$65.00

Tambourine, witch face, tin, T Cohn, 7", VG.................$42.00

Teddy Bear, 'The Devil Made Me Do It,' 9", unused, M ..$28.00

Treat Bucket, Buck Rogers head, EX.............................$40.00

Treat Bucket, gr plastic Hulk figure, 1970s, EX.............$22.50

Treat Bucket, yel, blk & red Popeye characters on yel plastic, 1970s, EX...$25.00

Trick or Treat Bags, 16-pc, 1950s, 7", unused, M...........$20.00

Whistle, jack-o'-lantern, witches, etc, rare, VG.............$28.00

Wax figures, Gurloy, ca 1950s, set of four, $80.00.

Halloween Costumes

During the fifties and sixties Ben Cooper and Collegeville made Halloween costumes representing the popular TV and movie characters of the day. If you can find one in excellent to mint condition and still in its original box, some of the better ones can go for over $100.00. MAD's Alfred E. Neuman (Collegeville, 1959-60) usually carries an asking price of $150.00 to $175.00, and The Green Hornet (Ben Cooper, 1966), $200.00. Even some from the seventies are collectible.

Admiral Ackbar, Don Post, mask only, MIB.................$125.00

Astronaut, 1962, complete, EX $25.00

Bart Simpson, Ben Cooper, complete, size 8, M, E3.........$10.00

Batman, Japan, mask only, celluloid, 1950s, M..............$125.00

Batman, Japan, w/cowl, mask, belt & cape, from 1989 movie, MIB, F1 ....$20.00

Batman, Morris Costumes, mask only, M, E3 ....$35.00

Beany (of Beany & Cecil), 1960s, EX, V1 ....$30.00

Beatles (Paul), Ben Cooper/NEMS, minor splits on mask, in 11x12" window box (no cellophane), EX (EX box), A $375.00

Beetlejuice, mask only, rubber, 1988, M $40.00

Barbie, Mattel, Collegeville, 1975, MIB, $14.00.

Big Boy (Dick Tracy), Don Post, mask only, latex, M, F1 .$30.00

Big Boy (Dick Tracy), mask only, plastic, M, F1 ....$10.00

Boss Hogg, Ben Cooper, 1982, MIB, N2 ....$35.00

Bunny (Bunny & Clyde), Collegeville, 1960s, complete, NMIB $68.00

Captain America, Ben Cooper, 1977, NMIB, T1 ....$15.00

Cat, unmk, blk celluloid mask w/leering grin & eyes, 4", EX, A...$190.00

Cone Head, mask, MIB $35.00

Creature, Ben Cooper, mask only, 1973, NM..................$18.00

Daffy Duck, Ben Cooper, 1962, NMIB $25.00

Daniel Boone, Collegeville, 1960s, MIB, H4..................$15.00

Doc, Einson-Freeman, paper, mask only, 1937, minor wear, o/w EX, M8...$20.00

Donny Osmond, Ben Cooper, 1977, MIB.......................$25.00

Dopey, Einson-Freeman, paper, mask only, 1937, EX, M8 .$25.00

Green Hornet, Ben Cooper, 1966, EX (EX-box), $175.00.

Ewok, Ben Cooper, complete, MIB $25.00

Farrah Fawcett, 1977, complete, EX $50.00

Flattop (Dick Tracy), mask only, plastic, M, F1................$10.00

Frankenstein, Ben Cooper, 1973, M (EX+ box) $50.00

Fred Flintstone, 1973, complete, EX $25.00

Girl from UNCLE, Halco, 1960s, litho box features Illya, Solo & Girl from UNCLE, EX+ (EX box), A $206.00

Gomez, Rubie's, sz 12, M, E3 ....$10.00

Grumpy, Einson-Freeman, paper, mask only, 1937, minor wear, M8 ....$20.00

Harry & the Hendersons, Morris Costumes, mask only, M, E3 ....$50.00

Hee Haw Country Bumpkin, Ben Cooper, 1976, NM (EX box), C1 ....$36.00

Huckleberry Hound, Ben Cooper, 1960, complete, EX $40.00

Hulk, mask only, zipper in bk of head, 1980s, NM $60.00

Humble Oil Tiger, suit & light, missing mask, 1960s, orig box, EX $12.50

I Dream of Jeannie, vinyl & cloth w/plastic head, 1974, EX (VG box), T6 ....$16.00

King Kong, Ben Cooper, 1976, MIB (cellophane window cracked on box), H4..$25.00

King Leonardo, Collegeville, 1961, NM (EX+ box), A....$80.00

Lamb Chop, Don Post, vinyl & plastic, sm, EX (cellophane torn on box), T6 ....$13.00

Little Orphan Annie, Ben Cooper, 1981, NMIB, P4........$15.00

Lone Ranger, missing mask, 1977, EX (VG box), I2............$8.00

M*A*S*H*, Hawkeye, vinyl w/plastic mask, 1981, med, EX (cellophane missing on box, o/w EX), T6.................$19.00

Mummy, Ben Cooper, 1963, bodysuit sealed in bag, M, +loose unused mask, M, T2..$60.00

P Pitstop (Wacky Races), 1970, NMIB..........................$38.00

Phantom, Collegeville, plastic mask w/nylon outfit, orig box, EX $45.00

Pinocchio, Gillette Blue Blade, paper, mask only, 1939, EX, M8...$15.00

Police Woman, Angie Dickinson, MIB, V1.....................$15.00

Predator, Morris Costumes, mask only, M, E3 ....$75.00

Pumpkinhead, Morris Costumes, mask only, M, E3..........$25.00

Road Runner, Collegeville, in 10x11" window display box w/many illus, 1973, M (EX+ box) T2 ....$30.00

Robocob, mask only, plastic, M, F1 ....$10.00

Shadow, Conde Nast, lg blk rayon cape w/slogans, 1973, 36", NM, C1 ....$36.00

Six Million Dollar Man, 1974, complete, EX...................$30.00

Space Ghost, Ben Cooper, sealed in orig bag (mask sold separately), 1965, scarce, M, T2..$62.00

Spaceman, Collegeville, 1950s, MIB, T1 ....$35.00

Spiderman, Ben Cooper, 1972, MIB $50.00

Spiderman, rain poncho w/hood, Ben Cooper, red plastic, 1976, 19x36", NM, C1 ....$27.00

Star Trek, Ferengi, Ben Cooper, 1987, MIB, from $20 to.$30.00

Star Trek, Klingon, Ben Cooper, 1975, M (VG box) $35.00

Star Trek, Lt Worf, Ben Cooper, 1987, MIB, from $20 to.$30.00

Star Trek, Spock, vinyl & cloth w/plastic head, 1975, med, EX (VG box), T6..$70.00

Star Wars, Battle Poncho, Ben Cooper, blk w/logo & hood, MIP, F1 ....$10.00

Star Wars, Buzz Off, Ben Cooper, MIB $30.00
Star Wars, C-3PO, Don Post, full face, MIP, F1 ....$45.00
Star Wars, Cantina Band Member mask, Don Post, full face,
    MIP, F1...$60.00
Star Wars, Chewbacca, Ben Cooper, MIB $40.00
Star Wars, Chewbacca mask, Don Post, full face, MIP, F1 .$96.00
Star Wars, Darth Vader mask, Don Post, full face, MIP, F1.$60.00
Star Wars, Stormtrooper mask, Don Post, full face, MIP, F1.$80.00
Star Wars, Wicket mask, Don Post, full face, MIP, F1 .....$72.00
Star Wars, Yoda mask, Don Post, full face, MIP, F1 ....$40.00
Strawberry Shortcake, 1980, sm, EX (cellophane torn on box),
    T6...$5.00

Superman, Ben Cooper, 1948, NMIB, $200.00.

SWAT, plastic & vinyl, 1975, NM (EX box), T6 ....$15.00
Tom Terrific, Halco, 1957, MIB $95.00
Troll, Van Dam, mask only, 12", I1 ....$100.00
Ultra Man, 1971, NM (EX box)......................................$75.00
Underdog, Collegeville, NM (EX+ box)...........................$72.00
Weird-Ohs, Digger, mask only $70.00
Witch from Snow White, Einson-Freeman, mask only, 1937,
    scarce, minor tape mks on bk, o/w EX, M8 ....$35.00
Witchiepoo, Collegeville, 1971, EX................................$65.00
Wizard of Oz, Straw Man, Ben Cooper, 1960s, missing light
    bulb & battery holder for mask, orig box (window torn),
    H4..$29.00
Wonder Woman, Ben Cooper, MIB $25.00
Woody Woodpecker, vinyl reinforced cloth, 1970, lg, VG+,
    T6..$6.00
Zorro, Ben Cooper, c WDP, 1960s, VG (cellophane missing
    on box) $45.00

Hartland Plastics, Inc.

Hartland Plastics, Inc., was formed in Hartland, Wisconsin, in the 1950s. The durable material used to make the figures was virgin acetate. Figures were hand painted with an eye for detail. The Western and Historic Horsemen, Minature Western Series, Authentic Scale Model Horses, Famous Gunfighter Series, and the Hartland Sports Series

of Famous Baseball Stars were a symbol of the fine workmanship of the 1950s. (There were also football, bowling, and religious statues.) Our advisor for this category is Terri Mardis-Ivers (I2).

Annie Oakley & Palomino, w/saddle, hat & gun, EX $175.00

Babe Ruth, replaced bat, EX, from $150.00 to $185.00.

Bat Masterson, w/cane, hat & pistol, EX, I2 ....$200.00
Bill Longley the Texan, missing horse & accessories, 6½",
    VG $37.50
Brave Eagle, w/horse, missing accessories, 9½", VG $75.00
Brave Eagle, w/horse & accessories, 9½", EX, I2.............$225.00
Bret Maverick, w/hat & guns, EX, I2 ....$170.00
Bret Maverick, w/horse, missing accessories, VG, I2 ....$50.00
Bret Maverick, w/horse, 5½", MOC................................$90.00
Bret Maverick, w/horse & saddle, hat & guns, NM, from
    $235 to..$300.00
Buffalo Bill, w/horse, US Mail saddle, hat & guns, EX, from
    $215 to..$245.00
Bullet, #700, 6", MIB..$75.00
Champ Cowboy, w/blk horse, red saddle & hat, EX.......$160.00
Champ Cowgirl, red shirt & wht pantskirt, NM..............$60.00

Chief Thunder Cloud, w/horse & accessories, NM, from $115
to $150.00
Chris Colt, missing accessories, EX, I2 ....$80.00

Cochise of Broken Arrow, 8" figure on 9" horse, with saddle, EX (VG box), $125.00.

Cochise, on blk & wht horse w/saddle, NM $100.00
Commanche Kid, w/horse, 8", M $75.00
Dale Evans, box only, EX $90.00
Dale Evans & Buttermilk, complete, EX, I2 ....$150.00
Dan Troop, no accessories, EX, I2................................$135.00
Davy Crockett, w/coonskin cap, frontier rifle, hunting knife, 7",
   on 8" horse w/accessories, EX (EX- box), A $500.00
Dick Groat, M, I2...$1,000.00
Don Drysdale, G $110.00
General Custer, w/horse, flag, hat, saddle & sword, EX, from
   $185 to $225.00
General Custer, w/horse, 9½", M $100.00
General George Washington, #815, on his war horse Ajax, com-
   plete, EX (NM box) $200.00
General Robert E Lee, w/horse, 9½", MIB.....................$250.00
Gil Favor, w/horse, 5½", MOC, from $50 to....................$85.00
Hoby Gilman, w/horse, 9½", EX $125.00
Horse, grazing mare, chestnut, A3................................$35.00
Horse, thoroughbred, buckskin, A3 ....$35.00
Horse, w/molded-on saddle & bridle, 6¼", EX................$15.00
Jim Bowie, w/horse & accessories, EX, I2 ....$150.00
Jim Hardie, w/horse, 5½", M, from $30 to.......................$50.00
Jim Hardie, w/horse, 9½", VG $50.00
Johnny McKay, w/horse, 9½", VG $100.00
Johnny Yuma, w/horse & accessories, EX, I2 ....$315.00
Lawman Gunfighter, w/hat & guns, complete, EX, I2....$160.00
Little Leaguer Bat Boy, 4", M, I2................................$265.00
Lone Ranger, w/horse, missing hat, 5½", VG, from $15 to .$25.00
Lone Ranger, w/horse, 9½", MIB.................................$275.00
Lucas McCain, w/horse, missing hat, 5½", VG, from $15 to ..$25.00
Lucas McCain, w/horse, 9½", EX $125.00
Matt Dillon, w/horse & accessories, 9½", MIB..............$250.00
Matt Dillon, 1950s, 7", w/orig box (rpr photocopy end flap),
   NM, A...$175.00
Matt Dillon's Horse, for sm figure, EX $22.50
Mickey Mantle, New York Yankees, EX $250.00

Maverick (James Garner) on horse, with saddle, NM, $235.00 to $300.00.

Paladin, w/horse, 9½", VG...$50.00
Paladin, w/horse & accessories, missing hat, sm, 5½", NM .$40.00
Polo Pony, gray, A3 ....$35.00
Roger Maris, NM $200.00

Tonto (Jay Silverheels) on horse, NM, $200.00.

Roger Maris, 25th-Anniversary edition, MIB $60.00
Roy Rogers, w/horse, missing accessories, 9½", VG $60.00
St Francis, 13" $55.00
Stan Musial, 25th-Anniversary, MIB $60.00
Tonto, w/horse, 9½", MIB..$275.00
Trigger, w/saddle, for lg figure, M $60.00
Turfking & Jockey (racehorse & jockey), w/saddle, EX, from
    $60 to $85.00
Ward Bond (Wagon Train), complete, NM $195.00
Westerner #5001, holding pistol over head, w/horse & hat, in
    scarce orig box (usually comes on card), NMIB, A .$195.00
Willie Mays, NM $240.00
Wyatt Earp, complete w/horse & hat, some pnt wear, 9½",
    EX..$60.00
Wyatt Earp, w/horse, saddle, hat & guns, 9½", NM, from $75
    to $100.00
Wyatt Earp, w/horse, 9½", MIB....................................$200.00

Horses

Horse riding being the order of the day, many children of the 19th century had their own horses to ride indoors; some were wooden while others were stuffed, and many had glass eyes and real horsehair tails. There were several ways to construct these horses so as to achieve a galloping action. The most common types had rocker bases or were mounted with a spring on each leg.

Hobby Horse, hide-covered w/wood rails, carved hooves, nose &
    mouth, glass eyes, 32x46", VG, A $250.00
Riding Horse, stuffed brn cloth w/fur mane, glass eyes, re-mtd on
    wood base w/hard rubber wheels, 28", G, A.............$130.00
Rocking Horse, pnt tin, w/jockey, on emb tin base, American,
    early, 7x7", EX, A $950.00

Rocking Horse, painted wood with glass eyes, leather saddle and horsehair tail, 52" long, G, A, $550.00.

Rocking Horse, pnt wood, dappled gray, w/tail & remnants of mane, stirrups, early 1900s, 24x49", some loose parts, A...$385.00

Hot Wheels

When they were introduced in 1968, Hot Wheels were an instant success. Sure, their racy style and flashy custom paint jobs were instant attention-getters, but what the kids loved most was the fact that they were fast! The fastest on the market! It's estimated that more than two billion Hot Wheels have been sold to date — every model with a little variation, keeping up with new trends in the big car industry. The line has included futuristic vehicles, muscle cars, trucks, hot rods, racers, and some military vehicles. Lots of these can still be found for very little, but if you want to buy the older models (collectors call them 'Red Lines' because of their red sidewall tires), it's going to cost you a little more, but many can still be found for under $25.00. By 1971, earlier on some models, black-wall tires had become the standard. A line of cars with Goodyear tires called Real Riders were made from 1983 until about 1987. Though recent re-releases have dampened the collector market somewhat, cars mint and in the original packages are holding their values and are still moving well. Near mint examples (no package) are worth about 40% to 50% (of MIP), excellent condition only about 25% to 35%. Collector pin-back buttons included in some of the packaging are worth from $3.00 to $5.00.

'31 Doozie, red line tires, orange, M, G3....................$20.00
'31 Ford Woody Classic, red line tires, lime, textured roof, M,
    G3...$25.00
'31 Ford Woody Classic, red line tires, metallic lime (unlisted
    color), NM+, W1...$21.00
'32 Ford Vicky Classic, red line tires, metallic orange, #6250,
    NM+, W1...$24.00
'34 Ford 3-Window, Real Riders, red w/flames, MBP, G3 .$15.00
'36 Ford Coupe Classic, red line tires, bl, MBP, G3.........$35.00
'36 Ford Coupe Classic, red line tires, metallic purple, NM+,
    W1..$16.00
'40 Woodie, blk walls, orange, 1980, NM+, A3...............$10.00
'40 Woodie, blk walls, yel, 1980, EX+, A3 ....$8.00
'40s Woodie, Real Riders, bl, MBP, G3...........................$20.00
'55 Chevy, blk walls, red & wht, 1986, MBP, A3 ....$35.00
'55 Chevy Nomad, Alive '55, red line tires, chrome, M,
    G3 ....$20.00
'55 Chevy Nomad Classic, red line tires, metallic bl, hood opens,
    NM+, W1...$34.00
'55 Chevy Nomad Classic, red line tires, metallic red, 1970,
    G+, A3...$25.00
'56 Hi-Tail Hauler, red line tires, orange, M, G3.............$25.00
'57 Chevy, red line tires, red, 1976, EX, A3 ....$5.00
'57 T-Bird Classic, red line tires, gold, NM, from $16 to ..$25.00
'63 Split Window Corvette, Real Riders, blk, M, G3 ....$20.00
'63 Split Window Coupe Corvette, blk walls, gray, 1980,
    NM+, A3...$6.00
'65 Mustang Convertible, wht walls, red, 1983, MBP, A3.$20.00
A-OK, blk walls, gr, 1978, NM+, A3 ....$12.00

Airport Rescue, blk walls, yel, 1981, NM, A3 .... $6.00

Ambulance, red line tires, gr, aqua & bl, NM, G3 .... $20.00

American Tipper, red line tires, red & wht, M, G3 .... $20.00

American Tipper, red line tires, wht, red & bl, 1976, NM+, A3 .... $15.00

American Victory, red line tires, bl, 1975, G+, A3 .... $10.00

American Victory, red line tires, bl, 1975, M, G3 .... $20.00

AMX/2, red line tires, magenta, M, G3 .... $30.00

Army Funny Car, blk walls, wht, 1982, NM, A3 .... $15.00

Backwoods Bomb, red line tires, gr, 1977, VG+, A3 .... $20.00

Beatnik Bandit, red line tires, lt bl, M, G3 .... $15.00

BMW M1, Real Riders, red, MBP, G3 .... $20.00

Braham Repco F1, red line tires, enamel gr, MBP, G3 ..... $25.00

Breakaway Bucket, red line tires, bl, 1974, G-, A3 .... $5.00

Bubble Gunner, blk walls, gr, 1978, G+, A3 .... $5.00

Bugeye, red line tires, lt bl, Shell Promo 1973, EX+, W1 . $22.00

Buzz-off, blk walls, gold, 1979, NM+, A3 .... $10.00

Buzz-off, red line tires, gold plated, M, G3 .... $20.00

California Cruiser, blk walls, silver, 1979, NM, A3 .... $10.00

Carabo, red line tires, lavender, EX, G3 .... $20.00

Chaparral 2G, red line tires, lt bl, orig spoiler, M, G3 ...... $20.00

Chevy Monza 2+2, red line tires, chrome, NM, G3 .... $20.00

Chief's Special, red line tires, red & lt bl, NM, G3 .... $25.00

Cobra Classic, Real Riders, bl, MBP, G3 .... $30.00

Cool 1 Dragster, red line tires, plum, wht & yel decal, NM+, W1 .... $29.00

Cord Classic, red line tires, bl, no roof or hood, NM, G3 . $40.00

Corvette Stingray, blk walls, gold, 1979, NM+, A3 .... $25.00

Corvette Stingray, blk walls, orange, 1980, NM+, A3 ...... $10.00

Corvette Stingray, blk walls, silver, 1978, NM+, A3 .... $25.00

Corvette Stingray, red line tires, red w/ribbons, M, G3 .... $25.00

Custom AMX, red line tires, orange, NM, G3 .... $25.00

Custom Barracuda, red line tires, purple, EX+, G3 .... $15.00

Custom Continental, red line tires, red & aqua, EX+, G3 . $10.00

Custom Corvette, red line tires, gold, NM, W1 .... $38.00

Custom Cougar, red line tires, metallic bl, NM+, W1 ...... $39.00

Custom Eldorado, red line tires, metallic gr, NM+, W1 ... $34.00

Custom Eldorado, red line tires, olive, NM, G3 .... $15.00

Custom Firebird, red line tires, gold, NM+, W1 .... $28.00

Custom Firebird, red line tires, orange, EX, G3 .... $20.00

Custom Fleetside, red line tires, metallic purple, NM+, W1 .... $39.00

Custom Mustang, red line tires, metallic lt gr, hood loose, NM+, W1 .... $39.00

Custom Police Cruiser, red line tires, blk & wht, NM, G3 . $35.00

Custom T-Bird, red line tires, bl, EX+, G3 .... $20.00

Custom VW, red line tires, brn, M, G3 .... $20.00

Custom VW, red line tires, metallic red, NM+, W1 .... $16.00

Demon, red line tires, bl, M, G3 .... $25.00

Deora, red line tires, lime, no boards, G+, A3 .... $10.00

Dixie Challenger, blk walls, orange, 1981, NM, A3 .... $6.00

Dodge D-50, Real Riders, metallic bl, NM+, W1 .... $4.50

Dodge D-50, Real Riders, wht, MBP, G3 .... $25.00

Dodge Rampage, Real Riders, red, MBP, G3 .... $15.00

Double Vision, red line tires, dk bl, 1973, NM-, W1 .... $56.00

Dream Van XGW, Real Riders, magenta, M, G3 .... $25.00

Dump Truck, red line tires, bl or gr, EX+, G3 .... $20.00

Dumpin' A, blk walls, yel, 1979, NM, A3 .... $10.00

Dune Daddy, red line tires, flourescent lime, 1973, NM, W1 .... $49.00

El Ray Special, red line tires, gr, NM, G3 .... $15.00

Emergency Squad, red line tires, red, NM+, G3 .... $15.00

Evil Weevil, red line tires, bl, EX, G3 .... $20.00

Ferrari 312P, red line tires, red enamel #60, M, G3 .... $20.00

Fire Chaser, blk walls, red, 1979, NM, A3 .... $5.00

Fire Chief Cruiser, red line tires, red, M, from $18 to $25.00

Fire Eater, blk walls, red, 1977, NM+, A3 .... $8.00

Fire Engine, red line tires, metallic red cab, M, G3 .... $35.00

Fire Engine, Old #5, 1980, 3", M, $6.00.

Firebird Hotbird, blk walls, gold, 1979, NM+, A3 .... $20.00

Ford Mark IV, red line tires, metallic gold, NM+, W1 .... $9.00

Ford Mark IV, red line tires, red enamel, NM, G3 .... $15.00

Formula Fever, Real Riders, yel, MBP, G3 .... $20.00

Formula PACK, blk walls, blk w/yel #8 decal, EX+, W1 .... $4.50

Formula PACK, red line tires, blk, 1976, G+, A3 .... $10.00

Formula 5000, red line tires, wht, 1976, VG+, A3 .... $10.00

Fuel Tanker, red line tires, wht, EX+, G3 .... $25.00

GMC Motor Home, blk walls, orange, 1977, NM, A3 ..... $12.00

Grasshopper, red line tires, magenta, M, G3 .... $25.00

Greased Gremlin, blk walls, red, 1979, VG+, A3 .... $15.00

Gremlin Grinder, red line tires, gr, M, G3 .... $30.00

Greyhound Bus, blk walls, silver, 1980, NM+, A3 .... $12.00

Greyhound Bus, 1970, 3", M, $15.00.

Gun Bucket, red line tires, olive, M, G3 .... $15.00

Hairy Hauler, red line tires, lime, M, G3 .... $25.00

Hare Opinion, blk walls, yel, 1979, NM, A3......................$6.00

Hare Splitter, blk walls, wht, 1979, NM+, A3 ....$8.00

Heavy Chevy, red line tires, gr, bl & red, NM, G3...........$20.00

Heavyweights, Dump Truck, red line tires, metallic brn, M, W1...$24.00

Heavyweights, Fire Engine, metallic red, orig ladder, wht interior, NM+, W1..$24.00

Heavyweights, Fuel Tanker, wht, MBP (sm crack in blister), W1...$135.00

Heavyweights, Moving Van, red line tires, metallic gr, customized w/US map decals, NM+, W1 ....$26.00

Heavyweights, Scooper, metallic lime, NM+, W1...........$49.00

Heavyweights, Team Trailer, metallic red, MBP, W1 ....$130.00

Hi-Tail Hauler, blk walls, bl, 1979, NM, A3.....................$8.00

Highway Patrol #12, blk walls, blk & wht, 1979, NM, A3 .$5.00

Hood, red line tires, magenta, NM, G3............................$20.00

Hot Heap, red line tires, purple, NM, G3 ....$20.00

Ice 'T,' red line tires, #6184, 1971, MBP, from $25 to......$30.00

Incredible Hulk, blk walls, yel, 2 rear windows, NM, W1...$9.50

Indy Eagle, red line tires, brn, NM, G3 ....$20.00

Indy Eagle, 1969, red line tires, with collector pin-back button, M (VG card), $28.00.

Inside Story, blk walls, yel, 1979, NM, A3.........................$8.00

Jack Rabbit Special, red line tires, wht w/blk interior, NM +, W1...$14.00

Jaguar XJS, blk walls, gold, XJS/Jag decal, NM, W1 ....$8.50

Jeep Scrambler, Real Riders, metallic bl, M, G3................$15.00

Jet Threat, red line tires, lime gr, no canopy, NM-, G3....$15.00

Khaki Kooler, red line tires, olive, NM, G3 ....$20.00

King Kuda, red line tires, chrome, M, G3 ....$45.00

Large Charge, blk walls, orange, 1979, NM, A3 ....$5.00

Large Charge, red line tires, chrome, M, G3....................$20.00

Lickety 6, blk walls, bl, 1978, NM+, A3 ....$10.00

Light My Firebird, red line tires, bl, MBP, G3 ....$35.00

Lightning Gold, Real Riders, yel, MBP, G3......................$15.00

Lola GT70, red line tires, metallic red, MBP (Canadian), W1...$19.00

Lotus Turbine, red line tires, bl, M, G3............................$15.00

Lowdown, red line tires, bl, flying low, NM, G3...............$30.00

Lowdown, red line tires, bl, 1976, G, A3 ....$10.00

Lowdown, red line tires, gold, 1977, EX, A3.....................$15.00

Mantis, red line tires, lime, M, G3 ....$15.00

Maxi Taxi, red line tires, yel, NM+, G3............................$30.00

Maxi Taxi, red line tires, yel, 1976, G+, A3 ....$10.00

McLaren M6A, red line tires, orange, M, G3.....................$20.00

Mercedes 280SL, red line tires, metallic aqua, NM, W1 ..$15.00

Mighty Maverick, red line tires, lime, M, G3....................$40.00

Minitrek, blk walls, wht, 1983, NM, A3............................$10.00

Mirada Stocker, blk walls, red, 1981, NM+, A3 ....$8.00

Mod Quad, red line tires, gold, 1969, NM+, A3................$18.00

Mongoose, red line tires, red w/decals, 1970, EX, A3 ....$25.00

Mongoose (no decals), red line tires, red, 1970, EX, A3...$15.00

Monte Carlo Stocker, red line tires, yel, #38, M, G3........$30.00

Moving Van, red line tires, bl w/gray trailer, NM, G3......$25.00

Mustang Boss Hoss, red line tires, chrome, M, G3............$35.00

Mustang Stocker, red line tires, chrome, orange & magenta, Ford/450 decals, NM+, W1 ....$49.00

Neet Streeter, blk walls, bl, 1976, NM+, A3 ....$15.00

Neet Streeter, red line tires, bl, M, G3.............................$30.00

Nitty Gritty Kitty, red line tires, metallic gr, MBP (Canadian), W1...$49.00

Nomad Classic, red line tires, lime & gold, M, G3 ....$35.00

Noodle Head, red line tires, red, M-, G3...........................$30.00

Odd Rod, blk walls, yel, flame decal, NM-, W1 ....$7.50

Olds 442, red line tires, metallic magenta, orig wing, decal residue, NM, W1 ....$199.00

P-911, red line tires, chrome w/gr & red stripes, M, G3 ...$25.00

P-928, Real Riders, red, M, G3..$12.00

Packin' Pacer, blk walls, yel, 1977, NM+, A3 ....$5.00

Paddy Wagon, blk walls, bl, 1977, NM+, A3 ....$8.00

Paddy Wagon, red line tires, bl, MBP (pack has lt wear), G3...$30.00

Paramedic Van, blk walls, yel, 1977, NM, A3 ....$15.00

Paramedic Van, red line tires, wht, M, G3........................$25.00

Path Beater, Real Riders, blk, MBP, G3............................$20.00

Pavement Pounder, Real Riders, gr, M, G3.......................$12.00

Peeping Bomb, red line tires, metallic gr, 1970, EX+, A3..$10.00

Pit Crew Car, red line tires, wht, orig decals & tools, EX, W1...$26.00

Poison Pinto, red line tires, gr, 1975, M, G3.....................$25.00

Police Cruiser-Olds, red line tires, wht, State Police, NM, G3...$35.00

Porsche 917, red line tires, lime gr, M, G3 ....$20.00

Power Pad, red line tires, chrome, M, G3.........................$20.00

Power Pad, red line tires, metallic red, orig top, NM+, W1 .$34.00

Power Plower, Real Riders, red, 'Brians' decal, MBP, G3 .$20.00

Prowler, blk walls, chrome, 1978, NM, A3 ....$15.00

Prowler, red line tires, chrome devil decal, MBP, G3.......$30.00

Python, red line tires, red, MBP, from $35 to $40.00

Racebait, blk walls, gold, 1979, NM+, A3 ....$20.00

Ranger Rig, blk walls, gr, 1975, NM, A3...........................$10.00

Ranger Rig, red line tires, gr, 1975, EX, A3.....................$12.00

Rash 1, Indy Style Racer, red line tires, metallic bl, NM, W1 ....$34.00

Red Baron, red line tires, metallic red w/spike & decal, NM, G3 ....$15.00

Rockbuster, blk walls, gr, 1980, NM+, A3 ....$8.00

Rockbuster, red line tires, chrome, M, G3 ....$25.00

Rockbuster, red line tires, yel, 1976, EX, A3....................$10.00

Rolls Royce SS, red line tires, silver w/dk interior, M, G3.$20.00

Ruby Red Passion, wht walls, red, 1991, MBP, A3 ....$25.00

S'Cool Bus, red line tires, yel, orig blower, cage, prop & decals (except blk stripes), EX, W1 ....$99.00

Science Friction, blk walls, wht, 1978, NM, A3 ....$8.00

Seasider, red line tires, metallic magenta, orig boat, NM+, W1 ....$49.00

Shelby Turbine, red line tires, metallic aqua, orig decals, NM+, W1 ....$10.00

Show Hoss II, Mustang Funny Car, blk walls, yel, orig seat, NM-, W1 ....$17.50

Showoff, red line tires, red, 1973, G+, A3 ....$25.00

Side Kick, red line tires, red, EX, G3.................................$35.00

Silhouette, red line tires, lime, 1967, EX, A3....................$8.00

Six Shooter Racer, 1970, Ex, $35.00.

Snake Funny Car, red line tires, yel, EX, A3/W1 ....$29.00

Snake II, red line tires, wht, NM+, G3 ....$35.00

Space Van (scene), blk walls, silver, 1979, NM+, from $15 to $25.00

Special Delivery, red line tires, bl w/decals, M, G3...........$35.00

Spiderman, blk walls, blk, 1979, NM+, A3 ....$10.00

Splittin' Image, red line tires, metallic orange, M, W1 .....$14.00

Spoiler Sport, blk walls, gold, 1979, NM+, A3 ....$20.00

Spoiler Sport, blk walls, wht, 1982, MBP, A3...................$15.00

Stagefright, blk walls, brn, 1978, NM, A3..........................$8.00

Steam Roller, red line tires, wht, 3 star decals, NM+, W1.$27.00

Street Rodder 4x4, red line tires, blk, M, G3 ....$25.00

Strip Teaser, red line tires, flourescent gr, Shell promo, 1973, NM, W1 ....$49.00

Sugar Daddy, red line tires, metallic red, orig decals, NM, W1...$23.00

Super Scraper, Real Riders, blk, 'Henry's' decal, MBP (rip in pack), G3...$15.00

Super Van, red line tires, blk, M, G3 ....$25.00

SWAT Van, blk walls, bl w/scene, 1979, NM+, A3.........$20.00

Swingin' Wing, red line tires, lime gr w/spots, MBP, G3..$30.00

T-bird Stocker, blk walls, wht, Valvoline/#21 decals, EX, W1 ....$7.50

T-Bucket, blk walls, yel, 1989, EX, A3 ....$5.00

T-Totaler, blk walls, blk, 1977, NM, A3...........................$20.00

T-4-2, red line tires, lime, M, G3 ....$50.00

Thor Van, 1978, MIP, F1 ....$15.00

TNT Bird, red line tires, metallic gr, orig decals, NM, W1.$24.00

Torino Stocker, blk walls, blk, 1979, NM, A3 ....$10.00

Torino Stocker, red line tires, red, #23 decal, M, G3 ....$25.00

Tough Customer Army Tank, red line tires, olive gr, NM+, W1 ....$14.00

Tri-Baby, red line tires, metallic red, NM+, W1 ....$6.00

Turbo Mustang, blk walls, orange or yel, 1981, NM+, A3 ....$8.00

Turbofire, red line tires, brn or bl, M, G3 ....$12.00

Twinmill, red line tires, lt gr, 1968, G+, A3 ....$6.00

Twinmill, red line tires, metallic gold, M, G3...................$20.00

Twinmill II, red line tires, chrome, M, G3........................$25.00

Vette Van, blk walls, blk, Vette Van tampo, NM, W1.......$4.50

VW, red line tires, orange, lady bug roof, EX, A3 ....$5.00

VW Beach Bomb, red line tires, M, G3 ....$50.00

Warpath, red line tires, red, 1969, NM, A3 ....$6.00

What 4, red line tires, metallic magenta, EX, W1 ....$34.00

Whip Creamer, red line tires, lime, M, G3 ....$20.00

Winnipeg, red line tires, yel, orange & bl decal, missing wing, VG, W1 ....$14.00

X-ploder, red line tires, dk gr, 1973, NM-, W1 ....$76.00

Z-Whiz, blk walls, gr, 1977, NM+, A3 ....$10.00

Sizzlers, Hot Wheels

Ford Mark IV, red line tires, gold, EX+, A3 ....$15.00

Gurney Eagle, red line tires, bl, EX+, A3 ....$15.00

Hot Wheels Sizzler Train, 1970s, MIB, T1 ....$145.00

Locomotive, blk walls, gold, EX+, A3...............................$15.00

Mustang, red line tires, gold, in box, EX+, A3.................$25.00

Sideburn, red line tires, blk, EX+, A3 ....$15.00

Straight Scoop, red line tires, orange, EX+, A3 ....$15.00

Accessories

Car Carrier Showcase Plaque, red or bl, 1969, new but dirty, MOC (NM card), W1 ....$39.00

Case, adjustable, 24-car, bl & wht cars on front, 1969, NM-, W1 ....$24.00

Custom Shop Showcase Plaque, red or yel, new but dirty, 1969, M (EX- card), W1 ....$29.00

Finishing Gate, 2-car w/flag, 1968, NM+, W1 ....$5.00

Hot Turns, lot of 2 90-degree turn tracks, EX+, W1..........$8.00

Lap Counter, 1970, M (EX+ box), W1 ....$14.00

Mongoose & Snake Drag Race Set, #6438, w/orig cars, 4 parachutes, starting & finishing gates, +more, NMIB (VG box), W1...$249.00

Rumbler, Rip Snorter, orig driver w/training wheels, NM+, W1 ....$39.00

Starting Gate, 2-car, 1967, NM, W1 ....$5.00

Supercharger, 1968, EX-, W1 ....$15.00

Track, 5 2-foot sections w/4 connectors, EX, W1 ....$9.00

Trestle Pak, 1969, M (EX box), W1 ....$10.00
Universal Clamps, lot of 2, NM, W1 ....$5.00

Housewares

Back in the dark ages before women's lib and career-minded mothers, little girls emulated mommy's lifestyle, not realizing that by the time they grew up, total evolution would have taken place before their very eyes. They'd sew and bake, sweep, do laundry, and iron (gasp!), and imagine what fun it would be when *they* were big like mommy. Those little gadgets they played with are precious collectibles today, and any child-size houseware item is treasured, especially those from the forties and fifties. Values are suggested for items in excellent condition unless noted otherwise.

Cleaning

Automatic Dishwasher, Marx, MIB $150.00
Automatic Dishwasher, Rosco, battery-op, MIB $350.00
Bissell Sweeper, oak w/stenciled gold & blk lettering, normal
    wear, 8", VG, A $35.00
Sad Iron, Dolly Dover $40.00
Sad Iron, Sensible #6 ....$130.00
Washing Machine, Dutch town graphics w/windmills & ships,
    10x9", G, A $25.00

Washer, 10"; washtub with board; iron, all red painted tin, $150.00 for the set.

Cooking

Bake Set, aluminum, orig Campbell Kid illus box, 1940s-50s,
    M $48.00

Bake-a-Cake Set, Wolverine, MIB $250.00
Betty Crocker Mini-Wave Oven, Kenner, NMIB $40.00
Busy Baker Pastry Set, Transogram, complete, 1957, MIB.$250.00
Cabinet & Table Combination, Wolverine, litho metal,
    1940s, MIB $100.00
Chafing Dish, brass, w/stand, 4¾" $45.00
Coffee Grinder, metal & wood, sm...................................$50.00
Cook Set, Mirro, Like Mother's, 16-pc, 1940s, MIB.......$450.00
Cutlery, Bo-Peep, MOC...$20.00
Doll-E-Do Dish Washing Set, Amsco, 1950s, M (VG box).$45.00
Ice Cream Freezer, White Mountain Junior, early 1900s,
    6½" $225.00
Iron & Ironing Board, Wolverine, MIB $75.00
Refrigerator, Japan, mc litho tin, litho interior of food & bever-
    ages, freezer door opens, orig box, 7", VG-EX, A.......$50.00

Refrigerator, Wolverine, 17", with toy food inside, EX, $65.00.

Teakettle, cast iron, Wagner, 3½", $140.00.

Refrigerator, Wolverine, litho metal, 1950s, MIB $100.00
Rolling pin, 1-pc wood $22.50
Sunbeam Mixer, w/2 bowls..$200.00
Waffle Iron, 3" base w/2¼" lid...$135.00

Serving

Akro Agate Play Time set, 7-pc, MIB, $140.00.

Baby Dish, Buffalo Pottery, mc transfer on ceramic, Dolly Din-
    gle-type boy & girl, minor crazing, 7½", VG, A $65.00
Cake Plate, Blue Willow, 5¼" $30.00
Caster set, 2 cruets, shaker, condiment jar in unmk metal stand,
    9½", EX, A..$150.00
Dishes, Akro Agate, Chiquita, transparent cobalt, 12-pc,
    MIB...$100.00
Dishes, mk Japan, rose design, 6 place settings w/casserole, plat-
    ter, shakers & coffeepot, M (VG box) $95.00
Dishes, wht w/gr trim, no mk, service for 6+teapot, sugar,
    creamer, 2 platters, soup tureen, VG, A $155.00
Pitcher, wht ironstone, 2"..$17.50
Tea Set, Blue Onion type, crossed swords on bottom, service for
    5, G, A $235.00
Tea set, caramel lustre w/scenes of children w/pets, teapot, sugar
    & creamer, 6 plates, 6 cups, 4 saucers, EX, A $85.00
Tea Set, Gaudy Staffordshire, Oyster pattern, teapot, sugar, creamer,
    4 plates, 1 orig cup & saucer +2 others, VG, A $360.00
Tea Set, ironstone w/rose-colored flowers, service for 5, mk
    Hawthorn, LP&Co, VG, A....................................$250.00
Tea Set, Little Bo-Peep, emb aluminum, 19-pc, MIB.......$35.00
Tea Set, Sunbonnet Babies, teapot, creamer, sugar bowl, 6 cups
    & saucers, cake plate, German, EX, A..................$1,000.00
Teapot, Sevres, ironstone, unmk, 5¼" $80.00
Waste Bowl, Ridgway's England, Humphrey's Clock, 1⅞" .$50.00

Sewing

Sewing Machine, Casige, Made in Germany, British Zone,
    VG+, P3 ....$50.00

**Casige #2, British Zone of Germany, NM, from $100.00
to $125.00.**

Sewing Machine, Jaymar, Sew Ette, complete w/attachments &
    instructions, late 1950s, MIB.......................................$80.00
Sewing Machine, Sew & Play, pk & wht plastic, w/battery-op
    pedal, EX..$25.00
Sewing Machine, Singer Sewhandy #20, MIB.................$98.00
Sewing Mate, yel & wht plastic, w/foot pedal, battery-op,
    NM $28.00

Miscellaneous

Adding Machine, Wolverine, ca 1937-38, 4½x9", MIB...$82.50
Chamber Set, porc w/gold floral, pitcher & bowl, chamber
    pot w/lid & bail, hair receiver, powder jar, open dish,
    EX, A $175.00
Doll Carriage, wood w/leather top & orig decor, 28x32" ..$400.00
Lamp, English, cased milk glass shade, metal base, clear chim-
    ney, 9½", VG, A..$100.00
Layette, Amsco, litho metal, complete w/accessories, M ..$175.00
My Merry Shoe Shining Set, Merry Mfg, dated 1953,
    MIB...$30.00

Wash set, Germany, 3½" pitcher, seven pieces, $175.00.

Nurse Kit, Transogram, 1967, MIB $10.00
Spinning Wheel, Remco, complete w/accessories, M (VG box) $50.00
Spinning Wheel, turned wood legs & features, appl wood decoration, 28", G, A $130.00
Weaving Loom, 1930s, NMIB..$60.00

Keystone

Though this Massachusetts company produced a variety of toys during their years of operation (ca 1920-late '50s), their pressed steel vehicles are the most collectible, and that's what we've listed here. As a rule they were very large, with some of the riders more than 30" in length.

Airmail Passenger Plane, mustard w/NP prop, red wheels w/rubber tires, sounds, 1929, 24x24x9½", A....................$900.00
American Railway Express Truck, blk cab, red chassis & wheels, dk gr screen-sided van, 26⅜", EX, A $1,650.00
Battleship w/Launching Glider, pnt wood & tin, no cannon shells, VG $40.00
Dump Truck, blk w/red chassis & wheels, working dump bed, rpr crank, lt rust, 27", G, A..$185.00
Dump Truck, closed cab w/lights, crank operated, worn/flaking pnt, rust on wheels & cab, 10½x8x27", VG, A.......$275.00
Dump Truck, gr cab, orange bed, steel wheels, electric headlights, emb Keystone on doors, 23½", G, A.............$110.00
Dump Truck, open cab, scissors-type mechanism, well worn, 7¼x8x26", G-, A..$150.00

Fire Department Ladder and Hose Truck, 28" long, D10, $1,250.00.

Fire Dept Ladder Truck, red, steel wheels, bell on hood, 2 orig ladders & hose w/brass nozzle, 27⅞", G, A $770.00
Fire Dept Water Truck, blk cab, orange tank on gr bed, red chassis & wheels, incomplete nozzle, 23¼", VG, A $1,375.00
Fire Dept Water Truck, blk cab w/gr tank, some pnt chipping, missing cover for tank, 27", G, A...........................$1,000.00
Fire Truck, red w/rubber tires, steers, parts missing, rstr, 28", VG-EX, A...$185.00
Fire Truck Water Tower, w/'Real Pump,' crank on front pumps water to hose, tower raises/lowers, 13x32", EX, A..$700.00

Greyhound Coast-To-Coast Bus Rider, hinged top, 22", D10, EX, $2,600.00.

Moving Van (Long Distance), blk, red van & wheels, Packard decal, yel label (unusual), orig box, 26½", VG+, A.$1,485.00
Moving Van (Long Distance), blk & orange w/red chassis, steers, rpt, rear doors missing, 26", G-, A................$450.00
Police Patrol Van, blk w/screened sides, red chassis & wheels, Packard decal on radiator, 27¾", EX, A $2,145.00
Pullman Car, ride-on capability, 26", VG, A................$440.00
Railroad Engine, ride-on capability, 23", VG+, A..........$110.00
Railroad Wrecking Car, 21", VG, A $275.00
Ride 'Em Dump Truck Rider, bright gr cab & wheels, red bed, removable seat, rubber tires, decal, 24½", VG, A....$358.00
Road Roller Rider, gray w/red wheels, roof (seat) & hdl, decal on right side, roof dent, wood hdl, 20", G-VG, A $550.00
Steam Shovel, gray, red & blk, wood hdl, old rpt, 20", G, A $121.00
Truck Loader, scoops on chain take load to funnel, decals ea side, 17x20", G, A $100.00
US Mail Truck, blk, gr & red, rear doors missing, 26", G .$300.00
US Mail Truck, blk cab, olive-gr screened van, red chassis & wheels, Packard decal, orig box, 26½", EX, A $1,155.00
US Mail Truck, blk cab, red chassis & wheels, dk olive screen sides, Packard decal, 26⅜", NM, A......................$1,760.00
Wrecker, open, no doors, considerable rpt, 11x27", G, A..$500.00

Lehmann

Lehmann toys were made in Germany as early as 1881. Their early toys were sometimes animated by means of an inertia-generated flywheel; later, clockwork mechanisms were used. Some of their best-known turn-of-the-century toys were actually very racist and unflattering to certain ethnic groups. But the wonderful antics they perform and the imagination that went into their conception have made them and all the other Lehmann toys favorites with collectors today. Though the company faltered with the onset of WWI, they were quick to recover and during the war years produced some of their best toys, several of which were copied by their competitors. Business declined after WWI. Lehmann died in 1934, but the company continued in business for awhile under the direction of Lehmann's partner and cousin, Johannes Richter.

Windups, Frictions, and Other Mechanicals

Alabama Coon Jigger, #695, blk-skinned jigger in blk jacket & red plaid pants atop mk base; NM (G box), M5 ......**$900.00**

Alabama Coon Jigger, EX, D10, $650.00.

Autobus, red with yellow striping and white top, 8", EX, $1,500.00.

Anxious Bride Nanni, litho & pnt tin, cloth & fur outfit, paper hanky, clockwork, working, 8½", G-VG, A $1,100.00

Autobus #590, red & beige litho tin dbl-decker open-top bus w/driver, rear stairway, seats atop, 8", EX $1,500.00

Balky Mule, clown in cart pulled by flocked mule, 7½", EX+ (EX box), A, $575.00.

Bucking Bronco, Wild West, pnt tin cowboy & horse on platform, EX+ (NM+ box), from $500 to $700.00

Bucking Bronco, Wild West; pnt & litho tin, 7", VG+, A .$385.00

Climbing Monkey, monkey climbs up string, 8", EX (G box), A...$265.00

Climbing Monkey, monkey climbs up string when finger loops are pulled; Pat 1892, 8", VG+ $135.00

Crawling Beetle, 3", M, D10, $300.00.

Crawling Beetle, litho tin, w/orig box, 4", EX, A $264.00

Dancing Sailor, pnt & litho tin, cloth clothes, 8", VG, A $275.00

Daredevil, man in gr jacket & gr & yel hat drives red cart pulled by zebra, 4½x7", EX, A.................................$375.00

Echo Motorcycle, #725, early, 9", G- $750.00

EPL-1 Zeppelin, litho tin, missing rear fin components, 7½", G, A..$132.00

EPL-1 Zeppelin, litho tin, 2 tabs missing, 2 tabs rpl, no celluloid fins, 7½", EX+, M5 ....$550.00

Galop Auto, litho tin, yel & bl w/red wheels & wht tires, working, 5¾", VG-EX, A $500.00

Garage & Sedan, litho tin, gr sedan, mc litho tin garage, working, G-VG, A...$525.00
Garage w/2 Cars, litho tin, w/up sedan & Galop race car, 6x7" garage, EX, A...$1760.00
Gustav the Miller, litho tin, moves on pole, cement bag drops on head at top of pole, 17", EX+ (NM box), A.......$580.00

Halloh Motorcycle, ca 1930s, 7x8", EX, D10, $2,400.00.

Hansom Cab, pnt & litho tin, maroon cab w/gray roof, working, 5¼", VG, A...$1100.00
Heavy Swell, litho tin man w/checked cloth coat holds cane, 8½", VG, A...$827.00
Hip-Hop Rabbit, friction, early 1960s, 3¼", MIB.............$25.00
Ito Limousine, litho tin, red & blk w/wht trim, clockwork, working, touch-up, 7", G-VG, A $550.00
Ito Limousine, red w/blk roof, 1913, 7", EX, A...............$725.00
Man Pushing Woman in Stroller Chair, litho tin, inertia toy, G+, A..$770.00
Mars Tricycle, w/man rider, pnt & litho tin, G+, A.......$440.00
Masayama (Rickshaw), pnt tin, inertia toy, G, A..........$440.00
Motorcoach, w/driver, pnt & litho tin, 5", G, A $300.00
Naughty Boy, in bl Victorian outfit holds steering rod of early auto, father's arm moves as if to hit him, NM (G box), A...$1500.00
OHO Automobile, open car, early 1900s style, Pat dates, mks, 3¾x4", G-, A $200.00
OHO Automobile, open car, EX....................................$500.00
Paddy Pig, man riding pig, EX+, A $1105.00
Paddy Pig, man riding pig, pig goes in circles, man goes sideways, man's cloth coat rpl, much rpt, 5½x5¼", G-, A $225.00
Performing Sea Lion, pnt tin, some rpt, 7", G, A $200.00
Quack-Quack, duck pulls cart carrying 3 sm ducks, 7", EX, A...$395.00
Rad Cycle (Anxious Bride), pnt & litho tin, w/up cycle w/rider, working, lt pnt chips, 8½", VG, A.........................$2500.00
Sea Lion, pnt tin, dk yel & gray w/red collar, clockwork, working, sm pnt chips, 7½", VG, A $60.00

Spiral Sailor, 2½" litho tin sailor spirals down tube, ca 1900, 14", A $440.00
St Vincent Warship, litho tin, red, gr & yel, clockwork, working, rpl parts, 13¾", G, A $200.00
Tap Tap Man w/Wheelbarrow, litho tin, 5½", VG, A ...$330.00
Tut-Tut, pnt & litho tin, wht w/red trim, clockwork, bellows mechanism, working, right arm missing, 6½", VG ..$800.00

Tut-Tut, man driving car and blowing horn, 6½", VG, A, $800.00.

Tut-Tut, pnt & litho tin, man in open car blowing horn, working 7", EX, A $1,760.00
UHU Amphibious Car, pnt tin body w/litho windshield & hood, pnt tin driver, clockwork, working, 9", VG, A $900.00
Velleda Car, litho tin, orange, wht & blk, driver in bl, clockwork, working, rear seats missing, 9½", VG, A $1,250.00
Zikra, #752, in cart pulled by bucking zebra, 7x5", EX, A..$535.00
Zirka, #752, zebra pulls cart w/driver, 7", NMIB, A $1,100.00

Lunch Boxes

When the lunch box craze began in the mid-1980s, it was only the metal boxes that so quickly soared to sometimes astronomical prices. But today, even the plastic and vinyl ones are collectible. Though most lunch box dealers agree, prices have become much more reasonable than they were at first, they're still holding their own and values seem to be stabilizing. So pick a genre and have fun. There are literally hundreds to choose from, and just as is true in other areas of character-related collectibles, the more desirable lunch boxes are those with easily recognized, well-known subjects — western heroes, TV, Disney and other cartoon characters, and famous entertainers. Thermoses are collectible as well. In our listings, values are just for the box unless a thermos is mentioned in the description. If you'd like to learn more about them, we recommend A *Pictorial Price Guide to Metal Lunch Boxes and Thermoses* and a companion book A *Pictorial Price Guide to Vinyl and Plastic Lunchboxes*, by Larry Aikins. For more pricing information, Philip R. Norman (Norman's Olde Store) has prepared a listing of hundreds of boxes, thermoses, and their variations. He is listed in the Categories of Special Interest under Lunch Boxes. Our advisor for this category is Terri Mardis-Ivers (I2).

Metal

A-Team, 1985, w/thermos, M, N2 ....$25.00
Adam-12, 1972, EX, N2 ....$49.00
Adam-12, 1972, w/thermos, VG, I2 ....$35.00
Addams Family, 1974, G-, N2 ....$19.00
Addams Family, 1974, w/thermos, VG-EX, from $70 to ..$85.00
Animal Friends, 1975, VG, N2 ....$16.00
Annie, 1981, w/hang tag, M, I2...$30.00
Annie, 1981, w/thermos, EX, I2 ....$15.00
Annie Oakley, Canadian, EX, M5 ....$190.00

Astronaut, domed top, American Thermos, VG+, I2, $110.00.

Astronaut, dome, w/thermos, NM, M5............................$210.00
Astronaut, 1960, dome, VG+, I2 ....$110.00
Auto Race, 1967, VG+, N2...$25.00
Back in 76, 1975, EX-, N2...$39.00
Barn, doors closed, dome, EX+, M5 ....$60.00
Barn, doors open, hay & animals, dome, EX+, M5...........$60.00

Batman, 1966, VG, T2, $70.00.

Batman, 1966, Batman & Robin on front, bk & all 4 side panels, VG, T2...$70.00
Batman, 1966, Canadian Aladdin kit, w/thermos, EX-, I2..$130.00
Battle Kit, 1965, VG, N2..$49.00
Battle of the Planets, 1979, VG, N2..................................$17.00
Battlestar Galactica, 1978, EX..$38.00
Bedknobs & Broomsticks, 1972, EX $40.00
Bee Gees (Barry), 1978, w/thermos, EX, from $35 to $45.00
Berenstain Bears, 1983, VG+, N2 ....$20.00
Beverly Hillbillies, Canadian, VG+, M5 ....$100.00
Bionic Woman, 1977, getting out of red car, w/plastic thermos, EX, C1 ....$39.00
Bionic Woman, 1978, running, VG+, I2 ....$32.00
Black Hole, 1979, w/thermos, EX, N2 ....$40.00
Blondie, 1969, VG, I2..$48.00
Boating, 1959, VG, I2...$138.00
Bobby Sherman, 1972, EX, C1 ....$72.00
Bonanza, 1963, VG, from $55 to $65.00
Bonanza, 1965, VG, from $68 to $72.00

Buck Rogers, 1979, embossed scenes, with thermos, EX, $45.00.

Buck Rogers in the 25th Century, 1979, VG+, I2 ....$25.00
Bugaloos, 1971, VG, I2..$64.00
Cabbage Patch Kids, 1984, KST, EX-, I2 ....$10.00
Cabbage Patch Kids, 1984, w/thermos, M, N2..................$20.00
Campus Queen, 1967, VG, N2...$19.00
Canadian Train, Canadian, 1970, NM, M5......................$38.00
Care Bear Cousins, 1985, w/thermos, VG+, I2 ....$5.00
Care Bears, EX, O1..$10.00
Casey Jones, 1960, dome, VG+, I2..................................$215.00
Charlie's Angels, 1978, w/thermos, EX-, I2 ....$40.00
Chuck Wagon, 1958, dome, EX-, I2 ....$142.00
Clash of the Titans, 1980, VG-, O1..................................$15.00
Clash of the Titans, 1980, w/plastic thermos, EX+, C1 ....$29.50
Cracker Jack, 1979, w/thermos, EX, N2 ....$50.00
Cyclist, 1979, EX, N2 ....$40.00
Dark Crystal, 1982, w/thermos, M, from $25 to...............$35.00
Davy Crockett, 1955, Canadian, VG............................$130.00
Denim Diner, 1975, dome, w/thermos, EX, I2 ....$32.00
Dick Tracy, 1967, Canadian, VG, M5 ....$95.00
Dick Tracy, 1967, VG+, N2..$50.00

Dick Tracy, 1967, w/EX thermos, NM, I2......................$130.00
Disco Fever, 1980, VG-, I2 ....$8.00
Disney Express, 1979, w/thermos, some rust inside, EX, I2 ....$14.00
Disney Firefighters, 1969, dome, EX+, M5 ....$110.00
Disney Firefighters, 1969, dome, EX-, I2 ....$99.00
Disney on Parade, 1970, VG+, N2 ....$37.00
Disney's Fox & the Hound, 1981, w/plastic thermos, EX+-NM, C1 ....$36.00
Disney's Magic Kingdom, 1980, w/thermos, EX, O1........$25.00
Disneyland Monorail, 1960, VG+, I2 ....$120.00
Dr Dolittle, 1967, Canadian, EX $80.00
Dr Dolittle, 1967, VG-, N2 ....$29.00
Dragon's Lair, 1983, VG+, N2 ....$20.00
Dukes of Hazzard, 1980, VG+, I2 ....$12.00
Dukes of Hazzard, 1980, w/thermos & tags, M, I2............$30.00
Dukes of Hazzard, 1983, G...$20.00
Dynomutt, 1976, VG-, from $27 to $33.00
Emergency, 1973, VG+, N2 ....$17.00
Emergency, 1973, w/thermos, NM $50.00
Emergency, 1973, w/thermos, VG+, I2 ....$28.00
Empire Strikes Back, 1980, swamp scene, w/thermos, VG+, I2 ....$22.00
ET, 1982, w/tags, M, I2 ....$28.00
Evel Knievel, 1974, VG+, from $20 to..............................$35.00
Evel Knievel, 1974, w/thermos, EX, from $50 to $75.00
Fall Guy, 1981, EX, N2...$15.00
Family Affair, 1969, EX-, I2 ....$65.00
Fat Albert & Cosby Kids, 1973, VG, from $12 to.............$28.00
Fireball XL-5, 1964, VG $95.00
Flintstones & Dino, 1962, G, N2 ....$28.00
Flintstones & Dino, 1962, VG, I2 ....$59.00
Flipper, 1967, VG+, I2..$75.00
Floral, 1970, NM, M5 ....$28.00
Flying Nun, 1968, VG+, I2..$59.00
Fox & the Hound, 1981, VG, from $15 to.........................$20.00
Fox & the Hound, 1981, w/thermos, EX, I2......................$24.00
Fraggle Rock, 1984, EX-, I2 ....$14.00
Fruit Basket, 1975, VG-, N2 ....$15.00
Funtastic World of Hanna-Barbera, 1977, Huckleberry Hound, VG $25.00
Funtastic World of Hanna-Barbera, 1977, w/Flintstones & Yogi, VG, from $22 to...$29.00
Gene Autry, 1954, VG+, I2...$155.00
Gentle Ben, 1968, w/thermos, VG+, I2 ....$75.00
Get Smart, 1966, w/thermos, EX.....................................$235.00
Ghostland, 1977, VG+, N2 ....$29.00
GI Joe, 1967, EX-, I2..$74.00
GI Joe, 1982, w/plastic thermos, EX, I2............................$11.00
Gomer Pyle USMC, 1966, VG+, N2 ....$79.00
Gomer Pyle USMC, 1966, w/thermos, VG, I2 ....$75.00
Goober & the Ghost Chasers, 1974, w/thermos, EX $45.00
Green Hornet, 1965, King Seeley, G-VG, A...................$135.00
Gremlins, 1984, EX, I2 ....$16.00
Gremlins, 1984, w/plastic thermos, VG, from $12 to $15.00
Guns of Will Sonnett, 1968, VG+, N2 ....$59.00
Gunsmoke, 1959, VG, I2 ....$90.00
Gunsmoke, 1973, VG, N2 ....$39.00

Gunsmoke, Matt Dillon, US Marshall, 1958, w/thermos, EX, $150.00.

Hair Bear Bunch, 1971, VG, I2..$29.00
Happy Days, 1976, w/thermos, VG-, N2 ....$15.00
Hardy Boys Mysteries, 1977, VG+, I2 ....$18.00
Harlem Globetrotters, 1971, VG+, I2 ....$23.00
Harlem Globetrotters, 1971, w/thermos, EX, I2................$48.00
He-Man & Masters of the Universe, 1984, EX, I2 ....$8.00
Heathcliff, 1982, VG, O1 ....$12.00
Heathcliff, 1982, w/thermos, M, N2.................................$20.00
Hector Heathcote, 1964, VG+, from $95 to....................$130.00
Hogan's Heroes, 1966, dome, EX+, M5...........................$150.00
Hogan's Heroes, 1966, dome, VG, I2...............................$100.00
Holly Hobbie, 1972, bl, standing sideways w/flowers, G, I2 ....$8.00
Holly Hobbie, 1975, profile w/flowers, VG+, I2 ....$13.00
Hopalong Cassidy, blk, w/thermos, VG $175.00
Hopalong Cassidy, red, w/thermos, G $85.00
Hot Wheels, 1969, VG+, N2 ....$25.00
How the West Was Won, 1978, no handle, VG-, I2........$17.00
How the West Was Won, 1978, w/thermos, EX, N2........$45.00
Howdy Doody, 1977, w/plastic thermos, VG $28.00
Huckleberry Hound & Friends, Quickdraw McGraw on bk, VG...$65.00
Inch-High Private Eye/Goober & the Ghost Chasers, 1974, VG, I2...$29.00
Incredible Hulk, 1978, no thermos, VG, N2.....................$14.00
Incredible Hulk, 1978, w/thermos, EX.............................$30.00
Indiana Jones & Temple of Doom, 1984, EX+, I2 ....$19.00
Indiana Jones & Temple of Doom, 1984, w/thermos, M, N2 ....$35.00
James Bond 007, 1966, VG- $55.00
Jet Patrol, 1957, EX, M5...$280.00
Joe Palooka, 1948, scarce, 7", EX+-NM, A.....................$120.00
Johnny Lightning, 1970, EX-, N2....................................$40.00
Jonathon Livingston Seagull, 1974, w/thermos, NM, T1 ....$100.00
Jungle Book, 1966, VG+, I2...$65.00
Junior Miss, 1966, w/thermos, VG, I2 ....$10.00
Junior Miss, 1978, w/girl in mirror, G+, I2 ....$9.00

Jetsons, 1960s, dome, w/thermos, EX, A, $650.00.

King Kong, 1977, NM, C1...$54.00
King Kong, 1977, w/thermos, VG, I2.............................$26.00
Korg 70,000 BC; 1975, VG+, O1......................................$40.00
Kroft Supershow, 1976, w/thermos, VG+, I2...................$38.00

Kung Fu, 1974, EX, from $30.00 to $35.00.

Kung Fu, 1974, w/thermos, EX $50.00
Land of the Giants, NM $125.00
Land of the Giants, 1968, VG+, N2 ....$69.00
Lawman, 1961, NM, M5 ....$125.00
Legend of the Lone Ranger, 1980, w/thermos, VG-, N2 ..$30.00
Little Dutch Miss, 1959, VG, N2 ....$60.00
Lone Ranger, 1954, EX, M5 ....$280.00
Looney Tunes TV Set, 1959, Warner Bros, VG, N2......$115.00
Major League Baseball, 1968, front EX+, bk VG, I2 ....$15.00
Man From UNCLE, 1966, G-, O1 ....$45.00
Marvel Comics Super Heroes, 1976, VG, O1 ....$18.00
Marvel Comics Super Heroes, 1976, w/thermos, NM, M5 .$60.00
Mary Poppins, 1964, VG, N2 ....$35.00
Masters of the Universe, 1983, w/thermos, VG $13.00
Mickey Mouse Club (cartoon), 1976, w/thermos, VG- $29.00
Miss America, 1972, VG+, N2...$30.00
Mr Merlin, 1981, EX, N2...$20.00

Ludwig von Drake in Disneyland, G, $65.00.

Mr Merlin, 1981, w/thermos, M, N2 ....$35.00
New Mickey Mouse Club, w/thermos, VG-VG+, from $30
    to...$35.00
Partridge Family, 1971, VG+, N2.....................................$29.00
Peanuts, 1976-79, red, Charlie Brown pitching & Snoopy
    marching, VG, T6 ....$10.00
Peanuts, 1980, yel, w/thermos, M, N2..............................$25.00
Pigs in Space, 1977, EX-, N2 ....$20.00
Pigs in Space, 1977, w/thermos, EX, N2 ....$40.00
Plaid, 1955, w/thermos, VG, O1 ....$28.00
Polly Pal, 1974, VG+, N2..$20.00
Popples, 1986, w/thermos, G $10.00

Play Ball Magnetic Game Lunch Kit, King-Seely Thermos
Co, no thermos, 1969, minor rust and denting, A, $50.00.

Racing Wheels, 1977, EX, N2 ....$50.00
Rat Patrol, 1967, VG, from $40 to $55.00
Return of the Jedi, 1983, VG, O1............................$22.00
Rifleman, 1961, VG, M5..$130.00
Robin Hood, 1974, VG, N2.......................................$25.00
Rough Rider, 1972, G+, N2 ....$15.00

Roy Rogers and Dale Evans, Double R Bar Ranch, 1953, w/thermos, EX, $150.00.

Roy Rogers & Dale Evans, 1955, 8 scenes on bk, G+, N2 ..$39.00
Scooby Doo, 1973, yel, w/thermos, EX, N2 ....$60.00
Secret Agent T, 1968, VG+, N2.....................................$35.00
Secret of Nimh, 1982, w/thermos, NM, N2 ....$25.00
Six Million-Dollar Man, 1974, VG+, N2 ....$15.00
Sleeping Beauty, 1960, Canadian, no hdl, VG, M5 ....$160.00
Snow White & the Seven Dwarfs, litho tin w/dbl hdls, mk Belgium, VG, T1 ....$345.00
Space Shuttle Orbiter Enterprise, 1977, VG-, O1 ....$25.00

Space: 1999, King-Seeley, no thermos, 1975, VG+, $29.00.

Space Shuttle Orbiter Enterprise, 1977, w/thermos, EX, N2 ....$50.00
Speed Buggy, 1973, VG, N2 ....$18.00
Star Trek, 1967, dome, NM $800.00
Street Hawk, 1985, VG+ $69.00
Super Friends, 1976, w/thermos, VG+, N2 ....$23.00
Superman, 1978, EX- $20.00
Tarzan, Canadian, EX...$85.00
Tom Corbett Space Cadet, 1952, EX, M5 ....$330.00
Tom Corbett Space Cadet, 1952, red, NM decal, VG, T1..$110.00
Train, 1970, CP Rail, M, N2 ....$35.00
Transformers, 1986, w/thermos, EX.............................$15.00
Traveler, 1962, bl w/red rims, G, N2.............................$19.00
Traveler, 1964, brn w/brn rims, VG+, N2.......................$29.00
Universal's Movie Monsters, 1979, VG+, N2...................$40.00
Voyage to the Bottom of the Sea, 1967, VG, I2 ....$85.00
Wagon Train, 1964, VG, N2..$65.00
Walt Disney World, 1972, EX-, N2................................$10.00
Waltons, 1973, G..$22.00
Washington Redskins, 1970, VG+, N2 ....$119.00
Weave Pattern, 1972, NM, M5 ....$32.00
Welcome Back Kotter, 1977, EX+, C1 ....$45.00
Wild Wild West, 1969, NM, A......................................$120.00
Woody Woodpecker, 1972, VG+, N2 ....$69.00
Yankee Doodles, 1975, EX-, N2 ....$20.00
Yogi Bear & Friends, 1963, EX+-NM, A $100.00

Zorro, 1958, w/thermos, EX, $190.00.

Plastic and Vinyl

A-Team, 1984, w/thermos, EX, I2 ....$8.00
A-Team, 1985, red, w/thermos, EX, I2 ....$8.00
Apple, 1985, cube, Lillian Vernon, EX-, I2 ....$40.00
Banana Splits, 1970, vinyl, w/metal thermos, NM, M5..$400.00
Barbie, 1971, vinyl, pk, w/thermos, EX, N2 ....$75.00
Barbie, 1988, Hollywood, pk, VG+, I2 ....$3.00

Barbie, 1989, Cool Time, pk, plain wht thermos w/pk cup, VG+, I2 ....$2.50
Barbie & Francie, 1965, vinyl, VG+, N2 ....$50.00
Barbie & Midge, 1963, vinyl, blk, EX-, I2.........................$71.00
Beany & Cecil, 1963, vinyl, KST, EX-, I2 ....$350.00

Bionic Woman, rare variation with flag, Canadian, M5, $100.00.

Bozostuffs, 1988, w/thermos, EX-, I2 ....$28.00
Cabbage Patch Kids, 1985, yel, w/thermos, EX-, I2 ....$5.00
California Raisins, 1988, Calrab, yel, w/plain thermos, EX, I2..$8.00
Capitol Critters, 1992, bl, w/plastic thermos, Steven Bochco/Aladdin, M, P4..$12.00
Captain Kangaroo, 1964, vinyl, red, w/thermos, EX-, I2 .$325.00
Care Bears, 1983, red, w/thermos, EX-, I2 ....$4.00
Dawn, 1970, vinyl, wht, w/thermos, EX-, I2 ....$150.00

Flintstones, A Day at the Zoo, Denny's, plastic, with thermos and Denny's Fun Book, 1989, NM, $50.00.

Donnie & Marie Osmond, 1976, vinyl, Aladdin, NM+, C1 ....$67.00
Dr Seuss, 1970, vinyl, w/thermos, EX-, I2 ....$150.00
Ed Grimmley, w/thermos, NM $12.00
Garfield, 1978, w/thermos, EX+, I2 ....$8.00
GI Joe, 1988, bl, w/thermos, VG, I2 ....$3.00
Gigi, 1962, vinyl, w/metal thermos, EX+, I2 ....$210.00
Go Bots, red, w/thermos, EX, I2 ....$4.00
Hot Wheels, 1984, red, EX, I2...$10.00
Inspector Gadget, 1983, w/thermos, EX, I2......................$11.00
Jem, 1986, purple, w/thermos, EX, I2 ....$4.00
Kermit the Frog, EX, O1 ....$28.00
Mam'zelle, 1971, vinyl, bl, VG, N2...................................$49.00
Mardi-Gras, 1971, vinyl, VG+, N2 ....$50.00
Ponytail Tid-Bit Kit, 1959, vinyl, gray, VG+, N2 ....$150.00

Return of the Jedi, 1983, plastic, EX, $12.00.

Return of the Jedi, w/thermos, EX, O1.............................$15.00
Ringling Bros & Barnum & Bailey, 1972, vinyl, Mattel, pk w/playset, EX+ $195.00
Rocketeer, 1991, bl, w/thermos, Disney/Aladdin, M, P4..$20.00
Roy Roger's Saddle Bag, vinyl, NM $195.00
Strawberry Shortcake, 1980, vinyl, pk checkered, EX-.....$25.00
SWAT, 1975, dome, VG+, T6..$8.00

Scooby Doo, w/thermos, plastic, Canadian, M5, $40.00.

Tic-Tac-Toe, 1970, vinyl, red, VG+, N2 ....$40.00
Tinkerbell, 1950s, vinyl, pk w/Tinkerbell & Fantasyland,
    unused, NM, A $225.00

Tinkerbell, Walt Disney Productions, vinyl, Aladdin, NM, A, $225.00.

Wonder Woman, 1977, vinyl, bl, VG+, N2 ....$45.00
Ziggy's Munch Box, 1979, vinyl, VG+, N2 ....$50.00

Thermoses

ABC Wide World of Sports, NM, $28.50.

Adam-12, 1972, standard version, plastic, EX, N2 ....$15.00
Addams Family, 1974, plastic, EX, N2 ....$17.00
Adventures of the Galaxy Rangers, 1986, plastic, EX, I2 ...$2.00
Angler, 1952, metal, tall, Aladdin, 3-cup, VG+, I2..........$32.00
Angler, 1952, metal, 12", EX, N2...................................$59.00
Archies, 1969, plastic w/glass liner, EX, N2 ....$30.00
Atom Ant, 1966, metal, EX-, I2 ....$35.00
Barbie, w/Midge, 1964, metal, Canadian, EX, M5 ....$30.00
Barbie, 1962, metal, blk, w/tan cup, tall, EX, I2...............$25.00
Battle Kit, 1965, metal, EX, N2......................................$39.00
Battle of the Planets, 1979, plastic, EX, N2 ....$20.00
Beatles Yellow Submarine, 1968, metal, surface rust, G,
    R2...$60.00
Belknap, metal, bl grass, ridged, w/bl bullet-shaped cup,
    EX, I2...$4.00
Birds, metal, Canadian, EX, M5 ....$26.00
Black Hole, 1979, metal, VG+ $22.00
Bonanza, 1965, metal, EX, from $50 to $65.00
Bozo the Clown, 1964, metal, NM, T1 ....$35.00
Buccaneer, 1957, metal, NM $55.00
Buck Rogers in the 25th Century, 1979, plastic, cup hdl gone,
    VG+, I2...$7.00
California Raisins, 1987, plastic, EX, N2 ....$8.00
Campus Queen, 1967, metal, EX, N2...............................$25.00
Campus Queen, 1967, metal, VG, O1 ....$12.00
Casper the Friendly Ghost, 1966, metal, King Seeley, may have
    wrong cap, VG, P4...$35.00
Chan Clan, 1973, plastic, NM, C1...................................$17.50
Charlie's Angels, 1978, plastic, EX, I2 ....$10.00
Chitty Chitty Bang Bang, 1968, metal, VG+, I2 ....$29.00
Corsage, 1963, metal, peach, rim, EX, N2.......................$25.00
Cutesy Barn, 1971, metal, M, N2 ....$65.00
Davy Crockett, 1950s, metal, Holtemp, NM-M, C1 ....$63.00
Disney Express, 1979, plastic, EX, I2 ....$5.00
Disney School Bus, 1960s, for dome-top, EX to NM $30.00
Disney School Bus, 1969, metal, EX, N2 ....$30.00
Disneyland Castle, 1957, metal, w/broken cup, EX, I2 .....$33.00
Disneyland Monorail, 1960, metal, EX $60.00
Donny & Marie, 1976, plastic, EX $15.00
Double Deckers, 1970, plastic w/glass liner, EX $30.00
Drag Strip, 1975, plastic, complete, VG, I2 ....$5.50
Dukes of Hazzard, 1980, plastic, EX, T6...........................$7.00
Emergency, 1973, plastic, NM, N2..................................$11.00
Evel Knievel, 1974, plastic, EX+, N2 ....$15.00
Firehouse, 1959, metal, EX, I2..$60.00
Flintstone's Pebbles & Bamm-Bamm, 1971, plastic, EX+,
    from $25 to..$30.00
Flintstones, 1962, metal, VG+, N2 ....$50.00
Flintstones, 1964, metal, EX, from $50 to.......................$60.00
Flintstones, 1971, plastic, fancy, NM, N2 ....$30.00
Flipper, 1967, metal, Canadian, NM, M5 ....$48.00
Flipper, 1967, metal, EX, N2 ....$39.00
Floral, metal, tall, peach background w/scattered floral arrange-
    ments of yel, lav, & wht flowers, EX, I2 ....$11.00
Fonz, 1978, metal, tall, still in wrapper, M, N2 ....$35.00
Game Birds, 1960, metal, 10", EX, N2 ....$39.00
Gentle Ben, 1968, metal, EX, N2....................................$38.00
GI Joe, 1967, metal, EX, N2 ....$39.00

Gigi, 1962, metal, EX...$30.00
Go Go, 1966, metal, EX $40.00
Green Hornet, 1966, metal, NM-M...............................$120.00
Gunsmoke, 1962, metal, VG, O1 ....$40.00
Hardy Boys Mysteries, 1977, plastic, EX, T6 ....$7.00
Harlem Globetrotters, 1971, metal, purple, EX, N2 ....$30.00
Harlem Globetrotters, 1971, metal, VG, from $14 to.......$22.00
Hector Heathcote, 1964, metal, EX, N2 ....$75.00
Hopalong Cassidy, 1950, metal, VG+, from $35 to $45.00
Hot Wheels, 1969, metal, EX, N2 ....$25.00
Indiana Jones, 1984, plastic, in wrapper, M, N2 ....$10.00
It's a Small World, 1954, metal, VG+, N2........................$30.00
It's About Time, 1967, metal, VG, N2 ....$50.00
Julia, 1969, metal, EX $30.00
Junior Miss, 1966, metal, yel background, EX, T6 ....$10.00
Kewtie Pie, 1964, metal, VG+, N2..................................$50.00
Land of the Giants, 1968, plastic, EX, J2 ....$25.00
Laugh-In, 1968, plastic, NM, J2 ....$30.00
Lidsville, 1971, plastic, EX..$25.00
Looney Tunes, 1977, plastic, NM...................................$15.00

Ludwig Van Drake, 1962, Aladdin, EX-, N2, $60.00.

MacPherson Plaid, 1964, metal, VG+, N2..........................$9.00
Marvel Super Heroes, 1983, plastic, EX, T6......................$5.00
Masters of the Universe, 1983, plastic, VG-, O1 ....$6.00
Mickey, Donald & Goofy, 1970s, plastic, EX-, T6.............$7.00
Mickey Mouse Club, 1962, metal, EX, N2......................$35.00
Mighty Mouse, 1979, plastic, EX, N2.............................$20.00
Monkees, 1967, metal, Canadian, VG+, M5 ....$25.00
NFL, 1976, metal, 13", VG+, N2....................................$29.00
Partridge Family, 1971, metal, King Seeley, lt rust & scratches,
    may have wrong cap, VG, P4 ....$25.00
Partridge Family, 1971, plastic, EX.................................$14.00
Peanuts, 1966, metal, EX, from $15 to $20.00
Peanuts, 1980s, plastic, yel, Charlie Brown w/Snoopy at dog-
    house eating cookies, EX, T6......................................$9.00
Plaid by Universal, 1959, metal, EX, N2..........................$40.00
Play Ball, 1969, metal, NM, N2 ....$30.00

Popeye, 1964, metal & plastic, several characters at harbor, 7",
    VG+, T2 ....$20.00
Princess, 1963, metal, EX, N2 ....$50.00
Punky Brewster, 1984, plastic, EX, N2 ....$12.00
Pussycats, 1968, plastic, EX, N2 ....$25.00
Red Roses, 1970, metal, EX, N2 ....$35.00
Rifleman, 1960s, metal, Canadian, VG+, M5..................$40.00
Road Runner, 1970, metal, EX, N2 ....$25.00
Robin Hood, 1956, metal, EX-NM..................................$40.00
Robin Hood, 1973, plastic, EX $15.00
Satellite, 1958, metal, VG+...$30.00
Secret Agent T, 1968, metal, NM-M, N2.......................$30.00
Shari Lewis w/Lambchop, 1963, metal, Mush Puppy & other
    characters, NM, C1 ....$72.00
Smurfs, 1983, plastic, EX, T6...$3.00
Space 1999, 1974, plastic, EX, O1 ....$10.00
Star Trek, 1979, plastic, EX, N2 ....$15.00
Strawberry Shortcake, 1980, plastic, EX, O1 ....$6.00
Super Friends, 1978, plastic, EX, N2 ....$10.00
Superman, 1967, metal, NM, N2 ....$35.00
Tarzan, 1966, metal, EX+, from $40 to $45.00
Tom Corbett Space Cadet, 1953, metal, EX...................$60.00
Twiggy, 1967, metal, NM, T1 ....$35.00
Universal's Movie Monsters, 1979, plastic, EX, N2 ....$12.00
Universal's Movie Monsters, 1979, plastic, NM, N2 ....$20.00
US Mail, 1969, plastic, standard version, NM, N2 ....$10.00
Voyage to the Bottom of the Sea, 1967, metal, NM-M, N2 ..$85.00
Waltons, 1973, plastic, EX+, N2 ....$20.00
Waltons, 1973, plastic, VG+, T6.....................................$9.00
Warner Bros, 1959, metal, VG+......................................$45.00
Welcome Back Kotter, 1976, plastic, VG $10.00
Woody Woodpecker, 1972, plastic, NM $40.00
World of Dr Seuss, 1970, plastic, EX...............................$30.00

Miscellaneous

Brown Bagger, canvas drawstring bag, 14", M, N2............$20.00
Dark Brown Brunch Bag, 1970s, leather, foam lined, EX,
    N2...$25.00
Denim Brunch Bag, 1970s, clump of strawberries, EX, N2 .$30.00
Don't Bug Me Ladybug, 1978, drawstring, EX, N2 ....$50.00
ET, the Extra Terrestrial; canvas drawstring bag, 14", M, N2...$50.00
I'm Brown Bagging It, canvas drawstring bag, 14", M,
    N2...$20.00
Leo Lion, 1978, drawstring, M, N2.................................$95.00

Terri's Toys & Nostalgia
Buy - Sell - Trade - Consignments Taken

Lunchboxes or thermoses and anything related to: Jetsons, Munsters, Flintstones, Lost In Space, Elvis, Beatles, KISS, Roy Rogers, Lone Ranger, Hopalong Cassidy, Green Hornet, Addams Family and other TV, cartoon, movie or music personalities. Toy vehicles, Games, Robots, Space toys, Breyer or Hartland animals or people. Tin toys, Wind-ups, Battery operated toys, Toy guns, Christmas catalogs, Advertising items, Coca-Cola, American made guitars, etc. Any toys, collectibles, or antiques considered.

1104 Shirlee
Ponca City, OK 74601

(405) 762-TOYS
or (405) 762-5174
No collect calls please

Lunch Bag, worm & apple, colorful canvas drawstring, 14", M, N2 ....$30.00

Peanut Butter & Jelly, canvas drawstring bag, 14", M, N2 ..$30.00

Peanuts, yel vinyl brunch bag, Snoopy & Woodstock dancing w/Charlie Brown watching, 1965, 8x8", EX, T6 ....$35.00

Pepsi, 1980s, wht, puffy, EX, N2 ....$20.00

Snoopy, 1970s, red tote bag, Snoopy sitting on big hot dog, in cellophane wrapper, 12x12", M, N2 ....$50.00

Snoopy Beach Bag, colorful drawstring canvas, 12x12", M, N2 ....$40.00

Speedy Turtle, 1978, drawstring, EX, N2 ....$50.00

Sun, insignia on front, 1980s, yel, puffy, EX, N2 ....$15.00

Take the Pepsi Challenge, 1980s, yel, puffy, EX, N2 ....$39.00

Wise Guy Owl, 1978, drawstring, M, N2 ....$95.00

Marbles

Antique marbles are divided into several classifications: 1) Transparent Swirl (Solid Core, Latticinio Core, Divided Core, Ribbon Core, Lobed Core, and Coreless); 2) Lutz or Lutz-type (with bands having copper flecks which alternate with colored or clear bands; 3) Peppermint Swirl (made of red, white, and blue opaque glass); 4) Indian Swirl (black with multicolored surface swirls); Banded Swirl (wide swirling bands on opaque or transparent glass); 6) Onionskin (having an overall mottled appearance due to its spotted, swirling lines or lobes: 7) End of Day (single pontil, allover spots, either 2-colored or multicolored); 8) Clambroth (evenly spaced, swirled lines on opaque glass); 9) Mica (transparent color with mica flakes added); 10) Sulphide (nearly always clear, colored examples are rare, containing figures). Besides glass marbles, some were made of clay, pottery, china, steel, and even semiprecious stones.

Most machine-made marbles are worth very little, but some may be worth from $10.00 up to $20.00, depending the colors that were used and how they are defined. Guineas (Christensen agates with small multicolored specks instead of swirls) often go for as much as $200.00. Mt. Peltier comic character marbles range from $60.00 to $80.00, except for Betty Boop and Kayo, which both go for about twice as much.

From the nature of their use, mint condition marbles are extremely rare and may be worth as much as three to five times more than one that is near-mint, while chipped and cracked marbles may be worth half or less. The same is true of one that has been polished, regardless of how successful the polishing was. If you'd like to learn more, Everett Grist has written three books on the subject that you will find helpful: *Antique and Collectible Marbles*; *Machine Made and Contemporary Marbles*; and *Everett Grist's Big Book of Marbles*.

Artist-Made, crown filigree & peppermints, contemporary, Bill Burchfield, 1", M, B8 ....$35.00

Artist-Made, end of day, contemporary, Jody Fine, 1½", M, B8 ....$35.00

Artist-Made, end of day & swirls w/lutz & mica, contemporary, Bill Burchfield, 1½", M, B8 ....$60.00

Artist-Made, Lutz-type, contemporary, Harry Boyer, 1⅝", M, B8 ....$50.00

Artist-Made, peppermint w/mica, contemporary, Mark Matthews, 1½", M, B8 ....$75.00

Artist-Made, single flower or 3 flowers, contemporary, Harry Boyer, 1½", M, B8 ....$50.00

Artist-Made, swirl, contemporary, Jody Fine, 1⅛", M, B8 .$15.00

Artist-Made, swirl or end of day, contemporary, Mark Matthews, 1½", M, B8 ....$60.00

Artist-Made, swirl or end of day w/lutz, aventurine or mica, contemporary, Rolf & Genie Wald, 1½", M, B8 ....$45.00

Artist-Made, swirls & ribbons, contemporary, Harry Boyer, 1¼", M, B8 ....$25.00

Artist-Made, swirls & ribbons, contemporary, Harry Boyer, 1⅝", M, B8 ....$50.00

Banded Lutz, clear base w/mica, 4 bl bands, extremely rare, 1¾", M, A $410.00

Banded Lutz, clear base w/4 yel bands, 1³⁄₁₆", NM, A $250.00

Banded Opaque, semiopaque wht base w/translucent pk bands, ¹¹⁄₁₆", NM, A $40.00

Banded Opaque, translucent, ½-⅞", M, B8 ....$400.00

Banded Opaque, wht w/gr stripes, ⁹⁄₁₆", M, A $60.00

Banded Opaque, wht w/2 sets of pk stripes, ¹¹⁄₁₆", M, A $80.00

Banded Swirl, cobalt w/wide bands of yel, red & wht, ¹¹⁄₁₆", NM, A $30.00

Banded Swirl, transparent gr w/translucent yel & wht stripes, ¹⁵⁄₁₆", NM, A $30.00

Blue Lace Agate, ½-⅞", M, B8 ....$25.00

Buddy Brand, 1940s, 30 marbles in orig pkg, VG.............$20.00

Cased Indian Lutz, amethyst mag-lite base w/bl, gr & wht slag-type stripes, rare, ⅞", G+, A $200.00

China, pnt, glazed, ½-⅞", M, B8, all colors, ea $15.00

Clambroth, blk opaque base w/wht & gray stripes, ¹³⁄₁₆", NM, A $80.00

Clambroth, opaque blk base w/wht stripes, ¹¹⁄₁₆", M, A.....$60.00

Clambroth, opaque wht base w/dk bl lines, ¾", NM, A .$140.00

Clambroth, semiopaque wht base w/alternating bl & red lines, EX+, A $60.00

Clambroth, semiopaque wht base w/turq lines, ¹⁵⁄₁₆", NM, A $110.00

Clambroth Swirl, ½-⅞", M, B8, all colors, ea $250.00

Comic Strip Characters, complete set of 20, Mt. Peltier Glass Company, M in 3x3½" box, A, $2,000.00.

Comic Strip, Andy, Annie, Bimbo, Herbie, Emma, Sandy, Skeezix, or Smitty, Peltier, M, B8, ea......................$125.00

Comic Strip, Betty Boop or Kayo, Peltier, M, B8 ....$200.00

Divided Core Swirl, variety of colored cores and outer strands, lot of three ranging from 1¼" to 1⅜" in diameter, NM, A, $240.00.

Divided Core Swirl, 2 pr of alternating 3-color inner bands, 4 sets of mc outer bands, 2", M, B8 ....$125.00

Divided Core Swirl, 2 pr of 3-color inner bands, 7 wht outer bands, 1¼", M, B8..$75.00

Divided Core Swirl, 3 red, wht & bl inner bands, 3 sets of wht outer bands, bl-tinted glass, 1¼", NM, B8 ....$80.00

Divided Core Swirl, 3 wide mc inner bands, 3 sets of yel & wht outer bands, 1⅞", NM, B8.......................................$150.00

Divided Core Swirl, 3 wide 4-color inner bands, 3 sets of yel & wht outer bands, 1¾", M, B8...................................$100.00

Divided Core Swirl, 4 wide mc inner bands, 3 sets of yel outer bands, tinted glass, 1¾", NM, B8 ....$175.00

Divided Core Swirl, 4 wide 3-color inner bands, 4 sets of mc outer bands, bl-tinted glass, 1⅞", NM, B8 ....$150.00

Divided Core Swirl, 4 wide 3-color inner bands, 4 sets of wht outer bands, 1⅝", M, B8 ....$175.00

Divided Swirl, 4 2-color inner bands, 2 sets of alternating yel & wht outer bands, bl-tinted glass, 1¾", M, B8 ....$125.00

End of Day, onionskin, wht core w/translucent salmon skin, bl & turq splotches, 1¾", NM+, A................................$110.00

End of Day, onionskin, 4-panel, opaque wht core, translucent red & wht panels, 1¹³⁄₁₆", EX+, A $85.00

End of Day, onionskin lutz, mc core, ¹¹⁄₁₆", NM, A $110.00

End of Day, onionskin lutz, pk & wht core, ⁹⁄₁₆", EX+, A .$85.00

End of Day, onionskin lutz, wht & gr core, ¹³⁄₁₆", NM, A .$95.00

End of Day, onionskin w/mica, opaque core w/transparent bl & red splotches, 1⁷⁄₁₆", EX+, A $110.00

End of Day, onionskin w/mica, opaque wht core covered w/semi-translucent mc stripes, ¹³⁄₁₆", NM, A $100.00

End of Day, peewee, onionskin w/lutz that floats in a seperate layer above the core, ½", M, A..................................$165.00

End of Day, peewee, ⅝-⅞", NM, B8 ....$25.00

End of Day, red, wht, yel, gr & bl, cloud type w/mica, 1⅝", M, B8...$550.00

End of Day, 4-panel onionskin w/mica, yel w/2 red & gr panels, 1⁹⁄₁₆", NM, A...$75.00

Goldstone, bl, ½-⅞", M, B8...$35.00

Goldstone, brn, ½-⅞", M, B8 ....$25.00

Indian, opaque blk base, pk, bl & gr edged in wht on 1 side, bl & gr edged in yel on the other, ¹¹⁄₁₆", NM, A $40.00

Indian, slag-type, aqua & wht lines on 1 side, mustard & red on the other, ¾", M, A...$90.00

Indian, slag-type, opaque blk base, red & wht stripes on 1 side, bl & wht on the other, ¹¹⁄₁₆", NM, A $80.00

Indian, slag-type, opaque blk base w/dk red bands, ¹¹⁄₁₆", NM, A $40.00

Indian Swirl, ½-⅞", M, B8, all colors, ea $125.00

Joseph's Coat, mc swirl, bl-tinted glass, ¹¹⁄₁₆", NM, A $55.00

Joseph's Coat, mc swirl, ¹¹⁄₁₆", NM+, A $25.00

Joseph's Coat, pastel swirl, bl-tinted glass, ¾", NM, A $40.00

Joseph's Coat, wht, bl, red & salmon swirl, bl-tinted glass, ¾", M, A $40.00

Latticinio Swirls, left to right: Error type with end-of-cane swirl from two separate canes, four multicolor outer bands, bottom with alternating pink and white bands, surface dings and chips, 1¾", G, A, $75.00; White core with alternating green and white bands that are covered by translucent pink, 2", NM, A, $150.00.

Latticinio Swirl, alternating yel & wht core w/4 wide mc outer bands, 1½", NM, B8 ....$100.00

Latticinio Swirl, alternating yel & wht core w/6 outer bands, 2", NM, B8 ....$125.00

Latticinio Swirl, wht core w/alternating bl & wht outer band, 1⅜", M, B8...$125.00

Latticinio Swirl, wht core w/alternating gr & wht outer bands under translucent pk, 2", NM, A $150.00

Latticinio Swirl, wht core w/alternating yel & orange outer bands, 1⅜", G+, A $25.00

Latticinio Swirl, wht core w/2 pr of 3-color outer bands, 1¾", G, B8..$100.00

Latticinio Swirl, wht core w/4 mc outer bands, 1½", NM, B8 ....$100.00

Latticinio Swirl, wht core w/4 wide outer bands, 2⅛", NM, B8 ....$150.00

Latticinio Swirl, wht core w/6 wide 2-color outer bands, bl tint to glass, 1⅝", NM, B8..$150.00

Latticinio Swirl, yel core in bl-tinted glass w/6 outer bands, 2¼", NM, B8 ....$200.00

Latticinio Swirl, yel core w/14 alternating strands of red & wht, 2", G, B8 ....$125.00

Latticinio Swirl, yel core w/6 red & wht outer bands, 1⅝", NM, B8 ....$100.00

Leopardskin, ½-⅞", M, B8 ....$25.00

Lutz, banded clear, ½-⅞", M, B8 ....$100.00

Lutz, banded opaque, ½-⅞", M, B8 ....$350.00

Lutz, clear w/bl swirl, ⅞", EX-, A $110.00

Machine-Made, Alox Agates, USA, boys playing marbles on header card, 1950s, M (EX pkg) $18.00

Machine-Made, aqua slag, Akro Agate, 9/16-11/16", M, B8 .....$8.00

Machine-Made, bag from Popeye set, Akro Agate, NM (worn bag), B8 ....$110.00

Machine-Made, blk w/electric orange swirl, Christensen Agate, ⅝", M, B8 ....$35.00

Machine-Made, Bogard & Sons, West Virginia, cat's eyes, shows cat on header card, 1950s, M (EX pkg) $16.00

Machine-Made, carnelian oxblood, Akro Agate, 9/16-11/16", M, B8 ....$100.00

Machine-Made, Cub Scout, yel & bl, Marble King, 9/16-11/16", M, B8 ....$5.00

Machine-Made, electric opaque red, American Christensen Agate, 11/16", M, B8 ....$45.00

Machine-Made, flame swirl, Christensen Agate, 9/16-11/16", M, B8 ....$50.00

Machine-Made, hybrid cat's eye, dk bl & gr vanes w/dk red edges, Vitro Agate, 15/16", NM, B1 ....$15.00

Machine-Made, hybrid cat's eye, Vitro Agate/Gladding-Vitro, 9/16-11/16", M, B8 ....$5.00

Machine-Made, lemonade & oxblood, Akro Agate, 9/16-11/16", M, B8 ....$75.00

Machine-Made, limeade corkscrew, Akro Agate, 9/16-11/16", M, B8 ....$20.00

Machine-Made, limeade corkscrew w/sm amount of oxblood, Akro Agate, ⅝", M, B8 ....$50.00

Machine-Made, lt aqua slag w/rotating wht spiral design, MF Christensen & Son, ⅝", M, B8 ....$50.00

Machine-Made, lt purple & yel Popeye corkscrew, Akro Agate, 9/16-11/16", M, B8 ....$40.00

Machine-Made, metallic stripe, Akro Agate, 9/16-11/16", M, B8 ....$20.00

Machine-Made, milky oxblood, Akro Agate, 9/16-11/16", M, B8 ....$15.00

Machine-Made, National Rainbo, opaque wht w/aventurine blk stripes under translucent red-brn, Peltier, 9/16", M, B8 .$125.00

Machine-Made, National Rainbo, Partiot or Liberty, Peltier, ⅝", NM, B8 ....$75.00

Machine-Made, National Rainbo, Peltier, ⅝", NM, B8 ...$50.00

Machine-Made, opaque wht w/red, gray & gr swirls, Christensen Agate, ⅝", M, B8 ....$60.00

Machine-Made, oxblood patch, Vitro Agate/Gladding-Vitro, 9/16-11/16", M, B8 ....$7.50

Machine-Made, oxblood swirl, Akro Agate, 9/16-11/16", M, B8 ....$20.00

Machine-Made, purple slag, melted pontil, ⅞", NM, B8 ....$40.00

Machine-Made, Rainbo, translucent wht w/4 red stripes, Peltier, ⅞", M, B8 ....$25.00

Machine-Made, red & bl Popeye corkscrew, Akro Agate, 9/16-11/16", M, B8 ....$60.00

Machine-Made, red & gr Popeye corkscrew, Akro Agate, 9/16-11/16", M, B8 ....$15.00

Machine-Made, red & wht, American Christensen Agate, ⅝", M, B8 ....$65.00

Machine-Made, ribbon-twist corkscrew, Akro Agate, 9/16-11/16", M, B8 ....$8.00

Machine-Made, sparkler, transparent clear base w/mc inner core, Akro Agate, ⅝", M, B8 ....$35.00

Machine-Made, Sun Brand, Japan, pictures cat on header card, 1950s, orig pkg, EX $15.00

Machine-Made, Sunburst, clear, Master Marble, 9/16-11/16", M, B8 ....$10.00

Machine-Made, Sunburst, opaque, Master Marble, 9/16-11/16", M, B8 ....$3.00

Machine-Made, Sunset, Peltier, 9/16-11/16", M, B8 ....$5.00

Machine-Made, Tiger, orange & blk, Marble King, 9/16-11/16", M, B8 ....$10.00

Machine-Made, translucent milky wht w/bl oxblood corkscrew design, Akro Agate, ¾", NM, B8 ....$50.00

Machine-Made, transparent brn slag w/single seam design, Christensen Agate, 15/16", NM, B8 ....$75.00

Machine-Made, transparent brn w/opaque wht swirls, MF Christensen & Son, 13/16", M, B8 ....$35.00

Machine-Made, transparent gr base w/translucent wht loops, melted pontil, 11/16", M, B8 ....$75.00

Machine-Made, transparent gr w/coral & gr swirl, Christensen Agate, 9/16", M, B8 ....$30.00

Machine-Made, transparent olive-brn w/single seam design, Christensen Agate, 13/16", M, B8 ....$30.00

Machine-Made, triple-twist corkscrew, Akro Agate, 9/16-11/16", M, B8 ....$10.00

Machine-Made, USA, full box, assorted, 1940s, EX+ (M box) $20.00

Machine-Made, USA, 35 in box w/Deco design, EX+ $14.00

Machine-Made, Wasp, red & blk, Marble King, 9/16-11/16", M, B8 ....$5.00

Machine-Made, 3-color Rainbo w/aventurine, Peltier, 9/16-11/16", M, B8 ....$125.00

Onionskin, peewee, ⅜-½", M, B8 ....$50.00

Onionskin, red, wht & bl, cloud type w/mica, 1⅝", G+, B8 ....$350.00

Onionskin, wht w/bl, red & gr specks, 1⅜", M, B8 ....$150.00

Onionskin, wht w/red & emerald specks, G+, 2", B8 .....$225.00

Onionskin, 4-lobe, yel, red & gr, 1⅞", NM, B8 ....$450.00

Onionskin, 4-panel, red, wht & bl, cloud type, 1⅞", G, B8 ....$200.00

Onionskin, 4-panel, red, wht & bl, 1⅞", M, B8 ....$250.00

Onionskin, 4-panel, red, yel, bl & wht, 1⅞", M, B8 ....$325.00

Onionskin, 4-panel, red, yel, gr & bl, 1⅝", NM, B8 ....$300.00

Peppermint Swirl, ½-⅞", M, B8, all colors, ea $125.00

Ribbon Core Swirl, dbl-core in red, wht & bl w/orange edges, yel outer bands, ¾", M, A $15.00

Ribbon Core Swirl, wht, blk & turq, ⅞", NM, A $20.00

Ribbon Core Swirl, ½-⅞", M, B8, all colors, ea $150.00

Ribbon Lutz, bl & yel edged in wht, 11/16", NM, A $90.00

Ribbon Lutz, vaseline gr & yel, transparent base, rare, 13/16", NM, A...$1,150.00

Solid Core, peewee, 5/8-7/8", NM, B8.................................$20.00

Solid Core Swirl, peewee, 3/8-1/2", M, B8 ....$35.00

Solid Core Swirl, red, wht, gr & bl core w/4 sets of gr-yel outer bands, 13/8", M, B8 ....$100.00

Solid Core Swirl, red, wht & bl lobed core, yel outer bands, 17/8", NM, B8...$150.00

Solid Core Swirl, wht core w/red, gr & bl bands, yel outer bands, 11/2", NM, B8...$125.00

Solid Core Swirl, yel core w/alternating red & gr, wht outer bands, gray-tinted glass, 2", G, B8............................$175.00

Solid Core Swirl, 3-section mc core, 3 sets of yel outer bands, bl-tinted glass, 11/2", NM, B8...................................$150.00

Solid Core Swirl, 4-lobe, opaque yel core w/alternating transparent gr & pk on lobe edges, 11/2", NM, A.....................$50.00

Sulphide, bear standing on mound of grass, 2", NM, B8.$150.00

Sulphide, camel on mound of grass, 21/8", NM, B8..........$175.00

Sulphide, cat reclining on a plaque, 13/4", NM, B8 ....$150.00

Sulphide, doe standing on mound of grass, 15/8", NM, B8 .$150.00

Sulphide, dog standing on mound of grass, 17/8", NM, B8 .$150.00

Sulphide, duck seated on mound of grass, 13/16", NM, A...$50.00

Sulphide, girl holding doll seated in upsidedown chair, 11/2", NM, B8...$350.00

Sulphide, girl kneeling in prayer, 2", M, B8.....................$450.00

Sulphide, girl seated on the ground reading a book, 2", M, A...$160.00

Sulphide, hen on light green nest, forest green and black details, 1½", polished M, A, $1,100.00.

Sulphide, hen on nest, 13/8", NM, B8 ....$150.00

Sulphide, lamb reclining on mound of grass, 11/2", M, B8 .$125.00

Sulphide, lg #8, 115/16", NM, A $170.00

Sulphide, male lion standing on mound of grass, 11/8", NM, B8...$100.00

Sulphide, peasant boy on stump w/legs crossed, 21/8", NM, B8...$450.00

Sulphide, peasant boy seated on a stump, 11/2", M, A $50.00

Sulphide, rabbit sprinting over grass, 17/8", NM, A $50.00

Sulphide, ram standing on mound of grass, hand painted, 13/4", M, A..$2,700.00

Sulphide, seated chimpanzee w/legs crossed holding an object, 113/16", EX+, A $85.00

Sulphide, spread-winged eagle, 13/8", M, A.....................$160.00

Sulphide, squirrel eating a nut, 13/8", M, A........................$80.00

Sulphide, standing billy goat, 17/8", EX+, A......................$50.00

Sulphide, standing rooster, 13/4", M, B8...........................$200.00

Sulphide, standing sheep, 17/8", NM, B8...........................$175.00

Sulphide, standing sheep dog, 2", NM, B8.......................$150.00

Sulphide, wart hog standing on mound of grass, 13/4", NM, B8...$175.00

Tigereye, bl, 1/2-7/8", M, B8...$35.00

Tigereye, golden brn, 1/2-7/8", M, B8 ....$30.00

Union Brand, Japan, shows owl on header card, 1950s, MIP...$22.00

Marx

Louis Marx founded his company in New York in the 1920s. He was a genius not only at designing toys but marketing them. His business grew until it became one the largest toy companies ever to exist, eventually expanding to include several factories in the United States as well as other countries. Marx sold his company in the early 1970s; he died in 1982. Though toys of every description were produced, collectors today admire his mechanical toys above all others. See also Advertising; Banks; Character Collectibles; Dollhouse Furniture; Games; Guns; Plastic Figures; Playsets; and other categories.

Battery-Operated

Alley the Roaring Stalking Alligator, 5 actions, MIB, L4.$475.00

Bangali Tiger, working, 1961, VG, C8.............................$50.00

Brewster the Rooster, plush rooster travels around, lifts head, opens beak & crows, 10", M (EX box), A.................$145.00

Walking Esso Tiger, tin, plush, and plastic, walks and growls, 1960s, 11½", NM (EX box), $300.00.

Buttons the Puppy w/Brain, 8 actions, 1950s, 12", NM, L4 ....$225.00

Chop Chop Helicopter, tin & plastic, ca 1966, M (EX box)...$125.00

Clang-Clang Locomotive, sounds & lights, early 1960s, 13", MIB $78.00

Flying Tiger Line Plane, tin & plastic, moves as props spin, wing tips light, rear section opens, 20" wingspan, EX, A .$330.00

Frankenstein, walker, rubber-like head, hard plastic hands, remote control, 12¾", EX (EX box), A....................$400.00

Fred Flintstone on Dino, purple and black plush with lithographed tin and plastic, 19", EX (VG box), L4, $750.00.

Great Garloo, gr plastic w/monster features, remote control, 5 actions, working, 1961-62, 18", EX+, A $273.00

Haunted House, litho tin, jumping blk cat, moving window shade, silhouette of ghost, etc, 1960s, 10", EX, A....$635.00

Ladder Fire Engine, MIB $425.00

Marx-a-Copter, plastic copter circles pylon, bombs sub & rescues men, missing tower, 1958, NMIB, P4 ....$125.00

Mighty Kong, gray plush, pnt tin & molded plastic, metal neck & handcuffs, working, orig box, 10¾", EX, A $475.00

Mighty Kong, plush over tin, walks, stops, beats chest & moves head, growls, neck & wrist shackles, 11½", MIB, A $650.00

Military Jet Plane, 1960s, 16", MIB, L4 ....$275.00

Moon Scout Helicopter, MIB, L4 ....$150.00

Nutty Mad Indian, litho tin, rubber, felt & plush, beats drum, sticks out tongue, orig box, 12", VG-EX, A $90.00

Nutty Mad Indian, MIB, L4 ....$250.00

Roadside Rest Service Station, litho tin, battery-op lights, 10x14", G+, A $198.00

US Navy Jeep & Searchlight Trailer, Willys navy bl jeep w/blk rubber tires, working, unused, 21", MIB, A $220.00

Walking Esso Tiger, missing hat, o/w NM, L4.................$200.00

Whistling Spooky Kooky Tree, litho tin trunk, rubber arms & nose, plastic leaves, 1950s, 14", NMIB.................**$1,600.00**

Whistling Spooky Kooky Tree, litho tin w/vinyl arms & nose, bump-&-go action, 1960s, 13", EX, A $750.00

Willys Jeep & Trailer, pressed steel & litho tin, sounds & lights, non-working, orig box, 22", VG-EX, A $170.00

Yeti the Abominable Snowman, plush over tin, walks, stops, screeches, raises arms, remote control, 11", MIB, A .**$925.00**

Pressed Steel

Army Transport Truck, canvas top, 4x13½", NM (EX box), A..$250.00

Army Truck w/2 Trailers & Cannon, olive drab w/blk wood wheels, metal hubcaps, fabric canopies, cannon fires, 32", VG, A $204.00

Auto Transport, bl w/plated grille, blk wood wheels w/red steel hubcaps, +coupe, roadster & loading ramp, 20⅝", VG, A $413.00

Auto Transport, red, wht & blk cab, wht trailer w/Deluxe Auto Transport decal, orig box, 16½", NM, A $230.00

Auto Transport, yel cab w/red trailer, Deluxe Auto Transport decals, +2 plastic cars & loading ladder, 22⅜", NM, A $182.00

Bus, red w/emb running dog on sides, plated grille, blk wood wheels, 5", VG, A $77.00

Car Carrier, gray, bl & red, NP grille, wood wheels, w/2 plastic cars, 13¾", EX, A $80.00

Coal Truck, red body w/front molded fenders, bl bed w/Lumar Coal stamped on sides, blk tires, red hubcaps, 11¼", G, A $39.00

Deluxe Pickup Truck, bl w/yel tailgate, plated grille, electric headlights, decals on doors, orig box, 14½", NM, A..........$495.00

Dump Truck, bl w/plated grille & bumper, red bed, blk wood wheels, 4 open windows in cab, 15¾", G, A $77.00

Dump Truck, Hi-Lift; lithoed, red, wht & blk, plastic wheels, dumping action, working, orig box, 12½", NM, A ..$160.00

Dump Truck, hydraulic, 1950s, 15", EX+ $150.00

Dump Truck, lt gr body w/4 molded fenders, plated trim, red bed, blk wood wheels, clockwork, working, 4¾", M, A $105.00

Dump Truck, red, running board, fenders & chassis, bl bed w/yel tailgate, blk steel wheels, 13¾", EX-, A $39.00

Dump Truck, red with cream dump bed, Bulldog decals on side, $65.00.

Dump Truck, red w/gr bed, plated grille, blk wood wheels, clockwork, 5¼", G, A..$66.00

Dump Truck, red w/yel bed & scoop, litho steel wheels, plated grille & trim, 20⅝", M, A..$165.00

Dump Truck, silver w/blk grille & bumper, Dept Street Cleaning stamped on side, blk wood wheels, 11", VG, A $149.00

Fire Chief's Car, red with yellow lettering, 1930s, 16", EX, D10, $450.00.

Fire Chief Coupe, red w/blk running boards & headlights, plated grille & bumpers, electric lights, w/up, 15", EX, A ..$385.00

Fire Chief Sedan, red w/4 molded fenders, Fire Chief stamped on doors, wood wheels, plated trim, 10", G, A $187.00

Fire Chief Siren Coupe, red w/plated grill, electric lights, blk rubber tires, non-working siren, w/up, 14", NMIB, A....$468.00

Fire Pumper, red body, blk chassis & benders, anodized gold boiler w/celluloid window, rubber tires, ca 1934, 9", EX, A...$77.00

Flatbed Truck, red cab w/4 molded fenders & Lumar Contractors decals on doors, yel bed, hoist winch, 19½", EX-, A...$39.00

Garbage Truck, wht w/blk & red litho letters on van, rear door slides open, litho tin wheels, 13⅜", EX-, A $220.00

Garden Truck, red w/molded front fenders, bl stake bed, blk wood wheels, red hubcaps, logo on cb insert, 11", EX, A $110.00

Gasoline Truck, gr w/Sinclair decal on ea side, plated grille, blk wood wheels, 17¾", VG, A $688.00

Guided Missile Truck, red, white, and blue, plastic antenna and missile, working missile mechanism, 18", EX (EX box), A, from $190.00 to $220.00.

Grocery Truck, red cab w/4 molded fenders, bl bed, plated grille & trim, +6 orig products, orig box, 14", NM, A $413.00

Grocery Truck, wht w/plated grille & trim, litho wheels, Marcrest Pure Milk decals, complete, 14", MIB, A........$413.00

Guided Missle Truck, lithoed, red, wht & bl, working missile mechanism, orig box, 18", EX, from $190 to $220.00

Jeep, bl w/yel windshield, red steering wheel, blk wheels w/red centers, electric headlights, 11¼", EX+, A $50.00

Joy Gasoline Trailer Truck, red, NP grille, wood wheels, clockwork, working, orig box, 14½", EX, A $200.00

Joy Gasoline Trailer Truck, red & yel, NP grille, wood wheels, clockwork, working, 14½", VG+, A $110.00

Joy Gasoline Truck & Trailer, bl w/4 molded fenders, detachable trailer, w/up motor, 15", MIB, A $440.00

Lumar Scoop & Dump End Loader, 1958, M...................$125.00

Magnetic Crane Truck, yel w/red roof on crane, plated grille & trim, crane rotates, battery-op winch, 15⅝", VG, A.$220.00

Milk Delivery Van, white with Cloverdale Farms on side, 10", VG+, $175.00.

Milk Truck, stake bed w/Marcrest decals on ea side, includes 3 glass milk bottles, 14", VG, A $85.00

Motor Market Truck, wht w/stamp mark on sides, plated grille & trim, blk wood wheels, red hubcaps on rear, 11", EX, A $99.00

Mystery Car, red w/4 molded fenders, plated grille & hood trim, wood wheels, spring mechanism, working, 10", VG-EX, A...$176.00

Pathe News Car, plated grill litho tin newsreel camera mtd on top, 10", VG, A $1,100.00

Pickup Truck, red w/4 molded fenders, plated grille, yel tailgate, electric headlights, 11⅛", VG, A $248.00

Police Coupe, gr w/yel litho letters, blk running boards & rubber tires, electric lights, w/up, rpl key, 15", VG, A $292.00

Power Road Grader, 1950s, 17½", NM $125.00

Rapid Express Pickup Truck, yel cab w/4 molded fenders, bl bed, plated trim, blk wood wheels, w/up, 8¾", MIB, A...$413.00

Search Light Truck, red w/silver bed & bumper, olive tool box (opens), plated grille, blk wood wheels, 9⅞", VG-EX, A $242.00

Sedan, gr w/4 molded fenders, rear spare tire, wood wheels, plated trim, dummy headlights, w/up, 9⅝", G, A $110.00

Stake Body Trailer, lithoed, gray, gr & blk, plastic wheels, Tri-City Freight decal, orig box, 19", NM, A.................$220.00

Stake Truck, bl w/plated grille, red bed, blk steel wheels, 14", EX, A $121.00

Stake Truck, bl-gray cab, gr bed, red fenders, plated grille, electric headlights, blk wheels, orig box, 10¾", M, A....$275.00

Stake Truck, blk cab w/plated grille, red fenders, yel bed, blk wood wheels, 10⅝", NM, A $220.00

Stake Truck, lithoed, red, yel & blk, rubber wheels, w/plastic farm animals, 13½", EX-NM, A $90.00

Stake Truck, pk cab, mint gr fenders, lavender bed w/chick & rabbit stamps, blk wood wheels, orig box, 10½", M, A ...$468.00

Stake Truck, red cab & chassis, bl bed, plated grille, red tailgate, blk wood wheels, 18¾", EX, A $105.00

Run To Reads Stake Truck, red with yellow bed, 1930s, M, D10, $550.00.

Steam Roller, chrome plated, ca 1940, 11⅜", EX, W1 .....$59.00

Van, tan w/Marx Coast To Coast rubber stamped on side, plated grille, blk wood wheels, 5¼", VG-EX, A....................$99.00

Water Tower Fire Truck, red w/yel tower & ladders, NP bumper, Bakelite wheels, w/up missing key, orig box, 14⅜", M, A $660.00

Willys Jeep Truck, red w/bl tailgate, dummy headlights, hood opens, yel wheels w/blk tires, orig box, 12⅞", M, A...$330.00

Windups, Frictions, and Other Mechanicals

Aerial Ladder Fire Truck, plastic w/rubber tires, friction, ca 1950s, MIB $95.00

Aeroplane (Bomber), bl & silver litho tin, 2 propellers, balloon tires, NM (G box) $400.00

Allstate Service Truck, friction, Emergency, bed w/crank-op winch, 4¾", NM (NM box), A...................................$65.00

Amos 'N Andy Fresh Air Taxi, litho tin, orange, blk & gr, clockwork, working, parts missing, 7¾", G, A.........$150.00

Amos 'N Andy Fresh Air Taxi, orig box, 8", NMIB, A..$2,000.00

Amos 'N Andy Fresh Air Taxi, w/windshield, 8", EX-, A.$1,000.00

Amos 'N Andy Taxi, litho tin figures & dog bounce as taxi moves, shakes & stops, windshield missing, 8", VG (NM box), A $1,300.00

Amos 'N Andy Walkers, litho tin, non-moving eye versions, orig arms swing & sway, complete, ea in box, EX+ (NM box), A $3,600.00

Amos 'N Andy Walkers, lithographed tin, blinking eyes, 11⅜", VG+ (G box), A, $1,900.00.

Andrew Brown FATC President, mc litho tin, Andy waddles forward, eyes move, working, 1 rpl arm, 11⅜", G+, A..$330.00

Arm Engineering Truck, friction, canvas bed cover, winch & boom assembly, w/insignia, 22", NM (EX- box), A.$220.00

Astro, litho tin, NM-M, T1...$345.00

Auto Mac Dump Truck & Driver, plastic w/blk rubber tires, 11½", EX (VG box), A...$201.00

Ballet Dancer, litho tin, blk, red & yel, hand-operated rod & gear mechanism, working, orig box, 5½", VG+, A..$170.00

Barrel Wagon, 2 donkeys pull wagon w/farmer driver, wagon lithoed w/barrels, 10", EX, A..................................$110.00

Be Bop Jigger, pnt yel plastic figure on mc litho tin drum base, clockwork, working, orig box, 10", EX, A...............$325.00

Bear Cyclist, orange w/red wheels, hands & legs move, 5¾x5½", VG (EX box), A...$225.00

Beat It the Komikal Cop Car, goes backwards & forward, circles, front end lifts, w/windshield, 7", NM (EX box), A.$1,700.00

Big Parade, soldiers, cannon & ambulance move along track, 1926, orig box, 24", VG, A $460.00

Big 3 Aerial Acrobats, litho tin, orig box taped & missing flaps, 18", VG, A...$247.50

BO Plenty, litho tin, gent in vest & tie w/striped pants holding baby, 8", VG+, A...$275.00

BO Plenty, mc litho tin, holds Baby Sparkle, waddles, hat bounces, 1930s, 9", M (NM+ box)..........................$450.00

Boat-Tail Racer 7-11, litho tin, yel w/blk trim & 7-11 in circle on sides, stamped tin driver, ca 1925, 12½", EX, A.$348.00

Buck Rogers Rocket Police Patrol, litho tin, advances w/noise & sparks, rare, 12", NMIB, A.....................................$2,801.00

Buck Rogers Rocket Police Patrol, litho tin, Buck firing from turret, advances w/sparking action, 12½", EX, A........$1,250.00

Buck Rogers Rocket Space Ship, litho tin, advances w/noise & sparks, 12", NMIB...$2,200.00

Buck Rogers Rocket Space Ship, litho tin, advances w/sparking action, EX (EX box), A...$1,100.00

Bulldog Mack Dump Truck, litho tin, 12", G, A...........$286.00

Busy Bridge, 24" long, EX, D10, $450.00.

Busy Delivery, litho tin w/cb arms & legs, clockwork w/erratic movement, working, 9", VG+, A $400.00

Busy Miners, litho tin, 2" coal cart w/2 men travel from station to mine entrance, 16", EX (NM box), A $348.00

Busy Miners, mc litho tin, clockwork, orig box (damaged flap), 16½", VG+, A $170.00

Butter & Egg Man, litho tin, yel & brn figure w/mc suitcase & duck, clockwork, working, 7¾", G-VG, A...............$375.00

Careful Johnnie, 1950s, NMIB, A...................................$335.00

Cargo Tractor, litho tin, red, rubber tires, plastic tools, clockwork, working, 14", EX, A..$300.00

Charleston Trio, jigger dances, little boy w/violin, dog w/cane jumps, lithoed audience watches, 1920, 9", NM (G box), A..$1,800.00

Charleston Trio, 3 Black minstrels atop roof, box missing 1 flap, EX+ (EX box), M5 ....$995.00

Charlie McCarthy and Mortimer Snerd Car, 16", NMIB, A, $4,800.00.

Charlie McCarthy & Mortimer Snerd Car, mc litho tin, heads spin & car changes direction, clockwork, working, 16", VG, A...$1,600.00

Charlie McCarthy Benzine Buggy, litho tin, orig box, 8½", VG, A...$725.00

Charlie McCarthy Benzine Buggy, litho tin, red wheels & steering wheel version, 1938, 7", NM (EX box), A $1,225.00

Charlie McCarthy Walker, litho tin, 8", VG, A $302.50

Climbing Bulldozer Tractor, red & yel Caterpillar w/driver, EX (EX box), A $195.00

Climbing Fireman, litho tin, red, yel & bl, clockwork, working, orig box (flap missing), 12½", VG-EX, A $200.00

Charlie McCarthy in His Benzine Buggy, lithographed tin, 8" long, EX in box, A, $1,320.00.

Climbing Fireman, plastic helmet, fireman w/comic face climbs ladder, fire litho on base, NM (G box), A $275.00

Convertible, litho tin, bl & sliver, clear plastic windshield & steering wheel, clockwork, non-working, 11", VG-EX, A $55.00

Coo Coo Car, litho tin w/butler driver, bounces, moves forward & backward, ca 1930, 8½", M (NM+ box), A $1,450.00

Coo Coo Car, runs in erratic manner, 5½x8", VG, A....$300.00

Cowboy Rider, horse-bk rider vibrates around as he spins lasso, left arm swings while holding gun, 7", MIB, A........$485.00

Crawler-Dump Truck, litho metal, red, wht & blk, blk fr, red wheels, dummy headlights, rpl rubber treads, 14½", VG, A $248.00

Dagwood Aeroplane, travels w/crazy action as Dagwood's head bobs around, character lithos, rpr box, 9", NM (VG box), A...$1,700.00

Dagwood the Driver, lithographed tin, eccentric clockwork, 8", EX (VG box), A, $1,100.00.

Dagwood the Driver, mc litho tin, clockwork, 8", EX (EX box), A..$1,500.00

Dan Dipsy Car, litho tin w/plastic nodding figure, ca 1950, orig box, 6", EX, A...$302.50

Dapper Dan Coon Jigger, litho tin, bl, yel & red porter jigs on brn trunk, clockwork, working, 10", VG, A $325.00

Dare Devil Flyer, #700, litho tin, includes plane, zeppelin & replica of Empire State Building, 1935, EX (EX box), A..$220.00

Dick Tracy Riot Car, litho tin, bl & yel, friction w/sparks & siren, working, 6½", EX- (G box), A $210.00

Dick Tracy Riot Car, litho tin, friction, character in ea window, orig box, 7", EX+ (EX box), A $375.00

Dick Tracy Squad Car, friction, 11", NM, $275.00.

Dick Tracy Squad Car, litho tin, friction, gr w/figure in ea window, battery-op roof light, 1950s, 11", VG+, A **$164.00**

Disney Airplane, litho tin, airliner w/Disney graphics, friction, props turn, working, 7½", VG-EX, A.....................$500.00

Disney Express, tin locomotive w/Mickey & Goofy engineers+3 cars w/Disney characters at windows, 12", VG+ (M box), A...$406.00

Disney Parade Roadster, mc litho tin, plastic figures, clockwork, working, mc orig box, 11", VG-EX, A $400.00

Donald Duck Dipsy Car, mc litho tin car w/plastic Donald, clockwork, working, orig box, 5½", VG-EX, A $400.00

Donald Duck Dipsy Car, tin w/plastic Donald, crazy actions, his head bobs around, 6", NM (VG box), A $695.00

Donald Duck Duet, litho tin, features Goofy & Donald, 1946, Goofy: 8", Donald: 3", EX (VG box), A $875.00

Donald Duck Duet, litho tin, tiny Donald Duck standing on sm drum, taller Goofy on lg drum, 10", EX, A $770.00

Donald Duck Duet, litho tin w/rubber ears, clockwork, working, Goofy missing ear, orig box, 10½", VG, A $450.00

Donald the Drummer, clockwork, working, 6", G-VG...$175.00

Donald the Drummer, pnt wht plastic, litho tin drum, clockwork, working, orig box, 9¾", VG-EX $350.00

Donald the Skier, pnt wht plastic, litho tin skis, clockwork, working, orig box, 10½", EX, A $400.00

Dora Dipsy Car, mc litho tin w/plastic Dora, forward & reverse w/crazy action, 6", EX+ (NM box), A $275.00

Drive-Ur-Self Car, advances, pull string to determine direction, w/orig string & key, 14", NM (EX box), A...........$1,200.00

Driver Training Car, tin w/plastic roof, travels & turns automatically, 1950s, 6½", NMIB, A $154.00

Dumbo Carousel, Disney, litho tin, 3 Dumbos w/rubber tails, umbrella top lithoed w/Mickey, Donald & Goofy, 7" dia, EX, A..$1,075.00

Farm Tractor & Trailer, litho tin, orange, yel & gr, clockwork, working, rubber treads, 16½", G+, A $45.00

FATC Amos Driver, litho tin, brn, orange & wht, Amos waddles, eyes move, working, 11⅛", G-VG, A $825.00

Ferdinand & Matador, litho tin, matador waving cape at bull on 4-wheeled base, 7", EX, A $450.00

Ferdinand the Bull, walks & spins tail, rubber horns, butterfly on bk, flower in mouth, 6", EX (EX box), A................$445.00

Fighting Tank w/Soldier, litho tin, soldier pops up from turret w/rifle & fires, 1930s, 10", VG, A $105.00

Fire Chief Car, litho tin, red w/yel lettering, friction, working, 11", VG, A..$70.00

Fire Chief Car, working roof light, siren sounds, 11", box w/great graphics, NM+ (EX+ box), A $240.00

Flash Gordon Rocket Fighter Ship, litho tin, red w/yel, wht & blk accents, needs flint for sparking action, 12", EX (VG box), A..$900.00

Flintstone Auto, pnt & litho tin, plastic figure, friction, working, 6¾", EX, A..$130.00

Flintstone Flivver (Fred), litho tin, w/vinyl head, friction, 1962, 7", NM+, A..$467.00

Flintstone Flivver (Fred), litho tin, friction, 1962, Japan, 7", EX, A..$304.00

Flintstones, see Hopping Barney Rubble, Hopping Fred (this section). See also Windups, Friction, and Other Mechanical.

Flippo the Jumping Dog, mc litho tin, flips when wound, 1930s, 4", EX+ (NM box), A...$200.00

Frankenstein, pnt tin & plastic, blk, gr & gray, clockwork, working, orig box, 5½", VG-EX, A $725.00

Funny Face Walker (Harold Lloyd knock-off), litho tin, sways bk & forth, forehead moves up & down, 10½", EX, A $350.00

Funny Flivver, driver's head turns, car goes bk & forth, 6x8", VG, A..$300.00

Funny Flivver, litho tin, funny figure in open car, ca 1925, 7", EX, A..$412.50

George the Drummer Boy, moving-eye version, bass drum, moving eyes, working, 9", VG, A..................................$155.00

George the Drummer Boy, moving-eye version, beats drum & plays cymbals, 9", NM, A $293.00

George the Drummer Boy, stationary eyes, 9", EX+ (EX-box), A $178.00

Golden Goose, lithographed tin, 1930s, MIB, D10, $300.00.

Gobbling Goose, plastic, goose pecks at ground while laying wooden golden eggs, complete w/eggs, 9", NMIB, A $154.00

Goofy, plastic, w/up tail, 1950s, 8", EX, V1 ....$65.00

Gorilla, vinyl, plush & gray pnt tin, clockwork, 3 actions & sound, working, orig box, 7½", EX-NM, A $260.00

Harold Lloyd Walker, expression changes, clockwork, working, rpl arms, 11", G-, A $110.00

Harold Lloyd Walker, expression changes, 1930s, some pnt chipping, o/w EX, 11" $600.00

Hawaiian Banjo, litho tin, complete w/instructions, early 1950s, NMIB $75.00

Hee-Haw, balky mule cart, litho tin, 10", EX, A $176.00

Hee-Haw, farmer drives his mule cart w/5 milk cans loaded in bk, 1925, 10½", NM (EX box), A $485.00

Helicopter Skyport, insert 9" copter into top of 9x11" tin terminal, turn crank for action, EX (NM box), A $283.00

Here Comes Charlie McCarthy, litho tin, red, wht & bl, clockwork, beats drum, 9", VG-EX, A $950.00

Honeymoon Express, litho tin, train circles 7x7" base, w/honeymoon cottage, tunnel & gates, EX (M box), A $227.00

Honeymoon Express, litho tin, train runs through countryside on 5½" dia base, ca 1920s, EX, A $120.00

Honeymoon Express, litho tin, 4" locomotive & cars circle 9" dia base, 3 tunnels & station house, c 1930, EX (NM box), A $265.00

Honeymoon Express, mc litho tin, sm train passes through 3 tunnels, clockwork, working, orig box, 9½", EX, A .$225.00

Honeymoon Express, streamlined train races around 9" dia base under 3 bridges, 1947, NM (G+ box), A $180.00

Honeymoon Express, lithographed tin, 1930s, very minor wear, A, $180.00.

Hop In Jalopy, litho tin, early automobile w/allover lettering, 7", G, A $77.00

Hopalong Cassidy, litho tin, blk & wht rider on mc base, clockwork, working, 11¼", G-VG, A $310.00

Hopping Barney Rubble, litho tin, brn & yel, clockwork, working, orig box, 3", VG-EX, A $575.00

Hey Hey Chicken Snatcher, Black man carries chicken as he is chased by dog, minor restoration, VG, 8¾", A, $900.00.

Hi-Yo Silver the Lone Ranger, litho tin, Silver vibrates, hands spin lasso & swing gun, 1938, 7", EX (EX+-NM box), A $650.00

Hi-Yo Silver the Lone Ranger, mc litho tin, clockwork, lasso spins, working, orig box, 7", VG, A $325.00

Hopping Corkie Corn, Munchie Melon, and Barnaby Banana, 1950s, MIB, D10, each $100.00.

Hopping Big Bad Wolf, mc litho tin, clockwork, working, orig box, 4", VG-EX, A $375.00

Hopping Calamity Clara, litho tin, yel, red & bl, clockwork, working, orig box, 3½", VG+, A $50.00

Hopping Fred Flintstone, litho tin, orange, tan & blk, clockwork, working, orig box, 3", VG-EX, A $550.00

Hopping George Jetson, litho tin, wht, brn, gr & bl, clockwork, working, 3½", VG (G box), A $425.00

Hopping George Jetson, 1963, 3½", NM (G- box), A....$875.00

Hopping Little Pig, mc litho tin, bricklayer costume, clockwork, working, orig box, 4", VG, A $175.00

Hopping Little Pig, mc litho tin, fiddler costume, working, orig box, 4", VG-EX, A $275.00

Hopping Little Pig, mc litho tin, flute player, orig box, 4", VG, A $175.00

Hopping Nutty Mad Indian, litho tin, yel, red, orange & brn, clockwork, working, orig box, 3½", VG, A..............$120.00

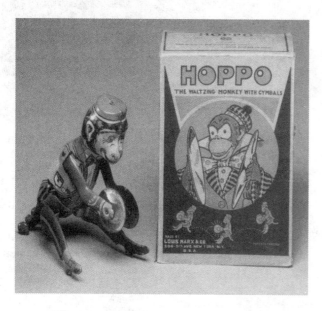

Hoppo the Waltzing Monkey, lithographed tin, 9½", EX, A, $350.00.

Huckleberry Hound, litho tin, friction, Huckleberry has vinyl head, 4", EX (EX box), A $239.00

Joe Penner & His Duck, litho tin, advances w/shuffling feet as his hat tips, 1934, 8", EX, A $500.00

Joe Penner & His Duck, mc litho tin figure in checked suit, clockwork, working, 8", VG-EX (EX box) $1,000.00

Jolly Joe Jeep, Joe wears plastic helmet, his head spins, machine guns turn, 6", NM+ (EX+ box), A $725.00

Joy-Rider, driver's head turns around, 7x5½", NMIB, A .$725.00

Jumpin' Jeep, shaded yel & gr litho tin w/brn & blk trim, clockwork, working, orig box, 5½", EX, A $240.00

Jumpin' Jeep, 4 soldiers, 2 w/machine guns, action box, 6", MIB, A..$385.00

Jumpin' Jeep, 4 soldiers travel in their jeep w/crazy car action, 5½", EX+, A $170.00

Liberty Bus, red litho tin w/blk letters, fenders & wheels, stamped driver, friction, 1920s, 5", EX+-NM, A $300.00

Lighted Train Set, mc litho tin & plastic, clockwork, orig 14½" box, VG-EX, A $45.00

Limping Lizzie, litho tin, early auto w/allover lettering, orig box, 7", VG $375.00

Limping Lizzie, 4x6¾", NM (NM box), A $600.00

Magic Garage, 6" litho tin car hits garage door, door opens & car enters, 1950s, 10x8" garage, EX+ (NM box), A $290.00

Main Street, trolleys & trucks move along track between buildings, traffic cop in center, play-worn, 24", A $275.00

Mechanical Gorilla (King Kong), tin, plush & plastic, walks, beats chest, opens/closes mouth, growls, 8", EX (NM box), A $450.00

Merry Makers, litho tin, w/marquee, 1 head loose, working, orig box (rpr), 9¼", G, A...$875.00

Merry Makers, litho tin, w/marquee, 4 motions, working, orig box, 9", VG, A $1,100.00

Merry Makers, litho tin version w/no backdrop & band leader sitting on piano, 9x9x5", NM................................$750.00

Mickey Mouse, plastic, tail spins, 1950s, NM, T1 ....$145.00

Mickey Mouse Express, plane with Mickey pilot circles 9" diameter base with train, 1940s, EX+ (NM box), A, $1,075.00.

Mickey Mouse Meteor Train Set, 11" engine, coal car, boxcar & caboose, bell ringing sounds, overall wear, G, A $475.00

Mickey the Musician, pnt blk plastic & litho tin, plastic & metal xylophone, clockwork, working, orig box, 11", EX, A...$450.00

Midget Climbing Fighting Tank, plastic tread hubs, detailed camo, 5", NM (EX box), A $170.00

Midget Racer, 1950s-style racer w/helmeted driver, exhaust pipe & brake lever, vivid box, 6", NM (EX box), A........$170.00

Mighty Kong, pnt tin, plush & plastic, clockwork, opens mouth, pounds chest & growls, working, 10½", VG-EX, A ...$90.00

Mighty Thor, vinyl, dances & jumps, working, 1968, 5", EX, H4 ....$39.00

Military Truck, litho tin w/canvas cover arched over truck bed, w/up disengaged, 10", VG, A $165.00

Milton Berle Carzy Car, litho tin w/plastic hat, 6", G....$225.00

Milton Berle Crazy Car, mc litho tin, red plastic hat, clockwork, working, orig box, 6¼", VG+ $395.00

Monkey Cyclist, litho tin w/cb arms on bl cycle, 6x6", EX (EX box), A $225.00

Moon Bug, yel head, blk & red striped body, NM, T1 ...$135.00

Moon Creature, litho tin, MIB, V1................................$175.00

Moon Mullins Handcar, litho tin, 6", VG, A $440.00

Mortimer Snerd's Hometown Band, litho tin, red, wht & bl, clockwork, beats drum, working, orig box, 9", EX.**$1,200.00**

Old Jalopy, lithographed tin, 7", VG, A, $150.00.

Mortimer Snerd's Hometown Band, lithographed tin, some scuffs, 8½", VG, A, $685.00.

Mortimer Snerd Tricky Auto, litho tin, Mortimer's head spins as auto moves to & fro & in circles, 1930s, EX+ (EX box), A..**$1,200.00**

Mortimer Snerd Walker, litho tin, c 1938 by McCarthy Inc, 8", NM **$250.00**

Motorcycle w/Sidecar, litho tin, 8½", G, A **$275.00**

Mowgli on a Stump, c Walt Disney, 1967, M **$75.00**

Musical Pluto, 3" Pluto travels around base under bridges, 8" sq base, correct generic box, M (EX+ box), A **$550.00**

Mystic Motorcycle, litho tin, policeman moves to edge of table & turns about, 1930s, 4", EX (NM box), A.............**$237.00**

Nutty Mad Tricycle, pnt celluloid figure, purple & blk litho tin tricycle, clockwork w/revolving bell, NMIB, A.......**$150.00**

Old Jalopy, advances w/swaying motion, allover graffiti, tin driver, 7", MIB, A...**$400.00**

Old Jalopy, litho tin, blk, yel & red, clockwork, working, 6¾", VG, A..**$150.00**

Old Jalopy, litho tin, 4 college boys in crazy car, orig box, 6", EX, from $270 to **$350.00**

Owl, brn & tan plush, clockwork, owl hoots, working, orig box, 7½", EX, A...**$90.00**

Party Pluto, pnt yel plastic, gr, red & blk w/rubber ears, clockwork, working, orig box (flap missing), 10", VG-EX, A...**$260.00**

Pecking Goose, working, EX pnt, 6x9", A $60.00

Pinched, mc litho tin, auto circles through bridges & buildings, motorcycle cop follows, working, 10" sq, VG, A $400.00

Pinched, truck moves in circle on 10x10" base w/2 bridges, tunnel & station house, cop stops truck, EX (NM box), A $1,900.00

Pinocchio & Figaro, mc litho tin figure w/blk & wht cat, clockwork, 2 motions, working, orig box, 8½", VG-EX, A $625.00

Pinocchio Acrobat, litho tin, Watch Him Go! lettered on base, 16", VG, A...$247.50

Pinocchio 1910 Studebaker, red, blk, bl, gold & silver plastic, 1960s, 4x3", NM, T2 ....$40.00

Planet Patrol Space Tank, litho tin, brn, bl & red w/wood wheels, clockwork, working, orig box, 10", EX, A...$325.00

Pluto, litho tin, yel, bl & red, lever action, working, ears missing, 9", G, A...$50.00

Pluto, plastic & metal, tail spins, 1950s, NM....................$75.00

Pluto & Donald Duck Duet, NM, M4...........................$175.00

Pluto Drum Major, Japan, litho tin, orig box, 6", VG+, A.$385.00

Police Cyclist, circles w/loud siren noise, w/orig key in envelope, 1930, 8½", NM (EX box), A $700.00

Police Siren Motorcycle, 1930s, MIB, D10, $750.00.

Police Motorcycle, mc litho tin, clockwork, working, 4½", G, A $130.00

Police Motorcycle & Sidecar, red cycle w/driver in bl, wood tires, 1930s, 3½", NM, A................................$200.00

Popeye, see also Walking Popeye

Popeye & Olive Oyl on Roof, litho tin, Popeye does the jig while Olive Oyl plays the accordion, 9", VG, A $660.00

Popeye Express, litho tin, Popeye twirls in airplane above 10" dia base, 1935, MIB......................................$1,850.00

Popeye Express w/Moving Parrot, working, very minor scuffs, 8x8", NM, A..$950.00

Popeye Express w/no Parrot, c King Features, litho tin, 8x8", NM (EX- box), A $2,250.00

Popeye Express w/Stationary Parrot, litho tin, legs move as he pushes wheelbarrow, 8½", VG+-EX, A....................$600.00

Popeye Express w/Stationary Parrot, litho tin, very minor scratches, 8x8", NM, A $800.00

Popeye Jigger, litho tin, EX, M5........................$575.00

Popeye the Champ, celluloid Popeye & Bluto on revolving litho tin platform, clockwork, working, orig box, VG, A $1,650.00

Popeye the Champ, 4" celluloid Popeye & Bluto stand in 7" sq tin ring, circle ring & move arms, 1930s, NMIB, A........$3,450.00

Popeye the Pilot, litho tin, Popeye in plane, 1940s, 8½", EX, M5...$600.00

Popeye the Pilot, litho tin plane, Popeye in cockpit, 1930s, 8", EX (EX box), A.....................................$1,045.00

Porky Pig, litho tin, standing w/umbrella, working, orig box, 8¼", G-VG, from $180 to $250.00

Porky Pig, standing w/umbrella, c Leon Schlesinger, scuffs on bk, non-working but complete, 8½", VG, A $145.00

Quickdraw McGraw Car, pnt tin & rubber, red, bl & brn, friction, working, 4", G+, A $55.00

Raceway, litho tin, w/2 4" cars, 2 keys & 16-pc track, 1930s, EX, W1..$329.00

Red Cap Porter, litho tin, red & bl porter w/yel bags, clockwork, working, orig box (flap missing), 8½", EX, A $600.00

Red Cap Porter, litho tin, 8½", EX, A $357.50

Roadster, litho tin, orange & bl, 12", VG+, A $550.00

Rock 'Em Sock 'Em Robots, 11" plastic robots in 14" sq ring, spring plunger activated, complete, MIB, A $310.00

Rocket Fighter, litho tin, rpl flint cover, 12", EX, A $412.50

Roll-Over Plane, litho tin, goggled pilot sits in cockpit, rod at bk turns plane, advances, 5½", VG+ (EX+ box), A $303.00

Roll-Over Pluto, litho tin, red, gr & yel w/rubber ears, clockwork, 1 ear missing, orig box (torn), 8", G-VG, A ..$210.00

Rookie Cop Motorcycle, travels in circle, falls over, rights itself, siren noise, 8½", EX (G box), A $385.00

Rookie Pilot, tin, ca 1940, VG.......................................$350.00

Rookie Pilot, yel & red litho tin, lg-headed pilot in cockpit, advances w/erratic motions, EX (VG+ box), A.......$556.00

Royal Bus Line, litho tin, red, yel & gr, EX $400.00

Royal Coupe, litho tin, 9", G, T3.................................$250.00

Royal Coupe, mc litho tin, rumble seat, plated bumpers & lights, orig box, 9", EX, A..$600.00

Siren Fire Chief Car, pnt & litho tin, gr & yel, clockwork w/siren, battery-op lights, 15", EX...........................$450.00

Skyhawk Airplane Tower, litho tin, 2 4" planes w/celluloid props fly above tower, battle scene, 1930s, 8", NM, A.......$233.00

Skyview Yellow Cab, litho tin w/driver & women passengers at windows, wood wheels, 1950s, 7", EX, A $99.00

Smokey Joe the Climbing Fireman, litho tin, bl, yel & red w/blk trim, clockwork, working, orig box, 12½", G+, A ..$280.00

Range Rider, Lone Ranger on Silver swings his lasso, 10x11", NMIB, A, $500.00.

Range Rider (Lone Ranger & Silver), litho tin, twirls lasso, rocker base, 1938, EX, A $265.00

Rapid Express Pickup Truck, tin & pressed steel, 1 decal complete, 2nd 75%, wood tires, 9", EX (G box), A $165.00

Smitty on Scooter, 8", VG, A, from $1,300.00 to $1,450.00.

Space Creature, rubber ears, blk antennae, yel cone-shaped body, walks, opens & closes mouth, sounds, 5½", EX, A $75.00

Space Man, vinyl head w/plastic arms, 1960s, 7", EX, H4 ....$110.00

Sparkling Climbing Tank, MIB $175.00

Sparkling Climbing Tractor, litho tin, plastic driver, clockwork, working, non-working sparker, orig box, 8", VG-EX, A $60.00

Sparkling Fighter, US Army plane advances on balloon tires, wing guns spark, 7", EX, A $240.00

Sparkling Highboy Climbing Tractor, no driver, NMIB .$200.00

Sparkling Rocket Fighter Ship (Flash Gordon), MIB, $1,450.00.

Sparkling Soldier, litho tin, brn w/red & blk trim, clockwork (crawls), orig box (top flap damage), 7½", EX, A....$230.00

Sparkling Space Tank, litho tin, slightly damaged orig box, 10", EX, A $330.00

Sparkling Tank 5A, litho tin, orig box slightly damaged, 10", EX, A $275.00

Sparkling Warship, litho tin w/depth charges, 14½", NM (G+ box), M5 ....$220.00

Speed Boy Delivery Motorcycle, 1930s, 10", M, D10, $650.00.

Speed Boy Delivery Motorcycle, litho tin, 10", VG+, A......$330.00

Steamroller, full-figure standing driver under canopy, 1930s, 6x8½", EX, A $350.00

Subway Express, mc litho tin, plastic tunnel, clockwork, working, orig 9½" box, EX, A $210.00

Superman Turnover Plane, bl plane, (rare color), 6x6", EX-, A $1,110.00

Superman Turnover Plane, gold & silver plane, Superman: EX, plane: VG, A $1,400.00

Superman Turnover Airplane, gold and silver plane, 6", EX-NM, A, $1,700.00.

Superman Turnover Tank, litho tin, blk, wht & bl w/chrome trim, clockwork, working, 4", VG, A $325.00

Tick & Tack the Tumbling Two, litho tin, orig box, 18", VG, A $209.00

Tidy Tim Street Cleaner, lithographed tin, EX-NM, D10, $650.00.

Tidy Tim, litho tin, figure pushing wheeled barrel, 9", VG+, A $412.50

Tiger Kart, friction, vinyl head, tiger advances on cart, MIB, A $150.00

Tiger Trike, plastic tiger rides trike w/bell noise, 4", MIB, A...$125.00

Tom Corbett Sparking Space Ship, bl, yel & red, clockwork w/sparking action & sound, working, orig box, 12", VG+, A...$550.00

Tom Corbett Sparking Space Ship, litho tin spaceship w/Tom & crew depicted in cockpit, 12", EX+ (VG+ box), A...$700.00

Tom Tom Jungle Boy, mc litho tin, red cloth shorts, rubber hands & blk hair, clockwork, working, orig box, 6½", EX, A...$150.00

Toyland Farm Products Wagon, litho tin, red, wht, bl & yel, clockwork, working, step missing, 9½", VG, A..........$95.00

Toyland Milk Wagon, litho tin, orange wheels, pulled by wht horse, working, orig box (parts missing), 9½", VG, A...$200.00

Toyland Milk Wagon, wagon w/red roof, brn horse, working, orig box (rpr flap), 10", EX, A...$325.00

Tri-Motor Army Bomber, litho tin w/pilot, co-pilot & crew at windows, props & wheels move, 1930s, rare, 24", EX, A...$775.00

Tricky Motorcycle, litho tin, police motorcyclist advances & turns, 4½", EX (NM box), A...$246.00

Tricky Taxi on Busy Street, taxi moves in all directions on 6x10" base, NM (G box), A...$550.00

Truck, bl litho tin, American Trucking Co & Padded Van, 3 stars on roof, Marx logo on hood, friction, 5" L, G, A...$95.00

Tumbling Monkey, litho tin, monkey spins head over heels between 2 chairs, 5", VG (EX box), A...$155.00

Tunnette Car w/Saxophone Player, litho tin, friction, ca 1960s, MIP...$75.00

Turnover Tank, litho tin, moves & rolls over, ca 1940-44, EX...$95.00

Turnover Tank #5, advances, flips over, 4", NM (EX+ box), A...$145.00

Twin Engine Bomber, litho tin, orig box, 18" wingspan, EX, A...$302.50

Uncle Wiggily & His Car, mc litho tin, clockwork, working, orig box, 7", EX, A...$825.00

Uncle Wiggily & His Car, mc litho tin, 1935, 8x6½", NMIB, from $1000 to...$1,300.00

Untouchables, target game, litho tin, .45 shoots at moving gangsters, EX- (G box), A...$120.00

Walking Popeye, litho tin, Popeye carries birdcages, clockwork, working, orig box (rough), 8", EX...$450.00

Walt Disney's Television Car, litho tin, friction, Disney character in ea window, 7", NMIB, A...$850.00

Wee Scottie, litho & flocked tin, advances as front legs move, 1930s, 5", EX, from $85 to...$120.00

Western Bucking Bronco, weight driven, plastic cowboy & horse, Woolworth, Hong Kong, 1966, 13", MIB, A..........$135.00

Whee-Whiz Auto Racer, 13" dish-like track moves up & down, 2 4" racers speed around, 1930s, EX (G box), A ..$1,900.00

Whee-Whiz Auto Racer, 4 1½" cars race around 13" dia dish-shaped track that rocks up & down, ca 1925, G+, A.$470.00

Whoopee Car, mc litho tin, eccentric clockwork, working, 8", G, A...$65.00

Wise Pluto, advances & turns at end of table, w/correct tail & ears, 1940s, 8", NM (EX box), A...$650.00

Wonder Cyclist, boy rides trike, moves handlebars to change direction, bell rings, 8", NM (EX+ box), A.............$550.00

Wonder Cyclist, red, yel, blk & bl litho tin, clockwork rings bell, working, orig box, 8½", VG, A...$230.00

Woopee Crazy Car, mc litho tin, complete w/trunk lid, ca 1930, EX+...$550.00

WWI Doughboy Tank, litho tin, camouflage pnt, pop-up soldier, clockwork, working, 10", G...$60.00

WWI Doughboy Tank, litho tin tank advances w/swiveling machine gun, pop-up soldier, 9½", NMIB...$245.00

WWI Sparkling Tank, litho tin, 8", VG, A...$143.00

Zippo the Climbing Monkey, litho tin, complete w/string & hooks, hat mk Zippo, 9½", EX (EX box), A...$516.00

Miscellaneous

Apollo Astronaut, HP plastic spaceman & accessories, on space illus card, 1970, complete, MOC, A...$110.00

Army Transport Truck & Cannon, litho tin, gr, yel & silver, canvas tarp, plastic wheels, orig 13¾" box, EX, A...$185.00

Atlas ICBM Rocket w/Launching Pad & Gantry, plastic, spring lever action, 13", NM (EX box), A...$55.00

Crop Duster Plane Set, plastic 5½" plane, push plunger, water sprays, 2 plastic figures, 7x6x3" tin hanger, MIB, A...$100.00

Deluxe Delivery Truck, tin w/separate grille pc, tin balloon tires, 1950s, 11", NM (EX box), A...$140.00

Disney Snap Eeze, EX (EX box), O1...$225.00

Fix-All Helicopter, Army gr plastic w/decals, 'easy to assemble & take apart,' no instructions, 1950s, EX (G box), A.....$45.00

Fix-All Wrecker & Hard Top Convertible, plastic, car: 9½", wrecker: 9", EX (VG box), A...$110.00

Hometown Meat Market, litho tin, 3-sided open front showing interior of meat market w/3 butchers, 5x2", NM (G box), A...$283.00

Hometown Movie Theatre, litho tin, turn knobs to 'show' movie, 1930, 5x2", NM (G box), A...$399.00

Hometown Police Station, litho tin, 3-sided w/open front showing interior of police station, 1930, 5x2", NM (EX box), A...$650.00

Kitty Kat (box only), toy has press-down tail action & ball between paws, complete, clean, NM, A...$58.00

Mustang Convertible, 1/64 scale, diecast, metallic bl, plastic tires, 1960s, 2⅜", EX, W1...$9.00

RCA Service Truck, wht plastic w/yel ladder, red decals, rear door opens, 8½", unused, NMIB, A...$120.00

Roadside Rest Service Station, litho tin, coffee stand, twin gas pump w/orig glass lights, accessories, 14x10", VG, A...$450.00

Upside Down Tumble Toy, tin, 3 clowns attached to rod tumble down chute, 1925, 10", EX (G box), A...$1,263.00

US Mail Truck, litho tin, red, wht & bl w/gold trim, plastic wheels, 12½", EX, A...$120.00

Wrecker, plastic, removable hood, complete w/2 spare tires & 8 loose tools in 4 compartments, EX...$125.00

Matchbox

The Matchbox series of English and American-made autos, trucks, taxis, Pepsi-Cola trucks, steamrollers, Greyhound buses, etc., was very extensive. By the late 1970s, the company was cranking out more than 5 million cars every week, and while those days may be over, Matchbox still produces about 75 million vehicles on a yearly basis.

Introduced in 1953, the Matchbox Miniatures series has always been the mainstay of the company. There were 75 models in all, but with enough variations to make collecting them a real challenge. Larger, more detailed models were introduced in 1957; this series, called Major Pack, was replaced a few years later by a similar line called King Size. To compete with Hot Wheels, Matchbox converted most models over to a line called SuperFast that sported thinner, low-friction axles and wheels. (These are much more readily available than the original 'regular wheels,' the last of which were made in 1969.) At about the same time, the King Size series became known as Speed Kings; in 1977 the line was reintroduced under the name Super Kings.

In the early '70s, Lesney started to put dates on the baseplates of their toy cars. The name 'Lesney' was coined from the first names of the company's founders. The last Matchboxes that carried the Lesney mark were made in 1982. Today many models can be bought for less than $10.00, though a few are priced much higher.

Another line that's become very popular is their Models of Yesteryear. These are slightly larger replicas of antique and vintage vehicles. Values of $20.00 to $60.00 for mint-in-box examples are average, though a few sell for even more. To learn more, we recommend *Matchbox Toys, 1948 to 1993*, by Dana Johnson. Our advisor for this category is Mark Giles (G2).

To determine values of examples in conditions other than given in our listings, based on MIB or MOC prices, deduct 5% if the original container is missing, 30% if the condition is excellent, and as much as 70% for a toy graded only very good.

Key:
LW — Laser Wheels (introduced in 1987)
reg — regular wheels (Matchbox Miniatures)
SF — SuperFast

1-75 Series

1-C, Road Roller, reg, 1958, 2⅜", MIB, J3 ....$45.00
1-E, Mercedes Truck, reg, orig canopy, MIB, W1 ....$12.50
1-K, Jaguar XJ6, SF, 1987, 3", MOC, J3 ....$2.00
2-B, Dumper, reg, 1957, 1⅞", MIB, J3..............................$50.00
2-D, Mercedes Trailer, reg, orig canopy, MIB, W1 ....$12.00
2-F, Jeep Hot Rod, SF, red, MIB......................................$15.00
2-G, Hovercraft, SF, avocado, blk hull, silver scoop, Rescue labels, MIB, W1 ....$10.00
2-H, S-2 Jet, SF, 1981, 2⅞", MOC, J3 ....$6.00
3-A, Cement Mixer, reg, 1⅝", MOC, from $35 to............$55.00
3-B, Bedford Tipper, reg, red dumper, M, G3 ....$20.00
3-D, Mercedes Ambulance, SF, red, MIB, A3 ....$15.00
3-E, Monteverdi Hai, SF, MIB, W1....................................$7.50

4-A, Massey Harris Tractor, reg, MIB, W1 ....$60.00
4-C, Triumph Motorcycle & Sidecar, reg, MIB................$50.00
4-F, Gruesome Twosome, SF, 1971, 2⅞", MOC, J3 ....$8.00
5-F, Seafire Boat, SF, 1975, 3", MOC, J3 ....$6.00
5-I, Peterbilt Petrol Tanker, SF, 1985, 3", MOC, J3 ....$3.00
6-E, Ford Pickup, SF, 1970, 2¾", MOC, J3 ....$10.00
6-K, Quarry Truck, replica of 6-A, 1993, 2⅛", MOC, J3 ....$3.00
7-A, Milk Float, reg, wht letters, driver, bottles, MIB, W1 ....$100.00
7-B, Ford Anglia, reg, 1961, 2⅝", MOC, from $25 to.......$45.00
7-D, Refuse Truck, reg, orange & gray, EX+, A3 ....$6.00
8-A, CAT Tractor, reg, yel w/silver trim, M.....................$25.00
8-E, Ford Mustang, reg, wht, NM, G3 ....$15.00
8-G, Ford Mustang Wildcat Dragster, SF, 1970, 2⅞", MOC, J3...$8.00
8-N, Airport Fire Tender, SF, 1992, 3", MOC, J3................$2.00
9-A, Dennis Fire Engine, reg, MIB....................................$60.00
9-E, AMX Javelin, SF, gr, MIB, A3....................................$10.00
9-H, CAT Bulldozer, SF, 1983, 2⅝", MOC, J3 ....$4.00
10-A, Mechanical Horse & Trailer, reg, gold trim, MIB, W1 ....$59.00
10-C, Sugar Container Truck, reg, 1961, 2⅝", MOC, J3..$50.00
10-H, Buick LeSabre, SF, 1987, 3", MOC, J3 ....$3.00
11-C, Jumbo Crane, reg, yel weight box, MIB $18.00
11-D, Scaffolding Truck, reg, w/scaffolding, M, W1.........$10.00
11-G, Car Transporter, SF, orange, blk base w/bl windows, red, yel & bl cars, MIB, from $5 to $6.00
11-I, IMSA Mustang, SF, 1983, 3", MOC, J3 ....$3.00
12-A, Land Rover, reg, gr, M, G3......................................$35.00
12-C, Land Rover, reg, bl, NM, A3....................................$12.00
12-D, Safari Land Rover (luggage on roof), SF, 1070, MOC, J3 ....$15.00
13-D, Dodge Wrecker, reg, yel & gr, NM, G3 ....$12.00
13-F, Baja Dune Buggy, SF, 1971, 2⅝", MOC, J3 ....$10.00
13-H, 4X4 Mini-Pickup, SF, roll bar, rally lights, 1982, 2¾", MOC, J3 ....$4.00
14-D, Iso Grifo, reg, EX, W1..$6.00
14-F, Rallye Royale, SF, 1973, 2⅞", MOC, J3....................$8.00
14-G, Minihaha, SF, red, M, A3 ....$10.00
14-K, Jeep Eagle/Laredo, SF, 1987, 2⅝", MOC, J3............$4.00
15-A, Prime Mover, reg, NM+, W1..................................$35.00
15-A, Truck Tractor, reg, dk orange, M, G3....................$30.00

15-E, Volkswagen 1500 Saloon with Superfast Wheels, 1970, 2⅞", MIB, $20.00.

15-G, Hi-Ho Silver VW Bug, SF, M, W1 ....$7.50

15-K, Saab 9000, SF, 1988, 3", MOC, J3.........................$4.00

16-A, Atlantic Trailer, reg, tan, NM $35.00

16-C, Scammell Mountaineer Snow Plow, reg, EX+ $15.00

16-H, Formula Racer 'Pirelli,' SF, 1984, 3", MOC, J3........$4.00

17-C, Tipper, reg, red & orange, EX, A3 ....$10.00

17-H, AMX Pro Stocker, SF, 1983, 2⅝", MOC, J3.............$6.00

18-D, CAT Crawler, reg, 1964, 2⅜", MOC, J3.................$30.00

18-G, Hondarora Harley-Davidson Motorcycle & Rider, SF, 1875, MOC, J3................................$8.00

19-D, Lotus Racer, reg, gr, M.......................................$15.00

19-G, Badger Cement Truck, SF, 1976, 3", MOC, J3.........$6.00

20-C, Chevy Impala Taxi w/driver, reg, 1965, 3", MOC..$15.00

20-C, Chevy Taxi, reg, yel, EX, A3.................................$10.00

20-D, Lamborghini Marzal, SF, red, NM, A3..................$12.00

20-G, Jeep Eagle/Laredo 4X4, SF, 1983, 2⅝", MOC, J3 .....$4.00

21-A, Long Distance Coach, reg, NM+, W1 ....$34.00

21-D, Concrete Truck, reg, red & yel, NM......................$10.00

22-A, Vauxhall Cresta Sedan, reg, MIB, from $40 to.......$45.00

22-C, Pontiac Grand Prix, red, 1964, VG, G2.................$7.00

22-C, Pontiac Grand Prix Sports Coupe, reg, NM, W1 ...$12.00

22-D, Pontiac Grand Prix, SF, 1970, 3", MOC, J3 ....$12.00

22-E, Intercity Commuter, SF, maroon, NM, A3 ....$12.00

22-G, Bigfoot Toyota Mini Camper, SF, 1983, 2¾", MOC, J3................................$4.00

23-A, Berkeley Cavalier, reg, bl, hitch, EX-....................$30.00

23-D, House Trailer Caravan, reg, pk, MIB, W1 ....$18.00

23-E, Atlas Truck, reg, 1975, 3", MOC, J3.......................$4.00

24-B, Weatherhill Hydraulic Excavator, reg, MIB, W1....$35.00

24-F, Shunter, SF, yel, VG..$3.00

24-K, Lincoln Town Car, reg, 1990, 3", MOC, J3 ....$2.00

25, Mod Tractor, SF, purple, M A3 ....$8.00

25-A, Dunlop Van, reg, decals, VG, from $12 to.............$15.00

25-C, BP Petrol Tanker, 1964, 3", MOC, $30.00.

25-H, Toyota Celica GT, reg, 1978, 3", MOC, J3 ....$4.00

26-B, Foden Concrete Truck, reg, orange barrel, VG, W1 .$15.00

26-E, Big Banger, reg, 1972, 2⅝", MOC, J3 ....$8.00

27-D, Mercedes 230SL Convertible, reg, NM, W1 ....$10.00

27-F, Lamborghini, Countach, SF, red, NM+, A3.............$6.00

27-H, Jeep Cherokee, SF, 1987, 2⅞", MOC, J3 ....$2.00

28-C, Jaguar MK10, reg, NM+ $20.00

28-E, Mack Dump Truck, SF, 1970, 2⅝", MOC, J3...........$8.00

28-G, Lincoln Continental Mark IV, SF, MIB $9.00

29-C, Fire Pumper, reg, red, NM $10.00

29-E, Racing Mini, SF, orange, stickers, NM+................$6.00

29-F, Shovel Nose Tractor, SF, 1976, 2⅞", MOC, J3 ....$3.00

30-B, 6-Wheel Crane, reg, silver w/gray hook, M, G3......$35.00

30-C, 8-Wheel Crane Truck, reg, MIB, W1 ....$12.50

30-F, Swamp Rat, reg, 1976, 3", MOC, J3.......................$6.00

31-A, American Ford Wagon, reg, yel, NMIB, from $35 to.$40.00

31-B, Ford Fairlane Station Wagon, reg, 1960, 2¾", MOC, J3................................$40.00

31-C, Lincoln Continental, reg, aqua, M, W1 ....$10.00

31-C, Lincoln Continental, reg, gr, EX, A3......................$8.00

31-E, Volks Dragon, SF, 1971, 2½", MOC, J3 ....$8.00

31-F, Caravan Camping Trailer, SF, NM+, W1 ....$3.00

32-B, E-Type Jaguar (XKE), reg, EX..............................$25.00

32-F, Field Gun, SF, 1978, 3", MOC, J3...........................$5.00

33-B, Ford Zephyr, reg, gr, EX $21.00

33-J, Ford Utility Truck, SF, 1989, 3", MOC, J3 ....$2.00

34-B, Volkswagen Camper, reg, lt gr, 1962, 2¼", MOC, J3 .$50.00

34-E, Formula 1, SF, yel, EX, A3.....................................$6.00

34-G, Chevy Pro Stocker, SF, wht, MIB..........................$6.00

35-A, Marshall Horse Box, reg, MIB, W1......................$60.00

35-B, Snow Trac, reg, red, cast lettering, MIB, G3..........$20.00

35-C, Merryweather Fire Engine, SF, red, M, A3 ....$10.00

35-G, 4x4 Pickup Camper, SF, 1986, 3", MOC, J3 ....$3.00

36-A, Austin A50 Sedan, reg, 1957, 2⅝", MOC, J3.........$45.00

36-C, Opel Diplomat, reg, gold, EX, A3..........................$8.00

36-E, Hot Rod Draguar, SF, pk, M, A3 ....$12.00

37-A, Coca-Cola Truck, reg, orig cases, lg letters, G+, W1 .$20.00

37-D, Cattle Truck, reg, yel & gray, NM, A3 ....$7.00

37-F, Soopa Coopa, SF, bl, MIB, A3 ....$15.00

37-J, Jeep 4x4, SF, w/roll cage & winch, 1984, 2⅞", MOC, J3................................$3.00

38-C, Honda Motorcycle & Trailer, reg, decals, yel trailer, G+ $9.00

38-G, Camper Pickup Truck, SF, 1980, 3", MOC, J3.......$12.00

39-C, Ford Tractor, reg, bl & yel, M, from $10 to $12.00

39-H, Ford Bronco II 4x4, SF, 1990, 3", MOC, J3 ....$2.00

39-J, Mercedes Benz, 1991, 3", MOC...............................$2.00

40-A, Bedford Tipper Truck, 1957, 2⅛", EX, $25.00.

40-B, Royal Tiger Coach, reg, silver & gray, M................$20.00

40-C, Hay Trailer, reg, 1967, 3¼", MOC, J3....................$15.00

41-A, Ford GT Racer, reg, wht, NMIB, G3 ....$15.00

41-E, Siva Spider, SF, 1972, 3", MOC, J3 ....$8.00

41-I, Jaguar XJ6, SF, 1987, 3", MOC, J3...............................$2.00

42-B, Studebaker Lark Wagonaire Station Wagon, reg, orig hunter & dog, NM+, W1 ....**$17.50**

42-C, Iron Fairy Crane, reg, MIB, W1 ....**$11.50**

42-E, Tyre Fryer, SF, 1972, 3", MOC, J3 ....$6.00

43-C, Pony Trailer, reg, orig horses still on tree, NM+, W1..**$17.50**

43-G, '57 Chevy, SF, 1979, 3", MOC, J3 ....$2.00

44-A, Rolls Royce Silver Cloud, reg, 1958, 2⅝", MOC, J3.**$40.00**

44-C, GMC Refrigerator Truck, reg, M, W1 ....**$10.00**

44-E, Boss Mustang, SF, 1972, 2⅞", MOC, J3..............$8.00

44-F, Passenger Coach Train Car, SF, red, NM+, W1.......$3.00

45-C, Ford Group 6, SF, dk red, EX+ **$12.00**

45-E, Kenworth COE Aerodyne, SF, 1988, 2¾", MOC, J3 .$3.00

46-A, Morris Minor 1000, reg, 1958, 2", MOC, J3 ....**$45.00**

46-B, Pickford's Removal Van, reg, gr, M, from $30 to **$40.00**

46-C, Mercedes 300SE, reg, bl, NM+................................**$10.00**

47-F, Pannier Tank Locomotive, SF, 1979, 3", MOC, J3 ...$4.00

48-B, Sports Boat & Trailer (plastic boat), reg, 1961, 2⅝", MIB, J3 ....**$25.00**

48-F, Sambron Jacklift Forklift, SF, yel blade, MIB, W1 ....$7.50

49-A, Army Halftrack Mark II Personnel Carrier, reg, 1958, 2½", MIB, J3 ....**$30.00**

49-B, Unimog, reg, tan & aqua, NM+, W1 ....**$11.50**

49-E, Crane Truck, SF, yel, EX+, A3 ....$4.00

49-I, Lamborghini Diablo, SF, 1992, 3", MOC, J3.............$2.00

50-B, John Deere Tractor, reg, NM, W1/A3 ....**$13.00**

50-B, Kennel Truck, reg, gr, MIB, G3.............................**$20.00**

50-G, Harley-Davidson Motorcycle, SF, 1980, 2¾", MOC, J3.............................$6.00

51-J, Camaro IROC Z, SF, 1985, 3", MOC, J3 ....$2.00

53-G, Flareside Pickup, SF, 1982, 2⅞", MOC, J3...............$4.00

54-A, Saracen Personnel Carrier, reg, NM+, W1 ....**$17.50**

54-B, S&S Cadillac Ambulance, reg, wht, NM, G3.........**$15.00**

54-D, Ford Capri, SF, pk, MIB, from $8 to......................**$10.00**

54-F, Motor Home, SF, 1980, 3¼", MOC, J3....................**$12.00**

55-D, Mercury Police Car, reg, wht, bl dome lights, labels, VG-, W1 ....$4.50

55-G, Hellraiser, reg, 1975, 3", MOC, J3..........................$6.00

56-B, Fiat 1500, reg, gr, EX...**$10.00**

56-B, Fiat 1500, reg, gr, MIB, G3 ....**$15.00**

56-C, Pininfarina, SF, gold, MIB, W1 ....**$15.00**

56-G, Peterbilt Tanker, reg, 1982, 3", MOC, J3.................$4.00

57-B, Chevy Impala, reg, 1961, 2¾", MIB, J3 ....**$35.00**

57-C, Land Rover Fire Vehicle, reg, red, NM, G3............**$10.00**

58-A, BEA Coach, reg, bl, clear decals, NM...................**$40.00**

58-E, Woosh-N-Push, reg, yel, MIB, A3 ....**$15.00**

58-F, Faun Dump Truck, SF, yel, EX+, A3......................$5.00

59-C, Fire Chief Galaxie, reg, red, EX, A3 ....**$10.00**

59-F, Planet Scout, reg, gr, M **$12.00**

59-I, Porsche 944, reg, 1991, 3", MOC, J3 ....$2.00

60-B, Site Hut Truck, reg, bl, NM+, A3 ....$6.00

60-D, Lotus Super 7, reg, 1971, 3", MOC, J3 ....$6.00

60-F, Mustang Piston Popper, SF, yel, MIB (1981 box), W1 .$7.50

61-A, Ferret Scout Car, reg, 1959, 2¼", MOC, J3.............**$35.00**

61-G, Nissan 300 ZX, 1900, 3", MIB, $2.00.

62-C, Mercury Cougar, reg, MIB, W1 ....**$15.00**

62-G, Corvette T-Roof, SF, 1980, 3", MOC, J3..................$5.00

63-E, Freeway Gas Tanker, SF, orange & wht, NM+, A3 ..$8.00

64-B, MG 1100 Sedan, reg, MIB, W1 ....**$12.50**

51-C, 8-Wheel Tipper Truck, Pointer and dog on side of bed, regular wheels, 1969, 3", MIB, $15.00.

52-B, BRM Racer, reg, bl, #5 labels, MIB, W1 ....**$15.00**

52-D, Police Launch, SF, 1976, 3", MOC, J3......................$6.00

53-C, Ford Zodiac Mark IV, reg, metallic silver & bl, MIB..**$15.00**

53-F, CJ-6 Jeep, SF, red & tan, MIB.................................$4.00

65-E, Airport Coach, 1977, MIB, $10.00.

64-D, Slingshot Dragster, SF, 1971, 3", MOC, J3 ....$6.00

64-E, MG1100, reg, gr, EX..$10.00

65-B, 3.4 Litre Jaguar, reg, red, MIB, G3.........................$35.00

65-C, Claas Combine, reg, red, NM, A3 ....$6.00

65-G, Indy Racer, SF, 1984, 3", MOC, J3.............................$2.00

66-B, Harley-Davidson Motorcycle w/Sidecar, reg, 1962, 2⅝",
MIB, J3 ....$50.00

66-C, Greyhound Bus, reg, amber windows, decals, M, W1.$12.00

66-E, Mazda RX500, SF, orange, NM+, from $8 to $10.00

66-I, Rolls Royce Silver Spirit, SF, 1988, 3", MOC, J3.......$2.00

67-B, VW 1600TL (Fastback), reg, MIB, W1....................$17.50

67-C, VW 1600 TL (Fastback), SF, lt purple, MIB, W1 ..$20.00

67-H, Lamborghini Countach LP500S, SF, 1987, 3", MOC,
J3 ....$2.00

68-B, Mercedes Coach, reg, orange, M, W1.....................$10.00

68-C, Porsche 910, SF, red, M, A3 ....$10.00

68-D, Cosmobile, SF, bl, MIB, A3 ....$15.00

68-G, Camaro IROC Z, SF, 1987, 3", MOC, J3...................$2.00

69-B, Hatra Tractor Shovel, reg, yel, NM, from $10 to....$15.00

69-D, Turbo Fury, SF, red, M, A3 ....$10.00

69-E, Armored Truck, Wells Fargo, SF, 1978, 2¾", MOC, J3.$8.00

70-B, Grit Spreader, reg, red & yel, M, G3 ....$10.00

70-D, Dodge Dragster, SF, 1971, 3", MOC, J3 ....$6.00

71-A, Austin 200 Gallon Water Tank (Army), reg, VG+,
W1..$12.50

71-B, Jeep Gladiator Pickup Truck, reg, 1964, 2⅝", MOC,
J3 ....$25.00

71-F, Cattle Truck (w/cows), SF, yel, EX $5.00

72-D, Hovercraft SRN6, SF, 1972, 3", MOC, J3 ....$15.00

72-F, Maxi-Taxi, SF, yel, tampo, MIB, W1.........................$5.00

73-F, Weasel Armored Vehicle, SF, 1974, 2⅞", MOC, J3..$8.00

74-A, Mobile Canteen Refreshment Bar, reg, 1959, 2⅝", MIB,
J3 ....$60.00

74-E, Cougar Villager Station Wagon, SF, gr, MIB, W1 ....$5.00

75-A, Ford Thunderbird, gray wheels, pk & gray, G $10.00

75-B, Ferrari Berlinetta, spoked wheels, 3", MIB, $40.00.

75-G, Ferrari Testarossa, reg, 1987, 3", MOC, J3................$2.00

King Size, Speed Kings, and Super Kings

K1-C, Weatherhill Hydraulic Shovel, 1960, 3¾", MIB, J3.$40.00

K2-B, KW Dart Dump Truck, 1964, 5⅝", MIB, J3 ....$25.00

K3-C, Massey Ferguson Tractor & Trailer, 1970, 8", MIB,
J3 ....$18.00

K4-D, Big Tipper, 1974, 4¾", MIB, J3 ....$25.00

K5-A, Foden Tipper Truck, 1961, 4¼", MIB, J3.............$30.00

K6-B, Mercedes Benz Binz Ambulance, 1968, MIB, J3 ....$20.00

K7-D, ZakSpeed Ford Mustang Turbo, 1989, 5", MIB, J3...$7.00

K8-E, Ferrari F40, 1989, 4¼", MIB, J3.............................$7.00

K9-B, Madator Combine Harvester, 1967, 5½", MIB, J3 .$20.00

K10-C, Car Transporter, 1976, 10½", MIB, J3.................$20.00

K11-A, Fordson Tractor & Farm Trailer, 1963, 6¼", MIB,
J3..$30.00

K11-D, Dodge Delivery Van, 1981, 5⅜", MIB, J3............$20.00

K12-C, Hercules Mobile Crane, 1975, 6⅛", MIB, J3.......$25.00

K13-A, Foden Ready-Mix Concrete Truck, 1963, 4½", MIB,
J3..$25.00

K14-C, Heavy Breakdown Truck, 1977, 5⅛", MIB, J3 .....$15.00

K15-A, Merryweather Fire Engine, 1964, 6", MIB, J3 ......$30.00

K16-B, Petrol Tanker, 1974, 11½", 1974, MIB, J3...........$25.00

K17-B, Scammell Articulated Container Truck, 1974, MIB,
J3..$25.00

K19-A, Scammell Tipper Truck, 1967, 4¾", MIB, J3.......$30.00

K20-B, Cargo Hauler & Pallet Loader, 1973, MIB, J3......$20.00

K21-A, Mercury Cougar, 1968, 4⅛", MIB, J3 ....$25.00

K22-C, SRN6 Hovercraft, 1974, 5", MIB, J3.....................$15.00

K24-A, Lamborghini Miura, 1969, 4", MIB, J3.................$15.00

K26-B, Cement Truck, 1980, 4", MIB, J3 ....$15.00

K27-A, Camping Cruiser, 1971, 4⅜", MIB, J3..................$15.00

K28-B, Skip Truck, 1978, 4⅜", MIB, J3 ....$15.00

K30-A, Mercedes C1.11, 1977, 4", MIB, J3 ....$15.00

K31-B, Peterbilt Refrigerator Truck, 1978, 12", MIB,
J3..$20.00

K36-A, Bandalero Custom Car, 1972, 4½", MIB, J3 ....$13.00

K38-B, Dodge Ambulance, 1980, 5⅜", MIB, J3.............$20.00

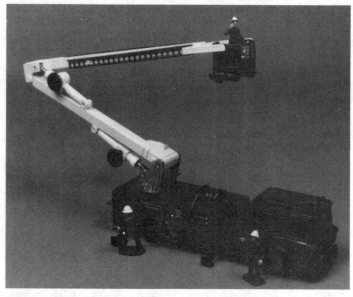

K39-B, ERF Simon Snorkel Fire Engine, 1980, MIB, $20.00.

K40-B, Pepsi Delivery Truck, 1980, 5⅜", MIB, J3 ....$15.00

K42-B, CAT Traxcavator Road Ripper, 1079, 5½", MIB,
J3 ....$15.00

K43-B, Log Transporter, 1981, 12⅝", MIB, J3 ....$20.00

K44-C, Bridge Transporter, 1981, 13⅛", MIB, J3 ....$55.00
K50-A, Street Rod, 1973, 4", MIB, J3 ....$55.00
K54-A, Javelin AMX, 1975, 4¼", MIB, J3 ....$12.00
K58-A, Corvette Power Boat Set, 10⅛", MIB, J3 ....$25.00
K64-A, Fire Control Range Rover, 1978, 4⅛", MIB, J3 ...$12.00
K70-A, Porsche Turbo 1979, 4⅝", MIB, J3 ....$12.00
K76-A, Volvo Ralley Set, 1981, 10⅝", MIB, J3 ....$25.00
K83-A, Harley-Davidson Motorcycle & Rider, 1981, 4⅜",
     MIB, J3 ....$12.00
K92-A, Helicopter Transporter, 1982, MIB, J3 ....$15.00
K98-A, Porsche 944, 1983, MIB, J3 ....$6.00
K107-A, Power Launch Transporter, 1984, MIB, J3.........$16.00
K111-A, Peterbilt Refuse Truck, 1985, MIB, J3 ....$10.00
K114-A, Mobile Crane, 1985, MIB, J3 ....$25.00
K121-A, Peterbilt Wrecker, 1986, MIB, J3 ....$8.00

K133-A, Iveco Refuse Truck, 1986, MIB, $10.00.

K134-A, Fire Spotter Airplane Transporter, 1986, MIB,
     J3 ....$20.00
K138-A, Fire Rescue Set, 1986, MIB, J3 ....$25.00
K142-A, BMW Police Car, 1987, MIB, J3 ....$8.00
K149-A, Ferrari Testarossa, 1988, MIB, J3 ....$6.00
K164-A, Range Rover, 1989, MIB, J3 ....$12.00
K168-A, Porsche 911, 1989, MIB, J3 ....$6.00
K171-A, Toyota 4x4 Hi-Lux, 1989, MIB, J3 ....$8.00

Models of Yesteryear

Y1-A, 1925 Allchin Traction Engine, M (NM box) $75.00
Y1-B, 1911 Ford Model T, red, blk hood, M (NM box), W1 .$29.00
Y1-C, 1936 SS100 Jaguar, gr, M (NM box), W1 ....$16.00
Y1-C, 1936 Jaguar SS100, 1977, MIB $25.00
Y2-B, 1911 Renault 2-Seater, 1963, MIB, J3 ....$25.00
Y2-C, 1914 Prince Henry Vauxhal, red, MIB, C6 ....$18.00
Y2-D, 1930 4.5 Litre Supercharged Bentley, 1984, MIB, J3.$18.00
Y3-A, 1907 London E Class Tramscar, red, cream roof, M (VG
     box), from $70 to $75.00
Y3-B, 1910 Benz Limo, metallic gr, blk roof, M, W1 ....$14.00
Y3-B, 1910 Benz Limousine, 1966, MIB, J3 ....$50.00

Y3-C, 1934 Riley MPH, metallic red, wht seats & radiator, silver
     24-spoke wheels, M, W1.......................................$19.00
Y3-D, 1912 Model T Ford Truck, Carnation, MIB..........$18.00
Y3-D, 1912 Model T Ford Truck, Texaco, MIB $18.00
Y4-B, 1960 Shand-Mason Horse-Drawn Fire Engine, 1960,
     MIB, J3 ....$125.00
Y4-C, 1909 Opel Coupe, wht, tan roof, M (EX box), W1 .$29.00
Y4-D, 1930 Duesenberg Model J, red, MIB......................$25.00
Y5, 1927 Talbot, 'Lipton's Tea,' gr, MIB, U1 ....$20.00
Y-5A, 1929 LeMans Bentley, gr, M (NM+ box), from $65
     to $70.00
Y5-C, 1907 Peugeot, yel, blk roof, M, W1 ....$22.50
Y5-D, 1927 Talbot Van, 1978, MIB, J3...........................$25.00
Y6-C, 1913 Cadillac, gold, dk red roof, seats & radiator, brass
     wheels, '1913' on base, M, W1 ....$24.00
Y6-C, 1913 Cadillac, 1967, MIB, from $35 to $40.00
Y6-D, 1920 Rolls Royce Fire Engine, 1977, MIB, J3.........$25.00
Y7, 1912 Rolls Royce, wht w/blk top & red trim, NM (EX
     box)...$25.00
Y7-B, 1913 Mercer Raceabout, 1961, MIB, J3 ....$35.00
Y7-C, 1912 Rolls Royce, gold w/dk red roof, M (NM box).$25.00
Y8-A, 1926 Morris Bullnose Cowley, tan w/gold trim & silver
     wheels, M (NM+ box), from $80 to $85.00

Y8-B, 1914 Sunbeam Motorcycle and Sidecar, 1962, MIB, $45.00.

Y8-B, 1914 Sunbeam Motorcycle & Sidecar, silver w/dk gr side-
     car, NM+, W1 ....$37.00
Y8-C, 1914 Stutz, 1969, MIB, J3 ....$35.00
Y9, Simplex-50, blk & yel, MIB $30.00
Y9-A, 1924 Fowler 'Big Lion' Showman's Engine, 1958, MIB,
     J3...$80.00
Y9-Bb, 1912 Simplex, yel, display facade box, 1986, M (VG
     box), G2 ....$70.00
Y10-B, 1928 Mercedes Benz 36/220, 1963, MIB..............$60.00
Y11, 1912 Packard, red, NM (EX box)..............................$24.00
Y11-A, 1920 Aveling & Porter Steam Roller, gr, blk flywheel &
     roof support, gold trim, M (NM box), from $65 to $70.00
Y11-B, 1912 Packard Landaulet, 1964, MIB, J3...............$30.00
Y12, 1912 Model T Ford, The Hoover, MIB, U1 ....$20.00
Y12-A, 1899 London Horse-Drawn Bus, red, M (NM+
     box) $95.00

Y12-A, 1899 London Horse-Drawn Bus, 1957, MIB, $95.00.

Y12-C, 1912 Model T Ford Truck, 1979, MIB, J3 ....$25.00

Y13-C, 1918 Crossley Coal & Coke Truck, red, blk roof & seats, red 12-spoke wheels, M (NM box), W1.....................$29.00

Y13-C, 1918 Crossley RAF Tender, 1973, MIB, J3 ....$30.00

Y14, Stutz Bearcat, gr & off-wht, MIB, U1 ....$20.00

Y14-B, 1911 Maxwell Roadster, turq w/blk roof, M (NM+ box), W1 ....$29.00

Y14-C, 1931 Stutz Bearcat, 1974, MIB, J3.......................$20.00

Y15, 1930 Packard Victoria, red & blk w/wht roof, MIB, U1 ....$20.00

Y16-A, 1904 Spyker, 1961, MIB, J3 ....$45.00

Y16-B, 1928 Mercedes Benz SS, red, MIB $15.00

Y16-C, 1960 Ferrari Dino 246/V12, MIB, C6..................$10.00

Y16-D, Scammell 100-Ton Truck w/Steam Engine, 1989, MIB, J3...$50.00

Y17, 1938 Hispano Suiza, gr, MIB, U1............................$18.00

Y18-B, 1920 Atkinson Steam Wagon, 1986, MIB, J3 ......$18.00

Y19-B, 1933 Auburn 851 'Boattail' Speedster, 1980, MIB J3...$20.00

Y20, 1937 Mercede Benz 540K, silver & blk, MIB, U1 ....$20.00

Y21-A, 1929 Ford Model A 'Woody' Wagon, 1981, MIB, J3.$20.00

Y22-A, 1930 Model A Ford, 'OXO,' MIB.........................$18.00

Y23-A, 1922 AEC Omnibus, Haug, MIB, from $20 to.....$24.00

Y23-B, 1930 Mack Tanker, 1989, MIB, J3........................$18.00

Y24, 1927 Bugatti T44, yel & blk, MIB, U1 ....$20.00

Y25, 1910 Renault Type AG, 'The Eagle Pencil Co,' MIB, U1...$18.00

Y26, 1918 Crossley Beer Lorry, 'Lowenbrau,' MIB............$18.00

Y27, 1922 Foden 'C' Steamwagon & Trailers, 'Frasers,' limited edition, MIB..$18.00

Y27, 1922 Foden Steam Lorry, 'Spillers,' limited edition, MIB, U1 ....$18.00

Y28, 1907 Unic Taxi, MIB, U1...$15.00

Y29, 1919 Walker Electric Van, 'Joseph Lucas, Ltd,' limited edition, MIB $30.00

Y30, 1920 Model AC Mack 'Acorn Storage Co,' MIB, U1 .$15.00

Y32-A, 1917 Yorkshire Steam Lorry, 1990, MIB, J3.........$18.00

Y37-A, 1931 Garret Stake Truck, 1990, MIB...................$18.00

Y40-A, 1931 Mercedes Benz T10, gray w/bl roof, MIB.....$18.00

Y41-A, 1932 Mercedes Truck, 1991, MIB, J3 ....$18.00

Y45-A, 1930 Bugatti Royale, 1991, MIB, J3 ....$18.00

Y47-A, 1929 Morris Light Van, Lindt Chocolate, MIB ...$18.00

Y61-A, 1933 Cadillac Fire Engine, 1992, MIB, J3 ....$18.00

Y63-A, 1939 Bedford KD Truck, 1992, MIB, J3 ....$18.00

Y65-A, 1992 Special Limited Edition Set, 1928 Austin, 1928 BMX Dixi, 1928 Rosengart, MIB, J3.......................$60.00

Y66-A, 1992 Special Limited Edition, Her Majesty Queen Elizabeth II's Gold State Coach, MIB, J3 ....$60.00

Skybusters

SB-12 Pitts Special; SB-27 Harrier; SB-24, F16A, MIB, $4.00 each.

Harrier, 'Marines,' gray & gr camouflage, MBP...................$6.00

Helicopter, 'Army,' Army gr, MBP, J1 ....$10.00

Learjet, 'US Air Force,' wht, MBP, J1 ....$6.00

Mirage F-1, '122-18,' orange, MIB, J1................................$6.00

Phantom, 'Marines,' gray & orange stripes, MBP................$6.00

Model Kits

Figure-type model kits have drastically increased in value over the past five to eight years, especially those made by Aurora

Y23-A, 1922 A.E.C. S type Omnibus, 1982, MIB, from $20.00 to $24.00.

during the 1960s. Though model kits were popular with kids of the fifties who enjoyed the challenge of assembling a classic car or two or a Musketeer figure now and then, when the monster series hit in the early 1960s, sales shot through the ceiling. Made popular by all the monster movies of that decade, ghouls like Vampirella, Frankenstein, and the Wolfman were eagerly built up by kids everywhere. They could (if their parents allowed them to) even construct an actual working guillotine. Aurora had other successful series of figure kits, too, based on characters from comic strips and TV shows as well as a line of sports stars.

But the vast majority of model kits were vehicles. They varied in complexity, some requiring much more dexterity on the part of the model builder than others, and they came in several scales, from 1/8 (which might be as large as 20" to 24") down to 1/43 (generally about 3" to 4"), but the most popular scale was 1/25 (usually between 6" to 8"). Some of the largest producers of vehicle kits were AMT, MPC, and IMC. Though production obviously waned during the late 1970s and early '80s, with the intensity of today's collector market, companies like Ertl (who now is producing 1/25 scale vehicles using some of the old AMT dies) are proving that model kits still sell very well.

As a rule of thumb, assembled kits (built-ups) are priced at about 25% to 50% of the lower end of the price range for a boxed kit. One mint in the box with the factory seal intact will often sell for up to 15% more than if the seal were broken. Condition of the box is crucial. For more information, we recommend *Aurora History and Price Guide* by Bill Bruegman.

Addar, Planet of the Apes, Dr Zira (1974) or General Aldo (1973), MIB (sealed), each $45.00.

Ace, Hughes OH-6 Cayuse #200, 1/85 scale, MIB (sealed), P4 ....**$4.00**

Action Kits International, Masque of the Red Death, MIB, E3 ....**$115.00**

Adams, Anti Aircraft Gun #K156, unassembled, C7 ....**$85.00**

Adams, Chuck Wagon #K235, 1958, 1/48 scale, NMIB (lt wear), P4 ....**$20.00**

Adams, Covered Wagon, 1958, 1/48 scale, believed complete, no instructions, EX+, D9 ....**$6.00**

Adams, Ranch Wagon #K232, unassembled, C7 ....**$15.00**

Addar, Lockheed F94C Starfire & North American F100 Super Sabre #902, 1976, 1/82 & 1/103 scale, MIB, P4...........**$8.00**

Addar, Planet of the Apes, General Aldo, 1973, MIB, C1/F3 ....**$36.00**

Addar, Scene in a Bottle Jail Wagon, 1975, missing background scene, unassembled (EX box), D9 ....**$19.00**

AEF, Queen Egg Chamber, MIB, E3 ....**$200.00**

AHM, Northrop 5B #FJ-4, unassembled (sealed box), C7..**$15.00**

AHM, 1905 Rolls Royce #K302, unassembled (sealed box), C7 ....**$20.00**

Airfix, Anne Boleyn #03542, Famous Women of History series, 1974, 1/12 scale, MIB, P4 ....**$15.00**

Airfix, Apollo Saturn V, 1960s, NMIB, J2.......................**$45.00**

Airfix, Boeing 727 #3173-6, MIB, C7 ....**$10.00**

Airfix, Bristol Beaufighter #283, unassembled, C7 ....**$5.00**

Airfix, B24J Liberator #5006-3, unassembled, C7.............**$10.00**

Airfix, Great Western Steam-Sail #802, unassembled, C7 .**$15.00**

Airfix, James Bond & Odd Job, 1966, 1/12 scale, all plastic, 6x9" box, EX (EX box), A **$185.00**

Airfix, James Bond 007 Aston-Martin DB-5, partially built (EX box), W1 ....**$159.00**

Airfix, Junkers JU-88 #1410, unassembled, C7.................**$10.00**

Airfix, Life Guard Trumpeteer #M206F, 1960s, 1/12 scale, in bag w/header, NMIP, P4 ....**$8.00**

Airfix, Lunar Module #393, unassembled, C7..................**$20.00**

Airfix, Starcruiser 1 (Gerry Anderson) #7100, 1979, 1/72 scale, MIB (sealed box w/sm warp), P4 ....**$35.00**

Airfix, The Mayflower, 1972, M (EX- box), D9 ....**$10.00**

Airline, Airspeed Oxford #7906, 1964, 1/72 scale, MIB, P4 ....**$20.00**

Airline, Hawker Sea Fury #4903, NMIB, P4....................**$10.00**

Airline, Hotspur II Glider #7904, 1964, 1/72 scale, MIB, P4 ....**$10.00**

Airline, Miles Master #4904, 1964, 1/72 scale, MIB (sealed), P4 ....**$10.00**

Airline, Morane Saulmier #4902, 1964, 1/72 scale, NMIB, P4 ....**$10.00**

Airline, Percival Proctor IV #4905, 1965, 1/72 scale, MIB, P3 ....**$12.00**

Airline, Westland Wallace, 1964, 1/72 scale, MIB, P4.....**$12.00**

AMT, Akron/Macon Blimp #T572, unassembled, C7 .....**$30.00**

AMT, Batwing, plastic, MIB (sealed), D4 ....**$12.00**

AMT, Budweiser Clydesdale 8-Horse Hitch, late 1970s-early 1980s, complete, M (EX sealed box), D9 ....**$25.00**

AMT, Flintstone's Rock Cruncher #497 or Sports Car #495, MIB, M5, each $45.00.

AMT, Kiss Van #2501, unassembled, C7..........................$75.00

AMT, Laurel & Hardy 1927 Ford Model T Touring #T461, 1/25 scale, NMIB (minor crushing), P4 ....$30.00

AMT, Munster Koach, 1964, 1/25 scale, assembled/pnt, 7" long, T2 ....$89.00

AMT, Munster Koach, 1965, 1/25 scale, NMIB.............$175.00

AMT, My Mother the Car, 1965, 1/25 scale, complete, M (EX+ box), D9 ....$47.00

AMT, Star Trek Enterprise Command Bridge Kit, 1975, MIB (sealed), C1..$72.00

AMT, Star Trek Exploration Set, w/phaser, tricorder & communicator, 1974, MIB, A $100.00

AMT, Star Trek Klingon Battle Cruiser, 1974, MIB, H4.$59.00

AMT, Star Trek Spaceship Set, set of 3: Romulan, Enterprise & Klingon, snap together w/stand, NM (G box), A $35.00

AMT, Star Trek USS Enterprise, 1968, orig 14x10" box, M (EX+ sealed box) $100.00

AMT, Star Trek USS Enterprise Gallieo & Shuttlecraft, 1974, MIB $85.00

AMT, 1947 Chevy Coupe #T149, unassembled, C7........$50.00

AMT, 1963 Chevy Impala #6723, some assembly, C7 .....$50.00

AMT, 1964 Grand Prix #6665, unassembled, C7...........$100.00

AMT, 1969 Lincoln #Y907, unassembled, C7.................$50.00

AMT/Ertl, Airwolf Helicopter, 1984, 1/48 scale, NMIB, from $15 to $24.00

AMT/Ertl, Ecto 1A, MIB, E3 ....$7.00

AMT/Ertl, Joker Goon Car, 1989, can be built 3 ways, NMIB (sealed), D9 ....$10.00

AMT/Ertl, Messerschmitt Bf-109G #8882, 1990, 1/48 scale, NMIB, P4 ....$5.00

AMT/Ertl, Monkeemobile, reissue, MIB, E3....................$40.00

AMT/Ertl, Peterbilt #359, 1/25 scale, M (NM box), from $15.00 to $25.00.

AMT/Ertl, Robo 1 Police Car, MIB, E3 ....$7.00

AMT/Ertl, Star Trek Next Generation Enterprise, MIB, E3.$14.00

AMT/Ertl, Star Trek Spaceship Set, MIB, E3 ....$8.00

AMT/Ertl, Star Trek: The Motion Picture Klingon Cruiser; MIB, E3 ....$10.00

AMT/Matchbox, Kenworth Aerodyne COE Tractor #5018, 1980, 1/25 scale, MIB, P4 ....$15.00

Argonauts, Cain, Robo-Cop 2; MIB, E3 ....$175.00

Aurora, Addams Family Haunted House #805, 1965, complete, w/instructions & sheet for windows, EX+ (EX+ box), A...$595.00

Aurora, Alfred E Neuman, 1965, has been started, missing some pcs (VG box), D9 ....$169.00

Aurora, Allosaurus, assembled, EX, J2................................$35.00

Aurora, Amazing Spider Man, Canadian, complete, NMIB, M5...$200.00

Aurora, American Astronaut, MIB, E3 ....$90.00

Aurora, Amzio Beach Diorama #339-200, 1968, 1/87 scale, pnt & assembled, near complete (jeep damaged), VG (VG box), P4 ....$30.00

Aurora, Anzio Beach, complete, unassembled, most pcs on tree, NMIB, M5 ....$100.00

Aurora, Anzio Beach Diorama #339-200, 1968, 1/87 scale, assembled & pnt, damage to jeep, VG (lt wear on box), A $25.00

Aurora, B-26D Martin Marauder #371-250, 1961, Famous Fighters series, 1/46 scale, MIB, from $60 to $80.00

Aurora, B-70 Bomber #370, unassembled, C7 ....$60.00

Aurora, Babe Ruth, 1965, 5" figures of umpire, catcher & Babe w/cb Yankee Stadium backdrop, MIB (sealed), T2 .$350.00

Aurora, Babe Ruth #862, assembled/pnt, C7 ....$150.00

Aurora, Barnstormers #200, unassembled, C7 ....$125.00

Aurora, Batcycle #810, Canadian, unassembled, C7 ......$350.00

Aurora, Batman, Comic Scenes series, 1974, MIB, E3 .....$65.00

Aurora, Batman, Comic Scenes series, 1974, unassembled, complete, M (EX box), D9 ....$55.00

Aurora, Batman #467, assembled, C7 ....$50.00

Aurora, Batman #467, unassembled, C7 ....$275.00

Aurora, Batmobile #486, unassembled, C7 ....$300.00

Aurora, Batplane, 1967, 1/60 scale, w/Batman & Robin, decals & display stand, 13x5" box, MIB, T2.......................$260.00

Aurora, Batplane, 1967, 1/60 scale, w/figures, stand & decals, assembled/nicely pnt, T2 ....$100.00

Aurora, Bell Huey #504, unassembled (sealed box) C7....$20.00

Aurora, Black Bear & Cubs #407, assembled, C7 ....$20.00

Aurora, Black Knight of Nurnberg, 1963, missing plume & pc of head, pnt lance (EX box), D9................................$12.00

Aurora, Black Knight of Nurnberg, 1963, 1/8 scale, metallic bl plastic German knight, Canadian, MIB, T2 ....$40.00

Aurora, Blue Knight of Milan, 1963, complete, NMIB (sealed), D9 ....$25.00

Aurora, Blue Knight of Milan, 1963, 1/8 scale, metallic bl plastic, Canadian, MIB, T2 ....$40.00

Aurora, Boeing F4B-4 FF #122-69, unassembled, C7 ....$40.00

Aurora, Bride of Frankenstein, assembled, E3.................$165.00

Aurora, Bride of Frankenstein, 1965, 1/10 scale, she on top of slab in laboratory, 13x7" box, unassembled (EX- box), T2...$995.00

Aurora, Captain Action, assembled, E3 ....$140.00

Aurora, Captain America, Canadian, box only, EX+, M5.$70.00

Aurora, Captain America, 1966, 1/12 scale, flat blk plastic Captain America running in battlefield, 13x4" box, MIB, T2..$400.00

Aurora, Captain Kidd, 1965, complete, w/US box & Canadian instructions, NMIB, D9 ....$73.00

Aurora, Cave, Prehistoric Scenes, 1971, 1st issue box w/Tyrannosaurus Rex, NMIB, D9..$65.00

Aurora, Cave, Prehistoric Scenes, 1972, 2nd issue box w/altered art, NMIB, D9...$50.00

Aurora, Cessna 310 #283, unassembled, C7 ....$25.00

Aurora, Chinese Junk, 1965, complete w/decals & instructions, NMIB, D9 ....$35.00

Aurora, Chitty Chitty Bang Bang, partly assembled, missing pcs (EX- box), D9 ....$43.00

Aurora, Creature From the Black Lagoon, Monsters of the Movies series, 1975, MIB from $190 to....................$240.00

Aurora, Creature From the Black Lagoon, 1969, MIB, H4 .$175.00

Aurora, Cro-Magnon Woman, MIB, E3 ....$35.00

Aurora, Customized Corvette #545, unassembled, C7 .....$35.00

Aurora, Cutty Sark, MIB, E3 ....$18.00

Aurora, D'Artagnan, 1965, 1/8 scale, plastic Musketeer w/sword, Canadian, MIB, T2 ....$200.00

Aurora, Dempsey vs Firpo, 1965, complete (EX box), D9....$79.00

Aurora, Dempsey vs Firpo, 1965, includes referee, 9x12" box, NMIB, T2 ....$130.00

Aurora, Denty Whoozis, 1968, w/sign: Caution: Engage brain..., 5x7" box, MIB, T2 ....$90.00

Aurora, Donovan 417 #843, unassembled, C7..................$85.00

Aurora, Douglas CD-8 Jet Mainliner United Airlines #387-2.49, 1959, 1/103 scale, MIB, P4 ....$65.00

Aurora, Douglas DC-10 American Airlines #366, 1970, 1/144 scale, MIB (sealed), P4 ....$20.00

Aurora, Douglas DC-8 Jetliner Eastern Airlines #388-2.49, 1960, 1/103 scale, MIB, P4 ....$85.00

Aurora, Douglas DC-8 United Jet Mainliner #367-2.49, 1959, 1/103 scale, MIB, A $34.00

Aurora, Dr Deadly #631, assembled, no base, C7 ....$35.00

Aurora, Dr Deadly's Daughter, MIB, E3 ....$115.00

Aurora, Dr Jekyll, Monsters of the Movies, 1975, 1/23 scale, about to drink serum, 5x8" box, MIB (sealed), T2 ..$120.00

Aurora, Dr Jekyll & Mr Hyde, Monster Scene Series, 1971, assembled, A..$100.00

Aurora, Dracula, Monsters of the Movies, MIB, from $185 to..$200.00

Aurora, Dracula, 1962, assembled, E3 ....$45.00

Aurora, Dracula, 1962, 1/8 scale (EX+ box), T2 ....$300.00

Aurora, Dracula Mom #656, unassembled, C7 ....$225.00

Aurora, Dracula's Dragster, 1964, NMIB, H4.................$395.00

Aurora, Esmerelda Whoozis, 1968, w/sign: My first mistake..., 5x7" box, MIB, from $65 to..$90.00

Aurora, F-4J Blue Angel #367, unassembled, C7..............$20.00

Aurora, Fairchild C-119A Flying Boxcar #393-2.49, 1960, 1/77, MIB, from $40 to $55.00

Aurora, Ferrari Berlinetta, 1/25 scale, MIB, J2..................$55.00

Aurora, Flying Reptile, MIB, E3/T7.................................$55.00

Aurora, Fokker D-VII #753, 1976, 1/48, MIB (sealed), P4 .$20.00

Aurora, Fokker D-7 #106, unassembled (sealed box), C7.$20.00

Aurora, Fokker D-7 Screwdriver #398, unassembled, no screws, C7 ....$100.00

Aurora, Fokker Eindecker FF #134-79, unassembled, C7 C7...$40.00

Aurora, Forgotten Prisoner of Castle Mare, 1964, M (EX Canadian box), H4 ....$275.00

Aurora, Frankenstein, Monster Scenes series, MIB, E3 ..$125.00

Aurora, Frankenstein, Monsters of the Movies, 1975, 1/12 scale, in shackles, holds club, climbs hill, MIB (sealed), T2 .....$280.00

Aurora, Frankenstein, 1961, NMIB $200.00

Aurora, German Wolf-Pack U Boat, 1961, complete, M (EX box), D9...$19.00

Aurora, Giant Bird, MIB, E3 ....$40.00

Aurora, Gladiator, unassembled, NMIB, J2 ....$150.00

Aurora, Godzilla #466, Glow-in-the-Dark, unassembled, C7...$200.00

Aurora, Green Beret, 1966, 1/12 scale, throwing hand grenade in Vietnam jungle diorama, MIB, T2........................$160.00

Aurora, Gruesome Goodies, Monster Scenes, MIB, E3 ....$95.00

Aurora, Guillotine, 1964, 1/15 scale, working, disassembled/ buffed, (NM Canadian box), T2 ....$500.00

Aurora, Hangin' Cage, MIB, E3 ....$80.00

Aurora, Hercules & the Lion, 1/8 scale, 1966, MIB (sealed), A..$475.00

Aurora, Hiller X18 #146, unassembled, no base, C7 ......$100.00

Aurora, Hulk, Canadian, NMIB, M5 ....$190.00

Aurora, Hulk, Comic Scenes series, MIB, E3....................$45.00

Aurora, Hulk, 1966, 1/12 scale, Hulk in a rage, bending girder, partial assembly, 13x4" box (NM box), T2............$350.00

Aurora, Hunchback of Notre Dame, 1963, built-up w/expert pnt, EX, D9 ....$55.00

Aurora, Hunchback of Notre Dame #461, Canadian, unassembled, C7..$175.00

Aurora, Invaders UFO, 1968, MIB, E3 ....$190.00

Aurora, Invaders UFO, 1968, 1/72 scale, orig issue, assembled/no pnt, T2..$70.00

Aurora, Invaders UFO, 1975, missing base & instructions (EX 2nd issue box), D9 ....$65.00

Aurora, James Bond 007, 1966, 1/8 scale, Bond w/gun stalking behind stone wall, NMIB, T2 ....$400.00

Aurora, Jerry West, Great Moments in Sports series, 1965, MIB (sealed), from $175 to $190.00

Aurora, Jesse James, 1966, complete, 20% pnt & 1 boot glued, missing instruction sheet (EX+ box), D9...................$99.00

Aurora, Jesse James, 1966, 1/8 scale, Jesse drawing gun, desert scene w/wanted poster, MIB, T2 ....$200.00

Aurora, Jimmy Brown, 1965, 1/13 scale, +2 team opponents & football field diorama, 12x9" box, MIB (sealed), T2..$240.00

Aurora, John F Kennedy, 1965, complete w/picture decal (unused) & flag (EX box), D9....................................$98.00

Aurora, Johnny Unitas, 1965, 1/13 scale, Unitas & 2 players in action, 12x9" box, NMIB, T2 ....$230.00

Aurora, Johnny Unitas #864, unassembled (damaged box), C7...$150.00

Aurora, King Kong, 1964, c RKO Pictures, Kong carries Fay through jungle, 7x13" box, M (EX+ box), T2 ....$950.00

Aurora, Klingon Battle Cruiser, MIB, E3........................$175.00

Aurora, Knights in Shining Armour Sir Kay, 1973, unbuilt w/silver metallic finish, w/instructions, (G box), D9 ....$38.00

Aurora, Land of the Giants, #816-150, 1968, 1/48 scale, little people fight snake w/safety pin, scarce (EX- box), T2 .....$485.00

Aurora, Land of the Giants #830, 1968, all plastic, 7x13" box, NMIB, A..$600.00

Aurora, Land of the Giants Spindrift, NMIB, H4 ....$450.00

Aurora, Lone Ranger, 1967, 1/10 scale, Lone Ranger on rearing Silver, 13x7" box, MIB (sealed), from $200 to $250.00

Aurora, Lone Ranger #188, Comic Scenes series, 1974, 1/12 scale, MIB (sealed), P4 ....$35.00

Aurora, Lost in Space Robot #418, assembled/pnt, C7 ..$400.00

Aurora, M-46 General Patton Tank #301-98, Famous Fighters series, 1956, 1/48 scale, MIB, P4 ....$70.00

Aurora, Man From UNCLE Napoleon Solo, 1966, partly pnt & glued (EX+ box), D9 ....$178.00

Aurora, Mr Deadly, MIB, E3 ....$85.00

Aurora, Mr Hyde, Monsters of the Movies, 1975, 1/12 scale, Hyde under street light, 8x5" box, MIB (sealed), T2.$90.00

Aurora, Mummy, Glow-in-the-Dark, 1972, made in England, M (EX+ box), D9 ....$65.00

Aurora, Mummy, 1963, 1/8 scale, based on Universal picture starring Boris Karloff, M (EX box), from $245 to $380.00

Aurora, Munitions Carrier & 8" Howitzer #333, some assembly, C7..$20.00

Aurora, Munsters Living Room #804, assembled, C7.....$450.00

Aurora, Nautilas #708, unassembled, C7 ....$15.00

Aurora, Neanderthal Man #729, Prehistoric scenes, 1971, 1/13 scale, M (G box), $24.00.

Aurora, Neanderthal Man, Prehistoric Scenes, MIB, H4.$39.00

Aurora, Odd Job, 1966, 1/8 scale, Odd Job throwing razor-edged derby, 13x5" box, unassembled (VG+ box), T2 ......$360.00

Aurora, Pain Parlor, Monster Scenes, MIB, E3................$100.00

Aurora, Pain Parlor, Monster Scenes, 1971, M (EX box), A $69.00

Aurora, Pan-Am Space Clipper, 1968, MIB, H4............$125.00

Aurora, Pendulum, MIB, E3 ....$75.00

Aurora, Penguin, 1/12 scale, all plastic, molded as Burgess Meredith, 1967, 13x4" box, MIB (sealed), A $700.00

Aurora, Phantom of the Opera, Glow-in-the-Dark, 1972, 1/8 scale, rocky base w/prisoner, 8x8" box, MIB, from $80 to..$120.00

Aurora, Phantom of the Opera, 1963, complete, M (EX+ box), D9..$269.00

Aurora, Phantom of the Opera, 1963, 1/12 scale, blk plastic, 13x4" box, MIB, T2...$450.00

Aurora, Piper Aztec C #282-70, 1/72 scale, MIB, P4........$20.00

Aurora, Piper Cherokee C 180 #281-70, 1/72 scale, MIB, P4..$20.00

Aurora, Prehistoric Scenes Tar Pit, 1971, complete, M (EX+ box), D9..$89.00

Aurora, Rat Patrol #340, complete, unassembled, most pcs on tree, NMIB, M5..$100.00

Aurora, Rat Patrol #340, HO, jeeps, tanks, soldiers, sand dunes, palm trees & accessories, MIB (sealed), T2 ....$230.00

Aurora, Rat Patrol #340, 1967, 1/87 scale, MIB, from $110 to..$135.00

Aurora, Red Knight of Vienna, 1963, 1/8 scale, metallic red plastic Austrian knight, MIB, T2 ....$70.00

Aurora, Robin #488, 1964, MIB, from $75 to.................$95.00

Aurora, Russian Stalin Tank #303, unassembled, C7.......$40.00

Aurora, Saratoga Carrier #702, unassembled, C7 ....$50.00

Aurora, Scout SE-5 #103-100 (WWI), 1963, MIB, P4.....$15.00

Aurora, Sealab #721, unassembled (sealed box), C7 ......$200.00

Aurora, Silver Knight of Augsberg, Famous Fighters series, 1956, Aurora Crown logo, 1st issue box, NMIB (sealed), D9...$65.00

Aurora, Silver Knight of Augsberg, 1963, complete, MIB (sealed), from $40 to...$50.00

Aurora, Sir Percival, Knights of Round Table, 1972, 1/8 scale, chrome-plated plastic, unassembled (EX box), T2 ....$60.00

Aurora, Sopwith Camel #102-79, Famous Fighters series, 1956, 1/48 scale, kit started, missing strut & wheel, G, P4..$10.00

Aurora, Sopwith Camel #751, 1976, 1/48 scale, MIB (sealed), P4..$20.00

Aurora, SPAD XIII #107-98, Canada, 1/48 scale, NMIB, P4 ....$75.00

Aurora, Spartacus, 1/8 scale, in battle pose on battlefield, 1964, MIB (sealed), from $300 to $350.00

Aurora, Spiderman, assembled, E3 ....$80.00

Aurora, Spiked Dinosaur #742, unassembled, C7 ....$60.00

Aurora, Steve Canyon, 1959, 1/8 scale, Steve in jet fighter uniform, 5x13" box, (EX box), T2.................................$250.00

Aurora, Superboy, Canadian, complete, some assembly, NMIB, M5...$125.00

Aurora, Superboy, Comic Scenes series, MIB, E3 ....$65.00

Aurora, Superboy, 1965, 1/8 scale, he & Krypto fighting dragon by cave, 13x5" box, NMIB, T2.................................$325.00

Aurora, Superman, Comic Scenes series, MIB, E3 ....$60.00

Aurora, Superman, 1963, 1/8 scale, Superman smashing brick wall, 13x5" Reeves rendition box, NMIB, from $225 to...$275.00

Aurora, Suzie Whoozis, MIB, E3 ....$75.00

Aurora, T-Rex, assembled, NM, J2 ....$110.00

Aurora, Tarzan, Canadian, complete, unassembled, most pcs on tree, NMIB, M5 ....$95.00

Aurora, Tarzan, Comic Scenes, 1974, MIB (sealed), C1 ..$69.00

Aurora, Tarzan, 1967, 1/11 scale, standing over lion, beating chest, 13x5" box, MIB, T2 ....$130.00

Aurora, Tiger Tank #324, unassembled, C7 ....$15.00

Aurora, Tonto, Comic Scene series, 1974, NMIB (sealed), D9/P4 ....$38.00

Aurora, Tonto, 1967, 1/10 scale, Tonto in desert scene w/eagle in tree, 13x7" box, MIB (sealed), T2 ....$250.00

Aurora, Tucumcari Hydrofoil, Young Model Builders Club series, 1974, NMIB, D9 ....$63.00

Aurora, Twelve O'Clock High B-17 Bomber Formation, 1965, MIB, A $275.00

Aurora, US Army Infantryman, factory assembled, E3.....$75.00

Aurora, US Marine, factory assembled, E3 ....$75.00

Aurora, US Navy Sea Lab II, 1969, built w/some pnt pcs, appears complete, missing instructions (EX box), D9.$85.00

Aurora, USS St Paul Baltimore Class Heavy Cruiser #703, 1972, 1/600 scale, MIB (sealed), P4 ....$15.00

Aurora, Vampirella, MIB, E3 ....$185.00

Aurora, Vampirella #638, unassembled, bagged, C7 ......$100.00

Aurora, Victim, MIB, E3 ....$95.00

Aurora, Victim, Monster Scenes, NMIB (sealed), M5 .....$80.00

Aurora, Voyage to the Bottom of the Sea Flying Sub, 1968, NMIB, H4...$200.00

Aurora, Voyage to the Bottom of the Sea Flying Sub, 1968, 1/60 scale, well assembled/some pnt, minus plastic stand, T2 ....$50.00

Aurora, Voyage to the Bottom of the Sea Seaview Submarine, 1966, missing 1 minor pc, NMIB, H4 ....$170.00

Aurora, Winchester 94 #551-79, Historic Rifles (ex-Best) series, 1/3 scale, MIB, A $62.00

Aurora, Witch, 1969, Glow-in-the-Dark, MIB, H4 ....$150.00

Aurora, Wonder Woman #479, assembled, C7 ....$250.00

Aurora, Woolly Mammoth, assembled, NM, J2...............$60.00

Aurora, WWII Sherman Tank #329, 1972, NMIB...........$10.00

Aurora, Zorro #801, 1965,
M(NM box), A, $215.00.

Aurora, Zorro #801, 1965, complete, M (EX+ box), D9 .$188.00

Aurora, Zorro #801, 1965, 1/12 scale, figure on rearing horse orig 13x7" box, MIB (sealed)....................................$300.00

Aurora, 155 Long Tom Gun #331-200, 1973, 1/48 scale, MIB, P4 ....$25.00

Aurora, 1963 T-Bird, MIB (sealed), T1 ....$25.00

Aurora, 2001: A Space Odessey, the Moon Bus; 1969, partial assembly & pnt, 1 pc missing, o/w complete (EX+ box), D9 ....$189.00

Aurora, 727 Boeing Eastern #351, unassembled, C7 ....$35.00

Aurora, 747 Air Canada #390, unassembled (worn box), C7..$30.00

Bachman/Fujimi, African Front Diorama #0881, 1/76 scale, NMIB (w/1 broken corner), P4 ....$15.00

Bandai, Baltan Seijin, MIB, E3..$10.00

Bandai, CE3K Spaceship #FA-130, unassembled, C7 ....$150.00

Bandai, Dr Slump 'Robbie,' MIB, E3................................$50.00

Bandai, Fieldwork Accessory No 1 Bricks #8229, 1/48 scale, MIB, P4..$3.00

Bandai, Galamon, MIB, E3...$10.00

Bandai, German Artillery No 5 #8245, 1/48 scale, MIB, P4 .$4.00

Bandai, German Infantry No 1 #8242, 1/48 scale, MIB (sealed), P4 ....$5.00

Aurora, Wonder Woman #479, 1965, MIB, from $400.00 to $500.00; Aurora, Land of the Giants #816, 1968, M (EX-box), T2, $485.00.

Bandai, Citroen DS 19 #740, NMIB, A, $245.00.

Bandai, German Infantry No 2 #8243, 1/48 scale, MIB (sealed), P4 ....$5.00

Bandai, Godzilla, 1/250 scale, MIB, E3 ....$15.00

Bandai, Mecha Godzilla, MIB, E3 ....$15.00

Bandai, Pegila, MIB, E3 ....$25.00

Bandai, Shado Interceptor, MIB, E3 ....$35.00

Bandai, Shado Mobile, MIB, E3 ....$15.00

Bandai, Star Blazer Space Cruiser #16, in orig 3½x6" box, MIB, F1 ....$10.00

Bandai, Star Blazer Fighter, MIB, E3 ....$12.00

Billiken, Creature From the Black Lagoon, MIB, E4/H4.$115.00

Billiken, Frankenstein, copyright 1959, MIB, O1/H4, $120.00.

Billiken, Godzilla, MIB, E3 ....$60.00

Billiken, Godzilla, 1986, from movie King Kong vs Godzilla, minor assembly, complete, orig box, EX+, D9 ....$43.00

Billiken, Laser Blast Alien, MIB, E3 ....$125.00

Billiken, Predator, MIB, E3 ....$95.00

Billiken, Saucerman, assembled, E3 ....$25.00

Billiken, Saucerman, MIB, H4 ....$80.00

Billiken, She-Creature, MIB, E3 ....$65.00

Billiken, Syngenor, MIB, E3..$200.00

Comet, Douglas F4D-1 Skyray #PL-5, 1/88, MIB, P4 ....$12.00

Comet, Lockheed F-104A Starfighter #PL-500, 1/62, MIB, P4 ....$18.00

Comet, Mitsubishi Zero A6M5 #1622-2.50, wood, partially assembled, not known if complete, 27½" wingspan, VG, P4 ....$10.00

Comet, NA F-100 Super Sabre #PL-2, 1/103, MIB, P4 .....$10.00

Craftmaster, Ox Team #952, wood, unassembled, C7 ......$25.00

Dark Horse, Dream Queen, MIB, E3 ....$225.00

Dark Horse, King Kong, MIB, E3 ....$75.00

Dark Horse, Predator, MIB, E3..$175.00

Delux Vacuform, Proteus, MIB, E3 ....$15.00

Eatex, Colt .45 Peacemaker #8007, 1981, 1/1 scale, MIB.$25.00

Eldon, Outhouse, Popular Hot Rodding Magazine series, 1969, 1/25 scale, NMIB (sealed), D9 ....$40.00

Empire, White House #1600 (ex-Marx), 1/87 scale, partially assembled, appears complete, VG, P4 ....$50.00

Entex, Boeing 747 Pan Am #8485J, 1/380 scale, NMIB, P4 ....$5.00

Entex, F-14 Tomcat #9010C, Supersonic series, 1/144 scale, MIB (sealed), P4 ....$5.00

Entex, F-15 Eagle #9010A, Supersonic series, 1/144 scale, MIB (sealed), P4 ....$5.00

Entex, Gee Bee Sportster #8463G, 1/48, MIB, P4 ....$20.00

Entex, Wankel Engine #8201, unassembled, C7...............$35.00

Ertl/Esci, Agusta-Bell Ab-205 #4029, 1/48, MIB, P4 ....$8.00

Ertl/Esci, Anti-Aircraft SDKfz 10/4 #8575, 1/35 scale, MIB (sealed), P4 ....$8.00

Ertl/Esci, Bell OH-58 Kiowa #8217, 1/48 scale, MIB (sealed), P4 ....$8.00

Ertl/Esci, F/A-18 Hornet #4072, 1/48 scale, MIB, P4 ....$10.00

Ertl/Esci, German Artillery Unit #8573, 1/35 scale, MIB (sealed), P4..$5.00

Ertl/Esci, German Smoke Unit #8570, 1/35 scale, MIB (sealed), P4 ....$5.00

Estes, Star Wars X-Wing Fighter Flying Rocket, 1978, orig 8x15" box, MIB (partially sealed), C1......................$36.00

Faller/Germany, Sikorsky S-58 #1058, 1/100 scale, MIB, P4 ....$10.00

Frog, Hampder #397P, unassembled, C7 ....$30.00

Frog, Macchi MC201 #158, unassembled, C7 ....$15.00

Fujimi/Testers, A-6A Intruder #333, 1/48 scale, MIB, P4 ...$10.00

Fundimensions, Alpha Moonbase, MIB, E3 ....$65.00

Fundimensions, Bionic Repair #1-0610, unassembled (sealed box), C7 ....$30.00

Fundimensions, Colossal Mantis, MIB, E3 ....$65.00

Fundimensions, Gigantic Wasp, MIB, E3 ....$65.00

Fundimensions, Six Million-Dollar Man Bionic Bustout, 1975, MIB, C1 ....$27.00

Fundimensions, Space 1999 Alien #1902, unassembled, C7 ....$50.00

Fundimensions, Tarantula, MIB, E3..................$65.00

Gaillow's, British SE-5 WWI Flying Model #104, wood, complete (?), VG, P4...................................$10.00

Gaillow's, Messerschmitt Bf-109 #401, wood, 1/25 scale (?), partially assembled, orig box, VG, P4................................$5.00

Geometric, Captain Picard, MIB, E3 ....$45.00

Geometric, Data, MIB, E3 ....$50.00

Geometric, Fiend Without a Face, MIB, E3........$65.00

Geometric, Leonardo Bust, MIB, E3 ....$100.00

Geometric, Lt Worf, MIB, E3.............................$50.00

Glencoe, Jupiter C #05103, 1990, 1/48 scale, Hawk reissue, MIB (sealed), P4..$8.00

Glencoe, Spacemen & Spacewomen #5907, 1991, 1/20 scale, reissues of 12 classic Archer figures, MIB (sealed), P4......................................$20.00

Golden Era, Sixth Finger, MIB, E3 ....$115.00

Graphitti, Death Statue, MIB, E3 ....$100.00

Graphitti, Lobo Statue, MIB, E3 ....$125.00

Graven Images, Judge Dredd, MIB, E3 ....$40.00

Graven Images, Killer McBash, MIB, E3............$40.00

Gunze-Sangyo, Pam-74C Dunc, MIB, E3 ....$25.00

Halcyon, Alien Armored Personnel Carrier, MIB, D4 .....$30.00

Halcyon, Alien Drop Ship, MIB, D4....................$40.00

Halcyon, Alien Warrior, vinyl, MIB, E3 ....$75.00

Halcyon, Alien Warrior w/Base & Egg, 1991, M (EX+ box), D9 ....$39.00

Halcyon, Alien 3 Facehugger, MIB, E3............$100.00

Halcyon, APC, MIB, E3 ....$25.00

Halcyon, Narcissus, MIB, E3 ....$35.00

Halcyon, Nostromo, MIB, E3 ....$165.00

Halcyon, Powerloader, MIB, E3 ....$50.00

Halcyon, Space Jockey, MIB, E3 ....$70.00

Hasegawa, F4U-1 Birdcage Corsair #C14, 1/72, MIB, P4.$10.00

Hasegawa, McDonnell Douglas A-4E/F Skyhawk #5002:2300, 1/32 scale, MIB, P4..................................$15.00

Hasegawa, Mitsubishi Ki-67 Hiryu (Peggy) #SM-7, 1/144 scale, MIB (sealed), P4.................................$6.00

Hasegawa, Nakajima J1N1-S Gekko (Irving) #SM-5, 1/44, MIB (sealed), P4..$4.00

Hasegawa, Nikajima Ki-49 Donryu (Helen) #SM-8, 1/144 scale, MIB (sealed), P4 ....$6.00

Hasegawa, P51D Mustang #101, unassembled, C7 ....$10.00

Hasegawa, Super Sager #JS-035, unassembled (sealed box), C7 ....$10.00

Hawk, Corporal US Army Tactical Guided Missle #554-130, 1969, 1/48 scale, NMIB, A $31.00

Hawk, Daddy, box only, M, E3.............................$30.00

Hawk, Digger, box only, M, E3.............................$25.00

Hawk, Drag Hag, MIB, E3 ....$80.00

Hawk, Endsville Eddie, assembled, E3.................$50.00

Hawk, Endsville Eddie, MIB, E3...........................$85.00

Hawk, Frantic Cats, MIB, E3................................$80.00

Hawk, Huey's Hot Rod #538, assembled, C7 ....$20.00

Hawk, Huey's Hot Rod #538, unassembled, C7................$40.00

Hawk, Killer McBash, MIB, E3 ....$135.00

Hawk, Lockheed T-33A #509, 1/48 scale, MIB, P4..........$16.00

Hawk, Lockheed TV-2 #512, 1/48, decals cut, missing instructions, VG, P4 ....$15.00

Hawk, Lockheed U2 #300, unassembled, no decals, C7...$10.00

Hawk, Silly Surfer Beach Bunny Catchin' Rays, MIB (sealed), J2..$110.00

Hawk, Silly Surfers #544-100, Hot Dogger & Surf Bunny Riding Tandem, all plastic, in 6x14" box, MIB, from $70 to..$90.00

Hawk, Spad XIII #617, unassembled, C7 ....$8.00

Hawk, Starfighter F-104 #504, unassembled, C7 ....$10.00

Hawk, T-33 Trainer #207, unassembled, C7.....................$10.00

Hawk, Thunderbird Totem Pole, MIB, E3 ....$45.00

Hawk, Weird-Ohs Davy the Way Out Cyclist, 1963, M (EX box), D9 ....$89.00

Hawk, Weird-Ohs Digger the Way Out Dragster, 1963, M (EX+ sealed box), D9 ....$95.00

Hawk, Weird-Ohs Francis the Foul, 1963, NMIB, C1......$42.00

Hawk, Weird-Ohs Leaky Boat Louie, box only, EX, J2 ....$35.00

Hawk, Weird-Ohs Leaky Boat Louie, the Vulgar Boatman; 1963, NMIB, D9 ....$113.00

Hawk, Weird-Ohs Sling Rave Curvette, 1963, MIB (sealed), C1 ....$42.00

Hawk, Woodie on Surfari, MIB, from $75 to.................$100.00

Heller, MIG 19 Farmer #L251, 1/72 scale, open box (crushed), sealed bag, NMIB, P4.................................$8.00

Heller, P51D Mustang #268, unassembled, C7 ....$5.00

Heller, Thunderbolt P47 #6084, unassembled, C7 ....$5.00

Hobby-Time, NAF-100A Super Sabre #2002, 1960, 1/51 scale, Vacuform flying kit, MIB, P4 ....$15.00

Horizon, Batman, MIB, $35.00 to $40.00.

Horizon, Bride of Frankenstein, unassembled, C7 ....$25.00

Horizon, Captain America, 1990, 1/6 scale, vinyl, complete, M (EX+ box), D9 ....$25.00

Horizon, Catwoman, MIB, E3 ....$35.00

Horizon, Dark Phoenix, MIB, from $15 to........................$25.00

Horizon, Dracula, 1980s, vinyl, complete w/molded vinyl cape, M (EX box), D9.....................................$25.00

Horizon, Hulk, MIB, E3.....................................$30.00

Horizon, Indiana Jones, MIB, E3.....................................$45.00

Horizon, Invisible Man, 1980s, complete w/2 heads & dk sunglasses, MIB, from $25 to.....................................$35.00

Horizon, Iron Man, MIB, E3.....................................$25.00

Horizon, Mole Man, MIB, E3.....................................$25.00

Horizon, Mole People, 1980s, all vinyl, M (EX+ box), D9 .$25.00

Horizon, Penguin, MIB, E3.....................................$40.00

Horizon, Robocop, 1989, vinyl, M (EX box), D9 ....$32.00

Horizon, Robocop 3, MIB, from $35 to.....................................$50.00

Horizon, Spiderman, MIB, from $15 to.....................................$25.00

Horizon, T-1000, MIB, E3.....................................$40.00

Horizon, T-800 Terminator Endoskeleton, MIB, E3 ....$40.00

Horizon, T-800 Terminator Endoskeleton, 1991, 1/5 scale, unassembled, complete (EX box), D9.....................................$32.00

Horizon, T-800 Terminator Schwarzenegger, 1991, 1/5 scale, vinyl, M (EX+ box), D9.....................................$25.00

Horizon, Tyrannosaurus Rex, MIB, E3.....................................$30.00

Horizon, Venom, 1992, 1/6 scale, vinyl, NMIB, D9 ....$35.00

Horizon, Wolverine, MIB, E3.....................................$25.00

Hudson Miniatures, 1910 Model T Turbo, wood, unassembled, C7.....................................$25.00

Hudson Miniatures, 1911 Buick Bug, wood, unassembled, C7.....................................$25.00

Imai, Angel, MIB, E3.....................................$5.00

Imai, Batmobile #B1397, unassembled, C7.....................................$50.00

Imai, Captain Black, MIB, E3.....................................$5.00

Imai, Colonel White, MIB, E3.....................................$5.00

Imai, Penelope's Car #B091, unassembled, C7.....................................$50.00

Imai, Sky-1, MIB, E3.....................................$20.00

Industro-Motive Corp (IMC), Lear Jet #401, 1/40, MIB, P4.$25.00

ITC, US Coast Guard Rescue Boat, 1950s, w/3 figures, unassembled (EX- box), T2.....................................$60.00

ITC, Yacht Atlantic #3719, unassembled/some pnt, C7 ..$50.00

JAM/Japan, Robocop #5, 1987, 5", MIB, F1.....................................$15.00

Johan, 62 Chrysler #4662, unassembled/pnt body, C7......$50.00

K&B, Breguet 14 #1141, unassembled, C7.....................................$50.00

K&B, DeHavilland DH-10A #1125, unassembled, C7.....$50.00

K&B, Fokker EV #1135-170, Collectors series, 1972, Aurora reissue, 1/48 scale, MIB (w/shrink-wrap), P4.............$35.00

K&B, Gotha GV Bomber #1126-300, Collectors series, 1972, Aurora reissue, 1/48 scale, MIB (sealed), P4.............$40.00

K&B, Sopwith Triplane #1100, unassembled, C7.....................................$45.00

Kabaya, Batman, 1989, 5", MIB, F1.....................................$15.00

Kabaya, Batmobile, 1989, 5", MIB, F1.....................................$15.00

Kaiyodo, Alien Queen, MIB, E3.....................................$275.00

Kaiyodo, Alien Warrior, MIB, E3.....................................$195.00

Kaiyodo, Freddy Krueger, MIB, E3.....................................$45.00

Kim Ito, Green Hornet, MIB, E3.....................................$115.00

Lehmann, DeHavilland DH-106 Comet Airplane #929, aluminum, 1960s, assembled, 5", NMIB, A.....................................$90.00

Lehmann, Primus-Tupolew TU 104 Airplane #930, aluminum, 1960s, assembled on display pole, 5", NMIB, A.........$90.00

Life-Like, Diplomat, Kooky Cycles series, 1971, M (EX box), D9.....................................$69.00

Life-Like, Flying Cloud #09370, 1/400 scale, Pyro reissue, MIB (sealed), P4.....................................$8.00

Life-Like, Pinta #09364, sm scale, Pyro reissue, w/sails, MIB (sealed), P4.....................................$8.00

Life-Like, Roman Chariot #09673, 1975, 1/48 scale, Miniature Masterpieces reissue, MIB, P4.....................................$8.00

Lindberg, Ankylosaurus, MIB, E3.....................................$5.00

Lindberg, Bobtail T, 1960s (?), partly assembled, appears complete, motorized kit (VG box, tape rpr), D9.............$22.00

Lindberg, British Battleship Prince of Wales #872, Snap Fit series, 1981, 1/1000, MIB (sealed), P4.....................................$6.00

Lindberg, Carvelle SE-210 Air France #454, 1/180 scale, MIB (sealed, w/window), P4.....................................$15.00

Lindberg, Cement Mixer #D278, Big Wheels, Snap Fit series, 1971, HO scale, MIB (sealed), P4.....................................$5.00

Lindberg, Chevrolet Van #D277:50, Snap Fit series, 1971, HO scale, MIB (sealed), P4.....................................$6.00

Lindberg, Destroyer Escort #753, unassembled, C7.........$20.00

Lindberg, DH Comet III BOAC #455, 1/180, MIB (sealed, w/window), P4.....................................$15.00

Lindberg, Dornier D017Z #577, unassembled, C7............$10.00

Lindberg, Douglas F4D-1 Skyray, 1/48 scale, MIB (sealed), P4.....................................$15.00

Lindberg, Dump Truck #1020, High Rollers, Snap Fit series, HO scale, MIB (sealed), P4.....................................$5.00

Lindberg, F-4D Phantom #596, 1975, 1/94 scale, MIB (sealed), P4.....................................$7.00

Lindberg, German Battleship Graf Spee #871, Snap Fit series, 1981, 1/800 scale, MIB (sealed), P4.....................................$6.00

Lindberg, German Blitz, complete, damaged instruction sheet, orig window box, EX, D9.....................................$11.00

Lindberg, Grumman Avenger #480, unassembled, C7.....$15.00

Lindberg, Hawk Hunter #536, 1/48 scale, MIB (sealed), P4.....................................$15.00

Lindberg, Hawk Hunter Black Arrows #564, 1/48 scale, MIB (sealed), P4.....................................$15.00

Lindberg, HMS Hood British Battlecruiser #763M, 1/400 scale, NMIB, P4.....................................$15.00

Lindberg, Kennedy PT 109 #7311:300, 1972, 1/60 scale, MIB, from $15 to.....................................$20.00

Lindberg, Mad Maestro, Monster Action Kit series, 1965, NMIB, H4.....................................$75.00

Lindberg, Mail Truck #D276:50, Snap Fit Series, 1971, HO scale, MIB (sealed), P4.....................................$6.00

Lindberg, Mighty Van Bus #1086, Van Go series, HO scale, sparkle-flake finish, chrome trim, MIB (sealed), P4 ..$10.00

Lindberg, Multistage Rocket #1001, assembled, C7.........$85.00

Lindberg, Navy Light Attack Bomber & Tractor #555, unassembled, C7.....................................$25.00

Lindberg, North American F-100 #528, 1/48 scale, partially assembled, non-pnt, complete, orig box, G, P4.........$12.00

Lindberg, Protoceratops, MIB, E3.....................................$5.00

Lindberg, Republic XF-91 Thunderceptor #513, 1/48 scale, open box, pilot warped, missing seat, o/w complete, NMIB, P4.....................................$10.00

Lindberg, Rockwell B-1 #2311, 1975, 1/150 scale, NMIB, P4..$8.00

Lindberg, Star Probe Space Shuttle, 1976, MIB (sealed), D9.....................................$18.00

Lindberg, Stuka Dive Bomber #306, unassembled, C7 .....$20.00

Lindberg, Tupelev TU-104 Aeroflot #456, 1/175 scale, MIB (sealed, w/window), P4 ....$15.00

Lindberg, US Coast Guard Coastal Patrol Boat, 1972, requires only minor assembly, EX+ (EX+ box), D9 ....$9.00

Lindberg, USCG Coastal Patrol Boat #7313:300, 1972, 1/80 scale, MIB, P4 ....$15.00

Lindberg, WWII German Bomber Junkers, 1975, w/scale engines, crew & movable controls, EX+, D9................$9.00

Lindberg, XKE Jaguar Mini-Lindy #4039, 1968, HO scale, NMIB, P4 ....$5.00

Lodella, El Eliminator, MIB, E3 ....$30.00

Lunar Models, Fly w/Two Heads, unassembled, C7........$100.00

Lunar Models, Invaders From Mars' Martian, resin sculpted by Randy Bowen, unbuilt, complete, no box, 7", D9......$59.00

Lunar Models, Vincent, MIB, E3 ....$65.00

Mad Labs, Alien, MIP, E3 ....$20.00

Mad Labs, Bride of Frankenstein, MIP, E3........................$20.00

Mad Labs, Famous Monsters Plaque, MIP, E3...................$25.00

Mad Labs, Mars Attacks Bust, MIP, E3 ....$30.00

Mad Labs, Super Deformed Ren & Stimpy, MIP, E3........$20.00

Mad Labs, Vampirella Plaque, MIP, E3..............................$25.00

Mandarin, Born Loser Napoleon, MIB, E3 ....$15.00

Marx, Fix-All Sports Car, 20-pc, assembled, 12", EX (NM box), A $90.00

Matchbox, Me Bf-190E Emil #PK-502, 1979, 1/32 scale, MIB, P4 ....$20.00

Max Factory, Female Guyer 2, MIB, E3 ....$65.00

Max Factory, Freddy Krueger, MIB, E3 ....$100.00

Max Factory, Gregole, MIB, E3...$45.00

Max Factory, Guyer, movie version, MIB, E3 ....$95.00

Max Factory, Vamore, MIB, E3...$45.00

Minicraft/Hasegawa, General Dynamics Convair F-106A Delta Dart #052, 1/72 scale, MIB, P4.................................$12.00

Minicraft/Hasegawa, Thunderbird F-105 Thunderchief #122, USAF Acrobatic Team series, MIB, P4 ....$12.00

Monogram, AH-1S Cobra Attack Helicopter, unassembled, T1 ....$10.00

Monogram, American Paratrooper #818, lead, unassembled, C7 ....$25.00

Monogram, Armored Half-Track (US-AA) #8215, Armor series, 1972, 1/35 scale, NMIB (w/wht background), P4 ....$10.00

Monogram, Attack Aircraft Carrier USS Kittyhawk, 1978, NMIB , D9 ....$9.00

Monogram, B-17G Flying Fortress #5600, unassembled, C7 ....$30.00

Monogram, B-58 Hustler #PA32, unassembled (open box), C7 ....$35.00

Monogram, Blue Thunder #6036, 1984, 1/32 scale, from movie, MIB (sealed), from $10 to $15.00

Monogram, Boeing SST Supersonic Transport #PA211, 1968, 1/400 scale, MIB (w/bl background), P4 ....$15.00

Monogram, Buck Rogers #6031, unassembled, complete, NMIB (worn), G5 ....$45.00

Monogram, Buggy Man Gobot, 1984, MIB, F1 ....$5.00

Monogram, C-47 Skytrain #P11, unassembled, C7 ....$45.00

Monogram, Curtiss P-40B Tigershark #PA96, 1964, MIB, P4 ....$20.00

Monogram, Days of Thunder Hardee's Lumina Stock Car #2926, 1/24 scale, MIB (sealed), P4 ....$5.00

Monogram, Douglas DC-3 TWA #P9-96, 1/90 scale, MIB, A $40.00

Monogram, Douglas DC-7 #P9, unassembled, C7 ....$75.00

Monogram, Dracula Universal Monster Luminator Kit, 1/8 scale, reissue of 1960s model, 1991, MIB, F1 ....$15.00

Monogram, Dragon Dinosaur, MIB, E3............................$10.00

Monogram, Dragon Wagon #6746, unassembled, C7.......$50.00

Mego, King Kong 'The Last Stand,' 1976, MIB, C1/T1, $45.00.

Monogram, 1934 Duesenburg, 1/24 scale, 1963, MIB, O1, $45.00.

Monogram, Duesenberg, 1963, 1/24 scale, mc w/chrome plating, 150 parts, EX+, D9 ....$19.00

Monogram, El Camino #2244, unassembled, C7 ....$25.00

Monogram, Elvira Macabre Mobile, 1988, 1/24 scale, NMIB (sealed), D9..$11.00

Monogram, Flap Jack #1143, Comedy Airplane series, 1989, battery-op, wings flap & guns move, MIB (sealed), P4 ...$10.00

Monogram, Flying Reptile, MIB, E3.................................$10.00

Monogram, Ford Tri-Motor Island Airlines #7592, 1975, 1/77 scale, MIB, P4 ....$25.00

Monogram, Frankenstein Universal Monsters Luminators Kit, 1/8 scale, reissue of 1960s model, 1991, MIB, from $10 to $15.00

Monogram, Futurista #PC108, unassembled, C7 ....$175.00

Monogram, General Dynamics F-16 #5401, 1976, 1/48, MIB, P4 ....$4.00

Monogram, Ghost of Red Baron #PC220, unassembled, C7 ....$200.00

Monogram, Giant Woolly Mammoth, 1987, 1/13 scale, reissue of old Aurora kit, NMIB (sealed), D9 ....$25.00

Monogram, Hawker Typhoon #PA213, unassembled, C7.$25.00

Monogram, Infantry Figures #8213, 1975, 1/35 scale, MIB (sealed), P4...$20.00

Monogram, Kitty Hawk, 1960, NMIB, J2 ....$40.00

Monogram, Land Rover #2279, 1981, 1/24 scale, MIB (bent from tight shrink-wrap), P4 ....$6.00

Monogram, Lee Tank #7536, 1973, 1/32 scale, MIB (wht background), P4 ....$10.00

Monogram, Lee Tank M3 #6503, 1983, 1/32 scale, MIB (sealed), P4 ....$8.00

Monogram, Luminator King Kong Neon Monster, MIB (sealed), T1 ....$50.00

Monogram, Miami Vice Daytona Spyder, 1984, 1/24 scale, hood opens, MIB, C1 ....$29.00

Monogram, Miami Vice Ferrari Testarossa #2756, MIB (sealed), A3 ....$15.00

Monogram, Mirage 2000 w/Exocet Missiles #5446, 1986, 1/48 scale, MIB, P4 ....$4.00

Monogram, Mork & Mindy Jeep, 1979, MIB (sealed), C1 .$22.00

Monogram, Mosquito Bomber #6064, Heritage Edition series, 1984, 1/48 scale, MIB (sealed), P4 ....$8.00

Monogram, M3-109E & Hawker Hurricane, Air Combat Series #4, #6082; 1988, 1/48 scale, NMIB, P4 ....$20.00

Monogram, Orient Express Hypersonic Airliner X-30 #1132, Snap Tite series, 1988, unknown scale, MIB (sealed), P4...$10.00

Monogram, OS2U Kingfisher #PA135, 1966, 1/48 scale, complete, NMIB (w/bl background), P4 ....$20.00

Monogram, P-38 Lighting #PA97, unassembled, C7........$30.00

Monogram, Roton Assault Vehicle, MIB, E3....................$8.00

Monogram, Royal T Convertible #6068, 1984, unknown scale, Go-Bots series, MIB (sealed), P4................................$15.00

Monogram, Shangri La #B5, wood, unassembled, C7.......$50.00

Monogram, Slot Racing Porsche 904 GTS, 1965, 1/24 scale, assembled, hand control, extra parts & instructions, EX, D9 ....$32.00

Monogram, Snoopy & His Bugatti #6894, unassembled (sealed box), C7...$75.00

Monogram, Stormpanzer 43 German Grizzly Bear #7506, 1973, Armor series, 1/32 scale, MIB, P4 ....$10.00

Monogram, Tyrannosaurus Rex, 1987, complete, bagged pcs, M (VG- box), D9 ....$39.00

Monogram, US Army Eager Beaver 2½ Ton Military Truck, 1950s, w/6 figures, 4-star logo, NMIB, T2.................$80.00

Monogram, US Army Miltary Jeep, 1950s, w/37mm anti-tank gun & 3 figures, minor assembly/pnt, unused decal (EX box), T2 ....$40.00

Monogram, USS New Jersey, 1976, NMIB (sealed), D9 ....$9.00

Monogram, Vietnam Memorial Statue, Three Fighting Men; 1988, 1/10 scale, bronze plastic, MIB (sealed), D9 ....$29.00

Monogram, Viper #6027, unassembled (worn box), C7 ...$35.00

Monogram, Wolfman, Monster Illuminator Kit, MIB, J2 ...$9.50

Monogram, Woody Wagon #PC 103, unassembled, C7...$30.00

Monogram, WWII German Battleship DKM Tirpitz, 1977, NMIB, D9 ....$9.00

Monogram, 1930 Ford Phaeton #PC64, minor assembly, C7 ....$35.00

Monogram, 1964 Pontiac GTO #2714, 1/24 scale, MIB (sealed), A3...$15.00

Monster Museum, Monster of Piedras Blancas, MIB, E3 .$55.00

MPC, Alien, from 1st movie, 1979, NMIB (sealed), C1 ..$105.00

MPC, B-Wing Fighter, MIB, E3....................................$10.00

MPC, Batman, MIB, E3..$35.00

MPC, Batman, 1984, MIB (sealed), C1 ....$45.00

MPC, Beverly Hillbillies TV Truck, 1968, may be built 2 ways, complete, orig box, EX+, D9................................$138.00

MPC, Bionic Woman's Bionic Repair Lab w/Oscar & Jamie, 1970s, MIB (sealed), C1 ....$29.00

MPC, Black Hole Cygnus, 1979, complete, NMIB (sealed), D9...$39.00

MPC, Black Hole Maximillian, 1979, complete, M (EX+ sealed box), D9 ....$33.00

MPC, Black Hole VINCENT #1-1981, 1979, 1/12 scale, MIB (sealed), P4 ....$35.00

MPC, Dark Shadows Barnabas Collins the Vampire, 1968, M (EX box), H4 ....$250.00

MPC, Dark Shadows Barnabas Collins the Vampire, 1968, 1/8 scale, in cape, w/cane, partially assembled (EX box), T2 ....$130.00

MPC, Dark Shadows Barnabas Vampire Van, 1969, 1/25 scale, w/coffin & Barnabas figure, nearly assembled/pnt (EX+ box), T2 ....$130.00

MPC, Dick Harrell's Camaro, NMIB, NM, J2 ....$68.00

MPC, Dukes of Hazzard Cooters Tow Truck, 1981, M (EX box), C1 ....$36.00

MPC, ESB, Encounter w/Yoda on Dagaboh; 1980, NMIB, C1 ....$39.00

MPC, Fonzie & His Bike #1-0634, unassembled, C7........$50.00

MPC, George Barris Ricksha, most pcs on tree, NMIB, M5 .$45.00

MPC, Good Guy Taxi #616, unassembled, C7.................$75.00

MPC, Hanover CL111A #5002, unassembled, C7 ....$15.00

MPC, Hot Curl the Surfer's Idol, 1960s, NMIB (sealed), from $45 to $75.00

MPC, Incredible Hulk, MIB, E3....................................$35.00

MPC, Incredible Hulk, 1978, MIB (sealed), C1 ....$45.00

MPC, Knight Rider, 1982, NMIB, C1 ....$22.00

MPC, Laser Warrior Phantom Intruder, MIB, E3............$10.00

MPC, Monkeemobile (PA), MIB, E3 ....$120.00

MPC, 'Pirates of the Caribbean,' Dead Men Tell No Tales, 1972, MIB (sealed), D9, $35.00.

MPC, Pilgrim Observer Space Station #9001, 1/100 scale, MIB, from $20 to...$40.00

MPC, Play It Again Sam #1-5052, unassembled, C7 .....$115.00

MPC, Snow Speeder, MIB, E3 ....$12.00

MPC, Space 1999 Alien Moon Vehicle #1-1902, 1978, 1/25 scale, NMIB, A $25.00

MPC, Space 1999 Hawk Attack Vehicle #1-1904, 1977, 1/72 scale, MIB (shrink-wrapped), A $92.00

MPC, Spiderman, 1978, snap-together assembly has been disassembled, sm rpr needed, pnt-free pcs (EX+ box), D9..$27.00

MPC, Star Wars A-Wing Fighter, ROTJ, 1983, NMIB (sealed), D9..$10.00

MPC, Star Wars B-Wing Fighter #I-1974, ROTJ, 1983, 1/144 scale, MIB (sealed), P4 ....$8.00

MPC, Star Wars C-3PO, 1977, complete, bagged pcs, M (EX+ box), D9 ....$23.00

MPC, Star Wars C-3PO #1-1935, ROTJ, 1983, 1/10 scale, MIB (sealed), P4 ....$10.00

MPC, Star Wars Darth Vader Action Model, 1978, bust type w/sounds & lights, NMIB (sealed), D9 ....$53.00

MPC, Star Wars Darth Vader Figure, 1979, complete, w/glow-in-dark light saber, NMIB (sealed), D9......................$28.00

MPC, Star Wars Darth Vader Star Destroyer, MIB, E3 ....$15.00

MPC, Star Wars Darth Vader TIE Fighter, 1977, M (EX sealed), EX sealed box) $50.00

MPC, Star Wars Darth Vader TIE Fighter, 1978, M (P box), D9 ....$19.00

MPC, Star Wars Darth Vader Van, 1979, 1/32 scale, NMIB, D9 ....$32.00

MPC, Star Wars Jabba the Hutt Throne Room #1-1928, ROTJ, 1983, 1/60 scale, NMIB (w/broken shrink-wrap), P4 .$15.00

MPC, Star Wars Luke Skywalker Van, 1979, 1/32 scale, glow-in-dark decals & rolling wheels, NMIB (sealed), D9......$32.00

MPC, Star Wars Luke Skywalker X-Wing Fighter, 1978, MIB, from $35 to...$45.00

MPC, Star Wars Millenium Falcon, ROTJ, 1983, MIB (sealed), A...$35.00

MPC, Star Wars Millenium Falcon, 1977, M (EX box), C1 ....$113.00

MPC, Star Wars Millenium Falcon, 1979, missing instructions, NM (EX box), D9...$45.00

MPC, Star Wars ROTJ, 3-pc set, MIB, E3 ....$15.00

MPC, Star Wars R2-D2 #1-1912, orig, unassembled (sealed), C7 ....$50.00

MPC, Star Wars R2-D2 #1-1934, ROTJ, unassembled (sealed), C7 ....$20.00

MPC, Star Wars R2-D2 Van, 1979, 1/32 scale, glow-in-dark decals & rolling wheels, M (EX+ box), D9 ....$29.00

MPC, Star Wars Speeder Bike, ROTJ, MIB, from $15 to..$20.00

MPC, Star Wars Speeder Bike, ROTJ, 1983, complete, M (EX box), D9 ....$10.00

MPC, Star Wars TIE Interceptor #I-1972, ROTJ, 1983, 1/48 scale, MIB (sealed), P4 ....$7.00

MPC, Star Wars X-Wing Fighter, ROTJ, 1983, NMIB (sealed), D9 ....$10.00

MPC, Strange Change Mummy, MIB, E3 ....$60.00

MPC, Strange Change Vampire #1-0901, MIB, C7/E3 ....$75.00

MPC, Superman, MIB, E3 ....$35.00

MPC, Sweat Hogs Dream Machine #1-0641, Welcome Back Kotter series, 1976, 1/25 scale, MIB, from $25 to $35.00

MPC, TJ Hooker Police Car #1-0676, 1982, 1/25 scale, MIB, P4 ....$22.00

MPC, Vampire's Midnight Madness, MIB, E3 ....$75.00

MPC, 1965 Dodge Monaco, 1/25 scale, MIB (sealed), H2 .$75.00

MPC, 1967 Bonneville #967, unassembled, C7 ....$60.00

MPC, 1972 Dodge Charger, 1/25 scale, MIB (sealed), H2.$120.00

Multiple, Painless False Teeth Extractor, MIB, E3 ....$55.00

Multiple, Ripley's Believe It or Not #981-100 Iron Maiden, 1966, 6x13" box, NMIB (sealed), A $245.00

Multiple, Rube Goldberg's Automatic Baby Feeder, 1965, 3 missing pcs, 2 glued pcs, w/2 cb signs (VG+ box), D9.......$19.00

Multiple, Rube Goldberg's Automatic Baby Feeder #955, unassembled, C7 ....$50.00

Multiple, Rube Goldberg's Signal for Shipwrecked Sailors, 1965, unassembled, missing 1 pc (EX+ box), D9.................$27.00

Multiple, World's Greatest Stage Illusions Disappearing Lady, fully operates when assembled, 1966, M (EX+ box), A $125.00

Multiple, World's Greatest Stage Illusions Float on Air, designed to fully operate when assembled, 1966, NMIB, A ...$125.00

Multiple, World's Greatest Stage Illusions Saw the Lady in Half, 1966, NMIB, A...$125.00

Nitto, Fireball, MIB, E3 ....$15.00

Nitto, Fledermaus, MIB, E3 ....$25.00

Nitto, Gogon, MIB, E3 ....$20.00

Nitto, Krote, MIB, E3 ....$22.00

Nitto, Pop-up Jeep, 1970s, 1/24 scale, motorized, MIB, C8..$25.00

Nitto, Porsche 928 #14049, 1/24 scale, MIB, P4 ....$6.00

Otaki, T-34 Tank #OT4-24, World Famous Tank series, 1/50 scale, motorized (included), MIB (sealed), P4 ....$15.00

Palmer, Corvette Stingray Convertible #574-39, 1/32 scale, NMIB (w/tape rpr), P4 ....$12.00

Palmer, Revolutionary War Cannon #7034, 1/32 scale, brass plated, MIB (sealed), P4...$10.00

Palmer, 1936 Ford 3-Window Coupe #251, 1/32 scale, NMIB, P4..$6.00

Paramount, Sussex Wagon VI, 1/30 scale, NMIB, P4.......$12.00

Palmer, Alaskan Timber Wolf 'Animals of the World,' late 1950s, EX box, D9, $10.00.

Pyro, Auburn Speedster #851, 8", M (EX box), O1, $85.00.

Palmer, Spirit of '76, late 1950s, unbuilt, VG+ box, D9, $55.00.

Paramount, The Lord Mayors' Coachman Horses, Harness & Postillion #2a, 1/30 scale, NMIB, P4..........................$12.00

Parks, Castro, Born Losers #803-100, from Hysterical Historical Greats, 14x6" box, NMIB (sealed), A........................$65.00

Parks, Hitler, Born Losers Series, 1960s, NMIB (sealed), D9..$139.00

Parks, Napoleon, Born Losers Series, 1965, 1/12 scale, Napoleon at Waterloo, 15x5" box, MIB, from $90 to..............$130.00

Plasticart, SE-210 Carvelle Air France #5006, 1/100 scale, damage to wing & decal sheet, complete, VG (VG box), P4...$10.00

Precision, Blue Marlin #F-101, unassembled, C7.............$15.00

Precision, Capt Kidd #M402, assembled, C7 ....$75.00

Precision, Capt Kidd #M402, unassembled, C7..............$100.00

Premier, Braddock Antique Gun (no #), 1/1 scale, most parts sealed in bag, complete, NMIB, P4 ....$12.00

Premier, Cadillac Type Model 1903 #104-39, 1950s, 1/32 scale, MIB (sealed), P4 ....$8.00

Premier, Packard Type Model 1900 #103-39, 1950s, 1/32 scale, MIB (sealed), P4 ....$8.00

Pyro, Buccaneer Pistol #C201-156, 1/1 scale, MIB, P4.....$20.00

Pyro, Burma River Pirate #C253, unassembled, C7 ....$15.00

Pyro, Deperdussian #P603, MIB, C7 ....$20.00

Pyro, Gertrude Thebaud #206, unassembled, C7.............$25.00

Pyro, HMS Victorious #376, 1960s, 1/1200 scale, NMIB, P4.$5.00

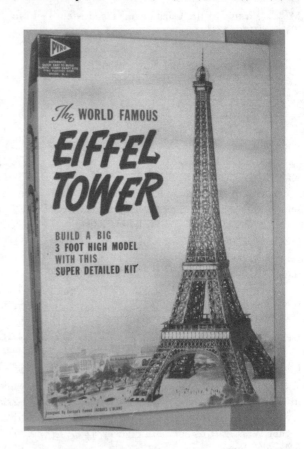

Pyro, Eiffel Tower, 1960s, unbuilt, most parts still on trees, EX, D9, $89.00.

Pyro, Italian Miquelet Lock Pistol #C226, 1967, 1/1 scale, VG (water damaged box), P4 ....$12.00

Pyro, Martin Handasyde 1911 #P602-100, 1/48 scale, MIB, P4..$10.00

Pyro, Medicine Man #272, unassembled, C7 ....$75.00

Pyro, Peacemaker .45 #231-1.29, 1960, 1/1 scale, NMIB, P4 ....$25.00

Pyro, Rolls Royce #C349, unassembled (sealed), C7 ....$10.00

Pyro, USS Constitution #C313-60, sm scale, MIB, P4.......$8.00

Pyro, Western 44 (gun) #200-1.29, 1960, 1/1 scale, NMIB, P4 ....$18.00

Pyro, Wyatt Earp US Marshal, Hugh O'Brien likeness, 1959, 12x4" box, M (EX+ box), A........................$73.00

Pyro, 1910 Bleriot Monoplane #P601, 1960s, M (VG+ sealed box), P3........................$15.00

Pyro, 1929 Mercedes-Benz SSk Sportwagon #C348, 1/32 scale, MIB, P4........................$5.00

Pyro, 1930 Packard Boat-Tail Roadster #C343, 1/32 scale, MIB, P4........................$5.00

Remco, Flintstone Motorized Paddy Wagon, M (EX box)..$250.00

Remco, Flintstones Yacht, plastic w/battery-op motor, NMIB, A........................$260.00

Renwal, Customized Service Truck #301:298, 1960s, 1/32 scale, MIB, A........................$60.00

Renwal, Human Skeleton #803, unassembled, C7..........$50.00

Renwal, Nike Launcher & Crew #550, Blueprint series, 1/32 scale, NMIB, from $35 to........................$50.00

Renwal, Polaris Launching Nuclear Sub Thomas Jefferson #618, 1950s-60s, 1/200 scale, kit started, orig box, EX+, D9.$23.00

Renwal, Polaris Launching Nuclear Sub Thomas Jefferson #653, 1950s, 1/200 scale, fires missiles, MIB, P4........$65.00

Renwal, Polaris Launching Nuclear Sub Thomas Jefferson #7100, 1950s, 1/200 scale, MIB, A........................$75.00

Renwal, USS Springield Light Cruiser #602, 1/500, 3 sm parts glued (restorable), VG (worn box), P4........$15.00

Renwal, Visible V-8 Engine, 1960s, 16x22" box, M (EX box), D9........................$49.00

Renwal, Walker Bulldog #M554, unassembled, C7..........$35.00

Renwal, 1965 Corvette Stingray #136-89, 1966, 1/48 scale, MIB (sealed), P4........................$20.00

Renwal, 8" Self-Propelled Howitzer #M551-298, Blueprint series, 1950s, 1/32 scale, NMIB, A........................$64.00

Revell, A-7A Corsair II, MIB (sealed), T1........................$10.00

Revell, Aerobee Hi Rocket S kit, 1958, MIB, J2..........$130.00

Revell, Alien Invader #8001, 1979, 1/144 scale, MIB (sealed), P4........................$15.00

Revell, American Airlines DC 7 #H219, unassembled, C7........................$75.00

Revell, Apollo Spacecraft Science Program #H1836-A, 1966, 1/96 scale, MIB, P4........................$35.00

Revell, Apollo 11 Lunar Module Tranquility Base, 1969, EX+, D9........................$22.00

Revell, Assault Tank M40-M41 SP Gun #H2104, 1976, 1/35 scale, MIB, P4........................$10.00

Revell, A38 Skywarrior #H256, unassembled (sealed), C7..$10.00

Revell, A5A Vigilanti #H134, unassembled (sealed), C7........................$10.00

Revell, B-17F Memphis Belle #H197, 1978, 1/48 scale, NMIB (minor wear), P4........................$20.00

Revell, Battleship HMS King George V, Battleship That Sank the Bismarck; 1974, complete, EX+, D9........................$9.00

Revell, Battleship USS Arizona, 1957, S kit, EX (EX box), D9........................$23.00

Revell, Battleship USS Arizona, 1971, M (EX+ box), D9..$9.00

Revell, Battleship USS Missouri, the Mighty MO; 1977, NMIB (sealed), D9........................$9.00

Revell, Beatnik Bandit, MIB, E3........................$20.00

Revell, Billy Carter's Redneck Power Pickup #H1385, 1978, 1/25 scale, MIB (sealed, w/lt warping), P4........................$20.00

Revell, Boeing P-26A Peashooter #H656, 1/72 scale, MIB, P4........................$12.00

Revell, Boeing 707 Astrojet American Airlines #H243, 1969, Jet Horizon series, 1/144 scale, NMIB, P4........................$40.00

Revell, Bomarc IM-99 #8602, unassembled, bagged, C7..$10.00

Revell, Bonanza #H1931, 1966, 1/7 scale, VG (1 box corner broken), A........................$80.00

Revell, Brother Rat Fink on a Bike, MIB (sealed)..........$65.00

Revell, California Highway Patrol Bike, Harley-Davidson, 1976, 1/8 scale, M (VG box), O1, $65.00.

Revell, Campbeltown Destroyer, 1971, MIB, P4, $10.00; Revell, PT-109 Kennedy #H310, unassembled, C7, $35.00.

Revell, Caravelle #H184, unassembled, C7........................$15.00

Revell, Carro De Bombeiro (Hose Reel) #H702, 1/48 scale, MIB, P4........................$22.00

Revell, Convair Altas ICBM #H-1622, 1958, 1/110 scale, some pc loose in box, NMIB (w/lt scuffs), A........................$198.00

Revell, Convair F-102A #H233-89, 1956, S kit, 1/78 scale, NMIB, A........................$31.00

Revell, Country Schoolhouse, plastic, orig box, T1..........$15.00

Revell, Cutty Sark #H364, 1960, 1/96 scale, VG (box w/tape rpr), P4........................$20.00

Revell, Cutty Sark #H393, Museum Classics series, 1/96 scale, NMIB, P4........................$30.00

Revell, Cutty Sark #5401, unassembled, C7 .... $15.00

Revell, Destroyer HMS Campbeltown #H450, 1971, MIB (sealed), P4 .... $10.00

Revell, Don 'The Snake' Prudhomme Rear-Engine Dragster #H1464, 1974, 1/25 scale, NMIB (plain wht, w/photo label), P4 .... $30.00

Revell, Don Garlits' AA Fuel Dragster, assembled, orig box, NM, J2 .... $45.00

Revell, Douglas DC-Y Mainliner United Flight 707 Airport Scene #H220-198, 1955, S kit, 1/122 scale, NMIB, A $200.00

Revell, Douglas DC-7 Mainliner United Flight 707 #H220:198, 1955, S kit, 1/122 scale, NMIB, P4 .... $385.00

Revell, Dr Seuss Birthday Bird, all plastic, Birthday Bird w/cake, w/letters to place on cake, 1960, scarce, MIB, A $216.00

Revell, Dr Seuss Cat in the Hat, all plastic, complete w/glue & brush, 1969, MIB, A $174.00

Revell, Dr Seuss Tingo the Noodle Topped Stroodle, NMIB, M5 .... $50.00

Revell, Dr Suess Norval the Bashful Blinket, 1960s, Zoo Kit series, missing 2 balls for antennas, H4 .... $70.00

Revell, DUNE Ornithopter #1775, MIB (sealed), P4 .... $25.00

Revell, DUNE Sand Crawler #1776, MIB (sealed), P4 .... $25.00

Revell, DUNE Sandworm #1778, MIB (sealed), P4 .... $25.00

Revell, Everything Is Go Friendship 7 Mercury Capsule & Atlas Booster, 1962, NMIB, A $50.00

Revell, F-4E Phantom & MIG 21 #4747, 1983, 1/32 scale, MIG started/missing decals, complete/unassembled Phantom, VG, P4 .... $12.00

Revell, F-89D Scorpion #H126, 1962, 1/80 scale, NMIB, P4 .... $15.00

Revell, F-94C Starfire #H123, Academy series, 1/55 scale, NMIB (minor damage), P4 .... $15.00

Revell, Fink Eliminator, reissue, MIB, E3 .... $15.00

Revell, Flash Gordon & Martian, MIB, from $150 to $190.00

Revell, Flight of the Intruder F-4J Phantom Jet, MIB (sealed), T1 .... $10.00

Revell, Fokker D-VIII #H632, unassembled, C7 .... $15.00

Revell, Frank Luke's SPAD XIII #H290:150, 1965, 1/27 scale, NMIB (sealed), P4 .... $25.00

Revell, Gemini Astronaut #H1837, unassembled, C7 ...... $50.00

Revell, Gene Snow's Snowman, assembled, orig box, EX, J2 . $45.00

Revell, German Battleship Bismark, Threat to the British Fleet; 1975, 1/570 scale, EX+, D9 .... $9.00

Revell, German Command Car Horch Kfz 15 #H2109, 1976, 1/35 scale, MIB, P4 .... $10.00

Revell, Global Van Lines Tractor & Trailer #T6018-98, 1959, 1/87 scale, tractor assembled, complete, orig box, G, P4 .... $10.00

Revell, Goodyear Blimp #H999, unassembled, C7 .... $25.00

Revell, Grumman F11F-1 Tiger #H249-89, 1/55 scale, S kit, NMIB, P4 .... $20.00

Revell, Jeb Allen's Praying Mantis Dragster, 1/16 scale, assembled, orig box, EX+, J2 .... $45.00

Revell, Lockheed Starfire #H201, unassembled, no decal, C7 .... $60.00

Revell, M-35 Military Truck #H537-129, 1958, 1/40 scale, S kit, MIB, P4 .... $70.00

Revell, M-56 Self-Propelled Gun #H540-98, 1958, S kit, 1/40 scale, MIB, A $40.00

Revell, Maintenance Shed, MIB, T1 .... $25.00

Revell, Martin PBM-5 Mariner (A Kikoler) #H175, 1/118 scale, NMIB (sealed), P4 .... $30.00

Revell, Martin P6M Seamaster #H244, 1/84 scale, S kit, damaged decals, complete, VG, P4 .... $30.00

Revell, Mayflower #H327, unassembled/some pnt, C7 ..... $20.00

Revell, Mickey Thompson US Marines, assembled, orig box, EX, J2 .... $45.00

Revell, Mr Gasser, orig edition, MIB, from $165 to $200.00

Revell, Mr Gasser, reissue, MIB, E3 .... $15.00

Revell, Operating Engine House #T9028, unassembled, C7.. $20.00

Revell, Oriano #H401, some assembly, C7 .... $25.00

Revell, P-40 Warhawk #6101, unassembled (sealed), C7 ... $5.00

Revell, Paul the Great McCartney, plastic, 1964, NM (EX+ box), A $241.00

Revell, Peter Pan Pirate Ship #H364, unassembled, C7. $100.00

Revell, Phantom & Voodoo Witch Doctor, 1965, 1/10 scale, 6x10" box, MIB, from $180 to $250.00

Revell, Polar Bear, 'Endangered Animals,' 1974, M (G-box), D9, $23.00.

Revell, Porsche 911 #H-1215, 1970, 1/25 scale, MIB, P4 ... $5.00

Revell, PT 109 Kennedy #H310, unassembled, C7 .... $35.00

Revell, Rat Fink, orig edition, MIB (sealed) $85.00

Revell, Rat Fink, reissue, MIB, E3 .... $15.00

Revell, Rat Fink, signed by Ed Roth, MIB, E3 .... $150.00

Revell, Rat Fink Drag Nut, 1963, NMIB, D9 .... $59.00

Revell, Republic F-84F Thunderstreak #H215-79, 1955, 1/54 scale, MIB, from $30 to $40.00

Revell, Robin Hood 1 #H945, unassembled, C7 .... $50.00

Revell, Russian T-34 Tank #H538-129, 1958, S kit, 1/40 scale, NMIB, from $50 to $60.00

Revell, R3Y-2 Tradewind #H 238-98, 1956, 1/168 scale, S kit, missing nose cap, o/w complete, NMIB, P4 .... $55.00

Revell, Snark #H1801, unassembled, C7 .... $50.00

Revell, Space Station, complete w/4 vehicles, 10 figures, decals, manual & accessories, unassembled, 1959, M (EX box), A $402.00

Revell, Stu-G IV Assault Gun Invasion Tank #H2118, 1976, 1/35 scale, MIB, P4 ....$10.00

Revell, Surf Fink, reissue, MIB, E3 ....$15.00

Revell, T-34 Russian Tank #H559, Model Builders of America Selection series, 1972, 1/40 scale, MIB (sealed), P4 ....$20.00

Revell, Tactical Missiles Set #H1812, 1956, S kit, 1/40 scale, w/Little John & dart missiles, MIB, A $37.00

Revell, Thermopylae Clipper Ship #H390, 1960, 1/96 scale, appears complete, NMIB (w/tape rpr), P4 ....$45.00

Revell, Tirpitz #H351, unassembled, C7 ....$25.00

Revell, Tom 'Mongoose' McEwen's Duster, 1/16 scale, assembled, orig box, EX+, J2 ....$45.00

Revell, US Army Tactical Missiles, 1958, NMIB, J2 ....$60.00

Revell, US Frigate Constitution Old Ironsides, 1966, complete, M (EX+ box), D9 ....$19.00

Revell, US Navy Oceanographic Office Lockeed P-3A Orion #4428, 1984, 1/144 scale, NMIB, P4 ....$5.00

Revell, USS The Sullivans' WWII Destroyer #5021, 1986, 1/306 scale, MIB (sealed), P4 ....$10.00

Revell, Vought F7U-3 Cutlass #H211-79, 1953, 1/59 scale, MIB, P4 ....$60.00

Revell, Westinghouse Atomic Power Plant #H 1550, 1961, 1/192 scale, 2nd issue, NMIB, A $350.00

Revell, William Barker's Sopwith Camel #H291-200, 1965, 1/28 scale, MIB, P4 ....$25.00

Revell, 1941 (The Movie) P-40 Flying Tiger #4506, 1979, 1/32 scale, MIB (sealed), P4 ....$40.00

Revell, 1957 Chevy #H1284, unassembled, C7 ....$25.00

Revell, 1957 Chevy Nomad, 1968, 1/25 scale, unbuilt, H2 .$25.00

Revell, 1960 Corvette, Model Builders Club of America series, 1/25 scale, M, A3 ....$25.00

Revell, 1969 Jaguar #H56, unassembled, C7 ....$25.00

Revell, 1983 Custom Chevrolet Camaro Berlinetta #7491, 1983, 1/16 scale, NMIB, P4 ....$15.00

Revell/Brazil, Corvair R3y-2 Tradewind (A Kikoler) #H178, 1/168 scale, MIB, P4 ....$35.00

Schuco, Bahama Sailboat #205-341, NM (EX box), A ..$152.00

Scientific, Sky-Master Rubber-Band Powered Sport Flyer #160-495, wood, partially assembled, complete (?), 44", G, P4 ....$5.00

Screamin', Betty Page in Orbit, MIB, E3 ....$80.00

Screamin', Freddy Krueger, MIB, E3 ....$30.00

Screamin', Friday the 13th's Jason, 1988, 1/4 scale, assembly & pnt started, complete (EX+ box), D9 ....$32.00

Screamin', Rocketeer, MIB, E3 ....$55.00

Screamin', Suburban Commando Mutant General Suitor, 1991, some trimmed pcs, complete (EX+ box), D9 ....$43.00

Screamin', Vampire, 1990, London After Midnight series, M (EX+ box), D9 ....$49.00

Screamin', Werewolf, 1988, 1/4 scale, soft vinyl, M (EX box), D9 ....$23.00

Shape of Things, Boobira, MIB, E3 ....$25.00

Shape of Things, Rock-a-Who, MIB, E3 ....$20.00

Strombecker, Chance Vought F8U-1 Crusader Glider #KB3, 1950s, unknown scale, vacuform, rubber-band launched, MIB, P4 ....$10.00

Strombecker, DeHavilland U1-A Otter EFM24-100, 1/25 scale, vacuform, MIB, P4 ....$18.00

Strombecker, Disney Satellite Launcher, 1957, NMIB, J2 .$160.00

Strombecker, Disneyland Rocket to the Moon, 1958, NMIB, J2 ....$220.00

Strombecker, US Navy Blimp #3723, unassembled, C7 .$100.00

Tamiya/MRC, German Army Officers #MM110, 1/35 scale, MIB (sealed), P4 ....$5.00

Tamiya/MRC, German Army Tank Crew #MM119, 1/35 scale, MIB (sealed), P4 ....$5.00

Testors, Davey, Grodies series, MIB, E3 ....$25.00

Testors, Digger, MIB, E3 ....$20.00

Testors, Freddie Flameout, Grodies series, MIB, E3 ....$30.00

Testors, Huey's Hut Rod, MIB, E3 ....$20.00

Testors, Killer McBash, MIB, E3 ....$35.00

Testors, Steel Pluckers, Grodies series, MIB, E3 ....$25.00

Testors, Top Gun F-5 Adversary, 1986, MIB (sealed), H4 ....$5.00

Tsukuda, Batman, MIB, E3 ....$95.00

Tsukuda, Endoskeleton, chrome, MIB, E3 ....$30.00

Tsukuda, Endoskeleton, 1/9th scale, MIB, E3 ....$20.00

Tsukuda, Ghost Buster's Marshmallow Man, 1984, complete w/2 different heads, M (EX+ box), D9 ....$123.00

Wave, Gaigan, MIB, E3 ....$125.00

Miscellaneous

Ad, Aurora Model Slot Car, full color, 1966 comic on bk, EX, W1 ....$10.00

Gordy's 1950's • 60's • 70's **CHARACTER TOYS & MODELS**

Selling/Buying/Trading

Illustrated Sales Catalog

U.S.A.
$2.00 3rd. class
$3.00 1st. class
$5.00 priority (2/day)

Foreign   **Canada**
$6.00 $4.00

P.O. Box 201 • Sharon Center, Ohio 44274-0201 U.S.A.
(216) 239-1657 • FAX (216) 239-2991

Home Of

Gordy's KIT BUILDERS Magazine

INTERNATIONAL Figure Kit Club

For Figure Kit Lovers

Aurora, Monster Colors Paint Set, 6 sm cans Humbrol enamel pnt, cb tray, on haunted house display, EX+ (EX+ box), A $880.00

Book, Color Treasury of Model Airplanes, Crescent, 1972, kit photos, hardcover, 9x12", G+, D9.............................$5.00

Book, How To Build Model Cars, 1969, hardcover, EX, W1 ..$9.00

Book, The Model Plane Annual, 1944, hardcover, EX, W1 .$24.00

Display, Revell-O-Rama Clouds Above the Coast, 1964, mc 3-D for 1/72 scale plane kits, MIP, D9 ....$35.00

Display, Revell-O-Rama Hidden Airstrip, 1964, mc 3-D cb for 1/72 scale plane kits, MIP, D9 ....$35.00

Musical Toys

Whether meant to soothe, entertain, or inspire, musical toys were part of our growing-up years. Some were as simple as a windup music box, others as elaborate as a lacquered French baby grand piano.

Blow-a-Tune, Kenner, 1949, crank hdl & blow to turn tune disk, w/Happy Birthday disk, M (EX box), D9 ....$23.00

Chime-A-Phone, tap bars to make sound, orig box, 7½x11¼", VG, A $20.00

Drum, Ohio Art, litho animal & children marching on tin, NM...$40.00

Electronic Organ #1200, Magnus Corp, MIB $125.00

Fido's Musical Doghouse, Ohio Art, 1950s, EX $57.50

Futureland Grand Piano #412, Mattel Creations, red & yel plastic, chromatically tuned, 1948, 12x9", MIB, P4 ......$125.00

Hot-Shots Jitter Board, 15x9" board & various instruments, lid endorsed by Hoosier Hot Shots, EX+ (VG+ box), A ..$80.00

Hurdy Gurdy, Verbena, red lacquered wood w/mc stencil & pnt details, turn crank for music, 15", G+, A $150.00

Hurdy Gurdy, Vicente Llinares, red lacquered wood w/stenciled grain, yel trim, in wood cart w/rubber tires, 31", VG, A $575.00

Islander Baritone Ukelele, French American Reeds Mfg, 1955, 29", MIB $100.00

Lyre, w/built in music box, 20", L5...................................$475.00

Merry Music Box, Mattel, litho tin, 1953, 8x6½", NM $50.00

Mickey & Thumper, Music Box, Schmid, as waltzing skaters, MIB $75.00

Piano, Ellis Britten & Eaton in gold scroll on front, 8 sq tapered legs, grain-painted, working, +stool, 23x28½", A....$775.00

Swissco Musical Shrine, w/rosary (missing) & glowing light, w/up plays Jesus My Lord, orig box, I2 ....$29.00

Whirl-a-Tune, Mattel, litho tin, 1951, MIB.....................$50.00

Xylophone, litho metal, w/orig sheet music, ca 1956, MIB.$28.00

Zither, German, complete w/tuning mechanisms & sheet music, 1965, 18", MIB $290.00

Noah's Ark

What Bible story is more delightful to children than Noah's? In the late 1800s, Bliss produced arks of various sizes along with animal pairs made of wood with applied paper lithographed details. Others imported from Germany had hand-carved or composition animals, some rather primitive, others wonderfully detailed. They're seldom found today at all, and when they are, the set is seldom complete.

Bliss, cb w/wood roof & hull, animals at window, no other animals, some paper loss, 22", G, A $400.00

Bliss, 9 animals, mk, 13", G...$400.00

Converse, emb & stenciled wood, hinged roof & side storage compartment, no animals, 18½", EX-, A $180.00

German, litho paper on wood, w/9 sm carved animals, 11", EX, A...$187.00

German, wooden w/wide assortment of animals under hinged rooftop, 1895, some rprs to animals, 15", A.............$985.00

Germany, pnt wood, w/27 simply carved animals & 2 people, slight damage, cloth hinges need rpr, boat: 7½x18", A.........$660.00

Wood ark stores 9 pr paper litho animals+5 extra sm animals, ea pr joined w/paper strips, VG, A $125.00

Wood w/Elastolin cover, pnt to resemble logs, hinged, lift-off roof, w/50+ compo & Elastolin animals, 24", G-VG, A......$600.00

Wooden ark with colorful paint on one-piece platform, with nearly one hundred painted composition and wooden animals and figures, 21" long, G-G+, A, $1,500.00.

Nodders and Bobbin' Heads

Nodders representing comic characters of the day were made in Germany in the 1930s. These were small doll-like figures approximately 3" to 4" tall, and the popular ones often came in boxed sets. But the lesser-known characters were sold separately, making them rarer and harder to find today. While the more common nodders go for $125.00 and under, Ambrose Potts, The Old Timer, Widow Zander, and Ma and Pa Winkle often bring about $350.00 — Happy Holligan even more, about $600.00. (We've listed the more valuable ones here; any German bisque nodder not listed is worth $125.00 or under.)

The concept of nodding and bobbin' heads was also used in many other applications, but it's the character nodders that are favorites of today's collector. Our advisor for German nodders is Doug Dezso (D6). See also Sports Collectibles.

Ambrose Potts, German, pnt bsk, NM...........................$350.00

Andy Gump, German, pnt bsk, NM $125.00

Aunt Mamie or Uncle Willie, German, pnt bsk, NM, ea..$350.00

Auntie Blossom, German, pnt bsk, NM.........................$150.00

Beetle Bailey, Lego, compo w/spring-mtd head, 1961, 8", NM, A...$182.00

Bill, Dock, Avery, Max, or Pop Jenks, German, pnt bsk, NM, ea...$200.00

Boy w/Cigar, standing on sq ashtray base, NM.................$65.00

Buttercup, German, pnt bsk, NM..$250.00

Chinaman, caricature figure, tape measure tab at side, NM.$50.00

Ching Chow, German, pnt bsk, 1930s, 4", NM..............$130.00

Chubby Chaney, German, pnt bsk, NM.........................$250.00

Corky, German, pnt bsk, NM..$475.00

Dog & Puppies, yel, 1960s, M...$32.50

Ferina, German, pnt bsk, NM...$350.00

Grandpa Teen, German, pnt bsk, NM.............................$350.00

Happy Homer Staggs, advertising item, NM.................$350.00

Happy Hooligan, German, pnt bsk, NM.........................$600.00

Harold Teen, German, pnt bsk, NM................................$150.00

Hula Dancer, Japan, compo, rpr, VG, I2.........................$19.00

I Only Said Putt Up, golfer w/ball in mouth, EX, I2.........$17.00

Junior Nebbs, German, pnt bsk, NM...............................$500.00

Lillums, German, pnt bsk, NM...$150.00

Little Annie Rooney, German, pnt bsk, only her arm 'nods,' NM..$250.00

Little Egypt, German, pnt bsk, NM..................................$350.00

Lord Plushbottom, German, pnt bsk, NM.......................$150.00

Ma or Pa Winkle, German, pnt bsk, NM, ea..................$350.00

Marjory, Patsy, Lilacs, or Josie, German, pnt bsk, NM, ea$400.00

Mary Ann Jackson, German, pnt bsk, NM.....................$250.00

Mickey Mouse, Marx, plastic, w/top hat, 1960s, 2", EX, M8..$25.00

Min Gump, German, pnt bsk, NM.....................................$150.00

Mr Bailey, German, pnt bsk, NM.....................................$150.00

Mr Bibb, German, pnt bsk, NM..$400.00

Mr Wicker, German, pnt bsk, NM....................................$250.00

Mummy Monster, Hong Kong, 1960s, MIP.....................$45.00

Mushmouth, German, pnt bsk, NM..................................$350.00

Mutt or Jeff, German, pnt bsk, NM, ea...........................$250.00

Nicodemus, German, pnt bsk, NM...................................$350.00

Old Timer, German, pnt bsk, NM.....................................$350.00

Our Gang Set, pnt bsk, orig 9x5" box, 6-pc, MIB, A..$1,210.00

Pat Finnegan, German, pnt bsk, NM...............................$400.00

Pete the Dog, German, pnt bsk, NM...............................$150.00

Rachel, German, pnt bsk, 1930s, NM.............................$135.00

Rudy or Fanny Nebbs, German, pnt bsk, NM, ea..........$250.00

Scottsman, Japan, compo, rpr, VG, I2.............................$19.00

Scraps, German, pnt bsk, NM..$250.00

Space Boy, compo, 1960s, EX...$87.50

Stewardess, Let's Fly United on sq base, EX.................$170.00

Twisters Couple, EX-, pr...$80.00

Widow Zander, German, pnt bsk, NM.............................$400.00

Winnie Winkle, German, pnt bsk, NM.............................$150.00

Optical Toys

Compared to the bulky viewers of years ago, contrary to the usual course of advancement, optical toys of recent years have become more simplified in concept. See also View-Master and Tru-View.

SVE Picturol Projection, patented October 1922, VG, $25.00. (Photo courtesy Kenn Norris.)

Cragstan TV-Z Junior 8mm Projector, w/4 movies (Our Gang, etc), I2..$35.00

Hanna-Barbera Talking Show Projector Slides, Kenner, 1971, MIP, C1...$29.00

Horiscope Panorama & History of American, Milton Bradley, w/lecture notes, orig box, 5x8", G, A....................$465.00

Kaleidoscope, blk paper on cb & brass, polished wood pedestal base, working, 14", VG-EX, A....................$300.00

Kaleidoscope, cb w/Disney graphics, older style, S1.........$60.00

Kaleidoscope, CG Bush, Pat 1873, blk paper over cb & brass, polished wood hand grip, 10", VG+, A.............$325.00

Kaleidoscope, CG Bush, Pat 1873, turned walnut base, 13¾", EX, A...$935.00

Kaleidoscope, Pixie Deluxe, Steven/Pixie, 4 interchangeable heads, 1964-73, 6x9" window box, NM (EX box), T2.$18.00

Kaleidoscope, psychedelic views, 1960s, NMIB...............$20.00

Magic Lantern, Ernst Planck, Germany, pnt tin w/oil burner, 10 slides, wood case w/labels, 8", VG, A...............$325.00

Magic Lantern, Ernst Planck #13, projector, oil lamp, lenses & 32 glass slides (some damaged), G, A...............$120.00

 WANTED

• German Comic Character Nodders – Junior Nebbs and Patsy

• Glass animal inkwells and candy containers

•Shafford Black Cats

• Tonkas

Doug Dezso

**864 Paterson Avenue
Maywood, New Jersey 07607
(201) 488-1311**

Magic Lantern, Germany, pnt & emb tin & brass, figure supports lens, w/3 disks & 7 slides, orig case, 14½", VG, A.......**$425.00**

Magic Mirror, McLoughlin, bends light to show litho paper image on mercury glass tube, orig wood box, EX, A...........**$1,500.00**

Marvel Super Heroes See-a-Show Viewer, Kenner, 1966, A..**$150.00**

Phantasmascope, Ackesmann, London, w/2 paper litho disks, creates image when spun before mirror, rpl hdl, G-VG, A **$85.00**

Wonder Wheel Kaleidoscope, Steven Manufacturing, 1975, NM, $8.00.

Paper Dolls

Turn-of-the-century paper dolls are seldom found today and when they are, they're very expensive. Advertising companies used them to promote their products, and some were printed on the pages of leading ladies' magazines. By the 1920s most paper dolls were being made in book form — the doll on the cover, the clothes on the inside pages. Because they were so inexpensive, paper dolls survived the Depression and went on to peak in the 1940s. Though the advent of television caused sales to decline, paper doll companies were able to hang on by making paper dolls representing Hollywood celebrities and TV stars. These are some of the most collectible today; even celebrity dolls from more recent years like the Brady Bunch or the Waltons are popular. Remember, condition is very important; if they've been cut out, even when they're still in fine condition and have all their original accessories, they're worth only about half as much as an uncut doll.

Alice in Wonderland, Dress the Mad Hatter in Bell-Bottoms!, 1976, uncut, M, P6 ....**$35.00**

Alice in Wonderland, Whitman, 1976, complete & unused, EX, M8..**$20.00**

Annette Funicello, Whitman, 1958, EX **$30.00**

Annie Oakley, Whitman #1960, w/Annie Oakley, Tagg & Lofty, cut out but complete, 1956, EX+ **$45.00**

Annie the Movie #4330, Milton Bradley, 1983, MIB.......**$12.50**

Archies, 1969, NMIB, J2 ....**$25.00**

Around the Clock w/Peg & Dot #980, Whitman, 1943, EX **$17.50**

Around the World w/Connie & Jean #1359, Saalfield, 1958, NM...**$17.50**

Baby Nancy, Her Nursery & Clothes #W966; Whitman, artist signed, 1935, EX **$55.00**

Annette, Whitman #1971, forty-eight costumes and accessories, ca 1960, uncut, M, $45.00.

Baby Sparkle Plenty Doll Book, Whitman, 1971, M **$25.00**

Baby Tender Love, Whitman #1960, 1971, uncut, 11x9", M **$5.00**

Baby Tender Love #1949, Whitman, NM **$12.00**

Ballet Dolls, Whitman, 1957, NM **$32.00**

Bed Knobs & Broomsticks, 1971, M, V1.........................**$20.00**

Betsy McCall Doll Book #4744, Whitman, 1971, M **$20.00**

Bette Davis, Merrill, 1942, complete, EX.......................**$45.00**

Betty Bonnet Goes to a Wedding, uncut, NM.................**$17.50**

Blondie, 4 dolls & dog, missing stand for dog, 1968, VG, T6 ....**$15.00**

Bonnie Braids #2724, Saalfield, cut, EX..........................**$20.00**

Bonnie Braids #2724, Saalfield, 1951, uncut, M **$50.00**

Brady Bunch, Whitman, Greg & Marsha dolls, cut, EX- (VG+ folder), C1..**$36.00**

Bride & Groom #1501, Western, 1988, EX.......................**$3.00**

Campus Queens, Saalfield, EX..**$6.00**

Charlie Chaplin, Merrimack, 1985, EX...........................**$3.50**

Charlie's Angels — Jill #110, Toy Factory, 14", 1977, MIB (sealed), C1 ....**$45.00**

Charlie's Angels — Jill #110, Toy Factory, 1970s, uncut, orig box, EX..**$20.00**

Charlie's Angels — Sabrina, 1977, complete, uncut, M...**$35.00**

Children From Other Lands #2089, Whitman, M...........**$12.50**

Chitty Chitty Bang Bang, 1968, EX+ (NM folder), C1....**$31.00**

Cinderella, Saalfield, ca 1960, M **$25.00**

Claudette Colbert #2451, Saalfield, 1943, EX **$44.00**

Cynthia Pepper as Margie Paper Doll Book, uncut, MIB, C1 .**$24.00**

Debbie Reynolds, 1960, complete, EX **$25.00**

Dennis the Menace Backyard Picnic Lg Paper Doll Book, 7 dolls, 29 costumes, 1960, M, V1..............................**$48.00**

Dionne Quints Cut-Out Set, 5 6" dolls, 90+ pcs, 1930s, EX+, C1 ....**$99.00**

Dionne Quintuplets Dolls #M3404, Merrill, 1936, 10x17", EX $45.00

Dionne Quintuplets Palmolive Premium Cut-Out Book, 1937, uncut, NM (EX-NM cover), C1 ....$36.00

Dolls of All Nations, Merrimack, 1980, EX $6.00

Dolly Dingle & Her Cousin Lucille, uncut, EX $25.00

Dolly Jean: Her Paper Dolls House, Furniture & Clothes #2173; Saalfield, by artist Fern Bisel Peat, 1938, EX $50.00

Doris Day #1952, Whitman, 1955, uncut, M $55.00

Dresses Worn by First Ladies of the White House #2164, Saalfield, artist signed, 1937, EX $60.00

Eight Little Playmates, Lowe, 1944, uncut, NM $12.50

Elizabeth Taylor Cut-Outs, Whitman, 1950s, NM doll, cut/uncut outfits, orig book w/half covers, NM, C1 ...$45.00

Ellie May Clampett, Watkins-Stratmore, 1960s, NM.......$32.50

Family Affair — Buffy, 1968, complete, M $40.00

Flintstones Punch-Out Paper Dolls, Fred & Wilma, Wonder Books, c 1974, M $35.00

Ginghams Visit Grandma #1987, Whitman, EX $10.00

Glamour Models #177, Stevens Publishing, 1960s, M, H4..$2.00

Gloria Jean, Saalfield, 1940, VG $37.50

Gone w/the Wind #3404, 1940, NM $350.00

Gone w/the Wind #3405, Merrill, 1940, EX....................$200.00

Good Neighbors #2487, Saalfield, NM $32.50

Grace Kelly, Whitman, 1955, NM, C1 ....$27.00

Happy Days Fonzie Paper Dolls, 14" doll, some cut, 1976, NMIB, C1 ....$31.00

Happy Kids Circus Is in Town #775, Burton Playthings, 1935, 10¾x17", NM $50.00

Happy Kids Present Your Own Quintuplets #275, Burton Playthings, 1935, 10¾x16¾", NM $45.00

Heart Family, Mattel, 1985, EX, from $4 to $7.00

Heart Family #1526, Western, 1985, EX $3.00

Hollywood Fashion Dolls #2242, Saalfield, cut, complete, EX $35.00

Infamous Women, Bellerophon, 1976, M $7.50

Janet & Jeanne #230C, Platt & Munk, 1937, EX $18.00

Jeanette MacDonald, Glorious Singing Star, Dolls & Costumes from Her Screen Plays #3460; Merrill, 1941, EX $45.00

John Wayne, 1981, M in folder $10.00

Julia, 1968, complete, M...$40.00

Julia, 4 dolls, 3 stands, 1970, VG+, T6.............................$15.00

Julia TV Show Paper Dolls, 1971, M................................$35.00

June Allyson, Whitman, 1956, EX $45.00

Katie's Country Store #7319F, Western, 1978, EX $3.50

Kopy Kate #1991, Whitman, 1971, EX $4.00

Laugh-In Paper Doll & Punch-Out Book, Saalfield, 1969, NM-M, C1 ....$81.00

Lennon Sisters #1991, Whitman, 1959, uncut, M...........$65.00

Li'l Abner & Daisy Mae #280, Saalfield, 1942, complete, NM $70.00

Little Lulu & Tubby Paper Dolls, Whitman, 1947, 10x13" book, NM, C1 ....$45.00

Little Women #5127, Artcraft, EX....................................$15.00

Littlest First Born #1964, Whitman, 1971, uncut, M..........$5.00

Lucille Ball, Saalfield, 1945, cut, complete, NM $65.00

Marilyn Monroe, dtd 1979, M in folder $10.00

Marilyn Monroe, Saalfield, 1954, litho hardcover w/dolls & stands, wardrobe sheet inside, 11x13", VG (NM cover), A $166.00

Mary Poppins, 1966, complete, M $40.00

Mary Poppins, 1973, uncut, M, J2 ....$30.00

Midge & Marge #1566, Merrill, 1951, NM $32.50

Miss America #1693, Western, 1990, EX $3.00

Mother Goose #4422, Artcraft, EX $12.00

My Fair Lady, Ottenheimer, 5 dolls, 1965, uncut, M........$27.50

Lennon Sisters, Whitman #1979, 1958, cut, EX-, $20.00.

National Velvet, Whitman #1958, ca 1961, uncut, M, $45.00.

Nancy & Sluggo Paper Doll Cut-Out Book, 1974, M.......$20.00
Nancy & the Professor Paper Doll Book, Saalfield, 1970, uncut, EX $35.00
Our New Baby #3428, Merrill, artist signed, 1937, EX $45.00
Paper Doll Family #985, Whitman, 1937, EX-.................$75.00
Paper Dolls of Early America #1983, Whitman, EX $8.00
Paper Dolls w/Costumes of 21 Nations #2179, Saalfield, 1938, EX...$35.00
Partridge Family Paper Doll Book, Artcraft, 1972, NM, from $35 to $50.00
Pat Boone #1968, Whitman, 1959, uncut, NM $75.00
Patty's Party #175, Stevens Publishing, 1960s, M, H4........$2.00
Peasant Costumes of Europe #900, Whitman, 1934, 10½x17", EX $40.00
Pebbles & Bamm-Bamm, Whitman, 1965, M $42.50
Pebbles Flintstone #1997, Whitman, early 1960s, NM $45.00
Pippi Longstocking, NM...$7.50
Prince Valiant & Princess Aleta, Saalfield, 1954, rare, EX+, A...$225.00
Princess Diana, Western, 1985, EX $5.00
Punky Brewster #1532, Golden Press, 1986, M.................$3.50

Ranch Family Cowboy/Cowgirl Dolls, Merrill #2584, 1957, NM uncut, $30.00.

Return to Oz, Golden, 1985, 5 dolls w/4 pgs of clothing, uncut, M (NM folder), A...$50.00
Robin Hood & Maid Marian, Saalfield, ca 1960, M.........$30.00
Rock Hudson #2087, Whitman, 1957, uncut, NM...........$60.00
Roy Rogers & Dale Evans #995, 1948, EX......................$60.00
Roy Rogers & Dale Evans at Double R Bar Ranch, Whitman, 1957, M...$48.00
Ruth Newton's Cut-Out Dolls & Animals #971, Whitman, 1934, 11x17", EX...$50.00
Sally & Jane, Lowe, 1964, NM......................................$12.50
Sassie #1972, Whitman, 1972, uncut, M..........................$7.50

Shirley Temple Dolls & Dresses #1761, Saalfield, authorized edition, 1937, in 10x15" book, EX $75.00
Shirley Temple Life-Like Paper Doll #1765, Saalfield, authorized edition, 1936, EX $150.00
Snow White, Whitman, 1974, M...................................$27.50
Snow White & the Seven Dwarfs #970, Whitman, authorized edition, 1938, 11½x17", EX $150.00
Sunshine Family #1995, Whitman, NM $7.50

Tender Love 'N Kisses, Whitman, Mattel, six uncut pages, 1978, NM, $4.00.

Tiny Thumbelina Cut-Out Book, Whitman, 1963, M, C1..$31.00
Tricia Nixon #4248, Artcraft, 1970, NM........................$16.00
Triplet Dolls #176, Stevens Publishing, 1960s, M, H4 ....$2.00
Twiggy, Whitman, 1967, M..$60.00
Valerie w/Growin' Pretty Hair, Whitman #1965, 1974, uncut, M..$5.00
Waltons, 1974, in 5x15" box, VG, N2 ....$29.00
Waltons Paper Doll Book, Whitman, 1975, 10x13" cover, M, C1 ....$39.00
Wedding of the Paper Dolls #3497, Merrill, 1935, EX......$60.00
Welcome Back Kotter, Toy Factory, 14" Gabe doll w/3 uncut sheets, 1976, MIB (sealed), C1....................................$27.00
Woody Woodpecker & Andy Panda, Artcraft, 1968, M ..$27.50
Yogi Bear & Girlfriend Cindy, Wonder Books, 1974, M..$25.00
1964 World's Fair Dress-Up Paper Doll Cut-Out Book, Spertus, M..$35.00

Paper Lithographed Toys

Following the development of color lithography, early toy makers soon recognized the possibility of using this technology in their own field. Both here and abroad, by the 1880s toys ranging from soldiers to involved dioramas of entire villages were being produced of wood with colorful and well-detailed paper lithographed surfaces. Some of the best known manufacturers were Crandall, Bliss, Reed, and McLoughlin. This style of toy remained popular until well after the turn of the century. See also Bliss; Boats; Circus; Doll Houses; Fisher-Price; Games; Noah's Ark; Puzzles.

Band Chariot with Thirteen Musicians and Driver, Reed's, ca 1895, 27½" long, A, $1,955.00.

Chicago Limited Train, with blocks, ca 1895, 46" long overall, EX, A, $2,195.00.

Cinderella Coach, Reed, paper on wood, 2 horses pull elaborate coach, 2 drivers, blocks missing, 26", A................$2,700.00
Fort Grant, paper litho on wood, 3 knock-down soldiers mtd behind wall of fort, 16¼", G-VG, A $700.00
Horse-Drawn Grocery Wagon, Groceries, Candy, etc on sides, w/roof, block-style horse, litho spokes, 9x21", VG, A $600.00
Horse-Drawn Open Air Trolley, Reed, paper on wood, Bowery & Central Park, seats swivel, 2 dappled horses, faded, 28", A...$2,900.00
Monkey Target Game, wood tree trunk w/squirrel, rnd target w/dangling monkey, may not be complete, 14", EX, A.$25.00
Nested Circus Blocks, Milton Bradley, litho on wood, set of 6 graduated sizes, 1910, 6x6x5¾", A $460.00

Old Lady in Shoe, pull toy, litho on wood, blk shoe w/mc figures, moderate paper loss, rpt, 9", P, A......................$70.00
Pretty Village Boat House Set, McLoughlin Bros, 6 folding buildings, props, figures, minor wear & damage, 12", VG, A...$200.00
Pretty Village Little Folks Hotel Set, McLoughlin Bros, 9 folding building, props, figures & plot sheet, 15", EX-, A....$250.00
US Mail Wagon, Gibbs #27, horse w/spotted body & jtd legs, enclosed red wagon, 1910, 12", A $200.00

Pedal Cars and Other Wheeled Goods

Just like Daddy, all little boys (and girls as well) are thrilled and happy to drive a brand new shiny car. Today both generations search through flea markets and auto swap meets for the cars, boats, fire engines, tractors, and trains that ran not on gas but pedal power. Some of the largest manufacturers of wheeled goods were AMF (American Machine and Foundry Company), Murray, and Garton. Values depend to a very large extent on condition, and those that have been restored may sell for upwards of $500.00, depending on year and model. Our advisor for this category is Nate Stroller. See also Clubs, Newsletters, and Publications.

Airplane, Single Engine; Toledo Mfg, yel w/red wing & striping, rpl wood prop, Falcon on side, 60", needs rpr, G orig, A $2,950.00
Airplane, Steelcraft, 1-engine, 3 rubber tires, blk w/wht striping, red wing tail w/wht stripes, rust, P pnt, 38", A $900.00

Pursuit Plane, painted and pressed steel with vinyl interior, working propeller, 46", restored, EX, from $2,500.00 to $3,000.00.

Big 4 Tractor & Trailer, Murray, pnt steel, yel, gr & blk, padded seat, dump lever, moderate rust, 68", G-VG............$250.00
Blitzen-Benz, Stearn, pnt & stenciled sheet metal & wood, gr & red w/gold trim, partial rpt, 46", G, A....................$750.00
Cabin Cruiser, handcrafted & pnt wood, red & bl, cabin lifts off to reveal motor mts (no engine), 63", VG, A..........$100.00

Cannonball Express Locomotive, Garton, pnt pressed steel, red body w/blk cab, yel cowcatcher, parts missing, 39", G, A $240.00

Car, '14 era, red w/some blk striping, crank makes clicking noise, spoked wheels, no rubber, rpl/damage, 42", A $300.00

Car, '25-30s era, balloon-type metal wheels lettered 'Trying,' 1 headlight, convertible top on bk, rpt, 36", G, A......$400.00

Car, '30s era, wood w/rubber-tired spoked wheels, roller derby type, 53", G, A...$300.00

Car, '30s-40s era, maroon w/metal hubcaps, rpt, 42", A .$300.00

Car, '35 era, pointed nose, rubber tires, bl w/NP grille, sloping bk, 40", G-P, A $300.00

Car, '50s era, all gr, rpt w/several dents, 37", A $325.00

Car, '50s era resembles Chevy, cream w/red stripe, plated bumpers, headlights, gear shift, red seat, worn/rpt, 44", A $475.00

Car, '60s era, red w/wht stripes, entire rpt, steering wheel needs to be reattached, 47", A $150.00

Car, American National, nameplate on dash, blk fenders, orange hood w/yel striping, tool box, 44", EX, from $5,500 to..$7,500.00

Car, American National, pnt sheet metal on wood chassis, bl w/yel trim, red wheels, wood grille, rstr, 46, G, A...$2,100.00

Car, Garton, pnt pressed steel coupe, gr body w/blk fenders, yel pinstriping & trim, 33½", VG, A.............................$425.00

Car, in the shape of a boat (no top), bl w/wht striping, rpt, 42", G, A..$300.00

Car, Murray, pnt pressed steel coupe, brn w/chrome steering wheel, windshield & bumpers, padded seat, rstr, 36", EX, A $525.00

Clipper Tricycle, solid CI chassis, padded wood seat, early, 48", G-VG, A...$250.00

Comet, Murray, 1949, rstr...$2,250.00

Dolphin Boat, Murray, 1958, rstr $700.00

Earth Mover, Murray, yel w/stripe & letters on side, rstr, ca 1959..$700.00

Fire Chief Car, AMF, complete, orig, M.......................$400.00

Fire Chief Car, Murray, all orig, 1959, EX $400.00

Fire Engine, American National, w/hose, reel, 2 ladders, lights front & bk, spotlight, bell, 64", rstr, appears M $5,500.00

Fire Truck, Murray, pnt pressed steel, red body w/gold trim, chrome steering wheel, windshield, mirrors work, 43", EX, A $750.00

Good Humor Ice Cream Truck, Murray, rstr $700.00

Grand Turismo, '50s era, Rosa on dash, cream & silver, antenna, steering wheel, spoked wheels, 44", G, A $250.00

Henley Rollabout, MC Henley & Son, US, pnt wood & steel scooter, 4 steel wheels, w/orig decal & booklet, 34", VG, A $200.00

Mercury Station Wagon, Murray, pnt pressed steel, red, wht & gold, pnt loss, rust, 47", G-, A $210.00

Nabisco National Biscuit Co Delivery Van, att Roberts, yel & red-orange, hard rubber tires, doors slide, 22¼", VG, A $215.00

Pedal Car, Boycraft, pnt pressed steel, red w/blk chassis, rpt, 38", G, A...$350.00

Pontiac Convertible, pnt pressed steel, maroon w/mustard top, pinstriping trim, red wheels, rstr, 39", EX, A...........$500.00

Pumper, Toledo, tin boiler & fuel compartment in bk, maroon, red & blk, rpl dash, pedal assembly gone, rpt, 60", G, A..$2,000.00

Pursuit Plane, pnt pressed steel w/blk vinyl interior, working prop, silver, red & bl, EX rstr, 46", from $2,500 to..........$3,000.00

Rebel Car, AMF, 1960s, complete, orig.........................$300.00

Renault, '33-34 era, sloping front, 4 rubber-tired wheels, hubs w/'Feredo,' worn/some rpt, 42", A $700.00

Skippy Desoto, Pioneer (?), red & cream, red bumper/wheels, taillights on side, all orig, rust, 38", A.....................$900.00

Spirit of St Louis Plane, pnt sheet metal, silver, red & bl, wood steering wheel, rpl stabilizers, 59", G, A...............$2,700.00

Station Wagon, #F641, 1950s, painted pressed steel, 44", VG, A, $350.00.

Studebaker Convertible, '50s era, Giordani, Bologna, Italy, rubber tires, working lights, orig box, 45", NM, A $1,600.00

Winner, pnt & stenciled sheet metal & wood, red, gr & yel, CI steering wheel & crank hdl, license plate, 44", G, A .$1,450.00

Wagons

Keith Simmons, unfinished wood w/pnt metal chassis & wheels, rpt red stenciled letters, 39", G, A..............................$80.00

Peerless, stenciled & pnt wood, yel & red w/red & blk letters, metal wheels, hard rubber tires, 43", VG, A............$290.00

Sheffield Coaster, pnt wood, gr w/sheet-metal wheels, 40", G, A $95.00

Teddy, stenciled and stained wood, spoked wood wheels, 43", G, A $375.00

Penny Toys

Penny toys were around as early as the late 1800s and as late as the 1920s. Many were made in Germany, but some were made in France as well. With a few exceptions, they ranged in size from 5" on down; some had moving parts, and a few had clockwork mechanisms. Though many were unmarked, you'll sometimes find them signed 'Kellermann,' 'Meier,' 'Fischer,' or 'Distler,' or carrying an embossed company logo such as the 'dog and cart' emblem. They were made of lithographed tin with exquisite detailing — imagine an entire carousel less than 2½" tall. Because of a recent surge in collector interest, many have been crossing the auction block of some of the country's large galleries. Our values are prices realized at several of these auctions. Our advisor for this category is Jane Anderson (A2).

#14 Chain Drive Racer, off-wht w/bl & red trim, brn driver, Germany, 4¼", VG, A $1,700.00

#32 Racer, mustard yel & orange w/gray wheels, Germany, 4½", G-VG, A..$275.00

Airplane, litho tin, yel & blk monoplane w/pilot, bird-tail end, early, 5", VG, A $120.00

Airplane, w/up, red & yel, prop spins as it advances, folding wings, balloon tires, Germany, 4", EX, A $70.00

Airplane #592, litho tin, olive-gr, brn & dk gr, Distler, 2¾", VG-EX, A $300.00

Airship, litho tin, yel w/spinning side props, 2 gondolas for pilot & passengers, Germany, 4½", VG, A.....................$275.00

Airship, litho tin w/red gondola & spinning side props, 3", G-VG, A $100.00

Ambulance, oversized spoke wheels, pnt lead figure, Germany, 4", VG, A $1,000.00

Ambulance, pulled by dappled horses, figure shown at window, Meier, 4⅝", G-VG, A...$450.00

Ambulance, pulled by 2 horses w/mounted soldiers, Meier, 4", NM, A $430.00

Ambulance, red, bl, orange & wht, passenger at rear window, Meier, 3⅜", G-VG, A...$250.00

Armored Car, emb litho tin, gray w/red & blk trim, lead gun, unmk, 3", G-G+, A $500.00

Automotive Pumper, red & gold w/figure, Meier, 3¼", G-, A.$210.00

Baby Carriage, mc litho tin, gr carriage body w/maroon trim & red wheels, Meier, 3⅜", VG-EX, A $426.00

Baby Carriage, w/flat figure of child inside, Fischer, 3¼", VG, A $325.00

Baby Tractor, dimensional farmer w/pipe in mouth as driver, lithoed gears, Kellerman (CKO), 3", EX, A..............$300.00

Baggage Handler, litho tin, man in gr coat, mk 240 on bl cart, 3", VG-EX, A $190.00

Bank, coin slot on roof, people & animals lithoed on sides, scallops in gable, Germany, 3", EX, A $295.00

Barrel Truck, brn barrels, Germany, 3½", VG, A $700.00

Beetle, on wheels, legs move, Germany, 3", NM, A $75.00

Begging Dog & Boy, depress plunger, dog leaps upward, boy steps bk, Meier, 3¾", EX, A $1,400.00

Bicycle Race, 6 cyclists under red canopy, gr base, Meier, 2½", VG-EX, A..$2,000.00

Black Jigger, dancer stands atop gr base, crank lever, unmk Germany, 3", NM, A $275.00

Black Man in Rocker, mc figure holds flowers & sits in rocker, 1 tab broken off figure, Germany, 1¾", G-VG, A $600.00

Blacksmith Gnomes, depress plunger, gnomes hammer, Meier, 4", VG, A $1,300.00

Boat, red & yel, flag ea end, 2-stacker, on wheels, Germany, 4½", NM, A..$395.00

Boxer Dog, brn w/red saddle, unmk, 2½", VG-EX, A.....$600.00

Boy at Desk, litho tin, figure in yel jacket, yel desk w/picture of locomotive, Germany, 2½", VG-EX, A $825.00

Boy in Wagon, yel wagon, bl & red outfit on boy, unmk, 2⅞", G-G+, A $1,200.00

Boy on Sled, yel sled, bl & red outfit, Meier, 3", G-, A..$350.00

Boy on Sled, yel sled, off-wht & brn clothes, Distler, 2½", G-G+, A...$500.00

Boy w/Rabbit, seated in ornate rocker, Meier, 2¾", VG, A $2,700.00

Cabin Cruiser, brn & wht, clockwork, working, missing part of rudder, Fischer, 4½", G-VG, A $20.00

Car, open, off-wht w/yel, red & gold trim, 2 female passengers w/driver, missing 1 headlamp, Meier, 4½", G, A.....$700.00

Carousel, figures on horses under red canopy, gr base, Meier, 2¾", G-VG, A from $400 to $600.00

Carousel Whistle, red & yel litho tin, 4 horses w/riders turn when bl tin whistle is blown, Kiko, 3¾", VG, A $170.00

Cat & Dog, depress plunger, cat rises, dog emerges, unmk, 4", VG, A..$1,300.00

Child in Highchair, Meier, opens to form chair and table with farm scene, 3¾", VG-EX, A, $225.00

Child in Chair, litho tin, yel chair w/spoked wheels, Germany, 2½", VG-EX, A $240.00

Chinaman w/Parasol, bl, red & yel outfit, parasol turns w/wheel, Distler, 3⅜", VG, A $1,300.00

Civilian Motorcycle, 3 wheels, yel & orange outfit, Kellermann, Germany, 3½", VG-EX, A $625.00

Climbing Monkey, litho tin, red & yel costume, climbs red ladder, weighted string, Germany, 6¾", VG-EX, A $170.00

Clipper Ship, candy container, sliding trap door reveals hidden compartment under platform, Meier, 3", G, A $550.00

Clown & Goat, depress plunger, clown steps bk & donkey kicks, Germany, 3¾", VG, A..$500.00

Clowns Tossing Ball, plunger activated, unmk, spring missing, 3¾", G-G+, A $1,150.00

Coach, dk gr & blk w/dappled horse, unmk, 4½", VG, A.$240.00

Coach, emb tin w/litho tin driver in footman dress, 1 dappled horse, Germany, 5½", G, A................................$350.00

City of London Police Ambulance, Fischer, lithographed tin, two passengers, 2¾", G, A, $1,300.00.

Galloping Bugler, Meier, lithographed tin, 3⅛", EX, A, $1,400.00.

Coach Car, red & yel, 3 passengers at windows, Meier, 3¼", VG, A $425.00

Coupe, litho tin, olive-gr & brn w/wht wheels, lt scratches, Fleischmann, 4½", VG, A $90.00

Cow, brn on gr base, 3¼", VG, A.....................................$375.00

Cross-Country Skier, off-wht sweater & brn pants, wood pole, Meier, 3½", G-VG, A.......................................$900.00

Dancer, Animated; moves when hdl in platform is turned, Germany, 3⅝", EX, A $275.00

Dbl-Decker Bus, yel & red w/gray wheels & trim, clockwork, 4¼", VG, A..$600.00

Delivery Wagon, candy container, bl & yel cart w/red wheels, sliding top on crate, Meier, 4⅝", VG-EX, A...........$325.00

Delivery Wagon, litho tin, yel w/wht wheels & bl interior, 1 gray horse, 5", VG-EX, A...$175.00

Delivery Wagon, orange & bl cart w/gray horse, Germany, 4¾", EX, A...$160.00

Donkey Cart, litho tin donkey w/inked tin cart, Germany, 4¾", VG, A...$110.00

Duck, head bobs & beak flaps when pushed, Germany, 2¾", VG, A $250.00

Duck on Platform, mc duck on gr platform, 1 rpl wheel, 3", G-VG, A $375.00

Early Auto, litho tin, red & tan, bl uniformed driver, friction, working, 3", VG-EX, A $250.00

Elephant Cart, litho tin, head nods, yel cart w/red wheels, 5", VG-EX, A..$150.00

Express Parcels Delivery Truck, brn & gray truck, yel & red cab, clockwork, non-working, 4", VG, A $550.00

Ferris Wheel, hand crank, Meier, 3⅝", VG+, A $3,700.00

Fighting Cocks, mc roosters on tan base, Meier, 4¼", VG, A $65.00

Fire Pumper, gold pumper w/red & wht chassis, bl uniformed figure, Distler, 3¼", G, A $210.00

Fire Pumper, horse-drawn, w/bell, fireman driver & passenger, Plank, 3¾", EX, A $435.00

Fire Pumper, litho tin w/gold trim, red engine, litho tin driver, stack missing, Meier, 3", G, A $100.00

Flying Hollander, bl, red & blk outfit, rocks when pushed, Germany, 3", VG-EX, A $1,200.00

Garage w/Autos, 3½x3½" pnt & litho tin garage, 2 3½" cars, Kellermann, VG-EX, A...$225.00

Girl in Goat Cart, bl & gr cart, red dress, unmk, 4", VG-EX, A...$750.00

Girl in Swing, gr & yel swing, orange dress, Distler, 2¾"", VG...$400.00

Girl at Desk, blue dress, yellow desk with picture of a clown, 2½", VG, A, $700.00.; Omnibus Grand Hotel, gray wheels and horse, minor scratches, 4¾", VG, A, $125.00.

Gnome & Rabbit, gnome on decorated egg rises to reveal hidden rabbit, Meier, 2½", G $2,600.00

Go-Round, mc litho tin, 4 flat horses w/riders under canopy, footed base, Meier, 2¾", G-VG, A.........................$350.00

Goat Cart, lady in seat of cart pulled by goat, Germany, 4", EX, A $485.00

Goose Nodder, Germany, 3½", NM, A.....................$175.00

Grand Hotel Omnibus, litho tin, red & yel w/gray horse, Meier, 5", EX, A $325.00

Hansom Cab, litho tin, blk cab w/red wheels, dappled horse, 4", EX, from $250 to $350.00

Hay Cart, litho tin, yel w/bl wheels, litho tin mule & driver, Germany, 6½", VG, A..$90.00

Hay Wagon, litho tin, red w/bl wheels, litho tin horse, Germany, 5¼", VG-EX, A...$110.00

Highchair, yel, animal pictures on tray surface, tray extends, Germany, 4", VG, A..$425.00

Hobby Horse, mc litho tin, gray horse on rockers w/outdoor graphics, 3¾", G, A $120.00

Hook & Ladder Truck, red, orange & yel, 5 passengers, clockwork, working, Germany, 4¼", VG, A $260.00

Horse Cart, dappled horse pulls flat red cart, Distler, 5", EX, A...$150.00

Horse-Drawn Wagon, wht horse & wheels, w/driver, Germany, 5", EX, A..$210.00

Horseless Carriage, prominent headlamps, friction flywheel, lt touch-up, Meier, 3½", G, A $300.00

Horseless Carriage, red & tan, driver, Meier, 2¾", G-VG, A $275.00

Horseless Carriage, red w/bl-gr interior, friction flywheel, 1 loose wheel, 2⅞", VG, A $500.00

Hose Reel Truck, red & gold truck w/bl uniformed figures, rpl hose, Meier, 3⅜", G-G+, A $575.00

Jockey on Rocking Horse, lg rockers, Meier, 3⅝", G-, A.$275.00

Ladder Truck, red & gold w/figures, Meier, 3⅜", G+, A..$210.00

Ladder Truck, red & yel w/figure, Germany, 2¾", NM, A.$800.00

Landau Coach, gr open coach w/red wheels, 1 dappled horse, 5", EX, A...$350.00

Limousine, gold & wht w/red trim, roof slides & rear door opens, Distler, 3", VG-EX, A..$350.00

Limousine, litho tin, olive gr w/blk top & wht wheels, 7 windows, Fleischmann, 4", VG, A $120.00

Limousine, red, yel & bl w/gold hood, 4 passengers, Meier, 3", EX, A...$800.00

Limousine, 2-door, off-wht & wht car w/gold trim, diecut passengers, friction flywheel, Meier, 4⅛", VG, A......$2,300.00

Lorry, gr, red & blk, driver in brn coat, Distler, 5¾", VG-EX, A...$250.00

Meteor Boat, yel & red w/eagle masthead, sailor stands at dbl-sided compass, Meier, 4¾", VG-EX, A $900.00

Military Motorcycle w/Sidecar, passenger w/sparking machine gun, balloon tires, Germany, 4", NM, A..................$200.00

Military Wagon, mc litho tin, yel wagon w/red wheels, 4 horses 2 w/riders, 6¼", EX, A..$325.00

Monkey Tooting Horn, Germany, lithographed tin, 3¼", EX, from $295.00 to $350.00.

Monkey Whistle, litho tin, red suit & hat, works at grinding bench when whistle blows, whistle end chewed, 4¼", VG, A..$130.00

Ocean Liner, Twin-Stack; red, wht & bl w/yel stacks, Germany, 4¼", VG, A..$250.00

Ocean Liners, Germany, lithographed tin, 4¾", VG, A, $300.00; 4¼", VG, A, $250.00.

Our Dumb Friends League No 14 Horse Ambulance, horse at window, 2 harnessed horses, Germany, 4", VG, A.......$2,200.00

Parrot Cage, litho tin, bl cage on red base, Meier, 3¾", VG-EX, A..$250.00

Passenger Boat, red, wht & bl w/yel stacks, Fischer, 4¼", G, A...$110.00

Passenger Boat, tin w/flywheel action, has flags & 2 stacks, Meier, logo emb between stacks, 4½", VG, A $265.00

Pecking Birds, pnt & litho tin birds in yel coop, crank hdl, pecking action, working, Germany, 2¼", VG-EX, A......$225.00

Phaeton Car, gold w/red & gr litho, open w/tan uniformed chauffeur, Germany, 3½", A $275.00

Phaeton Car, olive gr & blk, open, orig driver, 1912, 4½", A..$195.00

Policeman Motorcycle, red cycle w/yel driver, Kellermann, 3", EX, A...$750.00

Pool Player, red & gr table, player in blk suit, Kellermann, 4", VG, A...$60.00

Porter, pushing trunk w/opening lid, #240 on lid, Germany, 3x3", NM, A...$440.00

Pram, gr carriage w/red wheels, child w/toy clown, Germany, 3¼", VG-EX, A..$350.00

Pram, orange & blk pram w/emb flat figure under blanket, Germany, 3½", EX, A...$180.00

Rabbit on Wheeled Platform, brn w/red trim, Meier, 2½", VG, A...$375.00

Rabbits on Lg Rabbit, Meier, 2¾", VG-EX, A $2,300.00

Race Car w/Driver, tin, boxy style, Fischer, 1¼x4½", EX.$200.00

Red Cross Wagon, gray wagon w/red wheels & dappled horses, sliding tarpaulin, Meier, 4½", EX, A $850.00

Roadster, Civilian; w/driver, diecast, Plank, 3", EX, A...$350.00

Rowboat w/3 Oarsmen, wht wheeled base, axle on base rocks boat, Germany, 3½", EX, A $2,000.00

Saloon Car, litho tin, red & white w/yel trim, driver & 4 diecut passengers in windows, Meier, Germany, 4", EX+, A $1,350.00

Sawing Gnomes, depress plunger, gnomes saw, Meier, 4", VG, A...$375.00

Sewing Machine, litho tin, bl on red & yel base, crank hdl, 3¾", VG, A..$210.00

Soldier on Motorcycle, red & bl uniform, blk motorcycle, Ibense, 4", G, A $625.00

Speedboat w/Flag & Female Driver, tin, flag mk #5, Meier, 4½", VG, A...$550.00

Stake Body Truck, driver, sliding hood, unmk, 3¾", G, A..$170.00

Steamroller, gr boiler w/red & gold trim, gray wheels, unmk, 3", VG, A...$350.00

Sulky, litho tin, rider w/yel shirt, sulky w/red wheels, gray horse, 3¼", VG, A...$120.00

Supply Wagon, yel cart w/red wheels, Meier, 4¼", G, A.$150.00

Swing, dbl, figure in lg rocking gondola, Meier, 3¼", G+, A...$550.00

Taxicab, red, wht & bl, friction flywheel, Distler, 3⅛", G-VG, A $375.00

Touring Cars, Row 1: Distler, 4¼", VG-, A, $225.00; Fischer, elaborate detail, clockwork, 4½", VG+, A, $850.00. Row 2: Friction flywheel, 4", G, A, $210.00; Probably Distler, friction flywheel, 4¼", VG, A, $500.00.

Touring Car, bl, yel & wht, 4 passengers, friction flywheel, att Distler, 4¼", VG, A..........................$500.00

Touring Car, litho tin, cream w/red & yel accents, driver & 2 passengers, Meier, Germany, 4½", EX+, A..............$700.00

Woman Pushing Figure in Cart, lithographed tin, 3", $495.00.

Tractor, red & yel w/blk rubber treads, w/driver, Germany, 2¼", A...$110.00

Train, GC & Co N #905, locomotive & tender, passenger, box car, flat car w/lumber, 4-pc, Germany, total 11", EX, A $190.00

Train, tin, red engine & coal car w/yel passenger car mk No 100, no hitch, 6", EX+, M5...$110.00

Tugboat, red, gold & gr, friction flywheel, 3¾", G-VG, A.$160.00

Turtle, travels on wheels as legs & head move realistically, Chicago Concession premium, Germany, 2¾", EX ...$85.00

Vis-a-Vis Car, litho tin, red car w/bl uniformed driver, lg lead weight on bottom, Meier, 3", G, A $150.00

Water Truck, candy container, gr, red & wht, friction flywheel, sliding hood, Distler, 3¾", VG, A $300.00

Zeppelin, yel & blk balloon, bl propellers & red basket, 3", G+, A...$250.00

Pez Dispensers

Every few years a collecting phenomenon occurs, and none has been quite as intense in recent memory as the Pez craze. Pez was originally designed as a breath mint for smokers, but by the fifties kids were the target market, and the candies were packaged in the dispensers that we all know and love today. There is already more than three hundred variations to collect, and more arrive on the supermarket shelves every day. Though early on collectors seemed to prefer the dispensers without feet, that attitude has changed and now it's the character head they concentrate on. Feet were added in 1987, so if you were to limit yourself to only 'feetless' dispensers, your collection would be far from complete. Some dispensers have variations in color and design that can influence their values. Don't buy any that are damaged, incomplete, or that have been tampered with in any way; those are nearly worthless. For more information refer to *A Pictorial Guide to Plastic Candy Dispensers Featuring Pez* by David Welch and *Collecting Toys #6* by Richard O'Brien. Our advisor is Richard Belyski (B1). Values are for mint condition dispensers unless noted otherwise.

Angel, gold halo, yel hair, wht wings, on bl base, 1970s, B1 ....$15.00

Annie $50.00

Arlene, pk girl, w/feet, B1 ....$7.00

Astronaut, no feet, wht helmet, gr body, from $75 to $100.00

Barney Bear, B1...$30.00

Batgirl, soft head, no feet, MIP, B1 ....$65.00

Batman, no feet, MIP, O1...$15.00

Batman, w/feet, American, in cello bag, B1 ....$2.00

Bounder Beagle, w/feet, MOC, S4/B1.........................$8.00

Boy, w/feet, brn hair, B1...$8.00

Bugs Bunny, old, no feet, MIP, B1/O1, from $10 to $15.00

Bugs Bunny, w/feet, MOC $2.00

Bullwinkle, no feet...$175.00

Candy Shooter Gun, many color variations, from $60 to.$550.00

Capt America, no feet, MIP, B1 ....$30.00

Casper the Friendly Ghost, no feet, wht body...................$60.00

Charlie Brown, w/feet, American, in cello bag, M, B1 ....$3.00

Charlie Brown, w/feet, eyes closed, B1 ....$25.00
Charlie Brown, w/feet & frown, MIP, S4/B1......................$7.00
Clown, w/chin, no feet, B1 ....$40.00
Clown, w/feet, whistle head, MOC, S4 ....$6.50
Clown, yel collar, red nose & gr hat, from $50 to............$70.00
Cockatoo, no feet, bl face w/yel beak & red hair $30.00
Cool Cat, w/feet, B1 ....$25.00
Cop, w/feet..$45.00

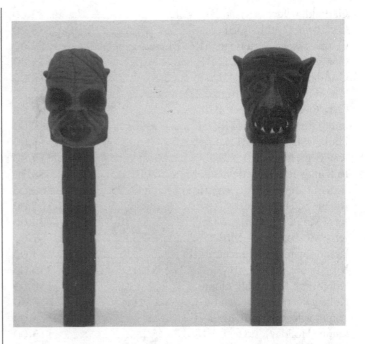

Diabolic and Zombie (Eerie Spectre Series), from $75.00 to $95.00 each.

Creature From the Black Lagoon, A (head and stem match), Universal Monsters, no feet, from $200.00 to $275.00.

Crocodile, no feet, w/gr face & red eyes, from $60 to $75.00
Daffy Duck, no feet, MIP, B1...$15.00
Daisy Duck (Webby), w/feet, MOC, S4 ....$8.50
Dalmation Pup, w/feet, B1 ....$25.00

Dispenser, Pez Box; no feet, from $500 to.......................$700.00
Dispenser, Regular; from $125 to $400.00
Doctor, w/feet..$65.00
Donald Duck, no feet, from $7 to....................................$15.00
Donald Duck, w/feet, from $1 to......................................$2.00
Donald Duck, yel beak, bl hat, on diecut base, 1960s, from $100
    to $120.00
Donald Duck's Nephew, w/feet, gr or bl hat, from $7 to...$12.00
Donald Duck's Nephew, w/feet, red hat $15.00
Donkey, gray, whistle head, B1, from $8 to......................$10.00
Donkey, w/feet, whistle head, MOC, S4/B1 ....$8.00
Dopey, no feet...$175.00
Dr Skull, no feet, B1 ....$10.00
Dr Skull, w/feet, remake, from $1 to.................................$2.00
Droopy Dog, no feet, plastic swivel ears, MIP, O1/B1 ......$15.00
Droopy Dog, w/feet, pnt ears, B1 ....$7.00
Duck, brn, w/feet, whistle head, B1 ....$20.00
Duck w/Flower, w/gr face, yel beak, red hair $45.00
Dumbo, no feet, bl head, yel hat......................................$35.00
Dumbo, no feet, gray head...$45.00
Dumbo, w/feet, bl head, B1..$23.00
Eerie Spectre Series, no feet, soft head, any, from $75 to .$95.00
Elephant, no feet, bl, w/hat, O1 ....$55.00
Elephant, no feet, orange head, bl hair, no hat..............$180.00
Elephant, no feet, orange head, w/hat, O1 ....$55.00
Engineer, no feet, EX...$40.00
Fireman, no feet, B1...$30.00
Foghorn Leghorn, w/feet, B1 ....$35.00
Fozzy Bear, w/feet, American, MIP, B1..............................$3.00
Frankenstein, no feet, from $150 to $175.00
Fred Flintstone, w/feet, American, in cello bag, B1 ....$3.00
Frog, w/feet, whistle head, B1 ....$40.00
Garfield, w/feet, B1 ....$3.00
Garfield, w/feet & teeth, B1 ....$12.00

Garfield, w/feet & visor, B1 ....$3.00
Girl, w/feet, yel hair, B1 ....$8.00
Gonzo, w/feet, American, MIP, B1 ....$3.00
Goofy, old, no feet, MIP, B1 ....$15.00
Gorilla, no feet, EX $45.00
Green Hornet, MIP, from $200 to $250.00
Gyro Gearloose, w/feet, B1 ....$7.00
Hulk, no feet, dk gr, MIP, B1 ....$20.00
Hulk, w/feet, lt gr, B1 ....$5.00
Icee Bear, w/feet, B1 ....$15.00
Indian, w/feet, whistle head, MOC, S4/B1 ....$6.50
Indian Chief, no feet, w/gr headdress, from $50 to $60.00
Indian Squaw, no feet $65.00
Jerry Mouse, no feet, pnt face, B1 ....$25.00
Jerry Mouse, w/feet, MIP $7.00
Kermit, w/feet, American, MIP, B1 ....$3.00
King Louie, no feet, B1 ....$30.00
Knight, no feet, w/blk plume $150.00
Kola, w/feet, whistle head, B1 ....$30.00
Lamb, w/feet, whistle head, B1 ....$25.00
Lamb (Holiday), no feet, B1/O1 ....$15.00
Lil Bad Wolf, no feet, B1 ....$30.00
Lion, no feet, orange, MIP, O1 ....$25.00
Lucy, w/feet, B1 ....$3.00
Maharasha, no feet, B1 ....$40.00
Make A Face, M on foreign card, A $2,600.00
Mary Poppins, bl base, 1960s, from $400 to $500.00
Merlin Mouse, w/feet, B1 ....$8.00
Mickey Mouse, no feet, NMIP, O1/B1 ....$15.00
Mickey Mouse, w/feet, MIP, from $1 to $2.00

Mimic (monkey w/ball cap), no feet, several available colors, B1, ea $35.00
Miss Piggy, American, MIP, B1 ....$3.00
Miss Piggy, w/feet & eyelashes, MIP, S4 ....$8.00
Monkey Sailor, no feet, B1 ....$35.00
Mowgli, no feet, from $25 to $35.00
Mr Ugly, no feet, B1 ....$23.00
Muscle Mouse (gray Jerry), w/feet, plastic nose, B1 ....$10.00
Muscle Mouse (gray Jerry), w/feet, pnt face, B1 ....$15.00
Nermal (gray Garfield), w/feet, B1 ....$7.00
Nurse, no feet, brn hair, lt bl body, from $65 to $75.00
One-Eyed Monster, no feet, orange head $35.00
Panda, no feet, diecut eyes, B1 ....$25.00
Panda, w/feet, remake, B1 ....$5.00
Panda, w/feet, whistle head, B1 ....$7.00
Papa Smurf, w/feet, MIP $10.00
Parrot, w/feet, whistle head, MOC, S4 ....$6.50
Peace Pipe, German, Calumets, 1970s, MIP, from $25 to .$35.00
Pebbles Flintstone, w/feet, American, in cello bag, B1 ....$3.00
Penguin, w/feet, whistle head, B1/S4 ....$7.00
Penguin (Batman's archenemy), no feet, soft head, O1 ....$65.00
Peter Pez, no feet $75.00
Peter Pez, w/feet, remake, B1 ....$5.00
Pilot, no feet, from $65 to $85.00
Pirate, no feet, B1 ....$35.00
Pluto, no feet, MIP, B1 ....$15.00
Police Style Whistle, no feet $25.00
Police Style Whistle, w/feet, American, in cello bag, B1 ....$3.00
Policeman, no feet, M, B1 ....$40.00
Pony, no feet, bl face, red reins & wht mane $65.00
Pony, no feet, orange head, wht mane, B1 ....$35.00
Popeye, no feet, w/removable pipe, red hat, MIP, B1 ......$45.00
Popeye, no feet, w/removable pipe, wht hat, MIP, B1 ......$40.00
Pumpkin, new, B1 ....$5.00
Pumpkin, no feet, old style, B1 ....$15.00
Pumpkin, w/feet, orange, remake, MIP, from $1 to $2.00
Rabbit, no feet, fat ears, pk head, B1 ....$15.00
Rabbit, no feet, fat ears, yel, B1 ....$10.00
Rhino, w/feet, whistle head, MOC, B1, from $7 to $10.00
Road Runner, no feet $20.00
Road Runner, w/feet, B1 ....$7.00
Rooster, w/feet, whistle head, B1 ....$22.00
Rooster, w/feet, wht or yel head, B1 ....$20.00
Rudolph, no feet, B1 ....$25.00
Santa Claus (B), from $85 to $110.00
Santa Claus (C), no feet, MIP, B1, from $5 to $15.00
Scrooge McDuck, no feet, B1 ....$25.00
Scrooge McDuck (B), w/feet, MOC, S4/B1 ....$8.00
Semi Tractor (truck), many variations, from $2 to $25.00
Sheik, no feet, B1 ....$40.00
Smurf, no feet $5.00
Smurf, w/feet $5.00
Smurfette, w/feet $10.00
Snoopy, w/feet, American, in cello bag, B1, from $1 to $3.00
Snow White, no feet, bl bow & collar $85.00
Snowman (A), no feet, B1/O1 ....$15.00
Snowman (B), w/feet, remake $2.00
Spaceman, no feet $100.00

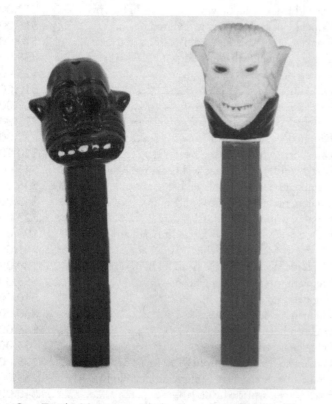

One-Eyed Monster, gorilla head, no feet, $35.00; Vamp (Eerie Spectre Series), from $75.00 to $95.00.

Santa Claus, full body, 1950s,
M, B1, $125.00.

Speedy Gonzales, w/feet, MOC, S4/B1.................................$8.00
Spiderman, no feet, MIP, B1 ....$15.00
Spiderman, w/feet, from $1 to..$2.00
Spike, w/feet, MOC, S4/B1..$6.50
Stewardess, no feet..$95.00
Sylvester, w/feet, cream whiskers, foreign version, B1 ....$5.00
Sylvester, w/feet, wht whiskers $2.00
Teenage Mutant Ninja Turtles, w/feet, 8 variations, ea,
    from $1 to $3.00
Thor, no feet..$150.00
Three-Piece Head, no feet $12.00
Three-Piece Head, w/feet, remake, from $1 to $2.00
Tiger, w/feet, whistle head, B1..$7.00
Tom (Tom & Jerry), w/feet, B1 ....$7.00
Tweety Bird, no feet, from $12 to......................................$15.00
Tweety Bird, w/feet, MOC, from $1 to..............................$2.00
Tyke, w/feet, B1 ....$7.00
Wile E Coyote, w/feet, MIP..$25.00
Winnie the Pooh, w/feet, B1 ....$25.00
Witch, no feet, regular, 1-pc orange head, blk body w/emb witch
    on side, from $150 to..$200.00
Wonder Woman, no feet, MIP, O1 ....$15.00
Wonder Woman, soft head..$75.00
Woodstock, w/feet, American, in cello bag, B1, from $1 to..$2.00
Woodstock, w/feet & pnt feathers, B1 ....$10.00
Zorro, w/logo, no feet, B1 ....$75.00
1950s Space Gun, from $150 to $300.00
1980s Space Gun, from $65 to $100.00

Miscellaneous

Box, Pez Peace Pipe Story Display, German issue, ca 1970s,
    empty, M, C6..$149.00
Puzzle, Ceaco, 125-pc, recalled for copyright infringement,
    1991, S4 ....$15.00
Puzzle, Springbok/PEZ, Hallmark, 500-pc, c 1992 ....$10.00
Two-Pack Box Set, Miss Piggy & Gonzo dispensers riding in
    paper litho car (box), complete w/12 candy pkgs, 1992,
    MIB, S4..$50.00
Visor, paper litho cb..$15.00
Yo-Yo, tin, premium, ca 1962-65, EX..............................$75.00

BOUGHT   SOLD

PEZ

CANDY DISPENSERS

For
FREE SALES LIST,
send SASE to:

RICHARD BELYSKI

P.O. Box 124
Sea Cliff, New York 11579
(516) 676-1183

Pin-Back Buttons

Pin-back buttons have been the means of asserting your loyalty to the political candidate of your choice; rooting for your favorite baseball team; advertising food items, cars, cigarettes, and beer; speaking out for causes ranging from peace and equality to saving the whales; and some were designed simply for amusement.

In the late forties and into the fifties, some cereal companies packed one in boxes of their product. Quaker Puffed Oats offered a series of movie star pin-backs, but probably the best known are Kellogg's Pep pins. There were 86 in all, so theoretically if you wanted the whole series as Kellogg hoped you would, you'd have to buy at least that many boxes of their cereal. Pep pins came in five sets, the first in 1945, three more in 1946, and the last in 1947. They were printed with full-color lithographs of comic characters licensed by King Features and Famous Artists — Maggie and Jiggs, the Winkles, and Dagwood and Blondie, for instance. Superman, the only D.C. Comics, Inc., character was included in each set. Most Pep pins range in value from $10.00 to $15.00 in NM/M condition; any not mentioned in our listings fall into this range. There are exceptions, and we've made sure they're evaluated below.

Nearly all pin-backs are collectible today with these possible exceptions: common buttons picturing flags of various nations, general labor union buttons denoting the payment of dues, and common buttons with clever sayings. Be sure that you buy only buttons with well-centered designs, well-alligned colors, no fading or yellowing, no spots or stains, and no cracks, splits, or dents. In the listings that follow, sizes are approximate. Our advisor for Kellogg's Pep Pins is Doug Dezso (D6).

Buster Brown, for Morton's Bread, each with a different ball player, Whitehead & Hoag Co. (lithographers), 1¼", A, $120.00 each.

Aircraft Warning Observer..............................$20.00
Aladdin, sneak preview promo, rectangular, 1992, M8 ....$10.00
Alfred E Neuman for President, lg.........................$45.00
Alien 3, movie promotion, M, E3.........................$3.00
All Star Game, Cleveland 1963, A........................$119.00
American & National All Star Game lettered in 5 rows in center, patriotic stars & stripes at perimeter, red, wht & bl, A..$28.00
American League in diecut banner over baseball w/St Louis Browns, red, wht & bl, w/tab, A...................$27.50
American League in diecut ribbon over baseball lettered Washington Nationals w/building, w/tab, A.............$28.00
Amsterdam Broom Co...................................$20.00
Andy Gump for President, mc on wht, lg...............$80.00
Babe Ruth Esso Boys Club lettered over background representing baseball, some wear, A.....................$40.00
Babe Ruth on wht lettered below waist-length portrait looking straight on, ball bat on shoulder, EX, A............$235.00
Baker, portrait in center, Phila Athletics, EX, A.........$44.00
Barney Google, Kellogg's, 1945-47 premium, NM, C1.....$16.00
Batman, Wha-Ram Stop Them w/Robin only, 1", EX, H4.$4.00
Batman & Robin Society, 1966..........................$20.00
Beauty & the Beast, heart shape, 1991, M8 ....$5.00
BO Plenty, Kellogg's, M.................................$30.00
Bob Bailey, Montreal Expo, red, wht & bl, A...........$20.00
Bond Bread, Floyd Bennett.............................$15.00
Brenda Star, Kellogg's, 1945, ⅞", NM, C1 ....$16.00
Bressler, ornate scrollwork fr, 1910, lt image, sm stain , oval, A.$125.00
Bringing Up Father, Kellogg's, 1945-47 premium, NM, C1 ....$29.00
Brown's Boys Club Member, Hornsby w/bat in center, dtd 1935, rare, A $135.00
Buck Rogers in the 25th Century lettered on ribbon around upper half of perimeter, Buck facing left, A.............$50.00
Buffalo Bill Plainsman lettered around perimeter of horseshoe, Bamby Bread, A.......................................$20.00
Bullet (Rin-Tin-Tin), Post Grape Nuts Flakes, 1953, lt rust on bk, VG, P4 ....$10.00

Captain Hook & Crocodile, 1990, 3", M8 ....$5.00
Champions 1929 above portrait of entire team, Cubs Team lettered below, oval, A $245.00
Charlie's Angels, metal, Farrah Fawcett posed in mauve swimsuit, 1977, 3", EX..$4.00
Chevrolet, Watch the Leader...........................$20.00
Chicago White Sox, pr of socks crossed in center, bl & wht, A...$22.00
Chicago White Sox lettered over background representing baseball, bats crossed above, A...........................$22.00
Chief Brandon, Kellogg's, ca 1945-47, ¾", EX+-NM, C1 ....$15.00
Chip 'N Dale Rescue Rangers, 1990s, 3", M8.............$5.00
Cole Bros Circus lettered over portrait of Ken Maynard, 1⅝", A...$90.00
Cubs above 2 facing bears w/ball bats over shoulders, ca 1929, A...$105.00
Curley Bradley, Tom Mix of Radio $25.00
Davy Crockett, w/horseshoe hanging from attached red ribbon $8.00
Davy Crockett lettered below bust portrait, ribbon & Western boot charm attached, red background.................$20.00
Dick Tracy, Kellogg's, NM $30.00
Dick Tracy Secret Service Patrol........................$25.00
Disney MGM Studios w/Mickey & Minnie (gold star), 1980s, 3", NM, M8..$6.00
Dizzy Dean, brass baseball, radio premium, 1930s, EX+, T1...$37.50
Dogers, Dixie Walker, w/ribbon & 'Our Bums' & ball dangles, A...$45.00
Dumbo, his name above his straight-forward face portrait, D-X lettered on his wide neck band, 1¼" $35.00
Dumbo 50th Anniversary, 1991, 3", M8 ....$5.00
Early Wynn, name in script by portrait, 300 Club lettered below, w/tab, scarce, A..$44.00
Eerie Magazine Fan Club, EX $10.00
El Squeako Mouse, 1950s, 1", EX-......................$25.00
Elmore Bicycles...$40.00
Epcot Dare Devil Circus, 1980s, 3", M8 ....$5.00
Ernie Banks Day, Aug 15, 1964, portrait on background representing baseball, A..$69.00
ET & Elliott, Universal Studios, 1982, 6", NM, D9..........$4.00
Famous Monsters Fan Club, Phantom of Opera at center .$20.00
Fat Stuff, Kellogg's, NM...............................$15.00

Felix the Cat, Kellogg's NM $75.00
Fenway Park, 1985, 75th Anniversary, diamond shaped, A.$20.00
Flash Gordon, Kellogg's, NM $30.00
Flattop, Kellogg's, NM....................................$15.00
Foxy Grandpa, brick building w/1 character in window, 2 sitting outside smoking, 2nd Year, minor flaws, scarce, 1¼".$30.00
Gene Autry lettered above portrait of Gene & Champion, Champion lettered below, lg star in background, 1⅝", A..$24.00
Giants, Carl Hubble around perimeter, portrait in center, 1937 Giants pennant-shaped ribbon attached, A.............$135.00
Giants, Dick Bartell, above & below portrait, A $20.00
Go Chicago lettered on diecut football, w/ribbon & football charm attached, early, A $29.00
Go White Sox Go, lettered in 3 lines over background representing baseball, A...$20.00
Good Sports Enjoy Ward's Sporties lettered around Cykes portrait, A...$133.00
Good Sports Enjoy Ward's Sporties lettered around Foxx portrait, lt stain, A..$150.00
Good Sports Enjoy Ward's Sporties lettered around Gehringer portrait, A...$160.00
Grape Nuts w/Trigger photo, EX..........................$18.00
Green Hornet, Official Agent; metal w/Green Hornet & Kato in Black Beauty, bl background, 1966, 4", EX+, T2.......$18.00
Green Hornet, Vari-View, flasher type, 1960s, 3", NM-M, C1...$36.00
Happy Birthday Donald Duck, 1934-84, 2½", M8 ....$7.00
Honey I Blew Up the Kids, rectangular, 1992, M8 ....$5.00
Hornsby, Certified's Ice Cream, Sold at Wrigley Field lettered around perimeter, rare, 1¼", A................................$440.00
I Am a Junior Celtics Rooter lettered around perimeter, Bob Cousy portrait in center, A....................................$55.00
I'm Keeping Fit w/Popeye, King Features/Green Duck, rare, 2⅞" $150.00
I'm Rooting for Jackie Robinson, Dodgers lettered around perimeter, portrait in center, very rare, A................$340.00
I've Seen The Cat-in-the-Hat..., ca 1958, 1½", M...........$35.00
Illinois vs Michigan 1947 Homecoming, edge stain, A $20.00
Jackie Gleason, Away We Go, w/ribbon & horseshoe, 1950s, EX, V1 ....$17.50

Jacqueline Kennedy, America's
First Lady, 3¾", A, $65.00.

Jackie Gleason, The Loud-Mouth, VIP Corp, 1955, 1¾", VG, P4 ....$25.00
Jackie Robinson, name lettered on lower perimeter, portrait on bl, rare, A..$90.00
Jerome (Dizzy) Dean lettered on lower perimeter below full-face portrait, A...$65.00
Jiggs, Kellogg's, NM $25.00
Joe Dimaggio, name lettered on lower perimeter, portrait on lt bl, scarce, A...$65.00
Joe Louis, World's Champion, words either side of full-length Joe in fighting stance, A................................$30.00
John Glenn, Around the World in 80 Minutes $20.00
Katzenjammer Kid Fritz or The Inspector, Kellogg's, 1944-45, ⅞", EX+-NM, C1.......................................$13.50

Kennedy/Johnson 44th Inauguration,
1961, ¾", A, $45.00.

Kellogg's Early Bird Breakfast Club $10.00
Lethal Weapon 3, M, E3....................................$2.00
Little Mermaid, 1980s, 3", M8.............................$5.00
Little Orphan Annie, Kellogg's, 1945, ⅞", NM $25.00
Little Orphan Annie, Radio Orphan Annie's Secret Society Booklet & Membership Decoder Pin, 1936, set of 2, NM+, A...$100.00
Lone Ranger, features early Lone Ranger riding Silver, 1940s, 1¼", NM, A...$80.00
Lone Ranger Club lettered above Lone Ranger on Silver, Dr West's Toothpaste, A.....................................$50.00
Mac, Kellogg's, NM $12.50
Maggie, Kellogg's, NM....................................$25.00
Mama Katzenjammer, Kellogg's, NM $25.00
Marilyn Monroe, Movie Star series, 1960s, 1¾", NM, C1...$18.00
Michael Jackson, metal, portrait of Michael in sunglasses & Nehru jacket, 2¼", EX+................................$2.00
Mickey Mouse, image under glass encased in hexagonal brass button, 1x1", EX, A.......................................$45.00
Mickey Mouse, name lettered above Mickey w/right foot resting on heel, ¾ left turn, 1930s, scarce, 1¼"....................$80.00
Mickey Mouse Club, copyright 1928-30 by WE Disney, 1¼", NM, A...$122.00

Mickey Mouse Club, orange w/lettering around entire perimeter, Mickey waving right hand, ¾ right turn, scarce, 1¼" .$125.00

Mickey Mouse's 60th Birthday Party, Special Guest at Disneyland, 1988, 3", NM, M8......$15.00

Mickey University, 1980s, 1¾", M8 ......$4.00

Minnesota Twins, crossed ball bats w/faces of twins in center, w/ribbon, ball & bat charms on chain, A......$20.00

Monkees, Raybert, 1", M......$3.50

Morton's Pennant Winner Bread, player's portrait in center, A......$225.00

Mutt & Jeff, cello, Tokio, sgn by Fisher, cigarette premium, early 1900s, ⅞", set of 4 different, NM, C1......$60.00

New York Giants lettered on background representing baseball, w/ribbon, bat & ball dangles, bl & wht, A......$45.00

New York Yankees, Chase, portrait in center, A......$27.50

NY Black Yankees lettered over backgound representing baseball, crossed bats at top, A......$40.00

Oliver & Co, 1988, 3", M8 ......$5.00

Pat Patton, Kellogg's, 1945-47, ¾", EX+-NM, C1 ......$15.00

Pee Wee Sez Stop, Tri-Country Service, Pee Wee running right in center, 1⅛", A......$25.00

Pete Rose, enameled diecut Pete swinging bat, A......$25.00

Peter Pan, Benay Albee, 1960s, 3½", NM, M8 ......$10.00

Phantom, Kellogg's, NM......$75.00

Philadephia Stars lettered in 2 lines on wide horizontal center band, A......$55.00

Pittsburgh Pirates, Tommy Leach, portrait in center, lg letters, A......$27.00

Popeye, Kellogg's, NM......$30.00

Popeye, w/St Louis Button Co paper label on bk, 1930s, NM, V1......$48.00

Preacher Roe, Dodgers, over waist-length portrait, arms above head, A......$65.00

Premier Helical Bicycles......$25.00

Prince Valiant, scarce, ⅞", NM, A......$95.00

Ray Milland, A Paramount Star, Quaker Puffed Wheat & Rice premium, 1 of series, 1950, ¾", VG, P4......$15.00

Rescuers Down Under, map background, rectangular, 1980s, NM, M8 ......$6.00

Rin-Tin-Tin......$10.00

Ringo Starr, metal, face w/signature, 1960s, 1¼", EX+.....$10.00

Rocketeers, Art Deco style, sq, 1990, M8......$4.00

Rocketeers, Disney, bursting through airplane background, oval, 1991, M, P4......$8.00

Rocketeers, Disney, sq w/movie poster art, 1991, M, P4.....$6.00

Roy Rogers, bl w/photo, 1950s, lg, NM, C1 ......$23.00

Roy Rogers, Roy's Guns, Post Grape Nuts Flakes, lt rust, 1953, VG, P4......$20.00

Santa, #16750 above outdoor scene, Meet Me at Hamburger's lettered around lower perimeter, 1⅝", A $125.00

Santa, Call Me Up at Wanamaker's, Santa facing forward w/phone, 1⅝", A......$65.00

Santa, I Am at the Bon Marche, Seattle, above Santa about to disappear down brick chimney, 1¼", A......$45.00

Santa, Meet Me at Marshall Fields, rare, 1⅝", A......$100.00

Santa, Merry Christmas Esso above waving Santa w/tree in left arm, 1¼", A......$70.00

Santa, Yes, I Am Staying at Yetter & Waters As Usual, Santa w/phone in center, 1⅝", A......$110.00

Santa in mc square on wht background, dtd 1915, 1", A..$22.00

Santa in open old-fashioned auto, 1¼", A......$100.00

Santa in oval at left, lady in 2nd on right, Hello! Little One, I Am at Fraser's lettered above & below, A......$270.00

Santa w/bag atop house by chimney, My Headquarters at Foster & Cochran's, 1¼", A......$95.00

Schaeffer Pianos, Best in the West......$25.00

Seattle Pilots lettered over ships wheel w/baseball in center, A......$24.00

Shirley Temple, My Friend above smiling face portrait on dk background w/wide horizontal central band, 1¼"......$50.00

Shirley Temple, pk, bl & wht celluloid w/photo of Shirley w/doll, 1940s, 1¼", EX+, C1 ......$21.00

Simpsons, Bart Under Achiever & Proud of It, Man!, Button-Up, 6", K1......$3.50

Simpsons, Bartman Avenger of Evil, Watch It, Dude; Button-Up, 6", K1......$3.50

Simpsons, Homer Simpson, No Problemo!; Button-Up, 1¾", K1......$1.00

Simpsons Family Portrait, Button-Up, 1¾", K1 ......$1.00

Simpsons Family Portrait, Button-Up, 6", K1 ......$3.50

Sixty Years w/You Mickey, 1988, 6", NM, M8......$12.00

Snoopy, as pilot, Millbrook Bread, 1½", M, H4 ......$2.00

Snoopy, wearing crown, Milbrook Bread, 1970, 1½", M, H4......$2.00

Snoopy, wearing crown, Milbrook Bread, 1970, 4", M......$4.00

Snow White Jingle Club, 1930s, NM, M8 ......$38.00

Snuffy Smith, Kellogg's, NM $15.00

Soupy Sales, 1965, 3"......$12.00

Spahnie at top, Sept 17, 1963 below, portrait over background representing baseball, red, wht & bl, A......$44.00

Squirt, EX......$15.00

Stan Musial, portrait on yel, name on lower perimeter, A.$40.00

Star Tours Disneyland, bl background, 1986, 3", M8......$6.00

Studebakers Really Rolling......$25.00

Superman, figural enameled silhouette, flag over head lettered Superman & American, 1⅝", A......$130.00

Superman, Kellogg's, 1945, ⅞", EX, C1......$15.00

Superman, Kellogg's, ⅞", NM......$35.00

Roy Rogers and Dale Evans, Charles Starret Famous Cowboy Series, black and white litho, 1¼", from $10.00 to $15.00 each.

Supermen of America lettered around perimeter band, ¾-length Superman turned slightly left in center, mc, 1¼", A .$25.00

Tarzan, Feldman's Safety Club, Tarzan running forward, 1¼" $225.00

Tarzan, 1974, 5", NM-M, C1..$17.50

Team Mickey Sports, rectangular, 1980s, M8 ....$4.00

Ted Williams lettered below portrait, w/ribbon & ball & glove charms attached w/chain, A.....................................$85.00

Tess Trueheart and Vitamin Flintheart, Kellogg's Pep Pins, $15.00 each.

Tilie the Toiler, Kellogg's, 1944-45, ⅞", NM, C1.............$15.00

Toasted Cream of Rye Flakes, Second Base lettered around perimeter, Good Ball Players Eat over ballplayer in center, A...$50.00

Tom Corbett, flasher type, Tom off center, ¾ right turn, looking upward, 1⅛", A...$22.00

Tom Mix, checkered bar pin w/disk dangle, no pin on bk, A...$25.00

Tom Mix for Vice President, rare, 1¼" $150.00

Totally Minnie, 1980s, 3", M8..$5.00

Townsend Gun Co & address below, Center Field lettered at top perimeter, ball player in center, A $90.00

Universal Monsters, set of 6: Creature, Wolfman, Dracula, Phantom of Opera, Frankenstein & Mummy, 1960s, ⅞", NM, C1...$54.00

University of Illinois 1963 Homecoming, bird's-eye view of stadium on oval, lt edge stain, A $28.00

Vitamin Flintheart, Kellogg's, 1945-47, ¾", EX, C1.........$15.00

Walt Disney Studios, features Mickey, 1980s, oval, M8 .....$4.00

Walt Disney World 10th Anniversary, 1981, 3½", M8 ......$5.00

Welcome Home lettered at top, Cardinal w/ball bat & gr branch in center, A...$68.00

Wimpy, Kellogg's, EX $15.00

Winkles Twins, Kellogg's, NM...$75.00

Wizard of Oz's Scarecrow, bl & orange on cello, Economy Novelty & Printing, El Mago de Oz (Spanish), ⅞", EX+, rare, A $86.00

Yankees, name on top of Uncle Sam hat superimposed over lg V, World's Series in top bars, 1953 Press at bottom, A...$275.00

Yankees & Uncle Sam hat on lg baseball, ribbon w/World Series extending out ea side, 1947, A..............................$500.00

Yankees Joe Di Maggio lettered around perimeter, portrait of young Joe in center, rare, A $150.00

Yellow Kid, #157, holding flag w/lg star, minor foxing, 1¼", A...$50.00

Yellow Kid, #2, standing, holding shirt out on sides, 1¼".$38.00

Yellow Kid, #22, standing w/pnt bucket in right hand, left raised holding pnt brush, 1¼" $38.00

Yellow Kid, playing baseball $65.00

Zorro, wht, red & blk litho metal, WDP/7-Up, M, P4........$5.00

101 Dalmations, 1990, 3", M8..$4.00

35 Years of Magic Disneyland, features Mickey, 1990, 3", M8...$5.00

Pipsqueaks

Pipsqueak toys were popular among the Pennsylvania Germans. Many featured animals made of painted papier-mache, some were on spring legs. All had bellows that produced a squeaking sound, hence the name. Early toys had bellows made from sheepskin. Cloth bellows followed, and on later examples, the bellows were made of paper.

Bird, gilt/mc pnt & wood composition, spring legs, on squeaking bellows base, some pnt wear, 1880s, 7¾", A $175.00

Bird, orange & bl, pecking from sm dish, standing on bellows (silent), sm crack, 1882, 7x2½", A...........................$170.00

Cat, painted composition, American, late 1800s, 7¾", EX, $600.00.

Cat, cloth over wood & compo w/glass eyes, ribbon at neck, orig label, 4" $100.00

Cat & Kitten, curled up mother, molded compo, bellows base (silent), 2x4½", A...$230.00

Cat w/2 Kittens, striped flocking, animated mouth, 7", VG $450.00

Chickens in Cage, door opens & papier-mache rooster pops up $85.00

Duck on Nest, pnt papier-mache, rpr, silent, 5¾" $425.00

Goose, spring legs, squeaks, glued rprs, 7" $165.00

Rabbit, haircloth, animated ears & glass eyes, silent, 9".$325.00

Rooster, papier-mache, spring legs, bellows base, 7", VG .$150.00

Plastic Figures

Plastic figures were made by many toy companies. They were first boxed with playsets, but in the early fifties, some became available individually. Marx was the first company to offer single figures (at 10¢ each) and even some cereal companies included one in boxes of their product. (Kellogg offered a series of 16 54mm Historic Warriors and Nabisco had a line of ten dinosaurs in marbleized, primary colors.) Virtually every type of man and beast has been modeled in plastic, today some have become very collectible and expensive. There are lots of factors you'll need to be aware of to be a wise buyer. For instance, Marx made cowboys during the mid sixties in a flat finish, and these are much harder to find and more valuable than the later, with a waxy finish. And the Marvel Super Heroes in the flourescent hues are worth about half as much as the earlier, light gray issue. Because of limited space, it isn't possible to evaluate more than a representative few of these plastic figures in a general price guide, so if you'd like to learn more about them, we recommend *Geppert's Guide* by Tim Geppert. See the Clubs and Newsletters section for information on how to order the *Plastic Figure & Playset Collector* magazine. Our advisor for this category is Mike Fredericks (F4). See also Playsets.

Action and Adventure

American Character, Action & Adventure series, coyote, M, H4...$10.00

American Character, Bonanza series, mountain lion, M, H4..$15.00

Archer, Spacemen, rifle across chest, gr, H5.....................$10.00

Archer, Spacemen, rifle across chest, wht, H5....................$6.00

Archer, Spacemen, right hand to head, wht, H5..............$10.00

Archer, Spacemen, standing w/ray gun, metallic gr, missing tip of gun, ca 1960s, 4", VG $3.50

Archer, Spacemen, w/radio in left hand, missing top of radio, H5 ....$6.00

Archer, Spacemen, woman w/pistol, orange, H5.............$10.00

Ideal, Super Heroes, Aquaman, 60mm, M $75.00

Ideal, Super Heroes, Joker, 60mm, purple, M...................$50.00

Ideal, Super Heroes, Wonder Woman, 1966, M...............$35.00

Marx, Ben Hur, donkey w/baskets on bk, lt bl soft plastic, NM, F5..$11.50

Marx, Ben Hur, gladiator w/long sword & round shield, H5 ....$8.00

Marx, Ben Hur, lady, bathing, gray, H5 ....$8.00

Marx, Ben Hur, slave driver, cream, H5............................$8.00

Marx, Ben Hur, slave woman w/vase, gray, H5 ....$8.00

Marx, Canadian Farm Set, 54mm, MIB.........................$550.00

Marx, Cavemen, standing w/spear or swinging club, rusty brn soft plastic, 6", NM+, F5...$10.50

Marx, Eskimos, 54mm, kayak boat, w/harpoon & rope, 2-pc, NM-M, F5..$8.50

Marx, Eskimos, 54mm, using spear & rope, flat powder bl soft plastic, EX, F5...$4.50

Marx, Explorers, 54mm, Arctic bush pilot holding helmet, flat lt gray, NM, F5 ....$7.50

Marx, Explorers, 54mm, filming w/motion picture camera, flat lt gray, NM, F5 ....$3.50

Marx, Explorers, 54mm, w/binoculars, flat lt gray, NM, F5..$5.50

Marx, Explorers, 54mm, w/flare gun, flat lt gray, NM, F5 ...$4.50

Marx, Jungle Jim or Daktari, adult & baby giraffe, pr, H5 ..$8.00

Marx, Jungle Jim or Daktari, alligator, H5 ....$6.00

Marx, Jungle Jim or Daktari, animal skin, H5 ....$5.00

Marx, Jungle Jim or Daktari, baby elephant, H5 ....$5.00

Marx, Jungle Jim or Daktari, cage trap w/forked stick, H5.$12.00

Marx, Jungle Jim or Daktari, canoe w/outrigger & 2 paddles, H5 ....$30.00

Marx, Jungle Jim or Daktari, gorilla, H5...........................$5.00

Marx, Jungle Jim or Daktari, hunter w/separate rifle, H5....$8.00

Marx, Jungle Jim or Daktari, leopard, H5 ....$4.00

Marx, Jungle Jim or Daktari, lion, H5 ....$4.00

Marx, Jungle Jim or Daktari, lion cub, H5.........................$3.00

Marx, Jungle Jim or Daktari, long log bowl, H5 ....$8.00

Marx, Jungle Jim or Daktari, lost hunter, H5 ....$12.00

Marx, Jungle Jim or Daktari, native, crouching w/separate spear, H5 ....$5.00

Marx, Jungle Jim or Daktari, native, kneeling w/separate drum, H5...$6.00

Marx, Jungle Jim or Daktari, native, throwing spear, w/separate spear & shield, H5 ....$7.00

Marx, Jungle Jim or Daktari, native chief w/top hat & cigar, H5...$12.00

Marx, Jungle Jim or Daktari, native drawing bow & arrow, H5 ....$5.00

Marx, Jungle Jim or Daktari, native policeman, marching, H5 ....$8.00

Marx, Jungle Jim or Daktari, native throwing spear (separate), H5..$5.00

Marx, Jungle Jim or Daktari, native w/molded spear, hand to cheek, H5 ....$5.00

Marx, Jungle Jim or Daktari, native w/staff, hand to head, H5 ....$4.00

Marx, Jungle Jim or Daktari, native witch doctor, Leopardhead, H5...$10.00

Marx, Jungle Jim or Daktari, spike trap w/trigger, H5.......$12.00

Marx, Jungle Jim or Daktari, zebra, H5............................$5.00

Marx, Jungle Jim or Daktari, 54mm, Tamba the Chimp, brn soft plastic, NM+, F5..$9.50

Marx, Man From UNCLE, Illya Kurakin or Napoleon Solo, steel bl, 6", NM+, F5.....................................$29.50

Marx, Man From UNCLE, Thrush agent w/pistol or giving karate chop, 6", NM+, F6..............................$24.50

Marx, Monsters, Creature, bl, H5......................$18.00

Marx, Monsters, Frankenstein, orange, H5......................$18.00

Marx, Monsters, Hunchback, orange, 1960s, 6", VG.......$25.00

Marx, Monsters, Mummy, orange, 1960s, 6", VG............$25.00

Marx, Monsters, Mummy, Universal Pictures, aqua-bl soft plastic, 6", NM, F5......................$19.50

Marx, Monsters, Phantom of the Opera, bl, gr or orange, 6", H5......................$18.00

Marx, Monsters, Wolfman, bl, H5......................$18.00

Marx, Moon Base, 54mm, 10 astronauts in 6 poses, silver soft plastic, EX-NM, F5......................$9.50

Marx, Pirate, 60mm, captain w/hand on pistol in belt, cream soft plastic, EX+, F5......................$6.50

Marx, Rex Mars Spacemen, 45mm, 19 different poses, bl vinyl, NM, F5......................$85.50

Marx, Rifleman, Lucas McCain & Mark, cream, character name on base, 1950, 2½", NM, A, pr......................$85.00

Marx, Robin Hood, 60mm, Friar Tuck, salmon soft plastic, NM, F5......................$8.50

Marx, Robin Hood, 60mm, knight shooting crossbow, silver, H5......................$15.00

Marx, Robin Hood, 60mm, knight w/club & shield, silver, H5......................$15.00

Marx, Robin Hood, 60mm, knight w/shield held overhead, H5......................$15.00

Marx, Robin Hood, 60mm, knight w/sword & knife, H5 .$12.00

Marx, Robin Hood, 60mm, knight w/sword & long axe, silver, H5......................$15.00

Marx, Robin Hood, 60mm, Little John, gr soft plastic, NM, F5......................$14.50

Marx, Robin Hood, 60mm, Maid Marion, gr soft plastic, scuffed nose, VG, F5......................$4.50

Marx, Robin Hood, 60mm, Merry Man, hand to mouth, dk brn soft plastic, NM, F5......................$7.50

Marx, Robin Hood, 60mm, Merry Man, lunging w/knife, dk brn soft plastic, NM, F5......................$7.50

Marx, Robin Hood, 60mm, Merry Man, w/raised staff, brn soft plastic, NM, F5......................$6.50

Marx, Space Patrol, 45mm, Carol Karlyle, rust vinyl, NM, F5......................$19.50

Marx, Space Patrol, 45mm, 9 spacemen in 8 poses, includes Buzz, Happy & pilot, orange vinyl, NM, F5......................$49.50

Marx, Spacemen, wht soft plastic, set of 8 different (w/alien), ca 1950s, NMIP, F5......................$119.50

Marx, Spacemen, 60mm, w/helmet & Geiger counter, walking, metallic bl, H5......................$25.00

Marx, Spacemen, 60mm, w/helmet & rifle, walking, metallic bl, H5......................$25.00

Marx, Tom Corbet Space Cadet, 45mm, standing w/hand on waist, gray vinyl, NM, F5......................$6.50

MPC, Hunters & Natives, native w/arms at sides, H5........$2.00

MPC, Hunters & Natives, native w/raised arms, H5..........$2.00

MPC, Pirates, club or shovel, H5......................$1.50

MPC, Pirates, flag, H5......................$3.00

MPC, Pirates, Hook, in long coat, H5......................$2.00

MPC, Pirates, Pegleg, w/parrot, H5......................$2.00

MPC, Pirates, pick, H5......................$1.50

MPC, Pirates, treasure chest w/lid, H5......................$2.00

MPC, Pirates, w/earrings & right arm raised, H5...............$2.00

MPC, Pirates, wearing beard, 1 raised arm, H5.................$2.00

Multiple, Monsters, Mummy & Grim Reaper, w/removable, interchangeable heads, 1964, 6", set of 2, MOC, A...$80.00

Multiple, Monsters, Wolfman & Frankenstein, Pop-Top series, removable head, 1964, 6", set of 2, MOC (8x9" card), A......................$80.00

Premier, Spacemen, standing akimbo, w/air hose or radio loop, metallic lt purple, ca 1950s, 3", VG......................$3.00

Timmee, Pirates, red & silver......................$3.00

Campus Cuties and American Beauties

Erie, Bathing Beauty, 75mm, standing & waving, peach hard plastic, broken finger, NM, F5......................$12.50

Marx, American Beauties, ballerina, ca 1955, F5 ....$15.50

Marx, American Beauties, full set of 8 different poses, peach hard plastic, ca 1955, w/orig pkg, NMIP-MIP, F5......$99.50

Marx, American Beauties, hula dancer, peach hard plastic, ca 1955, NM-M, F5......................$15.50

Marx, American Beauties, in bikini w/purse, ca 1955, F5.$15.50

Marx, American Beauties, reclining nude, peach hard plastic, rare promo, NM, F5......................$59.50

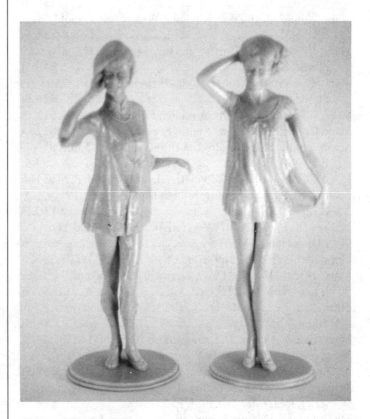

Marx, Campus Cuties: Dinner for Two and Nighty Night, 1964, from $10.00 to $15.00 each.

Marx, Campus Cuties, Lodge Party, 1st series, flesh pk, 6", NM, F5......................$8.50

Marx, Campus Cuties, Stormy Weather, NM.................$10.00

Marx, Campus Cuties, Twist Party, 2nd series, flesh pk, 6", NM+, F5......................$28.50

Comic, Disney, and Nursery Characters

Ideal, Gangsters, w/machine gun, red $5.00

Ideal, Super Heroes, Joker, gray, NM, F5 ....$48.50

Ideal, Super Heroes, Keyman, flourescent orange or gr, NM, F5 ....$58.50

Ideal, Super Heroes, Robin, w/cape, peach, NM, F5 ....$7.50

Lido, Disney, Zorro, blk soft plastic, NM+, F5 ....$6.50

Marx, Comic Strip, Archie or Jughead, 8", MOC, ea $25.00

Marx, Comic Strip, Archies, 60mm, Jughead, gr $8.00

Marx, Comic Strip, Blondie, Cookie, gr, H5 ....$8.00

Marx, Comic Strip, Blondie, Daisy, gr, missing tail, H5 .....$5.00

Marx, Comic Strip, Blondie, 1st issue, pk or gr, NM, F5, ea $6.50

Marx, Comic Strip, Blondie, 60mm, Alexander, gr, H5 .....$8.00

Marx, Comic Strip, Blondie, 60mm, Alexander, 1st issue, pk, NM, F5 ....$9.50

Marx, Comic Strip, Bringing Up Father, Jiggs, gr, H5 ......$10.00

Marx, Comic Strip, Bringing Up Father, 60mm, Maggie, cream or pk, EX+-NM, F5, ea $5.50

Marx, Comic Strip, Dick Tracy, Steve Katchem (driver), cream, 5", EX, F5 ....$28.50

Marx, Comic Strip, Li'l Abner, 60mm, Salomey the Pig, wht, NM, F5 ....$7.50

Marx, Comic Strip, Popeye, 60mm, Wimpy, pk, lt mold crease, EX+-NM, F5 ....$4.50

Marx, Comic Strip, Prince Valiant, 54mm, Aleta, silver soft plastic, NM, F5 ....$18.50

Marx, Comic Strip, Prince Valiant, 54mm, Boltar, cream soft plastic, NM, F5 ....$28.00

Marx, Comic Strip, Snuffy Smith, gr, H5 ....$12.00

Marx, Comic Strip, Snuffy Smith, Loweezy, pk, H5 ....$12.00

Marx, Comic Strip, Snuffy Smith, 60mm, Sutt Tatersall, tan, EX+-NM, F5 ....$4.50

Marx, Disney, Alice in Wonderland, set of 5: Alice, Mad Hatter, Queen & 2 rabbits, mk Holland on 2 pcs, 1950s, NM, A $120.00

Marx, Disney, Alice in Wonderland, 60mm, Mad Hatter or March Hare, NM, F5 ....$8.50

Marx, Disney, Bambi, 2nd series, cobalt bl, 6", NM+, F5 ...$6.50

Marx, Disney, Donald, Daisy, or any nephew, 60mm, 1st series, lt bl or flesh, NM, F5, ea $7.50

Marx, Disney, Donald Duck, flourescent gr soft plastic, 6", NM+, F5 ....$6.50

Marx, Disney, Dopey, 2nd series, cobalt bl, 6", NM-M, F5 .$4.50

Marx, Disney, Dumbo, 60mm, circus ringmaster, 1st series, lt bl or flesh, w/whip, NM, F5 ....$9.50

Marx, Disney, Dumbo, 60mm, Dumbo the baby elephant, 1st series, lt bl, w/feather, NM, F5 ....$14.50

Marx, Disney, Dumbo, 60mm, fireman clown, 1st series, cream, EX-NM, F5 ....$6.50

Marx, Disney, Dumbo, 60mm, singing clown, 1st series, flesh, NM, F5 ....$7.50

Marx, Disney, Fun on Wheels, Mickey Mouse or Donald Duck, HP, NM, F5 ....$6.50

Marx, Disney, Goofy, 60mm, 2nd series, pk, EX+, F5 ......$19.50

Marx, Disney, Mickey Mouse, 1st series, flourescent gr, pk, or red, 6", NM-M, F5, ea $2.50

Marx, Disney, Mickey Mouse, 60mm, mk Germany on bottom, factory pnt, ca 1955, NM, F5 ....$8.50

Marx, Disney, Minnie Mouse, 60mm, 1st series, flesh, NM, F5 ....$7.50

Marx, Disney, Morty Mouse, 60mm, mk Holland on bottom, factory pnt, ca 1955, NM, F5 ....$8.50

Marx, Disney, Peter Pan, 2nd series, cobalt bl, w/feather intact, 6", NM, F5 ....$8.50

Marx, Disney, Peter Pan, 60mm, set of 5, orig 12x3¾" box, NM, F5 ....$98.50

Marx, Disney, Peter Pan, 60mm, Smee, 1st series, cream or gr, NM, F5 ....$3.50

Marx, Disney, Pinocchio, set of 4: Pinocchio, Geppetto, Blue Fairy & Figaro, 1960, 3" tallest, NM, A $40.00

Marx, Disney, Pinocchio, 60mm, Jiminy Cricket, mk Holland on bottom, NM, F5 ....$8.50

Marx, Disney, Pluto, 1st series, flesh, w/tail intact, NM, F5 .$9.50

Marx, Disney, Pluto, 1st series, flourescent orange, 6", NM+, F5 ....$3.50

Marx, Disney, Snow White or Dopey, 60mm, mk Holland on bottom, NM, F5, ea $8.50

Marx, Disney, Tinker Bell, bl, 5", VG $20.00

Marx, Disney, Twistables, Goofy, like bendee w/wire arms & cloth outfit, complete & unbroken, NM, F5 ....$29.50

Marx, Disney, Zorro, 54mm, Don Alejandro or Don Diego, cream, NM, F5, ea $29.50

Marx, Disney, Zorro & Tornado, hard plastic, complete w/accessories, 1958, 7" Zorro, NMIB (EX-), A $432.00

Marx, Disney Playhouse, Alice, wht, H5 ....$15.00

Marx, Disney Playhouse, Bashful, bl, H5 ....$10.00

Marx, Disney Playhouse, clown in costume, bl, H5 ....$8.00

Marx, Disney Playhouse, Donald Duck or Daisy Duck, bl, H5, ea $10.00

Marx, Disney Playhouse, Dopey, cream, H5 ....$10.00

Marx, Disney Playhouse, Dopey, wht, H5 ....$9.00

Marx, Disney Playhouse, Figaro the Cat, wht, H5 ....$9.00

Marx, Disney Playhouse, Goofy, 6", H5 ....$5.00

Marx, Disney Playhouse, Grumpy, wht, H5 ....$9.00

Marx, Disney Playhouse, Hewey, Dewey, or Lewie, bl, H5, ea $8.00

Marx, Disney Playhouse, Jiminy Cricket, wht, H5 ....$10.00

Marx, Disney Playhouse, Mickey Mouse, bl, H5 ....$10.00

Marx, Disney Playhouse, Minnie Mouse, bl, 6", ...$10.00

Marx, Disney Playhouse, Morty or Monty, pk, H5 ....$8.00

Marx, Disney Playhouse, Peter Pan, 6", H5 ....$5.00

Marx, Disney Playhouse, Queen of Hearts, wht, H5 ....$12.00

Marx, Disney Playhouse, Wendy, wht, H5 ....$12.00

Marx, Disney Playhouse, White Rabbit, wht, H5 ....$10.00

Marx, Disneykins, Colonel Hathi, Jell-O premium, M $35.00

Marx, Disneykins, Donald Duck or Daisy, pnt, NM, F5, ea $7.50

Marx, Disneykins, Gepetto, HP, NM, F5 ....$7.50

Marx, Disneykins, Pecos Bill, pnt, NM, F5 ....$7.50

Marx, Disneykins, Peter Pan, pnt, NM, F5 ....$7.50

Marx, Disneykins, Shir Khan, 1968, M $25.00

Marx, Fairykins, complete set in book-type box, EX, V1 ..$185.00

Marx, Hanna-Barbara TV Tinykins, Mr Jinx & Pixie, 1960s, NM, C1, pr $27.00

Marx, Hanna-Barbara TV Tinykins, Snagglepuss, 1960s, NM, C1...$14.00

Marx, Hanna-Barbara's Flintstones, brontosaurus, lt gr styrene, 12" long, sm chip on tail, F5....................................$109.50

Marx, Hanna-Barbara's Flintstones, 60mm, Baby Puss, cream, NM, F5 ....$4.50

Marx, Hanna-Barbara's Flintstones, 60mm, Barney Rubble, cream, NM, F5 ....$4.50

Marx, Hanna-Barbara's Flintstones, 60mm, Bed Rock Fireman, powder bl soft plastic, NM, F5 ....$9.50

Marx, Hanna-Barbara's Flintstones, 60mm, Dino the Dinosaur, cream, EX+, F5...$2.50

Marx, Hanna-Barbara TV Tinykins, set of 3: Yogi, Boo Boo & Ranger Smith, 1960s, NM, C1 ....$36.00

Marx, Hanna-Barbara TV Tinykins, set of 4, Yogi Bear, Cindy Bear, Boo Boo & Ranger Smith, 3", M, A $50.00

Marx, Magic Marxie, lt brn, company mascot in presentation pose, given to distributors, 1950s, rare, 1½", M, A $83.00

Marx, Nursery Rhyme, Bo Peep, gr, H5..............................$9.00

Marx, Nursery Rhyme, Humpty Dumpty, gr, H5 ....$10.00

Marx, Nursery Rhyme, Jack Be Nimble, gr, H5 ....$8.00

Marx, Nursery Rhyme, Jack w/pail, H5 ....$8.00

Marx, Nursery Rhyme, Little Boy Blue, gr, H5 ....$9.00

Marx, Nursery Rhyme, Mary Had a Little Lamb, gr, H5.....$9.00

Marx, Super Heroes, Daredevil, flourescent orange, 6", NM+, F5 ....$18.50

Marx, Super Heroes, Daredevil, lt gray, 6", NM+-M, F5 ..$39.50

Marx, Super Heroes, Hulk, lt gray, 6", NM+-M, F5..........$39.50

Marx, Super Heroes, Spiderman or Thor, flourescent red, 6", NM+, F5 ....$18.50

Marx, Super Heroes, Spiderman or Thor, lt gray, 6", NM+-M, F5, ea..$39.50

Circus and Animals

Marx, Prehistoric Animals, Allosaurus, gr or gray, NM, F5 .$1.50

Marx, Prehistoric Animals, Kronosaurus, lt gr soft plastic, NM, F5 ....$12.50

Marx, Prehistoric Animals, Sphenagodon, gr, NM, F5.......$3.00

Marx, Prehistoric Animals, Trachodon, revised issue, gray, NM, F5 ....$1.50

Marx, Prehistoric Animals, Trachodon, 1st issue dk gray or gr, NM, F5 ....$3.50

Marx, Prehistoric Animals, Tyrannosaurus Rex, potbellied, lt gray soft plastic, NM, F5 ....$11.50

Marx, Super Circus Animals, camel, brn, H5 ....$5.00

Marx, Super Circus Animals, giraffe, brn, H5 ....$5.00

Marx, Super Circus Animals, gorilla, paws up, gray or gr, H5 ....$5.00

Marx, Super Circus Animals, lion, paw out, gray or gr, H5..$3.00

Marx, Super Circus Animals, monkey, hanging from front paws, H5 ....$3.00

Marx, Super Circus Animals, monkey, squatting w/hat, gray or gr, H5 ....$4.00

Marx, Super Circus Animals, performing dog w/cane, gray, H5 ....$3.00

Marx, Super Circus Animals, performing horse, gray or brn, H5 ....$4.00

Marx, Super Circus Animals, seal, w/ball on nose, gray, H5 ....$5.00

Marx, Super Circus Animals, sitting, w/seat, gray, H5........$8.00

Marx, Super Circus Animals, tiger, red or brn, H5 ....$4.00

Marx, Super Circus Bigtop, balloon vender, red, H5 ....$5.00

Marx, Super Circus Bigtop, boy w/bucket, red, H5 ....$4.00

Marx, Super Circus Bigtop, clown w/umbrella, yel, H5 ......$5.00

Marx, Super Circus Bigtop, elephant trainer, missing hook, yel, H5 ....$2.00

Marx, Super Circus Bigtop, fat woman, red, H5................$4.00

Marx, Super Circus Bigtop, father w/son, yel, H5 ....$5.00

Marx, Super Circus Bigtop, juggler, yel, H5 ....$5.00

Marx, Super Circus Bigtop, man hanging from knees, yel, H5 ....$4.00

Marx, Super Circus Bigtop, Nicky the Clown, 54mm, off-wht vinyl, NM, F5...$3.50

Marx, Super Circus Bigtop, popcorn vender, red, H5 ....$4.00

Marx, Super Circus Bigtop, Siamese twins, red, H5 ....$4.00

Marx, Super Circus Bigtop, strong man, yel, H5 ....$5.00

Marx, Super Circus Bigtop, sword swallower, yel, H5........$5.00

Marx, Super Circus Bigtop, tall man w/cane & hat, yel, H5 ....$5.00

Marx, Super Circus Bigtop, Tom Thumb w/cane, yel, H5..$5.00

Marx, Wild Life, Indian elephant, dk or lt gray hard plastic, hollow, 5", NM+-M, F5 ....$19.50

Marx, Wild Life, kudu (horned antelope), lt brn, horns & tail intact, M, F5 ....$12.50

Marx, Wild Life, lioness prowling, 60mm, creamy wht soft plastic, EX+, F5 ....$14.50

Marx, Wild Life, ostrich, 60mm, flat tan soft plastic, NM+, F5 ....$7.50

Marx, Wild Life, raccoon, flat chocolate brn soft plastic, NM+, F5..$2.50

Timmee, Prehistoric Animals, 35 dinosaurs, mc soft plastic, 1970s(?), MIP, P4 ....$15.00

Military and Warriors

Britains, Civil War, Confederate; officer, running w/pistol & sword, plastic on metal base, 1971, NM $5.00

Britains, Civil War, Union; mtd officer w/lg flag, rifle hanging downward to boot, plastic on metal base, 1971, NM ...$7.50

Britains, Herald Custer's 7th Calvary, officer w/pistol in right hand, all plastic, NM $3.50

Britains, Herald Custer's 7th Cavalry, advancing w/rifle, NM $3.50

Britains, Herald Custer's 7th Cavalry, bugler w/sword in left hand, all plastic, NM $3.50

Britains, Herald Guards, Horse; trumpeter, mk Hong Kong, all plastic, NM..$3.50

Britains, Herald Guards, infantryman, prone, firing rifle, all plastic, NM..$3.50

Britains, Herald Guards, Life; trumpeter, mk Hong Kong, all plastic, NM..$3.50

Britains, Herald Guards, mtd officer, sword at side, all plastic, NM..$35.00

Britains, Herald Guards, Queen's color bearer, marching, mk Hong Kong, all plastic, NM......................................$3.50

Britains, Herald Guards, Scots; marching bandmaster w/baton, all plastic, NM...$3.50

Britains, Herald Guards, standard bearer w/flag, mk Hong Kong, all plastic, NM...$3.50

Britains, Herald Indians, mtd, mk Hong Kong, all plastic, NM...$5.00

Britains, Herald Indians, mtd chief, holding spear & shield, all plastic, NM...$5.00

Britains, Herald Indians, w/bow & arrow, mk Hong Kong, all plastic, NM...$3.50

Britains, Herald Indians, w/tomahawk, all plastic, NM $3.50

Britains, Herald Knights, advancing w/pike, bl plume, all plastic, NM $3.50

Britains, Herald Knights, standing w/mace in right hand, shield in left, bl plume, all plastic, NM.....................................$3.50

Britains, Knights & Turks, mtd Turk w/lance & shield, plume on horse, plastic on metal base, 1971, NM $7.50

Britains, Knights & Turks, set of 6 different Turks, on foot w/weapons, plastic on metal base, 1971, M................$14.00

Britains, Knights & Turks, standing knight in full armor, purple plume on helmet, plastic on metal base, 1971, NM.....$3.50

Britains, Waterloo, British; infantryman holding flag in left hand & sword in right, plastic on metal base, 1971, NM $6.50

Britains, Waterloo, British; mtd, plastic on metal base, bl coat, wht trousers, blk hat & boots, 1971, NM.....................$9.50

Britains, Waterloo, British; mtd, w/sword, plastic on metal base, red coat w/gold sash & wht trousers, 1971, NM...........$9.50

Britains, Waterloo, French; mtd, w/sword, plastic on metal base, gr coat w/red sash, blk boots, 1971, NM.......................$9.50

Ideal, Knights, horse, stopping or running, H5 ....$20.00

Ideal, Knights, knight w/battle axe & shield, H5..............$15.00

Ideal, Knights, knight w/sword & shield out from body, H5 ....$12.00

Ideal, Knights, lance, H5 ....$10.00

Ideal, Knights, mtd, w/left or right leg forward, H5 ....$15.00

Ideal, Knights, queen w/rose, H5......................................$15.00

Italy, Knights, set of 28 different poses, ca 1970s, 2¼", MIP..$10.00

Lido, American Revolution, advancing w/rifle, H5 ....$3.00

Lido, American Revolution, drummer, H5 ....$3.00

Lido, American Revolution, officer, mtd or on foot, H5, ea .$4.00

Lido, American Revolution, walking w/flag, H5.................$4.00

Lido, King's Knights Set, 6 2" figures, 4 3½" horses, flag & 4 weapons, sealed, NMIB, A $65.00

Lido, Knights, flag, H5..$3.00

Lido, Knights, guard w/sword & shield, H5 ....$4.00

Lido, Knights, holding shield w/sword overhead, H5..........$4.00

Lido, Knights, lance w/pennant, H5...................................$2.00

Lido, Knights, mace or club, H5, ea....................................$1.00

Lido, Knights, mtd, w/shield at body, H5 ....$2.00

Lido, Knights, pole axe, H5 ....$2.00

Lido, Knights, silver hard plastic, detachable lance, mtd on rubber band-powered horse, 3", M, T2 ....$45.00

Lido, Knights, w/trumpet & pole axe, H5 ....$4.00

Marx, American Revolution, complete 17-pc set, pnt burgundy plastic, NMIP, F5..$44.50

Marx, American Revolution, 54mm, British Redcoat, running w/rifle, red, NM, F5..$3.00

Marx, American Revolution, 60mm, marching w/rifle on shoulder, wht soft plastic, NM, F5 ....$3.50

Marx, American Revolution, 60mm, marching w/rifle on shoulder, cream soft plastic, NM, F5 ....$5.50

Marx, American Revolution, 60mm, minuteman w/musket, cream soft plastic, NM, F5 ....$6.50

Marx, Captain Gallant & Foreign Legion, 54mm, 22 pcs, powder bl soft plastic, 1967, MIP (sealed bag), F5 ....$159.50

Marx, Civil War, Caisson wagon hitch, orig silver-gray pnt, NM, F5 ....$9.50

Marx, Civil War, Confederate; advancing w/rifle at waist, dk gray, H5 ....$3.00

Marx, Civil War, Confederate; kneeling & shooting, lt gray, H5 ....$4.00

Marx, Civil War, Confederate; loading rifle, dk gray, H5...$6.00

Marx, Civil War, Confederate; marching, dk gray, H5.......$3.00

Marx, Civil War, Confederate; running w/rifle, dk gray, H5...$4.00

Marx, Civil War, Confederate; shot, dropping rifle, dk gray, H5..$5.00

Marx, Civil War, Confederate; standing & shooting, dk gray, H5 ....$4.00

Marx, Civil War, Confederate; w/sword overhead, lt gray, H5..$4.00

Marx, Civil War, Confederate; 54mm, falling horse (no rider), gray or cream soft plastic, NM, F5, ea $29.50

Marx, Civil War, Confederate; 54mm, falling rider & horse, gray soft plastic, NM-M, F5................................$74.50

Marx, Civil War, Confederate; 54mm, stretcher bearer, lt gray soft plastic, NM, F5...$2.50

Marx, Civil War, Union; advancing w/rifle at waist, lt bl, H5 ....$3.00

Marx, Civil War, Union; cannoneer w/torch, lt bl, H5......$5.00

Marx, Civil War, Union; marching, lt bl, H5 ....$3.00

Marx, Civil War, Union; officer w/pistol, pointing, lt bl, H5 ....$4.00

Marx, Civil War, Union; prone, shooting rifle, lt bl, H5....$4.00

Marx, Civil War, Union; running w/rifle at waist, lt bl, H5..$3.00

Marx, Civil War, Union; standing & shooting, lt bl, H5 ...$4.00

Marx, Civil War, Union; w/pistol & bugle, lt bl, H5..........$4.00

Marx, Civil War, Union; w/ramrod, lt bl, H5 ....$4.00

Marx, Civil War, Union; 54mm, mtd, w/whip, bl soft plastic, F5 ....$2.00

Marx, Civil War, 24-pc set, dk brn soft plastic, NM, F5...$29.50

Marx, Germans, kneeling & aiming rifle, dk gray soft plastic (beware of Plastimarx reissue), 6", NM+, F5 ....$5.50

Marx, Germans, 54mm, advancing, rifle at waist, dk gray, H4 ....$1.50

Marx, Germans, 54mm, full set of 32 in 13 poses, dk gray soft plastic, NM+, F5...$32.50

Marx, Germans, 54mm, kneeling & firing rifle, dk gray, H5 ....$1.50

Marx, Germans, 54mm, lying dead w/MG rifle at waist, dk gray, H5...$2.00

Marx, Germans, 54mm, officer pointing down, dk gray, H5 ....$2.00

Marx, Germans, 54mm, running w/pistol, dk gray, H5.......$2.00

Marx, Germans, 54mm, running w/MG rifle, dk gray, H5..$2.00

Marx, Germans, 54mm, standing & firing rifle, dk gray, H5 .$2.00

Marx, Germans, 54mm, throwing grenade, dk gray, H5 .....$2.00

Marx, Germans, 54mm, w/binoculars, dk gray, H5 ....$2.00

Marx, Germans, 54mm, w/MG rifle at waist, dk gray, H5 ..$2.00

Marx, Germans, 54mm, walking w/bazooka at chest, dk gray, H5 ....$2.00

Marx, Germans, 54mm, walking w/MG rifle at shoulder, dk gray, H5 ....$1.50

Marx, Japanese, advancing w/bayoneted rifle or aiming rifle, caramel, 6", NM+, F5, ea..$7.50

Marx, Japanese, 54mm, advancing w/rifle at chest, tan or khaki, H5 ....$4.00

Marx, Japanese, 54mm, being shot, dropping weapon, tan or khaki, H5, ea...$3.00

Marx, Japanese, 54mm, crouching w/rifle, tan or khaki, H5, ea..$3.00

Marx, Japanese, 54mm, firing MG rifle from hip, tan or khaki, H5, ea...$4.00

Marx, Japanese, 54mm, kneeling w/radio & pistol, tan or khaki, H5, ea...$4.00

Marx, Japanese, 54mm, prisoner, hands behind neck, tan or khaki, H5, ea...$4.00

Marx, Japanese, 54mm, running w/flag, tan or khaki, H5, ea...$5.00

Marx, Japanese, 54mm, running w/knife, tan or khaki, H5, ea...$4.00

Marx, Japanese, 54mm, running w/sword & pistol, tan or khaki, H5, ea...$3.00

Marx, Japanese, 54mm, throwing grenade, tan or khaki, H5, ea...$3.00

Marx, Knights, tin case w/75 pcs, NM (EX+ case), F5 .....$89.50

Marx, Knights, 54mm, horse, running or walking, blk or cream, H5, ea...$6.00

Marx, Knights, 54mm, mtd, w/lance, H5 ....$2.00

Marx, Knights, 54mm, standing w/lance, H5 ....$2.00

Marx, Knights, 54mm, w/sword & shield, H5 ....$2.00

Marx, Knights, 60mm, w/crossbow or spear, silver soft plastic, NM, F5 ....$8.50

Marx, Original, German advancing w/left hand raised, 6", H5 ....$6.00

Marx, Original, German lunging forward, missing rifle tip, 6", H5 ....$4.00

Marx, Original, Japanese lunging w/rifle, missing bayonet tip, 6", H5 ....$4.00

Marx, Original, Japanese running w/pistol & knife, 6", H5 .$6.00

Marx, Original, Japanese standing & firing weapon, 6", H5 ....$6.00

Marx, Original, Russian clubbing w/rifle, 6", H5 ....$6.00

Marx, Original, Russian running w/automatic rifle, 6", H5..$6.00

Marx, Top Shelf, 60mm, Arab running w/rifle, rusty-brn soft plastic, EX+-NM, F5...$18.50

Marx, UN Soldiers on Parade, 60mm, Turkey, Canada, or Great Britain, pnt, M, ea...$65.00

Marx, US Dress Marine, 60mm, marching w/rifle, metallic bl soft plastic, NM-M, F5..$5.50

Marx, Vikings, blowing horn, w/spear in right hand, mint gr soft plastic, spear & horn intact, 6", NM+, F5.................$28.50

Marx, Vikings, 54mm, running w/knife & shield, H5........$2.50

Marx, Vikings, 54mm, w/axe, H5 ....$2.00

Marx, Vikings, 54mm, w/knife & club, H5 ....$2.00

Marx, Vikings, 54mm, walking w/sword, H5.....................$2.50

Marx, Warriors of the World, 1st series, set of 51 (49 different poses), MIB, V1 ....$300.00

Marx, West Point Cadets, 60mm, marching in overcoat, bl-gray or wht soft plastic, NM, F5, ea....................................$4.50

Marx, West Point Cadets, 60mm, marching w/rifle or sword, w/intact plume, NM, F5, ea...$4.50

Marx, WWI, US Doughboy; 60mm, marching in overcoat, NM, F5..$14.50

Marx, WWI, US Doughboy; 60mm, marching w/campaign hat, NM, F5...$14.50

Marx, WWII, Air Corps; 45mm, complete set of 11 poses, gray, MIP, F5..$21.50

Marx, WWII, Barracks Soldiers; 35mm, set of 10 in 8 poses, MIP, F5..$19.50

Marx, WWII, GIs; complete set of 6, 3½", NMIP, F5 ......$29.50

Marx, WWII, Marching GIs; 54mm, full set of 16 in 3 poses, NMIP, F5..$19.50

Marx, WWII, Paratroopers; 54mm, set of 2 w/2 different chutes, NM, F5..$19.50

Marx, WWII, US 48-star flag, for 60mm marching soldier, NM, F5 ....$4.50

Mattel, Guts!, set of 10: laser fighters w/super weapons, gray uniforms w/blk boots, visored helmets, ca 1986, MIP $12.50

Mattel, Guts!, set of 10: underwater demolition w/hi-tech weapons, dk bl wetsuits, ca 1986, MIP $12.50

Mattel, Guts!, set of 2: Green Berets, ca 1986, 2½", MIP...$5.00

MDM of France, French 1st Empire Artillery, 2 mtd soldiers, 4 horses, caisson & cannon, all on base, 1976, 8", NM .$25.00

MPC, Civil War, advancing w/left arm out, bl, H5 ....$2.00

MPC, Civil War, officer w/right arm up, bl or gr, H5, ea....$2.00

MPC, Civil War, wagon driver, seated, bl, H5....................$2.00

MPC, Civil War, walking, arms at sides, bl or gr, H5, ea....$2.00

Multiple, Brave Knights, set of 38, mc plastic, ca 1973, 2", MIP..$12.50

Timmee, Air Force, looking up w/binoculars, H5 ....$4.00

Timmee, Air Force, officer, reading papers, H5 ....$5.00

Timmee, Air Force, w/ammo belt, H5.................................$4.00

Timmee, Air Force, w/fire extinguisher, H5.......................$4.00

Timmee, Air Force, w/signal flags, H5................................$5.00

Nutty Mads

Marx, All-Heart Hogan, pk, M, H4 ....$35.00

Marx, All-Heart Hogan, purple, holds criminal by throat, 1963, 6", NM-M, A $30.00

Marx, Bullpen Boo-Boo, gr, Bullpen as pitcher for Podnuk Bums, 1963, 6", NM, A $30.00

Marx, Bullpen Boo-Boo, red, M, H4 ....$28.00

Marx, Chief Lost Tepee, avocado gr, Indian on horse, 1963, 6", NM-M, A $30.00

Marx, Chief Lost Tepee, flourescent red, EX $20.00

Marx, Dippy the Deep Diver, purple, Dippy scours ocean floor w/fish in hand, 1963, 6", M, A $30.00

Marx, Donald the Demon, gr, driving sm car, 1963, 6", NM-M, A $30.00

Marx, Freddy Flamout, turq bl, in jet plane, 1963, 6", NM-M, A $77.00

Marx, I Didn't Do It, lt bl bug-eyed child holding sawed-off table leg & hacksaw, Blame-It series, 1963, 6", NM, A $57.00

Marx, Manny the Reckless Mariner, off-lime gr, recklessly driving sm boat, 1963, 6", NM-M, A $30.00

Marx, Mudder, 3rd series, flourescent gr, missing frying pan, NM+, F5 ....$24.50

Marx, Rocko the Champ, purple, holding hand up in victory, 1963, 6", NM-M, A $30.00

Marx, Roddy the Hot Rod, lime gr, driving hot rod, 1963, 6", NM-M, A $30.00

Marx, Roddy the Hot Rod, pk, M, H4 ....$18.00

Marx, Suburban Sidney, lime gr, M, H4 ....$35.00

Marx, Waldo the Weightlifter, lt lime gr, trying to lift barbell, 1963, 6", M, A $30.00

Sportsmen, Dignitaries, and Civilians

Marx, ABC camera man, dark blue, 2½", $10.00.

Marx, American Civil War Leaders, General Grant, H5 ....$8.00

Marx, American Civil War Leaders, 54mm, Jefferson Davis, cream soft plastic, M, from $6 to $8.00

Marx, American Civil War Leaders, 54mm, Robert E Lee, cream soft plastic, M, from $6 to $8.00

Marx, American Civil War Leaders, 54mm, US Grant, cream soft plastic, NM, F5 ....$4.50

Marx, American Heroes, 60mm, Colonel Roosevelt, wht hard plastic, molded ⅛" short, NM, F5 ....$18.50

Marx, American Heroes, 60mm, General Bradley, wht hard plastic, sq base, NM, F5 ....$11.50

Marx, American Heroes, 60mm, General Marshall, wht hard plastic, sq base, NM, F5 ....$12.50

Marx, American Heroes, 60mm, General Spaatz, wht hard plastic, sq base, NM, F5 ....$11.00

Marx, American Heroes, 60mm, General Stillwell, wht hard plastic, sq base, NM, F5 ....$11.50

Marx, Civilians & Workmen, fireman w/extinguisher, wht soft plastic, 3¼", NM+, F5 ....$4.50

Marx, Civilians & Workmen, football player, wht, M $8.00

Marx, Civilians & Workmen, 35mm, motorcycle patrolman riding vintage Harley or Indian, F5 ....$2.50

Marx, Civilians & Workmen, 35mm, polo player, wht, M .$8.00

Marx, Civilians & Workmen, 35mm, 35 shopping center poses, creamy tan soft plastic, NMIP, F5 ....$24.50

Marx, Civilians & Workmen, 54mm, chauffeur, cream, NM+, F5 ....$9.50

Marx, Civilians & Workmen, 54mm, delivery man, cream, NM+, F5 ....$9.50

Marx, Civilians & Workmen, 54mm, 16 skyscraper poses, complete set, cream soft plastic, NMIB, F5 ....$129.50

Marx, Civilians & Workmen, 60mm, dollhouse father, cream or lt pk soft plastic, NM+, F5 ....$3.50

Marx, Famous Canadians, Jacques Cartier, pnt, Lipton Tea premium, EX, F5 ....$9.50

Marx, Famous Canadians, Samuel De Champlain, Lipton Tea premium, lt worn pnt, EX, F5 ....$9.50

Marx, Football Team, 54mm, 32 poses in red soft plastic, NMIB, F5 ....$79.50

Marx, Presidents & Politicals, Abraham Lincoln, H5 ....$8.00

Marx, Presidents & Politicals, Adlai Stevenson, '50s Presidential candidate, wht hard plastic, NM, F5 ....$19.50

Marx, Presidents & Politicals, FDR wearing Yalta cape, wht hard plastic, NM, F5 ....$12.50

Marx, Presidents & Politicals, Hubert Humphrey, factory pnt, MIP, F5 ....$2.50

Marx, Presidents & Politicals, Mendes-France, French Prime Minister, ivory hard plastic, NM, F5 ....$19.50

Marx, Presidents & Politicals, President Eisenhower w/hands at sides, NM, F5 ....$2.50

Marx, Presidents & Politicals, Richard M Nixon, wht hard plastic, NM, F5 ....$5.50

Marx, Presidents & Politicals, Robert F Kennedy, 1968 Presidential candidate, wht hard plastic, NMIP, F1 ....$14.50

Marx, Presidents & Politicals, set of 36, 1960s, NMOC (separate cards) $65.00

Marx, Queen Elizabeth II Coronation, Duke of Edinburgh, w/sword intact, NM, F5 ....$29.50

Marx, Queen Elizabeth II Coronation, Prince Charles, NM-M, F5 ....$19.50

Marx, Queen Elizabeth II Coronation, Princess Anne, NM, F5 .$19.50

Marx, Queen Elizabeth II Coronation, Princess Margaret, NM-M, F5 ....$19.50

Marx, Queen Elizabeth II Coronation, Put-together English Soldiers, 64-pc set builds 8 guards, complete, NM, F5 ....$29.50

Marx, Queen Elizabeth II Coronation, Queen Elizabeth II, NM, F5 ....$24.50

Marx, Queen Elizabeth II Coronation, Queen Mother, missing 1 point on crown, EX+, F5 ....$9.50

Marx, Religious, Cardinal Spellman, ivory hard plastic, NM, F5 ....$29.50

Marx, Religious, Jesus Christ, 1st version, w/left hand raised, ivory hard plastic, NM, F5 ....$24.50

Marx, Top Shelf, Untouchables' Eliot Ness & Al Capone, NMIP, F5 ....$32.50

Marx, Top Shelf, 60mm, Jackie Gleason as Ralph Kramden, wht hard plastic, sq base, NM, F5 ....$49.50

Marx, Top Shelf, 60mm, Jackie Kennedy, wht hard plastic, sq base, NM, F5 ....$49.50

Marx, Top Shelf, 60mm, Pinky Lee, c NBC, wht hard plastic, sq base, NM, F5 ....$49.50

Papco, Football Players, arms up, blocking pass, H5 ....$2.00

Papco, Football Players, center w/ball, H5 ....$2.00

Papco, Football Players, crouching lineman, H5 ....$1.50

Papco, Football Players, kicker, H5 ....$1.50

Papco, Football Players, quarterback, throwing ball, H5.....$2.00

Papco, Football Players, running to right or left, H5, ea $1.50

Western and Frontier

Britains, Cowboys, kneeling w/guns in both hands, plastic on metal base, 1971, NM $2.25

Britains, Cowboys, mtd, holding lariat w/hands, pistol in holster, plastic on metal base, 1971, NM $3.50

Britains, Cowboys, mtd bank robber w/bandana over face & carrying bag, pistol in hand, plastic on metal base, 1971, NM $3.50

Britains, Cowboys, mtd in buckskin clothes, holds rifle, rope on saddle horn, plastic on metal base, 1971, NM..............$3.50

Britains, Cowboys, standing w/guns, 2 ammo belts across chest, knife in belt, plastic on metal base, 1971, NM.............$2.25

Britains, Indians, on foot, holds spear over head w/right hand, left hand holds shield, plastic on metal base, 1971, NM $2.25

Britains, Indians, on foot, shooting bow & arrow, hatchet in belt, 2 feathers in hair, plastic on metal base, 1971, NM $2.25

Britains, Indians, on foot, wearing wolf headdress, holds spear, shield on bk, plastic on metal base, 1971, NM.............$2.25

Britians, Indians, mtd & wearing headdress, holds bow & arrow, plastic on metal base, 1971, NM $3.50

Gulliver (Brazil), Apache Camp figure set, on lg blister card, H5 ....$18.00

Gulliver (Brazil), Apache Camp figure set, in header bag, H5 ....$12.00

Gulliver (Brazil), Sioux, Sitting Bull, on lg blister card, H5 ....$2.00

Lido, Cowboy, rifle at body, H5...$2.00

Lido, Cowboys, kneeling w/pistol, H5 ....$2.00

Lido, Cowboys, standing, firing rifle, H5 ....$2.00

Lido, Cowboys, standing w/rope, H5 ....$2.00

Lido, Indians, chief, kneeling w/rifle, H5 ....$2.00

Lido, Indians, crawling w/tomahawk, H5 ....$2.00

Lido, Indians, medicine man w/tomahawk & shield, H5.....$2.00

Lido, Pioneers, w/rifle & knife, H5 ....$2.00

Lido, Western Horses, military saddle, walking, H5 ....$1.50

Marx, Alamo, Fort Apache or Ranch; flag pole, hitching rail or campfire, NM, F5 ....$2.50

Marx, Alamo, Fort Apache or Ranch; log peg, for tin building or wall, reddish-brn or dk brn, NM, F5 ....$5.00

Marx, Cavalry, aiming rifle, wide-brimmed hat, steel bl soft plastic, 6", NM+, F5 ....$9.50

Marx, Cavalry, bugler w/rifle at side, steel bl, 6", NM+, F5 .$9.50

Marx, Cavalry, 54mm, being shot, dropping pistol, H5 ......$3.00

Marx, Cavalry, 54mm, kneeling, shooting rifle, H5............$3.50

Marx, Cavalry, 54mm, mtd, blowing bugle, H5 ....$4.00

Marx, Cavalry, 54mm, w/rifle, blowing bugle, H5 ....$2.50

Marx, Cavalry, 54mm, w/sword, holding scabbard, H5.......$2.50

Marx, Cavalry, 54mm, clubbing w/rifle, H5 ....$2.50

Marx, Cavalry, 54mm, mtd, w/flag & pistol, H5 ....$4.00

Marx, Cavalry, 54mm, running w/sword, H5 ....$2.50

Marx, Cavalry, 60mm, dueling w/sword, metallic bl soft plastic, NM, F5 ....$8.50

Marx, Cavalry, 60mm, kneeling & aiming pistol, metallic bl soft plastic, EX+, F5 ....$8.50

Marx, Cavalry, 60mm, kneeling & aiming rifle, metallic bl soft plastic, NM, F5 ....$12.50

Marx, Cavalry, 60mm, officer w/sword & pistol, metallic bl soft plastic, NM, F5 ....$9.50

Marx, Cowboys, 60mm, 8 different rodeo poses, yel soft plastic, ca 1952, NMIP, F5 ....$29.50

Marx, Famous Frontier Americans, 54mm, Bullet, cream, NM, F5 ....$5.50

Marx, Famous Frontier Americans, 54mm, Flint McCullough, cream, NM, F5 ....$49.50

Marx, Famous Frontier Americans, 54mm, Pat Brady, walking w/hammer, wht vinyl, EX+-NM, F5 ....$2.50

Marx, Famous Frontier Americans, 54mm, set of 4: Roy Rogers, Dale Evans, Bullet & Pat Brady, cream, G-VG, F5......$2.00

Marx, Famous Frontier Americans, 60mm, Buffalo Bill, yel hard plastic, w/long rifle intact, NM, F5 ....$16.50

Marx, Famous Frontier Americans, 60mm, Daniel Boone, tan hard plastic, w/long rifle intact, NM-M, F5 ....$18.50

Marx, Famous Frontier Americans, 60mm, Davy Crockett, gray hard plastic, w/long rifle intact, NM-M, F5 ....$22.50

Marx, Famous Frontier Americans, 60mm, Davy Crockett, tan hard plastic, w/long rifle intact, NM-M, F5 ....$18.00

Marx, Famous Frontier Americans, 60mm, Davy Crockett, yel hard plastic, w/long rifle intact, NM, F5 ....$16.50

Marx, Famous Frontier Americans, 60mm, Lone Ranger & Tonto, cream, NMIP, F5 ....$24.50

Marx, Famous Frontier Americans, 60mm, Sitting Bull, w/peace pipe, yel hard plastic, NM, F5 ....$18.50

Marx, Famous Frontier Americans, 60mm, Wyatt Earp, cream, NM, F5 ....$24.50

Marx, Indians, throwing spear or w/war club & spear, pumpkin or rusty brn, beware of reissues, 6", NM+, F5, ea $3.00

Marx, Indians, 54mm, dancer w/drum & headdress, reddish brn, NM, F5 ....$2.00

Marx, Indians, 54mm, standing w/bow & arrow, reddish brn, NM, F5 ....$2.00

Marx, Indians, 54mm, tepee, gray soft plastic, NM, F5.......$6.50

Marx, Indians, 60mm, attacking w/raised tomahawk, lt gray soft plastic, EX+-NM, F5 ....$4.50

Marx, Indians, 60mm, chief w/knife & tomahawk, lt gray soft plastic, EX+-NM, F5 ....$3.50

Marx, Indians, 60mm, mtd w/knife & rifle, gray soft plastic, NM, F5 ....$3.50

Marx, Original, cowboy firing Winchester rifle from hip, 6",
    H5 ....**$5.00**

Marx, Original, cowboy w/2 drawn guns, 6", H5.................**$4.00**

Marx, Original, frontiersman w/knife & tomahawk, 6", H5..**$7.00**

Marx, Original, Indian chief w/spear & shield, 6", H5........**$5.00**

Marx, Original, Indian dancing w/spear & club, 6", H5 .....**$4.00**

Marx, Original, Indian throwing spear, 6", H5...................**$4.00**

Marx, Pioneers, running w/long rifle in left hand, caramel soft
    plastic, 6", NM, F5 ....**$12.50**

MPC, Cowboys, advancing w/left arm out, flesh, H5..........**$2.00**

MPC, Cowboys, walking, hands at side, flesh, H5 ....**$2.00**

MPC, Indians, chief, right arm up, red or bl, H5................**$2.00**

MPC, Indians, crawling, right arm up, gr, H5 ....**$3.00**

MPC, Indians, kneeling, shooting bow, red, H5 ....**$3.00**

MPC, Indians, mtd w/left arm up, red, H5 ....**$3.00**

MPC, Indians, walking, right hand to head, yel, H5 ....**$2.00**

MPC, Pioneers, kneeling & shooting, brn, H5 ....**$1.50**

MPC, Pioneers, mtd w/right arm up, brn, H5.....................**$1.50**

MPC, Pioneers, wagon driver, seated, brn, H5 ....**$1.50**

Timmee, Cowboys, advancing w/rifle, red or blk, H5, ea...**$3.00**

Timmee, Cowboys, mtd, shooting rifle, red, H5..................**$5.00**

Timmee, Cowboys, mtd, waving hat, red, H5 ....**$5.00**

Timmee, Cowboys, sheriff w/2 pistols, gr or yel, H5, ea......**$3.00**

Timmee, Cowboys, standing, shooting rifle, gr or yel, H5, ea.**$3.00**

Timmee, Indians, w/knife & rifle, red, H5 ....**$5.00**

Timmee, Indians, w/tomahawk & lance, red, H5 ....**$4.00**

Timmee, Indians, w/rifle in left hand, H5 ....**$3.00**

Timmee, Indians, squaw, sitting, red or brn, H5 ....**$4.00**

Timmee, Indians, standing, shooting bow, red or gr, H5, ea.**$3.00**

Timmee, Pioneers, advancing w/rifle at body, red, H5........**$3.00**

Timmee, Pioneers, clubbing w/rifle, yel, H5......................**$3.00**

Timmee, Pioneers, w/powder horn & rifle, gray, H5...........**$5.00**

Timmee, Pioneers, scout w/rifle in left hand, flesh, H5 ......**$3.00**

Timmee, Pioneers, standing & shooting rifle, flesh or yel, H5,
    ea...**$3.00**

Plasticville

From the 1940s through the '60s, Bachmann Brothers produced plastic accessories for train layouts such as buildings,
fences, trees, and animals. Buildings often included several
smaller pieces — for instance, ladders, railings, windsocks, etc.
— everything you could ever need to play out just about any sce-
nario. Beware of reissues.

Airport Administration Building, missing sm rotating wind-
    sock o/w complete w/railings, ladders, antenna, etc, M
    (VG box) **$45.00**

Airport Hanger, wht w/red overheads & bl roof, windsock, com-
    plete, M (VG box)...**$50.00**

Bank, very lt gray w/gr canopies, M (VG box)..................**$42.00**

Barn & Barnyard Animals, red barn & silo, wht roofing &
    fences, only 8 animals, barn complete, M, no boxes..**$26.00**

Billboards, gr w/signs for BC Apples, 3-pc, M **$8.00**

Cape Cod House, yel & wht w/dk brn roof, M (VG box)..**$23.00**

Church, wht w/gray roof, steeple w/cross on top, stained glass
    'paper insert' windows, complete (VG box)...............**$37.50**

Fence & Gate Set, MIB **$9.00**

Fire House, 2 overhead doors, M (VG box) **$37.50**

Footbridge, brn, M **$4.50**

Gas Station, lg version w/2 islands & color illus window inserts,
    M (VG box)..**$48.00**

Hospital, 2-story, wht w/bl roof & gray trim, 20 pcs of acces-
    sories, M (VG box)...**$68.00**

New England Ranch, wht house w/yel trim, brn roof, M (VG
    box)..**$34.00**

Outhouse, wht w/red trim, M...**$9.00**

Ranch House, pk w/wht & gray roof, M (VG box)...........**$35.00**

Schoolhouse, red w/wht trim, gray roof, complete w/steeple
    weather vane, M (VG box) **$42.00**

Street Sign, brn, M..**$3.00**

Switch Tower, brn w/gray roof & trim, M (VG box)........**$22.00**

Telephone Poles, brn w/cross support on top, 6 pcs, M......**$5.00**

US Post Office, complete w/exterior lamps, flag & flagpole, color
    illus window inserts, M (VG box) **$40.00**

Wishing Well, brn, M **$8.00**

5 & 10 Cent Store, cream w/red roof, complete w/color illus
    window inserts, M (VG box)...................................**$39.00**

Playsets

Louis Marx is given credit for developing the modern-age
playset, and during the fifties and sixties produced hundreds of
boxed sets, each with the buildings, figures, and accessories that
when combined with a child's imagination could bring any sce-
nario alive, from the days of Ben Hur to medieval battles,
through the cowboy and Indian era, and on up to Cape
Canaveral. Marx's prices were kept low by mass marketing
(through retail giants such as Sears and Montgomery Wards)
and overseas production. But on today's market, playsets are
anything but low-priced; some mint-in-box examples sell for
upwards of $1,000.00. But remember that a set that shows wear
or has even a few minor pieces missing is worth only about half
as much.

Africa Korps, Airfix, 1/32 scale, 29-pc, NMIB..................**$20.00**

Airport, T Cohn, complete, EX **$475.00**

Alamo #3534, Marx, NMIB..**$775.00**

American Airlines Astro Jet Port #4822, Marx, some missing
    pcs), VG (VG box)...**$110.00**

American Airlines International Jet Port #4810, Marx, com-
    plete, NMIB..**$250.00**

American West Indians, Airfix, 1/32 scale, 22-pc, MIB...**$50.00**

Apollo Lunar Station, MPC, complete, NMIB...............**$165.00**

Army & Air Force Training Center, Marx, NMIB........**$100.00**

Astro Base, Ideal, complete, NMIB................................**$300.00**

Atomic Cape Canaveral Missile Base #4525, Marx, NM
    (EX box) **$125.00**

Atomic Cape Canaveral Missle Base Set #2686, Marx, complete
    w/instructions, NM (EX box)................................**$215.00**

Attack Force, unknown mfg, complete set: 20 soldiers, jeep,
    fighter jet & howitzer, 1970s, MIP..........................**$6.00**

Auto-Rama Daytona Tri-Oval Stock Car Race, AC Gilbert
    #19070, NM (VG box)..**$82.50**

Batman's Wayne Foundation, Mego, NRFB...................$550.00

Battle Action Deluxe Combat Set, Ideal, w/4 spring-loaded dioramas, figures & accessories, 1965, scarce, NMIB, A $340.00

Battle Action Playset, Nasta, 40-pc set: 24x18" playmat, soldiers, tanks, planes, etc, plastic, ca 1980, M (EX box) $12.00

Battle Front, Toy Maker, 7 vehicles, cannon, bridge, tents, 25 soldiers & accessories, orig box, EX.....................$85.00

Battle of Bunker Hill, Multiple, complete w/2 cannons, emplacements, flag & 18 soldiers, plastic, ca 1975, MIB $15.00

Battle of the Blue & Gray #4762, Marx, NMIB $265.00

Battle of Waterloo, Giant Plastics, MOC, V1 ....$115.00

Battleground #4169, Marx, w/German & American tanks, soldiers & accessories, MIB.....................................$150.00

Battleground #4756, Marx, 1970s, complete, NMIB, from $120 to..$160.00

Blue & Gray Raid, Giant Plastics, MOC, V1 ....$55.00

Bonanza, Comansi, Spain, 1960s, NMIB1, A, $150.00.

Boot Camp #4645, Marx, EX $215.00

Cape Canaveral Missile Set #4524, Marx, complete, orig box, EX $145.00

Cape Canaveral Missile Set #4526, Marx, NMIB.............$80.00

Captain Gallant of the Foreign Legion #4730, Marx, EX.$600.00

Captain Video Space Port, T Cohn, litho tin building, walls & entrance gate, w/accessories & figures, 1952, MIB, A.$500.00

Castle of the Three-Headed Dragon, Helm, complete, EX (G box)...$70.00

Charge of the Light Brigade, Marx, HO scale, NM (EX box) $265.00

Civil War Centennial, Marx, lg version w/added accessories, NM (EX+ box) $875.00

Colonial Service Station, Marx, MIB $250.00

Construction Camp #4439, Marx, complete, EX (G box).$250.00

Construction Company, Mattel, MIB, T1 ....$15.00

Cragstan Fire Department Set, complete w/4 vehicles & accessories, NMIB...$275.00

Davy Crockett's Official Disney Alamo Gateway, Marx, litho metal, w/2 doors, EX, F5 ....$29.50

Davy Crockett Western Playset, Archer Plastics, 1 wagon wheel missing, 1950s, VG, T1 ....$95.00

Deluxe Santa Fe Trail, Multiple, complete, 1977, MIB (sealed)..$70.00

Disneyland Playset, Marx, EX (rpr box)..........................$600.00

Dixie Diners, Diner Playset, Tyco, 1988, NRFB, H4........$60.00

Dodge City, Ideal, litho tin & plastic, complete w/accessories, MIP $65.00

Doll House Family, Multiple, complete, 1963, MIB $35.00

F-Troop Ft Courage, Multiple, complete, NMIB...........$145.00

Fix-It Stagecoach, Ideal, NMIB....................................$78.00

Fonzie's Garage, Mego, MIB $75.00

Fort Apache, Marx, tin case w/85 pcs, NM, F5 ....$89.50

Fort Apache Stockade #3660, Series 2000, Marx, EX (G box)..$275.00

Fort Cheyenne, Ideal, complete, orig vinyl case, EX+ $95.00

Fort Cheyenne, Ideal, 15x15" fort, 14x14" Indian encampment & figures, appears complete, 1950s, w/carrying case, VG $45.00

Fort Comanche, T Cohn, litho tin, complete w/accessories, NMIB..$85.00

Fort Frontier, MPC, MIB..$25.00

Galaxy Command #4206, complete, NM (VG box) $70.00

Galaxy Lazer Team, Timmee, 25-pc set: figures, robots & monsters, mc solid plastic, ca 1970s, 2" tallest, MIP $12.50

Gallant Men Army #4634, Marx, M (NM box) $245.00

General Store, Marx, HO set, complete, M (G box)........$25.00

Growing Farm Playset, Marx/Sears, tin & plastic, NM (EX box)..$275.00

Guid-A-Traffic #6652, Marx, all plastic, w/up 4½" Buick, 4 buildings, animals, track, etc, incomplete, EX (EX box), A $75.00

Guns of Navarrone, Marx, complete, EX+ (EX box)........$70.00

Heritage Civil War Playset, Marx, mansion, figures & accessories, complete, NMIB...$280.00

Injector Western World, Mattel, 1968, MIB, from $125 to $165.00

Irrigated Garden, Marx, MIB (sealed)..............................$40.00

Jungle Battlefront, MPC, 8 vehicles, 25 figures & accessories, NM (VG box) $100.00

Jungle Wilderness, MPC, MIB......................................$125.00

Junior G-Men Finger Print Set, Hale-Nass Corp, code chart, magnifying lens, Capt badge, etc, complete, NM (NM box), A $98.00

Kennedy Airport, Remco, MIB $100.00

King Kong Magnetic Playset, MPC, instructions only, EX+, F5 ....$2.50

Lazy Days Farm Set, Marx, barn, chicken coop, 60+ animals & accessories, unassembled & complete, ca 1955, NMIP, F5 ....$195.50

Lost in Space Switch & Go Playset, Mattel, orig Sears shipping box, 1966, rare, NMIB, A $834.00

M*A*S*H Military Base, Ideal 60-pc, 1982, MIB, from $125 to $150.00

Marine Base, Ideal, litho tin & plastic, MIB....................$90.00

Medieval Castle, Marx, 25-pc w/arrows, NMIP, F5 ....$32.50

Medieval Castle #4709, Marx, litho tin & plastic, complete w/figures, accessories & instructions, NMIB............$190.00

Miniature Noah's Ark, Hong Kong, MIB........................$40.00

Miniature Noah's Ark, Marx, NMIB................................$65.00

Miniature Troll Village, Marx, NMIB $150.00

Missile Base, MPC, MOC..$55.00

Modern Farm Set #3931, Marx, MIB..............................$365.00

Modern Farm Set #3934, Marx, MIB..............................$175.00

Modern Ranch #4769, Marx, litho tin & plastic, MIB...$260.00

Modern Service Center #3471, Marx, litho tin w/plastic accessories, 1950s, complete, NM (NM box), A..............$340.00

Monster Battle Set, Bandai, vinyl, MIP, E3 ....$35.00

Moon Base, Marx, complete w/instructions, orig box, 1950s, EX, T1...$450.00

Multiple, Castle Attack, 1964, M (EX box).....................$45.00

Munchkinland, Mego, vinyl, 4" Munchkin Mayor doll, Dorothy's bed, unused sticker sheet, complete, 1976, M (EX box), A...$175.00

Nativity Scene, Marx, litho tin manger w/light, pnt figures & accessories, NMIB $150.00

NATO Infantry, Airfix, 1/32 scale, 14-pc, 1983, MIB $15.00

Noble Knights & Vikings' Giant Medieval Castle, Marx, complete, MIB, R4..$175.00

Okinawa War Game, Atlantic, HO scale, complete w/soldiers, vehicles, & accessories, 1945, MIB (minor crushing), H5...$35.00

One-Man Army, Gordy, complete set: 1 soldier, rifle, jet, howitzer, jeep & tank, dk gr plastic, ca 1976, MOC (7x12½")...$5.00

Pee-Wee's Playhouse, MIB (sealed) $100.00

Pet Shop, Marx, litho tin & plastic, complete w/accessories, NM (VG box)...$295.00

Police Station, plastic, orig box, EX, G1 ....$20.00

Prehistoric Playset, Marx, 12 figures, 38 dinosaurs, accessories & 20-pg booklet, 1971, NM (EX box).........................$165.00

Rex Mars Planet Patrol, Marx, 86 pc-set, orig box inserts, M (NM box)...$425.00

Rhine River Battleground, Marx, contents in orig bags, M (VG box)...$175.00

Robin Hood Castle Set, complete, M5, $400.00.

Robin Hood & His Merry Men, Marx, 22-pc, MIB........$150.00

Robot Hands & Face Mask #610, Kilgore, plastic & vinyl, 1951, complete, NM (EX box), A.......................................$228.00

Roy Rogers Mineral City, Marx, building, furniture, figures & accessories, complete, ca 1952, MIB $425.00

Roy Rogers Ranch #3980, Marx, cabin, jeep, 16 figures, orig accessories & instructions, NM (VG- box) $350.00

Roy Rogers Rodeo Ranch #3985, Marx, complete, ca 1952, NM (EX box) $140.00

Sand Castle Set, Transogram, complete w/figures & molds, 1956, MIB..$60.00

Silver City Frontier Town, Marx, complete, 1950s, EX .$240.00

Ski Patrol, MPC, MIB...$85.00

Soldiers of Fortune, Marx, 2-gun set, 24 targets, lg, orig box, EX, A...$140.00

Stagecoach Attack, Timpo, complete w/figures & accessories, NMIB...$58.00

Star Battle, Processed Plastic Co, 5-pc set: heroes, monsters & villians, mc solid plastic, ca 1970s, 4" tallest, MIP.....$12.50

Star Patrol w/Wing Rocket, Processed Plastic Co, 31-pc set, mc solid plastic, ca 1970s, 2" tallest, MIP $12.50

Steve Scout's High Adventure Scout Base, Kenner, 1974, NRFB, H4...$90.00

Steve Scout Warning From Thunderhead Weather Station, Kenner, High Adventure series, 1974, MIB (torn flap), H4...$28.00

Stor-All Station 7, Marx, MIB (sealed) $35.00

Superman, vinyl city w/19 stand-up figures, 1970s, NMIB, T1...$95.00

Swimming Pool, Marx, MIB...$55.00

Tom Corbett Space Academy, Marx, partial set, EX (EX in box), A, $400.00.

Tom Corbett Space Academy #7009, Marx, NMIB.......$650.00

Toy Circus, Revell, complete, EX $250.00

Ultraman City Playset, MIB (sealed) $25.00

US Armed Forces Battle Front, Multiple, lg set, NMIB .$185.00

US Armed Forces Training Center #4144, Marx, 75%, VG+...$90.00

US Armored Division, Timmee, complete set: tank, decals & 20 soldiers, ca 1970s, 2", MIP $6.00

US Army Artillery, Processed Plastic, complete 28-pc set: 26 soldiers, howitzer & jeep, gr, w/decals & flag, 1970s, MIP...$6.00

US Army Camp Training Center, Multiple, 1969, NMIB..$50.00

US Capitol, Master Builder, complete w/35 45mm presidents & instructions, NM (VG box).......................................$75.00

US Naval Base, T Cohn/Superior, complete set, 1954, MIB...$400.00

Vampire's Midnight Madness Haunted Mansion Kit, Walt Disney, MIB (sealed), T1...$85.00

Viking Ship, Renwal, complete, NMIB $160.00

Voice-Control Astronaut Base, Remco, MIB $50.00

Walt Disney World Main Street, NM, O1 ....$150.00

Walt Disney's Television Playhouse, Marx, NM (EX box), A, $575.00.

War of the Worlds, Archer, complete, rare, NMIB.....$1,400.00
Western Playtime, Archer, litho tin coach & wagon, complete, NMIB $50.00

Western Play Time Action Set, Archer Plastics, complete in poor box, 48-piece set, $35.00.

Western Town #2652, Marx, MIB..................................$265.00
Western Town #4229, Marx, G (EX box) $160.00
White House of the US, Marx, full set of Presidents, plastic, ca 1954, 35mm, NM (VG box), F5 ....$59.50
Wild West Play Scene, Britains, plastic figures w/backdrops & accessories, complete, 1970s, MIB.............................$75.00
World War I Air Aces, Remco, 1965, rare, NMIB, from $275 to $325.00
WWI Doughboy Playset, Remco, complete w/biplanes, tank & solders, w/cb backdrops & scenery, 1964, M (NM box), A $200.00

WWII British Commandos, Airfix, 1/32 scale, 28-pc, ca 1980, MIB..$30.00
WWII British Infantry, Airfix, 1/32 scale, 29-pc, MIB.....$40.00
WWII Russians, Airfix, 1/32 scale, 29-pc, MIB $35.00
X-500 Playset, Deluxe Reading, NMIB............................$65.00
Zorro Playset, official issue, orig 79¢ on card, missing ring, o/w complete, T1...$85.00
7th Cavalry, Airfix, 1/32 scale, 29-pc, MIB $50.00

Pressed Steel

Many companies were involved in the manufacture of pressed steel automotive toys which were often faithfully modeled after actual vehicles in production at the time they were made. Because they were so sturdy, some made as early as the 1920s have survived to the present, and those that are still in good condition are bringing very respectable prices at toy auctions around the country. Some of the better known manufacturers are listed in other sections. See also Buddy L; Keystone; Marx; Pedal Cars and Other Wheels Goods; Steelcraft; Structo; Tonka; Tri-Ang; Turner; Wyandotte.

Cars and Busses

Airflow, Cor-Cor, blk w/separate grille, electric lights w/bezels, Bakelite wheels, spare tire, 17", VG, A $1,375.00
Bus, Cor-Cor, gr w/rubber-tired red wheels, 1920s, some damage & rpr, pnt P, 23½", A...$275.00
Bus, Little Jim Playthings, maroon w/solid cream wheels, decals on roof, hood & sides, 24", EX, A $688.00
Chrysler Airflow, Cor-Cor, gr, rstr, 1930s, 16", M5 ....$1,350.00
Coupe, pk body w/burgundy roof, fenders & luggage rack, NP grille, electric lights, missing parts, 14", G, A..........$176.00
Electric Automobile, Knapp, open car, dk gr w/red spoked wheels, 2 bench-type seats, tiller steering, 11½", A.............$2,100.00
Electricar, KoKoMo, yel w/blk trim, NP grille, red wheels w/blk rubber tires, missing driver & 1 hubcap, 11½", VG, A .$99.00
Electricar the Auto Builder, KoKoMo, US, car & truck (may be reassembled), w/track, orig box, VG-EX, A $250.00
Graham Sedan, Cor-Cor, lt gr, plated grille, silver bumper, Bakelite wheels w/gr centers, 20½", VG+, A $1,540.00

Fire Chief's Roadster, Kingsbury, 10" long, 1930s, EX-, D10, $750.00.

Graham Sedan, Cor-Cor, navy bl, plated grille & hubcaps, Bakelite wheels, spare tire, rpl bumpers, 20½", G-VG, A $1,155.00

Model T, Nylint, 1960s, 10", M (VG box), N2 ....$35.00

Police Chief Siren Car, lt & dk gr litho body w/darker gr fenders, NP grille, electric headlights, rpl tires, 14", VG, A .$523.00

Racer, Deco style, bl w/plated silhouette driver, wht rubber tires w/Hubley-type hubs, 7¼", VG-EX, A $105.00

Racer #110, Oh-Boy, pnt & plated, windshield w/folding hinge, metal wheels, loose hinge, 20", G, A $180.00

Streamline Touring Sedan, gr, wood wheels, lt rust on roof, 6", G+, A $50.00

Yellow Taxi, orange-yel & blk, friction, non-working, pnt chips, 11", G-, A $80.00

Construction

Barber Green Gravel Loader, Model Toys, gr & blk, chain driven w/hand-op loading mechanism, orig label, 18", VG-EX, A..$120.00

Crane Truck, Little Jim Playthings, yel-gold & gr w/spoked steel wheels, rubber tires, boon may be repro, 28", VG-EX, A..$880.00

Excavator, Playboy, gr cab, red cabin w/blk roof, Marion decal on bk, missing bucket & 1 headlight, 24½", VG, A $165.00

Excavator, possibly Playboy, red w/blk fr, boom & shovel, red steel wheels, 19 gauge steel, 7", VG, A $154.00

Excavator, yel body, bl roof, blk boom, bucket & wheels, Construction Co decals on sides, chain mechanism, 8", VG, A..$203.00

Michigan Crane #T-24, Nylint, sm hinge pin rpl, o/w orig, VG++, P3...$135.00

Sand Loader, Moline, olive-gr & blk, crank & chain mechanism, chipped pnt, 18¾", G-VG, A $135.00

Steam Shovel, red & gray, 4-wheel platform, marked Riding Toy, 12x6¼x20", G-, A $65.00

Steam Shovel, Sturditoy, gr body, red chassis, blk boom & shovel, orig decals, missing door, needs restringing, G, A..$187.00

Tractor, Wilkins, 1930s, 8½" long, D10, $375.00.

Steam Shovel #502, Big Boy/Kelmet, blk w/red roof & boom, blk extension shovel, decal on boiler, 8½", G, A $248.00

Firefighting

American La France Fire Pumper, Doepke, mk Rossoyne, rubber tires, hose missing, 18½", VG, A................................$90.00

American La France Fire Pumper #7, Sturditoy, red, chemical fire version, long bumper version, working, 26", EX, A...$3,410.00

American La France Water Tower #9, Sturditoy, red, working water pump, headlights, long bumper, 33¼", EX, A...$2,200.00

American La France Water Tower Truck, Sturditoy, red, rubber tires, steers, rstr, 33", G, A.......................................$245.00

Automotive Pumper, Kingsbury, painted pressed steel and wood with rubber tires, 23", G-, A, $500.00.

Bulldog Chemical Fire Truck, Toledo Metal Wheel Co, red cab w/NP tanks, solid wheels, rnd decal on hood, G, A.$1,595.00

Bulldog Mack Jr Fire Truck, red, rubber tires, ladder retracts, hose reel works, steers, missing ladders, 25½", VG, A.........$350.00

City Fire Dept Truck, Little Jim Playthings, dk red, steel wheels, rubber treads, dents, missing parts, 23½", G-, A......$138.00

Fire Chief Siren Coupe, red w/decals on doors, plated grille, electric lights, blk rubber tires, orig box, 14", EX, A.......$413.00

Fire Ladder Truck, Kingsbury (molded into wht rubber tires), dbl ladder raises 40" & rotates, 'leather' seat, 35", VG, A $2,700.00

Fire Pumper, Scheible, pnt steel & wood, red, gr & gold, lt fender damage, pnt chips, 20", G, A $70.00

Fire Pumper/Hillclimber, Dayton (?), open, CI driver & 2nd standing on rear, tin boiler, flywheel, 7x14½", G-, A..........$300.00

Ladder Truck, Kingsbury, double ladder, white rubber tires, ca 1930, 35" long, VG, A, $2,760.00.

Fire Truck, Little Jim Playthings, red, decals on bed, yel stripe decal on hood, rpr steering bracket, 20", G-VG, A ...$88.00

Water Tower #9, Sturditoy, w/spout on end, hand-crank pump, pnt badly chipped, some wear, 12x32" (w/tower down), G, A $400.00

White Aerial Ladder Truck #510, Big Boy, red, steers, wood ladders, diamond decals, crank mechanism, 29½", G, A $550.00

White Aerial Ladder Truck #510, Big Boy/Kelmet, steers, solid wheels, rubber tires, wood ladders, 30", EX, A $1,430.00

White Ladder Truck #504, Big Boy/Kelmet, red, new aluminum canisters, rpl rubber tires & ladder, 26⅝", G, A $440.00

Trucks and Vans

American Express Truck #2, Sturditoy, lt gr w/screen sides, blk fenders, license #402, 26", G+, A $2,970.00

Antiaircraft Truck, Son-ny, USA #120 decal on hood, crank hdl raises & rotates cannon, spring fires marbles, 23", G-, A $523.00

Army Truck, Son-ny, antiaircraft gun on bk, khaki, mk USA #1120, open cab, 12x23", lt rust, overall G, A $250.00

Army Truck, Son-ny, USA decal on ea side of hood, removable cab roof, orig canvas cover, missing tailgage, 26", VG, A $605.00

Army Truck, Sturditoy, khaki, short bumper version, missing headlights & canvas top, 27", G+, A.....................$1,320.00

Brighton Place Dairy Delivery Van, pictures bull on sides, Selected Milk 10-15%..., 18", VG, A $650.00

Bunte Candies Dump Truck, Metalcraft, red cab, wht body, electric lights, balloon Goodrich tires, 4¼x12¼", VG, A $450.00

C-Cab Dump Truck, Son-ny, blk cab & chassis, orange bed & solid wheels, steers (loose), rpr, 25⅞", G, A $358.00

Cebasco Milk Truck, unknown mfg, red, wht & blk, steel hood, wood body, rubber tires, 8 tin cans, 24½", G-VG, A .$963.00

Circus Van, Giant, blk cab, cream cage w/litho inserts of animals, noisemaker crank, flaking pnt, 25¾", G-VG, A $1,320.00

City Co Milk Truck, blk hood & fenders, wht body, electric headlights, old rpt, 18", VG, A $231.00

City Delivery Moving Van, Playboy, bright gr w/wht trim, electric headlights & taillight, missing tailgate, 23", G, A $523.00

City Milk Co Truck, blk & wht, solid wheels, 17½", G-, A .$100.00

Clover Farm Stores Delivery Truck, Metalcraft, gr w/yel lettering, NP grille, electric headlights, 13⅜", EX, A ...$1,265.00

Coal Truck, Giant, red cab w/red striping, blk bed w/red striping, noisemaker crank at front, rstr, 24½", M, A $990.00

Coal Truck, Sturditoy (emblems on bk), separate coal chute, partial rpt, 10¾x8¼x27½", EX, A $2,700.00

Coal Truck #10, Sturditoy, blk on red chassis & wheels, short bumper version, missing headlights & side chute, 26", A $1,430.00

Coal Truck #6, Sturditoy, orange cab & wheels, red chassis, blk fenders, 2 removable dividers in bed, 26¼", EX, A $2,420.00

Construction Co Dump Truck #3, Sturditoy, lt gr cab & bed, red chassis & wheels, blk fenders, worn pnt, 27", VG+, A $1,100.00

Construction Co Dump Truck #5, Sturditoy, blk cab, gr bed, red chassis & wheels, short bumper version, worn pnt, G, A $715.00

Construction Co Steam Shovel, lt bl, wood wheels, scratches, 15½", G-G+, A...$30.00

Contractor's Truck, Bulldog, orange cab w/lt gr bed, solid wheels, decals (orig) placed over Gendron decals, G, A $908.00

CW Brand Coffee Delivery Truck, Metalcraft, red cab, gr box, silver wheels, 5¼x10¾", EX-VG, A $300.00

CW Coffee Wrecker, Metalcraft, blk cab & chassis, navy letters on orange bed, missing boom crank hdl, 10", VG, A $275.00

Dairy Truck & Trailer, Girard, cream & red, electric headlights, 2 orig batteries, orig box, 18¼", M, A $770.00

Delivery Truck, Kingsbury, crank wind, decal: Motor-Driven Truck, bl w/orange stake rack, rubber tires, 10x25", EX, A $4,250.00

Delivery Truck, Metalcraft, closed gr body & blk cab w/: Hardy's Salts, St Louis, metal wheels, 5¼x11¼", VG-EX, A..$900.00

Delivery Truck, Metalcraft (on sides of body), gr box, blk cab & fenders, some chipping/scratching/rust, 5x10¾", A.$275.00

Delivery Truck, Sturditoy, rpt gr & blk, steers, damage to roof & front, rear doors missing, 25", P, A..........................$175.00

Dump Truck, blk rubber tires, ca 1930s, 7", VG, W1 ......$39.00

Dump Truck, Cor-Cor, blk cab & chassis, red dump bed, Bakelite wheels w/red centers, dummy headlights, 23½", EX, A .$660.00

Dump Truck, Cor-Cor, blk w/apple-gr dump bed, Bakelite wheels, emb Cor-Cor Toys on radiator, 23⅛", VG, A $385.00

Dump Truck, Hydraulic; Keystone, label on side, cylinder/cables operate bk, crank in front, well worn, 10½x27", A .$800.00

Dump Truck, Master decal, red cab & chassis, yel bed, Bakelite wheels, 18¼", G-, A...$77.00

Dump Truck, Playboy, red cab, creamy-yel bed, blk steel wheels w/yel centers, electric headlights, 23⅛", VG, A $110.00

Dump Truck, Republic Toys, roof-top cab type, lever operated, considerable scratching/chipping/fading, 8x19½", G-, A $225.00

Dump Truck, Richmond, gr, plastic wheels w/plated metal hubcaps, hand-op dump lever, orig label, 11¾", G, A $55.00

Dump Truck, Richmond, red w/decal on hood, blk Bakelite wheels w/anodized gold tin hubcaps, dual rear tires, 12", EX, A $121.00

Dump Truck, Schieble, red cab & chassis, apple-gr dump bed, steel wheels w/blk tires, 20½", M, A $385.00

Dump Truck, Son-ny, blk, solid red wheels, blk fenders & tailgate, ca 1928, 25⅞", VG, A $468.00

Dump Truck, Sturditoy, closed roof cab, total rpt, 10½x8¼x27", A $625.00

Dump Truck #30, Emmets, blk cab & chassis, red bed w/decals, Bakelite wheels emb Emmets, 20½", G, A...............$605.00

Dump Truck #37, Wolverine, MIB..............................$450.00

Electric Truck, Kingston, gr, orange & blk, red wheels, blk rubber tires, +extra bed, missing headlights, 12⅛", VG, A $72.00

Erector White Express Truck, AC Gilbert, blk, red chassis, solid wheels, blk fenders, oval decals on bed, 25⅛", G-, A $110.00

Esso Stake Truck, Metalcraft, red w/wht bed, bl steel wheels, Goodrich tires, Buy at the Esso Sign, 13½", VG, A..$660.00

Express Truck, att Republic, blk cab & chassis, gray bed & wheels w/red centers, 24-gauge steel, 13", G, A $143.00

Express Truck, Metalcraft, red, Express in yel letters on navy stake bed, Goodrich tires, rpl grille, 12½", EX+, A..........$1,045.00

Federal Storage Moving Van, Playboy, gr & wht, electric lights, missing tailgate, 23", G, A..$468.00

Ford Econoline Dog Kennel Truck, Nylint, w/dogs, NMIB $165.00

Hardy's Salts Delivery Truck, Metalcraft, 5¼x11", G-, A .$65.00

Hardy's Salts Wrecker, Metalcraft, red body, boom in bk, 4x10¼", EX, A..$400.00

Heinz Pickles Truck, Metalcraft, electric lights, some pnt touch-up, 5x12", VG, A..$200.00

Heinz Pickles Truck #1, wht w/chartreuse wheels, Goodrich tires, electric headlights, 12", NM (VG box), A $908.00

Hercules Sr. Truck, Bandai, heavy gauge, 1969, 7½", $55.00.

Hoffman's Ice Cream Truck, Playboy, red cab, cream van, non-headlight version, w/3 tin cans, VG, A $440.00

Hood's Ice Cream Truck, Little Jim Playthings, red w/decals on van, decaled stripes on hood, 21⅝", P, A $165.00

Ice Truck, Lincoln, gr & yel w/letters decaled on sides, blk rubber tires, +glass 'ice,' 1949, 13", NM, A....................$400.00

Ice Truck, Lincoln, red w/gr bed, mc decals on sides & hood, sm pnt chips on fender, orig box, 13¼", NM, A $176.00

JC Penney Dump Truck, Little Jim Playthings, yel w/gr dump bed & wheels, rubber tires, 25", G-, A.....................$300.00

JC Penney Mack Dump Truck, Little Jim Playthings, red cab & solid wheels, khaki bed, 22¾", VG, A $440.00

JC Penney Mack Open-Cab Army Truck, Little Jim Playthings, khaki w/solid red wheels, canvas cover, 23", VG, A..$468.00

Jungle Wagon Ford Econoline Truck, Nylint, missing animals, 1960s, 12", NM, A3..$85.00

Kidd's Marshmallow Delivery Semi Truck, Nylint, 1970s, MIB, T1..$45.00

Kroger Food Express Truck, Metalcraft, orange w/plated wheels, 1st series grille, complete, 11", VG, A $385.00

Long Distance Moving Van, Son-ny, blk w/red van, decal ea side, solid wheels, drop tailgate, pnt loss, ca 1928, VG, A $825.00

Mack Dump Truck, Ezra Welding, w/yel wheels & rubber tires, 24", M, A..$325.00

Mobilgas Mack C-Cab Tank Truck, Les-Paul, red w/blk fenders & chassis, tandem axles w/dual wheels, 1988, 28½", NM, A $495.00

Moving Van, Cor-Cor, blk cab, fenders & chassis, royal bl body, gray wheels w/orange centers, 23½", VG-EX, A......$330.00

Moving Van, Son-ny, blk cab, orange van & solid wheels, blk fenders (bondo-type rpr), missing tailgate, 26", G-VG, A $660.00

National Dairy Ice Cream Truck, Playboy, loss to decals, red w/cream van, non-headlight version, 21½", G, A ...$143.00

Oil Co Tank Truck & Trailer, Sturditoy, red, headlights, long bumper, crank hdl, dual rear wheels, 33½", VG, A .$3,960.00

Oil Tanker, Sturditoy, red, spigot at rear, cap atop, on 6-wheel truck chassis, some scratches, 1929, 27", A $2,600.00

Pines Delivery Truck, Metalcraft, advertising on side, NRA decal on top, total rstr, 5¼x12", NM, A $175.00

Playboy Ice Cream Truck, Playboy, red cab, cream van, red wheels (1 cracked), 21½", G, A $231.00

Playboy Trucking Co Dump Truck, wht, rubber tires, pnt chips & scratches, rear gate missing, 19½", P, A.................$65.00

Playboy Trucking Co Wrecker #1, wht w/blk body, blk rubber tires (very poor), red hubs, 20", NM, A $523.00

Playboy Trucking Co Wrecker #2, Playboy, wht w/blk boom, non-headlight version, red wheels, rubber tires, 19", G-VG, A $215.00

Police Department Truck, Sturditoy, bl, bl wheels w/rubber tires, covered open cab, decals, headight gone, pnt P, 25", A $880.00

Police Patrol Van, blk cab, dk bl van w/screened sides, solid orange wheels, missing 1 brass handrail, 27¾", VG, A $1,320.00

Popcorn Truck, Ezra Welding, pnt w/varnished wood, plastic windows, yel trim & wheels, 20", EX, A $550.00

Pure Oil Co Truck, Metalcraft, bl w/NP radiator & bumpers, 3 lights on top, 2 NP headlights, Deco look, 4½x15", EX, A $1,050.00

Richfield Gasoline Truck, American National, original decals, 27", VG, A, $1,400.00.

Shell Motor Oil Stake Truck, Metalcraft, red cab & chassis, yel bed, electric lights, rpl grille, 12", G-, A $132.00

Shell Motor Oil Stake Truck, Metalcraft, red cab & chassis, yel bed, Goodrich tires, 12½", EX, A............................$880.00

Silvertown Pure Oil Co Oil Truck, plated grille & bumperettes, electric lights, 14⅞", G, A.........................$605.00

Sinclair Mack Truck Tanker & Trailer, Ezra Welding, gr w/yel wheels, rubber tires, 40", M, A...............................$500.00

Smile Stake Truck, red w/Drink Smile in ivory, electric headlights, Goodrich tires, steel wheels, 12⅜", VG+, A.$798.00

Stake Body Truck, streamlined, orange, wood wheels, 6", EX, A $25.00

Stake Body Truck, streamlined, red, rubber tires, 6", VG, A $40.00

Stake Truck, blk cab & chassis, orange bed & wheels, T-1929 license plate, decal on radiator, 22½", M, A............$660.00

Stake Truck, Cor-Cor, red body, blk cab & chassis, missing battery & headlights, 7¼x24", VG, A $100.00

Stake Truck, red & gr w/wooden wheels, 12½", EX, A $71.00

Stake Truck, red cab & chassis, tinplated grille, gr bed w/decals, Bakelite wheels, sm scratches, 11¼", NM, A..........$132.00

State Truck, finished in bl w/gold running boards, inertia drive, some pnt loss, 13", G, A...$187.00

Sunshine Biscuits Express Truck, Metalcraft, red cab & chassis, yel bed, dummy headlights, orig box, 11¾", G, A..$143.00

Sunshine Biscuits Van, Metalcraft, yel w/bl trim, electric lights, fenders over rear wheels, 5¼x3½x12¼", EX, A.......$450.00

Tank Truck, Les-Paul, red, aluminum wheels, front bumper, dummy headlights, fillable tank, ca 1980s, orig box, 25", M, A..$523.00

Telephone Service Truck, Lincoln Toys, dark green with yellow decals, 14", VG, M5, $200.00. (M: $450.00.)

Tractor w/Side-Dumping Hopper Trailer, red w/blk trailer fr, blk rubber tires w/red hubcaps, 11", NM, A...................$330.00

Tractor w/Removable Dump Trailer, Girard, red tractor w/orange trailer, blk rubber tires, red hubcaps, 11¼", NM-M, A $286.00

Tractor w/Removable Stake Bed Trailer, red w/blk rubber tires, red steel hubcaps, 10½", M, A $198.00

Tractor-Trailer, Kingsbury, w/CI drive, rubber tires, rpr trailer hook, 11¼", G-G+, A $150.00

Tractor-Trailer Tank Truck, red cab w/orange trailer, blk rubber tires w/red hubcaps, bell under cab, 11⅜", M, A $176.00

Traveling Store Truck, Sturditoys, original orange and black paint, rubber tires, minor repair and scratches, 26" long, G-, A, $450.00.

Traveling Store Truck, Sturditoy, orange & blk, rubber tires, steers, doors open, chassis rpr, 26", G-, A $450.00

US Army Truck, American National, drab olive w/blk striping, mk US Army #311 on sides, noisemaker crank, 26¾", G-, A...$743.00

US Mail Truck, Kiddies Metal Toys, pnt sheet metal, gr, red wheels, doors open (1 missing), 21½", VG-EX, A...$150.00

Van, Metalcraft, blk cab & chassis, Metalcraft St Louis in yel on gr body, dummy headlights, plated grille, 11", EX-, A $385.00

White Dump Truck, Burdette Murray, blk cab & fenders, gray bed, red chassis & wheels, crank mechanism, 25⅞", G, A...$715.00

White Dump Truck, Burdette Murray, blk w/red chassis & wheels, CI radiator & dual wheels, rpt, roof cut off, 26", G-, A...$220.00

White Dump Truck #501, Big Boy, blk body & bed, red chassis & wheels, crank mechanism, steel wheels, 25¾", EX, A $1,540.00

White King Delivery Truck, Metalcraft, red cab & chassis, yel box, 4x4x12", EX pnt, A $400.00

Whiting Milk Truck, Playboy, gr, Presenting a New...Product decal on sides, 3 milk glass bottles (Marx), 18", EX-, A..$1,018.00

Wix Filters Tractor-Trailer Promotional, Nylint, ca 1981, 21¼", MIB, W1 ....$69.00

Wrecker, Kingsbury, 1930s, 11" long, EX, D10, $425.00.

Wrecker, Metalcraft, blk cab & chassis, plated boom, wheels & grille, mk Towing & Repairs, missing hdl, 10", VG-EX, A...$385.00

Wrecker, Metalcraft, red cab & chassis, ivory bed w/Goodrich Silvertown Tires on sides, electric headlights, 12", VG, A...$286.00

Wrecker (Deco model), Metalcraft, red, ivory bed, mk Goodrich Silvertown Tires, electric headlights, 12¾", G-, A..$413.00

Wrigley's Spearmint Express Truck, rpt wheel hubs, rpr tire/wheel, allover wear, 9x23", G-G-, A.................$500.00

Miscellaneous

Locomotive, Hillclimber, pnt pressed steel, G.................$210.00

Motor Home, Nylint, EX..$125.00

Trolley Car, yel w/red roof, cast wheels, missing steering wheel & pentagrams/minor dents, 22", M5.......................$295.00

Wheelbarrow, red w/blk rubber tires, 7½", VG, W1.........$29.00

Trolley Car, Kingsbury, orange paint, 1930s, 10" long, EX, D10, $375.00.

Promotional Vehicles

Miniature Model T Fords were made by Tootsietoy during the 1920s, and though they were not actually licensed by Ford, a few of these were handed out by Ford dealers to promote the new models. In 1932 Tootsietoy was contacted by Graham-Paige to produce a model of their car. These 4" Grahams were sold in boxes as sales promotions by car dealerships as well as through the toy company's catalog. But it wasn't until after WWII that distribution of 1/25 scale promotional models and kits became commonplace. Early models were of cast metal, but during the 1950s, manufacturers turned to plastic. Not only was the material less costly to use, but it could be molded in the color desired, thereby saving the time and expense previously involved in painting the metal. Though the early plastic cars were prone to warp easily when exposed to heat, by the mid-'50s, they had become more durable. Some were friction powered, and others held a battery-operated radio. Advertising extolling some of the model's features was often embossed on the underside. Among the toy manufacturers involved in making promotionals were

National Products, Product Miniatures, AMT, MPC, and J-Han. Interest in fifties' and sixties' models is intense, and the muscle cars from the sixties and early seventies are also very collectible. The more popularity the actual model attained, the more popular the promotional is with collectors.

Check the model for damage, warping, and amateur alterations. The original box can increase the value by as much as 30%. Jo-Han has reissued some of their 1950s and 1960s Mopar and Cadillac models as well as Chrysler's Turbine Car. These are usually priced between $20.00 and $30.00. Our advisor for this category is Aquarius Antiques (A3).

1954 Pontiac, plastic w/metal undercarriage, blk, 2-door w/no interior detail, 7¾", VG...$50.00

1954-55 Corvette, plastic w/metal undercarriage, wht w/red interior, 6½", VG...$100.00

1955-56 T-bird, plastic, turq w/wht top & silver seat panels, friction, 8", VG..$20.00

1955-56 T-bird, plastic w/metal undercarriage, red w/red & wht interior, friction, 7¼", VG.....................................$65.00

1957 Chevy Belair Convertible, SMP, bronze w/2-tone interior, friction, NM...$130.00

1957 T-bird, AMT, plastic w/metal undercarriage, lt bl body w/wht & gold interior, friction, orig box, 7", VG, A .$45.00

1957 Thunderbird, plastic body with metal undercarriage, beige with cream and gold interior, friction, 7", VG-EX, A, $85.00.

1957 T-bird, red, MIB...$100.00

1957 T-bird Convertible, AMT, red w/chrome trim, EX+, A3..$45.00

1958 Corvette Roadster, plastic w/metal undercarriage, 1-pc body & interior, 6½", NM......................................$350.00

1958 Nomad Station Wagon, SMP, bl & wht, friction, NM $130.00

1958 Pontiac Bonneville, AMT, metallic bl, friction, NM $100.00

1958 T-bird, plastic w/metal undercarriage, wht over tan, gold seat panels, 8", VG+...$50.00

1958 T-bird, plastic w/metal undercarriage, wht over turq, gold seat panels, friction, 8", NM (VG box)....................$70.00

1959 T-bird Convertible, AMT, plastic w/metal undercarriage, copper w/gold seat panels, friction, 8", EX (VG box), A $35.00

1959 T-bird Convertible, plastic w/ metal undercarriage, yel top, wht seat panels, friction, 8", VG $20.00

1960 T-bird, plastic, wht over red, silver seat panels, 7½", NM (AMT illus box) $60.00

1960 T-bird, plastic w/metal undercarriage, pale yel, silver seat trim, friction, 8", EX $75.00

1961 Comet, silver, NM $65.00

1961 T-bird Convertible, AMT, plastic w/metal undercarriage, pale bl, silver seat trim, friction, 8", VG $90.00

1962 Corvette Roadster, plastic, off-wht w/silver seat trim & detailed undercarriage, friction, 6¾", VG..............$120.00

1962 T-bird Sport Roadster, plastic, blk w/silver seat panels, tonneau cap, detailed undercarriage, friction, 8", EX.........$170.00

1963 Ford Galaxie, cream, EX....................................$50.00

1963 T-bird, plastic, off-white, lift-out seat panels, detailed undercarriage listing features, 8", VG+, A $80.00

1963 T-bird Convertible, red w/tonneau cap, detailed undercarriage, friction, 8", EX $160.00

1964 T-bird, AMT, plastic, blk, detailed undercarriage, plain box, 8¼", EX...$100.00

1964 T-bird, radio, Philco, plastic, gold, not working, 8", VG...$25.00

1965 Corvette, plastic, silver, lt scratches, 6¾", VG $275.00

1965 Ford Fairlane 500, tan, 2-door hardtop, NM, A3.....$50.00

1965 Mustang, AMP, plastic, battery-op, 16", NMIB $175.00

1965 Mustang, plastic, bl, detailed undercarriage, minor scratches, 7", VG...$50.00

1965 Mustang Pace Car, plastic, off-wht coupe w/letters & stripes for Indy 500 Pace Car, mtd on wooden base, VG, A $110.00

1965 Mustang 2+2 Fastback, all plastic, red with detailed undercarriage, 7", VG, A, $60.00.

1965 T-bird, plastic, burgundy hard top, detailed undercarriage listing features, in Jo-Han box, 8", EX.....................$50.00

1965 T-bird, plastic, red, detailed undercarriage listing features, 8¼", VG...$20.00

1965 T-bird Convertible, plastic, detailed undercarriage listing features, 8", VG, A $130.00

1966 Mustang, plastic, red, detailed undercarriage listing features, 7¼", VG+..$70.00

1967, T-bird, radio, Philco, plastic, yel, not working, 8", VG .$15.00

1967 T-bird, plastic, avacodo, plain undercarriage, friction, not working, 8¼", VG+ $30.00

1967 T-bird Coupe, AMT, plastic, dk red, plain undercarriage, 8¼", EX $45.00

1968 Camaro Convertible, EX $50.00

1968 Corvette, plastic, red, detailed undercarriage, windshield cracked, missing 1 tail pipe extension, 7", G $110.00

1968 Corvette, plastic, silver w/gray interior, detailed undercarriage, VG...$250.00

1968 T-bird, AMT, plastic, bl, 8¼", NMIB $45.00

1970 Camaro, plastic, gr, detailed undercarriage, 7", VG, A $75.00

1970 El Durado, plastic body, yellow, MIB, D10, $125.00.

1970 Javelin, wht, MIB...$60.00

1970 Pontiac GTO, red, M.......................................$65.00

1974 Cadillac Eldorado, gold w/wht interior, right windshield post missing, A3...$25.00

1974 Corvette, plastic, red, detailed undercarriage, 7½", NM $150.00

1975 Corvette, plastic, orange flame, detailed undercarriage, 7½", NMIB...$100.00

1976 Corvette, plastic, metallic mahogany, detailed undercarriage, 7½", NMIB...............................$110.00

1977 Corvette, plastic, silver, detailed undercarriage, 7½", NMIB $75.00

1978 Chevrolet Monza 2+2, silver & bl, EX+, A3 ....$12.00

1978 Corvette, plastic, 1-tone silver (rare), detailed undercarriage, 7½", EX...$100.00

1978 Corvette, plastic, 1-tone silver (rare), detailed undercarriage, 7½", MIB...$150.00

1979 Corvette, plastic, red, detailed undercarriage, 7½", NMIB $30.00

1980 Corvette, plastic, yel, detailed undercarriage, 7½", NMIB $20.00

1981 Corvette, plastic, silver, detailed undercarriage, 7½", NMIB...$55.00

1984 Corvette, plastic, gray w/detailed undercarriage, 7", NMIB...$25.00

1985 Corvette, plastic, metallic bl w/gray interior, detailed undercarriage, 7", EX.....................................$15.00

1987 Corvette, plastic, red, detailed undercarriage, 7", NMIB...$20.00

1989 Corvette Convertible, plastic, blk, detailed undercarriage, 7", NMIB...$40.00

1990 Corvette Convertible, plastic, red, detailed undercarriage, 6¾", EX..$20.00

1990 Taurus Sho, Ertl, plastic, wht w/detailed undercarriage, 7¼", NMIB..$15.00
1991 Corvette ZR-1, AMT, plastic, Quasar bl, orig box, EX, A...$25.00

Pull Toys

Pull toys from the 1800s often were made of cast iron with bells that were activated as they moved along on wheeled platforms or frames. Hide and cloth animals with glass or shoebutton eyes were also popular, and some were made of wood. See also specific companies such as Fisher-Price.

Boy on Alligator, American, by NN Hill, CI, boy straddling alligator on 4-wheeled base w/bell, 6", G+, A $990.00
Buffalo Hunt, Fallows, rider on wht horse pursuing 3 buffalo, 1886, very worn pnt, 9", A.................................$1,495.00
Bull, hide covered, cvd mouth & nostrils, glass eyes, wood platform w/spoked wheels, normal wear, 10½", A.........$130.00
Butting Billys, American, Gong Bell, CI, 2 goats on 4-wheeled base w/center bell, 7½", G, A $1,155.00

Camel, Althof Bergmann, ca 1870s, 9", EX, D10, $6,500.00.

Clown & Pony, American, by Watrous, CI & sheet metal, 4-wheeled base, 10", VG, A $385.00
Clown on Donkey, American, by NN Hill, CI, 4-wheeled base w/bell on tale of donkey, 6", EX, A......................$1,155.00
Cow, leather-covered compo, glass eyes, mooing sound, missing 1 udder & horns, wooden platform, VG $260.00
Dog, American, pnt CI & sheet metal, 4-wheeled base w/bell, 6", VG+, A $440.00
Dog, pnt tin, brn dog, gr platform, wood wheels, pnt chips & wear, solder rpr, 9¾", G, A................................$110.00

Elephant, hollow molded compo w/pnt eyes, Indian riding on top, hinged panel opening in side, rpr, 17", G-, A...$200.00
Elephant, pnt tin, gray w/red howdah, spoked CI wheels, pnt chips, creases, 9", G, A $300.00
Flour Delivery Wagon, pnt & stenciled wood w/stuffed cloth sacks, 2 cloth-covered horses w/glass eyes, 24", VG, A...$575.00
Foxy Grandpa, American, by Gong Bell, CI, grandpa at helm of 3-wheeled base w/2 kids above front wheel, 7", VG+, A...$357.50
Goat, hide-covered w/glass eyes, wood horns, head activates noise, wood base w/iron wheels, 17", VG-EX, A $750.00
Horse & Cart, hide-covered horse w/felt blanket, mtd on wood base w/wheels, pulls pnt wood flat-bed cart, 27", G-G+, A $160.00
Horse & Rider, CI rearing horse on wheeled base w/bell, 30% pnt left, 6½", M5 ....$170.00
Horse w/Jockey, Fallows, jockey in red on blk horse w/gray mane, gr 4-wheeled platform (some rust), 7", A......$900.00

Horse-drawn Milk Wagon, Mason & Parker, ca 1895, 24" long, EX, D10, $2,700.00.

Horse-Drawn Streetcar, litho tin & pnt wood, yel & red w/gr base & roof, 2 pnt wood horses, 12", G, A.................$90.00
Jonah & the Whale Bell Ringer, CI, blk whale on 4-wheeled bl platform, 1895, 6½", A......................................$1,000.00
Kicking Mule, American, by Gong Bell, mule on 4-wheeled base w/bell, 8", VG+, A $632.50
Landau, American, Hubley, CI, coach rpt, 16", VG, A $1,540.00
Landing of Columbus, American, by J&E Stevens, pnt CI, gold & silver, Columbus on boat w/3 wheels & bell, 7", VG+, A...$440.00
Lion, pnt papier-mache, wool mane & underside, glass eyes, damage & rpr, 17", P-, A.......................................$100.00
Log Cart, American, Kenton, man seated on lg log pulled by 2 horses, 15", VG+, A $412.50
Man Washing Clothes, Eve Journal (NY), red, yel & bl pnt wood, 8", G+, A $30.00
Mary & Lamb, Fallows, pnt tin, bl & wht Mary, yel bell, 4-wheeled platform, chipped pnt, seam separated, 1890, 6½", A..$1,900.00

Lion on Platform, painted tin, ca 1880, 9" long, A, $1,000.00.

Monkey Bell Ringer, American, J&E Stevens, CI, monkey seated in 4-wheeled seat w/lg bell, extremely rare, 7", VG, A $2,640.00

Poodle Dog Bell Ringer, clown swivels on wheeled base, 1900, pnt chipped, 7½", A.............................$1,450.00

Pure Milk Cart, American, Mason & Parker, CI & sheet metal, paper labels, horse-drawn, labels & pnt worn, 23", G, A...$308.00

Seesaw, American, CI, 2 boys on seesaw w/4-wheeled base, 6", G, A..$275.00

Sheep, pnt emb tin w/red ball, emb tin base w/CI wheels, lt pnt loss & rust, 7½", G-VG, A.....................$280.00

Sparerib and Buttercup, Nifty, tin, ca 1920s, 8", NM, D10, $1,650.00.

St Claus Wagon, Germany, pnt wood, maroon & yel, cloth-covered horse w/glass eyes, wheeled wood base, 29", G-VG, A..$875.00

Train Engine, American, pnt tin, window stenciling on cab & fr, early, 1 air bag loose, usual pnt loss, 7x12", A.....$550.00

Tramp, Gong Bell, CI, figure moves chains from side to side to ring bell, 1900, pnt chipped, 6", VG+, A $850.00

Two Soldiers, American, Watrous, CI & sheet metal, 2 men on 4-wheeled base w/3 bells, 10", VG, A.....................$275.00

Two Tramps, American, by Gong Bell, CI, 2 tramps w/bells on 4-wheeled base, very rare, 6½", A..........................$550.00

Two-Horse Surrey, American, Hubley, CI w/steel & brass, 15", G, A...$495.00

Two-Seat Horse Trap, Pratt & Letchworth, 13", G+, A .$577.50

Water Tower, American, Hubley, CI, tower on wagon pulled by 3 horses, rare, 27", VG, A.......................................$440.00

Whoa Dar Caesar, American, NN Hill, CI, japanned finish, Black man on donkey on 4-wheeled base w/bell, 5¾", EX, A...$2,530.00

Puppets and Marionettes

Though many collectible puppets and the smaller scale marionettes were made commercially, others were handmade and are today considered fine examples of folk art and may often sell for several hundred dollars. See also Character Collectibles.

Black Woman, marionette, folk art carving, composition features, moving eyes, mouth, and breasts, in red sequined dress, 23", VG, A, $175.00.

Big Bad Wolf, Pelham marionette, EX, M9 ....$250.00

Bimbo Clown, Hazelle's marionette, compo, M9, minimum value...$35.00

Black Peppy, Hazelle's talking marionette, M, M9 ....$150.00

Buckaroo Bob, Hazelle's talking marionette, blk outfit, rare, EX, M9 ....$275.00

Calypso Boy, marionette w/bongo drum, barefoot, open & close eyes, movable mouth, 18", MIB, M9.......................$145.00

Caterpillar, Pelham marionette, MIB, M9 ....$95.00

Charlie Clown, Hazelle's talking marionette, MIB, M9 .$225.00

Chinese Gold Monkey, rod puppet, dressed in satin, open & close eyes, movable mouth, 24", M, M9..................$450.00

Cinderella, Pelham marionette, MIB, M9..........................$95.00

Cinderella Maiden, Hazelle's talking marionette, M, M9 ..$175.00

Clever Willie, Pelham marionette, trick clown, MIB, M9.$175.00

Clown, marionette, 1960s, NMIB, T1.............................$55.00

Compo head, papier-mache torso, partial wood arms, pull rings activate mouth, eyes, eyebrows & head, 26", VG, A.$325.00

Cop, Pelham marionette, movable mouth, MIB, M9 .....$120.00

Dick & Sally, Hazelle's marionette, EX, M9, pr................$85.00

Farmer, Pelham marionette, movable mouth, MIB, M9.$120.00

Fortune Teller, Hazelle's talking marionette, EX, M9 ....$150.00

Fritzi, Pelham marionette, MIB, M9..................................$60.00

Gepetto, Pelham marionette, MIB, M9 ....$125.00

Gomez Addams, hand puppet, 1968, VG, T1 ....$95.00

Hansel & Gretl, Hazelle's talking marionette, M, M9....$150.00

Indian, gender-changing marionette, M, M9 ....$75.00

Indian Brave, Hazelle's marionette, M, M9 ....$100.00

Jim-Bob & Suzy Pigtail, Curtis Craft marionette, 1950s, EX, M9, pr..$500.00

Jocko, unmk, EX, G4 ....$75.00

King & Queen, Pelham marionette, MIB, M9...............$175.00

Knight, Sicillian down-rod marionette, 40", EX, M9 .....$500.00

Little Boy Blue, Hazelle's marionette, compo, MIB, M9 .$275.00

Little Red Riding Hood, Hazelle's marionette, NM.........$35.00

Little Red Riding Hood Theatre, Germany, cloth-covered box's front drops down, 3 wood figures inside, 24x15x14", EX, A..$550.00

Lucifer, Effanbee marionette, EX, M9............................$350.00

Magician, folk art, compo head w/blk papier-mache top hat, jtd wood body, in blk & wht tuxedo & cape, 23", VG, A..$190.00

Man w/bald head, checked coat, wht vest, bl/wht pants; ugly lady in dress & pantaloons, hand cvd, ea 27", EX, A, pr $300.00

McBoozle, Pelham marionette, 1948, EX, M9 ....$125.00

Monk, Pelham ventriloquist, rod-control hands, M, M9.$250.00

Monkey, Pelham ventriloquist, M, M9 ....$200.00

Mortimer Snerd, hand puppet, 1944, orig box, G, M9 ...$150.00

Native Warrior, marionette, carries spear & shield, head cvd from coconut, 24", EX, M9......................................$200.00

Old Jocko, unmk, very worn, G4.....................................$45.00

Old Pappy, Hazelle's marionette, compo, MIB, M9........$275.00

Lion Tamer, marionette, folk art carving, composition head, jointed wood body, in circus attire, 25", VG, A, $70.00; Magician, marionette, folk art carving, composition head with black papier-mache top hat, jointed wood body, in tuxedo and cape, 23", VG, A, $190.00.

Woodsman, marionette, composition head with molded and painted features, glass eyes, leather boots, paint chips and losses, 19", G, A, $100.00.

Patty, skater marionette, Peter Puppet Playthings, orig box, EX, M9 ....$125.00

Peppy, Hazelle's talking marionette, M, M9 ....$150.00

Pink-Dressed Girl, Hazelle's marionette, compo hands, EX, M9 ....$75.00

Pirate, Pelham marionette, movable mouth, MIB, M9..$120.00

Prince Charming, Pelham marionette, MIB, M9 ....$95.00

Rosita the Gypsy, Hazelle's talking marionette, MIB, M9 .$350.00

Sailor, Hazelle's talking marionette, M, M9 ....$200.00

Sambo, Hazelle's marionette, compo, EX, M9 ....$275.00

Schoolmaster, Pelham marionette, movable mouth, MIB, M9...$120.00

Simple Simon, Hazelle's marionette, EX, M9 ....$95.00

Snake Charmer, Pelham marionette, w/snake, MIB, M9..$250.00

Soupy Sales, Knickerbocker, marionette, 1966, VG.........$90.00

Straw Man, Hazelle's marionette, M, M9.........................$70.00

Suzybell Clown, Hazelle's talking marionette, MIB, M9, minimum value $100.00

Tyrolean Girl, Pelham marionette, MIB, M9 ....$60.00

Voodoo Witch, Hazelle's marionette, M, M9 ....$125.00

Voodoo Witch, Hazelle's talking marionette, M, M9.....$200.00

Walter, Pelham ventriloquist, Sherlock Holmes-type hat, M, M9 ....$175.00

Warrior, Shirley & Williams marionette, wicked caricature of African tribal figure, 1940s, 30", EX, M9.................$600.00

Widow, fully jtd wood, molded compo & pnt features, nylon hair, blk dress, face soiled, 22", VG, A........................$25.00

Wild Bill Cody, Hazelle's talking marionette, M, M9 ....$275.00

Puzzles and Picture Blocks

Jigsaw puzzles have been around almost as long as games. The first examples were handcrafted from wood, and they are extremely difficult to find. Most of the early examples featured moral subjects and offered insight into the social atmosphere of their time. By the 1890s jigsaw puzzles had become a major form of home entertainment. Cube puzzles or blocks were often made by the same companies as board games. Early examples display lithography of the finest quality. While all subjects are collectible, some (such as Santa blocks) often command prices higher than games of the same period. Our puzzles advisor is Bob Armstrong (A4). See also Character Collectibles.

Allerford N Somerset, Russell, plywood, 254 interlocking pcs, color-line cut, complete, orig box, 1977, 9x9", EX, A4 ....$35.00

Animal Pets, Platt & Munk, set of 3, 1941, MIB..............$28.00

Autumn, Gebhard-GMC, plywood, 250 edge-interlocking pcs, 1930s, complete, orig box, 1930s, 10x12", EX, A4 ....$25.00

Basket of Flowers, Rollo Purrington, 214 interlocking pcs, complete, orig box, 1930s, 10x14", EX, A4 ....$28.00

Blacksmith Shop, plywood, 500 interlocking pcs, strip cut, complete, orig box, 1950s, 16x20", EX, A4 ....$30.00

Blossom Time, Hayter-Victory, plywood, 600 interlocking pcs, strip cut, complete, orig box, 1970s, 16x20", EX, A4..$60.00

Blown-Up Steamer, fire engine puzzle, Milton Bradley, paper litho on wood, complete, 1870s, VG (G box) $200.00

Battleship Picture Puzzle Cubes, McLoughlin Bros., full-color litho paper blocks, set of twenty for six different puzzles, G in wooden box, 12½" long, A, $85.00.

Blue Bonnet Hills, Will B Bean, plywood, 271 interlocking pcs, complete, 11x14", EX, A4 ....$35.00

Bluebirds Bring Happiness, plywood, 305 interlocking pcs, color line cut, complete, 1930s, 13x10", EX, A4 ....$45.00

Bowl of Flowers, Rollo Purrington, plywood, 245 interlocking pcs, complete, orig box, 1930s, 10x14", EX, A4 ....$30.00

Boy Diving Into Mountain Pool, plywood, 159 interlocking pcs, 2 rpl pcs, 1940s, 11x9", EX, A4 ....$20.00

Canal in Venice, Ken-Way, plywood, 200 interlocking pcs, 1 pc rpl, orig box, 1930s, 12x9", EX, A $30.00

Castle in the Air, Parker/Pastime, plywood, stories at hearth, 105 pcs (1 rpl), 1910s, 10x7", EX, A4 ....$20.00

Chase, Bradley-Piedmont, plywood, fox-hunt scene, 200 interlocking pcs, complete, orig box, 1930s, 9x12", EX, A4 ....$12.00

Cherry Blossoms, wood, Henry Smith artist, color-line cut, push-to-fit, 232 pcs, complete, 1920s, 12x17", P, A4 ....$25.00

Children Feeding Birds, plywood, cartoon, interlocking, strip cut, 180 pcs, complete, no box, foxing, 1920s, A4 ....$20.00

Cinderella Puzzle Blocks, Germany, color litho paper over wood, w/book, in box w/sliding lid, 11", G, A....................$175.00

Country Fair, Parker/Pastime, plywood, 200 interlocking pcs, color-line cut, complete, orig box, 1928, 12x10", EX, A4...$35.00

Couple Stepping Down to Sedan, masonite, 46 lg push-to-fit pcs, complete, 1950-60s, 11x9", EX, A4.......................$5.00

Cowboy in Corral, Jaymar, 1950s, A3 ....$5.00

Cozy Evening, Rollo Purrington, plywood, 75 interlocking pcs, complete, orig box, 1930s, 5x7", EX, A4....................$15.00

Cross Country Marathon, Milton Bradley, early 1900s, orig box, EX $42.50

Dissected ABC, J Ottoman, paper litho on cb, red & yel ABC puzzle, orig box (rpr), 13x18" assembled, G-VG, A..$110.00

Duel in the Sun, Jaymar, 300-pc, 1946, 14x22" picture, NMIB, P4..$45.00

Field Sparrow, plywood, Baird artist, 70 interlocking pcs, complete, 7x5", EX, A4 ....$12.00

Fire Engine Picture Puzzle, McLoughlin Bros., 67 jigsaw-cut paper litho pieces (near complete), paper litho cover on wooden 12" box, VG, A, $80.00.

Flowers of Holland, plywood, Van Vreeland artist, 60 interlocking pcs, complete, 1930s, 10x7", EX, A4.....................$7.00

Fox Hunters Outside Rising Sun Inn, plywood, 192 interlocking pcs, complete, 9x12", EX, A4.....................$15.00

French Village Scene, plywood, Geo Hann artist, 126 interlocking pcs, strip cut, complete, 9x7", EX, A4..................$10.00

Grazing Time, plywood, cows in pasture, 220 semi-interlocking pcs, complete, orig box, 1930s, 12x10", EX, A4........$20.00

Gretchen, plywood, woman at memorial, 296 interlocking pcs w/color-line cut, complete, 1933, 12x16", EX, A4....$45.00

Hay Stack, Straus, plywood, 100 interlocking pcs, strip cut, complete, orig box, 1950s, EX, A4.....................$5.00

Her Pride, Kingsbridge-Atlantic, plywood, 300 interlocking pcs, strip cut, complete, orig box, 10x13", EX, A4............$20.00

Hibiscus, Straus-Floral, plywood, bowl of flowers, 500 interlocking pcs, semi-strip cut, complete, 1940s, 16x20", EX, A4.................$25.00

House & Garden, plywood, Maud Hollyer, artist, edge-locking, 231 pcs, 2 pcs rpl, orig box, 1930s, 12x16", EX, A4...$30.00

I Know a Lovely Garden, Straus, plywood, 500 interlocking pcs, strip cut, complete, orig box, 1950s, 18x14", EX, A4..$30.00

Jersey, EL Clark, plywood, milkmaid w/cow & trophy, 246 push-to-fit pcs, complete, orig box, 1900s, 14x10", EX, A4..$40.00

Lady Seated in Red, plywood, 75 interlocking pcs, strip cut, complete, no box, 1930s, 10x8", EX, A4....................$12.00

Last Ray, plywood, edge-locking, 317 pcs, 1 pc rpl, w/box, rough plywood, foxing, 1920s, 12x16", G-, A4....................$25.00

Little Workers Picture Cubes, McLoughlin Bros, paper litho on wood, 10½x8x3", A................................$550.00

Locomotive, McLoughlin, made up, mtd, shrink wrapped, 1887, (G box), A...$440.00

Map of US, Madmar, wood, 1926, orig box, EX...............$25.00

Melton Breakfast, Straus, fox-hunt scene, plywood, 500 interlocking pcs, strip cut, orig box, 1940s, 16x20", EX, A4...$30.00

Murmuring Waters, Straus, plywood, 500 interlocking pcs, semi-strip cut, 2 pcs rpl, orig box, 1930s, 16x20", EX, A4..$25.00

New York Times Historic, Parker Bros, Abdication of King Edward VIII, 11x11" box, EX, T2.............................$15.00

New York Times Historic, Parker Bros, Sinking of Titanic, 11x11" box (rpr), EX, T2................................$24.00

Night Before Christmas Santa Puzzle, McLoughlin, w/6 patterns (torn), illus cb & wood box, 11x13½", A.............$1,100.00

Old Fashioned Mill, plywood, Andel Kader artist, 184 push-to-fit pcs, foxing, darkened, 1930s, 11x8", G-, A4........$15.00

Philadelphia Centenial, George Chinnock, litho paper, 5-tier, 1876, A...$1,250.00

Photo of Boy Fishing, plywood, 210 interlocking pcs, complete, 1930s, 13x10", G-, A4...............................$20.00

Picture Cubes, McLoughlin, 32 paper litho wood blocks, coaching, cowboys, Indian scenes, no patterns, wood box, VG, A......................................$265.00

Quick Action, Parker/Pastime, plywood, 200 interlocking pcs, color-line cut, complete, orig box, 1930s, 10x14", EX, A4...$35.00

Racing Sailboats, plywood, brn-toned photo image, 100 interlocking pcs, strip cut, complete, 1920s, 7x9", A4......$12.00

Rippling Mountain Stream, Madmar-Blue Ribbon, plywood, 200 interlocking pcs, complete, orig box, 1930s, 12x9", EX, A4...$25.00

Roadside Mill, Madmar Blue-Ribbon, plywood, C&I print, 200 interlocking pcs, complete, orig box, 1930s, 9x12", EX, A4...$25.00

Santa Claus Travels Cube Puzzle, McLoughlin, 20 blocks, w/patterns for 6 puzzles, orig box (rough), 10x13", VG, A...$575.00

Schuykill River, wood, 117 push-to-fit pcs, color-line cut, complete, early 1900s, 10x12", A4........................$20.00

Setting Sail, Madnar-Blue Ribbon, plywood, 800 interlocking pcs, complete, orig box, difficult, 1930s, 16x21", EX, A4...$90.00

Seventh Commandment, plywood, Leone Brachner, artist, 230 push-to-fit pcs, complete, orig box, foxing, 10x13", EX, A4..................................$25.00

Silent Teacher, Sherwin-Williams Paints, Samuel Crump paper box top label by W.J. Morgan Litho Co., VG in 16x12" box, A, $225.00.

Shadowland, plywood, night scene, edge-locking, 320 pcs, complete, w/box, rough plywood, 1920s, 16x12", A4.......$30.00

Sleigh Ride (Concord Bridge), plywood, 91 semi-interlocking pcs, complete, amateur cutter, 1930s, 8x8", EX, A4..$10.00

Spoils of War, plywood, story-telling scene, 645 interlocking pcs, 8 pcs rpl, 1930s, 16x20", EX, A4........................$60.00

Summer River Scene, Hayter-Popular, plywood, 350 interlocking pcs, strip cut, 1950s, complete, orig box, 12x16", EX, A4..$20.00

Sunset in Venice, wood, 85 push-to-fit pcs, complete, early 1900s, 5x9", EX, A4..$10.00

Treasured Memories, plywood, violin & books, 300 interlocking pcs, strip cut, complete, orig box, 1950s, 12x16", EX, A4...$20.00

Twilight Express Puzzle Box, five cars and locomotive make a 9-foot train, complete, EX (edge wear on box), A, $135.00.

Unconquered Places, plywood, edge-locking, 324 pcs, complete, w/box, 1920s, 12x16", rough plywood, foxing, G-, A4...$25.00

United States, Parker Bros, 53 edge-interlocking pcs, color-line cut, 1 pc rpl, 1915, 12x20", EX, A4....................$20.00

Vegas, HG, 1978, NMIB, C1...$16.00

Venetian Revelers, plywood, Moran artist, 140 interlocking pcs, complete, 1930s, 6x10", EX, A.................................$15.00

Venice at Sunset, Aldon L Fretts, plywood, Doran artist, 575 interlocking pcs, complete, orig box, 1932, 16x22", EX, A4...$90.00

Village Pond, Straus, plywood, winter scene, 500 interlocking pcs, strip cut, complete, orig box, 1950s, 16x19", EX, A4...$25.00

Vista by the Sea, Straus, plywood, 100 interlocking pcs, strip cut, complete, orig box, 1950s, 7x10", EX, A4.............$5.00

White Traditional House, plywood, 190 push-to-fit pcs, color-line cut, complete, 10x14", EX, A4....................$20.00

Winter Country Scene, plywood, 333 semi-interlocking pcs, color-line cut, complete, no box, tight, 15x18", EX, A4...$40.00

Winter in the Country..., R Chelsey, plywood, C&I print, 193 interlocking pcs, complete, orig box, 1971, 9x14", EX, A4...$43.00

Woodland Reflections, Straus, plywood, 500 interlocking pcs, strip cut, 1950s, 18x14", EX, A4................................$30.00

Washington Crossing the Delaware, McLoughlin Bros., early, EX in box with fine graphics, A, $300.00.

ARMSTRONG PUZZLES
15 Monadnock Road   Worcester, MA 01609

WOOD JIGSAW PUZZLES
Pre-1950 preferred
Incomplete, damaged accepted

BUY • SELL • COLLECT • DISPLAY

Call (508) 799-0644 (H)

Radios, Novelty

Many novelty radios are made to resemble a commercial product, and some of the more collectible, even though of recent vintage, are often seen carrying very respectable price tags. Likenesses of famous personalities such as Elvis or characters like Charlie Tuna house transistors in cases made of plastic that scarcely hint at their actual function. Others represent items ranging from baseball caps to Cadillacs. To learn more about this subject, we recommend *Collector's Guide to Tranistor Radios* by Sue and Marty Bunis and *Collecting Transistor Novelty Radios, A Value Guide*, by Robert F. Breed. Our advisors for this category are John and Sheri Pavone (P3).

Avon Skin So Soft Bottle, MIB...$50.00
Avon Skin So Soft Bottle, NM, S1....................................$35.00
Ball Cap, AM, NM, T1...$25.00

Batman, figure, NBC, VG, T1......................................$15.00
Beetle Bailey, EX...$45.00
Big Bird, face, transistor, S1....................................$20.00
Big Bird, JPI/Muppets Inc, vinyl & plastic seated figure,
    AM/FM, #SS1733, 1989, MIB, P4 ....$30.00
Blabber Mouse, AM, S1...$35.00
Blabber Mouth, S1..$47.00
Blabber Puppy, M, T1...$20.00
British Paints Four Seasons Paint Can, M..............$22.50
Bugs Bunny, 1976, missing battery cover, EX $10.00
Burger King, clips on belt, hamburger earphones, MIB $27.50
Cadillac Convertible, NMIB, T1/S1 ....$38.00
California Raisin Guy, AM/FM, MIB $85.00
Champion Spark Plugs Spark Plug, EX, T1 ....$125.00

Charlie McCarthy, Majestic, Bakelite case, 6x7x5", EX, $650.00.

Charlie McCarthy, Majestic, wht-pnt Bakelite case, pnt seated
    metal figure, working, damaged case, 7", P, A $160.00
Charlie the Tuna, MIB...$30.00
Classic Car, orig box, S1..$22.00
Coca-Cola Bottle, M $35.00
Coca-Cola Bottle, MIB...$47.50
Coca-Cola Upright Vending Machine, Enjoy Coke lettered on
    front panel, Hong Kong, NM, A $40.00
Coca-Cola Upright Vending Machine, plastic, red w/Drink
    Coca-Cola on wht panel across top, 1963, EX, A ...$120.00
Coca-Cola Vending Machine, Drink Coca-Cola w/contour logo
    in wht on red above wood panel, 1970s, EX+, A......$80.00
Coca-Cola Vendo Vending Machine, red & wht w/vertical row
    of bottles at left, 1965, EX+, A $80.00
Dick Tracy, wrist radio set, EX, M1...........................$67.50
Donald Duck, Disney, transistor, 1973, MIB, M4...........$60.00
Donald Duck, NM, T1...$35.00
Donny & Marie, red, 1977, S1 ....$30.00
Dr Pepper Can, AM/FM, 1980s, EX, T1 ....$17.50

Elvis Presley, full-figure doll in wht costume, S1 ....$60.00
Ernie the Keebler Elf, EX...$45.00
Football, on tee, mk Wilson, M.................................$17.50
French Phone, ivory, S1 ....$40.00
Garfield, MIP $65.00
Getty Oil Battery, VG+..$38.00
Ghostbusters, Dancing Slimer, Columbia Pictures/Justin, battery-
    op, moves to music, 1984-88, 12", MIB, from $35 to..$42.00
Ghostbusters, sq w/antenna, FM, on card, EX, T1 ....$10.00

Ghostbusters Marshmallow Man, Columbia Pictures/PI Concept 2000, AM, with night light, 1984-88, 7½", NMOC, P4, $25.00.

Ghostbusters Marshmallow Man, transistor, MIB, S1 ......$32.00
GI Joe, w/headset, NM, T1..$12.50
Globe, Fleetwood, gold, MIB.....................................$85.00
Grammy Phone 8, S1...$50.00
Green Giant's Little Sprout, 1970s, NMIB.....................$65.00
Guilders Fancy Mustard Bottle, EX+, T1 ....$55.00
Guitar, The Picker, NMIB..$45.00
Gulf Oil Can, EX $45.00
Gumby, Perma Toy #7015, AM/FM, M $35.00
Gumby & Pokey, gr & orange raised figures on ivory ground,
    AM, transistor, working, 4½x2¾" $20.00
Hamburger Helper's Helping Hand, M $40.00
Hamburger Helper's Helping Hand, MIB.......................$75.00

Hawaiian Punch, Punchy figure, plastic, 1970s, 6", M......$35.00

Heinz Ketchup Bottle, VG+ $35.00

Hi-Fi Stereo, w/2 speakers, S1 ....$22.00

Hopalong Cassidy, Arvin, Hoppy & Topper in rearing position, 1 leg up, 5x8", EX, A $550.00

Hopalong Cassidy, Arvin, red pnt metal case, emb pnt tin over paper face plate, 2 legs up, working, 8", G+, A........$200.00

Incredible Hulk, 1978, S1..$38.00

John Lennon, figure, 10", working, MIB.......................$100.00

Kitty Cat, Radio Shack, MIB, T1 ....$25.00

Knight Rider, AM, 1984, MIB, from $35 to.....................$50.00

Kraft Macaroni & Cheese Box, MIB $30.00

Lady Bug, orange, orig box, S1 ....$30.00

Lemon, orig box, M...$35.00

Lipton Cup-a-Soup, G-, T1 ....$25.00

Little John, toilet figure, NM......................................$38.00

Mask Command Center, orig box, S1 ....$15.00

Masters of the Universe, Mattel/Nasta-Powertronic, plastic, 2 faces, AM, 1984, NMIB, P4 ....$30.00

Michael Jackson, AM/FM, S1 ....$20.00

Mickey Mantle & Roger Marris, full-length ball player on front, A...$750.00

Mickey Mouse, #179, Concept 2000, portable AM, 1970s, NRFB..$45.00

Mickey Mouse, JPI/WD, Mickey Tronics FM #1008, 9-volt, tuner ears, 1989, MOC, P4......................................$15.00

Mickey Mouse, JPI/WD, Tronics AM Radio Music City, Mickey & Minnie at street sign, 8½", MIB, P4.......................$30.00

Mickey Mouse, seated in armchair, S1 ....$30.00

Pepsi-Cola Bottle, Made in Hong Kong, 8⅝x2¾", M, from $25.00-$35.00.

Mickey Mouse, 2-D face, transistor, orig pkg, S1 ....$20.00

Microphone, Realistic, S1 ....$75.00

Ork Egg, M (EX box)..$30.00

Oscar the Grouch, in garbage can, MIB, T1 ....$35.00

Overland Stagecoach, MIB..$50.00

Owl, ivory plastic & brass w/jeweled eyes, S1 ....$75.00

Panasonic, ball & chain, S1..$25.00

Pepsi-Cola Bottle, on rnd base, Bakelite, rpt label/cracked base, M5 ....$440.00

Pepsi-Cola Can, 1970s, NMIB, A $35.00

Pepsi-Cola Floor Cooler, bl plastic, bottle-cap knob, Ice Cold & oval Pepsi-Cola logo on front, 1950s, EX, A $160.00

Pepsi-Cola Floor Cooler, rectangular w/Pepsi logo on all sides, electric, 1967, NM, A $275.00

Pepsi-Cola Upright Vending Machine, Pepsi-Cola lettered on top panel, w/leather case, 1950s, 7", NM, A............$230.00

Pepsi-Cola Upright Vending Machine, Say (above) Pepsi (on bottle cap) Please (below), 1964, 7", NMIB, A.......$200.00

Pepsi-Cola Walkman type, VG $20.00

Phantom, Stewart/Hong Kong, Rolls Royce #22863, plastic car w/metal trim, AM, 1970s, MIB, P4 ....$65.00

Pinocchio, Disney, transistor, 1973, MIB, M4 ....$60.00

Polaroid 600 Camera, w/film pack, S1 ....$22.00

Polaroid 600 Filmpack, battery-op, MIB, T1....................$30.00

Popeye, transistor, 1973, MIB, M4 ....$60.00

Pound Puppy, MIB, from $18 to $22.00

Pratt & Lambert Paints Can, EX+, J2 ....$33.00

Raccoon, stuffed animal, S1 ....$18.00

Radio-Bot, Realistic, S1..$30.00

Raggedy Ann & Andy, VG, T1 ....$22.50

Raggedy Ann & Andy, 1973, MIB, M4 ....$70.00

Robot, MIB, T1..$15.00

Robot, silver & blk, w/headset, S1 ....$18.00

Rock Radio, AM/FM, orig box, S1 ....$30.00

Rocket, Minimann, plastic Germanium Radio shaped as missile, w/earphone, cord & antenna, 5", NMIB, A...............$55.00

Rolls Royce, car, NMIB, T1 ....$15.00

Shirt Tales, 2-D, AM, EX, T1 ....$25.00

Sinclair Gas Pump, S1 ....$35.00

Smurf Head, VG, T1 ....$12.50

Snoopy, full-figure outline, S1 ....$30.00

Snoopy, on doghouse, S1 ....$40.00

Spiderman, rnd w/logo, MIB, T1 ....$25.00

Stanley Tape Measure, walkman type, w/headphones, MIB .$57.50

Statue of Liberty, S1 ....$60.00

Sunkist Can, MIB, J2...$30.00

Sunoco Gas Pump, S1...$35.00

Tea Cup w/Saucer, orig box, M $35.00

Telephone, wall hanging w/crank, lg, S1 ....$45.00

Thunderbird, Philco, promotional item, missing knobs, 1964, EX, I2...$95.00

Toilet Paper Roll Holder, M..$20.00

Tony the Tiger, orig box, S1..$30.00

Town Crier Lantern, wood, metal & glass, transistor, 1958, S1...$150.00

Transformers Wrist Radio, AM, MIB, T1 ....$25.00

Tree Sweet Orange Juice Orange, w/3 gr leaves, dial on side, M...$55.00

U.S. Command Space Satellite 'Moon Radio,' Educational Electronics, 1950s, NM (EX box), A, $245.00.

Twix Candy Bar, w/hdl, NM, T1 .... $40.00
Wuzzel Butter Bear, transistor, S1 .... $25.00
Yogi Bear, head, NBC, EX, T1 .... $20.00
1917 Touring Car, Japan, early, S1 .... $55.00
1934 Stutz Bearcat, Japan, pewter finish, S1 .... $65.00

Ramp Walkers

The concept of ramp-walking toys is not new, though nearly all you'll see on today's market are of fairly recent manufacture. They date back to the 1870s, when the first cast-iron elephant walker was made by the Ives company. From the 1920s through the '40s, wood and composition ramp walkers were made in the USA as well as Czechoslovakia. One of the largest US producers was John Wilson of Pennsylvania. His 'Wilson Walkies' are approximately 4½" tall, and most are 2-legged.

The Marx company made plastic ramp walkers from the '50s through the early '60s. Some were produced in Hong Kong (but sold under the Marx logo), and some were sold by a subsidiary of Marx, the Chardmore Co.

Ramp walkers were made in three general sizes. The smaller ones measure about 1½" x 2" and are unpainted. The larger walkers are approximately 2¾" x 3" and 4" x 5", and may be either spray painted or painted by hand. Our advisor for this category is Randy Welch (W4); he is listed under Ramp Walkers in the Categories of Special Interest.

Ankylosaurus w/Clown, Marx, Animals w/Riders series ... $25.00
Asterix & Obelix, MOC $150.00
Baby, unmk, plastic, in Canadian Mountie uniform, lg $50.00
Baby Teeny Toddler, Dolls Inc, plastic baby girl, lg $50.00
Baby Walk-a-Way, Marx, plastic, lg $40.00
Band Drummers, European issue, NM $200.00
Baseball Player, w/ball & bat $30.00
Bear, unmk, plastic $15.00
Big Bad Wolf & 3 Pigs, plastic $90.00
Boy Walking Behind Girl, plastic, lg $45.00
Bull, unmk, plastic $15.00
Captain Flint, Long John Silvers, gr, w/plastic coin weight, 1989 .... $15.00
Chicks & Easter Egg, unmk, plastic $30.00
Chinamen w/Duck in Basket, unmk, plastic $30.00
Chipmunks, playing drum & horn $30.00
Choo-Choo Cherry, Kool-Aid, w/plastic coin weight $60.00
Clown, Wilson, wood & compo $30.00
Cow, plastic w/metal legs, sm $15.00
Cowboy, plastic w/weight, 1950s, EX, from $10 to $15.00
Cowboy, riding horse, plastic w/metal legs, sm $20.00
Dachshund, plastic $15.00
Dog, Czechoslovakian, wood & compo $20.00
Donald Duck & Goofy, Disney, plastic $40.00
Donald Duck w/Nephews in Wagon, Disney, plastic $35.00
Donald Duck w/Wheelbarrow, all plastic, 1960s, regular sz, EX $25.00
Donald Duck w/Wheelbarrow, plastic w/metal legs, sm ... $30.00
Dutch Boy & Girl, plastic $30.00
Elephant, plastic w/metal legs, sm $20.00
Eskimo, Wilson, wood & compo $60.00
Farmer w/Wheelbarrow, plastic $20.00
Figaro the Cat, w/ball, plastic $25.00
Flintstones, Fred & Barney Rubble, Hanna-Barbera, M, from $40 to $50.00
Flintstones, Fred & Wilma on Dinosaur, Marx, 1960s, M . $100.00

Hap and Hop, soldiers, 2¾", from $18.00 to $25.00.

Flintstones, Fred riding Dino, Marx, plastic, similar to Pebbles riding Dino..$75.00

Flintstones, Pebbles riding Dino, Marx, plastic, Pebbles glued onto Dino..$75.00

Frontiersman w/Dog..$75.00

Goofy Grape, Kool-Aid, w/plastic coin weight $60.00

Goofy Riding Hippo, Disney, plastic...................................$40.00

Horse, plastic, lg...$30.00

Horse, yel plastic w/rubber ears & string tail, lg...............$30.00

Horse w/Equestrian Rider, Marx, plastic, lg $40.00

House Painters, European issue, EX+.................................$150.00

Huckleberry Hound & Yogi Bear, EX+, O1 ....$39.00

Huckleberry Hound & Yogi Bear, Hanna-Barbera, plastic, M, from $50 to...$65.00

Indian Chief, Wilson, wood & compo $45.00

Indian Mother w/Baby on Travois..$75.00

Jetsons, Astro & George, Hanna-Barbera, Marx, NM....$100.00

Jetsons, Astro & Rosey Robot, Hanna-Barbera, Marx, M, from $100 to $125.00

Jiminy Cricket w/Cello, Disney, plastic, from $25 to........$30.00

Jolly Ollie Orange, Kool-Aid, w/plastic coin weight.........$60.00

Kangaroo & Baby...$25.00

Little King, King Features, MOC $75.00

Little King & Guard, King Features, M, from $60 to........$75.00

Little Red Riding Hood, Wilson, wood & compo.............$35.00

Mad Hatter & March Hare, Disney, plastic $40.00

Mamma Duck Leading 3 Ducklings, plastic $25.00

Mammy, Wilson, wood & compo..$35.00

Marty's Market Lady w/Shopping Cart $35.00

Mason Pig & Big Bad Wolf, Disney, plastic.......................$40.00

Mickey & Minnie Mouse, plastic w/metal legs, sm..........$40.00

Mickey & Minnie Mouse, w/picnic basket, Disney, plastic, regular sz $40.00

Mickey Mouse & Donald Duck, Marx, plastic, Mickey & Donald riding an alligator, 1960s, 4", NM, A $64.00

Mickey Mouse w/Roller, 1960s, EX $25.00

Milk Cow, Marx, MIB $55.00

Milk Cow, Marx, plastic, lg, NM...$40.00

Minnie Mouse, pushing baby carriage, plastic, EX, J2 ......$35.00

Monkey, Czechoslovakian, wood & compo $30.00

Native on Hippo, Marx, Animals w/Riders series.............$25.00

Nurse, Wilson, wood & compo $30.00

Nursemaid w/Baby in Stroller...$15.00

Olive Oyl, Wilson, wood & compo......................................$150.00

Oriental Couple, 1960s, NM $25.00

Penguin, Wilson, wood & compo..$25.00

Pig Couple w/Pig in Basket $35.00

Pigs (3), 1st dressed for school, 2nd in barrel carried by the carpenter, EX+, M5...$35.00

Pluto, Disney, EX+, M5 ....$27.00

Policeman, Czechoslovakian, wood & compo $35.00

Popeye, Irwin, celluloid, lg..$60.00

Popeye, w/spinach can wheelbarrow, King Features, plastic, M $35.00

Popeye, Wilson, wood & compo, lg $150.00

Popeye & Wimpy, Marx, plastic w/spring on heads, 4", M.$65.00

Pumpkin Couple, he in bk w/hands on her hips (in blk), she in gr, EX, M5..$34.00

Pinocchio, Elephant, and Donald Duck, all by Wilson, wood and composition, Disney characters: $150.00 each; Elephant: $30.00.

Pluto, yellow with black details, NM, $30.00.

Pumpkin Head Couple, faces on both sides, M.................$45.00

Rabbit, Wilson, wood & compo $40.00

Racehorse w/Jockey, Marx, NM, J2 ....$30.00

Reindeer...$25.00

Sailor, Wilson, wood & compo $30.00

Sailors (SS Shoreleave), any of 3 color variations, from $25 to...$30.00

Santa Claus, w/open gold sack..$45.00

Santa Claus, w/wht sack $40.00

Santa Claus, w/yel sack $35.00

Santa Claus, Wilson, wood & compo....................................$60.00

Santa Claus & Mrs Claus, faces on both sides $40.00

Santa Claus & Snowman, faces on both sides....................$40.00

Sheriff & Outlaw $50.00

Soldier, Wilson, wood & compo $25.00

Spark Plug (horse) $175.00

Tin Man Robot w/Cart..$100.00

Top Cat & Benny, Marx, 1950s, EX+, C1 ....$72.00

Wimpy, Wilson, wood & compo...$150.00

Wiz Walker Milking Cow, Charmore, plastic, lg.............$50.00

Wizard of Oz's Glinda, M $10.00

Reynolds Toys

Reynolds Toys began production in 1964, at first making large copies of early tin toys for window displays, though some were sold to collectors as well. These toys included trains, horse-drawn vehicles, boats, a steam toy, and several sizes of Toonerville trolleys. In the early 1970s, they designed and produced six animated cap guns. Finding the market limited, by 1971 they had switched to a line of banks they call 'New Original Limited Numbered Editions (10-50) of Mechanical Penny Banks.' Still banks were added to their line in 1980, and figural bottle openers in 1988. Each bank design is original; no reproductions are produced. Renolds' banks are in the White House and the Smithsonian as well as many of the country's major private collections. *The Penny Bank Book* by Andy and Susan Moore (Schiffer Publishing, 1984) shows and describes the first twelve still banks they produced. Our advisor for this category is Charlie Reynolds (R5). Values are given for mint condition banks.

Mechanical Banks

1M, Train Man, 1971, edition of 30.................................$250.00
2M, Trolley, 1971, edition of 30 ....$175.00
3M, Drive-In, 1971, edition of 10 ....$375.00
4M, Pirate, 1972, edition of 10.................................$225.00
5M, Blackbeard, 1972, edition of 10 ....$225.00
6M, Frog & Fly, 1972, edition of 10 ....$600.00
7M, Toy Collector, 1972, unlimited edition..................$450.00
8M, Balancing, 1972, edition of 10................................$350.00
9M, Save the Girl, 1972, edition of 10 ....$900.00
10M, Father Christmas, 1972, 1 made ea year at Christmas.$600.00
11M, Gump on a Stump, 1973, edition of 10 ....$650.00
12M, Trick Bank, 1973, edition of 10............................$450.00
13M, Kid Savings, 1973, edition of 10 ....$450.00
14M, Christmas Tree, 1973, edition of 10 ....$380.00
15M, Foxy Grandpa, 1974, edition of 10 ....$375.00
16M, Happy Hooligan, 1974, edition of 10 ....$435.00
17M, Chester's Fishin' Hole, 1974, edition of 10 ....$395.00
18M, Gloomy Bus, 1974, edition of 10 ....$425.00
19M, Kids Prank, 1974, edition of 10............................$425.00
20M, Mary & the Lamb, 1974, edition of 20.................$375.00
21M, Spook, 1974, edition of 10 ....$380.00
22M, Decoy, 1974, edition of 10 ....$325.00
23M, Decoy Hen, 1974, edition of 10.............................$325.00
24M, Comedy, 1974, edition of 10..................................$425.00
25M, Bozo, 1974, edition of 10 ....$285.00
26M, Reynolds Foundry, 1974, edition of 15...............$1,200.00
27M, Toonerville, 1974, edition of 10 ....$800.00
29M, Simple Simon, 1975, edition of 10 ....$385.00
30M, Humpty Dumpty, 1975, edition of 20...................$650.00
31M, Three Blind Mice, 1975, edition of 15 ....$475.00
32M, Clubhouse, 1975, edition of 10 ....$625.00
33M, Boat, 1975, edition of 10.......................................$600.00
34M, St Nicholas, 1975, edition of 50 ....$300.00
35M, Forging America, 1976, edition of 13 ....$650.00
36M, Suitcase, ca 1979, edition of 22 ....$425.00
37M, North Wind, ca 1980, edition of 23 ....$240.00

39M, Quarter Century, 25th Anniversary, ca 1982, edition of 25, $2,900.00.

40M, Columbia, ca 1984, edition of 25.........................$700.00
41M, Whirligig, ca 1985, edition of 30 ....$490.00
42M, Miss Liberty, ca 1986, edition of 36......................$425.00
42M, Miss Liberty on Pedestal, ca 1986, edition of 4 .....$600.00
43M, Auto Giant, ca 1987, edition of 30 ....$1,200.00
45M, Campaign '88, 1988, edition of 50 ....$1,500.00
46M, Hollywood, ca 1989, edition of 35 ....$400.00
48M, Williamsburg, ca 1991, edition of 25....................$400.00
49M, Duel at the Dome, 1992, edition of 50 ....$310.00

47M, Buffalos Revenge, ca 1990, edition of 35, $425.00.

50M, '92 Vote, 1992, edition of 50 ....$650.00
51M, Oregon Trail, 1993, edition of 50.........................$410.00

Still Banks

1S, Amish Man, ca 1980, edition of 50.........................$125.00
2S, Santa, 1980, edition of 50 ....$65.00
3S, Deco Dog, ca 1981, edition of 50.........................$70.00
4S, Jelly Bean King (Ronald Reagan), 1981, edition of 100 ....$225.00
5S, The Hag, 1981, edition of 50 ....$90.00
6S, Snowman, 1981, edition of 50.........................$90.00
7S, Mark Twain, ca 1982, edition of 50 ....$95.00
8S, Santa (thin), 1982, edition of 50 ....$125.00
10S, Redskins Hog, 1983, edition of 50.........................$95.00
11S, Lock-Up Savings Bank, ca 1983, edition of 50.........$45.00
12S, Miniature Bank Building, 1983, edition of 50 ....$75.00
13S, Santa in Chimney, 1983, edition of 50.........................$70.00
14S, Santa w/Tree (bank & doorstop), 1983, edition of 25.........................$325.00
15S, Redskins NFL Champs, 1983, edition of 35.............$90.00
16S, Chick, 1984, edition of 50.........................$50.00
17S, Ty-Up (bank & string holder), 1984, edition of 35 ....$85.00
18S, Tiniest Elephant, 1984, edition of 50 ....$40.00
19S, Baltimore Town Crier, ca 1984, edition of 50 ....$55.00
20S, Father Christmas Comes to America, July 4th, 1984, edition of 25 ....$270.00

21S, Campaign '84, 1984, edition of 100, $110.00.

22S, Santa '84, 1984, edition of 50 ....$100.00
23S, Reagan '85, 1985, edition of 100.........................$135.00
24S, Columbus Ohio '85, 1985, edition of 50.........................$55.00
25S, Austrian Santa (bank & doorstop), 1985, edition of 25.........................$260.00
26S, Halloween, 1985, edition of 50 ....$65.00

27S, Kriss Kringle (w/tree & candle decorations), 1985, edition of 20.........................$1,200.00
28S, Santa Coming to a Child, 1985, edition of 50........$150.00
29S, Halley's Comet, 1986, edition of 50.........................$150.00
30S, 20th Anniversary, 1986, edition of 86 ....$155.00
31S, Father Christmas (bank & doorstop), gr, 1986, edition of 25 ....$260.00
32S, Santa & the Reindeer, 1986, edition of 50.............$130.00
33S, Charlie O'Connor, 1987, edition of 50.........................$65.00
34S, Chocolate Rabbit, 1987, edition of 50.........................$65.00
35S, St Louis River Boat, ca 1987, edition of 60.............$55.00
36S, German Santa (bank & doorstop), 1987, edition of 25 ....$235.00
38S, Old Stump Halloween, 1987, edition of 50 ....$65.00
39S, Santa in Race Car, 1987, edition of 100.........................$75.00
40S, Technology Education, 1988, edition of 88.........................$50.00
41S, Super Bowl XXII Redskins, 1988, edition of 50........$70.00
42S, Easter Rabbit, 1988, edition of 50 ....$40.00
43S, Florida Souvenir, 1988, edition of 75.........................$80.00

44S, Father Christmas with Lamp (bank and doorstop), 1988, edition of 35, $225.00.

Robots and Space Toys

Space is a genre that anyone who grew up in the sixties can relate to, but whether you're from that generation or not, chances are the fantastic robots, space vehicles, and rocket launchers from that era are fascinating to you as well. Some emitted beams of colored light and eerie sounds and suggested technology the secrets of which were still locked away in the future. To a collector, the stranger, the better. Some were made of lithographed tin, but even plastic toys (Atom Robot, for example) are high on the want list of many serious buyers. Condition is extremely important, both in general appearance and internal workings. Mint-in-box examples may be worth twice as much as one mint-no-box, since the package art was often just as awesome as the toy itself.

Because of the high prices these toys now command, many have been reproduced. Beware! See also Marx.

#3 Rocket, MT, litho tin friction, advances, sparks, early 1950s, 6½", EX, A..$75.00
Acrobat #119, Kitachara, battery-op, MIB, L4 ....$525.00
Acumizer Shogun, TT/Japan, movable vinyl head, walks, swings arms, 9", NM (EX box), A $150.00
Airport Saucer, MT, 4 actions, 1960s, 8" dia, MIB, L4 ..$125.00
Apollo 11 American Eagle Lunar Module, EX+ (EX+ box), A..$180.00
Apollo 11 American Eagle Lunar Module, 7 actions, MIB, L4 ....$395.00
Apollo 11 Space Rocket, Japan, 1960s, NMIB, T1 ....$125.00
Apollo Space Patrol w/Satellite Ship, TPS, orig box, EX, L4 ....$175.00
Apollo X Moon Challenger, TN, 16", EX (EX box), O1.$150.00
Apollo X Moon Challenger, TN, 1960s, 16", MIB.........$235.00
Astro Base, NMIB, L4 ....$295.00
Astro Captain, Daiya, plastic astronaut walks as sparks show in his chest, 6", NM (EX+ box), A $240.00
Astro Dog, Yonezawa, plush & plastic, wearing bubble helmet & carrying NASA case & American flag, 10", NM (EX box), A $110.00
Astro-Sound Satellite Talking Space Toy, EX (VG box), O1 .$60.00
Astronaut, Marx, jtd arms & legs, w/equipment (80% complete), sold at NASA only, orig box, T1 ....$85.00
Astronaut, SY, w/up, gr, yel & pk (scarce color combination), chest sparks, 5½", NM, A..$145.00
Astronaut Robot, Daiya, bl, 1960s, 16", M $500.00
Astronaut Robot, Daiya, red, battery-op, w/oxygen tank & machine gun, missing antenna, NM $700.00
Atlas ICBM Missle Launcher w/Missiles & Flying Target, NMIB, L4 ....$675.00
Atom Rocket 7, MT, battery-op, advances, lights blink, sounds, tin astronaut under plastic dome, 1950s, 9", EX, A ..$125.00
Atomic Rocket, MT, battery-op, lights, sounds, antenna revolves, astronaut at controls, 1960s, 9", NM (EX box), A $650.00
Attacking Martian, blk w/red tin feet, chest opens, shoots, NM, M5 ....$150.00
Attacking Martian, SH, 7 actions, 11", MIB, L4 4.........$450.00
Automic Rocket w/Prop, MT, X201 rocket w/plastic satellite, 7½", NM (EX+ box), A...$150.00
Batman Billiken Robot, w/up, 1980s, MIB, T1...............$145.00
BBC Talking Dalek, Palitoy, red plastic w/emb details, 1975, 7", NM (EX box), A $412.00

Atomic Robot Man, Japan, lithographed and painted tin, aluminum arms, clockwork, 5", EX, A, $850.00.

Big Maxx Robot, battery-op, NMIB, L4 ....$200.00
Billy Blastoff Space Scout & Accessories, Eldon, battery-op, 1960s, MIB, L4 ....$400.00
Busy Robot, slight rust in battery box, arm sluggish, 12", EX+, M5 ....$185.00
Cape Canaveral Satellite Tracking Truck, rpl antenna, EX, L4...$200.00
Chief Robot Man, KO/Japan, tin, bump-&-go action, head turns, antenna spin w/clicking noise, battery-op, 12", EX, A $800.00
Clancy the Great, Ideal, plastic & vinyl, battery-op, makes chattering sound, non-working, 19½", orig box, VG, A...$75.00
Colonel Hap-Hazard Robot, Marx, 1960s, EX+, T1.......$750.00
Combattler Shogun Warrior, Japan, litho tin w/movable vinyl head, walks & swings arm, 9½", NM (G+ box), A..$150.00
Conehead, Japan, tin, 2 rubber bands swivel & revolve, ear antennae, battery boxes in legs, 13", VG, A............$400.00
Cragstan Astronaut, red, working, missing battery cover plate, NM $350.00
Cragstan Astronaut, red version w/man's face, w/instructions, NMIB, A..$3,200.00
Cragstan Flying Saucer w/Space Pilot, NMIB, L4 ....$275.00
Cragstan Launching Pad w/Rocket & Satellite, orig box, EX, L4...$375.00
Cragstan Mr Robot, litho tin & plastic, red, blk & yel w/plastic dome, battery-op, working, orig box, 11", EX, A $650.00
Cragstan Mr Robot, red version, working, EX+.............$325.00
Cragstan Mr Robot, wht version, non-orig head, 1960s, EX+, T1...$275.00
Creature Robot, figure, Robot House, MIP, E3 ....$95.00
Dino the Robot, SH/Japan, plastic, head splits open to reveal growling Dino dinosaur, 11", EX+ (EX box), A $726.00

Dux Astroman, West Germany, plastic, battery operated, 12", EX (NM box), A, $1,200.00.

Fighting Martian, S.H. mostly tin, battery operated, 11¼", original box, A, $150.00.

Dynamic Fighter Robot, Japan, working, 1960s, MIB, C8 .$85.00

Earth Man, w/sounding & blinking gun, EX (G box), A .$1,600.00

Earth Man Astronaut, TN, litho tin, remote control, carries space rifle, 9½", EX+ (VG box), A $1,700.00

Empire-Monster Robot, Tiawan, battery-op, working, MIB, C8 ....$45.00

Engine Robot, SH/Japan, battery-op, working, 1960s, MIB, C8 ....$85.00

Excavator Robot, SH/Japan, battery-op, 1960s, MIB, C8 .$95.00

Fighting Robot, SH/Japan, plastic w/litho tin chest plate, advances, stops, fires gun, sounds, 10", NM (EX- box), A $125.00

Fighting Space Man, SH, walks/arms swing, helmet light blinks/gun in chest fires, litho electronics, 12", NM (EX box), A $350.00

Fighting Space Man, SH/Japan, battery box is rusty, light not working on gun, 12", EX, M5 ....$170.00

Fighting Space Man, SH/Japan, pnt & litho tin w/plastic, battery-op lights & sound, working, orig box, 11", EX, A $275.00

Flash Space Patrol, NM (worn/taped box), A................$320.00

Flying Saucer, Y/Japan, tin & plastic, working, 1960s, MIB, C8 ....$95.00

Flying Saucer X-7, MT, half-figure litho tin astronaut under clear plastic dome, 8" dia, EX-NM, A $75.00

Friendship 7, SH, friction capsule advances as 3-D astronaut spins 360 degrees inside, 9½", EX, A..........................$85.00

Gama Space Tank, orig box, EX, A $300.00

Giant Robot, silver w/red feet & accents, battery-op, 17", EX+, M5 ....$340.00

Gigantor, Tin Toy Institute, litho tin, battery-op, 12½", MIB $370.00

Golden Sonic Spaceship, 19", NMIB.............................$175.00

Golden Sonic the Mysterious Spaceship, Tigrett, NMIB .$125.00

Great Garloo, Marx, gr plastic, pnt features & loincloth, battery-op, remote control, orig box, 22½", G, A $120.00

Gun Robot, box only, Japan, 1960s, T1 ....$50.00

Gun Robot, Taiwan, newer version, plastic & tin, 1970s, MIB, T1 ....$125.00

High-Wheel Robot, Japan, pnt tin & plastic, blk & red, clock-work w/sparking action, working, 9", MIB..............$395.00

Holdraketa Spaceship, friction, 16", EX (EX box), O1 .....$40.00

Hysterical Robot, Japan, plastic, working, 17", sm melt mk on bk side of base, T1 ....$145.00

Jetto the Air-Powered Robot, 1950s, MOC, T1 ....$15.00

Joker Billiken Robot, w/up, 1980s, MIB, T1 ....$145.00

Journey to the Moon, Y, plastic & tin, module travels on track from moon to space station, 36", NMIB, A $364.00

Jupiter Rocket, MS, litho tin, moves w/siren shound & stands up when it hits an object, mk MS, 9", EX (NM box), A .$100.00

King Ding, plastic, red, yel & blk, sm robot goes up & down in elevator, walks, movie on bk, 14", EX+, M5 ....$42.00

King Flying Saucer, KO, 3 actions, 1960s, 7½" dia, NMIB, A $150.00

King of Mars Robot, SH, battery-op, MIB $580.00

Laughing Clown Robot, battery-op, NM, L4................$325.00

Laughing Robot, Waco, plastic, bump-&-go, neck stretches as lights flash, laughs hysterically, battery-op, MIB, L4 .$495.00

Looping Space Tank, Daiya, 1960s, 8", NMIB, L4 ....$495.00

Lost in Space Robot, AHI, M, E3......................................$85.00

Lost in Space Robot, Remco, battery-op, orig box, EX, L4 .$325.00

Lost in Space Robot, Remco, bl version, MIB, L4..........$525.00

Lost In Space Robot YM-3, Yonezawa, w/up, 1982, 5", MIB, H4 ....$22.00

Lunar Explorer, MIB, L4...$575.00

Lunar Hovercraft, TPS, 8", EX (VG-EX box)................$325.00

Lunar Module, NMIB, L4...$275.00

Lunar Spaceman, Hong Kong, plastic (scarce maroon), walks, head lights, chest opens w/guns, 12", EX (EX box), A...$200.00

Lunar Spaceman, Hong Kong, pnt plastic body & face, clear plastic helmet, battery-op, working, orig box, 12", EX, A...$120.00

Lunar Traffic Control, MIB, A..$110.00

M-50 Spaceship, MT/Japan, working, 1960s, MIB, C8 ....$55.00

Magic Color Moon Express, SH, 4 actions, 1960s, MIB, from $150 to $185.00

Magic Mike II Robot, New Bright, MIP, E3 ....$15.00

Mars King, SH/Japan, advances on rubber treads, stops, raises arms, screeches, TV screen in chest, 10", EX (EX box), A...$350.00

Mars King, SH/Japan, litho tin, w/TV screen in chest, rubber treads, battery-op, working, orig box, 9¼", VG, A ..$270.00

Marvelous Mike Tractor, Saunders, pnt sheet metal, plastic figure w/decals, battery-op, working, orig box, 13", G, A...$160.00

Mechanic Robot Tho (symbol), tin & plastic, stops, rotates, gears in chest blink, sounds, 12", NM (EX+ box), A...$195.00

Mechanical Mighty Robot, Yonezawa, tin & plastic, 10½", EX (G box), A...$745.00

Lost in Space Robot, AHI/Azar Hamway, Hong Kong, plastic, battery operated, 1977, 10", O1, NMIB, $160.00.

Lunar-I, Scientific, actually fires, 13", NM (NM box), M5, $125.00.

Moon Astronaut, Japan, litho tin clockwork, red, white, blue, and silver, 8½", EX (EX box), A, $1,100.00.

Mechanical Robot, Japan, litho tin, yel, red & bl, yel plastic arms, clockwork w/sparking action, orig box, 6", VG-EX, A..$100.00

Mechanized Robot, Showa, 1950s, MIB......................$2,600.00

Mercury Explorer, TPS, 1960s, 8", MIB, L4..................$300.00

Mighty Robot, Japan, mc litho tin & plastic, clockwork w/sparker, working, orig box, 5¼", VG-EX, A, from $60 to...$80.00

Mighty Robot, Noguchi/Japan, 1960s, MIB..................$145.00

Mini Robotank TR2, battery-op, MIB, L4.......................$325.00

Mobile Satellite Tracking Station, Cragstan, litho tin, shows space scenes in side screen, 1950s, 8", NM (EX box), A...$615.00

Mobile Space TV Unit w/Trailer, Rosko, orig box, EX+, A...$2,200.00

Moon Astronaut, Japan, litho tin, red, wht & bl, clockwork, 2 motions w/noise, working, orig box, 8½", EX, A..$1,100.00

Moon Explorer, Ideal, 32", NMIB $85.00

Moon Explorer Vehicle, Gakken, vinyl astronaut in plastic bubble, lights, sounds, 11", EX, L4..............................$225.00

Moon Patrol Space Division #3, revolving radar mechanism, EX (EX- box), A $2,600.00

Moon Patroller, MIB, L4..$375.00

Moon Rocket, litho tin friction, vertical launch, automatic ladder release, orig box, 16", VG-EX, A.....................$250.00

Moon Rocket, Y, 1950s, MIB, L4.................................$325.00

Mr Machine, Ideal, orig version, 1960s, w/box, T1 ....$300.00

Mr Mercury, Marx, tin w/plastic arms, advances, bows, raises & lowers arms, grasps by remote, w/instructions, NMIB, A...$1,200.00

Mr. Robot, Cragstan, tin and plastic, battery operated, 11", original box, EX, A, $650.00.

Mr Robot, ATC/Japan, MIB.....................................$750.00

Mr Robot, Japan, litho tin, silver, bl, yel & red w/plastic arms & legs, clockwork, working, orig box, 7", VG-EX, A ..$325.00

Mr Robot the Mechanical Brain, Alps, pnt tin, silver, battery-op, bulbs flash, clockwork, working, orig box, 8", VG, A...$600.00

Mr Robot the Mechanical Brain, Alps, tin w/up, walks as red & gr lights flash at end of arms, 8", NM (EX box), A...$1,100.00

NASA Astro Captain, Daiya, 1960s, NM $250.00

NASA Control Center, MT/Japan, litho tin & plastic, 8x4", NMIB, A..$435.00

New Astronaut, MIB, L4..$130.00

New Space Capsule, SH, litho tin body mk United States & NASA, plastic dome, astronaut pops up, 8", EX (EX box), A...$243.00

New Space Refuel Station, WACO, litho tin NASA Space Station w/Jet Rocket Plane & satellite, 13", EX+ (EX box), A...$1,375.00

Nike Rocket, Masuya, friction, rocket advances, when it hits an object, it rises slowly, NM (M box), A $200.00

Non-Fall Moon Rocket, slight scratch, box w/some tape rpr, A...$330.00

Orbit Explorer, Japan, mc litho tin, clear plastic bubble w/man, clockwork, working, orig box, 7", VG-EX, A $525.00

Original Smoking Spaceman, Linemar, litho tin, walks, arms move, stops, eyes light, smokes, working, rare, 12", NM, A...$775.00

Out of This World Flying Saucer, Wilson 5" aluminum saucer circles around box, 1950s, NM (EX box), A...........$175.00

Pete the Spaceman, Bandai, MIB, L4 ....$195.00

Pioneer PX-3 Robot Dog, tin friction, 9", EX, O1 ....$45.00

Piston Action Robot, TN, remote control, maroon, EX (EX box) $1,500.00

Piston Robot, Japan, tin & plastic, working, 12", EX+, M5..$145.00

Planet Robot, KO, all tin, gray & red, w/up, 1955, minor wear, 9", EX, A..$450.00

Planet Robot, KO, pnt tin & plastic, w/up, red & blk, w/sparker, 1960s, working, orig box, 8¾", VG, A, from $200 to $300.00

Planet Y Space Station, TN, NM (VG box), A $300.00

R-35 Robot, battery-op, MIB $625.00

Radar Robot, battery-op, 12", EX (VG-EX), O1 ....$300.00

Ratchet Robot, TN, tin w/red-tinted plastic inserts in eyes & mouth, carries wrench in right claw, 8", VG, A $345.00

Robby the Robot, Japan, pnt tin w/red, blk & silver litho trim, battery-op, 2 motions, working, orig box, 12¾", EX, A $1,500.00

Robby the Robot, Japan, tin, blk, battery-op, lights & walks, 1960s, NM, T1 ....$1,450.00

Robby the Robot, Masadaya, vinyl, w/up, M, E3 ....$45.00

Robert the Robot, Ideal, battery-op, EX (damaged box), L4...$185.00

Robert the Robot, Ideal, silver & red plastic, turn crank, talker, working, orig box, 14", VG, A $110.00

Robot, Japan, litho tin, metallic bl w/blk & red highlights, coil antenna, clockwork, working, 6", G-, A $120.00

Robot, Yonezawa, litho tin w/metal easel-bk attachment for balance, 6", EX (EX box), A, from $700 to $800.00

Robot & Son, battery-op, MIB, L4 ....$550.00

Robot & Son, Marx, silver & red pnt plastic, battery-op, w/light & Morse code buzzer, non-working, orig box, G, A .$160.00

Robot Bulldozer, Japan, emb pnt tin body, metallic bl, rubber treads, remote control, battery-op, orig box, 7", VG-EX, A $400.00

Robot Captain, Yone/Japan, litho tin & plastic, walks, sparks come from chest, w/up, scarce, 6", VG+ (NM box), A $133.00

Robot Commando, Ideal, bl plastic w/red dome & trim, battery-op, remote control, 4 actions, complete, 1961, 15", NM, A $350.00

Robot Gun Car, Japan, litho tin, bl car w/red robot, battery-op, bump-&-go action, working, 7¾", G+, A $325.00

Robot Monster, Japan, pnt & litho tin w/plastic features, battery-op, working, orig box, 11½", EX, A $575.00

Robot on Tractor, Showa, battery-op, 1950s, MIB.........$700.00

Robot Super Space Commander, Hong Kong, plastic, battery-op, 1970s, orig box, T1 ....$85.00

Robot Supermoon Explorer, HK, 1970s, MIB...................$28.00

Robot Tractor, battery-op, pistons light, NMIB, L4 ....$475.00

Robot Warrior, Japan, pnt & litho tin w/plastic features, battery-op, working, damage on battery trap, 11¼", VG-EX, A $60.00

Robot 2500, battery-op, MIB, L4 ....$100.00

Robot 7, Korea, tin, w/up, 1970s, MIB, T1 ....$20.00

Robot-O-Matic Super Giant Robot, battery-op, MIB, L4..$375.00

Robotank Z, Japan, mc litho tin, plastic arms & dome, arms move, guns light, orig box (needs rpr), 10¼", EX, A $325.00

Rocket Man, Alps, litho tin & plastic, metallic gr & gray, remote control, battery-op, working, orig box, 13½", EX, A..$2,100.00

Rocket Missile, Cragstan, litho tin friction, USAF missile with rubber-tipped nose cone, 13", EX+ (EX+ box), A, $180.00.

Rotate Robot, Japan, pnt tin body, w/litho tin face, battery-op, 4 motions, working, orig box, 11½", EX, A $100.00

Rotate-O-Matic Super Astronaut, MIB, L4....................$275.00

Rotate-O-Matic Super Astronaut, SH/Japan, battery-op, 12", NM (EX+ box), M5 ....$200.00

Rotate-O-Matic Super Astronaut, silver version, MIB, L4 ....$375.00

Rotator Robot, SH, advances, stops, body swivels, 2 guns pop out & shoot w/lights & sounds, 12", NM (EX box), A..$265.00

Rudy the Robot, Remco, 1960s, NMIB, T1 ....$175.00

R2-D2, remote control, working, 8", EX+, M5 ....$60.00

Satellite Fleet, TPS, litho tin, 3 rotating saucers follow spaceship, 12", EX (NM box), A $325.00

Satellite Launching Truck, astronaut at controls under bubble dome, 4 plastic saucers on rod on bk, 12", EX (EX box), A $600.00

Saturn Robot, Tiawan, plastic, battery-op, working, 1970s, MIB, C8 ....$35.00

Solar X Rocket, TN, litho tin, battery-op, advances, sounds, litghts, stops & rises, 15", EX (NM box), A $167.00

SP-1 Space Car, Linemar, litho tin friction, tinted windows & futuristic designs, 7", EX, A....................................$130.00

Space Avenger, Japan, litho tin, bl, orange & red w/pnt plastic head, red vinyl cape, battery-op, orig box, 12", VG, A $575.00

Space Boy, Japan, mc litho tin track & figure, pnt vinyl head, clockwork, working, orig box, 12", EX, A...............$600.00

Space Bus, Bandai, NMIB, L4 ....$850.00

Space Capsule w/Floating Astronaut, Japan, litho tin & plastic, lights, sounds, bump-&-go, orig box, 9½", VG, A $95.00

Space Capsule w/Floating Astronaut, MIB, L4 ....$250.00

Space Cobra, Popy/Japan, 6¼", MIB $40.00

Space Cruiser, Japan, pnt tin, blk, working, 1 wheel re-soldered, orig box, 9", VG, A...$75.00

Space Dog, Cragstan, litho tin, red w/blk trim, friction, ears & mouth move, working, orig box, 6½", EX, A...........$750.00

Space Dog, KO, friction, robot-like dog makes engine noise, opens & closes mouth, coil spring tail, 7", EX, A $360.00

Space Explorer, Linemar, litho tin, bl-gray, dk bl, yel & red, friction w/sound, working, orig box, 6", VG-EX, A $700.00

Space Explorer, SH/Japan, advances, stops, chest opens & lighted space scene appears, sounds, 12", NM (EX box), A..$225.00

Space Explorer, Y, Japan, mostly tin, battery operated, original box, EX+, A, $900.00.

Space Explorer 1041, Yonezawa, MIB, L4 ....$1,200.00

Space Frontier Apollo 12, tin & plastic, revolving nose & tail, hatch opens to spaceman w/camera, 18", EX+ (VG+ box), M5...$150.00

Space Jet Ray Gun, tin & plastic, working, 9½", EX+, M5.**$30.00**

Space Lantern, Marbo, plastic globe filled w/info about universe, NM (EX+ box), A **$80.00**

Space Man litho tin, mk NASA on arm, 5½", EX (EX box), A...**$150.00**

Space Man Astronaut, MT, blinking helmet light, swinging arms, forward & reverse actions, 8", EX, A..............**$750.00**

Space Patrol, litho tin battery-op, flashing lights, 8", NM (EX+ box), A, $250.00; Planet-Y, litho tin with plastic space pilot behind clear plastic bubble, original box, 8½", EX, A, $200.00.

Space Patrol, MT, litho tin friction, bl w/red & yel accents, NASA emblem on tail, 7", EX+ (VG- box), A.......**$189.00**

Space Patrol Car, Linemar, violet, red, wht & yel, twirling antenna, sounds, working, orig box, 9½", VG-EX, A .**$550.00**

Space Patrol Walkie-Talkie Space-a-Phones, red & wht plastic w/string & holder, 1952, orig mailing box, NM, A...**$245.00**

Space Patrol X-16, Amico, saucer advances, will not fall off table, 8" dia, NM (EX+ box), A.............................**$250.00**

Space Patrol XII, tank, VG+, L4.................................**$185.00**

Space Patrol 2019 Saucer, MIB, L4.............................**$200.00**

Space Patrol 2019 Saucer, EX, L4 ....**$85.00**

Space Patrol 3 Saucer, Japan, metallic gr, red, orange & gray trim, flashing lights, working, orig box, 8" dia, EX, A **$190.00**

Space Patrol 3 Saucer, KO, EX, L4 ....**$125.00**

Space Robot, litho tin, silver, red, yel & bl, friction w/sound, working, orig box, 6", A **$210.00**

Space Rocket Blue Eagle, Masuya, 1950s, L4 ....**$175.00**

Space Rocket Patrol Car, Courtland, litho tin, yel, red, blk & wht, friction w/sparking, working, orig box, 7", VG-EX, A...**$95.00**

Space Rocket Solar X-7, TN, MIB, L4 ....**$195.00**

Space Satellite, litho tin w/up, metal rods hold rocket missile & satellite w/dog passenger, NM (EX box), A **$86.00**

Space Satellite Apollo, litho tin friction, astronauts, box mk Nr 562, 1950s, 4" dia, NM (NM box), A.....................**$200.00**

Space Scooter, MT, 4 actions, 1960s, M, C8.................**$200.00**

Space Ship SS-18, S&E, friction, ship w/litho tin astronaut under clear plastic dome, 9", EX, A **$70.00**

Space Ship X-5, MT, MIB, L4......................................**$95.00**

Space Ship X-8, battery-op, MIB, L4 ....**$475.00**

Space Ship X-8, Tada, litho tin, astronaut sits under clear plastic dome, 8x4", EX+ (VG+ box), A..............................**$326.00**

Space Shuttle, MT/Japan, working, 1960s, MIB, C8........**$55.00**

Space Station X-2, MIB, L4 ....**$175.00**

Space Tank, KO, 9", EX (EX box), O1 ....**$180.00**

Space Tank M-18, MT/Japan, NMIB, A **$350.00**

Space Tank M-18, MT/Japan, 3 actions, 1950s, VG, C8 .**$125.00**

Space Trip, MT, litho tin space vehicles navigate track & go under tunnel that catapults cars, complete, EX (EX box), A...**$450.00**

Space Vehicle, ball suspended above by stream of air, tin astronaut in orange suit at controls, 8", NM (EX box), A.**$300.00**

Space Vehicle Juggler, Schuco, from Brussels World's Fair, rare, L5...**$1275.00**

Space Walkman Robot, China, tin, battery-op, working, 1970s, MIB, C8 ....**$35.00**

Space Whale, Japan, litho tin, bl w/red, silver & yel trim, clockwork w/sparking, working, orig box, 9", EX, A.....**$1,300.00**

Space Whale, KO, Pioneer on striped red tail, w/whiskers, marble eyes spin, mouth opens, non-working, 8", o/w EX, A...**$380.00**

Space 1999 Eagle Spaceship, AHI, plastic w/metal axles, 1976, 7", EX, H4...**$20.00**

Space 1999 Moon Car, AHI, friction, yel w/2 spacemen, working, 1976, MOC, H4...**$45.00**

Spaceman, N/Japan, litho tin, silver w/bl, yel & red trim, clockwork w/sparking action, working, 5½", VG-EX, A **$65.00**

Spaceman, N/Japan, litho tin, walks & sparks from chest, 6" M (NM window box), A...**$110.00**

Sparking Robot, N/Japan, mc litho tin, transparent red plastic chest plate, clockwork, working, orig box, 6", EX, A.**$180.00**

Sparking Space Ranger, Elvin, litho tin friction, advances w/sparking action, 1950s, 7", NM (EX+ box), A.....**$400.00**

Sparky Robot, KO, Japan, windup, 8", original box, EX, $300.00.

Sparky Robot, KO, pnt tin, silver body w/red feet & ears, clockwork w/sparker, working, orig box, 7¾", G-VG, A..$160.00

Star Hawk Spaceship w/Zeroid, Ideal, MIB, L4 ....$95.00

Star Strider Robot, battery-op, MIB, L4 ....$225.00

Steele Robot, Marx, battery-op, MIB...............................$475.00

Super Sonic Space Rocket, NMIB, L4 ....$625.00

Super Space Capsule, 6 actions, M (EX box), from $200 to $275.00

Swinging Baby Robot, Japan, litho tin, orange, red, yel & bl, clockwork, working, touch-up, orig box, 6¼", VG-EX, A $450.00

Swinging Baby Robot, mechanical, scarce, NMIB, J2 ....$650.00

Talking Robot, HK, battery-op, working, 1970s, MIB, C8..$45.00

Television Spaceman, Alps, litho tin & plastic, gray-gr w/red antenna, battery-op, working, orig box, 14½", EX, A $500.00

Tobor I, vinyl, arms move, slot in chest, cracked near bottom of chest, 60", VG, T1 ....$275.00

Twirly-Whirly Rocket Ride, Alps, rocket spins, assembly runs & rises, lights flash, bell sounds, 13", NM (G+ box), A $650.00

Twirly-Whirly Rocket Ride, Alps, litho tin, bl w/mc trim, working, orig box (tape rpr), 13½", VG-EX, A $475.00

Two Stage Rocket Launching Pad, MIB, L4...................$525.00

UFO-O5 Space Ship, MT/Japan, working, 1960s, 7½", MIB, C8..$65.00

USA-NASA Apollo Space Ship, MT, battery-op, orig box, EX, L4..$185.00

USA-NASA Apollo Space Ship, MT, litho tin, full-body astronaut at controlls, 1 circles craft, bump-&-go, 9½", NMIB, A..$217.00

USAF Rocket Missile, Cragstan, litho tin w/rubber-tipped nose cone & red plastic engine windows, orig box, EX+, A $180.00

Venus Robot, Japan, litho tin & plastic, clockwork, working, orig box, 5½", EX, A...$200.00

Verbot R/C Robot, Tomy/Japan, battery-op, non-working, orig box, C8 ....$20.00

Walking Robot w/Spark, SY/Japan, tin w/up, walks w/sparking chest, 7", NM (EX box), A..$242.00

Winner #23 Rocket, Exelo, litho tin, travels on rubber track or on table, w/pilot, early '50s, 5½", EX (EX-NM box), A $200.00

X-7 Flying Saucer, Japan, tin litho, EX $110.00

X-9 Robot Driver, Japan, litho tin, bl & metallic gr w/mc trim, battery-op, erratic motions, working, 7½", VG+, A $675.00

Y-M-3, Masudaya, battery-op, talks, 16", MIB.................$90.00

Zerak the Blue Destroyer, Ideal, Zeriods series, 1 missing headlight, w/extra set of hands, 1968, 6½", EX, D9..........$35.00

Zeroid Robot, Ideal, Zintar, 1968, EX, H4 ....$25.00

Zobor, Ideal, 1968, MIB...$95.00

Zod the Enemy Robot Monster, motorized, MIB, D4 ....$10.00

Zoomer the Robot, Japan, pnt tin, silver & blk, battery-op w/light, working, 7½", VG-EX, A $400.00

Zoomer the Robot, Japan, rare blk & red version, 1950s, EX+, T1..$600.00

Miscellaneous

Activity Set, Space Science Drafting Kit, 1950s, NMIB $75.00

Astronaut Pilot Wings, 1963, MOC $25.00

Bendee, Alpha-7 Spaceman, Colorforms, w/helmet, no broken wires, sm tear in vinyl on left arm, NM-, F5 ....$84.50

Bendee, Xodiac, Man From Saturn Spaceman, Colorforms, worn pnt, no broken wires, EX, F5 ....$69.50

Book, coloring; Moon Rockets, 1950s, M $23.00

Book, coloring; Sky Rocket, Lowe, 50+ pgs, 8x11" softbound, 1959, unused, NM, T2 ....$15.00

Book, coloring; Zedo Into Space, 1950s, EX $20.00

Book, punch-out; Space Rockets, 1958, M, V1 ....$28.50

Book, Question & Answer Book About Space, Random House, EX..$4.00

Bubble Bath, Space Scouts Stardust, ea pkg features a plant, 1950s, boxed set of 20, 5x10", NM (EX box), A $162.00

Ceiling Light Shade, gold & wht space graphics on wht glass, ca early 1950, scarces, 13x13", M, A $68.00

Christmas Ornament, ceramic spaceship, Japan, 1960s, set of 3 different, 3" to 4", V1...$25.00

Clicker, Space Gun, plastic, w/whistle, 5", NM..............$20.00

Doll, Space Astronaut, Dakin type w/jtd arms & legs, unmk, 1950s, MIP, V1 ....$45.00

Doll, Space Scout, House of Dolls, 7" plastic, in jumpsuit, eyes open/close, in 6x10" window box, 1950s, EX (EX box), A $100.00

Drink Mixer, United Plastic Corp, rocket-shape container w/straw, 1952, 9", NM (NM box), A $85.00

Gum Card, Space Ventures, 1991, Moon-Mars series, emb, set of 36, M1 ....$65.00

Gum Card, Space Ventures, 1991, NASA photos, 1st series, set of 110, complete, M1 ....$50.00

Gum Card, Space Ventures, 1992, NASA photos, 2nd series, set of 110, complete, M1 ....$40.00

Gum Card, Space Ventures, 1992, NASA photos, 3rd series, set of 110, complete, M1 ....$18.00

Helmet, Ideal, orig box, EX..$125.00

Key Chain, yel plastic spaceman, 1950s, 2", M.................$15.00

Paint-By-Number Set, Space Traveler, unused, 1950s, V1..$98.00

Pajamas, boy's mc flannel w/spaceships & planets on bl ground, early 1950s, appears unused, scarce, M, A..................$73.00

Party Streamers, spaceship graphics, 1950s, NM, V1.......$19.50

Pencil Case, Rocket Patrol Deluxe, American Pencil, heavy cb w/litho paper space scene, 1950, 7x10", EX+, T2 ......$70.00

Pencil Case, Rocket Whiz, 1950s, EX $32.50

Pencil Topper, rubber astronaut head in space helmet w/visor up, sold through 25¢ gumball machines, 1960s, 1½", M, T2 ....$5.00

Pocketknife, mk Space Rocket, w/whistle, NM $45.00

Poster, Rand McNally, Historic Moon Landing, from mc photo taken by Apollo astronauts while on moon, 24x18", MIP, H4..$5.00

Target, Astro Ray, litho tin, 13", NM $25.00

Top, litho tin w/space graphics, 1950s, EX....................$45.00

Walkie-Talkies, QX-2, Remco, space model, MIB $60.00

Rubber Toys

Toys listed here are made of rubber or a rubber-like vinyl. Some of the largest producers of this type of toy were Auburn Rubber (Indiana), Sun Rubber (Ohio), Rempel (also Ohio), and Seiberling. Because of the very nature of the material, most rubber toys soon cracked, collapsed, or otherwise disintegrated, so they're scarce today. Character-related rubber toys are listed in the Character Collectibles.

Army Motorcycle, brn, blk & yel, sm tear near front wheel, 4¼", G, A $35.00
Boattail Racer, Sun Rubber, 3", VG, T1 ....$15.00
Boattail Racer, Sun Rubber, 6", VG, T1 ....$25.00
Boxer Baby, molded hair, robe & boxing gloves, 12", NM..$100.00
Cab-Over Box Truck, Arcor, red, blk rubber tires, ca 1946, 4⅛", VG, W1 ....$15.00
Cab-Over Stake Truck, Auburn, red w/blk rubber tires, ca 1930s, 4¼", VG, W1.............................$15.00
Cadillac Convertible, Auburn, yel w/wht tires, ca 1950s, 4½", VG+, W1 ....$17.50
Cop on Motorcycle, Auburn, gr w/wht plastic tires, ca 1950s, 4", EX, W1 ....$14.00

De Soto Airflow Car, Auburn Ruber, white rubber tires, 1937, 5", VG, $30.00.

Dog as Fireman, Serugo, molded w/hat, boots & fire hose wrapped around neck, squeaks, working, 1960s, 14", VG, H4 ....$20.00
Dragon, mk Made in Spain, pnt pk spots on wings, squeaks, 6", EX, H4 ....$10.00
Duck, Rempel, EX $25.00
Dump Truck, Auburn #352, 11", NM (EX box), A.........$39.00
Farm Animals, Auburn, plastic, 19-pc, MIP $20.00
Fire Truck, Auburn, blk, NM, A3 ....$35.00
Military Motorcycle w/Sidecar, Auburn, wht rubber tires, 3", G $45.00
Milky the Cow, Rempel, MIB $75.00
Open-Back Truck, Auburn, VG, T1 ....$20.00

Pickup Truck, Arcor, red, wht rubber tires, ca 1946, 4½", VG, W1 ....$15.00
Police Set #925, Auburn, 6x10" window box contains 2 3" policemen, 2 4" policemen on cycles, 2 vehicles, NMIB, A $75.00
Racer #566, Auburn, red Indy-style car w/yel wheels, goggled driver, 10½", NM (EX box), A...................$85.00
Road Grader, Auburn, missing blade, NM, A3 ....$30.00
Sedan, Rubber Fastback, blk, ca 1930-40s, 4", G, W1 ......$15.00
Slope-Back Car, Sun Rubber, VG, T1 ....$25.00
Train Set, molded, red, gr, blk & silver, orig 11¼" box, EX, A..$35.00
VW Bug, unknown maker, yel w/blk plastic tires, ca 1960s(?), 3⅝", M, W1 ....$19.00

Western Express, Auburn Rubber, 3-piece set, 18" overall length, NM, $50.00.

White Bus, Sun Rubber, red & silver w/wht rubber tires, 4", VG, W1 ....$15.00
1957 Ford Ranchero, Auburn, red & yel, hard plastic wheels, NM, A3 ....$20.00

Russian Toys

Many types of collectible toys continue to be made in Russia. Some are typical novelty windups such as walking turtles and pecking birds, but they have also made robots, wooden puzzles, trains, cars, trucks, and military vehicles that are exact copies of those once used in Russia and its Republics, formerly known as the Soviet Union. These replicas were made prior to June 1991, and are marked Made in the USSR/CCCP. They're constructed of metal and are very detailed, often with doors, hoods, and trunks that open. Our advisors for this category are Natural Way (N1) and David Riddle (R6). Values are given for mint-in-the box toys.

Replicas of Russian Vehicles

Armored Car, metal, 1/43 scale, orig box, R6 ....$12.00
Lada Auto Service Car, metal, 1/43 scale, hood & trunk open, orig box, R6.......................................$12.00
Lada Jeep 4x4, metal, 1/43 scale, orig box, R6 ....$12.00
Lada Sedan, metal, 1/43 scale, hood & trunk open, orig box, R6 ....$12.00
Lada Station Wagon, metal, 1/43 scale, hood & trunk open, orig box, R6.......................................$12.00
Lada 2121 Jeep 4x4 w/Trailer, metal, 1/43 scale, trunk, doors & hood open, orig box, R6 ....$18.00

Aeroflot (Soviet Airlines) Station Wagon, metal, 1/43 scale, trunk and four doors open, MIB, R6, $18.00.

Moon Buggy, windup, MIB, N1, $12.00; Robot, swings arms, walks forward with see-through moving chest, MIB, N1, $19.50.

Moskovitch Medical Sedan, metal, 1/43 scale, hood opens, MIB, R6, $10.00.

Moskvitch Aeroflot (Soviet Airlines) Station Wagon, metal, 1/43 scale, hood opens, orig box, R6 ....$12.00
Moskvitch Auto Service Car, metal, 1/43 scale, hood opens, orig box, R6..$12.00

Moskvitch Panel Station Wagon, metal, 1/43 scale, hood opens, orig box, R6...$12.00
Moskvitch Police Car, metal, 1/43 scale, hood opens, orig box, R6...$12.00
Moskvitch Sedan, metal, 1/43 scale, hood opens, orig box, R6...$10.00
Moskvitch Slant Back Sedan, metal, 1/43 scale, trunk & front doors open, orig box, R6.............................$12.00
Moskvitch Station Wagon, metal, 1/43 scale, hood opens, orig box, R6...$10.00
Moskvitch Taxi Sedan, metal, 1/43 scale, hood opens, orig box, R6...$10.00
RAF Ambulance Van, metal, 1/43 scale, bk & 3 doors open, orig box, R6...$18.00
RAF Police Van, metal, 1/43 scale, bk & 3 doors open, orig box, R6...$18.00

Volga Ambulance Station Wagon, metal, 1/43 scale, back and three doors open MIB, R6, $18.00.

Volga Police Sedan, metal, 1/43 scale, trunk, hood & 4 doors open, orig box, R6...$18.00
Volga Sedan, metal, 1/43 scale, trunk, hood & 4 doors open, orig box, R6...$18.00
Volga Station Wagon, metal, 1/43 scale, trunk, hood & 4 doors open, orig box, R6.................................$18.00
Volga Taxi Sedan, metal, 1/43 scale, trunk, hood & 4 doors open, orig box, R6...$18.00
Volga Taxi Station Wagon, metal, 1/43 scale, trunk, hood & 4 doors open, orig box, R6.............................$18.00
Zil Gorbi Limo, metal, 1/43 scale, hood, trunk & 4 doors open, orig box, R6...$20.00

Miscellaneous

Cast Metal, 1917 Revolution Soldiers Pulling Cannon, set of 10, N1 ....$25.00
Cast Metal, 1917 Russian Revolution Soldiers w/Rifles, set of 10, N1 ....$25.00
Metal, bird, w/up, N1...$4.50
Metal, car set, 6-pc, N1...$12.00
Metal, car track, w/up, F1 ....$19.50
Metal, chicken, N1 ....$4.50
Metal, dancing snow girl, N1.......................................$12.50
Metal, doll, Matryoshki, w/up, N1.............................$18.00

Metal, monster beetle, N1 ....$7.50
Metal, parking garage, N1..................................$15.00
Metal, pedal car, lg, N1 ....$295.00
Metal, train track, w/up, N1 ....$19.50
Metal, turtle, N1 ....$7.50
Military Belt, Army, N1 ....$39.00
Military Belt, Navy, N1 ....$39.00
Military Boots, N1 ....$69.00
Plastic, car on garage lift, N1 ....$8.00
Plastic, chicken inside an egg, w/up, N1............$4.50
Plastic, fighter jet, bl, N1 ....$7.00
Plastic, missile carrier, N1 ....$4.75
Plastic, tank, N1 ....$4.75
Plastic, woodpecker on a tree, w/up, N1...........$30.00
Plastic & Metal, doll swing, N1 ....$12.50
Plastic & Metal, moon buggy w/2 cosmos, w/up, F1 ....$12.00
Plastic & Metal, motorcycle w/sidecar, in display case, N1.$19.50
Plastic & Metal, robot, w/up, F1......................$19.50
Plastic & Metal, truck w/missile carrier body & 4 rockets, N1 ....$9.50
Wood, doll set, Lenin, Stalin, Kruschev, Brezhnev & Gorby, Matryoshki, made in China, N1.............$30.00
Wood, doll set, various sets of 5 or more, Matryoshki, made in Russia, N1, $75.00 up to.........................$195.00

Sand Toys

Included here are not only beach toys like sand pails and molds but also early toy dioramas enclosed in wood or paperboard boxes that became animated as the weight of the sand they contained shifted when they were tilted.

Pail, Chein, Disney, 1950s, 6½", EX, D9, $65.00.

Blacksmith Shop, Gernard Camagni, paper litho, 1800s, sand missing, needs work, 8x5x2½", A...........................$220.00
Box w/2 articulated paper figures behind glass window, early, 6x8x2½", EX, A.............................$300.00
Pail, Chein, mc circus graphics on litho tin, 6", NM.......$45.00
Pail, Germany, tin w/lithos of Steiff toy animals, 5¼", EX, A $60.00
Sand Castle Set, Transogram, molds, figures & accessories, complete, 1956, MIB $60.00

Sand Loader, Wolverine, M (G box), D9, $225.00.

Set, Regaline, plastic, complete w/pail, shovel & 2 molds, late 1950s, MOC.........................$32.00
Ship Wreck, German, hand-colored engraved paper covering on glass-fronted box, 6x5", G+, A................$55.00
Shovel, Tick Tock Toys, tin, diecut clock, illus w/boys playing in sand, NMIB, A $50.00
Southport Sandgrounder, English, printed wood figures w/paper labels on sand hopper & box lid, rare, ca 1890, 9", EX+, A $247.50
Windmill, German, hand-colored engraved paper in paper-covered red & glass-fronted box, 5½x6½", VG, A.........................$55.00

Santa Claus

To check values for battery-operated or windup Santa Claus toys, see those categories. See also Books.

Candy Container, papier-mache, unmk German, separates at waist, pnt features, fur beard & hair, orig suit, 10", EX, A $425.00
Doll, Japan, molded plaster face w/pnt features, wht cotton beard, red flannel suit w/wht trim, blk boots, 6¾", EX, A $75.00
Doll, molded stockinet cloth face w/pnt features, straw stuffed, blond hair & beard, minor wear, 26", G-, A $75.00

Candy container, papier-mache and cloth, wool beard, flannel clothes, Germany, 1920s, 15", EX, A, $1,200.00.

Jack-in-the-Box, Bradford, plastic, 1950s, EX $40.00

Puzzle Box, Milton Bradley, box lid features Santa surrounded by toys & elves, contains 1 of 3 puzzles, 9x13", EX, A ...$95.00

Santa, Belsnickle, molded compo nodder w/head mtd on wire rod, hollow body lifts off wood base, 12", G-VG, A.......$4,100.00

Santa, Belsnickle, papier-mache, red suit w/mica chips & gr cuffs, holding bl feather tree, mk Germany, 8", G, A $210.00

Santa, Belsnickle, pnt papier-mache & plaster, rare brn coat w/wht trim, gray beard, 13", EX, A $3,100.00

Santa, Belsnickle, pnt papier-mache & plaster, plush hood fringe & coat edge, wht coat w/clear mica, 13½", EX-, A..$1,450.00

Santa, Belsnickle, pnt papier-mache & plaster, plush trim on hat, dk yel coat w/dk mica, 10¾", VG, A $325.00

Santa Claus, German, cloth body w/papier-mache, holds Christmas tree sprig, push down to squeak, ca 1930, 8", M, A $85.00

Santa Claus, Noma, smiling, holding wreath & gifts, lights up, electric, 30x13", NMIB, A $50.00

Santa Claus Phone Bank, Santa Creation #3980, Japan, battery-op action, NMIB, A $757.00

Santa on House, Criterion Bell, mc litho tin w/electrically activated Santa, missing electric cord, minor pitting, G+, A........$55.00

Santa on Rocking Horse, pnt wood & papier-mache horse, compo Santa w/felt costume, 8", VG+, A................$230.00

Squeak Toy, Germany, compo Santa pops out of wood building, working, 11", EX, A...$325.00

Schoenhut

Albert Schoenhut & Co. was located in Philadelphia, Pennsylvania. From as early as 1872 they produced toys of many types including dolls, pianos and other musical instruments, games, and a good assortment of roly polys (which they called Rolly Dollys). Around the turn of the century, they designed a line they called the Humpty Dumpty Circus. It was made up of circus animals, ringmasters, acrobats, lion tamers, and the like, and the concept proved to be so successful that it continued in production until the company closed in 1935. During the nearly 35 years they were made, the figures were continually altered either in size or by construction methods, and these variations can greatly affect their values today. Besides the figures themselves, many accessories were produced to go along with the circus theme — tents, cages, tubs, ladders, and wagons, just to mention a few. Teddy Roosevelt's African hunting adventures inspired the company to design a line that included not only Teddy and the animals he was apt to encounter in Africa but native tribesmen as well. A third line featured comic characters of the day, all with the same type of jointed wood construction, many dressed in cotton and felt clothing. There were several, among them were Felix the Cat, Maggie and Jiggs, Barney Google and Spark Plug, and Happy Hooligan.

Several factors come into play when evaluating Schoenhut figures. Foremost is condition. Since most found on the market today show signs of heavy wear, anything above a very good rating commands a premium price. Missing parts and retouched paint sharply reduce value, though a well-done restoration is usually acceptable. The earlier examples had glass eyes; by 1920, eyes were painted on. Soon after that, the company began to make their animals in a reduced size. While some of the earlier figures had bisque heads or carved wooden heads, by the twenties, pressed wood heads were being used. Full-size examples with glass eyes and bisque or carved heads are generally more desirable and more valuable, though rarity must be considered as well.

During the 1950s, some of the figures and animals were produced by the Delvan company, who had purchased the manufacturing rights. A few of these are listed below. Consult the index for Schoenhut toys that may be listed in other categories. Our values reflect prices realized at auction.

Animals

Alligator, glass eyes, dk gr & yel, leather flippers missing, needs restringing, 13", G, A $170.00

Alligator, pnt eyes, leather feet, 1 toe missing, lt pnt chips, 12½", VG, A..$225.00

Alligator, pnt eyes, leather front feet, oilcloth bk feet, red pnt mouth w/teeth, 12½", EX, A.....................................$250.00

Brown Bear, glass eyes, open mouth, slight pnt scraping, 4", EX, A...$350.00

Brown Bear, pnt eyes, closed mouth, G pnt w/minor chipping & wear, 4", A...$300.00

Brown Bear, pnt eyes, top half of body dk, rope tail, 4½x7½", EX w/some rpt, A..$275.00

Brown Bear, Style II, glass eyes, leather ears & tail, rpt, 8", G+, A...$85.00

Brown Bear, Style III, glass eyes, leather ears, cord tail, rpt, rpl ears, 7¾", G, A $100.00

Brown Bear, Style V, pnt eyes, leather ears & tail, 7½", VG, A...$275.00

Buffalo, pnt eyes, leather horns, tail missing, needs restringing, 7½", G-VG, A...$100.00

Buffalo, Style IV, pnt eyes, leather horns & twine tail, lt scuffs, 7½", VG, A...$200.00

Buffalo, Style IV, pnt eyes, 1-pc molded head, leather horns, 1 horn & tail missing, flaking pnt, 7½", G-, A $70.00

Bulldog, pnt eyes, wht w/blk spots, leather ears, 3½x6", most pnt off face, wear/flaking, rare, A $350.00

Camel, 1-hump, pnt eyes, leather ears, rope tail, 6½x9", VG, A..$110.00

Donkey, Style II, glass eyes, dk muzzle, lt scuffs & scratches, mane loose, 10", VG, A..$40.00

Elephant, glass eyes, good pnt, tusks worn, lt wear, lg, G, from $100 to...$150.00

Elephant, pnt eyes, jtd hooves, rpl ears, trunk tip rpl, reduced, Delavan era, 6¼", VG-, A.......................................$30.00

Elephant, Style I, glass eyes, flowered blanket, 8½", G, A..$210.00

Elephant, Style III, pnt eyes, leather ears & trunk, tip of trunk missing, 8¾", G+, A $60.00

Felix, pnt blk intaglio eyes, leather ears (rpl), fine crazing, rpr to foot, pnt flaking, 7½", A.....................................$350.00

Giraffe, pnt eyes, fabric ears, rope tail, lt wear/rubs, pnt flaking from ears, 10x9", EX, A...$225.00

Giraffe, Style II, glass eyes, carved mouth groove, 10", VG, A...$600.00

Giraffe, Style IV, pnt eyes, leather ears, cord tail, surface abraisions, pnt chips, missing ear, 10", A...........................$75.00

Giraffe, Style IV, pnt eyes, molded head, pnt loss & cracks in mouth, detached front legs, 10", P, A $85.00

Goat, glass eyes, leather ears, horn, beard & tail, red nose & mouth w/pnt teeth, 4x8", VG, A $150.00

Goat, Style II, pnt eyes, leather beard, lt pnt chips, 7½", A...$100.00

Goose, pnt eyes (missing), wht w/dk stripes to indicate feathers, orange feet & legs, 6", pnt G-, cracks in wood, A ...$100.00

Gorilla, Style II, pnt eyes, carved ears, chip in fingertips of left hand, 8", VG, A $1,800.00

Camel, two humps, painted eyes, rope tail, molded ears, tail replaced, 6¾x7", G, A, $75.00; Elephant, glass eyes, rope tail, leather ears and tusks, end of trunk missing, 6x8½", G, $100.00.

Hippopotamus, painted eyes, leather ears, leather tail, 4½x10", G, A, $115.00; Billy Goat, painted eyes, leather ears and horns, leather beard, oilcloth tail, 5x8", VG, A, $50.00.

Cat, pnt eyes, gray & yel w/dk stripes, leather tail, molded ears, 3½x5", VG, A..$625.00

Cow, pnt eyes, orig leather collar & bell, rope tail, leather ears & horns, 5x9", VG, A.......................................$350.00

Cow, Style II, pnt eyes, molded head, leather ears & horns, missing horn & tail, 8¾", P, A..................................$90.00

Deer, glass eyes, leather ears, gr-brn, pnt loss, 6½", P, A .$180.00

Deer, glass eyes, leather tail, ears & antlers, 4½x7", VG, A...$975.00

Deer, Style I, glass eyes, leather antlers, gr-gray, EX, A..$1,250.00

Deer, Style III, pnt eyes, leather antlers, gr-brn, 7", G, A .$225.00

Hippopotamus, Style I, glass eyes, ball-&-socket neck joint, pnt wear, damage to leg, 9½", VG+, A $260.00

Horse, glass eyes, wht, leather saddle w/red fringe-trimmed platform attached, 6x9½", EX, A...................................$410.00

Horse, pnt eyes, brn leather ears, cloth bridle & reins, leather saddle, worn, pnt flaking, reduced, 4½x7", EX-, A..$105.00

Horse, pnt eyes, brn w/blk string tail, mane & hooves, leather saddle, fabric bridle, 4½x7", VG, A $65.00

Horse, pnt eyes, wht w/gray shadings, blk mane & tail, red platform on bk, parts of leather bridle, 4½x7", VG, A ..$100.00

Horse, Style I, glass eyes, dk w/wht mane & tail, 2-part head, minor pnt chips, 10", VG-, A $210.00

Hyena, Style II, pnt eyes, pnt loss in face & neck, 6½", G, A $1,150.00

Kangaroo, glass eyes, stenciled stripes, lt scratches & scuffs, 10½", VG, A $1,050.00

Kangaroo, Style II, pnt eyes, leather ears, orange-brn (no stripes), overall chips/nicks, crack/ear gone, 9", G-, A $275.00

Leopard, pnt eyes, brn spots on yel, rope tail, some pnt flaking, 3½x5½", A...$120.00

Leopard, Style II, pnt eyes, spotted woven cord tail, pnt loss at neck, lt chips on snout, 7½", G-VG, A $300.00

Lion, pnt eyes, molded/pnt mane & tail, pnt open-closed mouth w/pnt lower teeth, rope tail, 5x8", EX, A................$225.00

Lion, Style I, glass eyes, fur mane, lt pnt chips, mane worn, 7½", VG, A $525.00

Lion, Style III, glass eyes, carved mane and ears, rope tail, 7½" long, VG-EX, A, $550.00; Buffalo, Style III, glass eyes, leather horns, tail missing, VG-EX, A, $575.00.

Lion, Style IV, pnt eyes, molded head w/twisted twine tail, pnt chips, head EX, 7½", G-, A $55.00

Lion, Style IV, pnt eyes, molded wood head, lt pnt version, 8", VG-EX, A...$210.00

Monkey, pnt eyes, open-closed smiling mouth w/6 teeth, rope tail, red felt suit w/yel trim, matching hat, 8", VG, A.......$425.00

Monkey, Style II, 1-pc molded head, carved ears, sm pnt chips on face, 7½", G-VG, A..$225.00

Ostrich, glass eyes, blk & wht w/yel bill, lt wear/minor chipping & crack, 8x9", VG, A..$550.00

Pig, pnt eyes, blk leather ears, open mouth pnt red w/teeth, rope tail, lt wear, orig pnt, 3½x7½", EX, A.......................$80.00

Poodle, pnt eyes & whiskers, rope tail, molded ruff of hair over shoulders, curly hair on head, 5x8", EX, A $80.00

Poodle, Style III, intaglio eyes, cord tail, 7¼", G-VG, A.$110.00

Rabbit, Style II, pnt eyes, pnt loss on head & legs, needs restringing, 5", G-VG, A...$325.00

Rhinoceros, pnt eyes, molded head, leather ears & horn, cord tail, minor deterioration of horn, reduced, 6¾", VG, A $285.00

Rhinoceros, Style II, glass eyes, twine tail, gr-gray, sm scuffs under chin, 9", VG-EX, A....................................$575.00

Sea Lion, glass eyes, minor pnt chips, 7", EX-, A $1,800.00

Tiger, pnt eyes, open mouth w/pnt teeth, rope tail, 4x7¾", EX w/VG pnt, A...$300.00

Quacky Doodles, painted eyes and brows, yellow with orange legs and bill, red jacket, mouth opens and closes, 8½", G, A, $315.00; Danny Doodles, painted eyes, yellow with blue painted jacket, white vest, red lower body, orange bill, black wooden black top hat, 8", G-, A, $205.00.

Tiger, pnt eyes, rope tail, EX orig pnt, well-detailed pnt/modeling, 3½x5½", A..$250.00

Tiger, Style II, pnt eyes, molded head, spotted woven cord tail, heavy wear, damaged leg joint, 7½", P, A.................$70.00

Wolf, Style III, pnt eyes, leather ears, 1-pc head & neck, wood tail, minor pnt chips, 8", EX, A...............................$475.00

Zebra, cvd/pnt eyes, molded/pnt mane, leather ears, rope tail, good color & features, 5x8", EX, A.........................$220.00

Zebra, glass eyes, pnt on torso faded, 7", A....................$375.00

Circus and Accessories

Circus, pnt & jtd wood, 2 horses, 2 clowns, 2 elephants, props, tent, complete, orig 23x15" box, VG, A.................$500.00

Circus #20/32, pnt-eye animals & people, orig outfits, retied in orig box, EX, A...$800.00

Circus Ring & Tent #30/8, 18x24" wood base, red swing, sawdust floor, canvas tent, flags of all nations, curtains, EX, A...$700.00

Circus Wagon, pnt wood w/red & yel letters, hinged door, 10", VG-EX, A..$1,250.00

Exhibit Tent, fabric, open on all 4 sides, center pole attached to 7½" sq wood base board, flag atop, VG, A..............$350.00

Bandwagon, red, blue, gold, and silver, four bench seats with pegs for bandsmen, storage compartment, 15x20", EX, A, $7,000.00.

Humpty Dumpty Circus Cage Wagon, orange-red with blue-black bars and stenciled lettering, 12", VG-EX, A, $1,300.00.

Performance Cage, wire & tin, resoldered, 10" dia, G+, A ..$247.50
Ring Master's Whip, pnt wood & string, 4½", VG, A $45.00
Tent, Humpty Dumpty Circus on top, flag & 24x36" wooden base, w/center ring, curtains on bk, sawdust floor, 34", VG, A $900.00

People

Bandsmen, set of 6 complete w/instruments & clothing, EX, A $14,000.00
Barney Google & Spark Plug, pnt wood, cloth outfits, jtd, 7½" Barney w/orig label on foot, rpl ears, EX, A.............$475.00

Chinaman, pnt eyes, open-close mouth w/6 teeth, braided queue, orig wht pants & bl jacket, 8", VG, A..........$300.00
Clown, pnt eyes, orig clothes, dirt/wear, needs restringing, 9½", A $85.00
Farmer, pnt eyes, open-closed smiling mouth w/6 teeth, molded & pnt goatee, leather ears, pnt blk boots, 8", EX, A.$525.00
Foxy Grandpa, pnt compo head on jtd wood body, redressed & rpt, 8¾", EX, A $350.00
Hobo, pnt eyes, mustache, open-closed mouth w/6 teeth, leather ears, in bl & wht shirt, brn pants & jacket, 8", EX-, A $215.00
Hobo, pnt eyes, red & wht shirt, brn pants, tan felt jacket & hat, mustache & stubble, 5½", EX+, A $300.00
Lady Acrobat, pnt eyes & features, molded/pnt hair w/topknot, red tights, purple felt suit w/gold trim, 8", VG, A....$175.00
Lady Acrobat, Style II, molded 1-pc head, gr felt leotard w/gold paste & trim, rpr costume, touch-up on face, 8", G-, A...$55.00
Lady Bareback Rider, pnt eyes, brn hair w/topknot, red tights & shoes, gr felt top, pk skirt, early, 6½", EX, A $170.00
Lady Bareback Rider, pnt features, molded & pnt hair w/no top-knot, felt body suit, pk skirt, 6½", VG, A $65.00

Lady Circus Rider, Style V, bisque head, restored costume, 8", P-G, A, $110.00; Gent Acrobat, Style II, bisque head, 8", VG, A, $260.00.

Marionettes, set includes Hattie Pinn, Ty Pinn & Harry Pinn, clothespin limbs, yarn hair, VG, A $175.00
Milkmaid, pnt eyes, open-closed mouth w/wht between lips, molded & pnt hair, orig clothing & milk pail, 8", EX, A...$500.00
Milkmaid, Style I, 2-part head, plaid dress w/muslin apron & petticoat, touch-up on head, rpl bucket, 7½", VG-, A $450.00
Moritz, pnt features & hair, leather topknot, gr felt jacket (rpl), 8", some rpt, feet may have been rpl, A $65.00
Negro Dude, Style I, yel vest, coat missing, lt pnt wear, 9½", G, A $200.00

Negro Dude, Style III, pnt eyes, molded 1-pc head, wht hat, yel vest, red shirt, missing ears, 9", G, A $130.00

Pinn Family, clothespin-like arms & lower legs, yarn hair, tacked-on clothing, mk, 6 members, VG, A $575.00

Ringmaster, pnt eyes, mustache & goatee, wht suit w/tie & red felt jacket, 6½", VG, A................................$110.00

Ringmaster, Style II, 2-pc head, red coat w/yel vest, damaged hat, lt crazing on face, chipped beard, 8½", G, A $450.00

Ringmaster, Style V, 1-pc molded head, thumb & finger hands, pnt loss on face, 8½", G-, A $100.00

Teddy Roosevelt, two-part head, jointed elbows, thumb and finger hands, 8¾", EX, $1,500.00; Happy Hooligan, one-piece head, dowel thumb, repairs to shirt, VG, 8½", A, $850.00.

Miscellaneous

Catalog, *Illustrations of Schoenhut's Toys, the Humpty Dumpty Circus,* copyright 1918, EX, A, $300.00.

Alphies Blocks, #13N, zoo pictures 1st half of alphabet, dolls on 2nd, 13-pc, lt wear, 1 side of box missing, o/w EX, A .$450.00

Bungalow, yel w/wht trim, gr shutters, red roof, gray base, turn porch posts, 11x14x12½", EX, A $360.00

Hollywood Home Builder Set, c 1928, 'The Washington' on end of box lid, unplayed with (G box), A.......................$180.00

Indoor Golf Set, 2 sm golfers w/metal clubs attached to 36" poles, +greens, pond, terrain, etc, VG, A $675.00

Jolly Jiggers, molded & pnt compo, Dutch girl & boy outfits, heads mtd on wire & wood rods, wood base, 12x21", VG-EX, A $1,050.00

Little Village Builder, 4 unpnt wood buildings (approximately 28 pcs), cracks in wood, pencil damage, rough box, 15", A...$30.00

Man & Lady Golfers, from indoor golf Tommy Green game, Pat 1922, length w/shaft: 35½", A, pr $990.00

Metallophone, natural wood & metal, moderate wear, orig box damaged on corners, 11", G, A...................................$20.00

Milk Wagon, Fairmount Farms 'A' Milk on sides, no horse, rpl rear tailgate chains, 24" to end of shaft, EX, A........$950.00

Nursery Rhyme Set: Mary (8"), lamb (5x7") & desk (4½x5"), rpl slates, lt pnt wear, clothing faded/fragile, o/w EX, A .$700.00

Piano, baby grand; cherry-stained wood w/stenciled gold lettering on marquee, 12¾", VG, A....................................$70.00

Rolly Dolly, Schnickel-Fritz, papier-mache with painted features, open mouth with teeth, Patented Dec. 15, 1918, on label on bottom, EX, A, $925.00.

Piano, label on bk: Ten Ten Tennessee, I've Got Those Blues, gold stencil, w/up music box plays 2 tunes, 12x12", EX, A $245.00

Pick-Up Sticks, 1930, NMIB.................................$75.00

Rolly Dolly, baby clown, papier-mache, holds jester in right hand, 8½", EX, A..$625.00

Rolly Dolly, Buster Brown, papier-mache, orig cloth label, minor wear & abrasions, varnished, 6", VG, A $550.00

Rolly Dolly, clown, G pnt w/some wear & pitting, functional, 12" $250.00

Rolly Dolly, clown w/hat, papier-mache, chimes when rolled, damage along seam, varnished, 7½", G+, A $125.00

Rolly Dolly, Foxy Grandpa, papier-mache, overall crazing, minor damage, varnished, 9½", G-, A $400.00

Rolly Dolly, Happy Hooligan, papier-mache, pnt chips, neck damage, varnished, 4¾", G-, A $110.00

Rolly Dolly, rabbit, papier-mache, leather ears, cloth label, crazing & creases, varnished, 8½", G-, A $500.00

Rolly Dolly, rooster, papier-mache, minor crack in base, varnished, orig cloth label, 9", G, A $700.00

Rolly Dolly, Santa, papier-mache, hat rpr, other minor damage, varnished, 11½", P, A...$650.00

Rolly Dolly, Santa, papier-mache w/pnt features, label missing, seam has opened, 6½", EX, A..................................$750.00

Rubber Ball Shooting Gallery, lithographed paper on wood, cardboard targets, with original gun, ca 1901, 15x16¾", VG, A, $450.00.

Rubber Ball Shooting Gallery, Brownie-type figures & clowns, 15x16¾", VG, A...$450.00

Rubber Ball Shooting Gallery, litho paper on wood, w/orig gun, some paper components rpr, 15", G, A $330.00

Ski-Jumper Set, 27" ramp, man on skis w/metal wheels, G, in orig taped-together box, A $185.00

Thousand Face, turn blocks to make various changes in face, moderate wear, orig box (top missing), 9", G-, A $25.00

Train Set, blk engine, red cattle car w/blk wheels, red open car, blk open car, red caboose, wear/damage/rpr/losses, A .$55.00

Trinity Chimes (on lower front panel), 8 wooden keys play chime-like tones, working, 18x10", G, A..................$85.00

Slot Cars

Slot cars first became popular in the early 1960s. Electric raceways set up in retail storefront windows were commonplace. Huge commercial tracks with eight and ten lanes were located in hobby stores and raceways throughout the United States. Large corporations such as Aurora, Revell, Monogram, and Cox, many of which were already manufacturing toys and hobby items, jumped on the bandwagon to produce slot cars and race sets. By the end of the early 1970s, people were loosing interest in slot racing, and its popularity diminished. Today the same baby boomers that raced slot cars in earlier days are revitalizing the sport. Vintage slot cars are making a comeback as one of the hottest automobile collectibles of the 1990s. Want ads for slot cars appear more and more frequently in newspapers and publications geared toward the collector. As you would expect from their popularity, slot cars were generally well played with, so finding vintage cars and race sets in like-new or mint condition is difficult. Slot cars replicating the 'muscle' cars from the sixties and seventies are extremely sought after, and clubs and organizations devoted to these collectibles are becoming more and more commonplace. Large toy companies such as Tomy and Tyco still produce some slots today, but not in the quality, quantity, or variety of years past.

Aurora produced several types of slots: Screachers (5700 and 5800 number series, valued at $5.00 to $20.00); the AC-powered Vibrators (1500 number series, valued at $20.00 to $150.00); DC-powered Thunderjets (1300 and 1400 number series, valued at $20.00 to $150.00); and the last-made AMX SP1000 (1900 number series, valued at $15.00 to $75.00.) Our advisor for this category is Gary Pollastro (P5).

Complete Sets

Allstate, HO scale, Allstate by Lionel set #9544, orig box, G, P5 ....$95.00

AMT, 1/24 scale, Power Steering Race set #TR-190, MIB, P5 ....$450.00

Aurora, HO scale, Real Racing Set #1980, with red #1409 Alfa Romeo and #1415 Ford Mustang Mach I cars and 24-feet of track, EX, $250.00. (Photo courtesy Gary Pollastro.)

Atlas, HO scale, #5020 Riverside Enduro w/Corvette & Ford GT, bl & lime gr, orig box, EX, P5 ....$150.00

Aurora, HO scale, Formula I Racing set #1943, orig box, EX, P5...$195.00

Aurora, HO scale, Sears exclusive T-Jet set #1980, w/#1409 Alfa, red & #1409 Mach I, bl, orig box, EX, P5.......$250.00

Eldon, 1/24 scale, Power Pack '8' set #9545, orig box, EX, P5...$90.00

Gilbert, 1/32 scale, American Flyer Autorama #19080, Corvette, red, orig box, G, P5.......................................$200.00

Marx, 1/32 scale, International Sports Car set #22510, NMIB, P5 ....$100.00

Scalextric, set #31, MIB, P5 ....$400.00

Strombecker, 1/32 scale, #48-28004M, Wards Thunderbird Monza, orig box, G, P5 ....$150.00

Strombecker, 1/32 scale, #9930-2495, Highway Patrol...Race, Sparkling Hot Rod, Police w/light/sirens, orig box, EX, P5..$195.00

Strombecker, 1/32 scale, set #9945, MIB, P5 ....$295.00

Strombecker, 1/32 scale, set #9950, MIB, P5 ....$295.00

Tyco, A-Team Racing Sets, MIB $72.50

Tyco, Army Transport set, MIB $58.00

Tyco, Big Hauler Trucking set, MIB $50.00

Tyco, Big Rig Chase set, MIB..........................$50.00

Tyco, California Van set, MIB $38.00

Tyco, Challenge 100 set, MIB $35.00

Tyco, Dirt Bike Racing set, MIB $50.00

Tyco, Electric Trucking 70 set, MIB $75.00

Tyco, First Alert set, MIB................................$65.00

Tyco, HO scale, TycoPro Le Mans Stick Shift set #8113, orig box, G, P5 ....$80.00

Tyco, Motor City Trucking set, MIB $68.00

Tyco, Racing Hoppers set, MIB.......................$65.00

Tyco, Thunder Cats set, MIB $77.50

Tyco, TR-X 4-Car Racing set $35.00

Tyco, Trans-Formers Battle set, MIB $85.00

Tyco, U-Turn Chase set, MIB $44.00

Tyco, 2-in-1 Racing Wheels set, MIB $40.00

Slot Cars Only

AMT, 1/24 scale, Ford Galaxie, MIB, C5 ....$250.00

Aurora, HO scale, #1351 '63 Galaxie 500XL Convertible, T-Jet, yel, EX, P5 ....$100.00

Aurora, HO scale, #1353, '63 Fairlane, red, NM, C5 ....$50.00

Aurora, HO scale, #1355, '63 Thunderbird Roadster, red, M, C5...$75.00

Aurora, HO scale, #1356, Corvette, olive gr, NM, C5 .....$55.00

Aurora, HO scale, #1357, Buick Riviera, wht, NM, C5 ...$40.00

Aurora, HO scale, #1358, Jaguar XKE, olive gr, NM, C5.$45.00

Aurora, HO scale, #1359, Indy Racer, tan, M, C5............$35.00

Aurora, HO scale, #1361, Grand Prix Racer, yel, M, C5..$45.00

Aurora, HO scale, #1362, Mack Dump Truck, wht & gr, M, C5...$45.00

Aurora, HO scale, #1363, Mack Dump Truck, red & gray, M, C5...$75.00

Aurora, HO scale, #1364, International Tow Truck, tan, MIB, C5...$80.00

Aurora, HO scale, #1366, Hot Rod Coupe, red, NM+, C5 ....$55.00

Aurora, HO scale, #1367, Maserati, tan & blk, M, C5.....$45.00

Aurora, HO scale, #1368, Ferrari GT 250, red, M, C5 .....$42.00

Aurora, HO scale, #1370, AC Cobra, red, NM+, C5 ....$65.00

Aurora, HO scale, #1372, '65 Ford Mustang Hardtop, wht & blk, NM+, C5 ....$48.00

Aurora, HO scale, #1373, Mustang 2+2 Fastback, turq & blk, MBP, C5 ....$75.00

Aurora, HO scale, #1374, Ford GT, gr & wht, M, C5......$35.00

Aurora, HO scale, #1375, Cobra GT, red, MIB, C5 ....$35.00

Aurora, HO scale, #1376, Porsche 906, olive gr, NM, C5.$35.00

Aurora, HO scale, #1376, Porsche 906, yel, MIB, C5.......$30.00

Aurora, HO scale, #1377, Chaparral, yel w/roll cage, MIB, C5 ....$40.00

Aurora, HO scale, #1378, Lola GT, factory unfinished, M, C5 ....$45.00

Aurora, HO scale, #1378, Lola GT, red & wht, M, C5 ....$30.00

Aurora, HO scale, #1379, Toronado, wht, EX+, C5.........$75.00

Aurora, HO scale, #1380, Mako Shark, yel, NM, C5 ....$45.00

Aurora, HO scale, #1381, Dino Ferrari, gr & wht, M, C5 .$38.00

Aurora, HO scale, #1382, Ford J Car, bl & blk, MIB, C5.$35.00

Aurora, HO scale, #1382, Ford J Car, turq & blk, M, C5.$45.00

Aurora, HO scale, #1383, '67 Ford Thunderbird, tan, M, C5 ....$55.00

Aurora, HO scale, #1384, Black Beauty, blk, M, C5 ......$195.00

Aurora, HO scale, #1386, Ford XL500, gold chrome, speedline, M, C5 ....$40.00

Aurora, HO scale, #1387, Thunderbike, bl, EX+, C5.......$50.00

Aurora, HO scale, #1388, Camaro, red & blk, EX+, C5 ..$58.00

Aurora, HO scale, #1389, Cougar, yel, M, C5 ....$42.00

Aurora, HO scale, #1392, Candy Jaguar XKE, plated, peach, NM, C5 ....$45.00

Aurora, HO scale, #1396, Candy Cobra GT, red/candy pnt, NM, C5 ....$60.00

Revell, 1/24 scale, Corvette Stingray Model Car Racer #R3160:700, Fireball motor, SP 900 motor body, lightweight aluminum chassis, wheels, tires, and pickup, dated 1964, MIB, $195.00.

Aurora, HO scale, #1397, McLaren Elva, gr, M, C5.........$40.00

Aurora, HO scale, #1398, Dune Buggy Roadster, red, MIB, C5...$45.00

Aurora, HO scale, #1399, Dune Buggy w/top, wht, MIB, C5...$45.00

Aurora, HO scale, #1400, Mangusta (mongoose), yel, MIB, C5...$50.00

Aurora, HO scale, #1401, Willy's Gasser, gr, M, C5.........$60.00

Aurora, HO scale, #1401, Willy's Gasser, yel, M, C5.......$45.00

Aurora, HO scale, #1402, '67 Firebird, bl, M, C5.............$60.00

Aurora, HO scale, #1403, Cheetah, gr, M, C5...................$40.00

Aurora, HO scale, #1409, Alfa Romeo, red, M, C5..........$40.00

Aurora, HO scale, #1410, Chaparral 2F, '#1,' wht, MIB, C5...$32.00

Aurora, HO scale, #1411, Pontiac GTO, red & blk, MIB, C5...$165.00

Aurora, HO scale, #1412, F1 McLaren, red, MIB, C5......$50.00

Aurora, HO scale, #1413, Repco Brabham, gr, M, C5......$40.00

Aurora, HO scale, #1418, Wild One Camaro, '#2,' wht & bl, NM+, C5 ....$45.00

Aurora, HO scale, #1419, Wild One Cougar, '#3,' wht & red, M, C5...$40.00

Aurora, HO scale, #1430, Flamethrower Ford J, wht & bl, MIB, C5...$35.00

Aurora, HO scale, #1471, Tuff Ones Lola GT, yel, pk & wht, M, C5...$60.00

Aurora, HO scale, #1473, Dune Buggy Coupe, yel, M, C5.$30.00

Aurora, HO scale, #1477, Tuff Ones AMX, red, wht & bl, M, C5...$35.00

Aurora, HO scale, #1478, Tuff Ones Firebird, yel & blk, M, C5...$45.00

Aurora, HO scale, #1479, Tuff Ones Cougar, wht & yel, M, C5...$40.00

Aurora, HO scale, #1480, Tuff Ones Camaro, bl & yel, NM+, C5...$45.00

Aurora, HO scale, #1481, Tuff Ones Dino Ferrari, red, wht & gr, M, C5...$35.00

Aurora, HO scale, #1483, Sand Van Dune Buggy, pk & wht, M, C5...$35.00

Aurora, HO scale, #1484, Supermodified, bl, rpl chrome, NM, C5 ....$100.00

Aurora, HO scale, #1487, Good Humor Ice Cream Truck, wht, in special display pack, MIB, C5 ....$55.00

Aurora, HO scale, #1494 Flamethrower Ford GT, brn & wht, M, C5...$35.00

Aurora, HO scale, #1495, Flamethrower Cobra GT, bl w/wht stripe, special dome box, MIB, C5..........................$45.00

Aurora, HO scale, #1496, Flamethrower Snad Van, gr, M, C5 ....$35.00

Aurora, HO scale, #1541, Jaguar Convertible, bl, MIB, C5...$75.00

Aurora, HO Scale, #1542, Mercedes Benz 300SL-VIB, dk gray, red & blk, MIB, P5 ....$80.00

Aurora, HO scale, #1542, Mercedes Convertible, wht, NM+, C5...$55.00

Aurora, HO scale, #1544, '60 Thunderbird, red, M, C5 ...$75.00

Aurora, HO scale, #1544, '60 Thunderbird, yel & blk, M, C5...$70.00

Aurora, HO scale, #1545, Jaguar, hardtop, yel, M, C5 .....$75.00

Aurora, HO scale, #1545, Jaguar XK 140 Hardtop-VIB, bl, tan, MIB, P5...$90.00

Aurora, HO scale, #1546, Mercedes, hardtop, wht & blk, NM+, C5...$75.00

Aurora, HO scale, #1548, '62 Ford Sunliner Convertible-VIB, MIB, P5...$80.00

Aurora, HO scale, #1549, Galaxie Sunliner, red, NM+, C5 .$75.00

Aurora, HO scale, #1550, Ford Galaxie Station Wagon, yel, M, C5...$100.00

Aurora, HO scale, #1552, Galaxie Police car, tan w/wht (no stars), NM+, C5...$95.00

Aurora, HO scale, #1552, Hot Rod Coupe, yel, M, C5 ....$85.00

Aurora, HO scale, #1553, Hot Rod Roadster, gr, M, C5 .$100.00

Aurora, HO scale, #1554, Hot Rod Coupe-VIB, lemon yel & red, MIB, P5...$80.00

Aurora, HO scale, #1583, Mack Dump Truck, red & gray, NM, C5...$70.00

Aurora, HO scale, #1969, '57 Corvette Convertible, AFX, orange, NM, P5...$75.00

Aurora, HO scale, #5786, '76 Supervette Screacher, AFX, MIB, P5...$15.00

Aurora, HO scale, #6203, Porsche 934 Turbo #81, AFX, wht, MIB, P5...$20.00

Cox, Ferrari Formula I, 1/24 scale, 75% built but all in box, NMIB, C5...$65.00

Cox, Lotus 40, used, nice decals, EX, C5 ....$55.00

Cox, 1/24 scale, LaCucaracha, kit, unused, M, C5 ....$35.00

Dynamic, AC Cobra, body kit, no chassis, MOC, C5 ......$40.00

Eldon, 1/32 scale, #1093-12 Lotus, red, EX, P5................$35.00

Eldon, 1/32 scale, #1350 Chaparral, wht, G, P5 ....$15.00

Eldon, 1/32 scale, #1518-11B Dune Buggy, purple, EX, P5.$40.00

Garvic, 1/24 scale, Ocelot, red, EX, C5..............................$35.00

Lionel, 1/32 scale, BRM Racing Car Formula I, red or gr, M, C5 ....$25.00

Lionel, 1/32 scale, Cooper Racing Car, yel, M, C5...........$25.00

Lionel, 1/32 scale, Jaguar D, lt bl, some decal flaking, M, C5 ....$35.00

Lionel, 1/32 scale, State Police Car, bl, nonfunctional lights, M C5 ....$55.00

Monogram, Ferrari GTO, body kit, no chassis, MOC, C5 ..$45.00

Revell, 1/24, #R3160:700 Corvette Stingray, SP900 fireball motor, aluminum chassis, med bl, MIB, P5..............$195.00

Strombecker, 1/32 scale, #9535 AM GT Coupe #7, wht, MIB, P5 ....$50.00

Strombecker, 1/32 scale, #9575, Corvette Convertible, red, orig box, EX, P5...$60.00

Strombecker, 1/32 scale, #9590 Chettah #58, orange, MIB, P5 ....$50.00

Strombecker, 1/32 scale, #9620/595, Jaguar XKE, red, orig box, EX, P5...$60.00

Strombecker, 1/32 scale, Ford GT, yel, 1970s, MIB, C5...$25.00

Strombecker, 1/32 scale, Ford J Car, yel, MIB, C5...........$25.00

Strombecker, 1/32 scale, 6 Wheel Elf Formula, bl, M, C5 .$35.00

Tyco, HO scale, #7063, Mazda Miata MX-5, twin pack, red & gr, MIB, P5...$50.00

Tyco, HO scale, #8526, Corvette GT #4-Curve Hugger, bl & yel, MIB, P5...$25.00

Tyco, Ho scale, #8563, Corvette Silverstreak, #9 CH, chrome & pk, MIB, P5 ....$25.00

Tyco, HO scale, #8980T, Vette & Lamborgini, twin pack, blk & red, MIB, P5 ....$45.00

Tyco, HO scale, Canon Formula #2, 442 X2, wht, bl & yel, MIB, P5 ....$30.00

Tyco, US-1 Trucking, #3911 Fire Truck, red, MIB $47.50

Tyco, US-1 Trucking, #3941 Exxon Tank Trailer, MIB.....$9.00

Tyco, US-1 Trucking, #3942 Dupont Tank Trailer, MIB...$11.00

Tyco, US-1 Trucking, #3957 Army Jeep, olive drab, MIB..$22.50

Tyco, US-1 Trucking, Bordens Tank Trailer, MIB.............$9.00

Tyco, US-1 Trucking, Navajo Box Trailer, MIB $9.00

Tyco, US-1 Trucking, PIE Box Trailer, MIB $9.00

Tyco, US-1 Trucking, Redline Flatbed Trailer, MIB.........$7.50

Tyco, US-1 Trucking, Roadline Flatbed Trailer, MIB........$7.50

Tyco, US-1 Trucking, Shell Tank Trailer, MIB..................$9.00

Tyco, US-1 Trucking, Smith's Box Trailer, MIB...............$9.00

Accessories

Tyco, US-1 Trucking, #3410 Operating Crane Pipe Loader, MIB $14.00

Tyco, US-1 Trucking, #3415 Log-loading Bulldozer, MIB..$14.00

Tyco, US-1 Trucking, #3425 Gravel Truck Terminal, MIB $8.50

Tyco, US-1 Trucking, #3430 Freight Terminal, MIB.........$9.00

Tyco, US-1 Trucking, #3445 Garage, w/switch track, MIB.$11.00

Tyco, US-1 Trucking, #3450 Crate Loader, MIB...............$9.00

Tyco, US-1 Trucking, #3452 Gravel Unloading Site & Trailer, MIB $7.00

Tyco, US-1 Trucking, #3455 Auto Loader, MIB $9.00

Tyco, US-1 Trucking, #3460 Crate Unloader, MIB $7.00

Tyco, US-1 Trucking, Airport, w/Plane, MIB $28.00

Tyco, US-1 Trucking, Auto Unloader, MIB......................$9.00

Tyco, US-1 Trucking, Culvert Pipe Loader, MIB.............$8.50

Tyco, US-1 Trucking, Fire Station, w/switch track, MIB.$11.00

Tyco, US-1 Trucking, Pipe & Log Unloading Yard, MIB ..$6.50

Snow Domes

Snow domes are water-filled paperweights that come in several different styles. The earliest type was made in two pieces and consisted of a glass globe on a separate base. First made in the middle of the 19th century, they were revived during the thirties and forties by companies in America and Italy. Similar weights are being imported into the country today from the Orient. The most common snow domes on today's market are the plastic half-moon shapes made as souvenirs or Christmas toys, a style that originated in West Germany during the 1950s. Other shapes were made as well, including round and square bottles, short and tall rectangles, cubes and other simple shapes.

During the 1970s, figural plastic snow domes were especially popular. There are two types — large animate shapes themselves containing the snow scene, or dome shapes that have figures draped over the top. Today's collectors buy them all, old or new. For further information we recommend *Collector's Guide to Snow Domes* by Helene Guarnaccia, published by Collector Books.

Advertising

American Express Vacations, dome w/advertising against bl ground, '800' number on wht ftd base, EX $15.00

Coca-Cola, woman holding bottle of Coke, dk bl background w/wht ftd base, EX $12.00

Gordon Hart Truck Line, clear globe on blk trapezoid base w/gold lettering, shows Hart truck against cityscape, EX $40.00

IBM, dome w/wht prototype computer against lt bl European map, ftd base, EX $25.00

Maurer-Reifen Technic Service, dome w/penguin holding Uniroyal tire against wht w/bl advertising, wht ftd base, EX $12.00

Character

Barber the Elephant, storybook character by Jean de Brunoff, in dome on wht ftd base mk Barber in red, EX..............$15.00

Felix the Cat, Determined Productions, Standing Ovations, 1987, $15.00.

Little Mermaid, Bully, tall dome on rnd bl base mk Disney Collection, 1986, EX $18.00

Marilyn Monroe, Enesco, Marilyn in director's chair surrounded by memorabilia, glass dome on blk base w/signature, EX $35.00

Mickey Mouse, Bully, blk & wht Mickey in stride in dome on rnd blk base, 1977, EX $18.00

Paul Bunyan & His Blue Ox Babe, bl ground in dome on wht ftd base, EX..$15.00

Pluto, Kurt Adler, glass globe on rnd wood base, 1988, EX.$15.00

Snoopy, Willits, smiling Snoopy wearing red hat & scarf in dome on rnd red base w/wht plate mk Hup Hup Hup, 1966, EX...$20.00

Figurals

Alligator (seated), dk brn w/alligators on seesaw in globe belly, mk New Orleans, EX $12.00

Bats in My Belfry!, plastic, gray skull surrounding globe containing bats, orange base w/blk lettering, EX....................$16.00

Captain & Seaman, plastic, sailing ship in globe before sea captain in blk w/arm-around pipe-smoking seaman in brn, EX...$40.00

Christmas Tree, plastic, Santa in globe inserted in middle of decorated tree, EX...$25.00

Coffeepot, clear plastic w/boy playing in snow, EX...........$15.00

Girl w/Snowman, upper half of snowman atop clear globe contaiing only glitter next to girl in pk coat, EX $16.00

Lion, plastic, lion resting atop dome containing lion in jungle setting, wht base, mk African Lion Safari..., EX $18.00

Mickey Mouse, plastic, Mickey seated holding globe between legs, shows castle, EX.......................................$80.00

Santa & Mrs Claus Sitting Atop Chimney, plastic, red & wht w/4 choir boys against red ground in center, EX........$20.00

Santa w/Wrinkled Brow (standing), Santa w/bag against trees in globe belly, EX...$20.00

Snowman, Applause, ceramic, snowman smoking pipe w/snowman & 2 'bear' kids in globe belly, 1988, EX $18.00

Holidays and Special Occasions

Christmas, Santa on chimney in clear glass globe with green base, 1950s, $40.00. (Photo courtesy Nancy McMichael.)

Birthday, boy & girl holding up cake on platform mk Happy Birthday against bl ground in plastic dome on wht ftd base, EX...$8.00

Christmas, Santa & snowman on seesaw against bl ground in dome on wht ftd base, EX.....................................$8.00

Christmas, the Disney gang w/gifts around Christmas tree in clear globe, red base w/paper label mk Merry Christmas, EX..$10.00

Easter, Midwest Imports, rabbits in egg-shaped globe on rnd yel base, 1988, EX..$8.00

Halloween, Celebrations, pumpkin-shaped globe atop blk wood base, EX..$25.00

Halloween, wht light-up skull in glass globe w/glitter, blk base w/allover orange 'Boo' & star design, battery-op, EX..$22.00

Valentine's Day, red heart in cylinder shape w/flat bk, slot for personal photo, gold glitter, pk base, EX...................$14.00

Souvenirs

Alaska, pine trees before lake & mountains in dome on blk base w/Alaska lettered in wht, EX...............................$10.00

Calgary Zoo, name plaque & 2 resting tigers in grass against blk ground in dome on rnd blk base, EX $12.00

Gateway Arch, name plaque & river traffic under the Arch against dk bl ground in dome on wht ftd base, EX.....$15.00

Hoover Dam, name plaque & dam against bl ground in plastic dome on wht base, EX...$10.00

London, London Bridge & Parliament buildings against dk bl ground in dome on wht ftd base, EX $10.00

Nautilus Atomic Sub, glass, $50.00; War Between the States, plastic, $15.00. (Photo courtesy Nancy McMichael.)

New York World's Fair 1964-1965, name plaque & pastel Unisphere against NY City skyline in dome on wht ftd base, EX..$25.00

South Dakota, name plaque & buffalo standing before pine trees against bl ground in dome on wht base, EX $10.00

St Augustine, 3-masted ship against billowy cloud & bl sky in dome on wht plastic base w/name in blk script, EX $8.00

Miscellaneous

Ashtray, snow baby in glass globe on rnd blk Bakelite ashtray, EX...$70.00

German-Made Dome, red, yel & bl tractor-trailer against bl ground in plastic dome on wht ftd base, EX.................$8.00

Glass Dome, Masonic emblem in globe on wht trapezoid base lettered in bl, 1950s, EX.................................$35.00

Kaleidoscope, Silvestri, red w/wht snowflake design, clear center dome shows Santa & 2 kids, music box in bottom, EX...$30.00

Pencil Sharpener, Niagara Falls scene w/name plaque in plastic dome on yel ftd base w/sharpener, EX.................$12.00

Religious Dome, Crucifixion, 3 mourners at foot of cross, tall plastic dome on wht base, EX.................$10.00

Spinning Waterball Pin-On, lapel pin, China, M (VG card) $10.00

Soldiers

'Dimestore soldiers' were made from the 1930s until sometime in the 1950s. Some of the better-known companies who made these small-scale figures and accessories were Barclay, Manoil, and Jones (hollow cast lead); Gray Iron (cast iron); and Auburn (rubber). They're about 4" to 4½" high. They were sold in Woolworth's and Kresge's 5 & 10 stores (most for just five cents), hence the name 'Dimestore.' Marx made tin soldiers for use in target gun games; these sell for about $4.00. Condition is most important as these soldiers saw lots of action. They're most often found with much of the paint worn off. There were over 600 soldiers made, plus a number of others by minor makers such as Tommy Toy and All-Nu. Serious collectors should refer to *Collecting Toys* (1993) or *Toy Soldiers* (1992), both by Richard O'Brien, Books Americana.

Another very popular toy soldier has been made by Britains of England since 1893. They are smaller and more detailed than 'Dimestores,' and variants number in the thousands. O'Brien's book has over 200 pages devoted to Britains and other foreign makers.

You'll notice that in addition to the soldiers, many of our descriptions and values are for the vehicles, cannons, animals, etc., made and sold to accompany them. Note: Percentages in the description lines refer to the amount of original paint remaining, a very important worth-assessing factor. See also Plastic Figures.

Key:
ROAN — Regiments of All Nations

Barclay, aircraft carrier, no planes, all guns intact, very scarce, 94%, A1 ....$90.00

Barclay, antiaircraft gun truck, 2 men, new tires, 4", VG, P4 ....$35.00

Barclay, antiaircraft gunner, gr, M, A1.................................$21.00

Barclay, army truck, khaki, wht tires, 99%, A1.................$23.00

Barclay, at attention, cast hat, 100% pnt, A1.................$27.00

Barclay, at the ready, early version, 96%, A1.................$19.00

Barclay, bayonetting (no bayonet, thrusting with gun muzzle), cast helmet, M, $160.00; clubbing with rifle, cast helmet, M, $90.00.

Barclay, aviator, brn, 99%, A1 ....$17.00

Barclay, bazooka man, brn, 96%, A1.................................$14.00

Barclay, beer truck, red w/wht tires, no barrels, mk 'Beer' & 'Barclay #376' on inside, 1930s, 98%, A1.................$40.00

Barclay, bomb thrower, rifle off ground, tin helmet, VG, P4 ....$22.00

Barclay, Boy Scout cooking, scarce, 94%, A1.................$43.00

Barclay, Boy Scout saluting, scarce, 98%, A1.................$38.00

Barclay, boy skater, gr, bl, or orange & bl, 98%, A1.................$12.00

Barclay, bride, 99%, A1...$20.00

Barclay, bugler, gr, 98%, A1...$20.00

Barclay, bugler, khaki, early version, 94%, A1.................$17.00

Barclay, bull, reddish brn w/blk spots, 98%, A1.................$15.50

Barclay, bullet feeder, 98%, A1...$20.00

Barclay, cab for auto transport, no trailer or cars, red, 97%, A1...$14.00

Barclay, cadet officer, short stride, plume in hair intact, 90%, A1...$20.00

Barclay, cannon, elevated barrel, silver w/red wheels, 98%, A1...$19.00

Barclay, cannon, silver w/red spoked wheels, closed hitch, sm, 99%, A1...$18.00

Barclay, cannon car, gunner low, rpt, new tires, G, P4.....$25.00

Barclay, car carrier, early version w/wht tires, gr cab, bl slush-cast trailer, 2 sm cars, both red, 99%, A1, set.................$65.00

Barclay, cars, plastic wheels, sm, 99%, A1.................$8.00

Barclay, charging, cast helmet, long stride, rpt, G, P4.....$25.00

Barclay, charging, gr, M, A1...$21.00

Barclay, clubbing w/rifle, rusty tin hat, scarce, 93%, A1..$60.00

Barclay, cow lying down, M, A1...$14.00

Barclay, cowboy, w/lasso, rpt, G, P4.................................$15.00

Barclay, cowboy w/lasso, 100%, A1.................................$21.00

Barclay, cowboy w/tin brim hat, G, P4.................................$9.00

Barclay, crawling w/rifle, 94%, A1.................................$24.00

Barclay, dbl-decker car carrier: tractor, 96%; trailer, M; 4 cars, 99%; A1...$46.00

Barclay, delivery truck, red w/wht rubber tires, #309, 3", 95%, A1 ....$27.00

Barclay, doctor w/bag in brn, 94%, A1............................$18.00

Barclay, drum major, wht helmet, baton intact, very sm chip on bk of base, 97%, A1 ....$51.00

Barclay, dump truck, red cab, bl bed, 1960s, M, A1..........$15.00

Barclay, falling w/rifle, 99%, A1.....................................$35.00

Barclay, farm tractor, orange, lg blk metal wheels, scarce, 1930s, 95%, A1 ....$34.00

Barclay, field cannon w/lg rubber tires, spring action, khaki, mk 'Barclay' on the barrel, 98%, A1 ....$32.00

Barclay, fireman w/hose, 98%, A1...................................$29.00

Barclay, flagbearer, brn, 99%, A1 ....$19.00

Barclay, flagbearer, cast hat, 99%, A1 ....$24.00

Barclay, flagbearer, gr pot helmet, 97%, A1.....................$25.00

Barclay, flagbearer, long stride, tin hat, 99%, A1 ....$25.00

Barclay, flamethrower, gr, M, A1 ....$21.00

Barclay, girl on skis, bl, M, A1.......................................$20.00

Barclay, girl on sled, yel outfit, yel sled, sm dent in side of sled, 99%, A1 ....$17.00

Barclay, grazing cow, wht & tan, M, A1 ....$15.00

Barclay, horse, wht, 95%, A1..$11.00

Barclay, in gas mask w/rifle, tin hat, 97%, A1...................$21.50

Barclay, Indian on horse, 99%, A1...................................$34.00

Barclay, Indian w/bow & arrow, VG, P4...........................$12.00

Barclay, Indian w/bow & arrow, 99%, A1..........................$16.00

Barclay, Indian w/knife & spear, 97%, A1 ....$13.00

Barclay, Indian w/shield & tomahawk, 99%, A1 ....$15.00

Barclay, Japanese house for dish garden set, lg, 97%, A1..$39.00

Barclay, jockey on horse, gold horse, red shirt, #8, 99%, A1 .$28.00

Barclay, jockey on horse, silver horse, yel shirt, #8, 97%, A1 ....$26.00

Barclay, kneeling w/field phone, 92% pnt, A1.................$21.00

Barclay, knight w/shield, M, A1 ....$19.00

Barclay, little girl, in rocker, in red, 99%, A1 ....$20.00

Barclay, little girl in red, 98%, A1..................................$13.00

Barclay, machine gunner, prone, cast hat, 93%, A1 ....$22.00

Barclay, machine gunner kneeling, short stride, G, P4.....$18.00

Barclay, machine gunner kneeling, tin hat, maroon gun, 99%, A1 ....$22.00

Barclay, man, 99%, A1 ....$9.00

Barclay, man on skis, red, 99%, A1 ....$19.00

Barclay, man on sled, 98%, A1..$17.50

Barclay, marching, right shoulder arms, brn, M, A1 ....$17.00

Barclay, marching at slope arms, 97%, A1 ....$17.00

Barclay, marching w/gun slung over shoulder, M, A1.......$17.00

Barclay, marching w/pack, cast hat, scarce, 98%, A1 ......$40.00

Barclay, marching w/pack, tin hat, 97%, A1.....................$28.00

Barclay, marine, long stride, dk bl uniform, 96%, A1.......$34.00

Barclay, marine, 95%, A1..$17.00

Barclay, marksman, gr, M, A1 ....$21.00

Barclay, milkman, 97%, A1..$13.00

Barclay, minister holding hat, 99%, A1 ....$20.00

Barclay, minister walking, scarce, 93%, A1 ....$39.00

Barclay, monoplane, silver, tin overhead wing, wht rubber tires, mk 'Made in USA' on side, very scarce, 98%, A1 .....$98.00

Barclay, motor unit truck, khaki, wht rubber tires, peg hitch (bent), 98%, A1...$15.00

Barclay, moving truck, no decals, gr & silver, 99%, A1 ...$14.00

Barclay, naval officer, wht, long stride, 99%, A1 ....$22.00

Barclay, nurse, scarce, 96%, A1 ....$31.00

Barclay, officer, brn, 95%, A1 ....$13.00

Barclay, officer, khaki, early version, 97%, A1 ....$22.00

Barclay, officer, long stride, tin hat, 98% pnt, A1 ....$27.00

Barclay, officer, short stride, rpt, G, P4............................$15.00

Barclay, officer w/gas mask, cast hat, 97%, A1.................$22.00

Barclay, officer w/sword, M, A1......................................$24.00

Barclay, officer w/sword, tin helmet, long stride, G, P4....$18.00

Barclay, oil truck, red & bl, no decals, 1960s, 98%, A1....$15.00

Barclay, peeling potatoes, 96%, A1 ....$25.00

Barclay, pig, 93%, A1..$9.00

Barclay, pigeon dispatcher, missing sm part of pigeon, G, P4...$14.00

Barclay, pigeon dispatcher, 94%, A1................................$27.00

Barclay, pilot, 98%, A1..$21.00

Barclay, pirate, bl outfit, 97%, A1 ....$23.00

Barclay, racer 1931 Golden Arrow, no pnt, scarce, A1 ....$10.00

Barclay, range finder, 95%, A1 ....$25.00

Barclay, running w/rifle, cast hat, 97%, A1......................$27.50

Barclay, sailor, in wht, reddish hair, 94%, A1 ....$16.00

Barclay, sailor, in wht, long stride, 99%, A1 ....$25.00

Barclay, sailor marching, right shoulder arms, 94%, A1 ...$14.50

Barclay, Santa on sled, 93%, A1 ....$21.00

Barclay, seated machine gunner, early version 95%, A1 ..$18.00

Barclay, sentry, G, P4..$15.00

Barclay, sentry, 98%, A1 ....$22.00

Barclay, sheep lying down, M, A1 ....$12.50

Barclay, shoeshine boy, scarce, 99%, A1..........................$32.00

Barclay, side-dump truck, yel & bl, 1965, MBP, A1 ....$29.50

Barclay, skier in wht, no skis, 98%, A1 ....$29.50

Barclay, sniper kneeling, brn, 99%, A1............................$17.00

Barclay, soldier, bomb thrower, rifle off ground, tin hat, rusty helmet, 99%, A1..$28.50

Barclay, stretcher bearer, 96%, A1 ....$20.00

Barclay, surgeon w/stethoscope, 95%, A1 ....$26.00

Barclay, thrusting bayonet, tin hat, scarce, 98%, A1 ....$56.00

Barclay, tommy gunner, cast hat, 95%, A1 ....$31.50

Barclay, tommy gunner, gr, M, A1 ....$21.00

Barclay, tractor trailer, Allied Van Lines decals, orange tractor & trailer, 97%, A1..$24.00

Barclay, train conductor, 98%, A1 ....$12.50

Barclay, travel trailer only, no sedan, wht rubber tires, 95%, A1 ....$29.00

Barclay, tubist, wht helmet, scarce, 98%, A1 ....$57.00

Barclay, typist, no typewriter or table, 97%, A1 ....$36.00

Barclay, typist w/typewriter, no table, 99%, A1 ....$65.00

Barclay, US Army pursuit plane, red, fuselage notched for piggy-bk plane, 93%, A1 ....$28.00

Barclay, VW, bl, slightly larger than BV102, scarce, M, A1..$18.00

Barclay, w/antiaircraft gun, cast hat, M, A1.....................$29.50

Barclay, w/antiaircraft gun, sitting, cast hat, 97%, A1......$27.50

Barclay, w/gas mask, charging, tin hat, rusty helmet, 97%, A1...$23.00

Barclay, West Point Cadet, long stride, gray uniform, plume on cap intact, 97%, A1...$23.00

Barclay, wireless operator, VG, P4 ....$40.00

Barclay, 3-pc train set, blk plastic wheels, silver loco, gr tender, red passenger car, M, A1 ....$20.00

Barclay HO, brakeman, 98%, A1 ....$8.00

Barclay HO, conductor, 99%, A1 ....$10.00

Barclay HO, dining steward, 90%, A1.....................$5.00

Barclay HO, fireman, 98%, A1.............................$10.00

Barclay HO, hobo, M, A1...................................$9.00

Barclay HO, little boy, red shirt, tan pants, scarce, M, A1..$17.00

Barclay HO, little girl, scarce, 99%, A1 ....$16.00

Barclay HO, newsboy, dk gr, M, A1.......................$10.00

Barclay HO, policeman, 99%, A1............................$8.00

Barclay HO, porter, M, A1.................................$11.00

Barclay HO, redcap, 99%, A1...............................$9.00

Barclay HO, woman (no dog), M, A1........................$9.00

Barclay HO, woman w/baby, lt bl, scarce, 99%, A1.........$16.00

Britains, #1, Life Guards, mounted at the walk, some pnt chips & wear, VG, A $75.00

Britains, #2, Royal Horse Guards, mounted at the walk, 5-pc, EX, A $90.00

Britains, #17, Somerset Light Infantry at the ready, postwar, G+, B5 ....$98.00

Britains, #19, West India Regt, sq bases, EX, B5..............$19.00

Britains, #30, Drums & Bugles of the Line, drummer has chipped base, 6-pc, VG, A $100.00

Britains, #35, Royal Marines, marching at slope arms, 8-pc, EX, A $100.00

Britains, #48, Egyptian Camel Corps, re-tied in orig box, 6-pcs, EX, A $260.00

Britains, #66, Duke of Connaught's Lancers, postwar, set of 5, EX-, B5 ....$118.00

Britains, #116, Sudanese Infantry, at the trail, minor pnt chips, 8-pc, VG, A $350.00

Britains, #120, Coldstream Guards, kneeling, firing, postwar, EX-, B5 ....$94.00

Britains, #133, Russian Infantry at the trail, set of 8, G+, B5 ....$164.00

Britains, #134, Japanese Infantry, minimal mismatch, set of 8, G+, B5 ....$248.00

Britains, #135, Japanese Calvary, 1 slight mismatch, set of 8, G+, B5 ....$374.00

Britains, #145, Royal Army Medical Corps, Ambulance, gray wagon, 7-pc, EX, A $425.00

Britains, #146, Royal Army Service Corps, wagon w/2 horses, driver & 2 men, EX, A $325.00

Britains, #147, Zulus of Africa, 7-pc, EX, A..................$110.00

Britains, #154, Prussian Infantry, mismatch, G+, B5......$148.00

Britains, #164, Mounted Arabs, set of 8, G+, B5 ....$98.00

Britains, #169, Italian Bersaglieri, early postwar no officer, set of 8, EX-, B5 ....$124.00

Britains, #171, Greek Infantry, officer, EX-, B5 ....$38.00

Britains, #172, Bulgarian Infantry at the slope, G, B5 ......$34.00

Britains, #179, Cowboys, mtd & on foot, tied in orig box (no end label), EX, A $130.00

Britains, #182, 11th Hussers, Prince Albert's Own (dismounted), untied in orig ROAN box, minor chips, 8-pc, EX, A .$200.00

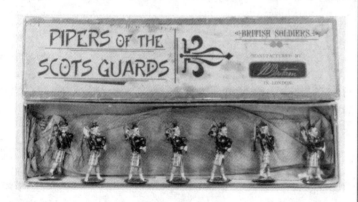

Britains, #69, Pipers of the Scots Guards, first version with oval bases, ca 1900, EX (G box), A, $550.00.

Britains, #193, Arabs of the Desert, ca 1920, EX (VG box), A, $1,600.00.

Britains, #74, Royal Welch Fusiliers, w/goat mascot, 8-pc, EX, A $110.00

Britains, #75, Scots Guards, prewar, sq bases, set of 8, G, B5 ....$98.00

Britains, #76, Middlesex Regiment, marching at the slope, 8-pc, EX, A $90.00

Britains, #77 Gorden Highlanders, marching at the slope, 5-pc, G-VG, A $50.00

Britains, #100, Empress of India Lancer in full dress, blk horse, EX-, B5 ....$34.00

Britains, #196 Greek Evzones, blk jackets, set of 8, EX-, B5 ....$118.00

Britains, #199 British Motor Machine Gun Corps, G+, B5 ....$64.00

Britains, #202, Togoland Warriors, w/bows & arrows, 8-pc, EX, A $110.00

Britains, #225, Kings African Rifle, 8-pc, EX, A...........$160.00

Britains, #228 US Marines, no officer, set of 8, G+, B5 .$108.00

Britains, #299, West Point Cadets, summer, postwar, set of 8, ROAN box, EX-, B5 ....$124.00

Britains, #717, Antiaircraft Gun, 1-pc, EX, A $70.00

Britains, #1258, Knights in Armor w/Squires, Herald & Marshall, 6-pc, VG-EX, A $250.00

Britains, #1349, Royal Canadian Mounted Police, pnt chips, 5-pc, VG, A $100.00

Britains, #1470, State Coach, King George & Queen, 8 horses, over-pnt, VG, A $110.00

Britains, #1475, Attendants to the State Coach, footmen, outriders & yeomen, 18-pc, VG-EX, A $230.00

Britains, #1527, Band of the Royal Air Force, 12-pc, VG-EX, A $525.00

Britains, #1542, New Zealand Infantry, Service Dress, marching at the slope, 8-pc, VG-EX, A $210.00

Britains, #1554, Royal Canadian Mounted Police, marching, 8-pc, VG-EX, A $110.00

Britains, #1631, Canadian Governor General's Horse Guards, 4-pc, VG+, A $55.00

Britains, #1633, Canadian Light Infantry, marching at the slope, 8-pc, VG, A $110.00

Britains, #1659, mtd knight w/maze, MIB, B5 ....$96.50

Britains, #1662, mtd knight w/lance, MIB, B5 ....$114.50

Britains, #1723, Royal Army Medical Corps Stretcher Bearer Unit, 9-pc, VG-EX, A $100.00

Britains, #1758, Royal Air Force Fire Fighters, 8-pc, VG-EX, A $425.00

Britains, #1759, Stretcher Party & Gas Decontamination Men, minor pnt loss, VG, A $400.00

Britains, #1791, Motorcycle Dispatch Riders, 4-pc, VG-EX, A $160.00

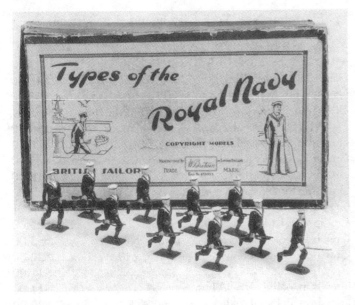

Britains, #1806 Royal Navy Bluejackets, EX (G- box), A, $1,900.00.

Britains, #1901, Capetown Highlanders, marching, 8-pc, VG-EX, A $130.00

Britains, #1911, Officers & Petty Officers of the Royal Navy, 7-pc, VG-EX, A $120.00

Britains, #2010, Airbourne Infantry, 7-pc, EX, A $100.00

Britains, #2011, Royal Air Force Officers, Flight Sergeants, Dispatch Rider, Aircraftsman, RAF Regiments, 22-pc, EX, A $300.00

Britains, #2071, Royal Marine Officer, at salute, marines presenting arms, 7-pc, VG, A $80.00

Britains, #2073, Royal Air Force, marching at the slope, w/officer, 8-pc, VG, A $100.00

Britains, #2080, Royal Navy, marching at the slope, w/officer, 8-pc, VG-EX, A $130.00

Britains, #2087, 5th Royal Inniskilling Dragoon Guards, 7-pc, VG-EX, A $160.00

Britains, #2090, Royal Irish Fusiliers, at attention, w/officers, 8-pc, VG-EX, A $150.00

Britains, #2092, Parachute Regiment, marching at the slope, 8-pc, VG-EX, A $160.00

Britains, #2094, State Open Landau, w/drivers, Queen, Prince Phillip & attendants, VG-EX, A $225.00

Britains, #2148, Fort Henry Guards, w/mascot, 7-pc, VG-EX, A $110.00

Britains, #9302, Attendants to the State Coach, outsiders & yeomen, 12-pc, G-VG, A $130.00

Britains, Arabs, mtd, 2 w/muskets, 3-pc, G-VG, A...........$80.00

Britains, boy on Shetland pony, G+, B5 ....$24.50

Britains, Bulgarian officer, G+, B5 ....$44.00

Britains, collie, blk & wht, G+, B5 ....$3.25

Britains, cow, blk & wht, G+, B5 ....$3.75

Britains, farmer w/walking stick, G+, B5 ....$4.50

Britains, girl w/feeding basket, EX, B5 ....$13.75

Britains, gorilla, EX-, B5 ....$9.75

Britains, Greek Evzone, red jacket, EX-, B5 ....$15.00

Britains, hare running, EX, B5 ....$4.75

Britains, Himalayan bear, EX, B5 ....$9.25

Britains, hippo, EX-, B5 ....$17.75

Britains, horse feeding, brn, EX, B5 ....$5.25

Britains, Indian elephant, young, EX, B5 ....$24.50

Britains, man w/wheelbarrow, G+, B5 ....$9.75

Britains, sheep walking, EX, B5 ....$3.00

Britains, shepherd w/crook, G+, B5 ....$9.75

Britains, stable lad, EX-, B5 ....$7.75

Britains, traffic policeman, postwar, G+, B5 ....$13.75

Britains, zebra, G, B5 ....$6.25

Courtenay, Alain, Lord of Montendre, H13, fully armored w/visorless helmet, red & gold trappings, 3⅛", EX, A.............$475.00

Courtenay, Black Prince, H6, blk armor, red & wht trappings, mk R Courtenay, minor chips, 3", VG-EX, A $350.00

Courtenay, Earl of Nassau, H1, bl robe w/gold trim, mk R Courtenay, lt chip on horse's hind leg, 5¼", VG-EX, A $400.00

Courtenay, John, King of France, #6, gold & wht tunic, mk R Courtenay, 1¾", EX, A..................................$170.00

Courtenay, John Lord Mohum, H12, gold & blk horse blanket, mk R Courtenay, lt pnt wear on horses ears, 3¼", EX, A $1,200.00

Courtenay, King Henry V, mtd in full gold armor, broadsword in movable right arm, mk R Courtenay, 3", VG-EX, A.$250.00

Courtenay, Lord de la Warr, #15, red shirt & shield w/heraldic bird, red plume on helmet, mk R Courtenay, 2¼", EX, A..................................$325.00

Courtenay, Louis Doria, delivering blow w/battle-axe, orange & wht shirt, mk R Courtenay, 2", EX, A $600.00

Courtenay, Sir Bartholomew Burghuren, #20, 1-eyed, red shirt mk R Courtenay, missing short sword hdl, 2⅜", VG-EX, A $240.00

Courtenay, Sir John Havering on horse with battle-axe in movable right arm, EX, A, $1,500.00.

Courtenay, Sir Miles Stapleton, Order of the Garter, standing knight w/off-wht shirt, red & bl cape, 2", EX, A $170.00

Courtenay, Sir Robert Dacre, #22, visorless helmet, red & wht shirt, mk R Courtenay, 2", EX, A $160.00

Courtenay, Thomas, Earl of Warwick, H12, red shirt & trappings, mk R Courtenay, right leg & base cracked, 3¼", VG, A $625.00

Dinky, #150B officer, w/binoculars, NM, F2 ....$20.00

Dinky, #150B Private, seated, EX, F2 ....$15.00

Dinky, #150C Private, standing, NM, F2 ....$20.00

Dinky, #150E NCO, walking, M, F2 ....$22.00

Dinky, #160B gunner, seated, EX, F2 ....$22.00

Dinky, #160D gunner, standing, EX, F2 ....$22.00

Dinky, #603 Private, driver, NM, F2 ....$15.00

Elastolin, #10 German officer, EX-, B5 ....$16.00

Elastolin, #14/12 Navy marching, G, B5 ....$25.00

Elastolin, #47/24 German w/schellenbaum, EX-, B5 ......$125.00

Elastolin, #60N German bandleader standing, EX-, B5....$45.00

Elastolin, #581 German kneeling throwing hand grenade, G, B5 ....$30.00

Elastolin, #628 German standing, shooting, EX-, B5........$30.00

Elastolin, #646/6 German medic marching, G, B5 ....$20.00

Elastolin, #649 Hindenburg, G, B5 ....$40.00

Elastolin, #650/3 Blomberg saluting, G+, B5 ....$50.00

Elastolin, #656/8 Red Cross dog, G, B5...........................$20.00

Elastolin, #659/1 German lying w/telephone, EX-, B5 .....$40.00

Elastolin, #662/32 German rubber boat w/2 men rowing, G+, B5 ....$275.00

Elastolin, #664/10N German lying w/lg machine gun, G+, B5...$40.00

Elastolin, #664/18 German kneeling w/shell, EX-, B5 ......$35.00

Elastolin, #664/3½ German standing w/binoculars & map, G, B5 ....$30.00

Elastolin, #664/56 German officer w/1 movable arm behind logs, G+, B5 ....$40.00

Elastolin, #664/7 German lying w/ammo belt, G, B5 ....$30.00

Elastolin, #664/8 German sitting w/rangefinder, G+, B5..$30.00

Elastolin, #665/7 German standing w/rangefinder, G+, B5..$35.00

Elastolin, New York City mounted policemen, ca 1829, set of four, G, A, $400.00.

Gama, tank, 'Med Tank MHG,' EX, B5............................$45.00

Gama, tank, American T65, G+, B5................................$65.00

Grey Iron, Battery F , bent over pulling lanyard, scarce, EX, A1...$8.50

Grey Iron, Battery F loader, bending, scarce, EX+, A1 ....$8.50

Grey Iron, Battery F shell stack, extremely scarce, EX, A1.$45.00

Grey Iron, Blk porter, scarce, 98%, A1 ....$18.00

Grey Iron, boy in summer suit, scarce, 97%, A1 ....$32.00

Grey Iron, Boy Scout saluting, early version, gr neckerchief, 98%, A1 ....$23.00

Grey Iron, boy w/life preserver, scarce, 98%, A1 ....$55.00

Grey Iron, bugler, orange puttees, 97%, A1 ....$22.00

Grey Iron, calf, 98%, A1..$11.00

Grey Iron, collie, 97%, A1 ....$11.00

Grey Iron, colonial soldier, port arms, 98%, A1 ....$27.00

Grey Iron, conductor, 96%, A1 ....$10.00

Grey Iron, engineer, aluminum, scarce, 98%, A1 ....$13.00

Grey Iron, Ethiopian, tribesman, pnt chips on face, scarce, 96%, A1 ....$65.00

Grey Iron, Ethiopian chief, scarce, 95%, A1.....................$77.00

Grey Iron, Ethiopian officer, sm pnt chips have rusted, very scarce, 89%, A1 ....$54.00

Grey Iron, Ethiopian soldier, charging, scarce, 94%, A1..$70.00

Grey Iron, farmer, 95%, A1...$12.50

Grey Iron, farmer's wife, 98%, A1 ....$15.00
Grey Iron, fence gate, scarce, 99%, A1 ....$28.00
Grey Iron, Foreign Legion, US Marine in bl, marching, scarce, 97%, A1 ....$52.00
Grey Iron, Foreign Legion, US Marine in bl, officer, scarce, 95%, A1 ....$55.00
Grey Iron, garage man, gr, 94%, A1 ....$16.00
Grey Iron, girl, 97%, A1 ....$18.00
Grey Iron, girl skipping rope, no rope, 92%, A1 ....$14.00
Grey Iron, girl w/sand pail, scarce, 99%, A1 ....$57.00
Grey Iron, goose, 98%, A1 ....$9.00
Grey Iron, Grey Clip aeroplane, no wing or pilots, very rare, EX+, A1 ....$55.00
Grey Iron, hired man digging, scarce, 97%, A1 ....$20.00
Grey Iron, Legion color bearer, 97%, A1 ....$29.00
Grey Iron, lifeguard chair, scarce, 93%, A1 ....$49.00
Grey Iron, man in traveling suit, brn, 98%, A1 ....$11.00
Grey Iron, old man seated, 99%, A1 ....$16.00
Grey Iron, old woman seated, lavender dress, 98%, A1....$16.00
Grey Iron, pirate w/sword, gr outfit, 94%, A1 ....$28.00
Grey Iron, policeman, 99%, A1 ....$20.00
Grey Iron, postman in gray, 97%, A1 ....$13.00
Grey Iron, Royal Canadian police, late version, 95%, A1.$32.00
Grey Iron, sheep, 99%, A1 ....$12.00
Grey Iron, ski trooper w/ repro skis, scarce, 99%, A1 ....$79.00
Grey Iron, Uncle Sam's Defenders, charging rifleman, 94%, A1..$6.00
Grey Iron, Uncle Sam's Defenders, seated machine gunner, 96%, A1 ....$7.50
Grey Iron, US Doughboy, bomber crawling, brn pistol, 98%, A1..$29.00
Grey Iron, US Doughboy, officer, early version, 93%, A1.$15.50
Grey Iron, US Doughboy, officer, 97%, A1 ....$16.00
Grey Iron, US Doughboy, shoulder arms, 97%, A1 ....$16.00
Grey Iron, US Infantry, charging, early version, 98%, A1.$21.00
Grey Iron, US Infantry, officer, 98%, A1 ....$20.00
Grey Iron, US Infantry, port arms, 98%, A1 ....$23.00
Grey Iron, US Infantry, shoulder arms, early version, 98%, A1..$17.50
Grey Iron, US machine gunner, orange puttees, brn gun, 97%, A1 ....$19.00
Grey Iron, US machine gunner, postwar silver gun, 95%, A1 ....$16.00
Grey Iron, US Naval officer in bl, 94%, A1....................$20.00
Grey Iron, US sailor in bl, 98%, A1 ....$24.00
Grey Iron, wounded on crutches, rpt, G........................$12.00
Lineol, #5/1, Hitler standing in party cap, EX-, B5.........$250.00
Lineol, #5/3M, Musolini w/movable arms, EX-, B5 ....$225.00
Lineol, #5/8/1 General giving army salute, G+, B5 ....$135.00
Lineol, #5/10 German officer w/arm akimbo, EX-, B5......$50.00
Lineol, #5/18M, Musolini mtd, G+, B5 ....$375.00
Lineol, #5/31 German advancing w/flag, G+, B5 ....$115.00
Lineol, #5/37B Danish gray w/rifle over shoulder, EX-, B5...$20.00
Lineol, #5/37T Danish brn marching w/backpack, EX-, B5 .$13.00
Lineol, #5/54 Danish gray w/bass drum, G+, B5 ....$24.00
Lineol, #5/66 Danish brn standing, shooting, EX-, B5......$15.00
Lineol, #5/66 German standing, shooting, G, B5 ....$20.00
Lineol, #5/77 German clubbing, EX-, B5 ....$35.00

Lineol, #5/79/2 Danish gray throwing hand grenade, G, B5 ....$20.00
Lineol, #5/79/2 German throwing hand grenade, G-, B5 .$15.00
Lineol, #5/88/2 Danish brn honor guard (unusual), EX-, B5 ....$45.00
Lineol, #5/100 German w/telegraph, G+, B5 ....$65.00
Lineol, #5/159 German lying w/rifle & ammo box, G+, B5.$40.00
Lineol, #5/163 Danish gray w/lt machine gun, EX-, B5 ...$35.00
Lineol, #5/181 German nurse w/bucket, EX-, B5............$45.00
Lineol, #5/184 German medic w/canteen, EX-, B5 ....$35.00
Lineol, #5/203 Danish brn carrying wounded, EX-, B5.....$42.00
Lineol, #5/250 & #5/241 mortar & shells, EX-, B5.........$100.00
Lineol, #5/370 Danish gray officer, EX-, B5 ....$12.00
Lineol, #5/370 German officer, EX-, B5 ....$20.00
Lineol, #5/2510 Danish gray officer mtd, G, B5 ....$50.00
Lineol, #7/2, Goering marching w/baton (no sword), G+, B5 ....$125.00
Lineol, #184/3 Indian w/spear & bow, yel & red, EX-, B5.$55.00
Lineol, #184/4 Indian standing, shooting bow, red, EX-, B5 ....$55.00
Lineol, #184/6 Indian kneeling, shooting bow, red, EX-, B5 ....$50.00
Lineol, #184/7 Indian w/tomahawk, lt gr, EX-, B5............$55.00
Lineol, #184/8 Indian crawling w/tomahawk, bl, B5 ....$55.00
Lineol, #184/9 Indian lying w/tomahawk, bl, B5 ....$55.00
Lineol, #184/10 Indian sitting w/pipe, red, EX-, B5..........$45.00
Lineol, #184/11 Indian woman w/papoose, tan & gr, EX-, B5 ....$65.00
Lineol, #184/26 cowboy standing, shooting, red & gr, EX-, B5 ....$55.00
Lineol, #184/28 cowboy clubbing, bl & gr, EX-, B5..........$55.00
Lineol, #184/29 cowboy sitting, tan & dk bl, EX-, B5 ......$55.00
Lineol, #184/30 prisoner tied to stake, EX-, B5 ....$145.00
Lineol, #184/34 cowboy w/2 revolvers, gray & gr, EX-, B5 .$55.00
Lineol, #184/35 cowboy surrendering, gray & gr, EX-, B5 .$60.00
Lineol, #184/42 campfire (electric), EX-, B5 ....$45.00
Lineol, #184/43 wigwams, G+, B5 ....$140.00
Lineol, #184/48 log cabin, EX-, B5 ....$375.00
Lineol, #649 Hindenburg, G, B5 ....$40.00
Lineol, #650/3 Blomberg saluting, G+, B5 ....$50.00
Lineol, #662/32 German rubber boat w/2 men rowing, G+, B5 ....$275.00
Manoil, antiaircraft gunner, 98%, A1 ....$39.00
Manoil, antiaircraft w/range finder, 97%, A1 ....$23.00
Manoil, aviation set #5/A, complete, very rare, EX, A1.$210.00
Manoil, aviator holding bomb, 97%, A1........................$37.00
Manoil, bazooka loader, 94%, A1............................$35.00
Manoil, bench, 93%, A1 ....$12.00
Manoil, blacksmith w/anvil, FW Woolworth price tag, 98%, A1 ....$25.00
Manoil, blacksmith w/wheel, 97%, A1 ....$27.00
Manoil, blk man digging, scarce, 99%, A1....................$32.00
Manoil, boy carring wood, 98%, A1............................$25.00
Manoil, boy w/beachball, scarce, 99%, A1 ....$57.00
Manoil, boy w/life preserver, scarce, 98%, A1 ....$55.00
Manoil, bugler, 2nd version, 99%, A1 ....$25.00
Manoil, cadet, right shoulder arms, wht uniform, 98%, A1 .$26.50
Manoil, caisson w/V-loop for support, 96%, A1 ....$27.00

Manoil, calf for ranch set, very scarce, 99%, A1 ....$24.00

Manoil, carpenter sawing lumber, scarce, 96%, A1 ....$32.00

Manoil, carrier w/bricks, 96%, A1.......................................$33.00

Manoil, colt, brn, rare color, 99%, A1 ....$29.00

Manoil, colt, maroon, 99%, A1 ....$27.00

Manoil, cook's helper w/ladle, sm dent bk of right leg, scarce, 97%, A1 ....$43.00

Manoil, cow grazing, 99%, A1...$15.00

Manoil, cowgirl rider, yel blouse, red pants, 97%, A1 ......$21.00

Manoil, darky eating watermelon, scarce, 98%, A1..........$97.00

Manoil, doctor in khaki, M, A1...$32.00

Manoil, drummer, hollow version, VG, P4 ....$40.00

Manoil, drummer, vertical drum, scarce, 97%, A1 ....$45.00

Manoil, ensign, wht w/gr base, pnt on base flaking o/w M, A1...$24.00

Manoil, farmer carrying pumpkin, 98%, A1 ....$28.00

Manoil, farmer cutting corn, 99%, A1................................$26.00

Manoil, farmer pitching sheaves, 99%, A1 ....$28.00

Manoil, farmer sowing grain, 99%, A1................................$24.00

Manoil, firing camouflaged antiaircraft gun, composition, very scarce, 85-88%, A1 ....$49.00

Manoil, flag bearer, hollow version, G, P4 ....$55.00

Manoil, flag bearer, 98%, A1...$30.00

Manoil, flagbearer, skinny, 97%, A1...................................$32.00

Manoil, girl in bl slacks, scarce, 98%, A1............................$55.00

Manoil, girl in traveling costume, 97%, A1 ....$11.50

Manoil, girl picking berries, scarce, 94%, A1....................$50.00

Manoil, goat, 98%, A1...$11.00

Manoil, grenade thrower, 3 grenades in pouch, 98%, A1 ...$28.00

Manoil, Indian w/hatchet, VG, P4 ....$75.00

Manoil, Indian w/knife, 97%, A1..$26.00

Manoil, lady w/churn, 97%, A1...$23.00

Manoil, lady w/pie, 98%, A1 ....$31.00

Manoil, Legion drum major, 99%, A1................................$27.50

Manoil, machine gunner, prone, no aperture, pack on bk, 97%, A1 ....$26.00

Manoil, machine gunner seated, 95%, A1 ....$35.00

Manoil, machine gunner w/helper, no aperture, 98%, A1 ....$28.50

Manoil, man dumping wheelbarrow, yel outfit, 97%, A1.$26.00

Manoil, man w/watering can, 97%, A1 ....$12.00

Manoil, mason laying bricks, 97%, A1................................$39.00

Manoil, nurse, 96%, A1..$26.00

Manoil, nurse w/bl bowl, 98%, A1 ....$22.00

Manoil, nurse w/red bowl, no hem in skirt, different headpiece, 96%, A1 ....$42.00

Manoil, observer, 99%, A1...$30.00

Manoil, officer, 2nd version, VG, P4 ....$20.00

Manoil, parade, FW Woolworth price tag, rifle tip bent, 98%, A1 ....$23.00

Manoil, parade, overseas cap, 99%, A1 ....$42.00

Manoil, parade, 5th version, 99%, A1 ....$22.00

Manoil, pirate w/2 pistols, red, 83%, A1 ....$18.00

Manoil, policeman, 96%, A1..$22.00

Manoil, sailor in wht, casting flaw in bk, 95%, A1 ....$20.00

Manoil, scarecrow w/top hat, 98%, A1 ....$25.00

Manoil, schoolteacher, rod intact, scarce, 96%, A1 ....$45.00

Manoil, searchlight, 98%, A1...$28.00

Manoil, sniper camouflaged, pnt flowers, 94%, A1..........$23.50

Manoil, sniper on 1 knee firing, 97%, A1 ....$36.00

Manoil, sniper standing, 98%, A1 ....$25.00

Manoil, sniper w/short thin rifle, scarce, 92%, A1...........$20.00

Manoil, soldier boxer, very scarce, 96%, A1 ....$95.00

Manoil, soldier juggling barrels of apples, scarce, 97%, A1.$78.00

Manoil, soldier w/rifle & pack marching, 99%, A1 ....$23.00

Manoil, stack of sheaves, 98%, A1 ....$21.00

Manoil, tommy gunner, 2nd version, 98%, A1................$29.00

Manoil, tractor, plain front, 99% A1 ....$23.00

Manoil, US Doughboy, bomber crawling, early version, brn puttees, belt, etc, 95%, A1...$17.50

Manoil, US Doughboy, charging, 96%, A1 ....$14.50

Manoil, US Doughboy, officer, 97%, A1 ....$15.50

Manoil, US Marine, early version, chip on cap, 83%, A1 ..$9.00

Manoil, US Marine, 2nd version, 99%, A1 ....$30.00

Manoil, water wagon, no number, 98%, A1 ....$25.00

Manoil, woman in bathing suit, scarce, 98%, A1 ....$55.00

Manoil, woman in traveling costume, 99%, A1...............$12.50

Mignot, Confederate Infantry, standing figures, 12 pieces, EX (G box), A, $190.00.

Manoil, wounded soldier, lying, G, P4 ....$16.00
McLoughlin Bros, Infantry Soldiers, pnt lead, flag bearer, drummer, 6 rifle carriers, 2 w/swords & 1 mtd, EX (EX box), A..$248.00

Sporting Collectibles

Baseball — the great American pastime — has given us hundreds of real-life sports heroes plus a great amount of collectible memorabilia. Baseball gloves, bats, game-worn uniforms, ephemera of many types, even games and character watches are among the many items being sought out today. And there are fans of basketball, football, and hockey that are just as avid in their collecting.

As you can see, many of our listings describe Kenner's Starting Lineup figures. These small plastic likenesses of famous sports greats were first produced in 1988. New they can be purchased for $5.00 to $8.00 (though some may go a little higher), but they have wonderful potential to appreciate. For instance, Nolan Ryan (card #94) is worth about $275.00 or so (MIB), John Stockton (card #72), even more — about $400.00. These are two of the top-prized figures, but on the average most from 1988 run from $25.00 to $50.00. Football and basketball series have been made as well, and in 1993 Kenner added hockey. If you're going to collect them, be critical of the condition of the packaging.

Bobbin' head dolls made of papier-mache were made in Japan during the 1960s up until about 1972, and we've listed some of these as well. They were about 7" high or so, hand-painted and then varnished. Some of them represent sports teams and their mascots. Depending on scarcity and condition, they'll run from as low as $35.00 up to $100.00, though there are some that sell for $300.00 or so. A few were modeled in the likeness of a particular sports star; these are rare and when they can be found sell in the $500.00 to $1,000.00 range. See also Character Clocks and Watches; Games; Pin-Back Buttons.

Alan Trammel vs Jose Canseco, figure, Starting Lineup, One on One series, MIP, F1..$20.00
Baltimore Oriole Player, nodder, Japan, M $85.00
Barry Sanders, figure, Starting Lineup, Football 1990, MOC, D4 ....$30.00

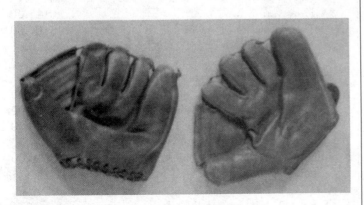

Bobby Doerr, baseball mitt, MacGregor, EX, $165.00; "Bob (Roberto) Clemente," baseball mitt, J.C. Higgins, EX, $95.00.

Boston Bruins Hockey Player, nodder, Japan, EX+, H4....$22.00
Charles Barkley, figure, Kenner, Starting Lineup, plastic, holds ball over head, ca 1988, 5½", MOC.........................$12.50
Cleveland Indians Player, nodder, Japan, M...................$100.00
Dallas Cowboy Cheerleaders, gum card set, Topps, 1981, 30 cards, complete, M1...$30.00
Dan Marino, figure, Kenner, Starting Lineup, 1992, NRFB..$25.00
Darryl Strawberry, Starting Lineup, Baseball 1990, MOC, D4..$6.00
Don Majowski, figure, Starting Lineup, Football 1990, MOC, D4..$6.00
Eddie Matthews, figure, Baseball Greats, MOC, D4 ....$10.00
Eddie Yost, glove & ball set, MIB....................................$85.00
Gary Carter vs Eric Davis, figure, Starting Lineup, One on One series, MIP, F1...$10.00
George Bell, figure, Starting Lineup, Baseball 1988, MOC, D4...$10.00
Hank Aaron, figure, Baseball Greats, MOC, D4.............$10.00
Hank Aaron, game, Eye Ball, A $65.00
Harlem Globetrotters, bendee, Lakeside, 1987, 9", M $10.00
Harlem Globetrotters, game, Mattel/Hanna-Barbera, based on cartoon show, 1971, MIP, C1..................................$17.50
Harlem Globetrotters, gum cards, Comic Images, 1992, set of 90, M1..$15.00
Harlem Globetrotters, program, 60th-Anniversary, M.....$10.00
Harlem Globetrotters, stickers, 1970, MIP....................$20.00
Isiah Thomas, figure, Kenner, Starting Lineup, mk Official NBA Product, ca 1988, MOC..$12.50
Jackie Robinson, candy container, Petito Studio, 1954, NM...$300.00
Jackie Robinson, game, Baseball, box has minor edge wear, A $670.00
Joe DiMaggio, baseball, signed, A $195.00
Joe Montana, figure, Kenner, Starting Lineup, 1988, M $65.00
Jose Canesco, figure, Starting Lineup, Baseball 1991, MOC, D4..$5.00
Kansas State Wildcat, nodder, 1969, MIB, T1.................$35.00
Kareem Abdul-Jabbar, figure, Kenner, Starting Lineup, in Los Angeles Lakers uniform, ca 1988, 6½", MOC...........$12.50
Ken Griffey Jr, figure, Kenner, Starting Lineup, Baseball 1991, MOC, D4 ....$10.00
Kirk Gibson, figure, Starting Lineup, Baseball 1990, MOC, D4..$6.00
Larry Bird, figure, Kenner, Starting Lineup, on base, ca 1988, 5", MOC..$12.50
Larry Johnson, figure, Kenner, Starting Lineup, 1992, NRFB...$75.00
Mario Andretti, gum cards, Collect-a-Card, 1992, 100 cards, complete, M1...$15.00
Michael Jordan, figure, Kenner, Starting Lineup, ca 1988, 5½", MOC, from $14 to $18.00
Michael Jordan, gift wrap set, Gibson, MIP $5.00
Michael Jordan, poster, Upper Deck, 1992, MIB.............$15.00
Mickey Mantle, Minute a Day Gym, in orig box, A.......$135.00
Mickey Mantle, pen, wood baseball bat w/facsimile signature, MIP, I2...$18.00

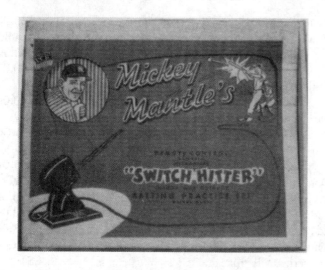

Mickey Mantle, Switch Hitter remote-control batting trainer, early 1960s, original box, EX, $400.00.

Muhammad Ali, decanter, 13", M (G box)......................$85.00
Muhammad Ali, figure, Mego, w/accessories, 3¾", MOC..$65.00
Muhammad Ali, poster, 1970s, 22x28", EX...................$65.00
Nolan Ryan, figure, Kenner, Starting Lineup, retirement, MIP..$40.00
Oakland A's Baseball Player, nodder, Japan, EX...............$55.00
Pittsburgh Steelers, nodder, Japan, EX, J2.....................$45.00
Rickey Henderson, Starting Lineup, Baseball 1988, MOC, D4..$10.00
Roger Clemens, figure, Starting Lineup, Baseball 1988, MOC, D4..$10.00
Roger Marris, game, Action Baseball, Pressman, NMIB...$85.00
Roger Marris, nodder, Japan, scarce, 9", A....................$400.00
Roy Campanella, figure, Big League, gold color, photo & stats on bk, orig pkg, NM, A.....................................$36.00
Ryne Sandberg vs Vince Coleman, Starting Lineup, One on One series, MIP, F1..$15.00
Shaq O'Neal, figure, Starting Lineup, 1993, MOC..........$35.00
Team Detroit Tigers, Starting Lineup, MIB, I2 ....$50.00
Ted Williams, figure, bsk, 500 Home Run Club, 7", MIB..$65.00
Troy Aikman, figure, Kenner, Starting Lineup, 1990, NRFB..$40.00
Ty Cobb, ball bat, child's, Official, dtd 1909, 28", A........$90.00
Wade Boggs vs Don Mattingly, Starting Lineup, One on One series, MIP, F1..$20.00
Walter Johnson, game, Baseball, w/postcard, rules, spinner & 10 tokens, box has wear, A.............................$270.00
Will Clark, figure, Kenner, Starting Lineup, swinging pose, 1988, MIP...$30.00

Star Trek

The Star Trek concept was introduced to the public in the mid-1960s via a TV series which continued for many years in syndication. The impact it had on American culture has spaned two generations of loyal fans through its animated TV cartoon series (1977), six major motion pictures, and Fox network's 1987

TV show, 'Star Trek, The Next Generation.' As a result of its success, vast amounts of merchandise, both licensed and unlicensed, have been marketed including jewelry, clothing, calendars, collector plates, comics, costumes, games, greeting and gum cards, party goods, magazines, model kits, posters, puzzles, records and tapes, school supplies, and a wide assortment of toys. Packaging is very important; an item mint and in its original box is generally worth 75% to 100% more than one rated excellent. Our advisor for this category is Craig Reid (R9). See also Character and Promotional Drinking Glasses; Fast-Food Collectibles; Halloween Costumes; Lunch Boxes; Models; Pin-Back Buttons.

Alien, Playmates, STNG, any other than Romulan or Ferengi, 1st series, 1992, MIP, ea, from $15 to.........................$18.00
Andorian, Mego, complete, 8", loose, EX, H4...............$250.00
Antican, Galoob, STNG, MOC, D8............................$45.00
Arcturian, Mego, The Motion Picture, 12", MIB, H4......$85.00
Benzite, Playmates, STNG, MOC, D8...........................$10.00
Beverly Crusher, Playmates, STNG, MOC, D4/D8..........$10.00
Borg, Playmates, STNG, MOC, from $7 to.....................$10.00
Borg, Presents, STNG, PVC, 1992, 4", MIP, F1.................$4.00
Chekov, Presents, vinyl w/stand, 1992, 11", MIP, F1.......$15.00
Cheron, Mego, complete, 8", loose, EX, H4....................$55.00
Data, Galoob, STNG, 1st series, bl face, MOC, from $100 to...$150.00
Data, Galoob, STNG, 2nd series, speckled face, MIP, from $25 to...$35.00
Data, Galoob, STNG, 3rd series, regular skin color, MOC, H4..$20.00
Data, Playmates, MOC, D4 ....$10.00
Data, Presents, vinyl w/stand, 11", MIB, F1 ....$15.00
Deanna Troi, Hamilton, MIB, E3.................................$15.00
Deanna Troi, Playmates, STNG, 1st series, 1992, MOC, from $20 to $25.00
Deanna Troi, Playmates, STNG, 2nd series, 1993, MIP, from $12 to $15.00
Deanna Troi, Presents, vinyl w/stand, 11", MIB, F1 ....$15.00
Decker, Mego, The Motion Picture, 1979, 3¾", MOC, D8/H4..$25.00
Decker, Mego, The Motion Picture, 1979, complete w/accessories, 3¾", VG..$10.00
Dr McCoy, Mego, complete, 8", loose, EX, H4................$50.00
Dr McCoy, Galoob, Star Trek V, 1989, 8", M (EX box), C1..$45.00
Dr McCoy, Mego, 8", MOC, from $75 to $100.00
Ferengi, Playmates, STNG, MIP $20.00
Geordi La Forge, Galoob, 1988, 4", MOC, from $15 to....$20.00
Geordi La Forge, Playmates, 1st issue, w/removable visor, 1992, MIP..$40.00
Gorn, Mego, 8", MOC (card opened & resealed), H4....$175.00
Guinan, Playmates, STNG, 1993, MIP..........................$15.00
Ilia, Mego, The Motion Picture, 1979, 3¾", MOC, H4....$20.00
K'Ehleyer, Playmates, STNG, MOC, D8 ....$10.00
Kirk, Knickerbocker, stuffed body w/vinyl head, 1979, 12", VG, H4..$10.00
Kirk, Knickerbocker, 1979, 12", EX+ (EX box), from $40 to...$45.00
Kirk, Mego, 8", MOC, from $40 to................................$60.00

Kirk and Spock, Mego, 7½", $25.00 each.

Kirk, Presents, vinyl w/stand, 1992, 11", MIP, F1 ....$15.00
Klingon, Mego, complete, 8", loose, EX, H4 ....$40.00
Klingon, Presents, STNG, PVC, 1992, 4", MOC, D4/F1 ...$4.00
Klingon, The Motion Picture, 12", M (NM box), H4 ....$125.00
Locutus, Playmates, STNG, MOC, D8 ....$10.00
Mugato, Mego, belt has caused fade mk on shirt, 8", loose, EX, H4 ....$150.00
Neptunian, Mego, 8", MOC (card opened & resealed), H4 ....$200.00
Picard, Galoob, STNG, MIP, from $15 to $20.00
Picard, Presents, PVC, 1992, 4", MIP, F1 ....$4.00
Picard, Presents, STNG, vinyl w/stand, 11", MIB, F1 ....$15.00
Q, Galoob, STNG, MOC, from $80 to $125.00
Riker, Galoob, STNG, 1988, 3¾", MOC, from $10 to $12.00
Romulan, Playmates, STNG, 1st series, 1992, MIP, from $28 to $35.00
Scotty, Ertl, Star Trek III, 1984, 3¾", MOC (sm dent on card bubble) $20.00
Scotty, Mego, complete, 8", loose, EX, from $35 to $50.00
Scotty, Mego, The Motion Picture, 1979, 3¾", loose, EX, H4 ....$12.00
Selay, Galoob, STNG, 1988, 4", MOC, from $40 to $60.00
Set: Star Trek III; Ertl, Kirk, Spock, Scotty & Klingon, 3¾", MOC, sold as set only, J4 ....$90.00
Set: STNG; Presents, PVC, 1992, 4", set of 8, M in separate pkgs, F1 ....$30.00
Skybok, Galoob, Star Trek V, 1989, 8", M (EX box), C1 ....$45.00
Spock, Mego, complete, 8", loose, EX $25.00
Spock, Mego, 8", MOC, from $50 to $60.00
Spock, Presents, PVC, 1992, 4", MIP, D4/F1 ....$4.00
Sulu, Presents, vinyl w/stand, 1992, 11", MIP, F1 ....$15.00
Talosian, Presents, vinyl w/stand, 1992, 11", MIP, F1 ......$15.00
Tasha Yar, Galoob, STNG, 1988, 3¾", MOC, from $20 to $25.00

Uhura, Mego, 8", MOC (1 corner of bubble dented on card), H4 ....$50.00
Worf, Galoob, STNG, 1988, 4", MOC, from $10 to $18.00

Playsets

Ferengi Fighter, Galoob, STNG, 1988, MIB, $35 to $50.00
Mission to Gamma VI, Mego, complete, very rare, MIB, from $700 to...$950.00
Star Trek Command Communication Console, Mego, 1976, orig 13x8x8" box, M (EX+ box) $80.00
Star Trek USS Enterprise Bridge, Mego, The Motion Picture, molded wht plastic, for 4" figures, 1980, NRFB, from $100 to...$175.00
Star Trek USS Enterprise Bridge, Mego, vinyl fold-out, w/chair, control panel, cb views, 1975, VG, T6 ....$30.00
Star Trek USS Enterprise Bridge, Mego, vinyl fold-out, 1975, NRFB (sealed) $220.00
Star Trek USS Enterprise Bridge, Mego, vinyl fold-out, 2 missing stools, 1975, EX, from $60 to $80.00

U.S.S. Enterprise Bridge Action Playset, Mego, for 8" figures, vinyl fold-out, 1975, M (EX box), $190.00.

Vehicles

Galileo Shuttlecraft, Galoob, STNG, MIP, from $30 to ..$45.00
Goddard Shuttlecraft, Playmates, STNG, MIP, from $35 to.$75.00
Klingon Warship, Corgi, Star Trek II, MIP, H4/O1 ....$18.00
Klingon Warship, diecast, 1979, 4", MOC, from $10 to...$20.00
Klingon Warship, Dinky, 1978, 9", MIB, from $85 to $100.00
Klingon Warship, Franklin Mint, pewter, w/stand, 1992, NM-M, from $125 to $175.00
Orion Wanderer #2522, Star Trek Miniatures, FASA gaming pc, 1981, MIP, from $5 to $8.00
USS Enterprise, Corgi, Star Trek II, MOC, from $18 to ..$20.00
USS Enterprise, Dinky, The Motion Picture, 1979, 3", MOC, from $10 to...$20.00
USS Enterprise, Ertl, Star Trek V, NMIP, from $15 to ...$20.00

USS Enterprise, Playmates, STNG, MIP, from $35 to $75.00

USS Larson Class Destroyer #2507, Star Trek Miniatures, FASA gaming pc, 1981, MIP, from $5 to $8.00

Miscellaneous

Action Fleet Mobile, Paramount/Mars Premium, 5 punch-out ships w/poster, unassembled, 1979, MIP (sealed envelope), P4 ....$20.00

Activity Set, Star Trek the Motion Picture Figural Paint Set, Whitling, Spock or Kirk figure, 1979, MOC, H4 ......$20.00

Album, Morris National, 1975, for gum cards & stickers, from $15 to $20.00

Bag, gray plastic w/abstract drawing of Enterprise on both sides, from April 1976 convention, EX, from $8 to.............$10.00

Belt Buckle, Paramount, 1979, M, from $6 to...................$10.00

Blueprints, complete set of Star Trek's USS Enterprise; Ballantine, 1975, set of 12, orig pouch, M, from $35 to.......$50.00

Book, Activity; Star Trek Action Toy Book, cutouts make toys, 1976, EX, T6...$15.00

Book, Comic; Star Trek V-The Final Frontier, DC Comics, #1 issue, 1989, M, F1...$5.00

Book, Enterprise Log, color comics, 224 pgs, 1976, EX, from $10 to $15.00

Book, Make Your Own Costume, patterns, 1979, EX+, T6 ....$12.00

Book, Star Fleet Medical Reference Manual, EX+-NM, from $60 to $75.00

Book, Star Fleet Technical Manual, Ballantine Books, 1st printing, 1975, hardcover, 8x11", w/letter, NM, from $50 to $75.00

Book, sticker; Jeopardy at Jutterdon, Whitman, 1979, NM, from $6 to $10.00

Book & Record Set, MIP (sealed), from $8 to $12.00

Calendar, Paramount Pictures, Ballantine Books, 1977, 24½" long (unfolded), NM, $10.00.

Book & Record Set, Peter Pan Records, 33⅓ rpm, from orig movie, 1979, EX, from $8 to................................$12.00

Cake Decorations, 20th Century Fox, 10 or 22-pc set, 1976, ea, MIP, from $10 to $20.00

Calendar, Ballantine, 1976, NMIB, T6........................$10.00

Calendar, Star Trek: TNG; 1992, M, E3........................$12.00

Cassette, Ideal, Pocket Flix, MIB $75.00

Coin, Chicago Land, Data, Worf & Geordi, silver, M, E3 ....$35.00

Coin, Chicago Land, Riker & Troi, silver, M, E3............$35.00

Communicator, Mego, Star Trek, set of 2, M (EX+ card), from $125 to...$160.00

Decanter, Mr Spock bust, 1979, MIB, from $40 to...........$50.00

Dictionary, Klingon language, M, from $5 to.....................$7.50

Display, Hallmark, for Galileo shuttlecraft ornament, M, minimum value $150.00

Game, Star Trek Color 'N Re-Color Game, Avalon, w/36x40" cloth, 1979, MIB (sealed), from $20 to.....................$28.00

Game, Star Trek Pinball, plastic, 14", VG+, from $25 to.$35.00

Game, Star Trek Super Phaser II Target Game, Mego, 1976, orig 8x10" box, M (EX+ box), from $40 to $60.00

Game, Star Trek Trivia, 1985, MIB, from $35 to $45.00

Globe, Enterprise form, lights, NM (EX box), O1 ....$55.00

Greeting Card, Captain Kirk, 1980, set of 6, MIP, from $8 to $12.00

Gum Card Box, STNG, Skybox, empty, M, from $2 to......$4.00

Gum Card Box, STNG, Skybox, w/set of 120, M, from $18 to $30.00

Gum Card Tin, Impel, 25th Anniversary, complete w/card sets & special cards, from $80 to.....................................$125.00

Gum Card Tin, Impel, 25th Anniversary, empty, M, E3..$20.00

Gum Cards, FTCC, from Star Trek IV movie, set of 60, from $20 to $30.00

Gum Cards, FTCC, 1984, from Star Trek III movie, 60 cards w/20 stickers, complete, from $30 to $40.00

Gum Cards, Impel, 1991, series 1, set of 160, from $18 to.$20.00

Gum Cards, Monty Gum, from Star Trek II movie, set of 100, from $60 to...$80.00

Gum Cards, Morris National, 1975, puzzle bk, set of 30, from $60 to $80.00

Gum Cards, Panini, 1989, STNG, set of 240 cards, M1 ...$55.00

Gum Cards, Topps, 1977, from TV series, 88 cards w/22 stickers, complete, M1..$295.00

Gum Cards, Topps, 1979, The Motion Picture, 88 cards w/22 stickers, complete, from $25 to.................................$35.00

Key Chain, Presents, Enterprise shape on chain, 1992, MIP, F1...$3.00

Lobby Card Set, STNG, Zanart, M, E3.........................$12.00

Magazine, Deep Space 9 #1, M, E3................................$6.00

Magazine, STNG #19, M, E3...$5.00

Magazine, STNG #8, M, E3...$4.00

Magazine, TV Guide, March 4, 1967, Leonard Nimoy & William Shatner on mc space background, EX, from $40 to $60.00

Magic Slate, mc illus at edges, 1978, EX, from $8 to $10.00

Magnet, Presents, Enterprise form, MIP, F1 ....$2.00

Medallion, commemorative issue, dtd Sept 6, 1966, w/chain & orig cellophane, M, M5 ....$35.00

Mug, Presents, Star Trek Collector, features Scotty, 1992, MIB, F1 ....$10.00

Napkins, illus of Kirk, Spock & McCoy, 1976, set of 8, MIP, from $3 to..$6.00

Necklace, Enterprise on chain, 1976, NMOC, V1 ....$18.50

Official Space Emblem, Paramount Pictures, 1975, MIP, $15.00.

Ornament, Shuttlecraft Galileo, Hallmark, MIB, from $25 to..$35.00

Ornament, Star Trek Starship USS Enterprise, Hallmark, NRFB, from $350 to...$400.00

Ornament, STNG USS Enterprise, Hallmark, 1993, MIB, from $35 to...$50.00

Paint-By-Number Set, Hasboro, features Kirk & Spock on alien planet, 1974, 12x19", M (NM box), from $50 to.......$65.00

Paint-By-Number Set, Hasbro, 11x11", M (NM box), from $30 to..$45.00

Paperweight, Presents, STNG Enterprise, MIB, F1.............$4.00

Patch, Star Fleet, NM (EX card), O1 ....$10.00

Pencil Topper, Presents, 1992, MIP, F1 ....$4.00

Phaser, Galoob, STNG, 1st issue, 1988, 3¾", MOC, from $35 to..$45.00

Phaser, Galoob, STNG, 2nd issue, 1988, 3¾", MOC, from $20 to..$35.00

Phaser, Mego, from Super Phaser II Target Game, blk plastic, light ray sets off buzzer, 1976, 8", VG, from $30 to....$45.00

Phaser, Playmates, STNG, MIP, E3 ....$12.00

Phaser, Star Trek Electronic Phaser Gun, Southbend, set of 2 w/copied instructions, orig 10x14" box, 1979, M (EX), from $75 to...$100.00

Phaser, Star Trek Phaser, Remco, 1975, M (M 8x11" box), from $50 to..$80.00

Phaser, Star Trek Phaser Ray Gun, AHI, 1976, MOC, H4..$30.00

Phaser, Star Trek Phaser Saucer Gun, AHI, shoots saucers, 1976, M (torn card), A...$35.00

Phaser, Star Trek Tracer, Ray, shoots jet disks, 1967, M (EX card), from $40 to...$50.00

Phaser Weapon, Star Trek Next Generation, Galoob, 1988, M on card, A, $30.00.

Plaque, Captain Picard, limited edition, 1988, M, T1 ....$125.00

Plaque, Presents, STNG, 1992, any of 5 characters or Enterprise, MIB, F1, ea...$13.00

Plate, Ernst, Data, by artist Suzie Morton, very short production run, 1989, MIB, from $200 to $250.00

Plate, Ernst, Picard, by artist Suzie Morton, very short production run, 1989, MIB, from $225 to........................$300.00

Playing Cards, Presents, complete, 1992, orig tin box, MIB, F1 ....$9.00

Postcard Book, complete set of 48, 1977, EX+-NM, from $18 to.$23.00

Program, Star Trek III, color photos, 1984, EX, T6 ....$5.00

Putty, Larami, The Motion Picture, bl plastic egg w/putty & transfer solution, 1979, MOC, from $10 to...............$15.00

Puzzle, HG, Battle on the Planet Romulon, 1974, NMIB, from $8 to..$12.00

Puzzle, Star Trek I, The Enterprise, 250-pc, 1979, 20x14", EX, T6..$15.00

Puzzle, Whitman, cartoon, 200-pc, 1978, 14x18", MIB, from $6 to..$10.00

Ring, 25th-Anniversary issue, 10k gold, 1991 ....$325.00

Snow Dome, Presents, w/Enterprise, 1992, MIB, F1 ....$8.00

Stamp Set, Star Trek 25th Anniversary issue, w/display case & orig mailer, M $40.00

Standee, Spock paper litho on cb, for US post office, Stamp Collecting Is Logical, 12", EX, from $10 to.....................$20.00

Standee, USS Enterprise, cb, 36", VG+.............................$20.00

T-Shirt, Deep Space 9, M, E3...$15.00

Tricorder, Mego, Star Trek, w/30-minute cassette, 1976, orig 8x10" box, MIB, A $125.00

TV Tray, Spock, from Star Trek the Motion Picture, 1979, EX $25.00

View-Master Set, Star Trek, The Omega Glory, 3-reel set w/booklet, 1968, MIP, from $35 to $45.00

Star Wars

The original 'Star Wars' movie was a phenomenal box office hit of the late 1970s, no doubt due to its ever-popular space travel theme and fantastic special effects. A sequel called 'Empire Strikes Back' (1980) and a third hit called 'Return of the Jedi' (1983) did just as well. As a result, an enormous amount of related merchandise was released — most of which was made by the Kenner Company. Palitoy of London supplied England and other overseas countries with Kenner's products and also made some toys that were never distributed in America. Until 1980 the logo of the 20th Century Fox studios (under whom the toys were licensed) appeared on each item; just before the second movie, 'Star Wars' creator, George Lucas, regained control of the merchandise rights, and items inspired by the last two films can be identified by his own Lucasfilm logo. Since 1987 Lucasfilm, Ltd., has operated shops in conjunction with the Star Tours at Disneyland theme parks.

In all, more than ninety action figures were designed. The last figures to be issued were the 'Power of the Force' series (1985), which though of more recent vintage are steadily climbing in value. A collector coin was included on each 'Power of the Force' card.

Original packaging is very important in assessing a toy's worth. As each movie was released, packaging was updated, making approximate dating relatively simple. A figure on an original 'Star Wars' card is worth more than the same character on an 'Empire Strikes Back' card, etc.; and the same 'Star Wars' figure valued at $50.00 in mint-on-card condition might be worth as little as $5.00 'loose.' For more information we recommend *Modern Toys, American Toys, 1930 to 1980*, by Linda Baker. Our advisor for this category is George Downes (D8).

Key:
ESB — Empire Strikes Back   POTF — Power of the Force
ROTJ — Return of the Jedi

Figures

A-Wing Pilot, Kenner, POTF, w/coin, 3¾", MOC, from $65 to $95.00

A-Wing Pilot, Kenner, 3¾", MOC (EX tri-logo card), D4/O1 ....$75.00

Admiral Ackbar, Kenner, 6th series, 1983, MOC, A $15.00

Amanaman, Kenner, POTF, MOC, D8 ....$95.00

Amanaman, Kenner, POTF, NM (EX card) $60.00

Anakin Skywalker, Kenner, 3¾", MOC (tri-logo card), D8/J4/T1 ....$35.00

AT-AT Commander, Kenner, ESB, 1980-82, 3¾", MOC, H4/O1 ....$20.00

AT-AT Commander, Kenner, ROTJ, 1983, 3¾", MOC, from $18 to $25.00

AT-ST Driver, Kenner, POTF, w/coin, MOC, from $20 to..$25.00

AT-ST Driver, Kenner, ROTJ, 1983, 3¾", MOC, from $15 to $20.00

B-Wing Pilot, Kenner, POTF, w/coin, MOC, from $12 to.$16.00

B-Wing Pilot, Kenner, ROTJ, 7th series, 1983, MOC (card split at slot), A $30.00

Barada, Kenner, POTF, w/coin, MOC, from $40 to $45.00

Ben Obi-Wan Kenobi, Kenner, ESB, 1983, MOC, from $40 to..$50.00

Ben Obi-Wan Kenobi, Kenner, POTF, 3¾", M(VG card), O1..$35.00

Ben Obi-Wan Kenobi, Kenner, Star Wars, 1977, 12", MIB, A $225.00

Bespin Security Guard, Kenner, ESB, Blk version, 1980-82, 3¾", MOC, from 20 to $30.00

Bespin Security Guard, Kenner, ESB, Caucasian version, 3¾", MOC (VG card), O1 ....$27.00

Bib Fortuna, Kenner, ROTJ, 3¾", M (VG card), O1........$22.00

Bib Fortuna, Sigma, pnt ceramic, MIB, D4 ....$20.00

Biker Scout, Kenner, POTF, w/coin, MOC, F1 ....$30.00

Biker Scout, Kenner, ROTJ, 1983, 3¾", MOC, from $18 to.$25.00

Boba Fett, Kenner, Star Wars, 13", MIB, A, $220.00.

Boba Fett, Kenner, ROTJ, MOC, D8.................................$50.00
Boba Fett, Kenner, Star Wars, 1977, 13", MIB, A..........$220.00
Boba Fett, Kenner, 13", loose, not complete, O1..............$65.00
Bossk, Kenner, ESB, 3¾", M (VG+ card), O1..................$25.00
Bossk, Kenner, ROTJ, MOC, from $25 to........................$35.00
C-3PO, Kenner, MOC (tri-logo card), D4........................$45.00
C-3PO, Kenner, POTF, removable limbs, w/coin, MOC, from
    $45 to...$75.00
C-3PO, Kenner, ROTJ, removable limbs, 3¾", M (VG+ card),
    O1..$20.00
C-3PO, Kenner, Star Wars, 1977, 12", EX......................$45.00
C-3PO, Kenner, Star Wars, 1977, 12", MIB, A..............$175.00
C-3PO, Kenner, Star Wars, 1977, 12", NM (VG+ box),
    O1..$135.00

Cloud Car Pilot, Kenner, ESB, 3¾", M (VG+ card), O1 .$22.50
Darth Vader, Kenner, POTF, w/coin, MOC, from $50 to .$65.00
Darth Vader, Kenner, ROTJ, 1983, MOC, from $18 to ...$25.00
Darth Vader, Kenner, 12", loose, missing saber, VG+, O1 .$45.00
Darth Vader, Kenner, 12", MIB $195.00
Darth Vader, Palitoy, MOC, J4.......................................$90.00
Death Squad Commander, Kenner, Star Wars, 3¾", MOC,
    J4..$90.00
Death Star Droid, ROTJ, MOC, D8 ....$40.00
Dengar, Kenner, ESB, 3¾", M (VG- card), O1...............$20.00
Dulok Shaman, Kenner, 1985, 3¾", MOC, H4 ....$10.00
Emperor, Kenner, ROTJ, 3¾", MOC, J4..........................$20.00
Emperor's Royal Guard, Kenner, ROTJ, 6th series, 1983,
    MOC $40.00
EV-9D9, Kenner, POTF, 3¾", MOC, from $85 to $100.00

Chewbacca, Kenner, 1978-80, 15", NM, from $60.00 to $85.00.

Chewbacca, Kenner, ROTJ, 3¾", MOC, from $25 to $35.00
Chewbacca, Kenner, Star Wars, w/ammo belt, 1977, 12", EX+,
    A..$30.00
Chewbacca, Kenner, Star Wars, 12", MIB.....................$150.00
Chief Chirpa, Kenner, ROTJ, 3¾", MOC, from $15 to ...$20.00

Ewok Action Figures, Kenner, 1984, Lucasfilm logo, M (EX box), $55.00.

Gamorrean Guard, Kenner, POTF, w/coin, MOC $100.00
Gamorrean Guard, Kenner, ROTJ, 1983, 3¾", MOC, H4 .$20.00

Greedo (Alien), Kenner, Return of the Jedi, 3½", MIP, from $20.00 to $30.00.

General Madine, Kenner, ROTJ, 1983, 3¾", MOC, from $12 to..$15.00

Han Solo, Kenner, ESB, Bespin outfit, 3¾", M (VG card), O1..$27.00

Han Solo, Kenner, POTF, Carbonite Chamber outfit, w/coin, MOC...$100.00

Han Solo, Kenner, ROTJ, Bespin outfit, MOC, D4.........$45.00

Han Solo, Kenner, ROTJ, Carbonite Chamber outfit, 3¾", M (EX tri-logo card), O1..................................$142.00

Han Solo, Kenner, ROTJ, trench coat, 3¾", MOC, from $25 to..$30.00

Han Solo, Kenner, 12", loose, EX, O1..........................$90.00

Han Solo, Kenner, 12", MIB, from $400 to...................$495.00

Han Solo, Palitoy, MOC, J4...$135.00

Han Solo, Sigma, pnt bsk, 1983, MIB, C1......................$45.00

IG-88, Kenner, ESB, 3¾", MOC, from $25 to.................$40.00

IG-88, Kenner, ROTJ, MOC, D8...................................$35.00

IG-88, Kenner, Star Wars, 15", rare, MIB, from $450 to..$600.00

Imperial Commander, Kenner, ESB, MOC, F1...............$40.00

Imperial Commander, Kenner, ROTJ, 3¾", MOC, O1....$17.00

Imperial Dignitary, Kenner, POTF, w/coin, MOC, from $40 to..$45.00

Imperial Dignitary, Kenner, ROTJ, MOC (tri-logo card), F1..$40.00

Imperial Gunner, Kenner, POTF, w/coin, MOC, D8.......$95.00

Imperial TIE Fighter Pilot, Kenner, ESB, 1983, MOC, A.$45.00

Imperial TIE Fighter Pilot, Kenner, ESB, 3¾", M (VG card, O1..$30.00

Jawa, Kenner, POTF, w/coin, 3¾", M (NM card), O1.....$55.00

Jawa, Kenner, ROTJ, 3¾", M (EX card), O1..................$30.00

Jawa, Kenner, Star Wars, posable, complete w/accessories, 1979, 12", EX..$50.00

Jawa, Kenner, Star Wars, 12", MIB, from $225 to..........$250.00

Jord Dusat, Kenner, Droid series, 3¾", 1985, MOC, from $10 to..$15.00

Kez Iban, Kenner, Droid series, MOC, T1....................$15.00

King Gorneesh, Kenner, NM (tri-logo card), D4...............$8.00

Klaatu, Kenner, ROTJ, MOC, T1..................................$12.00

Lady Gorneesh, Kenner, NMOC (tri-logo card), D4..........$6.00

Lando Calrissian, Kenner, POTF, General Pilot outfit, M (VG+ card), O1..$95.00

Lando Calrissian, Kenner, ROTJ, Skiff Guard outfit, 1983, 3¾", MOC, from $20 to...$25.00

Leia Organa, Kenner, POTF, combat poncho, 3¾", MOC, from $65 to..$85.00

Leia Organa, Kenner, ROTJ, Bespin gown, MOC, D4.....$50.00

Leia Organa, Kenner, ROTJ, combat poncho, MOC, from $25 to..$32.00

Leia Organa, Kenner, Star Wars, hair coming undone, complete except shoes, 1979, 11½", H4...............................$30.00

Leia Organa, Kenner, Star Wars, 1977, 11½", MIB, A...$245.00

Leia Organa, Sigma, pnt ceramic, MIB, D4....................$20.00

Lobot, Kenner, ESB, 1981, MOC, from $10 to...............$20.00

Logray, Kenner, ROTJ, 1985, MOC, F1........................$15.00

Luke Skywalker, Kenner, ESB, Bespin outfit, M (EX card), O1..$65.00

Luke Skywalker, Kenner, POTF, battle poncho, w/coin, MOC, from $55 to..$60.00

Luke Skywalker, Kenner, POTF, Imperial Stormtrooper outfit, w/coin, 3¾", M (VG card), O1................................$170.00

Luke Skywalker, Kenner, POTF, Jedi Knight outfit, w/coin, MOC..$55.00

Luke Skywalker, Kenner, POTF, X-Wing Fighter outfit, w/coin, MOC, D8..$75.00

Luke Skywalker, Kenner, ROTJ, as Jedi Knight, 3¾", MOC, from $30 to..$40.00

Luke Skywalker, Kenner, ROTJ, battle poncho, MOC (tri-logo card), F1..$60.00

Luke Skywalker, Kenner, ROTJ, Hoth Battle gear, 1983, MOC, A..$50.00

Luke Skywalker, Kenner, ROTJ, Imperial Stormtrooper outfit, MOC (foreign card), O1................................$130.00

Luke Skywalker, Kenner, ROTJ, X-Wing Pilot outfit, 3¾", M (VG+ card), O1..$20.00

Luke Skywalker, Kenner, 12", loose, EX, O1................$150.00

Luke Skywalker, Kenner, 12", MIB................................$225.00

Lumat, POTF, w/coin, MOC, D8...................................$25.00

Nien Nunb, Kenner, ROTJ, 7th series, 1983, MOC, A...$25.00

Nikto, Kenner, ROTJ, 1983, 3¾", MOC, from $15 to.....$25.00

Paploo, Kenner, POTF, w/coin, MOC, from $20 to........$30.00

Paploo, stuffed plush, lg, MIB.....................................$45.00

Patrol Dewback, Kenner, EX, O1/H4............................$10.00

Power Droid, Kenner, ROTJ, 3¾", M (VG+ card), O1....$25.00

Prune Face, Kenner, ROTJ, 1983, 3¾", MOC, from $12 to.$15.00

Rancor Keeper, Kenner, ROTJ, MOC, from $10 to.........$15.00

Rancor Monster, Kenner, ROTJ, 1983, 10", MIB (sealed), A..$35.00

Rebel Commander, Kenner, ESB, 3¾", M (VG card), O1.$27.00

Rebel Commando, Kenner, ROTJ, 3¾", MOC, J4..........$15.00

Ree-Yees, Kenner, ROTJ, 1983, 3¾", MOC, from $15 to.$20.00

Romba, Kenner, POTF, w/coin, MOC, F1......................$30.00

R2-D2, Kenner, Droid series, TV cartoon, 1985, rare, MOC, F1..$30.00

R2-D2, Kenner, MOC (worn Brazilian card w/tri-logo), D4..$22.00

R2-D2, Kenner, POTF, w/pop-up light saber, w/coin, 3¾", M (EX card), O1..$100.00

R2-D2, Kenner, ROTJ, w/sensor scope, 3¾", MOC, from $35 to..$50.00

R2-D2, Kenner, Star Wars, w/remote control, 1978, 8", M (EX box), A..$85.00

R2-D2, Kenner, Star Wars, 1978, 7½", M (EX+ box), A.$170.00

R2-D2, stuffed plush, EX, O1.......................................$20.00

R5-D4, Kenner, ROTJ, 3¾", M (VG card), O1...............$10.00

Security Scout, POTF, w/coin, M (NM card)..................$95.00

Snaggletooth, Kenner, ROTJ, 3¾", MOC, D8................$30.00

Squid Head, Kenner, ROTJ, 3¾", MOC, from $18 to......$25.00

Stormtrooper, Kenner, ESB, Hoth Gear outfit, 3¾", M (VG+ card), O1..$45.00

Stormtrooper, Kenner, 12", loose, EX, O1....................$95.00

Sy Snootles & the Rebo Band, Kenner, ROTJ, 1983, M (EX card), A..$45.00

Tauntaun, Kenner, NMIB (VG+), O1............................$25.00

Tauntaun, missing saddle & bridle, H4...........................$8.00

Teebo, Kenner, ROTJ, 1983, 3¾", MOC, F1/T1............$25.00

Thall Joben, Kenner, Droid series, MOC, F1/T1............$15.00

Tig Fromm, Kenner, Droid series, TV show, 1985, MOC, F1 ....$15.00
Tuskin Raider, ROTJ, MOC, D8 ....$35.00
Ugnaught, ROTJ, MOC, D8 ....$20.00
Walrusman, Kenner, 3¾", MOC, from $40 to $60.00
Wampa Snow Creature, Kenner, MIB, from $25 to $30.00
Warok, Kenner, POTF, w/coin, MOC, F1 ....$30.00
Warok, Kenner, ROTJ, MOC (tri-logo card), F1 ....$30.00
Weequay, Kenner, ROTJ, 1983, 3¾", MOC, from $15 to .$18.00
Wicket W Warrick, Kenner, ROTJ, 3¾", M (VG+ card), O1 ....$12.00
Wicket W Warrick, stuffed plush, EX, O1 ....$18.00
Yak Face, Kenner, 3¾", M (VG+ tri-logo card), O1 ......$140.00
Yoda, Kenner, ESB, 3¾", MOC, D8/O1 ....$35.00
Zuckuss, ROTJ, MOC, D8 ....$35.00
4-Lom, Kenner, ROTJ, MOC, F1 ....$25.00
8D8, Kenner, ROTJ, 7th series, 1983, MOC, A $20.00

Playsets

Bespin Control Room, Kenner, Micro Collection, 1982, NRFB, C1 ....$39.00
Bespin Freeze Chamber, Kenner, Micro Collection, for 3¾" figures, MIB, J4 ....$36.00
Bespin Gantry, Kenner, Star Wars, Micro Collection, 1982, MIB, A $45.00

Cantina Adventure Set, Kenner, Sears promo, 1977, EX (NM box), A, $180.00.

Cantina Adventure Set, Kenner/Sears, Star Wars, 1977, NM, no box $90.00
Creature Cantina, Kenner, EX (VG+ box), O1 ....$65.00
Darth Vader's Star Destroyer, Kenner, appears complete, 2 broken connectors on main structure, missing box, H4 ..$60.00
Death Star Escape, Kenner, Micro Collection, for 3¾" figures, MIB, J4 ....$30.00
Death Star Space Station, Kenner, Star Wars, partially assembled, snap together, 1977, 22" box, NM (EX box) ..$125.00
Degobah Action Playset, Kenner, ESB, EX (EX box), O1 .$45.00
Degobah Action Playset, Kenner, ESB, 1981, NRFB, A ..$75.00

Droid Factory, Kenner, Star Wars, 1977, complete, M (EX box), A $75.00
Droid Factory, Kenner, Star Wars, 1977, EX (VG- box), O1 ....$45.00
Ewok Village, Kenner, ROTJ, 1983, 21" box, NM (EX box), from $65 to $85.00
Hoth Generator Attack, Micro Collection, Kenner, 1982, MIB, C1 ....$80.00
Hoth Ion Cannon, Kenner, Star Wars, Micro Collection, MIB, D8 ....$55.00
Imperial Attack Base, Kenner, ESB, VG+ (VG box), O1 ....$45.00
Imperial Attack Base, Kenner, ESB, 1980, w/instruction book & used decals, VG+, D9 ....$35.00
Jabba the Hutt, Kenner, MIB, O1 ....$45.00
Rebel Command Center, Kenner, ESB, missing cb bk-drop scene, loose, H4 ....$10.00
Rebel Command Center, w/3 figures, EX, O1 ....$125.00
Turret & Probot Playset, Kenner, EX (VG+ box), O1 .....$65.00

Vehicles

AST-5, Kenner, Mini-Rigs series, MIB, from $15 to $22.00
AT-AT, Imperial All-Terrain Armored Transport; Kenner, ROTJ, 23" box, NM (EX box), A $95.00
B-Wing Fighter, Kenner, POTF, MOC $15.00
B-Wing Fighter, Kenner, ROTJ, 1984, 24" box, NM (EX box), A $60.00
B-Wing Fighter, Kenner, missing guns, ROTJ $14.00
CAP-2 Captivator, Kenner, Mini-Rigs series, EX (VG box), O1 ....$25.00
Darth Vader Star Destroyer, Kenner, ESB, MIB $125.00
Darth Vader TIE Fighter, Kenner, diecast, 1977, MOC, from $75 to $90.00
Darth Vader TIE Fighter, Kenner, Star Wars, 1983, NRFB, from $70 to $85.00
Droids Sidegunner, Kenner, Adventures of R2-D2 & C-3PO, 1985, NRFB, A $40.00

TIE Fighter, Kenner, 1980, MIB, from $60.00 to $85.00.

Ewok Woodland Wagon, Kenner, ROTJ, Mini-Rigs series, complete, M (EX box), A..$45.00

Imperial Cruiser, Kenner, Star Wars, diecast & plastic, 1979, 7", M (EX box), A..$140.00

Imperial Shuttle, Kenner, ROTJ, unassembled w/box inserts, 1984, NM (EX+ box), A $150.00

Imperial Trooper Transporter, battery-op, 6 buttons produced various sound effects, 5½x10½", G-VG $50.00

TIE Interceptor, Kenner, 1983, M (EX box), A, $65.00.

Jedi Tri-Pod Cannon, MIB, D8 ....$12.00

Landspeeder, Kenner, diecast, missing windshield, EX, H4 ....$15.00

Millenium Falcon Spaceship, Kenner, ESB, NRFB, H4 ....$200.00

Millenium Falcon Spaceship, Kenner, Star Wars, 1977, 23" long, NM (EX box), A, $120.00.

Millenium Falcon Spaceship, Kenner, ESB, partially assembled, 1979, NM (EX box, missing inserts), A...$125.00

PDT-8, Kenner, Mini-Rigs series, EX (VG box), O1 ...$15.00

Radar Laser Canon, Kenner, RTOJ, Mini-Rigs series, MIB, D4 ....$15.00

Rebel Armored Snowspeeder, Kenner, ESB, 1980-82, 12½", NMIB, H4..$70.00

Rebel Transport, Kenner, ESB, w/applied decals, NMIB, H4/O1 ....$70.00

Sand Skimmer, POTF, M (VG card) $60.00

Slave 1-Boba Fett's Spaceship, Kenner, ESB, w/Han Solo, 1980, M (EX box), A..$100.00

Speeder Bike, Kenner, MIB, from $25 to $35.00

TIE Fighter, Kenner, Star Wars, diecast & plastic, 1978, 4", MOC, A...$100.00

TIE Fighter, Kenner, Star Wars, Micro series, NM (EX card), O1 ....$65.00

Tri-Pod Laser Canon, Kenner, RTOJ, Mini-Rigs series, MIB, D4/T1 ....$15.00

Twin-Pod Cloud Car, Kenner, ESB, EX, H4....................$16.00

Vehicle Maintenance Energizer, Kenner, Mini-Rigs series, MIB, D4 ....$15.00

X-Wing Fighter, Battle Damaged; Kenner, Micro series, NM (VG+ card), 01 ....$75.00

X-Wing Fighter, Kenner, ESB, NRFB, H4......................$95.00

X-Wing Fighter, Kenner, Star Wars, diecast & plastic, 1978, 5", M (EX card), A..$125.00

Y-Wing Fighter, Kenner, ESB, NM (EX box), O1...........$65.00

Miscellaneous

Art Portfolio, Ralph McQuarrie's Return of the Jedi, M (sealed), D4...$20.00

Bank, R2-D2, 20th Century Fox, 1977, M, 8", $55.00.

Bank, Emperor's Royal Guard, EX, O1............................$15.00
Bank, Roman, pnt ceramic Darth Vader, MIB.................$95.00
Bank, Roman, pnt ceramic R2-D2, MIB.........................$70.00
Bank, Sigma, pnt ceramic Chewbacca, MIB, from $40 to .$55.00
Bank, Sigma, pnt ceramic Jabba the Hutt, MIB...............$50.00
Bank, Sigma, pnt ceramic Yoda, MIB, from $35 to...........$45.00
Bank, vinyl Princess Kaneesha, T1.................................$20.00
Bank, vinyl Wicket, MIB...$20.00
Banner, Star Wars Tour From Tokyo, T1 ....$10.00
Bedspread, bl cotton w/characters, 1977, twin sz, NM, C1 .$31.00
Belt Buckle, C-3PO & R2-D2, EX, O1 ....$12.00
Blueprints, Star Wars, MIP, D4.....................................$10.00
Book, activity; ESB, 1980, VG+, T6 ....$5.00
Book, coloring; Kenner, ROTJ, M..................................$8.00
Book, comic; ROTJ #1 & #2, MIP, T1, set $10.00
Book, comic; Star Wars, issue #1, 1977, M, F1 ....$16.00
Book, Dot-to-Dot Fun; ROTJ, softcover, T1....................$5.00
Book, ESB, w/pop-ups, T1...$15.00
Book, puzzle; Happy House, ROTJ, NM $40.00
Book, ROTJ, Random House, hardcover, T1.....................$5.00
Book, ROTJ Official Collector's Edition, photos, 64 pgs, soft-
    cover, 8x11", EX-NM, T6..$10.00
Book, The Red Ghost Ewok Adventure, from cartoon series,
    1985, MIP, F1 ....$10.00
Book & Record Set, Ewoks Join the Fight, 33⅓ rpm, 7",
    MIP $3.00
Book & Record Set, Read-Along Books, Star Wars, from orig
    movie, 24-pg book & 45 rpm record, 1977, M, from $5
    to $10.00
Book & Tape, ROTJ Read Along, NM (EX pkg), O1 ....$5.00
Book of Masks, ROTJ, NM, T1 ....$45.00
Bookmark, Random House, ROTJ, any of 16 different, M1,
    ea $3.00
Bowl, Deka, ESB, plastic, 20-oz, M $10.00
Calendar, ROTJ, 1984, M $12.50
Case, C-3PO, NMIP, O1 ....$35.00
Case, Chewbacca Bandolier Strap, NM (VG+ box), O1 .$25.00

Case, for laser rifle, NMIB (EX box), O1 ....$45.00
Case, Kenner, ESB, for action figures, 12x9x3", VG+, T6.$20.00
Case, vinyl Darth Vader, for action figures, T1.................$15.00
Child's Set, bowl & cup, ESB, plastic, NMIP, O1 ....$15.00
Child's Set, Sigma, w/mug, bowl & plate, M (EX box), A.$52.00
Clock, wall; 3-D Electronic Quartz Clock, Bradley, Star Wars,
    1982, M (EX box), A..$50.00
Collector Card, Wonder Bread, 1978, set of 16, complete,
    M1 ....$7.50
Collector Plate, Hamilton, Space Battle, MIB $150.00
Collector Plate, R2-D2 & Wicket, MIB.........................$95.00
Comb, Princess Leia, MIB $15.00
Cookie Jar, Roman, pnt ceramic R2-D2, MIB...............$150.00

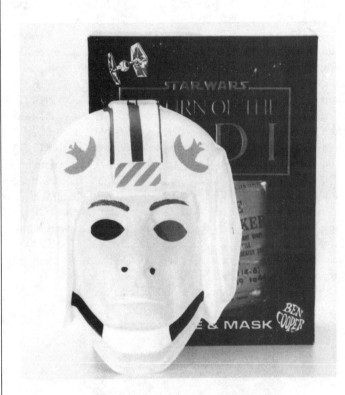

Costume, Luke Skywalker, MIB, $15.00.

Cup, Coca-Cola, soft plastic, #4 of 8, 1977, 5¼", T6.........$4.00
Curtains, Star Wars or ESB, M, D4, ea $10.00
Dixie Cup Lid, 1980, 1st or 2nd series, set of 40 different,
    M1 ....$20.00
Eraser, Darth Vader figure, MIP, from $3 to.....................$5.00
Felt-Tip Marker, Darth Vader, remove head to write, 1983, M,
    T6 ....$4.00
Figure, Sigma, pnt ceramic, Princess Leia, MIB $40.00
Figure, Sigma, pnt ceramic, Wicket, MIB $35.00
Figure Painting Kit, Craft Master, ESB, Princess Leia, Luke Sky-
    walker, Yoda or Han Solo, M (NM card), H4, any......$9.00
Figure Painting Kit, Craft Master, ROTJ, Admiral Ackbar or
    R2-D2 & C-3PO, MOC, H4 ....$9.00
Folder, Darth Vader w/Stormtroopers, 1977, VG+, T6 ......$5.00
Game, Adventures of R2-D2, MIB, from $25 to..............$35.00
Game, Battle at Sarlacc's Pit, MIB, F1 ....$15.00
Game, Duel at Death Star Race Set, Fundimensions, MIB.$250.00

Clock, talking alarm; Bradley, 1980, MIB, A, $65.00.

Game, Electronic Battle Command, Kenner, 1977, M (EX box), A $75.00

Game, Escape From Death Star, Kenner, 1977, NM, T2..$18.00

Game, ROTJ Play-for-Power Cards, MIB, T1 ....$12.50

Game, video; Atari 2600, Star Wars Jedi Arena, ROTJ or ESB, MIP, F1, any..$15.00

Game, Wicket the Ewok Food Gathering, NRFB, D4 ....$8.00

Game, Yoda the Jedi Master, Kenner, NRFB....................$25.00

Gift Wrap, ESB, MIP (sealed) $8.00

Gift Wrap, Star Wars, 1977, set of 2, MIP, F1 ....$20.00

Gum Card, English, 1979, 1st or 2nd series, 66 cards, complete, M1 ....$25.00

Gum Card, OPC, 1978, 1st or 2nd series, set of 66, M1 ...$25.00

Gum Card, OPC, 1978, 3rd series, set of 132, M1 ....$50.00

Gum Card, OPC, 1980, ESB, 1st series, set of 132, complete, M1..$18.00

Gum Card, Panini, 1978, set of 256, M1 ....$125.00

Gum Card, Topps, 1977, 1st series, set of 66, complete, M1 ....$28.00

Gum Card, Topps, 1977, 2nd series, set of 66, M1 ....$14.00

Gum Card, Topps, 1977, 3rd series, set of 66, M1 ....$14.00

Gum Card, Topps, 1977, 4th series, set of 66, M1 ....$17.50

Gum Card, Topps, 1977, 5th series, set of 66, M1 ....$17.50

Gum Card, Topps, 1980, ESB, 1st series, set of 132, complete, M1..$25.00

Gum Card, Topps, 1980, ESB, 3rd series, set of 88 cards w/22 stickers, complete, M1 ....$20.00

Gum Card, Topps, 1983, ROTJ, set of 132 w/66 stickers, complete, M1 ....$22.00

Jacket, Star Wars, blk & wht, sz 12, NM, O1 ....$38.00

Key Chain, Wicket figure, PVC, unlicensed, 1983, rare, 3", M, F1..$5.00

Lamp, R2-D2, VG+, O1 ....$75.00

Lamp, Windmill, Darth Vader ceramic bust, working, 1979, 12½", M, A $70.00

Laser Pistol, Kenner, Star Wars, Han Solo on box, 1977, 10", MIB, A $150.00

Laser Rifle, Kenner, Star Wars, 3-position style, 1977, 19", M (EX+ box), A $150.00

Light Saber, Kenner, Star Wars, flashlight w/inflatable sword, 1977, M (EX box), A $45.00

Napkins, ESB, 1980, set of 16, MIP, T6 ....$7.00

Night Light, ROTJ, Yoda head, MOC $10.00

Notebook, Jabba the Hutt on cover, spiral binding, NM....$3.50

Notebook Paper, mc star paper cover, 1977, VG+, T6.......$5.00

Paper Plate, ESB, 1980, 7" dia, set of 8, MIP, T6..............$7.00

Party Invitations, R2-D2 diecut, from orig movie, set of 8, 1977, MIP, F1 ....$5.00

Patch, Star Wars Lucasfilm Fan Club or ROTJ, M, D4, ea ...$5.00

Pencil Sharpener, ROTJ, w/scented eraser, 1983, M, T6....$4.00

Pencil Tray, Sigma, C-3PO, pnt ceramic, MIB, D4..........$25.00

Picture Frame, Sigma, C-3PO, pnt ceramic, MIB, D4 .....$25.00

Picture Frame, Sigma, Darth Vader, pnt ceramic, MIB, D4 ....$35.00

Picture Frame, Sigma, R2-D2, pnt ceramic, MIB.............$50.00

Pillow, Darth Vader & Boba Fett, ESB, EX, O1 ....$15.00

Pitcher, plastic, ROTJ/Coca-Cola, EX, O1 ....$12.00

Placemat Set, R2-D2 & C-3PO, ESB, NMIP, O1 ....$25.00

Play-Doh, Star Wars, MIB..$65.00

Poster, A Long Time Ago...Star Wars, 20th-Century Fox, cb litho, 1977, 24x38", NM, A $65.00

Poster, ESB Coming Soon to a Radio Near You, National Public Radio, 1982, 28x17", flat rolled, scarce, M, A $105.00

Poster, Montage, ESB, Han & Leia kissing, M, D4...........$10.00

Poster, Star Wars, 20th-Century Fox, 1977, 20x26", professionally matted, rare, M, A $100.00

Program, photos, 1977, 9x12", EX, T6 ....$20.00

Puppet, Yoda, EX, from $15 to $18.00

Puppet, Yoda, M (EX box)..$35.00

Puzzle, fr-tray; ROTJ, 1983, 11x8", EX+, T6......................$8.00

Puzzle, jigsaw; Kenner, Series I Space Battle, 1977, MIB (sealed), C1 ....$15.00

Puzzle, jigsaw; Luke Skywalker, 500-pc (4 missing), 15½x18", orig box, T6 ....$5.00

Puzzle, jigsaw; Star Wars III, Stormtroopers Stop the Land Speeder, 140-pc, orig box, 14x18", EX, D9/T6 ....$4.00

Rain Poncho, w/Star Wars logo, M, D4 ....$5.00

Record, ESB soundtrack, 33⅓ rpm, M in sleeve $20.00

Record, Star Wars Rebel Mission to Ord Mantel, 33⅓ rpm, 1983, M, F1 ....$10.00

Record, The Jedi Picture Disk album, 33⅓ rmp, Ewok on cover, 1983, EX, H4 ....$16.00

Record, The Story of Star Wars, 33⅓ rpm, 1978, EX, H4 .$12.00

Record, 20th-Century Records, 1977 soundtrack, w/Death Star Battle poster, EX, D9 ....$17.00

Record Tote, Star Wars, VG+, O1 ....$12.00

Salt & Pepper Shakers, Sigma, pnt ceramic R5-D4 & R2-D2, MIB, pr..$300.00

Shoelaces, Star Wars, MIP..$7.50

Soap Dish, Sigma, ceramic Landspeeder, MIB.................$60.00

Mask, Ewok, Don Post, rubber, 1983, $45.00.

Standee, C-3PO, cb, for store display, folded in middle for ship-
ping, 72", EX+...$45.00
Standee, Star Wars R2-D2 & C-3PO, litho cb, T1 ....$35.00
Sticker, General Mills, 1978, set of 18, w/wallet, M1 ....$50.00
Sticker, Topps, 1977, 1st series, set of 11, M1...................$20.00
Sticker, Topps, 1977, 2nd series, set of 11, M1 ....$6.50
Sticker, Topps, 1977, 3rd series, set of 11, M1 ....$30.00
Sticker, Topps, 1977, 4th series, set of 11, M1.................$10.00
Sticker, Topps, 1977, 5th series, set of 11, M1 ....$6.50
Sticker, Topps, 1980, ESB, 1st series, set of 33, complete,
M1...$50.00
Sticker, Topps, 1980, 2nd series, set of 33, complete, M1..$18.00
Sticker, Yoda, mc, 1983, 3½x5½", M, F1 ....$5.00
Stickpin, Darth Vader or C-3PO figure, pnt metal, EX, H4,
ea $3.00

**Teapot, Luke Skywalker on Tauntaun figural, 10½x9½",
M, $125.00.**

Teapot, Sigma, pnt ceramic, Luke Skywalker on Tauntaun,
MIB...$175.00
Toothbrush, Oral-B, Darth Vader figure, MIP (sealed) $8.00
Toothbrush, Star Wars, electric, MIB..............................$95.00
Toothbrush Holder, Sigma, pnt ceramic Snowspeeder,
MIB $40.00
Tote Bag, ROTJ graphics on bl ground, MIP, T1 ....$15.00
Transfer, Presto Magix, Battle of Endor, MIB, D4 ....$5.00
Transfer, Presto Magix, Deluxe Jabba Scene, MIB, D4 ....$10.00
Transfer Set, Presto Magix, set of 4: Asteroid Storm, Deck of
Star Destroyer, Dagobah Bog & Cloud City Battle, MIP,
F1 ....$15.00
Trash Can, litho tin w/ROTJ graphics, M, from $25 to....$35.00
Travel Bag, Ewoks pictured, MIB.....................................$15.00
Vase, Sigma, pnt ceramic Yoda, MIB...............................$50.00
Viewer, Star Wars, MIB, T1...$45.00

Steam Powered

During the early part of the century until about 1930,
though not used to any great extent, live steam power was used
to activate toys such as large boats, novelty toys, and model
engines. See also Boats.

Falk Five Steam Plant, no electrical cord, 1920-30, 14", 11x10"
base, EX+, M5 ....$475.00
Model Engine, Wilesco, tin & steel on metal base, 6x7x10", EX
(VG box), A $65.00
Model Engine, wood base, working & complete, 16x18½", G,
A..$575.00

Sausage Maker, Germany, ca 1910, EX, $250.00.

**Steam Pumper, lead chassis, hand-painted details, cop-
per finish on dome, 9¾", G-VG, A, $1,600.00.**

Steam Launch, Weeden, pnt boat w/tin boiler, oscillating cylinder, live steam, burner missing, pnt loss, 14", G-VG, A $350.00

Steam Propeller No 55, Union Mfg, pnt tin, blk, red, yel & gr, alcohol-fired boiler, steam, orig wood box, 19", VG-EX, A..$5,000.00

Woodcutters, Germany, tin litho, 1 man w/hand saw, 2nd w/power saw, 4½x4¼x9¼", EX, A $200.00

Steelcraft

These pressed steel vehicles were made during the late 1920s until sometime after 1935.

Army Scout, single engine, US insignia on wing tips, gr w/yel wing, tail & wheels, rpl screws, VG pnt, A $800.00

City Fire Dept Ladder Truck, GMC series, folding extension lg ladder, hose reel, bell, rubber tires, 26", G, A..........$633.00

Dairy Truck, red w/Bakelite wheels, Sheffield Farms on sides, electric headlights, NP grille, 18⅞", G-, A..............$220.00

Delivery Van, riding model, steers in front, electric lights, NP grille, Shuster's lettered on side, ca 1935, 18", G, A $275.00

Delivery Van #103, bl-gr cab, lt yel body w/City Delivery in gr letters, NP grille, red steel wheels, 19", VG-EX, A .$495.00

Delivery Van #103, gr cab, yel van w/City Delivery lettered on sides, NP grille, yel steel wheels, 19", G, A $165.00

Dump Truck, GMC series, blk w/solid red wheels, decal on dash, dome hubcaps, 2 rpl tires, 24¼", G, A $330.00

Dump Truck, Mack series, red cab, bed & wheels, blk fenders & chassis, lever-action dump, rpt, 26", VG, A $330.00

Dump Truck, scissors mechanism, GMC series, bl-gray cab, gray bed & wheels, narrow rubber tires, rpl parts, 26", G, A $358.00

Express Truck, GMC series, bl-gray body & fr, gray bed, red wheels, non-dumping, all orig parts, 25", G, A........$303.00

Graf Zeppelin, pnt pressed steel w/rubber tires, 30", VG, A $270.00

Intercity Bus, electric lights, battery compartment, original green paint, typical scratches, 6x24", A, $400.00.

Lockheed Sirius Airplane, 2-seater, wht enamel w/red wings, solid rubber wheels, electric lights, 21½x21¾", EX, A $1,100.00

Mail Truck, red w/gr van body, Mack Jr Performance Counts decals, rubber tires, missing part, 22½", G, A..........$523.00

Moving Van, GMC series, blk cab & fr, gr body, solid red wheels, decal on dash, dome hubcaps, 24¾", G-, A $853.00

Railway Express Van, Mack series, red cab & solid wheels, lt gr screened body, rubber tires, 24½", VG+, A..........$2,310.00

Steam Roller, blk w/red corrugated roof, red wheels, decals on sides, ca 1935, 16½", M, A $550.00

Steam Shovel #172, blk w/red roof, blk extension shovel & boom, decal on boiler, 1935, 8¾", EX, A................$138.00

Tank Truck, GMC series, blk body, gray tank, solid red wheels, Firestone treads, fillable, 25½", G-, A.....................$495.00

Tractor-Trailor Contractor Truck, GMC series, blk cab & chassis, gray bed, red steel wheels, 30", G, A $990.00

Tri-Motor Transport Plane, US Mail, w/orig canvas mailbag, partial rpt on top/tail, 23½x26½", A.........................$550.00

U.S. Mail Plane, orange and black, rubber tires on metal rims, working, 23½", G, A, $600.00.

Steiff

Margaret Steiff (Germany) made the first of her felt-stuffed toys in the late 1800s, marking them with a tag that carried a logo of an elephant in a circle. She changed to the bear logo in 1903 after her first teddy bear became such a popular seller. Excelsior and wool replaced the felt as stuffing, and when it became available, foam rubber was used. In addition to the tag, look for the 'Steiff' ribbon and the button inside the ear. For more information we recommend *Teddy Bears and Steiff Animals* by Margaret Fox Mandel.

Bambi, velvet & mohair, raised script button, 4", EX, G4 ..$65.00

Bambi, velvet & mohair, unmk, 9", EX, G4......................$85.00

Bear, mohair w/squeaker & glass eyes, jtd, w/Plexiglas showcase, 11¼", EX, A...$110.00

Bear Family, Collector's Edition 1982, mohair w/squeaker & glass eyes, set of 5, orig 16" box, EX, A $260.00

Bendy Zotty, long frosted tan mohair w/peach chest, open mouth, soft stuffed, non-jtd, unmk, 10", G4 ....$75.00

Bendy Zotty, long frosted tan mohair w/peach chest, open mouth, non-jtd, incised button, ear tag, 17", M, G4...$95.00

Berlin Bear, wht mohair, glass eyes, jtd arms & legs, Berlin chest banner & crown, 1960s, 7½", EX $65.00

Black Tom Cat (Halloween), raised script button, stock tag in ear, orig ribbon, 6x5", M, G4 ....$125.00

Bonzo (dog), lt brn velvet, bl glass eyes, pnt red nose, smiling w/red felt tongue out, music box inside, 13", EX, A...........$1,350.00

Bulldog, mohair w/velvet muzzle, unmk, 4", VG, G4.......$45.00

Camel, mohair w/velvet face & legs, raised script button, rope tail, 5½", EX, G4.................$95.00

Camel, mohair w/velvet legs & muzzle, raised script button, stock tag in ear, 10", EX, G4.................$125.00

Caribou, blond mohair with brown spots, felt antlers, 68" to top of antlers, A, $2,000.00.

Cat, unmk, mohair w/glass eyes, 6x8", very worn, G4......$45.00

Cock Puff, unmk, wool w/metal legs, 3", G4.................$25.00

Cocky, swivel head, velvet muzzle, raised script button, 5", EX, G4.................$75.00

Coco Baboon, chest tag, orig collar, 6", EX, G4.................$95.00

Coral Fish Puff, bl & gr wool, raised script button, stock tag, 2", M, G4.................$30.00

Cosy Teddy, lt brn w/beige felt paws, felt mouth, floss nose, jointed, 15½", EX.................$145.00

Country Mouse, wht w/red plastic eyes, gingham apron, felt hands, feet & tail, glass bead nose, w/button, 3¼", M, G4.................$85.00

Country Mouse, wht w/red plastic eyes, gold satin skirt, felt hands & feet, glass bead nose, w/button, 3¼", M, G4.................$85.00

Dangling Orangutan, incised button, stock tag in ear, rubber face, 22", M, G4.................$125.00

Donkey, tan & gray mohair w/blk mane & accents, button in ear, squeaker, US Zone, 13½", EX-, A.................$160.00

Dossy (cat), Dralon, incised button, stock tag in ear, chest tag, orig red shirt, 1965-77, 14", EX, G4.................$75.00

Duckling, swimming, unmk, swivel head, 5", G4.................$45.00

Elephant, incised button, stock tag in ear, red felt bib, 4", M, G4.................$55.00

Elephant, mohair, glass eyes, gr & red felt howdah, button in ear, bottom of feet stained, 11", VG, A.................$150.00

Floppy Lion, Dralon, baby toy, incised button, stock tag in ear, 7", G, G4.................$25.00

Floppy Poodle, baby toy, unmk, 9", EX, G4.................$55.00

Floppy Robby Seal, incised button, 14", VG, G4.................$55.00

Floppy Zotty Bear, baby toy, incised button, 7", EX, G4..$75.00

Floppy Zotty Bear, rattle in paw, raised script button, 10", G, G4.................$75.00

Friends of Christmas, bear in Santa costume in pnt wood sleigh w/1 deer, orig box, 17", NM, A.................$100.00

Frog, gr velvet, raised script button, 4", EX, G4.................$65.00

Froggy, incised button, stock tag in ear, 11", M, G4.........$95.00

German Shepherd, paw to tail, button in ear, 10x19", EX, $165.00.

Giraffe, velvet, raised script button, rope tail, 7", M, G4..$75.00

Goldy Hamster, Dralon, incised button, stock tag in ear, 7", VG, G4.................$35.00

Goldy Hamster, unmk, button hole, 5", VG, G4.................$50.00

Green Monkey, Dralon, baby toy, 9x7", VG, G4.................$50.00

Ground Squirrel, unmk, torn left ear, 5", G, G4.................$40.00

Jocko, Dralon, brass button, stock tag in ear, 1980s, 10", M, G4.................$40.00

Jocko, jtd, raised script button, 7", EX, G4.................$95.00

Jocko, raised script button, chest & ear tags, 11", M, G4..$125.00

Jocko, raised script button, chest tag, 3", M, G4.................$65.00

Joggi Hedgehog, brass button, stock tag in ear, chest tag, 7", M, G4.................$55.00

Jolanthe Pig, unmk, 6", M, G4 ....$65.00

Kitty, standing, gray & wht striped, raised script button, 5x6", G, G4 ....$65.00

Lamby, chest tag, orig ribbon & bell, soiled, 4", G4 ....$55.00

Lamby, unmk, 6x6", G, G4...........................$85.00

Lara the Parrot, old, lg, EX $225.00

Lion, standing, incised button, 7", EX, G4 ....$110.00

Loopy Wolf Puppet, incised button, stock tag in ear, chest tag, M, G4 ....$125.00

Lumpi Daschund, raised script button, remnant stock tag, 5x7", VG, G4 ....$75.00

Maxie Mole, unmk, missing shovel, 4", M, G4 ....$75.00

Molly Koala, gray w/off-wht chest, beige face, glass eyes, sits on hind legs, 15", EX $165.00

Monkey, wht, unmk, needs rpr, 11", G4 ....$45.00

Okapi, velvet, raised script button, 6x5½", EX, G4........$225.00

Peggy Penguin, unmk, 5", EX, G4.....................$65.00

Peky, incised button, stock tag in ear, 4", M, G4 ....$60.00

Peky, swivel head, raised script button, stock tag in ear, 8", EX, G4 ....$95.00

Pitou, orange Dralon, incised button, orig collar, 8", VG, G4 ....$55.00

Pony, Dralon, raised script button, 9x10", EX, G4............$55.00

Porcupines, Micki and Mecki, 10", $225.00 for the pair.

Rabbit, running, unmk, 9½", EX, G4.............................$125.00

Rabbit Family, Collector's Edition 1983, mohair w/glass eyes, set of 3, orig 15" box, EX, A $130.00

Monkey, glass eyes, felt hands and feet, tag in ear, 11", VG, $75.00.

Mopsey Puppy, swivel head, brass button, 5", M, G4........$55.00

Mountain Goat, unmk, 8", EX, G4 ....$95.00

Mungo Monkey, swivel head, unmk, worn tail, 11", G, G4 ..$75.00

Mungo Monkey Puppet, raised script button, stock tag in ear, EX, G4 ....$95.00

Nagy Beaver, unmk, 6", EX, G4 ....$65.00

Nelly Hen, Dralon w/plastic feet, brass button, stock & chest tags, 5", EX, G4....................................$50.00

Rabbit, Tami, with tag, 4x7½", $85.00.

Rabbit Puppet, incised button, stock tag in ear, orig ribbon, M, G4 ....$125.00

Rabbit Puppet, mohair, missing button, EX $40.00

Record Peter on Scooter, mohair, shoe button eyes, felt face & hands, squeaker mtd in rear, 7", G, A $90.00

Revue Suzi, raised script button, 5", EX, G4 ....$60.00

Rhino, chest tag, sm rpr horn, 12", VG, G4 ....$95.00

Robby Seal, unmk, 5x7", VG, G4 ....$75.00

Schlummi, br w/beige face, glass eyes, floss nose, lying down w/face between paws, no chest tag, 22½", EX $195.00

Slo Turtle, rubber shell, chest tag, 7", EX, G4 ....$75.00

Snobby Poodle, blk, collar w/tag, 4", worn, G4 ....$25.00

Snobby Poodle, blk, raised script button, stock tag on ear, chest tag, orig collar, 5", EX, G4 ....$60.00

Snobby Poodle, gray, jtd, raised script button, collar, 5", G, G4 ....$45.00

Snobby Poodle, lying, blk, raised script button, collar, 12", EX, G4 ....$95.00

Springer Spaniel, lying, open mouth, unmk, 13", VG, G4 ..$85.00

Squirrel, unmk, 5", VG, G4 ....$50.00

Tabby, sitting, jtd head, unmk, 4", G, G4 ....$65.00

Tapsy (bear cub), dk brn/ beige, googly eyes, standing on all fours, 7½x6", EX $55.00

Tapsy (cat), unmk, 5", M, G4 ....$65.00

Teddy Bear, blond mohair, shoe button eyes, fully jtd, excelsior stuffing, blank ear button, fur loss/moth holes, 14", A $1,650.00

Teddy Bear, blond mohair w/plain button in ear, shoe button eyes, fully jtd, floss mouth & nose, 10", VG-EX, A ..$850.00

Teddy Bear, curly blond mohair, shoe button eyes, fully jtd, ear button, 1905, hair loss/silent growler/damage, 23", A $2,200.00

Teddy Bear, jointed, stitched paws, button in ear, 9", $1,500.00.

Teddy Bear, lt yel mohair, shoe button eyes, fully jtd, excelsior stuffing, rpl pads, button missing, 24", G, A $700.00

Tessie Schnauzer, unmk, orig collar, worn, 4", G4 ....$35.00

Tiger, button in ear, 5x12", $125.00.

Tiger, lying, chest tag, 9", M, G4 ....$110.00

Tiger, running, chest tag, 4x10", EX, G4 ....$125.00

Tiger Puppet, incised button, stock tag in ear, EX, G4 .....$95.00

Valentine Bear, all orig w/tags & vest, 14", M $175.00

Wire Hair Fox Terrier, sitting, glass eyes, ear & collar buttons, some fiber loss, 4¼", A $220.00

Wittie Owl, rubber beak, raised script button, remnant of stock tag, 5", M, G4 ....$65.00

Stoves

Though size and weight alone deters many from owning even one full-size cast-iron stove, many collectors find salesman's samples and toy stoves satisfying alternatives, able to evoke the same feeling of hearth and home, but on a much more manageable scale.

Salesman' samples were often put on display in the hardware store window to entice potential buyers. These stoves were one-eighth scale or smaller and yet accurately reflected the details of larger kitchen stoves. Many were very ornate and carried names such as 'Rival,' Princess,' and 'Queen.' Toy stoves were made from the 1890s until the 1930s. They were one-sixteenth scale and were often enhanced with pots, kettles and a lifter for the stove's lids, and many of these had names as well.

Often a stove's cooking surface had four to six round lids or burners and one rectangular lid for the water reservoir. Some had high backs while others had only a tin smoke pipe. Earlier styles had three functional doors, the large oven door and a smaller one on the front, and a small door on the left, which on later models did not actually open. Many stoves had ornate skirts that were extended on the corners to form feet. Later stoves had backs and right sides of sheet steel, used to reduce the weight and make them cheaper to ship.

Stoves that are complete and in good condition (no breaks or cracks) are highly prized by collectors.

Baby, name emb on oven door, EX $350.00
Buck's Jr Range, St Louis MO, new body & pnt, recast parts, 26" $850.00
Dainty, Reading Stove Works, PA, 7x13x8", VG $150.00
Eagle, sm sz, EX...$200.00
Eclipse, EX $175.00
Karr, Qualified, bl porc w/nickel, Belleville IL, 1925, EX (reproduced in 1960s, same value for repro as for orig) $2,500.00
Little Fanny, minor rust, EX $300.00
Little Giant, unmk/unidentified, 7½x8½x11", EX orig ..$675.00
Little Willie, EX...$75.00
Queen, no shelves, 15" long, EX...............................$1,000.00
Queen, no shelves, 9" long, EX $500.00
Rival, no shelves, 12" long, EX $900.00

Rival, top warmers and oven, several accessories, 14", NM, $1,350.00.

Royal, sm sz, EX $200.00
The Pet, Young Bros, Albany NY, 10½x6x8½"..............$165.00
Triumph, Kenton Hardware, OH, 14x8½x19", G $195.00

Strauss

Imaginative, high-quality tin windup toys were made by Ferdinand Strauss (New York, later New Jersey) from the onset of World War I until the 1940s. For about fifteen years prior to his becoming a toymaker, he was a distributor of toys he imported from Germany. Though hard to find in good working order, his toys are highly prized by today's collectors, and when found in even very good to excellent condition, several are in the $500.00 and up range.

Air Devil Plane, litho tin, red, wht & bl w/orange rudder, working, 9½", G-VG, A $225.00
Alabama Coon Jigger, Tombo; litho tin, performs jig on stage, 1910, 10", M (NM box), A...................................$1,600.00
Alabama Coon Jigger, Tombo; litho tin figure on base, brn, yel, gr & orange, clockwork, working, 11", G, A $400.00
Clown Krazy Car, litho tin w/clown driver (may be replacement), balloons on side, 1920s, 8½", VG, A $414.00

Dandy Jim Clown Dancer, lithographed tin, mechanical, some scratches and wear, 10", VG, A, $450.00.

Dandy Jim Clown Dancer, does jig & plays cymbals on top of circus tent, 1921, 10", NM, A, ...$800.00
Dizzie Lizzie, litho tin w/colloquial sayings, w/driver, shakes, bounces & rattles, ca 1925, 8", G+ (NM box), A ...$595.00
Flying Zeppelin, tin, working, orig box has sm tear, NM...$400.00
Ham & Sam, black banjo player standing at piano, seated piano player, some wear, EX+, M5...................................$625.00

Inter-State Double-Decker Bus, gr & yel, working, 10½", G-VG,
A $625.00
Inter-State Double-Decker Bus, w/driver & rear platform,
6x10¾", w/up is nonexistent o/w EX, A $350.00
Jackie the Hornpipe Sailor, litho tin, figure standing on boat
base, 8", VG, A...$275.00
Jazzbo Jim, Black dancer on roof of cabin, EX.............$500.00
Jazzbo Jim, Black dancer on roof of cabin, roof faded, 10", G,
A $110.00
Jenny the Balking Mule, litho tin, farmer rocks bk & forth in
cart, mule kicks, 1920s, 9", EX+ (NM box), A........$419.00
Leaping Lena, litho tin, blk & wht, w/driver, clockwork, non-
working, hood ornament missing, 8", EX.............$325.00
Play Golf 'Just Like Daddy,' litho tin, 5" golfer on 7x21" base,
orig box mk No 110, EX (G+ box), A.....................$543.00

Rollo-Chair, lithographed tin, mechanical, working, 6½", NM (VG box), A, $2,300.00.

Santa Claus Sleigh, pulled by 2 reindeer, Santa & deer jump up
& down, 5½x11½", NM (P box), A.....................$1,500.00
Santa Claus Sleigh, pulled by 2 reindeer, Santa jumps up &
down, deer gallop, working, 6¼x12", EX, A............$700.00

Yell-O-Taxi, 7½", D10, NM, $850.00.

Structo

Pressed steel vehicles were made by Structo (Illinois) as early as 1920. They continued in business well into the 1960s, producing several army toys, trucks of all types, and fire-fighting and construction equipment.

Cadillac, red w/blk rubber tires, ca 1953, 6¼", EX, W1 .....$22.50

Delivery Truck, ca 1950s, MIB, $300.00. (Photo courtesy Continental Hobby House.)

Dump Truck, ca 1950s, MIB, $200.00. (Photo courtesy Continental Hobby House.)

Excavator Truck, lt bl-gray, dummy headlights, hood opens, Bakelite wheels & tires, plated headlights, 22⅛", G-, A $182.00
Excavator Truck, red cab w/NP grille (rpl), mint gr w/orange-
roofed excavator, Bakelite wheels w/whitewalls, 27", VG,
A $242.00
International Scout, turq & wht, w/2 interchangable tops, ca
1965, NM, A3...$125.00
Pile Driver, apple gr cab w/red roof & chassis, blk boom, CI hammer, decal on base, 20-gauge steel, 13¼", G, A........$121.00

Race Car, lg key in front, steers, w/up, working, 12½, VG, A..$275.00

Ready Mix Concrete Truck #700, NM (EX+ box), P3...$230.00

Road Grader, apple-gr chassis, red & blk trim, gray steel wheels w/red centers, steel hubcaps, 15⅜", EX-, A.............$523.00

Sandloader, yel & red pnt metal w/rubber loader, EX+, I2 .$32.00

Steam Shovel, orange, lt bl & blk, sm scratches, 18½", VG, A...$35.00

Firefighting

Aerial Fire Truck, red, chrome wheels w/blk tires, decals on doors & hood, detachable trailer, orig box, 26½", NM, A..$264.00

Fire Truck, red w/blk fenders, dummy headlights, Bakelite wheels, decal on hood, fillable tank, w/hose, 23½", P, A..$132.00

Pumper, red w/orange tank, steel wheels, brass pump behind cab, bell on cowl, CFD & Pumper decals, 1928, 21½", VG, A $660.00

Trucks and Vans

American Airlines Lift Truck, G......................................$75.00

Auto Transport, chrome-plated diecast cab, solid plastic wheels, pressed steel trailer, 3 vehicles, VG...........................$60.00

Dump Truck, orange cab, bed & chassis, steel wheels & tires, NP grille, electric headlights, decal, 19⅛", G, A.....$121.00

Fixed Bed Truck, olive gr w/blk fenders & chassis, Bakelite wheels, hinged tailgate, missing headlights, 22¼", P, A...$50.00

Flat Bed Truck, red & yel cab, red bed w/stake sides, yel fenders, dummy headlights, Bakelite wheels, 22¼", G-, A ...$550.00

Freeport Motor Express, stake sides, blk tires, 13", EX....$195.00

Motor Dispatch Truck, bl tractor trailer w/red airplane graphics, 23", VG, A...$900.00

Search Light Truck, olive gr, hood opens, battery-op search light swivels, aims up & down, blk wheels, 16", VG, A...$132.00

Sportsman Truck #311, MIB...$300.00

Truck, bl & wht, decals on doors, dummy headlights, Bakelite wheels, hinged lid on tool box, slot for boom, 21", G, A...$72.00

Truck w/Hydraulic Lift Tractor, rpt, 1950s, C8 ....$65.00

Vista Dome Horse Van, gold, 1966, 21", EX+, A3 ....$45.00

Wrecker, gray w/red hood, Structo Toys decal on sides, blk wood wheels, NP hubcaps, dummy headlights, 20¼", EX, A...$165.00

Wrecker, wht w/red boom, Bakelite wheels w/pnt whitewalls, electric headlights, NP grille, door decals, 19", VG, A..$242.00

Teddy Bears

Early bears have long snouts, jointed limbs, large feet and felt paws, long curving arms, and glass or shoe-button eyes. Most have a humped back and are made of mohair stuffed with straw or excelsior. Some of the most desirable were made early in the century by the Steiff company (see Steiff), but they don't necessarily have to be old to be collectible, and many choose to include toys, blocks, buttons, books, and other items dealing with teddies in their collections as well.

Herman, brn mohair w/glass eyes, inset shaved mohair snout, felt pads, loud growler, 1930s-40s, EX, G4 ....$450.00

10", Herman, Zotty, long brn mohair, squeaks, jtd, EX, A.$195.00

10", Schuco, Bigo Bello, tan mohair w/googly eyes, wire arms & legs, felt pads, red plaid pants, EX, G4 ....$75.00

11", blond mohair, long fur, glass eyes, embroidered nose & mouth, fully jtd, excelsior & cotton stuffed, 1930s, VG, A...$135.00

12", Made in England for Kaufmanns, golden yellow fur, jointed limbs, glass eyes, EX, A, $70.00.

14", English Merrythought (?), gold mohair w/glass eyes, canvas pads, some mohair loss, G4 ....$175.00

14", German, long lt tan mohair w/plastic eyes, worn felt arm pads, growler, rpl feet pads, 1940s, G, G4 ....$395.00

14", German, short gold mohair w/plastic eyes, long snout, leather pads, gruff expression, loud growler, 1940s, M, G4.......$195.00

14", Ideal, Sam, hump back, gold hair, shoe button eyes, straw stuffing, long snout, 1915, VG, A $345.00

14", Schuco, lt gold mohair, glass eyes, sheared snout & pads, flat-card soles, 1930s, worn, G4 ....$150.00

15", dk brn fur, fully jtd, straw filled, some wear to paws & foot pads, o/w EX $175.00

15x24", growler, glass eyes, on 4 CI wheels, top of his bk totally rpl, G-, A $300.00

19", Danish, short bristly wool plush w/amber glass eyes, dk brn felt pads, 1950s, M, G4...$395.00

19", gold-blond fur, jtd legs, arms & head, 1 eye missing, torn paws, fur wear, A $225.00

19", Schuco, gray mohair w/glass eyes, sheared snout & pads, stocky body, loud growler, flat-card soles, 1930s, VG, G4 ....$650.00

19", yel mohair, fully jtd, excelsior & kapok stuffing, embroidered nose etc, 1920s, fur loss/rprs/rpl eyes, A $165.00

23", Herman, brn mohair w/glass eyes, inset shaved mohair snout, felt pads, 1940s-50s, EX, G4 ....$650.00

23", tan fur, humpback, dressed in lederhosen, wear/some soil, A $150.00

24", Ideal, blond plush mohair, shoe button eyes, rust cloth & emboidered nose, jtd, accentuated hump, early, VG, A $1,200.00

24", German, cotton plush, large hump, glass two-tone eyes, embroidered nose, early, EX, $495.00.

Tekno

The Tekno company was formed in Denmark during the late 1920s. The toy vehices they made were of the highest quality, fully able to compete with the German-made Marklin toys then dominating the market. The earliest Tekno vehicles were made of tinplate, and though some were not marked at all, others were stamped with a number. The factory continued to expand until WWII broke out and restrictions made further building impossible. In 1940 the government prohibited the use of tinplate for toy production, and the company began instead to manufacture diecast vehicles in a smaller (1/43) scale. These were exported worldwide in great volume. Collectors regard them as the finest diecasts ever made. Due to climbing production costs and the resulting increases in retail prices that inevitably hurt their sales, the company closed in 1972. Tekno dies were purchased by Mercury Kirk Joal who used them to produce toys identical to the originals except for the mark.

#313 Falck Animal Ambulance, red (trailer), G, B5 ....$95.00
#321 Falck Utility Truck, red, tinplate, G, B5................$195.00
#331 Falck Wrecking Truck, red, G, B5 ....$195.00
#341 Falck Fire Engine, red, G, B5................................$225.00
#351 Falck Ambulance, red, bl wheels, G, B5 ....$400.00

#356A Porsche, $200.00. (Photo courtesy Continental Hobby House.)

#361 Falck Searchlight Truck, red w/blk fenders, G, B5 .$225.00
#371 Falck Generator Truck, red, G+, B5 ....$450.00
#381 Ambulance Plane, twin-engined, wht, G, B5.....$1,500.00
#401 Flying Fortress, silver, Soviet Union, extremly rare, G, B5 ....$195.00
#401 Flying Fortress, silver, US, G+, B5 ....$75.00
#402 Twin Engine Bomber BB1, silver, US, EX, B5.........$65.00
#403 1-Engine Fighter DSB1, wht w/red cross, EX, B5.....$60.00
#410, VW Van 'Taxa,' blk & rust, EX-, B5....................$120.00
#415 Ford Taurus Transit, wht & blk, 'Zonen,' MIB $60.00
#417 VW Van 'Rinso,' wht & gr, EX-............................$110.00
#421 Ford Taurus 1000 Pickup, bl & red, 'Ford,' MIB....$120.00
#422 Ford V8 Cement Truck, red & bl, G, B5 ....$65.00
#423 Ford V8 Garbage Truck, gr & red, G, B5 ....$45.00
#424 Packard Ambulance, 'Zonen,' wht, EX, B5............$195.00
#425 & 452 Volvo FB 88 Truck w/Trailer, MIB, B5 ......$120.00
#425 Ford Taxi, metallic bl, red wheels, rare, EX, B5.....$250.00
#427 Triangle Black Maria, dk gr, G+, B5 ....$95.00
#428 Ford V8 Wrecking Truck, red & blk, metal tires, very rare, G, B5..$175.00
#429 Ford Mercury, Firechief, 'Zonen,' red, EX, B5........$125.00

#431 Volvo Auto Transport, red, EX-, B5 ....$145.00

#434 Volvo Tank Truck, wht & gr, 'BP,' MIB, B5 ....$185.00

#442 Vespa Scooter, 2-seater, wht, EX-, B5 ....$60.00

#443 Vespa Scooter w/Sidecar, 1 seat, metallic gr, EX-, B5 .$75.00

#445 Scania Vabis Ladder Truck, red, EX, B5 ....$100.00

#453 Scania Vabis Cement Truck, G+, B5....................$195.00

#460 Tractor, red, G+, B5 ....$60.00

#462 Plow, for tractor, red & bl, G+ B5.........................$15.00

#463 Rake, for tractor, red, G+, B5 ....$15.00

#480 Ford V8 Tipping Truck, red, 'Zonen,' VG, B5 ....$35.00

#481 Ford V8 Wrecking Truck, 'Zonen,' red & blk, metal tires rare, G, B5 ....$150.00

#485 Triangel Ladder Truck, 'Zonen,' red & blk, EX, B5 .$110.00

#486 Triangel Fire Engine, 'Zonen,' dk red & blk, EX,B5 .$95.00

#488 Twin-Engine Plane, metallic bl, red cross, G-, B5 .$100.00

#719 Morris Oxford 1955, dk gr, G+, B5 ....$75.00

#720 Opel Record 1958, reddish brn, 'A&M,' rare, MIB, B5 ....$500.00

#725 Mercedes Benz 220 SE Fire Chief, red & blk, EX-, B5...$150.00

#731 Mercedes Benz 220 SE Ambulance, red & blk, EX (orig box), B5 ....$150.00

#732 Dodge Ambulance, red, 'Falck,' G+, B5.................$125.00

#734 Dodge Truck, w/barrels, red & bl, G+, B5 ....$65.00

#735 Dodge Flatbed Truck, red & bl, G, B5....................$65.00

#736 Dodge Beer Truck, wht w/red 'Tuborg,' EX-, B5......$95.00

#738 Dodge Coal Truck, blk, 'Kul & Koks,' G+, B5.........$95.00

#739 Dodge Truck, w/topper, yel & red, EX-, B5 ....$125.00

#741 Dodge Truck, w/logs & trailer, red & bl, G+, B5...$120.00

#746 Dodge Brick Truck, gr & red, G, B5......................$45.00

#760 Loading Lift, red, G+, B5...................................$55.00

#766 Caravelle, SAS, w/bottom of plastic box, EX, B5 ....$95.00

#785 Hawker-Hunter Jet-Fighter, silver, RAF, EX, B5...$125.00

#786 MIG Jet Fighter, olive, USSR, EX $125.00

#787 Super Sabre F100 Jet Fighter, silver, US, EX, B5...$125.00

#788 Super Mystery Jet Fighter, France, MIB, B5...........$145.00

#812 Cooper Norton #1, silver, EX, B5.........................$60.00

#813 Ferrari 750 Monza Racer, yel, GB flag #6, G+, B5...$75.00

#814 Jeep, w/driver, khaki, US star, MIB, B5 ....$60.00

#814K Cannon, for #814 Jeep, khaki, MIB, B5 ....$45.00

#814P Trailer for #814 Jeep, khaki, EX, B5.....................$45.00

#815 Sprite Musketeer Camping Trailer, ivory & lt gr, EX-, B5...$50.00

#819 VW 1200, 1960, yel, MIB, B5 ....$85.00

#824 MGA Coupe 1600, lt bl, EX (orig box), B5...........$170.00

#828 VW 1500, wht, VG-, B5....................................$10.00

#829 Lincoln Continental, off-wht, EX (orig box), B5 ..$135.00

#832 MG 1100 Ralley, wht, EX-, B5 ....$75.00

#833 Ford Mustang, metallic bl, MIB, B5 ....$145.00

#837 SAAB 99, lt gray, EX-, B5..................................$90.00

#851 Scania Vabis CR 76 Bus, wht & yel, 'KS,' MIB, B5.$120.00

#864 Forklift, yel, MIB, B5 ....$85.00

#912 Mercedes Benz LP 322 Garbage Truck, silver & gr, EX-, B5...$95.00

#914 Ford D800 Tipping Truck, red low side panels, MIB, B5..$45.00

#917 Ford D800 Lumber Truck, MIB, B5 ....$120.00

#926 Jaguar E, 1961, gray, EX, B5 ....$95.00

#926 Jaguar E, 1969, side windows up, silver & gray, EX-, B5..$95.00

#929 Mercedes Benz 230 SL, red & blk, EX, B5 ....$120.00

#930S Monza GT Coupe, chrome, MIB, B5...................$55.00

#934 Toyota 2000 GT, 1968, silver, MIB, B5 ....$60.00

#948 Military Truck, w/rocket, khaki, EX-, B5 ....$50.00

Harley-Davidson Motorcycle, blk rubber tires, steering & Harley decal, 3", EX (EX box), A $150.00

Junior Assembly Set, MIB, $275.00. (Photo courtesy Continental Hobby House.)

Volvo Carlsberg Truck, G, B5...$75.00

Volvo Express Fire Engine, red, 'Falck-Zonen,' EX, B5 ..$150.00

Telephones

Novelty phones representing a well-known advertising or cartoon character are proving to be the focus of lots of collector activity — the more recognizable the character the better. Telephones modeled after a product container are collectible too, and with the intense interest currently being shown in anything advertising related, competition is sometimes stiff and values are rising. Our advisors for this category are John and Sheri Pavone (P3).

Alvin (Chipmunk), Bagdassarian/Mode Productions, plastic, touch-tone, redial, mute, 1984, VG, P4 ....$30.00

Bart Simpson, Columbia Telecom, M, E3........................$25.00
Bart Simpson, 1980s, MIB, T1 ....$45.00

Batmobile Telephone Model BM-10, Columbia Telecommunication Group, Inc., DC Comics, 1990, MIB, $35.00.

Cabbage Patch Girl, Coleco, 1980s, EX-EX+, T1 ....$125.00
Charlie Tuna, MIB $35.00
Coca-Cola Can, M..$45.00
Crest's Sparkle Man, M $30.00
Crest's Sparkle Man, MIB, V1 ....$45.00
Garfield, eyes open & close, 1980s, VG-EX, T1 ....$35.00
Hawaiian Punch, 1980, R3...$150.00
Keebler Elf, 1980s, EX+, T1 ....$75.00
Kraft, bank, Cheesosaurus, R3...$12.00

Kraft Salad, figure, vinyl tomato head w/asparagus body, R3..$225.00
Life Savers, bendee, Multi-Products, 1967, R3 ....$150.00
Mario Bros, 1980s, MIB, T1 ....$45.00
Mickey Mouse, yel, red, blk & wht plastic w/faux wood base, 15", VG, A..$70.00
Ore-Ida Fast Fries, NM (NM box), T1 ....$125.00
Pillsbury's Poppin' Fresh, w/arms extended to hold receiver, plastic, 1980s, 14", M......................................$125.00
Pizza Man, 1980s, EX+, T1 ....$37.50
Raid Bug, MIB, minimum value......................................$150.00
Roy Rogers Western Telephones, Ideal, early working wall phones, battery-op, appears unused, 1950, MIB, A .$265.00
Snoopy & Woodstock, full figure, push-button type, lt stain, 14", EX-, P3..$20.00
Snoopy as Cool Joe, 1980s, MIB, T1 ....$55.00
Sunoco Gas Pump, bl, M $48.00
Tang Lips, on rnd base, very scarce, EX+, M5 ....$200.00
Ziggy, 1989, MIB, T1 ....$75.00
7-Up Spot, standing on blk checkered base, plastic, 1990, 12", M..$55.00

Tin Toys

Toys listed here are from the last decade of the 1800s up through the early years of this century. See also Battery Operated; Windups, Friction, and Other Mechanicals; and specific manufacturers.

Althof-Bergmann Express Wagon, 1870s, 18" long, D10, $4,500.00.

American Express Truck, gr w/Banner Toys World Over on both sides, labels on rear doors, 5x12", VG, A.................$150.00
Bear w/Boy on Platform, Fallows, pnt tin boy on emb cart, CI wheels, upright bear pulls cart, lt rpt, 5½", G-VG, A .$210.00
Broadway Trolley, Hull & Stafford, driver & conductor, horse missing, roof needs rpr, pnt loss/rpt, 9", A $550.00
Comet Engine w/Passenger Car, Am Tin, by George Brown, 9", G, A..$275.00
Covered Cart, pnt & stenciled gr cart, yel interior, CI wheels, pulled by wht horse, 7", VG, A $300.00
Dump Cart w/Horse, Am, by George Brown, pnt tin, red & blk trim, w/wht horse, removable tailgate, 12", G+, A..$412.50

Elephant on Rocker, Am, pnt tin, gray & red blanket, 8", G, A $159.50

Erie RR Horse Car, Bergman, pnt & lettered yel streetcar, CI wheels, pulled by wht horse, 7½", VG-EX, A $250.00

Express Wagon, pnt & stenciled red wagon, CI wheels, pnt tin driver, 2 pnt & emb horses on wheels, 18½", VG, A.$6,000.00

Fine Groceries Delivery Wagon, Am, orange w/gold stencil, yel horse, red saddle, blk roof, gr base, 7x14", EX $1,700.00

Fine Groceries Wagon, pnt & stenciled tin, gr & red w/CI wheels, brn trotting horse, touch-up on horse, 12", G-VG, A $550.00

Horse Cart, Am, George Brown, wht horse, gr 2-wheel cart, removable rear panel, horse resoldered, pnt worn, 12", A $230.00

Horse-Drawn Trolley, Am, pnt tin, trolley body w/emb design, 11", G, A..$302.50

Horseless Carriage, Fallows, 2-seater, blk open roadster, spoked wheels, string-op rear motor, rpl driver/wear, 8", A.$460.00

Prospect Park Omnibus, Althof-Bergmann, red, gray & beige w/stencil, rear entrance, 1 wht/1 gold horse, rstr, 17", A $13,800.00

Pure Milk Delivery Wagon, Fallows, open front, red & orange, horse-drawn (brn w/red saddle), rpr, 13", EX, A ..$1,400.00

Push Toy, Fallows, lg blk horse w/red & gold trim between 2 7" CI wheels, leather reins, rstr push pole, 30", A $2,100.00

Roundabout, 3 pnt tin boats w/drivers revolve on pnt & rtcl tin base, American flags at top, rpt/rstr, 24", G, A........$800.00

Street Railway Car, pnt tin, red & blk w/long open platform, 6 pnt compo passengers, CI wheels, lt rpr, 7¾", G-VG, A $200.00

Train, pnt & stenciled tin, red & bl locomotive, 2 bl coaches w/red roofs, CI wheels, coupler missing, early, 14", G, A $275.00

Train, pnt tin, orange, bl & blk locomotive w/3 coaches, CI wheels, hooks missing, pnt loss, early, 28", VG, A ..$300.00

Trotter, Fallows, pnt tin, brn horse pulls bell on CI wheels, working, lt pnt chips, 9", VG-EX, A $550.00

Trotting Horse Hoop Toy, Am, red blanket, bl hoop, very worn pnt, 6" dia, A $750.00

Water Wagon, George Brown, pnt tin, orange tank w/wht ends, CI wheels, wht horses pulling wagon, 6½", VG, A..$250.00

Yankee Notions Wagon, pnt & stenciled tin, red & blk, doors open, top hinged, 2 wht horses on wheeled base, 14", G-VG, A..$1,200.00

Tonka

Since the mid-forties, the Tonka Company (Minnesota) has produced an extensive variety of high-quality painted metal trucks, heavy equipment, tractors, and vans. Our advisor for this category is Doug Dezso (D6).

Airport Tractor, orange, MIB..............................$225.00

Allied Van Semi, #400, 1951, 23½", M $350.00

Boat Transport Semi, #41, 1959, 28", 5-pc, EX $550.00

Camper, #70, 1964, 9½", M..................................$175.00

Camper, 1973, MIB, M4...$50.00

Carnation Milk Delivery Van, #750, 1955, EX $475.00

Carnation Milk Truck, wht w/decals, plated bumpers, dbl rear doors, side door opens, rubber tires, 12⅛", VG........$350.00

CAT Cement Carrier, yel, M, L1............................$25.00

CAT Dumpster, yel, M, L1....................................$25.00

Cement Mixer Truck, #120, 1960, 15½", M................$200.00

Cement Mixer w/Turbine, MIB $150.00

Dragline & Semi Trailer, #44, 1959, 26¼", 3-pc, G.......$175.00

Dump Truck & Sand Loader, #116, 1961, 23¼", M......$140.00

Dune Buggy, 1970, VG..$50.00

Fire Engine, aerial ladder, 1960, MIB, M4 ....$575.00

Fire Pumper Truck, red and silver with gold lettering, ca 1953, 17½" long, NM (original box has end flap missing), A, $325.00.

Fire Truck, pnt pressed steel, red w/gold decals, rubber tires, working hose reel & hydrant, 17", VG, A $170.00

Fisherman Pickup, #110, 1960, 14", M $150.00

Forklift #2970, MIB $65.00

Green Giant Transport Semi, #650, 1953, 22¼", EX $200.00

International, Horse Transport, caramel, NM+, L1..........$18.00

Jeep Pumper, #425, 1963, 10¾", EX.......................$140.00

Jeep Universal, #249, 1962, 9¾", EX..............................$60.00

Jeepster, red with white plastic top, rubber wheels, 12¾" long, $75.00.

Jet Delivery, #410, 1962, 14", M $275.00

Lumber Truck, #998, 1956, 18¾", M $185.00

Military Jeep, #251, 1963, 10½", M............................$65.00

Minute Maid Delivery Van, #725, 1954, 14½", G.........$300.00

Nationwide Moving Semi, 1958, 24¼", M $240.00

Parcel Delivery Van, 1957, 12", EX $350.00

Pumper Truck w/Turbine, EX $100.00
Service Truck, EX..$75.00
Stake Truck, #56, 1964, 9½", EX $65.00
Steam Shovel, #50, 1947, 20¾", M..............................$125.00
Steam Shovel #50, missing treads, VG..........................$50.00
Suburban Pumper, #990, 1956, 17", M $300.00
Terminal Train, #720, 33⅜", 4-pc, EX..........................$175.00
Thunderbird Express Semi, 1957, 24", G.......................$125.00
Tractor-Carry-All Trailer, #130, 1949, 30½", G.............$90.00
Utility Dump Skooter, #301, 1962, 12½", M...................$100.00
VW Bug, orange, ca 1960s, 8⅝", EX, W1 ....$22.50
Winnebago, wht, 1970s, EX $100.00
Winnebago, 2-tone, 1973, M, M4 ....$70.00
Wrecker Truck, #250, 1949, 12½", EX $275.00
1961 Pickup Truck, red, NM..$120.00

Toothbrush Holders

Figural ceramic toothbrush holders have become very popular collectibles, especially those modeled after well-known cartoon characters. Disney's Mickey Mouse, Donald Duck, and the
Three Little Pigs are among the most desirable, and some of the
harder-to-find examples in mint condition sell for upwards of
$200.00. Many were made in Japan before WWII. Because the
paint was not fired on, it is often beginning to flake off. Be sure
to consider the condition of the paint as well as the bisque when
evaluating your holdings. Our advisor for this category is Marilyn Cooper (C9).

Andy Gump & Min, pnt bsk, standing arm in arm, mk FAS,
    Japan, 4x3¼", NM, A $85.00
Doc, figural, Doc Says Brush Your Teeth, EX, P6 ....$70.00
Donald Duck, bsk, tipping hat, mc, mk WED, prewar Japan,
    5x3", NM, A...$175.00
Donald Duck, pnt bsk, 2 co-joined Donald figures, prewar Japan,
    4½x3", NM+, A $325.00
Fiddler Pig, Genuine Walt Disney Copyright, made for British
    market, 4", EX, A...$45.00
Little Orphan Annie & Sandy, pnt bsk, on couch, prewar Japan,
    4x3¼", M, A $75.00
Little Orphan Annie & Sandy, pnt bsk, standing version, prewar
    Japan, 4x2", EX+, A $95.00
Lone Ranger, chalkware, 1940s, NM, V1.........................$88.00
Mickey, Minnie & Donald, pnt bsk, jtd arms, Donald in center,
    prewar Japan, 3½x5", EX, A...$300.00
Mickey, Minnie & Pluto, pnt bsk, sitting on couch, prewar
    Japan, 4x4½", NM+, A $240.00
Mickey & Minnie Mouse, bsk pie-eyed figures arm in arm,
    Japan, c WDE, 4½", EX, from $175 to $200.00
Mickey & Pluto, pnt bsk, Mickey helping Pluto blow his nose,
    prewar Japan, 3½x4½", NM+, A...............................$170.00
Minnie Mouse, pnt bsk, 1 jtd arm, mk WDE, prewar Japan, 5¼",
    NM+, A...$165.00
Moon Mullins & Kayo, pnt bsk, early, 4", EX..................$85.00
Skippy, ceramic, 5½", NM, V1..$110.00
Snow White, porc, standing figure, Great Britian, 6", NM,
    A..$200.00

**Mickey and Minnie Mouse, seated on couch, prewar Japan,
painted bisque, 3½", NM+, A, $240.00.**

Three Little Pigs, pnt bsk, center pig at brick piano, WD, prewar
    Japan, 4x3½", NM+, A $135.00
Three Little Pigs, pnt bsk, w/flute, violin & bass drum, WD
    Japan, 4x3½", NM+, A $110.00
Three Little Pigs, pnt bsk, w/flute, violin & bricks, prewar Japan,
    mk WD, 4x3½", EX, A..$100.00

Tootsietoys

The first diecast Tootsietoys were made by the Samuel
Dowst company in 1906 when they reproduced the Model T
Ford in miniature. Dowst merged with Cosmo Manufacturing in
1926 to form the Dowst Manufacturing Company and continued
to turn out replicas of the full-scale vehicles in actual use at the
time. After another merger in 1961, the company became
known as the Stombecker Corporation. Over the years, many
types of wheels and hubs were utilized, varying in both style and
material. The last all-metal car was made in 1969; recent Toosti-
etoys mix plastic components with the metal and have soft plastic wheels. Early prewar mint-in-box toys are scarce and command high prices on today's market. For more information we
recommend the *Collector's Guide to Tootsietoys* by David E.
Richter (Collector Books).

Ambulance, yel, 1950s, 4", EX, W1 ....$24.50
American La France, 1954, red, 3", NM, A3 ....$15.00
Army AA Canon, 6-wheeled version, rstr, EX $28.00
Army Truck & Trailer, 1970s, MOC, T1.........................$25.00
Bluebird Racer, wht, 3", EX $22.50
Boeing 707 Jet, silver, no landing gear, rstr, EX.............$33.00
Buck Rogers, Flash Blast Attack Ship, orig pnt, #1033, 4½", EX
    (EX box), A $350.00
Buck Rogers Flash Blast Attack Ship, rpt, orig box, 4½", EX,
    A..$150.00

Auto Transport, 1950, MIB, from $180.00 to $200.00.

Buck Rogers Venus Duo Destroyer, with original cord, 1937, MIB, $175.00.

Car & Ramp Set, #5798, complete w/6 cars & ramp, ea car 3½", NM (EX box), A $160.00
CAT Dozer, no blade, 4½", VG $27.50
Chevy Deluxe Panel Truck, red, 4", EX+........................$33.00
Chevy Fastback Sedan, red, 1940s, 4", EX, W1 ....$32.50
Chevy Monza, purple, 1970s, 2⅛", EX+, W1 ....$2.50
Chevy Panel, 1950, gr, 3", MIB, A3.................................$15.00
Dairy Delivery Truck, tan & blk w/gold grille, rubber tires, 3⅞", EX, A $170.00
Diamond T, Auto Transport, orange & red, EX $42.50
Dodge Pickup, gr & silver trim, 4", VG...........................$15.00
Fiat Abarth, metallic bl, 1970s, 2½", NM, W1 ....$3.00
Fire Station, MIB, T1 ....$28.50
Flash Gordon Spaceship, 1978, MOC, C1 ....$27.00
Ford Car, wht rubber tires, 1935, 3", VG, W1 ....$19.50
Ford Coupe, 1920s, 2½", EX+, W1..................................$29.00
Ford F-6 Stake Truck, red, 4", EX.................................$27.50
Ford Gasoline Tanker Truck, red, 1950s, 2½", G, W1........$2.50
Ford GT Race Car, metallic bl, 1960s, 2⅛", EX+, W1 ......$2.50
Ford Pickup, gray, 1949, 3", NM, A3 ....$12.00
Ford Ranch Wagon, red, 1954, 3", NM, A3.....................$10.00
Ford Semi Truck, missing trailer, red, 1950s, 1⅞", VG, W1...$2.50
Ford Stake Truck, red, 1949, 4", NM, A3 ....$12.00
Ford Thunderbird, yel, 1955, 3", NM, A3.......................$12.00
Ford Thunderbird Coupe, gr & cream, VG......................$22.50

Fleet #5700, 1942, largest: 6", NMIB, $200.00.

Ford 2-Door Sedan, bl, 1955, 3", G-, A3............................$5.00
Gas Tanker Truck, yel, blk rubber tires, 1940s, 3", VG, W1 ....$90.00
Horse Trailer, plastic, tan, G5 ....$5.00
Hot Rod, lt bl, 1960s, 2", EX, W1......................................$2.50
Hot Rod Pickup, gr, 1960s, 1⅞", VG, W1 ....$2.50

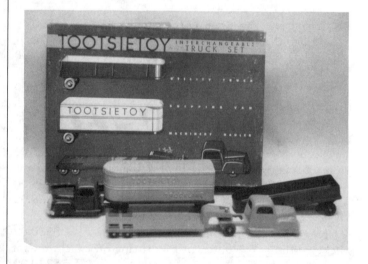

Interchangeable Truck Set #4900, 1955, MIB, D10, $350.00.

International Dump Truck, gr & yel, 1941, 6", VG, A3 ....$18.00
Jaguar Convertible Roadster, gr, blk rubber tires, 1950s, 3", NM, W1 ....$14.00
Jaguar Race Car, purple, 1960s, 2⅜", EX, W1 ....$3.00
Jeep, red, 1960s, 2¼", VG, W1 ....$2.50
Jeep CJ-7, snow plow, bl, NM $70.00
Jeep Pickup, orange, 1970s, 2⅛", EX, W1 ....$2.50

Jumbo Sedan, tin chassis, dk red, rare, 6", EX....................$90.00
Jumbo Torpedo Pickup, red w/silver trim, 6", EX............$33.00
Land Rover, gr, 1960s, 2¼", VG-, W1..............................$2.50
Mack Long-Distance Hauling Truck, red & blk, rubber tires, pnt
    chips on cab, 5½", VG-EX, A $85.00
Mamie & Uncle Willie Boat, NM $500.00
Mercedes 450SL, silver, 1970s, 2¼", NM+, W1................$2.50
Midgets, #0510, complete set of 8 cars, trucks, bus & plane,
    1930s, M (EX+ box), A...$235.00
Overland Bus Line, gr & blk, 3¾", VG-EX, A...............$130.00
Packard, gr & yel, 1956, 4", VG, A3 ....$15.00
Planes Set #7500, ea 4" to 5" wide, set of 8 in orig 15x10"
    lithoed box, EX (EX box), A.....................................$475.00
Porsche, orange, 1970s, 2⅜", VG, W1.............................$2.50

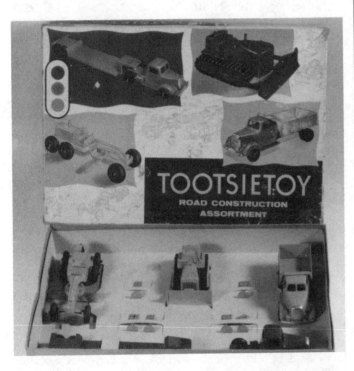

Road Construction Assortment #6000, 1956-58, MIB, $325.00. (Photo courtesy Continental Hobby House.)

Station Wagon, #1046, maroon & yel, 1939, 4", VG,
    W1 ....$29.00
Touring Sedan, orange & brn, gold grille, rubber tires, 4", EX,
    A $210.00
Tow Truck, gr, blk rubber tires, 1950s, 4½", missing boom, G,
    W1...$4.00
Train Set, Diesel; UP locomotive, 2 boxcars, coal car,
    caboose, tanker, ea 5", mk NYC-PA-Santa Fe, NM (EX
    box), A...$140.00
Train Set #5851, Limited, 4 Pullman cars, Santa Fe engine, in
    orig 8x14" box, G+ (G+ box), A $235.00
Triumph Convertible, gr plastic, EX-, P3........................$10.00
U-Haul Trailer, orange, decals, EX................................$22.00
VW Bug, red, 1960s, 2¼", VG, W1.................................$2.50
Wedge Dragster, blk, 1960s, 2½", VG, W1 ....$2.50
White Army Halftrack, rstr, 4", EX................................$33.00

Trains

Some of the earliest trains (from ca 1860) were made of tin or cast iron, smaller versions of the full-scale steam-powered trains that transversed America from the East to the West. Most were made to simply be pushed or pulled along, though some had clockwork motors.

Electric trains were produced as early as the late 19th century. Three of the largest manufacturers were Lionel, Ives, and American Flyer.

Lionel trains have been made since 1900. Until 1915 they produced only standard gauge models (measuring 2½" between the rails). The smaller O gauge (1¼") they introduced at that time proved to be highly successful, and the company grew until by 1955, it had become the largest producer of toys in the world. Until discontinued in 1940, standard gauge trains were produced on a limited scale, but O and 027 gauge models dominated the market. Production dwindled and nearly stopped in the mid-1960s, but the company was purchased by General Mills in 1969, and they continue to produce a very limited number of trains today.

The Ives company had been a major producer of toys since 1896. They were the first to initiate manufacture of the O gauge train and at first used only clockwork motors to propel them. Their first electric trains (in both O and #1 gauge) were made in 1910, but because electricity was not yet a common commodity in many areas, clockwork production continued for several years. By 1920 #1 gauge was phased out in favor of standard gauge. The company continued to prosper until the late 1920s when it floundered and was bought jointly by American Flyer and Lionel. American Flyer soon turned their interest over to Lionel, who continued to make Ives trains until 1933.

The American Flyer company had produced trains for several years, but it wasn't until it was bought by AC Gilbert in 1937 that it became successful enough to be considered a competitor of Lionel. They're best noted for their conversion from the standard 3-rail system to the 2-rail S gauge (⅞") and the high-quality locomotives, passenger, and freight cars they produced in the 1950s. Interest in toy trains waned during the space-age decade of the 1960s. As a result, sales declined, and in 1966, the company was purchased by Lionel. Today both American Flyer and Lionel trains are being made from the original dies by Lionel Trains Inc., privately owned.

Because of limited space, the only time we will use the number sign will be to indicate a set number. Numbers of individual pieces will not be preceded by the sign. For more information we recommend *Collecting Toy Trains, An Identification and Value Guide*, by Richard O'Brien. Our advisor for this category is Richard Trautwein (T3). See also Buddy L for that company's Outdoor Railroad.

Key:
b/c — boxcar	obv/c — observation car
bg/c — baggage car	st/c — stock car
fl/c — flat bed car	tk/c — tank car
loco — locomotive	/c — car

Cars

American Flyer, S ga, 24029 State of MA b/c, 24076 UP st/c, 24048 M&StL b/c, EX, A....................................$230.00

American Flyer, S ga, 24033 MP b/c, 24309 Gulf tk/c, 24619 caboose, EX-, A...$250.00

American Flyer, S ga, 24077 NP Pig Palace st/c, NM, A..$190.00

American Flyer, S ga, 24316 tk/c, 24124 gondola, 24058 Post b/c, 24052 banana/c, 24309 tk/c, EX, A....................$40.00

American Flyer, S ga, 24319 Penn salt tk/c, factory stamping error, EX, A $430.00

American Flyer, S ga, 24413 NP reefer w/sliding doors, 24216 UP hopper, 24109 gondola w/pipes, EX-, A $250.00

American Flyer, S ga, 24633 caboose, 24557 US Navy ft/c, 24116 Southern gondola, 24324 Hooker chemical tk/c, EX+, A...$350.00

American Flyer, S ga, 648 service, 948 track cleaner, 988 reefer, 640 hopper, 24757 Mounds w/pikemaster coupler, EX-, A..$50.00

American Flyer, S ga, 916 D&H gondola, 981 Central of GA, 988 MP reefer, 24550 Monon piggyback ft/c w/trailers, EX, A $270.00

American Flyer, S ga, 977 caboose, 928 NH ft/c w/lumber, 982 State of MA b/c, 919 CB&Q auto dump, EX-, A....$120.00

American Flyer, std ga, 4010 tk/c, 2-tone bl, minor touch-up, EX-, A...$500.00

American Flyer, 3006 log/c, 3010 tk/c, EX-, A $200.00

American Flyer/LTI, S ga, 9100, 9701, 48306, 9101, 48301, 48310, 9707, 48801, NMIB, A....................................$180.00

Buddy L, 1001 caboose, decals 1 side 80%, other side 100%, EX, A $850.00

Buddy L, 1002 b/c, decals 95%, faded, rstr couplers, EX, A...$1,000.00

Buddy L, 1003 tk/c, decals 85%, couplers worn, EX, A ..$850.00

Buddy L, 1004 st/c, red, decals 95%, couplers worn slightly, EX, A $700.00

Buddy L, 1005 coal/c, decals 95%, couplers missing, EX, A $800.00

Buddy L, 1006 fl/c, decals 50%, VG, A.........................$450.00

Dorfan, 600 gondola, 610 derrick, orig hook, EX, A $190.00

Dorfan, 604 tk/c (2), 601 b/c (2), 605 hopper, 600 gondolas (2), Seattle coaches (2), Boston coach, obv/c, EX-, A...$100.00

Hubley, 44 Narcissus coach, CI, red, EX-, A $300.00

Issameyer, 1 ga, coaches (4), litho & pnt tin, EX, A...$2,200.00

Ives, std ga, 199 derrick, dk gr tool box, brass plates, minor chipping, VG+...$325.00

Ives, 125 MKT b/c, 40% pnt; 125 C&GW, 90% pnt; EX, A $850.00

Ives, 130 combine, inside truck frames, yel w/red & blk striped roof, VG...$750.00

Ives, 130 combine, 129 coach, roofs flaking, EX-, A $65.00

Ives, 62 parlor, brn & blk roof; 60 Yale Harvard series bg/c, red, w/red & gray roof; EX-, A.....................................$95.00

Ives, 63 gondola, 67 caboose, 69 lumber/c, EX-, A $45.00

Ives, 64 PA b/c, red roof rpt; 64 NP b/c, 97% pnt; EX, A .$360.00

Ives, 70 caboose, red & peacock, brass trim, transitional, missing 1 coupler, EX-, A $60.00

Lionel, Baby Ruth (missing R), orig box, EX, G1 ....$55.00

Lionel BLT-92 Railway Express Agency-16237, 9½" long, NM, $50.00.

Lionel, candy companies, 9278, 9858, 9853, 9816, 9867, 9817, 9878, 9886, 9147, NMIB, A....................................$290.00

Lionel, fl/c w/no pipes, o/w EX, G1 ....$40.00

Lionel, HO ga, track cleaner, orig box, VG, G1 ....$55.00

Lionel, HO ga, 0847 exploding b/c, orig box, EX, G1 ......$20.00

Lionel, HO ga, 1349 launch-turbo missle, orig box, EX, G1 .$45.00

Lionel, Livingston passenger/c, silver, VG, G1 ....$55.00

Lionel, LV RR hopper, blk, EX, G1 ....$12.00

Lionel, NYC gondola, bl, EX, G1....................................$15.00

Lionel, O ga, 9802 Miller b/c, orig box, EX, G1 ....$39.00

Lionel, O ga, 9805 Grand Trunk, EX, G1 ....$39.00

Lionel, scrapper load, from 6817 scrapper/c, wheel hubs pnt silver, missing tip of stack, EX+, A..............................$110.00

Lionel, std ga, PA 15 tk/c, maroon & blk, 1-pc step, single rivet trucks, pnt long couplers, EX, A $125.00

Lionel, std ga, 12 gondola, gray w/pea gr trim, late coupler, EX, A $50.00

Lionel, std ga, 12 Lakeshore gondola, 13 st/c, long couplers, no pnt, single rivet trucks, emb rivet detail, EX-, A.....$200.00

Lionel, std ga, 16 NY, NH & HRR ballast, 12 PA gondola, both brn, early trucks, EX, A...$150.00

Lionel, std ga, 212 gondola, wine; 205 canisters, EX, A...$475.00

Lionel, std ga, 212 gondola, wine; 5 split barrels & early tool box, EX, A $375.00

Lionel, std ga, 214 b/c, yel & br, nickel trim, NM, A.....$950.00

Lionel, std ga, 215 Sunoco tk/c, brass, EX+, A...............$500.00

Lionel, std ga, 216 hopper, dk gr, brass, EX+, A............$375.00

Lionel United States Navy Submarine Car, 10" long, $65.00.

Lionel, std ga, 220 searchlight/c, terra cotta, blk, brass, NMIB, A..$425.00

Lionel, std ga, 310 bg/c, 309 Pullman, 310 obv/c, NMIB, A...$1,500.00

Lionel, std O ga, 6230 reefer, 6231 gondola, 6232 & 6239 b/cs, MIB, A...$210.00

Lionel, Toys R Us b/c, EX, G1 ....$40.00

Lionel, W Pacific b/c, silver, VG+, G1 ....$45.00

Lionel, X2458 Pennsylvania automobile/c, EX, G1 ....$39.00

Lionel, 54 ballast tamper, EX+, A................................$260.00

Lionel, 175 rocket launcher, orig box w/water stain, EX, A...$190.00

Lionel, 182 electromagnetic crane w/controller, orig box & instructions, EX+, A...$300.00

Lionel, 217 caboose, red & peacock, EX, A.................$125.00

Lionel, 400 PRR gondola, MIB, G1 ....$25.00

Lionel, 700 Pennsylvania caboose, MIB, G1..................$35.00

Lionel, 701 D&RG caboose, MIB, G1............................$35.00

Lionel, 806 cattle/cs (2), 804 tk/c, 805 b/c, EX, A $140.00

Lionel, 809 dump/c, 803 hopper, 902 gondola, EX+ (VG box), A...$110.00

Lionel, 814 reefer, ivory, bl, silver frame, some chips on 1 side, EX, A..$210.00

Lionel, 815 tk/c, gr w/brass; 815 Sunoco tk/c, silver & nickel w/brass plates; manual couplers, EX+, A................$230.00

Lionel, 816 hopper, 820 searchlight/c, EX- (G box), A .$180.00

Lionel, 1002 gondola, bl, EX, G1 ....$5.00

Lionel, 1005 Sunoco tk/c, EX, G1 ....$6.00

Lionel, 1679 Baby Ruth b/c, 1680 Shell tk/c, 1677 gondola, 2682 caboose, EX+, A...$150.00

Lionel, 1875W whistling coach, 6819 fl/c w/incomplete helicopter (orig box rough), 6464-275 State of Maine b/c, EX, A...$110.00

Lionel, 1951, 2023 UP Alco AA, 2421 Maplewood, 2422 Chatham, 2423 Hillside, orig boxes, EX, A.............$400.00

Lionel, 2400 Maplewood passenger/c, gr, EX, G1 ....$100.00

Lionel, 2412 astrodomes (2), 2414 coach, 2416 obv/c, NM (VG box), A...$500.00

Lionel, 2432 astrodomes, 2435 Elizabeth, 2434 Newark, red lettered, orig box missing 2 flaps, EX, A $280.00

Lionel, 2660 crane, plated, EX, A $90.00

Lionel, 2815 Shell tk/c, 1938-style couplers, decals strong, NM, A...$210.00

Lionel, 2820 searchlight/c, pea gr, 2812 gondola, Girard gr, both w/minor oxidation, EX-, A.................................$100.00

Lionel, 2820 searchlight/c, pea gr & nickel, EX+ (G box), A...$150.00

Lionel, 3461 log dump fl/c, EX, G1 ....$35.00

Lionel, 3470 target launcher w/3470-20 instruction packet unopened, 3349 turbo missile launcher, NMIB, A ...$220.00

Lionel, 3535 security caboose, 6512 cherrypicker, NMIB, A...$210.00

Lionel, 3620 searchlight/c, rpl blk hood, EX, G1 ....$30.00

Lionel, 3662-1 milk/c w/platforms, 6062 gondola, 6821 fl/c w/crates, 50 gang/cs (2), 6017 caboose, NM (boxes G-VG), A...$180.00

Lionel, 5717 ATSF bunk/c, MIB, G1................................$40.00

Lionel, 5733 bunk/c, M (EX box), 01...............................$40.00

Lionel, 5733 Lionel lines bunk/c, MIB, G1.....................$40.00

Lionel, 6014 Frisco b/c, M, A3 ....$15.00

Lionel, 6024 Shredded Wheat b/c, EX, G1 ....$25.00

Lionel, 6059 M&StL caboose, red, EX, G1 ....$10.00

Lionel, 6112 gondola, bl, no letters, EX, G1 ....$8.00

Lionel, 6112 gondola, blk w/4 canisters, EX, G1 ....$15.00

Lionel, 6119-50 caboose w/ladder, brn, EX, G1 ....$35.00

Lionel, 6151 range patrol fl/c, 6315 Gulf tk/c, EX, A $75.00

Lionel, 6314 Sante Fe Unibody passenger/c, MIB, G1 .....$46.00

Lionel, 6356 NYC st/c, orig box, EX, G1 ....$65.00

Lionel, 6419 caboose, tall stack, orig box, EX, G1 ....$50.00

Lionel, 6436 LV RR hopper, red, VG, G1 ....$24.00

Lionel, 6454 Erie b/c, orig box, EX, G1 ....$75.00

Lionel, 6456 gondola, maroon, EX, G1 ....$12.00

Lionel, 6460 Bucyrus Erie RR crane, NM, 01 ....$65.00

Lionel, 6462 gondola, blk, EX, G1 ....$10.00

Lionel, 6462 GRN gondola (N in 2nd panel), VG, G1....$20.00

Lionel, 6465 Sunoco tk/c, orig box, VG, G1 ....$12.00

Lionel, 6500 fl/c w/Bonanza airplane, NM (G box), A .$1,000.00

Lionel, 6520 searchlight/c, gr crackle head, EX, G1 ....$365.00

Lionel, 6530 firefighting instruction/c, 3428 operating mail/c w/bag, EX+, A $140.00

Lionel, 6560 crane, red, no # on frame, EX, G1 ....$60.00

Lionel, 6801 fl/c w/repro boat, EX, G1 ....$40.00

Lionel, 6802 girder fl/c, 6800 fl/c w/Bonanza airplane, yel over blk, EX+ (G box), A...$160.00

Lionel, 6807 fl/c w/military duck, 6803 fl/c w/tank only, missing truck supports, EX (G box), A.................................$210.00

Lionel, 6809 fl/c w/gun turret, truck & hospital, EX (G box), A...$220.00

Lionel, 6821 fl/c w/crates, EX, G1 ....$40.00

Lionel, 9064 C&O caboose, yel, EX, G1..........................$10.00

Lionel, 9140 Burlington gondola, EX, G1 ....$8.00

Lionel, 9141 Burlington North gondola, gr, EX, G1 ....$5.00

Lionel, 9148 Dupont 3-dome tk/c, NMIB, 01 ....$45.00

Lionel, 9462 Southern Pacific b/c, NMIB, G1 ....$25.00

Lionel, 9486 I Luv MI b/c, MIB, G1 ....$35.00

Lionel, 9700 Southern b/c, red, EX, A3 ....$25.00

Lionel, 16318 Lionel Lines fl/c, MIB, G1........................$21.00

Lionel, 16343 Burlington Coil, gondola, NMIB, G1 ....$23.00

Lionel, 16617 Chicago NW b/c, MIB, G1 ....$25.00

Lionel, 16622 CSX b/c, MIB, G1 ....$25.00

Lionel, 16651 Billboard reefer, NMIB, 01 ....$68.00

Lionel, 17605 Reading caboose, NMIB, G1.....................$60.00

Lionel, 17606, NYC caboose, MIB, G1 ....$69.00

Lionel, 17900 Sante Fe Unibody tk/c, MIB, G1 ....$46.00

Lionel, 17901 Chevron Unibody tk/c, MIB, G1 ....$46.00

Lionel, 19305 B&O Cheesie ore/c, MIB, G1 ....$49.00

Lionel, 19309 Seaboard Quad hopper/c, MIB, G1 ....$20.00

Lionel, 19313 B&O ore/c, MIB, G1 ....$17.00

Lionel, 19403 W Maryland gondola, MIB, G1 ....$28.00

Lionel, 19510 Pennsylvania st/c, MIB, G1......................$28.00

Lionel, 19515 Milwaukee st/c, MIB, G1 ....$28.00

Lionel, 19522 Guglielmo Marconi reefer, MIB, G1.........$22.00

Lionel, 19704 Western Maryland caboose, MIB, G1........$65.00

Lionel, 19811 Monon operating/c, MIB, G1 ....$58.00

Lionel, 87000 NYC b/c, MIB, G1 ....$42.00

Lionel, 87405 B&O gondola, MIB, G1 ....$32.00

Lionel, 87407 MKT gondola, MIB, G1 ....$32.00

Lionel, 87504 Union Pacific fl/c, MIB, G1 ....$29.00

Lionel, 87600 Alaska tk/c, MIB, G1 ....$39.00

Lionel, 87602 Gulf tk/c, MIB, G1 ....$39.00

Lionel, 87603 Borden tk/c, MIB, G1................................$39.00

Lionel, 87705 Great Northern caboose, MIB, G1 ....$45.00

Marklin, HO ga, DB TEE dining/c, NMIB......................$17.00

Marklin, HO ga, SNCF b/c, MIB $11.00

Marklin, HO ga, 390.6 freight bg/c ('50-51), VG (new box)..$11.00

Marklin, HO ga, 391.7 gondola w/USA-style trucks ('48-49), EX+ (new box) $37.50

Marklin, HO ga, 4093.4 DB bg/c, NMIB $17.00

Marklin, HO ga, 4094.3 DB dining/c, NMIB................$17.00

Marklin, HO ga, 4096.2 DB TEE, 1st CI coach, NMIB ...$17.00

Marklin, HO ga, 4098.2 DB TEE, CI express coach, NMIB $17.00

Marklin, HO ga, 4147 DB TEE, 1st CI Eurofima coach, NMIB..$17.00

Marklin, HO ga, 4157.2 DBP mail/c, orig box, EX+.........$12.00

Marklin, HO ga, 4402 NS b/c, MIB $9.00

Marklin, HO ga, 4405 CFL b/c, MIB $9.00

Marklin, HO ga, 4448 OBB tk/c 'OEVA,' hi-gloss, orig box, EX+ $9.00

Marklin, HO ga, 4508 DB reefer 'Kulwagen,' NMIB..........$9.00

Marklin, HO ga, 4533 DB reefer 'Pepsi,' NMIB................$9.00

Marklin, HO ga, 4646.6 DB tk/c 'Aral,' orig box, EX+.....$11.00

Marklin, HO ga, 4651 DB tk/c 'Shell,' NMIB................$22.50

Marklin, HO ga, 4742.2 DB Rolling Road/c w/Bauknecht truck, MIB $45.00

Marx, 3280 Sante Fe b/c, A3 ....$6.00

Marx, 5532 Allstate gondola, M, A3...............................$6.00

Pratt & Letchworth, CI, blk & gold engine w/lg stack, blk tender, yel NYC passenger/c, 1895, 25" overall, A.......$975.00

Tyco, HO ga, 327-14, ILL Central Gulf caboose, NMIB, 01..$2.00

Tyco, HO ga, 339A Sante Fe b/c, NM (EX box), 01 ....$3.00

Unknown, tin, yel pnt w/red stripes on side & top, 7½x21", G, A $65.00

Williams, passenger/c, bg/c, coaches (2), vistadome, obv/c in 2500 series style, gr stripe w/Southern mks, NM, A .$300.00

Locomotives and Tenders

American Flyer, HO ga, loco & 31045 diecast tender stamped Wabash, EX, A $275.00

American Flyer, wide ga, 4696 loco, 4694 tender, red plates, rewheeled, McCoy pickup plate, EX, A................$1,600.00

American Flyer, 21105 engine & coal/c, NM, 01 ....$46.00

Bassett Lowke Flying Scotsman, O ga, 410 loco, gr & blk litho, matching tender, BRR logo, VG $1,100.00

Beggs, loco & coach, live steam, litho paper on pasteboard, missing headlight & 3 handrails, EX-, A $750.00

Beggs, 3 loco, live steam, strong cartouch, orig wooden box, missing top, EX, A $950.00

Buddy L, 1000 steam loco & tender, loco w/silver pinstriping, bell & whistle, loco decals 97%, tender decals 95%, EX, A $1,800.00

Daniels, std ga, 608E switcher & tender, 0-6-0, slant-bk tender w/bk-up lights, EX, A $1,000.00

Buddy L Steam Locomotive and Tender, 1930s, M, D10, $1,250.00.

Ives, CI, loco, blk w/red wheels, gold piping, w/up motor, trackless, rpl bell, 1890s, 10", A $1,800.00

Ives, O ga, 4 loco, orig plates; 3rd series loco, clockwork, blk, red & gold trim; VG $90.00

Ives, std ga, 3237 loco, repro, M................................$350.00

Ives, 1 ga, 1129 loco, blk pnt CI, missing bell, some surface rust on wheels, G $825.00

Ives, 1 ga, 40 loco & tender, 3rd series loco, clockwork, blk, red & gold trim, repro harp, VG $1,700.00

Ives, 17 loco, clockwork, blk CI, red & gold trim, 4 boiler bands; 17 tender, EX-, A $100.00

Lionel, Pennsylvania 44-ton loco, NMIB, G1 ....$140.00

Lionel, std ga, 5 loco, 5 tender, EX, A $2,000.00

Lionel, std ga, 6 loco, thick rimmed; 7 tender; EX-, A $1,300.00

Lionel, std ga, 50 loco, dr gr & maroon, rewheeled, EX+, A $170.00

Lionel, std ga, 54 Special loco, highly polished, NMIB, A $1,600.00

Lionel, std ga, 392E loco, 384T tender, VG-, A $500.00

Lionel, std ga, 400E loco w/400T tender, blk & copper, NM (G boxes), A $2,700.00

Lionel Standard Gauge #408E Electric Locomotive, apple green, 7x16x4½", NM, A, $1,600.00.

Lionel, 58 Great Northern loco, rotary snowplow, NM (VG box), A...$310.00

Lionel, 211 TX Special Alco AA loco, EX+, A $150.00

Lionel, 212 Sante Fe dummy loco, red & silver, EX, A3 ..$50.00

Lionel, 215 Sante Fe Alco loco, powered unit, red & silver, EX, A3 ....$100.00

Lionel, 224E loco & 224W loco, prewar, EX, G1..........$175.00

Lionel, 225E loco & 2235W loco, gun metal, prewar, EX, G1..$650.00

Lionel #9E Electric Locomotive, 0-4-0 wheel configuration, 5¼x14¼x3¾", VG, A, $950.00.

Lionel, 226E loco, 226W tender (missing steps), ladder slightly bent, EX-..$400.00

Lionel, 249T tender only, Pennsylvania, EX, G1 ....$25.00

Lionel, 253 loco, slight fatigue to 1 casting, peacock, EX, A $85.00

Lionel, 256 loco, orange & brass, rubber stamped, EX-, A ..$325.00

Lionel, 637 loco (w/orig box), 773W tender, EX+, A $170.00

Lionel, 682 steam turbine, 2046-50 tender, EX-, A........$240.00

Lionel, 746 loco & 746W N&W loco, rpr, VG, G1.......$850.00

Lionel, 746 N&W loco, 746W short-stripe tender, NMIB, A $1,400.00

Lionel, 752E loco, silver w/blk rubber stamping, orig box, EX+, A $220.00

Lionel, 773 Hudson loco, 2426W tender, NMIB, A ...$2,700.00

Lionel, 1001 loco & Scout, 1948, 2-4-2, EX, G1 ....$45.00

Lionel, 1061 loco & 1061T loco, 0-4-0, EX, G1.............$425.00

Lionel, 2331 Virginia FM loco, blk stripe, 2 hairline cracks, NMIB, A $1,200.00

Lionel, 2333 NYC F3 AA units, some battery damage, missing porthole lenses, EX, A $525.00

Lionel, 2348 M&StL GP9 loco, missing 1 insert, NM, A.$425.00

Lionel, 2378AB Milwaukee Rd F3 loco, VG, G1 ....$950.00

Lionel, 2379 Rio Grande F3 AB loco, NMIB, A.........$1,350.00

Lionel, 8141 Pennsylvania steam loco, w/tender, M, A3..$55.00

Lionel, 8142 C&O diecast steam loco, 4-4-2, w/tender, makes sound of steam, M, A3 ....$75.00

Lionel, 8204 loco, C&O tender, 4-4-2, EX, G1 ....$65.00

Lionel, 8606 B&A Hudson loco, all orig, MIB, A $900.00

Lionel, 8851 loco & 8864 NH F3 ABA loco, 9272 NH bay-window caboose, MIB, A $400.00

Lionel, 8952 loco & 8059 PA F3 ABA loco, NM (VG boxes), A..$575.00

Lionel, 18000 loco & 19709 Pennsylvania loco, steam, 0-6-0, MIB, G1...$675.00

Lionel, 18001 Rock Island Berkshire loco, orig box, MIB, A $600.00

Lionel, 18011 loco & 17608 Chessie loco, tender, caboose, MIB, G1..$990.00

Lionel, 18103 Sante Fe 'B' loco, MIB, G1 ....$350.00

Lionel, 18303 Amtrak GG1 loco, MIB, G1 ....$380.00

Lionel, 18503 loco & 19707 Southern Pacific loco, MIB, G1 ....$325.00

Lionel, 18601 Great Northern loco, MIB, G1 ....$97.00

Lionel, 18607 Union Pacific loco, 2-6-4, MIB, G1 ....$162.00

Lionel, 18610 Rock Island loco, 0-4-0, MIB, G1............$175.00

Lionel, 18615 Grand Trunk West loco, MIB, G1..........$104.00

Lionel, 33000 Railscope loco, MIB, G1 ....$225.00

Marklin, HO ga, Diesel DB CL 212 loco, NMIB...........$140.00

Marklin, HO ga, Diesel DB CL 236 loco, NMIB..............$70.00

Marklin, HO ga, Diesel DB CL 260 loco, NMIB..............$70.00

Marklin, HO ga, Steam DB CL 78 2-6-2T loco, MIB $155.00

Marklin, HO ga, 3019.P diesel DB CL 218 loco, NMIB...$125.00

Marklin, HO ga, 3021.2 Diesel DB CL 220 loco, G (new box)...$55.00

Marklin, HO ga, 3038.2 Elok SN CF BB 9200 loco, NMIB..$140.00

Marklin, HO ga, 3039.4 Elok DB CL 110 loco, MIB......$155.00

Marklin, HO ga, 3040.2 Elok DB CL 140 loco, NM (rpl box)..$135.00

Marklin, HO ga, 3049.2 Elok DB CL 104 loco, NMIB ..$155.00

Marklin, HO ga, 3099.2 Steam DB CL 38 2-6-0 loco w/tender, MIB..$140.00

Marklin, HO ga, 3153.1 Elok DB CL 120 loco, orig box, EX...$120.00

Marklin, HO ga, 3173.1 Elok DB CL 120 loco, rare bl pnt, MIB...$740.00

Marklin, HO ga, 3340 Elok DB CL 110 loco, NMIB $165.00

Marklin, HO ga, 3665.3 Diesel DB CL 260 loco (w/Telex), digital, NMIB..$145.00

Marklin, RS900, O ga, clockwork, gr litho, wht pnt roof, missing key & 1 pantograph, working, VG...........$260.00

Marklin, Z ga, 8814 20th Anniversary Silver Tank loco, MIB...$420.00

Marklin, 1 ga, loco, clockwork, hand painted blk w/trim, EX-, A $1,400.00

Marx, 6000 Southern Pacific loco, tin plate, orange/silver stripe, powered unit w/dummy, A3 ....$45.00

McCoy, std ga, Cascade E2 loco, yel, 1 pantograph missing, MIB, A $700.00

Pnt wood w/CI wheels, red, gold, blk & wht, friction flywheel, 1 rpl stack, parts missing, 13", G-, A $55.00

Weaver, NP, 2-8-4 Berkshire loco & tender, MIB $875.00

Weaver, PRR, 4-6-0 G5 loco & tender, MIB $575.00

Welker & Crosbie, CI, loco, blk & red w/tall stack, bell, lamp & cow catcher, w/up 1880s, 11½", A.............$1,800.00

Williams, 4294 loco & Special tender, Big Boy, never ran, NMIB, A $900.00

Winner, std ga, 1035 loco, blk, orange frame w/copper trim, 10116T tender, litho, EX, A.......................$75.00

Sets

American Flyer, #2, CI loco, clockwork; 120 spotlight tender; 1108 PO bg/c; 1107 Jefferson; orig set box, EX+, A...$450.00

American Flyer, #3, 10 loco, clockwork, blk CI w/gold; 120 tender; 1108 bg/c; 1107 Pullman; 1107 coach; orig box, EX, A $600.00

American Flyer, #191, 13 loco, clockwork; 120 tender; 1108 bg/c; 1107 PA coach; orig set box, EX, A $375.00

American Flyer, #1101, 1095 loco, gr, yel w/cast pantographs; 1120 Seattle Pullmans (2), orig set box, EX, A $350.00

American Flyer, #1101, 1096 loco, 1108 bg/c; 1120 Seattle Pullman, EX (G set box), A $250.00

American Flyer, blk CI loco, clockwork; 120 tender; 1108 B&O bg/c; 1107 B&O coaches (2); EX, A $650.00

American Flyer #4654 Locomotive, Standard Gauge, with two orange lithographed cars, 32" long, VG, A, $525.00.

American Flyer, Burlington Zephyr, tin plate, 9900 electric loco, coaches (2), obv/c, EX-, A $110.00

American Flyer, CI loco, clockwork, 120 tender, 1108 bg/c, 1107 coach, EX+ (EX box), A $410.00

American Flyer, CI loco, 119 tender, 1108 bg/c, 1107 coach, orig set box, EX, A...$450.00

American Flyer, Hiawatha loco & tender, gondolas (2, 1 electric), fl/c w/lumber, Texaco tk/c, 1127 cabbose, EX, A $180.00

American Flyer, S ga, Rocket, 474 & 475 Rocket Pennsylvania Alco AA, 962 vistadomes (3), 963 obv/c, EX, A $850.00

American Flyer, S ga, Silver Streak, 405 Alco A unit, 660 combine, 661 coach, 662 vistadome, crackle chrome, VG, A..$130.00

American Flyer, S ga, 21085 loco & Reading tender, 24219 hopper, 24543 crane, 24546 boom tender (EX), remainder is NM, A $260.00

American Flyer, S ga, 2115 Docksider, 24003 Sante Fe plugdoor b/c, 24203 B&O hopper, 24603 caboose, EX, A $300.00

American Flyer, S ga, 293 loco & tender, 951 bg/c, 953 combine, 952 coach, 954 obv/c, EX-, A $300.00

American Flyer, S ga, 350 Royal Blue loco & tender, 642 b/c, 631 T&P gondola, 638 caboose, EX, A $150.00

American Flyer, std ga, Pocahontas, 4673 Shasta loco, 4340 club/c, 4341 coach, 4342 obv/c, EX, A.................$2,600.00

American Flyer, std ga, 4017 sand/c (orig box), 4012 machine, 4021 caboose, VG+, A $220.00

American Flyer, 429 loco, slant-bk AFL tender, 408 b/cs (2), 406 log/c, 411 caboose, EX+, A $550.00

American Flyer/LTI, S ga, B&M freight, 8350 GP7, 9003, 9703, 9104, 9203, 9402, NMIB, A..................................$600.00

American Flyer/LTI, S ga, Southern freight, 8458 GP9, 9704, 9303, 9105, 9204, 9004, 9403, NMIB, A.................$160.00

American Flyer/LTI, S ga, 8153 & 8154 B&O ABA, 9000, 9709, 9702, 9301, 9102, 9207, 9201, 9401, NMIB, A.......$290.00

American Flyer/LTI, 48009 GM GP7 Diesel, 48805, 49003, 48601, 48703, NMIB, A...$190.00

American/LTI, S ga, Wabash Diesel freight, 48100 PA-1 Diesel AA, 48603, 48502, 48503, 48505, 48800, 48702 (2), NMIB, A..$250.00

Bassett Lowke Train Set, O ga, 64193 loco; tender, British RR decals; 36721 low-sided goods wagon; 730273 brake van; EX...$500.00

Bing, O ga, PA Lines loco, 501 bg/c, 617 Pullman, 529 obs/c, VG $300.00

Bing, O ga, pnt CI loco, clockwork, no headlight; 1012 tender; 253 NYC coach; 617 PA parlor/c; 529 NYC obs/c, VG...$210.00

Bing, OO ga, 2-4-0 tank loco, pnt alligatored; coach & observation, all litho; orig set box rough, NM $250.00

Bing Train and Station, ca 1930s, train: 18" long, M, D10, $375.00.

Bing, trolley, O ga, yel & brn litho, clockwork, NM, A .$900.00

Bing Live Steam Train, 1 ga, 1902 loco, LNWR tender, 3rd class coach, VG $1,650.00

Buddy L, side dump/c, blk, decals 75%..........................$675.00

Buddy L, 1007 hopper/c, blk, decals 65%.......................$800.00

Burlington Zephyr, Western Coil, O ga, diecast, missing cb walkways, 1 window insert & 1 wheel set, decals 90%, VG..$425.00

Carette, O ga, live steam, pnt pinstriping, nickel rails, bg/c, coaches (2), EX, A $600.00

Coutland, #9000, WRR Lines, w/up, 3 pcs, 22" overall, NM (EX box), A..$125.00

Daniels, std ga, 4935 PA GG1, dbl motor; 1780 combine; 1781-82 coaches; 1783 diner/c; 1784 obv/c, Lionel latches; EX...$1,450.00

Daniels, std ga, 600E Hudson loco, NYC tender, rail chief/cs (4), vestibules (3), loco bell broken, EX, A...............$2,100.00

Dorfan, 52 loco, 601 b/c, 605 hopper, 604 tk/c, 607 caboose, EX, A...$220.00

Dorfan, 55 loco, clockwork, non-working; 160 tender; coaches (3); VG+, A..$270.00

German, O ga, 0-35 loco, wind-cutter cab, 2 #640 coaches, mk NYC, VG..$400.00

Hafner, #802, 100 loco, clockwork; PA tender; NW coach; NYC coach; orig set box rough, NM, A $750.00

Hafner, Century of Progress, clockwork, red & blk enameled tender, Overland Flyer bg/c, Pullman, obv/c, EX, A......$275.00

Hafner, Sunshine Special, broken clockwork, 118 tender, Sunshine Specials (2), EX+, A.....................................$270.00

Hafner, Sunshine Special, 1010 loco, clockwork, 2 coaches & observations, EX $575.00

Hoge, Tom Thumb, 9900 loco w/tender, 881 Pullman, 881 obv/c, litho powerhouse station transformer, EX, A...........$270.00

Hubley Passenger Train, NY Central & Hudson River Line, ca 1905, 51" long, EX, D10, $1,850.00.

**Hull & Stafford Passenger Train, 1870s, locomotive: 9"
long, each car: 9½" long, D10, $2,850.00.**

Ives, CI & tin plate w/up, blk steam engine, tender, b/c,
  Hiawatha passenger/cs, in red & blk tinplate, 1900, 26",
  A $575.00

Ives, Hero, pnt CI, 1-pc engine & tender, passenger car, gondola, 14", 3-pc set, G, A $350.00

Ives, std ga, #692, 3236 loco, missing whistle; 170 buffet/c; 171
  parlor/c; 172 obv/c; EX+ (EX box), A $320.00

Ives, std ga, Tiger, #1082R, 3236 loco, 184 club/c, 185 parlor/c,
  186 obv/c, EX (VG box) $3,500.00

Ives, std ga, 3236 loco, 194 Pennsylvania hopper/c, 191 coke/c,
  197 fl/c w/stakes, 195 caboose, set is dirty, G...........$525.00

**Ives #3241 Standard Gauge Passenger Train, with
buffet car #184 and observation car #178, original
box, EX, A, $1,100.00.**

Ives, 3250 loco, gr; 550 bg/c; 552 parlor/c; 551 chair; EX+, A..$90.00

Katz, 515 LTD, 515 loco, 515 b/c, track, EX (G box), A..$210.00

Kenton, floor train, pnt CI loco, sheet metal tender, coaches (3:
  1 red, 1 bl, 1 wht), all stamped Erie RR, EX, A $350.00

Krause, O ga, loco, clockwork, working; blk litho tender; coach;
  VG $170.00

Lionel, #3, 10 loco, clockwork; 120 tender; 1108 bg/c; 1107 Jefferson coach; 120 coach; EX, A $550.00

Lionel, #1672 service station, 8666 NP GP9, 9725 b/c, 9776 b/c,
  9267 hopper, 9869 reefer, 9177 coach, NMIB, A....$270.00

Lionel, #8560, #8470, C&O U36B diesel AA (no box), 6531
  (2), 9863/9265/9229/9747 (orig boxes), 9381 C&O
  caboose, EX, A $200.00

Lionel, #11500, 2029 loco, 234W tender, 6402, fl/c w/reels,
  6465 tk/c, 6175 hopper, 6014 reefer, 6257 caboose, NMIB,
  A $190.00

Lionel, #11758 1989 SS Desert King, MIB, G1 ....$249.00

Lionel, Congressional, 2360 GG1 loco, 2543 W Penn, 2544
  M Pitcher, 2542 B Ross, 2541 A Hamilton obv/c, EX+,
  A $1,050.00

Lionel, FF#4 W Maryland, MIB, G1 ....$425.00

Lionel, FF#5 Frisco, no coal/c, NMIB, G1 ....$490.00

Lionel, Flying Yankee, 616W loco, 617 coaches (2), 618 obv/c,
  gun metal & chrome, VG, A $350.00

Lionel, Golden State Arrow Set, NM (EX box), 01 ....$445.00

Lionel, Midnight Flyer Set, orig box, EX, 01 ....$115.00

Lionel, Nickel Plate Road, 8617 diecast loco, NPR tender, 6254
  gondola, 9137 hopper, 6419 caboose, EX, A.............$65.00

Lionel, OO ga, 001 loco & tender, 0016 hopper, 0014 Pennsylvania b/c, 0015 SUNX tk/c, 0017 caboose, transformer,
  NMIB, A $1,050.00

Lionel, OO ga, 004 Hudson loco, missing bell; 002T tender;
  0045 Shell tk/c (incomplete); EX-, A $210.00

Lionel, S ga, 0602 PA switcher, 0860-200 PA fl/c w/boom crane,
  0870 track maintenance/c, 0819/275 work caboose, NMIB,
  A $140.00

Lionel, Sante Fe aluminum passenger, 2353AA & 2531 locos,
  2532, 2533 (2), VG, G1 ....$675.00

Lionel, Scout, 1110 loco, 1001T tender, 1002 gondola, 1004 b/c,
  1007 caboose, conversion couplers, EX (P box), A ...$50.00

Lionel, std ga, Blue Comet, 400E loco, 400T tender, 420 Faye,
  421 Westphal, 422 Tempal, NMIB, A $6,800.00

Lionel, std ga, coal train, 318E loco, 516 hoppers (3), 517
  caboose, emb truck springs pnt silver, EX, A........$1,300.00

Lionel, std ga, 1911 loco, 112 gondolas (2), early, long pnt crin-
  kle couplers, EX, A..$1,700.00

Lionel, std ga, 1911 Special, 181 turbine, 180 coach, 182 obv/c,
  pnt mottled, EX, A..$3,500.00

Lionel, std ga, 33 loco (6-wheel), 35 Pullmans (6), 36 obv/c, blk
  w/red & brass trim, EX, A $1,200.00

Lionel, std ga, 38 loco, 114 CM&STP b/c, 112 Lakeshore gondola, 113 st/c, 116 ballast, 117 NYC & HR RR caboose, EX,
  A $390.00

Lionel, std ga, 8 loco, rpl wheels; 332 Pullman; 338 obv/c; orig
  boxes, EX+ (NM loco box), A $500.00

Lionel, std ga, 8 loco, 332 Pullman, 338 obv/c, orig boxes, EX,
  A $500.00

Lionel, std ga, 9E loco, 424 Liberty Belle, 425 Stephan Girard,
  426 Coral Isle, NMIB, A $6,500.00

**Lionel #38 Standard Gauge Freight Train, with orange
box car, green stock car and maroon caboose, 46" long,
G-VG, A, $250.00.**

Lionel, 027 ga, Mickey's World Tour, 1991, 27x54" oval track, MIB (sealed), A $175.00

Lionel, 8 loco, red & cream trim; 337 Pullman, olive w/red trim; EX, A $230.00

Lionel, 152 loco, 800 b/c, 802 st/c, 901 Lakeshore gondola, 801 Wabash caboose, orig box rough, EX, A $230.00

Lionel, 153 loco, 803 hopper, 804 tk/c, EX, A $230.00

Lionel, 156 loco, 820 b/cs (2), 822 caboose, VG-, A $210.00

Lionel, 248 loco, 804 tk/c, 831 lumber/c, 809 dump/c, 806 cattle/c, 807 caboose, EX-, A $200.00

Lionel, 249E loco, 265W tender, manual coupler, gun-metal nickel trim, EX, A $200.00

Lionel, 252 loco, 607 Pullman, 608 obv/c, cars are 2-tone gr, VG+ , A $120.00

Lionel, 254E loco, no reverse; 610 Pullmans (2); 612 obv/c; EX, A $200.00

Lionel, 254E loco, 820 searchlight, 816 hopper, 812 gondola, 817 caboose, EX, A $260.00

Lionel, 258 loco; 1689T tender, rubber stamped; 1680 tk/c; 1679 b/c; 1682 caboose; all w/manual couplers, EX, A.....$120.00

Lionel, 400 Budd/c, 2559 trailer, orig box, NM (VG- box), A $410.00

Lionel, 635 UP NW2 switcher, 6014 Frisco, 6076 hopper, 6167 UP caboose, EX, A $190.00

Lionel, 1065 UP Alco A, 6015 Sunoco tk/c, 6476-135 hopper (w/orig box), 6167 UP cabooses (2), EX, A.............$85.00

Lionel, 1662 Blk River, Toys R Us/c, EX, G1 ....$85.00

Lionel, 2020 turbine, 2046W tender, 6456 hopper, 2555 tk/c, 6014 Baby Ruth, 6465 tk/c, 6457 caboose, EX-, A ..$290.00

Lionel, 2032 Erie Alco AA, 6656 cattle/c, 6462 gondola w/drums, 6456 hopper, 6457 caboose, EX+, A $450.00

Lionel, 2332 GG1 loco, 2625 Irvington, 2627 Madison, 2628 Manhattan, EX (VG+ box), A $700.00

Lionel, 5484 Hudson, diecast tender, 1981 bg/c, 1982 combine, 1983 coach, 1980 obv/c, EX, A $340.00

Lionel, 5733 bunk/c, M (EX box), 01 ....$40.00

Lionel, 6424 fl/c carrier, NM, 01 ....$46.00

Lionel Blue Comet Set, Engine #400E: 18" long; twelve-wheeled tender: 12¼" long; observation car #422: 19" long; passenger car #420: 19" long; The Westphal #421: 19" long; NMIB, A, $5,665.00.

Lionel, 8100 N&W loco & tender, 7203 N&W diner, NMIB, A $800.00

Lionel, 8101 Chicago & Alton, 6 cars, MIB, G1 ....$950.00

Lionel, 8480 & 8481 F3 ABA, 9545 bg/c, 9546 combine, 9548 coach, 9549 coach, 7210 diner, 9547 obv/c, MIB...$1,250.00

Lionel, 8854 CP Rail GP9 in box, 6 assorted CP Rail b/c, 9149 fl/c w/trailer, 9057 caboose, EX, A $230.00

Lionel, 8904 Wabash loco & tender, 16314 piggyback fl/cs (2), 9376 & 9447 b/cs, NMIB; 16201 b/c, 9080 caboose, EX, A $160.00

Lionel, 8951 SP FM loco, 9581 bg/c, 9582 combine, 9583 & 9584 coaches, 9585 obv/c, NMIB, A $550.00

Marklin, HO ga, #2861 Rubenzug (Sugarbeet), MIB $185.00

Marklin, HO ga, #2890 DBP 500 Year Postal Anniversary Set, MIB..$215.00

Marklin, HO ga, #2916 Delta, Sm Freight Starter Kit, MIB..$150.00

Marklin, HO ga, #2922 Texas Western Starter Set, MIB..$12.50

Marklin, HO ga, #2964 Delta, Lg Freight Starter Set, MIB..$230.00

Marklin, HO ga, #84564 Five Hundred Years America Boxcar Set, MIB...$150.00

Marklin, O ga, R66-12910 loco, 4-wheel #9/9/10 loco, 16740 Shell tk/c, goodswagon, red & brn litho, blk roof, EX.........$725.00

Marklin, O ga, R890 loco & tender, clockwork, blk/red trim; 17230 coaches (3); 17269 bg/c; gr/yel; VG, A.........$150.00

Marx, #9625, 666 diecast loco, SP tender, 2532 tk/c, 13975 st/c, Erie fl/c, SP caboose, track, orig set box, EX, A.........$35.00

Marx, Gray Mercury, electric loco, NYC tender, mail coach, Toledo coach, Detroit obv/c, loco VG, cars EX, A....$85.00

Marx, mechanical, #886, Red Mercury, Mercury loco, NYC tender, Toledo coach, Detroit obs/c, NMIB, A $290.00

Marx, M10,000 UP electric loco, coaches (2), jeweled obv/c, red & silver litho, EX+, A $275.00

Marx, M10,000 UP electric loco, coaches (2), obv/cs (2), missing 1 tin wheel & axle, EX, A $90.00

Marx, red Comm Vanderbilt loco, clockwork w/whistle; NYC litho tender; Bogota; Monyclair; obv/c; EX-EX+, A..$75.00

Marx, UP10,000 (clockwork), coach, buffet, obv/c, red & silver w/dummy headlight, EX, A $80.00

McCoy TCA Set, std ga, General-style loco, TCA tender, advertising b/c, bg/c, combine, 2 coaches, obv/c, EX.........$290.00

MTH, std ga, 1764E loco, 1767 bg/c, 1766 Pullman, 11768 obv/c, NMIB...$750.00

Pride Lines Hiawatha, std ga, loco, tender, coach, Miniwaw, diner, Ishkoodah, Wenonah obv/c, EX+, A $700.00

Varney, std ga, Olympian, 3245R loco, 241 combine, 242 parlor/cs (2), 243 obv/c, NMIB, A.............................$1,700.00

Winner, #1005, 1035 loco, 1016 tender, 1011 Pullman, 1019 obv/c, missing transformer house, orig set box, G....$250.00

Accessories

American Flyer, refreshment stand & newsstand, part of 271 Whistle Stop set, wood & paper, EX, A $750.00

American Flyer, std ga, manual semaphores (4), block signal (2), w/1 activator insert, EX, A $160.00

American Flyer, 2222 crossing gate, orig box; 215 water tank & beacon light, orig box; NM, A $210.00

American Flyer, 237 station w/platform, 235 water tower & platform, EX+, A $270.00

American Flyer, 4265 tunnel, pnt papier-mache, NMIB, A...$50.00

American Flyer, 4267 tunnel w/telegraph poles, poles pnt CI, tunnel pnt papier-mache, NMIB, A $550.00

American Flyer, 568 Whistling billboards (2), 561 diesel horn billboard, 577 Whistling billboard, orig boxes, EX+, A...$180.00

Buddy L, track, straight sections (6), 1¾" L; curves (4); EX, A..$500.00

Ives, 113 station, litho w/ gray pnt roof (EX), 216 crossing gate, litho & pnt tin, NM, A........................$500.00

Ives, 114 station, litho, red pnt roof, brn base, orig box rpr, VG..$260.00

Ives, 115 freight station, early litho, missing base riser, EX..$325.00

Ives, 116 Union station, illuminated, brn roof on litho station, missing chimney, EX, A.........................$310.00

Ives, 201 Power Station, litho, terra cotta roof, blk chimney scratched, roof is factory rpt over litho, EX, A $1,000.00

Ives, 306 dbl lamppost, 305 single lamppost, both gr w/brass shades, EX, A..$120.00

Lionel, #86 telegraph post set, 85 telegraph posts (6), orange & red crossbars, litho insert, orig set box, EX, A $290.00

Lionel, #911 landscape villa, mustard, lt gr, gray base, EX+, A...$950.00

Lionel, automatic crossing gate, orig box, EX, G1 ....$32.00

Lionel, bumpers, std ga, 23 (2) in red, 25 (3, 2 blk & nickel, 1 blk & red), diecast, EX- (EX+ box), A $170.00

Lionel, crossing gates, orig boxes, 1 missing 2 flaps, EX+, A..$75.00

Lionel, JR bridge, orig box 27", EX, G1............................$25.00

Lionel, O ga, fire station, sm pc of roof peak missing, VG, A3...$10.00

Lionel, O ga, 042 manual switch, EX, pr, G1 ....$35.00

Lionel, OO ga, display layout, oval 3-rail track, landscaped tin, 48W station & advertising billboard, NM (VG box), A..$3,300.00

Lionel, station platforms (2), 1 w/broken fence section, EX, A...$240.00

Lionel, std ga, 103 bridge, 2 approaches, 3 center sections, EX (G- box), A..$150.00

Lionel, std ga, 219 derrick, ivory, red & apple gr, orig box, EX, A...$725.00

Lionel, 45 gateman, EX...$45.00

Lionel, 61 lampposts (3), 63 lamppost, orig bulbs, EX+, A .$450.00

Lionel, 91 circuit breakers (4, 1 orig box), 88 rheostats (3, orig boxes rough), 167 whistle controller, EX, A.............$80.00

Lionel, 92 floodlight tower, gray w/red base, NMIB, A ..$400.00

Lionel, 104 tunnel, pnt felt & compo, crack on top, EX+ (G box), A...$160.00

Lionel, 110 trestle set, NMIB, G1 ....$25.00

Lionel, 115 station, late colors, NMIB, A.......................$850.00

Lionel, 128 animated newsstand, NMIB, A...................$190.00

Lionel, 128 station & platform, 124 station in orig box w/wht label, early colors, NMIB, A $2,100.00

Lionel, 145 gateman, orig box, EX, G1 ....$35.00

Lionel, 154 crossing signal, EX, G1 ....$25.00

Lionel, 157 station platform, orig box, EX, G1 ....$70.00

Lionel, 163 target signal, EX, G1....................................$30.00

Lionel, 184 bungalows (2), litho gr roofs, 1 w/red awning, 1 w/alligatored chimney, EX+, A $190.00

Lionel, 197 radar tower w/insert, 193 blinking water tower, EX+ (VG box), A..$120.00

Lionel, 205 MoPac Alco AA units, EX-, A $85.00

Lionel, 214 girder bridge, orig box, EX, G1.....................$20.00

Lionel, 219 derrick, std ga, early colors, EX, A $130.00

Lionel, 252 crossing gate, EX, G1..................................$25.00

Lionel, 256 freight station, orig box, EX, G1 ....$40.00

Lionel, 260 bumper, red, orig box, EX, G1 ....$15.00

Lionel, 350 transfer table w/controller, rewired, EX, A ..$250.00

Lionel, 352 ice depot, red superstructure, NMIB, A.......$280.00

Lionel, 362 operating barrel loader w/3562-25 barrel/c, w/load & track trips, repro man, EX, A $150.00

Lionel, 397 coal loader, bl motor cover w/controller, NMIB, A...$140.00

Lionel, 437 switch tower, early colors, EX, A $460.00

Lionel, 438 signal tower, late colors, M, A $950.00

Lionel, 444 roundhouse section, VG..............................$775.00

Lionel, 450 signal bridge, orig box, EX, G1.....................$40.00

Lionel, 454 construction kit, 90% complete, w/instruction manual & inserts, orig box (veneer loose on top), EX, A.......$130.00

Lionel, 810 derrick, late colors, EX (G box), A.............$225.00

Lionel, 910 grove of trees, NMIB, A...........................$1,100.00

Lionel, 913 illuminated & landscaped bungalow, ivory w/gr roof, NMIB, A...$1,100.00

Lionel, 918 mountain, 2" crack at base, EX, A $350.00

Lionel, 927 lubricating & maintenance kit, incomplete, orange & bl box, A3...$10.00

Lionel, 1024 027 manual switches, orig box, EX, G1 ....$25.00

Lionel, 1033 transmitter, 90 watts, EX, G1......................$45.00

Lionel, 2117 block signal, MIB, G1.................................$24.00

Lionel, 2180 RR signs, MIB, G1.......................................$4.00

Lionel, 2256 station platform, NM, G1............................$20.00

Lionel, 2317 drawbridge, no steps, orig box, EX, G1 ....$65.00

Lionel, 2901 track clips, MIB, G1 ....$4.50

Lionel, 12710 engine house, MIB, G1..............................$23.00

Lionel, 12715 bumpers, lighted, MIB, G1 ....$5.00

Lionel, 12719 refreshment stand, animated, MIB, G1......$62.00

Lionel, 12720 girder bridge, MIB, G1................................$9.00

Lionel, 12735 diesel horn shed, MIB, G1.........................$32.00

Lionel, 12741 Intermodal crane, MIB, G1......................$189.00

Lionel, 12742 gooseneck lamps, MIB, G1........................$12.00

Lionel, 12770 arch under bridge, MIB, G1........................$19.00

Lionel, 12807 Little Caesar's truck, MIB, G1 ....$15.00

Lionel, 33002 railscope TV, MIB, G1 ....$88.00

Lionel, 82007 or 82008, right- or left-hand auto switch, MIB, G1...$42.00

Lionel, 6-12717 bumpers, lot of 3, MIB, A3......................$5.00

Lionel, 30-gal water tank, brn superstructure, gray base, EX, A...$160.00

Marklin, O ga, spring bumper, HP, EX $220.00

Marklin, O ga, 280 transformer, VG, A3 ....$20.00

Marklin, train station, pnt tin, w/telegraph room, waiting room etc, 1915, 7½x5x10¾", EX, A...............$1,000.00

Marklin, 1 ga, crossing gate, w/bell that rings, +signs, man & tree, NM, A $350.00

MTH, Hellsgate Bridge, early colors, M.........................$950.00

Schoenhut, house kits, 1915, pressed wood, tin doors & wooden inserts, lot of 3, EX-, A...$110.00

Train Station, Marklin, tin, bright colors, 7½x10¾x5", EX, A, $1,000.00.

Transformers

Made by the Hasbro Company, Transformers were introduced in the United States in 1984. Originally there were twenty-eight figures — eighteen cars known as Autobots and ten Decepticons, evil robots capable of becoming such things as a jet or a handgun. Eventually the line was expanded to more than two hundred different models, and more were produced in Japan that were never imported to the US. Transformers appeared in a series of animations, comic books, and a highly successful movie. The line was discontinued in 1990, but continued interest has spawned a number of fan clubs with chapters worldwide.

Because Transformers came in a number of sizes, you'll find a wide range of pricing. Original packaging can add as much as 30% to 40% to overall value. Many have snap-on parts and accessories, and to bring top price, these must be present. Paperwork is important as well. Our advisor for this category is David Kolodny-Nagy (K2).

Action Masters, Decepticon Bombshell, England, 1991, MIP $20.00

Action Masters, Decepticon Charger, England, 1991, MIP $15.00

Action Masters, Decepticon Slicer, England, battery-op, 1991, MIP $35.00

Action Masters, Decepticon Take-Off, England, 1991, MIP $15.00

Action Masters, Decepticon Thundercracker, England, 1991, MIP $30.00

Action Masters, Jazz, MOC, D4........................$7.00

Action Masters, Sprocket, Hasbro, 1989, MIP, F1 ....$30.00

Action Masters, Wheeljack, Hasbro, 1989, MIP, F1 ....$30.00

Action Masters Elites, Double Punch, England, 1991, rare, MIP, ...$24.00

Action Masters Elites, Omega Supreem, England, 1991, rare, MIP, ...$24.00

Action Masters Elites, Turbo Master, England, 1991, rare, MIP, ...$20.00

Action Masters Elites, Windmill, England, 1991, rare, MIP .$20.00

Aerialbot Leader, Silverbolt, complete, MIP $30.00

Autobots, Aquablast, England, 1993, MIP......................$22.00

Autobots, Circuit, England, 1991, MIP.........................$25.00

Autobots, Commander Optimus Prime, complete, NM (EX pkg), O1 ....$40.00

Autobots, Ground Assault Commander Roadbuster, MIP..$40.00

Autobots, Groundshaker, M $27.50

Autobots, Hot House, M $10.00

Autobots, Hydradread, England, 1993, MIP $22.00

Autobots, Inferno, MIB..$25.00

Autobots, Ironworks, M..$10.00

Autobots, Powerflash, England, 1991, MIP....................$15.00

Autobots, Rotorstorm, England, 1992, MIP....................$40.00

Autobots, Rumbler, England, battery-op, 1991, MIP, F1 .$35.00

Autobots, Sideswipe, England, 1991, MIP $22.00

Autobots, Spark, England, 1993, MIP...........................$45.00

Autobots, Tanker Truck, M $22.50

Autobots, Thunderclash, England, 1992, MIP.................$60.00

Autobots, Tracks, England, 1991, MIP $22.00

Battle Patrol, Japanese issue, 1991, MIP $20.00

Bludgeon, US issue, 1988, MOC.................................$25.00

Cars, Bluestreak, Hasbro, 1984, MIB............................$45.00

Cars, Inferno, MIB..$40.00

Cars, Ironhide, 1st series, 1984, MIB...........................$30.00

Cars, Mirage, Hasbro, 1st series, MIB..........................$45.00

Cars, Skids, MIB $55.00

Constrictors, Barrage, M...$65.00

Decepticons, City Commander, NM (VG box), $20.00.

Constrictors, Blaster, MIB $50.00
Constrictors, Bonecrusher, M $20.00
Constrictors, Crane, MIB $20.00
Constrictors, Inferno, MIB $40.00
Constrictors, Scavenger, Hasbro, MIB $20.00
Constrictors, Scrapper, M $20.00
Constructicons, Bonecrusher, Hasbro, MIP, F1 .... $10.00
Constructicons, Mixmaster, Hasbro, MIP, F1 .... $10.00
Constructicons, Scavenger, MOC $10.00
Decepticons, Air Strike Patrol Control, set of 4, MIB $15.00
Decepticons, Airwave, M $10.00
Decepticons, Aquafend, England, 1993, MIP $22.00
Decepticons, Colossus, England, 1993, MIP $45.00
Decepticons, Falcon, England, 1992, MIP $25.00
Decepticons, Greaspit, M $10.00
Decepticons, Jetstrom, England, 1993, MIP $22.00
Decepticons, Skydive, England, 1992, MIP $25.00
Decepticons, Skyquake, England, 1992, MIP $60.00
Decepticons, Skywalker, M $32.00
Decepticons, Snare, England, 1992, MIP $25.00
Decepticons, Stalker, England, 1992, MIP $40.00
Decepticons, Talon, England, 1992, MIP $25.00
Dinobots, Slag, MIB $35.00
Dinobots, Swoop, Hasbro, MIB $70.00
Insecticons, Barrage, MIB $75.00
Insecticons, Bombshell, Hasbro, 1984, MIP, D4/F1 .... $15.00
Insecticons, Kickback, Hasbro, 1984, MIP, D4/F1 .... $15.00
Insecticons, Ransack, Hasbro, MIB $70.00
Insecticons, Shrapnel, Hasbro, 1984, MIP, D4/F1 .... $15.00
Jets, Megatron, Hasbro, 1st series, MIB $175.00
Jets, Ramjet, Hasbro, MIB $45.00
Jets, Thrust, Hasbro, MIB $45.00
Jets, Thundercracker, Hasbro, 1st series, MIB $55.00
Jumpstarters, Blitzwing, M $28.00
Legends, Bumblebee, M $28.00
Legends, Grimlock, M $35.00
Legends, Jazz, M $35.00
Legends, Starscream, M $38.00
Micromasters, Air Patrol, MOC, D4 .... $8.00
Micromasters, Autobot Hothouse Station, Hasbro, 1988, MIP, F1 .... $10.00
Micromasters, Autobot Ironworks Station, Hasbro, 1988, MIP, F1 .... $10.00
Micromasters, Autobot Off-Road Patrol, Hasbro, 1988, set of 4, MIP, F1 .... $15.00
Micromasters, Autobot Race Car Patrol, Hasbro, 1988, set of 4, MIP, F1 .... $15.00
Micromasters, Construction Patrol, MOC, D4 .... $8.00
Micromasters, Decepticon Air Strike Patrol, Hasbro, 1988, complete set of 4, MIP, F1 .... $15.00
Micromasters, Decepticon Airwave Station, Hasbro, 1988, MIP, F1 .... $10.00
Micromasters, Decepticon Greasepit Station, Hasbro, 1988, MIP, F1 .... $10.00
Micromasters, Race Track Patrol, MOC, D4 .... $8.00
Mini Autobot, Seaspray, Hasbro, 1985, MIP, F1 .... $10.00
Mini-Car, Beachcomber, 1985, MIB $20.00
Mini-Car, Brawn, 2nd series, 1985, MIB $35.00

Mini-Car, Bumblebee, Hasbro, yel, MIB $50.00
Mini-Car, Cliffjumper, Hasbro, red, 1985, MIB $45.00
Mini-Car, Cosmos, 1985, MIB $10.00
Mini-Car, Powerglide, 1985, EX $8.00
Mini-Car, Seaspray, Hasbro, 1985, MIB $20.00
Omega Supreme, Hasbro, MIB $175.00
Optimus Prime, M $125.00
Perceptor, Hasbro, MIB $40.00
Predicons, Tantrum, complete, NM (VG-EX box), O1 ... $20.00
Pretender, Doubleheader, US issue, 1988, MOC $15.00
Pretender, Longtooth, hovercraft w/shell, US issue, 1988, MOC $15.00
Pretender, Octopunch, US issue, 1988, MOC $20.00
Pretender, Pincher, US issue, 1988, MOC $15.00
Protectobot Leader, Hot Spot, complete, NM (VG-EX box), O1 .... $18.00
Quickmix, 1987, MIB $10.00
Quickswitch, Hasbro, NM $37.50
Rumbler, European issue, 1991, MIB (French & German box) $35.00
Runamucker, 1986, MIB $25.00
Scattershot, M $25.00
Slicer, European issue, 1991, MIB (French & German box) . $35.00
Sparkler Minibots, Cindersaur, Hasbro, 1987, MIP, F1 .... $10.00
Sparkler Minibots, Fizzle, Hasbro, 1987, MIP, F1 .... $10.00
Sparkler Minibots, Flameater, Hasbro, 1987, MIP, F1 ...... $10.00
Sparkler Minibots, Guzzle, Hasbro, 1987, MIP, F1 .... $10.00
Sparkler Minibots, Sizzle, Hasbro, 1987, MIP, F1 .... $10.00
Sparkler Minibots, Sparkstalker, Hasbro, 1987, MIP, F1 .. $10.00
Stranglehold, US issue, 1988, MOC $20.00
Targetmaster, Landfill, Hasbro, 1987, MIP, F1 .... $10.00
Whirl, Hasbro, MIB $80.00

Miscellaneous

Gum Card Set, Milton Bradley, 1985, 192 cards w/24 stickers, complete, M1 .... $48.00
Sticker Book, Diamond, Made in Italy, MIP, F1 .... $5.00
Stickers, Diamond, Italy, 1986, mc set of 7, MIP, F1 .... $1.00
Voice Synthesizer, Nasta, Deception Enemy, w/headphones, 1986, MIB, F1 .... $20.00
Voice Synthesizer, Nasta, Heroic Autobot Electronic Voice, makes you talk like robot, 1986, MIP, F1 .... $15.00

Tri-Ang

Tri-Ang vehicles were made in England of heavy gauge steel; some of the later models had diecast components.

Anti-Aircraft Gun Truck, apple-gr cab & base, blk cannon w/red base, blk rubber tires, decal on roof, 9¾", M, A $198.00
Brick Lorry, bl & wht w/diecast front, w/28 wood bricks, orig box, 12½", EX-NM, A $70.00
Dump Truck, blk & red w/decals, NP grille & bumper, logo on radiator, rubber tires, friction, 19½", G-, A $55.00
Dump Truck, red w/plated grille, 4-spoke dummy steering wheel, rubber tires, decal on bed, 20-gauge, 19", G, A $132.00

Dump Truck, red-orange w/wht grille, bl steel wheels w/rubber tires, disk dummy steering wheel, new rivets, 19", VG, A $94.00

Greenline Bus, rubber tires, chrome grille, 1956, 23", MIB, A, $550.00.

Rubbish Truck, 1930s, D10, $150.00.

Tip Lorry, gr & red w/diecast front, working dump bed, orig box, 13", EX-NM, A $55.00
Wrecker, bright red w/blk grille, steel wheels w/narrow rubber tires, dummy steering wheel, decal on roof, 17", EX-NM, A..$633.00

Turner

The Turner Company made large-scale pressed-steel vehicles from the twenties on up to the 1940s.

Army Truck, olive gr, plated grille, decals on cab, US Army Signal Corp decal on sides, canvas top, 19¼", G-VG, A.$88.00
Dump Truck, Mac truck style, gr dump body, 4 in-line wheels w/rubber tires, worn, 8x26", EX-, A $150.00

Dump Truck, seat-style cab, headlights & dump body, part of mechanism missing, rpl screws/wheels, EX pnt, 12x31", A $375.00
Dump Truck, short-bed style, yel cab, apple gr fenders & chassis, red dump bed, Bakelite wheels, 22⅛", G, A $132.00
Dump Truck #42648, red cab & chassis w/gr bed, plated grille, headlights & hubcaps, Bakelite wheels, box, 27", NM, A $605.00
Flatbed Truck & Excavator, wht truck cab w/plated grille, gr fenders & bed, orange & yel excavator, 18½", VG, A $275.00

Lincoln Sedan, green with black roof and hood, old poor repaint, wrong wheels, 1920s, 28", M5, $2,700.00.

Lincoln Sedan, gr-gray w/blk striping & roof, rubber tires w/logo, yel int, possible rpt, 10½x27", G, A $4,250.00
Open Roadster, gray w/gr fenders & red top, chipped pnt, 18", G-VG, A $240.00
Packard Dump Truck, inertia drive, orig rubber wheels, 19", G+, A $440.00
Truck, red cab, yel bed, wood dual wheels w/plated hubcaps, hinged tailgate, missing part of bumper, 19", EX-, A ..$248.00

View-Master and Tru-Vue

View-Master, the invention of William Gruber, was introduced to the public at the 1939–1940 New York World's Fair and the Golden Gate Exposition in California. Since then, View-Master reels, packets, and viewers have been produced by five different companies — the original Sawyers Company, G.A.F (1966), View-Master International (1981), Ideal Toys, and Tyco Toys (the present owners). Because none of the non-cartoon single reels and three-reel packets have been made since 1980, these have become collectors' items. Also highly sought after are the 3-reel sets featuring popular TV and cartoon characters, and from the viewpoint of a person who is basically a View-Master collector, the crossover interest from the character-collectible field results in prices they consider extremely high. Our ranges reflect both aspects.

Until 1945, single reels were dark blue with a gold sticker in the center or a combination of blue and tan. They came in attractive gold-colored envelopes. Since print runs were low, these early singles are much more desirable than the white ones that were produced by the millions from 1946 until 1957. Three-reel packets, many containing story books, were introduced in 1955, and single reels were phased out. Nearly all viewers are very common and have little value except for the very early ones, such as the Model A and Model B. Blue and brown versions of the Model B are especially rare. Another desirable viewer, unique in that it is the only focusing model ever made, is the Model D. Our advisor for this category is Roger Nazeley; he is listed under View-Master in the section entitled Categories of Special Interest.

#1004, Spiderman, 3-reel set, 1980s, MOC......................$8.00

#1036, Masters of the Universe, 3-reel set, 1983, MOC.....$3.00

#1039, Charlie Brown, It's Your First Kiss, 3-reel set, 1980s, MOC..$8.50

#1046, Masters of the Universe #2, 3-reel set, 1985, MOC .$3.00

#1050, Princess of Power, 3-reel set, 1985, MOC, from $5 to $8.00

#1059, Jem, 3-reel set, 1986, MOC $7.00

#4047, Michael Jackson's Thriller, 3-reel set, 1984, MOC .$12.00

#4055, Gremlins, 3-reel set, MOC, D4.................................$5.00

#4067, Wrestling Superstars, 3-reel set, 1985, MOC $5.00

#4074, Pee Wee's Playhouse, 3-reel set, MOC....................$8.00

#4086, Who Framed Roger Rabbit, 3-reel set, 1988, MOC, from $10 to $15.00

#4092, Legend of Indiana Jones, 3-reel set, 1989, MOC.....$6.00

#950, Gene Autry, Sawyers, 1950, 1 reel only, Gene Autry & His Wonder Horse, 1950, EX+..................................$3.00

#975, Tarzan Rescues Cheeta, single reel w/booklet, 1950, NM, from $3 to $5.00

A-071, Expo '67, General Tour; Sawyers-GAF, 3-reel set, MIP...$50.00

A-074, Expo '67, Night Scenes & La Ronde; Sawyer-GAF, 3-reel set, MIP..$50.00

A-170, California State Tour, 3-reel set, MIP $20.00

A-172, San Francisco, 3-reel set, MIP (sealed).................$12.00

A-173, San Diego Zoo, 3-reel set, MIP (sealed).................$6.00

A-179, Tomorrowland, Disneyland; 3-reel set, MIP (sealed), from $10 to...$12.50

A-203, Death Valley, 3-reel set, MIP, from $10 to $20.00

A-241, Universal Studios, 3-reel set, MIP (sealed)...........$17.00

A-306, Yellowstone National Park, 3-reel set, 1948, MIP ..$6.00

A-361, Grand Canyon National Park, Sawyers, 3-reel set, MIP...$10.00

A-363, Painted Desert & Petrified Forest National Monument in Arizona, 3-reel set, no date, MIP $7.00

A-425, NASA's Manned Spacecraft Center, GAF, 3 reels & 16-pg booklet, NMIP, T2..$15.00

A-595, Ohio Sights, 3-reel set, 1954, MIP.......................$12.00

A-648, Statue of Liberty, 3-reel set, MIP $9.00

A-650, New York, The Empire State; 3-reel set, 1956, MIP...$12.00

A-652, Rockefeller Center, 3-reel set, 1958, MIP............$18.00

A-655, Niagara Falls, 3-reel set, 1958, MIP $12.00

A-657, Coney Island, 3-reel set, 1956 MIP......................$20.00

A-671, New York World's Fair, General Tour; Sawyer, 3-reel set, 1964, NMIP..$25.00

A-761, Atlantic City Sights, 3-reel set, 1957, MIP $30.00

A-960, Florida, The Peninsula State; 3-reel set, #955, MIP.$12.50

A-969, Cypress Gardens' Floral Paradise, GAF (w/zip code), 3-reel set, T6...$3.00

A-970, Performancer Parrot Jungle in Miami, 3-reel set, 1955, MIP..$6.00

A-988, Bush Gardens in Tampa, Florida; GAF, 3-reel set, MIP..$9.00

A-991, Weeki Wachee, Spring of Live Mermaids; 3-reel set, 1971, MIP..$20.00

B-316, Sword in the Stone, 3-reel set, MIP (sealed)...........$8.00

B-317, Goldilocks & the 3 Bears, GAF, 3-reel set w/booklet, 1970s, MIP...$8.00

B-362, Winnie the Pooh, Sawyers, 5x5" mc envelope & 16-pg booklet, features claymation puppets, 1964, NM.......$12.00

B-372, Peter Pan, 3-reel set, still figures, Disney, 1957, MIP, from $17 to...$20.00

B-376, Mary Poppins, 3-reel set, MIP (sealed), M4 ....$10.00

B-393, James Bond Live & Let Die, 3-reel set w/booklet, MIP, from $15 to...$25.00

B-405, Smokey Bear, 3-reel set, MIP (sealed), M4 ....$10.00

B-462, Roy Rogers, King of the Cowboys; 3-reel set w/booklet, NM (EX+ pkg)...$25.00

B-465, Lone Ranger, Mystery Rustler; 3-reel set, 1956, MIP...$25.00

B-468, Johnny Moccasin w/Jody McCrea, 3-reel set, 1956, MIP, from $15 to...$25.00

B-469, Zorro, 3-reel set, MIP, from $25 to $40.00

B-472, Lassie & Timmy & the Runaway Mule, GAF, 3-reel set, 1958, MIP, from $10 to...$15.00

B-473, Wild Bill Hickok, 3-reel set, NMIP, from $20 to ..$30.00

B-473, William Tell, 3-reel set, 1959, MIP.......................$25.00

B-474, Lassie & Timmy, 3-reel set, MIP (sealed), from $17 to $20.00

B-478, Mod Squad, 3-reel set w/booklet, MIP $25.00

B-480, Lassie Look Homeward, 3-reel set, MIP (sealed), from $10 to..$20.00

B-483, Voyage to the Bottom of the Sea, 3-reel set w/EX viewer, 1966, NMIP, from $35 to $45.00

B-484, Man From UNCLE, 3-reel set w/booklet, 1966, MIP, from $20 to...$45.00

B-485, Flipper, 3-reel set w/booklet, MIP, from $8 to.......$11.00

B-488, Green Hornet, 3-reel set w/booklet, 1966, MIP, from $45 to..$75.00

B-489, Lassie Rides the Log Flume, 3-reel set, 1968, MIP, from $10 to...$15.00

B-491, Time Tunnel, 3-reel set, 1966, MIP, from $25 to .$40.00

B-492, Batman, Catwoman's Purrfect Crime; 3-reel set, 1966, from $20 to...$30.00

B-492, Batman, GAF, 3-reel set, 1976, MIP (sealed), from $8 to $12.00

B-493, Monkees, 3-reel set w/booklet, 1967, MIP, from $25 to $50.00

B-494, Land of the Giants, GAF, 3-reel set w/booklet, 1968, MIP, from $40 to...$65.00

B-495, Flying Nun, 3-reel set w/booklet, MIP, from $15 to..$25.00

B-497, Laugh In, 3-reel set w/booklet, 1968, MIP (sealed), from $20 to..$30.00

B-498, Daktari, 3-reel set w/booklet, NMIP.....................$25.00

B-498, Daniel Boone, 3-reel set w/booklet, 1965, MIP (sealed), from $15 to..$22.00

B-501, Lovebug, 3-reel set, MIP (sealed), M4...................$15.00

B-503, Dark Shadows, 3-reel set, from $60 to..................$75.00

B-504, Lancelot Link, 3-reel set w/booklet, MIP, from $12 to..$20.00

B-505, Mission Impossible, 3-reel set, 1967, MIP.............$20.00

B-506, Million-Dollar Duck, 3-reel set, MIP (sealed), from $15 to...$25.00

B-507, Planet of the Apes, 3-reel set w/booklet, MIP, from $25 to...$35.00

B-513, Top Cat, 3-reel set w/booklet, 1962, MIP, from $15 to..$25.00

B-516, Popeye, 3-reel set, MIP (sealed)............................$6.00

B-517, Disney on Parade, 3-reel set, MIP (sealed)...........$12.00

B-520, Pebbles & Bamm-Bamm, 3-reel set, MIP, from $7 to..$12.00

B-524, Mickey Mouse Club Mouseketeers, GAF, 3-reel set, 1956, MIP, from $25 to..$40.00

B-525, Donald Duck & Flying Saucer Pilots, GAF, 3-reel set, MIP...$12.00

B-526, Mighty Mouse Meets Powerful Puss, GAF, 3-reel set w/booklet, 1958, MIP (sealed), from $12 to..............$20.00

B-528, Mickey Mouse, 3-reel set, 1958, MIP, from $15 to.$25.00

B-531, Bugs Bunny, the Chiseler; Daffy Duck, Moonman; Bugs & Porky, TV Trouble; GAF, 3-reel set, 1959, EX, from $9 to..$20.00

B-532, 101 Dalmations, 3-reel set, MIP (sealed), from $12 to..$17.00

B-533, Casper the Ghost, 3-reel set, MIP (sealed), from $8 to..$10.00

B-537, Blondie & Dagwood, Sawyers, 3-reel set, 1966, MIP, from $20 to..$25.00

B-538, Beep Beep Roadrunner, 3-reel set, MIP (sealed), M4..$10.00

B-539, Dennis the Menace, 3-reel set w/booklet, 1967, MIP, from $4 to..$10.00

B-548, Charlie Brown's Summer Fun, GAF, 3-reel set w/booklet, 1972, MIP, from $8 to....................................$10.00

B-550, Shazam, 3-reel set, MIP (sealed).........................$8.00

B-555, Star Trek, Mr Spock's Time Trek; 3-reel set, 1974, T6..$20.00

B-559, Six Million-Dollar Man, 3-reel set w/booklet, 1974, MIP (sealed), from $8 to...$20.00

B-560, Captain Kangaroo, 3-reel set, MIP (sealed).........$15.00

B-564, Curiosity Shop, 3-reel set, 1971, MIP, from $10 to.$15.00

B-568, Brady Bunch, 3-reel set w/booklet, 1972, MIP......$15.00

B-569, Partridge Family, 3-reel set, 1971, MIP.................$33.00

B-570, Beverly Hillbillies, 3-reel set, 1963, MIP..............$45.00

B-572, Julia, 3-reel set w/booklet, 1969, MIP, from $10 to .$15.00

B-573, Nanny & the Professor, 3-reel set w/booklet, 1970, MIP..$25.00

B-574, Archie, 3-reel set w/booklet, MIP (sealed).............$8.00

B-579, Land of the Lost, 3-reel set, MIP (sealed), from $8 to..$11.00

B-581, Tom Corbett Space Cadet, 3-4331 set w/booklet, from $25 to...$45.00

B-583, Flash Gordon, In the Planet Mongo; 3-reel set, 1976, MIP, from $8 to...$15.00

B-586, Happy Days, The Not Making of a President; 3-reel set w/booklet, MIB (sealed), from $10 to......................$15.00

B-589, Gunsmoke, The Rat Trap; 3-reel set, GAF, 1972, MIP, from $15 to..$25.00

B-590, Captain Kangaroo, 3-reel set, 1957, MIP..............$15.00

B-590, Hawaii Five-O, 3-reel set, MIP (sealed), from $15 to..$20.00

B-591, Search, 3-reel set w/booklet, 1973, NM (EX pkg).$20.00

B-592, Partridge Family, 3-reel set, talking, MIP (sealed), M4..$25.00

B-593, Adam 12, 3-reel set, MIP (sealed).......................$18.00

B-596, Waltons, 3-reel set w/booklet, 1972, MIP (sealed), from $10 to...$15.00

B-597, Emergency, 3-reel set w/booklet, 1973, MIP, from $10 to..$18.00

B-605, Little Yellow Dinosaur, 3-reel set, MIP (sealed), M4...$10.00

B-615, Strange Animals of the World, 3-reel set, 1958, MIP .$11.00

B-662, US Spaceport, GAF, 3-reel set w/16-pg booklet of JFK Space Center in Florida, 1965, NMIP........................$9.00

B-770, A Day at (Ringling Bros Barnum & Bailey) the Circus, 3-reel set, 1952, MIP..$12.50

B-780, Coronation of Elizabeth II, Sawyers, 3-reel set w/booklet, 1953, MIP, from $15 to......................................$25.00

B-790, War Between the States, Sawyer, authentic blk & wht stereograph repros from 1863-64, 3-reel set, MIP, from $27 to...$35.00

B-901, Wonders of the Deep, Sawyers, 3-reel set w/booklet, 1950s, NMIP...$12.00

BB-450, Mannix, Enter Tami Okada; 3-reel set, 1974, MIP (sealed)..$25.00

BB-452, Rookies, 3-reel set w/booklet, 1975, MIP (sealed), from $20 to...$30.00

BB-453, SWAT, 3-reel set w/booklet, 1975, MIP (sealed), from $15 to...$20.00

BB-526, Mighty Mouse, 3-reel set, GAF, 1970s, EX (VG pkg) $5.00

FT-8, Little Black Sambo, in orig envelope, 3-reel set, 1948, EX..$8.00

H-11, Spiderman, 3-reel set, MIP...................................$12.00

H-2, Dr Shrinker & Wonderbug, Krofft Supershow #1, 3-reel set w/booklet, 1977, MIP, from $8 to.............................$25.00

H-21, Main Street, Disney World; 3-reel set, MIP (sealed).$8.00

H-22, Frontierland, Disney World, 3-reel set, MIP (sealed) .$8.00

H-24, Liberty Square, 3-reel set, MIP (sealed)..................$8.00

H-44, Iron Man, Spell of the Black Widow; 3-reel set w/booklet, MIP (sealed)..$8.00

H-56, Mr Magoo, 3-reel set, 1977, MIP...........................$8.00

J-1, Buck Rogers, 3-reel cartoon version set w/booklet, 1978, MIP (sealed), from $8 to..$12.00

J-10, Grizzley Adams, Life & Times of; 3-reel set, 1978, MIP.$10.00

J-11, M*A*S*H, Major Topper; 3-reel set w/booklet, 1978, MOC...$10.00

J-13, Happy Days, Requiem for a Malph; 3-reel set w/booklet, MIP (sealed)...$15.00

J-14, Wizard of Oz, The Wiz; 3-reel set w/booklet, from Broadway musical, 1978, MIP (sealed) $20.00

J-20, Laverne & Shirley, 3-reel set, 1978, MIP (sealed), from $6 to $15.00

J-21, Little Orphan Annie, 3-reel set, MIP, M4.................$10.00

J-26, Incredible Hulk, 3-reel set, 1978, MIP $10.00

J-47, Close Encounters of the Third Kind, 3-reel set w/booklet, 1977, MIP, from $9 to $25.00

J-78, Superman, The Movie; 3-reel set w/booklet, 1978, MIP, from $12 to...$20.00

K-22, Dr Strange, 3-reel cartoon version set w/booklet, 1979, MIP (sealed) $10.00

K-35, Black Hole, 3-reel set w/booklet, 1979, MIP (sealed), from $10 to $20.00

K-37, Winnie the Pooh, GAF, 3-reel set w/booklet, 1979, MIP (sealed)..$10.00

K-57, Star Trek, The Motion Picture; 3-reel set, 1979, MIP..$8.00

K-68, James Bond Moonraker, 3-reel set w/booklet, 1979, MIP (sealed), from $12 to..$18.00

K-71, KISS, 3-reel set w/booklet, 1979, MIP, from $22 to.$30.00

K-76, Eight Is Enough, 3-reel set w/booklet, 1980, MIP (sealed), from $8 to...$16.00

L-15, Buck Rogers, Real Photo version, 3-reel set, 1979, MIP $20.00

L-17, Dukes of Hazzard, 3-reel set w/booklet, 1980, MIP (sealed), from $6 to...$18.00

L-27, Jetsons, 3-reel set w/booklet, 1981, MIP (sealed) $4.00

L-32, Vote I Go Pogo, 3-reel set w/booklet, 1980, MIP....$10.00

L-6, Flintstones, Sawyers, 3-reel set w/booklet, 1962, MIP (sealed), from $15 to...$25.00

M-1, Museum of Science & Industry, 3-reel set, MIP (sealed)..$14.00

TJ-029, Mickey Mouse, 3-reel set, talking, MIP (sealed)..$12.00

Windups, Friction, and Other Mechanicals

Windup toys represent a fun and exciting field of collecting. Our fascination with them stems from their simplistic but exciting actions and brightly colored lithography, and especially the comic character or personality-related examples are greatly in demand by collectors today. Though most were made during the years of the thirties through the fifties, they carry their own weight against much earlier toys and are considered very worthwhile investments. Various types of mechanisms were used — some are key wound while others depend on lever action to tighten the mainspring and release the action of the toy. Tin and celluloid were used in their production, and although it is sometimes possible to repair a tin windup, experts advise against investing in a celluloid toy whose mechanism is not working, since the material is usually too fragile to withstand the repair.

Many of the boxes that these toys came in are almost as attractive as the toys themselves and can add considerably to their value. We have included friction toys in this category as well as other types of mechanicals. Our advisor for this category is Richard Trautwein (T3). See also Chein; Lehmann; Marx; Strauss.

American

Aero Speeder, Buffalo, litho tin, planes w/celluloid propellers, spring-loaded helical screw action, orig box, 10", G, A $209.00

Airplane, Girard, tin w/bull's-eye wing decals, pilot in cockpit, w/complete decal, 12½", EX-, A $325.00

Ambulance, Wyandotte, plastic, friction, w/siren & stretcher, early, 9", EX $125.00

Amusement Park, Wyandotte, Ferris wheel, go-round & plane ride, lever & spring mechanism, working, 11½x16", VG, A $300.00

Artillery Truck, Kingsbury, steers, gun swivels & raises, EX $1,100.00

Battleship, Wyandotte, 4 sets of guns (1 set sparks), prop spins, scarce, 14½", EX, A $180.00

Bicycle and Rider, American, ca 1900, 6", D10, $650.00.

Biplane, Schieble, yel w/pnt tin pilot, rudder swivels, prop turns, working, 15", G-VG, A $325.00

Black Boy on Tricycle, Stevens & Brown, various materials, cloth clothes, motor housing rpt, 11", G, A $1,650.00

Black Jigger, Automations, jtd wood figure on wood box, cloth clothes, Pat Sept 23, 1873, 11", VG+, A $660.00

Black Man w/Cart, G Levy, litho tin, advances as legs move, ca 1920, scarce, 7", EX+-NM, A...................................$380.00

Bombo the Monk, Unique Art, orig box water damaged, 9½", EX, A $121.00

Boy on Soap Box Scooter, B&R, pull-cord mechanism, 8", VG, A $302.50

Brudder Bones, seated Black minstrel doll, Secor, CI & other materials, cloth clothes, clockwork, 10", VG, A $11,550.00

Bus, Dayton, 2-tone orange-yel & blk, friction, non-working, 26", G-, A $260.00

Capitol Hill Racer, Unique Art, litho tin, spring pushes car up & down, working, orig box (end torn), 16", VG-EX, A $150.00

Carousel, Althof-Bergmann, cloth, tin, wire & wood, bsk doll turns crank, very rare, 20x18" dia, rstr, VG+, A ..$4,070.00

Caterpillar Tractor, Cortland, #6100, litho tin w/rubber treads, full-figure driver, 5½", NM (NM box), A $115.00

Charlie Chaplin Mechanical Walking Toy, B&R, litho tin, CI feet, orig arms, orig worn box, VG.....................$1,600.00

Checker Cab, Courtland, #4000, driver lithoed in 3 windows, 7", NMIB, A $130.00

Children on See-Saw, Irwin, 2 actions, ca 1955-56, 4½", EX...$75.00

Circus Shooting Gallery, Ohio Art, tin, working, 1950s, EX, C8 ....$65.00

Clown Motorcycle w/Acrobat Monkeys, Wyandotte, litho tin, 10" dia, EX, A $302.50

Commando Joe, Ohio Art, crawling soldier, early 1950s, M, (VG box) $150.00

Coupe, Girard, gr w/orange fenders & bumpers, electric lights, w/up motor, w/orig bulbs & battery cover, 14", NM, A...$440.00

Coupe, Scheible, blk & red w/yel wheels, friction, working, 1 headlight missing, 17½", G-, A, from $125 to.........$175.00

Coupe w/Rumble Seat, Kingsbury, lavender & purple, operating front headlamp, lt pnt scratches, motor skips, 12½", A..$250.00

Crawling Soldier, Ohio Art, litho tin, 8", EX, A............$110.00

Curve-Dash Oldsmobile, Acme, pressed steel, rubber tires, cloth upholstered seat, clockwork mechanism, 11", EX, A $220.00

Dancing Cinderella & Prince, Irwin, pnt plastic figures, working, orig box, 5", EX, A $110.00

Deco Roadster, Wyandotte, red w/4 molded fenders, blk wood wheels, working, 9⅞", G-, A $83.00

Donald Rocket, litho tin Donald atop rocket holding handlebar, 1950s, 7", EX (EX box), A $751.00

Double Black Dancers, Ives, jtd wood figures on base, red cloth outfits, clockwork, 10", VG+, A $495.00

Drum Major, Wolverine, yel & bl w/blk & wht highlights, working, faded, scratches, lt pitting, 13½", G-, A.............$65.00

Extension Ladder Truck, Wilkins, metal & wood, 10", VG+, A..$440.00

Finnegan, Unique Art, litho tin, figure w/luggage cart, 14", luggage cutouts on box, 14", VG (NM box), A............$248.00

Fire Chief Car, Lupor, friction, fireman litho in ea window, mk Co #7, siren, 7", NMIB, A....................................$140.00

Fire Chief Car, Lupor, litho tin, red & wht, friction, w/siren, working, 8½", VG-EX, A.......................................$55.00

Fire Engine w/Fire Fightin' Fireman, Nosco, friction, plastic, w/12 accessories, 1950s, 8", MIB, A $40.00

Fire Pumper, Kingsbury, steering wheel missing, well used, pnt only fair, working, 6½x9½", A $195.00

Five Jolly Darkies, Reed, litho paper on wood, crank action, paper darkened, hdl rpl, 9", G, A $165.00

Flying Zeppelin, aluminum, never had pnt, w/up propeller, minor dents, 16", EX (P box), A $375.00

Frankensycle, Ideal, Scare Cycle series, EX (VG box), T1..$85.00

Gad Jet Racer, Allan Sales Co., Los Angeles, 7½", MIB, $275.00.

Doin' the Howdy Doody, Unique Art, lithographed tin, working, 8¼", VG-EX (G box), A, $1,250.00.

Galloping Horse Pulling Wagon, man driver, Ives, 1870s, EX, D10, $6,500.00.

Doin' the Howdy Doody, Unique Art, mc litho tin, Howdy dances to Buffalo Bill's playing, clockwork, working, 8", G, A $650.00

Donald Duck & Pluto Handcar, Lionel, pnt metal w/compo figures, clockwork, 10", G, A $357.50

Gertie Goose, Unique Art, litho tin, goose bounces around while pecking at the ground, 9", A $146.00

GI Joe & His Jouncing Jeep, Unique Art, circles w/crazy action, 1944, 7", EX, A.....................................$150.00

GI Joe & His Jouncing Jeep, Unique Art, colorful orig box, 7", EX, A, from $200 to $300.00

GI Joe & His Jouncing Jeep, Unique Art, mc litho tin, clockwork, working, 6½", VG, A.....................................$110.00

G.I. Joe and His K-9 Pups, Unique Art, lithographed tin, original box, 9", EX, A, $285.00.

Giant Ride, Ohio Art, litho tin w/plastic seats, Ferris wheel spins, bell sounds, midway scenes on base, 17", EX, A $283.00

Golden Arrow Race Car, Kingsbury, pressed steel, missing side panels, 1 tire & tail fin, clockwork, working, P, W1..$345.00

Hansom Cab, Converse, 2 passenger w/rear motor, driver at rear, yel spoked wheels, 1895, 8½x10½", A.....................$345.00

Hillbilly Express, Unique Art, litho tin, 3" train engine travels from station house to end & bk, 16", EX (NM box), A........$237.00

Hood & Ladder Truck, Turner, pnt & litho tin, red, gold & blk, friction, non-working, missing parts, 12½", G-, A.....$30.00

Hook & Ladder Truck, Scheible, red, friction, working, rear ladder support missing, 20", G-, A $60.00

Hopalong Cassidy Shooting Gallery, ATC/USA, hit moving outlaws, shoots bb's, 22x14", NMIB, A $400.00

Hopalong Cassidy Shooting Gallery, ATC/USA, litho tin, shoot revolving figures w/gun, 1950s, 15", EX- (EX box), A .$283.00

Howdy Doody & Buffalo Bob at Piano, Unique Art, litho tin, Bob plays piano & Howdy dances, NM (NM box), A.....$2,000.00

Howdy Doody & Buffalo Bob at Piano, Unique Art, litho tin, Howdy dances while Buffalo Bob plays piano, EX (VG box), A $900.00

Humphrey Mobile, Wyandotte, litho tin, clockwork, working, chimney missing, 8½", G, A....................................$180.00

Ice Cream Scooter, Courtland, mc litho tin w/rubber wheels, clockwork (bells ring), working, orig box, 6½", VG-EX, A..$230.00

Injun Chief, Ohio Art, crawling Indian w/tomahawk, 7½", NM, A $100.00

Jazzbo Jim, Unique Art, Jim dances & plays banjo atop cabin, 10", NM (EX box), A...$800.00

Jazzbo Jim, Unique Art, mc litho tin, clockwork, mechanism runs, figure won't dance, 10¼", VG, A...................$300.00

Jazzbo Jim, Unique Art, 1 tall & 1 short minstrel atop cabin roof, not working/slight fading on 1 side, VG+, M5 ....$345.00

Jocko the Golfer, B&K, litho tin, pull-cord mechanism, orig box separated, figure flaking, 6½", G, A $412.50

Jungle Pete the Mechanical Alligator, Automatic Toy, litho tin alligator advances w/snapping jaws, 15", NM (EX box), A..$145.00

Kid Sampson, B&R, litho tin, man swings mallet, strikes bell to test strength, 1921, 9", EX, A $1,400.00

Kid Special, B&R, boy on yel & cycle w/red wheels, 1920s, 6", box w/repro flap, EX (EX box), A $585.00

Kid Special, B&R, litho tin, yel, red & bl, rear string-wind clockwork, 2 motions, working, 6½", VG, A...........$200.00

Kiddy Cyclist, Unique Art, 9", NM, D10, $275.00.

Kiddy Cyclist, Unique Art, blond boy pedals trike w/erratic motion & ringing bell, 7x8", EX (EX box), A $365.00

Kiddy Cyclist, Unique Art, mc litho tin, working, orig box (tape rpr), 7", VG, A $300.00

Ladder Truck, Kingsbury, steel & CI, rubber tires, wood ladder, clockwork, working, 18½", G+, A................................$80.00

Li'l Abner & His Dogpatch Band, Unique Art, Abner dances, Daisy at piano, Pappy Yokems at drums, 9", MIB, A............$1,400.00

Li'l Abner & His Dogpatch Band, Unique Art, Mammy atop piano, Pappy on drums, EX (EX box), A, from $550 to $690.00

Li'l Abner & His Dogpatch Band, Unique Art, mc litho tin, clockwork, 4 motions, working, orig box (tape rpr), 7", VG, A..$470.00

Li'l Abner & His Dogpatch Band, Unique Art, 4 characters at piano & drums, 8½", VG, A $345.00

Limousine, Scheible, pnt pressed steel, dk bl w/yel wheels, friction, working, bumper missing, 17", G, A.................$190.00

Lincoln Tunnel, Unique Art, cars, bridges, terminals & policeman, orig box, 24", VG, A $345.00

Loop De Loop Carnival, Wolverine #30, litho tin w/carnival scene, car races through center track, 19", NM (VG box), A $480.00

Mammy, Lindstrom, shakes bk & forth & sideways, 8", EX, from $175 to...$200.00

Man From Mars, Irwin, red plastic, missing antenna, EX .$295.00

Man From Mars, yel plastic w/rubber antenna, rare color, EX (EX box), A $525.00

Man on the Flying Trapeze, Wyandotte, litho tin, athlete swings, twists & turns on trapeze, box mk #516, 9x3x5", EX+, A...$190.00

Marching Drum Major, Wolverine, litho tin, red & bl uniform, yel drum w/red & blk trim, rnd base, 1930s, 13½", EX, A..$183.00

Mechanical Bear, Ives, various materials, fur-covered bear on wood box w/paper label, box lid missing, 8", VG+, A $605.00

Mechanical Billiard Table, Ranger Steel, litho tin, 2 men shooting pool at 5x10" table, men: 5½", EX (G box), A..$253.00

Mechanical Boxers, Ives, CI, compo & wood, 2 figures on base, tattered cloth clothes, extremely rare, 11", G, A .$3,740.00

Mickey & Minnie Mouse Handcar, Lionel, O ga, w/circle track, loose spring, non-working, 7½", G, A......................$350.00

Mickey Mouse Circus Train w/Mickey Barker, Lionel, litho tin, 1930s, VG+, A...$1,450.00

Mickey Mouse Handcar, Lionel, wheels/tails rpl, 6x8", o/w NM (VG box), A...$850.00

Mickey Mouse Handcar, Lionel, composition figures, 7" long, NM (NM box), A, $2,300.00.

Monkey Shines, Emporium, weight driven, monkey carries coconuts down trunk of palm tree, 1950, 18", NM (EX box), A $220.00

Motor Ambulance, Kingsbury, pnt tin w/CI driver, plated steering wheel, bell rings (non-working), working, 6¾", G, A $450.00

Motorcycle Cop & Car, Automatic Toy, molded plastic car w/motorcycle cop on string, orig box (rpr), 12", EX, A $100.00

Open Auto, Scheible, pnt pressed steel, gray w/bl fenders & red gas tank, pnt tin driver & passenger, 11", G, A.......$500.00

Operation Airlift, ATC, escort plane circles & buzzes transport plane, prewar, slight box rpr, 16x10", NM, A..........$200.00

Orio Tailspin Pup, spinning action, tail also spins, 1930s, 5x4", MIB, A..$65.00

Pan-Gee the Funny Dancer, CE Carter, litho tin, 10", VG, A $357.50

Panama Pile Driver, Wolverine, pnt & litho tin, seated figure rides wheeled lift, marble powered, orig box, 15", VG, A $35.00

Peter Rabbit Chick-Mobile, Lionel, compo Peter pumps handcar w/basket, pressed steel base, 1930s, 9", EX, from $650 to...$700.00

Peter Rabbit Chick-Mobile, Lionel, pnt compo figure & basket, steel chassis, clockwork rings bell, rpl eye, 10", VG, A $440.00

Playland Roller Coaster Shoot the Shoots, Cragston, yel & red litho tin track w/mc cars, 11x22", EX+ (VG+ box), A $188.00

Pool Players, Wyandotte, litho tin, 14", VG+, A $143.00

Race Car, Kingsbury, pnt tin, metallic gr, emb wht rubber tires, front wheels trn (some rust), 1932, 20", A...............$275.00

Racer, Lupor, #597, red & yel litho tin w/fire-breathing dragon images, blk rubber wheels, 11½", VG (VG+ box), A $128.00

Railroad Handcar, Girard, litho tin, w/2 workmen, 6", VG, A $121.00

Rap & Tap in a Friendly Scrap, Unique Art, litho tin, Red Mike & Smiling Jack in boxing ring, 1920s, 6", VG+ (EX box), A..$513.00

Red Devil Racer, Budwill, red litho tin w/yel accents, half-figure in cockpit, break lever on hood, 8", EX (VG box), A $330.00

Robot Bus #300, Woodhaven Metal Stamping, litho sides, silver roof, blk rubber tires, working, orig box, 14⅜", NM, A..$231.00

Rocking-R-Ranch See-Saw, Courtland, litho tin, ca 1955-57, 6x18", M, (VG box) $215.00

Rodeo Joe in His Yipee-I-Aaay Jouncing Jeep, Unique Art, Joe & car rock bk & forth, 8x10", EX $200.00

Rodeo Joe in His Yipee-I-Aaay Jouncing Jeep, Unique Art, 9x8", NMIB, A...$350.00

Runabout Auto, Hafner, sheet metal, rubber tires, cloth upholsted seat, clockwork mechanism, rare, 7", G, A.......$110.00

Runabout Auto, Ives, pnt CI, missing clockwork mechanism, 7", G, A...$330.00

Runabout Truck w/Metal Canopy, Acme, rubber tires, clockwork mechanism, top rpt & soldered, 11", VG, A...$605.00

Sea Plane, Ohio Art, red, wht, bl & yel, actually works on water, 10x6", NM, A...$145.00

Shopping Betty, holds shopping bags, circles & spins, 8x3½", VG+, A..$140.00

Single Boy Trapeze Toy, litho tin, 12", G.........................$44.00

Sky Rangers, Unique Art, tin, working, EX....................$195.00

Sky Rangers, Unique Art, 6" w/up airplane climbs & circles around lithoed lighthouse, w/instructions, NM (G+ box), A..$600.00

Snare Drummer, Wyandotte, litho tin, 13", G, A...........$110.00

Soldier, Lindstrom, litho tin, olive gr, red & orange, clockwork, working, 6½", VG, A..$140.00

Speed Boat, Lindstrom, w/driver, prop spins, 7½", EX, A.$120.00

Speed King (boy on soap box scooter), Wyandotte, litho tin, 6", VG, A..$187.00

Stake Truck, Girard, bl & red, blk wood wheels w/red hubcaps on rear, plated grille & trim, working, 11¼", VG-EX, A..$165.00

Stake Truck, Kingsbury, pnt tin, olive w/rubber tires, working, 10¾", G-VG, A...$450.00

State Police Car, Courtland, litho tin, bl & wht, friction, working, orig box, 7", EX, A..$110.00

Stutz Racer, Gilbert, litho tin, yel car w/driver & plated grille, crank hdl, working (gear slips), 9", VG, A..............$475.00

Sunbeam Racer, litho tin, 1930s, EX, T3.......................$795.00

Sweeping Betty, Lindstrom, tin, ca 1930s, 8", EX..........$195.00

Sweeping Mammy, Lindstrom, litho tin, brn, yel, red & wht, clockwork, working, 8", VG+ (VG box), A.........................$280.00

Sweeping Mammy, Lindstrom, red dress, wht apron, yel stockings, 1930s, 8", NM (NM box), A............................$450.00

Teddy Bear Bicycle Aerialist, Gilbert, litho tin, colorful image of a Roosevelt bear, 7", EX, A..$187.00

Train Engine, Boss emb on side, early, 5½x3x7¾", EX, A..$500.00

Tricky Trolley, Mattel, red plastic w/yel trim, w/litho tin passengers, early 1950s, 4½x7½", EX......................................$85.00

Truck #1300, Courtland, M (EX+ box)..........................$250.00

U.S. Mail Electric-Type Delivery Truck, Gilbert, lithographed tinplate, ca 1916, 8¼" long, VG, A, $550.00.

US Mail Delivery Truck, early style, bl w/driver, crank in front, may have had bk door, wear/rust/tears, 5½x8", G-, A..........$150.00

US Mail Delivery Truck, Gilbert, 1916 era, blk & yel, w/driver, Parcel Post on side, red spoked wheels, 8¼", VG, A..$550.00

Walt Disney's Cinderella & Prince, Irwin, plastic, 1950s, 5½", NM (EX box), A...$255.00

Thimble Drome Race Car #63, Cox/Champion, M (VG box), D10, $850.00.

Thunderbolt Racer, Kingsbury, red & silver, w/driver, blk rubber tires, 1938, 18", VG, A...$400.00

Tiger Steam Engine, Ives, pnt tin, clockwork mechanism, 10", G, A..$825.00

TJ Hooker LCPD Police Car, Fleetwood, friction, MOC, H4...$8.00

Town Car, Girard, dk bl & blk, ivory seat, plated grille & trim, blk wood wheels, friction, non-working, 6", NM, A..$154.00

Winner Motorcycle, American, lithographed tin, friction, 1960s, 8", MIB, D10, $175.00.

Yellow Taxi, Mohawk, pnt tin, yel & blk, clockwork, working, G, A..$70.00

Zilotone, Wolverine, litho & pnt steel, orange & bl, clockwork, working, w/6 disks, 9", VG, A...................................$325.00

English

#7 Racer, litho tin, red w/Dunlop Fort tires, litho tin driver, working, lt rust, 12½", G-VG, A.............................$190.00

Broderick Crawford Highway Patrol Siren Car, Welsotoy, lithographed tin, friction, NM (G box), A, $385.00.

Broderick Crawford Highway Patrol Car, Welsotoy, 11", Chief shown on box, VG (G box) $195.00

Chad Valley Racing Car, Chad Valley, litho tin, red & wht, clockwork, working, orig box, 11½", EX, A.............$200.00

Chief Dan Mathews Siren Car, Welsotoy, litho tin, wht & bl w/rubber wheels, friction w/siren, orig box, 11", VG-EX, A..$340.00

Clown Riding Stubborn Ass, litho tin clown on donkey w/rubber ears, 6½", EX (G+ box), A................................$275.00

Disneyland Skating Rink, Mettoy, litho tin, w/decal, plastic figures, friction, working, orig box, 6", VG-EX, A.......$200.00

Double-Decker Bus, Brimtoy, litho tin, clockwork, non-working, 4½", VG, A...$50.00

Ford Royal Mail Van, Minic, litho tin, 100% decals, 3½", EX+ (NM box), A $165.00

G-A MTY Passenger Plane, twin engine, slight wear & scuffs, 18x20", EX, A...$300.00

Gyro Cycle, Tri-Ang, various metals w/celluloid figure, gyroscope action, orig box, 8", EX, A $286.00

Hawk Speedboat, Sutcliffe, w/decals & windshield, orig key, flag & keyhole cover, 1950s, 12½", NM (EX box), A......$85.00

Hi-Wing Monoplane, litho tin, British bull's eye on wings, balloon tires, 1930s, 17" wingspan, VG+, A $175.00

Inverted Clown, Wells, litho tin, stars & crescent moons on pants, clockwork, working, orig box, 4¾", VG-EX, A...$110.00

Jupiter Ocean Pilot Cruiser, Sutcliffe, metal, separate pilot plaque on deck, orig key, 9½", NM (EX box), A.....$105.00

Lady Penelope's Fab I Car, J Rosenthal, pk plastic w/authentic detail, friction, 1960s, 10", M (NM box), A.............$225.00

Motor Car #3, Meccano, 2-seater, boat-tailed, yel & red, lg head-lamps, driver in wht w/red helmet, 12", VG, A......$1,000.00

Open Limousine, Wells, litho tin, bl & yel w/blk trim, clock-work, working, 9", VG-EX, A $170.00

Police Patrol Motorcycle, Mettoy, detailed litho tin w/spoked Dunlop balloon tires, 1930s, 8", EX, A $425.00

Rodeo Joe, unusual English version, lithographed tin, EX (EX box), A, $380.00.

Rodeo Joe Git Along Lil' Doggie, cowboy driving red crazy car, cowboy's hat has indentations on all sides, 7x7", NMIB, A...$375.00

Sedan, Mettoy, yel & red litho tin, blk balloon tires w/yel hubs, moves forward, 9", EX+, A......................................$204.00

Stubborn Ass w/Clown Rider, litho tin, donkey has rubber ears, 6½", EX (G box), A..$275.00

Super Skyliner, Mettoy, litho tin, red, yel w/bl trim, w/up motor turns prop & wheels, working, 16¾", VG, A...........$325.00

French

Bowler, Martin, 1880s, EX, D10, $1,500.00.

Auto Miracle, Brevete #2002, litho tin, 8 different movements, full-figure driver, 5½", NM (EX box), A.................$288.00

Boy on Scooter, Bonnet, pnt tin, cloth clothes, VG, A..$3,300.00

Cakewalk Dancer, Martin, pnt tin, cloth clothes, rare, 8", G-, A..$3,740.00

Clown Orchestra, Bonnet, pnt tin, lever-action toy, cloth clothes, 10", G, A...$440.00

Clowns w/Chairs, various materials, compo heads, cloth clothes, 2 are articulated, third has clockwork, 20", G, A..$1,870.00

Convertible Auto, Citroen, gr w/blk fenders, Michelin tires, headlights, '30s style, rpl door/canvas/fr, 15", G, A..$900.00

CR 9 Monoplane, litho tin, red & gray plane w/pnt rudder, prop turns, working, 14", VG-EX, A.................$200.00

Delivery Boy, Martin-Bonnet, pnt tin, boy pushing 2-wheeled cart w/box, cloth clothes, 8½", VG, A.................$385.00

Delivery Man, Martin, pnt & litho tin, inertia toy, man pulling 2-wheeled cart, 6", EX, A.................$467.50

English Bobby, Martin, pnt tin w/wire & lead, cloth clothes, walking action, 8", G, A.................$2,310.00

English Trap, Martin, pnt tin, inertia toy, man pulling 2-wheeled cart w/2 girls, ca 1892, 7", VG+, A........$3,410.00

Extension-Ladder Truck, JEP, litho tin, 12", VG+, A....$522.50

Fiddler, Martin, in top hat & checked pants, NM, L5 .$1,550.00

Fire Truck, JEP, tin, 7", EX.................................$350.00

Girl Skipping Rope, Saut De Corde, girl moves as wheel turns, friction, litho label on orig box, 4x3½x7½", EX, A.$500.00

Hansom Cab, Martin, pnt tin, bl w/red wheels, 9", VG+, A...$495.00

Horse Race Game, pnt metal, 8 horses circle track, lever action, working, fabric-covered wood box, 10½" sq, G, A ..$275.00

Irish Mail, Bonnet, pnt tin, mailman in motor trike, rpl motor cover, spring skips, 7½", G-, A.................$38.50

La Joyeuse Grenouille (The Joyful Frog), Joustra, litho tin singing frog w/banjo, rubber feet, 4¼", NM (EX+ box), A...$77.00

Lady Piano Player, Martin, pnt tin w/wire & lead figure, cloth clothes, 5", G, A...$907.50

Lady w/Baby, Martin, pnt tin w/wire & lead, cloth clothes, lady rocks baby, 8", G+, A.................$4,620.00

Les Auto Transports Road Tractor, Martin-Bonnet, pnt tin, 6½", G, A...$110.00

Les Auto Transports w/Trailer, Martin-Bonnet, pnt tin, complex clockworks, w/orig paper instructions, 13", VG, A..$687.50

Lion Nodder on Rock, Decamps, papier-mache w/cloth & fur, wood base, clockwork mechanism, 15", G+, A $247.50

Male Piano Player, Martin, pnt tin, cloth clothes, 5" , G .$176.00

Man Climbing Ladder, FM, clockwork, bl coat, gray pants, blk shoes, brn lint hair, metal ladder, orig box, 8", G, A $800.00

Mme Crainquebille, pnt tin & compo, orange, gr, red & bl, clockwork, working, orig box (end flap damage), 6", EX, A $400.00

Moto-Police, SFA, litho tin, policeman in sidecar w/sparking machine gun, balloon tires, 1930s, 4", EX (EX box), A $375.00

Motorcycle & Sidecar w/Rider, mk 756, litho tin, 4", VG, A $67.00

Mysterious Ball, Martin, litho tin ball spirals up platform where figure emerges, clockwork, working, 13¾", VG, A..$750.00

Nautilus Submarine, JEP, pnt metal, gray & wht, working, brass plugs for access to motor & drain, 16", EX, A $150.00

Orange Vendor, Martin, pnt tin, cloth clothes, walking action, 6", VG+, A...$1,375.00

Organ Grinder, SIJIM, litho tin w/wire & lead, compo head, dual hand action, 9¼", VG+, A.................$1,155.00

Paris Tokio Biplane, litho tin, yel w/red trim, litho tin pilot, w/up prop, rpl rudder, non-working, 7¾", VG, A....$850.00

Performing Bear, Martin, pnt tin w/brn felt-type cloth covering body, VG+, A...$577.50

Pousse Pousse, red, pnt tin & compo, red, bl & yel, clockwork, working, orig box (end flap damage), 6½", EX, A ...$325.00

Rabbit in Cabbage, Decamps, various materials w/fur-covered rabbit, rabbit pops up & shakes ears, clockwork, 8", G, A $770.00

Railway Porter, Martin, pnt tin, inertia toy, man pushing 2-wheeled cart w/box, 5½", VG, A $825.00

Limousine, Georges Carrette, hand-painted tin, clockwork non-working, 8½" long, G+, A, $3,300.00.

Seaplane with Pilot, J.E.P. lithographed tinplate, keywind, ca 1935, 9x13½x10", A, $2,185.00.

Ruban Bleu #O Speed Boat, JEP, pnt metal, bl & wht w/cast metal pilot, working, detached rudder, 12", VG-EX, A.....................$140.00

Ruban Bleu #1 Speed Boat, JEP, pnt metal, red & bl w/cast metal pilot & removable deck, orig box, 13½", VG-EX, A.....................$250.00

Sack Race, Martin, pnt tin w/cloth clothes, boy in gunnysack, rare, 6½", G+, A.....................$4,400.00

Smasher of Plates, Martin, pnt tin, Dutch girl in bl dress & wht apron wobbles to spill plates, 6½", G, A.....................$522.50

Speed Boat #4, JEP, pnt tin, red & wht w/cast metal pilot, working, rpt figure & windshield, 17", VG, A.....................$350.00

Springing Lion, Decamps, fur-covered papier-mache, clockwork, 16", VG, A.....................$209.00

Springing Tiger, Decamps, fur-covered papier-mache, clockwork, 16", VG, A, from $350 to.....................$450.00

Squirrel on Treadmill, squirrel runs in wire cage mtd to building, gr platform base, clockwork, working, 8½", G-VG, A.....................$100.00

Street Sweeper, Martin, pnt tin w/wire & lead, cloth clothes, 7", G-, A.....................$1,870.00

Strongman, Martin, pnt tin w/wire & lead, cloth clothes, rare, 7½", G-, A.....................$4,070.00

Swimming Doll (Ondine), Martin, wood & other materials w/celluloid head, clockwork, 9", VG+ A.....................$154.00

Walking Poodle, Decamps, fur-covered compo & papier-mache, walks & turns head, clockwork mechanism, 11", EX, A.....................$330.00

Wood Pigeon, Bonnet, pnt tin, 8", G, A.....................$852.50

German

Airplane Carousel, Doll & Cie, 4 airplanes fly around gr canopy-top carousel, early flag atop, 1920, 9x9x10", A....$1,000.00

Airplane on Rail Car, Bing, pnt tin, 8", G+, A.....................$286.00

Airplane w/Flying Saucers, W Germany, litho tin, 3 propped disks on plane launches as plane moves, 8", EX (NM box), A.....................$72.00

Airship R-100, Tipp, litho & emb tin, silver w/blk trim, prop rpt, working, 13½", VG, A.....................$275.00

Alpine Climber, Technofix, no key, 1950s, T1.....................$150.00

American Yellow Cab, pnt & litho tin, bl & yel-orange, mk Lenox 530 on rear, doors open, clockwork, working, 7½", G, A.....................$180.00

Army Staff Car, Hauser, camo colors, 2 soldiers in front seat, 8", 7" cannon behind, 2 figures gone/non-working, G, A.....................$650.00

Automatic Loader, Technofix, mc litho tin, clockwork, working, orig box (1 tab torn), 28", EX, A.....................$75.00

Automobile, Bing, gray w/blk top & trim, taxi-like appearance, front wheels turn left or right, 3⅜x5½", VG, A.....................$200.00

Touring Car with Four Passengers, Carrette, hand-painted and lithographed tin, clockwork, 8¼", VG, A, $4,700.00.

Violinist, Martin, pnt tin w/wire & lead, cloth clothes, top hat, 8", G+, A.....................$495.00

Walking Elephant, Decamps, leather-covered papier-mache, articulated front legs, 15", VG+, A.....................$440.00

Black Girl With Broom, M, D10, $350.00.

Baby the Monkey Cyclist, Arnold, litho tin, brn, red, yel & bl, clockwork, working, 4", VG+, A $160.00

Barney Google Riding Spark Plug, Nifty, litho tin, complete/orig, 7", EX+, A.................................$2,450.00

Barney Google Riding Spark Plug, Nifty, litho tin, some tab retainers missing, G, A $550.00

Baron Limousine #540, litho tin, MIB.........................$150.00

Bear Winding Music Box, pnt tin w/straw-stuffed bear, plink-plunk music mechanism in barrel, 7", VG, A..........$467.50

Beetle, mc litho tin, walks & flaps wings, 1895, 4", EX+ (NM+ box), A $515.00

Billy Goats Butting Heads, Einfalt, litho tin, 8½", VG+, A...$632.50

Bird, flaps wings & tail, 4½x7", EX-NM, A $100.00

Black Boy & Dog, litho tin, orange, brn, wht & bl, clockwork, touch-up, 6½", G-, A $210.00

Black Figure, joined silhouette on canister base w/hand crank, goes up & down & does jig, 8", EX, A $200.00

Black Man Versus Wht Man, litho tin, clockwork, L5..$2,450.00

Boat-Tail Racer, litho tin, orange w/driver, working, 10½", VG, A $325.00

Bowing Man on Base, Gunthermann, pnt tin, 8", G-, A.$231.00

Boxing Elephant, Schuco, gray felt, 1935, sluggish w/up, 8", A $750.00

Boy Drinking Beer, Schuco, pnt tin & cloth, brn hair, brn suit, gr hat, bl ceramic mug, working, 5", EX-, A $120.00

Boy on Sled, Hess, litho tin, friction, working, 6", G-VG, A $375.00

Boy w/Hoop & Bell, Gunthermann (?), pnt tin, boy on 2-wheeled cart, 8", G, A.................................$330.00

Cabrino 359, CKO, car converts to convertible w/driver or hard-top, lever activated, tin balloon tires, 6", NMIB, A...$416.00

Camouflage Cycle w/Soldiers, Kellerman, litho tin, 2 full-figure soldiers w/rifles, non-working, 6", G, A $384.00

Carousel, Gunthermann, musical, pnt fair, some retouching, 1800s, 15½", A $825.00

Carousel w/4 Figures on Horses & Pigs, Gunthermann, M, L5...$1,475.00

Cat Drummer, Gunthermann, ca 1910, 7", EX+, D10, $600.00.

Charlie Chaplin Dancer, litho tin Charlie on base, crank lever for action, scarce, EX, A $2,125.00

Chicken Fight, Einfalt, 2 chickens facing each other on 2-wheeled platforms, 8½", VG+, A.............................$412.50

Chrysler Convertible, pnt tin, orange & wht, compo figures, friction, working, orig box (tape rpr), 11", EX, A....$350.00

Circus Clowns, mc litho tin, 2 clowns seated on platform facing ea other playing drums & cymbals, 1948, scarce, VG, A ..$525.00

Circus Elephant on Tricycle, US Zone, litho tin, umbrella spins from trunk as he moves in circle, 8", NM, A $92.00

City Traffic, Technofix, remote control, 3 w/up cars navigate board, 21x15", NMIB, A $120.00

Civilian Cycle, Tippco, litho tin, full-figure driver w/helmet & goggles, non-working, 8", EX, A $476.00

Carousel, painted tin clockwork, 1890s, EX, D10, $3,200.00.

Clown & Donkey Cart, Gama, mc litho tin, umbrella twirls, lever-action clockwork, working, sm pnt chip, 8", VG, A..$95.00

Clown Accordionist, Gunthermann, pnt tin w/compo head, cloth clothes, plink-plunk music movement, 14", VG, A...$2,530.00

Clown Artist, Vielmetter, litho tin, crank activates clown who then draws the Bismarck, extra drawing cams, 5", EX, A..$2,640.00

Clown Base Violinist, Gunthermann, stained & pnt tin, crank action, plink-plunk music movement, 8½", VG, A.$1,430.00

Clown Clarinetist, Gunthermann, pnt tin, plink-plunk music movement, 6½", G-, A...$385.00

Clown Doing Splits, Gunthermann, pnt tin, cloth clothes, 9", G-, A...$165.00

Clown Harpist, Gunthermann, pnt tin w/lead harp, cloth clothes, plink-plunk music movement, 12", G, A.$2,530.00

Clown Musicians, Gunthermann, pnt tin, clarinetist & violinist on base, plink-plunk music movement, 10", G, A..$1,100.00

Clown on Pig, Gunthermann, pnt tin, 7", G+, A...........$770.00

Clown on Rocking Horse, pnt compo head on wood body & horse, wood rockers, working, 7½", EX, A...............$250.00

Clown See-Saw, Gunthermann, pnt tin, plink-plunk music movement, 10", G-, A...$715.00

Clown Twirling Bells, Gunthermann, pnt & litho tin, clown behind star w/bells on points, 9", VG, A.............$1,100.00

Clown w/Dog Jumping Into Flaming Hoop, TPS, EX $200.00

Clown w/Drum, Schuco, 4¾", EX....................................$160.00

Clown w/Drum & Cymbals, Schuco, MIB......................$595.00

Clown w/Fiddle, Schuco, litho tin, cloth clothes, 4½", NM, L5...$225.00

Clown w/Fiddle, Schuco, pnt features, metal ft, 4½", NM (M box), A..$430.00

Clown w/Poodle, Gunthermann, pnt tin, poodle rotates as clown strums, plink-plunk music movement, 8½", G, A...$1,375.00

Clown w/Trained Pig, litho tin, pig jumps up as platform moves, 6", VG, A..$825.00

Clown w/Violin, Schuco/US Zone, tin & cloth clown, 4¼", NM (G box), A..$275.00

Clowns (2) w/Revolving Hoop, litho tin, hoop resoldered, 3½", G, A...$275.00

Clowns w/Ball & Banjo, Gunthermann, pnt tin, clown strums as other rotates ball on feet, plink-plunk music, 9", G, A...$1,705.00

Columbia Battleship, Hess, pnt tin, rolls & rocks, working, lt scratches & rust, 8", G-VG, A $160.00

Coney Island, Technofix, complete, VG (incomplete box), T1 ....$165.00

Cowboy, Technofix, eyes & body move side to side, NM (VG box), A..$300.00

Cowboy on Horse, GNK/US Zone, tin, MIB.................$135.00

Cowboy w/Pistol, Technofix/US Zone, mc litho tin, movable eyes, shoots gun, working, 9", EX, A.........................$150.00

Crawling Clown, Gunthermann, litho tin, 8", G, A $385.00

Curt Monkey, mc litho tin, 9", MIB...............................$65.00

Cyclon Motorcycle w/Sidecar, mk To-Et-Co, litho tin, 7", VG, A...$880.00

Donald Duck, Schuco, litho tin w/plastic arms, beak & feet, vibrates about, mouth opens & closes, 6", EX+ (NM box), A..$370.00

Donald Rocket, litho tin w/plastic head, 1950s, orig box, 7", EX, A..$725.00

Double Acrobats in Hoops, Gunthermann, pnt tin, plink-plunk music movement, 9" dia, G-, A.................................$605.00

Dual Racing Cars, PN, drivers lithoed in windows, cars attached by rod, leader changes as they advance, 5", NMIB, A..$135.00

Duck, lg, pnt tin, wings flap, 7", G, A...........................$132.00

Early Bi-Wing Airplane, Gunthermann, litho tin & celluloid, w/pilot sitting on wing, ca 1910, 8", VG+, A..........$860.00

Early Runabout, Hauser, pnt & stenciled pressed steel, orange w/spoked wheels, rubber tires, 7¼", G-VG, A $125.00

Ebo, Pao-Pao Peacock; mc emb litho tin, fine details, non-working bellows, clockwork, working, 9", VG, A $17,000.00

Elephant Rolling Ball, Gunthermann, pnt & litho tin, 7", G+, A..$1,017.50

Erratic Baggage Handler, US Zone, mc litho tin, clockwork, working, orig box (rough), 6", VG-EX, A................$300.00

Express Boy Porter, compo & tin boy pushes tin suitcase, legs move, scarce red version, 3", EX+ (scarce NM box), A $258.00

Express Boy Porter, compo porter pushes litho tin trunk mk Express, 1950s, 3", EX, A $166.00

Felix Walker, Nifty, 1920s, 7½", EX, D10, $1,150.00.

Famous Juggler, cloth-over-tin clown w/plastic head juggles 3 sets of plates, 1950s, 8", NM (EX box), A **$300.00**

Famous Juggler, pnt plastic head & balance rings, cloth outfit, clockwork, working, orig box, 8½", VG-EX, A **$210.00**

Felix on Cart, Gunthermann, pnt & litho tin, yel cart w/3 red wheels, working, 6¾", VG, A..................................**$275.00**

Felix the Cat Scooter, Nifty, 8", NM (EX box), A......**$1,000.00**

Ferris Wheel, Muller & Kadeder (?), pnt tin, plink-plunk music movement, rpl motor fan on reverse, 15", VG, A **$1,595.00**

Figure-Eight Roller Coaster, pressed lt metal & wire w/2 litho tin w/up cars, orig box damaged, 38", VG+, A **$275.00**

Fire Chief Car, Lupor, friction, fireman litho in ea window, mk Co #7, siren, 7", NMIB, A......................................**$140.00**

Fire Ladder Tuck, Kellerman, litho tin, red & silver, clockwork, working, orig box (torn flap), 5½", VG, A **$130.00**

Fisherman w/Ball, Levy, litho tin, fisherman standing on octagonal base, rpl uprights, 6", G, A **$341.00**

Fishing Fred, mc litho tin, clockwork, working, orig box, 6", EX, A **$190.00**

Flotilla, Hess, pnt tin battleship pulls 5 sm wheeled ships, working, 8", VG, A..**$500.00**

Foot-Tapping Banjo Player, Gunthermann, pnt tin, plink-plunk music movement, 6½", G-, A **$1,155.00**

Frog on Swing, Gunthermann, pnt tin, 8⅓", G-, A........**$385.00**

Frosch Flipo, Schuco, gr felt over metal, frog hops & swims, EX, G4 ....**$125.00**

Gama Tank, litho tin, olive gr, wht & blk, compo driver, clockwork, man pops up from turret, working, 5¼", EX, A .**$120.00**

Garage w/Telephone, Schuco, car inside, 1930s, M, D10, $325.00.

Garage w/2 Cars, Bing, litho tin, w/up cars, 6x8" garage, G+, A **$440.00**

Girl Jumping Rope, mk SH, bsk head & legs, cloth clothes, 12", EX, A **$467.50**

Girl Skating, litho tin, 3-D girl w/ice skates advances on wheeled base, 1930s, 8", EX, A **$522.00**

Girl w/Donkey, Gunthermann (?), pnt tin, girl cracks whip, 7½", VG, A...**$357.50**

Hand-Standing Clown, US Zone, balances on hands, moves bk & forth, well detailed, 5", EX-, A **$140.00**

Harold Lloyd Bell, litho tin, depress plunger, face expression changes, working, 6½", VG, A...............................**$110.00**

Harold Lloyd Bumper Car, litho tin, fantasy horse on bk of car, 5½x3½", NM, A **$16,000.00**

Helibus Helicopter, Arnold, crank action lifts & flies as props spin, minor blade rpr, worn box, EX, A **$140.00**

Hi-Way Henry, c Oscar Hitt, litho tin, 1 support for clothesline above car broken, dirty, 8½x10", A **$3,050.00**

Holiday Camp, litho tin track w/2 w/up cars moving around track & activating elements in campground, 9x28", VG, A **$220.00**

Honeymoon Express, litho tin w/homemade wood bottom, crank lever, train runs track, mk MIG, 1920s, 4½" sq, EX-, A .**$275.00**

Howdy Doody the Live Acrobat, Arnold, pnt compo w/cloth clothes, 1950s, 15x9x4" trapeze w/10" Howdy, EX+ (EX box), A **$1,400.00**

Hudson Car, Tippco, 9¾", NM **$250.00**

Irish Mail, Greppert & Kelch, litho tin, 4", VG+, A......**$187.00**

Jack Sprat & Wife Dancers, Gunthermann, pnt tin, 6½", G, A...**$412.00**

Jackie Coogan, litho tin, bl, red & yel outfit w/blk shoes, clockwork, eyes move, working, retouch, 7", G-, A **$225.00**

Jaguar XK120 Sport Coupe, aluminum, orig key shaped like policeman, 1¾x2x6", M (G- box), A.......................**$200.00**

Jiggs Bumper Car, litho tin, fantasy horse on bk of car, ca 1920s, very rare, 5½x3½", NM, A **$10,000.00**

Jimmy, Arnold, W Germany, lever action, composition Jimmy performs on trapeze, NM (G box), A.......................**$100.00**

Johnny the Clown, Lindstrom, clown in red & yel suit vibrates when wound, 1930, 8", EX+, A...............................**$160.00**

Juggling Clown, Schuco/US Zone Germany, cloth, tin & plastic clown spins 4 balls at front, 5", M, A **$90.00**

Jumbo the Elephant, US Zone, olive gr, orange & yel, working, damaged leg opening, minor pitting, 4¼", G, A **$60.00**

Jupiter Hot Air Balloon, Lehmann, litho tin string climber, man in basket waves American flag, non-working, 6", VG+, A **$2,310.00**

KLM Flying Dutchman DC-6, Arnold/W Germany, litho tin w/spinning plastic props (4), late 1950s, 12" wingspan, NMIB, A...**$266.00**

Kneeling Clown, Gunthermann, pnt tin, rocks on hands & knees, working, 5", EX, A.......................................**$950.00**

Ladder Truck, Germany, litho tin, crank-op ladder, blk rubber tires, 6 litho tin fireman, working, 12½", G, A........**$175.00**

Ladder Truck, litho & plated tin, w/5 fireman & lever-action ladder, working, 4½", VG, A...................................**$150.00**

Limousine, Bing, 1930s, 6", EX+, D10, $425.00.

Lady w/Baby, Gunthermann, pnt tin, lady swings baby up in arms, rare, 7", G+, A $1,265.00

Lift Garage, Technofix, litho tin & plastic, 3 cars ride elevator, drive circle & repeat, 15x11", MIB, A $190.00

Limousine, Moko, litho tin, gray & blk, pistons move, 1 wheel missing, 8", G-VG, A $475.00

Limousine, pnt & litho tin, 2-tone gr w/blk roof, litho tin driver, clockwork, working, doors & parts missing, 12", G, A $525.00

Limousine, Tipp, litho tin, red & yel, yel & blk uniformed driver, clockwork, working, 8¼", G-VG, A.............$160.00

Loading Crane, Gely, mc litho tin, clockwork, 4 position control lever, working, 19½", VG, A $80.00

Mac 700 Motorcycle, Arnold, litho tin, red cycle (scarce color), 2 levers allow actions, 7½", EX+-NM, A $1,150.00

Maggie & Jiggs, lithographed tin, working, 7", VG, A, $1,150.00.

Man at Grindstone, litho tin, 4" VG, A $77.00

Man in Donkey Cart, Gunthermann, pnt & litho tin, hand-inked inventory number, 10½", VG+, A.................$495.00

Man Pushing Luggage Cart, pnt tin, 6½", G+, A $302.50

Man Smoking Pipe, gr farmer's hat, blk coat, wht pants, brn shoes, working, 7", EX, A $55.00

Man w/Suitcase, Distler, litho tin, 7½", VG, A $440.00

Mary Had a Little Lamb, Schuco, 1930, L5 ....$475.00

Mechanical Skier, Moschokowitz, litho tin, bl on wheeled skis, working, 7", VG, A $2,300.00

Mercedes Benz 300, Pragmeta/US Zone, chrome w/wht rubber tires, 1 headlight missing, ca 1945-49, EX+, T1 ......$185.00

Mercedes Roadster, Distler, pnt tin, red w/gearshift, working, orig box, 10", EX-NM, A...$425.00

Mercedes 190SL, Motex #188, Schuco, tin w/blk rubber tires, red w/wht top, rear plate mk 1088, 8½", NM (NM box), A $563.00

Mercedes 190SL, Schuco #2095, tin red convertible w/plastic interior, orig key, steering wheel & cable, 8½", NMIB, A..$695.00

Mickey Mouse Hurdy Gurdy, Distler, litho tin, missing Minnie figure & left arm on Mickey, 6", G-, A $330.00

Mickey Mouse Jazz Drummer, Nifty, pnt litho tin, pie-cut eyes, spring-loaded mechanism, 6¾", G-VG, A............$1,400.00

Mickey Mouse Slate Dancer, extremely rare, ca 1931, 6½", NM, A, $26,500.00.

Mickey Mouse Sparkler, Nifty, diecut litho tin, blk & wht w/red & bl cellophane, spring-loaded plunger, 5½", VG, A $1,200.00

Micro Racer 1047 Porsche, Schuco, gray, working, EX $95.00

Mikifex Mouse, Schuco, leather over metal, non-working, missing tail, G, G4 ....$30.00

Minstrel Concertina & Clarinet Players, Gunthermann, pnt tin, plink-plunk music movement, 9", G, A $1,540.00

Minstrel Muscians, Gunthermann, pnt tin, lute & tamborine players, plink-plunk music movement, 8½", G, A..$1,210.00

Model T Ford, Bing, litho tin w/woman driver, spoked wheels, spare tire mtd at bk, ca 1920, 6", VG+, A $500.00

Monkey Acrobat, w/up mechanism in stuffed cloth body, 11", G A $165.00

Monkey Drummer, Schuco, pnt tin face w/cloth, brn hair, gr shirt & blk pants, non-working, minor pitting, 4¼", VG-, A...$90.00

Monkey Drummer, US Zone, cloth over tin, mk on feet, drums w/metal sticks, EX (G box), A $335.00

Monkey on Horseback Carousel, Gunthermann (?), pnt tin, plink-plunk music movement, rpl flag, 7", VG, A..$1,980.00

Monkey on Tricycle, Arnold, litho tin, working, slight chips on legs & wheels, EX+, M5 ....$115.00

Monkey on Tricycle, Bing, mohair, glass eyes, gr felt jacket, red cloth pants, metal cycle, 10", VG, A $500.00

Monkey Playing Violin, Schuco, pnt tin w/cloth, brn hair, gr shirt & red pants, working, hole in pants, 4¼", VG, A $100.00

Monkey Violinist, Schuco, litho tin, cloth clothes, 4½", EX, A..$176.00

Monkey w/Umbrella, Gunthermann, pnt tin, 6", G-, A..$132.00

Moon Mullins & Kayo Deluxe Hand Car, Nifty, 1930s, D10, $650.00.

Motorcycle, Arnold, U.S. Zone Germany, lithographed tin, 7½", NMIB, A, $600.00.

Motorcycle & Sidecar, CKO, litho tin, gray & blk cycle, olive uniforms, w/up, spark action, working, 4", EX-VG, A..$375.00

Motorcycle Racer, Technofix, litho tin, orange, brn & gray, clockwork, working, orig box, 7", EX, A.................$300.00

Motorcycle Racer, Technofix, red, yel & mc, moves in circles, slight wear, 4x7", EX, A...$240.00

Motorcycle w/Driver, Arnold, rider stands/gets off/stands by cycle/gets bk on, 5x3x8" box, NM (EX+ box), A....$650.00

Mountain Express, Einfelt, litho tin track & w/up train car, 43", EX, A...$132.00

Mystery Car, West Germany, litho tin, red, bl & yel, clockwork car travels around & through garage, orig box, 5", VG, A...$65.00

Nickel Toy Truck, litho tin w/driver, stake sides, 6-spoke wheels, 5¼", NM, A...$430.00

Oarsman, Arnold, pnt tin, red & wht rowboat w/compo figure, working, 8", G, A..$90.00

Oldsmobile Radio Car #4012, Schuco, litho tin, mechanism w/push lever, plays music, complete, 6", EX+ (NM+ box), A $535.00

Opening Door Limo, Orobr, litho tin, moustached driver at wheel, ca 1920, 6", EX, A....................................$900.00

Over & Under Track Toy, Technofix, litho tin toy folds out to 41", vehicle navigates track, 1950s, EX (G+ box), A.$170.00

Paak-Paak Duck Pulling Ducklings, Lehmann, litho tin, VG, A $231.00

Packard Convertible, highly detailed, 11", NM, J2 ....$225.00

Parachutist, pnt compo w/cloth hands, spring mechanism, working, orig box, 10", EX, A $225.00

Peacock, mk Ebo, litho tin, working, G+, A.................$110.00

Performing Sea Lion Le Paoque, Lehmann, pnt features, flippers move, 7½", EX (G+ box), A $365.00

Pick Pick Chicken, Schuco, yel mohair over metal, working, EX, G4 ....$95.00

Pig Playing Violin, Schuco, felt over tin, (may be 1 of The Three Little Pigs), 4½", EX+, M5 ....$200.00

Plane Tower, Technofix, litho tin, 2 4½" planes w/celluloid props spin above tower, 8", EX (EX box), A...........$194.00

Pointing Dog, friction, crouching dog advances, ca 1910, 7", VG+, A $100.00

Pool Player, pnt tin, clockwork mechanism, 10", G+, A ..$253.00

Race Car, Mercedes, Schuco, 1970s, MIB, D10, $110.00.

Porter Pushing Trunk in Wheelbarrow, Stock, litho tin, 6", EX, A $412.50

Porter Riding Baggage Cart, litho tin, 5½", EX, A $132.00

Puss-in-Boots, GNK, litho tin w/plastic legs & feet, complete w/feather in cap, metal cane & purse, 5", EX+ (VG box), A $115.00

Reversible Interurban Train, litho track & w/up train, car 30", EX, A $231.00

Rolli Bicycle, red, gr, cream & brn litho tin, 8", MIB.....$130.00

Rotating Swing Ride, Muller & Kadeder, litho tin, rpl flag, 10", G+, A..$605.00

Round-E-Go Zeppelin Ride, Muller & Kadeder, 13", G, A **$1,485.00**

Rudy the Ostrich, Nifty, pnt & tin litho, rpt on head, beak dented, G-, A..$302.50

Sixmobil, Gescha, pnt tin, bl, clockwork, working, 8½", VG-EX, A $250.00

Skip Rope Girl, girl spins wire rope over head & under feet as she advances, 4¾", EX, A..$125.00

Sky Rocket, litho tin, missile circles platform, dual levers control height & start-&-stop action, EX+ (EX box), A $167.00

Slugger Champions, Western Germany, orig box, EX, A.$150.00

Smitty Scooter, Nifty, ca 1920s, 10", NM, D10, $2,500.00.

Stork Circling Chimney, Adebar, litho tin w/celluloid & plastic components, w/orig box, 14", EX, A $253.00

Street Sweeper Man, Kellerman, litho tin, 7", VG, A....$264.00

Sulky Racer, pnt compo driver & horse, plastic horse legs, clockwork, working, 6½", VG-EX, A..$60.00

Swimmer Man, Issmayer, pnt tin (pnt loss heavy on bk), non-working, 2x1½x7", A..$125.00

Swimming Clown, pnt tin, possible rpt, 5½", G, A........$275.00

Tango, dancing couple, pnt tin, working, minor chips, NMIB..**$1,700.00**

Three Ducks, pnt tin, rocking action simulates swimming, 6", EX, A $715.00

Toonerville Trolley, Borgeflot, red & yel, fading & play wear, 1925, 5", A..$600.00

Toonerville Trolley, Nifty, complete/orig but dirty, 7x5½", VG, A $500.00

Touring Car, Bing, red w/brn seats, gold striping & driver, wheel rpr, sometimes works, EX pnt, 4x3½x9½", VG, A ..$550.00

Toy Vendor, monkey swings under toy box, he raises & lowers toys on a string (including Mickey Mouse), 6½", NM, A $950.00

Toy Vendor, monkey w/moving eyes swings, dangles toys on string, working, 6½", VG, A $375.00

Tractor, Distler, litho tin, red wheels, w/figure, working, 7", EX, M5..$450.00

Tranport Carrier & Trailer, Tipp & Co, w/8 Nazi soldiers, +2nd trailer w/mtd cannon, chain drive, overall 22", EX, A $800.00

Traveling Salesman, litho tin & paper, fine details, clockwork, swings arm, orig box, 4½", EX, A..$500.00

Trumpet Player, TN, Blk musician kicks foot, rocks to & fro, 10", EX (G+ box), A $365.00

Twin Racers, W Germany, litho tin, 2 5" cars attached w/cord move & switch position, EX+ (NM box), A $127.00

Two Bears, fur-covered, 1 on rocker & 1 ringing bell, both wearing muzzles, clockwork, 13", EX, A $495.00

Undersea Diver, Bing, pnt metal, clockwork, 8", VG+, A.$198.00

US Army Tank, Gama, rubber treads, orig key, 4x7½", NM (G box), A..$275.00

Varianto #3010/0 Truck, US Zone, plastic bed, 3-speed controls, w/garage, wire track & key, 4½", M (EX box), A..$130.00

Varianto #3010/0 Limo, Schuco/US Zone, w/all accessories, Schuco key, instructions & tracks, MIB, A $160.00

Vendemaus Mouse, Schuco, velvet over metal, working, missing tail, G4..$65.00

Walking Dog, Lehmann, litho tin, 6½", G, A $522.50

Walking Rooster, flocked tin rooster walks & pecks at ground, kicks leg & scratches, early, 5", EX (NM box), A ...$314.00

Walt Disney's Three Little pigs, Schuco, cloth over tin, pig plays fiddle & vibrates, 5", EX (NM box), A....................$487.00

What's Wrong Car, Distler, stops, driver's head rises, he looks bk, car moves forward, driver faces front, 7", EX, A $835.00

Zigzag Motor Trike, litho tin, folding cloth top, 7", G, A..**$1,430.00**

Italian

Clown on Mule, litho tin, gray & yel mule w/orange & bl clown on red tricycle, clockwork, working, 6½", VG-EX, A $575.00

Ferrari, Founderpress, pnt cast aluminum, red w/lift-off top, rubber-band drive at front, 21", EX, A......................$2,800.00

Happy Holligan in Cart Pulled by Donkey, Ingap, litho tin, 4x7", EX, A......................$900.00

Military Motorcycle w/Sidecar, litho tin, missing 1 tab , 5", G, A......................$605.00

Motorcycle w/Sidecar, Ingap, driver, passenger in sidecar, 3¾x5¼", EX, A......................$650.00

Japanese

#18 Racer, KSG, litho tin w/tin driver & hinged rear spoiler, blk rubber tires, friction, 11", EX, A......................$75.00

Acrobat Skier, tin, twirls skis, goes forward & then somersaults, EX......................$50.00

Acrobatic Artie, Occupied Japan, NMIB, T1......................$95.00

Air Terminal Baggage Cart, litho tin, driver rears bk to tip up front of cart, 6", EX, A......................$220.00

Aircraft Carrier Coral Sea, Bandai, friction, 7 tin jets on deck, radar antenna, 4 guns, 15", NM (EX box), A......................$245.00

American Air DC-3, Yone, red, wht, silver & bl, classic twin engine, 9x7", EX+, A......................$245.00

American Airlines DC-3, Acorn, friction, silver & red w/plastic props, 13x14", NM (VG box), A......................$95.00

American Airlines DC-7, Bandai, friction, litho tin, wing & tailfin mk N309AA, 9x11" wingspan, EX+, A......................$176.00

American Circus Truck, K, friction, cab w/litho clown on roof pulls 2 animal cages, 1950s, 19", EX, A......................$435.00

Amphibian Army Vehicle, friction, rotating machine guns, ca 1950s, EX, W1......................$82.00

Animal Barber Shop, TPS, litho tin rabbit barber shaves customer, 5", NM (EX box), A......................$403.00

Antiaircraft Jeep, w/driver & 2 soldiers firing antiaircraft guns, tin friction w/siren, 7½", VG (VG box), A......................$70.00

Antique Truck, pnt tin, gray, wht, red & yel, friction, working, orig box, 6½", VG-EX, A......................$35.00

Astronaut Fighting Jeep, Daiya, twin-mounted rear guns swivel, 7", NM (EX box), A......................$675.00

Atomic Drive Jet Racer, litho tin, red, tan, silver & bl, friction w/smoke & flame, working, orig box, 8½", EX, A......................$425.00

Auto Carrier, tin, friction, w/6 tin public service cars (police, taxi, etc), ca 1960-70s, 15", M (NM box), W1......................$89.00

Auto Carrier, tin, friction, w/6 tin race cars, ca 1960-70s, M (NM box), W1......................$69.00

Auto Racer, San-Ei, mc litho tin motorcycle mk #10, w/rider, friction, 6", EX+ (EX box), A......................$98.00

Autobus, pnt tin, bl, tan & red, litho tin dasher, rubber tires, friction, non-working, 12", VG-EX, A......................$25.00

Autocycle, Alps, detailed mc litho tin w/rider, friction, 4½", M (NM box), A......................$200.00

Automatic Racing Game, Haji, 3 1½" litho tin race cars w/garage, push lever for race action, 1950s, EX (NM box), A......................$400.00

B-50 Boeing Superfortress, Y, litho tin, 4 spinning props activated by wheels, friction, 19" wingspan, EX+, A......................$412.00

Babes in Toyland Go Mobile, Linemar, litho tin, yel, red, blk & wht w/pnt vinyl head, friction, orig box, 6", VG-EX, A......................$210.00

Babes in Toyland Soldier, Linemar, litho tin, 7", EX, from $200 to......................$250.00

Baby Carriage, pnt celluloid & plastic, red, yel, bl & pk, clockwork w/revolving umbrella, orig box, 6½", VG-EX, A......................$55.00

Baby Race Car, Cragston, litho tin w/blk rubber tires, friction, mk Rocket & 39, 3½", NM (EX box), A......................$115.00

Baby Walking in Stroller, litho tin w/vinyl head, arms & legs, 6", VG......................$45.00

Ball-Juggling Clown, cloth over tin, celluloid face, holds 2 transparent balls that rattle, scarce, 6", EX, A......................$95.00

Ball-Playing Giraffe, litho tin w/rubber ears, clockwork, orig box, 8½", G-VG, A......................$230.00

Ball-Playing Giraffe, TPS, ball bounces off giraffe's hooves up & down a wire, EX+ (EX box), A......................$380.00

Barking Dog, litho tin, silver w/blk, bl & red trim, friction, mouth opens, working, 6", VG-EX, A......................$250.00

Basketball Player, litho tin, orange, gr, red & bl, w/2 plastic basketballs, working, orig box, 8", VG-EX, A......................$60.00

Batman, Billiken, litho tin, 1989, MIB......................$95.00

Batman Batcopter, AHI, friction, 1976, MOC, C1......................$54.00

Batman in Batmobile, Yanoman, vinyl Batman w/movable arms in red tin car w/bats & Batman lettered on sides, NMIB, A......................$1,450.00

Batman on Trike, plastic cycle w/fancy litho tin hubs, celluloid Batman w/felt cape, bell rings, 4½", NM, A......................$400.00

Batmobile (new style), Apollo, plastic, MIB......................$35.00

Bear & Pig Ball Toss, mc litho tin, stationary figures w/clockwork arms toss ball, 19", VG-EX, A......................$80.00

Bear & Row Boat, mc litho tin, clockwork, working, orig box (tape rpr), 10", VG-EX, A......................$210.00

Bear Golfer, litho tin, yel, blk & red, clockwork, working, orig box, 7¼", VG-EX, A......................$220.00

Bear Playing Ball, mc litho tin w/rubber ears, clockwork, working, orig box (partially crushed), 19", VG-EX, A......................$270.00

Begging Dog, TN, plush over tin, Victory decal on ribbon around neck, 5½", NM (EX box), A......................$45.00

Begging Roll-Over Pluto, Linemar, yel plush, rubber tail & tin eyes, clockwork, touch-up, orig box, 6½", VG-EX, A......................$130.00

Bell Cycle Monkey, Suzuki, celluloid monkey on mc litho tin tricyle, revolving & sounding bell, 4", NM (EX box), A......................$66.00

Bell Cycle Rabbit, Suzuki, M......................$225.00

Bengali Tiger, Japan, 1960s, 7", EX, T1......................$95.00

Bestmaid Baby Car, litho tin, celluloid & cloth, clockwork, 2 motions, working, orig box, 6", VG-EX, A......................$65.00

Big Chief Indian, litho tin w/cloth clothes, head moves, raises tomahawk, walks, 7", VG+ (EX+-NM box), A......................$138.00

Big Joe Chef, litho tin, red, wht, bl & yel, clockwork, working, orig box, 6½", EX, A......................$50.00

Big League Hockey Player, litho tin, red, yel & bl w/aluminum puck & stick, clockwork, working, orig box, 6", EX, A......................$325.00

Big Top Circus Juggling Clown, Alps, pnt compo head, rubber hands, cloth outfit, tin body, twirls 5 balls, 11", NMIB, A......................$700.00

Black Boy Drummer, pnt celluloid w/wood cap, eyes vibrate as head turns, clockwork, working, 7¼", VG-EX, A......................$525.00

Billy the Ball Blowing Whale, K0, NM (VG box), from $80.00 to $125.00.

Black Musician Car, friction, music notes & musicians allover, 1955 on rear plate, 7", EX, A $245.00

Bleating Pig, CM/Occupied Japan, celluloid, vibrates as head bobs, sounds, 5", MIB, A $167.00

Boy on Swing, celluloid, EX, D10, $200.00.

BMW Isetta, litho & pnt tin, orange & tan w/silver trim, rubber tires, friction, working, orig box, 4¾", EX, A...........$275.00

Bobbing-Head Santa, rubber head, cloth suit, litho tin sign, clockwork, bell rings, 7", G-VG, A...........$30.00

Bouncing Dolly Ball, TPS, girl on knees uses arm to bounce tin litho ball, she has vinyl head, 6", EX+ (EX box), A ..$90.00

Boxer Dog, Linemar, plush over tin, nodding head & tail, bell around neck jingles, 6", NM (EX box), A.................$51.00

Boxing Kids, pnt celluloid figures w/jtd arms, pnt tin base, clockwork, 2 motions, working, orig box, 5", VG-EX, A .$210.00

Boxing Monkey, plush & litho tin monkey on base w/punching bag, 6", NM (EX+ box), A $98.00

Boy Carrying Suitcase, Occupied Japan, pnt celluloid & tin, clockwork, working, 4", VG, A $40.00

Boy on Pony, Occupied Japan, pnt celluloid boy on pnt tin horse w/leather tail, clockwork, working, 5¼", VG-EX, A .$40.00

Brick Orion Sedan, TN, friction, siren sound, 8½", NM (EX box), A...$110.00

British Tank, mc litho tin, friction w/cap action, 6", G, A .$15.00

Bronco Bill, celluloid cowboy twirls wire lasso as tin horse vibrates & tail spins, prewar, 6", VG (EX box), A.....$91.00

Bubbling Boy, San, litho tin, lowers head, blower dips into pan & he blows bubbles, no solution, 8", EX+ (NM box), A...$134.00

Buck Rogers Walking Twiki, Mego, head turns as he walks, 1979, MIB, C1 ....$75.00

Bucking Bronco, brn & gold horse rears up & down as tail spins, 6x6", MIB, A...$50.00

Buick, tin, friction, working, early 1950s, lg, EX, C8........$95.00

Buick Century Ambulance, Bandai, wht pnt tin, friction, missing 1 hubcap, ca 1958, 8", NMIB, W1 ....$35.00

Buick Invicta, Linemar, litho tin, red & silver, flip-top concealed in trunk, friction, working, orig box, 9", VG, A $90.00

Buick LeSabre Futuristic Car, friction, 1950s style, 8", EX, A..$765.00

Buick Sedan, pnt tin w/litho tin interior, friction, moving wipers & sound, 16", VG-EX, A....................................$65.00

Bulldozer, friction, 1950s, G, C8 ....$40.00

Bullwinkle Car, KO, he steers, rocks bk & forth, bumper-type car, characters lithoed on sides, 5½", EX, A $275.00

Bump 'N Go Fire Chief Camaro, Tayio, MIB.................$90.00

Bump 'N Go Love Bug Volkswagon Beetle, Tayio, MIB ..$90.00

Bump 'N Go Volkswagon Bug, KO, red, 7", NM (EX+ box), M5 ....$87.00

Bump Car w/Pop-Up Clown, litho tin car, clown wears cloth suit, friction, EX (EX box), A $100.00

Bunny Family Parade, TPS, litho tin, mother & 3 babies move forward & spin, 13", EX (EX box), A.......................$78.00

Bunny Jockey, M..$135.00

Busy Mouse, TPS, litho tin mouse & base w/kitchen scene, 6x9", NM (VG box), from $75 to....................................$125.00

Cadillac, early 1950s, red w/tin tires, makes engine noise, friction, 7", M (NM box), A...$100.00

Cadillac, 1959, Bandai, lt bl litho tin, plastic steering wheel & windshield, friction, 11¼", EX- (NM box), A $525.00

Cadillac Old Timer Convertible, 1933, Bandai, tin w/blk rubber tires, fold-down windshield, 8", EX+ (VG box), A....$85.00

Cadillac Sedan, Bandai #781, tin friction, Cadillac rear plate, blk rubber tires, 10½", NM (EX box), A..................$325.00

Cadillac Sedan, late 1950s, Bandai, rubber wheels, friction, 11", EX $248.00

Cadillac Sedan, pnt tin, off-wht w/pk & bl litho tin interior, friction, working, orig box, 9", EX, A $120.00

Cadillac Sedan, 1950, Marusan, litho tin interior, friction, working, orig box, 11¼", EX+, A........................$600.00

Cadillac Sedan, 1950, Marusan, litho tin interior, friction, working, orig box, 11¼", VG+, A........................$425.00

Cadillac Sedan, 1960s, Schuco, litho tin interior, bl windshield, 21½", G, A..$250.00

Calypso Joe the Drummer, Linemar, litho tin native figure w/rubber hands beats drum & rocks, 6", NM (EX box), A..........$368.00

Calypso Joe the Drummer, litho tin, brn, yel, red & gr w/plush trim, clockwork, working, orig box, 5½", VG, A.....$325.00

Canary Roller, mk CK, litho tin, bird in cage, bellows simulate bird chirping, 5½", EX+, A $176.00

Candy Loving Canine, TPS, litho tin, flips pc of candy in mouth, 6", NM (EX box), A...........................$128.00

Car w/Sailboat & Boat Trailer, tin friction, boat mk No 7 Blue Bird, car: 6½", trailer: 7", EX (EX box), A...........$152.00

Casper Ghost Turnover Tank, Linemar, mc litho tin, clockwork, working, orig box, 3¾", EX, A $450.00

Cat w/Butterfly, off-wht fur w/brn spots & orange ribbon around neck, legs move, orig box & key, EX..........................$85.00

Central RR Train, friction, siren sounds, wheel assembly moves, 3x8½", MIB, A.....................................$75.00

Champ on Ice, 3 mc litho tin skating bears, clockwork, working, orig box, 8½", EX, A.............................$750.00

Champs, Wakourva, pnt wood, jtd boxers on base, string tension action, working, orig box, 5¼", VG-EX, A..............$150.00

Cherry Cook, Occupied Japan, EX......................$125.00

Chevrolet Corvair, early 1960s, HS, friction, plastic windshield, detailed interior, early 1960s, 9½", NM (EX box), A $175.00

Chevrolet Corvair, early 1960s, Schuco, litho & pnt tin, wht, brn & bl, friction, orig box, 9½", EX, A..................$140.00

Chevrolet w/Bk Motion, SKK, controlled by lever at rear fender, 5", NMIB, A $85.00

Chick, friction, movable wings, 3", VG+, P3..................$65.00

Chicken Feeder, Toyodo & Co, litho tin, non-working, spring sprung, VG...$95.00

Chico the Cha-Cha Monkey, Alps, cloth, plush & litho tin, dances & shakes maracas, 8½", NMIB, A..................$89.00

Chico the Cha-Cha Monkey, Alps, litho tin, plush & mc cloth, clockwork, non-working, orig box, 8½", VG-EX, A..$25.00

Chrysler Imperial Sedan, 1958, Bandai, friction, plastic windshields & steering wheel, 9½", NM (EX box), A.....$225.00

Circling Helicopter, MT, w/celluloid blades in rear (rare), lithoed pilot & passenger in window, 7", NM (EX box), A...$150.00

Circus Boy, TN, moves head, rings bell, M (NM box), A $240.00

Circus Bus, litho tin, circus graphics, friction, working, orig box, 9", EX, A...$75.00

Circus Car, litho tin, wht, red, gr & bl, rubber tires, friction, clown tumbles, working, orig box, 8¼", VG+, A .$1,000.00

Circus Car, mc litho tin, clockwork w/air motor for styrofoam ball, working, orig box, 4¾", VG-EX, A $75.00

Circus Clown, TN, litho tin w/celluloid arms & head, waddles & rings bell, 5", NM (EX box), A $125.00

Circus Clown Aerial Tightrope Walker, I, litho tin & cloth, pipe in his mouth, hand over hand across rope, 8", NMIB, A..$245.00

Circus Crown, K, clown w/celluloid head rocks as cylinder spins above head, 6", NM (EX box), A..............................$75.00

Circus Cyclist, litho tin, red & yel w/cloth outfit, clockwork, bell rings, working, orig box, 6½", VG, A................$625.00

Circus Parade, mc litho tin, clockwork, working, orig box, 11½", VG, A..$190.00

Circus Parade, TPS, 11", MIB, from $450 to $500.00

Circus Seal, TN, plush seal spins balls on nose & flippers, 6x5", MIB, A...$85.00

Clarabell Howdy Doody Delivery, Linemar, mc litho tin tricycle & figure, friction, working, orig box, 5½", G, A......$300.00

Climbing Pirate, TPS, litho tin, string climber, 6", VG, A.$71.50

Climbo the Climbing Clown, TPS, litho tin w/cloth pants, 7", VG+, A..$125.00

Clown, MT, celluloid w/pnt face, cloth outfit, walks on tin hands, 9", NM (EX box), A.....................................$222.00

Clown Balancing Act, pnt papier-mache head w/cloth outfit, clockwork, working, 11", VG+, A.............................$270.00

Clown Drummer Boy, mk Sugimoto Tokyo, cloth w/celluloid head & arms, plays drum, head moves, prewar, 12", EX (NM box), A...$725.00

Clown Horse Trainer, Japan Tokyo Shei, litho tin, appears to be pre-WWII, rare, 7", VG, A..................................$797.50

Clown Jalopy Cycle, mc litho tin, friction, head bobs, working, 8½", EX, A..$325.00

Clown Jalopy Cycle, TPS, when cycle hits object, front wheel comes off & clown's head pops up, 9", NM (EX box), A...$745.00

Clown Juggler w/Monkey, TPS, litho tin, circus monkey spins on chair atop clown's nose, 9½", NM (VG box), A $625.00

Clown Making the Lion Jump Through Hoop, TPS, litho tin, flaming (red felt) hoop, orig box, 5x6", NM (EX+ box)..$300.00

Clown Musician, TN, cloth-over-tin clown behind podium w/litho fox, lifts hat, rabbit appears, 7", NM (EX+ box), A $750.00

Clown on Roller Skates, litho tin, yel, blk & red, clockwork, working, orig box, 6", VG-EX, A $275.00

Clown Trainer & His Acrobat Dog, TPS, poodle jumps through flaming (felt) hoop, orig box, 4½", EX+, from $220 to...$280.00

Clown Unicyclist, litho tin w/cloth outfit, clockwork, 3 motions, working, 5½", VG, A...$120.00

Clown Unicyclist, red & wht striped jacket, bl & wht polka-dotted pants, arms & legs animated, 6", NM, A...........$230.00

Cock Fighting, litho tin, MIB $125.00

Cock-A-Doodle, TPS, mc tin litho rooster w/celluloid-like tail & comb, rocks & sings, 8", NM (EX+ box), A........$138.00

Collie Dog, 1960s, NMIB, T1.............................$75.00

Combat Tank on Battle Front, TPS, tank moves along lithoed battle scene, 14x6", MIB, A $135.00

Concrete Mixer Truck, Cragstan, Toymaster/Japan, friction, 8¼", MIB, $65.00.

Coney Island Scooter, KO, 6", NMIB, $175.00.

Consolidated Freightways Tractor/Trailer, litho tin, silver, red & gr, friction, working, orig box, 20½", EX, A $275.00

Construction Jeep, litho tin, gray & yel, friction, w/sheet metal parts for trailer construction, 7½", EX, A....................$60.00

Continental Mark III Convertible, pnt tin, wht w/yel & red litho tin interior, friction, orig box, 11½", VG-EX, A.......$425.00

Continental Super Special, litho tin, bl, pnt compo driver, friction, working wipers, orig box, 13½", EX, A.............$400.00

Continental Trailways Silver Eagle Bus, Kyoei, friction, blk rubber tires, lithos in windows, 15", EX+ (EX box), A ...$95.00

Corvette, 1960, Y, friction, bucket seats, plastic windshield, metallic bl, 8", NM (EX box), A.............................$285.00

Cowboy on Horseback, Haji, litho tin, horse gallops as cowboy holds gun in right hand, 8", NM, A $85.00

Cowboy Whirling Lasso, Alps, litho tin, MIB $265.00

Cragstan Antique Fire Engine, TN, friction, 1960s, MIB, C8.$65.00

Crawling Baby, Alps/Occupied Japan, celluloid baby, fabric clothes, 5", in box w/Mickey Mouse toy litho, EX (G+ box), A $110.00

Crawling Baby, Suzuki, celluloid w/pnt features, cloth outfit, 4½", NM (NM box), A $35.00

Crysler Imperial Convertible, Japan, pnt & litho tin, maroon, bl seats, friction, working, orig box, 8½", VG, A.........$160.00

Crysler Imperial Convertible, pnt tin, red w/wht & bl litho tin interior, friction, working, orig box, 8¼", NM, A ...$275.00

Crysler Sedan, Alps, pnt tin, shaded brn & blk w/litho tin interior, friction, lt touch-up, orig box, 7½", VG-EX, A..$165.00

Cubby the Reading Bear, Alps, gray plush w/wht nose & ears, in gr cloth overalls & litho tin shoes, 1950s, 7", NM, A..$40.00

Curls Baby (Blk Baby), pnt celluloid & cloth, clockwork, working, w/orig label on head, orig box, 5", EX, A..........$170.00

Daddy & Kid Turn Turtles, AOKI, daddy nods, baby hangs onto dad's shell, 6", EX (G+ box), A...............................$120.00

Dancing Couple, Occupied Japan, MIB $95.00

Dancing Couple, Occupied Japan, pnt celluloid, clockwork, working, orig box (flaps missing), 4½", VG-EX, A....$55.00

Dancing Duck, litho tin, plush & felt, clockwork, walks, spins cane & opens mouth, working, 6¾", VG-EX, A........$20.00

Dancing Sam, mc litho tin figure on revolving base, working, orig box, 8¾", EX, A...$170.00

Dandy, Mukini, litho tin, carnival clown-like man walks & tips his hat, 6", NM (EX box), A...................................$330.00

Dino the Dinosaur, Linemar, purple litho tin, walks w/swaying motion, mouth action, clicking noise, 1962, 8", VG, A $500.00

Dino the Dinousaur, Linemar, litho tin, purple, blk & gr, clockwork, working, touch-up at tail, orig box, 7½", EX, A .$950.00

Disney Character Carousel, Linemar, litho tin canopy & base, celluloid figures, clockwork, orig box, 7", VG-EX, A $900.00

Disney Flivver, Linemar, litho tin car w/mc Disney characters, clockwork, working, 5¾", VG-EX, A......................$180.00

Disney Parade Roadster, Linemar, 4 plastic Disney characters inside, 11", EX+, A...$325.00

Donald Duck the Drummer, Linemar, lithographed tin, 7", NMIB, A, $1,025.00.

Disney's Babes in Toyland Cart & Soldier, Linemar, litho tin, soldier w/vinyl head, friction, 1961, NM, A............$238.00

Dog, brn fur w/ribbon around neck, mouth opens, body moves, mk, VG...$105.00

Dog & Shoe, celluloid dog shakes old litho tin shoe, lg 8" version, NM, A...$85.00

Donald Duck Acrobat Toy, Linemar, celluloid & wire, Donald Duck rotates over wire bar, 9", VG, A....................$247.50

Donald Duck Quack Quack Car, MT, friction, vinyl head, characters lithoed along sides, 13", EX+, A.................$270.00

Donald Duck Tricycle, Linemar, celluloid Donald on trike w/bell on bk, 3½", EX (EX- box), A $575.00

Donald Duck Tricycle, Linemar, litho tin, orig box, 4", NM, A..$685.00

Donald Duck w/His 3 Nephews, Linemar, litho tin, Donald pulls nephews as they move to & fro, 11", NM (EX+ box), A..$1,610.00

Donald Duck w/His 3 Nephews, Linemar, mc litho tin w/rubber guns, clockwork, working, orig box, 11", G-VG, A.$700.00

Donald Duck w/Whirling Tail, Linemar, he moves erratically as tail twirls, WDP, complete w/rubber tail, 4½", NMIB, A..$490.00

Donald Duck, w/Whirling Tail; Linemar, litho tin, yel, red, wht & bl, w/red paper umbrella, clockwork, orig box, 5", VG, A..$225.00

Donkey, gray fur w/bee on rear end, ears & tail flip around & he tries to hit bee, working, VG.............................$62.50

Donkey Band Wagon, pnt & litho tin, red, yel, bl & brn, rubber ears, friction, working, orig box, 8", VG, A.............$210.00

Donkey Clown, CK, celluloid clown spins paper cube over head, litho tin donkey vibrates & spins tail, 8½", NM, A..$171.00

Douglas Sky Rocket, Bandai, mk Navy B-335 on tail fin, litho tin pilot in cockpit, 17½", EX (EX box), A.............$220.00

Drinking Monkey, he twists his hips & brings his arms up w/jug in hand, 7¾", EX-...$40.00

Drive Car, mc litho tin, friction, w/chasing dog, working, touch-up on hood, 6", VG, A...$160.00

Drum Major, litho tin w/celluloid head & arms, plays drum, prewar, 4½", EX+ (EX box), A.................................$185.00

Drummer Bear, Toyland Toys, plush bear w/litho tin drum, 6½", NM (NM box), A...$77.00

Drummer Boy, celluloid, in red & wht striped shirt plays drum, 2x4x2" wood base, prewar, 10½", EX, A, from $200 to..$275.00

Drummer Boy, celluloid boy w/animated arms, cloth outfit, pnt features, on 3x4" wood base, prewar, 10", NM (EX box) $450.00

Drummer Elephant w/Winky Eyes, TN, M....................$150.00

DS19 Citroen Convertible, pnt tin, metallic red w/yel & red litho tin interior, friction, working, orig box, 9", EX, A..$275.00

Easter on Parade, tin & celluloid, rabbit pulls sleigh w/ducklings & newly hatched chick in basket, 8", MIB, A.........$116.00

Eastern Airlines 727, friction, siren sounds as plane moves, 12x11", NM-, A...$75.00

Educational Pet Pooch, TPS, litho tin, turn numbered dial & graduation cap, will nod same number, 4½", MIB, A..$70.00

Elephant, plush, gray w/brn howdah & litho tin tusks, clockwork, 3 motions, working, orig box, 7½", VG-EX, A..........$40.00

Excalibur Car, Bandai, mystery action, MIB, C8.............$95.00

F-100 Super Sabre Jet, Y, litho tin, friction, scarce, 1950s, EX (G box), A..$147.00

F-9F Jet Fighter, friction, red, bl & yel, sparks, 6x6", NMIB, A...$95.00

Fairchild C-120 Pack Plane, M, tin w/plastic doors on nose (cracked), w/2" jeep & tank, 16" wingspread, EX+ (NM box), A...$550.00

Fairchild US Air Force C120 Pack Plane, metal props activated by wheels, plastic nose doors, 16", EX, A.................$375.00

Fat Sedan, litho tin w/blk rubber tires, friction, yel tinted headlights & metal hood ornament, 10", EX, A.............$120.00

Ferdinand Bull, Linemar, tail & head move, G, L5........$175.00

Fiat Convertible, Usagiya, friction, bl w/emb rear-mtd spare tire on trunk, blk rubber tires, 6¼", NM (EX box), A ...$125.00

Fiat Sedan, Usagiya, friction, bl w/spare tire on trunk, blk rubber tires, 6¼", NMIB, A...$125.00

Fire Car, litho tin, red, yel & bl, friction, w/siren, working, orig box (torn lid), 6½", VG, A $130.00

Fire Car, SSS, friction, mk Josteele FD above rear plate, 4 firemen hang onto sides, 6¼", NM (NM box), A.........$135.00

Fire Chief Car, Alps, litho tin, friction, ca 1950s, 4¼", EX, W1..$24.50

Fire Chief Car, litho tin, red w/silver, wht & yel trim, friction, working, orig box, 7½", VG-EX, A....................$130.00

Fire Engine, litho tin, silver, red & yel w/bl trim, clockwork, self-extending ladder, working, 3¾", EX, A.....................$70.00

Fire Marine Dept Fireboat F-100, Marusan, w/3 3-D fireman, American flag, EX (EX box), A $330.00

Fire Truck, litho tin, red, yel & bl, rubber tires, friction, bell rings, working, 7½", VG-EX, A.................................$100.00

Fishing Bear, mc litho tin w/cloth net & rubber ears, clockwork, working, orig box, 7¾", EX, A $220.00

Fishing Monkey on Whale, mc litho tin, clockwork, 3 motions, orig box, 9", VG-EX, A...$400.00

Fishing Monkey on Whale, TPS, litho tin monkey & whale w/2 fishes, whale rocks as fish fins move, 9", EX (NM box), A...$500.00

Flintstones Hauler and Trailer, Linemar, Hanna-Barbera, lithographed tin, friction, 1961, 12" long, MIB, A, $3,200.00.

Flintstone on Tricycle (Fred), Linemar, litho tin & plastic, repro box, rpl handlebar, working, EX, M5 ....$200.00

Flintstone on Tricycle (Wilma), Linemar, EX, J2 ....$265.00

Flintstone on Tricycle (Wilma), Linemar, w/bell, 1962, NM, A $413.00

Flintstone Pals on Dino (Barney), Linemar, vinyl-headed Barney holds reins as Dino waddles forward, sounds, 9", VG, A $315.00

Flintstone Pals on Dino (Fred), Linemar, 8", NM, D10, $375.00.

Flintstone Pals on Dino (Fred), Linemar, litho tin, 1962, 8", EX $250.00

Flintstone Pals on Dino (Fred), Linemar, litho tin, working, orig box, 8", VG-EX, A $450.00

Flintstone Turn-Over Tank, Linemar, tank advances, Fred lifts tank causing it to roll over, NM, A $720.00

Flippo Dog, Linemar, mc litho tin, clockwork, working, adjustable spring-tension mechanism, orig box (torn), 4", EX, A $75.00

Ford Custom Ranch Wagon, Bandai, painted tin with lithographed tin interior, friction, 11¾", EX (VG+ box), A, $350.00.

Ford, 1933, CK, balloon tires, prewar, 7¼", G-G+, A $660.00

Ford Convertible, 1955, Haji, friction, 8", EX, M5.........$155.00

Ford Fairlane Station Wagon, friction, ca 1957, 14", NM $275.00

Ford Fairlane 500 Skyliner, pnt tin, bl & tan w/litho tin interior, friction, working, orig box, 10¾", EX, A $450.00

Ford Fastback, 1966, Haji, friction, opening doors, undercarriage details, 8½", NM+, A $120.00

Ford Fire Dept Station Wagon, Shudo, tin, friction, ca 1960-70s, 7½", M (NM box), W1...$63.00

Ford Hwy Patrol Police Car, Taiyo, tin, ca 1960, 10½", NMIB, W1 ....$35.00

Ford Skyliner, 1958, K, tin, friction, turn spare tire & top retracts, 9¾", NM (EX box), A $325.00

Ford Skyliner, 1958, TN, friction, roof slides out of trunk to convert to hardtop, 7½", EX, A $185.00

Ford Sunliner Convertible, 1962, litho tin, red, silver, gray & yel, friction, working, orig box, 9¾", EX, A $140.00

Ford Yellow Cab Taxi, Marusan, friction, M $750.00

Ford 2-Door Hardtop, 1955, friction, red & wht, 8", EX+, A $165.00

Frankenstein, Robot House, litho tin, 9", MIB.................$80.00

Freight Ways Tractor & Trailer, Linemar, friction, 9½", EX+ (VG box) $200.00

Frosty Bar Truck, litho tin, wht w/orange, brn & bl trim, rubber tires, friction, bell rings, orig box, 7¼", EX, A $300.00

Furry Dog, wht & gray fur, head moves, lifts leg up & then legs move, EX..$72.50

Furry Rabbit, wht fur w/red & blk ears, little legs move, w/key, EX...$80.00

Futuristic Car, Meiko, friction, plastic see-through roof, 8½", EX, A $200.00

Gasoline Truck, friction, litho tin, red w/Gasoline lettered in yel, 7", NMIB, M5 ....$48.00

Gay 90's Cyclist, TPS, clockwork, litho tin, 1950s, 7", EX (EX box), from $275 to..$290.00

Girl on Donkey, celluloid, revolving umbrella w/dangling balls, bobbing donkey's head, 4-wheel base, working, 6", NM, M5 ....$175.00

Girl w/Chickens, TPS, blond in scarf, long dress & apron feeds chickens attached to rod in front of her, 5½", EX, A.$275.00

Godzilla Egg, Takara, 1988, MIB.....................................$45.00

Good Humor Ice Cream Truck, litho tin, wht w/gr & red trim, friction, working, orig box, 4½", EX, A $300.00

Good Humor Ice Cream Truck, litho tin, wht w/mc trim, rubber tires, retractable roof, friction, orig box, 8", VG-EX, A..$700.00

Goofy, Linemar, litho tin, head goes up & down as tail spins, orig box, 5", VG+, A..$357.50

Goolies Monster Car, Yone, litho tin, Universal Monster at ea window, eye headlights, 4½", NM (EX+ box), A $300.00

Grandpa's New Car, Y, Grandpa & front end of car shakes & rattles, 1950s, 5½", NM (EX box), A.......................$345.00

Grandpa's New Car, Y, litho tin w/Grandpa bouncing in seat, moves forward, 5½", NM, A..$225.00

Great Magician, TN, litho tin fox in tuxedo w/cane & top hat, plays card trick at table, 1950s, 8", NM, A $180.00

Greyhound Bus, Cragstan, friction, MIB........................$75.00

Greyhound Scenic Cruiser, pnt & litho tin, bl & wht, friction, working, orig box, 12½", EX, A $120.00

Greyhound Senicruiser Bus, ATC, friction, blk rubber tires, roof rack, sounds, 11½", EX (EX box), A $90.00

Greyhound Senicruiser Bus, Daiya, friction, blk rubber tires, sounds, 1950s style, 8½", NM (EX box), A...............$70.00

Gyrodyne, Haji, litho tin, friction, EX $65.00

Ham 'N Sam, Linemar, one plays piano while the other dances, 4x5x6" box, EX (G box), A $1,300.00

Happy Car, Alps, Buick-style convertible w/side portholes, blk rubber tires, plaid bucket seats, 8½", NM (EX box), A...$120.00

Happy Hippo, litho tin, brn w/yel & gr trim, clockwork, working, orig box, 5½", VG-EX, A $500.00

Happy Life, Alps, celluloid girl rocks in beach chair under umbrella, duck by her side, 6x5" tin base, NM (EX box), A $535.00

Happy Life, celluloid girl in rocker under spinning umbrella, duck spins, 4x6" carnival illus base, 9½", EX, A $300.00

Happy Skaters, TPS, lithographed tin, rubber ears, 1950s, 6½", NM (EX box), from $250.00 to $310.00.

Happy Speed Car Trolley, Hadson, litho tin w/electric cable connection on top, recessed windows, friction, 1950s, VG+, A $220.00

Happy the Violinist, tin litho clown w/long legs in red & wht striped pants, plays violin, 9", NM (EX+ box), M5 .$250.00

Happy Times, Kuramochi, tin w/celluloid girl in rocking chair, boat in lap, celluloid umbrella, duck, 5x6½", EX, A..$95.00

Harley-Davidson Auto Cycle, TN, lithographed tin, friction, original box, 9", EX, A, $480.00.

Hawaiian Dance, celluloid, dk-skinned girl dances hula, sm crease in arm, prewar, 9", o/w M, A $103.00

Henry on Elephant, celluloid, elephant w/moving head & flapping ears lifts Henry w/trunk, orig box, EX+, A ...$1,950.00

Henry on Trapeze, Borgfeldt/pre-war Japan, lithographed tin, EX (VG+ box), A, $495.00.

Henry on Trapeze, celluloid, Henry performs acrobatic tricks on high bar, 4", VG (VG box), A $380.00

Honeymoon Express, Linemar, NMIB $225.00

Hopping Crow, Linemar, litho tin, EX............................$65.00

House Trailer w/Cadillac, SSS, friction, 9½" trailer, sun roof & doors open, 8" car fits inside, 1954, NM (G+ box), A .$235.00

Howdy Doody & Clarabell, Linemar, mc litho tin, Howdy dances, Clarabell plays piano, clockwork, working, 5½", G-, A..$650.00

Howdy Doody Clock-A-Doodle, Bandai/Kagran, Howdy on swing below, moving hands, Flub-A-Dub eats, 9", NM (NM box), A $3,000.00

Huckleberry Hound Aeroplane, Linemar, c Hanna-Barbera, litho tin & vinyl, friction, 1961, 10", MIB, A $979.00

Huckleberry Hound Aeroplane (Yogi Bear Version), Linemar, litho tin w/vinyl-headed Yogi, friction, 1961, NMIB, A $1,900.00

Huckleberry Hound Ford Convertible, Linemar, bl tin w/litho interior, vinyl Huck at wheel, 1961, 9", VG, A.......$723.00

Hunter Truck, YH, friction, Wild Beast Hunting on animal cage, hunter & lion fight at bk door, 9", NM (G+ box), A...$120.00

Hustling Bulldozer, litho tin, red, gr, bl & yel, friction, working, orig box, 6¼", EX, A......................................$35.00

I Like Ice Cream Monkey, NGT/MM, brn plush w/litho tin face, stretches tongue to lick cone, 1950s, 7", NMIB, A....$83.00

Ice Cream Cycle, litho tin wht w/red & bl trim, crank friction action, working, orig box, 6¼", EX, A $350.00

Ice Cream Truck, litho tin, rubber tires, friction, bell rings, canopy retracts, working, touch-up, orig box, 8", VG, A..$325.00

Ice Cream Vendor, litho tin, wht w/red, bl & yel trim, crank friction mechanism, working, orig box, 7", EX, A...$325.00

Ice Cream Vendor, Occupied Japan, tin & celluloid, 4x3½", EX $125.00

Impala, 1962, litho tin, gr w/tan roof, clockwork, working, orig box, 7½", EX, A..$90.00

Indian Police Cycle, litho tin, gr & red w/mc trim, friction w/siren, working, orig box, 6", VG-EX, A...............$825.00

Inverted Clown, litho tin head, cloth outfit & pnt celluloid ball, clockwork, working, 8", VG, A, from $225 to........$285.00

Ironing Monkey, TN, plush monkey w/rubber hands & face, litho tin ironing board, w/orig box, 6½", NM+, A $98.00

Isetta, Bandai #588, litho tin, friction, red & wht w/blk rubber tires, mk Isetta 700, 6", EX+ (EX+ box), A $390.00

Isetta, pnt tin, 2-tone gr w/litho tin interior, friction, working, orig box, 6½", EX-NM, A.................................$300.00

Jaguar Convertible, litho tin, red w/blk plastic tires, friction, orig box, 6", EX+ (VG+ box), A.................................$156.00

Jazzbo Jim, Linemar, mc litho tin, clockwork, working, orig box (warped), 6½", VG, A.....................................$1,050.00

Jenny the Balking Mule, mule pulling farmer in cart, 6x9", NM (EX box), A...$300.00

Jet Plane, friction, pilot ejects, 10", M (NM box) $150.00

Jock-O-Panda, MIB..$95.00

Joe the Xylophone Player, Linemar, litho tin clown in cloth outfit, 5", NM (EX box), from $600 to........................$800.00

Jolly Cub Carriage, plush mama bear rocks litho tin carriage w/cub holding Fairyland balloon, 6½", NM (NM box), A..$67.00

Jolly Penguin, MT, tin & cloth, orig box, 5", L5 ....$125.00

Juggling Clown, Alps, compo head, mc cloth outfit & litho tin balance balls, clockwork, working, orig box, 7¾", EX, A $775.00

Juggling Clown, CK, litho tin, travels in circle as arms move, ball circles on nose, prewar, 7", VG+, A..................$200.00

Juggling Popeye & Olive Oyl, Linemar, he juggles her as she sits in chair, 9", NM (NM box) $3,400.00

Jumbo w/Howdah, litho tin, elephant walks as hunter bobs bk & forth, 6", EX, A..$357.50

Jumping Clown, Mikini, litho tin, holds felt cloth & metal cane, jumps, dances & tips hats, 6½", NM (EX box), A...$216.00

Jumping Rabbit, litho tin w/plush ears & tail, M...........$150.00

Jumping Zebra, MS, jumps around w/monkey rider holding his hat, 7", NM (EX box), A..$150.00

Jumpy Bambi, Linemar, litho tin, brn, tan & gray, hand-tension wire mechanism w/voice, working, orig box, 5½", EX, A...$190.00

Kentucky Stagecoach, litho tin w/passenger in ea window, friction, full-figure driver holding reins, 1950s, 9", NM, A..$100.00

Kikaitaiso Gym Toy, celluloid girl performs on highbar, prewar, nice box art, 7", NM (EX box), A..............................$95.00

King Jet Car, TKK, rpl dome/no driver, EX+, M5 ....$225.00

Knitting Cat, TN, plush, cat w/ball of yarn goes through realistic knitting motions, 6", NM (EX box), A $66.00

Knitting Minnie, Linemar, mc litho tin & cloth, rubber ears, clockwork, working, 7½", VG-EX, A.......................$575.00

Ko-Ko Sandwich Man, litho tin w/pnt vinyl head, cloth outfit w/paper ad sign, clockwork, working, 7", EX, A $110.00

Ko-Ko Sandwich Man, TN, litho tin & vinyl w/cloth outfit, wears cb sign that reads Eat At Joe's..., 7", NM (EX+ box) $225.00

Kobe Lute Player, pnt wood, knob lever action, 4", EX+, A...$357.50

Kobe Sake Drinker, pnt wood, knob lever action, w/orig box, 4", VG, A..$357.50

Kobe Xylophone Player, pnt wood, knob lever action, retains paper label mk Nunobiki Doll, 4", EX+, A..............$357.50

Lincoln Futuristic XL-500, friction, plastic see-through roof, detailed interior, 7½", NM, A.................................$375.00

Little Monkey Artist, plush monkey paints, moving from easel to canvas, 6½", MIB, A..$150.00

Little Suzy Driving Her Sports Car, Kanto, red litho tin w/blk rubber tires, friction, 7", NMIB, A.............................$231.00

Load-Lift Tractor, litho tin, brn, orange & bl, rubber tires, friction, working, orig box (torn lid), 7¼", EX, A...........$35.00

Lotus Elan (GT Car Series), Bandai, red tin w/blk plastic top, plastic tires & steering wheel, friction, 8", NMIB, A.$67.00

Louie in His Dream Car, Linemar, litho tin w/celluloid Louie driving, friction, 1950s, 5", NM (EX box), A $458.00

Lucky Monkey Playing Billiards, mc litho tin, clockwork, working, orig box, 6", VG, A $220.00

Lucky Monkey Playing Billiards, TPS, litho tin, monkey hits celluloid ball & lifts his head, 4½", NM (EX box), A..$500.00

M-4 Tank, mc litho tin, friction, working, 7½", G-VG, A $10.00

Magic Circus, TPS, plastic & litho tin, skating monkey & seal on platform, pull lever for action, NM (NM box), A $242.00

Major Tooty, Alps, litho tin, vinyl & cloth, rocks, blows whistle, plays tune on drum, 13", EX+-NM (M box), A.......$160.00

Mama Rabbit Pushing Baby Carriage, CK, mc celluloid, twirling parasol w/hanging balls above carriage, 7x5", NM, A.$132.00

Man & Monkey on Motorcycle, litho tin, flat spot on drive wheel, 6", VG+, A..$170.50

Mariachi Bear, 1970s, NM, T1 ....$45.00

Marionette Theatre, Bestmaid, tinplate with cardboard roof and celluloid dancers, ca 1938, 10x10x4", A, $4,400.00.

Mars Race Car, w/driver, Yonezawa, litho tin, friction, mk #8, 5", NM (NM box), A $127.00

Mary & Her Little Lamb, CK, mc celluloid Mary on wheeled base pulls celluloid lamb on separate base, 6", EX (NM box), A..$225.00

Mary Open Car, mc litho tin, friction, working, orig box, 7", EX, from $25 to..$40.00

Mercedes Benz, pnt tin, red, w/litho tin interior, clear plastic hood, friction & battery op, orig box, 8½", VG, A..$300.00

Mercedes Benz 220S, pnt tin, blk, orange & red litho tin interior, friction, lever-action jack, orig box, 11¾", EX, A......$250.00

Mercedes Benz 300 SL Coupe, pnt tin, silver & blk w/mc litho tin interior, friction, working, orig box, 8¼", EX-NM, A $140.00

Mercury w/Siren, Bandai, friction, lithoed inside rear window w/luggage & magazines, rubber tires, 6½", NMIB, A.$85.00

Merry Ball Blower Circus Car, KO, litho tin, balances styrofoam ball in stream of air above, 5x5", NM (NM box), A $150.00

Merry Cockyolly See-Saw, SY, litho tin, 2 chicks on base rock & make eating motion, 5x6", NM (NM box), from $325 to...$425.00

Merry-Go-Round Truck, TN, tin, advances w/bell noise as merry-go-round turns w/3 kids on horseback, 1957, 8", A...$145.00

MG Midget, Bandai, friction, flip-down windshield, litho spoked wheels, tin steering wheel, 8", NM (EX box), A $200.00

Mickey & Minnie Acrobats, pnt celluloid figures on wire trapeze, working, orig box (torn), 11½", EX, A $375.00

Mickey & Minnie Swinging Exibition Flights, pnt celluloid w/wire frame, clockwork, working, orig box, 13½", NM, A $775.00

Mickey Mouse, Linemar, litho tin, blk, red, yel & wht, rubber ears, clockwork, working, 5¾", EX, A.....................$175.00

Mickey Mouse, Running Mickey on Pluto; Occupied Japan, c WDP, celluloid, w/tin wheel, 5x6", NM (NM box), A $7,000.00

Mickey Mouse Acrobat, Linemar, c WDP, celluloid Mickey, w/flag, 6" to top of trapeze, EX (EX box), A $650.00

Mickey Mouse Dipsy Car, Linemar, mc litho tin, clockwork, working, 5½", VG, A..$275.00

Mickey Mouse Mousexeteers Moving Van, Linemar, opening rear doors, 13", EX (EX box), A $875.00

Mickey Mouse Riding Pluto, Linemar, c WDP, Pluto's tail/their ears orig, some discolor/corrosion, 5x7", VG+, A....$750.00

Mickey Mouse Tricycle, Linemar, celluloid w/pnt features, pedal motion & ringing bell, 4x4", M (NM box), A.........$625.00

Mickey Mouse Tricycle, Linemar, mc litho tin w/celluloid Mickey, clockwork, working, orig box, 3¾", VG, A..$425.00

Mickey Mouse Whirligig, Borgfeldt, c WED, celluloid, Mickey on ball under parasol, both spin, 9", NM (EX box), A...$5,000.00

Mickey Mouse Zylophone Player, Linemar, he moves bk & forth as he plays, w/tail, 7", NM (EX box).....................$1,400.00

Mickey Mouse Zylophone Player, Linemar, litho tin, w/rubber tail & nose, clockwork, orig box (torn), 6⅜", VG, A.......$625.00

Mickey Mouse Zylophone Player, Linemar, litho tin w/rubber tail (rpl), moves, plays, 7", EX, A...........................$582.00

Mighty Aircraft Carrier, NS, litho tin, helicopter & 2 jets on deck, blades spin, friction, 9", VG (EX+ box), A $90.00

Mike Mallard the Climbing Fireman, Linemar, litho tin, Mike climbs up ladder & slides down, 1950s, orig box, NM, A...$346.00

Milk Drinking Bear, pours milk into cup & lifts to mouth, NM $80.00

Minnie Mouse Knitting in Rocking Chair, Linemar, 7", VG-EX, A..$400.00

Minnie Mouse Knitting in Rocking Chair, Linemar, mc litho tin, cloth w/rubber ears, clockwork, orig box, 6¾", EX, A $775.00

Miss Bruin the Typist, Kanto, litho tin girl w/vinyl head & blond hair, 5½", NM (NM box), A...........................$91.00

Miss Busy-Bee the Typist, Kanto, vinyl head, 5½", NMIB, A $115.00

Mobil Tanker, litho tin, friction, working, orig box, 9½", EX, A...$100.00

Model A Ford, mostly tin, friction, 1960s, EX, C8 ....$45.00

Model T Convertible, MT, tin, friction, lever action, 1960s, M, C8...$45.00

Model T Sedan, MT, tin, friction, lever action, 1960s, M, C8...$45.00

Monkey Baseball Catcher, mc litho tin, scarce, 1950s, 7", VG, A...$206.00

Monkee-Mobile, painted plastic and lithographed tin, friction (non-working), original box, 12", EX, A, from $300.00 to $350.00.

Monkey Basketball Player, TPS, litho tin monkey bends over & shoots underhand into basket, 8", NM (EX box), A $342.00

Monkey Batter, litho tin, bl, brn, red & gr w/rubber tail, clockwork, 4 motions, working, orig box, 7", EX, A $475.00

Monkey Cycle, Bandai, monkey on Comic Circus cycle rings & lifts bell, eyes pop out of head, 5", NM (EX box), A $220.00

Monkey the Sheriff, litho tin, plush, bl cloth pants & plastic guns, clockwork, sounds, working, orig box, 7", EX, A..........$60.00

Monkey w/Cymbals, brn fur, red cap, orange ears, flush face, cymbals clap & body jumps, VG $80.00

Monkey w/Field Glasses, tin, working, MIB, C8..............$75.00

Motorcycle, w/driver w/goggles, litho tin, 5", VG, A........$88.00

Motorcycle w/Sidecar, 2 figures, No 2 printed on sidecar, sparks, L5 ....$425.00

Mountain Climber, litho tin & cloth, yel, red, gr & orange, pull tension climbing action, orig box, 6½", EX, A........$170.00

Moving Elephant, Occupied Japan, mc celluloid, nods head, vibrates about, tail spins, ears move, bell rings, 6", MIB, A..$175.00

Moving Gun Police Car, TN, advances as gun rotates, friction, 1950s, EX (EX box), A..$120.00

Mr Caterpiller, TPS, mc litho tin in 3 sections w/spring antenna, advances in swiveling motion, EX+ (EX+ box), A $132.00

Mr Dan Hot Dog Eating Man, TN, litho tin & vinyl, lifts hot dog to mouth, chews & wipes mouth, 7", M (NM box), A..$75.00

Mr Dan the Coffee-Drinking Man, TN, working, 1960s, MIB, from $75 to..$85.00

Music Hall, Linemar, plush dog sits at piano, hits keys & plays tune, 6", EX (NM box), A..$304.00

Musical Bunny w/Xylophone, plush bunny seated atop litho tin barrel, 9", NM (EX box), A..$95.00

Musical Clown, TN, working, MIB, C8..$75.00

My 3 Friends, litho tin swing w/pnt celluloid figures, clockwork, 3 motions, working, touch-up, orig box, 10", VG-EX, A.$120.00

Mystery Police Cycle, mc litho tin, crank friction mechanism, working, orig box, 6¼", VG, A $225.00

National DC-8, Linemar, friction, silver, bl & red, sparking action, slightly scuffed box, 16x16", NM, A............$120.00

Naughty Boy, litho tin, gr, bl & brn, bulging eyes, clockwork, working, 5¼", VG, A...$325.00

Naughty Dog, KT, celluloid dog w/pnt features shakes litho tin boot, 7½", NM (EX+ box), from $175 to $225.00

New Cadillac Sedan, tin litho, bl w/wht top, plastic steering wheel, front & rear windshields, 9¼", EX+ (EX box), A $300.00

Ninkimono, Modern Toy, celluloid hands & face, lg wood shoes, balances pole on forehead, prewar, 13", NMIB, A ..$250.00

Northwest Airlines Strato-Cruiser, Alps, litho tin w/blk balloon rubber tires, 1950s, 18½" wingspan, EX (EX box), A..$523.00

Ocean Speed Boat, litho tin, gr outboard w/sound, friction, crank hdl, working, orig box, 11", EX, A $70.00

Old Fashioned Car #6, Modern Toys, litho tin, red, bl & blk, lever action, working, orig box, 5¼", VG, A $35.00

Oldsmobile, pnt tin, red & pk w/litho tin interior, friction w/siren, working, orig box, 13", VG-EX, A.............$400.00

Olive Oyl Ballet Dancer, Linemar, NM (EX box), D10, $650.00.

Olive Oyl on Tricycle, feet go up & down, bell rings, rpt arms/feet, needs some rpr, 4x2x3½", A....................$250.00

Olive Oyl Roadster, Linemar, tin friction, yel w/blk rubber tires, Olive Oyl has long flowing hair, 8", EX, A..............$545.00

Open Car #70, MT, friction, bright bl Jaguar-like vehicle w/driver & passenger, 6", NMIB, A $180.00

Open Sleigh, MT, litho tin & plastic, 2 Husky dogs pulling Eskimo in sleigh, 15", EX (EX box), A $367.00

Oscar the Seal, TPS, in cloth carnival attire, twirls celluloid device attached to his nose, 5", EX+ (EX box), A...$100.00

Over the Hill, Alps, litho tin, 3" racer navigates track & catapults from lower to upper level, 23", EX (EX box), A.........$159.00

Pan Am 747 Jumbo Jet, TT, friction, red, wht & bl, box has sm stain, 15x13", NM, A $75.00

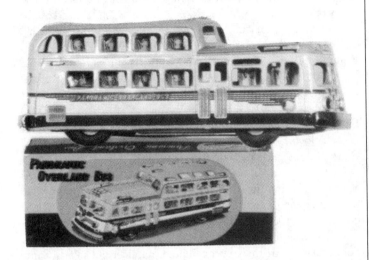

Panoramic Overland Bus with Black Rider, Marusan, lithographed tin, friction, 12½", NMIB, A, $545.00.

Pango-Pango African Dancer, litho tin, brn, yel & red, clockwork, working, orig box, 6", EX, A $165.00

Patrol Car, mc litho tin, crank friction, working, right rear wheel damaged, lt touch-up on bottom, 6", VG, A...............$40.00

Patrol Plane, litho tin w/plastic prop activated by blk rubber tires, friction, 14" wingspan, EX (EX-NM box), A $78.00

Percy Penguin, TN, litho tin, friction, Percy on skis advances as wings flap, mouth opens, squeaks, 5", NMIB, A......$155.00

Picnic Dog, Yonezawa, plush, vinyl & litho tin, wears sign around neck that reads Vacation Today, 5½", NM (NM box), A...$60.00

Pinocchio, Walking; Linemar, litho tin w/rubber nose, arms move & head nods as he advances, 1960s, 6", MIB, from $650 to...$800.00

Pinocchio, Walking; Linemar, mc litho tin, clockwork, working, orig box, 5¾", EX, A..$425.00

Pioneer Spirit Covered Wagon, 3-D driver whips team of horses, battery-op lanterns, 11", EX+, A.............................$145.00

Pirate, mc litho tin w/rubber sword, clockwork, working, orig box, 6", VG-EX, A..$260.00

Piston Action Bulldozer, TN, litho tin, friction w/battery-op lighted piston action, NM (EX box), A....................$100.00

Plane Tower, ATC, lever action, 2 4" planes (Firebird & Comet) spin around tower, satellite atop, 12", NM (EX box), A...$330.00

Playful Animal Swing, mc litho tin, clockwork, working, orig box, 6", VG-EX, A..$210.00

Pluto, Playful; Linemar, head nods, rubber tail twirls, 6", EX (EX box), A..$425.00

Pluto, Stretchy; Linemar, litho tin, orange & gr, rubber ears & tail, clockwork, working, orig box, 7½", VG, A $400.00

Pluto, Walking; Linemar, yel & blk plush, clockwork, working, plush soiled, rubber tail missing, 6", G, A.................$35.00

Pluto, Walking; Linemar, yel plush, rubber tail & ears w/litho tin eyes, clockwork, working, orig box, 5½", EX, A...$95.00

Pluto Drum Major, Linemar, litho tin, orange, red & gr w/rubber ears, clockwork w/squeaker, working, 6", VG, A.....$270.00

Pluto Drum Major, Linemar, litho tin w/rubber tail & ears, blows horn & rings bell, 6¼", NM (NM box), A, from $450 to...$500.00

Pluto Pulling Cart, Linemar, tin w/rubber tail & orig ears, friction, EX, A...$527.00

Pluto Unicyclist, Linemar, litho tin w/rubber ears & tail, pedals unicycle, working, orig box, 5½", EX, A.................$475.00

Pluto Wagon, Linemar, litho tin, blk, red & yel, friction, working, w/orig paper label, 8½", EX, A.........................$270.00

Plymouth Fury, ca 1958, Bandai, yel & fr, friction, missing wheels, 8¼", G, W1...$39.00

Plymouth Fury, 1958, Bandai, litho tin w/plastic windshield, bench seat interior, friction, 8½", EX, A $202.00

Plymouth Station Wagon, Bandai, friction, Plymouth in raised letters by bk gate, rubber tires, 8½", EX (EX box), A...$237.00

Plymouth Valiant, pnt tin, blk & bl, red & gray litho tin interior, clockwork, working, orig box, 7¼", VG-EX, A.........$120.00

Plymouth w/Siren, Ichiko, litho tin w/blk plastic tires, red w/wht top, friction, 6½", EX+ (EX box), A.........................$150.00

Police Auto, litho tin, bl, wht & yel, friction w/siren, working, orig box, 8", EX, A..$60.00

Police Auto Motorcycle, mc litho tin, friction, working, orig box, 7¾", EX, A...$75.00

Police Department Patrol Helicopter, tin, friction, 10", EX, J2...$38.00

Police Helicopter, S&E, litho tin, w/tin pilot & co-pilot, props spin, engine sounds, friction, 11", EX (EX box), A....$65.00

Police Motorcycle, litho tin w/red & wht helmeted man, plastic side wheels, sounds, friction, 9", EX (NM window box), A..$94.00

Police Motorcycle & Driver, litho tin, 6½", VG+, A.....$150.00

Police Patrol Motorcycle, TN, racing cycle, sparks show through side windows, driver crouches, sounds, 8", NM (M box), A...$175.00

Poor Peter, pnt celluloid w/cloth outfit, clockwork, working, orig box (rough), 5¾", VG-EX, A.................................$625.00

Popeye, celluloid, c King Features 1929, shakes, head moves up & down, 8", NMIB, A...$1,500.00

Popeye Basketball Player, Linemar, c King Features, 9", M- (NM box), A...$3,800.00

Popeye Cyclist, Linemar, on high-wheeler, all orig, 7x4", NM (VG box), A..$3,200.00

Popeye Roller-Skater, Linemar, litho tin w/cloth pants, wood pipe, clockwork, working, orig box, 6¼", EX, A...$1,000.00

Popeye the Acrobat, Linemar, litho tin w/rocker base, Popeye hits Bluto while swinging from highbar, 12½", NMIB, A...$4,250.00

Popeye the Traveler, Modern Toy, pnt compo w/fabric suitcase, working, 6", VG, A...$475.00

Popeye Tricycle, Linemar, tin & celluloid, working, bell rings, 4x3", NM (EX box), A..$2,250.00

Popeye Turnover Tank, Linemar, mc litho tin, clockwork, working, orig box (flap missing), 4", VG, A...................$450.00

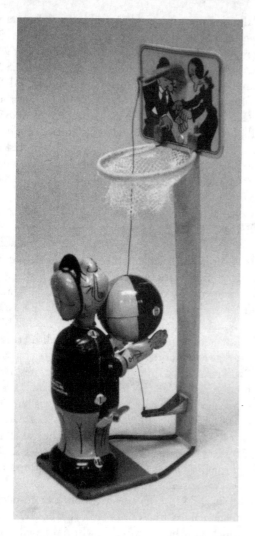

Popeye Basketball Player, Linemar, 1950s, NM, D10, $1,850.00.

Popeye Turnover Tank, Linemar, silver version, 4x3", NM (EX box) $1,500.00

Popeye Unicyclist, Linemar, litho tin, cloth pants, wood pipe, clockwork, working, retouch, orig box, 5½", VG, A.$1,350.00

Popeye Unicyclist, Linemar, litho tin/cloth trousers (stains), missing wood pipe bowl, 6", EX (EX box), A $2,000.00

Porter, MT/Occupied Japan, celluloid, Blk man w/bags, walks & head moves, 5½", M (NM+ box), A $546.00

Prehistoric Animal (dinosaur), Linemar, litho tin, yel & gr, clockwork w/sound, working, orig box, 8", EX, A ...$425.00

R-102 Airship, litho tin, gr dirigible w/plastic prop, working, orig box, 9½", EX, A...$375.00

R-26 Dragon Speedboat, litho tin, orange, red, blk & gr, friction, skiing action, working, 14", VG-EX, A....................$150.00

Rabbit Drummer, Alps, litho tin, beats drum w/vibrating motion & shakes head, 9", EX, A $393.00

Rabbit w/Balloons, 1960s, MIN, T1 ....$65.00

Rabbit w/Doghouse, celluloid, 1950s, VG, T1 ....$65.00

Racing Car w/Piston Action, OKK, friction, dual tin litho drivers, 10", NM (G box), A..................................$175.00

Rambler, Bandai, friction, bl w/wht top, VG+ (VG box), M5..$125.00

Rocket Racer, MT, friction, EX $165.00

Rocking Dog, litho tin, rocks & swings lariat, working, orig box (tape rpr), 6", VG, A $75.00

Roger Rabbit, MIB, D4/T1, from $40 to $50.00

Rolls Royce, pnt tin, gray, bl & wht litho tin interior, friction, working, orig box, 8½", EX, A $160.00

Round Motorcycle, mc litho tin, friction, working, w/spring-cable racetrack, orig box, 4¾", VG-EX, A..............$250.00

Round-Up Ride, litho tin w/celluloid riders, 3 cars rotate around sq carnival-type ride, 6½x6½", VG+, A $825.00

Rowing Boat, mc litho tin boat w/figure, clockwork, working, touch-up, orig box, 8", VG, A..................................$230.00

Sam the Strolling Skeleton, litho tin, wht w/gray, yel & bl trim, clockwork, working, orig box, 5½", VG-EX, A $300.00

Santa Claus, Alps, litho tin w/vinyl head, 10", ca 1955, MIB..$100.00

Santa Claus, mc litho tin, clockwork, bell rings, Santa waves sign, head turns, working, 6", VG-EX, A.................$130.00

Santa Claus, Occupied Japan, celluloid, bag over shoulder, waddles around & nods head, 3½", NM (EX box), A....$175.00

Santa Claus Christmas Eve, celluloid, reindeer pulls early Santa on sled as bell rings, prewar, 6", VG- (EX box), A ..$105.00

Santa on Skis, mc litho tin, clockwork, working, missing ski pole ring, 5¾", G, A $35.00

Santa on Skis, mk KSK, litho tin, orig box, EX, A.........$198.00

School Line Bus, Marusan, litho tin, bold graphics, friction w/siren, working, orig box, 7½", EX, A....................$400.00

Scottie Dog, blk fur w/bone in mouth, works, mk Made in Japan, VG $70.00

Seal, litho tin, moves fins & ball, NM $90.00

See-Saw Cats on Cat House, CK, 2 celluloid cats rock bk & forth under umbrella atop wood-like house, 11", EX, A..$345.00

Sharp Shooter, Alps, celluloid soldier crawls, stops, fires & continues, 8", MIB, A.......................................$77.00

Shoes Dog, MT, Occupied Japan, celluloid dog grabs & shakes litho tin shoe, 4", NMIB, A..................................$85.00

Singing Canary, Alps, celluloid on tin legs, holds paper leaf in mouth, vibrates & sings, 4", EX+ (M box), A $65.00

Siren 1902 Ford Jalopy, Linemar, friction, allover graffiti, convertible w/2 celluloid riders, 8¼", NM (G+ box), A $180.00

Skating Chef, TPS, lithographed tin, clockwork, VG-EX, 6", A, from $325.00 to $400.00.

Skating Bear, litho tin w/cloth pants & rubber ears, clockwork, working, 6", VG, A..$110.00

Skating Dogs, litho tin, dog on wheels pulls 2 skating dogs, working, 9½", EX, A...$75.00

Skating Hobo Clown, TPS, litho tin w/cloth clothes, advances in erratic circular motions, 5½", EX, A...................$273.00

Skippy the Tricky Cyclist, TPS, litho tin, clown in circus outfit, 6", EX (EX box), A, from $210 to...........................$235.00

Sky-View Taxi w/Siren, Linemar, friction, rates on doors, separate roof plate, siren sounds, 5", EX- (G box), A.....$120.00

Smarty Pants, litho tin w/vinyl head, raises bottle & drops pants, MIB...$125.00

Smiling Dandy, mc litho tin w/blk plush hair & rubber cane, clockwork, 3 motions, working, orig box, 6", EX, A.$250.00

Smiling Sam the Carnival Man, Alps, litho tin clown in cloth outfit, vibrates & twirls cane, 9", EX, A $207.00

Sniffing Rooting Pig, TN, lt orange plush w/red cloth collar & tin ears, ears, tail & snout move, 1960s, 6", M (NM box) $46.00

Sniffy Puppy, TN, litho tin, puppy wiggles his nose & wags his tail, advances w/nonfall action, MIB, A $70.00

Snow White Van Trailer, Linemar, friction, she & dwarfs lithoed on trailer, 2 rear doors open, 13", NMIB, A $2,000.00

Soldier Shooting Gun, tin, 5", EX+, J2 ....$85.00

Speed King Racer, w/driver, Maruya Toys, #61, tin friction, blk rubber tires, 11", EX (EX box), A $136.00

Speed Lion Cycle, litho tin, brn w/gr, orange & red, friction, sparks & siren, working, orig box, 5½", EX, A.........$350.00

Speedy Donkey, pnt tin & celluloid, gr, red & bl, clockwork, bell rings, working, w/orig label, orig box, 7", VG-EX, A $150.00

Spin-A-Roo, Alps, carnival vehicle travels bk & forth w/wild action, 6", NM+, A $160.00

Spirit of St Louis, litho tin w/fancy rubber design behind propeller, mk X-2 Ryan NYP on tail fin, 12", EX, A $226.00

Sports Car, friction, 8", MIB, D10, $325.00.

Sprite Day Cruiser, Sutcliffe, metal w/rubber closure, 1950s, 9½", NM (EX box), A $87.00

Stream-Liner Express Train, silver litho tin w/red accents, friction, 13", EX+ (VG box), A.....................................$60.00

Strolling Cat in Dress, pnt celluloid & cloth, clockwork, working, split seam in head, 4", G, A.............................$20.00

Submarine, anchor trademark, tin w/litho tin America flag, lg gun on deck, 12", paper litho on box, EX (EX box), A...$275.00

Super Fire Engine, K, mc litho tin, detailed engine w/telescopic ladder, blk rubber tires, friction, 13", EX (NM box), A $107.00

Super Sonic Racer, tin, friction, w/orig tag, ca 1950s, NMIB...$145.00

Superman Turn-Over Tank, Linemar, litho tin, figure lifts gr tank, working, 4", G, A.....................................$110.00

Superman Turn-Over Tank, Linemar, litho tin, gr w/yel & bl trim, clockwork, working, 3¾", VG, A..................$300.00

Susie the Ostrich, TPS, litho tin, Susie pulling clown in cart, scarce, 5½x5½", NM (EX box), A $950.00

Suzy Bouncing Ball, TPS, litho tin w/vinyl head, bounces tin ball attached by wire, arms move, 5", EX (NM box), A...$88.00

T-Bird Convertible, Japan for Sears, pnt tin, red & wht, friction, operable windows, working, orig box, 15", VG, A...$130.00

Take-Off Airport, TPS, 3x3" Fighter N-100 circles above airport & city lithographed on tin base, NM (EX box), A..$159.00

Tambourine Clown, rocks from side to side, bell-jingling sound, 7½", EX+, A...$200.00

Tap Dancer, Alps, pnt celluloid, litho tin & cloth, red coat, checked pants, clockwork, working, orig box, 8¼", EX, A $525.00

Teddy Bear, lt brn fur w/orange ribbon around neck, legs & head moves, original box & key, VG.............................$110.00

Teddy's Cycle, Occupied Japan, EX $125.00

Televi Jeep, friction, M..$75.00

Texas Sporting Convertible, Indian chief lithoed on sides, mtd cowboy on trunk, siren sounds, 6", NM (G box), A $100.00

Thirsty Monkey, plush & litho tin monkey on tree trunk, pours & drinks in realistic motion, 6", NM (NM box), A ..$70.00

Tortoise Piggyback Race, mc litho tin, clockwork, working, orig box, 6", VG-EX, A $120.00

Touchdown Pete, TPS, litho tin football player in red & bl uniform, wht & red helmet, scarce, 5", EX+ (VG+ box), A..$493.00

Toyland Elf, 2 actions, early 1960s, M $85.00

Toyota Corolla 1100, pnt tin, bl w/red & yel litho tin interior, friction, working, orig box, 10", EX, A $140.00

Tramp of Lady & the Tramp, Linemar, fur-covered tin, tail spins, legs move, EX, M8.......................................$100.00

Transport Van, SSS, friction, Express Freight on side, opening rear door, 9", NMIB, A...$90.00

Traveling Boy, Alps, celluloid boy walks w/tin suitcase, 4½", EX+ (M box), A...$111.00

Traveller Monkey w/Camera, Alps, plush & cloth w/litho tin feet, 6½", NM (NM box), A $99.00

Tri Cycling Clown, MT, vinyl head, cloth suit w/red jacket & striped pants (rare version), 12", NM (EX box), A .$750.00

Tri Cycling Clown, MT, vinyl head, red & wht polka-dotted suit, 12", NM (EX box), A $650.00

Tricycle, Occupied Japan, litho metal, 2½", EX $90.00

Trombone Player, Linemar, litho tin, 5½", NM (EX box), A...$308.00

Trumpet Player, TN, Blk man w/vinyl face & cloth clothes on litho tin base, EX+ (EX box), A $455.00

Tumbling Clown, cloth & celluloid, pnt features, performs somersalts, 5½", EX+ (VG+ box), A.....................$200.00

Turkey, Alps, litho tin & plush, brn, yel & gr, clockwork, sounds, working, orig box, 7", EX, A.........................$80.00

Turkey, mc litho tin, clockwork, walks as tail feathers fan out, working, orig box, 4½", VG, A $145.00

Turn-Over Circus Plane, Yone, litho tin, clown pilot w/headgear, 4" wingspan, EX (EX box), A.........................$165.00

TWA Jet Airliner, Japan, friction, 1970s, 14", T1..........$135.00

Uncle Sam, CK, mc celluloid, arms & googly eyes move as hat appears to fly off, prewar, 6½", G+ (NM box), A....$231.00

Upsy Down Clown, Alps, litho tin clown on motorcycle w/Gus lettered on seat, friction, 1950s, 6¼", NM (EX box), A $775.00

US Air Force F-105A, AAA, litho tin w/rubber needle nose cone, pilot in cockpit, friction, 10", EX, A $63.00

US Army Helicopter, Marusan, tin pilot, aircraft advances, props turn, rear rises & it turns, 8", M (NM box), A...........$100.00

US Military Ambulance, Cragstan, friction, ca 1955, 6", MIB $68.00

Vacation Land Airplane Ride, mc litho tin, boats & planes revolve around tower, clockwork, orig box, 5¼", VG-EX, A $80.00

Valiant Convertible, Yonezawa, red tin body w/litho interior, blk rubber tires, working wipers, 9", EX+ (VG+ box), A $175.00

Volkswagen Micro-Bus, Cragstan, pnt tin, red & metallic gray w/litho tin interior, friction, orig box, 8", EX-NM, A..$230.00

Volkswagon Bug, friction, bl, not working, 8", M5..........$50.00

Volkswagon Bug, tin, red & wht, blk rubber tires, working, ca 1960s, 2⅝", NM, W1 ....$19.00

Volkswagon Bug Police Car, Aoshin, tin, friction, multi-action, ca 1970s, M (NM box), W1 ....$54.00

Volkswagon Ice Cream Van, Taiyo, litho tin, friction, ice cream bars & polar bears on ea side, 9", NM (VG box), A.$167.00

Wabbling Pelican, MT, pnt celluloid, advances in wobbling motion as beak moves up & down, 4½", NM (EX box), A $78.00

Waggles the Dog, Alps, litho tin, tail spins in operation, 3¼", NM (VG box), A..$87.00

Walking Bear, Occupied Japan, MIB...........................$140.00

Walking Collie, Alps, plush, 5½", NM (NM box), A $35.00

Walking Drummer Clown, MM, litho tin & cloth, beats drum & holds rubber horn, 11", EX (NM box), A $365.00

Walking Mule, working, EX, C8 ....$65.00

Walking Pet Tortoise, litho tin, gr, yel, red & orange, clockwork, 3 motions, working, orig box, 6½", VG, A $85.00

Walking Wimpy, celluloid w/pnt features, carries cane, moves up & down while swaying, 1940s, 7", EX+, A $340.00

Wandering Chimpanzee, Occupied Japan, M.................$185.00

Wild Roaring Bull & Boy, Mikuni, litho tin, bull advances as boy is dragged from behind, 9", NM (EX box), A ...$152.00

World Circus Truck, friction, litho paper cylinder revolves showing animals, seal & clown on top, 9", EX (EX- box), A...$235.00

XV-3 Bell Helicopter, Linemar, litho tin, twin rotors, friction, working, orig box, 8", EX, A $120.00

Xylophone Clown, Linemar, litho tin w/brn cloth jacket, clockwork, working, 5", G+, A.......................................$130.00

Yearling, TN, deer w/bow tie, rubber ears, advances by hopping, toy & box mk Occupied, 6", NM (G box), A..........$120.00

Spanish

Airflow Car, Paya, 13", VG+-EX $300.00

Auto Gyro, Rico, litho tin, bl & wht plane, wheels & prop turn, working, 9", VG, A...$375.00

Bugatti Racer, Paya, new issue, steers, working, orig box, 18½", M, A $150.00

Felix the Cat Pulled by Mule, litho tin, key wind through spokes of cart, ca 1920s-30s, very rare, 7x4", NM..........$13,500.00

Mickey & Felix Sparkler, Isla, ea lights cigar from candle, rpl mechanism, rpl tin pcs in bk, 6x5", EX, A $10,000.00

Motorcycle & Rider, RSA, non-working, 6½", EX, A ...$325.00

Tom & Jerry Crazy Track, 2 cars w/vinyl-headed Tom & Jerry navigate 11x16" track, 1950s, 12x17" box, NM (EX box), A..$875.00

Train, Paya, engine, tender, car & caboose, 1930s, L5 .....$39.00

Wyandotte

Though the Wyandotte Company (Michigan) produced toys of all types, included here are only the heavy-gauge pressed-steel cars, trucks, and other vehicles they made through the 1930s and '40s. See also Aeronautical; Boats; Character Collectibles; Windups, Friction, and Other Mechanicals.

Cars and Busses

Airstream-Styled Coupe, red w/4 molded fenders, plated grille & bumper, wht rubber tires, 5", VG, A $61.00

Boat-Tail Speedster, lt gr w/gold stripping (probably added), wht rubber tires, lt rust spots, 5⅞", EX, A $198.00

Boat-Tail Speedster, red w/4 molded fenders, yel wood wheels, electric headlights, 20-gauge steel, 8⅝", VG-EX, A $220.00

Bus, lt bl w/plated grille, blk wood wheels, stamped mk on left side, 5¼", VG, A $105.00

Bus, wht cab w/litho grille, lt bl coach w/Coast To Coast Bus Line decals, rubber tires, wood hubs, 24", VG-EX, A..........$495.00

Cord, '30s era, yel w/red top, Deco styling, rubber tires, friction drive (non-working), 4x13", G, A $175.00

Cord w/Trailer, red car w/yel roof & plated bumper, wood wheels, rear door opens, blk floor board, rpl parts, 24", G, A $468.00

Coupe, caramel w/4 molded fenders, plated grille & bumpers, wht rubber tires, electric headlights, 9", EX, A........$198.00

Coupe, red w/4 blk fenders, wht rubber tires, electric headlights (tabs missing), orig box (rpl ends), 8¼", NM, A $286.00

LaSalle Sedan, apple gr, wht rubber tires, blk steel belly pan, plated trim, dummy headlights, rpl tires, 15¾", EX, A $468.00

LaSalle Sedan & Trailer, gr w/plated grille, wht rubber tires, blk steel belly pan, dummy headlights, 15½", EX-NM, A $880.00

Packard & Trailer, prewar (door opens on trailer), rpl wheels, orig pnt, 25", EX, A $500.00

Sedan, lt bl w/4 molded wheel covers, silver grille, blk tires, 5¾", VG-EX, A $83.00

Station Wagon, 24", EX $300.00

Streamline Touring Sedan, bl w/gray front grille, plastic wheels, 6", VG+, A $35.00

Firefighting

Fire Chief Cord Coupe, red, blk belly pan, blk rubber tires w/red wood hubs, spring mechanism, non-working, 13", G-VG, A $209.00

Fire Chief Hook & Ladder Truck, NMIB..........................$75.00

Hook & Ladder Truck, litho tin, red, yel & blk, rubber tires, orig decals, orig box (damaged flap), 8½", VG, A.............$60.00

Trucks and Vans

Ambulance, ivory w/Ambulance Wyandotte Toys decal on sides, rear door opens, blk belly pan, wood wheels, 11", G, A $121.00

Army Supply #42 Corps, litho tin w/cloth cover, balloon tires, separate headlights & trim, 1939, 17", VG+ (EX box), A $393.00

Circus Truck, 11", VG, A..$300.00

Dairy Farm Truck & Trailer, pnt pressed steel, 1 litho tin stake body panel, rubber tires, 25", VG, A........................$200.00

Delivery Truck, red & gr w/plastic tires, rear door opens, dent in right fender & bumper, 17", VG, A $50.00

Dump Truck, apple gr body, blk chassis, wht rubber tires w/red wood hubs, electric headlights, 1 tire rpl, 15", G-VG, A $72.00

Dump Truck, bl cab w/yel grille & lights on red fr, apple-gr trailer on yel fr, sm chip on roof, 17", NM, A..........$110.00

Dump Truck, blk rubber tires, ca 1930s, 6", G, W1..........$34.00

Dump Truck, gr cab, red bed, Wyandotte Toys balloon tires, push lever dumping action, 1940, 11", EX, A..........$180.00

Dump Truck, lt bl cab w/plated grille, red bed, blk chassis, rubber tires w/red wood hubs, 21", EX, A......................$193.00

Dump Truck, missing rear axle, ca 1930s, 12", G, W1......$39.00

Dump Truck, orange, wht tires on red wood hubs, 19-gauge steel, 15⅛", VG-EX, A $66.00

Dump Truck, red cab & bed, blk fenders & chassis, red wood wheels, wht rubber tires, electric headlights, 15", EX, A $61.00

Dump Truck, red cab w/yel grille, gray scoop, yel & red litho bed, yel wheels, tilting tailgate, 11½", G, A $55.00

Dump Truck, red w/inset silver grille, blk Bakelite wheels, stamped mk on sides, 6", EX-NM, A..........................$39.00

Express Truck, bl & yel w/wood tires, ca 1930s, 23½", VG, W1 ....$179.00

Express Truck, red cab w/plated grille, apple-gr trailer, blk chassis & wheels, non-detachable trailer, 17", VG-EX, A $105.00

Fire Truck, w/bell & orig ladders, complete, 11½", EX (EX box)..$185.00

Gardner's Truck, gr, yel & blk litho w/decals, rubber tires, +pnt wheelbarrow, shovel & orig box, 10¼", M (VG box, A $358.00

Gasoline Truck, orange, plated grille & bumper, blk rubber tires, tailgate opens, 10¾", EX, A, from $120 to.............$140.00

Ice Truck, red cab & chassis, Toytown Ice Co Crystal Clear on sides, wht wheels, 11⅞", EX, A $171.00

Medical Truck, wht w/molded front fenders, Medical Corps & cross decal on sides, wht tin wheels, 11¾", EX, A...$176.00

Moving Van, red cab, apple-gr chassis, dk bl trailer, dummy headlights, blk rubber tires, orig box, 24¾", NM, A.........$633.00

Moving Van, red cab, blk chassis, bl trailer, litho grille, spare tire mtd on rear, tailgate drops, 24¾", EX, A $495.00

Oil Tanker, ca 1930s, 10", G, $145.00.

Railway Express Agency Truck, red & bl, NP grille, litho tin cargo box, rubber wheels, 12", VG-EX, A $150.00

Semi-Trailer Express Truck #830, litho bl, silver & blk cab, red fr, non-detachable yel trailer, orig box, 17¼", M, A $413.00

Shady Glen Stock Ranch Tractor Trailer, ca 1950s, 17", EX...$185.00

Stake Truck, red & blk, rubber tires (incomplete), 9½", G, A $25.00

Stake Truck, red cab & gr bed on blk fr, blk rubber tires w/red hubs, electric headlights, plated grille, 15", VG, A ...$66.00

Stake Truck, red cab w/bl grille, apple gr bed, blk chassis & wood wheels, pnt loss, 12½", A..................................$28.00

Stake Truck, red w/blk fenders, yel wood wheels, decals on doors, lt rust, 15", VG-EX, A $300.00

Sunshine Dairy Farms Truck, red cab, yel, wht & bl bed, yel wheels, ad insert in bed, 12", unused, NM (EX box), A $585.00

Tow Truck, litho, gr & wht w/pinstriping, red plastic wheels, tools missing, orig box, 15", VG-EX, A $160.00

Van, red cab w/plated grille & dummy headlights, yel van w/rear door, blk belly pan, missing plating, 17½", EX, A $242.00

Wrecker, red cab w/molded fenders, plated grille, ivory bed w/Official AAA Service decal, red wheels, 12", EX, A.........$330.00

Yo-Yos

Yo-Yos are starting to attract toy collectors, especially those with special features such as Hasbro's 'Glow-Action' and Duncan's 'Whistler.' For more information contact Lucky Meisenheimer, who is listed under Yo-Yos in the section entitled Categories of Special Interest. (Mr. Meisenheimer is a collector; he does not sell yo-yos.)

Alox Mfg, Flying Disk, wood, ca 1950s, 2⅛", M..............$35.00
Duncan, Baseball, 1965, MOC, J2.........................$8.00
Duncan, Beginners & Juniors, wood, ea.....................$5.00
Duncan, Butterfly, wood, M.............................$10.00
Duncan, Cattle Brand, logo on simulated wood, ca 1965, NM...$22.50

Duncan, Five Jewel, wood, M............................$50.00
Duncan, Four Jewel, M.................................$25.00
Duncan, Glow Imperial, red letters on cream, w/logo, ca 1965, EX..$20.00
Duncan, Jumbo Award, wood, M $30.00
Duncan, Satellite Lighted, battery-op, ca 1965-68, MOC $25.00
Duncan, Strings, Official Egyptian Fibre Strings, MIP $10.00
Duncan, Tournaments, M, from $8 to.....................$20.00
Duncan, Whistler, 1950s, NMOC........................$35.00
Fli-Back, gr, plastic sparkle, 1960s, T1 ....$3.00
Hasbro, Glow-Action, dtd 1968, MOC $45.00
Life Saver, wood promo, M..............................$22.00
Orbit, CL Land, plastic satellite & Earth, on 4x6" display card, 1969, unused (NM card), T2...........................$10.00
Whirl King, Standard Model, red & bl w/gold logo, 1950s, 3", M...$35.00
Yogi Bear, gr & brn plastic, VG, T6......................$3.00
Yogi Bear, Justen, 1976, MOC, C1.......................$18.00

Duncan, Beginners Whirl King, MIP, $8.00.

Dealer Codes

Most of our description lines contain a letter/number code just before the suggested price. They correspond with the names of the following collectors and dealers, many of whom sent us their current selling list last spring. If you're interested in buying an item in question, don't hesitate to call or write them. We only ask that you consider the differences in time zones, and try to call at a convenient time. If you're corresponding, please send a self-addressed, stamped envelope for their reply. Because our data was entered several months ago, many of the coded items will have already sold, but our dealers tell us that they are often able to restock some of the same merchandise over and over. Some said that they had connections with other dealers around the country and might be able to locate a particular toy for you. But please bear in mind, that because they may have had to pay more to restock their shelves, they may also have to charge a little more than the price quoted in their original sales list.

If you have lists of toys for sale that you would like for us to use in the next edition, please send them to us at Huxford Enterprises Inc., 1202 7th Street, Covington, IN 47932, by January 1995.

(A1)
Stan and Sally Alekna
724 Oceanfront Dr.
Neptune Beach, FL 32266
904-249-4831

(A2)
Jane Anderson
Rt. 1, Box 1030
Saylorsburg, PA 18353

(A3)
Aquarius Antiques
Jim and Nancy Schaut
P.O. Box 10781
Glendale, AZ 85318-0781
602-878-4293

(A4)
Bob Armstrong
15 Monadnock Rd.
Worcester, MA 01609

(B1)
Richard Belyski
P.O. Box 124
Sea Cliff, NY 11579
516-676-1183

(B2)
Larry Blodget
Box 753
Rancho Mirage, CA 92270

(B3)
Bojo
Bob Gottuso
P.O. Box 1203
Cranberry Twp., PA 16033-2203
phone or FAX 412-776-0621

(B4)
Dick Borgerding
RJB Toys
720 E Main
Flushing, MI 48433
313-659-9859

(B5)
Bertel Bruun
P.O. Box 400
59 Shore Rd.
Westhampton, NY 11977
phone or FAX 516-288-0581

(B6)
Jim Buskirk
175 Cornell St.
Windsor, CA 95492
707-837-9949

(B7)
Danny Bynum
12311 Wedgehill Ln.
Houston, TX 77077-4805
713-972-4421 or 713-531-5711

(B8)
Stanley A. & Robert S. Block
P.O. Box 51
Trumbull, CT 06611
203-261-3223 or 203-775-0138

(B9)
Joe Bodnarchuk
62 McKinley Ave.
Kenmore, NY 14217
phone or FAX 716-873-0264

(C1)
Casey's Collectible Corner
HCR Box 31, Rt. 3
N Blenheim, NY 12131
607-588-6464

(C2)
Mark E. Chase
Collector Glass News
P.O. Box 308
Slippery Rock, PA 16057
412-946-2838

(C3)
Ken Clee
Box 1142
Philadelphia, PA 19111
215-722-1979

(C4)
Arlan Coffman
1223 Wilshire Blvd., Ste. 275
Santa Monica, CA 90403
310-453-2507

(C5)
Joe Corea
New Jersey Nostalgia Hobby
401 Park Ave.
Scotch Plains, NJ 07076
908-322-2676 or FAX 908-322-4079

(C6)
Cotswold Collectibles
P.O. Box 249
Clinton, WA 98236
206-579-1223 or FAX 206-579-1287

(C7)
James P. Crane
15 Clemson Ct.
Newark, DE 19711
302-738-6031

(C8)
Mike Czerwinski
825 Vista Cir.
Brea, CA 92621
714-990-4851

(C9)
Marilyn Cooper
8408 Lofland Dr.
Houston, TX 77055
713-465-7773.

(D1)
Allen Day
Yesterday's Toys
P.O. Box 525
Monroe, NC 28810

(D2)
Marl Davidson
5705 39th St. Circle East
Bradenton, FL 34203
813-751-6275
FAX 813-751-5463

(D3)
Larry DeAngelo
516 King Arthur Dr.
Virginia Beach, VA 23464
804-424-1691

(D4)
John DeCicco
57 Bay View Dr.
Shrewsbury, MA 01545
508-797-0023

(D5)
Dennis & George Collectibles
Dennis O'Brien
George Goehring
3407 Lake Montebello Dr.
Baltimore, MD 21218
410-889-3964

(D6)
Doug Dezso
864 Patterson Ave.
Maywood, NJ 07607

(D7)
Ron and Donna Donnelly
Saturday Heroes
P.O. Box 7047
Panama City Beach, FL 32413
904-234-7944

(D8)
George Downes
Box 572
Nutley, NJ 07110
201-935-3388

(D9)
Gordy Dutt
P.O. Box 201
Sharon Center, OH 44274-0201
216-239-1657 or FAX 216-239-2991

(D10)
Dunbar's Gallery
Leila and Howard Dunbar
76 Haven St.
Milford, MA 01757
508-634-8697 or FAX 508-634-8696

(E1)
Eccles Bros., Ltd
R.W. Eccles
R.R. #1, Box 253-D
Burlington, IA 52601
319-752-3840 (days) or 319-753-1179
(evenings); FAX 319-753-5933

(E2)
Perry R. and Donna Eichor
703 N Almond
Simpsonville, SC 29681
803-967-8770

(E3)
Alan Edwards
Toys From the Crypt
P.O. Box 3294
Shawnee, KS 66203
913-383-1242

(F1)
Figures
Anthony Balasco
P.O. Box 19482
Johnston, RI 02919
401-946-5720 or FAX 401-942-7980

(F2)
Paul Fideler
20 Shadow Oak Dr., Apt. #18
Sudbury, MA 01776
617-386-0228 (24 hours)

(F3)
Paul Fink's Fun and Games
P.O. Box 488
59 S Kent Rd.
Kent, CT 06757
203-927-4001

(F4)
Mike Fredericks
145 Bayline Cir.
Folsom, CA 95630
916-985-7986

(F5)
Fun House Toy Co.
G.F. Ridenour
P.O. Box 343
Bradfordwoods, PA 15015-0343
412-935-1392 (FAX capable)

(F6)
Donald Friedman
660 W Grand Ave.
Chicago, IL 60610

(F7)
Finisher's Touch Antiques
Steve Fisch, proprietor
10 W Main St.
Wappingers Falls, NY 12590
914-298-8882 or FAX 914-298-8945

(G1)
Gary's Trains
R.D. #2, Box 147
Boswell, PA 15531
814-629-9277

(G2)
Mark Giles
510 E Third St.
Ogalala, NE 69153
308-284-4360

(G3)
Robert Goforth
4061 E Castro Vly. Blvd.
Ste. 224
Castro Valley, CA 94552
510-889-0397 or FAX 510-581-0397

(G4)
Glass Circus Antiques
Milt and Libby Sternberg
412 W San Mateo
Santa Fe, NM 87505

(H1)
The Hamburgs
Happy Memories Antique Toy Co.
P.O. Box 1305
Woodland Hills, CA 91365
818-346-9884 or 818-346-1269
FAX 818-346-0215

(H2)
Rick Hanson
Trader Rick
P.O. Box 161
Newark, IL 60541
815-695-5135

(H3)
George Hardy
1670 Hawkwood Ct.
Charlottesville, VA 22901
804-295-4863 or FAX 804-295-4898

(H4)
Jerry and Ellen L. Harnish
110 Main St.
Bellville, OH 44813
phone or FAX 419-886-4782

(H5)
Lee Harris
5903 Watson Lane
Fredericksburg, VA 22407
703-786-8162

(H6)
Phil Helley
Old Kilbourne Antiques
629 Indiana Ave.
Wisconsin Dells, WI 53965
608-254-8770

(H7)
Jacquie and Bob Henry
Antique Treasures and Toys
Box 17
Walworth, NY 14568
315-986-1424

(H8)
Homestead Collectibles
Art and Judy Turner
R.D. 2, Rte. 150
P.O. Box 173-E
Mill Hall, PA 17751
717-726-3597 or FAX 717-726-4488

(I1)
Roger Inouye
2622 Valewood Ave.
Carlsbad, CA 92008-7925

(I2)
Terri Ivers
1104 Shirlee Ave.
Ponca City, OK 74601
405-762-8697 or 405-762-5174
FAX 405-765-5101

(J1)
Bill Jackameit
200 Victoria Dr.
Bridgewater, VA 22812
703-828-4359 (Monday-Thursday,
7 PM – 9 PM EST)

(J2)
Ed Janey
2920 Meadowbrook Dr. SE
Cedar Rapids, IA 52403
319-362-5213

(J3)
Dana Johnson Enterprises
1347 NW Albany Ave.
Bend, OR 97701-3160
503-382-8410

(J4)
David S. Jones
P.O. Box 1703
Bethlehem, PA 18016-1703
215-694-9713

(J5)
Just Toys
Hwy. 30
Standwood, IA 52337
319-945-6693

(K1)
K-3 Inc.
Bendees Only; Simpson Mania
2335 NW Thurman
Portland, OR 97210
503-222-2713

(K2)
David Kolodny-Nagy
3701 Connecticut Ave. NW #500
Washington DC 20008
202-364-8753

(L1)
Jean-Claude Lanau
740 Thicket Ln.
Houston, TX 77079
713-491-6034
(after 7:00 PM, CST)

(L2)
John and Eleanor Larsen
523 Third St.
Colusa, CA 95932
916-458-4769 (after 4 PM)

(L3)
Gary Lassin
P.O. Box 747
Gwynedd Valley, PA 19437
215-361-5100

(L4)
Tom Lastrapes
P.O. Box 2444
Pinellas Park, FL 34664
813-545-2586

(L5)
Stephen Leonard
Box 127
Albertson, LI, NY 11507
516-742-0979

(L6)
Kathy Lewis
Chatty Cathy's Haven
187 N Marcello Ave
Thousand Oaks, CA 91360
805-499-7932

(L7)
Terry and Joyce Losonsky
7506 Summer Leave Ln.
Columbia, MD 21046-2455
301-381-3358

(M1)
Mark and Val Macaluso
3603 Newark Rd.
Marion, NY 14505
315-926-4349 or FAX 315-926-4853

(M2)John McKenna
801-803 W Cucharres
Colorado Springs, CO 80918
719-630-8732

(M3)
Lucky Meisenheimer
7300 Sand Lake Commons Blvd.
Orlando, FL 32819
407-354-0478

(M4)
Bill Mekalian
550 E Chesapeake Cir.
Fresno, CA 93720
209-434-3247

(M5)
Mike's General Store
52 St. Annes Rd.
Winnipeg, Manitoba, Canada R2M-2Y3
204-255-3463 or FAX 204-253-4124

(M6)
Paul David Morrow
13550 Foothill Blvd. #28
Sylmar, CA 91342
818-898-9592

(M7)
Judith A. Mosholder
R.D. #2, Box 147
Boswell, PA 15531
814-629-9277

(M8)
The Mouse Man Ink
P.O. Box 3195
Wakefield, MA 01880
phone or FAX 617-246-3876

(M9)
Steven Meltzer
670 San Juan Ave. #B
Venice, CA 90291
310-396-6007

(M10)
Gary Metz
4803 Lange Ln. SW
Roanoke, VA 24018
703-989-0475

(N1)
Natural Way/DBA Russian Toy Co.
820 Massachusetts
Lawrence, KS 66044
913-841-0100

(N2)
Norman's Olde & New Store
Philip Norman
126 W Main St.
Washington, NC 27889-4944
919-946-3448

(O1)
Olde Tyme Toy Mall
105 S Main St.
Fairmount, IN 46928
317-948-3150

(P1)
Parkway Furniture & Gift Shop
603 Volunteer Parkway
Bristol, TN 37602
615-968-1541

(P2)
Dawn Parrish
9931 Gaynor Ave.
Granada Hills, CA 91343-1604
818-894-8964

(P3)
The Toy Cellar
John and Sheri Pavone
29 Sullivan Rd.
Peru, NY 12972

(P4)
Plymouth Rock Toy Co.
P.O. Box 1202
Plymouth, MA 02362
508-746-2842
FAX 508-830-1880

(P5)
Gary Pollastro
4156 Beach Dr. SW
Seattle, WA 98116
206-935-0245

(P6)
Judy Posner
R.D. 1, Box 273
Effort, PA 18330
717-629-6583

(R1)
John Rammacher
1610 Park Ave.
Orange City, FL 32763-8869
904-775-2891

(R2)
Rick Rann, Beatlelist
P.O. Box 877
Oak Park, IL 60303
708-442-7907

(R3)
Jim Rash
135 Alder Ave.
Pleasantville, NJ 08232
609-646-4125

(R4)
Robert Reeves
1253 Jedburg Rd.
Summerville, SC 29483
803-688-4673

(R5)
Reynolds Toys
Charlie Reynolds
2836 Monroe St.
Falls Church, VA 22042
703-533-1322

(R6)
David E. Riddle
P.O. Box 13141
Tallahassee, FL 32308
904-877-7207

(R7)
Jay Robinson, The Chicago Kid
P.O. Box 529
Deerfield, IL 60015
708-940-7547

(R8)
Bill Rugg
2405 14th Ave.
Marion, IA 52302
319-377-5176

(R9)
Craig Reid
P.O. Box 881
Post Falls, ID 83854
509-536-3278 (6-10 pm PST)

(S1)
Sam Samuelian, Jr.
700 Llanfair Rd.
Upper Darby, PA 19082
215-566-7248

(S2)
Mary Ann Sell
3752 Broadview Dr.
Cincinnati, OH 45208

(S3)
Greg and Lisa Slote
P.O. Box 20224
Port Washington, NY 11050
516-767-1638

(S4)
SLX Toys
7233 Michael Rd., Apt. #1
Orchard Park, NY 14127-1406
716-674-0432

(S5)
Sue Sternfeld
90-60 Union Tpke.
Glendale, NY 11385

(S6)
Bill Stillman
Scarfone & Stillman Vintage Oz
P.O. Box 167
Hummelstown, PA 17036
717-566-5538

(S7)
Nate Stroller
960 Reynolds Ave.
Ripon, CA 95366; 209-599-5933

(S8)
Steve Santi
19626 Ricardo Ave.
Hayward, CA 94541; 510-481-2586

(T1)
John Thurmond
Collector Holics
15006 Fuller
Grandview, MO 64030; 816-322-0906

(T2)
Toy Scouts, Inc.
Bill Bruegman
137 Casterton Ave.
Akron, OH 44303
216-836-0668 or FAX 216-869-8686

(T3)
Richard Trautwein
437 Dawson St.
Sault Ste. Marie, MI 49783; 906-635-0356

(T4)
Three Stooges Fan Clubs, Inc.
P.O. Box 747
Gwynedd Valley, PA 19437
215-654-9466

(T5)
Bob and Marcie Tubbs
31 Westwood Rd.
Fairfield, CT 06432-1658
203-367-7499

(T6)
TV Collector
P.O. Box 1088
Easton, MA 02334
502-238-1179

(T7)
'Tiques
Maxine and Stuart Evans
7 Rittner Ln.
Old Bridge, NJ 08857
908-679-8212
FAX 908-679-1090

(U1)
Unique Collections
938-A Halona St.
Honolulu, HI 96817
808-848-7366 or 808-488-1626

(V1)
Norm and Cathy Vigue
62 Bailey St.
Stoughton, MA 02072
617-344-5441

(W1)
Dan Wells Antique Toys
P.O. Box 6751
Louisville, KY 40206
502-896-0740 before 9:00 PM EST

(W2)
Ron Wiener
1200 Packard Bldg.
111 S 15th St.
Philadelphia, PA 19102
215-977- 2266
or 215-977-2346

(W3)
Nathan Willensky
5 E 22nd St., Suite 24C
New York, NY 10010
212-982-2156

(W4)
Randy Welch
1100 Hambrooks Blvd.
Cambridge, MD 21613
410-228-5390

(Y1)
Henri Yunes
971 Main St.
Apartment #2
Hackensack, NJ

Categories of Special Interest

Action Figures

Publishes newsletter, Headquarters Quarterly; specializes in 1964 Hasbro GI Joes
Joe Bodnarchuk
62 McKinley Ave.
Kenmore, NY 14217
Phone or FAX 716-873-0264

Also GI Joe, Star Wars and Super Heroes
John DiCicco
57 Bay View Dr.
Shrewsbury, MA 01545
508-797-0023

Captain Action, Star Wars, Secret Wars, and other character-related Western, TV, movie, comic, or paperback tie-ins
George Downes
Box 572
Nutley, NJ 07110
201-935-3388

Figures
Anthony Balasco
P.O. Box 19482
Johnston, RI 02919
401-946-5720 or FAX 401-942-7980

GI Joe, Captain Action, and other character-related TV, advertising, Marx and Mego figures; send $1 for sales catalog
Jerry and Ellen Harnish
110 Main St.
Bellville, OH 44813
Phone or FAX 419-886-4782

Also science fiction, movie, TV, and comic figures and accessories
David S. Jones
P.O. Box 1703
Bethlehem, PA 18016-1703
215-694-9713

Advertising

Also character
Dennis & George Collectibles
Dennis O'Brien
George Goehring
3407 Kake Montebello Dr.
Baltimore, MD 21218
410-889-3964

Gary Metz
4803 Lange Ln. SW
Roanoke, VA 24018
703-989-0475

Also general line
Mike's General Store
52 St. Annes Rd.
Winnipeg, Manitoba,
Canada R2M 2Y3
204-255-3463
FAX 204-253-4124

Also plastic toys and radio, movie, or TV tie-ins
The Toy Cellar
John and Sheri Pavone
29 Sullivan Rd.
Peru, NY 12972

Aernonautical Toys

Also pull toys
Perry and Donna Eichor
703 N Almond
Simpsonville, SC 29681
803-967-8770

Banks

Ertl; sales lists available
Homestead Collectibles
Art and Judy Turner
R.D. 2, Rte. 150
P.O. Box 173-E
Mill Hall, PA 17751
717-726-3597
FAX 717-726-4488

Parkway Furniture and Gift Shop
603 Volunteer Pky.
Bristol, TN 37602
615-968-1541

Penny banks (limited editions): new, original, mechanical, still, or figural; also bottle openers
Reynolds Toys
Charlie Reynolds
2836 Monroe St.
Falls Church, VA 22042
703-533-1322

Barbie and Friends

Also wanted: Mackies, holiday and porcelain as well as vintage Barbies; buying and selling ca 1959 dolls to present issues
Marl Davidson
5705 39th St., Circle East
Bradenton, FL 34203
813-751-6275
FAX 813-751-5463

Battery-Operated Toys

Also tin windup and friction cars; repairs on battery-op toys; collects broken toys for parts
Mike Czerwinski
825 Vista Cir.
Brea, CA 92621
714-990-4851

Tom Lastrapes
P.O. Box 2444
Pinellas Park, FL 34664
813-545-2586

Also general line
Mike Roscoe
3351 Lagrange
Toledo, OH 43608
419-244-6935

Boats and Toy Motors

Also Japanese wood toys
Dick Borgerding
RJB Toys
720 E Main St.
Flushing, MI 48433
313-659-9859

Books

Specializing in Little Golden Books and look-alikes; author of Collecting Little Golden Books, Volumes I and II. Also publishes news letter, Poky Gazette, primarily for Little Golden Book collectors
Steve Santi
19626 Ricardo Ave.
Hayward, CA 94541; 510-481-2586

Building Blocks and Construction Toys

Arlan Coffman
12223 Wilshire Blvd., Ste. 275
Santa Monica, CA 90403
310-453-2507

Richter's Anchor (Union) Stone Building Blocks
George Hardy
1670 Hawkwood Ct.
Charlottesville, VA 22901
804-295-4863 or FAX 804-295-4898

Candy Containers

Jeff Bradfield
Corner of Rt. 42 and Rt. 257
Dayton, VA 22821
703-879-9961

Doug Dezso
864 Patterson Ave.
Maywood, NJ 07607
201-488-1311

Cast Iron

Pre-war, large scale cast iron toys and early American tinplate toys
John McKenna
801-803 W Cucharres
Colorado Springs, CO 80918
719-630-8732

Any taxi cab item
Nathan Willensky
5 E 22nd St., Ste. 24C
New York, NY 10010
212-982-2156 or FAX 212-995-1065

Character and Promotional Glasses

Especially fast foods and sports glasses; publisher of Collector Glass News
Mark E. Chase
P.O. Box 308
Slippery Rock, PA 16057
412-946-2838

Character Clocks and Watches

Also radio premiums and decoders, P-38 airplane-related items from World War II, Captain Marvel and Hoppy items, Lone Ranger books with jackets, selected old comic books, toys and cap guns; buys and sells Hoppy and Roy items
Bill Campbell
Kirschner Medical Corp.
1221 Littlebrook Ln.
Birmingham, AL 35235
205-853-8227 or FAX 405-658-6986

Character Collectibles

Dolls, rock 'n' roll personalities (especially the Beatles), related character items, and miscellaneous toys
BOJO
Bob Gottuso
P.O. Box 1203
Cranberry Twp., PA 16033-2203
Phone or FAX 412-776-0621

1940s-'60s character items such as super heroes, TV and cartoon items, games, playsets, lunch boxes, model kits, comic books, and premium rings
Bill Bruegman
Toy Scouts, Inc.
137 Casterton Ave.
Akron, OH 44303
216-836-0668 or FAX 216-869-8686

TV, radio, and comic collectibles; sports and non-sports cards; silver and golden-age comics
Casey's Collectible Corner
HCR Box 31, Rt. 3
N Blenheim, NY 12131
607-588-6464

California Raisins (PVC); buying collections, old store stock and closeouts
Larry DeAngelo
516 King Arthur Dr.
Virginia Beach, VA 23464
804-424-1691

Early Disney, Western heroes, premiums, and other related collectibles
Ron and Donna Donnelly
Saturday Heroes
P.O. Box 7047
Panama City Beach, FL 32413
904-234-7944

Especially bendee figures and the Simpsons
K-3 Inc.
Bendees Only; Simpson Mania
2335 NW Thurman
Portland, OR 97210
503-222-2713

The Three Stooges
Gary Lassin
P.O. Box 747
Gwynedd Valley, PA 19437
215-361-5100

Especially Disney; send $5 for annual subscription (6 issues) for sale catalogs
The Mouse Man Ink
P.O. Box 3195
Wakefield, MA 01880
Phone or FAX 617-246-3876

General line
Olde Tyme Toy Mall
105 S Main St.
Fairmount, IN 46928
317-948-3150

Especially pottery, china, ceramics, salt and pepper shakers, cookie jars, tea sets, and children's china; with special interest in Black Americana and Disneyana; illustrated sale lists available
Judy Posner
R.D. #1, Box 273
Effort, PA 18330
717-629-6583

Buying, selling, and trading original Beatles memorabilia
Rick Rann, Beatlelist
P.O. Box 877
Oak Park, IL 60303
708-442-7907

Special interest in Star Trek, Aurora Slot Cars, and Halloween Costumes
Craig Reid
P.O. Box 881
Post Falls, ID 83835
509-536-3278 (6-10 pm PST)

Also battery-ops, character clocks, and novelties
Sam Samuelian, Jr.
700 Llanfair Rd.
Upper Darby, PA 19082
215-566-7248

Wizard of Oz memorabilia; quarterly mail/Phone bid auctions available for $2; always buying Oz
Bill Stillman
Scarfone & Stillman Vintage Oz
P.O. Box 167
Hummelstown, PA 17036
717-566-5538

General line
John Thurmond
Collector Holics
15006 Fuller
Grandview, MO 64030
816-322-0906

General line
'Tiques
Maxine and Stuart Evans
7 Rittner Ln.
Old Bridge, NJ 08857
908-679-8212 or FAX 908-679-1090

Tinplate toys and cars, battery-op toys, and toy trains
Richard Trautwein
437 Dawson St.
Sault Ste. Marie, MI 49783
906-635-0356

TV, movie, rock 'n' roll, comic character, commercials, radio, theater, etc., memorabilia of all kinds; Send $2 for sale catalog. We are not interested in buying items. All inquires must include SASE for reply unless ordering catalog
TV Collector
P.O. Box 1088
Easton, MA 02334
508-238-1179 or FAX by pre-set agreement

Games, premiums, cartoon personalities, Dick Tracy, Popeye, Buck Rogers, Flash Gordon, Tarzan, Lone Ranger, and others
Norm and Cathy Vigue
62 Bailey St.
Stoughton, MA 02072
617-344-5441

Especially Disneyana and Roger Rabbit
Yesterday's Toys
Allen Day
P.O. Box 525
Monroe, NC 28810

Chinese Tin Toys

Also buying and selling antiques, old toys and collectibles; custom refinishing and quality repairing
Finisher's Touch Antiques
Steve Fisch, proprietor
10 W Main St.
Wappingers Falls, NY 12590
914-298-8882 or FAX 914-298-8945

Dakins

Jim Rash
135 Alder Ave.
Pleasantville, NJ 08232

Diecast

Also pressed steel trucks and comic character toys
Aquarius Antiques
Jim and Nancy Schaut
P.O. Box 10781
Glendale, AZ 85318-0781
602-878-4293

Send $3 for fully illustrated catalog of cars, soldiers, planes, parts, etc.
Eccles Bros., Ltd.
R.R. 1, Box 253-D
Burlington, IA 52601
319-752-3840 (days) or 319-753-1179
FAX 319-753-5933

Especially Dinky; also selling reproduction parts and decals for various diecast brands
Paul Fideler
20 Shadow Oak Dr., Apt. #18
Sudbury, MA 01776
617-386-0228 (24 hours)

Especially English-made toy vehicles
Mark Giles
510 E Third St.
Ogalala, NE 69153
308-284-4360

Hot Wheels, Matchbox, Dinky, and Corgi
Robert Goforth
4061 E Castro Vly. Blvd.
Ste. 224
Castro Valley, CA 94552
510-889-0397
FAX 510-581-0397

Especially Matchbox and other small-scale cars and trucks
Bill Jackameit
200 Victoria Dr.
Bridgewater, VA 22812
703-828-4359 (Monday-Thursday, 7PM – 9PM EST)

Author/publisher of Matchbox Blue Book, Hot Wheels Blue Book, and Collecting Majorette Toys price guides (prices updated yearly)
Dana Johnson Enterprises
1347 NW Albany Ave.
Bend, OR 97701-3160
503-382-8410

Especially Nascar, banks, farm toys, and haulers
Just Toys
Hwy. 30
Standwood, IA 52337
319-945-6693

Especially Dinky; also obsolete French, German, Italian, and English-made vehicles
Jean-Claude Lanau
740 Thicket Ln.
Houston, TX 77079
713-491-6034

Ertl, banks, farm, trucks, and construction
John Rammacher
1610 Park Ave.
Orange City, FL 32763-8869
904-775-2891

All types; also action figures such as GI Joe, Johnny West, Matt Mason, and others
Robert Reeves
1253 Jedburg Rd.
Summerville, SC 29483
803-688-4673

Especially Soviet-made toys (marked USSR or CCCP)
David E. Riddle
P.O. Box 13141
Tallahassee, FL 32308
905-877-7207

Hot Wheels, Matchbox, and all obsolete toy cars, trucks, and airplanes
Dan Wells Antiques Toys
P.O. Box 6751
Louisville, KY 40206
502-896-0704

Unique Collections
938-A Halona St.
Honolulu, HI 96817
808-848-7366
FAX 808-488-1626

Dolls

Chatty Cathy and Mattel; author of book: Chatty Cathy Dolls, An Identification and Value Guide; has repair service
Kathy Lewis
Chatty Cathy's Haven
187 N Marcello Ave.
Thousand Oaks, CA 91360
805-499-7932

Liddle Kiddles and other small dolls from the late '60s and early '70s
Dawn Parrish
9931 Gaynor Ave.
Granada Hills, CA 91343-1604
818-894-8964

Liddle Kiddles, GI Joe, Barbie, and '60s TV character toys
Greg and Lisa Slote
P.O. Box 20224
Port Washington, NY 11050
516-767-1638

Dollhouse Furniture

Renwal, Ideal, Marx, etc.
Judith A. Mosholder
R.D. #2, Box 147
Boswell, PA 15531
814-629-9277

Dollhouses

Tin and fiberboard dollhouses and plastic furniture from all eras
Bob and Marcie Tubbs
31 Westwood Rd.
Fairfield, CT 06432-1658
203-367-7499

Fast Food

All restaurants and California Raisins
Ken Clee
Box 1142
Philadelphia, PA 19111
215-722-1979

McDonald's only, especially older or unusual items
John and Eleanor Larsen
523 Third St.
Colusa, CA 95932
916-458-4769

McDonald's; Illustrated Collector's Guide to McDonald's® Happy Meals ® Boxes, Premiums, and Promotionals ($9.50 postpaid).
Terry and Joyce Losonsky
7506 Summer Leave Lane
Columbia, MD 21046-2455
410-381-3358

Games

Victorian, cartoon, comic, TV, and nostalgic themes
Paul Fink's Fun & Games
P.O. Box 488
59 S Kent Rd.
Kent, CT 06757
203-927-4001

Paul David Morrow
13550 Foothill Blvd. #28
Sylmar, CA 91342
818-898-9592

Gas-Powered Toys

Airplanes, cars, and boats
Danny Bynum
12311 Wedgehill Ln.
Houston, TX 77077-4805
713-972-4421
or 713-531-5711

GI Joe

Also diecast and Star Wars
Cotswold Collectibles
P.O. Box 249
Clinton, WA 98236
206-579-1223
FAX 206-579-1287

Guns

Pre-WWII American spring-air BB guns, all Red Ryder BB guns, cap guns with emphasis on Western six-shooters; especially wanted are pre-WWII cast iron six-guns
Jim Buskirk
175 Cornell St.
Windsor, CA 95492
707-837-9949

Specializing in cap guns
Happy Memories Antique Toy Co.
The Hamburgs
P.O. Box 1305
Woodland Hills, CA 91365
818-346-9884 or 818-346-1269
FAX 818-346-0215

Also model kits, toy soldiers, and character toys and watches; character watch service available
Plymouth Rock Toy Co.
P.O. Box 1202
Plymouth, MA 02362
508-746-2842 or FAX 508-830-1880

Lunch Boxes

Norman's Olde and New Store
Philip Norman
126 W Main St.
Washington, NC 27889-4944
919-946-3448

Also characters such as cowboys, TV shows, cartoons, and more
Terri's Toys
Terry Ivers
1104 Shirlee Ave.
Ponca City, OK 74601
405-762-8697 or 405-762-5174
FAX 405-765-5101

Marionettes and Puppets

Steven Meltzer
670 San Juan Ave. #B
Venice, CA 90281
310-396-6007

Marx

Figures, playsets, and character toys
G.F. Ridenour
Fun House Toy Co.
P.O. Box 343
Bradfordwoods, PA 15015-0343
412-935-1392 (FAX capable)

Model Kits

Store displays, catalogs, paper for plastic model kits, and non-sports cards
James P. Crane
15 Clemson Ct.
Newark, DE 19711
302-738-6031

Specializing in figures and science fiction
Gordy Dutt
P.O. Box 201
Sharon Center, OH 44274-0201
216-239-1657 or 216-239-2991

Also action figures, monsters (especially Godzilla and Japan automated toys), Star Trek, and non-sports cards
Alan Edwards
Toys From the Crypt
P.O. Box 3294
Shawnee, KS 66203
913-383-1242

1/25th scale car kits and promotionals
Rick Hanson
Trader Rick
P.O. Box 161
Newark, IL 60541
815-695-5135

Character, space, monster, Western, radio and cereal premiums and toys; GI Joe, Captain Action, tin toys, and windups
Ed Janey
2920 Meadowbrook Dr. SE
Cedar Rapids, IA 52403
319-362-5213

Also slot cars, Matchbox, car and airplane catlogs and magazines
Bill Rugg
2405 14th Ave.
Marion, IA 53202
319-377-5176

Non-Sport Trading Cards

Send $1 for our 40-page catalog of non-sport cards ca 1970 to date; dealers send large SASE for our 10-page wholesale and close-out list
Mark and Val Macaluso
3603 Newark Rd.
Marion, NY 14505
315-926-4349
FAX 315-926-4853

Pedal Cars

Also specializing in Maytag collectibles
Nate Stroller
960 Reynolds Ave.
Ripon, CA 95366
510-481-2586

Penny Toys

Jane Anderson
Rt. 1, Box 1030
Saylorsburg, PA 18353

Pez Candy Dispensers

Richard Belyski
P.O. Box 124
Sea Cliff, NY 11579

Trading, buying, and selling since 1991
SLX Toys
7233 Michael Rd., Apt. #1
Orchard Park, NY 14127-1406
716-674-0432

Plastic Figures

Also Dakins, cartoon and advertising figures, and character squeeze toys
Jim Rash
135 Alder Ave.
Pleasantville, NJ 08232
609-649-4125

Promotional Vehicles

'50s and '60s models (especially Ford); also F&F Post Cereal cars
Larry Blodget
Box 753
Rancho Mirage, CA 92270

Puzzles

Wood jigsaw type, from before 1950
Bob Armstrong
15 Monadnock Rd.
Worcester, MA 01609

Specializing in advertising puzzles
Donald Friedman
660 W Grand Ave.
Chicago, IL 60610
708-656-3700

Ramp Walkers

Specializing in walkers, ramp-walking figures, and tin windups
Randy Welch
1100 Hambrooks Blvd.
Cambridge, MD 20783
410-228-5390

Russian and East European Toys

Wooden Matrioskha dolls, toys of tin, plastic, diecast metal; military theme and windups
Natural Way/DBA Russian Toy Co.
820 Massachusetts
Lawrence, KS 66044
913-841-0100

Sand Toys

Jane Anderson
Rt. 1, Box 1030
Saylorsburg, PA 18353

Slot Cars

Especially HO scale from the 1960s to the present; also vintage diecast
Joe Corea
New Jersey Nostalgia Hobby
401 Park Ave.
Scotch Plains, NJ 07076
908-322-2676 or FAX 908-322-4079

Specializing in slots and model racing, '60s-'70s; especially complete race sets in original boxes
Gary Pollastro
4156 Beach Dr. SW
Seattle, WA 98116
206-935-0245

Soldiers

Barclay, Manoil, Grey Iron, Jones, dimestore types, and others; also Sirrocco figures
Stan and Sally Alekna
724 Oceanfront Dr.
Neptune Beach, FL 32266
904-249-4831

Lineol, Elastolin, Heyde, Brigader, Britains; also Tekno model cars and airplanes
March of Time Antique Toys
Bertel Bruun
P.O. Box 400
59 Shore Rd.
Westhampton, NY 11977
Phone or FAX 516-288-0581

Space Toys

Also Star Trek, science fiction, and dinosaurs
Mike Fredericks
145 Bayline Cir.
Folsom, CA 95630
916-985-7986

Steiff

Also Schuco
Milt and Libby Sternberg
Glass Circus Antiques
412 W San Mateo
Santa Fe, NM 87505

Particularly bears; also Schucos and dolls
Bunny Walker
Box 502
Bucyrus, OH 44820
419-562-8355

Tonka

Also candy containers and German nodders
Doug Dezso
864 Patterson Ave.
Maywood, NJ 07607

Toothbrush Holders

Also Pez
Marilyn Cooper
8408 Lofland Dr.
Houston, TX 77055

Trains

Lionel, American Flyer, and Plasticville
Gary's Trains
R.D. #2, Box 147
Boswell, PA 15531
814-629-9277

Also Fisher Price, Tonka toys, and diecast vehicles
Bill Mekalian
550 E Chesapeake Cir.
Fresno, CA 93720
209-434-3247

Electric or windup types; also windup vehicles
Jay Robinson
The Chicago Kid
P.O. Box 529
Deerfield, IL 60015
708-940-7547

Also other Marklin (German) toys made before 1960 and especially those from before 1915
Ron Wiener
1200 Packard Bldg.
111 S 15th St.
Philadelphia, PA 19102
215-977-2266
or 215-977-2346

Transformers

Specializing in Transformers, Robotech, and any other robots or Japanese animated items
David Kolodny-Nagy
3701 Connecticut Ave. NW #500
Washington, DC 20008
202-364-8753

Trolls

Roger Inouye
2622 Valewood Ave.
Carlsbad, CA 92008-7925

View-Master

Roger Nazeley
4921 Castor Ave.
Phil., PA 19124
FAX 215-288-8030

Mary Ann Sells
3752 Broadview Dr.
Cincinnati, OH 45208

Windups

Especially German and Japan tin toys, Cracker Jack, toothbrush holders, radio premiums, pencil sharpeners, and comic strip toys
Phil Helley
Old Kilbourne Antiques
629 Indiana Ave.
Wisconsin Dells, WI 53965
608-254-8770

Also pressed steel toys, battery-ops, candy containers, dolls and children's things, games, soldiers, Noah's ark, space, robots, etc.
Jacquie and Bob Henry
Antique Treasures and Toys
Box 17
Walworth, NY 14568-0017
315-986-1424

Also Black Americana
Stephen Leonard
Box 127
Albertson, LI, NY 11507
516-742-0979

Yo-Yos

Lucky Meisenheimer
7300 Sand Lake Commons Blvd.
Orlando, FL 32819
407-354-0478

Clubs, Newsletters, and Other Publications

There are hundreds of clubs, newsletters, and magazines available to toy collectors today. Listed here are some devoted to specific areas of interest. You can obtain a copy of many newsletters simply by requesting a sample.

Action Toys Newsletter
P.O. Box 31551, Billings, MT 59107
406-248-4121

American Game Collectors Assn.
49 Brooks Ave.
Lewiston, MA 04240

American International Matchbox Collectors & Exchange Club News-Monthly
Dottie Colpitts
532 Chestnut St.
Lynn, MA 01904; 617-595-4135

Anchor Block Foundation
908 Plymouth St.
Pelham, NY 10303; 914-738-2935

Antique Advertising Association
P.O. Box 1121
Morton Grove, IL 60053; 708-446-0904

Antique & Collectors Reproduction News
Mark Cherenka
Circulation Department
P.O. Box 71174
Des Moines, IA 50325; 800-227-5531.
Monthly newsletter showing differences between old originals and new reproductions; subscription: $32 per year

The Autograph Review (newsletter)
Jeffrey Morey
305 Carlton Rd.
Syracuse, NY 13207; 315-474-3516

Autographs & Memorabilia
P.O. Box 224
Coffeyville, KS 67337; 316-251-5308.
6 issues per year on movie and sports memorabilia

Barbie Bazaar (magazine)
5617 Sixth Ave., Dept NY593
Kenosha, WI 53140;
414-658-1004 or FAX 414-658-0433.
6 issues for $25.95

Barbie Talks Some More!
Jacqueline Horning
7501 School Rd.
Cincinnati, OH 45249

The Baum Bugle
The International Wizard of Oz Club
Fred M. Meyer
220 N 11th St.
Escanaba, MI 49829

Berry-Bits
Strawberry Shortcake Collectors' Club
Peggy Jimenez
1409 72nd St.
N Bergen, NJ 07047

Beyond the Rainbow Collector's Exchange
P.O. Box 31672
St. Louis, MO 63131

Big Little Times
Big Little Book Collectors Club of America
Larry Lowery
P.O. Box 1242
Danville, CA 94526; 415-837-2086

Bojo
P.O. Box 1203
Cranberry Township, PA 16033-2203;
412-776-0621 (9 am to 9 pm EST).
Issues fixed-price catalog containing Beatles and Rock 'n' Roll memorabilia

Buckeye Marble Collectors Club
Betty Barnard
472 Meadowbrook Dr.
Newark, Oh 43055; 614-366-7002

Bulletin
Doll Collectors of America
14 Chestnut Rd.
Westford, MA 01886; 617-692-8392

Bulletin of the NAWCC
National Assn. of Watch and Clock Collectors, Inc.
Thomas J. Bartels, Executive Director
514 Poplar St.
Columbia, PA 17512-2130
717-684-8621 or FAX 717-684-0878

Canadian Toy Collectors Society
Gary A. Fry
P.O. Box 636
Maple, Ontario, Canada L6A 1S5

The Candy Gram
Candy Container Collectors of America
Douglas Dezso
864 Paterson, Ave.
Maywood, NJ 07607; 201-845-7707

Captain Action Collectors Club
P.O. Box 2095
Halesite, NY 11743; 516-423-1801.
Send SASE for newsletter information

Cast Iron Toy Collectors of America
Paul McGinnis
1340 Market St.
Long Beach, CA 90805

Cat Collectors Club
33161 Wendy Dr.
Sterling Heights, MI 48310.
Subscription: $18 per year

Cat Talk
Marilyn Dipboye
31311 Blair Dr.
Warren, MI 48092; 313-264-0285

Century Limited
Toy Train Collectors Society
160 Dexter Terrace
Tonawanda, NY 14150; 716-694-3771

Coca-Cola Collectors Club International
P.O. Box 49166
Atlanta, GA 30359. Annual dues: $25

Collecting Tips Newsletter
% Meredith Williams
P.O. Box 633
Joplin, MO 64802;
417-781-3855 or 417-624-2518.
12 issues per year focusing on fast-food
collectibles

The Cookie Jar Collector's Club News
Louise Messina Daking
595 Cross River Rd.
Katonah, NY 10536
914-232-0383 or FAX 914-232-0384

Cookie Jarrin' with Joyce:
The Cookie Jar Newsletter
R.R. 2, Box 504
Walterboro, SC 29488

Dark Shadows Collectibles Classified
Sue Ellen Wilson
6173 Iroquois Trail
Mentor, OH 44060; 216-946-6348.
For collectors of both old and new series

Dionne Quint Collectors Club
Jimmy Rodolfos
P.O. Box 2527
Woburn, MA 01888; 617-933-2219

Doll Investment Newsletter
P.O. Box 1982
Centerville, MA 02632

Doll News
United Federation of Doll Clubs
P.O. Box 14146
Parkville, MO 64152

Dunbar's Gallery
76 Haven St.
Milford, MA 01757;
508-634-8697
FAX 508-634-8698.
Specializing in quality advertising, Halloween, toys, coin-operated machines;
holding cataloged auctions occasionally,
lists available

Ephemera News
The Ephemera Society of America, Inc.
P.O. Box 37, Schoharie, NY 12157
518-295-7978

The Ertl Replica
Ertl Collectors Club
Mike Meyer, Editor
Hwys 136 & 20
Dyersville, IA 52040; 319-875-2000

FLAKE, The Breakfast Nostalgia Magazine
P.O. Box 481
Cambridge, MA 02140; 617-492-5004.
Bimonthly illustrated issue devoted to one
hot collecting area such as Disney, etc.,
with letters, discoveries, new releases, and
ads; single issue: $4 ($6 foreign); annual:
$20 ($28 foreign); free 25-word ad with
new subscription

Friends of Hoppy Club and Newsletter
Laura Bates
6310 Friendship Dr.
New Concord, OH 43762-9708
614-826-4850

Game Times
American Game Collectors Assn.
Joe Angiolillo, Pres.
4628 Barlow Dr.
Bartlesville, OK 74006

Garfield Collectors Society Newsletter
% David L. Abrams, Editor
744 Foster Ridge Rd.
Germantown, TN 38138-7036; 901-753-1026

Gene Autry Star Telegram
Gene Autry Development Assn.
Chamber of Commerce
P.O. Box 158
Gene Autry, OK 73436

Ginny Doll Club News
Jeanne Niswonger
305 W Beacon Rd.
Lakeland, FL 33803; 813-687-8015

Gone With the Wind Collectors Club
Newsletter
8105 Woodview Rd.
Ellicot City, MD 21043; 301-465-4632

Good Bears of the World
Terri Stong
P.O. Box 13097
Toledo, OH 43613

Grandma's Trunk
P.O. Box 404
Northport, MI 49670.
Subscription: $8 per year for 1st class or
$5 per year for bulk rate

Headquarters Quarterly, for GI Joe Collectors
Joe Bodnarchuk
62 McKinley Ave.
Kenmore, NY 14217-2414

Hello Again
Old-Time Radio Show Collector
Jay A. Hickerson
P.O. Box 4321
Hamden, CT 06514;
203-248-2887
FAX 203-281-1322.
Sample copy upon request with SASE

Highballer for Toy Train collectors
% Lou Bohn
109 Howedale Dr.
Rochester, NY 14616-1543

Hobby News
J.L.C. Publications
Box 258
Ozone Park, NY 11416

Holly Hobbie Newsletter
Helen McCale
Route 3, Box 35
Butler, MO 64730

Hopalong Cassidy Newsletter
Hopalong Cassidy Fan Club
P.O. Box 1361
Boyes Hot Springs, CA 95416

Ideal Doll & Toy Collectors Club
P.O. Box 623
Lexington, MA 02173; 617-862-2994

International Figure Kit Club
Gordy's
P.O. Box 201
Sharon Center, OH 44274-0201
216-239-1657 or FAX 216-239-2991

International Wizard of Oz Club Inc.
P.O. Box 95
Kinderhook, IL 62345

Kit Builders & Glue Sniffers
Gordy's
2103 Sharon Copley Rd.
Medina, OH 44256; 216-239-1657

Madame Alexander Fan Club Newsletter
Earl Meisinger
11 S 767 Book Rd.
Naperville, IL 60564

Marble Mania
Marble Collectors Society of America
Stanley Block
P.O. Box 222
Trumbull, CT 06611; 203-261-3223

Martha's Kidlit Newsletter
Box 1488A
Ames, IA 50010.
A bimonthly publication for children's
books collectors. Subscription: $25 per year

Matchbox USA
Charles Mack
62 Saw Mill Rd.
Durham, CT 06422; 203-349-1655

McDonald's® Collecting Tips
Meredith Williams
Box 633
Joplin, MO 64802.
Send SASE for information

McDonald's® Collector Club
Joyce & Terry Losonsky
7506 Summer Leave Ln.
Columbia, MD 21046-2455; 301-381-3358.
Authors of *Illustrated Collector's Guide to
McDonald's® Happy Meal® Boxes, Premi-
ums, & Promotions©* with updated 1994 val-
ues; available for $9.50 (includes postage)

McDonald's® Collector Club Newsletter
% Tenna Greenberg
5400 Waterbury Rd.
Des Moines, IA 50312; 515-279-0741

Model & Toy Collector Magazine
Toy Scouts, Inc.
137 Casterton Ave.
Akron, OH 44303
216-836-0668 or FAX 216-869-8668

Modern Doll Club Journal
Jeanne Niswonger
305 W Beacon Rd.
Lakeland, FL 33803

The Mouse Club East (Disney collectors)
P.O. Box 3195
Wakefield, MA 01880.
Family membership: $25 (includes
newsletters and 2 shows per year)

The Mouse Club (newsletter)
Kim and Julie McEuen
2056 Cirone Way
San Jose, CA 95124
408-377-2590
FAX 408-379-6903

Movie Advertising Collector (magazine)
George Reed
P.O. Box 28587
Phil., PA 19149

NAOLH Newsletter
National Assn. for Outlaw & Lawman
History
Hank Clark
P.O. Box 812
Waterford, CA 95386; 209-874-2640

NAPAC Newsletter
National Assn. of Paper and Advertising
Collectors
P.O. Box 500
Mt. Joy, PA 17552; 717-653-4300

National Fantasy Fan Club
(for Disney collectors)
Dept. AC, Box 19212
Irvine, CA 92713.
Membership: $20 per year, includes newslet-
ters, free ads, chapters, conventions, etc.

National Headquarters News
Train Collectors Assn.
300 Paradise Ln.
Strasburg, PA 17579

Novelty Salt and Pepper Club
% Irene Thornburg, Membership Coordinator
581 Joy Rd.
Battle Creek, MI 49017.
Publishes quarterly newsletter & annual
roster. Annual dues: $20 in USA,
Canada, & Mexico; $25 for all other
countries

Paper Collectors' Marketplace
470 Main St., P.O. Box 128
Scandinavia, WI 54977; 715-467-2379.
Subscription: $17.95 (12 issues) per year
in USA; Canada and Mexico add $15
per year

Paper Doll News
Ema Terry
P.O. Box 807
Vivian, LA 71082

Paper Pile Quarterly
P.O. Box 337
San Anselmo, CA 94979-0337
415-454-5552.
Subscription: $12.50 per year in USA &
Canada

Peanuts Collector Club Newsletter
Peanuts Collector Club
Andrea C. Podley
P.O. Box 94
N Hollywood, CA 91603

The Pencil Collector
American Pencil Collectors Soc.
Robert J. Romey, Pres.
2222 S Millwood
Wichita, KS 67213; 316-263-8419

Pepsi-Cola Collectors Club Newsletter
Pepsi-Cola Collectors Club
Bob Stoddard
P.O. Box 1275
Covina, CA 91722; 714-593-8750.
Membership: $15

The Plastic Candy Dispenser Newsletter
Sue Sternfeld
90-60 Union Turnpike
Glendale, NY 11385.
Information on Pez containers

Plastic Figure & Playset Collector
5894 Lakeview Ct. E
Onalaska, WI 54650

The Pokey Gazette — A Little Golden Book
(newsletter)
Steve Santi
19626 Ricardo Ave.
Hayward, CA 94541; 510-481-2586

Positively PEZ
Crystal and Larry LaFoe
3851 Gable Lane Dr., Apt. 513
Indianapolis, IN 46208

Quint News
Dionne Quint Collectors
P.O. Box 2527
Woburn, MA 01888; 617-933-2219

Record Collectors Monthly (newspaper)
P.O. Box 75
Mendham, NJ 07945;
201-543-9520 or FAX 201-543-6033

Roy Rogers-Dale Evans Collectors Assn.
Nancy Horsley
P.O. Box 1166
Portsmouth, OH 45662

Schoenhut Newsletter
Schoenhut Collectors Club
Robert Zimmerman
45 Louis Ave.
W Seneca, NY 14224

The Shirley Temple Collectors News
8811 Colonial Rd.
Brooklyn, NY 11209.
Dues: $20 per year; checks paybable to Rita
Dubas

The Silent Film Newsletter
Gene Vazzana
140 7th Ave.
New York, NY 10011
Subscription $18, send $2.50 for sample
copy

The Silver Bullet
Terry and Kay Klepey
P.O. Box 553
Forks, WA 98331; 206-327-3726.
Subscription $10 per year, sample issue
$4; also licensed mail-order seller of mem-
orabilia and appraiser

Smurf Collectors Club
24ACH, Cabot Rd. W
Massapequa, NY 11758.
Membership includes newsletters. LSASE
for information

Steiff Life
Steiff Collectors Club
Beth Savino
% The Toy Store
7856 Hill Ave.
Holland, OH 43528
419-865-3899 or 800-862-8697

The Television History Magazine
William J. Flechner
700 E Macoupin St.
Staunton, IL 62088; 618-635-2712

Toy Collector Club of America
(for Ertl toys)
P.O. Box 302
Dyersdille, IA 52040; 800-452-3303

Toy Dish Collectors
Abbie Kelly
P.O. Box 351
Camillus, NY 13031; 315-487-7415

Toy Gun Collectors of America Newsletter
Jim Buskirk, Editor & Publisher
175 Cornell St.
Windsor CA 95492; 707-837-9949.
Published quarterly, covers both toy and
BB guns. Dues: $15 per year

Toychest
Antique Toy Collectors of America, Inc.
2 Wall St., 13th Floor
New York, NY 10005; 212-238-8803

Toys & Prices (magazine)
700 E State St.
Iola, WI 54990-0001
715-445-2214 or FAX 715-445-4087.
Subscription: $14.95 per year

Transformer Club
Liane Elliot
6202 34th St., NW
Gig Harbor, WA 98335

The Trade Card Journal
Kit Barry
86 High St.
Brattleboro, VT 05301; 802-254-2195.
A quarterly publication on the social and
historical use of trade cards

Trainmaster (newsletter)
P.O. Box 1499
Gainesville, FL 32602
904-377-7439 or 904-373-4908
FAX 904-374-6616

Troll Monthly
5858 Washington St.
Whitman, MA 02382
800-858-7655
or 800-85-Troll

Turtle River Farm Toys
Rt. 1, Box 44
Manvel, ND 58256-9763

The TV Collector
Diane L. Albert
P.O. Box 1088
Easton, MA 02334-1088
508-238-1179.
Send $3.50 for sample copy

View-Master Reel Collector
Roger Nazeley
4921 Castor Ave.
Phil., PA 19124; 215-743-8999

Western & Serials Club
Rt. 1, Box 103
Vernon Center, NM 56090
507-549-3677

The Working Class Hero
(Beatles newsletter)
3311 Niagara St.
Pittsburgh, PA 15213-4223.
Published 3 times per year; send SASE for
information

The Wrapper
Bubble Gum & Candy Wrapper Collectors
P.O. Box 573
St. Charles, IL 60174; 708-377-7921

The Yellow Brick Road Fantasy Museum
& Gift Shop
Rt. 49 & Yellow Brick Rd.
Chesterton, IN 46304
219-926-7048

DON'T MISS YOUR CHANCE
TO REACH THOUSANDS OF TOY COLLECTORS

TO RESERVE YOUR AD SPACE FOR THE NEXT EDITION
PLEASE CONTACT HUXFORD ENTERPRISES *IMMEDIATELY*

RATES
(Ad Size)

FULL PAGE	7½" wide x 9¾" tall –	$750.00
HALF PAGE	7½" wide x 4½" tall –	$400.00
QUARTER PAGE	3½" wide x 4½" tall –	$250.00
EIGHTH PAGE	3½" wide x 2¼" tall –	$150.00
(or business card)		

*NOTE: The above rates are for **camera ready copy only** – Add $50.00 if we are to compose your ad. These prices are net – no agency discounts allowed. Payment in full must accompany your ad copy.*

All advertising accepted under the following conditions:

1. The Publisher will furnish advertising space in sizes and at rates as set forth in this rate sheet upon full payment in advance of its annual advertising deadline as set forth herein.

2. Submission of Copy. The publisher shall have the right to omit any advertisement when the space allotted to Advertiser in a particular issue has been filled. In addition, the Publisher reserves the right to limit the amount of space the Advertiser may use in any one edition.

3. Content and Design. Publisher reserves the right to censor, reject, alter, or refuse any advertising copy at its sole discretion or disapprove any advertising copy in accordance with any rule the Publisher may now have, or may adopt in the future, concerning the acceptance of advertising matter, but no intentional change in advertising copy will be made without the prior consent of the Advertiser.

4. Publisher's Liability for Deletions. Publisher's liability for failure of the Publisher to insert any advertisement in their books shall be limited to a refund of the consideration paid for the insertion of the advertisement or, at Advertiser's option, to such deleted advertisement being inserted in the next edition.

5. Copyright and Trademark Permission. Any Advertiser using copyrighted material or trademarks or trade names of others in its advertising copy shall obtain the prior written permission of the owners thereof which must be submitted to the Publisher with the advertising copy. Where this has not been done, advertising will not be accepted.

Half Page	
Quarter Page	**Eighth Page**

Make checks payable to:

HUXFORD ENTERPRISES
1202 7th St.
Covington, IN 47932

NOEL BARRETT
ANTIQUES & AUCTIONS

Box 1001 • CARVERSVILLE, PA 18913
215-297-5109 • FAX 297-0457

PERSONALIZED SERVICE
QUALITY CATALOGING
FIRST RATE PROMOTION

BACK ISSUE CATALOGS WITH PRICES REALIZED FOR SALE

We are known for the quality of our catalogs, many of which have become price and identification guides in their fields. We have a limited supply of back numbers for sale. All are supplied with post-sale price-keys as well as pre-sale estimates.

THE TOM ANDERSON COLLECTION: APRIL 1991 The finest collection of American clockwork toys ever sold at auction. More than 60 classic toy are pictured in full color, plus American tin toys, Christmas items, folk art and country store fixtures. More than 20 pages of color. Issue price $20. now $12.00

SIEGEL COLLECTION OF GAMES & TOYS: JUNE 1992 The definitive game auction - more than 700 items described - over 200 games pictured in color plus numerous lithographed toys, blocks and puzzles also pictured in color - plus optical toys, Christmas toys, penny toys, etc. -- 32 pages of color plus full color covers. Price: $22.00

SPILHAUS COLLECTION: MECHANICAL TOYS: JULY 1993
500 toys from this renowned collection: mechanicals,
Schoenhut, automata, etc. 8 pages color, -- $12.00

HAROLD WILLIAMS COLLECTION OF PRESSED STEEL:
NOVEMBER 1992 - near definitive collection of large
pressed steel toys: Buddy L, Keystone, Steelcraft,
Kingsbury, etc. plus 120 windups. --- $22.00

PRESSED STEEL PLAYTHINGS - RALSTON COLLECTION:
NOVEMBER 1993 - 450 pressed steel toys large and
small all pictured in color. -- $25.00

   PRESSED STEEL COMBO: order both for $37.00

Send orders to:
BARRETT AUCTION CATALOGS • PO Box 1001
CARVERSVILLE, PA 18913

THE GOTTSCHALK COLLECTIONS

AUTOMOTIVE TOYS AT AUCTION: APRIL 6 & 7 1990 - The classic book on Automotive toys by Lillian Gottschalk is Out of Print. But the entire book is reproduced in this catalog together with many toys not in book. 700 items pictured in black and white: cast iron, tin, and steel. Price $20.00

STEAM TOYS & OTHER TOYS: JUNE 2, 1990 - 500 items: comprehensive collection of steam engines and accessories, plus American tin, clockwork toys, & aeronautical toys. Issue price: $20 -- now $12.00

AUTOMOBILIA AT AUCTION: OCTOBER 3, 1989 - 400 items: auto mascots, gas globes, pedal cars, signs, ceramics., etc. issue price: $18.00, now $10

Buy set and get illustrated sales list : GOTTSCHALK IV - OCTOBER 1990 - automotive toys, Steelcraft Trucks, etc., - 530 lots - 100 items pictured.

   COMPLETE GOTTSCHALK SET: $40.

Please include $3.00 for postage and handling.

Jeff Bub Auctioneer

Antiques and Fine Arts

1658 Barbara Dr. • Brunswick, Ohio 44212

(216) 225-1110 • (216) 273-5772 Fax

Experienced in all phases of disposal of large collections
and single pieces of antique toys and other antiques

Over the years we have had great success auctioning these and other fine toys at market prices or above.

C. 1890 Automata

C. 1935 Borgfeldt Mickey the Bandleader

Dooling Brothers Gas-Powered Racer

Shand Mason Horse Drawn Fire Engine

Contact us today to maximize the advertising of your items
at our next antique toy or antique auction.

Riding around looking for that right way to sell your prized toy collection?

You only have to look as far as:

Collectors Auction Services

We offer:

☞   National & International exposure of your collection.

☞   Extensive keyed in mailing list of high end buyers.

☞   Fully computerized auction for quick error free operations.

☞   Extremely competitive commission fees.

☞   Discrete transactions always.

RR 2 Box 431 Oakwood Rd. Oil City, PA 16301

Ph (814) 677-6070 Fax (814) 677-6166

Mark Anderton/Dir.

Continental Hobby House

Route 1 L.S. N 9399

P.O. Box 193

(414) 693-3371

Sheboygan, WI 53082

Fax: (414) 693-8211

Dealers in Antique Toys

Vehicles: Autos, Trains, and Planes

Character: Disney, TV, and Comic

Military: Tanks, Soldiers, and Jeeps

Misc.: Steam, Windup, Battery Operated

And Many More…

Send your want lists

76 Haven Street., Milfurd, MA 01757

508-634-8697 Days

508-473-8616 Evenings & Weekends

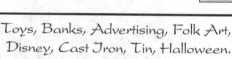

DUNBARS GALLERY

Toys, Banks, Advertising, Folk Art, Disney, Cast Iron, Tin, Halloween. All Items Guaranteed Mail Order Our Speciality

Please Call or Write With Wants — More than 500 Toys, Banks, Halloween Items In Stock.

NEW WORLDS RECORD

FOR A COMIC CHARACTER TOY AT AUCTION

$29,150 was realized for this rare Mickey Mouse 6-1/2" high Slate Dancer sold at our August 3 & 4, 1993 auction. It was part of the famous Michael Del Castello collection of San Francisco. The Mickey Slate Dancer along with numerous other very rare comic character, cast iron, early tin toys and dolls, were highly competed for by bidders all over North America and Europe. Each year we conduct special catalogued toy & doll auctions which are highly promoted here and abroad. All items are illustrated and come with a complete guaranteed catalogue description. If you are considering selling items, please call us.

We also conduct special catalogued sales of antique firearms, antique advertising, rare glass and lamps, important Americana, Victoriana and estates. We travel all over North America for consignments and would be happy to discuss the sale of your collection. All inquiries are held in the strictest of confidence and without obligation.

28 YEARS IN THE AUCTION BUSINESS

Rt. 201, Skowhegan Rd.
P.O. Box SC-830
Fairfield, ME 04937
Tel: (207) 453-7125
Fax: (207) 453-2502

CALL TODAY

Toy consultants: Douglas Wengal & Joe Olimpio & Doll consultant: Elizabeth Smith

Ask about our innovative new **"TRADE UP PROGRAM"** which may allow you to upgrade your collection with a minimal or no cash outlay.

Upcoming Sales at Christie's

**Antique Toys from the Collection of
Lawrence Scripps Wilkinson (Part II), November 1994**

Antique Toys & Collectibles, December 1994

Auctions are to be held in our galleries at Christie's East,
219 East 67th Street, New York, New York 10021.
For further information, please contact the Collectibles
Department at 212/606-0543. For catalogues, please
telephone Christie's Publications at 800/395-6300.

Shown on facing page: Mikado Bank, Kyser & Rex Co., very rare and excellent condition –
5 in. base. Sold at Christie's New York on December 18, 1993 for $63,000.
This page: A Fisher-Price lithographed paper-on-wood Mickey Mouse and Pluto Band, circa
1935 – 12 in. x 4 in. x 11 in. Sold at Christie's New York on November 20, 1993 for $2,300.

CHRISTIE'S

Before you consign to any auction company, be certain you are *making the right choice*.
Ask the questions that could mean the difference between a *successful* return on your investment
or another *horror story to pass along to your friends.*

QUESTIONS....	others	McMasters
• Do they have *years of experience and specialized knowledge?*	?	yes
• Are their policies and professional fees provided in *writing?*	?	yes
• Are they *members of UFDC?*	?	yes
• Are they *members of the National and State Auctioneer Association?*	?	yes
• Do they *personally pick-up and pack* your collection?	?	yes
• Do you receive a *complete list* at the time of pick-up?	?	yes
• Are catalog *descriptiions complete enough* to encourage absentee bidding?	?	yes
• Are your items sold *without reserve* to assure larger auction attendance?	?	yes
• Are your items sold with *no buyer's premium* to promote higher prices?	?	yes
• Do you receive *payment after each sale* (not after the entire collection is sold)?	?	yes
• Have their catalogues *won National and State awards for excellence?*	?	yes

Let's be honest.... we have heard "horror" stories of other auction companies. At McMasters, we pride ourselves
in genuinely caring about our customers and their collection. We have 18 years of experience and have built our
business on being honest and fair with our customers. When you decide to sell your collection or estate,
we encourage you to "shop around".... *then come to us for peace of mind.*

5855 Glenn Highway • P.O. Box 1755 • Cambridge, Ohio 43725

James E. McMasters, Auctioneer, Member OAA, PAA, NAA • Shari McMasters, Member UFDC

Office: 614-432-4419 • Fax: 614-432-3191

 McMasters .... the difference .... Integrity.

Call us TODAY at 1-800-842-3526 to be placed on our mailing list and receive free announcements of our upcoming monthly auctions!
• *Mention this ad and receive $5.00 of McMasters Money FREE* •

Mike's General Store

In Business Since 1979
Specializing in:
TOYS - ADVERTISING - TINS

Our shop, which is located 8 hours north of Minneapolis, is crammed full of interesting and unique pieces of nostalgia and collectibles. We buy and sell worldwide. We purchase one item or complete collections. We can travel anywhere to do so. If you have anything for sale, call us.

MAIL ORDER CATALOGS

We provide a full color catalog featuring over 500 items. All original and old. Advertising, tins and toys. Along with the catalog, we include a mini auction of over 100 items. Catalogs are printed every spring and fall, at a cost of $6.00 each or 4 issues for $20.00.

MIKE'S GENERAL STORE
52 ST. ANNES ROAD
WINNIPEG, MANITOBA
CANADA R2M 2Y3

PH: 1-204-255-3463 • FAX: 1-204-253-4124

DEBBY & MARTY KRIM'S
NEW ENGLAND AUCTION GALLERY

P.O. BOX 2273 T, WEST PEABODY, MA 01960   TEL: (508)535-3140   FAX: (508)535-7522

BID BY MAIL, BID BY PHONE, BID BY FAX FROM THE COMFORT OF YOUR HOME OR OFFICE
HUNDREDS OF ANTIQUE AND COLLECTIBLE TOYS, GAMES, AND CHARACTER ITEMS TO CHOOSE FROM

SUBSCRIBE NOW

SINGLE ISSUE: $8.   ANNUAL (4 ISSUES): $30.   FOREIGN: $40.

NEW ENGLAND AUCTION GALLERY IS ALWAYS BUYING TOYS, GAMES & CHARACTER COLLECTIBLES
PLEASE CALL, WRITE, OR FAX US IF YOU HAVE COLLECTIBLES TO SELL

Thank you for making 1993 another record year!

Richard Opfer Auctioneering will conduct several catalogued auctions for 1994, featuring fine Toys, Dolls, Antique Advertising, Country Store items as well as monthly "Eclectic Collectors" Auctions.

We are consistently bringing top prices for quality toys, advertising and collectibles.

We offer complete catalogued auction services for the large collection or the individual consignment. Please call us with your specific needs.

Our monthly "Eclectic Collectors" Auction is a series of non-catalogued auctions which will include collectibles from Toys to Black Americana to Advertising to Dolls to Pens to Paper Ephemera or Radios — Anything Collectible!

Ives Hippodrome Chariot
$90,200
Sold: December 5, 1991

Call to be placed on our mailing list for monthly "Eclectic Collectors" Auctions. We'll send you a flyer highlighting details of each auction.

We are also pleased to offer the following services: Consultation / Appraisals
Collection Management / Acting Agent for Private Treaty Sales / Agent Representation at Auctions

OA Richard Opfer
Auctioneering, Inc.

1919 Greenspring Drive / Timonium, Maryland 21093 / (410) 252-5035 / Fax 252-5863

•BUY
•SELL
•TRADE

Open 10 to 6
7 days a week

Olde Tyme **Toy Mall**
Fairmount, IN

105 S. Main
Fairmount, IN 46928
(317)948-3150

CAPTAIN ACTION

✶ Tin Windups ✶ Cast Iron ✶ Lead and Plastic Soldiers
✶ Raggedy Ann Booth ✶ Mego Figures ✶ Hartland ✶ Marx Monsters ✶ Personality
✶ Radio Premiums ✶ Old Toy Stock ✶ Figures Battery Toys ✶ Slot Cars ✶ Banks
✶ Bicycles ✶ Cap Pistols ✶ Character Toys ✶ Comics ✶ Construction Sets ✶ Disneyana
✶ Dolls ✶ Doll Furniture ✶ Farm Toys ✶ Fast Food ✶ Games ✶ Air and Pop Guns
✶ Lunch Boxes ✶ Marbles ✶ Models ✶ Pedal Cars ✶ Playsets ✶ Trains ✶ Robots ✶ Space
Toys ✶ Sports ✶ Star Wars ✶ Star Trek ✶ Diecast (Matchbox, Hot
Wheels, Corgi) ✶ Promotion Cars ✶ Lots of Boxed Big Jim Fig-
ures ✶ Cap Guns ✶ Batman
✶ Large Selection of GI Joe
and accessories
✶ Price Guides

STAR TREK

GIJOE

STAR WARS

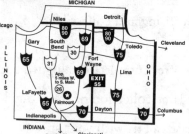

We welcome want lists and we are doing mail order!

Booths, Showcases, and Glass Front Shelves are still available for quality dealers. Our monthly rates are very reasonable and our commission is a low 5%. Our mall will continually be heavily advertised, and our in-house staff handles ALL THE SALES!

Come visit us in Fairmount, Indiana, the hometown of James Dean.
Always Buying Toy Collections

Toy Shop 1993

Finest Mechanical

ANTIQUE TOYS

Please send $5
for always
up-to-date
fully illustrated
catalog

S. Leonard
Box 127, Albertson, LI, NY 11507
(516) 742-0979

CALLING ALL COLLECTORS!

If you are thinking of either buying or selling, Collection Liquidators Auction Service & Sales is the place for you.

Specialists in Antique Toys, Character Collectibles & Black Americana, we hold three to four Absentee Mail auctions per year, each one offers hundreds of quality collectibles for every level of collector, and unique to the industry, our catalog price is deductible from your successful bid.

We are the only auction house in America which offers, along with a vast assortment of toys & related character collectibles, a large selection of quality Black Americana in <u>each and every sale</u>.

Both buyers and consignors benefit from our personalized approach to providing individualized customer service.

Call or write today and subscribe for our fully illustrated catalogs that size, describe, and condition each and every item (includes prices realized). Send $9.00 ($14 foreign) for a single issue or $24.00($38. foreign) for the next three.

COLLECTION LIQUIDATORS
341 LAFAYETTE STREET SUITE 007
NEW YORK, NY 10012
212-505-2455

Set A Course for Financial Independence! Let the Lloyd Ralston Gallery Sell Your *Whole* Collection for You.
Not to OnePerson, but to Hundreds of Live Bidders from All Over the World.

We Are Now Accepting Toy and Train Consignments for Our 1994 auctions. Pleasing Collectors for 30 years.

LLOYD RALSTON TOYS • 173 POST ROAD, FAIRFIELD, CT 06430
Call Glenn, Jeff or Mark at 203-255-1233 • FAX 203-256-9094

We have the best names in Antiques and Fine Arts in Boston.

Cartier and Gloria Lieberman. Americana and Stephen Fletcher. Boudin and Colleene Fesko. These are just a few of the superb names in antiques and highly respected antique specialists that you will discover at Skinner.

Art Deco Onyx and Diamond Wristwatch, Cartier, Paris, sold for $16,500

Gloria Lieberman, Skinner Specialist in Fine Jewelry

Impressionist Painting "Trouville" by Eugene Boudin (French 1824-1898), sold for $198,000

We have 20 of the country's most knowledgeable antique experts on staff, specializing in a variety of fields from European and American furniture and paintings to oriental rugs to toys and dolls.

Whatever your interest, our Skinner experts are there to help you with appraisals, consignments or simply to answer your questions. No other New England auction house can offer you the thirty years of experience and expertise that we do.

Stephen Fletcher, Skinner Specialist in American Furniture and Decorative Arts

And now with our new expanded gallery at The Heritage On The Garden in Boston's Back Bay, you can browse through our auction exhibitions whenever you like.

So for the fine quality antiques and fine arts you're looking for, plus the expert advice you can't find anywhere else, just remember one name. Ours.

Colleene Fesko, Skinner Specialist in American and European Paintings

Federal Mahogany Inlaid Secretary and Bookcase Sold for $46,000

SKINNER

Auctioneers and Appraisers of Antiques and Fine Art

The Heritage On The Garden, 63 Park Plaza, Boston, MA 02116, Tel. 617-350-5400, FAX 617-350-5429
357 Main Street, Bolton, MA 01740, Tel. 508-779-6241, FAX 508-779-5144

MUDDY RIVER TRADING CO.
Vintage and Antique Advertising
Tin • Paper • Cardboard • Procelain
Country Store Items

Gary Metz
703-989-0475

4803 Lange Lane, S.W.
Roanoke, VA 24018

ALWAYS WANTING TO BUY
Collections • Signs in quantity • Coca Cola • Die-Cuts • Stand Ups
Any single great sign or item priced from $500 to $25,000

MY SERVICES INCLUDE:
1) Buying old advertising of every description.
2) Finding and filling customer wants in advertising.
3) Auction promotion and presentation.
4) Single item or collection liquidation through consignment, on a fee or net basis.
5) Restaurant decor services.
6) Anything related to the buying, selling, or trading or antique advertising — we can talk.

Classic Tin Toy Company

Route 1 L.S. N 9399
P.O. Box 193
Sheboygan, WI 53082

Restoration Services

Manufacturers of Fine Quality
Replacement Parts for Toys and Trains

From parts to total restoration

Catalog — Write for details
Tel: (414) 693-3371
Fax: (414) 693-8211

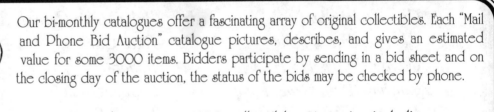

Our bi-monthly catalogues offer a fascinating array of original collectibles. Each "Mail and Phone Bid Auction" catalogue pictures, describes, and gives an estimated value for some 3000 items. Bidders participate by sending in a bid sheet and on the closing day of the auction, the status of the bids may be checked by phone.

Specializing in over 100 collectible categories including:

⌐ Disneyana ⌐ Comic Character Items ⌐ Toys ⌐ Radio Premiums
⌐ Western & Space Hero Items ⌐ Early Radio & TV Items ⌐ Advertising
Collectibles ⌐ Presidential Campaign Items ⌐ Pinback Buttons of All Types
⌐ Sports ⌐ Movie Items ⌐ Aviation ⌐ Bicycles ⌐ Automotive ⌐ World War I & II
⌐ Patriotic Items, World's Fairs ⌐ Ephemera ⌐ Shirley Temple & Related Doll Items ⌐ Gum Cards
⌐ Elvis ⌐ The Beatles and Most Forms of American Popular Culture

We would like to show you what is available —
$7.50 Sample Auction — 1 Catalogue
$20.00 — 3 Catalogue Subscription
$30.00 — 5 Catalogues (1 Year)
(overseas: $30.00 for 3 issues)

Since 1967
America's Premier
Mail & Phone Bid
Auction

HAKE'S AMERICANA
PO BOX 1444 (DEPT. 181), YORK, PA 17405 (717) 848-1333

SMITH HOUSE TOYS

4 Phone & Mail Auctions Yearly

1-207-439-4614 Ph.   1-207-439-8554 Fax

P.O. Box 336
Eliot, Maine 03903

Supplying Dealers & Collectors Worldwide for 8 Years

Categories of toys that will be in each of our quarterly catalogs is listed. Every toy is pictured in beautiful color with conditions and descriptions.

Airplanes	*German Tin W/U*
American Tin W/U: Prewar	*Battery Operated*
Black Toys	*Hanna Barbera Toys*
1950's TV Related	*Japan W/U's: Prewar, Occupied*
Character Watches	*Motorcycles*
Cap Guns	*Penny Toys*
Circus/Carnival	*Premiums: Cereal, Radio*
Clowns: Tin W/U's	*Race Cars*
Comic Character Toys	*Robots*
Cowboy: Roy, Gene, Hoppy	*Schuco Toys*
Disney: 1930's	*Space Toys*
Fisher-Price: Pre 1960	*Tootsietoys: Boxed*
Flash Gordon	*Trucks*
Superman	*Buck Rogers*

All items are in superb condition, most with boxes. Become one of our very satisfied customers and subscribe today to our quarterly catalogs.

Many toy reference books use Smith House's prices in their guides. Subscribers will receive our prices realized. We travel the world to bring to you the finest toys we can find. Each catalog will include approximately 300 items.

Subscription rate: per catalog – U.S.A. $8.00 Canada $9.00 Foreign $10.00
Yearly – Jan., April, July, Oct. $30.00 U.S.A./Canada $35.00 Foreign

Visit us at the Atlantique Shows in A.C. NJ, Booth #337

Books on Antiques and Collectibles

This is only a partial listing of the books on antiques that are available from Collector Books. All books are well illustrated and contain current values. Most of the following books are available from your local book seller, antique dealer, or public library. If you are unable to locate certain titles in your area, you may order by mail from COLLECTOR BOOKS, P.O. Box 3009, Paducah, KY 42002-3009. Customers with Visa or MasterCard may phone in orders from 8:00 – 4:00 CST, M – F – Toll Free 1-800-626-5420. Add $2.00 for postage for the first book ordered and $0.30 for each additional book. Include item number, title, and price when ordering. Allow 14 to 21 days for delivery.

BOOKS ON GLASS AND POTTERY

1810	American Art Glass, Shuman	$29.95
1312	Blue & White Stoneware, McNerney	$9.95
1959	Blue Willow, 2nd Ed., Gaston	$14.95
3719	Coll. Glassware from the 40's, 50's, 60's, 2nd Ed., Florence	$19.95
3816	Collectible Vernon Kilns, Nelson	$24.95
3311	Collecting Yellow Ware – Id. & Value Gd., McAllister	$16.95
1373	Collector's Ency. of American Dinnerware, Cunningham	$24.95
3815	Coll. Ency. of Blue Ridge Dinnerware, Newbound	$19.95
2272	Collector's Ency. of California Pottery, Chipman	$24.95
3811	Collector's Ency. of Colorado Pottery, Carlton	$24.95
3312	Collector's Ency. of Children's Dishes, Whitmyer	$19.95
2133	Collector's Ency. of Cookie Jars, Roerig	$24.95
3723	Coll. Ency. of Cookie Jars-Volume II, Roerig	$24.95
3724	Collector's Ency. of Depression Glass, 11th Ed., Florence	$19.95
2209	Collector's Ency. of Fiesta, 7th Ed., Huxford	$19.95
1439	Collector's Ency. of Flow Blue China, Gaston	$19.95
3812	Coll. Ency. of Flow Blue China, 2nd Ed., Gaston	$24.95
3813	Collector's Ency. of Hall China, 2nd Ed., Whitmyer	$24.95
2334	Collector's Ency. of Majolica Pottery, Katz-Marks	$19.95
1358	Collector's Ency. of McCoy Pottery, Huxford	$19.95
3313	Collector's Ency. of Niloak, Gifford	$19.95
3837	Collector's Ency. of Nippon Porcelain I, Van Patten	$24.95
2089	Collector's Ency. of Nippon Porcelain II, Van Patten	$24.95
1665	Collector's Ency. of Nippon Porcelain III, Van Patten	$24.95
1447	Collector's Ency. of Noritake, 1st Series, Van Patten	$19.95
1034	Collector's Ency. of Roseville Pottery, Huxford	$19.95
1035	Collector's Ency. of Roseville Pottery, 2nd Ed., Huxford	$19.95
3314	Collector's Ency. of Van Briggle Art Pottery, Sasicki	$24.95
3433	Collector's Guide To Harker Pottery - U.S.A., Colbert	$17.95
2339	Collector's Guide to Shawnee Pottery, Vanderbilt	$19.95
1425	Cookie Jars, Westfall	$9.95
3440	Cookie Jars, Book II, Westfall	$19.95
2275	Czechoslovakian Glass & Collectibles, Barta	$16.95
3882	Elegant Glassware of the Depression Era, 6th Ed., Florence	$19.95
3725	Fostoria - Pressed, Blown & Hand Molded Shapes, Kerr	$24.95
3883	Fostoria Stemware - The Crystal for America, Long	$24.95
3886	Kitchen Glassware of the Depression Years, 5th Ed., Florence	$19.95
3889	Pocket Guide to Depression Glass, 9th Ed., Florence	$9.95
3825	Puritan Pottery, Morris	$24.95
1670	Red Wing Collectibles, DePasquale	$9.95
1440	Red Wing Stoneware, DePasquale	$9.95
1958	So. Potteries Blue Ridge Dinnerware, 3rd Ed., Newbound	$14.95
3739	Standard Carnival Glass, 4th Ed., Edwards	$24.95
3327	Watt Pottery – Identification & Value Guide, Morris	$19.95
2224	World of Salt Shakers, 2nd Ed., Lechner	$24.95

BOOKS ON DOLLS & TOYS

2079	Barbie Fashion, Vol. 1, 1959-1967, Eames	$24.95
3310	Black Dolls – 1820 - 1991 – Id. & Value Guide, Perkins	$17.95
3810	Chatty Cathy Dolls, Lewis	$15.95
1529	Collector's Ency. of Barbie Dolls, DeWein	$19.95
2338	Collector's Ency. of Disneyana, Longest & Stern	$24.95
3727	Coll. Guide to Ideal Dolls, Izen	$18.95
3822	Madame Alexander Price Guide #19, Smith	$9.95
3732	Matchbox Toys, 1948 to 1993, Johnson	$18.95

3733	Modern Collector's Dolls, 6th series, Smith	$24.95
1540	Modern Toys, 1930 - 1980, Baker	$19.95
3824	Patricia Smith's Doll Values – Antique to Modern, 10th ed.	$12.95
3826	Story of Barbie, Westenhouser, No Values	$19.95
2028	Toys, Antique & Collectible, Longest	$14.95
1808	Wonder of Barbie, Manos	$9.95
1430	World of Barbie Dolls, Manos	$9.95

OTHER COLLECTIBLES

1457	American Oak Furniture, McNerney	$9.95
3716	American Oak Furniture, Book II, McNerney	$12.95
2333	Antique & Collectible Marbles, 3rd Ed., Grist	$9.95
1748	Antique Purses, Holiner	$19.95
1426	Arrowheads & Projectile Points, Hothem	$7.95
1278	Art Nouveau & Art Deco Jewelry, Baker	$9.95
1714	Black Collectibles, Gibbs	$19.95
1128	Bottle Pricing Guide, 3rd Ed., Cleveland	$7.95
3717	Christmas Collectibles, 2nd Ed., Whitmyer	$24.95
1752	Christmas Ornaments, Johnston	$19.95
3718	Collectible Aluminum, Grist	$16.95
2132	Collector's Ency. of American Furniture, Vol. I, Swedberg	$24.95
2271	Collector's Ency. of American Furniture, Vol. II, Swedberg	$24.95
3720	Coll. Ency. of American Furniture, Vol III, Swedberg	$24.95
3722	Coll. Ency. of Compacts, Carryalls & Face Powder Boxes, Mueller	$24.95
2018	Collector's Ency. of Granite Ware, Greguire	$24.95
3430	Coll. Ency. of Granite Ware, Book 2, Greguire	$24.95
1441	Collector's Guide to Post Cards, Wood	$9.95
2276	Decoys, Kangas	$24.95
1629	Doorstops – Id. & Values, Bertoia	$9.95
1716	Fifty Years of Fashion Jewelry, Baker	$19.95
3817	Flea Market Trader, 9th Ed., Huxford	$12.95
3731	Florence's Standard Baseball Card Price Gd., 6th Ed.	$9.95
3819	General Store Collectibles, Wilson	$24.95
3436	Grist's Big Book of Marbles, Everett Grist	$19.95
2278	Grist's Machine Made & Contemporary Marbles	$9.95
1424	Hatpins & Hatpin Holders, Baker	$9.95
3884	Huxford's Collectible Advertising – Id. & Value Gd., 2nd Ed	$24.95
3820	Huxford's Old Book Value Guide, 6th Ed.	$19.95
3821	Huxford's Paperback Value Guide	$19.95
1181	100 Years of Collectible Jewelry, Baker	$9.95
2216	Kitchen Antiques – 1790 - 1940, McNerney	$14.95
3887	Modern Guns – Id. & Val. Gd., 10th Ed., Quertermous	$12.95
3734	Pocket Guide to Handguns, Quertermous	$9.95
3735	Pocket Guide to Rifles, Quertermous	$9.95
3736	Pocket Guide to Shotguns, Quertermous	$9.95
2026	Railroad Collectibles, 4th Ed., Baker	$14.95
1632	Salt & Pepper Shakers, Guarnaccia	$9.95
1888	Salt & Pepper Shakers II, Guarnaccia	$14.95
2220	Salt & Pepper Shakers III, Guarnaccia	$14.95
3443	Salt & Pepper Shakers IV, Guarnaccia	$18.95
3890	Schroeder's Antiques Price Guide, 13th Ed.	$12.95
2096	Silverplated Flatware, 4th Ed., Hagan	$14.95
2348	20th Century Fashionable Plastic Jewelry, Baker	$19.95
3828	Value Guide to Advertising Memorabilia, Summers	$18.95
3830	Vintage Vanity Bags & Purses, Gerson	$24.95

Schroeder's ANTIQUES Price Guide

. . . is the #1 best-selling antiques & collectibles value guide on the market today, and here's why . . .

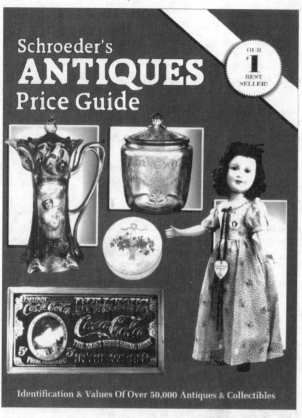

Schroeder's
ANTIQUES
Price Guide

OUR **1** BEST SELLER!

Identification & Values Of Over 50,000 Antiques & Collectibles

8½ x 11, 608 Pages, $12.95

• More than 300 advisors, well-known dealers, and top-notch collectors work together with our editors to bring you accurate information regarding pricing and identification.

• More than 45,000 items in almost 500 categories are listed along with hundreds of sharp original photos that illustrate not only the rare and unusual, but the common, popular collectibles as well.

• Each large close-up shot shows important details clearly. Every subject is represented with histories and background information, a feature not found in any of our competitors' publications.

• Our editors keep abreast of newly developing trends, often adding several new categories a year as the need arises.

If it merits the interest of today's collector, you'll find it in *Schroeder's*. And you can feel confident that the information we publish is up to date and accurate. Our advisors thoroughly check each category to spot inconsistencies, listings that may not be entirely reflective of market dealings, and lines too vague to be of merit. Only the best of the lot remains for publication.

Without doubt, you'll find
SCHROEDER'S ANTIQUES PRICE GUIDE
the only one to buy for
reliable information and values.

COLLECTOR BOOKS
A Division of Schroeder Publishing Co., Inc.